MW01053899

Criminal Procedure:
The Post-Investigative Process

Criminal Procedure: The Post-Investigative Process

FIFTH EDITION

Neil P. Cohen

(Late) W.P. Toms Professor of Law and Distinguished Professor of Law

The University of Tennessee College of Law

Stanley E. Adelman

Visiting Professor of Law (Retired)

University of New Mexico School of Law

University of San Francisco School of Law

Leslie W. Abramson

Frost Brown Todd Professor of Law

University of Louisville Louis D. Brandeis School of Law

Michael O'Hear

Professor of Law

Marquette University Law School

Wayne A. Logan

Gary & Sallyn Pajcic Professor of Law

Florida State University College of Law

Carolina Academic Press

Durham, North Carolina

ISBN 978-1-5310-0920-5
e-ISBN 978-1-5310-0921-2
LCCN 2018954462

Carolina Academic Press, LLC
700 Kent Street
Durham, North Carolina 27701
Telephone (919) 489-7486
Fax (919) 493-5668
www.cap-press.com

Printed in the United States of America

To Leroy and Mindy
S.E.A.

To Sam, Shel, and Will
L.W.A.

To Jennifer, Lauren, Daniel, and Owen
M.O.

To Meg, Anna, and Charlotte
W.A.L.

To the memory of Neil, our enduring guiding light
S.E.A., L.W.A., M.O., W.A.L.

Contents

Preface to the Fifth Edition

Historically, the course that most law schools call "Criminal Procedure" focused on vital Fourth, Fifth, and Sixth Amendment issues, but paid scant attention to the subject matter of this book – the equally vital aspects, both practical and theoretical, of the criminal adjudication process.

Happily, in recent years, law schools have added a separate course on criminal adjudication, and placed it on a co-equal footing with the traditional "Crim. Pro." course. In recognition of the importance of requiring demonstrated competence in this area of law practice, bar examiners around the nation have also begun testing for knowledge of the criminal adjudication process. It is no exaggeration (and no disrespect to the traditional Criminal Procedure course) to call this book, and the course it is intended for, "the real criminal procedure."

This Fifth Edition continues the previous editions' focus on both the theoretical and practical aspects of the "bail to jail" aspects of American criminal procedure. We have deliberately chosen to give special emphasis to many practice-related issues, such as motion practice, the form and content of indictments and other pleadings, the impact of various parts of the system on the guilty plea process, and ethical dilemmas facing lawyers (both prosecution and defense) and judges in criminal cases. Ability to navigate through these real-life (and frequently occurring) practice issues is every bit as essential as the formal mastery criminal law and rules of criminal procedure to providing students with the necessary knowledge and skills to serve as competent and ethical practitioners, be they prosecution or defense lawyers.

Criminal adjudication is one of the most rapid developing areas of the law, accounting for approximately twenty percent of the U.S. Supreme Court's decisions in recent years. Keeping current is of vital importance to students, practitioners, and of course, to us. Each year, shortly after the close of the Supreme Court's term, we prepare a cumulative annual supplement incorporating important new decisions from SCOTUS and lower federal and state courts, as well as recent scholarship that we find helpful and illuminating. Carolina Academic Press publishes our annual supplements on its website (at no additional cost) prior to each fall semester, in time to assure that students and teachers will have available the most up-to-date set of materials in this area of the law.

We have discontinued the practice from earlier editions and supplements of reproducing verbatim the full text of the Federal Rules of Criminal Procedure, which are easily available from other sources on line. Their omission, except where we have deemed including the exact text to be crucial, has helped us to reduce the length of this book so that teachers, with perhaps a few judicious omissions, can cover its wide-ranging content in one semester of study.

Substantively, the Fifth Edition continues our detailed focus on the most important recent trends, upheavals, and hotly debated issues in adjudicatory criminal procedure, including:

- The fairness (or not) and the effectiveness (or not) of the grand jury as both "a sword and a shield";
- Prosecutors' duty to disclose materially exculpatory evidence, and remedies for *Brady* violations;
- Defense counsel's obligations under *Frye* and *Lafler* to provide competent advice and effective assistance to clients in the plea-bargaining process;
- Continually evolving post-*Crawford* case law under the Sixth Amendment Confrontation Clause;
- Application of the *Apprendi-Booker* line of cases to sentencing decisions;
- The steady decrease in the availability and use of the death penalty nationwide; and
- The near-total disappearance of habeas corpus as an effective post-conviction remedy. As we observe in Chapter 17, the Supreme Court has reached a solid consensus in recent years, that habeas lies only to correct blatant misapplications of the Court's constitutional precedents and not as an easily available second round of appeals. That battle is now over.

Just before we were to begin work on this new edition, we lost our original lead author, Professor Neil Philip Cohen, W.P. Toms Distinguished Service Professor of Law at the University of Tennessee College of Law, to an untimely passing. We have missed Neil's warmth, his guidance, his quick wit, his sharp intellect, and his commitment to excellence, but we hope that this book will continue to live up to his high standards. As a camp counselor in his late teens, Neil was known to his campers as "Captain Neil." He spent a lifetime inspiring campers, students, scholars, and teaching colleagues throughout the United States. His loss to us, and to the legal academy, is inestimable. We dedicate this and all future editions and supplements of this book to the honor and the memory of our own Captain Neil.

To our teaching colleagues who have taught from earlier editions of this book and to attorneys who have kept it on their bookshelves as a practice reference, welcome back. We hope you find this edition to be worthy of the earlier editions begun by Professor Cohen and our other original co-author, the late Professor Don Hall of Vanderbilt University Law School. We have tried to maintain their clarity of analysis, structure, and just plain good writing, and adapt these strengths to evolving doctrinal law in the electronic era of legal scholarship and law practice. To our new readers, welcome to our world! To both our newer and more "experienced" readers, we look forward to receiving your thoughts, comments, suggestions, and yes, your criticisms.

Stanley E. Adelman
Leslie W. Abramson
Michael O'Hear
Wayne A. Logan

October 2018

Acknowledgments

Without the invaluable assistance of many, many colleagues, students, and administrative assistants, this book would not have been possible.

For assistants on the first two editions, we remain grateful for the research assistance of Chad Riddle, Esq., a former student at the University of Tennessee College of Law, and to Morgan Gire., Patricia Judd, Esq., Eric McCord, Esq., and Michael Sherman, Esq., former students at Vanderbilt Law School, and for the outstanding administrative assistance of Sonya Fowler at the University of Tennessee and Nan Paden at Vanderbilt Law School.

For the Third Edition, we remain grateful for the research assistance of our former students Stuart White, Esq., and Chow Xie, Esq., of Brooklyn Law School, and Mianette Layne, Esq., of the University of Arkansas School of Law, and for the administrative assistance of Fredd Brewer of Albany Law School.

For the Fourth Edition, we appreciate the research assistance of Mary Susan Lucas Reference Librarian at Charlotte School of Law, Preston Hilton, Esq., formerly of Charlotte School of Law; Sydney Scarce of Charlotte School of Law; Robin David Rice of the University of Louisville School of Law; Nicholas Maggipinto and Hal Berman of Brooklyn Law School; and Gabrielle Alexander, Katie Finch, Adrienne Garcia, Winston Francisco School of Law; and the invaluable administrative assistance of Monica Oberthaler of Charlotte School of Law.

For the Fifth Edition, we thank Professor Suzanne Mawhinney and Library Research Assistant Javkhlan Enkhbayar of the University of San Francisco School of Law, and research assistants Lance Duroni, Mitchell Kiffmeyer, Allison Mignon, and Darrin Pribbernow of the Marquette University Law School, all of whom provided crucial research and technical assistance.

Our editors through the years at Carolina Academic Press and previously at LexisNexis, most especially Biz Ebben, our editor since the Third Edition who has been a constant for us in a sea of change, and CAP Book Designer Kathleen Soriano Taylor, have also contributed immeasurably to the quality of our final product.

Our deans and colleagues at our respective schools have also generously supported this endeavor in numerous ways, for which we also remain grateful.

We humbly thank them all.

Criminal Procedure:
The Post-Investigative Process

Chapter 1

Overview of the Criminal Justice System

A. Introduction

This book deals with a part of the criminal justice system: what happens between a suspect's arrest and the final disposition of the case via sentencing, direct appeal, or collateral (usually habeas corpus) review. The process itself is often complicated, varies considerably among jurisdictions, and depends to some extent on whether the crime charged is a misdemeanor or felony. Some procedural steps are rarely or never used in misdemeanor cases. Moreover, much of the criminal justice process is informal; precise legal rules play a surprisingly minor role in the routine processing of a typical case. The cast is large, consisting of defendants, victims, witnesses, police, prosecutors, defense lawyers, judges, and probation and parole officers.

This chapter provides a general overview of common features and factors that influence the criminal justice system and of the stages of the adjudicatory process covered later in this book. Obviously, a brief summary cannot be accurate for all jurisdictions. The attempt is to describe what would happen in a typical case in most American jurisdictions. Later chapters of this book provide a more detailed analysis of this process.

B. General Features

Despite some significant differences in the criminal justice systems of American jurisdictions, there are common features that heavily influence the way the system handles actual cases. A few of these commonalities are described below.

[1] Overworked Participants and Overcrowded Facilities

Every component of the criminal justice system purports to be overworked and underfunded. Police argue that they have too many duties, too many miles to patrol, too much paperwork, and too many lawbreakers to catch. Prosecutors, defense counsel, and judges maintain that they cannot try all the criminal cases assigned them. Many probation and parole officers have caseloads that make effective community supervision difficult, if not impossible. Jails and prisons are often so overcrowded that large numbers of additional prisoners cannot be sentenced to harsh penalties and incarcerated under conditions that would satisfy the constitutional restraints on punishment. In 2011, for example, federal prisons were operating at 139% of capacity.[1] Recent surveys have also found that state prison populations exceed maximum capacity.[2] These shortages of resources have a substantial impact on the criminal justice system's capacity to prosecute and punish criminals.

In order to meet such demands, vast and ever-increasing sums of money are spent each year on state and federal criminal justice systems. In 1982, federal, state, and local governments spent less than $36 billion on their criminal justice systems.[3] By 2006, federal, state, and local expenditures on police, courts, and corrections had exceeded $214 billion.[4] Of the $214.5 billion spent in 2006, about $99 billion was spent on police protection, $46.9 billion on judicial and legal costs, and $68.7 billion on corrections.[5] A 2013 report by the Administrative Office for the United States Courts indicates that the annual cost of incarceration in a federal prison is almost $28,000 (a daily cost of $79.16) per inmate, while the cost of probation supervision is just under $3,347 (a daily cost of $9.17) per person under supervised release.[6]

Correctional populations (including persons either incarcerated or under community supervision), and their corresponding costs, grew phenomenally in recent decades, but have shown a significant decrease in the past few years. From 1980 to 2006, total federal, state, and local expenditures on corrections increased from about $7 billion to almost $69 billion,[7] and the number of adults under correctional supervision, including probation and parole, increased from 1.8 million to about 7 million.[8] In 2015, more than 2.1 million persons were incarcerated in federal and state prisons or local jails.[9] In addition, just under 3.8 million persons were on probation, and approximately 870,500 were on parole.[10] In 2012, local jails supervised some 64,000 persons in the community through electronic monitoring, work release, or other alternative programs.[11]

After peaking in 2007, the United States correctional population has declined steadily. The 2.1 million estimate of incarcerated persons in 2015, referenced above, represents the lowest levels of incarceration nationwide since 2004. What has widely been described as an "Era of Mass Incarceration" beginning in the decades following federal sentencing reform legislation in the 1980s (discussed in Chapter 17) appears to be abating somewhat.

As the number of persons under correctional supervision grew drastically in those decades, crime has decreased significantly since 1993. Between 1997 and 2016, the estimated number of violent crimes decreased from 1,636,096 to 1,248,185,[12] and property crimes decreased even more dramatically, from 11,588,475 to 7,919,035 during the same period.[13] What kinds of inferences do you think can be drawn from the at least arguable anomaly of increased use of incarceration in times of decreasing crime?

Even with recent declines in correctional populations, the "system" remains hard-pressed to keep up with the demands placed on it. It is simply not feasible to prosecute and defend every case to the theoretical limits, and to apprehend and punish each law violator. As a result, jurisdictions have adapted to resource limits by adopting many shortcuts and "exit ramps," both formal and informal, throughout the criminal justice process.

[2] Discretion

A key aspect of the American criminal justice system is *discretion*, defined for our purposes as the legal power to make decisions with little specific direction or review from higher authorities or other branches of government. American criminal law gives the police, victim, defendant, prosecutor, judge, and defense lawyer all considerable discretion, most of which is exercised informally, in carrying out their functions. As discussed throughout this book and especially in Chapter 2, at many stages in the criminal justice process there is the discretion to "throw out" a case or to permit it to go to the next stage, or to not initiate a criminal case at all. The victim, for example, may or may not elect to report a crime to the police. In 2015, an estimated 9.5% of all violent crimes and 71.3% of property crimes were not reported by victims to police.[14] Once a report is made, the police may decide that there is too little evidence to justify an arrest, or may often choose, within their discretion, either to arrest a suspect or to issue a summons or citation in lieu of arrest.

After police make an arrest, the prosecutor has broad discretion in deciding whether or not to prosecute. The prosecutor may decide not to prosecute if there is inadequate proof to prosecute or he or she believes that somehow public policy would not be served by prosecution. The prosecutor also has broad discretion in determining which crimes and at what level of severity to charge, and which people to charge. For example, if two people commit a bank robbery, the prosecutor must decide whether to charge both of them with both robbery and conspiracy to rob the bank, or with only one of these offenses. This judgment may be based on a number of factors, such as the accused's criminal record, the severity of the crime, the role the victim played in the crime, the impact of prosecution on the accused and the victim, the need for deterrence, the likelihood of conviction, the need to obtain the defendant's cooperation in prosecuting other criminal suspects, and the availability of prosecutorial and correctional resources.

Similarly, the judge has immense discretion in criminal cases. He or she may decide to set a high or low bail, or not to require any form of bail or security at all while criminal charges are pending. Before trial, the judge may decide to have multiple defendants tried together ("joined") or separately ("severed") (see Chapter 8). At trial, the judge may cut off testimony from either side that the judge believes is redundant or irrelevant, and after conviction, the judge usually has considerable discretion in imposing the sentence.

The grand jury (see Chapter 7), if used, also has discretion in carrying out its duties. Although in theory, it must indict if it finds probable cause to believe that the defendant has committed a crime, the grand jury may decide not to indict, despite the existence of probable cause, for reasons of policy or sympathy, or based on its own notions of fairness and justice. It may also conduct its own investigation and issue an indictment for someone unsuspected by the police prior to the grand jury's investigation.

Often these exercises of discretion are poorly documented or not documented at all and are virtually unreviewable by higher judicial authority. While discretion at any stage of the process may be subject to abuse, discretion has the advantage of providing the actors in the system with a flexible process to deal with both unusual fact situations and inadequate resources. For example, a shortage of police officers or jail beds may cause some patrol officers to exercise their discretion and not charge someone with public drunkenness. The time and resources needed to arrest, process, and incarcerate the drunk offender may be needed for more important tasks. Some jurisdictions are attempting to control and structure this exercise of discretion by issuing written directives that provide police officers with guidance on how to deal with specific situations such as domestic violence and drunk driving. These directives often operate to limit or reduce an officer's discretion not to arrest if probable cause is present.

[3] Race and Gender

The roles that race and gender play in the criminal justice system are too complex to allow for complete discussion here, but they are among the most important social issues (some would say *the* most important) in contemporary criminal justice. To some extent these concerns are bottomed on data that show significant racial and gender differences in a number of relevant areas. An analysis of the basic statistics raises serious questions about the differential impact that the criminal justice system plays in the lives of different segments of the American community.

[a] Victimization

Race and gender are reflected in victimization data. Generally, blacks are more likely than whites to be victims of violent crime, other than murder. In 2015, the rate (per 1,000 persons age 12 and older) of victimization for violent crimes other than murder was about 17.4 for white persons, 22.6 for black persons, and 16.8 for Hispanic persons.[15] Whites are slightly more likely to be victims of murder or nonnegligent manslaughter.[16] Persons tabulated as "Other," including persons of two or more races, experienced higher rates of violent crimes than persons of other races.[17] Generally, whites are slightly less likely than blacks to be victims of property crime. In 2011, the estimated rate per 1,000 households of all property crimes was 130.2 when the head of household was white and 158.0 when the head of household was black.[18]

Most crime is intra-racial. In 2011 a study of murders and nonnegligent manslaughters that involved one offender and one victim, of the 2,950 crimes committed by black offenders, 2,459 victims were black. Of 3,062 crimes committed by white offenders, 2,777 victims were white.[19]

As for gender, males have historically been more likely than females to be victims of violent crimes. However, this trend reversed in 2015, with 15.9 males (per 1,000 persons age 12 or over), compared with 21.5 females, reported as being victims of violent crime other than murder.[20] Males are also much more likely than females to be the victims of homicide.[21] In 2011, 78% of murder victims were male.[22] However, females are far more likely to be victims of rape/sexual assault.[23]

[b] Arrest and Conviction

Most adults arrested in the United States are white and male. In 2009, almost 70% of persons, age 18 or over, arrested were white, 28% were black, and less than 2.5% were other races.[24] Seventy-five percent of persons arrested were male.[25] Most adults convicted of felonies are also white males. In federal courts, in 2010, 86.8% of those convicted were men, 27.6% were white, 20.7% were black, 48.1% were Hispanic, and 3.6% were other races.[26] As to ethnicity, 57.4% of convicted offenders were non-Hispanic and 42.6% were Hispanic.[27] In state courts in 2004, about 83% of persons convicted of felonies were male, 60% were white, 38% were black, and 2% were another race.[28] As of January 2018, 93.2% of federal inmates were male, 58.4% were white, and 37.9% were black.[29]

[c] Sentencing

The average length of sentences imposed on federal offenders is longer for blacks and males than for whites and females. In the period from federal fiscal year 2012 to 2016, of offenders sentenced to federal prison, black male offenders received sentences on average 19.1% longer than similarly situated white male offenders.[30] Female offenders convicted of violent offenses received median sentences of 46 months, and males received sentences of 63 months.[31]

Generally, the median sentences imposed in the other categories of offenses, such as property offenses, reflect the same trend. Sentencing factors that are not directly related to race or gender, such as the extent or severity of a defendant's previous criminal record, may explain some demographic differences in the length of sentences.

In the federal system, the issue of race is especially obvious for drug sentences. In 2015, 49.5% of federal prisoners were incarcerated for drug offenses.[32] In 2010, 78.5% of persons sentenced for crack cocaine in federal court were black, 7.3% white, 13.1% Hispanic, and 1.1% other.[33]

Since in the federal system sentences for offenses involving crack cocaine are longer than the sentences for offenses involving powder cocaine, many critics have argued that, in this and in other ways, the federal criminal justice system singles out blacks for the harshest drug sentences. In *Kimbrough v. United States*, 552 U.S. 85 (2007), the Supreme Court approved the practice of departing downward from the federal sentencing guidelines (discussed more fully in Chapter 16) to lessen this disparity. Further, recent changes in those guidelines have somewhat reduced the crack/powder sentencing disparity.

[4] The Prevalence of Guilty Pleas

Despite the widespread belief that criminal cases are routinely fought out in dramatic courtroom confrontations between a zealous prosecutor and a dedicated defense lawyer, the truth is that very few criminal cases go to trial. In virtually every American jurisdiction, approximately 96.8% of the criminal cases are disposed of by a guilty plea.[34] This is a process in which the defendant pleads guilty, neither side presents much if any proof, and the judge typically imposes a sentence that has been negotiated by the prosecution and defense. The judge, who usually agrees with whatever "deal" has been worked out in plea bargaining, may know little about the case or the defendant and may spend no more than a few minutes on the case before accepting the plea.

Because the deal must be acceptable to both prosecution and defense, it ordinarily involves give-and-take by the prosecutor and defense lawyer. The deal may involve concessions on the charges, the sentence, or both. For example, if the defendant is charged with three burglaries, the prosecution may agree to a deal in which the defendant pleads guilty to one burglary count and the other two are dismissed. The defendant is pleased because he or she will not risk a long cumulative sentence for three offenses. The prosecution is satisfied because the defendant will serve some prison time (or be placed on probation, if the prosecution finds that agreeable) and scarce prosecutorial resources will not have to be used on trying three cases. Another model is sentence bargaining, in which the prosecution and defense agree on the sentence that the judge should impose. At the sentencing hearing, both lawyers will advise the judge that they believe that a certain sentence, for example a five-year prison term, is appropriate. Usually the court will accept this recommendation and impose the agreed upon sentence.

As discussed in Chapter 11, views differ sharply, both among criminal justice practitioners and in society in general, as to whether plea bargaining, on the whole, is a good thing, a bad thing, or a "necessary evil." While the practice of plea bargaining has been severely questioned as both allowing the guilty to escape the full measure of justice and unduly pressuring the innocent to give up the right to trial by jury and other procedural protections, it has the advantages of allowing prosecution and defense to arrive at a shared assessment of what result is "just" in a given case, and also allows "the system" to process a large number of cases in a short period of time. A 2010 study of dispositions in federal courts found that the median time between filing charges and disposition was 6.1 months when there was a guilty plea and 15.3 months when there was a jury trial.[35]

[5] Differences Between Felonies and Misdemeanors

The American criminal justice system typically classifies a crime as either a felony or a misdemeanor. The obvious difference between the two is the maximum possible sentence. Ordinarily, a felony is punishable by incarceration in a state penal institution for a year or more, and a misdemeanor is punishable by a sentence of less than a year in a local or county jail or house of correction. There are other differences as well. Because a felony carries a substantial possible sentence, some procedural protections are only applicable to prosecutions for felonies. For example, in some jurisdictions a grand jury indictment is required only for felonies, but not for misdemeanors. Similarly, the federal constitutional right to trial by jury attaches to all felonies, but only to misdemeanors carrying a potential sentence of more than six months incarceration.

[6] The Cast: Lawyers and Others

The criminal justice system is comprised of many people with quite different training and responsibilities.

[a] Law Enforcement

The police constitute the "street" embodiment of the criminal justice system. They not only begin the processing of a criminal case, they also investigate it, testify (usually for the prosecution), and sometimes even staff the jails. In 2011 there were just over 1,000,000 full-time county and local law enforcement employees.[36] About 12% of the sworn officers were women.[37] In spite of the significant and dangerous responsibilities that police officers undertake, their salaries tend to be quite low. In 2007, the mean starting salary for entry-level local police officers in cities with populations of more than 10,000 people was about $38,000.[38]

[b] Prosecution

The prosecutor is the lawyer who is a government employee and represents the interests of the government and, in an indirect way, the victim. Ordinarily, the prosecutor maintains close ties with the local police, who assist the prosecutor by doing most or all of the investigation in criminal cases. Sometimes the prosecutor will also assist in training police officers, counseling them on search and arrest warrants and other legal matters, and conducting difficult investigations where legal expertise is needed. The prosecutor also plays a crucial, some would say controlling, role in the presentation of cases to the grand jury for indictment and in furnishing the grand jury with legal guidance.

In 2005 there were more than 78,000 people employed in various capacities in state and local prosecutors' offices.[39] Most prosecutors do not spend their entire professional career in this capacity. After a few years as a prosecutor, many go into private law practice, often representing criminal defendants or civil litigants, which may be far more lucrative than service as a prosecutor. New prosecutors often start out drawing up criminal complaints or handling minor cases, perhaps misdemeanors or traffic offenses. Over time, with more experience, they are given responsibility for more serious criminal matters, including felony trials and grand jury proceedings.

In the federal system, each district has a United States Attorney, appointed by the President (upon confirmation by the Senate) and who serves at the pleasure of the President. The United States Attorney recommends to the Attorney General the appointment of Assistant United States Attorneys. Unlike the United States Attorney, however, they receive civil service protection. Federal prosecutions are usually conducted by an Assistant United States Attorney, although the Justice Department or another federal agency may also participate in or even conduct the prosecution in some situations.

The head prosecutor for a state judicial district or county is almost always an elected official and is usually a full-time prosecutor. Their exact titles vary; the most common are District Attorney, County Attorney, Commonwealth Attorney, Prosecutor, Solicitor, and Prosecuting Attorney. Most serve a four-year term and appoint assistant prosecutors. While most prosecutors are full-time government employees, sometimes, especially in rural areas, assistant prosecutors may be hired to prosecute on a part-time basis.

[c] Defense

Right to counsel. Under the Sixth Amendment to the United States Constitution, the criminal defendant is entitled to be represented by counsel before being sentenced to incarceration of any length, *see, e.g., Scott v. Illinois*, 440 U.S. 367 (1979), or to probation if the defendant may be incarcerated for violating the conditions of probation, *see Alabama v. Shelton*, 536 U.S. 654 (2002). In such cases, counsel must be provided free of charge to indigent defendants.

Appointed defense counsel. Defense lawyers may be either public employees or private lawyers. If a public employee, the defense counsel will usually be a public defender. Most commonly, the head public defender is elected or appointed and the assistant public defenders are appointed by the head public defender. Many public defenders are recent law school graduates with little experience who work for fairly low salaries. If the office is large, the novice public defender may handle misdemeanor or traffic cases, then move up to more difficult assignments after gaining some hands-on experience.

Retained defense counsel. Private defense counsel in criminal cases often come from small firms or are solo practitioners. Often their practice includes areas other than criminal law. In many jurisdictions, a relatively small number of criminal defense lawyers handle a large number of criminal cases. Sometimes a county will have no public defender or will need defense services beyond those provided by the public defender. In this situation the county may contract with a criminal defense lawyer or firm to provide defense services to some or all indigents in that county, often at a very modest hourly rate.

Lawyer's fee. If a private lawyer is retained or hired to represent a non-indigent defendant, very often the lawyer will require that all or a large part of the fee be paid in cash and in advance. After a client is convicted, the unsuccessful criminal defendant often will refuse or be unable to pay the defense lawyer. In 2004 and 2006, some 80% of state felony defendants (in large counties) were represented by public defenders or assigned counsel.[40] White collar defendants were far more likely than violent offender defendants to have private defense counsel. Interestingly, the studies have found guilty plea and conviction rates to be almost identical irrespective of whether defense counsel was retained or appointed, and that state inmates who used appointed counsel had *shorter* sentences than those with retained counsel. *Id.* Why do you think this is the case?

[d] Judiciary

Judges in criminal cases range from specialists, who only handle criminal cases and may have been criminal practitioners before coming to the bench, to generalists who handle both criminal and civil cases and come to the bench from broadly diverse prior legal backgrounds. In the federal system, as of 2010 there were 678 district judgeships authorized.[41] In the same year there were 167 circuit (appellate) judgeships.[42] While virtually all state judges are lawyers, in a few jurisdictions judges at the lowest court level (such as Justice of the Peace) might not be.

Criminal cases often involve more than one tier of court. For example, preliminary matters (such as bail, warrants, and preliminary hearings) may be resolved by a judge of the lowest court level. Sometimes, as in the federal system, this person is referred to as a *magistrate* (or *magistrate judge*). Subsequent proceedings may be conducted exclusively or primarily by a judge of the court of general jurisdiction. Appeals usually go to the next higher court, although in capital cases sometimes the intermediate appellate courts are bypassed.

[e] Probation and Parole

Probation and parole officers also play an important role in criminal cases. These civil servants often possess at least a bachelor's degree and must undergo regular updating and training during the work year. Frequently, probation officers will prepare a *presentence report* to provide the judge with information about the offense and the offender. If the defendant is placed on probation, a probation officer will supervise the offender, perhaps by meeting with him or her on a weekly or monthly basis. After incarceration and service of a specified fraction of the maximum sentence, the offender may be placed on parole or supervised release, where his or her activities will be supervised by a parole officer.

Inadequate resources have caused some probation departments to be terribly understaffed. In 2009, in the Federal Probation System, some 5,000 probation officers supervised just over 124,000 persons.[43] Parole departments experience the same shortages of resources and understaffing as do probation departments.

[7] The Scene: Federal and State

By far, most criminal proceedings take place in state and local courts. In 2010, for example, 89,741 people were convicted in federal courts.[44] In 2006, more than

1.1 million felony convictions occurred in state courts.[45] Additional convictions occurred in various municipal courts. State courts as a general rule have jurisdiction to prosecute the vast bulk of crimes that evolved from the common law; federal criminal prosecution occurs far less frequently, usually pertaining to offenses against federal property, federal personnel, or a federal agency, or involving bank robbery or complex criminal enterprises or large-scale interstate drug or weapons trafficking.

In recent decades, as Congress has taken a more active interest in crime control, federal criminal jurisdiction has expanded somewhat into areas that were traditionally matters of state law enforcement, a trend that some, including the late Chief Justice William H. Rehnquist, have decried as "creeping federalization" of our criminal laws. For certain offenses which Congress has brought within federal jurisdiction, there may be a choice between prosecution by either federal or state authorities, or there may even be both federal and state prosecutions for the same offenses, without violating the Double Jeopardy prohibition of the Fifth Amendment. This topic is discussed more extensively in Chapter 15. There may be major differences and consequences to a defendant between being prosecuted in a state or a federal jurisdiction, both procedural (e.g., right to indictment or not) and substantive (e.g., potentially great differences in severity of sentence if the defendant is convicted).

C. Stages of the Criminal Process

[1] Complaint

At an early stage of most criminal proceedings, a complainant (a citizen or law enforcement officer who knows or believes that a crime was committed) will sign, under oath, a *complaint*, which is a formal charge of criminal activity. The complaint will often briefly describe the basic facts of the crime, indicate what offense is being charged, and sometimes cite the relevant section of the criminal code believed to be violated. Usually a lower level judge, sometimes called a *magistrate*, must also sign the complaint. If the complaint provides a sufficient basis to show probable cause to believe a crime was committed and the defendant committed it, the magistrate may issue an arrest warrant authorizing law enforcement officers to take the accused person into custody. Chapter 4 deals with the complaint in criminal cases.

[2] Custody

When a police officer has probable cause to believe a person has committed a criminal offense, the officer may arrest the suspect, or (typically in the case of a traffic infraction or other minor offense) may serve the suspect with a *summons*, sometimes called a *citation*. The summons provides formal notice of the charge(s) and orders the suspect to appear in court at a stated time. Failure to appear in court at the time stated on the summons may result in a court-issued *bench warrant* for the suspect's arrest, and possible additional charges of *contempt* or *failure to appear.* The decision whether to arrest or issue a summons for a lesser offense falls within the officer's *discretion. Atwater v. City of Lago Vista,* 532 U.S. 318 (2001).

In serious cases and some minor ones, the first step in a criminal prosecution is usually arrest of the accused by law enforcement officers. In 2011, there were more than 9.5 million non-traffic arrests in the United States.[46] The arrest may occur at the crime scene immediately after the crime or may occur days or years later after a substantial investigation. Depending on the circumstances, the arrest may occur with or without a warrant. The validity of the arrest may be important in assessing the admissibility of evidence obtained during the arrest (the law of arrest, including the many complex Fourth Amendment issues, is beyond the scope of this book).

Booking process at jail. Generally, when a suspect is arrested and taken into custody, he or she will be transported to the police station and *booked.* During this administrative process, jail officials obtain and record information about the accused. The booking process may involve fingerprinting and photographing, a search of the suspect's clothing and belongings, an inventory of the possessions in the person's pocket, purse, and packages, the issuance of prison clothing to wear while incarcerated, the opportunity for the accused to make one or more telephone calls, and sometimes even a lineup and an interrogation by a police officer. During the booking process, police also run the suspect's fingerprints and other identifying information through national databases, to see if the suspect is wanted by other authorities for other criminal offenses, escape from prison, probation or parole violation, or immigration offenses. In *Florence v. Board of Chosen Freeholders of County of Burlington*, 566 U.S. 318 (2012), the Supreme Court, by a 5–4 vote, upheld the practice of strip-searching newly received detainees, even those detained for minor offenses, in order to deter and detect the presence of contraband in pretrial detention facilities. Similarly, the Court also held that police may take a DNA sample using a mouth swab when a person is arrested for a serious crime is booked. *Maryland v. King*, 569 U.S. 435 (2013).

Release from custody. If the accused is taken into custody, as discussed more fully in Chapter 5, different persons (i.e., *bail commissioners* or judges) will determine whether and under what conditions the accused will be released from custody until the case is disposed of by trial or other means. A 2006 study of state felony defendants in the 75 largest counties found that 58% were released from custody following an arrest.[47] Eighteen percent of released felons failed to appear in court as scheduled.[48]

In the federal system, in 2004, a pretrial detention hearing was held in 56.1% of the cases. Of those, almost 79% resulted in pretrial detention.[49] In that year, federal releasees committed no violations while on release in 80.2% of the cases.[50] Only 2.2% of those released by federal courts failed to appear.[51]

Station house bail. Frequently, jail officials are authorized to use *station house bail* to release the arrestee. The jailor, or some other officer authorized to receive bail payments, will determine the financial conditions of release by consulting a written schedule that applies to all similar cases. For example, the bail schedule may authorize the sheriff to release alleged shoplifters upon payment of $250. This sum is designed to guarantee that the offender will show up for trial. If the offender is unsuccessful in obtaining station house bail, the issue of release becomes a judicial matter. The arrestee will soon be brought before a judge or magistrate who will decide the conditions of release. These may include posting an amount of money or satisfying other release conditions (such as staying within the county, or surrender of the defendant's passport to the court).

Professional bond services. In some jurisdictions professional bail *bondspersons* are available to post amounts required as bail. Bondspersons earn a fee, usually approximately 10% of the bail amount, in exchange for their promise to pay the court the total amount of bail if the offender does not appear for trial. In the shoplifting hypothetical above, the offender would pay the bondsperson 25 dollars as a fee. The bondsperson would then sign a promise (i.e., *bond*) to pay the full $250 if the offender does not appear for trial. If the offender appears for trial, he or she does not get back the $25; this sum represents the bonding company's fee for its services. In cases where the defendant does not appear for trial (usually referred to as "*defaulting*" or "bail jumping"), the judge has the discretion to order the bonding company to pay the court clerk the entire sum of the bond ($250 in the above example). But if the bonding company can produce the defaulter within a reasonable time after the court date, many courts will routinely "reward" the bonding company by not ordering it to pay the amount of the bond. This system provides bonding companies with a financial incentive to locate defaulting criminal defendants.

In some jurisdictions, the bail bondsperson is replaced by a "cash bail" system in which the defendant posts 10% of the bail amount with a court clerk. If the defendant appears at trial and at all other required court proceedings, he or she gets back all or almost all of the 10% paid to the clerk. If the defendant fails to appear as required, the court can issue an order forfeiting the 10% already paid and decreeing that the defaulter owes the remaining 90% as a penalty for not appearing at the scheduled hearing. An arrest warrant will also be issued under these circumstances. Failure to appear may also be prosecuted as a separate crime.

[3] Initial Appearance

Soon after arrest, a criminal accused is brought before a judge, usually one presiding over the lowest level court in the jurisdiction. Ordinarily this hearing, frequently called an *initial* (or first) a*ppearance* or an *arraignment*, as discussed in Chapter 4, is brief and relatively informal. Here the accused is formally notified of the charges and advised of basic constitutional rights, and various routine procedural matters are resolved. An attorney may be appointed if, as is often the case, the accused is indigent. The issue of bail is addressed if the accused is still in custody. At the initial appearance, or at any later time while charges are pending, the judge may also review and alter the conditions of release, and either allow the accused to be released pending trial or set more stringent release conditions or revoke bail if additional favorable or unfavorable information comes to the court's attention. Finally, the judge will set a date for the next step, usually a preliminary hearing, to be held in a week or two.

If the defendant has been arrested without an arrest warrant, a common occurrence throughout the country, the judge at the initial appearance may have an additional task (also discussed in Chapter 4): to determine whether there is probable cause to detain the accused. Since the lack of a warrant means that no judge has assessed whether there is probable cause to deprive the accused of his or her freedom, the judge must decide this question and either issue an arrest warrant or make a finding of probable cause if the accused is to remain in custody. This judicial determination is required by the Supreme Court decision in *Gerstein v. Pugh*, 420 U.S. 103 (1975), and is sometimes made at the defendant's initial appearance, or may sometimes be made earlier by the judge, *ex parte*.

Often the initial appearance lasts only a few minutes. A number of initial appearances may be scheduled at the same time and held one after the other. Depending on the jurisdiction defense counsel may or may not be present, and the prosecutor may address only the issue of release conditions. Often the court will assign counsel to an indigent defendant at the initial appearance. No evidence is taken other than information needed to determine probable cause, the conditions of release, or eligibility for appointed counsel.

In some locales the initial appearance is conducted by videoconference. The defendant is physically located in a room at the jail and the judge is situated in the courthouse. A video camera and monitor at both locations allow the participants to see and speak with one another. This procedure reduces both the expense of transporting defendants from jail to court, and the risk of an escape attempt before, during, or after the initial appearance.

[4] Preliminary Examination

Probable cause. A criminal accused is often entitled to a *preliminary examination* (or preliminary hearing), which is an adversary proceeding presided over by a judge (without a jury) and conducted by a criminal defense attorney and a prosecutor. This proceeding is discussed in Chapter 6. The usual purpose of this proceeding is to determine whether there is *probable cause* to believe that (1) a crime was committed and (2) the accused committed it. This probable cause determination is designed to ensure that citizens do not have to endure the rigors and expenses of a criminal trial if there is not enough proof to show probable cause. The probable cause standard is less demanding than the burden of proving guilt beyond a reasonable doubt at trial, but still generally requires the prosecution to show that the defendant, more likely than not, committed the crime(s) charged. Jurisdictions differ as to whether the formal rules of evidence or a less restrictive set of evidence principles apply in preliminary examinations.

Entitlement to examination. Whether a particular defendant is entitled to a preliminary examination varies considerably among the jurisdictions and may depend on the particular procedural posture of the case. In many jurisdictions the defendant is entitled to a preliminary examination unless a grand jury has already issued an indictment. If, as explained below, the jurisdiction permits use of an *information* (formal charge by the prosecutor) rather than an indictment, the defendant is usually entitled to a preliminary examination after the prosecutor signs the information.

If probable cause is found at the preliminary examination, in many jurisdictions the case is *bound over* or transferred to the grand jury. If probable cause is not found, the case is dismissed by the preliminary examination judge, but ordinarily the prosecutor can still present the case to the grand jury anyway. If the grand jury then issues an indictment, the case will be scheduled for trial. It is also possible that the judge, after conducting the preliminary examination, may find probable cause for a lesser crime (perhaps a misdemeanor instead of a felony) than the one initially charged.

Strategy at preliminary examination. Because the probable cause standard is not as rigorous as the burden of proving guilt beyond a reasonable doubt at trial, it is relatively rare that probable cause is not found. Accordingly, often defense counsel will not make a serious effort to use the preliminary examination to have all or some of the charges dismissed or reduced. Instead, the defense lawyer will focus on discovering information about the prosecution's case. Although the defense has the option of calling witnesses, usually the defense will call no witnesses and instead will spend its time cross-examining prosecution witnesses to discover their knowledge of the case and evaluate their likely credibility as witnesses if the case should go to trial. This enables the defense to learn about the prosecution's case without disclosing much, if anything, about the defense's strategy and proof.

[5] Information or Grand Jury Indictment

In perhaps half the American jurisdictions, a criminal case (or at least a felony) can only be tried if the grand jury has returned an *indictment*, discussed in Chapter 7. If the jurisdiction does not utilize a grand jury or the defendant waives indictment by a grand jury, the prosecutor can proceed by *information*. An information is a formal charge by the prosecutor, stating that a named person is charged with committing a specified crime.

Organization. The grand jury is a group of 13–23 citizens usually selected from the same large group of eligible jurors (the jury pool) as the petit or trial jury. One model of the grand jury mandates that at least 12 votes (out of a larger number of grand jurors) in favor of an indictment are necessary for the indictment to be issued; the decision need not be unanimous. A survey of federal grand juries found that in 2010 the average federal grand jury session was attended by approximately 20 grand jurors, lasted almost five hours, and indicted 7.6 persons.[52]

Foreperson. The foreperson or leader of the grand jury chairs the sessions and reports to the judge on behalf of the grand jury. Sometimes, the foreperson must sign the indictment on behalf of the grand jury members.

Functions. The grand jury has several functions. Its primary function, by design, is to serve as a check on prosecutorial abuse by screening cases that do not have enough merit to justify continued processing through the criminal justice system. The test is whether there is probable cause to believe that (1) a crime was committed and (2) the defendant committed it. If the grand jury finds that probable cause is present, a *true bill* or indictment is issued. If probable cause is not found, a *no true bill* is returned and the case is dismissed, but often it can be resubmitted to the same or a different grand jury if the prosecution wants to try again for an indictment.

Ordinarily, the prosecuting attorney serves as counsel to the grand jury, facilitates the issuance of subpoenas for witnesses, documents, and other physical evidence; prepares cases for it to consider, instructs the grand jury on the applicable law, may recommend whether to issue or not issue an indictment, and drafts indictments for the grand jury to vote on. This close contact between prosecutor and grand jury has led many people to argue that the grand jury does not really fulfill its intended function of shielding citizens against meritless charges, but is rather a "rubber stamp" for the prosecution. This allegation is supported by studies that show that grand juries issue an indictment in approximately 95% of the cases brought before them. A number of states have done away with the fiction of grand jury independence and protection and either abolished it altogether or severely curtailed its use, allowing the prosecutor instead to initiate criminal charges by filing an information with the court.

The second function of the grand jury is to investigate possible violations of the criminal law. A member of the grand jury, the prosecutor, or a private citizen may suggest that the grand jury investigate a person, place, or business for possible criminal activity. If the grand jury chooses to launch this probe, it may use its power to issue *subpoenas* to compel people to testify and bring records and other things with them to the grand jury. If the grand jury finds probable cause to believe that a crime has been committed, it can issue a *presentment*, which is a formal allegation that a named person or business has committed a crime. The presentment serves exactly the same function as an indictment. Indeed, in many jurisdictions the term "presentment" is not used; the grand jury issues indictments only.

A third function of the grand jury is to oversee some public facilities or activities. In some jurisdictions, for example, the grand jury inspects certain public facilities, such as jails, and issues a report of its findings to a judicial or executive officer. The report can provide the basis for corrective action to eliminate problems identified by the grand jurors.

Secrecy. One of the unusual features of the grand jury is *secrecy.* In almost all jurisdictions the grand jury operates away from the public eye. Its sessions are closed to the public, the identity and testimony of witnesses are often secret, and grand jurors are often barred from disclosing matters they have discussed.

Subpoenas and immunity. Another important aspect of the grand jury is its legal authority to issue subpoenas, orders compelling a person to testify before or bring materials to the grand jury. A person disobeying a subpoena may be held in *contempt* of court, which can be punished by a fine or even incarceration. The grand jury in many jurisdictions may also grant or request witnesses *immunity* to encourage or require testimony from people who fear that their testimony may incriminate themselves. A grant of immunity means, in most instances, that the government cannot use the person's grand jury testimony as evidence against that person in a later criminal prosecution. Accordingly, a person granted immunity cannot refuse to testify by invoking the Fifth Amendment's privilege against self-incrimination. The immunity essentially satisfies the witness's Fifth Amendment rights by, in theory, removing the possibility of compelled self-incrimination, for the testimony cannot be used as direct or indirect evidence to incriminate the witness.

Schedule. The grand jury usually meets over a period of months or even years, but the sessions are often held many days apart. For example, a grand jury may meet one day a month for six months. The prosecutor routinely presents each case to the grand jury.

Evidence. Usually only evidence supporting the existence of probable cause is presented, but sometimes, even though not constitutionally required, countervailing evidence is also made known to the grand jury. No judge attends grand jury sessions, and usually the formal rules of evidence are not used. An indictment may be based, at least in part, on hearsay.

[6] Arraignment and Plea

If a grand jury issues an indictment or if a case is initiated by information, the accused is brought before a judge for an *arraignment*, which is much like the initial appearance which follows the defendant's arrest. At this brief hearing, usually a prosecutor and defense lawyer will be present. The defendant will be informed of the charges (i.e., of the contents of the indictment or information) and given a chance to plead. There may be several options: guilty, not guilty, not guilty by reason of insanity (sometimes part of a "not guilty" verdict rather than a separate plea), *nolo contendere* ("I do not wish to contest the charges and I agree to be punished as if I pled guilty but I do not admit guilt"), and perhaps others.

If the defendant decides to plead guilty (either at the arraignment or at any later time), the judge will inform the defendant of the consequences of the plea, including the waiver of various rights, and then almost always will accept the plea. The defendant may then be sentenced or a decision on sentencing will be postponed until a later date. More often than not, however, the defendant offers a plea of not guilty at the arraignment.

If the defendant pleads not guilty, the court will set a date for trial. At this time, questions of bail or other conditions of release can be, but usually are not, revisited. A defendant in jail awaiting trial may request a reduction in the amount of bail or some other order that will permit him or her to be released until the trial. The prosecution may ask for additional conditions of release or even for the revocation of release on bail.

[7] Motions

Either before or during trial, a party (usually the defense) may file one or more *motions* with the court. A motion, discussed more fully in Chapter 9, is a request for a court order. The motions may address virtually any issue. Some pretrial motions (generally referred to as *dispositive motions*) may seek to dismiss charges on grounds such as statute of limitations, double jeopardy, or a fatal flaw in the indictment, while other motions seek to gain some tactical advantage at or before trial, e.g., to order discovery, or to limit the evidence that will be used at trial.

Motions *in limine*, made just before the start of trial, may seek to limit or preclude certain lines of questioning at trial, or to affect the order or the manner in which witnesses and evidence will be presented. Motions made during trial may, for example, ask the court to dismiss some or all of the charges at the conclusion of the prosecution's case, to strike or exclude evidence or testimony, or, in extreme circumstances, to declare a mistrial.

While many motions are written, others, especially ones made during the heat of trial, are oral. Sometimes the other side will file a written response to a written motion. The court may hold a hearing on the motion and will then issue an order denying or granting all or part of it.

[8] Discovery

While discovery in civil cases is often extensive, it is usually quite limited in criminal cases, as discussed more fully in Chapter 10. The rules of criminal procedure often mandate that relatively few items be disclosed to the other side, although the Constitution requires that the prosecution disclose some information that will assist the defense. Interrogatories and depositions are rare or nonexistent in criminal cases. Accordingly, in lieu of formal discovery opportunities, both the defense and prosecution will use each hearing and motion to learn about the other side's case. In addition, in some jurisdictions there are informal discovery practices that give the two sides greater access to information than would be required by the rules of criminal procedure. Some prosecutors have an *open file* policy that gives defense lawyers full access to all or most information available to the prosecutors.

[9] Pretrial Conference

Days or even weeks before trial, the judge may convene a pretrial conference to clarify the issues and resolve various procedural matters, such as discovery problems and scheduling. Although in many jurisdictions this practice is permissible because of the judge's inherent authority to manage the case, some jurisdictions have enacted a rule of procedure specifically addressing the pretrial conference. Federal Rules of Criminal Procedure, Rule 17.1 provides, "On its own, or on a party's motion, the court may hold one or more pretrial conferences to promote a fair and expeditious trial." A few statutes even require a pretrial conference in unusual situations.

The exact content of the pretrial conference differs from judge to judge. To encourage candor, Rule 17.1 provides that admissions made by the defendant or defense counsel during pretrial conferences are not admissible against the defendant unless reduced to writing and signed by both the defendant and defense counsel. A pretrial conference is not authorized under Rule 17.1 if the defendant is not represented by counsel. Rule 43(b)(3) of the Federal Rules of Criminal Procedure suggests that the defendant need not be present at a pretrial conference.

[10] Trial

At trial, the defendant will usually be represented by retained or appointed counsel while the government will be represented by a lawyer from the prosecutor's office. Criminal trials ordinarily do not last very long. In 2010, for example, approximately 77% of federal criminal trials took 1–2 days, while only 0.2% took 10 days or more.[53] The general format of the trial follows.

[a] Right to Jury Trial or Trial by a Judge

If the case goes to trial, in any but the most minor cases the defendant is entitled to have a jury decide guilt or innocence. *See* Chapter 13. However, some defendants, for a variety of possible reasons, choose to waive their right to a trial by jury and have their guilt or innocence determined by a judge. A trial conducted by a judge sitting without a jury is often referred to as a *bench trial.*

[b] Jury Selection

Traditionally the trial (or *petit*) jury is comprised of 12 citizens, although in a few jurisdictions juries of less than 12 (but more than five) are used in some or all criminal cases. Often one or more alternate jurors are selected to serve if one of the regular jurors must be replaced because of illness or some other reason. In almost all states the jury verdict must be unanimous either to convict or acquit; however, this is not a constitutional requirement. The jury is selected from a *jury pool* or *venire*, a large number of possible jurors selected by some random process. The actual jury, of 12 persons or less, is selected from this larger group through a process called *voir dire*, during which the judge and often the lawyers for both prosecution and defense question jurors to determine possible bias and competence to serve. Although there is no single method of winnowing the total number of potential jurors down to the needed number, both the prosecutor and defense counsel are permitted to challenge and exclude some jurors.

Challenges. During the selection process, potential jurors may be excluded either *for cause* or by a *peremptory challenge.* A challenge for cause is determined by the judge, who may disqualify a potential juror for such reasons as a physical or mental inability to serve, a problem with devoting adequate time to jury duty, or for potential bias which may include a relationship to one of the parties or lawyers. A peremptory challenge, on the other hand, is made by either the defense or prosecuting attorney for any reason, other than race and gender. There are no limits on the number of challenges for cause, but there are significant numerical limits on peremptory challenges. For example, a state statute may provide each side with eight peremptory challenges. Often trial lawyers will use their experience and instinct as guidance in using a peremptory challenge to exclude a potential juror.

Pay. Jurors are paid for their services, although the amount is hardly adequate. As of October 2013, juror fees were $40–$50 per day for each federal juror.[54] In a recent survey of juror fees payable in each state, the fees paid to each juror ranged from $5 to $50 per day.[55]

[c] Swearing in the Jury

A jury is usually "sworn in" after it is selected. This entails having the jurors repeat a short oath that obligates them to be fair, listen to all sides, and obey the law. It is at this juncture that *jeopardy* attaches (see Chapter 15 for full discussion of Double Jeopardy issues).

[d] Initial Jury Instruction

Sometimes the jury is then given an introductory instruction by the judge. This brief lecture may thank the jurors for their service, inform them of their duties, and perhaps describe in general terms what is going to happen, and, in some locales, outline the law to be applied in the case.

[e] Opening Statement

Each side ordinarily will make an opening statement, outlining the evidence and theory it will present. Traditionally the prosecution goes first, followed by the defense, although the defense may choose to defer its opening statement until the prosecution has rested its case. Many judges encourage short opening statements on the theory that the evidence, not the opening statement, is the important information for the trier of fact.

[f] Prosecution's Case

The prosecution presents its *case in chief* first. It will call witnesses and present evidence and testimony (through *direct examination*) that, the prosecution hopes, will prove each element of the crime(s) charged beyond a reasonable doubt. After each of these witnesses testifies for the prosecution, the defense has the opportunity to *cross examine* the witness. The prosecution may then be permitted to ask additional, but limited, questions on *redirect* exam. Sometimes the defense can then ask more questions on *recross* examination.

[g] Defense Motion to Dismiss

After the prosecution has presented its witnesses and any physical evidence and has rested its case, the defense lawyer may make an oral motion to dismiss all or part of the charges. The defense may argue that the prosecution's witnesses have not proven an element of one or more of the offenses charged. While this motion is usually unsuccessful, sometimes the judge will grant the motion and dismiss or reduce some or all of the alleged offenses.

[h] Defense's Case

If the motion to dismiss does not end the trial, the next step is for the defense to present its case. The defense counsel may introduce witnesses and other evidence to counter a prosecution witness's testimony or to prove some issue, such as an affirmative defense, not addressed by the prosecution. For example, the prosecution may present proof that a homicide was an intentional killing of the defendant's enemy. The defense may offer evidence that the killing was in self-defense. The prosecution has the right to cross-examine defense witnesses, including the defendant him- or herself if the defendant should choose to testify.

The defendant is not obligated to testify or to present any defense at all, and may choose to simply argue to the jury (or judge) that the prosecution has failed to prove the defendant's guilt beyond a reasonable doubt.

[i] Other Proof

After the defense has presented its case, the court may permit the prosecution to put on more evidence in *rebuttal* to counter that presented by the defense. The usual order of direct, cross, redirect, recross, etc. is used. If the defense needs to put on proof to counter the state's rebuttal proof, the court may permit *surrebuttal* evidence to be introduced. Rarely will the judge exercise his or her discretion to permit proof after surrebuttal.

[j] Closing Arguments

After both sides have presented their proof and cross-examined the other side's witnesses and rested, each side is permitted to make a closing argument. Ordinarily, each side will thank the jury for its patience, summarize the proof its side has offered, and minimize the probative value of some or all the proof presented by the other side. Usually, the prosecution will make the first closing argument, the defense will make the second, and, in many jurisdictions, the prosecution will have a brief chance to make a final argument responding to the defense counsel's closing remarks.

[k] Jury Instructions

Following the closing argument, the judge gives the jury its instructions or *jury charge*. This lecture informs the jury of its responsibilities, jury procedures, and the applicable law. For example, in a case involving a homicide the jury may be told about such matters as the burden of proof, the jury's role in ascertaining the facts, the selection of a foreperson, and the definitions of the crimes with which the accused is charged.

Opportunity to propose or oppose instructions. Usually counsel for both sides will have an opportunity to suggest instructions for the judge to use in the jury charge. These suggested instructions are presented to and ruled on by the judge prior to closing argument, so that counsel can find out before making the final argument how the judge will charge the jury. Sometimes the charge is also "reduced to writing" and a copy is given to each juror to use during the deliberations. The correctness (or not) of jury instructions is often a key issue for appeal, so it is of great importance that both sides make timely requests for charges that they think are appropriate, and objections and exceptions to jury charges that they believe may be in error. Failure to object to an allegedly erroneous charge will usually result in a waiver of the issue on appeal.

[l] Jury Deliberations

The jury will then "retire" or go to the jury room, usually located near the courtroom. Only the jurors are permitted in this room. Often the first step is for the jury to select a *foreperson* to organize the deliberations and represent the jury in communications with the judge. In some jurisdictions, the foreperson may be chosen by lot, or may be appointed by the judge.

More information. Sometimes during its deliberations the jury may feel that it needs more information. For example, after an hour of discussion about the case the jury may discover that individual jurors have different recollections about the content of a particular witness's testimony or different interpretations of several words in the jury instructions. The foreperson will communicate this in writing to the judge who ordinarily will convene a hearing to resolve the issues. Counsel for both sides and the defendant will be present. The judge will then respond to the jury's request, usually after receiving suggestions from both sides. Sometimes the court will refuse to answer an improper question, perhaps even instructing the jury not to consider the issue raised by the question. For other questions, the judge may order the stenographer to read to the jury some or all of the testimony of a witness, or the court may repeat or explain the part of the jury instruction that is confusing.

Unanimity. In most but not all jurisdictions, the jury decision must be unanimous. A conviction occurs if all 12 (sometimes fewer) jurors find the defendant guilty beyond a reasonable doubt. In these jurisdictions, if all 12 vote that the state has not proved each element of the crime beyond a reasonable doubt, the defendant is acquitted and the charges are dismissed. In some jurisdictions, however, a jury may return a verdict of guilty or not guilty on a less-than-unanimous vote.

Burden of proof. The burden of proof on defenses such as insanity or self-defense is more complex, with several variations. The defendant may, in some jurisdictions, be required to both offer proof ("*burden of production*") and persuade the trier of fact ("*burden of persuasion*") as to the existence of a defense. Where the burden of proof regarding an affirmative defense is placed on the defendant, the usual standard of proof is for the defendant to establish the defense by a "preponderance of the evidence." Another model that some states use for certain defenses is that the defendant must first raise the defense by offering some evidence to support it (sometimes called the "*burden of going forward*"), and then the burden shifts to the prosecution to disprove the defense beyond a reasonable doubt.

Hung jury. If after extensive deliberation the jury cannot reach a verdict (commonly referred to as a *hung jury*), the judge then declares a *mistrial* and the prosecution is usually free to try the case again at a later date. The Double Jeopardy Clause does not bar a retrial following a hung jury. Statistics show that criminal trials almost always result in a conviction.

[m] Announcement of Jury Verdict

Once the jury has made a decision, all jurors return to the courtroom where the foreperson informs the judge of the decision. The jury's written decision will be signed by the foreperson or all jurors, depending on the jurisdiction. Either the foreperson or the judge will announce the verdict to the defendant and everyone else in the court room. Usually the defendant and defense counsel will stand when the verdict is disclosed. Sometimes the jurors are polled. This means that each juror is asked in open court whether the announced guilty verdict reflects his or her own vote.

If the defendant is acquitted, in the usual case he or she is immediately released from custody and is free to return home unless the defendant is also facing other untried charges. If the jury finds the defendant guilty, the judge will again consider the issue of bail or custody pending sentencing and appeal.

[11] Sentencing Hearing

In the typical case, there will be a delay between a jury verdict of guilty (or a defendant's guilty plea) and the imposition of sentence, as discussed in Chapter 16. During this time a probation or other court officer may prepare a *presentence report*, which provides data about the offense and the offender. This social history may be based in part on information supplied by the defendant and defense counsel. Ordinarily the defendant will be given access to all or most of the presentence report, and may even submit a more favorable or inclusive report for the court's consideration. The police officers involved in the case may also be asked for their version of the offense.

Hearing. If no agreement has been reached between the prosecution and defense, the judge will often conduct a full sentencing hearing. The prosecution and defense will be permitted to offer proof and arguments on the proper sentence, although the strict rules of evidence that apply at trial typically do not apply at the sentencing hearing. The defendant is also permitted to speak ("*allocution*"). In some jurisdictions, the crime victim (or a family member of a deceased victim) is permitted to describe the crime's effect upon the victim or survivors through the presentation of a written *victim impact statement* or by addressing the court directly ("*victim allocution*"). The judge may also read the sentencing report and hear from the probation officer who prepared it. Finally, the judge will impose sentence on the defendant. The range of permissible sentences extends from non-custodial to custodial to capital, depending on the offense and the jurisdiction.

[12] Non-Custodial Sentences

Unless the defendant has been convicted or has pleaded guilty to a crime that carries mandatory incarceration, the judge may see fit to place the defendant on *probation* or impose a fine or some other obligation on the defendant if the judge does not believe that the facts of the case or the defendant's prior history require a sentence of incarceration. A defendant placed on probation must abide by the conditions of probation that the court has imposed, and probation may be revoked and the defendant incarcerated if the defendant commits a serious violation of probation conditions. Similarly, a defendant who willfully fails to pay a fine that he or she can afford to pay may also be incarcerated. Often fines are imposed as a condition of probation, and willful failure to pay may be grounds to revoke probation. Other non-custodial sentences may require that the defendant make restitution to the victim or perform a certain number of hours of specified community service.

[13] Custodial Sentences

Defendants sentenced to imprisonment usually serve their sentence at a penal facility determined by the state or county correctional agency. Prisoners may be assigned to a variety of possible correctional facilities, from maximum (or even recently-developed "supermax" prisons) to minimum security. For any sentence other than to death or life without parole, the convicted prisoner usually will not serve the entire sentence ordered by the court. Although jurisdictions vary considerably, most have an administrative process that shortens the sentence for good behavior or work while in prison, participation in education and other rehabilitative programs (so-called *good time* deductions), and perhaps even because the prison is so overcrowded that bed space must be made available for new arrivals.

[14] Parole and Other Supervised Release

Most jurisdictions also use *parole*, which authorizes a parole board or commission to evaluate a prisoner's likely success on the street and to release him or her, in appropriate cases, before the end of the sentence. Statutes ordinarily determine when a prisoner becomes eligible to be considered for parole. For example, a law may provide that prisoners committing a certain class of felony are parole-eligible after serving 50% of the sentence.

A parolee usually works at a job and must satisfy a number of specific conditions, such as maintaining employment, reporting regularly to a parole officer, remaining within the state, living at a certain place, limiting (or eliminating) the use of alcohol, and avoiding violations of the law. Failure to adhere to these conditions can lead to a parole revocation hearing before the parole board or a hearing officer and a return to prison for all or part of the unexpired sentence.

Some jurisdictions, including the federal government, have eliminated parole. A prisoner must serve all or virtually all of the sentence imposed by the judge, minus good time deductions. After release from prison, however, ex-prisoners in non-parole jurisdictions usually are required to have a short period of supervised release where they are counseled and monitored by a counselor under conditions that are similar to parole supervision. Violations of the conditions of supervised release, however, are handled by the sentencing judge rather than by a parole board.

[15] Direct Appeal

If the defendant is dissatisfied with the verdict, he or she has a right to a direct appeal to the next highest court in the jurisdiction; see Chapter 17. Usually the defendant will file a notice of appeal with the trial court. The case is then transferred to the appellate court for resolution. In most states this means that the state intermediate appellate court where a panel of (usually, three) judges hears the appeal. While the defendant usually has a right to file this appeal and have the case decided by the appellate court, frequently the appellate court can decide the issue summarily without hearing oral argument if the appellate briefs—documents detailing the legal arguments for each side—are deemed sufficient.

If an oral argument is held, usually there will be no decision immediately. The appellate judges will deliberate for a few days or sometimes months, and then render a written opinion. If the decision is adverse to the defendant (usually affirming the conviction and sentence), in most states the accused may seek a rehearing from the same court, perhaps this time before all the state or circuit's appellate judges (an *en banc* hearing), not just a panel of three appellate jurists.

If the defendant is dissatisfied with the intermediate appellate court's decision, usually he or she can ask the state supreme court to review the case. Often, however, that court does not have to accept the case; it may decline to review the matter, leaving intact the decision of the appellate court. If the appeal involves the United States Constitution, the defendant may also seek review from the United States Supreme Court.

If an appellate court decides that a serious error committed at trial, at sentencing, or in pre-trial proceedings impaired the defendant's right to a fair trial, it will reverse the conviction and/or sentence. Certain reversals are accompanied by an order from the appellate court that the defendant receive a new trial (or a new pretrial hearing, if that was the source of the erroneous conviction), while other reversals mandate that the indictment or information be dismissed and the defendant released from custody and spared any further criminal proceedings.

[16] Collateral Attack

After direct appeals have been exhausted, the defendant may consider bringing a *collateral attack* on the conviction (see Chapter 17). In most states this can be pursued in state court. If a constitutional violation is alleged, a state conviction may also be challenged collaterally in federal court through a petition for a *writ of habeas corpus* seeking the defendant's immediate release from allegedly unlawful confinement, but only after the habeas corpus petitioner has first exhausted all available state remedies on the issue presented. A collateral attack is a procedure used to ensure that people convicted of crimes are not punished and confined wrongfully. Because such proceedings often involve a rehash of issues already resolved at trial or on direct appeal, a number of procedural hurdles must be surmounted before a successful collateral attack may be brought. Because of these procedural requirements and because of the strong presumption of correctness given to the original conviction and subsequent direct appellate review, collateral challenges rarely succeed in reversing a conviction or sentence. Supreme Court decisions and congressional legislation in recent years (discussed in Chapter 17) have combined to significantly restrict the availability of federal habeas corpus review for state prisoners, and to make prisoners' chances of succeeding in obtaining habeas relief ever more unlikely.

[17] Executive Clemency

Constitutions and statutes routinely permit the jurisdiction's highest executive officer (a state governor or the President of the United States) or an executive department board to grant a convicted offender executive clemency. The clemency power includes the power to *pardon* an offender and to *commute* a sentence. A pardon remits any penalty resulting from conviction, possibly including not only release from imprisonment, but also restoration of any other collateral penalties, such as loss of a public license or civil rights. The mere fact of having a misdemeanor or felony conviction may, in many instances (depending on the law of the jurisdiction), subject the offender to such "collateral disabilities" as ineligibility to vote, possess a firearm, serve on a jury, or hold a professional license, or being required to register as a sex offender.

A pardon, however, does not by itself remove or expunge a conviction completely. The pardoned offender is still technically guilty of the offense for which he or she was originally convicted—it has been said that a pardon "forgives, but does not forget, the fact of guilt." *Randall v. Florida Dep't of Law Enforcement*, 791 So. 2d

1238 (Fla. Dist. Ct. App. 2001). A pardon may be granted because a governor or the president believes that the accused was erroneously convicted, or for humanitarian reasons such as removing civil disabilities that resulted from a proper conviction.

A commutation reduces the sentence, sometimes changing a sentence of death to one of life imprisonment, or shortening a deserving prisoner's sentence to "time served." A commutation may be granted to reward extraordinary or exemplary conduct while in prison (for example, to a prisoner who risked his own life to save other prisoners' lives in a prison fire), or simply where a governor or president feels that justice requires mitigation of the court-imposed sentence.

Under one common model, the offender applies for executive clemency to a board that recommends whether it should be denied or granted. The jurisdiction's highest executive officer (the President or Governor) then decides whether to accept or reject the board's recommendation. Another model is for the offender to apply directly to the executive's office where some internal administrative structure is in place to evaluate the requests. A third model involves a petition to and decision by an executive branch board, such as a Pardon Board or the Parole Board.

Although many prisoners covet executive clemency and believe they are entitled to it, the overwhelming majority of such applications are denied.[56]

Endnotes

1. U.S. Gov't Accountability Office, GAO-12-743, Bureau of Prisons: Growing Inmate Crowding Negatively Affects Inmates, Staff, and Infrastructure (2012), *available at* http://www.gao.gov/assets/650/648123.pdf.

2. University at Albany, Hindelang Criminal Justice Resource Center, *Sourcebook of Criminal Justice Statistics* [online] (hereinafter, "*Sourcebook*"), *available at* http://www.albany.edu/sourcebook. Table 1.102. *Sourcebook* tables and charts cited in this chapter are updated from time to time, and were most recently visited in February 2018.

3. *Id.*, Table 1.2.2003 at http://www.albany.edu/sourcebook/pdf/t122003.pdf.

4. *Id.*, Table 1.2.2006 at http://www.albany.edu/sourcebook/pdf/t122006.pdf.

5. *Id.*

6. http://www.uscourts.gov/news/2013/07/18/supervision-costs-significantly-less-than-incarceration-federal-system.

7. *Sourcebook*, Table 1.2.2006, note 4, *supra*.

8. U.S. Dep't of Justice, NCJ 250374, Bureau of Justice Statistics: Correctional Populations in the United States, (December 2016), Figure 1, *available at* http://bjs.gov/content/pub/pdf/cpus15.pdf.

9. *Id.*, "Highlights."

10. *Id.*, Table 2.

11. *Sourcebook*, Table 6.15.2012, http://www.albany.edu/sourcebook/pdf/t615202.pdf.

12. U.S. Dep't of Justice, Federal Bureau of Investigation: Uniform Crime Reports, 2016 Crime in the United States, *available at* http://www.fbi.gov/crime-in-the-u.s.-2016/topic-pages/tables/table-

13. *Id.*

14. U.S. Dep't of Justice, NCJ 250180, Bureau of Justice Statistics: Criminal Victimization, 2015 (revised 2018), *available at* http://bjs.gov/content/pub/pdf/cv15.pdf (hereinafter, Criminal Victimization, 2015), Table 5.

15. *Id.*, Table 7.

16. *Sourcebook*, Table 3.129.2011, *available at* http://www.albany.edu/sourcebook/pdf/t3129 2011.pdf.

17. Criminal Victimization, 2015, Table 7.

18. *Sourcebook*, Table 3.22.2008, *available at* http://www.albany.edu/sourcebook/pdf/t322 2008.pdf.

19. *Sourcebook*, Table 3.129.2011, *available at* https://www.albany.edu/sourcebook/pdf/t3129 2011.pdf.

20. Criminal Victimization, 2015, Table 7, *available at* https://bjs.gov/content/pub/pdf/cv15 .pdf. ojp.usdoj.gov/content/pub/pdf/cv11.pdf.

21. *Sourcebook*, Table 3.129.2011, note 19, *supra*.

22. *Id.*, at Table 3.122.2011, *available at* http://www.albany.edu/sourcebook/pdf/t31222011.pdf.

23. *Id.*, at Table 3.16.2010, *available at* http://www.albany.edu/sourcebook/pdf/t3162010.pdf.

24. U.S. Census Bureau, Statistical Abstract of the United States (2012) (information no longer available at Census Bureau website).

25. *Id.*

26. *Sourcebook*, Table 5.26.2010, *available at* Criminal Justice Statistics, at http://www.albany .edu/sourcebook/pdf/t5262010.pdf.

27. *Id.*, at Table 5.18.2003, *available at* http://www.albany.edu/sourcebook/pdf/t5182003.pdf.

28. *Id.*, at Table 5.45.2006, *available at* http://www.albany.edu/sourcebook/pdf/t5452006.pdf.

29. Federal Bureau of Prisons, Statistics: Inmate Race (updated as of March 24, 2018), http:// www.bop.gov/about/statistics/statistics_inmate_race.jsp.

30. U.S. Sentencing Commission, *Demographic Differences in Sentencing: An Update to the 2012* Booker *Report*, *available at* https://www.ussc.gov/sites/default/files/pdf/research-and-publications /research-publications/2017/20171114_Demographics.pdf.

31. *Sourcebook*, Table 5.21.2003, *available at* https://www.albany.edu/sourcebook/pdf/t521 2003.pdf.

32. U.S. Dep't of Justice, NCJ 250229, Bureau of Justice Statistics: Prisoners in 2015 (2016), Table 10, *available at* https://www.bjs.gov/content/pub/pdf/p15.pdf.

33. *Sourcebook*, Table 5.39.2010, *available at* https://www.albany.edu/sourcebook/pdf/t539 2010.pdf.

34. This percentage is even greater for convictions in U.S. District Courts, where 96.8% of dispositions were the result of guilty pleas in 2010, and only 3.2% resulted from trials. *Sourcebook*, Table 5.34.2010, *available at* https://www.albany.edu/sourcebook/pdf/t5342010.pdf.

35. *Id.*, Table 5.43.2010, *available at* https://www.albany.edu/sourcebook/pdf/t5432010.pdf.

36. *Id.*, Table 1.68.2011, *available at* https://www.albany.edu/sourcebook/pdf/t1682011.pdf.

37. *Id.*

38. *Id.*, Table 1.69.2007, *available at* https://www.albany.edu/sourcebook/pdf/t1692007.pdf.

39. *Id.*, Table 1.85.2005, *available at* https://www.albany.edu/sourcebook/pdf/t1852005.pdf.

40. Thomas H. Cohen, Who's Better at Defending Criminals? Does Type of Defense Attorney Matter in Terms of Producing Favorable Case Outcomes? 15 (2011) [citing data from Carolyn Wolf Harlow, *Defense Counsel in Criminal Cases*, Bureau of Justice Statistics Nov. 2000], *available at* http://ssrn.com/abstract=1876474.

41. *Sourcebook*, Table 5.8.2010, *available at* https://www.albany.edu/sourcebook/pdf/t58 2010.pdf.

42. *Id.*, Table 5.55.2010, *available at* https://www.albany.edu/sourcebook/pdf/t5662010.pdf.

43. *Id.*, Table 6.7.2010, *available at* https://www.albany.edu/sourcebook/pdf/t672010.pdf.

44. *Id.*, Table 5.24.2010, *available at* https://www.albany.edu/sourcebook/pdf/t5242010.pdf.

45. *Id.*, Table 5.44.2006, *available at* https://www.albany.edu/sourcebook/pdf/t5442006.pdf.

46. *Id.*, Table 4.7.2011, *available at* https://www.albany.edu/sourcebook/pdf/t472011.pdf.

47. *Id.*, Table 5.54.2006, *available at* https://www.albany.edu/sourcebook/pdf/t5542006.pdf.

48. *Id.*, Table 5.56.2006, *available at* https://www.albany.edu/sourcebook/pdf/t5562006.pdf.

49. *Id.*, Table 5.14.2004, *available at* https://www.albany.edu/sourcebook/pdf/t5142004.pdf.

50. *Id.*, Table 5.16.2004, *available at* https://www.albany.edu/sourcebook/pdf/t5162004.pdf.

51. *Id.*

52. *Id.*, Table 1.94.2010, *available at* https://www.albany.edu/sourcebook/pdf/t1942010.pdf.

53. *Id.*, Table 5.42.2010, *available at* https://www.albany.edu/sourcebook/pdf/t5422010.pdf.

54. *Juror Pay*, U.S. Courts, http://www.uscourts.gov/FederalCourts/JuryService/JurorPay.aspx.

55. Gregory E. Mize, Paula Hannaford-Agor & Nicole L. Waters, Center for Jury Studies, The State-of-the-States Survey of Jury Improvement Efforts: A Compendium Report 11–12 (2007), *available at* http://www.ncsc-jurystudies.org/~/media/Microsites/Files/CJS/SOS/SOSCompendiumFinal.ashx.

56. *Sourcebook*, Table 5.72.2010, *available at* http://www.albany.edu/sourcebook/pdf/t5722010.pdf (clemency applications for federal offenses).

Chapter 2

The Decision to Begin Formal Criminal Proceedings

A. Introduction

Once there is reason to believe that a crime has been committed, numerous individuals may exercise discretion in ways that will have an impact upon a suspect. Initially, for example, a crime victim may elect not to report a criminal offense because he or she perhaps thought the matter too trivial to justify official intervention. Similarly, a police officer may decide to resolve what would otherwise be a criminal matter through an informal warning to the would-be defendant. And even where both the victim and police proceed with vigor, the prosecutor can likewise exercise discretion in numerous ways with respect to the accused.

The initial decision to proceed with a criminal charge against an individual is one that should not be taken lightly. The financial costs incurred in mounting a prosecution or a defense to a criminal charge can be quite substantial. Moreover, in addition to suffering reputational harm, the accused will very often be detained in a jail, which can be intimidating and at times unsanitary, with time spent in detention often negatively affecting family relations and employment status. *See, e.g., Cooper v. Dupnik*, 963 F.2d 1220 (9th Cir. 1992) (after erroneous arrest for rapes and robberies, defendant lost his job and was evicted from his apartment).

While the criminal justice system provides mechanisms to screen cases that should not proceed to trial (principally the preliminary examination and grand jury review, discussed in Chapters 6 and 7), this chapter examines the exercise of discretion and explores both informal and formal means of influencing or restricting discretionary powers. After discussing the concept of discretion and the judiciary's acceptance of it as part of the American criminal justice system, this chapter deals with the exercise of discretion by three actors: the victim, the police, and the prosecutor.

B. Discretion in General

Existence of and Need for Discretion

The discretionary power of law enforcement officers is largely unrestrained in any legal sense. Of course, that power is not unique to law enforcement; indeed, it is a characteristic of many aspects of the American legal system. For example, a tort victim may or may not pursue a legal remedy. In the criminal arena, Professor Kenneth Culp Davis, the preeminent scholar of discretion in the criminal justice system, wrote the leading book, *Discretionary Justice: A Preliminary Inquiry* (1969), which is still insightful and well worth reading for anyone interested in low-visibility facets of criminal justice system decision-making.

Professor Davis noted that police personnel virtually always have an array of options when faced with criminality. One choice is whether to effectuate an arrest or refrain from making an arrest at all. Similarly, prosecutors may elect not to prosecute a case even when the evidence is strong, such as when the accused is dying of a terminal illness or will cooperate in convicting far more important criminals.

> [These choices create a] power of selective enforcement. Such power goes to selection of parties against whom the law is enforced and selection of the occasions when the law is enforced. Selective enforcement may also mean selection of the law that will be enforced and of the law that will not be enforced; an officer may enforce one statute fully, never enforce another, and pick and choose in enforcing a third.
>
> Selective enforcement obviously may be just or unjust, depending upon how the selections are made. Theoretically possible is a system of enforcement in only a fraction of the cases in which enforcement would be appropriate, with discretionary selections made in such a way that all the cases prosecuted are more deserving of prosecution than any of the cases not prosecuted.

Id. at 162, 163, 167.

C. Victim Discretion

Crime victims play a basic gatekeeper role in the criminal justice system. Unless criminal misconduct is observed by an officer, the system relies upon victims to bring misconduct to the attention of police. Whether this occurs depends on a number of factors, but one thing criminologists have long known is that criminal victimization often goes unreported: that there exists a "dark figure of crime." The discrepancy becomes apparent when one considers official data collected by police and reported to the Federal Bureau of Investigation, reflected in the federal Uniform Crime Report (UCR), and victimization surveys based on population samples, such as the National Crime Victimization Survey (NCVS). According to the 2015 NCVS, it was estimated that 46.55% of violent crimes and 34.6% of property-related crimes were reported to police. J.L. Truman & R.E. Morgan, U.S. Dept. of Justice, Criminal Victimization, 2015, Tech. Report, NCJ 250180. Moreover, victim non-reporting varies considerably within the broad crime categories; nearly 62% of robberies were reported to police, whereas only 32.5% of rapes and sexual assaults were reported. For a helpful overview of the issue, *see* Mark Berg & Ethan Rogers, *The Mobilization of Criminal Law*, 13 Ann. Rev. L. & Soc. Sci. 451 (2017).

Assuming a victim wishes to report, he or she might pressure police to arrest a suspect, may attempt to persuade the officer not to make the arrest, or might be ambivalent about the arrest decision. In responding to victim preferences, police officers may or may not show deference to the victim, depending upon variables, including:

1. Whether or not the victim was a "wrongdoer" in the alleged criminal event.
2. Whether the victim and the alleged offender are related by friendship, marriage, family, or contract.
3. The victim's possible underlying motive for seeking an arrest.
4. The seriousness of the underlying crime.

In addition to playing a significant role at the arrest stage, crime victims also influence the prosecutor's decision whether to prosecute. Based upon his field study, Professor Hall reported:

> [I]f the crime charged is a misdemeanor or non-serious felony, chances are good that the case will be dismissed if the victim so desires unless specific circumstances other than the victim's desires predominate. With the exception of the crime of rape, however, the reluctant victim's desires will not be heeded by the prosecutor in a serious felony case.

Donald J. Hall, *The Role of the Victim in the Prosecution and Disposition of a Criminal Case*, 28 Vand. L. Rev. 931, 952 (1975). Hall relates that prosecutors had varying opinions about the victim's influence on the choice of charge. They agreed, however, that they listen attentively to the victim who desires to "overcharge" in a serious felony case but not to the victim who desires similarly overcharging in a misdemeanor case. Victims desirous of undercharging experience more success with misdemeanors than with serious crimes.

A number of factors unique to the individual victim may account for the way discretion is exercised by prosecutorial officials. Such factors include age and stature in the community. One author concluded that perhaps the single most important variable in this context is whether the victim and defendant were strangers to one another at the time of the offense:

> Prosecutors and judges view stranger crimes as more serious offenses than crimes involving a prior relationship between victim and offender; but they concentrate their resources on stranger crimes, too, because it is so much harder to get a conviction in prior relationship cases. The reason, quite simply, is that when they know the offender, victims often refuse to press charges, to testify against the offender, or to cooperate with the prosecutor in other ways.

Charles E. Silberman, Criminal Violence, Criminal Justice 359–60 (1978). Silberman also observed that police and prosecutors tend to view prior-relationship crimes as less serious than those involving strangers.

It has been argued that victims should play an even greater role in criminal cases. *See, e.g.*, Sarah N. Welling, *Victims in the Criminal Process: A Utilitarian Analysis of the Victim's Participation in the Charging Decision*, 30 Ariz. L. Rev. 85 (1988). Numerous commentators and policymakers have championed the so-called "Victims' Rights" movement that fosters this goal. *See, e.g., Victims' Rights Symposium*, 11 Pepp. L. Rev. 1 (1984) and *Follow-Up Issue on Victims' Rights*, 17 Pepp. L. Rev. 1 (1989).

This movement has prompted the enactment of a number of state and federal statutes, many of which ensure that crime victims have an opportunity to be active participants in some phases of the criminal case. In Florida, for instance, the court must advise crime victims that among other rights they have the right to "be informed . . . [t]o be present . . . [t]o be heard . . . at all crucial stages of criminal proceedings . . . [and] [t]o consult with the state's attorney's office in certain felony cases regarding disposition of the case." Fla. Stat. §960.0021(2). Moreover, several states have amended their constitutions to afford crime victims a variety of rights. *See, e.g.*, Cal. Const., art. I, §28 ("Marsy's Law," enumerating a variety of rights, enforceable by victims or their attorneys); *see also generally* Douglas A. Beloof, *The Third Wave of Crime Victims' Rights: Standing, Remedy, and Review*, 2005 B.Y.U. L. Rev. 255, 350–54 (2005).

In 2004 Congress passed the Crime Victims' Rights Act, 18 U.S.C. §3771, which included a list of victims' rights that included the right to be "reasonably heard" at any public proceeding involving "plea" and "sentencing," as well as the reasonable right to "confer" with the federal prosecutor. The crime victim has standing to assert these rights and a court can issue a mandamus order to compel compliance. Many of these "rights" are included in Rule 60 of the Federal Rules of Criminal Procedure. Professor Paul Cassell argues that the rights of crime victims should be even more specific to require the court, before accepting a plea, to consider the views of any victim present in the courtroom, and the prosecutor to consider the victim's views "in developing any proposed plea agreement." Paul G. Cassell, *Treating Crime Victims Fairly: Integrating Victims into the Federal Rules of Criminal Procedure*, 2007 Utah L. Rev. 861. Do you think this approach is sensible? Does it undercut the prosecutor's traditional discretion in the plea process? For further discussion of the issue, *see* Dana Pugach & Michal Tamir, *Nudging the Criminal Justice System into Listening to Crime Victims in Plea Agreements*, 28 Hastings Women's L.J. 45 (2017).

Should a crime victim be given this kind of explicit influence over the handling of the defendant's case? If, as a policy matter, you believe that crime victims should be given such a voice, will this policy possibly lead to disparate treatment of similarly situated defendants? Would a prosecutor be as forceful in presenting the views of a particular victim if he or she knew that the victim was disinclined to urge harsh treatment of the defendant? For a discussion of these and other issues raised by victim participation statutes, *see* Donald J. Hall, *Victims' Voices in Criminal Court: The Need for Restraint*, 28 AM. CRIM. L. REV. 235 (1991).

D. Police Discretion

[1] Generally

Because "full" enforcement of the law (especially regarding minor offenses) is neither practical, for resource reasons, nor desired (do we want police to always detain us when we jaywalk?), discretion figures centrally in policing. Indeed, it is fair to say that because police make far more discretionary determinations in individual cases than any other class of administrators, they are "among the most important policy-makers of our entire society." KENNETH CULP DAVIS, DISCRETIONARY JUSTICE 222 (1969). One of the most comprehensive studies in which the exercise of discretion by police has been described and catalogued is WAYNE R. LAFAVE, ARREST: THE DECISION TO TAKE A SUSPECT INTO CUSTODY 9–10 (1965):

> Many persons whose conduct apparently violates the criminal law are not arrested. In some instances this may be explained by the fact that there is no legislative purpose to enforcing some statutes which are obsolete or drafted in overly general or ambiguous terms. In other instances the failure to make arrests results from the obvious fact that the resources available to law enforcement agencies make impossible the full enforcement of the existing substantive criminal law. A significant number of decisions not to arrest are unrelated to either legislative intent or resource allocation. Illustrative is the failure to arrest an informant as a reward for information.

For various reasons, as noted above, some persons who have likely violated substantive criminal laws will not be subjected to arrest. On the other hand, some individuals will be arrested for purposes other than prosecution. LaFave cites the example of arresting intoxicated persons and then releasing them when they become sober. Thereafter, the case is not prosecuted. In that instance, the underlying reason for arrest is the well-being of the individual. Similarly, certain types of offenders are arrested for the purpose of confiscation of equipment with little thought given to successful criminal prosecution (e.g., suspected gamblers).

Notwithstanding the many ways in which police exercise discretion, LaFave asserts that "the police have failed to evaluate carefully such enforcement policies or even to acknowledge that such practices exist. Rather, most departments attempt to maintain the existing stereotype of the police as ministerial officers who enforce all of the laws, while they actually engage in a broad range of discretionary enforcement."

In light of concerns raised by Davis, LaFave, and others, attempts have been made to address ways in which police discretion can be limited or controlled. One of the earliest detailed proposals emerged in 1973 from the *National Advisory Commission on Criminal Justice Standards and Goals, Report on Police*. The Commission urged the adoption of guidelines to limit the exercise of discretion by police in conducting investigations. With regard to alternatives to arrest, the Commission recommended guidelines that should:

> 1. establish the limits of discretion by specifically identifying, insofar as possible, situations calling for the use of alternatives to continued physical custody;
>
> 2. establish criteria for the selection of appropriate enforcement alternatives;
>
> 3. require enforcement action to be taken in all situations where all elements of a crime are present and all policy criteria are satisfied;
>
> 4. be jurisdiction-wide in both scope and application; and
>
> 5. specifically exclude offender lack of cooperation, or disrespect toward police personnel, as a factor in arrest determination unless such conduct constitutes a separate crime.

Six years later, the American Bar Association approved STANDARDS FOR CRIMINAL JUSTICE, THE URBAN POLICE FUNCTION, which recommended that police departments formulate and adopt administrative regulations to guide the exercise of their discretion. The rulemaking process should "give the highest priority to the formulation of administrative rules governing the exercise of discretion, particularly in the areas of selective enforcement, investigative techniques, and enforcement methods." Standard 1-4.3 (2d ed. 1980 § Supp. 1996).

Many law enforcement agencies have adopted rules. Professor LaFave calls this a "most encouraging development," noting that rulemaking improves police performance in four major ways: (1) it enhances the quality of police decisions by promoting the decision-making authority in responsible and capable hands; (2) it ensures fair and equal treatment of citizens as rules reduce the influence of bias; (3) it increases visibility of police policy decisions; and (4) on the assumption that rules made by police are most likely to be obeyed by police, it offers the best hope for getting police officials to obey and enforce constitutional norms. Wayne R. LaFave, *Constitutional Rules for Police: A Matter of Style*, 41 SYRACUSE L. REV. 849, 867, 868, 873 (1990).

At least two concerns emanate from the police department creation and use of rules, one theoretical and the other practical. On theoretical grounds, administrative rulemaking by police agencies has been criticized as a usurpation of legislative authority, on the ground that police are charged with enforcing the law, not devising conditions under which it is to be enforced. *See* Ronald J. Allen, *The Police and Substantive Rulemaking: Reconciling Principle and Expediency*, 125 U. PA. L. REV. 62 (1976). The practical concern is that to date the Supreme Court has refused to tie determinations of Fourth Amendment reasonableness to police violation of department rules. *See Whren v. United States*, 517 U.S. 806 (1996).

Finally, it should not go unmentioned that police can exercise discretion in contexts other than street patrol. In a few jurisdictions, they actually enjoy a degree of prosecutorial discretionary authority with respect to less serious offenses, deciding whether and what charges to file, and actually prosecuting cases. *See, e.g.*, Nikolas Frye, Note, *Allowing New Hampshire Police Officers to Prosecute: Concerns with the Practice and a Solution*, 38 New Eng. J. Civ. & Crim. Confinement 339 (2012). What concerns, if any, are prompted by allowing police to exercise this discretionary authority? For instance, are police officers subject to the same ethics rules as members of the bar? Does the policy amount to the unauthorized practice of law?

[2] Racial Profiling

A persistent concern in the discretionary enforcement decisions of police is racial profiling, in which police make discretionary decisions on the basis of profiles entirely or largely based on race. One study of state police searches along I-95 found that 63% of those stopped and searched were African-American and only 29% were white, though only 18% of the drivers on the road were African-American. John Knowles et al., *Racial Bias in Motor Vehicle Searches: Theory and Evidence*, 109 J. Pol. Econ. 203 (2001). The study's findings are consistent with numerous other studies conducted of traffic stops conducted in recent years. *See generally* Frank R. Baumgartner et al., Suspect Citizens: What 20 Million Traffic Stops Tell Us About Policing and Race (2018).

Moreover, outside the motor vehicle context, data about "stop, question and frisk" in New York City showed that in 2011 almost 700,000 people were stopped and frisked by police; weapons were found in about one of each 1,000 frisks. Almost all (90%) of individuals targeted were minority males and a similar percentage (88%) of detentions discovered no evidence of criminal wrongdoing. Jeffrey Bellin, *The Inverse Relationship between the Constitutionality and the Effectiveness of New York City's "Stop and Frisk,"* 94 B.U. L. Rev. 1495, 1498 (2014); *see also Floyd v. City of New York*, 959 F. Supp. 2d 540 (S.D.N.Y. 2013) (holding that the practice violated plaintiffs' Fourth and Fourteenth Amendment rights).

Concluding that the data show that police use racial profiling in deciding whom to stop, question, and search, many states have formally outlawed the practice and mandate that law enforcement departments keep statistics to monitor the use of this practice. Some jurisdictions require police departments to make regular reports about racial profiling practices in the jurisdiction. Many also specifically prohibit racial profiling and require police officers to undergo training to combat it. On reform efforts on the issue more generally, see Kami Chavis Simmons, *Beginning to End Racial Profiling: Definitive Solutions to an Elusive Problem*, 18 Wash. & Lee J. Civ. Rts. & Soc. Just. 25 (2011).

Notes

1. *Racial profiling and efficiency.* Some economists question whether the data actually show improper racial profiling, arguing that race may be a proper factor in some discretionary police decisions. *See* Yoram Margalioth & Tomer Blumkin, 24 Yale L. & Pol'y Rev. 317 (2006) ("profiling is always efficient, helping the police to

mitigate the screening problem when criminal activity varies across racial groups"). If criminal activity is not equal across race lines, is racial profiling justifiable as an efficient way of assigning scarce law enforcement resources? Assuming *arguendo* that it is, is it fair in a diverse, democratic society?

2. *Airport security after September 11.* Would your view change if the context were airport security rather than road or street crime? Should it be permissible for airport security personnel to focus their attention on people who appear to be of Middle Eastern descent or whose passport or background suggests they may be from that area of the world? Is there a difference in the goal of screening at airports and of stopping drivers suspected of traffic violations?

3. *State efforts to limit racial profiling.* In *Comm. v. Gonsalves*, 711 N.E.2d 108 (Mass. 1999), the Massachusetts Supreme Judicial Court held that under the state constitution's protection from unreasonable searches and seizures, police officers in routine traffic stops must have a reasonable belief that the officer or someone else's safety is in danger before ordering a driver out of a vehicle. Concurring, Justice Ireland observed:

> I write separately, however, to stress the dangers posed by unfettered police power to order individuals out of automobiles without any justification. The grant of such power is certainly, as the majority notes, "a clear invitation to discriminatory enforcement of the rule." This is precisely the type of power "that art. 14 [of the Massachusetts Constitution] was adopted to guard against," because, in the words of James Otis, it "'places the liberty of every man in the hands of every petty officer.'" The widespread public concerns about police profiling, commonly referred to as "DWB—driving while black," has been the subject of much discussion and debate both across the country and within the Commonwealth. [United States Supreme Court decisions] which permit automobile exit orders during any traffic stop "may also pose unique hardships on minorities" and could be a "clear invitation to discriminatory enforcement." Prohibiting the police from ordering people out of automobiles without any justification is a much needed step in the right direction to cure such abuses.

4. *Implicit bias.* In recent years, commentators drawing from the teachings of social psychology have asserted that police decisions can at times be motivated by implicit, not explicit, racial bias. *See, e.g.*, L. Song Richardson, *Implicit Racial Bias and Racial Anxiety: Implications for Stops and Frisks*, 15 Ohio St. J. Crim. L. 73 (2017). According to Professor Richardson, "research in the field of social psychology over the past four decades repeatedly demonstrates that most individuals of all races have implicit, i.e., unconscious, racial biases linking Blacks with criminality and Whites with innocence. These associations can lead to systematic and predictable judgment errors concerning who is and is not suspicious." *Id.* at 75.

5. *Data-based policing.* Finally, in keeping with the broader increase in the use of "big data" by governmental agencies and private industry alike, police departments have gravitated toward use of algorithms to determine when and where to deploy

officers. Police departments, for instance, rely on data of past arrests in particular locations to engage in "hot spot" policing. The data-based analytical approach has been lauded for its capacity to neutralize possible discriminatory exercises of police discretionary authority. However, critics have argued that the approach, while seemingly bias-free and objective, can simply reflect past systemic discriminatory policing practices, and replicate them. *See, e.g.*, Margaret Hu, *Algorithmic Jim Crow*, 86 FORDHAM L. REV. 633 (2017); David Weisburd, *Does Hot Spots Policing Inevitably Lead to Unfair and Abusive Police Practices, or Can We Maximize Both Fairness and Effectiveness in the New Proactive Policing?*, 2016 U. CHI. LEG. FORUM 661.

6. *Underenforcement of criminal laws.* Most often, public concern about police practices focuses on over-enforcement of laws, such as in the context of racial profiling vis-à-vis motorists (e.g., "driving while black"). Critics maintain, however, that poor, predominantly African-American communities also suffer from underenforcement of criminal laws, evidenced for instance in high percentages of reported yet unsolved crimes. *See, e.g.*, Alexandra Natapoff, *Underenforcement*, 75 FORDHAM L. REV. 1715 (2006). According to one commentator, the practice gives rise to "legal cynicism" in such communities, which regard themselves as "essentially stateless—unprotected by the law and its enforcers and marginal to the making of American society." Monica C. Bell, *Police Reform and the Dismantling of Legal Estrangement*, 126 YALE L.J. 2054, 2057 (2017).

[3] Domestic Violence: A Case Study

As the materials above make clear, police officers have broad discretion with regard to the initial decision to arrest a suspect. In domestic violence cases, the exercise of this discretion raises some unique questions about the scope and effect of police decision-making. If police are summoned to a private residence in which domestic violence has recently occurred, it is not uncommon for the battered individual (assuming that both parties do not appear to be equally culpable) to urge that the alleged batterer not be arrested.

It is widely believed that many police officers will not arrest unless the victim expresses clearly his or her desire for arrest of the offending party. Moreover, in many locales police are not authorized to arrest for a misdemeanor assault unless the officer personally witnesses the crime. Finally, in the past, it was not uncommon for police to take a hands-off view, letting the parties "work it out" or to perhaps have a "cooling off period," encouraging one or both of the parties to perhaps take a walk around the block.

[a] Statutory Efforts

Recognizing that battery is criminal in nature and can cause serious harm, including escalation to death, governments came to require arrests in certain domestic violence situations. Some state statutes, including the ones below, provide that the arrest decision does not depend on the victim's noted request or desire.

Many also permit the officer to make the arrest as long as the officer has probable cause to do so, irrespective of whether the officer personally witnessed the crime.

Mandatory arrest. One variety of arrest provisions requires the officer to make an arrest if there is probable cause to do so (mandatory arrest). The Nevada provision is illustrative:

> Nev. Rev. Stat. § 171.137: "[A] peace officer shall, unless mitigating circumstances exist, arrest a person when he has probable cause to believe that the person to be arrested has, within the preceding 24 hours, committed a battery upon his spouse, former spouse, any other person to whom he or she is related by blood or marriage, a person with whom he or she was is or was actually residing, a person with whom he or she has had or is having a dating relationship, a person with whom he or she has a child in common, the minor child of any of those persons or his or her minor child. . . . A peace officer shall not base a decision whether to arrest a person pursuant to this section on the peace officer's perception of the willingness of a victim or a witness to the incident to testify or otherwise participate in related judicial proceedings."

Preferred arrest. Another variety of domestic violence arrest statutes makes arrest the preferred option (presumptive arrest or "preferred" arrest). The Tennessee statute is explicit:

> Tenn. Code Ann. 36-3-619: "If a law enforcement officer has probable cause to believe that a person has committed a crime involving domestic abuse, whether the crime is a misdemeanor or felony, or was committed within or without the presence of the officer, the preferred response of the officer is arrest. . . . A law enforcement officer [in a domestic abuse case] shall not base a decision regarding whether to arrest a person pursuant to this section on the peace officer's perception of the willingness of a victim or a witness to the incident to testify or otherwise participate in related judicial proceedings."

While research shows that mandatory and preferred arrest laws substantially increase the likelihood that the officer will *arrest* one or more of the participants in the incident, do you think either approach will affect the number of domestic violence *incidents*? If so, is one preferable? Does it matter that one reason for the increase in arrests is that more females are being arrested under these laws?

[b] Impact of Statutory Efforts

Are these statutes likely to restrict the exercise of police discretion in any meaningful way? Do they reflect "good" public policy?

It has been reported that the number of police departments encouraging or requiring their officers to make arrests in domestic violence cases has significantly increased. This increase follows a finding in an experimental program in Minneapolis in the 1980s that arrest is an effective deterrent to domestic violence. However, subsequent research has shown complex trends:

1. Mandatory arrest reduces domestic violence in some cities but increases it in others.

2. Mandatory arrest reduces domestic violence among employed people but increases it among unemployed people.

3. Mandatory arrest reduces violence in the short run but may increase it in the long run. Indeed, while "intimate partner" homicides have decreased in the years since mandatory and preferred arrest statutes were enacted, in "states with mandatory arrest laws the homicides are about 50 percent higher today [2007] than they are in states without the laws." Radha Iyengar, *The Protection Battered Spouses Don't Need*, N.Y. Times, Aug. 7, 2007.

4. Mandatory arrest has no more deterrent effect on domestic violence than does separation or counseling.

R Gilles, *The Politics of Research: The Use and Misuse of Social Science Data—the Cases of Intimate Partner Violence*, 45 Family Ct. Rev. 42 (2007).

Mandatory arrest statutes still allow police to use their discretion, sometimes resulting in the arrest of both parties. In response, many states have enacted provisions directing police to arrest only the primary physical aggressor or the party not acting in self-defense. The issue of dual arrests is being discussed in police stations across the country, concerning inter alia the impact of dual arrests on children living in the home. *See* Elizabeth Schneider et al., Domestic Violence and the Law (2007); David Hirschiel, *Domestic Violence Cases: What Research Shows About Arrest and Dual Arrest Rates* (National Institute of Justice, July 25, 2008).

Do you think police should be *required* to arrest a suspected abuser if they have probable cause to do so? Only *encouraged* to do so? What effect would such a requirement have on the number of reported abuse incidents? Could it actually discourage victims from calling the police? Should remedies such as counseling or mediation be an alternative to arrest? An alternative to prosecution? For more on the effects of arrest-related policies, *see, e.g.*, Margaret E. Johnson, *Changing Course in the Anti-Domestic Violence Legal Movement: From Safety to Security*, 60 Vill. L. Rev. 145, 166–68 (2015). For an argument in favor of more victim autonomy being afforded in some domestic violence cases, *see* Kimberly D. Bailey, *Lost in Translation: Domestic Violence, "The Personal Is Political," and the Criminal Justice System*, 100 J. Crim. L & Criminology 1255 (2010).

E. Prosecutorial Discretion

[1] Generally

[a] Ethical Restrictions

Prosecutors, both state and federal, have the extraordinary power to determine whether an individual should be charged with a crime. As Justice Robert Jackson once observed, "The prosecutor has more control over life, liberty and reputation than any other person in America. His discretion is tremendous." Robert Jackson, *The Federal Prosecutor*, 24 J. Am. Jud. Soc'y 18, 18 (1940).

Public prosecutors occupy a dual role of representing the government as an advocate while also seeking the objective of impartial justice. Under the American Bar Association's Model Rules of Professional Conduct, for example, a prosecutor is obligated to "refrain from prosecuting a charge that the prosecutor knows is not supported by probable cause." Model Rules of Prof'l Conduct r. 3.8(a). *See also* Model Code of Prof'l Responsibility DR 7-103(A) (same). The most recent ABA Standards provide that a prosecutor should not bring charges if she believes that the defendant is innocent, regardless of the strength of the evidence. 2015 ABA Prosecution Standards, Stnd. 3-4.3(d); *see also id.* (stating that prosecutor should seek or file charges only when she "reasonably believes that the charges are supported by probable cause, the admissible evidence will be sufficient to support the conviction beyond a reasonable doubt, and that the decision to charge is in the interests of justice"). Moreover, a "prosecutor should not file or maintain charges greater in number or degree than can reasonably be supported with evidence at trial and are necessary to fairly reflect the gravity of the offense or deter similar misconduct." *Id.* Stnd. 3-4.4(d). The Standards, moreover, state that prosecutors should "consider the possibility of a noncriminal disposition, formal or informal, or a deferred prosecution or other diversionary disposition." *Id.* Stnd. 3-4.4(f).

In short, prosecutors are to function as "ministers of justice," whose job, as the ABA Model Rules of Professional Conduct state, require that defendants be "accorded procedural justice, that guilt is decided upon the basis of sufficient evidence, and that special precautions are taken to prevent and to rectify the conviction of innocent persons." Model Rule 3.8, *supra*, Comment. As the Supreme Court put it many years ago, a prosecutor's client is "not an ordinary party to a controversy" but "a sovereignty whose obligation to govern impartially is as compelling as its obligation to govern at all, and whose interest, therefore, in a criminal prosecution is not that it shall win a case, but that justice shall be done." *Berger v. United States*, 295 U.S. 78, 88 (1935).

The aforementioned lofty language aside, in reality prosecutors function as bureaucratic managers, whose duties and decisions vary depending on the jurisdiction, turning such issues as resources, case volume, and crime control policy preferences. As important, in our adversary system of criminal justice, where conviction rates and sentences often serve as benchmarks for success, it should not be unexpected that a securing a "win" is not always synonymous with justice being done in an individual case.

While in some cases it can be relatively easy to determine the charge to be filed against an individual, a number of variables might influence the decision. First and foremost, as suggested by the Rules of Professional Conduct, is the question whether there is enough evidence to support a prosecution for a particular offense.

Even if ample evidence exists, however, a prosecutor may elect to bypass prosecution because of what are believed to be legitimate reasons for not subjecting a defendant to that process. Sometimes a prosecutor will forego prosecution if the defendant agrees to meet certain conditions. For example, a prosecutor may decide not to prosecute an individual found in possession of a small amount of marijuana in exchange for that person's agreement to "stay clean for six months." Or a prosecutor could disagree with the wisdom of invoking a particular criminal provision or its application in a particular case and engage in "nullification" by refusing to prosecute all or some cases. *See* Roger Fairfax, Jr., *Prosecutorial Nullification*, 52 B.C. L. Rev. 1243 (2011) (arguing prosecutorial nullification is inevitable when prosecutors are given wide discretion but suggesting screening applicants for prosecution positions and providing guidelines to control this discretion).

On the other extreme, the maximum possible charge (or any number of charges) may be sought against an individual in order to bolster the prosecutor's position in later plea bargaining sessions, discussed more fully in Chapter 11. *See, e.g.*, United States v. Kupa, 976 F. Supp. 2d 417, 420 (E.D.N.Y. 2013) ("[T]o coerce cooperation... prosecutors routinely threaten ultra-harsh, enhanced mandatory sentencing that *no one*—not even the prosecutors themselves—thinks are appropriate.").

Choice of forum (discussed in the next chapter) is another key issue affected by prosecutorial discretion. Criminal misconduct might be susceptible of prosecution in more than one locality in a given state, more than one state, and even in either or both state or federal courts. The impact of this decision can be quite significant. Jurisdictions can differ significantly in their laws and procedures and punishments, including with respect to the death penalty. Should a defendant, arrested for a homicide in a non-capital jurisdiction, be able to challenge his case being prosecuted in federal court where he can face capital charges? *See, e.g., United States v. Acosta-Martinez*, 252 F.3d 13 (1st Cir. 2001) (concluding that federal capital charges against defendants can be prosecuted in Puerto Rico, a non-capital jurisdiction).

In short, prosecutorial discretion hinges on a multitude of considerations and functions, for better or worse, as a "black box." Marc L. Miller & Ronald F. Wright, *The Black Box*, 94 Iowa L. Rev. 125 (2008).

[b] Other Considerations

Prosecutors are subject to very few constraints in exercising their discretion. If a prosecutor decides not to charge a criminal offense, there is little that can be done to challenge that decision, as will be discussed *infra*. In many jurisdictions, the political process may be the only effective means of "disciplining" an elected prosecutor. However, experience suggests that political accountability exercises little, if any, influence on prosecutorial policies and practices. *See* Ronald F. Wright, *How Prosecutor Elections Fail Us*, 6 Ohio St. J. Crim. L. 581 (2009). At the same time, when a prosecutor elects to pursue criminal charges, courts generally recognize a rebuttable presumption that the prosecution has been undertaken in good faith and in compliance with constitutional mandates. Indeed, prosecutors enjoy absolute immunity from liability based on the decision to file charges and the trying of cases. *Imbler v. Pachtman*, 424 U.S. 409 (1976).[1]

Professor LaFave has referred to broad prosecutorial discretion as "one of the most striking features of the American system of criminal justice." Wayne R. LaFave, *The Prosecutor's Discretion in the United States*, 18 Am. J. of Comp. Law 532 (1970). In deciding whether or not to prosecute, he has identified "common explanations" that drive the necessity for selective enforcement. They are (1) legislative "overcriminalization," (2) limitations in available enforcement resources, and (3) a need to individualize justice. With respect to resources, for instance, deciding to file a capital charge against an individual, and actually litigating the case, has a very significant budgetary impact on an office, which can negatively affect wherewithal to prosecute other cases. In light of the knowledge deficit among voters regarding the operation of prosecutors' offices, should prosecutors standing for reelection be required to disclose costs of cases prosecuted and all cases not prosecuted where an arrest was made and sufficient evidence existed to support prosecution? According to one author, doing so would provide the electorate with "concrete, monetized evidence of prosecutorial priorities" and afford a meaningful way to monitor prosecutorial operations. *See* Russell M. Gold, *Promoting Democracy in Prosecution*, 86 Wash. L. Rev. 69 (2011).

It might also be that a prosecutor may reject a case that he or she believes "would not be in the public interest." For example, the prosecutor may believe that the crime is too trivial, that the defendant has already suffered enough, is seriously ill, or will provide information in another, more important, case. Prosecutors also consider the defendant's "convictability" because they do not like to lose cases. Local ambivalence regarding the prosecution and conviction of individuals possessing small amounts of marijuana, manifest in juries refusing to convict, for instance, might factor into a prosecutor's charging calculus.

Several trends have intensified the power of the prosecutor in the American criminal justice system. First, by legislating numerous overlapping provisions in criminal codes, states have passed the decision of how to characterize allegedly criminal conduct to the prosecutor. Second, because of sheer volume, the system is more dependent upon plea bargaining. Finally, the creation of presumptive sentencing guidelines has increased the importance of the initial charging decision because the sentences available to the court are almost always determined by the charging decision. Robert L. Misner, *Recasting Prosecutorial Discretion*, 86 J. Crim. L. & Criminology 717 (1996). So, too, has the increase in the number of laws requiring

1. It is worth noting, however, that prosecutors are entitled to only qualified immunity for statements made to the media and for conduct during the investigation of an uncharged crime. *Buckley v. Fitzsimmons*, 509 U.S. 259 (1993).

a mandatory minimum sentence vis-à-vis particular misconduct, which can afford prosecutors latitude in their charging decisions.

As noted above, resources often factor into charging decisions. As penal facilities have become increasingly overcrowded—and hence more expensive to run—in recent years, and the collateral consequences of convictions for individuals have ballooned (e.g., losing access to student loans), some have urged that prosecutors should consider the broader systemic impact of their individual charging decisions. *See e.g.*, ABA Prosecution Stnd. 3-1.2(f) (stating that a prosecutor should be a "problem-solver" who is "responsible for considering broad goals of the criminal justice system"); Roger A. Fairfax, Jr., *The "Smart on Crime" Prosecutor*, 25 Geo. J. Legal Ethics 905 (2012); Babe Howell, *Prosecutorial Discretion and the Duty to Seek Justice in an Overburdened Criminal Justice System*, 27 Geo. J. Legal Ethics 285 (2014); Eisha Jain, *Prosecuting Collateral Consequences*, 104 Geo. L.J. 1197 (2017). Should prosecutors take such a broad view or should they simply focus on "doing justice" in each case? Does your opinion change in light of evidence that changes in prosecutorial practices in recent years may have been a prime factor in what has been termed the nation's problem with "mass incarceration"? *See* John F. Pfaff, Locked In: The True Causes of Mass Incarceration and How to Achieve Real Reform 71–74 (2017); Lisa Griffin & Ellen Yaroshefsky, *Ministers of Justice and Mass Incarceration*, 30 Geo. J. Legal Ethics 301 (2017).

The ABA Prosecution Standards provide a lengthy list of factors for prosecutors to consider when exercising their charging discretion, even if a charge satisfies minimal charging requirements:

(i) The strength of the case;

(ii) The prosecutor's doubt that the accused is in fact guilty;

(iii) The extent or absence of harm caused by the offense;

(iv) The impact of prosecution or non-prosecution on the public welfare;

(v) The background and characteristics of the offender, including any voluntary restitution or efforts at rehabilitation;

(vi) Whether the authorized or likely punishment or collateral consequences are disproportionate in relation to the particular offense or the offender;

(vii) The views and motives of the victim or complainant;

(viii) Any improper conduct by law enforcement;

(ix) Unwarranted disparate treatment of similarly situated persons;

(x) Potential collateral impact on third parties, including witnesses or victims;

(xi) Cooperation of the offender in the apprehension or conviction of others;

(xii) The possible influence of any cultural, ethnic, socioeconomic or other improper biases;

(xiii) Changes in law or policy;

(xiv) The fair and efficient distribution of limited prosecutorial resources;

(xv) The likelihood of prosecution by another jurisdiction; and

(xvi) Whether the public's interests in the matter might be appropriately vindicated by available civil, regulatory, administrative, or private remedies.

2015 ABA Prosecution Standards, Stnd. 3-4.4. Applying the foregoing, what should be the charging outcome in the following cases? (The essential facts of these Problems are set forth in H. Richard Uviller, *The Virtuous Prosecutor in Quest of an Ethical Standard: Guidance from the ABA*, 71 Mich. L. Rev. 1145, 1157–58 (1973).)

Problem 2-1. "I Never Forget a Face"

An elderly person is suddenly grabbed from behind in a dimly lit alley by a young male who shows a knife and takes the victim's wallet. The entire incident lasts no more than 30 seconds. Several days later, the victim spots the defendant in the neighborhood and has him arrested by the nearest police officer. Although the prosecutor presses him hard, the victim swears that his identification of the defendant is correct. The defendant's appearance is not unusual, the victim never saw the defendant before the crime, and the victim also admits that he cannot identify the perpetrator's voice because nothing was said. Certain about his identification, though, he insists that in those few moments of terror his attacker's face was "indelibly engraved on his memory." The defendant may have an alibi: his mother apparently will testify that the defendant was home watching television at the time of the crime (evidence which is not readily credited). Does the prosecutor have enough information to decide whether to prosecute? If not, what information is lacking?

Problem 2-2. Dropsy Syndrome

Defendant, charged with illegal possession of a small amount of cocaine, has indicated to defense counsel a readiness to plead guilty. Defendant claims, however, that the police found the cocaine in an illegal search of his automobile trunk and therefore it should be suppressed. The police officer claims to have retrieved the drugs after the defendant threw them from the window of the vehicle at the police officer's approach. The prosecutor, based on personal experience, suspects that this officer sometimes seeks to avoid the strictures of the exclusionary rule by using the "law of abandonment" (or "dropsy" testimony) to justify what would otherwise be an illegal search and seizure.

1. If the prosecutor believes this officer may testify falsely, what steps should the prosecutor take?

2. Even if the prosecutor suspects the officer may lie, should the prosecutor accept the plea offer if the defendant had a lengthy drug record? What if this were the first offense charged against the defendant?

3. Should the prosecutor lend weight to the fact that the presiding judge has signaled in a prior case that he was skeptical of the arresting officer's veracity?

[2] Challenges to the Exercise of Discretion

[a] Decision Not to Charge

When the legislature enacts a statute that makes certain conduct a crime, it can be assumed that the legislature intends—at least in broad terms—that the statute will be enforced in appropriate cases. It sometimes is the case, however, that the legislature may approve of a law for symbolic or political reasons, but have little actual desire or expectation that such a law will be enforced fully. Criminal laws related to so-called "victimless" crimes, such as gambling or prostitution, may fall into this category. Laws prohibiting adultery or cohabitation likewise attract little or no prosecutorial attention, perhaps remaining in statutory codes because legislators are wary of the political risk of being associated with condoning such behaviors.

Even where full enforcement of criminal statutes is desired by the legislature, however, such enforcement may be nearly impossible. Some of the more obvious reasons for this are limited numbers of police, prosecutors, courts, and jail facilities. And, as with police discretionary decisions, "full enforcement" of the criminal code is neither desired nor possible. For a historical overview of prosecutors' discretionary power, *see* Carolyn Ramsey, *The Discretionary Power of "Public" Prosecutors in Historical Perspective*, 39 Am. Crim. L. Rev. 1309 (2002).

In short, prosecutorial refusal to charge is a foundational reality in the criminal justice system. *See, e.g.*, Alexandra Natapoff, *Misdemeanors*, 85 S. Cal. L. Rev. 1313, 1330 (2012) ("In some jurisdictions, prosecutors decline to prosecute as many as half of all misdemeanor arrests."). When a criminal law goes unenforced, the one person most likely to complain is the crime victim. What remedy is available to have law enforcement authorities enforce the law? Consider, in this context, the following classic case.

Inmates of Attica Correctional Facility v. Rockefeller

477 F.2d 375 (2d Cir. 1973)

Mansfield, Circuit Judge:

This appeal raises the question of whether the federal judiciary should, at the instance of victims, compel federal and state officials to investigate and prosecute persons who allegedly have violated certain federal and state criminal statutes. Plaintiffs in the purported class suit, which was commenced in the Southern District of New York against various state and federal officers, are certain present and former inmates of New York State's Attica Correctional Facility ("Attica"), the mother of an inmate who was killed when Attica was retaken after the inmate uprising in September 1971, and Arthur O. Eve, a New York State Assemblyman and member of the Subcommittee on Prisons. They appeal from an order of the district court ... dismissing their complaint. We affirm.

The complaint alleges that before, during, and after the prisoner revolt at and subsequent recapture of Attica in September 1971, which resulted in the killing of 32 inmates and the wounding of many others, the defendants, including the Governor of New York, the State Commissioner of Correctional Services, the Executive Deputy Commissioner of the State Department of Correctional Services, the Superintendent at Attica, and certain State Police, Corrections Officers, and other officials, either committed, conspired to commit, or aided and abetted in the commission of various crimes against the complaining inmates and members of the class they seek to represent. It is charged that the inmates were intentionally subjected to cruel and inhuman treatment prior to the inmate riot, that State Police, Troopers, and Correction Officers (one of whom is named) intentionally killed some of the inmate victims without provocation during the recovery of Attica, that state officers (several of whom are named and whom the inmates claim they can identify) assaulted and beat prisoners after the prison had been successfully retaken and the prisoners had surrendered, . . . that personal property of the inmates was thereafter stolen or destroyed, and that medical assistance was maliciously denied to over 400 inmates wounded during the recovery of the prison. [The inmates also alleged that abusive conduct would continue to occur unless the responsible state officers were prosecuted.]

The complaint further alleges that Robert E. Fischer [a special prosecutor appointed by the Governor] . . . to investigate crimes relating to the inmates' takeover of Attica and the resumption of control by the state authorities, ". . . has not investigated, nor does he intend to investigate, any crimes committed by state officers." Plaintiffs claim, moreover, that because Fischer was appointed by the Governor he cannot neutrally investigate the responsibility of the Governor and other state officers said to have conspired to commit the crimes alleged. It is also asserted that since Fischer is the sole state official currently authorized under state law to prosecute the offenses allegedly committed by the state officers, no one in the State of New York is investigating or prosecuting them. . . .

As a remedy for the asserted failure of the defendants to prosecute violations of state and federal criminal laws, plaintiffs request relief in the nature of mandamus (1) against state officials, requiring the State of New York to submit a plan for the independent and impartial investigation and prosecution of the offenses charged against the named and unknown state officers, and insuring the appointment of an impartial state prosecutor and state judge to "prosecute the defendants forthwith," and (2) against the United States Attorney, requiring him to investigate, arrest and prosecute the same state officers for having committed the federal offenses defined by 18 U.S.C. §§ 241 and 242 [involving infringing rights secured by the United States Constitution or laws]. . . .

With respect to the defendant United States Attorney, plaintiffs seek mandamus to compel him to investigate and institute prosecutions against state officers, most of whom are not identified, for alleged violations of 18 U.S.C. §§ 241 and 242. . . . Federal courts have traditionally and, to our knowledge, uniformly refrained from overturning, at the instance of a private person, discretionary decisions of federal prosecuting authorities not to prosecute persons regarding whom a complaint of criminal conduct is made. . . .

The primary ground upon which this traditional judicial aversion to compelling prosecutions has been based is the separation of powers doctrine.

> Although as a member of the bar, the attorney for the United States is an officer of the court, he is nevertheless an executive official of the Government, and it is as an officer of the executive department that he exercises a discretion as to whether or not there shall be a prosecution in a particular case. It follows, as an incident of the constitutional separation of powers, that the courts are not to interfere with the free exercise of the discretionary powers of the attorneys of the United States in their control over criminal prosecutions. *United States v. Cox*, 342 F.2d 167, 171 (5th Cir.), *cert. denied*, 381 U.S. 935 (1965).

. . . In the absence of statutorily defined standards governing reviewability, or regulatory or statutory policies of prosecution, the problems inherent in the task of supervising prosecutorial decisions do not lend themselves to resolution by the judiciary. The reviewing courts would be placed in the undesirable and injudicious posture of becoming "superprosecutors." In the normal case of review of executive acts of discretion, the administrative record is open, public and reviewable on the basis of what it contains. The decision not to prosecute, on the other hand, may be based upon the insufficiency of the available evidence, in which event the secrecy of the grand jury and of the prosecutor's file may serve to protect the accused's reputation from public damage based upon insufficient, improper, or even malicious charges. *In camera* review would not be meaningful without *access* by the complaining party to the evidence before the grand jury or United States Attorney. Such interference with the normal operations of criminal investigations, in turn, based solely upon allegations of criminal conduct, raises serious questions of potential abuse by persons seeking to have other persons prosecuted. Any person, merely by filing a complaint containing allegations in general terms (permitted by the Federal Rules) of unlawful failure to prosecute, could gain access to the prosecutor's file and the grand jury's minutes, notwithstanding the secrecy normally attaching to the latter by law.

Nor is it clear what the judiciary's role of supervision should be were it to undertake such a review. At what point would the prosecutor be entitled to call a halt to further investigation as unlikely to be productive? What evidentiary standard would be used to decide whether prosecution should be compelled? How much judgment would the United States Attorney be allowed? Would he be permitted to limit himself to a strong "test" case rather than pursue weaker cases? What collateral factors would be permissible bases for a decision not to prosecute, e.g., the pendency of another criminal proceeding elsewhere against the same parties? What sort of review should be available in cases like the present one where the conduct complained of allegedly violates state as well as federal laws? With limited personnel and facilities at his disposal, what priority would the prosecutor be required to give to cases in which investigation or prosecution was directed by the court?

These difficult questions engender serious doubts as to the judiciary's capacity to review and as to the problem of arbitrariness inherent in any judicial decision to order prosecution. On balance, we believe that substitution of a court's decision to compel prosecution for the U.S. Attorney's decision not to prosecute, even upon an abuse of discretion standard of review and even if limited to directing that a prosecution be undertaken in good faith, would be unwise. Plaintiffs urge, however, that Congress withdrew the normal prosecutorial discretion for the kind of conduct alleged here by providing in 42 U.S.C. § 1987 that the United States Attorneys are "authorized *and required* . . . to institute prosecutions against all persons violating any of the provisions of [18 U.S.C. §§ 241 and 242]" (emphasis supplied), and, therefore, that no barrier to a judicial directive to institute prosecutions remains. This contention must be rejected. The mandatory nature of the word "required" as it appears in § 1987 is insufficient to evince a broad Congressional purpose to bar the exercise of executive discretion in the prosecution of federal civil rights crimes. . . .

Such language has never been thought to preclude the exercise of prosecutorial discretion. . . . Nor do we find the legislative history of § 1987 persuasive of an intent by Congress to depart so significantly from the normal assumption of executive discretion. . . . [The court also rejected similar claims against state defendants.]

Notes

1. *Judicial reluctance to interfere with prosecutor's discretion.* State and federal prosecutors serve as public officials, and they are charged with the responsibility of enforcing relevant criminal statutes. As the *Attica* decision indicates, courts refuse to interfere except in extraordinary cases. *See, e.g., United States v. Lighty*, 616 F.3d 321, 369 (4th Cir. 2010) (decision to prosecute is within the "special province" of the executive branch). But why would a court refuse to review the prosecutor's decision by an abuse of discretion standard or at least require the decision to be made in good faith?

2. *Civil settlement in Attica.* While "criminal remedies" were denied the victims in *Attica*, the New York Times reported on January 5, 2000, that the inmates would be receiving a settlement of $12 million from the State of New York ($4 million of which was for lawyers' fees) and that the award "is believed to be the biggest ever in a prisoners' rights case."

3. *What could Congress have done?* If the court in *Attica* was correct in deciding that Congress did not intend to restrict the exercise of prosecutorial discretion, how could Congress draft a statute to effectuate "full" enforcement of a specific statute? *Cf.* Alexander Zendeh, Note, *Can Congress Authorize Judicial Review of Deferred Prosecution and Nonprosecution Agreements? And Does It Need To?*, 95 Tex. L. Rev. 1451 (2017).

4. *Standing.* Challenges to prosecutorial discretion are virtually impossible by people other than the person being prosecuted. The Supreme Court has noted that this "Court's prior decisions consistently hold that a citizen lacks standing to contest the policies of the prosecuting authority when he himself is neither prosecuted nor threatened with prosecution." *Linda R.S. v. Richard D.*, 410 U.S. 614 (1973).

5. *Appoint special prosecutor?* Given some of the concerns expressed regarding the control of prosecutorial discretion, should a court be authorized to appoint a *special prosecutor* to consider instituting criminal charges? The special prosecutor is a person with the legal authority to prosecute but is unaffiliated with the prosecutor's office that has declined to pursue the case. Some jurisdictions authorize this appointment in unusual cases when the usual prosecutor cannot or will not pursue a case. *See, e.g.*, Colo. Stat. § 16-5-209 (person seeking appointment of special prosecutor may file affidavit in trial court alleging "unjustified refusal" of prosecutor "to prosecute any person" for a specific crime; court may appoint special prosecutor (or order the prosecutor to file criminal charges) if, after a hearing, the court finds the refusal to prosecute was "arbitrary or capricious" and "without reasonable excuse").

6. *An intra-executive branch conflict.* Prosecutors, and of course state governors, are both part of the executive branch of government. In Florida, an interesting intra-branch conflict arose when a publicly elected state prosecutor refused to seek the death penalty in a high-profile case in which the defendant allegedly killed his pregnant ex-girlfriend and a police officer, based on her office's policy to not seek death in any case. In response, the Governor of Florida reassigned the defendant's case and other potentially death-eligible cases to a prosecutor in another district within the state. The Governor cited his duty under the Florida Constitution to "take care that the laws be faithfully executed" and his statutory authority to reassign "if, for any . . . good and sufficient reason, the Governor determines that the ends of justice would be best served." The local prosecutor challenged the reassignment and the Florida Supreme Court ultimately sided with the Governor, holding that the local prosecutor's "blanket refusal" to bring capital charges qualified as a "good and sufficient reason" for the Governor's action, and that the prosecutor "exercised no discretion at all." *Ayala v. Scott*, 224 So. 3d 755 (Fla. 2017).

Prosecutors, however, generally retain and use enormous power to refuse prosecution, especially with regard to less serious offenses. *See, e.g.*, Stephanie Clifford & Joseph Goldstein, *Brooklyn Prosecutor Limits When He'll Target Marijuana*, N.Y. Times, July 8, 2014 (discussing policy whereby arrestees with no or minimal criminal histories and not found smoking marijuana in public will not face charges).

7. *State legislative efforts to control prosecutorial discretion.* Finally, if courts are not allowed to control prosecutorial discretion, what would happen if the legislature attempts to control prosecutorial discretion? For example, and as discussed below, in domestic violence situations many states mandate or "prefer" that cases be prosecuted if there is probable cause to do so. Courts often do not read the statutes literally, treating them as inconsistent with the general rule giving police and prosecutors discretion. *See, e.g., Town of Castle Rock, Colo. v. Gonzalez*, 545 U.S. 748 (2005) (Colorado law requiring police to "use every reasonable means to enforce

a restraining order" does not alter the traditional rule that police have discretion to enforce the restraining order in a particular situation); *Chicago v. Morales*, 527 U.S. 41, 62 (1999) (ordinance providing that police "shall order" people to disperse in specific circumstances does not deprive police of their traditional discretion in deciding whether to enforce the ordinance).

Sometimes prosecution is discouraged rather than encouraged by statute. In Texas, for example, the legislature passed a law requiring prosecutors (who are considered judicial officers) to first consult with the Texas Commission on Environmental Quality (an executive agency) before bringing any criminal charges against a permit holder for criminal violations. *See* Suzanne M. Jost, Comment, *Unconstitutional Delegation of Prosecutorial Discretion in Texas: The Pollution of Environmental Pollution Deterrents,* 36 St. Mary's L. J. 411 (2005).

8. *Prosecutorial discretion and grand juries.* Assume a grand jury decides to hand down a "true bill" (a criminal indictment) against an individual, specifying criminal charges. Must a prosecutor accede to the grand jury's determination? Should deference be accorded, based on the structural role played by grand juries (see Chapter 7)? *See United States v. Navarro-Vargas*, 408 F.3d 1184 (9th Cir. 2005) ("The prosecutor has no obligation to prosecute the [grand jury's] presentment, to sign the return of an indictment, or even to prosecute an indictment properly returned."). What about the converse: can a prosecutor, in a jurisdiction that does not require an indictment, decide to file charges when a grand jury refuses to indict?

[b] Decision to Charge: Desuetude

The *Attica* case addressed the issue of selective non-enforcement of a viable criminal statute. Victims filed a lawsuit to require prosecution in a specific situation. In contrast, in some cases a statute will have gone unenforced (i.e., no prosecutions will have occurred) for many years only to surface in a specific prosecution. In this instance, the defendant will now be the complaining party, as illustrated in the next case.

State v. Paul Blake, Prosecuting Attorney of Fayette County

584 S.E.2d 512 (W. Va. 2003)

[The petitioner operated a pawnshop for 10 years. Shortly after he went out of business, he was indicted for violation of W. Va. Code § 61-3-51 (1981). The statute required people in the business of buying precious metals or gems for non-personal use to (1) obtain and retain documentary proof that the seller owned the items and (2) list each such purchase, including information about the seller, in a permanent record book open to inspection by law enforcement. Violation is a felony with a maximum sentence of two years. The petitioner requests that the prosecuting attorney be prohibited from proceeding against him or that the circuit court be prohibited from proceeding to trial. We issue a writ prohibiting the circuit court from proceeding to trial.]

The petitioner contends, in this original action of prohibition, that W. Va. Code §61-3-51 (1981) has fallen into desuetude due to nonuse and lack of enforcement. Desuetude is defined as

1. Lack of use; obsolescence through disuse.

2. The doctrine holding that if a statute or treaty is left unenforced long enough, the courts will no longer regard it as having any legal effect even though it has not been repealed. Black's Law Dictionary 458 (7th ed. 1999).

> Stated more clearly, the doctrine of desuetude, the concept that a statute may be void because of its lack of use, is founded on the constitutional concept of fairness embodied in federal and state constitutional due process and equal protection clauses. In other words, "the problem [of applying, or refusing to apply, the rubric of desuetude] must be approached in terms of that fundamental fairness owed to the particular defendant that is the heart of due process." *United States v. Elliott*, 266 F. Supp. 318, 326 (S.D.N.Y. 1967).

The seminal case in West Virginia regarding desuetude is *Comm. on Legal Ethics v. Printz*, 187 W.Va. 182, 416 S.E.2d 720 (1992). In . . . *Printz*, this Court held that:

Penal statutes may become void under the doctrine of desuetude if:

(1) The statute proscribes only acts that are *malum prohibitum* and not *malum in se*;

(2) There has been open, notorious and pervasive violation of the statute for a long period; and

(3) There has been a conspicuous policy of nonenforcement of the statute.

We believe all three elements are satisfied in this case.

First, we must distinguish between crimes that are *malum prohibitum* [a crime only because made so by statute and not necessarily inherently immoral, such as littering] and crimes that are *malum in se* [a crime that is inherently immoral, such as rape or murder]. Crimes that are *malum in se* will not lose their criminal character through desuetude, but crimes that are *malum prohibitum* may. . . . The defense attorney . . . argued that "this kind of statute is clearly *malum prohibitum*. The whole distinction between *malum in se* and *malum prohibitum* makes it clear. This statute is not anything that came up through the common law or something that is inherently wrong." . . . We agree [that it is *malum prohibitum*].

Second, there must be an open, notorious, and pervasive violation of the statute for a long period before desuetude will take hold. In the case before us, the defense argued that the statute had been violated "for the entire period of time the statute has been in place[.]" The assistant prosecutor did not contest this contention, but rather argued that the statute was not old enough to fall into desuetude. Finally, there is no doubt that a conspicuous policy of nonenforcement exists in Fayette County. . . . [T]he Sheriff of Fayette County . . . testified that he believes W.Va. Code §61-3-51 has never been enforced in the county since its inception in 1981. . . .

Richard Kemp, an investigator, did a survey of businesses in Fayette County which pawn or purchase gems or precious metals, to see if they have been following the provisions of 61-3-51. The State stipulated Mr. Kemp would report that no business in Fayette County was making such report.

. . . [T]he petitioner argues that W.Va. Code § 61-3-51 has fallen into desuetude and, consequently, he cannot be reindicted and tried for failure to conform to the requirements of the statute. . . .

. . . [Citing *Printz,* the court agreed that a law that was not prosecuted in 20 years is unfair to the one person selectively prosecuted under it.] Because W.Va. Code § 61-3-51 (1981) has fallen into desuetude, the petitioner cannot be made to stand trial for violating the statute. The . . . indictment fails and must be dismissed.

Notes

1. *Does type of crime matter?* Why did the *Blake* court care whether the crime was *malum prohibitum* or *malum in se*? Could the answer be based, at least in part, on the concept of fair warning? Some jurisdictions apply desuetude to both categories of crimes.

2. *Other constitutional arguments.* Desuetude, though a separate non-constitutional defense, raises a number of constitutional issues that, today, are usually the focus of the defense. *Blake* noted that "fundamental fairness" is at the heart of not enforcing old or scarcely or never-invoked criminal laws. Often this is explained as a concern about fair warning that the conduct may be punished criminally. Since fair warning is protected by the Due Process Clause, desuetude cases are frequently presented as due process violations. Another rationale, resembling a substantive due process approach, is that the statute serves no modern purpose. Another is that it lends itself to improper selective enforcement, an Equal Protection argument. More generally, it has been argued that "longstanding nonenforcement implies a lapse in democratic support for the law itself, making it fundamentally unfair to impose the prohibition on individual defendants without further legislative action to renew the law's force." Zachary S. Price, *Reliance on Nonenforcement*, 58 Wm. & Mary L. Rev. 937, 1016 (2017).

3. *Desuetude in the courts.* Desuetude is rarely a successful defense. Indeed, it is a civil law doctrine that was not part of English law. Many American jurisdictions do not recognize it as a possible criminal defense. *See, e.g., State v. Nease*, 80 P. 897 (Or. 1905) (fact that statute never applied in particular manner in 40 years does not bar its enforcement); *Lee v. Seitz*, 1930 Tenn. App. LEXIS 139 (1930) (nonenforcement does not destroy statute's validity which has same effect as if enforced strictly). Instead, these jurisdictions focus on whether enforcing a long-dead statute would violate some constitutional provision, such as the due process guarantee of fundamental fairness. *See, e.g., United States v. Elliott*, 266 F. Supp. 318 (S.D.N.Y 1967) (refusing to apply desuetude to statute barring injury to property—here a bridge in Zambia—belonging to a foreign government; though law had not been enforced since enacted in 1917, policy underpinning still valid—to stop interference in foreign relations—and no fair notice problem because blowing up a bridge

in another country has never been accepted by community mores). *See generally* Note, *Desuetude,* 119 HARV. L. REV. 2209 (2006).

4. *Minimal enforcement.* Enforcement within any remotely recent time also is fatal to a desuetude defense. *See, e.g., Leonard v. Robinson*, 477 F.3d 347 (6th Cir. 2007) (statute enforced within last 10 years).

[c] Decision to Charge: Abuse of Discretion

A defendant may challenge prosecutorial discretion in bringing criminal charges.

State v. Bell

69 S.W.3d 171 (Tenn. 2002)

We granted this appeal to determine the following [issue] . . . whether the district attorney general abused his discretion by failing to consider and weigh evidence favorable to the defendant before denying the defendant's request for pretrial diversion. . . . After a thorough review of the record and relevant authority, we hold that when the district attorney general denies pretrial diversion without considering and weighing all the relevant factors, including substantial evidence favorable to the defendant, there is an abuse of prosecutorial discretion. . . . [T]he proper remedy . . . [is] for the district attorney general to consider and weigh all of the relevant factors to the pretrial diversion determination. . . .

BACKGROUND

The defendant, Johnnie Bell, was charged with vehicular homicide and aggravated assault [resulting] from a collision between a tractor-trailer driven by Bell and a minivan driven by Mrs. Lois Bacon [in which Bacon was killed and her passenger was injured.]. . . . After being charged, Bell applied for pretrial diversion. . . .

In the pretrial diversion report, Bell stated that he felt terrible about the victim's death but that the accident was unavoidable, and he was not negligent. Officer Jerry Mowell reported that Bell was truthful and cooperative during the investigation and showed extreme remorse for the accident. . . .

According to the pretrial diversion report, Bell was 34 years old at the time of the accident. He had been married for thirteen years and had three children. Bell graduated from high school and served seven years in the army before receiving an honorable discharge. . . . At the time he was interviewed, Bell worked as a releasing agent for Auto Rail Services, and a representative of the company characterized him as a good employee.

The pretrial diversion report also indicated that Bell paid a fine following a conviction for defective equipment in 1994. Additionally, Bell reported incurring two speeding tickets in Ohio and having a following-too-closely offense in Louisiana. Bell reported that although he had back problems, he was in good physical health and excellent mental health. . . . [Bell did not use alcohol or drugs.]. . . . In a letter dated March 26, 1999, the district attorney denied Bell's request for pretrial diversion, noting the following reasons:

> 1. The defendant takes no responsibility for his actions and blames the victim in this case.... The lack of acceptance of responsibility on behalf of the defendant shows that he would be a poor candidate for rehabilitation.
>
> 2. The defendant admits to having two speeding tickets and one conviction for following too closely. There is evidence that the defendant was following too closely to the victim of this fatality. The defendant has violated the motor vehicle rules in the past but chose to drive dangerously again.
>
> 3. The defendant had no hesitation in acting recklessly and did endanger several motorists other than the victims. Other motorists were in danger of serious bodily injury. Diversion would depreciate the seriousness of these crimes.
>
> 4. The defendant has an unstable work history as a truck driver. He has been terminated twice and all of his jobs have been of short duration. The defendant would be a poor candidate to complete any probationary period.
>
> 5. The driver was driving a large semi-truck. The victim was driving a Dodge Caravan. The officer states that the victim was killed in part by the fact that the defendant was following too closely. The defendant should have reasonably known of his vehicles [sic] potential for deadly force. Fatalities by large trucks are a growing problem in our community and in our nation....

[The trial and appellate courts upheld the denial of diversion.]

ANALYSIS

Under the pretrial diversion program, the district attorney general is permitted to suspend a prosecution against a qualified defendant for a period of up to two years.... A person who is statutorily eligible for pretrial diversion [as is Bell] is not presumptively entitled to diversion. Rather, the district attorney general has the sole discretion to determine whether to grant pretrial diversion to one who is statutorily eligible. In order for the district attorneys general "to properly exercise the discretion vested in them by the pretrial diversion statute," this Court has established several objective considerations:

> When deciding whether to [place the defendant on pretrial diversion]... a prosecutor should focus on the defendant's amenability to correction. Any factors which tend to accurately reflect whether a particular defendant will or will not become a repeat offender should be considered. Such factors must, of course, be clearly articulable and stated in the record in order that meaningful appellate review may be had. Among the factors to be considered in addition to the circumstances of the offense are the defendant's criminal record, social history, the physical and mental condition of a defendant where appropriate, and the likelihood that pretrial diversion will serve the ends of justice and the best interest of both the public and the defendant.

In cases where the district attorney general denies an application for pretrial diversion, the denial must be written and must discuss all of the relevant factors considered and the weight accorded to each factor. . . . In addition, the denial statement must identify factual disputes between the evidence relied upon and the application filed by the defendant.

. . . With these principles in mind, we turn to the facts of this case. The district attorney general denied pretrial diversion because Bell failed to take responsibility for his actions, has a record of traffic offenses, acted recklessly, endangered persons other than the victims, and has an unstable work history. The district attorney general also cited a need to deter irresponsible driving by tractor-trailer drivers. The district attorney general, however, failed to consider evidence favorable to Bell, such as his honorable discharge from the United States Army, stable marriage of thirteen years, high school diploma, and lack of a history of drug or alcohol abuse. Moreover, the district attorney general failed to set forth this favorable evidence in writing, weigh it against the other factors, and reach a conclusion based on the relative weight of all of the factors.

This Court has stated unequivocally that the district attorney general has a duty to exercise his or her discretion by focusing on a defendant's amenability for correction and by considering all of the relevant factors, including evidence that is favorable to a defendant. . . .

Accordingly, we now reiterate the well-established rule that the district attorney general, when denying pretrial diversion, must consider all relevant factors, including evidence favorable to the defendant, must weigh each factor, and must explain in writing how the decision to deny pretrial diversion was determined. We [hold] . . . that the district attorney general abused his discretion by failing to satisfy these requirements in this case. [Remanded.]

Notes

1. *An unusual case. Bell* is an unusual case where the appellate court found the prosecutor had committed an abuse of discretion in making a discretionary decision as to the sanction to seek. The usual rule is that the prosecutor's decision is found not to be an "abuse of discretion" even when the appellate court disagrees with it.

2. *Does* Bell *depend on use of specific factors?* Could the *Bell* result be the product of the court's adoption of specific factors to be addressed by the prosecutor in deciding whether to approve a petition for diversion? This is an unusual structure since courts ordinarily do not require a prosecutor to assess specific facts or explain their reasoning when making discretionary decisions.

3. *Prosecutors and office-related factors.* Research suggests that the personality of individual prosecutors, their age and extent of experience on the job, the degree of supervisory office culture and political pressures, on the chief elected prosecutor can affect charging prosecutors. Ronald F. Wright & Kay L. Levine, *The Cure for Young Prosecutors' Syndrome*, 56 Ariz. L. Rev. 1065 (2014) (concluding, based on

survey of prosecutors in eight different offices, that prosecutors tend to become less adversarial and more proportional and pragmatic over the course of their careers).

4. *Pretextual prosecutions.* It can be the case that government authorities have reason to believe that an individual has engaged in serious criminal wrongdoing but lack sufficient evidence to prosecute on that legal basis. They do, however, have evidence that the individual has engaged in less serious criminal activity and file charges on that basis. Perhaps the most famous historical instance of the scenario is the federal prosecution of gangster Al Capone in the 1930s. Capone was convicted of federal tax evasion and died in prison. While Capone was kept off the streets, did his pretextual prosecution come at a cost?

According to two commentators, the answer is yes:

> There is a strong social interest in non-pretextual prosecution, and that interest is much more important than the "fairness to the defendants" argument that has preoccupied the literature on the subject. Criminal charges are not only a means of identifying and punishing criminal conduct.... When a prosecutor gets a conviction... for an unrelated lesser crime than the one that motivated the investigation the signals are muddied.... Another audience gets a muddied signal: would-be criminals. Instead of sending the message that running illegal breweries and bribing local cops would lead to a term in a federal penitentiary, the Capone prosecution sent a much more complicated and much less helpful message: If you run a criminal enterprise, you should keep your name out of the newspapers and at least pretend to pay your taxes.... When crimes and charges do not coincide, no one can tell whether law enforcers are doing their jobs. The justice system loses the credibility it needs, and voters lose the trust they need to have in the justice system.

Daniel Richman & William J. Stuntz, *Al Capone's Revenge: An Essay on the Political Economy of Pretextual Prosecution*, 105 COLUM. L. REV. 583 (2005).

[d] Decision to Charge: Overlapping Statutorily Authorized Penalties

In some instances, a state or federal criminal defendant is subject to prosecution under more than one statute for a single criminal act. The prosecutor will choose which one to pursue. If the more severe law is used as the basis for a prosecution, the defense may challenge that decision on both due process and equal protection grounds.

United States v. Batchelder

442 U.S. 114 (1979)

JUSTICE MARSHALL delivered the opinion of the Court.

[Batchelder, a convicted felon, was charged with violating 18 U.S.C. § 922(h). This statute makes it a felony for any person previously convicted of a felony "to receive any firearm . . . which has been shipped . . . in interstate . . . commerce." He received the maximum authorized sentence of five years' imprisonment. He was not charged under a separate statute making it a felony punishable by two years' imprisonment for a convicted felon to "receive, possess or transport" a firearm. 18 U.S.C. § 1202(a). The Court of Appeals affirmed the conviction but remanded for sentencing; it held that since the two statutes are identical as applied to a convicted felon who receives a firearm, the maximum allowable sentence was two years' incarceration under § 1202. Justice Marshall delivered the opinion for a unanimous Court, ruling that the Court of Appeals erred in reducing the five-year sentence to two years. The U.S. Supreme Court found that the two statutes were unambiguous and that they were "fully capable of coexisting."]

. . . That this particular conduct may violate both Titles does not detract from the notice afforded by each. Although the statutes create uncertainty as to which crime may be charged and therefore what penalties may be imposed, they do so to no greater extent than would a single statute authorizing various alternative punishments. So long as overlapping criminal provisions clearly define the conduct prohibited and the punishment authorized, the notice requirements of the Due Process Clause are satisfied. This Court has long recognized that when an act violates more than one criminal statute, the Government may prosecute under either so long as it does not discriminate against any class of defendants. . . . Whether to prosecute and what charge to file or bring before a grand jury are decisions that generally rest in the prosecutor's discretion. . . . Contrary to the Court of Appeals' assertions, a prosecutor's discretion to choose between §§ 922(h) and 1202(a) is not "unfettered." Selectivity in the enforcement of criminal laws is, of course, subject to constitutional constraints [such as equal protection.]

And a decision to proceed under § 922(h) does not empower the Government to predetermine ultimate criminal sanctions. Rather, it merely enables the sentencing judge to impose a longer prison sentence than § 1202(a) would permit and precludes him from imposing the greater fine authorized by § 1202(a). More importantly, there is no appreciable difference between the discretion a prosecutor exercises when deciding whether to charge under one of two statutes with different elements and the discretion he exercises when choosing one of two statutes with identical elements. In the former situation, once he determines that the proof will support conviction under either statute, his decision is indistinguishable from the one he faces in the latter context. The prosecutor may be influenced by the penalties available upon conviction, but this fact, standing alone, does not give rise to a violation of the Equal Protection or Due Process Clause.

Notes

1. *Great disparity in sentences.* The sentencing disparity in the *Batchelder* case does not seem to be an extreme one in relative terms. Assume that a state legislature defined the offense of burglary in two separate statutes, one of which authorized a maximum period of incarceration of five years, while the other authorized

a maximum sentence of 30 years. Should a defendant prosecuted under the second statute be granted any relief, assuming that he or she cannot demonstrate impermissible selective prosecution?

2. *Ambiguity in punishment.* Overlapping statutes must be carefully examined to ascertain whether there is ambiguity regarding the choice of punishment. In *United States v. Trout*, 68 F.3d 1276 (11th Cir. 1995), a federal statute (the "Anti-Drug Abuse Amendments Act") prescribed two different punishments for the same offense. Because the government conceded that the statute was ambiguous, the appellate court upheld the district court's sentence under the "lesser punishment" section, observing that "the rule of lenity directs [the court] to apply the lesser penalty when a statute presents an ambiguous choice between two punishments."

3. *Charge decision affecting procedural options.* The prosecutor's discretion is routinely upheld even, as in *Batchelder*, when the decision will eliminate some of the defendant's procedural advantages. *See, e.g., Evans v. United States*, 779 A.2d 891 (D.C. 2001) (right to jury trial eliminated by prosecutor's choice of charges); *People v. Caster*, 2011 N.Y. Misc. LEXIS 3779 (Aug. 2, 2011) (eligibility for diversion).

[e] Decision to Charge: Selective Prosecution Limit

Although prosecutors enjoy enormous discretion in their decisions to file charges, their authority is not totally exempt from limits. One limit is that prosecutors cannot selectively single out individuals for prosecution, when they do so on impermissible grounds.

Even though there is a widely recognized presumption that every criminal prosecution is undertaken in good faith, a defendant may challenge his or her prosecution on selective prosecution grounds. The defendant will be required to meet a relatively heavy burden of proving facts sufficient to satisfy two requirements: (1) others similarly situated have not been prosecuted; and (2) the decision to prosecute was based on impermissible considerations, such as race, religion, political affiliation, or the exercise of constitutional rights. While the most important United States Supreme Court decisions were announced later (*Wayte v. United States*, below), two earlier cases are deserving of consideration.

Yick Wo v. Hopkins

118 U.S. 356 (1886)

[Yick Wo was found guilty of violating a San Francisco ordinance, which provided:

> Sec. 1. It shall be unlawful, from and after the passage of this order, for any person or persons to establish, maintain, or carry on a laundry within the corporate limits of the city and county of San Francisco without having first obtained the consent of the board of supervisors, except the same be located in a building constructed either of brick or stone.

His uncontested claim was that at the time of his conviction, there were about 320 laundries in the city, of which about 240 were owned by Chinese. Pursuant to the ordinance, he and 200 of his countrymen petitioned the board of supervisors for permission to continue their laundry business. Each of their petitions was denied, yet virtually all of those who were not Chinese were granted their petitions.

The United States Supreme Court held this a violation of the Fourteenth Amendment equal protection guarantee.]

... [T]he facts shown establish an administration directed so exclusively against a particular class of persons as to warrant and require the conclusion that, whatever may have been the intent of the ordinances as adopted, they are applied by the public authorities charged with their administration, and thus representing the state itself, with a mind so unequal and oppressive as to amount to a practical denial by the state of that equal protection of the laws which is secured to the petitioners, as to all other persons, by the broad and benign provisions of the Fourteenth Amendment to the Constitution of the United States. Though the law itself be fair on its face, and impartial in appearance, yet, if it is applied and administered by public authority with an evil eye and an unequal hand, so as practically to make unjust and illegal discriminations between persons in similar circumstances, material to their rights, the denial of equal justice is still within the prohibition of the constitution....

The present cases, as shown by the facts disclosed in the record, are within this class. It appears that both petitioners have complied with every requisite deemed by the law, or by the public officers charged with its administration, necessary for the protection of neighboring property from fire, or as a precaution against injury to the public health. No reason whatever, except the will of the supervisors, is assigned why they should not be permitted to carry on, in the accustomed manner, their harmless and useful occupation, on which they depend for a livelihood; and while this consent of the supervisors is withheld from them, and from 200 others who have also petitioned, all of whom happen to be Chinese subjects, 80 others, not Chinese subjects, are permitted to carry on the same business under similar conditions. The fact of this discrimination is admitted. No reason for it is shown, and the conclusion cannot be resisted that no reason for it exists except hostility to the race and nationality to which the petitioners belong, and which in the eye of the law is not justified. The discrimination is, therefore, illegal, and the public administration which enforces it is a denial of the equal protection of the laws, and a violation of the Fourteenth Amendment of the Constitution.

Oyler v. Boles

368 U.S. 448 (1962)

Oyler, serving a life sentence under a West Virginia habitual criminal statute [providing a mandatory life sentence upon a third conviction for a crime punishable by confinement in a penitentiary], claimed a denial of equal protection, alleging:

> Petitioner was discriminated against as an Habitual Criminal in that from January, 1940, to June, 1955, there were six men sentenced in the Taylor County Circuit Court who were subject to prosecution as Habitual

> offenders, Petitioner was the only man thus sentenced during this period. It is a matter of record that the five men who were not prosecuted as Habitual Criminals during this period all had three or more felony convictions and sentences as adults, and Petitioner's former convictions were a result of Juvenile Court actions.

Justice Clark, writing for a five-member majority, affirmed the denial of a writ of habeas corpus:

> ... We note that it is not stated whether the failure to proceed against other three-time offenders was due to lack of knowledge of the prior offenses on the part of the prosecutors or was the result of a deliberate policy of proceeding only in a certain class of cases or against specific persons. The statistics merely show that according to penitentiary records a high percentage of those subject to the law have not been proceeded against. There is no indication that these records of previous convictions, which may not have been compiled until after the three-time offenders had reached the penitentiary, were available to the prosecutors. Hence the allegations set out no more than a failure to prosecute others because of a lack of knowledge of their prior offenses. This does not deny equal protection due petitioners under the Fourteenth Amendment....
>
> Moreover, the conscious exercise of some selectivity in enforcement is not in itself a federal constitutional violation. Even though the statistics in this case might imply a policy of selective enforcement, it was not stated that the selection was deliberately based upon an unjustifiable standard such as race, religion, or other arbitrary classification. Therefore grounds supporting a finding of a denial of equal protection were not alleged....

[Chief Justice Warren and Justices Douglas, Black, and Brennan dissented on different grounds. They expressed no opinions relevant to the equal protection issue.]

Wayte v. United States

470 U.S. 598 (1985)

Justice Powell delivered the opinion of the Court.

The question presented is whether a passive enforcement policy under which the Government prosecutes only those who report themselves as having violated the law, or who are reported by others, violates the First and Fifth Amendments.

[Wayte was charged by the federal government with failure to register for the draft. He claimed that he had been singled out for criminal prosecution because of his vocal opposition to the registration system.[2]

2. On August 4, 1980, for example, petitioner wrote to both the President and the Selective Service System. In his letter to the President, he stated: "I decided to obey my conscience rather than your law. I did not register for your draft. I will never register for your draft. Nor will I ever

Six months later, petitioner sent a second letter to Selective Service:

> Last August I wrote to inform you of my intention not to register for the draft. Well, I did not register, and still plan never to do so, but thus far I have received no reply to my letter, much less any news about your much-threatened prosecutions. I must interpret your silence as meaning that you are too busy or disorganized to respond to letters or keep track of us draft-age youth. So I will keep you posted of my whereabouts.

He also stated that, although he would "be traveling the nation ... encouraging resistance and spreading the word about peace and disarmament," he could be reached at his home address in Pasadena, California. Wayte moved to dismiss his indictment on the ground of selective prosecution, asserting that he and other vocal non-registrants were identified for prosecution because of their exercise of First Amendment rights. He offered evidence that more than 650,000 persons had failed to register. Yet, only a dozen or so men had been prosecuted, all of whom were "vocal opponents of draft registration." The district court dismissed his indictment on the ground that the government had failed to rebut Wayte's prima facie case of selective prosecution. The court of appeals reversed, holding that Wayte failed to establish that the government focused its investigation on him because of his protest activities. While Wayte had shown that the government was aware that a "passive enforcement system" would result in prosecutions primarily of vocal objectors, there was no evidence of impermissible governmental motivation. The appellate court also found two legitimate explanations for the government's enforcement system: (1) identities of non-reported non-registrants were not known and (2) non-registrants who expressed refusal to register made clear their intentional violation of the law.] ...

It is appropriate to judge selective prosecution claims according to ordinary equal protection standards. Under our prior cases, these standards require petitioner to show both that the passive enforcement system had a discriminatory effect and that it was motivated by a discriminatory purpose.... All petitioner has shown here is that those eventually prosecuted, along with many not prosecuted, reported themselves as having violated the law. He has not shown that the enforcement policy selected nonregistrants for prosecution on the basis of their speech. Indeed, he could not have done so given the way the "beg" policy was carried out. The Government did not prosecute those who reported themselves but later registered. Nor did it prosecute those who protested registration but did not report themselves or were not reported by others. In fact, the Government did not even investigate those who wrote letters to Selective Service criticizing registration unless their letters stated affirmatively that they had refused to comply with the law.... The Government, on the other hand, did prosecute people who reported themselves or were reported by

---

cooperate with yours or any other military system, despite the laws I might break or the consequences which may befall me." In his letter to the Selective Service System, he similarly stated: "I have not registered for the draft. I plan never to register. I realize the possible consequences of my action, and I accept them."

others but who did not publicly protest. These facts demonstrate that the Government treated all reported nonregistrants similarly. It did not subject vocal nonregistrants to any special burden. Indeed, those prosecuted in effect selected themselves for prosecution by refusing to register after being reported and warned by the Government.

Even if the passive policy had a discriminatory effect, petitioner has not shown that the Government intended such a result....

Petitioner also challenges the passive enforcement policy directly on First Amendment grounds. In particular, he claims that "[e]ven though the [Government's passive] enforcement policy did not overtly punish protected speech as such, it inevitably created a content-based regulatory system with a concomitantly disparate, content-based impact on nonregistrants." ... This Court has held that when, as here, "'speech' and 'nonspeech' elements are combined in the same course of conduct, a sufficiently important governmental interest in regulating the nonspeech element can justify incidental limitations on First Amendment freedoms." *United States v. O'Brien*, 391 U.S. 367. Government regulation is justified "if it is within the constitutional power of the Government; if it furthers an important or substantial governmental interest; if the governmental interest is unrelated to the suppression of free expression; and if the incidental restriction on alleged First Amendment freedoms is no greater than is essential to the furtherance of that interest." In the present case, neither the first nor third condition is disputed.

There can be no doubt that the passive enforcement policy meets the second condition. Few interests can be more compelling than a nation's need to ensure its own security.... First, by relying on reports of nonregistration, the Government was able to identify and prosecute violators without further delay. Although it still was necessary to investigate those reported to make sure that they were required to register and had not, the Government did not have to search actively for the names of these likely violators. Such a search would have been difficult and costly at that time. Indeed, it would be a costly step in any "active" prosecution system involving thousands of nonregistrants. The passive enforcement program thus promoted prosecutorial efficiency. Second, the letters written to Selective Service provided strong, perhaps conclusive evidence of the nonregistrant's intent not to comply—one of the elements of the offense. Third, prosecuting visible nonregistrants was thought to be an effective way to promote general deterrence, especially since failing to proceed against publicly known offenders would encourage others to violate the law....

We conclude that the Government's passive enforcement system together with its "beg" policy violated neither the First nor Fifth Amendment. Accordingly, we affirm the judgment of the Court of Appeals....

[Justice Marshall, with whom Justice Brennan joins, dissents, arguing that the real issue is whether Wayte may discover government documents concerning selective prosecution, an issue addressed in the next case.]

Notes

1. *Plaintiff's evidence. Wayte* states that a plaintiff in a selective prosecution case must prove both discriminatory purpose and discriminatory effect. How would a plaintiff gather the necessary information? Who would be the witnesses? What data should be gathered? Where would it come from? How much would it cost to obtain the necessary information?

2. *Discovery.* The issue of discovery addressed by the *Wayte* dissenters is frequently an important pretrial issue in selective prosecution cases. What factual showing must be made by a complaining defendant in order to obtain information from the government regarding its charging decision? The United States Supreme Court answered that question in the following case.

United States v. Armstrong[1]

517 U.S. 456 (1996)

CHIEF JUSTICE REHNQUIST delivered the opinion of the Court.

In this case, we consider the showing necessary for a defendant to be entitled to discovery on a claim that the prosecuting attorney singled him out for prosecution on the basis of his race. We conclude that respondents failed to satisfy the threshold showing: They failed to show that the Government declined to prosecute similarly situated suspects of other races.

[In April 1992, respondents were charged with conspiracy related to the distribution of more than 50 grams of crack cocaine and certain firearms offenses. They filed a motion for discovery, alleging that they were victims of selective prosecution based upon race. Accompanying this motion was an affidavit prepared by a paralegal stating that in every one of the 24 crack cocaine cases closed by that office during 1991, the defendant was black. Over government objection, the district court granted the motion and ordered the government to: (1) provide a list of all cases in the last three years in which the government charged both cocaine and firearms offenses, (2) identify the race of the defendant in those cases, (3) identify levels of law enforcement involved in those cases, and (4) explain its criteria for deciding to prosecute those defendants. The government moved for reconsideration, submitting affidavits to explain why the respondents had been charged and why the respondents' "study" failed to support the inference that blacks had been singled out for prosecution. The district court denied the motion "for reconsideration and the Ninth Circuit Court of Appeals affirmed that order, holding that a defendant is not required to demonstrate that the government has failed to prosecute others who are similarly situated."]

... A selective-prosecution claim is not a defense on the merits to the criminal charge itself, but an independent assertion that the prosecutor has brought the

---

1. This case is also discussed in Chapter 10 as it relates to discovery under Rule 16.

charge for reasons forbidden by the Constitution. Our cases delineating the necessary elements to prove a claim of selective prosecution have taken great pains to explain that the standard is a demanding one. These cases afford a "background presumption," that the showing necessary to obtain discovery should itself be a significant barrier to the litigation of insubstantial claims.

A selective-prosecution case asks a court to exercise judicial power over a "special province" of the Executive. ... [A] "presumption of regularity supports" their prosecutorial decisions and, "in the absence of clear evidence to the contrary, courts presume that they have properly discharged their official duties." [citations omitted.]

... The requirements for a selective-prosecution claim draw on "ordinary equal protection standards." The claimant must demonstrate that the federal prosecutorial policy "had a discriminatory effect and that it was motivated by a discriminatory purpose." To establish a discriminatory effect in a race case, the claimant must show that similarly situated individuals of a different race were not prosecuted.

The similarly situated requirement does not make a selective-prosecution claim impossible to prove. [The court then discusses the *Yick Wo* case.]

... Having reviewed the requirements to prove a selective-prosecution claim, we turn to the showing necessary to obtain discovery in support of such a claim. If discovery is ordered, the Government must assemble from its own files documents which might corroborate or refute the defendant's claim. Discovery thus imposes many of the costs present when the Government must respond to a prima facie case of selective prosecution. It will divert prosecutors' resources and may disclose the Government's prosecutorial strategy. The justifications for a rigorous standard for the elements of a selective-prosecution claim thus require a correspondingly rigorous standard for discovery in aid of such a claim. The parties, and the Courts of Appeals which have considered the requisite showing to establish entitlement to discovery, describe this showing with a variety of phrases, like "colorable basis," "substantial threshold showing," "substantial and concrete basis," or "reasonable likelihood." However, the many labels for this showing conceal the degree of consensus about the evidence necessary to meet it. The Courts of Appeals "require some evidence tending to show the existence of the essential elements of the defense," discriminatory effect and discriminatory intent. *United States v. Berrios*, 501 F.2d 1207, 1211 (2d Cir. 1974).

... In this case we consider what evidence constitutes "some evidence tending to show the existence" of the discriminatory effect element. The Court of Appeals held that a defendant may establish a colorable basis for discriminatory effect without evidence that the Government has failed to prosecute others who were similarly situated to the defendant. We think it was mistaken in this view. The vast majority of the Courts of Appeals require the defendant to produce some evidence that similarly situated defendants of other races could have been prosecuted, but were not, and this requirement is consistent with our equal protection case law.

... In the present case, if the claim of selective prosecution were well founded, it should not have been an insuperable task to prove that persons of other races were being treated differently than respondents. For instance, respondents could have investigated whether similarly situated persons of other races were prosecuted by the State of California and were known to federal law enforcement officers, but were not prosecuted in federal court. We think the required threshold—a credible showing of different treatment of similarly situated persons—adequately balances the Government's interest in vigorous prosecution and the defendant's interest in avoiding selective prosecution. In the case before us, respondents' "study" did not constitute "some evidence tending to show the existence of the essential elements of" a selective-prosecution claim. The study failed to identify individuals who were not black, could have been prosecuted for the offenses for which respondents were charged, but were not so prosecuted. This omission was not remedied by respondents" evidence in opposition to the Government's motion for reconsideration. The newspaper article, which discussed the discriminatory effect of federal drug sentencing laws, was not relevant to an allegation of discrimination in decisions to prosecute. Respondents' affidavits, which recounted one attorney's conversation with a drug treatment center employee and the experience of another attorney defending drug prosecutions in state court, recounted hearsay and reported personal conclusions based on anecdotal evidence. The judgment of the Court of Appeals is therefore reversed, and the case is remanded for proceedings consistent with this opinion.

Justice Stevens, dissenting.

... The Court correctly concludes that in this case the facts presented to the District Court in support of respondents' claim that they had been singled out for prosecution because of their race were not sufficient to prove that defense. Moreover, I agree with the Court that their showing was not strong enough to give them a right to discovery, either under Rule 16 or under the District Court's inherent power to order discovery in appropriate circumstances. Like Chief Judge Wallace of the Court of Appeals, however, I am persuaded that the District Judge did not abuse her discretion when she concluded that the factual showing was sufficiently disturbing to require some response from the United States Attorney's Office. Perhaps the discovery order was broader than necessary, but I cannot agree with the Court's apparent conclusion that no inquiry was permissible.

The District Judge's order should be evaluated in light of three circumstances that underscore the need for judicial vigilance over certain types of drug prosecutions. First, the Anti-Drug Abuse Act of 1986 and subsequent legislation established a regime of extremely high penalties for the possession and distribution of so-called "crack" cocaine.... Second, the disparity between the treatment of crack cocaine and powder cocaine is matched by the disparity between the severity of the punishment imposed by federal law and ... [the lower sentences] imposed by state law for the same conduct.... The majority of States draw no distinction between types of cocaine in their penalty schemes; of those that do, none has established as stark a differential as the Federal Government.... Finally, it is undisputed that the brunt of the elevated federal penalties falls heavily on blacks.... The extraordinary severity of the imposed penalties and the troubling racial patterns of enforcement give rise to a special concern about the fairness of charging practices for crack offenses. Evidence tending to prove that black defendants charged with distribution of crack in the Central District of California are prosecuted in federal court, whereas members of other races charged with similar offenses are prosecuted in state court, warrants close scrutiny by the federal judges in that District. In my view, the District Judge, who has sat on both the federal and the state benches in Los Angeles, acted well within her discretion to call for the development of facts that would demonstrate what standards, if any, governed the choice of forum where similarly situated offenders are prosecuted.

[The separate concurring opinions by JUSTICES SOUTER, GINSBURG and BREYER are omitted.]

Notes

1. *Selective prosecution in a nutshell. Armstrong* makes it clear that there is a presumption of regularity for prosecutorial decisions and, absent objective proof to the contrary, courts presume that prosecutorial decisions have been properly discharged. To prevail on what the *Armstrong* Court termed its "rigorous standard," the accused must address the twin issues of discriminatory effect and discriminatory purpose. Specifically, selective prosecution requires that the defendant establish that he or she was treated differently from other similarly situated people (discriminatory effect). To show effect, there must be a showing, in a race-based case, that "similarly situated individuals of a different race were not persecuted." *Armstrong*, 517 U.S. at 465. Further, the accused must show that the differential treatment was based on an impermissible consideration (discriminatory purpose) such as race or religion, intent to inhibit or punish the exercise of constitutional rights, or malicious or bad faith intent to injure him. *Diesel v. Town of Lewisberg*, 232 F.3d 92, 103 (2d Cir. 2000). The difficulty in finding proof of these elements is a main reason that selective prosecution claims rarely succeed. As the late Professor William Stuntz observed, the decision creates a "classic Catch-22 situation: Armstrong's claim couldn't win without more information, yet Armstrong could get that information only if he had a winning claim without it." WILLIAM J. STUNTZ, THE COLLAPSE OF AMERICAN CRIMINAL JUSTICE 120 (2011).

A review of the case law reveals that a successful claim is very rare. *See, e.g., Commonwealth v. Bernardo B.*, 900 N.E.2d 834 (Mass. 2009) (granting relief, and allowing discovery, in case where underage male claimed that he was selectively prosecuted for statutory rape because of his gender, compared to underage females); *cf. In re Welfare of B.A.H.*, 829 N.W.2d 431 (Minn. Ct. App. 2013) (underage boys aged 13 and 14 engaged in sexual misconduct with one another but only one was prosecuted; held, violated equal protection since similarly situated people not treated alike; no discussion of discriminatory purpose).

2. *Is a single event sufficient?* Must there be a long-standing practice of non-prosecution under the *Wayte* standard, or would it be permissible to establish such a claim based upon a single event? Consider the following case.

During a private party at a club, female nude dancers allegedly engaged in sexual conduct with male patrons in return for money. Four police officers arrested and prosecuted the four female performers, but did not seek to arrest any of the 50 to 75 men who "fondled the women performers and thrust money at them." Two officers testified that "they understood the focus of the investigation to be on the female dancers." The female defendants moved for dismissal of all charges, claiming that they could not be convicted of prostitution because of discriminatory prosecution. The government responded that the male patrons were not similarly situated with the female performers because (1) the women engaged in a larger number of criminal law violations and (2) the women received financial benefit from their actions. The government also responded that any gender-based discrimination occurred because the small number of police officers were forced to focus their resources on the smallest, most manageable group—the female performers. The Wisconsin Court of Appeals rejected the government's argument, noting that both the patrons and performers could have been convicted under the language of the Wisconsin statute:

> The plain language of that statute criminalized the behavior of both the payor and the payee. It is persuasive that the goals of both general and specific deterrence in this case would have been better served by the arrest of some of the large number of local citizens involved in illicit behavior than by the arrest of a small number of out-of-towners. Because the police intentionally focused their investigation on only the female violators, the trial court properly dismissed the criminal charges.

State v. McCollum, 464 N.W.2d 44 (Wis. Ct. App. 1990). Was *McCollum* properly decided according to the *Wayte* standard?

3. *Outrageous intent supplanting lack of discriminatory effect?* In a selective prosecution claim, can outrageous discriminatory intent be sufficient to compensate for a lack of discriminatory effect? The Sixth Circuit Court of Appeals held in *United States v. Jones*, 159 F.3d 969 (6th Cir. 1998), that a black defendant was entitled to discovery based upon unprofessional behavior by white police officers even though the defendant failed to establish a showing of discriminatory effect. The officers, who had arrested the defendant, had printed pictures of the defendant and his wife on the shirts worn by officers during the arrest, and one officer had sent the defendant a postcard from Mexico taunting him about his chances of acquittal at his upcoming trial.

Upon remand, and "voluminous discovery regarding local law enforcement practices," the trial court denied defendant's motion to dismiss his indictment, which the Sixth Circuit upheld on appeal. While the court found evidence of discriminatory intent, it concluded that the defendant failed to show that "similarly situated non-African-American defendants were not recommended for federal prosecution based on their race." *United States v. Jones*, 399 F.3d 640, 645–46 (6th Cir. 2005).

4. *Similarly situated.* The Fourth Circuit Court of Appeals, clarifying *Armstrong's* similarly situated requirement for selective prosecution claims, held that people are similarly situated if "their circumstances present no distinguishable legitimate prosecutorial factors that might justify making different prosecutorial decisions with respect to them." *United States v. Olvis*, 97 F.3d 739, 744 (4th Cir. 1996). The two black defendants in *Olvis* did not meet the high threshold burden for obtaining discovery where they claimed that the state had failed to indict similarly situated white conspirators in a crack cocaine conspiracy. The court found that the white conspirators presented prosecutorial profiles significantly different from those of the black defendants. For example, one white conspirator offered to go undercover and there was not sufficient evidence to prosecute the second. As for the defendants, by contrast, one was the alleged head of the organization and the other was prosecuted for committing perjury before the grand jury and for having refused to cooperate with law enforcement authorities.

5. *Impact of* Armstrong. For an insightful discussion of the way in which *Armstrong* has acted as a barrier to the establishment of selective prosecution claims, *see* Anne Bowen Poulin, *Prosecutorial Discretion and Selective Prosecution: Enforcing Protection After* United States v. Armstrong, 34 AM. CRIM. L. REV. 1071 (1997). Because *Armstrong* limits the ability of a defendant to obtain discovery, Professor Poulin urges the enlistment of all branches of government to eliminate selective prosecution in the judicial system. While *soft enforcement*, defined as the impact of an open judicial process on the voluntary behavior of both the government and the public, serves as the most effective protector of the right against selective prosecution, the key to exercising that right is discovery:

> In most cases, *Armstrong* imposes a strict requirement that an aggrieved defendant requesting discovery prove the existence of a control group (other similarly situated violators who have not been prosecuted), making it unlikely that a defendant will win discovery. However, the decision signals that there may be an exception to the control group requirement if the defendant presents evidence of improper motive. The courts should respond to that signal and grant discovery, not only if the defendant proves direct expressions of improper motive, but also if the defendant produces other evidence that indicates improper motive, such as proof of departure from regular procedures or pretextual conduct.

Id. at 1124.

6. *Uncovering discriminatory charging decisions outside of formal discovery.* It is important to recognize that *Armstrong* addresses only the entitlement to discovery, not the merits of a claim. Assuming that *Armstrong* is a significant barrier to uncovering discriminatory charging decisions, are there other ways to discover those practices? Professor Andrew Leipold suggests that race-based decision making in official discretion can be reduced through the use of racial impact studies and information-gathering studies on discretionary police and prosecutor decisions. Andrew D. Leipold, *Objective Tests and Subjective Bias: Some Problems of Discriminatory Intent in the Criminal Law*, 73 CHI.-KENT. L. REV. 559, 590 (1998). Another commentator, however, argues that defendants will have a nearly impossible burden of satisfying the *Armstrong* standard where they are complaining that similarly situated whites are not prosecuted at all. He describes the following case:

> Proof problems arise when a crime is minor enough that, absent selective prosecution, it is not prosecuted at all. As one example, imagine that a federal official, motivated by racial animus, concentrates health and safety inspections on (the few) food distribution businesses owned by African Americans, Asian Americans, or Latinos. The official prosecutes a number of these minorities for criminal violations of the Food, Drug, and Cosmetic Act but prosecutes no white owners. At the time, suppose the relevant state, relying on federal efforts, brings no criminal prosecutions for these kinds of violations. Under *Armstrong* this startling racial gap would not be sufficient to permit a district court to order discovery unless the defendants can first show that similarly situated but unprosecuted whites also violated the statute. But given the difficulty of detecting such violations in private facilities—that is, after all, the whole reason for authorizing agents to conduct surprise inspections—how can a black defendant, acting without such power, prove that his white counterparts are also violating the law? Realistically, he can't.

Richard H. McAdams, *Race and Selective Prosecution: Discovering the Pitfalls of* Armstrong, 73 Chi.-Kent L. Rev. 605, 617–19 (1998).*

7. *Wealth as criterion.* In California, Oregon, Pennsylvania, and South Carolina, prosecutors have solicited and accepted private financing through voluntary contributions from the business community in order to pay costs of criminal prosecutions in certain types of cases (essentially white-collar crime prosecutions). In his article, *Private Financing of Criminal Prosecutions and the Differing Protections of Liberty and Equality in the Criminal Justice System*, 23 Hastings Const. L.Q. 551, 670 (1997), Professor Joseph Kennedy postulates that the result of such private financing will be a "two-tiered criminal justice system" with the best efforts and resources going to the privately financed cases:

> [P]rivate financing serves economic efficiency and the interests of victims selectively, at best, and inevitably at the expense of equality interests whose importance has not been appreciated fully. Private financing in any of its likely forms threatens equality of treatment by potentially biasing the prosecutor in favor of the contributors. Such a practice sacrifices the equality of the prosecutor's choices in order to enlist the financial support of victims who have both a direct interest in the prosecution and the money to further that interest. Ultimately, the overall benefit of that support to society does not justify the damage done to the legitimacy of government prosecutions.

Even if funds for hiring private lawyers to serve as prosecutors come from public rather than non-public sources, there are strong arguments against the practice. Can you identify them? Are there any advantages of using a private lawyer to prosecute criminal cases (which includes making discretionary decisions whether to prosecute and which crimes to pursue)? *See generally* Roger A. Fairfax, Jr., *Delegation of the Criminal Prosecution Function to Private Actors*, 43 U.C. DAVIS L. REV. 411 (2009). Also, consider the English system, where the same barristers sometimes prosecute and sometimes defend criminal cases. Might such a system, if it were ever adopted in the United States, produce prosecutors and defenders who practice with a better balanced sense of justice (and with less of an edge of self-righteousness that sometimes affects criminal practitioners on both sides), rather than seeing themselves as belonging to the prosecution or defense "camp?" Or is it better to have a system where both prosecutors and defenders act as ultra-zealous advocates?

8. *Selective prosecution and capital cases.* Given the high stakes of capital litigation, should the demanding proof regime of *Armstrong* be relaxed? The result in *United States v. Bass*, 536 U.S. 862 (2002) (per curiam) suggests that the answer is no. In *Bass*, the Supreme Court overruled the Sixth Circuit Court of Appeals' holding that discovery regarding the government's capital charging practices was warranted. Bass presented considerable statistical evidence in support of his contention of racial bias, showing *inter alia* disparity in the percentages of white versus black defendants receiving non-death pleas. The Court reversed, stating that Bass failed to submit relevant evidence showing that similarly situated defendants were treated differently: the statistics provided said "nothing about charges brought against similarly situated defendants." *Id.* at 864.

[f] Decision to Charge: Vindictive Prosecution Limit

Once a prosecutor has made the basic decision to charge the defendant with a criminal offense, the next question is the precise charge or range of charges to be filed against that individual. The charging decision involves not only a consideration of "degrees" of liability within a certain crime (murder first degree versus manslaughter, aggravated robbery versus simple robbery), but also the question whether multiple counts or multiple offenses should be charged. An individual who breaks into a home at night, steals property, and threatens to assault the homeowner, may be charged with (1) burglary, (2) theft, or (3) assault, or with any combination of those three offenses. Again, the circumstances of the case and matters related to characteristics of the defendant may influence a prosecutor to charge "the maximum" or something of lesser magnitude.

A defendant may seek to have charges dismissed because of prosecutorial vindictiveness, the second chief limit on prosecutorial discretion. The Due Process Clause prohibits the prosecution from punishing a defendant for exercising a protected statutory or constitutional right. *See, e.g.*, United States v Stokes 124 F.3d 34, 45 (1st Cir. 1997). Consider, in this context, the following decision by the United States Supreme Court, which alleges prosecutional vindictiveness in response to a defendant's demand for a jury (as opposed to a judge) trial.

United States v. Goodwin

457 U.S. 368 (1982)

[The facts of this case are best summarized in JUSTICE BRENNAN's dissenting opinion: Respondent was originally charged with several petty offenses and misdemeanors—speeding, reckless driving, failing to give aid at the scene of an accident, fleeing from a police officer, and assault by striking a police officer—arising from his conduct on the Baltimore-Washington Parkway. Assuming that respondent had been convicted on every count charged in this original complaint, the maximum punishment to which he conceivably could have been exposed was fines of $3,500 and 28 months in prison. Because all of the charges against respondent were petty offenses or misdemeanors, they were scheduled for trial before a magistrate, who was not authorized to conduct jury trials. In addition, the case was assigned to a prosecutor who, owing to inexperience, was not even authorized to try felony cases. Thus the Government recognized that respondent's alleged crimes were relatively minor, and attempted to dispose of them in an expedited manner. But respondent frustrated this attempt at summary justice by demanding a jury trial in Federal District Court. This was his right, of course, not only under the applicable statute, but also under the Constitution.

Respondent's demand required that the case be transferred from the Magistrate's Court in Hyattsville to the District Court in Baltimore, and that the prosecution be reassigned to an Assistant United States Attorney, who was authorized to prosecute cases in the District Court. The new prosecutor sought and obtained a second, four-count indictment, in which the same conduct originally charged as petty-offense and misdemeanor counts was now charged as a misdemeanor and two felonies: assaulting, resisting, or impeding a federal officer with a deadly weapon, and assault with a dangerous weapon.

[Respondent was convicted of a felony.] If we assume (as before) that respondent was convicted on all of these charges, his maximum exposure to punishment had now become fines of $11,500 and 15 years in prison. Respondent's claim below was that such an elevation of the charges against him from petty offenses to felonies, following his exercise of his statutory and constitutional right to a jury trial, reflected prosecutorial vindictiveness that denied him due process of law.]

JUSTICE STEVENS delivered the opinion of the Court.

... The imposition of punishment is the very purpose of virtually all criminal proceedings. The presence of a punitive motivation, therefore, does not provide an adequate basis for distinguishing governmental action that is fully justified as a legitimate response to perceived criminal conduct from governmental action that is an impermissible response to noncriminal, protected activity. Motives are complex and difficult to prove. As a result, in certain cases in which action detrimental to the defendant has been taken after the exercise of a legal right, the Court has found it necessary to "presume" an improper vindictive motive. Given the severity of such a presumption, however—which may operate in the absence of any proof of an improper motive and thus may block a legitimate response to criminal conduct—the Court has done so only in cases in which a reasonable likelihood of vindictiveness exists.

In *North Carolina v. Pearce*, 395 U.S. 711 (1969), the Court held that neither the Double Jeopardy Clause nor the Equal Protection Clause prohibits a trial judge from imposing a harsher sentence on retrial after a criminal defendant successfully attacks an initial conviction on appeal. The Court stated, however, that "[i]t can hardly be doubted that it would be a flagrant violation [of the Due Process Clause] of the Fourteenth Amendment for a state trial court to follow an announced practice of imposing a heavier sentence upon every reconvicted defendant for the explicit purpose of punishing the defendant for his having succeeded in getting his original conviction set aside." The Court continued:

> Due process of law, then, requires that vindictiveness against a defendant for having successfully attacked his first conviction must play no part in the sentence he receives after a new trial. And since the fear of such vindictiveness may unconstitutionally deter a defendant's exercise of the right to appeal or collaterally attack his first conviction, due process also requires that a defendant be freed of apprehension of such a retaliatory motivation on the part of the sentencing judge.

In order to assure the absence of such a motivation, the Court concluded:

> [W]henever a judge imposes a more severe sentence upon a defendant after a new trial, the reasons for his doing so must affirmatively appear. Those reasons must be based upon objective information concerning identifiable conduct on the part of the defendant occurring after the time of the original sentencing proceeding. And the factual data upon which the increased sentence is based must be made part of the record, so that the constitutional legitimacy of the increased sentence may be fully reviewed on appeal.

In sum, the Court applied a presumption of vindictiveness, which may be overcome only by objective information in the record justifying the increased sentence.

In *Blackledge v. Perry*, 417 U.S. 21 (1974), the Court confronted the problem of increased punishment upon retrial after appeal in a setting different from that considered in *Pearce*. Perry was convicted of assault in an inferior court having exclusive jurisdiction for the trial of misdemeanors. The court imposed a 6-month sentence. Under North Carolina law, Perry had an absolute right to a trial *de novo* in the Superior Court, which possessed felony jurisdiction. After Perry filed his notice of appeal, the prosecutor obtained a felony indictment charging him with assault with a deadly weapon. Perry pleaded guilty to the felony and was sentenced to a term of five to seven years in prison.

. . . The Court held that the opportunities for vindictiveness in the situation before it were such "as to impel the conclusion that due process of law requires a rule analogous to that of the *Pearce* case." It explained:

> A prosecutor clearly has a considerable stake in discouraging convicted misdemeanants from appealing and thus obtaining a trial *de novo* in the Superior Court, since such an appeal will clearly require increased expenditures of prosecutorial resources before the defendant's conviction becomes final, and may even result in a formerly convicted defendant's going free. And, if the prosecutor has the means readily at hand to discourage such appeals—by "upping the ante" through a felony indictment whenever a convicted misdemeanant pursues his statutory appellate remedy—the State can insure that only the most hardy defendants will brave the hazards of a *de novo* trial.

The Court emphasized in *Blackledge* that it did not matter that no evidence was present that the prosecutor had acted in bad faith or with malice in seeking the felony indictment. As in *Pearce*, the Court held that the likelihood of vindictiveness justified a presumption that would free defendants of apprehension of such a retaliatory motivation on the part of the prosecutor. . . .

There is good reason to be cautious before adopting an inflexible presumption of prosecutorial vindictiveness in a pretrial setting. In the course of preparing a case for trial, the prosecutor may uncover additional information that suggests a basis for further prosecution or he simply may come to realize that information possessed by the State has a broader significance. At this stage of the proceedings, the prosecutor's assessment of the proper extent of prosecution may not have crystallized. In contrast, once a trial begins—and certainly by the time a conviction has been obtained—it is much more likely that the State has discovered and assessed all of the information against an accused and has made a determination, on the basis of that information, of the extent to which he should be prosecuted. Thus, a change in the charging decision made after an initial trial is completed is much more likely to be improperly motivated than is a pretrial decision. In addition, a defendant before trial is expected to invoke procedural rights that inevitably impose some "burden" on the prosecutor. Defense counsel routinely file pretrial motions to suppress evidence; to challenge the sufficiency and form of an indictment; to plead an affirmative defense; to request psychiatric services; to obtain access to government files; to be tried by jury. It is unrealistic to assume that a prosecutor's probable response to such motions is to seek to penalize and to deter. The invocation of procedural rights is an integral part of the adversary process in which our criminal justice system operates.

. . . In declining to apply a presumption of vindictiveness, we of course do not foreclose the possibility that a defendant in an appropriate case might prove objectively that the prosecutor's charging decision was motivated by a desire to punish him for doing something that the law plainly allowed him to do. In this case, however, the Court of Appeals stated: "On this record we readily conclude that the prosecutor did not act with actual vindictiveness in seeking a felony indictment." ... Respondent does not challenge that finding. Absent a presumption of vindictiveness, no due process violation has been established.

[JUSTICE BRENNAN dissented, arguing that Goodwin's claim should be analyzed as follows:]

... Did the elevation of the charges against respondent pose a realistic likelihood of "vindictiveness?" *See Blackledge v. Perry*, 417 U.S., at 27. Is it possible that "the fear of such vindictiveness may unconstitutionally deter" a person in respondent's position from exercising his statutory and constitutional right to a jury trial? *See North Carolina v. Pearce, supra*, 395 U.S. at 725. The answer to these questions is plainly "Yes."

The Court suggests ... that the distinction between a bench trial and a jury trial is unimportant in this context. Such a suggestion is demonstrably fallacious. Experienced criminal practitioners, for both prosecution and defense, know that a jury trial entails far more prosecutorial work than a bench trial.... And there is always the specter of the "irrational" acquittal by a jury that is unreviewable on appeal. Thus it is simply inconceivable that a criminal defendant's election to be tried by jury would be a matter of indifference to his prosecutor. On the contrary, the prosecutor would almost always prefer that the defendant waive such a "troublesome" right. And if the defendant refuses to do so, the prosecutor's subsequent elevation of the charges against the defendant manifestly poses a realistic likelihood of vindictiveness.

Notes

1. *Presumption of vindictiveness present: post-trial. (Blackledge).* As *Goodwin* notes, the Supreme Court has recognized a presumption of vindictiveness in two post-trial situations. First, in *North Carolina v. Pearce,* when a defendant is convicted and sentenced, appeals, receives a new trial, and then is given a more severe sentence than in the first proceeding. This is an example of judicial vindictiveness (see Chapter 17). The second context regarding vindictiveness concerns prosecutorial decision making, where *Blackledge v. Perry*, 417 U.S. 21 (1974), is the seminal decision. *Blackledge* teaches that a presumption of vindictiveness arises when the defendant exercises a right to appeal to a higher court, pursuant to state law, and the prosecution files a more serious charge. A prosecutor's attempt to penalize a defendant's valid exercise of constitutional or statutory rights violates the Due Process Clause; the presumption arises because it is difficult to divine prosecutors' motives in such situations and due process is jeopardized by the mere appearance of vindictiveness. *Id.*

A presumption of vindictiveness, however, can be overcome if the government can show "that it was impossible to proceed on the more serious charge at the outset." *Id.* For an instance of a successful rebuttal by the government in this regard, see *United States v. York*, 933 F.2d 1343 (7th Cir. 1991) (defendant successfully appeals murder conviction and is then charged with obstruction of justice based on subsequent willingness to inform police of defendant's actions).

2. *Presumption of vindictiveness absent: pretrial stage. (Goodwin).* In *Goodwin* the Supreme Court refused to apply a presumption of vindictiveness in a pretrial setting, but indicated that there may be cases where the presumption would be applied pretrial when the accused can provide "objective" proof of a prosecutorial decision based on improper motive. The "objective" proof may be difficult to gather. As the Fifth Circuit Court of Appeals noted:

> If any objective event or combination of events...should indicate to a reasonable minded defendant that the prosecutor's decision to increase the severity of charges was motivated by some purpose other than a vindictive desire to deter or punish appeals, no presumption of vindictiveness is created.

United States v. Molina-Iguado, 894 F.2d 1452, 1453 (5th Cir. 1990).

In the plea context, a presumption of vindictiveness "does not arise from plea negotiations when the prosecutor threatens to bring additional charges if the accused refuses to plead guilty to pending charges. The Due Process Clause does not bar the prosecutor from carrying out his threat." *United States v. Muldoon*, 931 F.2d 282 (4th Cir. 1991). For further discussion of the issue, *see* Doug Lieb, Note, *Vindicating Vindictiveness: Prosecutorial Discretion and Plea Bargaining, Past and Future*, 123 Yale L.J. 1014 (2014).

3. *Vindictiveness toward people other than the defendant.* Should the *Pearce* presumption of vindictiveness apply to events that do not necessarily involve vindictiveness toward the individual defendant? Assume, for example, that a particular defense attorney has been publicly critical of policies in the local district attorney's office. Thereafter, evidence is adduced to suggest that prosecutors are being especially aggressive in charging and prosecuting defendants represented by that attorney. Should the defendant be entitled to protest that practice on the ground that the prosecutor is "punishing" the defendant because of the defense lawyer's "sins"?

4. *Appellate review.* Assume that the defendant is indicted and then obtains a change of venue to another district. A superseding indictment is obtained in the latter district in which new substantive counts are added to the original counts. The defendant moves to dismiss the new counts on prosecutorial vindictiveness grounds, but the trial judge denies the motion. Is that decision immediately appealable, or must the defendant reserve appellate review until after trial on the merits? In *United States v. Hollywood Motor Car Co., Inc.*, 458 U.S. 263 (1982), the Supreme Court held that federal appellate courts have no jurisdiction to review such an interlocutory order and, therefore, the defendant must postpone appellate review of that issue until after trial. (Note: This issue also arises in the context of speedy trial claims, which are discussed in Chapter 12.)

Although as seen above there is a clear presumption in favor of the propriety of prosecutorial discretion, courts do not always find in favor of the prosecution.

United States v. Jenkins

504 F.3d 694 (9th Cir. 2007)

The United States appeals the district court's dismissal of an indictment of Sharon Ann Jenkins for alien smuggling. The ground of dismissal was the appearance of vindictive prosecution.

Jenkins was apprehended twice for attempting to cross the U.S.-Mexico border while driving a vehicle containing undocumented aliens. Both times, Jenkins stated that she had been paid to drive the car across the border. She was not charged with any crime. Almost three months later, Jenkins was apprehended while attempting to cross the border as a passenger in a vehicle containing marijuana. She stated that she had been paid to drive the car, which she believed contained illegal aliens, across the border. Jenkins was charged with importation of marijuana. At trial, she testified in her own defense and maintained that she believed the vehicle in which she had been a passenger contained illegal aliens because she had been paid on two previous occasions to smuggle aliens. While the jury was deliberating, the government filed alien smuggling charges against Jenkins in connection with her first two border apprehensions.

The district court found that the prosecutor's conduct created the appearance of vindictive prosecution because the alien smuggling charges were brought only after Jenkins exercised her right to testify in her own defense at her separate marijuana smuggling trial. We affirm. We conclude that, because the government could have prosecuted Jenkins for alien smuggling well before she presented her theory of defense at the marijuana smuggling trial, the timing of the charges created the appearance of vindictiveness. The government's assertion that its case against Jenkins was much stronger after her in-court admission does not suffice to dispel the appearance of vindictiveness. We therefore conclude that the indictment should be dismissed....

The government violated Jenkins's right to due process of law if it filed the alien smuggling charges to penalize her for exercising a protected statutory or constitutional right. *See United States v. Goodwin*, 457 U.S. 368 (1982). Jenkins may establish prosecutorial vindictiveness by producing direct evidence of the prosecutor's punitive motivation towards her. Alternatively, she is entitled to a presumption of vindictiveness if she can show that the alien smuggling charges were filed because she exercised a statutory, procedural, or constitutional right in circumstances that give rise to an appearance of vindictiveness. This case involves the latter situation, as the record contains no direct evidence of the government's improper motivation.

A. Whether the filing of alien smuggling charges created the appearance of vindictiveness

To establish a presumption of vindictiveness, Jenkins need not show that the prosecutor acted in bad faith or that he maliciously sought the alien smuggling indictment. Rather, she must demonstrate a *reasonable likelihood* that the government would not have brought the alien smuggling charges had she not elected to testify at her marijuana smuggling trial and present her theory of the case. The mere appearance of prosecutorial vindictiveness suffices to place the burden on the government because the doctrine of vindictive prosecution "seeks[s] to reduce or eliminate apprehension on the part of an accused" that she may be punished for exercising her rights.

... The case before us presents an unusual situation because the government's alien smuggling case essentially was open and shut even before Jenkins testified in court.... In these circumstances, the government's decision to press charges only after Jenkins asserted a reasonably credible defense to the marijuana importation charges raises, at the very least, a "reasonable or realistic likelihood" that the government's decision was motivated by a retaliatory purpose. We therefore conclude that the government's conduct created the appearance of vindictiveness.

We are sensitive to the government's concern that the dismissal of charges resulting from a defendant's in-court admission may hamstring prosecutorial efforts. This might be a different case if the government had not been equipped with Jenkins's previous admissions at the time of her in-court testimony. But the government had more than enough evidence to proceed with the alien smuggling charges prior to Jenkins's decision to testify. We therefore find it appropriate to place the burden on the government to justify its course of conduct....

B. Whether the government rebutted the presumption of vindictiveness

The presumption of vindictiveness raised by the prosecutor's decision to file alien smuggling charges against Jenkins must be overcome by objective evidence justifying the prosecutor's action. The prosecution must show that the additional charges did not stem from a vindictive motive, or were justified by independent reasons or intervening circumstances that dispel the appearance of vindictiveness.

The government argues that, even if the content of the evidence against Jenkins was available all along, the evidence was stronger once Jenkins testified in court.... [W]e find the government's explanation unpersuasive. As the district court noted, it was not necessary to wait to file charges until Jenkins took the witness stand and confessed under oath: cases for illegal alien smuggling in this district are proven on much less than that....

We also are unconvinced by the government's argument that it brought the alien smuggling charges precisely because bringing them after trial would have seemed vindictive. From the moment she was apprehended for smuggling marijuana, Jenkins maintained that she believed she was smuggling aliens and pointed to her October apprehensions. There was no reason for the government to think that she would not continue with this defense at trial. If the government had been concerned with appearing vindictive, it could have filed the alien smuggling charges in January, when Jenkins first asserted that she did not know she was smuggling marijuana. We therefore conclude that the justifications offered by the government do not suffice to dispel the appearance of vindictiveness created by the timing of the alien smuggling charges.

Notes

1. *Presumption of vindictiveness.* Note that, unlike *Goodwin*, the *Jenkins* court recognized a presumption of vindictiveness because the defendant showed that new charges were filed because she exercised a right (here, to testify in her own defense) "in circumstances that give rise to an appearance of vindictiveness." The remedy was to dismiss the indictment for the *new* charges. This amounted to a presumption of vindictiveness applied in a *pretrial* setting, a result raised as a possibility in *Goodwin.*

2. *Declining to plead guilty.* As noted *supra*, no presumption arises when a prosecutor in a jurisdiction threatens to bring more serious charges and does so. What if a *federal* prosecution is begun because the defendant declined to plead guilty to *state* charges for the same conduct? In *United States v. Gray*, 382 F. Supp. 2d 898 (E.D. Mich. 2005), the defendant was charged under state law with possession of a firearm by a convicted felon. When he refused to plead guilty to state charges, the state charges were dropped, and he was charged with a federal offense for the same conduct. The state plea he rejected would have subjected him to 24 months of incarceration, but the federal indictment upped the possible sentence to 57–71 months. The federal court refused to dismiss the federal case or to remand the case to state court, finding that the filing of federal charges did not constitute vindictive prosecution in violation of due process. Rejecting the argument that the defendant was being penalized for rejecting the plea and waiving many constitutional rights, the District Court held that in the "give and take" of plea bargaining, there is no element of punishment as long as the defendant is free to accept or reject the prosecutor's offer. Do you agree that the defendant was not punished for asserting his right to a trial?

[3] Other Potential Limits on Prosecutorial Discretion

[a] Separation of Powers

While separation of powers doctrine is usually cited as a significant reason why courts (part of the judicial branch) give prosecutors (part of the executive branch) significant leeway in deciding which criminal charges to bring, occasionally courts invoke separation of powers to *restrict* the exercise of a prosecutor's broad discretion. *See, e.g., United States v. Hamm*, 659 F.2d 624 (5th Cir. 1981) (noting that because courts retain sentencing discretion, they have the power to supervise prosecutorial conduct in the sentencing process).

Under Federal Sentencing Guidelines, federal prosecutors may seek a sentence reduction based on the prosecutor's representation that a defendant has substantially cooperated with law enforcement officials. Some commentators suggest that this aspect of the federal legislation may pose a due process issue by "transferring much of the responsibility of sentencing from impartial judges to prosecutors, without providing standards to guide the prosecutors' discretion." Bennett L. Gershman,

The Most Fundamental Change in the Criminal Justice System, 5 Crim. J. 3 (1990). *See also* Cynthia Lee, *Prosecutorial Discretion, Substantial Assistance, and the Federal Sentencing Guidelines*, 42 UCLA L. Rev. 105 (1994).

In *United States v. Cobbins*, 749 F. Supp. 1450 (E.D. La. 1990), defendants were tried and convicted of using and carrying firearms in relation to a drug trafficking crime. This offense carried a mandatory, consecutive five-year term under the Federal Sentencing Guidelines. Defendants argued that the prosecutor's decision to include the gun count along with the drug cases determined, at least in part, their sentences and that this violated due process by giving the prosecutor an improper role in the sentencing decision. The United States district court rejected the claim (there having been no showing that the charges were selected arbitrarily or in bad faith), observing that under the Federal Sentencing Guidelines there is a "de facto transfer" of some of the responsibility for sentencing from courts to prosecutors. Nonetheless, this shift of power was found to be a legitimate policy choice by Congress that did not, in and of itself, violate due process.

[b] Internal Guidelines or Standards

It has long been noted that prosecutors—executive branch actors—who oversee what are in effect agencies, might, like other agency actors, be subject to rules and guidelines to inform and control their discretionary authority. *See, e.g.*, Kenneth C. Davis, Discretionary Justice 57–59, 220–21 (1969) (arguing that courts should require prosecutors and other criminal justice "administrators" to adopt administrative rules to regulate their discretion). The ABA Prosecution Standards recommend that prosecutors establish internal guidelines and office policies. *See* 2015 ABA Prosecution Standards, Stnd. 3-2.4(a). Prosecutors "should seek to develop general policies to guide the exercise of prosecutorial discretion, and standard operating procedures for the office." *Id.*

New Jersey is one jurisdiction where guidelines have taken hold, based on the state supreme court's mandating them in cases involving mandatory drug sentences. *See* Ronald F. Wright, *Prosecutorial Guidelines and the New Terrain in New Jersey*, 109 Penn. St. L. Rev. 1087 (2005). As a result, prosecutors must complete a worksheet specifying the reasons for and size of a deviation from a mandatory term, any aggravating and mitigating factors, and any other sentencing considerations. In Florida, the Prosecuting Attorneys Association adopted written guidelines prescribing criteria for determining whether to charge an individual as a habitual offender. Reasons for deviation must be specified and filed with the court and the Association. R. Michal Cassidy, *(Ad)Ministering Justice: A Prosecutor's Ethical Duty to Support Sentencing Reform*, 45 Loy. Chi. U. L. Rev. 981, 1021–22 (2014).

Perhaps the best-known example of guidelines is found in the United States Attorneys' Manual. *See* https://www.justice.gov/usam/title-9-criminal. For example, the Manual specifies when an interstate auto theft should be prosecuted by federal rather than state authorities ("Because of various other prosecutive priorities, only a portion of the individual theft cases involving exceptional circumstances will qualify for Federal prosecution." *Id.* § 9.61.112.

Prosecutorial guidelines have come to play a particularly important role in the white-collar crime context. There, it has become increasingly common for prosecutors, especially in the federal system, to rely upon them when entering into "deferred prosecution" and "non-prosecution" agreements with corporations. For more on this important and quite complex area of the law, *see* Samuel W. Buell, *Why Do Prosecutors Say Anything? The Case of Corporate Crime*, 96 N.C. L. Rev. 823, 832–36 (2018).

There are sound reasons in support of guidelines, which can promote accountability and transparency. However, are there separation of powers arguments against them, in principle? Should it matter that a prosecutor's office is in effect second-guessing the viability of a legislative determination? Also, is there any argument that guidelines—which signal a willingness to not prosecute or prosecute less harshly, and provide guiding criteria—might undercut general and/or specific deterrence? Finally, in the end, do guidelines have practical importance, providing a basis to challenge a prosecutor's failure to adhere to guidelines in a specific case? *See, e.g., United States v. Caceres*, 440 U.S. 741 (1979) (defendant cannot enforce internal rules of law enforcement agency). For more on external and internal checks on prosecutorial discretion, *see* Stephanos Bibas, *Prosecutorial Regulation Versus Prosecutorial Accountability*, 157 U. Pa. L. Rev. 959 (2009).

F. Role of Defense Counsel

Until a criminal case is formally begun, often there is relatively little that a defense attorney can do to assist his or her client. Indeed, the defendant may not even be aware of a criminal investigation until it is too late—meaning, that an information has been filed by a prosecutor or an indictment has been issued by a grand jury. In cases in which the defense attorney knows of a pending criminal investigation, however, it may be very helpful to the client to pursue a course of action designed to discourage the prosecution from moving forward. Furthermore, as discussed earlier, pre-charge bargaining with the United States Attorney may have a significant impact upon the defendant's sentence under Federal Sentencing Guidelines. In addition, as any good defense counsel will tell you, a major goal is to head off being charged in the first instance.

Where a criminal investigation is occurring in the corporate or commercial context, it has been reported that with increasing frequency the target defendant's first notice of a federal investigation is not by way of a grand jury subpoena, but through federal investigators in the workplace. The investigator may be representing any one of several federal agencies, including the FBI, IRS, Postal Service, or the Departments of Labor, Defense, Transportation, or Health and Human Services. In this context, the following advice provided several years ago still rings true:

> Counsel should attempt to determine the scope of the investigation and, specifically, determine whether the company or any of its officials are targets. Once counsel has established contact with the regional counsel of the investigating agency or the Assistant U.S. Attorney in charge of the investigation, it is imperative that a conference be scheduled with this individual. . . . A line of communication must be kept open with the government attorney, even though his or her position will become adversarial. At this point, the government attorney holds all the cards. Company counsel may want to declare war, and tell the government that the company will fight on all grounds. This may be the case, but the company cannot fight without information, and the government attorney is the best source.

The authors conclude with the following observation:

> If the company keeps abreast of the investigation and makes an early and informed assessment of the extent of its liability, it may be able to head off possible criminal and civil proceedings altogether.

Vaira & Backstrom, *Agents on Your Doorstep: Managing the Government Investigation*, 2 Corp. Crim. Liab. Rep. 33 (1988).

Many defense attorneys have echoed these sentiments in a broader context, encouraging involvement in a pending criminal case as soon as possible, particularly in the pre-indictment phase. Not only will the defense lawyer be in a position to influence the very decision to prosecute, but it is also possible that the prosecutor may disclose, at least in part, his or her theory of the case or an assessment of the prospective defendant's culpability. Such an "early warning" discovery process can also be helpful in preparation for representation of one's client before an investigative grand jury. Finally, it has been noted that some criminal investigations are governed by internal procedures for review of the exercise of discretion in seeking grand jury indictments. With access to such information, counsel's ability to dissuade presentation of the case to the grand jury may be enhanced.

Early and aggressive intervention by defense counsel is recommended by the American Bar Association's Standards Relating to the Defense Function. The two pertinent Standards in this regard are as follows:

> **American Bar Association, Standards for Criminal Justice (3d ed. 1993)**
> **Standard 4-4.1. Duty to Investigate** (a) Defense counsel should conduct a prompt investigation of the circumstances of the case and explore all avenues leading to facts relevant to the merits of the case and the penalty in the event of conviction. The investigation should include efforts to secure information in the possession of the prosecution and law enforcement authorities. The duty to investigate exists regardless of the accused's admission or statements to defense counsel of facts constituting guilt or the accused's stated desire to plead guilty. (b) Defense counsel should not seek to acquire possession of physical evidence personally or through use of an investigator where defense counsel's sole purpose is to obstruct access to such evidence.

Standard 4-6.1. Duty to Explore Disposition Without Trial (a) Whenever the law, nature, and circumstances of the case permit, defense counsel should explore the possibility of an early diversion of the case from the criminal process through the use of other community agencies.

Notes

1. *How aggressive?* How "aggressive" should the defense lawyer be at the pre-indictment stage? Is there not a risk that the defense attorney's vigorous advocacy will "boomerang"?

2. *Approval of victim.* Should the defense attorney attempt to contact the crime victim for the purpose of obtaining a victim's support of "diversion of the case from the criminal process" under Standard 4-6.1? From a policy perspective, should contact with a crime victim in this fashion be discouraged? Communications between victims and defense attorneys in the pretrial setting will be explored further in Chapter 10.

Chapter 3

Place of Prosecution: Venue and Related Concepts

A. Venue

The physical location, or *venue*, of criminal proceedings can be very important to their outcome. In most cases, however, the appropriateness of the location chosen by the prosecution is clear and uncontested. For instance, assume that a bank robbery occurs in Washington County, State X. For most people involved in the crime and its investigation and prosecution, the most convenient location for the trial is the courthouse in Washington County. Many, if not most, witnesses probably live in or near that county. The investigating police officers and the prosecuting lawyers from that area will find it convenient to do their work there since the crime scene and witnesses will be close to their offices and staff. The defendant may also live in that county and therefore have family, character witnesses, and a lawyer who also reside nearby. Routinely, the charge would be filed, and the trial scheduled and held, in a courthouse in Washington County, and no one would think about the issue.

But sometimes the facts are more complex. What if the defendant lived in a different county or state than Washington County, State X? It could be more convenient for the defendant if the trial were held in his or her home county rather than in Washington County where the crime occurred. The defendant's character witnesses and family attorney would be closer to the courthouse. Moreover, what if the crime had generated a lot of media attention in Washington County? The defendant may fear that the Washington County jurors would have heard or read this publicity and perhaps formed an opinion about guilt before they heard any evidence in the case. To reduce the risk of a trial before a guilt-prone jury, the defendant may prefer to have the case tried in a county other than Washington County.

In unusual situations, the prosecution may also prefer that the case be tried in another county. Perhaps the accused is from a highly respected Washington County family. The prosecution may suspect that the jury will be prone to believe the accused because of the family's stature in the community. This concern could be alleviated if the trial were held in another area. Similarly, a prosecutor may prefer trial outside Washington County in order to accommodate a victim or another key prosecution witness who lives elsewhere.

More difficult questions may arise as the facts become more intricate. For example, perhaps there were two perpetrators in the Washington County bank robbery.

One of them lived in Lincoln County, the other in Jefferson County. The two talked about the crime on the phone while at home each night. The bank robbery was planned in detail in Kent County where they both worked. They stole the "getaway" car in Hamilton County, obtained the gun in Cobb County, and hid the money in an abandoned shack in Florence County. After hiding the money, they fled to Belton County, State Y, where they were arrested. Where did the crime occur? Although the bank was located in Washington County, State X, other facets of the crime were carried out in six other counties and one other state. Could the joint trial of the two defendants be held in Lincoln County where one of them lived and used the telephone to discuss the crime with the other defendant? In Cobb County where they obtained the gun used in the robbery? In Belton County, State Y, where they fled and were apprehended?

These questions implicate the law of venue, which will be the principal topic of this chapter. As a legal concept, venue overlaps with the concepts of *jurisdiction* and *vicinage*, which will be discussed more briefly at the end of the chapter.

[1] Basic Principles

The law of venue determines where criminal charges may be filed and litigated. The key legal principles are derived from constitutional provisions, statutes, and rules of criminal procedure. In many cases, the governing legal principles indicate that there is only one permissible venue. In other cases, there may be multiple permissible venues; in such cases, prosecutors are generally free to select whichever venue they think would be most advantageous.

Federal and state courts have separate venue laws. In the federal system, venue rules focus on the *judicial district.* The federal system is divided into 94 districts. Some districts cover an entire state, while others cover just a portion of a state. Federal venue laws limit which of the 94 districts may be selected by federal prosecutors as the place where a given case will be litigated.

State court systems are also subdivided, normally along county lines. Typically, then, state venue laws focus on the county of prosecution. Although state venue laws operate on a different geographical scale from federal, analogous principles tend to inform the venue limitations at both levels of government.

In general, venue lies at the *locus delicti*—that is, the place where the crime was committed. This principle is embodied in not just one, but two, sections of the United States Constitution. Article III, § 2 of the United States Constitution provides:

> The trial of all Crimes . . . shall be held in the State where the said Crimes shall have been committed; but when not committed within any State, the Trial shall be at such Place or Places as the Congress may by Law have directed.

Similarly, the Sixth Amendment states:

> In all criminal prosecutions, the accused shall enjoy the right to a . . . trial . . . by an impartial jury of the State and district wherein the crime shall have been committed, which district shall have been previously ascertained by law. . . .

Federal Rule of Criminal Procedure 18, another important venue provision, echoes the same *locus delicti* principle.

The Article III and Rule 18 venue provisions relate to the operation of the federal courts only. Similarly, the United States Supreme Court has never held that the pertinent Sixth Amendment requirement is incorporated into the Due Process Clause of the Fourteenth Amendment, and lower courts generally find it to be inapplicable to state prosecutions. *See, e.g., People v. Thomas*, 274 P.3d 1170 (Cal. 2012). Nevertheless, most states follow the federal lead and authorize a trial in the county or district where the crime occurred.

Determining where a given crime occurred is in part a factual question, but it may also require some statutory interpretation. After all, crimes are defined by statute. It is only by analyzing the relevant statutory language and identifying the elements of the charged offense that we can know exactly what actions and results constitute that offense—that we can know, in other words, when and where the charged offense was begun, and when and where it was completed. These questions—central to applying the *locus delicti* test—are not difficult to answer in most cases, but they can be quite tricky in some.

The Supreme Court has not always followed a clear, consistent path in resolving difficult venue questions in the federal system. Consider the following two decisions.

United States v. Cabrales

524 U.S. 1 (1998)

Justice Ginsburg delivered the opinion of the Court.

This case presents a question of venue, specifically, the place appropriate for trial on charges of money laundering. . . .

I

In a three-count indictment returned in the United States District Court for the Western District of Missouri, Cabrales, as sole defendant, was charged with the following offenses: conspiracy to avoid a transaction-reporting requirement, in violation of 18 U. S. C. §§ 371, 1956(a)(1)(B)(ii) (Count I); conducting a financial transaction to avoid a transaction-reporting requirement, in violation of § 1956 (a)(l)(B)(ii) (Count II); and engaging in a monetary transaction in criminally derived property of a value greater than $10,000, in violation of § 1957 (Count III). The indictment alleged that, in January 1991, Cabrales deposited $40,000 with the AmSouth Bank of Florida and, within a week's span, made four separate withdrawals of $9,500 each from that bank. The money deposited and withdrawn was traceable to illegal sales of cocaine in Missouri.

Cabrales moved to dismiss the indictment in its entirety for improper venue. On recommendation of the Magistrate, the District Court denied the motion as to Count I, the conspiracy count, based on the Government's assertions that Cabrales "was present in Missouri during the conspiracy, lived with a conspirator in Missouri, and participated in various activities in Missouri in furtherance of the conspiracy." Also on the Magistrate's recommendation, the District Court granted the motion to dismiss Counts II and III, the money-laundering counts, because the deposit and withdrawals occurred in Florida and "[n]o activity of money laundering . . . occurred in Missouri."

On the Government's appeal, the Eighth Circuit affirmed the District Court's dismissal of the money-laundering counts. The conspiracy charge was not part of the appeal, and that count remains pending in the Missouri District Court.

. . .

II

Proper venue in criminal proceedings was a matter of concern to the Nation's founders. Their complaints against the King of Great Britain, listed in the Declaration of Independence, included his transportation of colonists "beyond Seas to be tried." The Constitution twice safeguards the defendant's venue right. . . . Rule 18 of the Federal Rules of Criminal Procedure, providing that "prosecution shall be had in a district in which the offense was committed," echoes the constitutional commands.

We adhere to the general guide invoked and applied by the Eighth Circuit: "[T]he *locus delicti* must be determined from the nature of the crime alleged and the location of the act or acts constituting it." *Anderson*, 328 U.S., at 703. Here, the crimes described in Counts II and III are defined in statutory proscriptions, 18 U.S.C. §§ 1956(a)(1)(B)(ii), 1957, that interdict only the financial transactions (acts located entirely in Florida), not the anterior criminal conduct that yielded the funds allegedly laundered.

Congress has provided by statute for offenses "begun in one district and completed in another"; such offenses may be "prosecuted in any district in which [the] offense was begun, continued, or completed." 18 U.S.C. § 3237(a). The Government urges that the money-laundering crimes described in Counts II and III of the indictment against Cabrales fit the § 3237(a) description. We therefore confront and decide this question: Do those counts charge crimes begun in Missouri and completed in Florida, rendering venue proper in Missouri, or do they delineate crimes that took place wholly within Florida?

Notably, the counts at issue do not charge Cabrales with conspiracy; they do not link her to, or assert her responsibility for, acts done by others. Nor do they charge her as an aider or abettor in the Missouri drug trafficking. . . .

Whenever a defendant acts "after the fact" to conceal a crime, it might be said, as the Government urges in this case, that the first crime is an essential element of the second, and that the second facilitated the first or made it profitable by impeding its detection. But the question here is the *place* appropriate to try the "after the fact" actor. As the Government recognizes, it is immaterial whether that actor knew where the first crime was committed. The money launderer must know she is dealing with funds derived from "specified unlawful activity," here, drug trafficking, but the Missouri venue of that activity is, as the Eighth Circuit said, "of no moment."

Money laundering, the Court of Appeals acknowledged, arguably might rank as a "continuing offense," triable in more than one place, if the launderer acquired the funds in one district and transported them into another. But that is tellingly not this case. In the counts at issue, the Government indicted Cabrales "for transactions which began, continued, and were completed only in Florida." Under these circumstances, venue in Missouri is improper.

The Government identified *Hyde v. United States, 225* U.S. 347 (1912), and *In re Palliser,* 136 U.S. 257 (1890), as the two best cases for its position that money launderers can in all cases be prosecuted at the place where the funds they handled were generated. Neither decision warrants the ruling the Government here seeks.

In *Hyde,* the defendants were convicted in the District of Columbia of conspiracy to defraud the United States. Although none of the defendants had entered the District as part of the conspiracy, venue was nevertheless appropriate, the Court ruled, based on the overt acts of a co-conspirator there. 225 U.S., at 363. By contrast, the counts at issue in this case allege no conspiracy. They describe activity in which Cabrales alone, untied to others, engaged.

In re Palliser concerned a man who sent letters from New York to postmasters in Connecticut, attempting to gain postage on credit, in violation of then-applicable law. The Court held that the defendant could be prosecuted in Connecticut, where the mail he addressed and dispatched was received. 136 U.S., at 266–268. The *Palliser* opinion simply recognizes that a mailing to Connecticut is properly ranked as an act completed in that State. *Cf.* 18 U.S.C. § 3237(a) ("Any offense involving the use of the mails ... is a continuing offense and ... may be ... prosecuted in any district from, through, or into which such ... mail matter ... moves.").... Cabrales, however, dispatched no missive from one State into another. The counts before us portray her and the money she deposited and withdrew as moving inside Florida only.

Finally, the Government urges the efficiency of trying Cabrales in Missouri, because evidence in that State, and not in Florida, shows that the money Cabrales allegedly laundered derived from unlawful activity. Although recognizing that the venue requirement is principally a protection for the defendant, the Government further maintains that its convenience, and the interests of the community victimized by drug dealers, merit consideration.

But if Cabrales is in fact linked to the drug-trafficking activity, the Government is not disarmed from showing that is the case. She can be, and indeed has been, charged with conspiring with the drug dealers in Missouri. If the Government can prove the agreement it has alleged, Cabrales can be prosecuted in Missouri for that confederacy, and her money laundering in Florida could be shown as overt acts in furtherance of the conspiracy. . . .

We hold that Missouri is not a place of proper venue for the money-laundering offenses with which Cabrales is charged. For the reasons stated, the judgment of the Court of Appeals for the Eighth Circuit is [affirmed].

United States v. Rodriguez-Moreno

526 U.S. 275 (1999)

JUSTICE THOMAS delivered the opinion of the Court.

This case presents the question whether venue in a prosecution for using or carrying a firearm "during and in relation to any crime of violence," in violation of 18 U.S.C. § 924(c)(1), is proper in any district where the crime of violence was committed, even if the firearm was used or carried only in a single district.

I

During a drug transaction that took place in Houston, Texas, a New York drug dealer stole 30 kilograms of a Texas drug distributor's cocaine. The distributor hired respondent, Jacinto Rodriguez-Moreno, and others to find the dealer and to hold captive the middleman in the transaction, Ephrain Avendano, during the search. In pursuit of the dealer, the distributor and his henchmen drove from Texas to New Jersey with Avendano in tow. The group used Avendano's New Jersey apartment as a base for their operations for a few days. They soon moved to a house in New York and then to a house in Maryland, taking Avendano with them.

Shortly after respondent and the others arrived at the Maryland house, the owner of the home passed around a .357 magnum revolver and respondent took possession of the pistol. As it became clear that efforts to find the New York drug dealer would not bear fruit, respondent told his employer that he thought they should kill the middleman and end their search for the dealer. He put the gun to the back of Avendano's neck but, at the urging of his cohorts, did not shoot. Avendano eventually escaped through the back door and ran to a neighboring house. The neighbors called the Maryland police, who arrested respondent along with the rest of the kidnapers. The police also seized the .357 magnum, on which they later found respondent's fingerprint.

Rodriguez-Moreno and his codefendants were tried jointly in the United States District Court for the District of New Jersey. Respondent was charged with, *inter alia,* conspiring to kidnap Avendano, kidnaping Avendano, and using and carrying a firearm in relation to the kidnaping of Avendano, in violation of 18 U.S.C. § 924(c)(1). At the conclusion of the Government's case, respondent moved to dismiss the § 924(c)(1) count for lack of venue. He argued that venue was proper only in Maryland, the only place where the Government had proved he had actually used a gun. The District Court denied the motion, and the jury found respondent guilty on the kidnaping counts and on the § 924(c)(1) charge as well. He was sentenced to 87 months' imprisonment on the kidnaping charges, and was given a mandatory consecutive term of 60 months' imprisonment for committing the § 924(c)(1) offense.

On a 2-to-l vote, the Court of Appeals for the Third Circuit reversed respondent's § 924(c)(1) conviction. *United States* v. *Palma-Ruedas,* 121 F.3d 841 (1997). A majority of the Third Circuit panel applied what it called the "verb test" to § 924(c)(1), and determined that a violation of the statute is committed only in the district where a defendant "uses" or "carries" a firearm. *Id.,* at 849. Accordingly, it concluded that venue for the § 924(c)(1) count was improper in New Jersey even though venue was proper there for the kidnaping of Avendano....

II

...

As we confirmed just last Term, the "'*locus delicti* [of the charged offense] must be determined from the nature of the crime alleged and the location of the act or acts constituting it.'" *United States* v. *Cabrales,* 524 U.S. 1, 6–7 (1998) (quoting *United States* v. *Anderson,* 328 U.S. 699, 703 (1946)). In performing this inquiry, a court must initially identify the conduct constituting the offense (the nature of the crime) and then discern the location of the commission of the criminal acts.[2] ...

At the time respondent committed the offense and was tried, 18 U.S.C. § 924(c)(1) provided:

> "Whoever, during and in relation to any crime of violence ... for which he may be prosecuted in a court of the United States, uses or carries a firearm, shall, in addition to the punishment provided for such crime of violence ... be sentenced to imprisonment for five years ..."

The Third Circuit, as explained above, looked to the verbs of the statute to determine the nature of the substantive offense. But we have never before held, and decline to do so here, that verbs are the sole consideration in identifying the conduct that constitutes an offense. While the "verb test" certainly has value as an interpretative tool, it cannot be applied rigidly, to the exclusion of other relevant statutory language. The test unduly limits the inquiry into the nature of the offense and thereby creates a danger that certain conduct prohibited by statute will be missed.

In our view, the Third Circuit overlooked an essential conduct element of the § 924(c)(1) offense. Section 924(c)(1) prohibits using or carrying a firearm "during and in relation to any crime of violence ... for which [a defendant] may be prosecuted in a court of the United States." That the crime of violence element of the

2. The Government argues that venue also may permissibly be based upon the effects of a defendant's conduct in a district other than the one in which the defendant performs the acts constituting the offense. Because this case only concerns the *locus delicti,* we express no opinion as to whether the Government's assertion is correct.

statute is embedded in a prepositional phrase and not expressed in verbs does not dissuade us from concluding that a defendant's violent acts are essential conduct elements. To prove the charged § 924(c)(1) violation in this case, the Government was required to show that respondent used a firearm, that he committed all the acts necessary to be subject to punishment for kidnaping (a crime of violence) in a court of the United States, and that he used the gun "during and in relation to" the kidnaping of Avendano. In sum, we interpret § 924(c)(1) to contain two distinct conduct elements—as is relevant to this case, the "using and carrying" of a gun and the commission of a kidnaping.[4]

Respondent, however, argues that for venue purposes "the New Jersey kidnapping is completely irrelevant to the firearm crime, because respondent did not *use* or *carry* a gun *during* the New Jersey crime." In the words of one *amicus,* § 924(c)(1) is a "point-in-time" offense that only is committed in the place where the kidnaping and the use of a gun coincide. We disagree. . . . A kidnaping, once begun, does not end until the victim is free. It does not make sense, then, to speak of it in discrete geographic fragments. Section 924(c)(1) criminalized a defendant's use of a firearm "during and in relation to" a crime of violence; in doing so, Congress proscribed both the use of the firearm *and* the commission of acts that constitute a violent crime. It does not matter that respondent used the .357 magnum revolver, as the Government concedes, only in Maryland because he did so "during and in relation to" a kidnaping that was begun in Texas and continued in New York, New Jersey, and Maryland. In our view, § 924(c)(1) does not define a "point-in-time" offense when a firearm is used during and in relation to a continuing crime of violence.

. . . The kidnaping, to which the § 924(c)(1) offense is attached, was committed in all of the places that any part of it took place, and venue for the kidnaping charge against respondent was appropriate in any of them. (Congress has provided that continuing offenses can be tried "in any district in which such offense was begun, continued, or completed," 18 U.S.C. § 3237(a).) Where venue is appropriate for the underlying crime of violence, so too it is for the § 924(c)(1) offense. As the kidnaping was properly tried in New Jersey, the § 924(c)(1) offense could be tried there as well. [Reversed]

[The dissenting opinion of Justice Scalia, in which Justice Stevens joined, is omitted.]

---

4. By way of comparison, last Term in *United States* v. *Cabrales,* 524 U.S. 1 (1998), we considered whether venue for money laundering, in violation of 18 U.S.C. §§ 1956(a)(I)(B)(ii) and 1957, was proper in Missouri, where the laundered proceeds were unlawfully generated, or rather, only in Florida, where the prohibited laundering transactions occurred. As we interpreted the laundering statutes at issue, they did not proscribe "the anterior criminal conduct that yielded the funds allegedly laundered." *Cabrales,* 524 U.S., at 7. The existence of criminally generated proceeds was a circumstance element of the offense but the proscribed conduct—defendant's money laundering activity—occurred "'after the fact' of an offense begun and completed by others." *Ibid.* Here, by contrast, given the "during and in relation to" language, the underlying crime of violence is a critical part of the § 924(c)(1) offense.

Notes

1. *Competing tests.* The approach used by the Court to determine where the crimes were committed in *Cabrales* and *Rodriguez-Moreno* is often called the "nature of the offense" test. It may be contrasted with the more rigid "verb test" that was employed by the Third Circuit in *Rodriguez-Moreno.* Can you articulate the difference between these tests? In *Rodriguez-Moreno,* the Supreme Court indicated that federal courts should not use the verb test—or at least not in such an inflexible way as the Third Circuit did. However, state courts, in applying their venue rules, do not necessarily have to follow the Supreme Court's admonition.

2. *Distinguishing the cases.* Venue was proper in *Rodriguez-Moreno,* but not in *Cabrales.* How did the *Rodriguez-Moreno* Court distinguish *Cabrales*? See footnote four of the Court's opinion. Does that aspect of the Court's reasoning help to clarify the "nature of the offense" test? Does the test seem likely to yield consistent, predictable results in the lower courts?

3. *Constitution versus statute.* Are *Cabrales* and *Rodriguez-Moreno* constitutional cases? As often happens in venue decisions, the Court seemed to blur the line between constitutional and statutory analysis. In both cases, the Court quoted the venue provisions of Article III and the Sixth Amendment. The Court also cited Rule 18 in both cases. The Rule requires prosecution "in a district where the offense was committed," unless "a statute or these rules permit otherwise." The Court seemed to assume (not unreasonably) that the general *locus delicti* analysis for Rule 18 purposes is the same as it is for constitutional purposes. Notice, however, that Rule 18 recognizes the possibility that a statute may "permit otherwise"—that is, provide for venue in a district that is not "where the offense was committed." For instance, imagine that Congress, in the interest of better accommodating crime victims, passes a law authorizing the prosecution of § 924(c)(1) cases in any district in which a victim resides. Such a law might in some cases require courts to engage in a distinct analysis of statutory and constitutional venue constraints, with the possibility that a statutorily permissible venue would be rejected on constitutional grounds. (For instance, what if Avendano, the victim in *Rodriguez-Moreno,* had been visiting Houston from his home in Boise at the time of his kidnapping? Could the defendant have been charged in the District of Idaho?) However, in *Cabrales* and *Rodriguez-Moreno,* the government was not relying on any special venue statutes that raised constitutional concerns. The Court could thus perform its venue analysis without clearly distinguishing between constitutional and statutory rules.

4. *Section 3237(a).* Although Congress has enacted a number of venue laws, the most generally applicable and practically important is likely 18 U.S.C. § 3237(a), which provides that:

> any offense against the United States begun in one district and completed in another, or committed in more than one district, may be inquired of and prosecuted in any district in which such offense was begun, continued, or completed.

> Any offense involving the use of the mails, transportation in interstate or foreign commerce, or the importation of an object or person into the United States is a continuing offense and, except as otherwise expressly provided by enactment of Congress, may be inquired of and prosecuted in any district from, through, or into which such commerce, mail matter, or imported object or person moves.

The government tried unsuccessfully to rely on § 3237(a) in *Cabrales*. Why did the Court not find the statute to be applicable? How did the statute figure into the Court's reasoning in *Rodriguez-Moreno*? Note the tendency of the § 3237(a) analysis to dovetail with the constitutional *locus delicti* analysis.

5. *State law.* Most states have adopted statutes that are similar to § 3237(a) in order to deal with crimes that have in some sense occurred in more than one county or judicial district. *See* WAYNE R. LAFAVE ET AL., CRIMINAL PROCEDURE § 16.1(d) (4th ed. 2015). Thus, like their federal counterparts, state prosecutors are able to choose in some cases from among multiple legally permissible venues. In addition, as in the federal system, states have adopted a host of more specific statutes in order to handle venue questions regarding particular offenses or particular circumstances. *See, e.g.*, CAL. PENAL CODE § 782 (for offense committed on boundary of two or more judicial territories or within 500 yards thereof, prosecution may be in either territory); KAN. STAT. ANN. § 22-2613 (bigamy can be tried in the county where the invalid marriage ceremony was performed or in any county in which the bigamous cohabitation occurred); MICH. COMP. LAWS ANN. § 762.3 (West) (if it appears to attorney general that a felony was committed within the state and it is impossible to determine the county, the crime may be prosecuted in any county designated by attorney general); MO. ANN. STAT. § 541.035 (Vernon) (the crime of failure to file a mandatory report can be tried in the county of the residence of the person failing to file); OR. REV. STAT. § 131.325 (if offense was committed in the state but it cannot be determined in which county it was committed, trial may be held in county where defendant resides or, if no fixed residence, in county where defendant was apprehended or to which defendant was extradited).

6. *Venue within a district.* Section 3237(a) focuses on the *district* of prosecution, but many federal districts have multiple courthouses located in different cities. In some cases, the government and/or the defendant may care a great deal about which specific courthouse within the district is the place of prosecution. Rule 18 provides some guidance on this point: "The court must set the place of trial within the district with due regard for the convenience of the defendant and the witnesses, and the prompt administration of justice."

7. *Count by count.* In *Cabrales*, the Supreme Court held that Missouri was an improper venue for Counts II and III, but seemed to assume that Missouri would be fine for Count I. What exactly did Count I charge, and why was it distinguished for venue purposes from the other two counts? Note that venue must be assessed count by count. Just because one charge against a defendant is permissible in a particular venue does not mean that the government can add every related charge it has against the defendant to the same case in the same district. (The topic of joinder of offenses in one case is considered in more detail in Chapter 8.)

8. *Continuing crimes.* Often, in deciding whether a particular venue is within the *locus delicti*, a court will have to decide whether the charged offense was a "continuing crime" or a "point-in-time crime." Any offense, of course, will have various elements. Once all the elements are present, we can say that the crime has been committed. However, that does not necessarily mean that the crime is *over.* If an offense is continuing in nature, then the defendant continues to commit the crime until something happens to end it. In this way, the defendant's subsequent movement across district lines—even if he or she has performed all of the elements of the offense in the first district—may create a new venue option for the government. In *Rodriguez-Moreno*, the Supreme Court held that kidnapping is just such a continuing crime. Whether a given offense is continuing in nature presents a problem of statutory interpretation—occasionally, a rather tricky one at that. *See, e.g., State v. Thompson*, 284 P.3d 559 (Or. Ct. App. 2012) (since failure to register as a sex offender is not a continuing crime, venue will not lie anywhere the defendant was present after failing to register, but rather is in the county where the defendant was when his deadline to register passed).

Another notable example of a continuing crime comes from *United States v. Cores*, 356 U.S. 405 (1958). In that case, the defendant, a non-American crew member of a ship that landed in Philadelphia, failed to leave the country within 29 days, as he was required to do by his immigration permit. Later, he was prosecuted for violation of a federal statute making it a crime to "willfully remain" in the United States after the expiration of a conditional entry permit. Apparently, after his arrival in Philadelphia, the defendant went to New York for a year. He was then apprehended and charged in Connecticut after leaving New York. However, the charge was dismissed by the district court on venue grounds since the entry permit had long expired before the defendant entered Connecticut.

On appeal to the Supreme Court, the defendant argued that the offense was completed the moment his permit expired. The government, on the other hand, maintained that the crime was a continuing crime that could be prosecuted in any state where the accused was found. The Supreme Court agreed with the government, holding that the essence of the crime is "remaining" after the permit has expired. Accordingly, venue was permissible in any district where the crewman willfully went more than 29 days after his entry into the United States.

9. *What about convenience?* The "nature of the offense" test used in *Cabrales* and *Rodriguez-Moreno* is rather formalistic, focusing as it does on the statutory language that defines the charged offense. The test leaves little room for consideration of what venue would be most convenient for the defendant or anyone else involved in the case. What interests do you suppose are intended to be served by the venue provisions of the Constitution? By Rule 18? Does the *locus delicti* principle seem the best way to further these interests?

10. *Substantial contacts test.* In the 1980s, a few of the lower federal courts adopted a "substantial contacts" test for resolving venue disputes. *See, e.g., United States v. Williams*, 788 F.2d 1213 (6th Cir. 1986). Somewhat less formalistic than the approach you have seen in *Cabrales* and *Rodriguez-Moreno*, the substantial contacts test required courts to consider not only the nature of the crime charged, but also "the suitability of each district for accurate fact-finding." However, the Supreme Court's disregard of the test in *Cabrales* and *Rodriguez-Moreno* has cast doubt on its validity, even in the minority of circuits that once endorsed it. In the following decision, you can see the Third Circuit attempting to make some sense of all of the conflicting case law on the substantial contacts test. You can also see how the *locus delicti* concept is put under pressure in the Internet age.

United States v. Auernheimer

748 F.3d 525 (3d Cir. 2014)

Chagares, Circuit Judge.

This case calls upon us to determine whether venue for Andrew Auernheimer's prosecution for conspiracy to violate the Computer Fraud and Abuse Act ("CFAA"), 18 U.S.C. § 1030, and identity fraud under 18 U.S.C. § 1028(a)(7) was proper in the District of New Jersey.... Because we conclude that venue did not lie in New Jersey, we will reverse the District Court's venue determination and vacate Auernheimer's conviction.

I.

A.

[Defendant Auernheimer and his co-conspirator Spitler discovered a flaw in an AT&T website that allowed them to collect the email addresses of 114,000 iPad users. In order to do this in an automated fashion, they jointly developed an "account slurper" program that submitted false identifying information to the AT&T website.]

While Spitler's program was still collecting email addresses, Auernheimer emailed various members of the media in order to publicize the pair's exploits. Some of those media members emailed AT&T, which immediately fixed the breach. One of the media members contacted by Auernheimer was Ryan Tate, a reporter at *Gawker*, a news website. Tate expressed interest in publishing Auernheimer's story. To lend credibility to it, Auernheimer shared the list of email addresses with him. Tate published a story on June 9, 2010 describing AT&T's security flaw, entitled "Apple's Worst Security Breach: 114,000 iPad Owners Exposed." The article mentioned some of the names of those whose email addresses were obtained, but published only redacted images of a few email addresses and ICC–IDs.

Evidence at trial showed that at all times relevant to this case, Spitler was in San Francisco, California and Auernheimer was in Fayetteville, Arkansas. The servers that they accessed were physically located in Dallas, Texas and Atlanta, Georgia.

Although no evidence was presented regarding the location of the *Gawker* reporter, it is undisputed that he was not in New Jersey.

B.

Despite the absence of any apparent connection to New Jersey, a grand jury sitting in Newark returned a two-count superseding indictment charging Auernheimer with conspiracy to violate the CFAA, 18 U.S.C. § 1030(a)(2)(C) and (c)(2)(B)(ii), in violation of 18 U.S.C. § 371 (count one), and fraud in connection with personal information in violation of 18 U.S.C. § 1028(a)(7) (count two, commonly referred to as "identity fraud"). To enhance the potential punishment from a misdemeanor to a felony, the Government alleged that Auernheimer's CFAA violation occurred in furtherance of a violation of New Jersey's computer crime statute, N.J. Stat. Ann. § 2C:20–31(a).

[After Auernheimer's motion to dismiss the indictment on venue grounds was denied, he was convicted by a jury and appealed.]

III.

A.

... Venue [for count one] would be proper in any district where the CFAA violation occurred, or wherever any of the acts in furtherance of the conspiracy took place.

The charged portion of the CFAA provides that "[w]hoever ... intentionally accesses a computer without authorization or exceeds authorized access, and thereby obtains ... information from any protected computer ... shall be punished as provided in subsection (c) of this section." 18 U.S.C. § 1030(a)(2)(C). To be found guilty, the Government must prove that the defendant (1) intentionally (2) accessed without authorization (or exceeded authorized access to) a (3) protected computer and (4) thereby obtained information. The statute's plain language reveals two essential conduct elements: accessing without authorization and obtaining information.

New Jersey was not the site of either essential conduct element. The evidence at trial demonstrated that the accessed AT&T servers were located in Dallas, Texas, and Atlanta, Georgia. In addition, during the time that the conspiracy began, continued, and ended, Spitler was obtaining information in San Francisco, California, and Auernheimer was assisting him from Fayetteville, Arkansas. No protected computer was accessed and no data was obtained in New Jersey.

This is not the end of our analysis, however, because the Government did not just charge Auernheimer with conspiracy to commit an ordinary violation of the CFAA, but also with conspiring to violate the CFAA in furtherance of a state crime. The Government can increase the statutory maximum punishment for a subsection (a)(2) violation from one year to five years if it proves one of the enhancements contained in § 1030(c)(2)(B). The enhancement relevant here provides for such increased punishment if "the offense was committed in furtherance of any criminal or tortious act in violation of the ... laws of ... any State." ...

The New Jersey statute allows for criminal liability "if the person purposely or knowingly and without authorization, or in excess of authorization, accesses any . . . computer [or] computer system and knowingly or recklessly discloses, or causes to be disclosed any data . . . or personal identifying information." N.J. Stat. Ann. § 2C:20–31(a). Its essential conduct elements are accessing without authorization (or in excess of authorization) and disclosing data or personal identifying information.

Here, none of the essential conduct elements of a violation of the New Jersey statute occurred in New Jersey. As discussed, neither Auernheimer nor Spitler accessed a computer in New Jersey. The disclosure did not occur there either. The sole disclosure of the data obtained was to the *Gawker* reporter. There was no allegation or evidence that the *Gawker* reporter was in New Jersey. Further, there was no evidence that any email addresses of any New Jersey residents were ever disclosed publicly in the *Gawker* article. The alleged violation of the New Jersey statute thus cannot confer venue for count one.

Just as none of the conduct constituting the CFAA violation or its enhancement occurred in New Jersey, none of the overt acts that the Government alleged in the superseding indictment occurred in New Jersey either. The indictment listed four overt acts: writing the account slurper program, deploying the account slurper program against AT&T's servers, emailing victims to inform them of the breach, and disclosing the emails addresses obtained to *Gawker*. The co-conspirators collaborated on the account slurper program from California and Arkansas and deployed it against servers located in Texas and Georgia. The Government offered no evidence whatsoever that any of the victims that Auernheimer emailed were located in New Jersey, or that the *Gawker* reporter to whom the list of email addresses was disclosed was in the Garden State.

Because neither Auernheimer nor his co-conspirator Spitler performed any "essential conduct element" of the underlying CFAA violation or any overt act in furtherance of the conspiracy in New Jersey, venue was improper on count one.

B.

[By similar reasoning, the court also found venue improper as to count two.]

IV.

. . .

The Government argues that we need not rely on the essential conduct elements test mandated by *Cabrales* and *Rodriguez–Moreno* because we have "adopted" a "substantial contacts test." Under this approach, frequently employed by the Court of Appeals for the Second Circuit, a number of factors help to determine whether venue was proper, including "the site of the defendant's acts, the elements and nature of the crime, the locus of the effect of the criminal conduct, and the suitability of each district for accurate factfinding." *United States v. Reed*, 773 F.2d 477, 481 (2d Cir. 1985). The Government contends that venue is proper in New Jersey because about four percent (approximately 4,500 of 114,000) of the email addresses obtained from AT&T's website belonged to New Jersey residents, thereby satisfying the "locus of the effect[s]" consideration. *See id.*

It is far from clear that this Court has ever "adopted" this test. . . .

Even if it could be said that we perhaps tacitly endorsed this test once almost thirty years ago, the test operates to limit venue, not to expand it. Cases from the Court of Appeals for the Second Circuit make this clear. The test "does not represent a formal constitutional test," but rather is merely "helpful in determining whether a chosen venue is unfair or prejudicial to a defendant." *United States v. Saavedra*, 223 F.3d 85, 93 (2d Cir. 2000). To satisfy this test, there must be "more than 'some activity in the situs district'; instead, there must be 'substantial contacts.'" *United States v. Davis*, 689 F.3d 179, 186 (2d Cir. 2012) (quoting *Reed*, 773 F.2d at 481). There "must be some sense of venue having been freely chosen by the defendant." *Id.* (alteration and quotation marks omitted). If a defendant argues that the chosen venue is constitutionally infirm but that it did not result in any hardship to him, the court only determines the *locus delicti* and does not then analyze whether there were "substantial contacts." *See United States v. Magassouba*, 619 F.3d 202, 205 n.2 (2d Cir. 2010). This test thus serves to limit venue in instances where the *locus delicti* constitutionally allows for a given venue, but trying the case there is somehow prejudicial or unfair to the defendant.

Even assuming that the substantial contacts test is viable within our Circuit, it cannot serve as a sufficient basis for conferring venue. The Government argues only that it has minimally satisfied one of the four prongs of the test—the "locus of the effect of the criminal conduct." There was no evidence at trial that Auernheimer's actions evinced any contact with New Jersey, much less contact that was "substantial." The Government has not cited, and we have not found, any case where the locus of the effects, standing by itself, was sufficient to confer constitutionally sound venue.

Undoubtedly there are some instances where the location in which a crime's effects are felt is relevant to determining whether venue is proper. *See Rodriguez-Moreno*, 526 U.S. at 279 n.2 (reserving the issue of whether venue may also be permissibly based on the location where a crime's effects are felt). But those cases are reserved for situations in which "an essential conduct element is itself defined in terms of its effects." [*United States v.*] *Bowens*, 224 F.3d [302,] 311 [(4th Cir. 2000)]. For example, in a prosecution for Hobbs Act robbery, venue may be proper in any district where commerce is affected because the terms of the act themselves forbid affecting commerce. *See* 18 U.S.C. § 1951(a). . . .

Sections of the CFAA other than § 1030(a)(2)(C) do speak in terms of their effects. For example, § 1030(a)(5)(B) criminalizes intentionally accessing a computer without authorization and recklessly causing damage. Because that crime is defined in terms of its effects—the damage caused—venue could be proper wherever that occurred.

Congress, however, did not define a violation of § 1030(a)(2)(C) in terms of its effects. The statute simply criminalizes accessing a computer without authorization and obtaining information. It punishes only the actions that the defendant takes to access and obtain. It does not speak in terms of the effects on those whose information is obtained. The crime is complete even if the offender never looks at the information and immediately destroys it, or the victim has no idea that information was ever taken....

V.

Venue issues are animated in part by the "danger of allowing the [G]overnment to choose its forum free from any external constraints." [*United States v.*] *Salinas*, 373 F.3d [161,] 169–70 [(1st Cir. 2004)]. The ever-increasing ubiquity of the Internet only amplifies this concern. As we progress technologically, we must remain mindful that cybercrimes do not happen in some metaphysical location that justifies disregarding constitutional limits on venue. People and computers still exist in identifiable places in the physical world. When people commit crimes, we have the ability and obligation to ensure that they do not stand to account for those crimes in forums in which they performed no "essential conduct element" of the crimes charged.... [Reversed]

Notes

1. *Conspiracy.* Where is venue proper in a conspiracy case? As far as we can tell, Auernheimer has never at any time in his life left the state of Arkansas. Could he nonetheless be charged in California, where Spitler resides? Could Spitler, for his part, have been charged in Arkansas?

2. *Permissible venues.* What were the "essential conduct" elements of count one? Based on the Third Circuit's assessment of these elements, what are all of the places where Auernheimer could have been properly prosecuted?

3. *Venue in the Internet age.* It can be hard to conceptualize "where" a computer crime occurs. In *Auernheimer*, the Third Circuit tries to anchor its venue analysis in the physical reality of a server. Unlike the Internet, which seems to exist everywhere and nowhere, a server does have a discrete, identifiable location. But does that location necessarily supply a fair place for prosecution? It is only the very rare Internet user who gives any conscious thought to the location of the servers that are being accessed online. Would not a server-based venue seem rather arbitrary in many cases?

4. *Substantial contacts test.* What exactly is the substantial contacts test? Does it remain a valid part of venue analysis in the Third Circuit? Do you prefer this test to the formalism of *Cabrales* and *Rodriquez-Moreno*?

5. *Actions versus effects.* In a conventional victimizing offense, the defendant's key actions normally occur more or less at the same time and place as the victim's injury or loss. Sometimes, however, *actions* and *effects* do occur in different jurisdictions. We've seen that actions can provide a basis for venue, but what about effects? Does the *locus delicti* include the place where a victim experiences harm, even if the defendant performed no actions in that locale? In *Rodriguez-Moreno*, the Supreme Court

raised the question, but did not answer it. (See footnote 2 of the Court's opinion.) How does the Third Circuit answer the question in *Auernheimer*?

[2] Offenses Committed Outside any County, District, or State

Sometimes a crime occurs in an area other than a clearly defined district or county. For example, a crime may occur in the middle of a lake that separates two counties or states. Or it may occur on the high seas. Where is venue? Both constitutional and statutory provisions address these issues.

For federal crimes, recall that Article III, § 2 of the United States Constitution provides that a federal crime committed in no state shall be tried "at such Place or Places as the Congress may by Law have directed." U.S. Const., Art. III, § 2. Congress has exercised this authority in 18 U.S.C. § 3238:

> The trial of all offenses begun or committed upon the high seas, or elsewhere out of the jurisdiction of any particular State or district, shall be in the district in which the offender, or any one or two or more joint offenders is arrested or is first brought; but if such offender or offenders are not so arrested or brought into any district, an indictment or information may be filed in the district of the last known residence of the offender or of any one of two or more joint offenders, or if no such residence is known the indictment or information may be filed in the District of Columbia.

The "first brought" provision was applied in the prosecution of the notorious would-be "shoe bomber," Richard Reid, who attempted to blow up a plane over the Atlantic Ocean. The flight, originally destined from Paris to Miami, was diverted to Boston, the nearest major international airport, and Reid was subsequently tried and convicted in the United States District Court for the District of Massachusetts.

States have also enacted statutes establishing the venue in no-district cases. *See, e.g.*, 720 Ill. Comp. Stat. Ann. 5/1-6(e) (Smith-Hurd) (venue of offense committed on navigable waters bordering Illinois is in any county adjacent to the body of navigable water).

[3] Litigating Venue

If a defendant contests venue, then the government must prove the facts necessary to show that venue is proper. However, venue is not a "substantive element" of a crime that must necessarily be proven to the jury beyond a reasonable doubt.

Standard of proof. When venue must be proven, the rule in the federal system, as in some states, is that the government need only satisfy the preponderance of the evidence standard. *See, e.g., Auernheimer*, 748 F.3d at 533. In other states, however, the government does bear the higher beyond-a-reasonable-doubt burden that normally applies to the proof of offense elements. *See* Wayne R. LaFave et al., Criminal Procedure § 16.1(g) (4th ed. 2015).

Could venue be established by judicial notice? For example, could the trial judge in King County simply take judicial notice that the Safety Bank on West Broadway in Central City is located in King County? Alternatively, could venue be established by defense counsel's stipulation? *See Muldrow v. State*, 744 S.E.2d 413 (Ga. Ct. App. 2013) (no to judicial notice, yes to stipulation).

Who decides: jury or judge? Once again, jurisdictions are divided. In the federal system and some state systems, the jury is given the ultimate responsibility for determining whether venue is proper. In a few states, though, the judge serves in this role and will conduct a pretrial evidentiary hearing if necessary to resolve factual disputes relating to venue. *See* LaFave et al., *supra*, § 16.1(g); Lorraine Donnelly, Note, *Proper Venue as a Jury Issue in Federal Criminal Cases*, 76 Temp. L. Rev. 883 (2003).

Waiver. Since venue provisions are designed to assist the accused, he or she can waive them. Sometimes a waiver has been inferred when the defendant did not object to the lack of venue or move for a change of venue. Note that this is a more relaxed standard than usual for waiver of a constitutional right, which usually requires an affirmative showing of a knowing and voluntary waiver. *See, e.g., United States v. Carreon-Palacio*, 267 F.3d 381 (5th Cir. 2001) (extensive discussion of venue procedures); *Turner v. Commonwealth*, 345 S.W.3d 844 (Ky. 2011) (defendant waived venue issue by not making a motion to transfer venue). Venue "occup[ies] a lesser station in the hierarchy of constitutionally-derived rights." *United States v. Perez*, 280 F.3d 318, 328 (3d Cir. 2002).

Acquittal. On rare occasions the government gets sloppy and forgets to prove venue or does not present adequate proof of it. The accused may then be entitled to an acquittal. *See, e.g., State v. Hampton*, 983 N.E.2d 324 (Ohio 2012) (acquittal on basis of insufficient proof of venue is final verdict not appealable by state); *Muldrow v. State*, 744 S.E.2d 413 (Ga. Ct. App. 2013) (venue in a particular county is not established by proof that a crime occurred on a given street or city without proof that the street or city was in that county).

Harmless error. When trial courts make venue errors, the usual remedy is for the appellate court to acquit the accused or require a new trial with proper venue. However, there are a few cases where the doctrine of harmless error is applied. Even though venue was wrong, the conviction is upheld as long as the accused received a fair trial and there was no miscarriage of justice. *People v. Houthoofd*, 790 N.W.2d 315 (Mich. 2010) (in Michigan a defendant has no state constitutional right to a particular venue; violation of the statutory right is assessed under the harmless error rule). *But see Auernheimer*, 748 F.3d at 538 ("[W]e are skeptical that venue errors are susceptible to harmless error analysis.").

[4] Transfer of Venue

Although the Sixth Amendment and court rules establish that venue lies in the district (or county) where the crime occurred, sometimes the accused or the prosecution would like the venue changed. The person seeking this will file a Motion for a Change (or Transfer) of Venue. As a general principle, though, courts are reluctant to grant a venue change. If the request is made because of concerns about an inability to obtain a fair trial in the original venue, the judge in that venue may be unwilling to admit that he or she cannot provide a fair trial. Additionally, some courts may believe that the local populace has a right to have the case tried where the crime occurred.

Rule 21 of the Federal Rules of Criminal Procedure permits the accused to file a Motion for Transfer. Note that the transfer request may be based on three grounds: prejudice against the defendant (Rule 21(a)), convenience of the parties or victim or witnesses (Rule 21(b)), or the interest of justice (Rule 21(b)). Since venue is a right conferred on the federal defendant, the government cannot obtain a change of venue to another district without the defendant's consent. The defendant's consent to a change is viewed as a waiver of venue rights. The government's consent is not necessary.

All states authorize a transfer of venue if necessary to ensure that the defendant receives a fair trial. However, only a minority of states provide for transfer on grounds of convenience. Similarly, states are divided over whether and under what circumstances a prosecutor may obtain a transfer over the defendant's objection. *See* WAYNE R. LAFAVE ET AL., CRIMINAL PROCEDURE § 16.3 (4th ed. 2015).

[a] Transfer Because of Prejudice

Rule 21(a) requires a transfer if there is so much prejudice in the original locale that the defendant cannot obtain a fair trial. Ordinarily, the prejudice is caused by hostile pretrial media coverage. When pretrial publicity is the culprit, it raises several serious issues. These include the defendant's right to a fair trial by an impartial jury and to have the case tried pursuant to the usual venue rules, and the media's right to press freedom as well as the citizens' right to have a trial in their area.

When the court finds that the defendant cannot obtain a fair and impartial trial because of prejudice, it *must* transfer the proceeding under Rule 21(a). This could occur in cases that have attracted a lot of media attention. The accused may believe that a fair trial is impossible in the district where there is venue. Perhaps the media has depicted the defendant as guilty, disclosed inadmissible evidence, or caused outrage about the crime.

Under Rule 21, this transfer may occur only when requested by the accused (who thereby waives the right to be tried in a certain locale), but in some states the court may transfer venue for prejudice upon the motion of either the defendant or the state. *See, e.g.*, MONT. CODE ANN. § 46-13-203.

Skilling v. United States

130 S. Ct. 2896 (2010)

Justice GINSBURG delivered the opinion of the Court.

In 2001, Enron Corporation, then the seventh highest-revenue-grossing company in America, crashed into bankruptcy. We consider in this opinion ... did pretrial publicity and community prejudice prevent Skilling from obtaining a fair trial?

I

[Enron, with headquarters in Houston, Texas, was one of the world's leading energy companies. Skilling was chief executive officer until he resigned from Enron. The company's stock, which had traded at $90 per share in August 2000, plummeted to pennies per share in late 2001.] On July 7, 2004, a grand jury indicted Skilling, Lay [Enron's founder], and Richard Causey, Enron's former chief accounting officer . . . [for] "a wide-ranging scheme to deceive the investing public, including Enron's shareholders, . . . about the true performance of Enron's businesses by: (a) manipulating Enron's publicly reported financial results; and (b) making public statements and representations about Enron's financial performance and results that were false and misleading."

Skilling and his co-conspirators, the indictment continued, "enriched themselves as a result of the scheme through salary, bonuses, grants of stock and stock options, other profits, and prestige."

. . . In November 2004, Skilling moved to transfer the trial to another venue; he contended that hostility toward him in Houston, coupled with extensive pretrial publicity, had poisoned potential jurors. To support this assertion, Skilling, aided by media experts, submitted hundreds of news reports detailing Enron's downfall; he also presented affidavits from the experts he engaged portraying community attitudes in Houston in comparison to other potential venues.

The U.S. District Court for the Southern District of Texas . . . denied the venue-transfer motion. Despite "isolated incidents of intemperate commentary," the court observed, media coverage "ha[d] [mostly] been objective and unemotional," and the facts of the case were "neither heinous nor sensational." Moreover, "courts ha[d] commonly" favored "effective voir dire . . . to ferret out any [juror] bias." Pretrial publicity about the case, the court concluded, did not warrant a presumption that Skilling would be unable to obtain a fair trial in Houston.

[Virtually all of the 400 prospective jurors completed a 77-question, 14-page questionnaire that asked about their sources of news and exposure to Enron-related publicity, beliefs concerning Enron and what caused its collapse, opinions regarding the defendants and their possible guilt or innocence, and relationships to the company and to anyone affected by its demise. The parties agreed to exclude, in particular, "each and every" prospective juror who said that a preexisting opinion about Enron or the defendants would prevent him or her from impartially considering the evidence at trial.]

[Before trial] . . . Skilling renewed his change-of-venue motion, arguing that the juror questionnaires revealed pervasive bias and that news accounts of Causey's guilty plea further tainted the jury pool. . . . The District Court again declined to move the trial. . . . But the court promised to give counsel an opportunity to ask follow-up questions and it agreed that venire members should be examined individually about pretrial publicity. The court also allotted the defendants jointly 14 peremptory challenges, 2 more than the standard number. . . . In all, the court granted one of the Government's for-cause challenges and denied four; it granted three of the defendants' challenges and denied six. The parties agreed to excuse three additional jurors for cause and one for hardship.

... Before the jury was sworn in, Skilling objected to the seating of six jurors. He did not contend that they were in fact biased; instead, he urged that he would have used peremptories to exclude them had he not exhausted his supply by striking several venire members after the court refused to excuse them for cause. The court overruled this objection.

... Following a 4-month trial and nearly five days of deliberation, the jury found Skilling guilty of 19 counts, ... and not guilty of 9 insider-trading counts. The District Court sentenced Skilling to 292 months' imprisonment, 3 years' supervised release, and $45 million in restitution.

On appeal ... the Fifth Circuit initially determined that the volume and negative tone of media coverage generated by Enron's collapse created a presumption of juror prejudice. The court also noted potential prejudice stemming from Causey's guilty plea and from the large number of victims in Houston....

The Court of Appeals stated, however, that "the presumption [of prejudice] is rebuttable," and it therefore examined the voir dire to determine whether "the District Court empanelled an impartial jury." The voir dire was, in the Fifth Circuit's view, "proper and thorough." Moreover, the court noted, Skilling had challenged only one seated juror—Juror 11—for cause.... In sum, the Fifth Circuit found that the Government had overcome the presumption of prejudice and that Skilling had not "show[n] that any juror who actually sat was prejudiced against him." ...

II

... Skilling's fair-trial claim thus raises two distinct questions. First, did the District Court err by failing to move the trial to a different venue based on a presumption of prejudice? Second, did actual prejudice contaminate Skilling's jury?

A

...

2

... We begin our discussion by addressing the presumption of prejudice from which the Fifth Circuit's analysis in Skilling's case proceeded. The foundation precedent is *Rideau v. Louisiana*, 373 U.S. 723 (1963).

Wilbert Rideau robbed a bank in a small Louisiana town, kidnaped three bank employees, and killed one of them. Police interrogated Rideau in jail without counsel present and obtained his confession. Without informing Rideau, no less seeking his consent, the police filmed the interrogation. On three separate occasions shortly before the trial, a local television station broadcast the film to audiences ranging from 24,000 to 53,000 individuals. Rideau moved for a change of venue, arguing that he could not receive a fair trial in the parish where the crime occurred, which had a population of approximately 150,000 people. The trial court denied the motion, and a jury eventually convicted Rideau. The Supreme Court of Louisiana upheld the conviction.

We reversed. "What the people [in the community] saw on their television sets," we observed, "was Rideau, in jail, flanked by the sheriff and two state troopers, admitting in detail the commission of the robbery, kidnapping, and murder." "[T]o the tens of thousands of people who saw and heard it," we explained, the interrogation "in a very real sense was Rideau's trial—at which he pleaded guilty." We therefore "d[id] not hesitate to hold, without pausing to examine a particularized transcript of the voir dire," that "[t]he kangaroo court proceedings" trailing the televised confession violated due process.

We followed *Rideau*'s lead in two later cases in which media coverage manifestly tainted a criminal prosecution. In *Estes v. Texas*, 381 U.S. 532 (1965), . . . [t]he media's overzealous reporting efforts, we observed, "led to considerable disruption" and denied the "judicial serenity and calm to which [Billie Sol Estes] was entitled."

Similarly, in *Sheppard v. Maxwell*, 384 U.S. 333, (1966), news reporters extensively covered the story of Sam Sheppard, who was accused of bludgeoning his pregnant wife to death. "[B]edlam reigned at the courthouse during the trial and newsmen took over practically the entire courtroom. . . . We upset the murder conviction because a "carnival atmosphere" pervaded the trial.

In each of these cases, we overturned a "conviction obtained in a trial atmosphere that [was] utterly corrupted by press coverage"; our decisions, however, "cannot be made to stand for the proposition that juror exposure to . . . news accounts of the crime . . . alone presumptively deprives the defendant of due process." *Murphy v. Florida*, 421 U.S. 794 (1975).

3

Relying on *Rideau*, *Estes*, and *Sheppard*, Skilling asserts that [there is presumed prejudice so] we need not pause to examine the screening questionnaires or the voir dire before declaring his jury's verdict void. We are not persuaded. Important differences separate Skilling's prosecution from those in which we have presumed juror prejudice.[14]

First, we have emphasized in prior decisions the size and characteristics of the community in which the crime occurred. In *Rideau*, for example, we noted that the murder was committed in a parish of only 150,000 residents. Houston, in contrast, is the fourth most populous city in the Nation: At the time of Skilling's trial, more than 4.5 million individuals eligible for jury duty resided in the Houston area. Given this large, diverse pool of potential jurors, the suggestion that 12 impartial individuals could not be empaneled is hard to sustain.

---

14. Skilling's reliance on *Estes* and *Sheppard* is particularly misplaced; those cases involved media interference with courtroom proceedings during trial. Skilling does not assert that news coverage reached and influenced his jury after it was empaneled.

Second, although news stories about Skilling were not kind, they contained no confession or other blatantly prejudicial information of the type readers or viewers could not reasonably be expected to shut from sight. Rideau's dramatically staged admission of guilt, for instance, was likely imprinted indelibly in the mind of anyone who watched it.

Third, unlike cases in which trial swiftly followed a widely reported crime, over four years elapsed between Enron's bankruptcy and Skilling's trial. Although reporters covered Enron-related news throughout this period, the decibel level of media attention diminished somewhat in the years following Enron's collapse.

Finally, and of prime significance, Skilling's jury acquitted him of nine insider-trading counts. . . . It would be odd for an appellate court to presume prejudice in a case in which jurors' actions run counter to that presumption.

4

Skilling's trial, in short, shares little in common with those in which we approved a presumption of juror prejudice. . . . In this case . . . news stories about Enron did not present the kind of vivid, unforgettable information we have recognized as particularly likely to produce prejudice, and Houston's size and diversity diluted the media's impact.

Nor did Enron's "sheer number of victims," trigger a presumption of prejudice. Although the widespread community impact necessitated careful identification and inspection of prospective jurors' connections to Enron, the extensive screening questionnaire and follow-up voir dire were well suited to that task. And hindsight shows the efficacy of these devices; jurors' links to Enron were either nonexistent or attenuated.

Finally, although Causey's "well-publicized decision to plead guilty" shortly before trial created a danger of juror prejudice, the District Court took appropriate steps to reduce that risk. The court delayed the proceedings by two weeks, lessening the immediacy of that development. And during voir dire, the court asked about prospective jurors' exposure to recent publicity, including news regarding Causey. Only two venire members recalled the plea; neither mentioned Causey by name, and neither ultimately served on Skilling's jury. . . . Persuaded that no presumption arose,[18] we conclude that the District Court, in declining to order a venue change, did not exceed constitutional limitations.

B

[There was also no actual prejudice] . . . Reviewing courts are properly resistant to second-guessing the trial judge's estimation of a juror's impartiality, for that judge's appraisal is ordinarily influenced by a host of factors impossible to capture

18. The parties disagree about whether a presumption of prejudice can be rebutted, and, if it can, what standard of proof governs that issue. Because we hold that no presumption arose, we need not, and do not, reach these questions.

fully in the record—among them, the prospective juror's inflection, sincerity, demeanor, candor, body language, and apprehension of duty.... We consider the adequacy of jury selection in Skilling's case, therefore, attentive to the respect due to district-court determinations of juror impartiality and of the measures necessary to ensure that impartiality.

2

Skilling deems the voir dire insufficient because, he argues, jury selection lasted "just five hours," "[m]ost of the court's questions were conclusory[,] high-level, and failed adequately to probe jurors' true feelings," and the court "consistently took prospective jurors at their word once they claimed they could be fair, no matter what other indications of bias were present." Our review of the record, however, yields a different appraisal.[21]

... [T]he District Court initially screened venire members by eliciting their responses to a comprehensive questionnaire drafted in large part by Skilling. That survey helped to identify prospective jurors excusable for cause and served as a springboard for further questions put to remaining members of the array. Voir dire thus was, in the court's words, the "culmination of a lengthy process." ...

The District Court conducted voir dire, moreover, aware of the greater-than-normal need, due to pretrial publicity, to ensure against jury bias. At Skilling's urging, the court examined each prospective juror individually, thus preventing the spread of any prejudicial information to other venire members. To encourage candor, the court repeatedly admonished that there were "no right and wrong answers to th[e] questions." The court denied Skilling's request for attorney-led voir dire.... The parties, however, were accorded an opportunity to ask follow-up questions of every prospective juror brought to the bench for colloquy. Skilling's counsel declined to ask anything of more than half of the venire members questioned individually, including eight eventually selected for the jury, because, he explained, "the Court and other counsel have covered" everything he wanted to know.

Inspection of the questionnaires and voir dire of the individuals who actually served as jurors satisfies us that, notwithstanding the flaws Skilling lists, the selection process successfully secured jurors who were largely untouched by Enron's collapse....

The questionnaires confirmed that, whatever community prejudice existed in Houston generally, Skilling's jurors were not under its sway. Although many expressed

---

21. In addition to focusing on the adequacy of voir dire, our decisions have also "take[n] into account ... other measures [that] were used to mitigate the adverse effects of publicity." We have noted, for example, the prophylactic effect of "emphatic and clear instructions on the sworn duty of each juror to decide the issues only on evidence presented in open court." Here, the District Court's instructions were unequivocal; the jurors, the court emphasized, were duty bound "to reach a fair and impartial verdict in this case based solely on the evidence [they] hear[d] and read in th[e] courtroom." Peremptory challenges, too, "provid[e] protection against [prejudice]"; the District Court, exercised its discretion to grant the defendants two extra peremptories.

sympathy for victims of Enron's bankruptcy and speculated that greed contributed to the corporation's collapse, these sentiments did not translate into animus toward Skilling. When asked whether they "ha[d] an opinion about ... Jeffrey Skilling," none of the seated jurors and alternates checked the "yes" box. And in response to the question whether "any opinion [they] may have formed regarding Enron or [Skilling] [would] prevent" their impartial consideration of the evidence at trial, every juror—despite options to mark "yes" or "unsure"—instead checked "no." ...

The District Court, moreover, did not simply take venire members who proclaimed their impartiality at their word. As noted, all of Skilling's jurors had already affirmed on their questionnaires that they would have no trouble basing a verdict only on the evidence at trial. Nevertheless, the court followed up with each individually to uncover concealed bias. This face-to-face opportunity to gauge demeanor and credibility, coupled with information from the questionnaires regarding jurors' backgrounds, opinions, and sources of news, gave the court a sturdy foundation to assess fitness for jury service. The jury's not-guilty verdict on nine insider-trading counts after nearly five days of deliberation, meanwhile, suggests the court's assessments were accurate.

3

... In sum, Skilling failed to establish that a presumption of prejudice arose or that actual bias infected the jury that tried him.... We therefore affirm the Fifth Circuit's ruling that Skilling received a fair trial.

[The concurring opinions of JUSTICES ALITO and SCALIA are omitted, as is the dissenting opinion of JUSTICE SOTOMAYOR, which was joined by JUSTICES STEVENS and BREYER.]

Notes

1. *Actual v. presumed prejudice.* The *Skilling* Court, like many courts, categorizes prejudice as *actual* or *presumed*. For presumed, "we simply cannot rely on jurors' claims that they can be impartial." *State v. Kingman*, 264 P.3d 1104, 1112 (Mont. 2011). If the defendant demonstrates that prejudice should be presumed, then there may be no need for the court to comb the trial record for evidence that the particular jurors selected were, in fact, biased against the defendant. There is disagreement, though, about whether a presumption of prejudice can be rebutted, as indicated in footnote 18 of the *Skilling* opinion. *See also* Andrew Mayo, *Non-Media Jury Prejudice and Rule 21(a): Lessons from Enron*, 30 REV. LITIG. 133 (2010) (arguing for rebuttable presumption for media pretrial publicity but irrebuttable presumption for non-media prejudice (prejudice based on effects of the crime in the community)).

Courts rarely find presumed prejudice sufficient to trigger a venue change. They have described the presumed-prejudice situation as "rarely applicable" and the necessary standard of proof as "extremely high," involving an atmosphere "utterly corrupted by press coverage" or a "circus atmosphere or lynch mob mentality." *Rideau*, *Sheppard*, and *Estes* are the most-cited cases involving the presumption of prejudice. Review the facts of the cases as described in *Skilling* and you can see how profoundly harmful the publicity must be to trigger this presumption. *See also United States v. Casellas-Toro*, 807 F.3d 380 (1st Cir. 2015) (presuming prejudice when there was "'massive' and 'sensational' publicity blanketing the community for two years before trial," including "extensive reporting" of the defendant's conviction in another, related case; court assumed without deciding that presumption was rebuttable, but found that government "has not met its burden to show Casellas was tried by an impartial jury").

2. *How likely must prejudice be under Rule 21(a)?* Rule 21(a) requires a transfer of venue when the court is "satisfied" that the defendant cannot obtain a fair and impartial trial in the venue. Often the standard of "satisfied" is interpreted as meaning that the court must find a *reasonable likelihood* or *reasonable certainty* that there cannot be a fair trial.

3. *Empirical findings about pretrial publicity.* Social scientists have extensively studied the impact of pretrial publicity on jurors' perceptions. The overwhelming result is that jurors are affected by exposure to pretrial publicity. One author noted that research has shown that jurors' views are shaped by the jurors' knowledge of inadmissible evidence, a prior arrest record, a confession, performance on a lie detector, negative facets of a defendant's character, and "emotional" publicity (arousing an emotional reaction, as provided by a graphic description of a homicide victim's injuries), all information provided by out-of-court publicity. Vineet R. Shahani, Note, *Change the Motion, Not the Venue: A Critical Look at the Change of Venue Motion*, 42 Am. Crim. L. Rev. 93, 101 (2005).

4. *Possible remedies other than venue change for hostile pretrial publicity.* When pretrial publicity interferes with an accused's rights to a fair trial by an impartial jury, there are a number of possible remedies. One is for the court to grant a continuance to permit the media attention to extinguish. Another remedy is to use the jury selection process to winnow out persons who were too affected by the publicity or to sequester the jurors to protect them from the media coverage. When pretrial publicity is an issue, trial judges routinely allow potential jurors to be questioned about their exposure to the publicity and the impact of the publicity on their impartiality. Many judges also instruct jurors to ignore pretrial publicity in their deliberations on the case. Sometimes the trial court will consider a change of venue only after an unsuccessful attempt to seat an untainted jury.

5. *Burden of proof.* Ordinarily the defendant has the burden of establishing that hostile publicity makes a venue change necessary. Sometimes there is an express presumption that the jury in the locale of the crime can provide a fair trial. *See, e.g., Swisher v. Commonwealth*, 506 S.E.2d 763 (Va. 1998).

6. *Source of pretrial publicity.* Often neither the prosecution nor defense is responsible for the damaging pretrial publicity. However, if the victim or prosecution was at fault in generating the publicity, courts are more inclined to transfer venue. *See, e.g., State v. Lee*, 976 So.2d 109 (La. 2008).

7. *Public's right to local venue.* Some commentators argue that the members of a community have a right to see that a defendant from their community is tried locally. *See, e.g.,* Steven A. Engel, *The Public's Vicinage Right: A Constitutional Argument,* 75 N.Y.U. L. Rev. 1658 (2000). *See also People v. Thomas,* 274 P.3d 1170 (Cal. 2012) (venue rules protect the interests of the community in which a crime or related activity occurs by vindicating the community's right to sit in judgment on crimes committed within its territory). How much weight do you think should be given the community's interests in venue decisions?

8. *Fair trial impossible but no venue change.* Note that while *Rideau* indicates that the criminal defendant may have a right to a change of venue in situations where the media has created an overwhelmingly hostile environment, the case does not hold that the accused *must* request a venue change in this situation. What if the hostile publicity has risen to the level that *Rideau* finds sufficient for a constitutional violation, but the accused does not want a change of venue and yet demands a fair trial by an impartial jury as guaranteed by the Sixth Amendment and the Due Process Clause? Should the accused have to waive the right to venue in order to assert the crucial right to a fair trial? Can a change of venue be forced on the accused in order to protect the accused's right to a fair trial?

The usual judicial response to this unusual dilemma is to avoid it by finding that a fair trial is possible in the original place of venue (perhaps by granting a continuance and liberal jury voir dire to ensure impartiality). In rare circumstances, on the other hand, a court may dismiss the charges because there is no place that satisfies normal venue rules where a fair trial is possible. But, of course, this extreme remedy is a last resort. As was said in *United States v. Abbott Laboratories,* 505 F.2d 565, 572 (4th Cir. 1974), *cert. denied,* 420 U.S. 990 (1975):

> Although a change of venue under Rule 21 cannot be imposed on a defendant against his will, the availability of a change of venue as a corrective device undergirds the requirement that a defendant, who declines to request a change of venue but who seeks dismissal of an indictment against him because of allegedly prejudicial pretrial publicity, demonstrates the existence of actual prejudice far more convincingly than was done in the case at bar. A defendant who has unused means [i.e., a motion for a change of venue] to protect his rights [to a trial by an impartial jury] should not lightly be granted the extreme remedy of dismissal of the charges against him on less than a conclusive showing that the unused means would be ineffective.

In a few states, the defendant's venue rights are not absolute; the government may obtain a change of venue when necessary to empanel a fair and impartial jury. *See Sailor v. State,* 733 So. 2d 1057 (Fla. App. 1999); *State v. House,* 978 P.2d 967 (N.M. 1999) (state given change of venue to county with fewer Native Americans; noting since 1851 New Mexico has policy of allowing change of venue request by either side).

9. *Impartial jury unavailable.* A related issue arises when massive publicity makes it impossible to obtain an impartial jury anywhere in the country (for federal

crimes) or state (for state offenses). Even if the accused is willing to request a change of venue for the purpose of securing an impartial jury, the efforts may be fruitless. Imagine a trial if Adolf Hitler had somehow been arrested in the United States and was charged in an American court with a violation of American homicide law for his part in the Holocaust, or if Osama Bin Laden had been captured and tried in connection with the thousands of deaths that took place on 9/11. In such high visibility, emotionally charged cases, it is arguable that the case would have to be dismissed because a fair trial before an impartial jury is simply impossible. *See State v. Banks*, 387 N.W.2d 19 (S.D. 1986) (defendant has right under South Dakota law to be tried by impartial jury in county where crime occurred; if an impartial jury cannot be secured in that county, there can be no lawful conviction). Can you imagine the public outcry if a dismissal of charges against a genocidal mass murderer were to be ordered because it was impossible to find an impartial jury anywhere?

Such an argument was raised, unsuccessfully, in the case of Timothy McVeigh, tried for the 1995 bombing of the Murrah Building in Oklahoma City. Because of the intense emotional impact of the bombing on the community, the District Court judge transferred the case from Oklahoma to Denver, Colorado. Thereafter, McVeigh argued that because of massive national coverage by the media, the case should be dismissed or, in the alternative, a lengthy continuance should be granted to permit the media attention to diminish. In denying the motion, the trial judge took a number of measures to ensure that jurors would remain impartial, including lengthy questionnaires in the selection process and detailed instructions admonishing the jurors to set aside any preconceived impressions they might have. The appellate court concluded that the trial court ruled correctly, noting that the defendant failed to make "the strong showing that would be necessary for the court to presume prejudice as a result of the publicity." *United States v. McVeigh*, 153 F.3d 1166 (10th Cir. 1998).

10. *Transfer of jury.* One solution to the problem of a jury tainted by local publicity is to select a *foreign jury* from another area and then transport the jurors to the original venue of the offense. Under this model, the jury should have less exposure to the local media coverage and the accused will have a trial in the locality of the crime. In federal cases, the district court judge has discretion to select jurors from areas other than the one in which the crime occurred so long as the jurors reside within the federal district where the crime occurred. *See, e.g., United States v. Ford*, 958 F.2d 372 (6th Cir. 1992) (jury selected from Jackson, Tennessee, then transported to Memphis for trial; publicity concerns justify intra-district transfers). Many states also permit the use of foreign jurors if the accused waives venue. *See, e.g., State v. Harris*, 716 A.2d 458 (N.J. 1998); *see also Harris v. Ricci*, 607 F.3d 92 (3d Cir. 2010) (Supreme Court has not decided validity of use of foreign jury to ameliorate harmful pretrial publicity).

[b] Transfer for Convenience or in the Interests of Justice

A defendant may seek a transfer for reasons other than adverse publicity. Rule 21(b) recognizes that a transfer may be appropriate, upon the motion of the defendant, for either the convenience of the parties or witnesses or in the interests of justice. Courts faced with a motion under Rule 21(b) use a factor approach.

Platt v. Minnesota Mining & Manufacturing Co.

376 U.S. 240 (1964)

JUSTICE CLARK delivered the opinion of the Court.

[The defendant, Minnesota Mining and Manufacturing Company, was indicted for several antitrust violations for efforts to monopolize commerce in pressure-sensitive tape and other products. The indictment was issued by a federal grand jury in the Eastern District of Illinois. It was agreed that the indictment could have also been returned in the District of Minnesota and several other districts.

The defendant filed a motion under Rule 21(b), based on the "interests of justice," to transfer the case from the Eastern District of Illinois to the District of Minnesota where it had its headquarters. The District Court denied the motion on the grounds that the factors of convenience, expense, and early trial, together with the probability that it "would be more difficult (for the Government) to get a fair and impartial jury in the Minnesota District," meant that "the interests of justice" would not be promoted by a transfer.

The Court of Appeals found that the trial judge had treated the factor of a fair and impartial trial as the "most important item" in his decision and that this was not an appropriate criterion. It concluded that in addition to "the essential elements of convenience, expense and early trial, constituting 'interest of justice' in a civil case," a criminal case was "impressed with the fundamental historical right of a defendant to be prosecuted in its own environment or district. . . ." Upon reviewing the record, the Court of Appeals substituted its own findings for those of the trial judge and ordered the case transferred from Illinois to Minnesota.]

. . . We believe that the Court of Appeals erred in ordering the transfer. . . .

. . . The Court of Appeals found, in contradiction to the finding of the District Court, that a trial in the Eastern District of Illinois would result in unjustifiable increased expenses to the respondent of "at least $100,000, great inconvenience of witnesses, serious disruption of business and interference of contact between the (respondent's) executives and its trial attorneys. . . ." It also found that respondent had no office, plant, or other facility in the Eastern District and that there was less congestion in the docket of the Minnesota District than in the Eastern District of Illinois. The court concluded that this was a "demonstration by proof or admission of the essential elements of convenience, expense and early trial, constituting 'interest of justice' in a civil case," which, augmented by the additional consideration that this was a criminal action, compelled the granting of the motion to transfer.

. . . [T]he Court of Appeals placed particular weight on the trial judge's finding that it "would be more difficult to get a fair and impartial jury in the Minnesota District than in the Eastern District of Illinois." The Court of Appeals stated that this finding, if true (which it doubted), "would not justify a refusal to make a transfer otherwise proper under rule 21(b) . . ." and concluded that "it would be an unsound and dangerous innovation in our federal court system for a judge in any district to appraise or even speculate as to the efficacy of the operations of a federal court of concurrent jurisdiction in another district. It follows that no order in any way based upon such reasoning can stand, even under the guise of an exercise of discretion."

. . . The trial judge in his memorandum decision listed a number of items as pertinent in the determination of whether the case should be transferred to Minnesota "in the interest of justice" as required by Rule 21(b). As Chief Judge Hastings pointed out in his dissent, these "factors were (1) location of corporate defendant; (2) location of possible witnesses; (3) location of events likely to be in issue; (4) location of documents and records likely to be involved; (5) disruption of defendant's business unless the case is transferred; (6) expense to the parties; (7) location of counsel; (8) relative accessibility of place of trial; (9) docket condition of each district or division involved; and (10) any other special elements which might affect the transfer."

It appears that both parties and the Court of Appeals agree that the first nine factors enumerated were appropriate. As we have noted, the Court of Appeals struck the fair and impartial jury finding as not being a proper factor and the Government does not challenge that action here. . . . This leaves before us the question of whether the Court of Appeals erred in considering the motion to transfer de novo on the record made in the District Court and ordering transfer to the District of Minnesota.

. . . The District Court's use of an inappropriate factor did not empower the Court of Appeals to order the transfer. The function of the Court of Appeals in this case was to determine the appropriate criteria and then leave their application to the trial judge on remand. . . . Here, however, the Court of Appeals undertook a de novo examination of the record and itself exercised the discretionary function which the rule commits to the trial judge. . . .

Since the trial court must reconsider the motion, effective judicial administration requires that we comment upon the erroneous holding of the Court of Appeals that criminal defendants have a constitutionally based right to a trial in their home districts. . . . As we said in *United States v. Cores*, 356 U.S. 405, 407 (1958): "The Constitution makes it clear that determination of proper venue in a criminal case requires determination of where the crime was committed. . . . The provision for trial in the vicinity of the crime is a safeguard against the unfairness and hardship involved when an accused is prosecuted in a remote place." The fact that Minnesota is the main office or "home" of the respondent has no independent significance in determining whether transfer to that district would be "in the interest of justice," although it may be considered with reference to such factors as the convenience of records, officers, personnel and counsel. [Reversed]

[The concurring opinion of Justice Harlan is omitted.]

Notes

1. *Government's interest.* Recall that Rule 21(b) authorizes a transfer "[f]or the convenience of the parties, any victim, and the witnesses, and in the interest of justice." Note also that in *Platt* venue was appropriate in either the Eastern District of Illinois or the District of Minnesota (as well as several other districts). Apparently the prosecution decided to seek the indictment in Illinois rather than Minnesota. The defendant corporation wanted to move the case to Minnesota, its home base. The *Platt* Court seems to suggest that the trial court could not consider the *government's* interest in an impartial jury. Why not? Isn't the government entitled to a fair trial? Doesn't the "interest of justice" by definition include the likelihood of a fair trial?

2. *Pretrial publicity and Rule 21(b).* While Rule 21(a) specifically addresses pretrial publicity and mandates a venue change if the court finds the defendant is unlikely to get a fair and impartial trial, the court may also order a venue change for hostile publicity under Rule 21(b). One author summarized the cases as suggesting that courts apply the "interests of justice" standard by looking at five factors: the nature and extent of pretrial publicity, the size and demographic composition of current and potential trial venues, the nature and gravity of the offense, the interests of the defendant and the victim, and the existence of any government-sponsored publicity. Vineet R. Shahani, Note, *Change the Motion, Not the Venue: A Critical Look at the Change of Venue Motion,* 42 Am. Crim. L. Rev. 93, 108 (2005).

3. *Choice of new location.* Note that Rule 21 does not indicate to which district the case should be transferred. Nowhere does the rule indicate that the new location must be one suggested by the defendant. Many state statutes provide similar flexibility, but some are more specific. *See, e.g.,* Ala. Code § 15-2-24 (new venue must be nearest county free from the reasons mandating the change). Do you favor a rule restricting the new location of the trial? A recent trend is for states to authorize the court to consider the racial composition of the venues to which the trial could be transferred. If the defendant is not guaranteed a trial of any particular racial composition, does it make sense to allow the judge to consider the racial composition of potential trial sites?

4. *Victim's preferences.* Courts deciding whether to order a venue change often may take into consideration the victim's interests. Rule 21 and some states require this. *See, e.g.,* N.J.S.A. § 52:4B-36 (victims entitled to have inconvenience to their participation in court proceedings minimized to fullest extent possible).

5. *Limit on number of venue changes.* Rule 21 contains no limit on the number of times venue can be changed. Some state laws do. *See, e.g.,* Ala. Code § 15-2-24 (only one venue change permitted). On rare occasions the reasons for a venue change are no longer valid. Some state statutes specifically authorize the court in the new venue to return the case to the original venue after holding a hearing on the issue. *See, e.g.,* Cal. Penal Code § 1033.1.

[c] Timing and Content of Transfer Motions

Because a successful motion for a change of venue has a significant impact on the court calendar as well as that of the other participants in the trial, the motion should normally be made as early in the proceedings as feasible. Indeed, some such motions have been denied because, in part, they were not filed pretrial, *see, e.g., State v. Gaines*, 316 S.W.3d 440 (Mo. Ct. App. 2010), or only shortly before the trial was to begin, *see, e.g, Cornette v. Commonwealth*, 2013 Ky. Unpub. LEXIS 12. Yet in some cases defense counsel may prefer not to proceed with the motion until after the *voir dire* process has explored jurors' exposure to the publicity since this process may provide counsel with the strongest support for a venue change.

By way of contrast, a motion to acquit because of improper venue has fewer time limits than one to transfer venue. Since the court may not be able to assess whether the state met its burden regarding venue any earlier, it may be appropriate to wait to file a motion to acquit for failure to prove venue until sometime midtrial. *See, e.g., United States v. Robinson*, 167 F.3d 824 (3d Cir. 1999); *see also United States v. Biao*, 51 F. Supp. 2d 1042 (S.D. Cal. 1999) (motion to dismiss for lack of venue may be brought before close of government's case, but must be raised before trial if claim is that the indictment is defective on its face).

Normally, a defendant's motion to transfer venue is made with a *trial* in mind—the defendant is concerned about getting an impartial jury, or wants the trial to take place somewhere that is convenient for his or her witnesses, or is motivated by some other trial-related consideration. Sometimes, though, a defendant may request a transfer when there is no expectation that a trial will occur. Even if the proceedings are essentially limited to a guilty plea hearing and a sentencing, the defendant may still regard one venue as more convenient or strategically helpful than another. For instance, if the defendant committed a crime in one district, but lives in another, the defendant may prefer to have the sentencing occur in the district of residence, which will normally facilitate attendance and participation by family members and friends.

Rule 20 of the Federal Rules of Criminal Procedure can provide for transfer in such cases. The rule specifically authorizes a defendant to request a transfer from the district of the crime to another district where the accused was arrested, held, or is present. *See also* Fla. Stat. Ann. § 910.035 (West) (transfer to county where defendant was arrested or is held). The defendant's request for a change of venue is viewed as a waiver of the ordinary rule requiring venue at the location of the crime. The government's interests are safeguarded in the transfer process since the United States Attorneys for both districts must agree to the transfer.

As for the content of a transfer motion, the exact facts that must be proved vary according to the theory of the motion. For example, if the change of venue is sought under Rule 21(a) because adverse publicity has so polluted the jury pool that it will be impossible to select an impartial jury, the venue motion must include sufficient facts to raise a serious question on this issue. One way to do this is to include an appendix that reproduces the newspaper and other articles about the defendant and the trial. If funds permit, defense counsel may also want to commission a trial consultant to conduct a study of community attitudes. The results of this could also be included in the appendix to the venue motion. *See generally* Edward R. Shohat & Pamela I. Perry, *International Drug Cartels: Miami Vice or Government Spice*, 40 Am. U. L. Rev. 849 (1991).

Many courts have begun to rely on public opinion surveys to ascertain the effect of pretrial publicity. *See* Vineet R. Shahani, Note, *Change the Motion, Not the Venue: A Critical Look at the Change of Venue Motion*, 42 Am. Crim. L. Rev. 93 (2005). In fact, one court actually denied a change of venue primarily due to a defendant's failure to submit a public opinion survey despite his producing a quantity of media coverage. *See State v. Erickstad*, 620 N.W.2d 136 (N.D. 2000).

[d] Multiple Parties and Multiple Counts

Questions of venue become difficult if there are multiple parties with different views of the proper or best venue for a joint trial or if there is one defendant facing several counts who believes that the venue should not be the same for all counts. In such cases the trial court may grant a severance of defendants or counts pursuant to Rules 8, 13, or 14 of the Federal Rules of Criminal Procedure. However, as discussed in Chapter 8 below, courts are often disinclined to grant such a severance because a joint trial of multiple defendants and counts usually saves judicial and prosecutorial resources.

Problem 3-1. Byrds of a Feather

Karen Byrd-Forrester and Kyle Byrd are 29-year-old twins. Although they were born in Miami, Karen moved to Chicago six years ago. Kyle remained in Miami with the rest of the family. Karen and Kyle were engaged in a scam involving fraudulent mortgages. They talked on the phone almost daily about their "deals" and traveled as necessary to carry them out. Since Karen was an accountant, she kept the records of their deals in her professional office in Chicago.

Federal law authorized the United States Department of Housing and Urban Development (HUD) to insure mortgages for certain condominiums. A person who lived in the condominium could get a mortgage that covered 97 percent of the cost, while a non-occupant person could get only an 85 percent mortgage. Karen and Kyle paid Oliver Stohn $1,500 to buy a condo with money from a 97 percent HUD-insured loan, then immediately to sell the condo to Karen and Kyle for the original purchase price. In order to qualify for the federal mortgage insurance, Stohn signed an application (drafted by Karen) in which Stohn stated that he would personally live in the condominium, located in Virginia just outside Washington, D.C., although in truth he never had any intent to do so. The mortgage documents were actually signed in a motel room in Maryland, then taken to Virginia where they were submitted to the lending bank, First Virginia Bank and Trust. After the bank processed and approved the loan, the papers were mailed to the HUD office in Washington, D.C., for approval.

Since the mortgages were assumable, Stohn immediately sold the condominium and the government-insured mortgage to Karen and Kyle. This scheme gave Karen and Kyle a 97 percent government-insured mortgage (minus the $1,500 fee), although they were non-occupant owners and entitled to no more than an 85 percent mortgage.

Karen and Kyle were indicted for (1) conspiracy to commit offenses against the United States, and (2) making a false statement in violation of 18 U.S.C. § 1001:

> [W]hoever, in any matter within the jurisdiction of the executive, legislative, or judicial branch of the Government of the United States, knowingly and willfully—
>
> (1) falsifies, conceals, or covers up by any trick, scheme, or device a material fact;
>
> (2) makes any materially false, fictitious, or fraudulent statement or representation; or
>
> (3) makes or uses any false writing or document knowing the same to contain any materially false, fictitious, or fraudulent statement or entry;
>
> shall be fined under this title [and/or] imprisoned not more than 5 years. . . .

1. Note that Karen and Kyle are charged with two offenses. List all possible locations where there is venue for the conspiracy charge. Which would the government prefer? Karen? Kyle?

2. Where is venue for the false statement charge? Which would the government prefer? Karen? Kyle?

3. Assume that the government chose the federal district in Virginia as the locale for the trial. Assume further that the media in the Washington-Virginia area had launched a blistering campaign against mortgage fraud. There are daily articles in the local papers and regular features about the case on local television stations. You represent Karen. Would you seek a change of venue under Federal Rules of Criminal Procedure, Rule 21? To where? Could you get the case tried in Chicago? What would you include in your Motion to Change Venue? Would you file an Affidavit? What would you expect the judge to do with your Motion?

4. Assume that Kyle's lawyer does not agree with the concept of a venue change and does not request one for Kyle. If the district judge agrees that there should be a venue change for Karen because of hostile publicity, can the judge order one for Kyle as well?

5. Although the government chose Virginia for the case, it now prefers Washington, D.C., where the HUD records and officials are located. Can the government obtain a venue change under Rule 21?

B. Jurisdiction and Vicinage: Other Limitations on the Place of Litigation

The concept of jurisdiction overlaps, and is often confused, with that of venue. "Jurisdiction" refers to a given court's power to hear a particular case. Whether or not a court has jurisdiction is a function of several different considerations. First, there is a geographic component to the analysis, which often echoes the venue analysis. A state cannot normally criminalize conduct that occurs entirely beyond its territorial boundaries and that has no effects within its borders. The state's courts would have no jurisdiction over such wholly extraterritorial conduct. Note how the rules of territorial jurisdiction and venue interact: the former indicate which *states* can be the place of prosecution for a given crime, while the latter further localize the prosecution to particular *counties* or *districts* within a state. Note also that territorial jurisdiction is defined a bit more expansively for the federal system, permitting prosecution in some circumstances of conduct that occurred entirely outside the United States. *See generally* Wayne R. LaFave et al., Criminal Procedure § 16.1(a) (4th ed. 2015). Second, by statute, court rule, or constitution, some courts have jurisdiction over only certain types of criminal cases. For example, in many states some courts have jurisdiction to try misdemeanors and/or city ordinance violations, but not felonies. Third, a court must have jurisdiction over the defendant's person. As you may know, there is a voluminous body of case law on personal jurisdiction in civil cases. By comparison, personal jurisdiction is only very rarely an issue in criminal cases, and it is not entirely clear whether or how the governing legal principles might differ in the civil and criminal contexts. The sparse case law mostly arises from the criminal prosecution of foreign corporations in the United States. *See, e.g., United States v. Maruyasu Industries Co., Ltd.*, 229 F. Supp. 3d 659 (S.D. Ohio 2017).

The concept of *vicinage* also relates in important, and sometimes confusing, ways to that of venue. "Vicinage" refers to the locale from which jurors are chosen. Vicinage and venue almost always go together—if the venue of a particular trial is a certain county, then the normal expectation is that the jurors will be selected from that same county. In theory, though—and occasionally in practice—venue and vicinage may diverge. For instance, we noted earlier in this chapter that one potential remedy for prejudicial pretrial publicity in a particular venue would be to select jurors from another county or district where there was less publicity.

State and federal constitutions give defendants vicinage rights, which are worded in a variety of different ways. *See* LaFave et al., *supra*, § 16.1(b). In the federal system, the Sixth Amendment language quoted earlier in this chapter, while often discussed as a venue provision, is more accurately characterized as a vicinage rule: "the accused shall enjoy the right to a . . . trial . . . by an impartial jury of the State and district wherein the crime shall have been committed." Use of the same *locus delicti* concept means that, in federal cases, the venue and vicinage analysis will normally point to the same district or districts. In some states, however, venue and vicinage laws are not so closely aligned with one another. This may create some difficulties, for instance, if the defendant has a right to a jury selected from one county, but venue also lies in a different county that the prosecution regards as more convenient or strategically advantageous. Trying the defendant in the latter county might then require "importing" jurors from the defendant's preferred county.

Professor Brian Kalt has identified an odd quirk of the federal vicinage right that seems to create a zone of impunity for felonies committed entirely within a small portion of Yellowstone National Park. *The Perfect Crime*, 93 Geo. L.J. 675 (2005). Federal law establishes exclusive federal jurisdiction over any crimes committed in Yellowstone. This means that such crimes may not be prosecuted in state courts. Federal law further establishes that the District of Wyoming includes all of Yellowstone, including relatively small parts of the park that are actually located in Idaho and Montana. Kalt invites us to imagine a murder committed in the Idaho section of Yellowstone. Rule 18 indicates that venue would lie in the district where the crime was committed (Wyoming), but Article III—which speaks in terms of states, not districts—would override Rule 18 and require that the trial be held in Idaho. The real problem, though, comes from the Sixth Amendment, which speaks in terms of *both* states and districts. Our hypothetical murderer would have a constitutional right to jurors who come from the state where the crime occurred (Idaho) and who also come from the district where the crime occurred (Wyoming). In other words, the Sixth Amendment seems to require jurors who live in that small portion of Yellowstone where the District of Wyoming overlaps with Idaho. Yet, that territory, encompassing about 50 square miles, has no residents, and hence no potential jurors. Could this be the one part of the United States in which—as a matter of constitutional law—a person could literally get away with murder?

Chapter 4

Complaint and Initial Appearance

Once a police officer, prosecutor, or private citizen has decided to "press charges," a formal *complaint* serves as the initial charging document, and alleges that a named (or described, but not named) person committed a specified crime.

A. The Complaint

The complaint serves two functions: it begins the formal criminal processes by charging the defendant with a crime, and it provides the basis for an arrest warrant. Often, both occur at the same time.

[1] Begin Formal Process

The first function of a complaint can be important because it both notifies the accused of the allegations and facilitates the initial appearance, discussed below. It also may stop or "toll" the running of the statute of limitations, discussed in Chapter 12.

The exact impact of the complaint as a charging instrument varies among jurisdictions and may depend on whether the crime charged is a misdemeanor or felony. The complaint typically serves as the only formal charging document throughout misdemeanor cases. There may be no indictment to replace it. For felonies, on the other hand, the complaint usually will be the first formal charge, but it may be replaced later in the process by a grand jury indictment or prosecutor's information, discussed in Chapter 7. Accordingly, some states require greater specificity in misdemeanor complaints than in felony complaints. *See, e.g.*, Pa. R. Crim. P. 504(6)(a) and (b) (complaint must include citation to law violated in a "summary" case, but no such requirement in "court" cases; both types of complaints must contain "a summary of the facts sufficient to advise the defendant of the nature of the offense charged.").

In a jurisdiction in which the complaint is replaced by an indictment or information, the importance of the complaint wanes considerably as the case proceeds further into the criminal justice process. Indeed, in these jurisdictions the case can be initiated by an indictment or information, thus eliminating the need for a complaint to be filed.

The American Law Institute's Model Code of Pre-Arraignment Procedure (1975), commentary on Section 340.1, recommends that all offenses—even misdemeanors—be formally prosecuted by indictment or information. Therefore, the practice of prosecuting a misdemeanor on the complaint (made with little, if any, pretrial screening) would be eliminated if such a recommendation were adopted. Some jurisdictions require that "citizen complaints" be reviewed by a prosecutor who has the authority to screen out ill-founded complaints. What arguments could be advanced for allowing the prosecution of misdemeanors on the basis of the complaint, alone?

[2] Basis for Arrest Warrant

The second function of the complaint is to serve as the written basis for an arrest warrant. This function is so important that it has even been described as the principal function of the complaint. Although the law of search and seizure as governed by the Fourth Amendment is beyond the scope of this book, a few basic principles will help explain the role of the complaint in the arrest warrant process. It is clear that an arrest warrant must be based on probable cause, which may be established by a sworn affidavit presented to the judge issuing the warrant.

The sworn complaint can provide the magistrate with sufficient information to demonstrate the existence of probable cause. If the complaint (and perhaps other documents) establish probable cause to arrest, the magistrate or judge who signs the complaint may simultaneously issue an arrest warrant. These principles are embraced in Rule 4 of the Federal Rules of Criminal Procedure.

[3] Procedures

Despite the importance of the complaint and the fact that it is routinely described in criminal procedure rules, there are relatively few rules or decisions providing much information about the complaint process. Often a court clerk will have form copies of a complaint that a person, called a *complainant*, fills out and signs under oath. Sometimes, police departments maintain copies of the general form. Rule 3 of the Federal Rules of Criminal Procedure now authorizes complaints to be filed electronically in the federal system as provided in more detail in Rule 4.1.

The rules of criminal procedure give little guidance about the form and content of a complaint. However, Rule 3 and similar state rules require that the complaint be minimally descriptive of the accused, the alleged crime, and the victim. As an illustration, Rule 3 is brief and general: "The complaint is a written statement of the essential facts constituting the offense charged."

United States ex rel. Savage v. Arnold

403 F. Supp. 172 (E.D. Pa. 1975)

The foundation of relator's criminal complaint is 18 U.S.C. § 242 which deals with the willful violation of civil rights under color of law. The named defendants include 2 unknown City of Philadelphia Police Officers, 2 unknown City of Philadelphia Detectives, 1 unknown City of Philadelphia Police Official, the Police Commissioner of Philadelphia, as well as the City and County of Philadelphia, the Commissioner of Corrections of Pennsylvania, and the Commonwealth of Pennsylvania.

For present purposes, it is enough to summarize the allegations of the complaint as follows: it is charged that since October 17, 1963, the defendants, at various times and in various combinations, have conspired to falsely arrest relator without probable cause, and subsequently cause him to be brought to trial, convicted and imprisoned for nearly seven years, and thereafter conspired to deny relator's attempts to obtain postconviction relief until he was awarded a new trial, and ultimately, following a finding that his arrest was illegal and the suppression of evidence, the case against him was dismissed on October 9, 1970.

Several defects are apparent under even the most liberal reading of relator's complaint, which necessitate that it be rejected. First, and most importantly, the complaint fails to state "the essential facts constituting the offense charged." Fed.R.Crim. P. 3. Despite the long listing of abuses and deprivations which the relator alleges he suffered, the conduct of the defendants is described only in conclusory fashion without a factual basis. There are no facts to show willfulness on the part of any of the named defendants, nor to establish the alleged conspiracy. Furthermore, at least as to the "unknown" defendants, . . . there is no adequate identification of the defendants to allow issuance of arrest warrants. The use of a warrant where the name of the defendant is unknown can be permitted only where it contains "any name or description by which [the defendant] can be identified with reasonable certainty." Fed.R.Crim.P. 4(b) (1). To do otherwise would clearly violate not only the language of Rule 4(b), Federal Rules of Criminal Procedure, but would likewise fail to meet the requirements of the Fourth Amendment of the United States Constitution.

Although presumably the arrest and other police records of this case would reveal the identity of these unknown defendants, the complaint on which relator seeks to proceed is nonetheless defective. Lastly, it must be noted that relator's complaint, as presented, runs head on into the five-year statute of limitations applicable to the offense he would charge. 18 U.S.C. § 3282. The operative events which relator describes occurred in 1963 and allegedly continue to the present time. Regardless of the confusion as to which of the defendants participated in the alleged conspiracy or continued to participate throughout the period of time, no "overt acts" after 1969 are alleged, even accepting the conclusory nature of all of the allegations made. Nothing is averred beyond that time except relator's own bald statement that the conspiracy to violate his constitutional rights continued and is continuing to this day. Even measuring the limitation period from the time when the last "overt act" in furtherance of the alleged conspiracy was committed, it is clear that the criminal proceeding relator seeks to commence would be barred by the statute of limitations.

Notes

1. *Essential facts.* In order to satisfy the requirement of Rule 3 that the complaint state "the essential facts constituting the offense," what additional facts should the complainant have included in the complaint?

2. *Content differs if used for arrest warrant.* Note that the complaint in *Arnold* was attacked on several grounds, including allegations that the prosecution was barred by the statute of limitations and that the complaint was inadequate to serve as the basis for an arrest warrant. Should the contents of a complaint differ when it is used *only* to begin the prosecution and not as the basis for an arrest warrant?

3. *Contrast with notice pleading.* Contrast Rule 3 with what you learned from your Civil Procedure course about pleading in a civil action. How would you compare the Rule 3 requirement that a criminal complaint be factually specific with the predominant system of *notice pleading* instituted under the Federal Rules of Civil Procedure? With that system in light of the Supreme Court's decisions in *Bell Atlantic Corp. v. Twombly*, 550 U.S. 544 (2007) and *Ashcroft v. Iqbal*, 556 U.S. 662 (2009) (complaint must have enough factual specificity to meet the standard of "plausibility")?

4. *State statutes on content of complaint.* In some jurisdictions, a statute or court rule describing the complaint process provides more detail about the form the complaint is to take. Occasionally, it is quite specific. Pennsylvania, for example, requires that the complaint contain 10 separate items, and all complaints sought by private citizens must be submitted via affidavit to a prosecutor for approval. Pa. R. Crim. P. 504 and 506. If the prosecutor does not approve, then the affiant may seek review by a judge.

5. *Oath.* The only other typical requirement is that the complaint must be made under oath. An unsigned, unsworn complaint is void. Note, however, that the rules of criminal procedure do not place limits on who can sign as the complainant. Since there is no requirement that the person signing the complaint have personally observed the crime, virtually anyone can sign a criminal complaint to initiate criminal proceedings. Presumably, the complainant can base the allegation upon hearsay. Obviously, the victim of the crime can do it. Frequently, a police officer will sign the complaint.

6. *Citizen complainant.* The usual rule is that a citizen has a right to file a request for a complaint, but has no right to have the case prosecuted fully by the district attorney or even to have the judge issue the complaint. *See, e.g., Victory Distributors v. Ayer Div. of Dist. Court*, 755 N.E.2d 273 (Mass. 2001) (citizen has right to file criminal complaint and judges must act on it, but judge need not issue the complaint and district attorney may decline to prosecute it).

7. *Prosecutor's approval.* Jurisdictions frequently add other requirements. As noted above, often a prosecuting attorney must also sign the complaint. The Federal Rules of Criminal Procedure have been interpreted as requiring that an Assistant United States Attorney sign a criminal complaint. A citizen has no right to file a federal criminal complaint absent the prosecutor's signature. Because courts are reluctant to interfere with prosecutorial discretion, the United States Attorney's failure or refusal to sign a complaint is virtually unreviewable in federal court. *See e.g., Lewis v. Gallivan*, 315 F. Supp. 2d 313 (W.D.N.Y. 2004) (no citizen has a constitutional

right to bring a criminal complaint; citizen lacks standing to contest policies of the prosecuting attorney when the citizen himself is not being prosecuted or threatened with prosecution); *Freeman v. Murray*, 163 F. Supp. 2d 478 (M.D. Pa. 2001) (no constitutional violation if prosecutor refuses to sign a criminal complaint, because complainant has other forms of relief available such as civil actions for malicious prosecution or abuse of process).

8. *Judge as complainant.* Some jurisdictions provide a check on the prosecutor's exercise of discretion by authorizing a court to commence a formal prosecution if the district attorney refuses to do so or is unavailable to issue a complaint. *See, e.g,* Wis. Stat. Ann. § 968.02(3) (if there is probable cause, judge may issue complaint if prosecutor refuses to do so).

9. *Officer as Complainant.* In a handful of jurisdictions, police officers do more than merely arrest individuals, with or without warrants. They actually file charges sometimes and prosecute low-level offenses. Is this objectionable in principle? In practice? Who, after all, knows the case best—the arresting officer or the prosecutor? Yet is there anything problematic about vesting both arresting and charging discretion in one executive branch decision matter? For more on the issue, *see* Andrew Horwitz, *Taking the Cop Out of Copping a Plea: Eradicating Police Prosecution of Criminal Cases*, 40 Ariz. L. Rev. 1305 (1998).

10. *Double Jeopardy inapplicable.* Since the complaint is issued in an early stage of the criminal process, the Double Jeopardy Clause does not apply. *See* Chapter 15. Accordingly, a faulty or erroneous complaint can be withdrawn and a better one issued. If the complaint is faulty and not corrected, the effect of the error depends on the circumstances. If the complaint served as the basis for an arrest warrant, the arrest could be deemed illegal, with all the attendant consequences. On the other hand, if the faulty complaint was not used as support for an arrest warrant and was used only to begin the prosecution, the harmless error rule will most likely mean that the mistake will not cause an appellate reversal. A subsequent proper indictment or information will be viewed as "curing" any defect in the complaint. However, a new or amended complaint may be dismissed if the court finds it was the product of an effort to harass the defendant by repeated prosecutions for the same offense.

11. *Motion practice.* Even though a faulty complaint will most likely be "cured" by a subsequent indictment or information, defense counsel may still choose to attack it with a Motion to Dismiss. The motion can be based on any ground, such as the statute of limitations, insufficient description of the offense, or violation of a grant of immunity. If the motion is successful, it will have the effect of ending the prosecution, though perhaps only temporarily. A byproduct of the Motion to Dismiss, however, is that it enables defense counsel to convey the message that the prosecution is in for a major, time-consuming battle if the case is pursued. The prosecutor may choose to dismiss a borderline charge or offer a lenient plea bargain rather than face the likely time commitment necessary to take the case to trial. (For more on motion practice, see Chapter 9.)

B. The First Hearing: The Initial Appearance

If a criminal suspect is arrested, with or without a warrant, he or she is ordinarily brought to the police station or jail and "booked." The booking process is an administrative mechanism designed to obtain information about the accused for purposes of record keeping and checking for outstanding warrants. The suspect may be fingerprinted and photographed as part of the procedure. The suspect may also be interrogated about the crime for which he or she was arrested, and perhaps other unsolved offenses as well.

After (or sometimes before) this process is completed, the accused suspect is brought before a judicial officer. In federal cases, this proceeding is called the *initial appearance* before the magistrate, but some jurisdictions describe it as the *first appearance* or even the *preliminary arraignment.*

[1] Purposes of Initial Appearance

The initial appearance serves a number of purposes, ranging from the provision of basics information to decisionmaking of considerable importance to both the accused and the prosecution.

[a] Provide Information to Accused

A key function of the initial appearance is more ministerial than adversarial in nature. It involves providing the accused with important information about future proceedings and the accused's basic constitutional rights. At the initial appearance, the accused is formally notified of the charges and, in some jurisdictions, is given a copy of the complaint. [**Note**: At the initial appearance, the "suspect" or "accused" formally becomes a criminal "defendant." From this point forward, this book will use the terms "accused" and "defendant" interchangeably.] Also, the defendant is informed of relevant constitutional and statutory rights, such as the right to remain silent, the privilege against self-incrimination, the right to a preliminary examination, and the right either to retain counsel or, if indigent, to have counsel appointed. Pretrial release may be considered if the defendant is still in custody. In juvenile cases, the initial appearance also ensures that the child's parents or guardians have been notified.

[b] Appoint Counsel

If the defendant is indigent and wants counsel, the judge presiding over the initial appearance may appoint counsel or begin the administrative process of having a lawyer appointed. The court may first have to determine whether the defendant is actually indigent and therefore qualified to receive free counsel. This procedure may require the defendant to complete a questionnaire about his or her employment, assets, liabilities, and familial responsibilities. The judge also may ask a series of questions about the defendant's resources. In some jurisdictions, representatives of the public defender's office or private lawyers attend initial appearances and are appointed at that time to represent indigent defendants. However, as a general rule counsel are not present at this early stage, despite its importance—for instance, in determining whether bail is appropriate and if so, its amount. *See generally*, Douglas L. Colbert, *Prosecution Without Representation*, 59 Buff. L. Rev. 333 (2011).

An anomaly in the Federal Rules of Criminal Procedure is contained in Rule 44(a), which specifically gives the accused a right to counsel at the initial appearance. Since counsel is ordinarily appointed at this hearing, Rule 44 is not taken literally to require appointment of counsel *before* the initial appearance. However, in *Rothgery v. Gillespie County*, 554 U.S. 191 (2008), the Supreme Court held that the initial appearance triggers attachment of the Sixth Amendment right to counsel requiring appointment of counsel at or within a reasonable time after the initial appearance.

[c] Schedule Future Proceedings

A third function of the initial appearance is to schedule future proceedings, such as the preliminary hearing. Often, a statute or court rule will prescribe the maximum delay between the initial appearance and the preliminary hearing. *See, e.g.*, Fed. R. Crim. P. 5.1(c) (preliminary examination required within 14 days after initial appearance if defendant is in custody, 21 days if not in custody).

Since often the defendant will not have counsel at the initial appearance, the court may delay resolving some issues for a few hours or days until counsel is retained or appointed and can attend the hearing. These issues include a decision on release conditions or a hearing to assess whether the defendant is mentally competent. If a date for a later proceeding is set at the initial appearance, it is probably a "soft" date that is easily changed once counsel is appointed or retained and has a chance to check his or her calendar.

[d] Make Release Decision

If the accused is in jail at the time of the initial appearance, another important function is to determine whether the accused should be released pending trial. There are actually two facets of this process. First, if no judge has assessed whether there is probable cause to detain the accused, the judge at the initial appearance may have to resolve that issue pursuant to the Supreme Court's decision in *Gerstein v. Pugh*, discussed below. Second, if a judge or grand jury has found probable cause (and therefore the accused is lawfully held in custody), the judge at the initial appearance may explore various methods of release on bail or other procedures, discussed in Chapter 5. Sometimes, however, the pretrial release decision is scheduled at a different time and, in some cases, a different judge hears that matter.

[i] *Gerstein* Probable Cause Determination

As discussed briefly in Chapter 1 and in detail in Chapter 6, a criminal defendant actually is likely to encounter two types of pretrial proceedings before judicial officers: the initial appearance and the preliminary examination (also called the "preliminary hearing" in many jurisdictions). In addition, in accordance with the Supreme Court's decision in *Gerstein v. Pugh*, 420 U.S. 103 (1975), there may need to be a determination that the warrantless arrest of a defendant was based on probable cause. This "*Gerstein* determination" thus tests the validity of the defendant's initial detention. Rather than have three separate hearings, judges often combine the *Gerstein* determination with the initial appearance. On rare occasions the *Gerstein* determination, the initial appearance, and the preliminary hearing are all combined into one proceeding.

The issue in *Gerstein* was whether a person arrested without a warrant and held in jail for trial under a prosecutor's information is constitutionally entitled to a probable cause determination by a judicial officer. The two defendants in *Gerstein* were arrested pursuant to a Florida law that permitted a criminal proceeding to be initiated by an information, which is a formal, written allegation by a prosecutor that a particular person has committed one or more specified crimes. Because under Florida law the filing of an information authorized an arrest, the person accused in an information could be arrested and held in jail for a substantial period solely on the basis of a prosecutor's decision. Under this procedure, no judge promptly assessed whether there was probable cause to detain the accused, although this issue could be addressed a month or so later at the arraignment or preliminary hearing.

The Supreme Court in *Gerstein* noted that "the standards and procedures for arrest and detention have been derived from the Fourth Amendment and its common law antecedents." Under the Fourth Amendment, an arrest must be based on probable cause, defined as sufficient proof to cause a prudent person to believe the defendant has committed an offense. Reasoning that "the detached judgment of a neutral magistrate is essential if the Fourth Amendment is to furnish meaningful protection from unfounded interference with liberty," the Supreme Court held in *Gerstein* that the Fourth Amendment requires that a neutral and detached judicial officer must determine probable cause before a person can be subjected to an extended restraint of liberty after a warrantless arrest.

"Hearing" procedures. Rejecting the notion that a fully adversarial hearing is essential to this probable cause determination, the *Gerstein* Court held that the required judicial finding of probable cause may be made in an informal, non-adversary *ex parte* proceeding on the basis of oral or written hearsay testimony. Thus the judge may make the *Gerstein* determination not necessarily from a courtroom, but from home in the middle of the night or from the country club in the middle of a round of golf, on the basis of information provided over the phone or via an email or text message. The accused is not entitled to confront or cross-examine adverse witnesses at this proceeding. For these reasons, the phrase "*Gerstein* determination" is probably a more accurate description of what takes place than the term "*Gerstein* hearing." The Court in *Gerstein* indicated that it may be desirable for the judicial officer to make the probable cause determination at the suspect's initial appearance or at a preliminary hearing held soon after arrest.

Timing of Gerstein determination: The 48-hour burden shift. Gerstein requires that all states provide "prompt" determinations of probable cause for detained criminal suspects arrested without a warrant, but the Court in that case set no precise time requirements for this determination. In *County of Riverside v. McLaughlin*, 500 U.S. 44 (1991), the Supreme Court held that such determinations ordinarily must occur within 48 hours of arrest. The Court explained:

> This is not to say that the probable cause determination in a particular case passes constitutional muster simply because it is provided within 48 hours. Such a hearing may nonetheless violate *Gerstein* if the arrested individual can prove that his or her probable cause determination was delayed unreasonably. Examples of unreasonable delay are delays for the purpose of gathering additional evidence to justify the arrest, a delay motivated by ill will against the arrested individual, or delay for delay's sake. In evaluating whether the delay in a particular case is unreasonable, however, courts must allow a substantial degree of flexibility. Courts cannot ignore the often unavoidable delays in transporting arrested persons from one facility to another, handling late-night bookings where no magistrate is readily available, obtaining the presence of an arresting officer who may be busy processing other suspects or securing the premises of an arrest, and other practical realities.
>
> Where an arrested individual does not receive a probable cause determination within 48 hours, the calculus changes. In such a case, the arrested individual does not bear the burden of proving an unreasonable delay. Rather, the burden shifts to the government to demonstrate the existence of a bona fide emergency or other extraordinary circumstance. The fact that in a particular case it may take longer than 48 hours to consolidate pretrial proceedings does not qualify as an extraordinary circumstance. Nor, for that matter, do intervening weekends. A jurisdiction that chooses to offer combined proceedings must do so as soon as is reasonably feasible, but in no event later than 48 hours after arrest.

Id. at 56–57. *See also Bryant v. City of New York*, 404 F.3d 128 (2d Cir. 2005) (detention beyond 48 hours is presumptively unreasonable).

Justice O'Connor wrote the *McLaughlin* opinion for a five-Justice majority. Justice Marshall, joined by Justices Blackmun and Stevens, wrote a short dissenting opinion, arguing that the probable cause hearing should be held immediately after completion of the administrative steps in the arrest process. Justice Scalia, also dissenting, argued forcefully for a rule that would set the limit at 24 hours in most cases. He concluded his dissent by asserting that the majority had repudiated one of the Fourth Amendment's core applications—judicial determinations of probable cause—which will result in the incarceration of presumptively innocent people.

Notes

1. *A.L.I. Code of Pre-Arraignment Procedure.* Justice Scalia's dissent in *McLaughlin* cited the American Law Institute's Model Code of Pre-Arraignment Procedure. Under § 310.1, persons in custody must be brought before a magistrate within 24 hours of arrest. Interestingly, however, the A.L.I.'s Model Code does not require that a probable cause determination occur at the first appearance. Rather, the defendant is advised of the right to counsel. If the defendant desires to be represented by a lawyer, the hearing is adjourned for 48 hours. The second hearing (characterized as the "adjourned session of the first appearance") then takes place and the judge makes the requisite "reasonable cause" determination. In what way does the A.L.I. procedure go beyond the requirements of *Gerstein* and *McLaughlin?* In what way does it fall short of the *Gerstein/McLaughlin* guarantee?

2. *Remedy.* What is the remedy for a *Gerstein* violation? In *Gerstein*, the Supreme Court made it clear that the unlawful pretrial detention (where there has not been a prompt determination of probable cause) will not invalidate a subsequent conviction. It is possible, however, that the failure to bring the accused before a magistrate in a reasonably prompt fashion may jeopardize the admissibility of pre-appearance confessions and consensual searches. The so-called *McNabb-Mallory* rule is discussed, below.

3. *Waiver of time limits.* The defendant may make a knowing and intelligent waiver of *Gerstein's* time limits. *Commonwealth v. Jackson*, 855 N.E.2d 1097 (Mass. 2006).

[ii] Conditions of Release

Assuming that there is probable cause to detain a suspect, the judge at the initial appearance may have to make a decision about whether release from confinement is appropriate. This decision is discussed more fully in Chapter 5. If the defendant has been released by jail personnel on "station house" bail, the judge at the initial appearance will ordinarily confirm the release decision already made, although the prosecution may request more stringent release conditions and the defense may ask for less stringent ones. If the defendant is still in custody at the time of the initial appearance, the court may conduct a release hearing at that time or may delay the matter for a day or two until the defendant has had the chance to confer with appointed or retained counsel, subject, of course, to *McLaughlin* constraints.

[2] Procedures

The initial appearance is likely to be the defendant's first opportunity to appear before a judicial officer. The proceeding is usually of short duration (often lasting only a few minutes) and the defendant will be given little, if any, opportunity to discuss the charge with the magistrate.

Use of video. An increasing number of states now permit the "appearance" to occur "in person or by electronic audio-visual device," *e.g.*, Fla. R. Crim. P. 3.130(a), or by "two-way closed-circuit television." Ill. Code Crim. P. § 109-1(a). Federal Rule 5(f) permits videoconferencing with the defendant's permission.

When videoconferencing is used, the defendant may be taken to a room in the jail equipped with a monitor and a video camera. The judge is located in a similar room in another building, perhaps a courthouse miles away. Ordinarily the video technology allows each to see and talk with the other. The session may be videotaped to memorialize the proceeding.

[a] Felony-Misdemeanor Distinctions

Both the content and importance of the initial appearance may turn upon the felony-misdemeanor distinction. In federal cases and in most states, more detailed initial appearance procedures exist for misdemeanor cases. For example, some jurisdictions expressly permit the criminal accused to plead guilty at the initial appearance in a misdemeanor case. In specific federal misdemeanor cases, the magistrate judge also is empowered to take guilty pleas. *See* Fed. R. Crim. P. 58(b)(3)(A). The entry of a plea at the initial appearance turns that proceeding, in effect, into an arraignment (pleas of guilty, not guilty, or *nolo contendere* are discussed more fully in Chapter 11).

[b] Timing

In federal criminal cases and in approximately one-half of the states, statutes or court rules provide that the defendant must appear before the magistrate "without unnecessary delay." The federal provision is contained in Rule 5 of the Federal Rules of Criminal Procedure, discussed below. This requirement of a prompt hearing serves several purposes—to minimize the likelihood of a coerced confession, to apprise the defendant of his or her rights, and to perform a number of routine administrative and scheduling functions.

While this standard may suggest an almost immediate appearance in court, it is possible that an accused person will be held in custody several days before making this appearance. This delay is especially likely to occur in a smaller community in which a magistrate may be available only during the five-day work week. Some states now prescribe exact time limits, ranging from 24 to 72 hours as the maximum allowable time span within which the accused must be brought before a magistrate. *See* Wendy L. Brandes, *Post-Arrest Detention and the Fourth Amendment: Refining the Standard of* Gerstein v. Pugh, 22 Colum. J. L. & Soc. Prob. 445 (1989). Of course, *McLaughlin* mandates a *Gerstein* determination within 48 hours of a warrantless arrest in most cases, but remember that the often *ex parte Gerstein* determination is not necessarily an initial appearance.

[c] Federal Rule 5

Rule 5 of the Federal Rules of Criminal Procedure mandates an initial appearance for almost all persons arrested for both felonies and misdemeanors, irrespective of whether the arrest was with or without an arrest warrant. Rule 5(a)(1)(A) and (B) require the defendant to be brought before a magistrate "without unnecessary delay." This standard involves a case-by-case review of a number of factors, such as the length of the delay, reasons for the delay, and whether an involuntary confession was obtained. The rule also includes language regarding the defendant's right to a preliminary examination. That is the subject of Chapter 6 and is covered also in Rule 5.1 of the Federal Rules of Criminal Procedure.

Arrest in another district. What happens if a person is arrested in a district other than that in which the offense was committed and in which the trial will be held? Rule 40(a) provides that in some such situations the person must be taken without unnecessary delay before the nearest available federal magistrate judge, in accordance with Rule 5. Rule 5 states that a person must be brought before a federal magistrate judge or a state or local officer, which could mean one in the state or district of arrest rather than the one where the charges are pending.

Without unnecessary delay. Is the "without unnecessary delay" standard too vague? Would it be better to adopt the *McLaughlin* 48-hour rule for both the initial appearance and the *Gerstein* determination?

[d] Remedy: Dismissal of Charges?

What is the remedy for an unreasonably delayed initial appearance? Almost all federal courts have held that the right to timely initial appearance is procedural, not substantive, and therefore Rule 5 violations do not require dismissal of an indictment, even for extensive delays in holding the initial appearance. *See, e.g., United States v. Dyer*, 325 F.3d 464, 470 n.2 (3d Cir. 2003). In *United States v. Osunde*, 638 F. Supp. 171 (N.D. Cal. 1986), however, the court characterized a 106-day delay between arrest and initial appearance as a "flagrant violation" of Rule 5 which warranted dismissal with prejudice. Other federal courts have not followed *Osunde*.

[e] Remedy: Exclusion of Evidence?

The primary remedy for violation of Rule 5 is the exclusion of evidence obtained during the period of this impermissible delay.

[i] Searches and Seizures

Failure to hold a prompt initial appearance can lead to the exclusion of evidence obtained through a search conducted during a period of unnecessary delay. An unnecessarily delayed hearing may cause consent-to-search to be invalidated. *See, e.g., United States v. Iribe*, 806 F. Supp. 917 (D. Colo. 1992), *rev. in part*, 11 F.3d 1553 (10th Cir. 1993) (consent-to-search held valid).

[ii] Confessions

McNabb-Mallory Rule. The remedy for a delayed initial appearance is that confessions obtained before the hearing may be excluded as evidence at trial. According to the so-called "*McNabb-Mallory* rule," derived years before *Gerstein* from the cases of *Mallory v. United States*, 354 U.S. 449 (1957), and *McNabb v. United States*, 318

U.S. 332 (1943), statements made by suspects during a period of unnecessary delay in bringing them before a magistrate are inadmissible at a federal trial. *McNabb-Mallory* excluded the statements whether or not they were given voluntarily, and irrespective of the presence or absence of a voluntary waiver of Fifth Amendment rights. As one court explained:

> [T]he protection of the right of an accused to prompt production before a judicial officer following arrest will be most effectively accomplished by a per se exclusionary rule. Not only is such a rule calculated to deter unlawful detentions and to preserve the integrity of the criminal justice system, but it is likely to assure more certain and even-handed application of the prompt presentment requirement. . . .

Johnson v. Maryland, 384 A.2d 709, 717 (Md. 1978).

This *McNabb-Mallory* exclusionary rule was based upon the Supreme Court's supervisory authority over criminal justice in federal courts. It was not mandated by the United States Constitution, and applied whether the accused was arrested with or without an arrest warrant.

Since the *McNabb-Mallory* exclusionary rule is not binding upon states, the vast majority of state courts have rejected it and instead use a "totality test" to determine the admissibility of a confession under these circumstances. In these jurisdictions, a statement given by a suspect who has not been promptly presented to a judicial officer is not, per se, inadmissible; delay in presenting the suspect is simply one factor in evaluating the overall voluntariness of the confession. *See, e.g.*, *People v. Cipriano*, 429 N.W.2d 781 (Mich. 1988) (extensive discussion); *Seales v. State*, 90 So. 3d 37 (Miss. 2012) (unnecessary delay, alone, will not result in suppression of evidence or reversible error where defendant was informed of his rights and made a voluntary and knowing waiver).

Federal statute—The six-hour "safe harbor." Congress reacted negatively to the *McNabb-Mallory* rule in 1968 and enacted 18 U.S.C. § 3501(c). This statute overturned one facet of *McNabb-Mallory*. It distinguished between delays of up to six hours and those of longer duration.

The statute established a rule that virtually insulated confessions from attack on the basis of delays of six hours or less between arrest and confession. This is the so-called "safe harbor" provision. This statute provides that a custodial confession "shall not be inadmissible [in federal court] solely because of delay in bringing [the accused] before a magistrate" if the confession was made voluntarily and within six hours (or more if reasonably necessary because of transportation requirements) of arrest. 18 U.S.C. § 3501(c).

Survival of McNabb-Mallory: Corley v. United States. Despite the seeming demise of the *McNabb-Mallory* rule via the enactment of § 3501, the Supreme Court held in *Corley v. United States*, 556 U.S. 303 (2009), that Congress merely intended to *limit* the rule to custodial confessions that take place more than six hours after arrest, but not to abrogate the rule entirely. The Court in *Corley* reaffirmed the common law basis of *McNabb-Mallory*—to require that arrestees be "presented" by police to a magistrate as soon after arrest as possible, in order to protect against extended custodial interrogations conducted in secret. Further, the Court laid down a somewhat brighter line rule to govern the admissibility of post-arrest custodial confessions:

> If the confession came within [six hours after arrest], it is admissible, subject to the other Rules of Evidence, so long as it was "made voluntarily and . . . the weight to be given [it] is left to the jury" [quoting from § 3501]. If the confession occurred before presentment and beyond six hours, however, the court must decide whether delaying that long was unreasonable or unnecessary under the *McNabb-Mallory* cases, and if it was, the confession is to be suppressed.

556 U.S. at 322.

Some courts have found delays beyond six hours to be reasonable under the circumstances. *See, e.g., United States v. Rivera Ruiz*, 797 F. Supp. 78 (D.P.R. 1992) (10-hour delay between arrest and confession held permissible because extra time was needed to continue boat investigation and because defendant's arrest occurred at sea). In determining reasonableness, courts look at such facts as transportation and distance to the magistrate, the availability of the magistrate, the need for routine processing and lodging, and any medical or family matter that affected the delay.

Motive for delay. The government's motive is also a factor in determining reasonableness of delay. In *United States v. Wilbon*, 911 F. Supp. 1420 (D.N.M. 1995), there was a delay of 38 and one-half hours between the defendant's arrest and the initial appearance. Additionally, the U.S. District Court determined that the FBI agent intentionally exploited the delay for the purpose of obtaining a "last minute" confession. Therefore, the court held that under § 3501 the confession must be suppressed "regardless of voluntariness" as "an appropriate means to deter similar misconduct in the future."

Federal-state issues. The federal statute clearly applies to a person arrested on federal charges, but does it also apply to someone arrested on *state* charges who is in state custody but interrogated by federal agents concerning a possible federal criminal violation? In *United States v. Alvarez-Sanchez*, 511 U.S. 350 (1994), the United States Supreme Court answered that question "no." The defendant's conviction was upheld, as was the admissibility of the confession used in the federal criminal case, even though more than 48 hours had elapsed between his arrest and interrogation by federal officials. The Court noted that the defendant was under arrest on state charges at the time when he made inculpatory statements to Secret Service agents and that there was no evidence of a "collusive arrangement" between state and federal agents.

Rule 5, like 18 U.S.C. § 3501, also applies only to a person in federal custody. What should be the result, however, if federal and state authorities have a "working arrangement" designed to have a person arrested by state authorities so that federal authorities could conduct an interrogation unimpeded by Rule 5? *See, e.g.*,

Anderson v. United States, 318 U.S. 350 (1943) (strikers unlawfully arrested and held by state authorities, and interrogated by federal agents; confession held inadmissible because it was the product of an impermissible "working relationship" between state and federal officers); *United States v. Roberts*, 928 F. Supp. 910 (W.D. Mo. 1996) (defendant's arrest and detention by state authorities held improper pretext for sole purpose of furthering federal criminal investigation).

The defendant has the burden of establishing collusion between state and federal officers.

Chapter 5

Custody and Release Pending Trial

A. Introduction

When a criminal suspect is taken into custody, a number of events, both formal and informal, occur prior to final case disposition (whether by voluntary dismissal, guilty plea or trial). The time between arrest and final disposition may be from several days to many months. Occasionally, several years will elapse between arrest and trial. Perhaps one of the most extreme examples is that of Raymond Buckey, who was detained without bail for almost four years. Ultimately, he was either acquitted of his charges or his trials ended in mistrials. *See* Marc Miller & Martin Guggenheim, *Pretrial Detention and Punishment*, 75 MINN. L. REV. 335, 335–38 (1990).

The suspect may avoid being taken into custody in some circumstances. Sometimes a police official will release a defendant by means of a *citation release*. This procedure involves giving the defendant a "ticket" or written order to appear in court on a specified date. It is employed in minor cases, such as traffic violations, and it results in the immediate release of the defendant at the time of the issuance of the citation (sometimes referred to as a non-custodial arrest).

If the defendant is taken to the police station for booking, a law enforcement official may permit the immediate release of the defendant. This is done either by way of a modified citation release or by posting bail according to a bail schedule, discussed later in this chapter. Persons charged with less serious offenses are sometimes released. In the case of felony charges, however, the accused faces a more formidable challenge in obtaining freedom prior to case disposition. Generally, a judicial officer must decide whether the defendant will be released, and, if so, under what conditions.

B. Competing Policies and Concerns

[1] Society's Need for Pretrial Detention

[a] Appearance at Proceedings

The traditional justification for detention of a suspect after arrest is that it guarantees presence of the defendant at his or her upcoming trial and other proceedings. *See Stack v. Boyle*, 342 U.S. 1, 4 (1951) ("The right to release before trial is conditioned upon the accused's giving adequate assurance that he will stand trial and submit to sentence if found guilty.").

[b] Prevent Destruction or Alteration of Evidence

Similarly, to the extent that society is worried about the defendant's ability to unfairly or inappropriately "alter" evidence (through intimidation of witnesses, for example), pretrial incarceration increases the likelihood of a full and fair fact-finding process.

[c] Prevent Future Harm

A third and more recent rationale in favor of pretrial detention is that it protects society from possible further criminal harm that may be inflicted by the defendant prior to trial (thus the expression "preventive detention").

This rationale has proved controversial for several reasons. First, because the defendant awaiting trial is presumed innocent, this justification rings of "punishment" prior to a criminal conviction.[1] Similarly, protecting society from future criminal acts of the defendant rests upon a speculative or predictive judgment as to the defendant's likelihood to commit further criminal acts. While we may intuitively believe that a particular suspect will commit offenses prior to trial, are we capable of making that judgment in a reliable way?

In the past, pretrial risk assessments were mainly based on the subjective determinations of judges and pretrial services personnel. Of late, however, individual risk assessments, based on actuarial risk assessment instruments that consider a variety of factors, are increasingly being used. However, to the extent that risk can be reliably forecast, what should be the degree of risk that would warrant denial (or granting) of release? For more on the use of actuarial risk instruments and the risk "cut point," *see* Sandra G. Mayson, *Dangerous Defendants*, 127 YALE L.J. 490 (2018).

[d] Terrorism: The PATRIOT Act and Other Laws

The threat of terrorism has prompted several legal issues involving detention. Since September 11, 2001, Congress has enacted laws intended to fight the threat of terrorism. The primary vehicle is the 2001 PATRIOT Act, a title that stands for Providing Appropriate Tools Required to Intercept and Obstruct Terrorism. The Act encompasses many topics, such as wiretapping, freezing assets, immigration, and pretrial detention. One provision authorizes the Attorney General to detain any alien whom the Attorney General certifies is engaged in any activity that endangers the national security of the United States or is involved in other anti-government pursuits and is therefore deportable. The alien must be subjected to deportation proceedings or charged with a crime no later than seven days after detention begins. 8 U.S.C. § 1226a.

---

1. For arguments in favor of preventive detention of dangerous individuals *see, e.g.*, Ronald J. Allen & Larry Laudan, *Deadly Dilemmas III: Some Kind Words for Preventive Detention*, 101 J. CRIM. L. & CRIMINOLOGY 781 (2011); Christopher Slobogin, *The Civilization of the Criminal Law*, 58 VAND. L. REV. 121, 122 (2005).

A high-profile outgrowth of the federal government's power under the Act concerns the detention of foreign nationals apprehended in Afghanistan after September 11, 2001, and taken to the American prison in Guantanamo Bay, Cuba. The plaintiffs in *Rasul v. Bush*, 542 U.S. 466 (2004), were nationals of countries that were not engaged in a formal war with the United States, denied any terrorist acts, and had not been charged with any crimes. The Supreme Court held that federal courts had jurisdiction in cases challenging the legality of the detentions at Guantanamo. A similar result occurred when the Court held that a United States citizen, captured in Afghanistan but held in the United States and categorized by the government as an "enemy combatant," had a due process right to challenge the factual basis for the detention by bringing the case before a neutral decision maker. *Hamdi v. Rumsfeld*, 543 U.S. 507 (2004).

Another terrorist-related detention issue is the use of the statute permitting the detention of material witnesses allegedly involved in terrorist activity. *See generally* R.V. Stevens, *Keeping the U.S.A. Patriot Act in Check One Material Witness at a Time*, 81 N.C. L. Rev. 2157 (2003).

Detention of non-citizens suspected of engaging in crimes presents another question. The Supreme Court has held that the government can detain aliens who have been convicted of a serious crime and are awaiting deportation. *Demore v. Kim*, 538 U.S. 510 (2003).

[2] Defendant's Interest in Freedom Pending Trial

We should never overlook the quite obvious fact that at this stage of a criminal case, guilt beyond a reasonable doubt has not been established, though there may have been an arrest warrant based on a finding that there is probable cause that the defendant committed a crime. The presumptively innocent defendant, then, arguably is entitled to freedom prior to a finding of guilt beyond a reasonable doubt. *See United States v. Salerno*, 481 U.S. 739, 755 (1987) (recognizing that "[i]n our society liberty is the norm, and detention prior to trial or without trial is the carefully limited exception.").

Beyond this principle, practical reasons militate in favor of pretrial release. It is well-known that pretrial detention has very significant negative consequences for individuals. Even being detained for a few days can jeopardize one's housing, employment, or custody of children, and jails are not always especially sanitary or safe. Detention can also affect case outcomes, impairing the ability of individuals to assist in the investigation and preparation of their cases. *See* Shalia Dewan, *When Bail Is Out of Defendant's Reach, Other Costs Mount*, N.Y. Times, June 10, 2015; Nick Pinto, *The Bail Trap*, N.Y. Times Mag., Aug. 13, 2015. Detention is also thought to play a major role in inducing guilty pleas, often regardless of actual guilt, with convictions having major negative impact on individuals' lives on the outside. Alexandra Natapoff, *Misdemeanors*, 85 S. Cal. L. Rev. 1313, 1316–17 (2012). *See also* Andrew D. Leipold, *How the Pretrial Process Contributes to Wrongful Convictions*, 42 Am. Crim. L. Rev. 1123, 1130 (2005).

The U.S. Court of Appeals for the Third Circuit recently addressed what it saw as the inequities of the money bail system. *See Curry v. Yacehra*, 835 F.3d 373 (3d Cir. 2016). Defendant Curry, upon learning that a warrant was out for his arrest relating to his purported theft from a Wal-Mart store, and wanting to assert his innocence, contacted police, but was thereafter arrested. Unable to afford bail, Curry was jailed for several months, during which time he missed the birth of his child and lost his job. Fearing that he would lose his home and car, Curry pled nolo contendere, and was released. He thereafter sued local officials for malicious prosecution and other claims, which were rejected by the federal trial court. Before reaching the merits of Curry's appeal, the Third Circuit stated:

> The broader context of this matter is disturbing, as it shines a light on what has become a threat to equal justice under the law. That is, the problem of individuals posing little flight or public safety risk, who are detained in jail because they cannot afford the bail set for criminal charges that are often minor in nature . . . It seems anomalous that in our system of justice the access to wealth is what often determines whether a defendant is freed or must stay in jail. Further, those unable to pay who remain in jail may not have the "luxury" of awaiting a trial on the merits of their charges; they are often forced to accept a plea deal to leave the jail environment and be freed.
>
> Consider [Curry's] alleged circumstances. The [complaint] charges that Curry collected items worth a total of $130.27 at a Wal-Mart and used a receipt found in the parking lot to return the items for cash. . . .
>
> Ultimately, he pled nolo contendere in order to return home. Curry has maintained his innocence. . . . Nevertheless, as part of [his plea], Curry must pay restitution of $130.27 to Wal-Mart and the costs of prosecution. He was sentenced to probation for two years . . . Moreover, . . . Curry's nolo contendere plea operates as a procedural bar requiring dismissal of his malicious prosecution claim. . . . Thus, Curry's inability to post bail deprived him not only not only of his freedom, but also of his ability to seek redress for the potentially unconstitutional prosecution that landed him in jail in the first place.

Id. at 376–77.

In short, critics maintain that money bail, intended to serve as a basis to secure freedom, instead serves as a chronic impediment to it, and does so unfairly by discriminating against indigent individuals, and often without regard to the ostensible purposes of bail. As one commentator wrote, pessimistically:

> [E]nsuring that no one is held in jail based on poverty would, in many respects, necessitate a complete reordering of criminal justice. The open secret is that in most jurisdictions bail is the grease that keeps the gears of the overburdened system turning. Faced with the prospect of going to jail for want of bail, many defendants accept plea deals instead . . . If even a small fraction of those defendants asserted their right to trial, criminal

> courts would be overwhelmed. By encouraging poor defendants to plead guilty, bail keeps the system afloat.

Pinto, *The Bail Trap*, *supra*.

[3] The Monetary Cost of Pretrial Detention

Feeding, housing, and providing needed medical care for pretrial detainees is expensive. New York City, for instance, spends nearly $45,000 per pretrial detainee a year. According to the U.S. Department of Justice, pretrial detainees in state and local facilities cost roughly $9 billion annually. To the extent that the detainee population includes those who pose neither a risk of flight nor a danger to the community, and who simply remain in detention due to lack of money, critics maintain that the expenditures are unwise and unfounded. *See* Liana M. Goff, Note, *Pricing Justice: The Wasteful Enterprise of America's Bail System*, 82 Brooklyn L. Rev. 881, 896–97 (2017). For more on the issue of the monetary consequences, from a cost-benefit perspective, *see* Shima Baradaran Baughman, *Costs of Pretrial Detention*, 97 B.U. L. Rev. 1 (2017).

C. History of Bail

The relevant language of the Eighth Amendment in the United States Constitution provides "excessive bail shall not be required." This clause was adopted almost verbatim from the Virginia Declaration of Rights of 1776, which itself was derived from the English Bill of Rights of 1689. Chief Judge Newman, writing for the District of Columbia Court of Appeals in *United States v. Edwards*, 430 A.2d 1321, 1326–27 (D.C. 1981), described the history of English bail as follows:

> The English bail system developed out of the ancient Anglo-Saxon forms of sureties into early common law bail. By the thirteenth century, . . . the sheriff exercised a broad and ill-defined discretionary power to bail the King's prisoners committed to his custody. This power was widely abused by sheriffs who extorted money from individuals entitled to release without charge and who accepted bribes from those who were not otherwise entitled to bail. The first statutory regulation of bail . . . sought to curb such abuses by carefully enumerating which offenses were bailable and which were not.
>
> Further limitations on the discretion to grant bail were enacted to cure defects in the law which the Stuarts exploited to deny release to particular prisoners. Procedural abuses by the Stuarts [eventually] led to the . . . Habeas Corpus Act of 1679, which closed the procedural loopholes by firmly establishing a means for enforcing the rights of bail and habeas corpus. When, thereafter, the protections of the Habeas Corpus Act were circumvented by the practice of setting prohibitively high bail, the excessive bail clause was drafted into the Bill of Rights of 1689, in order to correct

> this injustice. In sum, the excessive bail clause was developed as a specific remedy for judicial abuse of the bail procedure as otherwise established by law, and did not, in and of itself, imply any right to bail.

For more on the history of bail in the United States, *see* Matthew J. Hegreness, *America's Fundamental and Vanishing Right to Bail*, 55 ARIZ. L. REV. 909 (2013).

D. Constitutional Constraints

The Eighth Amendment bans "excessive bail" but does not explicitly guarantee a right to bail.[2] As will be seen later in this chapter, federal legislation precluding bail has been upheld by the United States Supreme Court. While many state constitutions duplicate the Eighth Amendment *verbatim*, others create an explicit right to bail, absent particular circumstances. For example, the Florida Constitution provides that "unless charged with a capital offense or an offense punishable by life imprisonment and the proof of guilt is evident or the presumption is great, every person charged with a crime . . . shall be entitled to pretrial release on reasonable conditions. If no conditions of release can reasonably protect the community from risk of physical harm to persons, assure the presence of accused at trial, or assure the integrity of the judicial process, the accused may be detained." Fla. Const. art. I, § 14. *See also, e.g.,* Cal. Const. art. I, § 12(b) (court can refuse release if it "finds based on clear and convincing evidence that there is a substantial likelihood that the person's release would result in great bodily harm to others").

E. Forms of Release Pending Trial

If it is determined that the defendant should be released prior to trial, a variety of conditions can be imposed. Generally, the judge making the pretrial release decision has considerable discretion in selecting a particular form of release. Note, however, that the Bail Reform Act of 1984, discussed below, mandates that federal defendants be released "on personal recognizance, or upon execution of an unsecured appearance bond in an amount specified by the court" unless it is determined that either form of pretrial release will not reasonably assure appearance of the defendant at trial or will endanger the safety of the community. 18 U.S.C. § 3142(b).

Today, a form of "money" bail is by far the most common condition imposed on pretrial release. Jessica Eaglin & Danyelle Solomon, Brennan Ctr. for Justice, *Reducing Racial and Ethnic Disparities in Jails* 19 (2015). The use of money bail in the

---

2. It is worth noting that the U.S. Supreme Court has never formally held that the "excessive bail" portion of the Eighth Amendment applies to the states (via Fourteenth Amendment incorporation doctrine), although it has implied that the prohibition is a fundamental right. *See Schilb v. Kuebel*, 404 U.S. 357 (1971).

United States increased by 32% between 1992 and 2006, and the average amount of bail set grew by $30,000 during that time as well. Justice Policy Inst., *Bail Fail: Why the U.S. Should End the Practice of Using Money for Bail* 10–16 (2012). The majority of individuals are detained because they cannot afford to pay relatively small amounts of bail. In New York City, for instance, 46% of misdemeanor defendants could not secure release due to an inability to post bail of $500 or less. Crystal S. Yang, *Toward an Optimal Bail System*, 92 N.Y.U. L. Rev. 1399, 1401 (2017)(citing sources). Concern exists, moreover, that the money bail system reflects and perpetuates not only socio-economic but also racial inequalities in the criminal justice system, based on data showing higher rates of detention among African-Americans and Hispanics. *Id.*

A bond can be forfeited if any of the terms of release are violated. *See* Fed. R. Crim. P. 46(f)(1). It can be the case, as a result, that forfeiture occurs even if the defendant appears as required, based on violation of one or more other conditions of release.

[1] Full Cash Bond

After a judge sets a dollar amount of bail, the defendant must post the full amount in cash with the court in order to be released from custody. If the defendant appears in court as scheduled, he or she gets back all the deposited money. If she fails to appear, the court can order a forfeiture of the full cash bond. For example, a person charged with aggravated robbery may be required to post bond in the amount of $25,000. Upon payment of this full amount to the court, the defendant will be released from jail. The full $25,000 will be returned to the defendant when he or she appears at trial.

A study of state pretrial release of felony defendants in the 75 largest counties found that only three percent of those released pending trial posted a full cash bond. Bureau of Justice Statistics, U.S. Dept. of Justice, *Pretrial Release of Felony Defendants in State Courts* (2007).

Because of concerns that the money used to post bond was obtained through illegal activities, such as drugs or gambling, the court may inquire into its source and conduct a hearing on the issue. *See United States v. Nebbia*, 357 F.2d 303 (2d Cir. 1966). If the defendant does not account for the money or the hearing shows its source was illegal, the court may refuse to accept the money in satisfaction of the bond. The prosecution may engage in considerable discovery during this hearing. *See also, e.g.,* Fla. Stat. § 903.046(2)(h) (stating that when deciding release, bail amount, and other conditions, the court "should carefully consider the utility and necessity of substantial bail in relation to the street value of the drugs or controlled substances involved.").

[2] Deposit Bond

With a deposit bond, the defendant is required to deposit a percentage of the full bond (usually 10%) with the court. Failure to appear could result in an order that the remaining amount of the bond (usually 90%) be paid by the defendant. Appearance at court often results in a return of the initial 10% deposit, but the court may retain a small percentage of that amount for administrative costs (often 10% of the initial 10% amount, or 1% of the total amount). Assuming the aggravated robbery defendant faces the same $25,000 bond, this procedure allows the defendant to deposit $2,500 with the court to secure immediate release. If the defendant fails to appear for trial, the court may order the defendant to pay the remaining $22,500. If the defendant appears as scheduled, however, the court will refund all of the initial $2,500 deposit, less an appropriate administrative fee (10% of the initial deposit, or $250).

A study of state pretrial release of felony defendants in the 75 largest counties found that only 6% of those released pending trial posted a deposit cash bond. Bureau of Justice Statistics, U.S. Dept. of Justice, *Pretrial Release of Felony Defendants in State Courts* (2007).

[3] Surety Bond

[a] Professional Bond Companies

This is the most common form of bail in which a third party, usually a bail bonding company, signs a promissory note to the court for the full bail amount and then charges the defendant a percentage of that full amount as a fee. The "surety" ordinarily must meet statutory or court-ordered criteria to ensure its financial soundness. Nationally, there are about 14,000 commercial bail agents who secure the release of two million defendants annually. Bureau of Justice Statistics, U.S. Dept. of Justice, *Pretrial Release of Felony Defendants in State Courts* (2007). At least four states (Illinois, Kentucky, Oregon, and Wisconsin) do not allow commercial bail businesses. *Id.* In 2018, California became the first state to abolish "cash bail" altogether (effective October 2019). Thomas Fuller, *California Is the First State to Scrap Cash Bail*, N.Y. Times, Aug. 28, 2018.

Usually, the fee assessed by the company is 10% of the total bond. If the defendant fails to appear in court as scheduled, the court can order the bonding company to pay the full bail amount to the court. Many bond companies require the defendant to post collateral to ensure that the company is protected from loss if the defendant absconds.

Often the court will give the bond company time to locate and return the defendant to court. If the company is successful in obtaining the defendant's presence in court, the judge may reward the company by refusing to require it to pay the amount of the bond. Indeed, in some locales the bond company can obtain a refund of a forfeited bond it has paid if, perhaps years after a defendant absconded, the company locates and returns him or her to court. In the event bond is forfeited, a surety can, in certain circumstances, seek a remission of forfeited funds. The Ninth Circuit identified the following as factors for a court to consider when deciding whether to remit forfeiture of a bond:

> (1) the defendant's willfulness in breaching the release condition; (2) the sureties' participation in apprehending the defendant; (3) the cost, inconvenience, and prejudice suffered by the government; (4) mitigating factors; (5) whether the surety is a professional or a member of the family or a friend; and (6) the appropriateness of the amount of the bond. Not all of the factors need to be resolved in the government's favor.

United States v. Amwest Surety Ins. Co., 54 F.3d 601, 603 (9th Cir. 1995).

There is also authority for the court to relieve the bond company of its contractual duty to pay the bond in the interests of "justice." *See, e.g.*, Fed. R. Crim. P. 46(f)(2) (no forfeiture ordered if "justice does not require forfeiture" of bond amount). This could occur if a defendant absconded before trial, triggering forfeiture by the bond company, but then was soon apprehended by police in another jurisdiction.

If the defendant makes all scheduled court appearances and otherwise complies with conditions imposed, he or she receives no refund of the initial 10% fee paid for the surety bond. The bond company retains this as its fee for its service. By contract, the accused is legally obligated to reimburse the bond company for any money the company has to pay to the court. Sometimes the bond company requires the defendant to find a guarantor—someone who agrees to reimburse the company if it cannot locate the accused and must pay the bond amount to court.

[i] Authority to Recapture

One of the most controversial aspects of the commercial surety industry is the bonding company's broad authority to recapture the defendant. Using "skip tracers" (or "bounty hunters"), bond companies sometimes make substantial efforts to locate and return absconding offenders. While some states have placed statutory restrictions on the extent of the bonding company's power to arrest, the authority remains largely unrestrained. It has long been held that an American court has the jurisdictional authority to try a defendant even though the defendant's presence was obtained by a forcible abduction. In *Frisbie v. Collins*, 342 U.S. 519 (1952), Justice Black noted that "[t]here is nothing in the Constitution that [permits] a guilty person rightfully convicted to escape justice because he was brought to trial against his will."

Even though bounty hunters effectively serve as an adjunct to government-paid law enforcement officers, they are not always deemed state actors for purposes of imposing liability for violations of constitutional rights. *See* John L. Watts, *Tyranny by Proxy: State Action and the Private Use of Deadly Force,* 89 Notre Dame L. Rev. 1237, 1258–59 (2014) (noting that while several courts have deemed bounty hunters state actors when they assist police, courts have refused to extend liability in its absence).

[ii] Policy Arguments

Many reformers have called for the abolition of the commercial surety industry. *See* Standards for Criminal Justice § 10-1.4 (3d ed. 2007) (compensated sureties should be abolished) (second edition commentary stated that the commercial bond business is "one of the most tawdry parts in the criminal justice system"). One argument is that law enforcement officers, not a for-profit business, should be responsible for locating and returning absconding defendants. Abusive arrests by bond company agents are cited in support of this argument. A second argument is that a prisoner's freedom should not be dependent on whether a for-profit business will guarantee a bond. Some critics also condemn bonding companies for excessive profits and corruption (such as bribing jailors or court personnel to recommend a particular bond company). Critics also argue that bail bonding companies actually reduce an offender's incentive to appear in court by minimizing the personal financial impact of violating bail conditions.

Defenders of bond companies argue that they save taxpayer dollars by reducing the prison population and shouldering some responsibility for ensuring that criminal defendants show up for trial or are returned to court if they abscond. This saves both correctional and police resources.

Some empirical studies, however, have found that professional bonding companies are responsible for returning few of the people who are captured after missing a scheduled court date. *See, e.g.*, STANDARDS FOR CRIMINAL JUSTICE § 10-5.5 (3d ed. 2007). In addition, it is not uncommon for governments to fail to demand that companies pay the full amount of the bond owed, as required. Instead, they might demand payment of only a portion, for example, 5% (with companies pocketing half of the 10% put up by the defendant), or fail to recover any money at all. *See* Laura Sullivan, *Bail Burden Keeps U.S. Jails Stuffed with Inmates*, Nat. Pub. Radio, Jan. 21, 2010 (noting arrearages in several states and that the practice in Lubbock, Texas is to not require company payment of bonds, quoting local prosecutor that "bond companies play an important purpose" and that demanding more money might put them out of business); Kevin Krause & Ed Timms, *Bail Bondsmen Owe Dallas County $35 Million in Uncollected Default Judgments*, DALLAS MORNING NEWS, July 2, 2011.

Of late, significant reform efforts directed at reducing the use of money bail have been undertaken by many states. The efforts have understandably fostered significant resistance from private bail providers. In New Jersey, which in 2017 instituted major reform, opponents have provided support in a lawsuit filed by the mother of a murder victim alleging that the reforms resulted in the release of an individual who allegedly killed her son. Ariel Scotti, *Dog the Bounty Hunter Joins Bail Reform Lawsuit Against Chris Christie*, N.Y. DAILY NEWS, Aug. 1, 2017.

[b] "Community Bail Funds"

It is important to note that for a large segment of the detainee population money bail, even if a court deems it appropriate, is not an option. It is often the case, for instance, that bonds in comparatively modest amounts, say $500, are not worth the trouble for bond companies and they refuse to act as sureties. Or if bond is set at a higher amount, a detainee might not be able to obtain the customary 10% needed to secure release under surety auspices. Every day, many thousands of indigent detainees must therefore remain in jail, experiencing the negative consequences noted at the outset, simply because they are poor. *See, e.g.*, Paul Heaton et al., *The Downstream Consequences of Misdemeanor Pretrial Detention*, 69 Stan. L. Rev. 711, 733 (2017) (noting that 53% of Houston misdemeanor defendants were detained pretrial from 2008–2013). On a daily basis, more than 450,000 individuals are detained because they have not posted money bail. Todd D. Minton & Zhen Zeng, U.S. Dep't of Justice, Bureau of Just. Statistics, *Jail Inmates at Midyear* 2014 (2015). According to another study, nine of ten pretrial felony detainees remain in jail because they cannot afford their bail. Ram Subramanian et al., *Incarceration's Front Door: The Misuse of Jails in America* 32 (Vera Institute of Justice, July 29, 2015), https://storage.googleapis.com/vera-web-assets/downloads/Publications/incarcerations-front-door-the-misuse-of-jails-in-america/legacy_downloads/incarcerations-front-door-report_02.pdf.

In response, a number of community organizations have instituted efforts to collect money for use in posting bail for indigent detainees. *See* Jocelyn Simonson, *Bail Nullification*, 115 Mich. L. Rev. 585 (2017) (discussing funds established in Massachusetts; Brooklyn, the Bronx, and Queens, New York; and Nashville, Tennessee). According to Professor Simonson, the funds in effect nullify a judge's bail determination because "each time a community bail fund pays for a stranger, the people in control of the fund reject a judge's determination that a certain amount of the defendant's personal money was necessary for the defendant's release." *Id.* at 588. "Community bail funds vary enormously in how they function—some are run by mobilized grassroots groups intent on abolishing the criminal justice as we know it, while others are more of a private, pretrial-services agency, making sure that their neighbors return to court on time." *Id.* at 589. In essence, Professor Simonson notes, "bail funds consist of a revolving pool of money: bail funds post bail for someone, and if that defendant returns to court the bail fund receives the money back; the bail fund can then use that money anew." *Id.* at 600.

[4] Unsecured Bond

This is considered to be the least restrictive financial release condition. The defendant is released from custody upon promising to pay the bond amount if he or she fails to appear in court. Initially, however, the defendant pays no money to the court, and no money changes hands if the defendant appears as scheduled. This is a preferred option in some states and in federal courts. *See* 18 U.S.C. § 3142(b). However, a study of state pretrial release of felony defendants in the 75 largest counties found that only four percent of those released pending trial posted an unsecured bond. Bureau of Justice Statistics, U.S. Dept. of Justice, *Pretrial Release of Felony Defendants in State Courts* (Nov. 2007).

[5] Release on Recognizance (R.O.R.)

The court releases the defendant on the personal promise that the defendant will appear in court as required. Some jurisdictions attach conditions to the R.O.R.

release, such as restricting travel or maintaining employment. In order to encourage the use of R.O.R., a number of jurisdictions have enacted laws creating a presumption of this form of release. Standards for Criminal Justice § 10-5.1(a) (3d ed. 2007) (commentary refers to 23 jurisdictions). R.O.R. is a preferred option in some states and in federal courts. *See* 18 U.S.C. § 3142(b).

A study of state pretrial release of felony defendants in the 75 largest counties found that 20 percent of those released pending trial were released on their own recognizance. Bureau of Justice Statistics, U.S. Dept. of Justice, *Pretrial Release of Felony Defendants in State Courts* (2007).

Does a defendant, thought to not pose a public safety risk, have a right to electronic monitoring, in lieu of detention? For an argument in the affirmative, *see* Samuel R. Wiseman, *Pretrial Detention and the Right to Be Monitored*, 123 YALE L.J. 1344 (2014).

[6] Citation Release

Often, a person arrested for a minor criminal offense (such as a traffic violation) is given a "citation" by the arresting officer. The citation orders the offender to appear for trial on a specific date. The defendant is not taken to a police station, is not required to make an initial court appearance, and suffers no serious deprivation of freedom. Many studies recommend the use of citation release whenever possible as a means of reducing unnecessary incarceration and saving police and correctional resources. *See, e.g.*, ABA Standards for Criminal Justice § 10-2.1 (3d ed. 2007) (citations should be used "to the maximum extent consistent with the effective enforcement of the law"). Some jurisdictions now mandate the use of citation release. *See* Cal. Penal Code § 853.6(a)(i) (mandating citation release for misdemeanors unless one or more statutory conditions met).

If the defendant is taken to a police station for booking, the police may decide to release him or her without court involvement; this is referred to as "stationhouse release," which is another form of citation release. Another form of "at-station" release involves utilization of a bail schedule, by which a police official is permitted to receive money bail (either full cash bond or surety bond) according to a schedule calibrated to the crime allegedly committed by the defendant.

[7] Conditional Release

In addition to, or in place of, other pretrial release mechanisms, some jurisdictions provide for the release of a defendant subject to one or more conditions that are thought to assure the defendant's appearance at trial or to further safeguard the community while the defendant is free. These conditions may include restrictions on travel (including wearing a locating device), avoiding contact with identified individuals (such as witnesses or the victim), periodic reporting to law enforcement agencies, remaining in custody of a designated person, and undergoing medical treatment (including in-patient psychiatric care) or schooling. A comprehensive list of such conditions appears in § 3142(c) of the Bail Reform Act of 1984. Violation of a condition of release can lead to arrest and confinement pending trial or to citation for contempt of court.

A study of state pretrial release of felony defendants in the 75 largest counties found that 8% of those released pending trial were released on conditional release. Bureau of Justice Statistics, U.S. Dept. of Justice, *Pretrial Release of Felony Defendants in State Courts* (2007).

Many courts have adopted the practice of conditioning pretrial release on the suspect's consent to warrantless searches and drug tests by government officials. Some authorities have held that this condition, despite the defendant's "consent," violates the Fourth Amendment unless the search is based on probable cause. *See United States v. Scott*, 450 F.3d 863 (9th Cir. 2006). *See also* Andrew J. Smith, Note, *Unconstitutional Release: A Pyrrhic Victory for Arrestees' Privacy Rights Under* United States v. Scott, 48 Wm. & Mary L. Rev. 2365 (2007).

[8] Property Bond

Many states statutorily authorize defendants who are eligible for bail to post a property bond in lieu of the full cash bond. Some states specify that the property must have a market value of at least twice the amount of bail, *e.g.*, Cal. Penal Code § 1298, while other states require that the value of the property be at least one and one-half times the amount of bail, Tenn. Code Ann. § 40-11-122(1). States also vary with respect to deed and disclosure requirements.

A study of state pretrial release of felony defendants in the 75 largest counties found that only one percent of those released pending trial were released on a property bond. Bureau of Justice Statistics, U.S. Dept. of Justice, *Pretrial Release of Felony Defendants in State Courts* (2007).

F. Pretrial Detention and Release: Facts and Figures

According to a Bureau of Justice Statistics study of state felony defendants in the largest counties from 1990–2004, more than 58% of all felony defendants were released prior to case disposition. Bureau of Justice Statistics, U.S. Dept. of Justice, *Pretrial Release of Felony Defendants in State Courts* (2007). The comparable federal release rate for federal defendants was 36%. While various forms of pretrial release are available, generally the accused obtains release either by posting bail (a money amount designed to insure the defendant's subsequent court appearance) or by some form of non-financial release. Thirty percent of those released secured a "financial" release (surety bond, full cash bond, or deposit bond), while 32% secured a "non-financial" release (release on recognizance, conditional, or unsecured bond). *Id.* Only 6% of all felony defendants were held without bail. Driving-related offenses resulted in the highest release rate (73%), while murder defendants were least likely to be released prior to trial (19%). Other release percentages for specific offenses were rape (53%), robbery (44%), burglary (49%), and drug sales (63%). *Id.*

Bail was set at a high amount or denied altogether in cases where the charges were for serious felony offenses. For example, 80% of murder defendants had either a high bail amount or were detained without bail. *Id.*

Among felony defendants, 62% were released prior to disposition of their case and 38% were detained. Of the 38% detained, 6% were denied bail and 32% had bail set but could not find the financial resources to post the required amount. *Id.*

When bail was set, the higher the bail amount the less likely the defendant would be released on bail. Thus, the median amount of bail for detained defendants was $15,000, while it was $5,000 for those able to be released. The mean (average) numbers were more striking: $58,400 (detained) compared with $11,600 (released). When bail was set at $100,000 or more, release occurred in about 10% of the cases. By contrast, with bail set at under $5,000, 70% of the defendants in the study obtained pretrial release. *Id.* The study found that approximately 75% of all felony defendants who secured release prior to trial made all scheduled court appearances. *Id.*

Looking at race, the study found that 68% of white arrestees were released, while 62% of blacks and 55% of Hispanics were released. The study noted that the low rate for Hispanics may be due to immigration "holds" causing defendants to be held pending further processing on immigration issues. *Id.*

G. The Bail Hearing

The bail hearing, which may occur at the defendant's initial appearance or separately, is relatively informal. Often this is the first opportunity for both the government and the accused to present arguments related to (1) whether the accused should be released pending trial, and (2) if release is deemed appropriate, the terms and conditions, which may include the specific dollar amount of bail. In cases in which a "stationhouse release" decision has been previously made, if either the government or the accused is dissatisfied with the amount or conditions of release, the court may be asked to review those matters at the initial appearance or at any other time.

Pretrial release service agency. A number of jurisdictions have established a pretrial release service agency to assist in the release process. Agency staff may interview new jail prisoners to gather data about the prisoner's history and likely conduct if released. The agency may also run programs to supervise and assist persons on pretrial release. These duties may include employment counseling, regular monitoring, and even transportation to court. *See generally* ABA Standards for Criminal

Justice § 10-1.10 (3d ed. 2007) (recommending that all jurisdictions provide a pretrial services agency).

Counsel. Because a bail hearing is not typically thought of as a "critical stage" of a criminal case, the Sixth Amendment right to counsel does not require states to provide counsel to indigents at hearings. Only a relatively small number of states elect to do so. Paul Heaton et al., *The Downstream Consequences of Misdemeanor Pretrial Detention*, 69 STAN. L. REV. 711, 773–77 (2017); *see also* Douglas L. Colbert, *Do Attorneys Really Matter? The Empirical and Legal Case for the Right of Counsel at Bail*, 23 CARDOZO L. REV. 1719 (2002). A study in Baltimore reported that defendants represented by counsel at bail hearings were two and one-half times more likely than unrepresented defendants to be released on their own recognizance; even if not released, they were four times more likely to receive a reduction in the amount of bail. *See* Colbert, *supra*.

Thus, at the bail hearing, where the defendant's liberty is at stake, "the prosecutor is expected to serve as law enforcer and defense attorney at the same time." Sandra Guerra Thompson, *Do Prosecutors Really Matter? A Proposal to Ban One-Sided Hearings*, 44 HOFSTRA L. REV. 1161, 1162 (2016). If counsel is not present when a decision is made to detain the defendant, the issue may be revisited later when counsel becomes available.

Hearing. At the bail hearing, both sides may present evidence, including live witnesses and documentary proof. The rules of evidence generally do not apply. The hearing may be somewhat informal and will rarely last longer than a few minutes.

Sometimes judges announce decisions without giving their reasons, although it is recommended that judges be required to give reasons for any decision other than release on the offender's promise to return. *See, e.g.*, Standards for Criminal Justice § 10-5.1 (3d ed. 2007).

Some jurisdictions require regular reports to the judge on the status of prisoners unable to meet the conditions of release. This is designed to provide a review to ensure that efforts are being made to secure the offender's release or to expedite the proceedings and minimize pretrial detention. It is not uncommon to provide an expedited trial for offenders unable to obtain pretrial release.

Judges can have considerable discretion in deciding the amount of bail. One commentator has noted that judges sometimes go beyond the language of bail statutes in order to achieve objectives other than guaranteeing a defendant's future appearance in court:

> First, some judges view bail as a punitive measure and set bail at a high level in the belief that the defendant has committed the crime and deserves detention or at least temporary economic hardship. Second, others view bail as a means to implement preventive detention. Bail is set at an amount which is beyond the economic means of defendants in order to protect society from those who would, in the judge's view, commit crimes while free during the pretrial period.

Paul B. Wice, Bail and Its Reform: A National Survey 5 (1973). A judge, for personal and professional reasons, might be risk-averse when it comes to releasing defendants; suffice it to say, no judge relishes the negative attention generated by a violent crime committed by a released individual.

A judge's bail decision is subject to review by the same or an equivalent judge or one from a higher court. Either the prosecutor or the defendant may request the review. Research has shown significant variation among individual judges with regard to affording release opportunity on money bail for similarly situated defendants and differences in the amount of bail imposed. Crystal C. Yang, *Toward an Optimal Bail System*, 92 N.Y.U. L. Rev. 1399, 1461–65 (2017) (discussing results from study of Miami-Dade and Philadelphia courts); *see also id.* at 1465–67 (discussing results indicating significant variations based on race of defendants).

Professor H. Richard Uviller's thought-provoking book, The Tilted Playing Field: Is Criminal Justice Unfair? (1999), devotes a chapter to the issue of bail. He describes bail as "[a] nasty, miserable business that defies all pretense of reason and good judgment." Expressing wonder that judges don't "show their palms in despair every time a bail call is presented to them," he describes the bail decision as "casual, impulsive, largely idiosyncratic, totally arbitrary, wildly variable, and without any possibility of objective verification." *Id.* at 166.

Role of victim. The usual rule is that the victim of crimes plays no role in the decision about release from detention. However, the federal Crime Victims' Rights Act, 18 U.S.C. § 3771 changes this by giving victims the right to timely notice of any public court proceeding involving "any release" of the accused. It also states that the victim has the right to be "reasonably heard" at a public proceeding involving release and to confer with the prosecutor. Since 1996, states have adopted VINE systems—Victim Information and Notification Everyday—to alert victims of the suspect's release.

Allowing the victim an opportunity to be heard during a bail hearing might have therapeutic value, but is a bail hearing the appropriate stage in a criminal prosecution for this to occur? In a hearing determining pre-trial release, there are "at least three matters to which the victim's statement might have been relevant or material . . . : the strength of the case against Defendants, the seriousness of the crimes they are alleged to have committed, and the reasonable apprehension of personal danger to the victim." *United States v. Marcello*, 370 F. Supp. 2d 745, 747 (N.D. Ill. 2005).

Although the Crime Victims' Rights Act envisions that a victim who is improperly denied her opportunity to be reasonably heard may enter "a motion to re-open a plea or sentence," 18 U.S.C.A. § 3771(d)(5), the federal statute does not specify the effect of such a denial upon a bail hearing decision. At least one court has proceeded with the bail hearing in the absence of the victim, while reserving the right to reconsider its determination upon motion by the excluded victim. In *United States v. Turner*, 367 F. Supp. 2d 319 (E.D.N.Y. 2005), the alleged victims had not received proper notice of the bail hearing, the district judge held the hearing as scheduled, but provided each alleged victim a record of the hearing and the opportunity for the alleged victims after the hearing to seek reconsideration of the determination, because the only available alternative, adjourning the hearing, would result in a greater period of incarceration for the defendant without a ruling on the defendant's eligibility for pre-trial release.

Problem 5-1. Clyde's Plight

Clyde Hopkins, a 26-year old male, was charged with burglary of a home in the daytime. The offense allegedly occurred August 3. He was arrested August 10, and was in possession of a very small amount of cocaine at the time of his arrest. His record shows one prior conviction for burglary two years ago, resulting in a suspended sentence, and one conviction for possession of cocaine 18 months ago, resulting in a jail sentence of 60 days. Hopkins lives with his mother (with whom he has lived all of his life), is presently unemployed, and is a high school graduate. He has worked as a dishwasher in several local restaurants, but has lost each job for failing to report to work on schedule. He has not had steady employment in six months. Hopkins was previously placed on parole after serving his jail term and apparently established an excellent record while on parole, which was successfully completed three months ago. He was also released on money bail in his two prior cases and appeared for trial in each case according to schedule.

Under state law the maximum sentence that could be imposed is eight years' incarceration (assuming prior convictions for burglary and possession of cocaine). In all likelihood, even if the defendant were to receive that sentence, he would be released on parole in approximately two years.

1. As prosecutor, what arguments would you make in support of a recommendation that Mr. Hopkins not be released on bail? Assuming that the court decides to release the accused, what amount would you recommend for bail? What conditions would you advocate?

2. As defense counsel, what arguments would you make in favor of releasing Hopkins on bail (or, perhaps even on personal recognizance)? Assuming that the judge has decided to release the accused, what should be the appropriate bail amount? If the judge were considering a "release on conditions" plan, what conditions would you advocate as defense counsel?

3. *Variation No. 1.* Assume that Clyde Hopkins is a first-time offender (meaning no record of prior arrests or convictions). Also assume that he has no permanent residence in the community and has described himself as "homeless." Also assume that at least three credible witnesses identified Hopkins as he left the victim's home immediately after commission of the alleged burglary. What relevance, if any, do each of these facts have with respect to the bail decision?

4. *Variation No. 2.* Assume that immediately after his arrest, Hopkins sent a letter to Ms. Adams, the burglary victim. She has turned the letter over to the prosecutor. The letter reads as follows:

Dear Ms. Adams,

I don't know why you think I am the man who stole property from your house. People have been accusing me of things all my life, and I do not know what I've done to deserve that kind of treatment. I am asking you to call the district attorney and tell her to drop these charges. Some people say I have a temper. When people don't do what I ask them to do, sometimes I get really mad.

Sincerely,

Clyde Hopkins

a. If you were the judge in a jurisdiction in which the bail statute provided that the sole issue in determining bail was "assuring the presence of the defendant at trial," would your decision with respect to the amount of bail be influenced by your knowledge of this letter?

b. Assume that your jurisdiction authorizes denial of bail (i.e., preventive detention) where there is clear and convincing evidence of "future dangerousness" or "likely intimidation of witnesses." The Assistant District Attorney has recommended preventive detention based upon all the facts of this case, including the letter. As defense attorney, what arguments would you make in opposition to that motion?

Notes

1. *Master bail schedules.* Many jurisdictions use *bail schedules* (sometimes known as *master bail schedules*), a system by which bail is set by the court or jail officials at a specified amount depending upon the alleged offense committed by the defendant. The system is quick and efficient because it requires virtually no exercise of discretion by the judicial officer. The use of a schedule means that the only factor considered is the identity of the alleged offense; hence, circumstances of the individual defendant (community ties, assets, etc.) are usually irrelevant, though sometimes criminal history is considered. With this uniformity, schedules are thought to limit the threat of arbitrary decisions, perhaps based on inappropriate factors such as race or gender, or the variable preferences of individual judges.

The United States Supreme Court, in addressing the issue of what is "excessive" under the Eighth Amendment, has said that "the fixing of bail for any individual defendant must be based upon standards relevant to the purpose of assuring the presence of that defendant." *Stack v. Boyle*, 342 U.S. 1, 5 (1951). Although intended to help individuals to secure quicker release without waiting for a formal judicial hearing, which might take days, bail schedules have been the subject of widespread criticism. In principle, they arguably contradict the *Stack* principle, and result in unwarranted detention of individuals. Bail schedules, it has been asserted, are at once prone to under- and over-detention:

> Regular use of bail schedules often unintentionally fosters unnecessary detention of misdemeanants, indigents, and nondangerous defendants

> because they are unable to afford the sum mandated by the schedule. . . . On the other hand, bail schedules permit dangerous or risky defendants to purchase release without judicial review or other conditions tailored to prevent danger or flight.

Lindsey Carlson, *Bail Schedules: A Violation of Judicial Discretion?*, 26 Crim. Justice 12, 17 (2011). According to the American Bar Association:

> Financial conditions should be the result of an individualized decision taking into account the special circumstances of each defendant, the defendant's ability to meet the financial conditions and the defendant's flight risk, and should never be set by reference to a predetermined schedule of amount fixed according to the nature of the charge.

ABA, *Criminal Justice Standards, Pretrial Release* § 10-5.3(e) (2007).

In many cases, the amount of bail (even if comparatively modest) is set at an amount that virtually ensures pretrial incarceration of the accused. A master schedule could certainly have that result. Similarly, a judge may purposely set high bail to achieve the goal of pretrial detention. Conversely, however, the financially secure defendant is likely able to obtain pretrial release if the amount of bail is arbitrarily based only on the nature of the alleged offense. In both instances (virtually automatic incarceration or pretrial release), the interests of the accused and society are inadequately protected.

2. *Amount of bail.* Cases litigating the amount of bail produce few rules or patterns. In cases involving drug offenses and particularly violent crimes, appellate courts rarely hold that bail amounts are excessive. *See, e.g., United States v. Auriemma*, 773 F.2d 1520 (11th Cir. 1985) ($1,000,000 bail was reasonable where defendant was charged with importation of 800 pounds of cocaine and related drug offenses, even though numerous factors suggested a low risk of flight (Florida resident for 27 years, married with four children and an employment history)); *Ex parte Willman*, 695 S.W.2d 752 (Tex. App. 1985) (defendant was indicted for delivery of some 2,000 grams of cocaine and faced a possible punishment of confinement for life and a fine not to exceed $250,000; bail set at $300,000; court noted that sometimes financial backers in drug cases are willing to forfeit bond money).

3. *Constitutional challenges.* Laws and policies governing the availability and amount of bail are frequently challenged in court. In *ODonnell v. Harris County, Texas*, 892 F.3d 147 (5th Cir. 2018), a decision with potentially broad ramifications, the Fifth Circuit unanimously granted injunctive relief to arrestees challenging a system governed by bail schedules. The court found that the system violated the equal protection and due process rights of petitioners, indigent misdemeanor arrestees who were denied release due to their inability to pay. With respect to the equal protection claim in particular, the court stated:

> In sum, the essence of the [claim] can be boiled down to the following: take two misdemeanor arrestees who are identical in every way. . . except

> that one is wealthy and one is indigent. Applying the [defendants'] current custom and practice, with their lack of individualized assessment and mechanical application of the secured bail schedule, both arrestees would almost certainly receive identical secured bail amounts. One arrestee is able to post bond, and the other is not. As a result, the wealthy arrestee is less likely to plead guilty, more likely to receive a shorter sentence or be acquitted, and less likely to bear the social costs of incarceration. The poor arrestee, by contrast, must bear the brunt of all of these, simply because he has less money than his wealthy counterpart.

Id. at 163.

4. *Factors in bail reduction.* If a defendant cannot meet the financial conditions previously set, he can ask the court to lower the amount. When a defendant files a motion to reduce the amount, he does not have to be released; the judge may either consider reducing bond or decide that no other condition of release will assure appearance. *See, e.g., Luyao v. Mascara*, 815 So. 2d 748 (Fla. Dist. Ct. App. 2002) (following the local bond schedule for each charge, the total amount of bail for a medical doctor charged with drug trafficking was set at $1,890,000; petition for habeas corpus was granted because the amount was excessive in light of the defendant's financial circumstances); *Reeves v. State*, 923 N.E.2d 418 (Ind. Ct. App. 2010) ($1,500,000 bail amount reversed as excessive in securities fraud case; trial court set an amount 100 times greater than prescribed for the class of felony charge but failed to articulate any connection between the amount and statutory factors). *But see Hernandez v. State*, 669 S.E.2d 434 (Ga. Ct. App. 2008) (bail amount of $1,000,000 in drug trafficking case held not excessive when defendant was not United States citizen and presented no evidence that he was in the United States legally).

5. *Factors in determining excessive bail.* Recall that the Eighth Amendment bans "excessive bail." That a defendant cannot satisfy a financial condition does not render a financial condition excessive when the record shows that detention is based on protecting the safety of the community. *See, e.g., United States v. Fidler*, 419 F.3d 1026 (5th Cir. 2005). In *Fidler*, the condition of posting a $300,000 property bond was upheld, even though the defendant was unable to afford that amount, because the defendant's hostile and possibly threatening statements to likely witnesses raised a "real risk that he might intimidate or threaten prospective witnesses or jurors."

6. *Skips.* People released on bail who abscond are often called *skips* (or *defaulters*). They are subject to arrest and prosecution for the original crime as well as for a separate offense called *bail jumping. See, e.g.,* 18 U.S.C. § 3146. This crime ordinarily reaches people who, released on bail or another mechanism, knowingly or willfully fail to appear at a proceeding in violation of the terms of their release. Ordinarily the defendant may defend by proving that "uncontrollable circumstances" caused the nonappearance.

According to one scholar, it is important to distinguish between the risk of flight and risk of nonappearance in court, as the two occurrences entail different kinds of behavior and risks. "Flight risk is properly assigned to defendants who are expected to flee a jurisdiction. This is a small, and arguably shrinking, subcategory of a much larger group of defendants who pose risks of nonappearance." Lauryn P. Gouldin, *Defining Flight Risk*, 85 U. Chi. L. Rev. 677, 683 (2018). Likewise, it is important to distinguish between flight risk and dangerousness. *See* Lauryn P. Gouldin, *Disentangling Flight Risk from Dangerousness*, 2016 B.Y.U. L. Rev. 837.

7. *Illegal immigrants.* An Arizona law barring pretrial release for serious felony arrestees who are illegal immigrants was upheld against an equal protection challenge as appropriate to prevent flight from the jurisdiction. *Hernandez v. Lynch*, 167 P.3d 1264 (Ariz. Ct. App. 2007). Do you agree with this approach to denial of pretrial release?

H. Bail Reform Act of 1984: Introduction

The Bail Reform Act of 1984 numbers among the most significant and controversial federal laws adopted regarding the adjudicatory process. The provision not only follows the traditional view and allows pretrial detention of defendants who will not likely appear at trial, it also permits the detention of defendants thought to present a risk of harm to society.

In *United States v. Salerno*, 481 U.S. 739 (1987), the Supreme Court by a 6–3 vote upheld the constitutionality of the Bail Reform Act. The petitioners challenged the Act on two grounds: (1) Fifth Amendment due process, in that pretrial detention amounted to being punished without adjudication of guilt and (2) the Eighth Amendment, in that pretrial detention on the basis of a judicial finding of dangerousness constituted excessive bail. The Court rejected the due process claim by finding that the detention was regulatory (not punitive) in character, provided procedural protections to guide its application, and that ultimately the deprivation of liberty was outweighed by the government's interest in community safety. With respect to the Eighth Amendment claim, the Court concluded that "[n]othing in the text of the Bail Clause limits permissible Government considerations solely to questions of flight." *Id.* at 754. When the government's only interest is ensuring appearance in court, "bail must be set by a court designed to ensure that goal, and no more." *Id.* at 755. However, "when Congress has mandated detention on the basis of a compelling interest other than prevention of flight, as it has here, the Eighth Amendment does not require release on bail."

As you consider the Bail Reform Act, keep in mind the overall significance of the legislation, summarized as follows:

> The Bail Reform Act of 1984 attempts to solve the problem of the infliction of harm on innocent victims by defendants who have been released pending trial. Congress acknowledges that the measures it enacted to address this problem substantially depart from the principles which previously guided the bail system. The Act's new procedures are preventive in

> nature, authorizing detention of defendants who are determined to present an intolerable risk of committing future criminal acts before trial. In such instances, Congress has determined that the safety of the community outweighs the right of these defendants to be free until proven guilty at trial, a right which until now was generally assumed not to be subject to a balancing of interests approach. By legislatively authorizing such preventive measures, Congress has led the courts into an area which up until now they were unwilling to go, having previously limited [pretrial detention] to situations where the defendant had threatened the integrity of the judicial process.

Kenneth Frederick Berg, *The Bail Reform Act of 1984*, 34 Emory L.J. 685, 739 (1985).

Notes

The federal Bail Reform Act is lengthy and complex. The following questions should help you understand some of its most important features.

1. *Appearance and safety.* The Bail Reform Act is designed to "reasonably assure" (i) "the appearance of the person as required" and (ii) that the person will not "endanger the safety of any other person or the community."

Appearance refers to attendance at any proceeding the defendant is ordered to attend. The "safety" concerns are quite broad, reaching particular individuals (such as potential witnesses or the victim) or the community (such as continuing drug activity or violent crimes). Which of the two concerns (appearance or safety) do you think the court is more likely to be able to predict accurately?

2. *Least restrictive form of release.* Under § 3142(c)(1)(B), conditions of release must be the least restrictive that will satisfy the appearance and safety requirements. Could any condition require the accused to waive or forfeit a constitutional right? *See, e.g., United States v. Kills Enemy*, 3 F.3d 1201 (8th Cir. 1993) (submit to warrantless drug search as condition of release). *See generally* ABA Standards for Criminal Justice, Pretrial Detention, Standard 10-1.2 (3d ed. 2007) (recommending least restrictive alternative that will reasonably assure appearance and safety).

Conditions are deemed proper if they are related to statutory appearance or safety concerns. Circuit courts have held, however, that there are some conditions judicial officers may not impose. *See, e.g., United States v. Scott*, 450 F.3d 863 (9th Cir. 2006) (error in conditioning pretrial release on defendant's consent to random drug testing); *United States v. Gundersen*, 978 F.2d 580 (10th Cir. 1992) (error in requiring indigent defendants to reside at halfway house as condition of bail solely because of their indigency).

3. *When pretrial detention authorized.* Section 3142(e) authorizes pretrial detention if "no condition or combination of conditions will reasonably assure" appearance and public safety. Section 3142(c)(1)(B)(xiv) contains a catch-all provision authorizing the court to fashion "any other condition that is reasonably necessary." Does this mean that there can be no pretrial detention if safety and court appearance

would be likely if the police assigned a police officer to follow the accused everywhere? *See United States v. Tortora*, 922 F.2d 880 (1st Cir. 1990) (heroic measures not required before pretrial detention authorized).

4. *Duration of pretrial detention.* The Bail Reform Act sets no time limit on pretrial detention. Several limits exist, however. The Speedy Trial Act, discussed in Chapter 12, indirectly provides limits by mandating that certain procedures be held within a certain number of days. For example, in theory at least, a trial should be started within 100 days of arrest. 18 U.S.C. § 3161.

Another limit—though lacking any definite standards—is due process. Case law suggests that at some point the government's interest in pretrial detention would give way to the defendant's interest in freedom. *See, e.g., United States v. Infelise*, 934 F.2d 103 (7th Cir. 1991) (holding that two-year detention did not violate due process based on case complexity, multiple defendants, and defense motions); *United States v. Archambault*, 240 F. Supp. 2d 1082 (D.S.D. 2002) (due process violated; 20-month delay with disposition many months away; there was release plan, and delay not caused by defendant).

5. *Public safety.* The Bail Reform Act authorizes pretrial detention if necessary to protect "the safety of any other person and the community." 18 U.S.C. § 3142(e). What threats to public safety are considered? Only crimes of violence? What if the court believes the defendant, if released, is likely to sell drugs? Commit burglaries? Obstruct justice? Take drugs?

6. *Detention hearing.* Section 3142(f) deals with the detention hearing.

a. *Motion practice.* In some situations, the hearing is initiated by a motion filed by the government. In others, either the government or the court can order a detention hearing.

b. *Timing.* Section 3142(f) deals with the detention hearing procedures. When must the detention hearing be held? If a continuance is granted, what happens to the accused? If § 3142(f)'s time limits are violated, the accused is not necessarily entitled to be released. *See United States v. Montalvo-Murillo*, 495 U.S. 711 (1990).

c. *Defendant's rights.* What rights does the accused have at this hearing? What about the right to issue subpoenas? *See United States v. Hurtado*, 779 F.2d 1467 (11th Cir. 1985) (court can deny some subpoenas; should grant one if necessary to rebut presumption). Have counsel? Testify? Present evidence? Cross examine government witnesses? (Yes to all.) However, the accused does not have the right to cross-examine witnesses who are not called by the government to testify. *United States v. Winsor*, 785 F.2d 755 (9th Cir. 1986).

d. *Evidence rules.* Considering that the accused's liberty is at stake, why do the rules of evidence not apply?

e. *Proof.* The government bears the burden to prove by a preponderance of the evidence that the defendant is a flight risk, whereas the government must prove by clear and convincing evidence that the defendant poses a public safety risk. 18

U.S.C. § 3142(f)(2)(B). What accounts for these varied proof burdens? What kinds of information might the government adduce to satisfy the respective standards? What information might defense counsel seek to muster? *See, e.g., United States v. Abad*, 350 F.3d 793 (8th Cir. 2003) (upholding determination that defendant posed a flight and public safety risk).

f. *Crime of violence.* The attorney for the government may move for a detention hearing if the case involves "a crime of violence" under § 3142(f)(1)(A). In 18 U.S.C. § 3156(a)(4) a *crime of violence* is defined to mean

> (A) an offense that has as an element of the offense the use, attempted use, or threatened use of physical force against the person or property of another; or (B) any other offense that is a felony and that, by its nature, involves a substantial risk that physical force against the person or property of another may be used in the course of committing the offense.

See, e.g., United States v. Ingle, 454 F.3d 1082 (10th Cir. 2006) (felon in possession of firearm not crime of violence, but cases split); *United States v. Reiner*, 468 F. Supp. 2d 393 (E.D.N.Y. 2006) (child porn possession is crime of violence). A review of cases shows that crimes of violence also include such offenses as arson, armed robbery, providing materials support to terrorist organizations, and possession of a sawed-off shotgun.

7. *Appeal of release decision.* The Federal Bail Reform Act authorizes both the government and the defendant to appeal a court's detention decision. 18 U.S.C. § 3145.

8. *Modification and revocation.* The court has the authority to modify the release conditions if there is new information or changed circumstances. 18 U.S.C. § 31452(c)(3). It can also revoke the decision to release the accused, though this authority should be exercised "with circumspection." *Bitter v. United States*, 389 U.S. 15 (1967).

9. *Academic critique.* The Bail Reform Act of 1984 has been the subject of intensive academic criticism. *See, e.g.*, Albert W. Alschuler, *Preventive Pretrial Detention and the Failure of Interest-Balancing Approaches to Due Process*, 85 Mich. L. Rev. 510 (1986); Marc Miller & Martin Guggenheim, *Pretrial Detention and Punishment*, 75 Minn. L. Rev. 335 (1990).

10. *Denial of bail for dangerousness usually upheld.* A review of rulings by the federal courts indicates that decisions to deny federal criminal defendants bail on grounds of predicted dangerousness are generally upheld. Identifiable danger to the community includes economic harm regarding the propensity to commit future economic crimes. *See, e.g., United States v. Reynolds*, 956 F.2d 192 (9th Cir. 1992); *United States v. Madoff*, 556 F. Supp. 2d 240 (S.D.N.Y. 2009).

11. *Absence of harm.* The most successful arguments attack bail denials based upon the absence of actual physical harm to third parties or threats to witnesses. For example, in *United States v. King*, 849 F.2d 485 (11th Cir. 1988), a United States district court in Florida had issued a pretrial detention order based upon allegations that the defendant, King, was a "leader" of a high volume and extremely profitable

cocaine distribution scheme. Detention was ordered based upon both risk of flight and risk of dangerousness. The Eleventh Circuit Court of Appeals affirmed the order, notwithstanding the absence of evidence of prior physical harm or threats made by the defendant against witnesses who might testify against her at trial. With respect to detention based upon risk of flight, King presented evidence that she did not pose a likelihood of flight because she was aware of the imminence of the grand jury indictments six months prior to the time that her indictment actually was returned. Accordingly, that fact, coupled with the fact that she chose to retain counsel to contest the charges, manifested "her true intent with respect to flight." The appellate court was unpersuaded by this evidence, observing that this contention was "not sufficient to overcome the statutory presumption and other evidence adduced at the hearings." *See also, e.g., United States v. Stone*, 608 F.3d 939 (6th Cir. 2010) (willingness to commit violence against girlfriend supports bail denial because it evidences violent tendency); *United States v. Orena*, 986 F.2d 628 (2d Cir. 1993) (gang war participant denied bail because of danger of continued participation in violent crimes).

12. *Drug cases.* Similarly, other cases suggest that defendants accused of large-quantity drug crimes (for which the Bail Reform Act carries a presumption in favor of detention) may be detained without bail based upon a prediction of future dangerousness, even in the absence of specific evidence related either to prior physical violence or actual threats to witnesses. *See, e.g., United States v. Gebro*, 948 F.2d 1118 (9th Cir. 1991).

[1] Implementation of Bail Reform Act of 1984

The Bail Reform Act of 1984 has resulted in the detention of a much higher percentage of people in jail awaiting trial for federal crimes. Based upon information collected in a study of pretrial incarceration in federal cases, one year before and after the Bail Reform Act went into effect, the percentage of federal defendants incarcerated until trial increased from 24% to 29%. The likelihood of being held until trial was 21% higher for violent offenses involving firearms, 20% for more serious drug offenses, 26% higher for other drug offenses, and 63% higher for defendants who caused injury. Defendants held without bail increased from 2% to 19%, while those required to post financial bail decreased from 44% to 27% (meaning pretrial detention has been substituted for money bail in some cases). The reason for incarceration pending trial changed. Before the Act, 93% of those held in jail were there for failure to meet bail conditions. After the Act, 65% were held on pretrial detention. Bureau of Justice Statistics, *Pretrial Release and Detention: The Bail Reform Act of 1984* (1988).

Released defendants. Given the statutory preference for nonfinancial conditions of release, it is not surprising that a large percentage (71%) of federal defendants obtain their release using an unsecured appearance bond or personal recognizance, instead of financial conditions. Federal female defendants (65%) are released pretrial more frequently than males (31%) across all major offense categories. Defendants younger than age 17 and older than age 40 are more likely to be released pretrial than defendants ages 18 to 39. Black and Hispanic defendants are less likely than white defendants to be released pretrial for all major federal offense categories, with the gap especially large for drug offenses, where white defendants are more likely to be released pretrial than black defendants by a gap of 60% to 36%. Thomas H. Cohen, *Pretrial Release and Misconduct in Federal District Courts, 2008–2010*, Bureau of Justice Statistics, U.S. Department of Justice (2012), http://www.bjs.gov/content/pub/ascii/prmfdc0810.txt.

Detained defendants. In 2013, the United States Department of Justice published a report of pretrial detention for defendants arrested between fiscal years 1995 and 2010. The number of defendants with cases disposed in federal district courts increased by 120%, from 45,635 in 1995 to 100,622 in 2010. [For the Bureau of Justice Statistics, a defendant is a person with a case disposed in the federal courts, while a disposition involves the act of terminating the defendant's case through a guilty plea, or through a trial conviction, dismissal, or acquittal.] From 1995 to 2010, the percentage of all federal defendants who were detained pretrial increased from 59% to 76%. The percentage of federal defendants detained for the duration of the case increased from 46% in 1995 to 64% in 2010. Thomas H. Cohen, *Pretrial Detention and Misconduct in Federal District Courts, 1995–2010*, U.S. Dep't of Justice, Office of Justice Programs, Bureau of Justice Statistics (2013), http://www.bjs.gov/index.cfm?ty=pbdetail&iid=4595.

Other notable findings in the study included:

- The number of defendants who were detained at any time in the pretrial process increased by 184%, from 27,004 in 1995 to 76,589 in 2010.
- Growth in pretrial detentions was primarily due to immigration caseloads, which increased by 664%, from 5,103 cases in 1995 to 39,001 in 2010.
- The percentage of immigration defendants who were detained pretrial increased from 86% in 1995 to 98% in 2008, and then declined to 88% in 2010.
- The percentage of drug defendants detained pretrial increased from 76% in 1995 to 84% in 2010.
- While weapons caseloads almost tripled between 1995 and 2010, the percentage of weapons defendants detained pretrial increased from 66% to 86% during the same period.
- For defendants released pretrial, the percentage committing pretrial misconduct peaked in 2006 at 22% and then declined to a percentage (17%) similar to that in 1995.

As expected, defendants with serious or lengthy criminal histories had the highest percentages of pretrial detention. In 1995, 39% of defendants had no prior arrests and that percentage decreased to 28% by 2010. Of those defendants with no prior arrests, 47% of them were detained pretrial in 1995, but that percentage increased to

64% by 2010. In 1995, 26% of all arrested defendants had five or more prior arrests, with that percentage increasing to 37% by 2010. In that 15-year period, defendants with five or more prior arrests who were detained pretrial increased from 79% in 1995 to 85% in 2010. *Id.*

I. Special Cases and Circumstances

[1] Capital Cases

Almost all jurisdictions, either by constitution or statutory provision, deny a person accused of a capital offense the right to release. As earlier noted in Part D, sometimes there is an additional requirement that bail can be denied if "proof of guilt is evident or the presumption is great." *E.g.*, Fla. Const. art. 1, § 14. In a jurisdiction with this rule, the judge in a capital case deciding a motion for release on bail must assess the strength of the government's case against the accused. While defense counsel may have little reason to expect a favorable ruling on the motion to release a capital defendant on bail, the bail hearing will afford counsel some discovery of the government's case. Considering the relatively limited right to pretrial discovery in criminal cases, discussed in Chapter 10, the bail hearing in a capital case may provide useful information not otherwise obtainable prior to trial. Irrespective of the rules applied, it is safe to say that virtually no accused capital offenders are actually released on bail.

[2] Juvenile Cases

In some jurisdictions, procedures are the same for children and adults. *See, e.g.*, Fla. Stat. § 903.06 ("Minors may bind themselves by a bond to secure their release on bail in the same manner as persons sui juris"). Other jurisdictions have special provisions concerning release of a juvenile to his or her parents. *See, e.g.*, Pa. C.S.A. § 6326 ("A person taking a child into custody . . . shall notify the parent, guardian or other custodian of the apprehension of the child . . . [and] shall release the child to [same] upon their promise to bring the child before the court when requested by the court.").

A number of unique issues can arise in juvenile cases, which suggest that the "regular" adult bail system should not apply fully to minors. Typically, juveniles are not legally competent to enter a contract with bonding companies. Unless the juvenile's parents are willing to secure bond, no release will occur. Additionally, if the juvenile's parents will not care for the child or if a court predicts continued harm in the home situation, the child probably will not be allowed to return home pending adjudication. The only alternative at that point is a form of pretrial detention unless the law allows placement with a relative or in foster care, or the court elects to allow the child to live alone or with a friend.

What should be done in the case of a juvenile charged with a serious felony and who also is deemed to be dangerous to society? In *Schall v. Martin*, 467 U.S.

253 (1984), the United States Supreme Court upheld a preventive detention statute applicable to juvenile court cases. In an opinion written by Justice Rehnquist, the Court made a number of observations that would be repeated a few years later in *Salerno*, discussed earlier in this chapter. Recognizing that the protection of the community from crime is a legitimate state objective, the Court found that interest sufficient to outweigh the juvenile's interest in freedom from restraint. And as the Court found later in *Salerno*, it concluded that the preventive detention statute was not being used or intended as punishment:

> First of all, the detention is strictly limited in time. If a juvenile is detained at his initial appearance and has denied the charges against him, he is entitled to a probable-cause hearing to be held not more than three days after the conclusion of the initial appearance or four days after the filing of the petition, whichever is sooner. If the Family Court judge finds probable cause, he must also determine whether continued detention is necessary.
>
> ... Detained juveniles are also entitled to an expedited factfinding hearing.
>
> ... The conditions of confinement also appear to reflect the regulatory purposes relied upon by the State. When a juvenile is remanded after his initial appearance, he cannot, absent exceptional circumstances, be sent to a prison or lockup where he would be exposed to adult criminals.

Id. at 269–270.

Justices Marshall, Brennan and Stevens dissented, arguing that the harm to minors outweighed the public purpose advanced by this statute.

J. Ethical Issues

Pretrial release can raise ethical issues for lawyers. In significant part, concerns can stem from the typically one-sided nature of bail hearings: as noted earlier, counsel is very often not afforded the defendant at this early stage of the proceedings. A prosecutor and judge (and sometimes only a judge) are present. In the event defense counsel is not present, the prosecutor must assuredly serve as an advocate for the government, yet according to one commentator, also must serve "as a surrogate defense attorney." Sandra Guerra Thompson, *Do Prosecutors Really Matter?: A Proposal to Ban One-Sided Bail Hearings*, 44 Hofstra L. Rev. 1161, 1162 (2016). In the context of pretrial release, the American Bar Association has adopted the following standard for prosecutors:

> (a) The prosecutor should favor pretrial release of a criminally accused, unless detention is necessary to protect individuals or the community or to ensure the return of the defendant for future proceedings.
>
> (b) The prosecutor's decision to recommend pretrial release or seek detention should be based on the facts and circumstances of the defendant and the offense, rather than made categorically. The prosecutor should consider

> information relevant to these decisions from all sources, including the defendant.
>
> (c) The prosecutor should cooperate with pretrial services or other personnel who review or assemble information to be provided to the court regarding pretrial release determinations.
>
> (d) The prosecutor should be open to reconsideration of pretrial detention or release decisions based on changed circumstances, including an unexpectedly lengthy period of detention.

Am. Bar Assoc., Criminal Justice Standards for the Prosecution Function, Stnd. 3-5.2 (4th ed. 2015).

The Standards also speak to the duties of defense counsel. Once again, to the extent counsel is made available at the pretrial detention stage, the Standards provide that:

> (a) In every case where the client is detained, defense counsel should discuss with the client, as promptly as possible, the client's custodial or release status, and determine whether release, a change in release conditions, or less restrictive custodial conditions, should be sought. . . .
>
> (b) Counsel should investigate the factual predicate that has been advanced to support detention and custodial conditions, and not assume its accuracy.
>
> (c) Once counsel has sufficient command of the facts, counsel should approach the prosecutor to see if agreement to release or a change in release or custodial conditions can be negotiated and submitted for approval by the court.
>
> (d) If the prosecutor does not agree, counsel should submit to the court a statement of facts, legal argument, and proposed conditions if necessary, to support the client's release or a reduction in release or custodial conditions.
>
> * * *
>
> (g) Counsel should reevaluate the client's eligibility for release, or for reduced release or custodial conditions, at all significant states of a criminal matter and when there is any relevant change in facts or circumstances. Counsel should request reconsideration of detention or modification of conditions whenever it is in the client's best interests.

Am. Bar Assoc., Criminal Justice Standards for the Defense Function, Stnd. 4-3.2 (4th ed. 2015).

If a defendant has been released pending trial, what happens if he or she does not appear as scheduled? The ethical rules are strangely silent on the issue whether defense counsel must disclose the whereabouts of his or her client. The issue depends on the scope of the attorney's obligation of confidentiality. The American Trial Lawyer's Code of Conduct (issued in 1982 and thus far not formally adopted by any jurisdiction) reads confidentiality broadly. In an illustrative case, this Code states clearly that a lawyer, representing a client who has "jumped bail" and absconded, would commit a disciplinary violation by revealing the client's whereabouts. American Trial Lawyers Foundation, The American Lawyer's Code of Conduct, Illustrative Cases 1(h).

The American Bar Association's Model Rules of Professional Conduct takes a *permissive* approach to a lawyer's actions in such situations. Model Rule 1.6 permits an attorney:

> to reveal information relating to the representation of a client to the extent that the lawyer reasonably believes necessary, [*inter alia*], to prevent reasonably certain death or substantial bodily harm; to prevent the client from committing a crime or fraud that is reasonably certain to result in substantial injury to the financial interests or property of another and in furtherance of which the client has used or is using the lawyer's services; to prevent, mitigate or rectify substantial injury to the financial interests or property of another that is reasonably certain to result or has resulted from the client's commission of a crime or fraud in furtherance of which the client has used the lawyer's services; . . . to comply with other law or a court order.

Model Rules of Prof'l Conduct Rule 1.6 (2012). However, in all of these instances, the choice to reveal such information belongs to the attorney. Do you agree with the American Trial Lawyers Foundation's approach? Do you agree with the Model Rule's permissive standard? Would it matter whether absconding was a crime? Would it matter that the missing client is accused of a property crime or a violent crime?

Chapter 6

The First Evidentiary Hearing: The Preliminary Examination

A. Introduction

In many criminal cases, the defendant has a *preliminary examination* or, as it is sometimes called, a *preliminary hearing*, a *probable cause hearing*, an *examining trial*, a *PX*, a *prelim*, or a *bindover hearing*. Although whether and when this hearing occurs varies from case to case and jurisdiction to jurisdiction, typically the defendant will first have had an initial appearance, discussed in Chapter 4, during which the presiding judge or magistrate assesses the validity of any arrest and detention, informs the defendant of various rights, and schedules the preliminary examination in a few days or weeks. Occasionally, the initial appearance and preliminary examination are combined in one hearing.

The preliminary examination, an adversarial proceeding, is distinct from a "*Gerstein*" hearing that, while also assessing the existence of probable cause, typically occurs earlier (within 48 hours of arrest) and is non-adversarial in nature. *Gerstein* hearings are limited in their scope, simply testing the state's authority to lawfully detain an arrestee (who has been arrested without a warrant, based upon a probable cause determination by police), typically without defense counsel present. A preliminary examination, on the other hand, is intended to assess the validity of the charge(s) filed against a defendant, and defense counsel—the provision of which is assured by the Sixth Amendment—can take an active role in questioning witnesses put on by the government.

[1] Overview

As discussed more fully below, the primary purpose of the preliminary examination is to determine whether there is probable cause to send the case on for further proceedings. Weak cases, according to theory, should be screened out of the system so that the defendant and often the defendant's family do not have to suffer the many financial and emotional harms that accompany criminal prosecution. Of course, the preliminary examination also serves many other functions, some more important than the screening function. The screening function may have little actual relevance in the typical criminal case where the government's proof is so strong that probable cause is obviously present.

The preliminary examination resembles a bench trial. The defendant will be represented by counsel and the local prosecutor will present the government's case by calling one or more witnesses, who testify under oath. The defense may or may not elect to call witnesses or offer a defense. Typically, formal rules of evidence are not followed and the judge can base her probable cause determination on unlawfully secured evidence.

[2] Relationship to Grand Jury

If the judge in the preliminary examination finds sufficient probable cause that the crime occurred and the defendant committed it, the judge will make a formal finding that probable cause exists. Often this is referred to as a "bindover," meaning that the judge will bind (or turn) the case over to the grand jury or, in jurisdictions with a limited or nonexistent grand jury system, for an information (a formal accusation prepared and filed by the prosecutor) and trial.

It should be noted that the crime(s) bound over for further proceedings are not necessarily the same as those included in the initial complaint, discussed in Chapter 4. Sometimes the judge may bind over charges that were proven by probable cause at the preliminary hearing, even though they differed from those in the complaint. For an in-depth discussion of the importance of this "subconsitutional" check on prosecution authority, including state and federal law on the availability of the examinations and their governing provisions, see Andrew Manuel Crespo, *The Hidden Law of Plea Bargaining*, 118 Colum. L. Rev. 1303, 1340, 1352 (2018).

[a] Jurisdictions Where Grand Jury Indictment Is Unnecessary

Preliminary hearing after information filed by prosecutor. Roughly two-thirds of the states permit felony prosecutions to be brought by either an "information," filed by a prosecutor, or by a grand jury indictment (though several "information states" require indictment for death or life sentence cases). In these jurisdictions, charges most commonly result from the filing of an information, which is much more efficient and less resource-intensive for prosecutors than going before a grand jury.

When an information is filed, the defendant is entitled to a preliminary hearing to assess whether the charges are supported by probable cause. If probable cause is found, the case is scheduled for trial. In the event a case is initiated by a grand jury indictment, usually no preliminary examination will be held because the grand jury itself made a finding of probable cause to support the charge.

Information after preliminary hearing. If no information was filed before the preliminary hearing, often one must be filed after the hearing and before trial. Some locales limit the permissible scope of the information to those charges for which probable cause was found at the preliminary hearing or to charges "related to" the bound-over charges. Thus, in these jurisdictions the preliminary hearing may limit the scope of subsequent formal charges.

[b] When Grand Jury Is Used

In those jurisdictions using the grand jury, usually the next step after a preliminary hearing is for the grand jury, discussed in Chapter 7, to consider the case. As strange as it may seem, the grand jury will then make a second, seemingly redundant, probable cause determination, returning an indictment only if the proof establishes probable cause to believe a crime was committed and the defendant was the culprit.

[3] Often the Only Adversarial Proceeding

The preliminary examination can be a very important procedural facet of a criminal case. Not only does it present the accused with an opportunity to learn about some of the prosecution's case and to attempt to have the case dismissed or charges reduced, it also may be the only adversary hearing that occurs in the entire case. Recall that the vast majority of criminal defendants in state and federal court eventually plead guilty. At the plea hearing (see Chapter 11), the defendant waives the right to trial and other related constitutional rights, and must aver that there exists a factual basis for the charge(s) to which the defendant will plead. Very often, the terms of the plea bargain have been agreed to by the prosecution and defense prior to the plea hearing. The judge's acceptance of the plea and ratification of the plea agreement are most often a mere formality (except that, as discussed in Chapter 11, the judge must take pains to ensure that the guilty plea is entered knowingly, intelligently, and voluntarily). Thus, the preliminary examination may actually have been the only opportunity for the defendant and the presiding judge alike to hear an adversarial presentation of the case and assess the strength of the prosecution's evidence. For an in-depth discussion of the importance of this "subconstitutional check" on prosecutors constitutional authority, see Andrew Manual Crespo, *The Hidden Law of Plea Bargaining*, 118 Colum. L. Rev. 1303, 1340–52 (2018).

[4] Preliminary Hearing as "Critical Stage"

Coleman v. Alabama

399 U.S. 1 (1970)

Mr. Justice Brennan announced the judgment of the Court and delivered the following opinion.

Petitioners were convicted in an Alabama Circuit Court of assault with intent to murder in the shooting of one Reynolds after he and his wife parked their car on an Alabama highway to change a flat tire.

... Petitioners ... argue that the preliminary hearing prior to their indictment was a "critical stage" of the prosecution and that Alabama's failure to provide them with appointed counsel at the hearing therefore unconstitutionally denied them the assistance of counsel.

II

Mr. Justice Douglas, Mr. Justice White, and Mr. Justice Marshall join Part II.

... This Court has held that a person accused of crime "requires the guiding hand of counsel at every step in the proceedings against him," *Powell v. Alabama*, 287 U.S. 45, 69 (1932), and that that constitutional principle is not limited to the presence of counsel at trial. "It is central to that principle that in addition to counsel's presence at trial, the accused is guaranteed that he need not stand alone against the State at any stage of the prosecution, formal or informal, in court or out, where counsel's absence might derogate from the accused's right to a fair trial." *United States v. Wade*, 388 U.S. 218, 226 (1967). Accordingly, "the principle of *Powell v. Alabama* and succeeding cases requires that we scrutinize any pretrial confrontation of the accused to determine whether the presence of his counsel is necessary to preserve the defendant's basic right to a fair trial as affected by his right meaningfully to cross-examine the witnesses against him and to have effective assistance of counsel at the trial itself. It calls upon us to analyze whether potential substantial prejudice to defendant's rights inheres in the particular confrontation and the ability of counsel to help avoid that prejudice." *Id.* at 227. Applying this test, the Court has held that "critical stages" include the pretrial type of arraignment where certain rights may be sacrificed or lost, and the pretrial lineup....

The preliminary hearing is not a required step in an Alabama prosecution. The prosecutor may seek an indictment directly from the grand jury without a preliminary hearing. The opinion of the Alabama Court of Appeals in this case instructs us that under Alabama law the sole purposes of a preliminary hearing are to determine whether there is sufficient evidence against the accused to warrant presenting his case to the grand jury and, if so, to fix bail if the offense is bailable. The court continued:

> ... At the preliminary hearing ... the accused is not required to advance any defenses, and failure to do so does not preclude him from availing himself of every defense he may have upon the trial of the case. Also *Pointer v. State*, 380 U.S. 400 (1965) bars the admission of testimony given at a pretrial proceeding where the accused did not have the benefit of cross-examination by and through counsel. Thus, nothing occurring at the preliminary hearing in absence of counsel can substantially prejudice the rights of the accused on trial.

This Court is of course bound by this construction of the governing Alabama law. However, from the fact that in cases where the accused has no lawyer at the hearing the Alabama courts prohibit the State's use at trial of anything that occurred at the hearing, it does not follow that the Alabama preliminary hearing is not a "critical stage" of the State's criminal process.... Plainly the guiding hand of counsel at the preliminary hearing is essential to protect the indigent accused against an erroneous or improper prosecution. First, the lawyer's skilled examination and cross-examination of witnesses may expose fatal weaknesses in the State's case that may lead the magistrate to refuse to bind the accused over. Second, in any event, the skilled interrogation of witnesses by an experienced lawyer can fashion a vital impeachment tool for use in cross-examination of the State's witnesses at the trial, or preserve testimony favorable to the accused of a witness who does not appear at the trial. Third, trained counsel can more effectively discover the case the State has against his client and make possible the preparation of a proper defense to meet that case at the trial. Fourth, counsel can also be influential at the preliminary hearing in making effective arguments for the accused on such matters as the necessity for an early psychiatric examination or bail.

The inability of the indigent accused on his own to realize these advantages of a lawyer's assistance compels the conclusion that the Alabama preliminary hearing is a "critical stage" of the State's criminal process at which the accused is "as much entitled to such aid (of counsel) . . . as at the trial itself." *Powell v. Alabama*, 287 U.S. at 57.

III

Mr. Justice Black, Mr. Justice Douglas, Mr. Justice White, and Mr. Justice Marshall join Part III.

There remains, then, the question of the relief to which petitioners are entitled.

. . . We accordingly vacate the petitioners' convictions and remand the case to the Alabama courts for such proceedings not inconsistent with this opinion as they may deem appropriate to determine whether such denial of counsel was harmless error and therefore whether the convictions should be reinstated or a new trial ordered.

[Omitted are the concurring opinions of Justices Black, Douglas, and White; the concurring and dissenting opinion of Justice Harlan; and the dissenting opinions of Chief Justice Burger and Justice Stewart.]

Notes

1. *Critical stage.* Because, according to the Supreme Court, the preliminary hearing is a "critical stage" of the criminal process that serves a number of important functions, such that it triggers the right to counsel under the Sixth Amendment, should it be constitutionally required by the due process guarantee of a fair trial? If so, every state would have to have a preliminary hearing (or the equivalent) as part of its criminal procedures.

2. *Function of counsel.* In *Coleman*, the Supreme Court recognized that counsel at an Alabama preliminary hearing serves many important functions. Most of these are "unofficial" in that no rule of criminal procedure specifically assigns them as functions of counsel. The functions of counsel listed in *Coleman* are to: (1) expose weaknesses in the prosecution's evidence so the case can be dismissed; (2) preserve helpful testimony and fashion impeachment evidence for use at trial; (3) discover the prosecution's case to assist in trial preparation; and (4) make arguments on such matters as bail and the need for psychiatric evaluation. Has *Coleman* elevated these

functions to the status of constitutional rights, so that the defendant cannot be denied the opportunity (within reasonable limits) to use the preliminary examination for discovery, evidence preservation, and gathering information for impeachment at trial?

3. *Benefits of counsel. Coleman* deals with some possible advantages accruing from a preliminary examination where the defendant is represented by counsel. Are there other advantages that the *Coleman* Court ignored? Did *Coleman* ignore some harms that could occur if the defendant has a preliminary examination without benefit of a defense lawyer?

4. *Harmless error.* You will recall that the principal purpose of the preliminary examination is to determine whether there is probable cause to charge the defendant with a criminal offense. There appears to be no challenge in the *Coleman* case to the fact that petitioners, later at trial, were found guilty beyond a reasonable doubt of assault with intent to murder. Given a conviction, in what way could it be argued that denial of counsel at the preliminary examination constituted anything other than harmless error?

B. Functions and Strategies

The preliminary examination serves a number of functions, some obvious and others quite subtle. The strategy a lawyer adopts for the hearing depends on the functions the hearing is to serve in the case.

[1] Screening

There is general agreement that the primary function of the preliminary examination is to protect individuals from having to defend themselves against charges that are insubstantial or are brought carelessly or maliciously. The charges are dismissed if the preliminary hearing judge finds the government did not establish probable cause to believe that the defendant committed a crime. Federal Rule of Criminal Procedure 5.1(f), for instance, provides that "[i]f the magistrate judge finds no probable cause to believe an offense has been committed or the defendant committed it, the magistrate judge must dismiss the complaint and discharge the defendant. A discharge does not preclude the government from later prosecuting the defendant for the same offense."

The preliminary examination thus performs a screening function—sifting out weak cases that should be dismissed in an already overcrowded criminal justice system. According to an important study of the preliminary hearing, "[t]he pretrial screening decisions are designed not only to save the government and the accused from incurring unnecessary expense, but also to protect the accused from unfounded and malicious allegations, thereby avoiding the anxiety and embarrassment of trial."

Deborah Day Emerson & Nancy L. Ames, The Role of the Grand Jury and the Preliminary Hearing in Pretrial Screening 3 (National Institute of Justice 1984). The preliminary examination may also spare the accused from unwarranted pretrial detention.

Logically, if the prosecution cannot offer enough proof to satisfy the probable cause standard, then there is too little justification to retain the case in the criminal justice system, since it would be unlikely that the state could later satisfy the higher trial standard of proof beyond a reasonable doubt. Certainly the state would have to offer more convincing proof at trial than it presented at the preliminary examination.

Tactical considerations. If the defense strategy at the preliminary examination is to seek a dismissal or reduction of charges, counsel should vigorously object to inadmissible evidence and aggressively cross-examine prosecution witnesses. In unusual cases, defense counsel pursuing this strategy may even elect to offer proof and consider recommending that the client testify at the preliminary examination. Often this defense proof is offered only after defense counsel has tried unsuccessfully to have the case dismissed at the end of the prosecution's side of the case.

However, if, as is often the case, a finding of probable cause appears to be a foregone conclusion, then the preliminary hearing becomes more useful to the defense as a discovery vehicle than as a screening device.

[2] Discovery

Although the screening function is everywhere given as the primary (or even the sole) purpose of the preliminary examination, experienced prosecutors and criminal defense lawyers realize that another critical function is discovery by the defendant.

Limited discovery. Formal discovery is quite limited in criminal cases in virtually every jurisdiction (see Chapter 10). Usually such devices as interrogatories and depositions are either unavailable or severely limited in criminal cases. *See, e.g.*, Fed. R. Crim. P. 15 (depositions available only in extraordinary circumstances to preserve testimony). Moreover, informal discovery opportunities may also be severely limited. For example, crime victims and investigating police officers may refuse to talk with defense counsel about the crime. This means that defense counsel could first learn about their testimony when the victim or officer testifies on direct examination during the trial. The use of the preliminary examination as a discovery tool is less effective if, as discussed below, the jurisdiction permits probable cause to be established by hearsay. In such jurisdictions, one witness may summarize the testimony of many people who will not testify in person at the preliminary examination.

Tactics to obtain discovery at preliminary examination. Since this dearth of information makes it difficult to prepare for trial, defense counsel (and sometimes the prosecution) will use the preliminary examination as a vehicle to learn about the other side's case. One way is for defense counsel to listen carefully to (and sometimes cross-examine) the prosecution witnesses who testify at the preliminary examination. A related, and sometimes dangerous, way is for the preliminary hearing defense counsel to call as *defense* witnesses those people who are likely to testify for the prosecution at trial but will not be called as prosecution witnesses at the preliminary examination. This may be especially appealing if the witness has refused to talk with defense counsel during the investigation of the case. Many judges dislike this tactic and will only allow the defense to call as witnesses at a preliminary hearing those persons "whose proposed testimony would be reasonably likely to establish an affirmative defense, negate a crime element, or impeach prosecution evidence." *People v. Erwin*, 20 Cal. App. 4th 1542 (1993).

In questioning prosecution witnesses, often defense counsel will probe rather than challenge, trying to get as much information as possible from each prosecution witness. For example, counsel for the defense may ask prosecution witnesses to give the names and addresses of everyone they know who has information about the event (to help locate new defense witnesses and be better prepared for unknown prosecution witnesses); to relate the witness's own history of drugs, criminal convictions, and psychological problems (to use to impeach the witness at trial); and to describe in minute detail the facts the witness knows about (to facilitate preparation for trial, perhaps by spotting a slight inconsistency or vagueness).

There are many risks when the defense lawyer calls a likely prosecution witness as a defense witness at a preliminary hearing. Unless the judge permits the witness to be declared a hostile witness, defense counsel may be limited to non-leading questions, while the prosecutor will be permitted to reshape the direct testimony by asking leading questions on cross examination. And, of course, the defense lawyer could inadvertently provide the prosecution with the name and testimony of a most helpful prosecution witness.

Jencks Act (Fed. Crim. P. Rule 26.2). Another opportunity for discovery in federal cases by both sides is provided by the so-called Jencks Act or Rule 26.2 of the Federal Rules of Criminal Procedure. *See* Fed. R. Crim. P. 5.1(h) & 26.2(g)(1). (Rule 26.2 is discussed further in Chapter 10.) This rule, also applicable at trial, gives either side the right to examine and use any statement of a testifying witness that relates to the subject of the testimony and is in the possession of the party calling that witness. The statement must be made available, however, only *after* the witness has testified at the preliminary examination, but of course can be provided earlier. Thus, if the prosecution calls an eyewitness to testify at a preliminary hearing, after that witness has testified the prosecution, under Rule 26.2, must give the defense lawyer access to any statement the eyewitness made that is relevant to the testimony. The prosecution can avoid this obligation by electing not to call the eyewitness as a witness at the preliminary examination. Rule 5.1(h) also gives the judge the discretion to not require the production of these statements "for good cause shown."

Limiting "fishing expeditions." At some point the judge or prosecutor may attempt to stop what may be characterized as a defense "fishing expedition," citing the basic rule that the preliminary examination is not designed to provide discovery. *See, e.g.*, Cal. Penal Code § 866 (preliminary examination "shall not be used for purposes of discovery"). Often this argument is made after the prosecutor believes that he or she has offered sufficient proof to satisfy the probable cause standard. If the court agrees, defense counsel then will have to curtail questions that have virtually nothing to do with the presence or absence of probable cause. A typical judicial endorsement of the anti-fishing expedition view has been stated as follows:

> The mission of the hearing is an investigation into probable cause for further proceedings against the accused. It does not include discovery for the sake of discovery. To be sure, the evidence the Government offers to establish probable cause is by nature also discovery for the accused. So also is information adduced on cross-examination of Government witnesses on the aspects of direct-examination testimony tending to build up probable cause. In those senses, some discovery becomes a by-product of the process of demonstrating probable cause. But in no sense is discovery a legitimate end unto itself.

Coleman v. Burnett, 477 F.2d 1187, 1199–1200 (D.C. Cir. 1973).

Because it is no secret that the preliminary examination can help the defense learn about the prosecution's evidence and strategy, the prosecutor will often offer only a bare-bones case at the preliminary examination so that the defense receives only minimal discovery. Commonly, for example, the prosecution's case at the preliminary examination will consist of only a small number of the witnesses it plans to use later at trial. Sometimes only one prosecution witness will testify. Similarly, the defense usually offers few or no witnesses of its own, and may try not to disclose its theory of the case and its likely defenses.

[3] Preserve Testimony

The preliminary examination also serves to preserve testimony for use at trial. A preliminary examination will routinely satisfy the former testimony hearsay exception, permitting a record (or even memory) of the preliminary examination testimony to be used as proof in the later trial if the witness who testified at the preliminary examination becomes unavailable to testify at the later trial and the defendant had an opportunity to cross examine the witness at the hearing. *See, e.g.*, Fed. R. Evid. 804(b)(1). The Confrontation Clause is also satisfied by this use of the preliminary examination. *Crawford v. Washington*, 541 U.S. 36 (2004).

The prosecution in particular may utilize the preliminary examination to preserve testimony if, for example, a prosecution witness is dying or, for any number of reasons, the prosecution suspects the witness may not testify at trial despite being subpoenaed to do so. Of course, in these same cases the defense may prefer that the witness not testify at the preliminary examination so that the witness's testimony at that proceeding cannot be used later at trial if the witness is unavailable at trial. This could occur, for example, if a key government witness were terminally ill. If the witness does not testify at the preliminary examination and dies before trial, the prosecution may be barred from using the witness' statements to the police as evidence at trial. In those few jurisdictions that do not require a formal record of preliminary examinations, counsel must ensure that a proper record is made if the evidence is to be preserved for later use. A stenographic or audio record may also aid in the use of information discovered during the hearing. An indigent defendant may have to file a motion to have the government pay the costs of the transcription.

[4] Test or Prepare Witness

Sometimes the preliminary examination will serve as a testing ground for witnesses. Counsel for either side can use the hearing to assess whether a particular witness comes across well or poorly, or is even willing to testify at all. The mere experience of testifying at the preliminary examination can also help the witness become more effective at trial. The preliminary examination can serve as a dry run so that at trial the witness is not answering questions for the first time. This may be especially important for the witness who will be vigorously cross-examined at trial and can benefit from a lifelike practice session. If a witness performs poorly, counsel will have time to better prepare the witness to testify at trial.

[5] Facilitate Later Impeachment

Witnesses at the preliminary examination are usually less prepared than those at trial because lawyers (usually the prosecution) spend less time "working up" the case at the early stages. This means that defense counsel at the preliminary examination may be successful in eliciting contradictory statements or perhaps ambiguous or ambivalent shadings to questions on cross-examination. At the least, counsel may be able to pin down a preliminary examination witness so that the witness may be impeached at trial if he or she deviates from the preliminary examination testimony. Of course, this cross-examination may also cause a witness to become a better trial witness who is even more convinced of the accuracy of his or her observations.

[6] Solidify Identification

The preliminary hearing can also be used, particularly by the prosecution, to solidify a witness's identification of the accused. The process of viewing and identifying the accused during the preliminary hearing provides the witness with an additional opportunity to feel comfortable with the identification that will be sought during the subsequent criminal trial. The obvious danger that an identification made during a preliminary examination could be improperly suggestive prompted the United States Supreme Court to hold that a criminal defendant has a Sixth Amendment right to counsel at a preliminary examination where the victim will make an in-court identification of the alleged offender. In *Moore v. Illinois*, 434 U.S. 220, 229–30 (1977), the Supreme Court observed:

> It is difficult to imagine a more suggestive manner in which to present a suspect to a witness for their critical first confrontation than was employed in this case. The [rape] victim, who had seen her assailant for only 10 to 15 seconds, was asked to make her identification after she was told that she was going to view a suspect, after she was told his name and heard it called as he was led before the bench [at the preliminary examination], and after she heard the prosecutor recite the evidence believed to implicate petitioner. Had petitioner been represented by counsel, some or all of this suggestiveness could have been avoided.

[7] Send Message to Witness

Some attorneys use the preliminary examination as a vehicle to communicate with a witness. During direct or cross-examination, counsel will let the witness know that certain subjects will be explored or that the cross-examination will be detailed and hostile. This may induce the witness to rethink his or her testimony. Of course it may also alert the witness or witness' counsel about weaknesses in the testimony and provide an opportunity to eliminate or at least minimize the weakness at the subsequent trial. Can an ethical lawyer use this opportunity to intimidate a witness so that the witness will change testimony or decline to testify at trial?

[8] "Reality Therapy" for Defendant

A criminal defendant may actually or apparently be convinced that he or she has a viable defense or that the prosecution's case is weak. Conversely, the defendant may believe that the prosecution's case is overwhelming. In either event, the defense or prosecution may use the preliminary examination to help demonstrate to the client the strength or weakness of the prosecution or defense's case. For example, the victim may testify at the preliminary hearing and appear as a credible, convincing witness or as an unsure, weak one. This "reality therapy" may convince the defendant to be honest with defense counsel or to rethink the defendant's response to plea bargain offers.

[9] Affect Plea Bargaining

Because the overwhelming number of criminal defendants, including those who have a preliminary examination, will eventually plead guilty, the preliminary examination may have an important impact on plea negotiations. One way is that it may help either side assess its likely success if the case were to go to trial. For example, the preliminary examination may apprise the defense that the prosecution witnesses are quite strong or quite weak. In either event, the defense will have new information to use in forming its plea bargaining strategy and in deciding whether to accept or reject a plea. And, as noted above, it may provide "reality therapy" for the defendant who has steadfastly disbelieved defense counsel's assessment of the prosecution's case. Overwhelming caseloads may lead some prosecutors to offer more lenient sentences to offenders who save the prosecution time by waiving the preliminary examination.

[10] Affect Bail Decision

The preliminary examination may also affect the bail decision. By the time of the preliminary examination, it is likely that a decision will already have been made on whether the defendant will remain in custody until the trial. The conditions of release will have been set and often satisfied. But the initial bail decision may have been made on little information and can always be reopened by either the defense or prosecution on the basis of new data. If such information is presented at the preliminary examination, the judge is authorized to alter the initial release decision. For example, if the prosecution's preliminary examination proof turns out to be quite weak and a conviction is doubtful, the court may lower the defendant's money bond or alleviate some of the harsh release conditions. On the other hand, if a preliminary examination witness testifies that the defendant has close associates who live in another country and has secreted a good bit of money, the judge may increase the amount of the bond or forbid release entirely.

[11] Diversion

In some jurisdictions a court may use the preliminary examination to have the defendant enter a diversion program which, if successfully completed, will result in a dismissal of the charges. The defendant may be required to waive the preliminary examination in order to participate. Peggy Fulton Hora, et al., *Therapeutic Jurisprudence and the Drug Treatment Court Movement*, 74 Notre Dame L. Rev. 439, 495 (1999).

C. Procedures

Although the preliminary examination is an adversary hearing, it differs in many ways from a criminal trial.

[1] Governing Rules

The preliminary examination is routinely described in general terms in a jurisdiction's rules of criminal procedure. These rules usually describe at least some of the procedures that are applicable. Federal Rule of Criminal Procedure 5.1(e), for instance, provides that: "the defendant may cross-examine adverse witnesses and may introduce evidence but may not object to evidence on the ground that it was unlawfully acquired. If the magistrate judge finds probable cause to believe an offense has been committed and the defendant committed it, the magistrate judge must promptly require the defendant to appear for further proceedings."

[2] Entitlement

Since there is no federal constitutional right to a preliminary examination, jurisdictions vary considerably in their approach to providing the defendant access to a preliminary examination. To a large extent the issue depends on whether the jurisdiction utilizes the grand jury. As noted earlier, most states permit a prosecution to be pursued by either an indictment or an information. As discussed in Chapter 7, an *indictment* is a finding by a grand jury that there is probable cause to believe a crime occurred and the defendant is the person who committed it. An information is the same, except it represents a finding by the prosecuting attorney rather than by a group of citizens who constitute the grand jury.

With the exception of the practice in a few states, the right to a preliminary examination is restricted to felonies. Paul G. Cassell & Thomas E. Goodwin, *Protecting Taxpayers and Crime Victims: The Case for Restricting Utah's Preliminary Hearings to Felony Offenses*, 2011 UTAH L. REV. 1377, 1383 (noting that only five states allow preliminary examinations for misdemeanors of some kind).

Effect of indictment. Typically, as Federal Rule of Criminal Procedure 5.1(a) exemplifies, a defendant has a right to a preliminary examination unless there has been an indictment. Once a grand jury has issued an indictment usually the defendant is no longer entitled to have a preliminary examination. *See* 18 U.S.C. § 3060(e). The grand jury's decision that there is probable cause to indict is deemed sufficient to protect the defendant's interest in having weak cases removed from the system. In jurisdictions following this model, the prosecutor can prevent the defendant from having a preliminary examination by submitting the case to the grand jury before there has been a preliminary examination. Some prosecutors have even requested a delay in the scheduled date of the preliminary examination in order to enable the grand jury to consider the case first. If the grand jury issues an indictment, the preliminary examination is then canceled.

Equal protection. Obviously, the preliminary examination, which is adversarial, affords the defendant many advantages unavailable if the hearing is replaced by a grand jury indictment, which is the product of a secret, nonadversarial procedure virtually unregulated by the judiciary. In *Hawkins v. Superior Court*, 586 P.2d 916 (Cal. 1978), the California Supreme Court held that California's equal protection guarantee gives the indicted citizen a right to a post-indictment preliminary examination if there was no such examination before the indictment. This procedure equalized the rights of all criminal defendants by providing them all with the opportunity to have a preliminary examination. *Cf. State v. Sanabria*, 474 A.2d

760 (Conn. 1984) (state constitution mandates preliminary hearing in most serious cases). *Hawkins* has been widely rejected by other state courts. In California, public outcry against *Hawkins* resulted in an amendment to the California Constitution that barred a post-indictment preliminary hearing. *See Bowens v. Superior Court (People)*, 820 P.2d 600 (Cal. 1991). Despite the demise of *Hawkins* in California (*Hawkins* was eventually abrogated by the California Supreme Court itself, *Strauss v. Horton*, 207 P.3d 48 (Cal. 2009)), considering the fact that the preliminary hearing actually does provide the accused with many benefits, wasn't *Hawkins* correct in recognizing that defendants deprived of the hearing because of a prior indictment are at a considerable disadvantage? Is the disadvantage so important that it creates an equal protection violation?

Use of grand jury. Studies show that prosecutors vary considerably in the percentage of cases taken directly to the grand jury. One report showed that in one large county a preliminary hearing was scheduled in a majority of cases, while in another large county of the same state the preliminary hearing was scheduled infrequently (6% of the cases) and the grand jury was relied upon as a replacement. Deborah Day Emerson & Nancy L. Ames, The Role of the Grand Jury and the Preliminary Hearing in Pretrial Screening 32, 41 (1984). Some prosecutors, as a matter of policy, prefer to take all felony cases directly to the grand jury and thereby deprive defendants of the opportunity for a preliminary hearing. This practice of "direct indictment" may seem harsh, but it does not violate any constitutional rights of a defendant because, as previously discussed, there is no federal constitutional right to a preliminary examination.

Preliminary examination after information. As noted above, in some jurisdictions the prosecutor has the option of using the grand jury or relying on an information. Because the issuance of an information requires no real screening by anyone outside the prosecutor's office, virtually all states permitting prosecution by information give the accused the right to a preliminary examination, at least in felony cases, if an information is used in lieu of a grand jury. If probable cause is found at this preliminary hearing, the case is "bound over" for trial. Of course, if an indictment rather than information is obtained in these jurisdictions, the defendant usually loses the right to have a preliminary examination, but may still be entitled to a so-called *Gerstein* determination, discussed in Chapter 4, to assess the validity of pretrial detention. *Gerstein v. Pugh*, 420 U.S. 103 (1975).

[3] Timing

Many jurisdictions specify that the preliminary examination must be held a certain number of days after arrest or after the initial appearance. For example, Federal Rule 5.1(c) and many similar state provisions provide that the preliminary examination must be held no later than 14 days after the initial appearance if the defendant is in custody and not more than 21 days if not in custody. *See also* 18 U.S.C. § 3060(b); Cal. Penal Code § 859b (not less than two days or more than 10, with exceptions;

complaint dismissed if preliminary hearing not held within 60 days). These deadlines can be waived with the defendant's consent. Sometimes the time limits can be extended by the judge for good cause. *See, e.g.*, 18 U.S.C. §3060(c) (extraordinary circumstances exist and delay is indispensable to the interests of justice). Both prosecution and defense may also—and frequently do—request a continuance.

[4] Length

Preliminary hearings usually are fairly brief. Although available studies on the question are rather dated, they suggest that hearing times averaged from 30 to 45 minutes. Deborah Day Emerson & Nancy L. Ames, The Role of the Grand Jury and the Preliminary Hearing in Pretrial Screening 52 (1984); Kenneth Graham & Leon Letwin, *The Preliminary Hearings in Los Angeles: Some Field Findings and Legal-Policy Observations*, 18 U.C.L.A. L. Rev. 636 (1971); Janet A. Gilboy, *Prosecutors' Discretionary Use of the Grand Jury to Initiate or to Reinitiate Prosecution*, 1984 A. Bar Found. Res. J. 1, 22 (preliminary hearing in ordinary murder case in Chicago takes 20–30 minutes).

[5] Waiver

If the defendant is entitled to a preliminary examination, ordinarily he or she may elect to waive the proceeding and proceed directly to a later stage, perhaps the grand jury, arraignment, trial, or sentencing hearing. The waiver must be knowing, intelligent, and voluntary.

Procedures. Ordinarily the waiver must be in writing and is formalized in open court. A small minority of jurisdictions mandate that defense counsel approve any such waiver. *See Esparaza v. State*, 595 So. 2d 418 (Miss. 1992) (defense counsel approval of waiver required by statute). There is little judicial guidance on the standards of waiver of the preliminary examination. The ordinary standard for waiver of important rights is that the waiver must be knowing, intelligent, and voluntary. In some jurisdictions, however, a waiver is inferred if the defendant proceeds further into the criminal justice system without requesting a preliminary examination. *See, e.g., Flowers v. Wyrick*, 732 F.2d 659 (8th Cir. 1984), *cert. denied*, 469 U.S. 848 (1984) (guilty plea constitutes waiver of objection to lack of preliminary examination or does not appear for the scheduled examination); *State v. Kenney*, 973 S.W.2d 536 (Mo. Ct. App. 1998) (lack of preliminary examination waived once defendant proceeds to trial without making objection); *People v. Abbott*, 638 P.2d 781 (Colo. 1981) ("implied waiver" found).

Tactical considerations. As discussed above, there are many tactical considerations in the decision whether to waive the preliminary examination. Because of the many advantages to the defense, many experienced criminal defense lawyers caution against waiver of a preliminary examination. But waiver may make sense in certain situations when the costs of the hearing exceed its benefits. Sometimes, the defendant will waive the preliminary examination as part of a deal with the prosecutor who agrees to accept a more lenient sentence in exchange for not having to spend time preparing for and conducting the preliminary examination, or who agrees to recommend release on bail if the preliminary examination is waived.

A preliminary examination could also be waived by the defense in cases where it would serve no purpose, such as where the facts are undisputed. Another ground is when the preliminary examination would actually be harmful to the defense. Perhaps it would provide too much information to the prosecution, solidify the testimony of a weak prosecution witness, preserve the testimony of an important prosecution witness who may not appear at trial, alert the prosecution to the fact the accused is charged with less serious crimes than the proof would establish, cause a witness (perhaps the victim) to get angry and become resolved to harm the defense's interests at trial, or breed too much adverse publicity that can compromise the likelihood of a fair trial or will cause an unacceptable level of embarrassment to the defendant or the defendant's family, or will induce a reconsideration of an earlier decision to release the offender on favorable bail conditions.

[6] Evidence and Witnesses

Rules of evidence. Although a preliminary examination is an adversary proceeding, jurisdictions differ in whether the formal rules of evidence apply. Of course the rules of privilege apply in all jurisdictions. A few jurisdictions also apply the full range of evidence rules so that whatever evidence is admissible at the preliminary examination would also be admissible at trial. Most, however, apply a watered-down set of evidence rules, admitting evidence that would not necessarily be admissible at a criminal trial. *See, e.g.,* Fed. R. Evid. 1101(d)(3) (rules of evidence except for privileges do not apply at preliminary examination). Hearsay, by the same token, is also often admissible. *See, e.g.,* Cal. Penal Code § 872(b) (at preliminary examination experienced law enforcement officer may relate hearsay statements); N.Y. Crim. Proc. L. § 180.60(8) (hearsay reports of experts and some sworn statements that court finds "sufficiently reliable" admissible at preliminary examination); Wis. Stat. § 970.038 ("A court may base its finding of probable cause . . . in whole or part on hearsay"). Indeed, in some jurisdictions the finding of probable cause may be based entirely on hearsay.

Exclusionary rule. Many statutes or criminal procedure rules also provide that the rule excluding unconstitutionally obtained evidence does not apply at a preliminary examination. *See, e.g.,* Federal Rule of Criminal Procedure 5.1(e) (defendant may not object to the introduction of evidence at the preliminary hearing on the ground that it was unlawfully acquired).

Policy issues. Lax evidence rules at the preliminary examination raise several interesting questions about the role of the preliminary examination as a screening device. There are good reasons why the preliminary hearing should adhere to the same evidence rules as the trial court. Indeed, if the purpose of the preliminary examination is to screen out weak cases, why admit less reliable evidence at the preliminary hearing than at trial? If at the preliminary examination the state cannot establish probable cause by producing evidence that conforms with the constitution and the rules of evidence, can it meet the higher standard of proof beyond a reasonable doubt later at trial when it must adhere to the higher evidence rules?

On the other hand, there are also reasons why the lower standard makes sense. It is well established that the grand jury likewise can consider evidence that does not comply with some constitutional provisions or the rules of evidence. If the preliminary examination uses the rules of evidence but the grand jury does not, would prosecutors be more inclined to use the grand jury in lieu of the preliminary hearing? If so, the preliminary examination's role as a protection against unwarranted prosecution would be greatly diminished. In addition, what impact would formalizing the admissibility of evidence have on the already overwhelmed workload of some prosecutors?

Witnesses, cross-examination, and documentary evidence. Witnesses at preliminary examinations routinely testify under oath and virtually all witnesses can be excluded ("*sequestered*") from the courtroom during testimony by other witnesses. Indeed, in some jurisdictions the general public can also be excluded during some or all of the preliminary examination in narrowly circumscribed circumstances where no other reasonable alternative can protect the defendant's interests in a fair trial. *See Press-Enterprise Co. v. Superior Court*, 478 U.S. 1 (1986) (preliminary examinations in California may be closed to the public only if there are specific findings that defendant's right to a fair trial would be prejudiced by publicity and that reasonable alternatives to closure will not adequately protect defendant's rights).

Both the defense and the prosecution ordinarily have the right to subpoena and to examine and cross-examine witnesses at the preliminary examination. Because the court is only assessing the existence of probable cause, some judges will exercise their discretion to cut off the cross-examination of prosecution witnesses once the state's proof has established probable cause. This is especially likely to occur if the judge believes that defense counsel is pursuing discovery rather than attempting to establish lack of probable cause. All witnesses, including the defendant, may assert their Fifth Amendment right to refuse to answer incriminating questions at the preliminary hearing. Although the defendant has the right to testify (by statute and perhaps constitution) or not testify (by statute and Fifth Amendment) at the preliminary examination, usually the defendant will not take the stand. If it is more likely that the defendant would have the case thrown out if he or she testifies at the preliminary examination, why do most criminal defendants still refuse to testify at this proceeding?

Problem 6-1. To Speak or Not to Speak

Kyle French had always been a bit strange. He had few friends, and was frequently observed talking to himself. He was known to be willing to fight anyone at any time, particularly when he was drunk. A month ago, Kyle got in a fight with Seth

Joiner at the Star Tavern. Joiner claims that he drew his knife to protect himself from French, and that he was then shot by French. No one witnessed the fight or the events preceding it. Defendant French maintains that he is not sure what happened, but thinks that Joiner called him names and attacked him with a knife. French has been charged with assault.

The preliminary hearing is scheduled for today. You are defense counsel. Should your client testify if you plan to argue that:

(1) he did not shoot Joiner? or

(2) he was insane at the time of the assault? or

(3) he shot Joiner in self-defense?

Empirical data. Research has shown that most preliminary hearings involve relatively few witnesses. One study of two populous Arizona counties reported that the average preliminary hearing involved two witnesses. If someone other than a law enforcement official testified, that person was likely to be the victim or an eyewitness. Approximately 99% of the witnesses were called by the prosecution. Rarely did either side introduce physical or documentary evidence at the preliminary hearing. Deborah Day Emerson & Nancy L. Ames, The Role of the Grand Jury and the Preliminary Hearing in Pretrial Screening 52–53, 57 (1984).

[7] Probable Cause

The preliminary examination determines whether at the time of the proceeding there is *probable cause* to believe (1) that a crime was committed, and (2) that the defendant committed the crime. The government has the burden of proof. Although there is no precise meaning for the term "probable cause," all jurisdictions agree that it requires less convincing proof than the "beyond the reasonable doubt" standard used in criminal trials. The judicial decisions are sparse and often unhelpful in defining the standard of proof.

People v. Ayala

770 P.2d 1265 (Colo. 1989)

Erickson, Justice:

The prosecution appeals the dismissal of an information charging defendant Anselmo Hijinio Ayala with theft by receiving. At the conclusion of the preliminary hearing, the information was dismissed by the trial judge because of the failure of the prosecution to establish probable cause that Ayala committed the crime charged. We affirm.

... Ayala and Anthony Wayne Johnson saw a 1983 Chevrolet Camaro in a field near the house where Ayala and Johnson were living. A man who was removing the parts from the Camaro identified himself as "Mike Klark." The affidavit of Officer Zabukovic, the investigating officer, states that Ayala told him that "Klark" informed him and codefendant, Anthony Johnson, that the Camaro belonged to "Klark's" brother, and that his brother had had problems with the automobile and that they were "stripping the vehicle out." Officer Zabukovic testified at the preliminary hearing that Ayala and Johnson told him that the Camaro was partially dismantled when they arrived at the lot and the dashboard and other items had been removed. "Klark" told Ayala and Johnson that they could purchase the automobile for $800. Ayala and Johnson returned to their home and obtained money to purchase the car, and both defendants contributed $400 to make up the $800 purchase price. They did not receive a title to the vehicle at that time. Both defendants told the police that at the time of the purchase, "Klark" gave them a phone number and said to call him to obtain the title to the Camaro. Nothing in the record establishes the precise extent of the disassembly or the condition of the Camaro when Ayala and Johnson first saw it.

Shortly thereafter, Ayala and Johnson were using a cutting torch to take the Camaro apart when a fuel line was cut causing the Camaro to go up in flames. The defendant called the fire department and cooperated in the subsequent police investigation. The police investigation disclosed that the automobile was stolen. After the police concluded that the identity and telephone number provided to Ayala and Johnson by "Mike Klark" were fictitious, a theft by receiving charge was filed.

A preliminary hearing is a screening device to determine whether there is probable cause to believe that the defendant committed the crime charged.... Greater evidentiary and procedural latitudes are permitted at a preliminary hearing because it is not a mini-trial. The sole issue at a preliminary hearing is whether probable cause exists to bind the accused over for trial.

To meet the standard of probable cause, there must be evidence sufficient to induce a person of ordinary prudence and caution conscientiously to entertain a reasonable belief that the defendant committed the crime charged. The evidence must be viewed in the light most favorable to the prosecution, and all inferences must be resolved in favor of the prosecution. The testimony of the investigating officer and the owner of the used car lot established the time of the theft and that the price set for the sale of the Camaro was $7,995. After hearing the testimony and the arguments of counsel, the trial court found that probable cause was not established and said:

> [THE COURT]: I appreciate what the standards are for the People to have this case bound over for trial at this stage of the proceedings.... The only evidence I have before me is that the vehicle was stolen. There's no indication that either Mr. Johnson or Mr. Ayala had anything to do with that consistent with that time period. Again, the only evidence ... as to how the parties came to have this car was that they contacted a person who was in a field parting the vehicle out and that the vehicle was partly dismantled at that time. And while I'm not saying that that is a perfectly plausible explanation as to what happened, that's what I have before me. It isn't a situation in which somebody came up to them and said, "Do you want to buy this

car," came by peddling the car or that the car was in good driving condition or fairly good driving condition or the same kind of condition as it came off the lot. The only evidence is that the car was being parted out and I don't know to what extent that was. The offense here requires not only a knowing act but also a specific intent. And I simply don't think that there's enough evidence, regardless of what reasonable suspicions there might be, I don't believe that there's enough evidence to bind the case over.

Based upon the evidence and the testimony I've heard, the case is dismissed for lack of probable cause. Mr. Ayala is discharged from his bond and the case is dismissed.

Section 18-4-410(1), 8B C.R.S. (1986), states, in part:

[A] person commits theft by receiving when he receives, retains, loans money by pawn or pledge on, or disposes of anything of value of another, *knowing or believing* that said thing of value has been stolen, and when he *intends* to deprive the lawful owner permanently of the use or benefit of the thing of value. (Emphasis added.)

It was incumbent [on] the prosecution to establish that Ayala, knowing and believing that the Camaro was stolen, intended to deprive the lawful owner of the Camaro. The record contains only the testimony of the owner of the used car lot and the investigating officer. The testimony establishes that the Camaro was priced at $7,995 on the used car lot at the time it was stolen. The remaining testimony describes the condition and the circumstances which led to the acquisition of the Camaro by Ayala and Johnson. The Camaro was inoperable and partially dismantled when it was purchased by Ayala and Johnson. Nothing in the record establishes whether $800 was an unreasonable price to pay for the partially dismantled and inoperable Camaro. Nothing appears in the record to show that Ayala and Johnson stole the vehicle. Therefore, as a basis for reversal we are asked to infer that a Camaro that had a price tag of $7,995 when stolen was worth more than $800 when acquired by the defendants. We must then infer that the purchase price caused Ayala to know or believe that the automobile was stolen. In *Tate v. People*, 125 Colo. 527, 247 P.2d 665 (1952), we said:

Presumption and inferences may be drawn only from facts established, and presumption may not rest on presumption or inference on inference . . . and this rule is doubly applicable in criminal cases.

Id. at 541, 247 P.2d at 672.

In *People v. Tumbarello*, 623 P.2d 46 (Colo. 1981), a theft by receiving case, we held that a "defendant's state of mind may be inferred from his conduct or from the circumstances of the case." *Tumbarello* is factually distinguishable from this case. In *Tumbarello*, the prosecution presented evidence that an undercover officer sold defendant goods which the officer represented as "hot" and "ripped off." From that evidence it could be reasonably inferred that defendant knew the goods were stolen.

Here, by contrast, any effort to infer that Ayala knew the Camaro was stolen would necessitate drawing an inference upon an inference.

As evidenced by the investigating officer's affidavit, both Ayala and Johnson gave independent and virtually identical accounts of the automobile purchase. There was no competent evidence presented at the hearing that Ayala knew or believed that the Camaro was stolen or that he intended to permanently deprive the lawful owner of the use of the automobile. The Camaro had been partially dismantled and was not operational at the time of the sale and had to be towed to a garage next to the Ayala and Johnson residence. Accordingly, the prosecution failed to establish that Ayala or Johnson knew the Camaro was stolen and had the requisite mens rea to commit theft by receiving when they took possession of the Camaro.

The prosecution claims that because the ownership of the automobile was transferred without title, it may be inferred that Ayala must have known the vehicle was stolen. Although Colorado requires the seller of a motor vehicle to transfer title to the vehicle at the time of sale, failure to deliver a certificate of title does not prevent the acquisition of ownership rights by the parties to the transaction. The mere fact that Ayala did not receive a certificate of title when he purchased the automobile does not establish probable cause that Ayala knew the vehicle was stolen.

Nothing in the record reflects an abuse of discretion by the trial court and the judgment of dismissal is accordingly affirmed.

Vollack, Justice, dissenting:

I respectfully dissent from the majority's affirmance of the trial court's dismissal of the information filed against the defendant.

The probable cause determination which must be met at a preliminary hearing requires sufficient evidence to induce a person of ordinary prudence and caution to a reasonable belief that the accused committed the crime charged. The prosecution is not required to present evidence sufficient to support a conviction. It is not for the trial judge at a preliminary hearing to accept the defendant's version of the facts over the legitimate inferences which can be drawn from the People's evidence, and a defendant's state of mind can be inferred from his conduct, or from the circumstances of the case.

The evidence presented at a preliminary hearing must be viewed in the light most favorable to the prosecution. The issue is not the defendant's innocence or guilt; the issue at a preliminary hearing is whether the evidence is sufficient to induce a person of ordinary prudence and caution to a reasonable belief that the defendant committed the crimes charged.

Applying these principles, I do not agree with the majority's conclusion that "the prosecution failed to establish that Ayala had the mens rea required to commit theft by receiving." The owner of the used car dealership testified at the preliminary hearing that the sale price of the 1983 Camaro at his lot was $7995. Even though the vehicle was only three years old when stolen, the defendant was given the opportunity to purchase it from a stranger, with no supporting paperwork, for $800. Acquisition of recently stolen property at a ridiculously low price from an unknown person is itself sufficient to support an inference that the one acquiring the property knew the property was stolen. *United States v. Prazak*, 623 F.2d 152, 154–55 (10th Cir.), *cert. denied*, 449 U.S. 880 (1980). Reviewing the testimony in the light most favorable to the prosecution, I would conclude that the prosecution met its burden of establishing probable cause. Based on the testimony at the preliminary hearing, I would let the jury assess the witnesses' credibility and decide whether the requisite mens rea has been established beyond a reasonable doubt. . . .

Notes

1. *Definition of probable cause. Ayala* joins many jurisdictions in holding that probable cause means "there must be evidence sufficient to induce a person of ordinary prudence and caution conscientiously to entertain a reasonable belief that the defendant committed the crime charged." This differs markedly from the trial jury's role of finding guilt only if proof rises to the level of establishing guilt beyond a reasonable doubt. Is the *Ayala* court's test sufficiently rigorous to protect the accused from unwarranted prosecutions? What would be wrong with applying the "beyond the reasonable doubt standard" to *both* the preliminary examination and the subsequent criminal trial?

As one commentator has observed, the probable cause "burden is not only lower than the prosecutor's burden at trial, but also significantly lower than a *civil plaintiff's* burden at trial." Ion Meyn, *The Unbearable Lightness of Criminal Procedure*, 42 Am. J. Crim. L. 39, 61 (2014). In light of this, should the bindover standard be heightened and, if so, what should it be? What consequences might flow from such a change?

Historically, grand jury indictments were the means to initiate prosecutions, with preliminary examinations gaining currency only in the mid- to late nineteenth century. According to one commentator, the probable cause standard to bind over cases and issue indictments arose more or less at the same time, at the expense of the exacting requirement that the government establish a "prima facie" case of guilt:

> In information states, magistrates thus took over the grand jury's screening function. . . .
>
> When jurisdictions added the review of informations to the preliminary hearing agenda, they had to choose a standard. They could use the probable cause standard applicable to arrest, or they could use the prima facie standard, which, at least in the earliest days of information charging, still dominated the grand jury context. They overwhelmingly chose probable cause.

William Ortman, *Probable Cause Revisited*, 68 Stan. L. Rev. 511, 543 (2016).

2. *Tilt toward prosecution? Ayala* follows the traditional view in indicating that the proof process at the preliminary examination is tilted in favor of the prosecution. *Ayala* states the common view that at a preliminary examination the "evidence

must be viewed in the light most favorable to the prosecution, and all inferences must be resolved in favor of the prosecution." It has also been held that there is a presumption that the state will strengthen its case at trial. A related maxim was noted in *State v. Dunn*, 359 N.W.2d 151, 155 (Wis. 1984) (followed in *State v. Anderson*, 695 N.W. 2d 731 (Wis. 2005)):

> We stress that a preliminary hearing is not a proper forum to choose between conflicting facts or inferences, or to weigh the state's evidence against evidence favorable to the defendant. That is the role of the trier of fact at trial. If the hearing judge determines after hearing the evidence that a reasonable inference supports the probable cause determination, the judge should bind the defendant over for trial. Simply stated, probable cause at a preliminary hearing is satisfied when there exists a believable or plausible account of the defendant's commission of a felony.

Accord People v. Northey, 591 N.W.2d 227 (Mich. Ct. App. 1998) (probable cause requires belief that evidence at preliminary examination is consistent with defendant's guilt); *State v. Hendricks*, 586 N.W.2d 413 (Minn. Ct. App. 1998) ("Probable cause exists where facts would lead a person of ordinary care and prudence to hold an honest and strong suspicion that the person under consideration is guilty of a crime"). One especially low standard is "some rational ground for assuming the possibility that he or she committed an offense." *Thompson v. Superior Court*, 91 Cal. App. 4th 144 (2001). Considering the relatively low standard (probable cause) used in these proceedings, and the use of hearsay and evidence subject to possible suppression later in the case, can preliminary examinations truly be seen as being designed to protect the accused from baseless criminal prosecutions? Why should the tables be tilted so much in favor of the prosecution?

3. Note that the dissent in *Ayala* believed that probable cause had been established. Does the dissent or majority view best serve the primary purpose of the preliminary examination? With which do you agree?

In other words, do you believe that the evidence adduced at the proceeding was, or was not, sufficient to justify an inference that Ayala had "the mens rea required to commit theft by receiving?" Should the ultimate facts in this case, including Ayala's mental state, be determined by the preliminary hearing judge or by a jury?

4. *Changing the Ayala facts.* Is the real problem with *Ayala* that the prosecution failed to offer adequate proof? Would the outcome have been different if the following facts had been established:

a. A witness reported that Ayala and Johnson "dashed" home to get the money and then, with money in hand, ran back to the field where the car was being stripped by "Klark."

b. An expert on used cars testified that from Ayala's description of the car when Ayala and Johnson bought it for $800, the partially stripped car had a value of at least $2,000. Would your view change if the value were $5,000?

c. Would it matter whether Ayala knew nothing about cars? What if he were an expert on used cars? What if Ayala knew nothing about cars but Johnson was an expert on the value of used cars?

5. *Prosecution remedies.* Note that *Ayala* involves the unusual procedural posture of an appeal by the *prosecution* to a dismissal of charges in a preliminary hearing. In many locales, the prosecution could seek the same result (a finding of probable cause) by convening another preliminary hearing before the same or a different judge (perhaps with additional proof) or by seeking an indictment.

Problem 6-2. Probable Cause of What, and against Whom?

Berger was charged with possession with intent to deliver 1,000 tablets of pentazocine (Talwin) in violation of the drug laws. He was arrested by a police officer who came to his apartment after a neighbor complained of a noisy party. The officer knocked on the door and was invited in by one of the guests who answered the door. There were four adults and two minors obviously having a party. Everyone was in the living room. Three dozen cans of beer (some opened, some not) were on the kitchen table. In the bedroom the guests' coats were stored on the bed. On the top of the dresser was an open box containing the 1,000 pills. It was established that Berger was the only person who lived in the apartment, but his girlfriend stayed there occasionally. Berger's clothes were in the dresser and closet.

At the preliminary hearing, all six people testified that they did not know anything about the drugs.

If you were the judge, would you find that probable cause had been established as to Berger? His girlfriend? Anyone else in the apartment at the time? This issue comes up with some frequency in drug cases where multiple occupants of cars or dwellings have been arrested and the court must determine if probable cause has been established as to all, some, or none of the occupants.

[8] Empirical Studies

Studies show that almost all preliminary hearings end in a finding of probable cause, although jurisdictions do vary in this regard. *See, e.g.*, Deborah Day Emerson & Nancy L. Ames, The Role of the Grand Jury and the Preliminary Hearing in Pretrial Screening 68 (1984) (probable cause not found in 3–6% of cases in two Arizona counties); Kenneth Graham & Leon Letwin, *The Preliminary Hearings in Los Angeles: Some Field Findings and Legal-Policy Observations*, 18 U.C.L.A. L. Rev. 636, 719–724 (1971) (probable cause not found in 8% of 200 California cases in study; authors estimate approximately 90% of preliminary hearings result in bindover to grand jury in California).

[9] Motion Practice

Despite the informality of preliminary examinations in many jurisdictions, experienced lawyers often consider making various motions before, during, and after the proceeding. Pre-hearing motions may seek to affect preliminary hearing procedures, such as the exclusion of witnesses from the courtroom during the proceeding except when they are testifying, or to have inadmissible evidence barred from the proceeding. Pretrial motions may also request more fundamental relief, such as dismissal of some or all charges, because of the statute of limitations, double jeopardy, or the court's lack of jurisdiction over the cases or some of the charges.

During or immediately after the presentation of evidence at the preliminary examination, the defense lawyer may make one or more motions, usually orally. Counsel may ask for all or some of the charges to be dismissed for any number of reasons. Most often the motion will assert that the charges are unproven (no probable cause), unconstitutionally vague, or based on unconstitutionally secured evidence. Another motion may ask that one or more charges be reduced to allege the commission of less severe crimes. Perhaps counsel will concede that the proof established probable cause for a lesser crime, such as public intoxication, but will argue that it was not sufficient for a more serious offense, such as driving while intoxicated. Defense counsel may also move for a reduction in the amount of bail, while the prosecution may ask that it be increased.

Failure to move to dismiss charges at or after a preliminary examination may be viewed as a waiver of the issue. *See, e.g., State v. Mays*, 85 P.3d 1208 (Kan. 2004) (failure to file motion to dismiss charges waives issue of untimely preliminary examination).

[10] Effect of Decision

The preliminary examination is held at such an early stage of the criminal process that the double jeopardy guarantee does not apply. As discussed in Chapter 15, jeopardy attaches only once the actual trial begins. This means that the judge's decision at the preliminary examination is not a final resolution. In most jurisdictions that retain the grand jury, a dismissal in a preliminary hearing does not bar a subsequent grand jury indictment. Thus, if the judge at the preliminary examination dismisses the case and orders the defendant's release from custody because the state did not offer sufficient proof to meet the probable cause standard, the prosecutor can still take the case to the grand jury. If the latter issues an indictment, the case will proceed to trial. Similarly, if the judge at the preliminary examination rejects some of the charges or reduces their severity, the grand jury can restore the original charges or even indict for new ones.

One study of Chicago homicide cases found that the prosecution presented the case to the grand jury in half the cases where no probable cause was found at the preliminary examination. Surprisingly, an indictment was returned in 97% of these cases that had been first rejected in the preliminary examination. One explanation for the high success rate before the grand jury is that the prosecution may have presented stronger evidence to the grand jury than it did to the judge at the preliminary examination. Another possibility is that the grand jury's standards for probable cause were lower than that of the judge at the preliminary examination, or that the prosecution's influence over the grand jury is so great that it can get an indictment virtually any time it seeks one. Looking at the ultimate disposition of the cases that were rejected in the preliminary examination but revived with a grand jury indictment, the same study found that only 54% of the first-rejected cases produced a guilty verdict after trial. In contrast, the study found a trial conviction rate of 74% for the cases where the preliminary examination found probable cause. Janet A. Gilboy, *Prosecutors' Discretionary Use of the Grand Jury to Initiate or to Reinitiate Prosecution*, 1984 AM. BAR FOUND. RES. J. 1, 26.

After a preliminary examination judge issues a decision, an appeal is often possible, though rarely successful. Reviewing courts routinely affirm the probable cause determination unless there was an "abuse of discretion." One court stated that "every legitimate factual inference" must be drawn to uphold a magistrate's finding of probable cause at a preliminary hearing. *People v. Scott*, 76 Cal. App. 4th 411 (1999).

In some jurisdictions where there is no grand jury, a finding of probable cause at the preliminary examination can be appealed to the court of general jurisdiction that will eventually preside over the trial of the case. But once there is a criminal conviction following an erroneous "bindover" at the preliminary hearing, courts will virtually never reverse the conviction because of the error. Usually the "harmless error" standard is used to defeat the appeal. Some courts go further, holding that a valid conviction by the trial court cures any error in the preliminary examination and bars appellate reversal for any such error.

A finding of no probable cause is rarely appealed by the prosecution to a higher court, but the prosecutor may elect to refile the complaint and request another preliminary hearing in the same or a different court with jurisdiction to hold preliminary examinations. The California Supreme Court explained in *People v. Wallace*, 93 P.3d 1037, 1043 (Cal. 2004):

> A deficiency of proof at a preliminary hearing frequently reflects a temporary state of affairs. The prosecution may discover and proffer additional proof by the time a second preliminary hearing is held or by the time the case proceeds to trial.

Refiling could be barred if the new charges are designed to harass the defendant or if the defendant is prejudiced by them. *See, e.g., Commonwealth v. Carbo*, 822 A.2d 60 (Pa. Super. Ct. 2003).

Ordinarily another preliminary examination hearing on exactly the same evidence is possible. In some jurisdictions the state may appeal an unsuccessful preliminary hearing and, if it loses again on appeal, convene another preliminary examination only if there is additional evidence not presented at the first such hearing. *See, e.g., State v. Huser*, 959 P.2d 908 (Kan. 1998); *State v. Zahn*, 180 P.3d 186 (Utah Ct. App. 2008) (due process bars prosecutor from refiling criminal charges dismissed at a preliminary examination unless prosecutor can show new or previously unavailable evidence has surfaced or that other good cause justifies refiling). One study found that 10% of the dismissed cases were refiled. Kenneth Graham & Leon Letwin, *The Preliminary Hearings in Los Angeles: Some Field Findings and Legal-Policy Observations*, 18 U.C.L.A. L. REV. 636, 730 (1971).

Chapter 7

The Grand Jury

A. Introduction

The grand jury is a group of citizens who review cases to determine whether there is probable cause to believe that a crime was committed by the defendant. Despite the historic importance of the grand jury, the Supreme Court has not required that states use grand juries (i.e., the "grand jury clause" of the Fifth Amendment has not been imposed upon the states via incorporation). As a consequence, while the grand jury is an important part of federal criminal procedure, its use and procedures vary considerably among the states. Also, as discussed later in this chapter, the actual utility of the grand jury as a limit on possible government overreach remains the subject of considerable debate.

[1] Functions

The grand jury is both a "shield" and a "sword." As a shield, the grand jury is intended to act as a buffer between the defendant and the government seeking to prosecute him, with the grand jurors guarding against possibly unfounded criminal accusations. As a sword, it can function as an investigative body to gather information and determine whether a formal criminal charge should be brought.

[a] Grand Jury as Shield

The grand jury has been praised as a body that protects "the innocent against hasty, malicious, and oppressive public prosecutions." *Ex parte Bain*, 121 U.S. 1, 12 (1887). In cases where a grand jury refuses to indict a defendant because of insufficient evidence, it protects that person "from an open and public accusation of crime, and from the trouble, expense, and anxiety of a public trial." *Id.*

[b] Grand Jury as Sword

The grand jury can also investigate possible criminal activity and initiate criminal charges when appropriate. In this capacity the grand jury serves as a sword, an inquisitorial body that enjoys investigative powers, including authority to issue subpoenas. The individual or entity that is the subject of grand jury investigation ordinarily has no right to appear or to present arguments with respect to the determination of probable cause, the required standard of proof to issue an indictment (also known as a "true bill"). For discussion of how probable cause came to be the accepted charging standard (as opposed to a "prima facie case" of guilt), *see* William Ortman, *Probable Cause Revisited*, 68 STAN. L. REV. 51 (2016). According to the author, at this time only two states (New York and New Jersey) use a grand jury charging standard that is more demanding than probable cause. *Id.* at 547 n.201.

[c] Independence or Rubber Stamp

It is often contended that grand juries are not "independent" and that they essentially act as rubber stamps for prosecutors. Because it is typically the case that no judge or defense counsel is present during the course of a grand jury proceeding, public prosecutors not only control what charges might be brought against the target of a grand jury proceeding, they also control what evidence and information is considered by grand jurors. The California Supreme Court echoed this point of view in *Hawkins v. Superior Court*, 586 P.2d 916, 919 (Cal. 1978), when it stated:

> The prosecuting attorney is typically in complete control of the total process in the grand jury room: he calls the witnesses, interprets the evidence, states and applies the law, and advises the grand jury on whether a crime has been committed. The grand jury is independent only in the sense that it is not formally attached to the prosecutor's office; though legally free to vote as they please, grand jurors virtually always assent to the recommendations of the prosecuting attorney, a fact borne out by [empirical data].
>
> . . . Today, the grand jury is the total captive of the prosecutor who, if he is candid, will concede that he can indict anybody, at any time, for almost anything, before any grand jury. . . .

Grand jury independence is an issue that continues to be debated. Some commentators agree with the view that grand juries are not in fact independent, with one even going so far as to consider them as "an arm of the prosecution." Gregory T. Fotus, *Reading Jurors Their Rights: The Continuing Question of Grand Jury Independence*, 79 IND. L.J. 323, 324 (2004). For an argument that the disconnect between the rhetoric and reality of the grand jury is one of the central and important features of the modern federal criminal justice system, *see* Niki Kuckes, *The Useful, Dangerous Fiction of Grand Jury Independence*, 41 AM. CRIM. L. REV. 1 (2004).

Other commentators, however, have characterized the *Hawkins* opinion as overstated, pointing out that it should come as no surprise that a group of persons hearing only one side of a case will likely agree with that side. In this sense, perhaps the grand jury's real function is to compel the government to present a defensible case before a formal charge is brought. But some even question that argument. *See* Andrew D. Leipold, *Why Grand Juries Do Not (and Cannot) Protect the Accused*, 80 CORNELL L. REV. 260 (1995). Professor Leipold characterizes the grand jury as a shield that works poorly, attributing grand jury failings to jurors' lack of competence to perform their tasks, leading inevitably to deference to prosecutorial direction and decision. He concludes:

> [A]lthough the framers of the Bill of Rights considered grand juries an important protector of individual liberty, time and close scrutiny have shown that they are not. Despite the mechanical support voiced by courts for the institution, once the focus is placed on the jurors themselves, and their inability to perform the task assigned to them, it becomes clear that grand juries will not dissuade prosecutors from bringing unfounded charges, nor do they alter the charging decisions in any significant respect. In almost all cases, a criminal defendant would be just as well off without the grand jury as he is with it.

Id. at 323.

[2] Use of Grand Juries

In addition to the federal criminal system, where grand juries are used to charge most crimes, 48 states and the District of Columbia use grand juries to some extent. In 19 states, a grand jury indictment is required in all felony matters, in four states an indictment is required only for especially serious felonies, such as murder. In 25 states, a grand jury indictment is not required, and criminal charges can be filed by means of either a grand jury indictment or an "information" filed by a prosecutor alone. Ric Simmons, *Re-examining the Grand Jury: Is There Room for Democracy in the Criminal Justice System?*, 82 B.U. L. Rev. 1, 19 & nn.85–87 (2002). As the following discussion highlights, however, variations can exist regarding when a matter must be reviewed by a grand jury.

[a] Federal Use

The Fifth Amendment to the United States Constitution provides that "[n]o person shall be held to answer for a capital, or otherwise infamous crime, unless on a presentment or indictment of a grand jury. . . ."

The phrase "infamous crimes" in the Fifth Amendment has been construed to apply to all felonies. This means that a federal felony prosecution must be the product of a grand jury indictment or presentment unless waived by the defendant. A federal misdemeanor offense does not require an indictment, though a federal prosecutor may choose to seek one. Gabriel J. Chin & John Ormanda, *Infamous Misdemeanors and the Grand Jury Clause*, 102 Minn L. Rev. 1911 (2018).

A *presentment* is a formal charging document issued by a grand jury in cases that have been initiated by the prosecutor's office. The more common charging instrument is the *indictment*, a document issued by a grand jury in cases brought to its attention by the prosecutor. The indictment and the presentment have the same legal effect since both are approved by the grand jury. This similarity occasionally produces a blurring in the distinctions between these two concepts.

The fact that the federal defendant's entitlement to grand jury review is enshrined in the Bill of Rights underscores its intended role as a protective device in the federal system. As discussed below, individuals selected for grand jury duty sit for a designated period, often several months, usually hearing multiple case presentations from prosecutors. In 2010, for example, federal courts impaneled 784 grand juries and convened 9,227 grand jury sessions. Each session averaged just under five hours and indicted an average of more than seven people per session. A total of 186,194 persons (about 20 per session) served as federal grand jurors. Bureau of Justice Statistics, Sourcebook of Criminal Justice Statistics Online, Table 1.94, available at www.albany.edu/sourcebook/pdf/t1942009.pdf. A total of 49,144 criminal cases were filed that year against 69,245 defendants. *Id.* at Table 5.9, available at www.albany.edu/sourcebook/pdf/t592009.pdf.

[b] State Use

While the Fifth Amendment makes the grand jury an inherent part of federal criminal processes, this guarantee does not apply to state prosecutions. *See Hurtado v. California*, 110 U.S. 516 (1884) (California not obligated to prosecute by indictment). Accordingly, a number of states now use an information in lieu of an indictment. An *information* is the counterpart of an indictment except that it is drafted and signed by a prosecutor, not by a judge or grand jury, and it is filed in court.

Less than half of the states today *require* grand jury review for all felonies. A number of state constitutions do not make any reference to grand jury proceedings (e.g., Massachusetts and Michigan), while others extend the right to indictment to all felony cases, using language very similar to that of the Fifth Amendment (see, e.g., New York, Ohio, and Texas).

The "middle ground" state constitutional provisions permit the government to initiate criminal proceedings either by indictment or information (e.g., California and Illinois). In Arkansas and Oklahoma, the vast majority of felony prosecutions are initiated by information rather than indictment, and the grand jury has been relegated to being a back-up alternative where a judge or prosecutor is persuaded of the need in a particular case for the charging decision to come from outside the prosecutor's office.

There are also other approaches to grand jury use. In Florida, the right to grand jury review is triggered only when the defendant "shall be tried for a capital crime," thereby allowing other felony prosecutions to proceed either by indictment or information. Fla. Const. art. 1, § 15. Illinois has a unique constitutional provision, expressly authorizing the state legislature to "abolish the grand jury or further limit its use." Ill. Const. art. 1, § 7.

If a prosecutor can choose to file an information or seek an indictment from a grand jury, do you think that use of a grand jury might be preferable for particular kinds of cases? For instance, if presented with a felony burglary complaint and a complaint of police excessive force, would one case be more likely to be submitted to a grand jury than the other?

For a more detailed discussion of grand jury procedures at the state level, *see* Sara Beale et al., Grand Jury Law and Practice § 1.5 (2d ed. 2017) [hereinafter cited as Beale et al., Grand Jury Law and Practice].

[c] Waiver

If a criminal defendant is entitled to a grand jury indictment as a precondition to a criminal trial, he or she is also entitled to waive the indictment process and to proceed by information. *See, e.g.*, Fed. R. Crim. P. 7(b). The waiver must be "voluntary and intelligent" and it is routinely made in writing. Some jurisdictions also require that the waiver occur in open court. *See generally* Roger A. Fairfax, Jr., *The Jurisdictional Heritage of the Grand Jury Clause*, 91 Minn. L. Rev. 398 (2006) (providing a history of the grand jury guarantee and evolution of permitting waiver of the right).

There are several reasons why a criminal defendant might find it advantageous to waive a grand jury indictment. Perhaps the most prevalent is to expedite the trial process. An accused who wants a prompt trial or a quick resolution involving a guilty plea may save several months of pretrial delay by waiving the grand jury process. This could be important to an individual who is in jail, yet believes he or she will be acquitted at trial or simply wants the case concluded. Waiver might also be motivated by concern that a witness might be unavailable if a trial were delayed. Finally, some prosecutors will sweeten a plea offer if the defendant will waive indictment, saving the prosecution the time and effort involved in presenting the case to the grand jury.

[3] Legal Powers

To fulfill its roles as both a sword and a shield, a grand jury possesses considerable legal powers. First, it may use subpoenas to require witnesses to testify or produce physical evidence. Second, its power is backed by the authority of the court, which can hold an uncooperative grand jury witness in contempt. Third, the grand jury operates in almost total secrecy, thereby facilitating the investigative role largely free of public oversight and accountability. Fourth, while grand jury witnesses are allowed to assert various constitutional rights (most notably, the Fifth Amendment self-incrimination privilege), the grand jury may seek a grant of immunity that forces the witness to disclose incriminating information (subjecting the witness to contempt if she refuses).

[4] Relationship to Preliminary Examination

Recall that a significant number of states permit the prosecutor to select whether to use the grand jury or an information. When an information (formal charges prepared and filed by the prosecutor without grand jury involvement) is used, the defendant usually is entitled to a preliminary examination where a judge assesses whether there is probable cause to believe the defendant committed a certain crime. *See* Chapter 6 (Preliminary Examinations). If the judge at the preliminary examination finds no probable cause, the defendant is discharged. The same result occurs if the grand jury finds no probable cause and refuses to issue an indictment. Whether discharge occurs through magistrate determination or the decision of a grand jury (a "no true bill"), neither form of disposition is final because the double jeopardy clause does not attach until the criminal trial on the merits begins. *See* Chapter 15 (Double Jeopardy). Ordinarily, the government can elect to re-initiate the prosecution either by presenting the case for the first or second time to a grand jury or by filing a new information and presenting the case at a second preliminary examination.

It is likely that the cases that are dismissed at a preliminary examination or that are no-true-billed by a grand jury are weak. A study in Cook County, Illinois, found that one-fourth of preliminary examinations resulted in discharge of the accused after a judicial finding of no probable cause. In approximately one-half of those discharged cases, the government reinitiated prosecution by grand jury indictment. As to those reinitiated cases, there was a significantly higher chance that they would result in acquittals or dismissals at the trial level. Additionally, it was found that those defendants were more likely to demand trial than to plead guilty, "which is another indication that reinitiated cases might be weaker, since there might be strong incentives in weak cases for defendants to seek a review of their cases." Janet A. Gilboy, *Prosecutors' Discretionary Use of the Grand Jury to Initiate or to Reinitiate Prosecution*, 1984 Am. Bar Found. Res. J. 1, 9.

Preliminary examinations and grand jury proceedings differ in critically important ways, which can account for different outcomes. A preliminary examination is adversarial in nature, with defense counsel present and able to cross-examine witnesses. A grand jury is not adversarial, it is more inquisitorial in nature: defense counsel typically is not present and witnesses are not subject to cross-examination. The *Hawkins* opinion, cited earlier, described these differences:

> [At a grand jury hearing] the defendant has no right to appear or be represented by counsel, and consequently may not confront and cross-examine the witnesses against him, object to evidence introduced by the prosecutor, make legal arguments, or present evidence to explain or contradict the charge. If he is called to testify, the defendant has no right to the presence of counsel, even though, because of the absolute secrecy surrounding grand jury proceedings, he may be completely unaware of the subject of inquiry or his position as a target witness. This remarkable lack of even the most basic rights is compounded by the absence from the grand jury room of a neutral and detached magistrate, trained in the law, to rule on the admissibility of evidence and ensure that the grand jury exercises its indicting function with proper regard for the independence and objectivity so necessary if it is to fulfill its purported role of protecting innocent citizens from unfounded accusations, even as it proceeds against those who it has probable cause to believe have committed offenses.

Hawkins v. Superior Court, 586 P.2d 916, 918 (Cal. 1978).

[5] Secrecy

Grand jury proceedings are conducted in secret, subject to a few exceptions. The identities of grand jurors are not publicly disclosed and grand jurors (and prosecutors) are not allowed to divulge matters related to proceedings. While courts and legislatures occasionally permit disclosure under very specific circumstances, the rule of secrecy promotes the following interests: (1) avoids embarrassment to persons who are investigated but not charged; (2) prevents leaks of information to prospective defendants; and (3) reduces the danger that a grand jury witness will be threatened or harassed by a target of the grand jury. *See* Mark Kadish, *Behind the Locked Door of an American Grand Jury: Its History, Its Secrecy, and Its Process*, 24 Fla. St. U.L. Rev. 1 (1996). Secrecy violations can result in civil or criminal contempt of court. *See, e.g.*, Fed. R. Crim. P. 6(e)(7).

In *United States v. Procter & Gamble*, 356 U.S. 677, 682 (1958), the Supreme Court affirmed the notion that secrecy encourages witnesses "to step forward and testify freely without fear of retaliation." Subsequently, however, the Court recognized that there may be circumstances in which transcripts of grand jury proceedings might be disclosed:

> Parties seeking grand jury transcripts . . . must show that the material they seek is needed to avoid a possible injustice in another judicial proceeding, that the need for disclosure is greater than the need for continued secrecy, and that their request is structured to cover only material so needed. Such a showing must be made even when the grand jury whose transcripts are sought has concluded its operations. [T]he courts must consider not only the immediate effects upon a particular grand jury, but also the possible effect upon the functioning of future grand juries. Persons called upon to testify will consider the likelihood that their testimony may one day be disclosed to outside parties. Fear of future retribution or social stigma may act as powerful deterrents to those who would come forward and aid the grand jury in the performance of its duties. Thus, the interests in grand jury secrecy, although reduced, are not eliminated merely because the grand jury has ended its activities.

Douglas Oil Company of California v. Petrol Stops Northwest, 441 U.S. 211, 222 (1979).

In federal courts, the Jencks Act allows a defendant to obtain transcripts of grand jury testimony provided by a government trial witness when the testimony relates to matters explored on direct examination of the witness. 18 U.S.C. 3500(b) (2012). Such disclosure can occur after motion by the defendant and, if permitted by the court, is provided after the witness has testified at trial. *Id.*

It is important to note that *witnesses* who testify in grand jury proceedings are not generally subject to this secrecy obligation. The Advisory Committee Note to Federal Rule of Criminal Procedure 6(e) reasons that the exception is warranted because "[t]he seal of secrecy on witnesses seems an unnecessary hardship and may lead to injustice if a witness is not permitted to make a disclosure to counsel or to an associate." Fed. R. Crim. P. 6(e), advisory committee's note 2 (1944). In the federal system, while the rules do not require secrecy of grand jury witnesses, a governmental request (rather than a requirement) that a witness not disclose the existence of a grand jury subpoena is permissible. *See United States v. Bryant*, 655 F.3d 232,238 (3d Cir. 2011) (holding that "[m]erely requesting that witnesses practice discretion [in speaking to others outside the proceeding] does not violate a defendant's due process right" to access witnesses).

As indicated in *Bryant*, a primary concern with secrecy is that it potentially impairs the ability of a defendant to mount a defense, and thereby "undermines the fundamental fairness" of an ensuing criminal trial. *See id.* ("Generally, because witnesses 'belong' neither to the defense nor to the prosecution, both must have equal access to witnesses before trial."). Is there an argument that the minority approach, imposing a secrecy obligation on witnesses, also violates First Amendment freedom of speech or press (if the witness is a journalist)?

In *Butterworth v. Smith*, 494 U.S. 624 (1990), a news reporter testified before a grand jury about alleged wrongdoing in the local police and prosecutors' offices, and later sought to write a book on the issue, after the grand jury refused a public corruption indictment. The Supreme Court invalidated Florida's blanket secrecy law on First Amendment grounds, writing that "[t]he invocation of grand jury interests is not some talisman that dissolves all constitutional protections." *Id.* at 630. The Court acknowledged that the law protected individuals from having unproven allegations publicly exposed but, "absent exceptional circumstances, reputational interests alone cannot justify the proscription of truthful speech." *Id.* at 634. "[I]nsofar as the Florida law prohibits a grand jury witness from disclosing his own testimony after the term of the grand jury has ended, it violates the First Amendment. . . ." *Id.* at 626. Does this mean that the reporter was still denied the right to disclose anything else about his testimony before the grand jury, such as particular questions asked by grand jurors or exhibits that were referenced? For more on the question, *see* R. Michael Cassidy, *Silencing Grand Jury Witnesses*, 91 Ind. L.J. 823 (2016).

For discussion of changes to Rule 6(e) of the Federal Rule of Criminal Procedure in the wake of September 11, 2001, and the USA PATRIOT Act of 2001 and the resultant sharing of grand jury materials relating to intelligence matters with other federal intelligence, immigration, and defense agencies, *see* Lori E. Shaw, *The USA PATRIOT Act of 2001, the Intelligence Reform and Terrorism Prevention Act of 2004, and the False Dichotomy Between Protecting National Security and Preserving Grand Jury Secrecy*, 35 Seton Hall L. Rev. 495 (2005).

B. Selection of Grand Jurors

Grand jurors are selected in a different way from petit jury members used in criminal trials (see Chapter 13). Unlike petit (i.e., trial) jurors, for instance, citizens who serve on grand juries are not typically subject to extensive voir dire prior to being selected for service. The following discussion examines the methods used in the federal and state systems.

[1] Federal System

The selection of federal grand jurors is governed by the Jury Selection and Service Act of 1968, 28 U.S.C. §§ 1861–1869, and is discussed in greater detail in Chapter 13. Rule 6 of the Federal Rules of Criminal Procedure also contains provisions pertaining to the selection of grand jurors.

In general terms, this statute requires that federal jurors be selected in a random fashion in order to guarantee that they represent a fair cross section of society. Various exemptions from jury service are recognized. Each federal judicial district must adopt a plan governing the manner in which jurors' names are to be drawn. Both the government and the defense may move for dismissal of an indictment on the ground of "substantial failure to comply with [the Act]." 28 U.S.C. § 1867. The Supreme Court has held that an indictment may be dismissed because of an Equal Protection Clause violation in the selection of grand jurors. *See, e.g.*, *Vasquez v. Hillery*, 474 U.S. 253 (1986) (dismissal based on racial discrimination in empanelment). (Empanelment of jurors is discussed further in Chapter 13.)

With regard to challenges, Rule 6(b)(1) of the Federal Rules of Criminal Procedure provides that "[e]ither the government or a defendant may challenge the grand jury on the ground that it was not lawfully drawn, summoned, or selected, and may challenge an individual juror on the ground that the juror is not legally qualified." The rule further provides, however, that a "party may move to dismiss the indictment based on an objection to the grand jury or on an individual juror's lack of legal qualification, unless the court has previously ruled on the same objection under Rule 6(b)(1). . . .The court must not dismiss the indictment on the ground that a grand juror was not legally qualified if the record shows that at least 12 qualified jurors concurred in the indictment." Fed. R. Crim. P. 6(b)(2).

[2] State Systems

Many states follow the federal model by requiring that grand jurors be selected according to a random process. In some states, however, a *key person* system is used. Selectors (usually either jury commissioners or judges) are given discretion to select private citizens they believe are qualified for grand jury service.

Qualifications of those who may be selected as grand jurors vary from state to state, but it has been observed by the United States Supreme Court that the key person system is the method most susceptible to abuse. This is significant because an equal protection challenge is more likely to succeed where underrepresentation of a cognizable group results from such a selection process. *See* Beale et al., Grand Jury Law and Practice, *supra*, § 3:6.

Challenges to the selection or composition of the grand jury may be brought by (1) persons eligible to serve as grand jurors, (2) the defendant whose case has been or will be heard by the grand jury, and (3) the government attorney. The usual method is a motion to dismiss the indictment. A defendant, for example, can challenge the exclusion of potential jurors of his own or any other race. *See Campbell v. Louisiana*, 523 U.S. 392 (1998) (holding that a white defendant has standing to raise both equal protection and due process objections to discrimination against black persons in the selection of grand jurors). On the other hand, witnesses called to testify before the grand jury have not been accorded the right to challenge the selection of the grand jury. *Blair v. United States*, 250 U.S. 273 (1919).

Courts have recognized the following kinds of challenges: (1) qualifications of prospective grand jurors, (2) composition of the grand jury panel on constitutional bases (equal protection and due process), and (3) failure to comply with statutory selection requirements. For an extended analysis of challenges in each of these categories, including citations to state and federal cases, see BEALE ET AL., GRAND JURY LAW AND PRACTICE, *supra*, Ch. 3.

C. Procedures

[1] Size and Vote

Grand juries range in size from as few as seven to as many as 23 persons (as noted above, Fed. R. Crim. P. 6 requires 16 to 23 jurors). Often a majority vote is required for return of an indictment. In the federal system, 12 affirmative votes are needed to indict. If there is a finding of insufficient probable cause to charge a defendant, the grand jury returns what is often called a *no true bill.*

[2] Foreperson

While the empaneling court ordinarily appoints one of the jurors to serve as foreperson, in some jurisdictions the grand jurors themselves select the foreperson. The foreperson is usually charged with the responsibility of swearing witnesses, chairing the deliberations, signing indictments, and sometimes keeping records of votes and organizing the process.

[3] Duration of Term

In the federal system, a grand jury may sit for up to 18 months and may be extended for six months more. The terms of state grand juries vary widely, from as little as 10 days to a maximum of 18 months. This does not necessarily mean that the grand juror will be devoting "full time" to the jury process. The juror may be called upon to meet one particular afternoon each week, for example.

Special grand jury. Both state and federal laws authorize the court to impanel *special grand juries* to deal with specific matters, such as an antitrust or organized crime investigation. *See e.g., Alwan v. Ashcroft*, 388 F.3d 507 (5th Cir. 2004) (special grand jury to investigate a specific terrorist group). Special grand juries are also authorized to address unresolved cases when a regular grand jury faces a backlog.

[4] Oath of Office

All jurisdictions require that grand jurors be sworn by the judge assigned to supervise the grand jury or by the clerk of the court. The form of the oath utilized in almost all jurisdictions, state and federal, is as follows:

> Do you . . . solemnly swear that you shall diligently inquire into and make true presentation or indictment of all such matters . . . as shall be given you in charge or otherwise come to your knowledge, touching your grand jury service; to keep secret the counsel of the [government], your fellows and yourselves; not to present or indict any person through hatred, malice or ill will; nor leave any person unrepresented or indicted through fear, favor, or affection, nor for any reward, or hope or promise thereof; but in all your presentments and indictments to present the truth . . . to the best of your skill and understanding?

BEALE ET AL., GRAND JURY LAW AND PRACTICE, *supra*, § 4:4.

[5] Hearings

No judge is present during grand jury hearings. The proceedings are preserved by audio equipment or stenographers in most locales.

Typically, grand jurors are assisted by a prosecuting attorney who, as noted earlier, essentially controls the grand jury's focus and its investigative inquiries. The person who is the target or object of the grand jury probe ordinarily has no right to testify or be present in the grand jury room. Sometimes he or she does not know that the grand jury is investigating the person's possible criminal activity. Even when the person being investigated is permitted to testify before the grand jury, he or she is ordinarily not entitled to representation by counsel in the grand jury room (although counsel can be nearby outside the room and available for consultation). The obvious consequence is that the defendant cannot confront or cross-examine witnesses, object to evidence, or make any legal arguments relevant to the grand jury's decision whether to file an indictment.

[a] Role of Judge

The judge's role in the day-to-day functioning of the grand jury is quite limited. Initially, the judge administers the oath to grand jurors and is usually the person who also "charges" or informs the grand jurors about their responsibilities and duties. Federal judges instruct grand juries about the limits of their powers (e.g., to only address federal law violations, not state law), their procedures, the evidence they will hear, their independence, how they are to deliberate and vote, and their obligations regarding secrecy. *See* Beale et al., Grand Jury Law and Practice, § 4.5 (model charge to federal grand jurors). *See also United States v. Caruto*, 627 F.3d 759 (9th Cir. 2010) (rejecting claim that deviatiion from model charge was prejudicial).

Once the grand jury begins its work, the judge plays no direct role in the proceedings and is not present in the grand jury room, but may be asked to intervene if issues arise, such as whether a particular evidentiary privilege should apply (e.g., spousal).

Judges do, however, possess broad discretionary power over the grand jury process. This control can occur in several ways:

> [The judge] has the power to order the grand jury into existence; conversely, unless otherwise provided by statute, [the judge] has complete discretion to refuse to call a grand jury. [The judge] may dismiss the grand jury ... at any time after it is called. [The judge] may deny requests to issue subpoenas ... and, after the grand jury submits its findings, [the judge] may quash for cause any indictments returned, expunge reports or any surplusage in the indictment, and divulge the records of the secret grand jury proceedings upon a showing of "particularized need."
>
> As a practical matter, perhaps the most important of these powers is the judge's control over the issuance and enforcement of subpoenas. It allows [the judge] to maintain a degree of contact with the proceedings and to scrutinize them to a limited extent. But because of traditional restraints against interference with the scope of grand jury investigations, many trial judges have been hesitant to refuse to issue and enforce subpoenas.

Robert T. Brice, *Grand Jury Proceedings: The Prosecutor, the Trial Judge, and Undue Influence*, 39 U. Chi. L. Rev. 761, 768 (1972). *See also* Anna Offit, *Ethical Guidance for a Grander Jury*, 24 Geo. J. Legal Ethics 761 (2011) (calling for increased *judicial* oversight with grand juries).

Sealing an indictment. Judges have the authority to seal indictments returned by the grand jury. The judge can order that the indictment be sealed for a period to ensure that the defendant does not learn of the charges, reducing the risk, for instance, that the target flees before being arrested. Or, the judge may seal an indictment to guard against potential witness intimidation or tampering. *See, e.g., United States v. Ellis*, 622 F.3d 784 (7th Cir. 2010) (sealing the indictment was reasonable to protect the identity, security, and testimony of witnesses).

[b] Role of Prosecutor

Lawyer for the grand jury. The prosecutor initiates almost all cases handled by a grand jury. While the grand jury has the authority in many jurisdictions to investigate any matter on its own initiative, this occurs in relatively few cases. Keeping in mind that the prosecutor is the only official government "actor" and probably the only lawyer in the grand jury room, he or she also serves as the grand jury's legal adviser. The prosecutor usually suggests to the grand jury the identity of the witnesses to be summoned, may actually issue the subpoenas for the grand jury, and may conduct the examination of witnesses. In the event a witness invokes the Fifth Amendment self-incrimination privilege, the prosecutor makes the initial decision whether to propose a grant of immunity to that witness in exchange for testimony. The prosecutor also might interpret the evidence for the grand jurors and advise them whether there has been a sufficient showing of probable cause to believe that a crime was committed.

Discretion not to prosecute an indictment. In many jurisdictions, including the federal system, the prosecutor has the discretion to refuse to prosecute an indictment issued by a grand jury. This is part of the prosecutor's general discretion to determine which charges to pursue. Prosecutorial discretion is discussed in Chapter 2.

Rubber stamp? As noted earlier, critics of the grand jury often argue that grand jurors fail to serve as a bulwark against government overreach because they simply do the bidding of prosecutors. As an advocate for the government, the prosecutor's presentation to the grand jury is designed to urge the grand jurors to agree with the prosecutor's "case." This prosecutorial overzealousness has been condemned by the American Bar Association. *See* CRIMINAL JUSTICE STANDARDS FOR THE PROSECUTION FUNCTION § 3-4.5(a) (4th ed. 2015) (in presenting case to a grand jury, "in light of its *ex parte* character, the prosecutor should respect the independence of the grand jury and should not preempt a function of the grand jury, mislead the grand jury, or abuse the processes of the grand jury"). It has been argued that the grand jury would be more independent if it had its own lawyer. *See* Thaddeus Hoffmeister, *The Grand Jury Legal Advisor: Resurrecting the Grand Jury's Shield*, 98 J. CRIM. L. & CRIMINOLOGY 1171 (2008).

An old adage provides that grand jurors would "indict a ham sandwich" if requested by a prosecutor. Data showing that an overwhelming proportion of prosecutorial requests do result in indictment would tend to support the adage. *See* Bureau of Justice Statistics, *Federal Justice Statistics 2010*, tbl 2.3 (2013), https://www.bjs.gov/content/pub/pdf/fjs10.pdf (indicating that federal grand juries declined to indict in only 11 of more than 162,000 cases in 2010).

One context where indictment filing rates are not high concerns instances of alleged police misconduct. In several high-profile recent instances, for instance, involving the shooting death of Michael Brown in Ferguson, Missouri, and the death by asphyxiation of Eric Garner in New York City, both unarmed, state grand juries refused to indict officers. Although the decisions not to indict generated considerable public outrage and concern, such refusals are in fact quite common. *See* Roger A. Fairfax Jr., *The Grand Jury's Role in the Prosecution of Unjustified Police*

Killings—Challenges and Solutions, 52 Harv. C.R.-C.L. L. Rev. 397, 400 (2017) (noting that "it appears that these contemporary cases mimic historical patterns in police violence cases. Indeed, grand juries almost never indict police officers in these types of cases."). In response to significant public criticism, the prosecutor in the Michael Brown case took the highly unusual step of releasing transcripts of the grand jury proceeding. *Id.* at 49 n.5. *See also* Frank O. Bowman III, *Vox Populi: Robert McColloch, Ferguson, & the Roles of Prosecutors and Grand Juries on High-Profile Cases*, 80 Mo. L. Rev. 1111 (2015).

Exculpatory evidence. Approximately one-quarter of the states require that a prosecutor inform the grand jury of exculpatory evidence, at least under some circumstances. Beale et al., Grand Jury Law and Practice, *supra*, § 4:17. The American Bar Association adopts this approach by recommending that "[a] prosecutor with personal knowledge of evidence that directly negates the guilt of a subject of the investigation should disclose that evidence to the grand jury." Criminal Justice Standards for the Prosecution Function, *supra*, § 3-4.6(e). *See also U.S. Attorneys' Manual* § 9-11.233 (2015) (requiring disclosure to grand jury of any "substantial evidence that directly negates the guilt of a subject of the investigation."). This could mean, for example, that a prosecutor would be obligated to inform grand jurors of evidence raising the possibility that a killing occurred in self-defense.

It can be argued, however, that no such duty should be placed upon a prosecutor because the grand jury's role is inquisitorial, focusing only upon the question whether there is probable cause to believe that a crime occurred. The "defendant's side" of the case is more appropriately left for consideration at trial. Indeed, *Brady v. Maryland* (see Chapter 10, Discovery) requires that exculpatory material be disclosed to defendants before trial.

In the federal criminal trial context, the United States Supreme Court has refused to dismiss an indictment on the ground that the prosecution failed to disclose exculpatory evidence to the grand jury. *See United States v. Williams*, 504 U.S. 36 (1992). In other words, while federal prosecutors might be ethically obliged by internal policy to reveal exculpatory material to the grand jury (see U.S. Attorney's Manual, *supra*), they are not constitutionally required to do so. *United States v. Navarro*, 608 F.3d 529, 537 (9th Cir. 2010).

Notes

1. *Directly negating guilt.* What kind of evidence "directly negates the guilt" of the subject of the investigation (the standards noted above)? Would evidence that would impeach the testimony of a main government witness? Strong evidence in support of a defense of insanity?

2. *Grand jury requests exculpatory information.* Assume that the grand jury requested that the prosecutor provide it with information as to the defendant's version of the facts. If the prosecutor fails to provide that information and the grand jury indicts the defendant, should that be grounds for dismissal of the indictment?

3. *Denying evidence to second grand jury after first refuses to indict.* Assume that certain evidence presented to a previous grand jury apparently led that grand jury not to indict the defendant. The prosecutor, now presenting the case to a second grand jury, fails to present that same evidence to the grand jury, as a result of which a "true bill" issues. Have the defendant's constitutional rights been infringed? If so, in what way?

4. *Prosecuting in the face of substantial evidence negating guilt.* If a prosecutor is aware of substantial evidence that would tend to negate guilt, should she seek an indictment with the knowledge that the case will probably not result in conviction? While our intuitive answer to this question should be no, it has been suggested that prosecutors sometimes utilize the grand jury to obtain an indictment in such cases. They might do so because of (1) public pressure to prosecute, (2) a sense that the grand jury process, itself, will generate the desired sanction (e.g., possible loss of reputation if made public), or (3) a desire to secure a conviction through plea bargaining. *See* Janet A. Gilboy, *Prosecutors' Discretionary Use of the Grand Jury to Initiate or to Reinitiate Prosecution*, 1984 AMER. BAR FOUND. RES. J. 1.

If a prosecutor were to engage in this kind of behavior, would he or she be acting in a professionally ethical way? *See* CRIMINAL JUSTICE STANDARDS FOR THE PROSECUTION FUNCTION, *supra*, § 3-4.6(a) ("A prosecutor should not seek an indictment unless the prosecutor reasonably believes the charges are supported by probable cause and that there will be admissible evidence sufficient to support the charges beyond a reasonable doubt at trial."). The *Standards*, moreover, impose upon the prosecutor an affirmative obligation to "advise a grand jury of the prosecutor's opinion that it should not indict if the prosecutor believes the evidence presented does not warrant an indictment." *Id.* According to Professor Uviller, a prosecutor serves as the "people's lawyer" who should disclose exculpatory information and be more concerned with doing justice than securing an indictment. H. Richard Uviller, *The Neutral Prosecutor: The Obligation of Dispassion in a Passionate Pursuit*, 68 FORDHAM L. REV. 1695, 1707 (2000).

5. *Defense counsel's options with exculpatory evidence.* Assume you are a defense attorney who has an important piece of exculpatory written evidence you would like the grand jurors to have when they consider whether to return an indictment against your client. What can you do? Should you give it to the prosecutor with a request that the evidence be submitted to the grand jury? Send it to the judge with this same request? Mail a copy of the evidence directly to the foreperson and/or each grand juror (presuming the names and addresses of the grand jurors can be obtained from the court clerk)? *See* CRIMINAL JUSTICE STANDARDS FOR THE PROSECUTION FUNCTION, *supra*, § 3-4.6(e) ("The prosecutor should relay to the grand jury any request by the subject or target of an investigation to testify before the grand jury, or present other non-frivolous evidence claimed to be exculpatory.").

6. *Dismiss without prejudice.* When a court dismisses a potential criminal case "without prejudice" what does this mean? This is the usual remedy for a faulty indictment. Why would defense counsel bother to file a motion to dismiss an indictment if the likely remedy is dismissal without prejudice, allowing the indictment to be refiled at a later date?

7. *Internal policies requiring submission of exculpatory evidence.* Of course a prosecutor is free to present exculpatory evidence to a grand jury. Internal prosecution policies may require it. *See, e.g.*, U.S. Attorney's Manual 9-11.233, *supra*.

8. *State rejection of* Williams. Some state courts have rejected *Williams* and have exercised their supervisory powers to require prosecutors to present exculpatory evidence to grand juries. In *Johnson v. Superior Court*, 539 P.2d 12 (1975) the California Supreme Court construed a state statute allowing the grand jury to hear evidence favorable to the defendant as implicitly requiring the prosecutor to inform jurors of evidence "reasonably tending to negate guilt." In *State v. Hogan*, 676 A.2d 533 (N.J. 1996), the New Jersey Supreme Court reasoned that a prosecutor has a duty to present exculpatory evidence to a grand jury when it "squarely refutes an *element* of the crime in question." The victim in *Hogan* recanted her testimony to investigators and later claimed that she did so because of death threats against her and her daughter. The court held that the prosecutor did not have a duty to disclose this evidence to the grand jury because it was not sufficiently reliable to be clearly exculpatory. *See also Trebus v. Davis*, 944 P.2d 1235, 1239 (Ariz. 1997) ("The county attorney is not obligated to present all exculpatory evidence to the grand jury absent a request by the grand jury, but must present only 'clearly exculpatory' evidence. . . . Clearly exculpatory evidence is evidence of such weight that it might deter the grand jury from finding the existence of probable cause.").

[c] Role of Target

[i] Subpoena Target

Consistent with the grand jury's broad investigative powers, a grand jury can call any individual before it as a witness. When subpoenaed, unless a privilege applies, a person has no right to refuse to testify and must respond truthfully to questions posed by grand jurors or prosecutors. Generally, this rule also applies to an individual who may be characterized as a "target" or "subject" (or perhaps "putative defendant") of the grand jury investigation.

The terms *subject* and *target* are often used interchangeably. Both refer to an individual who either could become an indicted defendant or, more narrowly, is a focus of the grand jury's attention for possible indictment. Federal prosecutors have attempted to distinguish between a subject and a target. To them, a subject is "a person whose conduct is within the scope of the grand jury's investigation." A target is "a person as to whom the prosecutor or the grand jury has substantial evidence linking him/her to the commission of a crime and who, in the judgment of the prosecutor, is a putative defendant." Beale et al., Grand Jury Law and Practice, *supra*, § 6.23.

Whether one is a target (or subject) is important because a minority of jurisdictions do not permit the prosecution to use the grand jury's subpoena authority to force either a subject or a target to appear.

Need a target be informed that they are the target of a grand jury proceeding? The ABA *Standards* so recommend, stating that:

> [u]nless there is a reasonable probability that it will facilitate the flight of the target, endanger other persons, interfere with an ongoing investigation, or obstruct justice, the prosecutor should give notice to a target of a grand jury investigation, and offer the target an opportunity to testify before the grand jury.

Criminal Justice Standards for the Prosecution Function, *supra*, § 3-4.6(f).

[ii] Target's Right to Appear

But what if the target (or a person who perceives that the grand jury may be investigating his or her behavior) wants to testify before the grand jury? *United States v. Williams,* the Supreme Court decision noted above, stated the traditional rule that no individual—including a target—has a right to testify before the grand jury. *United States v. Williams*, 504 U.S. 36, 52 (1992). Similarly, no witness, including a target, has a right to cross-examine other witnesses or to present evidence, but a prosecutor may present evidence or witnesses suggested by a target or other witness. While this principle does not prohibit any individual from requesting such an appearance or to present evidence, it is within the grand jury's discretion to grant or deny the request.

A few states believe this is unfair and afford the target of a grand jury proceeding the right to appear and testify. Perhaps the most protective provision is a New York statute requiring that an indictment be voided if the target is not afforded the right to testify. N.Y. Crim. Proc. Law § 190.50(5)(c). The ABA *Standards* similarly provide that "[t]he prosecutor should honor . . . a reasonable request from a target or subject who wishes to testify before the grand jury." Criminal Justice Standards for the Prosecution Function, *supra*, § 3-4.6(f).

Compelling a target to testify before a grand jury, however, is another matter. The ABA *Standards* state that "[i]f the prosecutor concludes that a witness is a target of a criminal investigation, the prosecutor should not seek to compel the witness's testimony before the grand jury absent immunity." *Id.* § 3-4.6(f).

[iii] Procedures When Target Appears

Assume that a target is subpoenaed to appear before the grand jury. Is a target witness entitled to different treatment from any other witness? The federal government and a minority of state jurisdictions mandate that *target warnings* be given to such individuals. Such warnings may include advice that (1) the individual is a target of the grand jury investigation, (2) the witness has no right to refuse to answer a question, except that the Fifth Amendment self-incrimination privilege may apply, (3) anything said by the witness may be used in a subsequent legal proceeding, and (4) the witness may have a reasonable opportunity to confer with retained counsel outside the grand jury room. The ABA *Standards* provide that "[p]rior to taking a target's testimony, the prosecutor should advise the target of the privilege against self-incrimination and obtain a voluntary waiver of that right." Criminal Justice

Standards for the Prosecution Function, *supra*, § 3-4.6(g). The general rule, however, is that a subject or target appearing before the grand jury will be treated as any other witness and afforded no particularized warnings or special protections. *See, e.g., United States v. Mandujano*, 425 U.S. 564 (1976) (*Miranda* warnings do not have to be given to a grand jury witness).

If a target's request to testify voluntarily is granted, he or she may be required to waive any Fifth Amendment rights prior to testifying. *See, e.g.,* U.S. Attorney's Manual 9-11.152 (must also be represented by counsel or validly waive counsel).

[iv] Wisdom of Target's Appearance

In the minority of jurisdictions that afford the target witness an opportunity to appear before the grand jury, is it always advisable for the target to do so? Strategically, this may pose a very difficult question for the target witness and her counsel. The testimony before the grand jury may persuade it not to indict. On the other hand, the target witness has a responsibility to answer questions truthfully, except where protected by the privilege against self-incrimination or another limit. Since the target witness may inadvertently answer a question under circumstances when a self-incrimination claim could have been asserted, the testimony may establish probable cause. Similarly, as the proceedings are on the record and under oath, even seemingly insignificant responses could be used for impeachment purposes at a subsequent trial.

[v] Privileges Potentially Available to a Target or Witness

As discussed at length later in this chapter, a target of a grand jury investigation or a witness summoned to appear might be able to invoke the Fifth Amendment privilege against self-incrimination, and thereby avoid having to provide testimony or documents to the grand jury. Other privileges also potentially apply, however, such as the attorney-client privilege, the adverse spousal testimony and confidential marital communications privileges, and the patient-psychotherapist privilege. Whether a privilege can be invoked is determined by the judge supervising the grand jury proceeding.

[d] Role of Defense Attorney

[i] Prior to Grand Jury Hearing

Sometimes, and especially in white-collar crime cases, an individual has some reason to believe that he or she is, or soon will be, the subject of a grand jury investigation and consults an attorney before an indictment is issued. Even though the grand jury process is outside of the lawyer's control, it would be a mistake to conclude that there is nothing the lawyer can do on behalf of the client.

The defense attorney's first mission may be to persuade the prosecutor not to seek an indictment against the client. This may entail making a presentation of facts or legal theories to convince the prosecutor that a formal charge would be ill-advised. Similarly, defense counsel may succeed in urging the prosecutor to limit the indictment in various ways (i.e., fewer counts or a lesser offense). In exchange, the client may agree to cooperate with the government, which may have the effect of shifting the focus to other culpable parties. Cooperation at this stage also could benefit the client at the sentencing phase of the case. Defense counsel can also request that the prosecutor submit certain exculpatory evidence to the grand jury. Finally, defense counsel should begin gathering information about the investigation in order to assist in trial preparation.

[ii] During Grand Jury Hearing: Minority Rule

Some states now permit witnesses' attorneys to be present to a limited extent during grand jury proceedings. Massachusetts, for example, provides that counsel can be present but "shall make no objections or arguments or otherwise address the grand jury or the prosecuting attorney." Mass R. Crim. P. 5. Similarly, Michigan rules provide that the lawyer "not participate in the proceedings other than to advise the witness." Mich. R. Crim. P. 6.005.

The right to counsel in the grand jury room is usually restricted to retained attorneys; states do not ordinarily provide for state-funded attorneys for indigent witnesses. A small number of states provide counsel to indigent witnesses called to testify before grand juries, while others appear to limit that provision to witnesses against whom the state may be seeking an indictment.

Prosecutors generally oppose provisions that permit a defense attorney to be present in the grand jury room. They argue that the lawyer will jeopardize grand jury secrecy and disrupt the grand jury process by making objections, requesting delays, and conducting lengthy legal examinations of witnesses. Do you agree that these concerns are sufficient to keep witness lawyers out of the grand jury room? Do the Michigan and Massachusetts provisions noted above constitute tenable compromises?

[iii] During Grand Jury Hearing: Majority Rule

In most states and in the federal system, witnesses must enter grand jury rooms alone while their retained attorneys wait outside the grand jury room. The witness desiring to consult with counsel during the grand jury proceedings ordinarily will write down the question, request permission to leave the room, consult with counsel in the corridor outside the grand jury room, and then return and respond to the question. The scenario is repeated with each question. One rationale for this awkward and time-consuming practice is that the grand jury is non-adversarial. Its sole task, it is argued, is to determine whether there is probable cause to indict; the presence of counsel would not aid in meeting that objective.

A number of issues are litigated in the context of the majority no-counsel-present rule. First, since it is well established that a grand jury witness has the right to consult with counsel, the witness must be afforded the right to leave the grand jury room at reasonable times to consult with their lawyer. *See, e.g., Gilbert v. Connecticut*, 131 F.3d 793 (9th Cir. 1997). On the assumption that a non-immunized witness has more to fear in terms of self- incrimination than one who has received immunity, some courts have suggested that the non-immunized witness should have broader power to interrupt the grand jury proceedings to confer with counsel. *Matter of Lowry*, 713 F.2d 616 (11th Cir. 1983).

Perhaps the most difficult issue to resolve is the question under what circumstances consultation with counsel becomes unreasonable or obstructionist. A prosecutor or the grand jury foreperson may try to restrict a witness's frequent consultations with counsel. If the witness refuses to obey such a command, the prosecutor can seek a contempt of court order against the witness. If the judge determines that the witness is engaging in consultation either to obstruct the grand jury's investigation or for frivolous reasons, the judge may cite the witness for contempt of court.

[e] Admissibility of Evidence

Given the non-adversarial nature of the grand jury investigative process, rules governing the presentation and admissibility of evidence at trial are relaxed in grand jury hearings, though privileges can still apply in full force. Additionally, as indicated above, courts are hesitant to convert grand jury proceedings into "mini-trials." They believe that extending evidentiary challenges to the grand jury context could impede investigations and sacrifice the traditional rule of grand jury secrecy.

Notwithstanding these concerns, many legislatures and courts impose some restrictions on the evidence admissible in grand jury proceedings. A few states follow relatively strict rules of evidence in grand jury proceedings. *See, e.g.*, N.Y. Crim. Pro. § 190.30(1). However, in New York, prosecutors have the authority to make rulings regarding "the competency of a witness to testify or upon the admissibility of evidence." *Id.* § 190.30(6).

Other states do not follow the rules of evidence, but prohibit indictments that are based, for instance, solely on inadmissible evidence. Most states and the federal government, however, recognize relatively few limitations (other than privileges) on the kinds of evidence admissible before the grand jury. Beale et al., Grand Jury Law and Practice, *supra*, §§ 4:19, & 4:20.

One key evidentiary issue, grand jury consideration of hearsay evidence, which would be inadmissible at trial, was addressed by the United States Supreme Court in the following case.

Costello v. United States

350 U.S. 359 (1956)

Mr. Justice Black delivered the opinion of the Court.

We granted certiorari in this case to consider a single question: "May a defendant be required to stand trial and a conviction be sustained where only hearsay evidence was presented to the grand jury which indicted him?"

[Defendant was indicted for willfully attempting to evade payment of income taxes by understating his income. The only witnesses before the grand jury were the government investigators who summarized the results of interviews with witnesses and the content of various documents.]

... The Fifth Amendment provides that federal prosecutions for capital or otherwise infamous crimes must be instituted by presentments or indictments of grand juries. But neither the Fifth Amendment nor any other constitutional provision prescribes the kind of evidence upon which grand juries must act....

If indictments were to be held open to challenge on the ground that there was inadequate or incompetent evidence before the grand jury, the resulting delay would be great indeed. The result of such a rule would be that before trial on the merits a defendant could always insist on a kind of preliminary trial to determine the competency and adequacy of the evidence before the grand jury. This is not required by the Fifth Amendment. An indictment returned by a legally constituted and unbiased grand jury, like an information drawn by the prosecutor, if valid on its face, is enough to call for trial of the charge on the merits. The Fifth Amendment requires nothing more.

Petitioner urges that this Court should exercise its power to supervise the administration of justice in federal courts and establish a rule permitting defendants to challenge indictments on the ground that they are not supported by adequate or competent evidence.... It would run counter to the whole history of the grand jury institution, in which laymen conduct their inquiries unfettered by technical rules. Neither justice nor the concept of a fair trial requires such a change. In a trial on the merits, defendants are entitled to a strict observance of all the rules designed to bring about a fair verdict. Defendants are not entitled, however, to a rule which would result in interminable delay but add nothing to the assurance of a fair trial.

Mr. Justice Burton, concurring.

I agree with the denial of the motion to quash the indictment. In my view, however, this case does not justify the breadth of the declarations made by the Court. I assume that this Court would not preclude an examination of grand-jury action to ascertain the existence of bias or prejudice in an indictment. Likewise, it seems to me that if it is shown that the grand jury had before it no substantial or rationally persuasive evidence upon which to base its indictment, that indictment should be quashed. To hold a person to answer to such an empty indictment for a capital or otherwise infamous federal crime robs the Fifth Amendment of much of its protective value to the private citizen....

Notes

1. *Exclusionary rule—Inapplicable in grand jury. Costello* provides that hearsay testimony is admissible, even though a fact-finder could not consider the testimony in a trial. A different question arises when police have obtained evidence in violation of the Fourth or Fifth Amendment and now seek to use or rely upon that evidence in presenting a case for grand jury consideration. Again, presuming the evidence was subject to suppression, it would not be considered by the fact-finder in assessing guilt at trial.

This evidence, too, can be considered by grand juries in their decision to indict. *See United States v. Calandra*, 414 U.S. 338 (1974). In *Calandra*, a witness testifying before a grand jury sought to refuse to answer questions on the ground that they were based upon evidence obtained from an unlawful search. The Court responded that the exclusionary rule does not apply to grand jury proceedings. Therefore, the witness had no right to refuse to answer the questions. Using a balancing approach, the Court noted that extending the exclusionary rule to the grand jury "would unduly interfere with the effective and expeditious discharge of the grand jury's duties." And while the purposes behind the exclusionary rule (deterrence of police misconduct) might be advanced by extending the rule to the grand jury proceeding, that benefit would be "uncertain at best."

The *Calandra* exception to the exclusionary rule for Fourth Amendment violations also extends to evidence obtained in violation of the Fifth Amendment's self-incrimination clause. *United States v. Blue*, 384 U.S. 251 (1966).

2. *Exclusionary rule—Applicable in grand jury.* The exclusionary rule does apply in a few narrow contexts in grand jury proceedings. As discussed later, an indictment can be dismissed if it was based directly or indirectly on immunized testimony of the person who was indicted. An indictment has also been dismissed for violation of the Speech and Debate Clause. *See In re Grand Jury Subpoenas*, 571 F.3d 1200 (D.C. Cir. 2009) (grand jury subpoena for Congressman's attorneys who represented him during congressional ethics hearing was properly quashed because the hearing was a legislative function).

The Foreign Intelligence Surveillance Act (FISA) requires courts to "suppress the evidence which was unlawfully obtained or derived from electronic surveillance." 50 U.S.C.A. § 1806(g). However, FISA has been deemed inapplicable to grand jury proceedings. *See In re Grand Jury Subpoena (T-112)*, 597 F.3d 189, 194 (4th Cir. 2010).

3. *Voluntary application of exclusionary rule.* The U.S. Justice Department has internal rules barring federal prosecutors from presenting to grand juries evidence "against a person whose constitutional rights clearly have been violated . . . which the prosecutor personally knows was obtained as a direct result of the constitutional violation." U.S. Attorney's Manual 9-11.231. How important is the word "clearly" in the practical impact of this rule?

4. *State variations.* A few states disagree with *Calandra* and bar indictments based solely on evidence obtained in violation of the constitution. BEALE ET AL., GRAND JURY LAW AND PRACTICE, *supra*, § 4:21.

5. *Evidence rules and function of grand jury.* If a grand jury relies upon hearsay testimony, as in *Costello*, or evidence inadmissible at trial, such as in *Calandra*, has it truly performed its "shield" function in serving as a buffer between the government and the accused? Can it accurately assess either the defendant's culpability or the strength of the prosecution's case?

What bearing, if any, should allowing grand jurors to consider evidence that is ultimately inadmissible have on a prosecutor's decision to bring a case to the grand jury? Earlier it was noted that a prosecutor might have collateral reasons to bring such a case. Do the outcomes in *Calandra* and *Costello* change your view?

United States Attorneys are instructed that they may use hearsay evidence in grand jury proceedings but the evidence should "be presented on its merits so that the jurors are not misled into believing that the witness is giving his or her personal account." U.S. Attorneys' Manual 9-11-232. To the extent that you disagree with *Costello*, do you think this adequately ameliorates the situation?

6. *Impact of stricter evidence rules.* If stricter evidentiary rules were to apply to grand juries, to what extent would (or should) the target be entitled to a transcript of the grand jury proceeding to determine whether the indictment was properly issued? If this were allowed, how could grand jury secrecy be preserved?

[f] Subpoena Power

The grand jury's (actually the prosecutor's) power to issue subpoenas is a potent investigative tool to obtain both tangible and testimonial evidence. A *subpoena ad testificandum* is an order compelling the named witness to appear and testify before the grand jury. A *subpoena duces tecum* is an order for the witness to appear and produce certain specified records before the grand jury.

Unlike an arrestee who is interrogated in a police station, one who has been subpoenaed has no general right to refuse to cooperate, although the Fifth Amendment privilege against self-incrimination is available to both the arrestee and the subpoenaed person.

Testimony before the grand jury will be given under oath, which means that false testimony can result in a perjury conviction. A subpoenaed witness who refuses without justification (usually based on the Fifth Amendment privilege) to give testimony may be held in contempt and jailed for the duration of the grand jury's term, or until the witness purges himself of contempt by complying with the subpoena and testifying.

As discussed earlier in this chapter, many states do not require grand juries or have limited their required use. In the federal system and in states that retain the grand jury, it is usually the prosecutor, acting on behalf or in the name of the grand jury, who issues subpoenas or moves to have a recalcitrant witness held in contempt by a judicial officer.

In non-grand jury states, the prosecutor initiates charges directly via an information and typically has the power to summon witnesses to appear and produce documents at a designated date and time. The Arkansas statute, conferring investigatory subpoena power directly on the prosecutor, is illustrative:

Arkansas Code, § 16-43-212.

Criminal proceedings—Issuance of subpoenas pursuant to investigations

(a) The prosecuting attorneys and their deputies may issue subpoenas in all criminal matters they are investigating and may administer oaths for the purpose of taking the testimony of witnesses subpoenaed before them. Such oath when administered by the prosecuting attorney or his or her deputy shall have the same effect as if administered by the foreman of the grand jury. The subpoena shall be substantially in the following form:

The State of Arkansas to the Sheriff of ____________________ County: You are commanded to summon [name of person] to attend before the Prosecuting Attorney at [date]__________________, A.D. 20________________. M., and testify in the matter of an investigation then to be conducted by the said Prosecuting Attorney growing out of a representation that [name of suspect] has committed the crime of ________________ in said County. Witness my hand this __________________, A.D. 20________________.

____________________.

____

Prosecuting Attorney

By

____

Deputy Prosecuting Attorney

(b) The subpoena provided for in subsection (a) of this section shall be served in the manner as provided by law and shall be returned and a record made and kept as provided by law for grand jury subpoenas. . . .

Note

As explained earlier, the witness has the affirmative duty to assert the Fifth Amendment self-incrimination privilege, if applicable. The witness must be cautious to avoid making an "unwitting waiver," in which the witness who voluntarily discloses some facts to the grand jury cannot assert the privilege to refuse to answer questions about the details of those facts. *See, e.g.*, *Rogers v. United States*, 340 U.S. 367 (1951) (federal courts have uniformly held that, where incriminating facts have been voluntarily revealed, the privilege cannot be invoked to avoid disclosure of the details). The Supreme Court later reaffirmed *Rogers*, noting that "there is no unfairness in allowing cross-examination when testimony is given without invoking the privilege." *Mitchell v. United States*, 526 U.S. 314 (1999). *See also* Leslie W. Abramson, *Witness Waiver of the Fifth Amendment Privilege: A New Look at an Old Problem*, 41 Okla. L. Rev. 235 (1988).

[g] Jurisdiction, Relevance

Assume a witness is subpoenaed to appear before the grand jury and the witness believes that the grand jury has no jurisdiction over the matter being investigated, or asserts that the testimony sought is irrelevant to the matter being considered by the grand jury. Is the witness permitted to refuse compliance on either basis? In *Blair v. United States*, 250 U.S. 273 (1919), the United States Supreme Court held that neither is a valid basis to resist compliance.

[h] Reasonableness

Can an individual or entity subpoenaed to provide evidence to a grand jury resist on the basis that the information sought is purportedly irrelevant to the grand jury's inquiry? Federal Rule of Criminal Procedure 17(c) authorizes a court to quash or modify a grand jury *subpoena duces tecum* "if compliance would be unreasonable or oppressive." The definition of the standard was addressed by the U.S. Supreme Court in *United States v. R. Enterprises*, 498 U.S. 292 (1991). In *R. Enterprises*, a grand jury investigating alleged interstate transportation of obscene materials issued a *subpoena duces tecum* commanding companies to produce materials, and the companies sought to quash the subpoena on the basis of irrelevance and the First Amendment. The Court upheld the lower courts' rejection of the motion, stating:

> The grand jury occupies a unique role in our criminal justice system. It is an investigatory body charged with the responsibility of determining whether or not a crime has been committed . . . The function of the grand jury is to inquire into all information that might possibly bear on its investigation until it has identified an offense or has satisfied itself that none has occurred.
>
> A grand jury subpoena is thus much different from a subpoena issued in the context of a prospective criminal trial, where a specific offense has been identified and a particular defendant charged. . . . [T]he Government cannot be required to justify the issuance of a grand jury subpoena by presenting evidence sufficient to establish probable cause because the very purpose of requesting the information is to ascertain whether probable cause exists. . . .
>
> The investigatory powers of the grand jury are nevertheless not unlimited. Grand juries are not licensed to engage in arbitrary fishing expeditions, nor may they select targets of investigation out of malice or an intent to harass. In this case, the focus of our inquiry is the limit imposed on a grand jury by Federal Rule of Criminal Procedure 17(c), which governs the issuance of *subpoenas duces tecum* in federal criminal proceedings. The Rule provides that "the court on motion made promptly may quash or modify the subpoena if compliance would be unreasonable or oppressive." . . .
>
> We begin by reiterating that the law presumes, absent a strong showing to the contrary, that a grand jury acts within the legitimate scope of its authority. . . . Consequently, a grand jury subpoena issued through normal channels is presumed to be reasonable, and the burden of showing unreasonableness must be on the recipient who seeks to avoid compliance. . . . Drawing on the principles articulated above, we conclude that where, as here, a subpoena is challenged on relevancy grounds, the motion to quash must be denied unless the district court determines that there is no reasonable possibility that the category of materials the Government seeks will produce information relevant to the general subject of the grand jury's investigation. Respondents did not challenge the subpoenas as being too indefinite nor did they

> claim that compliance would be overly burdensome. The Court of Appeals accordingly did not consider these aspects of the subpoenas, nor do we.

Id. at 299–301.

A party seeking to quash a subpoena, however, very often is unaware of the exact nature of the grand jury's inquiry, imposing a burden on the party's ability to contest reasonableness. Mindful of this challenge, the Court stated:

> a court may be justified in a case where unreasonableness is alleged in requiring the Government to reveal the general subject of the grand jury's investigation before requiring the challenging party to carry its burden of persuasion. . . . In cases where the recipient of the subpoena does not know the nature of the investigation, we are confident that district courts will be able to craft appropriate procedures that balance the interests of the subpoena recipient against the strong governmental interests in maintaining secrecy, preserving investigatory flexibility, and avoiding procedural delays.
>
> For example, to ensure that subpoenas are not routinely challenged as a form of discovery, a district court may require that the Government reveal the subject of the investigation to the trial court in camera, so that the court may determine whether the motion to quash has a reasonable prospect for success before it discloses the subject matter to the challenging party.

Id. at 301–02.

Concurring, Justice Stevens (joined by Justices Marshall and Blackmun) took issue with the standard of reasonableness specified by the Court:

> Federal Rule of Criminal Procedure 17(c). . . . requires the district court to balance the burden of compliance, on the one hand, against the governmental interest in obtaining the documents on the other. . . . [T]he Court has attempted to define the term "reasonable" in the abstract, looking only at the relevance side of the balance. Because I believe that this truncated approach to the Rule will neither provide adequate guidance to the district court nor place any meaningful constraint on the overzealous prosecutor, I add these comments . . .
>
> The moving party has the initial task of demonstrating to the Court that he has some valid objection to compliance. This showing might be made in various ways. Depending on the volume and location of the requested materials, the mere cost in terms of time, money, and effort of responding to a dragnet subpoena could satisfy the initial hurdle. Similarly, if a witness showed that compliance with the subpoena would intrude significantly on his privacy interests, or call for the disclosure of trade secrets or other confidential information, further inquiry would be required. Or, as in this case, the movant might demonstrate that compliance would have First Amendment implications. . . .

For the reasons stated by the Court, in the grand jury context the law enforcement interest will almost always prevail, and the documents must be produced. I stress, however, that the Court's opinion should not be read to suggest that the deferential relevance standard the Court has formulated will govern decision in every case, no matter how intrusive or burdensome the request. . . .

I would only add that further inquiry into the possible unreasonable or oppressive character of this subpoena should also take into account the entire history of this grand jury investigation, including the series of subpoenas that have been issued to the same corporations and their affiliates during the past several years.

Notes

1. *Rule 17(c).* As noted in *R. Enterprises*, "reasonableness" is a key limit on a subpoena. Under Rule 17(c) of the Federal Rules of Criminal Procedure, a court may quash or modify any subpoena found to be unreasonable or oppressive. According to one commentator,

> The subpoena's reasonableness comes into question only when the subpoenaed party, who bears the burden of proof, desires to quash. In order to fulfill the reasonableness requirement, the subpoena must state with particularity the materials relevant to the investigation and span a reasonable period of time. The "reasonable period of time" limitation requires that the subpoena bear "some relation" to the subject matter of the investigation. Courts have upheld subpoenas covering time spans ranging from four to twenty-seven years. Other factors bearing on reasonableness include the volume of subpoenaed records, the disruptive impact on the subpoenaed party, and the cost of compliance.

Susan L. Boccardi et al., *Grand Jury Subpoena and Secrecy*, 28 AM. CRIM. L. REV. 749, 753–54 (1991).

2. *Scope of the relevancy issue.* As discussed in *R. Enterprises*, the relevancy issue applies to the possibility of quashing categories of documents, not individual documents. *See also In re Grand Jury Proceedings*, 616 F.3d 1186 (10th Cir. 2010) (a court considers the relevancy of each category or subcategory of a subpoena's document requests, not specific documents).

3. *Identity of person subpoenaed; lawyers and members of media.* Another limit is based on the identity of the person receiving the subpoena. In *United States v. Klubock*, 832 F.2d 664 (1st Cir. 1987), the court held that prior judicial approval was necessary before serving a subpoena upon an attorney to provide evidence regarding the attorney's own client. *See also* U.S. ATTORNEYS' MANUAL 9-11.255 (prior approval of Assistant Attorney General needed for grand jury subpoena of an attorney for information related to the representation of a client). Do you agree with this special treatment of lawyers? Should there be a similar rule for physicians? Legislators?

Members of the media? (Note that the U.S. Attorneys' Manual requires permission of an *Assistant* Attorney General to subpoena a lawyer, but mandates that of the *Attorney General* for a member of the news media. *See id.*)

4. *Probable cause.* The *subpoena duces tecum* requires that the subpoenaed party produce records, physical evidence, or both. While a search warrant requires probable cause for a search and seizure under the Fourth Amendment, no such probable cause requirement applies to a grand jury's *subpoena duces tecum.* A grand jury may decide to request documents based upon uncorroborated and unsubstantiated tips or rumors. In addition to documentary evidence, the recipient of a *subpoena duces tecum* may be forced to appear before a grand jury to be photographed, to have a hair sample taken, or to appear in a line-up.

Some states impose restrictions upon grand jury powers of this kind. For example, the Illinois Supreme Court relied upon its state constitution in holding that a grand jury subpoena for "non-invasive" physical evidence (appearance in line up, fingerprint, voice or handwriting exemplars) must be predicated on some showing of individualized suspicion and relevance. A grand jury subpoena for "invasive" physical evidence (pubic hair or blood sample) must be based on the higher standard of probable cause, but the grand jury need not first obtain a search warrant. *People v. Watson*, 825 N.E.2d 257 (Ill. 2005). What, if any, practical problems are likely to surface under the Illinois rule?

5. *Voice and handwriting exemplars.* Grand jury witnesses may also be compelled to provide voice recordings or handwriting exemplars. In both instances, a witness may believe either that the Fourth Amendment or Fifth Amendment protects the witness from having to comply with such orders. The United States Supreme Court, however, has held otherwise. In *United States v. Dionisio*, 410 U.S. 1 (1973), the Court reasoned that compelled production of a voice exemplar did not violate the Fifth Amendment because self-incrimination does not protect the "compelled display of identifiable physical characteristics."

Similarly, the *Dionisio* Court held that the Fourth Amendment guarantee against unreasonable searches and seizures was not infringed because "no person can have a reasonable expectation that others will not know the sound of his voice." The companion case of *United States v. Mara*, 410 U.S. 19 (1973), involving orders to produce handwriting exemplars, was resolved in like fashion under the *Dionisio* rationale. In his dissenting opinion, Justice Marshall characterized the Court's decisions as serving "only to encourage prosecutorial exploitation of the grand jury process."

6. *Subpoenas for digital information.* Subpoenas for electronically stored information provide new challenges for the application of traditional grand jury subpoena standards. As one commentator noted, "neither the document creator nor the prosecution knows precisely what records might exist: because of the networking of digital storage, third parties are now significantly more likely to possess digital data, such as personal communications and stored documents, created by others." Joshua

Gruenspecht, *"Reasonable" Grand Jury Subpoenas: Asking for Information in the Age of Big Data*, 24 HARV. J. L. & TECH. 543 (2011).

7. *Procedures to challenge subpoena.* As indicated in *R. Enterprises*, any person challenging a grand jury subpoena may file a Motion to Quash, but the complainant must overcome the initial presumption of regularity in order to prevail. If the judge denies the motion, the subpoenaed party may appeal the decision only after refusing to comply with the order and being held in contempt. The following is a list of some objections that may be raised in a Motion to Quash a subpoena:

a. The *subpoena duces tecum* is too sweeping and indefinite to be regarded as reasonable. Sometimes, the argument is made that compliance with the subpoena would be "oppressive."

b. The witness may assert that materials or testimony are protected from disclosure because of a legal privilege, such as those protecting communications between attorneys and clients, spouses, physicians or psychotherapists and patients, and priests and confessors.

c. Notwithstanding *R. Enterprises*, the witness may assert that the subpoena was obtained by prosecutorial misconduct through abuse of the grand jury or interference with the independence of the grand jury's performance.

d. The witness may object that the government is using the subpoena power to elicit evidence for use in a civil proceeding, as noted in *United States v. Procter and Gamble*, 356 U.S. 677 (1958). Lower courts have differed considerably, however, about the application of the *Procter and Gamble* standard. Because white-collar crime statutes often include civil penalty provisions, many defendants find themselves involved in both criminal and civil proceedings. For a review of some of the difficult issues that can arise in parallel proceedings, *see* D. Grayson Yeargin & Lindsey Nelson, *The Pitfalls of Parallel Proceedings* (ABA Section of Litigation-Criminal Litigation, Apr. 4, 2012), http://apps.americanbar.org/litigation/committees/criminal/email/winter2012/winter2012-0402-pitfalls-parallel-proceedings.html.

e. If a grand jury continues to investigate a case after an indictment has been issued, the witness may assert that the subpoena power is being used to obtain evidence for trial. A number of courts have condemned this practice. *See, e.g., United States v. United States Infrastructure, Inc.*, 576 F.3d 1195 (11th Cir. 2009).

f. The witness may allege the subpoena was issued in bad faith for the purpose of "harassment." One commentator has suggested that calling a witness before the grand jury solely to "trap" the witness into committing perjury is a form of unreasonable harassment. *See* Bennett L. Gershman, *The "Perjury Trap,"* 129 U. PA. L. REV. 624 (1981).

g. The witness may assert what is now the most frequently litigated constitutional claim in the context of a *subpoena duces tecum*: the Fifth Amendment self-incrimination privilege, which is addressed in the next section.

D. The Fifth Amendment: Self-Incrimination

When a witness is asked to testify before a grand jury, he or she may assert that the questions require a response that may be self-incriminating. If the witness wants the protection of the Fifth Amendment's self-incrimination guarantee, the witness must claim the privilege. In most jurisdictions neither the prosecutor nor the grand jury is obliged to "warn" the witness in advance of the questioning that the witness has a self-incrimination privilege or that an incriminating response could be used as evidence against that person. Indeed, the United States Supreme Court has indicated that *Miranda* warnings need not be given to a witness who appears before the grand jury. *United States v. Mandujano*, 425 U.S. 564 (1976). The Constitution also does not mandate that the witness be told he or she is the target of the grand jury probe, though in this situation the prosecution may be wise to give the witness the *Miranda* warnings. *United States v. Washington*, 431 U.S. 181 (1977).

To successfully assert a Fifth Amendment privilege, three things must be established. First, it must be shown that the government is "compelling" compliance with its order or demand. Second, the material or information compelled must be "testimonial" in nature. And third, since the Fifth Amendment privilege is personal, the protection extends only to incrimination of oneself by oneself.

[1] Compelled Disclosure

A person who produces documents in response to a *subpoena duces tecum* is deemed "compelled" to do so. However, as will be seen in the cases of *Fisher* and *Doe I*, discussed later in this Chapter, where records or papers are voluntarily prepared, there is no compulsion involved with respect to the preparation, as distinguished from the production of the items.

[2] Testimonial

The government can compel the production of certain types of physical evidence without implicating the Fifth Amendment because such evidence is deemed non-testimonial. On the other hand, most statements, whether written or oral, are considered testimonial because they may disclose facts or information that comes "from the individual's mind." As the following case demonstrates, while the distinction between physical evidence (deemed non-testimonial) and statements (testimonial) is generally accurate, it falls short of defining precisely the parameters of the testimonial requirement.

Doe v. United States (Doe II)

487 U.S. 201 (1988)

Justice Blackmun delivered the opinion of the Court.

This case presents the question whether a court order compelling a target of a grand jury investigation to authorize foreign banks to disclose records of his accounts, without identifying those documents or acknowledging their existence, violates the target's Fifth Amendment privilege against self-incrimination.

Petitioner, named here as John Doe, is the target of a federal grand jury investigation into possible federal offenses arising from suspected fraudulent manipulation of oil cargoes and receipt of unreported income. Doe appeared before the grand jury pursuant to a subpoena that directed him to produce records of transactions in accounts at three named banks in the Cayman Islands and Bermuda. Doe produced some bank records and testified that no additional records responsive to the subpoena were in his possession or control. When questioned about the existence or location of additional records, Doe invoked the Fifth Amendment privilege against self-incrimination.

The United States branches of the three foreign banks also were served with subpoenas commanding them to produce records of accounts over which Doe had signatory authority. Citing their governments' bank-secrecy laws, which prohibit the disclosure of account records without the customer's consent, the banks refused to comply. The Government then filed a motion with the [District Court] . . . that the court order Doe to sign 12 forms consenting to disclosure of any bank records respectively relating to 12 foreign bank accounts over which the Government knew or suspected that Doe had control. The forms indicated the account numbers and described the documents that the Government wished the banks to produce.

The District Court denied the motion, reasoning that by signing the consent forms, Doe would necessarily be admitting the existence of the accounts. The District Court believed, moreover, that if the banks delivered records pursuant to the consent forms, those forms would constitute "an admission that [Doe] exercised signatory authority over such accounts." The court speculated that the Government in a subsequent proceeding then could argue that Doe must have guilty knowledge of the contents of the accounts. Thus, in the court's view, compelling Doe to sign the forms was compelling him "to perform a testimonial act that would entail admission of knowledge of the contents of potentially incriminating documents," and such compulsion was prohibited by the Fifth Amendment. The District Court also noted that Doe had not been indicted, and that his signing of the forms might provide the Government with the incriminating link necessary to obtain an indictment, the kind of "fishing expedition" that the Fifth Amendment was designed to prevent.

The Government sought reconsideration. Along with its motion, it submitted to the court a revised proposed consent directive that was substantially the same as that approved by the Eleventh Circuit in *United States v. Ghidoni*, 732 F.2d 814 (11th Cir.), *cert. denied*, 469 U.S. 932 (1984). The form purported to apply to any and all accounts over which Doe had a right of withdrawal, without acknowledging the existence of any such account.[2]

---

2. The revised consent form reads: "I, ____________________, of the State of Texas in the United States of America, do hereby direct any bank or trust company at which I may have a bank

... We granted certiorari to resolve a conflict among the Courts of Appeals as to whether the compelled execution of a consent form directing the disclosure of foreign bank records is inconsistent with the Fifth Amendment. We conclude that a court order compelling the execution of such a directive as is at issue here does not implicate the Amendment.

... The execution of the consent directive at issue in this case obviously would be compelled, and we may assume that its execution would have an incriminating effect.

The question on which this case turns is whether the act of executing the form is a "testimonial communication." ... An examination of the [prior decisions] indicates the Court's recognition that, in order to be testimonial, an accused's communication must itself, explicitly or implicitly, relate a factual assertion or disclose information. Only then is a person compelled to be a "witness" against himself.

... The difficult question whether a compelled communication is testimonial for purposes of applying the Fifth Amendment often depends on the facts and circumstances of the particular case.

... The consent directive itself is not "testimonial." It is carefully drafted not to make reference to a specific account, but only to speak in the hypothetical. Thus, the form does not acknowledge that an account in a foreign financial institution is in existence or that it is controlled by petitioner. Nor does the form indicate whether documents or any other information relating to petitioner are present at the foreign bank, assuming that such an account does exist.... The form does not even identify the relevant bank. Although the executed form allows the Government access to a potential source of evidence, the directive itself does not point the Government toward hidden accounts or otherwise provide information that will assist the prosecution in uncovering evidence....

Given the consent directive's phraseology, petitioner's compelled act of executing the form has no testimonial significance either. By signing the form, Doe makes no statement, explicit or implicit, regarding the existence of a foreign bank account or his control over any such account. Nor would his execution of the form admit the authenticity of any records produced by the bank....

Finally, we cannot agree with petitioner's contention that his execution of the directive admits or asserts Doe's consent. The form does not state that Doe "consents" to the release of bank records. Instead, it states that the directive "shall be

---

account of any kind or at which a corporation has a bank account of any kind upon which I am authorized to draw, and its officers, employees and agents, to disclose all information and deliver copies of all documents of every nature in your possession or control which relate to said bank account to Grand Jury 84-2, empaneled May 7, 1984 and sitting in the Southern District of Texas, or to any attorney of the District of Texas, or to any attorney of the United States Department of Justice assisting said Grand Jury, and to give evidence relevant thereto, in the investigation conducted by Grand Jury 84-2 in the Southern District of Texas, and this shall be irrevocable authority for so doing...."

construed as consent" with respect to Cayman Islands and Bermuda bank-secrecy laws. Because the directive explicitly indicates that it was signed pursuant to a court order, Doe's compelled execution of the form sheds no light on his actual intent or state of mind. The form does "direct" the bank to disclose account information and release any records that "may" exist and for which Doe "may" be a relevant principal. But directing the recipient of a communication to do something is not an assertion of fact or, at least in this context, a disclosure of information. In its testimonial significance, the execution of such a directive is analogous to the production of a handwriting sample or voice exemplar: it is a nontestimonial act. In neither case is the suspect's action compelled to obtain "any knowledge he might have."

... Because the consent directive is not testimonial in nature, we conclude that the District Court's order compelling petitioner to sign the directive does not violate his Fifth Amendment privilege against self-incrimination. Accordingly, the judgment of the Court of Appeals is affirmed.

Justice Stevens, dissenting.

A defendant can be compelled to produce material evidence that is incriminating. Fingerprints, blood samples, voice exemplars, handwriting specimens, or other items of physical evidence may be extracted from a defendant against his will. But can he be compelled to use his mind to assist the prosecution in convicting him of a crime? I think not. He may in some cases be forced to surrender a key to a strongbox containing incriminating documents, but I do not believe he can be compelled to reveal the combination to his wall safe—by word or deed.

The document the Government seeks to extract from John Doe purports to order third parties to take action that will lead to the discovery of incriminating evidence. The directive itself may not betray any knowledge petitioner may have about the circumstances of the offenses being investigated by the grand jury, but it nevertheless purports to evidence a reasoned decision by Doe to authorize action by others. The forced execution of this document differs from the forced production of physical evidence just as human beings differ from other animals.

If John Doe can be compelled to use his mind to assist the Government in developing its case, I think he will be forced "to be a witness against himself." The fundamental purpose of the Fifth Amendment was to mark the line between the kind of inquisition conducted by the Star Chamber and what we proudly describe as our accusatorial system of justice. It reflects our respect for the inviolability of the human personality.... In my opinion that protection gives John Doe the right to refuse to sign the directive authorizing access to the records of any bank account that he may control.

Notes

1. In the view of the *Doe II* majority, the compelled disclosure of a person's signature on a consent form directing a bank to release bank records was not testimonial in nature because it did not qualify as an assertion of fact that the records actually existed. Responding to the dissent, the majority explained in a footnote:

> We do not disagree with the dissent that "[t]he expression of the contents of an individual's mind" is testimonial communication for purposes of the Fifth Amendment. We simply disagree with the dissent's conclusion that the execution of the consent directive at issue here forced petitioner to express the contents of his mind. In our view, such compulsion is more like "be[ing] forced to surrender a key to a strongbox containing incriminating documents" than it is like "be[ing] compelled to reveal the combination to [petitioner's] wall safe."

Do you agree that the consent directive is like "being forced to surrender a key to a strongbox" rather than being "compelled to reveal the combination to one's wall safe?" Does that distinction seem meaningful for self-incrimination purposes?

2. Assume that the Fifth Amendment protects against compelled disclosure of the "combination to the safe." Could a grand jury require that the owner of such a safe sign a "consent directive" to blow open the safe?

3. With respect to the dissenting opinion by Justice Stevens, should the Fifth Amendment be interpreted to protect the individual from being "compelled to use his mind to assist the government in developing its case?" If this were the proper standard, could a witness appearing in a lineup be compelled to repeat words (ostensibly being used only for identification purposes)?

4. In *Pennsylvania v. Muniz*, 496 U.S. 582 (1990), the Supreme Court held that a drunk driving suspect's answer to a question regarding the date of his sixth birthday was testimonial; because it was given in custody without *Miranda* warnings, it was inadmissible. The Court distinguished *Doe II*, noting that "the compelled execution of the consent directive did not force [him] to express the contents of his mind, but rather forced [him] only to make a nonfactual statement." Muniz, by contrast, was required to make a testimonial response to a question, from which the incriminating inference of impaired mental faculties stemmed.

[3] Self-Incriminatory

[a] In General

The Fifth Amendment protects an individual from being compelled to provide self-incriminating information that could be used against him or her in a criminal prosecution. With respect to the risk of self-incrimination, the Supreme Court has stated that it must

> be *perfectly clear*, from a careful consideration of all the circumstances in the case, that the witness is mistaken, and that the answers *cannot possibly* have such tendency to incriminate.... [The privilege] extends to answers that would themselves support a conviction ... but likewise embraces those which would furnish a link in the chain of his claim of evidence needed to prosecute.

Hoffman v. United States, 341 U.S. 479, 488 (1951). *See also Kastigar v. United States*, 406 U.S. 441 (1972) (privilege protects against compelled disclosure "that the witness reasonably believes could be used in a criminal prosecution or could lead to other evidence that might be used").

The Fifth Amendment privilege does not protect the witness from providing information that would be considered embarrassing or that could incriminate or otherwise harm a third party. Nor does it apply if the information in question would negatively affect a party in a pending or future civil case. (However, the privilege can be raised in a civil case if it would self-incriminate in a criminal case.) Given that sometimes there will be uncertainty regarding whether a response will be legally incriminating, sometimes a grand jury witness will seek to assert the self-incrimination privilege when the answers are perhaps not covered by the privilege. This is a question for the court, charged with overseeing the operation of the grand jury, to decide. In *Hoffman*, the Court described how such a review is to be undertaken:

> [The privilege] must be confined to instances where the witness has reasonable cause to apprehend danger from a direct answer. . . . To sustain the privilege, it need only be evident from the implications of the question, in the setting in which it is asked, that a responsive answer to the question or an explanation of why it cannot be answered might be dangerous because injurious disclosure could result. The trial judge in appraising the claim "must be governed as much by his personal perception of the peculiarities of the case as by the facts actually in evidence." . . .

Hoffman, 341 U.S. at 486.

The privilege is personal in nature, and protects only against incrimination of oneself. Therefore, Jones has no Fifth Amendment protection from production by Smith of evidence that will prove incriminating to Jones. Indeed, the Fifth Amendment "is designed to prevent the use of legal process to force from the lips of the accused individual the evidence necessary to convict him or to force him to produce and authenticate any personal documents or effects that might incriminate him." *United States v. White*, 322 U.S. 694, 698 (1944). (The extent of coverage enjoyed by non-individuals, such as partnerships and corporations, is discussed later in this Chapter.)

[b] Business Records Possessed by Third Parties

Couch v. United States

409 U.S. 322 (1973)

MR. JUSTICE POWELL delivered the opinion of the Court.

[Petitioner, owner of a restaurant, gave her business records to her accountant for use in preparing Petitioners' tax returns. An I.R.S. agent, investigating possible tax crimes, issued a summons to the accountant after the accountant had refused the agent's request to see Petitioners' records. After finding that the accountant had, at Petitioner's request, delivered the papers to the Petitioner's attorney, the agent sought enforcement of the summons. Petitioner intervened, claiming that her ownership of the records warranted a Fifth Amendment privilege "to bar their production."]

The question is whether the taxpayer may invoke her Fifth Amendment privilege against compulsory self-incrimination to prevent the production of her business and tax records in the possession of her accountant. Both the District Court and the Court of Appeals for the Fourth Circuit held the privilege unavailable.

... In the case before us the ingredient of personal compulsion against an accused is lacking. The summons and the order of the District Court enforcing it are directed against the accountant. He, not the taxpayer, is the only one compelled to do anything. And the accountant makes no claim that he may tend to be incriminated by the production.

... The divulgence of potentially incriminating evidence against petitioner is naturally unwelcome. But petitioner's distress would be no less if the divulgence came not from her accountant but from some other third party with whom she was connected and who possessed substantially equivalent knowledge of her business affairs. The basic complaint of petitioner stems from the fact of divulgence of the possibly incriminating information, not from the manner in which or the person from whom it was extracted. Yet such divulgence, where it does not result from coercion of the suspect herself, is a necessary part of the process of law enforcement and tax investigation.

... Petitioner further argues that the confidential nature of the accountant-client relationship and her resulting expectation of privacy in delivering the records protect her, under the Fourth and Fifth Amendments, from their production. Although not in itself controlling, we note that no confidential accountant-client privilege exists under federal law, and no state created privilege has been recognized in federal cases. Nor is there justification for such a privilege where records relevant to income tax returns are involved in a criminal investigation or prosecution. In *Boyd v. United States*, 116 U.S. 616 (1886), a pre-income tax case, the Court spoke of protection of privacy, but there can be little expectation of privacy where records are handed to an accountant, knowing that mandatory disclosure of much of the information therein is required in an income tax return. What information is not disclosed is largely in the accountant's discretion, not petitioner's. Indeed, the accountant himself risks criminal prosecution if he willfully assists in the preparation of a false return. His own need for self-protection would often require the right to disclose the information given him. Petitioner seeks extensions of constitutional protections against self-incrimination in the very situation where obligations of disclosure exist and under a system largely dependent upon honest self-reporting even to survive. Accordingly, petitioner here cannot reasonably claim, either for Fourth or Fifth Amendment purposes, an expectation of protected privacy or confidentiality....

Mr. Justice Brennan, concurring.

I join the opinion of the Court on the understanding that it does not establish a per se rule defeating a claim of Fifth Amendment privilege whenever the documents in question are not in the possession of the person claiming the privilege. In my view, the privilege is available to one who turns records over to a third person for custodial safekeeping rather than disclosure of the information, to one who turns records over to a third person at the inducement of the Government, to one who places records in a safety deposit box or in hiding; and to similar cases where reasonable steps have been taken to safeguard the confidentiality of the contents of the records.*

The privilege cannot extend, however, to the protection of a taxpayer's records conveyed to a retained accountant for use in preparation of an income tax return, where the accountant is himself obligated to prepare a complete and lawful return. . . .

Mr. Justice Douglas, dissenting.

I cannot agree with the majority that the privilege against self-incrimination was not available to the petitioner merely because she did not have possession of the documents in question and was not herself subject to compulsory process. . . . The decision today sanctions yet another tool of the ever-widening governmental invasion and oversight of our private lives. . . .

[The dissent of Justice Marshall is omitted.]

[c] Lawyers and Client's Documents

Fisher v. United States

425 U.S. 391 (1976)

Mr. Justice White delivered the opinion of the Court.

In these two cases we are called upon to decide whether a summons directing an attorney to produce documents delivered to him by his client in connection with the attorney-client relationship is enforceable over claims that the documents were constitutionally immune from summons in the hands of the client and retained that immunity in the hands of the attorney.

[Taxpayers, who were under investigation for possible civil or criminal tax violations, secured documents from their accountants pertaining to preparation of their tax returns. They thereafter provided these documents to the lawyers they retained

* In some of these instances, to be sure, the person claiming the privilege would not himself have been the subject of direct Government compulsion. And there is no doubt that the Fifth Amendment is concerned solely with *compulsory* self-incrimination. But surely the availability of the Fifth Amendment privilege cannot depend on whether or not the owner of the documents is compelled personally to turn the documents over to the Government. If private, testimonial documents held in the owner's own possession are privileged under the Fifth Amendment, then the Government cannot nullify that privilege by finding a way to obtain the documents without requiring the owner to take them in hand and personally present them to the Government agents. . . .

to assist in the investigation. The lawyers then refused to comply with summonses served upon them by the Internal Revenue Service.]

... The taxpayer's privilege under [the Fifth] Amendment is not violated by enforcement of the summonses involved in these cases because enforcement against a taxpayer's lawyer would not "compel" the taxpayer to do anything and certainly would not compel him to be a "witness" against himself.

... In *Couch v. United States*, 409 U.S. 322 (1973), we recently ruled that the Fifth Amendment rights of a taxpayer were not violated by the enforcement of a documentary summons directed to her accountant and requiring production of the taxpayer's own records in the possession of the accountant. We did so on the ground that in such a case "the ingredient of personal compulsion against an accused is lacking."

Here, the taxpayers are compelled to do no more than was the taxpayer in *Couch*. The taxpayers' Fifth Amendment privilege is therefore not violated by enforcement of the summonses directed toward their attorneys. This is true whether or not the Amendment would have barred a subpoena directing the taxpayer to produce the documents while they were in his hands.

The fact that the attorneys are agents of the taxpayers does not change this result.... Nor is this one of those situations ... where constructive possession is so clear or relinquishment of possession so temporary and insignificant as to leave the personal compulsion upon the taxpayer substantially intact. In this respect we see no difference between the delivery to the attorneys in these cases and delivery to the accountant in the *Couch* case.

[It is contended] that if the summons was enforced, the taxpayers' Fifth Amendment privilege would be, but should not be, lost solely because they gave their documents to their lawyers in order to obtain legal advice. But this misconceives the nature of the constitutional privilege. The Amendment protects a person from being compelled to be a witness against himself. Here, the taxpayers retained any privilege they ever had not to be compelled to testify against themselves and not to be compelled themselves to produce private papers in their possession.

... The Court of Appeals for the Fifth Circuit suggested that because legally and ethically the attorney was required to respect the confidences of his client, the latter had a reasonable expectation of privacy for the records in the hands of the attorney and therefore did not forfeit his Fifth Amendment privilege with respect to the records by transferring them in order to obtain legal advice. It is true that the Court has often stated that one of the several purposes served by the constitutional privilege against compelled testimonial self-incrimination is that of protecting personal privacy. But the Court has never suggested that every invasion of privacy violates the privilege.

... We cannot cut the Fifth Amendment completely loose from the moorings of its language, and make it serve as a general protector of privacy—a word not mentioned in its text and a concept directly addressed in the Fourth Amendment.

... Our above holding is that compelled production of documents from an attorney does not implicate whatever Fifth Amendment privilege the taxpayer might have enjoyed from being compelled to produce them himself. The taxpayers in these cases, however, have from the outset consistently urged that they should not be forced to expose otherwise protected documents to summons simply because they have sought legal advice and turned the papers over to their attorneys. The Government appears to agree unqualifiedly. The difficulty is that the taxpayers have erroneously relied on the Fifth Amendment without urging the attorney-client privilege in so many words. They have nevertheless invoked the relevant body of law and policies that govern the attorney-client privilege. In this posture of the case, we feel obliged to inquire whether the attorney-client privilege applies to documents in the hands of an attorney which would have been privileged in the hands of the client by reason of the Fifth Amendment.

... Since each taxpayer transferred possession of the documents in question from himself to his attorney in order to obtain legal assistance in the tax investigations in question, the papers, if unobtainable by summons from the client, are unobtainable by summons directed to the attorney by reason of the attorney-client privilege. We accordingly proceed to the question whether the documents could have been obtained by summons addressed to the taxpayer while the documents were in his possession. The only bar to enforcement of such summons asserted by the parties or the courts below is the Fifth Amendment's privilege against self-incrimination.

... Accordingly, we turn to the question of what, if any, incriminating testimony within the Fifth Amendment's protection, is compelled by a documentary summons.

A subpoena served on a taxpayer requiring him to produce an accountant's work papers in his possession without doubt involves substantial compulsion. But it does not compel oral testimony; nor would it ordinarily compel the taxpayer to restate, repeat, or affirm the truth of the contents of the documents sought. Therefore, the Fifth Amendment would not be violated by the fact alone that the papers on their face might incriminate the taxpayer, for the privilege protects a person only against being incriminated by his own compelled testimonial communications. The accountant's work papers are not the taxpayer's. They were not prepared by the taxpayer, and they contain no testimonial declarations by him.

... The act of producing evidence in response to a subpoena nevertheless has communicative aspects of its own, wholly aside from the contents of the papers produced. Compliance with the subpoena tacitly concedes the existence of the papers demanded and their possession or control by the taxpayer. It also would indicate the taxpayer's belief that the papers are those described in the subpoena. The elements of compulsion are clearly present, but the more difficult issues are whether the tacit averments of the taxpayer are both "testimonial" and "incriminating" for purposes of applying the Fifth Amendment. These questions perhaps do not lend themselves to categorical answers; their resolution may instead depend on the facts and circumstances of particular cases or classes thereof. In light of the records now before us, we are confident that however incriminating the contents of the accountant's work papers might be, the act of producing them—the only thing which the taxpayer is compelled to do—would not itself involve testimonial self-incrimination.

It is doubtful that implicitly admitting the existence and possession of the papers rises to the level of testimony within the protection of the Fifth Amendment. The papers belong to the accountant, were prepared by him, and are the kind usually prepared by an accountant working on the tax returns of his client. Surely the Government is in no way relying on the "truth-telling" of the taxpayer to prove the existence of or his access to the documents. The existence and location of the papers are a foregone conclusion and the taxpayer adds little or nothing to the sum total of the Government's information by conceding that he in fact has the papers.

... Whether the Fifth Amendment would shield the taxpayer from producing his own tax records in his possession is a question not involved here; for the papers demanded here are not his "private papers." We do hold that compliance with a summons directing the taxpayer to produce the accountant's documents involved in these cases would involve no incriminating testimony within the protection of the Fifth Amendment....

Mr. Justice Marshall, concurring in the judgment.

... The Fifth Amendment basis for resisting production of a document pursuant to subpoena, the Court tells us today, lies not in the document's contents, as we previously have suggested, but in the tacit verification inherent in the act of production itself that the document exists, is in the possession of the producer, and is the one sought by the subpoena.

This technical and somewhat esoteric focus on the testimonial elements of production rather than on the content of the evidence the investigator seeks is ... contrary to the history and traditions of the privilege against self-incrimination both in this country and in England, where the privilege originated. A long line of precedents in this Court, whose rationales if not holdings are overturned by the Court today, support the notion that "any forcible and compulsory extortion of a man's ... private papers to be used as evidence to convict him of crime" compels him to be a witness against himself within the meaning of the Fifth Amendment to the Constitution.

[The concurring opinion of Justice Brennan is omitted.]

Note

There has been significant litigation over the "constructive possession" or "clearly temporary relinquishment of possession" exceptions raised in both *Couch* and *Fisher.* Under these doctrines, an individual who is not in actual possession of a document that is subpoenaed from another may invoke the Fifth Amendment because the party being subpoenaed either is in constructive possession of the document or has received possession so temporarily that the subpoena's compulsion actually falls upon the non-subpoenaed party. The Tenth Circuit has interpreted this doctrine to apply to situations "in which the records sought remain within the actual physical control of the party asserting the constitutional privilege even though they may be placed with another party for custodial safekeeping." *United States v. Silvestain*, 668 F.2d 1161, 1164 (10th Cir. 1982).

After *Fisher*, three specific doctrines are pertinent to the analysis of Fifth Amendment challenges to compelled evidentiary productions. These doctrines are the Collective Entity Rule, Required Records Doctrine, and Act of Production Doctrine.

[4] The Collective Entity Rule

The Fifth Amendment protects a "person" from being compelled to be a "witness against himself." Over time, the Supreme Court has been asked to interpret the Amendment's definitional scope (and hence protective coverage). As early as 1906, in *Hale v. Henkel*, 201 U.S. 43 (1906), the Court recognized that the privilege against self-incrimination is unavailable to corporations that, as fictive legal creatures of the state, are subject to the state's "visitatorial" powers to monitor and investigate its activities. Years later, the Court made clear that a corporation must submit its books and papers when properly ordered, and that "the visitatorial power which exists with respect to the corporation of necessity reaches the corporate books, without regard to the conduct of the custodian." *Wilson v. United States*, 221 U.S. 361, 385 (1911). In *United States v. White*, 322 U.S. 694 (1944), the Court extended the class of entities lacking the Fifth Amendment privilege from corporations to unincorporated entities (a labor union). It also made clear that an individual acting "in a representative capacity" (that is, on behalf of a collective entity) cannot claim a personal Fifth Amendment privilege with respect to "entity" materials. In *Bellis v. United States*, 417 U.S. 85 (1974), the Court held that a partner in a small law firm cannot invoke his personal privilege against self-incrimination to justify his refusal to produce financial records of the partnership.

Notes

1. *What is a collective entity?* The Supreme Court has stated that "an individual cannot rely upon the privilege to avoid producing the records of a collective entity which are in his possession in a representative capacity, even if these records might incriminate him personally." *Bellis*, 417 U.S. at 88. There has been considerable lower court litigation regarding the foregoing rule, known as the Collective Entity Rule. A variety of things have been deemed collective entities, not "natural individuals" entitled to enjoy the Fifth Amendment privilege: corporations, unincorporated associations, partnerships, and law firms. *See, e.g., In re Grand Jury Subpoena Issued June 18, 2009*, 593 F.3d 155 (2d Cir. 2010) (*Bellis* applies to the papers of a one-person professional corporation).

In *United States v. Doe (I)*, 465 U.S. 605 (1984), the Court distinguished *Bellis* and held that a sole proprietorship was entitled to Fifth Amendment protection. The Court reasoned that a sole proprietorship is not considered an entity distinct from the individual. Yet, a few years later, in *Braswell v. United States*, 487 U.S. 99 (1988), the Court held that a corporation wholly owned and operated by an individual was not entitled to Fifth Amendment protection.

It is important to note that less formalized arrangements may be deemed not to be a "collective entity" for purposes of the privilege against self-incrimination. As one court noted:

> [W]hen two or more persons act in concert to conduct some manner of business and attempt to exploit the benefits of a collective entity, the purported entity will be treated as a validly constituted entity for the purpose of the collective entity doctrine. As a consequence, any of the persons conducting business through the purported collective entity can be ordered to produce documents of the entity in a representative capacity.

United States v. O'Shea, 662 F. Supp. 2d 535 (S.D.W. Va. 2009). For further discussion of the Collective Entity Rule, *see, e.g.*, Lila L. Inman, Note, *Personal Enough for Protection: The Fifth Amendment and Single-Member LLCs*, 58 Wm. & Mary L. Rev. 1067 (2017).

2. *Personal, business, and mixed documents.* Courts have also examined the issue of what entity documents are protected by the Fifth Amendment notwithstanding the Collective Entity Rule. Documents can be classified as personal (or "intimate personal"), business, or mixed business and personal (such as appointment books and calendars). Personal documents, though located in the workplace, are not covered by the entity rule. Most courts addressing this issue find that mixed documents are corporate and therefore outside the privilege. *See United States v. MacKey*, 647 F.2d 898 (9th Cir. 1981).

At times, the analysis can be quite fact-specific. One federal district court, for instance, distinguished between desk calendars and pocket calendars, holding that the former had to be produced, while the latter did not. The court stated that any purely private notations in the desk calendars could be protected. Yet "an officer's diary is a corporate record if it is used to record entertainment expenses and is actually submitted to the company for use as the proof required by the Internal Revenue Code" and "the officer cannot change the nature of the document by including private and personal matters in the diaries." *In re Grand Jury Subpoena Duces Tecum dated April 23, 1981*, 522 F. Supp. 977, 982 (S.D.N.Y. 1981).

[5] The Required Records Doctrine

In *Wilson v. United States*, 221 U.S. 361 (1911), the Court held that the Fifth Amendment does not apply to "records required by law to be kept." In a later case, the Court specified the three questions to be addressed under the doctrine:

> First, the purposes of the United States' inquiry must be essentially regulatory; second, information is to be obtained by requiring the preservation of records of a kind which the regulated party has customarily kept; and

> third, the records themselves must have assumed "public aspects" which render them at least analogous to public documents.

Grosso v. United States, 390 U.S. 62, 67–68 (1968); *see also In re Grand Jury Subpoena*, 696 F.3d 428, (5th Cir. 2012) (discussing the tension between doctrine and Fifth Amendment privilege). For more on the required records doctrine, *see* Daniel M. Horowitz & Stephen K. Wirth, *The Death and Resurrection of the Required Record Doctrine*, 86 Miss. L.J. 813 (2017).

[6] Act of Production Doctrine

The Supreme Court has acknowledged that the act of production of evidence in responding to a subpoena may have incriminating aspects unrelated to the contents of the document itself. Specifically, the Court has noted that the act of producing a document can incriminate an individual in one of three ways. First, production can concede the very existence of the evidence demanded. Second, producing the document acknowledges that the subpoenaed document is in the party's possession or control. Third, the act of production can be used for authentication purposes.

Braswell v. United States

487 U.S. 99 (1988)

Chief Justice Rehnquist delivered the opinion of the Court.

This case presents the question whether the custodian of corporate records may resist a subpoena for such records on the ground that the act of production would incriminate him in violation of the Fifth Amendment. We conclude that he may not.

[A grand jury issued a subpoena to the president of two Mississippi corporations, both of which had three directors: Petitioner, his wife and his mother. The subpoena required petitioner to produce books and records of the two corporations. It also provided, however, that petitioner was not required to testify and that he could deliver the records to the agent serving the subpoena.]

There is no question but that the contents of the subpoenaed business records are not privileged. Similarly, petitioner asserts no self-incrimination claim on behalf of the corporations; it is well established that such artificial entities are not protected by the Fifth Amendment. Petitioner instead relies solely upon the argument that his act of producing the documents has independent testimonial significance, which would incriminate him individually, and that the Fifth Amendment prohibits Government compulsion of that act.

... Had petitioner conducted his business as a sole proprietorship, *United States v. Doe*, 465 U.S. 605 (1984), would require that he be provided the opportunity to show that his act of production would entail testimonial self-incrimination. But petitioner has operated his business through the corporate form, and we have long recognized that, for purposes of the Fifth Amendment, corporations and other collective entities are treated differently from individuals. This doctrine—known as the collective entity rule—has a lengthy and distinguished pedigree.

... [T]he Court has consistently recognized that the custodian of corporate or entity records holds those documents in a representative rather than a personal capacity. Artificial entities such as corporations may act only through their agents, and a custodian's assumption of his representative capacity leads to certain obligations, including the duty to produce corporate records on proper demand by the Government. Under those circumstances, the custodian's act of production is not deemed a personal act, but rather an act of the corporation. Any claim of Fifth Amendment privilege asserted by the agent would be tantamount to a claim of privilege by the corporation—which of course possesses no such privilege.

... Although a corporate custodian is not entitled to resist a subpoena on the ground that his act of production will be personally incriminating, we do think certain consequences flow from the fact that the custodian's act of production is one in his representative rather than personal capacity. Because the custodian acts as a representative, the act is deemed one of the corporation and not the individual. Therefore, the Government concedes, as it must, that it may make no evidentiary use of the "individual act" against the individual. For example, in a criminal prosecution against the custodian, the Government may not introduce into evidence before the jury the fact that the subpoena was served upon and the corporation's documents were delivered by one particular individual, the custodian. The Government has the right, however, to use the corporation's act of production against the custodian. The Government may offer testimony—for example, from the process server who delivered the subpoena and from the individual who received the records—establishing that the corporation produced the records subpoenaed. The jury may draw from the corporation's act of production the conclusion that the records in question are authentic corporate records, which the corporation possessed, and which it produced in response to the subpoena. And if the defendant held a prominent position within the corporation that produced the records, the jury may, just as it would had someone else produced the documents, reasonably infer that he had possession of the documents or knowledge of their contents. Because the jury is not told that the defendant produced the records, any nexus between the defendant and the documents results solely from the corporation's act of production and other evidence in the case.[11]

---

11. We reject the suggestion that the limitation on the evidentiary use of the custodian's act of production is the equivalent of constructive use immunity barred under our decision in *Doe*. Rather, the limitation is a necessary concomitant of the notion that a corporation custodian acts as an agent and not an individual when he produces corporate records in response to a subpoena addressed to him in his representative capacity. We leave open the question whether the agency rationale supports compelling a custodian to produce corporate records when the custodian is able to establish, by showing for example that he is the sole employee and officer of the corporation, that the jury would inevitably conclude that he produced the records.

Consistent with our precedent, the United States Court of Appeals for the Fifth Circuit ruled that petitioner could not resist the subpoena for corporate documents on the ground that the act of production might tend to incriminate him. The judgment is affirmed.

[Justice Kennedy, with whom Justice Brennan, Justice Marshall, and Justice Scalia join, dissenting, omitted.]

United States v. Hubbell

530 U.S. 27 (2000)

Justice Stevens delivered the opinion of the Court.

The two questions presented concern the scope of a witness' protection against compelled self-incrimination: (1) whether the Fifth Amendment privilege protects a witness from being compelled to disclose the existence of incriminating documents that the Government is unable to describe with reasonable particularity; and (2) if the witness produces such documents pursuant to a grant of immunity, whether 18 U.S.C. §6002 prevents the Government from using them to prepare criminal charges against him.

This proceeding arises out of the second prosecution of respondent, Webster Hubbell, commenced by the Independent Counsel appointed in August 1994 to investigate possible violations of federal law relating to the Whitewater Development Corporation. The first prosecution was terminated pursuant to a plea bargain. In December 1994, respondent pleaded guilty to charges of mail fraud and tax evasion arising out of his billing practices as a member of an Arkansas law firm from 1989 to 1992, and was sentenced to 21 months in prison. In the plea agreement, respondent promised to provide the Independent Counsel with "full, complete, accurate, and truthful information" about matters relating to the Whitewater investigation.

The second prosecution resulted from the Independent Counsel's attempt to determine whether respondent had violated that promise. In October 1996, while respondent was incarcerated, the Independent Counsel served him with a subpoena duces tecum calling for the production of 11 categories of documents before a grand jury sitting in Little Rock, Arkansas. [The appendix described the documents, and all of those requested were limited to the dates "January 1, 1993, to the present." (November 9, 1996, the required date of appearance). Examples include "any and all documents reflecting, referring, or relating to Webster Hubbell's schedule of activities, including all calendars, appointment books, diaries, records of reverse telephone toll calls, credit card calls, telephone message slips, other telephone records, minutes, databases, electronic mail messages, travel records, itineraries, tickets for transportation of any kind, payments, bills, expense backup documentation, schedules, and/or any other document or database that would disclose Webster Hubbell's activities."]

On November 19, he appeared before the grand jury and invoked his Fifth Amendment privilege against self-incrimination. In response to questioning by the prosecutor, respondent initially refused "to state whether there are documents within my possession, custody, or control responsive to the Subpoena." Thereafter, the prosecutor produced an order, which had previously been obtained from the District Court pursuant to 18 U.S.C. § 6003(a), directing him to respond to the subpoena and granting him immunity "to the extent allowed by law." Respondent then produced 13,120 pages of documents and records and responded to a series of questions that established that those were all of the documents in his custody or control that were responsive to the commands in the subpoena, with the exception of a few documents he claimed were shielded by the attorney-client and attorney work-product privileges.

The contents of the documents produced by respondent provided the Independent Counsel with the information that led to this second prosecution [for] ... various tax-related crimes and mail and wire fraud. The District Court dismissed the indictment relying, in part, on the ground that the Independent Counsel's use of the subpoenaed documents violated [the grant of immunity through] § 6002 because all of the evidence he would offer against respondent at trial derived either directly or indirectly from the testimonial aspects of respondent's immunized act of producing those documents. Noting that the Independent Counsel had admitted that he was not investigating tax-related issues when he issued the subpoena, and that he had "learned about the unreported income and other crimes from studying the records' contents," the District Court characterized the subpoena as "the quintessential fishing expedition."

The Court of Appeals vacated the judgment and remanded for further proceedings. The majority concluded that the District Court had incorrectly relied on the fact that the Independent Counsel did not have prior knowledge of the contents of the subpoenaed documents. The question the District Court should have addressed was the extent of the Government's independent knowledge of the documents' existence and authenticity, and of respondent's possession or control of them. ...

On remand, the Independent Counsel acknowledged that he could not satisfy the [independent knowledge] ... standard prescribed by the Court of Appeals and entered into a conditional plea agreement with respondent. In essence, the agreement provides for the dismissal of the charges unless this Court's disposition of the case makes it reasonably likely that respondent's "act of production immunity" would not pose a significant bar to his prosecution. The case is not moot, however, because the agreement also provides for the entry of a guilty plea and a sentence that will not include incarceration if we should reverse and issue an opinion that is sufficiently favorable to the Government to satisfy that condition. Despite that agreement, we granted the Independent Counsel's petition for a writ of certiorari in order to determine the precise scope of a grant of immunity with respect to the production of documents in response to a subpoena. We now affirm.

... More relevant to this case is the settled proposition that a person may be required to produce specific documents even though they contain incriminating assertions of fact or belief because the creation of those documents was not "compelled" within the meaning of the privilege. . . . It is clear, therefore, that respondent Hubbell could not avoid compliance with the subpoena served on him merely because the demanded documents contained incriminating evidence, whether written by others or voluntarily prepared by himself.

On the other hand, we have also made it clear that the act of producing documents in response to a subpoena may have a compelled testimonial aspect. We have held that "the act of production" itself may implicitly communicate "statements of fact." By "producing documents in compliance with a subpoena, the witness would admit that the papers existed, were in his possession or control, and were authentic." Moreover, as was true in this case, when the custodian of documents responds to a subpoena, he may be compelled to take the witness stand and answer questions designed to determine whether he has produced everything demanded by the subpoena. The answers to those questions, as well as the act of production itself, may certainly communicate information about the existence, custody, and authenticity of the documents. Whether the constitutional privilege protects the answers to such questions, or protects the act of production itself, is a question that is distinct from the question whether the unprotected contents of the documents themselves are incriminating.

. . . Compelled testimony that communicates information that may "lead to incriminating evidence" is privileged even if the information itself is not inculpatory. It is the Fifth Amendment's protection against the prosecutor's use of incriminating information derived directly or indirectly from the compelled testimony of the respondent that is of primary relevance in this case.

Acting pursuant to 18 U.S.C. § 6002, the District Court entered an order compelling respondent to produce "any and all documents" described in the grand jury subpoena and granting him "immunity to the extent allowed by law."

. . . The "compelled testimony" that is relevant in this case is not to be found in the contents of the documents produced in response to the subpoena. It is, rather, the testimony inherent in the act of producing those documents.

. . . The Government correctly emphasizes that the testimonial aspect of a response to a subpoena duces tecum does nothing more than establish the existence, authenticity, and custody of items that are produced. We assume that the Government is also entirely correct in its submission that it would not have to advert to respondent's act of production in order to prove the existence, authenticity, or custody of any documents that it might offer in evidence at a criminal trial; indeed, the Government disclaims any need to introduce any of the documents produced by respondent into evidence in order to prove the charges against him. It follows, according to the Government, that it has no intention of making improper "use" of respondent's compelled testimony.

The question, however, is not whether the response to the subpoena may be introduced into evidence at his criminal trial. That would surely be a prohibited "use" of the immunized act of production. But the fact that the Government intends no such use of the act of production leaves open the separate question whether it has already made "derivative use" of the testimonial aspect of that act in obtaining the indictment against respondent and in preparing its case for trial. It clearly has.

It is apparent from the text of the subpoena itself that the prosecutor needed respondent's assistance both to identify potential sources of information and to produce those sources. Given the breadth of the description of the 11 categories of documents called for by the subpoena, the collection and production of the materials demanded was tantamount to answering a series of interrogatories asking a witness to disclose the existence and location of particular documents fitting certain broad descriptions . . . Entirely apart from the contents of the 13,120 pages of materials that respondent produced in this case, it is undeniable that providing a catalog of existing documents fitting within any of the 11 broadly worded subpoena categories could provide a prosecutor with a "lead to incriminating evidence," or "a link in the chain of evidence needed to prosecute."

Indeed, the record makes it clear that that is what happened in this case. The documents were produced before a grand jury sitting in the Eastern District of Arkansas in aid of the Independent Counsel's attempt to determine whether respondent had violated a commitment in his first plea agreement. . . . It is abundantly clear that the testimonial aspect of respondent's act of producing subpoenaed documents was the first step in a chain of evidence that led to this prosecution. . . . It was only through respondent's truthful reply to the subpoena that the Government received the incriminating documents of which it made "substantial use . . . in the investigation that led to the indictment."

For these reasons, we cannot accept the Government's submission that respondent's immunity did not preclude its derivative use of the produced documents because its "possession of the documents [was] the fruit only of a simple physical act—the act of producing the documents." It was unquestionably necessary for respondent to make extensive use of "the contents of his own mind" in identifying the hundreds of documents responsive to the requests in the subpoena. . . .

In sum, we have no doubt that the constitutional privilege against self-incrimination protects the target of a grand jury investigation from being compelled to answer questions designed to elicit information about the existence of sources of potentially incriminating evidence. That constitutional privilege has the same application to the testimonial aspect of a response to a subpoena seeking discovery of those sources. . . . On appeal and again before this Court, the Government has argued that the communicative aspect of respondent's act of producing ordinary business records is insufficiently "testimonial" to support a claim of privilege because the existence and possession of such records by any businessman is a "foregone conclusion" under our decision in *Fisher v. United States*. This argument both misreads *Fisher* and ignores our subsequent decision in *United States v. Doe*.

. . . Whatever the scope of [the foregone conclusion doctrine discussed in *Fisher*], this "foregone conclusion" rationale, the facts of this case plainly fall outside of it.

While in *Fisher* the Government already knew that the documents were in the attorneys' possession and could independently confirm their existence and authenticity through the accountants who created them, here the Government has not shown that it had any prior knowledge of either the existence or the whereabouts of the 13,120 pages of documents ultimately produced by respondent. The Government cannot cure this deficiency through the overbroad argument that a businessman such as respondent will always possess general business and tax records that fall within the broad categories described in this subpoena. The *Doe* subpoenas also sought several broad categories of general business records, yet we upheld the District Court's finding that the act of producing those records would involve testimonial self-incrimination.

Given our conclusion that respondent's act of production had a testimonial aspect, at least with respect to the existence and location of the documents sought by the Government's subpoena, respondent could not be compelled to produce those documents without first receiving a grant of immunity. . . .

Accordingly, the indictment against respondent must be dismissed.

Justice Thomas, with whom Justice Scalia joins, concurring.

Our decision today involves the application of the act-of-production doctrine, which provides that persons compelled to turn over incriminating papers or other physical evidence pursuant to a subpoena duces tecum or a summons may invoke the Fifth Amendment privilege against self-incrimination as a bar to production only where the act of producing the evidence would contain "testimonial" features. I join the opinion of the Court because it properly applies this doctrine, but I write separately to note that this doctrine may be inconsistent with the original meaning of the Fifth Amendment's Self-Incrimination Clause. A substantial body of evidence suggests that the Fifth Amendment privilege protects against the compelled production not just of incriminating testimony, but of any incriminating evidence. In a future case, I would be willing to reconsider the scope and meaning of the Self-Incrimination Clause.

The Fifth Amendment provides that "[n]o person . . . shall be compelled in any criminal case to be a witness against himself." The key word at issue in this case is "witness." The Court's opinion, relying on prior cases, essentially defines "witness" as a person who provides testimony, and thus restricts the Fifth Amendment's ban to only those communications "that are 'testimonial' in character." None of this Court's cases, however, has undertaken an analysis of the meaning of the term at the time of the founding. A review of that period reveals substantial support for the view that the term "witness" meant a person who gives or furnishes evidence, a broader meaning than that which our case law currently ascribes to the term. If this is so, a person who responds to a subpoena duces tecum would be just as much a "witness" as a person who responds to a subpoena ad testificandum.

. . . This Court has not always taken the approach to the Fifth Amendment that we follow today. The first case interpreting the Self-Incrimination Clause—*Boyd v.*

United States—was decided, though not explicitly, in accordance with the understanding that "witness" means one who gives evidence. In *Boyd*, this Court unanimously held that the Fifth Amendment protects a defendant against compelled production of books and papers. And the Court linked its interpretation of the Fifth Amendment to the common-law understanding of the self-incrimination privilege.

But this Court's decision in *Fisher v. United States*, rejected this understanding, permitting the Government to force a person to furnish incriminating physical evidence and protecting only the "testimonial" aspects of that transfer. In so doing, *Fisher* not only failed to examine the historical backdrop to the Fifth Amendment, it also required . . . a difficult parsing of the act of responding to a subpoena duces tecum.

None of the parties in this case has asked us to depart from *Fisher*, but in light of the historical evidence that the Self-Incrimination Clause may have a broader reach than *Fisher* holds, I remain open to a reconsideration of that decision and its progeny in a proper case.

[The dissent of JUSTICE REHNQUIST is omitted.]

Notes

1. *Unanswered questions.* The *Hubbell* decision leaves several questions unanswered. Professor Robert Mosteller, for example, characterizes the decision as a "major reformulation of act of production doctrine." He notes:

> How protective the courts [after *Hubbell*] will prove to be when the issue is the target's possession of an item rather than its existence and how incrimination analysis will play out as to possession are the major puzzles remaining after *Hubbell*. Resolution of these issues will likely be interconnected. The Court's conclusion either will allow the anti-inquisitorial sentiment of *Hubbell* to invalidate subpoenas demanding that targets produce evidence that could incriminate them or will permit the Court to distinguish subpoenas for documents, where production might continue in a limited fashion, from other more facially incriminating items of physical evidence, whose compelled surrender appeared to greatly trouble the courts in *Hubbell*.

Robert P. Mosteller, *Cowboy Prosecutors and Subpoenas for Incriminating Evidence: The Consequences and Correction of Excess*, 58 WASH. & LEE L. REV. 487, 547, 548 (2001). *See also* Mark A. Cowen, *The Act-of-Production Privilege Post-*Hubbell: United States v. Ponds *and the Relevance of the "Reasonable Particularity" and "Foregone Conclusion" Doctrines*, 17 GEO. MASON L. REV. 863 (2010) (arguing that courts err by focusing "too much on the prior knowledge of the government and too little on the actual testimonial character of the production itself").

If the Thomas/Scalia "originalist" view in *Hubbell* should prevail in some future case (i.e., that *Boyd* was right and *Fisher* and its progeny are wrong, and that the Fifth Amendment protects not only against testimonial use of the act of production but also, more broadly, against compulsory production of the documents themselves), it is quite possible that the Court will substantially rework this whole area of the law. Do you agree with the views of Justices Thomas and Scalia in *Hubbell*?

2. *State deviations.* The Supreme Judicial Court of Massachusetts has declined to follow the reasoning of *Braswell*, deeming it "a fiction." *Commonwealth v. Doe*, 544 N.E.2d 860, 861–62 (Mass. 1989). In *Doe*, it was held that the custodian of corporate records could invoke his state constitutional self-incrimination claim when the act of production would be personally self-incriminating. It may be interesting to note that the Massachusetts constitutional provision in question provided that "no subject shall . . . be compelled to accuse, or furnish evidence against himself." Mass. Const. part 1, art. XII.

Is there anything fundamentally unfair, in your view, about compelling corporate officers (in the absence of any corporate privilege against self-incrimination) to produce company records where they as individuals, rather than the business entity, are the true target of the investigation?

3. *Contents of documents.* While the Fifth Amendment today generally provides no protection for private documents, there may be certain unique documents which are so personal in nature that they might qualify for some Fifth Amendment protection. For instance, the Court has never ruled on the issue of the Fifth Amendment protection as it pertains to a personal diary.

4. *Location v. production.* While a corporate custodian of records cannot assert a Fifth Amendment privilege in order to avoid production of documents, a custodian, not in possession of the documents, is protected by the privilege against self-incrimination from being compelled to testify about the documents' location. *In re Grand Jury Subpoena Dated April 14, 1996 v. Smith*, 87 F.3d 1198 (11th Cir. 1996). The court reasoned that unlike the act of production, testimony regarding the location of records requires the witness to disclose the contents of her mind.

5. *Production of people.* The act of production doctrine applies to people. In *Baltimore City Dep't of Soc. Servs. v. Bouknight*, 493 U.S. 549 (1990), the Supreme Court held that a mother given protective custody of a child through a protective services order could not invoke the Fifth Amendment to refuse production of the child. However, the state could not make evidentiary use of producing the child, such as admission of possession, existence, or identity of the child.

6. *"Foregone conclusion" doctrine.* Over the course of several opinions the Court has created what has come to be known as the "foregone conclusion" doctrine. As the *Fisher* Court described it:

> [When the] Government is in no way relying on the "truth-telling" of the taxpayer to prove the existence of or his access to the documents . . . [t]he existence and location of the papers are a foregone conclusion and the taxpayer adds little or nothing to the sum total of the Government's information by conceding that he in fact has the papers. Under these circumstances

> by enforcement of the summons "no constitutional rights are touched. The question is not one of testimony but one of surrender."

Fisher v. United States, 425 U.S. 391, 411 (1976) (citations omitted). In other words, the production of documents is not testimonial if the contents of the documents are already known by the government. *Id.*

Problems 7-1 to 7-4. Subpoenas Galore

7-1. The President of ABC, Inc., has moved to quash a *subpoena duces tecum* served upon the President's secretary. The subpoena directs the secretary to appear before the grand jury and produce the following materials and documents in the secretary's possession: the President's and the secretary's Rolodexes; and the secretary's appointment book, desk calendar, and business expense receipts (received from the President, but left in the secretary's files). What specific argument should be made by the President? How should the prosecuting attorney respond?

7-2. A restaurant owner has moved to quash a subpoena to produce a list of all customers who have paid by credit card in the restaurant in the previous two months. On what basis should the motion be filed? What should be the outcome?

7-3. A robbery suspect moves to quash a subpoena directing a bank manager to produce the contents of the suspect's safety deposit box in a specified branch of the bank. On what basis should the robbery suspect move to quash? How should the prosecuting attorney respond?

7-4. A homicide suspect has moved to quash a subpoena directing her suspected accomplice to produce the key to a vault in the accomplice's basement. It is believed that the vault contains weapons used by the suspect and her accomplice to commit the murder. What should be the result?

[7] Immunity

If a grand jury witness makes a legitimate claim of a Fifth Amendment privilege, the government has two choices. First, it can honor the privilege and proceed no further with the particular line of inquiry. Second, it can consider granting the witness immunity, as a result of which the witness may be compelled to respond. If the witness does not thereafter respond, the court can hold the witness in contempt.

The possibility of an immunity grant can be initiated either by the witness (with or without counsel) or by the government attorney. Sometimes the prosecuting attorney may request a "proffer" (a preview of the witness's testimony) for the purpose of judging the desirability of the immunity grant. Since this step is not technically protected by a grant of immunity or an evidentiary privilege, defense counsel should enter into a stipulation or agreement that statements made in the course of such a proffer will not constitute admissions and will not be admissible in court.

[a] Informal Immunity

Prosecutors. Immunity may be conferred in a process that is either informal or formal. *Formal immunity* is granted by a judge who issues an order pursuant to a statute. *Informal immunity* is conferred by the prosecutor without technical compliance with immunity statutes. Under the latter, a prosecutor will make an informal promise—perhaps even in the context of plea bargaining—that cooperation will result in non-prosecution of the witness. This informal agreement, sometimes known as *pocket immunity*, may have the same effect as a statutory grant of immunity: testimony is given and the witness is not prosecuted. There are some significant legal differences, however. Since the grant is informal, the witness cannot be held in contempt for refusing to testify. A witness who wants to enforce a pocket immunity agreement will rely on the due process clause or contract principles.

Police. What is the legal effect of an immunity/non-prosecution agreement between a suspect and police officials? A number of jurisdictions hold that unless there is compliance with statutory immunity procedures, such an agreement has no binding effect. *See, e.g., Tabor v. State*, 971 S.W.2d 227 (Ark. 1998).

[b] Formal Immunity and Contempt

To confer statutory immunity, the prosecuting attorney must apply for a formal grant of immunity from a judge. If the court grants the request, the government calls (or recalls) the witness to testify before the grand jury.

A grant of immunity should be formalized in writing and on the record to protect the witness's interests. Courts virtually never confer "constructive immunity" on a witness who did not follow the statutory immunity procedures. *See United States v. Doe*, 465 U.S. 605 (1984).

If the immunized witness continues to assert the self-incrimination privilege, the court will issue a summons requiring the witness to show cause (explain) why the witness refused to testify. If the witness fails to *show cause*, the court will issue a second order compelling the witness to answer the grand jury's questions. If the witness continues to assert the self-incrimination privilege, the witness may then be held in contempt of court.

While both civil and criminal contempt sanctions are available, most courts invoke *civil contempt*. Under the usual rules for this form of contempt (*e.g.*, 28 U.S.C. § 1826), the witness is jailed until he or she agrees to testify or until the grand jury term is over. To hold a person in civil contempt, clear and convincing evidence must show (1) the existence of a valid order of which the person had actual or constructive knowledge, (2) that order was in the moving party's favor, (3) the person's conduct violated the terms of the order, and (4) the moving party suffered harm as a result of the person's conduct. *In re Grand Jury Subpoena*, 597 F.3d 189 (4th Cir. 2010). Some state statutes restrict civil contempt orders in various ways.

Criminal contempt involves punishing the witness for violation of a court order. Contrary to civil contempt, punishment for criminal contempt is not necessarily rescinded when the witness complies with the subpoena or order to testify. Ordinarily, the person convicted of criminal contempt will be sentenced to a short jail term and/or a fine. When a grand jury witness refuses to testify, *Harris v. United States*, 382 U.S. 162 (1965), e.g., held that a trial court must proceed against that witness under Fed. R. Crim. P. 42(a), which contains notice and hearing provisions. The sentence for criminal contempt should be reasonably related to the seriousness of the conduct. *See United States v. Halliday*, 665 F.3d 1219 (10th Cir. 2011) (10-month sentence was reasonable after witness texted a friend about his childish behavior before the grand jury).

[c] Factors in Conferring Immunity

What factors or circumstances should a prosecutor consider in determining whether to seek a grant of immunity? Assume that a state grand jury is investigating a conspiratorial drug case in which the leader is being sought. A witness suspected of criminal involvement in a drug enterprise appears before the grand jury. It is not known, however, whether that individual is actually involved or what role that individual may have played in the larger scheme. The grant of immunity under these circumstances may lead to the discovery of more serious criminal wrongdoing on the part of other offenders. Yet there is also a possibility that these leads may go nowhere. In either event, a criminal offender has been granted immunity and may be shielded from criminal prosecution.

Assume a grand jury issues subpoenas to a number of witnesses, each of whom may have knowledge of a drug scheme. How soon in the investigation should grants of immunity be considered? The immunity grant to an individual witness may well be helpful in building a case against other members. On the other hand, an early grant of immunity may have been inadvertently extended to the drug kingpin. Consequently, the real grand jury target has been immunized from criminal prosecution.

The Witness Immunity Act of 1970, 18 U.S.C. §§ 6001–6005, states that the grant of immunity must be based upon a determination that:

> (1) the testimony or other information from such individual may be necessary to the public interest and (2) such individual has refused or is likely to refuse to testify or provide other information on the basis of his privilege against self-incrimination.

How helpful is this language in guiding a prosecutor to seek immunity in the kinds of cases described above? Consider the advice offered by an appellate judge:

> Do not give up more to make a deal than you have to. This is a temptation to which too many prosecutors succumb. If you have to give up anything at all, a plea to a lesser number of counts, a reduction in the degree of a crime, or a limitation on the number of years that an accomplice will serve

> is frequently sufficient to induce an accomplice to testify; and it sounds better to jurors when they discover that both fish are still in the net. Total immunity from prosecution should be used only as a last resort.

Stephen S. Trott, *Words of Warning for Prosecutors Using Criminals as Witnesses*, 47 HASTINGS L.J. 1381, 1392 (1996). *See also* Miriam Hechler Baer, *Cooperation's Cost*, 88 WASH. U. L. REV. 903 (2011) (exploring the costs/benefits of criminal cooperation, by which prosecutors offer criminal defendants reduced sentences in exchange for assistance in arresting other suspects).

[d] Transactional and Use Immunity

There are two forms of immunity: *transactional immunity* and *use immunity.* Many states use the transactional immunity grant, which means that a witness cooperating under such an immunity order cannot be prosecuted "for or on account of any transaction, matter, or thing concerning which he may testify or produce evidence." Once the witness has testified pursuant to the grant of transactional immunity, the witness cannot be charged with any crimes related to that testimony. Some defense lawyers characterize transactional immunity as a "total bath."

Use immunity, the immunity grant utilized in federal criminal cases and in many other states, provides less protection than transactional immunity. A typical use immunity statute provides: "No testimony or other information compelled under the immunity order (or any information directly or indirectly derived from such testimony or other information) may be used against the witness in any criminal case, except a prosecution for perjury, giving a false statement, or otherwise failing to comply with the order." 18 U.S.C. § 6002.

For considerable time there was debate over whether use immunity or transactional immunity provided enough protection to satisfy the constitutional demands of the Fifth Amendment. In *Kastigar v. United States*, 406 U.S. 441 (1972), the Supreme Court held that use immunity is "coextensive with the privilege and suffices to supplant it." As a result, to pass constitutional muster, a jurisdiction need only offer use immunity to a witness.

Notes

1. Kastigar *hearing.* In *Kastigar*, the court stated that a criminal prosecution brought after a grant of use immunity requires the prosecutor to shoulder a "heavy burden" of proving lack of taint. The prosecutor must demonstrate that the incriminating evidence being relied upon was derived from legitimate sources independent of the witness's immunized testimony. The so-called "taint" or "*Kastigar*" hearing requires that the government establish a separation between the immunized testimony and the evidence being relied upon to establish guilt of the defendant. Once the prosecutor establishes that a witness has not been affected by immunized testimony, the burden of going forward shifts to the defense to contest the prosecution's proof. The general view is that the government's standard of proof is a

preponderance of evidence, a surprisingly low standard considering the "heavy burden" the government bears.

2. *Government procedures to preserve options.* Prosecutors use various procedures to satisfy the heavy burden imposed by *Kastigar.* One method is to collect all evidence against the witness in written form and present this to a court prior to the receipt of the immunized testimony. This is called "canning" the evidence. Another is to have the criminal matter prosecuted by a government attorney who had no personal involvement in the immunity grant process and who has not read or otherwise been apprised of the specifics of the immunized testimony.

3. *State-federal issues.* Is it proper for a witness in a state criminal proceeding who has been granted use immunity from state prosecution to invoke the privilege against self-incrimination based upon the fear of a subsequent federal prosecution?

In *Murphy v. Waterfront Commission of New York Harbor,* 378 U.S. 52 (1964), witnesses persisted in refusing to testify based upon their fear of federal prosecution and they were held in contempt. Recognizing that if a witness could not assert the privilege in such circumstances, the witness could be "whipsawed into incriminating himself under both state and federal law," the Court held that a state witness may not be compelled to give testimony which could be incriminating under federal law "unless the compelled testimony and its fruits cannot be used in any manner by federal officials in connection with a criminal prosecution against him." The Court held that the privilege protects state witnesses against incrimination under federal as well as state law, and federal witnesses against incrimination under state as well as federal law.

If a jurisdiction grants *transactional immunity,* on the other hand, that jurisdiction may not bar another one from pursuing criminal charges. But the other jurisdiction may not use evidence or the fruit of evidence obtained through the immunity given by the first jurisdiction.

4. *Foreign country issues.* Can a witness in a federal proceeding invoke the privilege against self-incrimination based upon his fear of prosecution by a foreign nation? In *United States v. Balsys,* 524 U.S. 666 (1998), Balsys, a resident alien, was subpoenaed to testify about his wartime activities between 1940 and 1944 and his immigration to the United States. Balsys claimed the privilege against self-incrimination, based upon fear of prosecution by a foreign country, and he contended that this entitlement arose because of a real and substantial fear that his testimony could be used against him by Lithuania or Israel in a criminal prosecution for Nazi war crimes. Rejecting the claim, the United States Supreme Court held that fear and concern regarding foreign prosecution was beyond the scope of the self-incrimination clause.

5. *State variations.* A small number of states have ruled that under their state constitutional self-incrimination provisions, use immunity statutes are unconstitutional (i.e., transactional immunity is constitutionally mandated). In so holding, for example, the Alaska Supreme Court in *State v. Gonzalez,* 853 P.2d 526, 530 (Alaska 1993), stated:

> In a perfect world, one could theoretically trace every piece of evidence to its source and accurately police the derivative use of compelled testimony. In our imperfect world, however, the question arises whether the judicial process can develop safeguards to prevent derivative use of compelled testimony that satisfy [the Alaska Constitution]. Because we doubt that workaday measures can, in practice, protect adequately against use and derivative use, we hold that [the use immunity statute] impermissibly dilutes the [state Constitutional self-incrimination protection].

6. *Immunity for defense witnesses?* While immunity is customarily a tool used by government prosecutors to secure testimony for their case, prosecutors also have the power to grant immunity to defense witnesses. Perhaps unsurprisingly, however, they seldom do so, as immunity would at once help the defense in the immediate trial and limit the prosecution of witnesses. In response, and in light of the reality that defense counsel lack power to confer immunity, courts in some instances have directly granted immunity or threatened to dismiss the prosecution's case if it does not extend an offer of immunity to a defense witness. *See* Alison M. Feld, *Defense Witnesses Need Immunity Too: Why the Supreme Court Should Adopt the Ninth Circuit's Approach to Defense-Witness Immunity*, 49 New Eng. L. Rev. 23 (2015).

The next case illustrates how difficult it can be for the prosecution to demonstrate an absence of taint.

United States v. North

910 F.2d 843 (D.C. Cir. 1990)

[Marine Corps Lieutenant Colonel Oliver North, a member of President Ronald Reagan's National Security Staff, testified under a grant of use immunity before the United States Congress. Thereafter, North was indicted on various criminal charges, and eventually convicted on three of twelve counts. The Court of Appeals reversed the convictions because the district court erred in failing to hold a full hearing as required by *Kastigar.*]

North's primary *Kastigar* complaint is that the District Court failed to require the IC [Independent Counsel] to demonstrate an independent source for each item of evidence or testimony presented to the grand jury and the petit jury, and that the District Court erred in focusing almost wholly on the IC's leads to witnesses, rather than on the content of the witnesses' testimony. North also claims that the IC made an improper nonevidentiary use of the immunized testimony (as by employing it for purposes of trial strategy), or at least that the District Court failed to make a sufficient inquiry into the question. North also protests that his immunized testimony was improperly used to refresh the recollection of witnesses before the grand jury and at trial, that this refreshment caused them to alter their testimony, and that the District Court failed to give this question the careful examination it deserved. In our discussion here, we first consider alleged nonevidentiary use of immunized testimony by the IC. We will then proceed to consider the use of immunized testimony to refresh witnesses' recollections. Finally, we will address the distinction between use of immunized testimony as a lead to procure witnesses and use insofar as it affects the substantive content of witnesses' testimony.

Assuming without deciding that a prosecutor cannot make nonevidentiary use of immunized testimony, we conclude that the IC here did not do so and that the District Court's inquiry and findings on this issue are not clearly erroneous. Thus, we do not decide the question of the permissibility or impermissibility of nonevidentiary use. However, contrary to the District Court, we conclude that the use of immunized testimony by witnesses to refresh their memories, or otherwise to focus their thoughts, organize their testimony, or alter their prior or contemporaneous statements, constitutes evidentiary use rather than nonevidentiary use. The District Court on remand is to hold the searching type of *Kastigar* hearing described in detail below, concerning North's allegations of refreshment. Finally, because the District Court apparently interpreted *Kastigar* as prohibiting the government only from using immunized testimony as a lead rather than using it at all, we hold that the District Court's truncated *Kastigar* inquiry was insufficient to protect North's Fifth Amendment right to avoid self-incrimination.

. . . The convictions are vacated and the case is remanded to the District Court. On remand, if the prosecution is to continue, the District Court must hold a full *Kastigar* hearing that will inquire into the content as well as the sources of the grand jury and trial witnesses' testimony. That inquiry must proceed witness-by-witness; if necessary, it will proceed line-by-line and item-by-item. For each grand jury and trial witness, the prosecution must show by a preponderance of the evidence that no use whatsoever was made of any of the immunized testimony either by the witness or by the Office of Independent Counsel in questioning the witness. This burden may be met by establishing that the witness was never exposed to North's immunized testimony, or that the allegedly tainted testimony contains no evidence not "canned" by the prosecution before such exposure occurred. Unless the District Court can make express findings that the government has carried this heavy burden as to the content of all of the testimony of each witness, that testimony cannot survive the *Kastigar* test. We remind the prosecution that the *Kastigar* burden is "heavy" not because of the evidentiary standard, but because of the constitutional standard: the government has to meet its proof only by a preponderance of the evidence, but any failure to meet that standard must result in exclusion of the testimony.

If the District Court finds that the government has failed to carry its burden with respect to any item or part of the testimony of any grand jury or trial witness, it should then consider whether that failure is harmless beyond a reasonable doubt. If the District Court concludes that the government's failure to carry its burden with respect to that particular witness or item is harmless beyond a reasonable doubt, the District Court should memorialize its conclusions and rationales in writing. If the government has in fact introduced trial evidence that fails the *Kastigar* analysis, then the defendant is entitled to a new trial. If the same is true as to grand jury evidence, then the indictment must be dismissed. . . .

Notes

1. *Prosecution's difficult position.* Can the prosecution actually satisfy the *North* decision's rigorous requirements? Imagine a case where a witness confesses to a government agent, then repeats the same confession under a grant of use immunity. Under the *North* test, could the agent satisfy *Kastigar* and be permitted to testify about the first conversation?

Because of a fear that the *North* test could not be satisfied, the charges were eventually dropped against Oliver North. For a fascinating insider's view of the Oliver North trial, *see* JEFFREY TOOBIN, OPENING ARGUMENTS: A YOUNG LAWYER'S FIRST CASE: UNITED STATES V. OLIVER NORTH (1991).

2. North *modified.* The *North* decision excerpted above was later slightly modified to ease the government's *Kastigar* burden. *United States v. North*, 920 F.2d 940 (D.C. Cir. 1990), *cert. denied*, 500 U.S. 941 (1991). Nevertheless, the second *North* decision repeated the rule that *Kastigar* was violated when a prosecution witness's testimony before a grand or petit jury is shaped, directly or indirectly, by compelled testimony, irrespective of how or by whom the witness was exposed to the compelled testimony. The prosecutor's bad motives or fault were not necessary to establish a *Kastigar* violation. A vigorous dissent by Chief Judge Wald argued that the majority opinion made it so difficult to satisfy *Kastigar* that it essentially turned use immunity into transactional immunity.

3. *Variations of* North. Some courts have rejected *North* as requiring the prosecution to shoulder too great a *Kastigar* burden. In *United States v. Koon*, 34 F.3d 1416 (9th Cir. 1994), for example, the court held that the government meets its *Kastigar* burden by proving that each matter as to which the witness will testify is derived from a source independent of the immunized testimony. The government need not show that the witness has neither shaped nor altered his or her testimony in any way as a result of that exposure. The *Koon* court noted that the latter requirement would essentially bar the witness from testifying in cases where the witness was exposed to the immunized testimony because it would be virtually impossible to prove there was no indirect effect of that exposure.

E. Indictment

[1] Purpose

The central purpose of the indictment is to notify the defendant of the precise crime or crimes allegedly committed by the defendant. In *Hamling v. United States*, 418 U.S. 87, 117–18 (1974), the Supreme Court articulated the following test for determining the legal sufficiency of an indictment:

> An indictment is sufficient if it, first, contains the elements of the offense charged and fairly informs a defendant of the charge against which he must defend, and, second, enables him to plead an acquittal or conviction in bar of future prosecutions for the same offense. It is generally sufficient that an indictment set forth the offense in the words of the statute itself, as long as "those words of themselves fully, directly, and expressly, without any uncertainty or ambiguity, set forth all the elements necessary to constitute the offense intended to be punished." [The language of the statute may be used], but it must be accompanied with such a statement of the facts and circumstances as will inform the accused of the specific offense.

[2] Contents

The basic purpose of an indictment is to apprise a defendant of the criminal charge(s) that the grand jury deemed warranted, based on the facts and law presented to it in the hearing. Federal Rule 7, for instance, provides that an indictment:

- Must contain a statement of essential facts constituting the offense;
- Provide the factual statement in a way that is "plain, concise, and definite";
- Be signed by an attorney for the government;
- Provide citation to the law(s) allegedly violated; and
- Indicate which property, if any, is possibly subject to forfeiture.

Fed. R. Crim. P. 6(c) adds another element. It provides that a federal indictment must be signed by the foreperson of the grand jury.

States have similar provisions with respect to the required contents of indictments. In addition, a number of states use *indictment forms*. This procedure permits a "fill-in-the-blank" approach to indictment drafting. While technically grand jurors could draft their own indictments, in many jurisdictions prosecutors routinely prepare indictments prior to the presentation of evidence, hoping (and expecting) that the grand jury will concur with the prosecutor's proposed charge. In this sense, the "rubber stamp" accusation leveled at grand juries appears literally true.

The requisite specificity of an indictment can vary in accord with the facts of a particular case. In *United States v. Resendiz-Ponce*, 549 U.S. 102 (2007), the Supreme Court stated that while "an indictment parroting the language of a federal statute is often sufficient," certain crimes "must be charged [in the indictment] with greater specificity" in order to provide fair notice and ensure that the conviction arose out of the same theory of guilt presented to the grand jury. *See also United States v. Villarreal*, 707 F.3d 942 (8th Cir. 2013) ("An indictment is fatally insufficient when an essential element of the crime is omitted.").

Specificity requirements vary considerably from state to state. A leading treatise summarizes some of the general rules as follows:

> As courts repeatedly note, "an indictment [or information] must not only contain all the elements of the offense charged, but must also provide the accused with a sufficient description of the acts he is alleged to have committed to enable him to defend himself adequately." Precisely how much factual specificity is needed to meet that standard will necessarily vary from one case to another. Relevant factors include the nature of the offense, the likely significance of particular factual variations in determining liability, the ability of the prosecution to identify a particular circumstance without a lengthy and basically evidentiary allegation, and the availability of alternative procedures for obtaining the particular information. It generally is agreed that the issue is not whether the alleged offense could be described with more certainty, but whether there is "sufficient particularity" to enable the accused to "prepare a proper defense."

WAYNE R. LAFAVE ET AL., 5 CRIMINAL PROCEDURE § 19.3(b), at 276 (4th ed. 2017) (citations omitted).

Problem 7-5. Overkill

Defendants, Vicki Lynn Kennedy and William Hargis, have been joined together in a one-count indictment. The defendants had an ongoing feud with their next door neighbor Joseph Bean, who objected to the couple living together without being legally married. The indictment accuses them of killing Bean, when both of them aimed automatic machine gunfire at the windows and doors of Bean's living area. Count one accuses the two defendants of murder "by intentionally killing Joseph Bean or by wantonly killing Joseph Bean with extreme indifference to human life."

Does the aforementioned murder indictment adequately inform defendants of the alleged crime, when the indictment specifies alternative theories upon which the state may rely in proving murder? Should the government be required to "elect" its legal theory prior to trial?

Notes

1. *Motion practice.* Assume that both defendants have legally sound objections to the indictment, but fail to make appropriate motions prior to trial. What are the consequences of such inaction? Rule 12 of the Federal Rules of Criminal Procedure provides that several specified defense claims must be raised before trial and that failure to do so constitutes a waiver. Among the specific matters that must be raised before trial is "a motion alleging a defect in the indictment or information—but at any time while the case is pending, the court may hear a claim that the indictment or information fails to invoke the court's jurisdiction or to state an offense...." FED. R. CRIM. P. 12(b)(3)(B).

This rule was designed to prevent the defense from "sandbagging." That is, a defense attorney consciously foregoing an objection regarding the language of the indictment prior to trial. After conviction, defense counsel would call the court's attention to the alleged defect in the hopes of obtaining a new trial.

2. Assume that the prosecutor desires to amend one or more of the indictments to correct what he or she believes to be a deficiency in the pleading language. Can she do so? How? Is additional information needed to answer this question?

[3] Amending an Indictment

Federal Rule of Criminal Procedure 7(e) provides that "[u]nless an additional or different offense is charged or a substantial right of the defendant is prejudiced, the court may permit an information to be amended at any time before the verdict or finding." However, if an indictment is involved, the prosecutor does not possess that authority. This interpretation is based on the early case of *Ex parte Bain*, 121 U.S. 1 (1887), prohibiting amendment of an indictment except by resubmission to the grand jury. *Bain* does not prevent a federal prosecutor from amending an indictment as to form (e.g., misspellings), but it does prevent a prosecutor from amending an indictment substantively.

Surplusage. In *United States v. Miller*, 471 U.S. 130 (1985), the Court interpreted *Bain* to allow for the striking of surplusage (irrelevant material that is not essential for a valid indictment) from an indictment by the court without resubmission to the grand jury. *See also* Fed. R. Crim. P. 7(d) (on defendant's motion, court may strike surplusage from indictment). A defendant may ask that surplusage be struck so that the jury, which may be read or informed of the indictment at the start of the trial, does not learn of the irrelevant allegations. For example, an indictment may contain background information alleging new, uncharged criminal activity. Surplusage is discussed further below.

State variations. While a number of states allow a prosecutor to amend both an information and an indictment, federal courts and a significant number of states continue to adhere to the "old" rule that an indictment cannot be amended by the prosecutor.

[4] Bill of Particulars

A party who needs more information about the crime than is alleged in the indictment may seek a *bill of particulars*, which is obtained through a motion requesting the court to order the government to provide additional facts about the crime. More specifically, the purpose of the bill of particulars is to give the defendant enough additional information to prepare for trial, avoid unexpected facts or legal theories at trial, and assert a double jeopardy bar for the same offense. *See, e.g., United States v. Moyer*, 674 F.3d 192 (3d Cir. 2012); *United States v. Beasley*, 688 F.3d 523 (8th Cir. 2012).

Federal Rule of Criminal Procedure 7(f) provides that "[t]he court may direct the government to file a bill of particulars. The defendant may move for a bill of particulars before or within 14 days after arraignment or at a later time if the court permits. The government may amend a bill of particulars subject to such conditions as justice requires." The rule, however, articulates no standard regarding either the granting or denial of a motion for a bill of particulars. Its only details when the motion must be filed.

It is difficult to discern the proper relationship between the bill of particulars and constitutional principles governing adequacy of the content of the indictment. Additionally, it has been noted by many courts that a bill of particulars is not intended to serve as a substitute for discovery, is not designed to provide the accused with specifications of factual evidence, and does not cure an otherwise invalid indictment.

If the government provides a bill of particulars, the trial proof must conform to the bill of particulars. The defendant may rely on the facts alleged in the bill of particulars in preparing for trial and presenting its defense. The government may amend the bill of particulars as long as it does not prejudice the defendant.

The grant or denial of a bill of particulars lies within the discretion of the trial court. *See, e.g., United States v. Huggans*, 650 F.3d 1210 (8th Cir. 2011). Often a judge will refuse to order a bill of particulars because the indictment is deemed adequate and the defendant is simply seeking discovery, perhaps beyond that authorized in criminal cases. In addition, many judges do not want to limit the government's flexibility by forcing the government to specify some of the issues or theories it will prove at trial. In order to establish that the trial court abused its discretion by denying a motion for a bill of particulars, a defendant must show actual surprise at trial and substantial prejudice to his or her rights.

A defendant will seek a court-ordered bill of particulars by motion. The motion should request specific information, such as the date or exact location of the crime. Often defense counsel will include an affidavit describing why the information is needed. The government may respond by providing all, some, or none of the requested information and giving an explanation when it does not fully comply with the motion.

The bill of particulars is an important procedural device in complex white-collar crime cases. In *United States v. Bortnovsky*, 820 F.2d 572 (2d Cir. 1987), for instance, defendants were charged with conspiring to defraud certain government entities by submitting false and inflated insurance claims. They requested a bill of particulars, identifying which insurance claims for burglary losses were allegedly fraudulent and which invoices were falsified. Following conviction, the Second Circuit Court of Appeals found error in the trial court's refusal to grant the motion. The Court noted that the denial of the bill of particulars forced the defendants to explain circumstances surrounding eight actual burglaries and to deal with a large amount of unnecessary documents. Therefore, the bill of particulars was "vital to [defendants'] understanding of the charges . . . and to the preparation of a defense."

Problem 7-6. Tell Me More

Paul Lawrinson was indicted for gross sexual imposition upon a minor in violation of state law. Desiring more specificity, Lawrinson filed a bill of particulars, requesting that the government specify the date on which the alleged offense occurred. The trial judge granted the motion, whereupon the prosecution filed a bill of particulars stating that "the offense in the indictment occurred between January 1, 201X, and January 31, 201X."

1. If the indictment specifically alleges one single act of "gross sexual imposition," is the response provided by the bill of particulars sufficient? Should there also be specification with respect to the time of day and location of the alleged offense?

2. Assume that Lawrinson intends to rely upon an alibi defense. He is able to account for his whereabouts for much of the time during the period January 1 through January 31. In light of this allegation, should a more specific bill of particulars be granted?

3. Assume that the state's attorney, in response to the motion for a bill of particulars, contends that no additional information is available in the prosecutor's file. Therefore, it is asserted that a more detailed bill of particulars cannot be provided. Assume, however, that the police statement received from the victim's mother contained information that pinpointed the date of the alleged offense as either January 24 or January 25. Should the prosecutor's office be held to the level of knowledge established by information available to it in police reports?

4. Assume that a more specific bill of particulars is granted and the government states that the alleged offenses occurred on January 24 or 25. The defendant now alleges an alibi defense for these two days. If the case proceeds to trial and the victim's mother testifies that the alleged attack may have occurred "anywhere between the 20th and 27th" of January, is the government now limited to proving that the offense occurred either on January 24 or January 25?

5. Assume that a more specific bill of particulars is not granted (meaning that the time period during which the alleged attack occurred is alleged to be January 1 through January 31). If witnesses testify that the alleged crime occurred January 18, in what way has the defendant been prejudiced in his ability to defend himself? Could prejudice be established in light of rules of criminal discovery that may require the defendant to give pretrial notice of his intention to rely on an alibi defense? If the judge grants a continuance so that the defendant can prepare his alibi defense for the specific date of January 18, does this "cure" any error in failing to grant the motion for a more specific bill of particulars?

6. Assume that the defendant is accused of various sexual assaults upon a minor and that the information states that the offenses occurred "on various dates between approximately June 2006 through July 2006." Should a trial judge's denial of the defendant's motion for a bill of particulars (for specific dates of said crimes) be upheld if the judge finds that the prosecutor had no knowledge of specific dates? In *State v. Vumback*, 819 A.2d 250 (Conn. 2003), the Connecticut Supreme Court held that the bill of particulars should have been granted because the state did not use its best efforts to provide a narrower time frame in order to allow the defendant to defend against the crimes charged. Interestingly, the Court nonetheless concluded that the conviction must be affirmed because the defendant failed to establish that the trial judge's error prejudiced his defense. Specifically, because Vumback had access to information concerning the dates of the charged offense (via the police report and the victim's physician), he failed to show that the information "was necessary to his defense." *Id.* at 258.

[5] Variance

Assume that an indictment alleges that Defendant A committed the crime of first-degree murder by means of shooting his victim in the head with a. 22 caliber pistol. The government later discovers that the defendant killed his victim with a .45 caliber pistol. If before trial the government was concerned that the indictment for Defendant A was problematic because of the misidentification of the weapon, it could replace it with a *superseding indictment* issued by a grand jury. But what if the government did not discover the error until the middle of trial when an expert witness testified about the weapon? The error in the indictment could be deemed a *fatal variance.*

[a] Limits of Variance

The defendant may assert that there is a "fatal variance" between the language of the indictment and the proof at trial (sometimes termed a "constructive amendment"). That is, the defendant was on notice that the government would prove its case according to the specifics of the charging document, but the proof at trial was at variance with the facts alleged in the indictment. How is a court to judge whether the degree of variance is permissible? According to Federal Rule of Criminal Procedure 52(a), "Any error, defect, irregularity or variance that does not affect substantial rights must be disregarded." This standard was explicated in *Berger v. United States*, 295 U.S. 78, 82 (1935):

> The true inquiry . . . is not whether there has been a variance in proof, but whether there has been such a variance as to "affect the substantial rights" of the accused. The general rule that allegations and proof must correspond is based upon the obvious requirements (1) that the accused shall be definitely informed as to the charges against him, so that he may be enabled to present his defense and not be taken by surprise by the evidence offered at the trial; and (2) that he may be protected against another prosecution for the same offense.

See also Martin v. Kassulke, 970 F.3d 1539 (6th Cir. 1992) (providing a helpful overview of differences between fatal and nonfatal variances).

There are times when inclusion of surplus language in the indictment is both fair and unfair to the accused. For example, if a defendant is charged with growing and producing marijuana in violation of federal law, the amount or quantity of the marijuana is not relevant to an element of that offense; reference to the quantity is not essential and may be prejudicial to the defendant. *See, e.g., United States v. Caldwell*, 589 F.3d 1323 (10th Cir. 2009) (variance relating to evidence of drug quantity not prejudicial because drug quantity was not an element of offense). On the other hand, fatal variances can occur when a defendant is charged with committing a crime on a specific date but the proof at trial showed that the offense was committed prior to that date. *See, e.g., United States v. Ross*, 412 F.3d 771 (7th Cir. 2005).

[b] Procedures to Address Variance

A variance, unlike a bill of particulars, is an issue that rarely can be addressed prior to trial. While the bill of particulars is designed to afford a remedy for the individual who does not have adequate information about what the government intends to prove at trial, the variance problem only occurs at such time as proof becomes inconsistent with the language of the indictment. Sometimes, through pretrial discovery, the defense attorney may anticipate a factual variance. Moreover, a prosecutor may be in possession of information that suggests the possibility of a variance argument occurring at trial. When this occurs, the prosecutor may seek amendment of the indictment by withdrawing the indictment and presenting it to another grand jury.

[c] Prejudice

When the proof at trial is at significant variance with the language in the indictment, an argument can be made that the crime of conviction is not the one charged by the grand jury in the indictment. Some courts refer to this kind of case as one in which the charging terms are altered such that an "unconstitutional amendment of the indictment" occurs. *See United States v. Attanasio*, 870 F.2d 809 (2d Cir. 1989) (noting that the Fifth Amendment grand jury guarantee is violated when evidence and jury instructions modify the essential elements set forth in the indictment to such an extent that the conviction offense is different from that charged in the indictment).

The central question facing courts is the extent to which proof at trial varies from the language of the indictment. Simply stated, a variance occurs where the evidence at trial establishes facts different from those alleged in the indictment. Not all variances, however, are "fatal." A fatal variance is considered to be one in which the defendant suffers prejudice. This usually means that the defendant has been deprived of an adequate opportunity to prepare a defense or that he or she may be exposed to a risk of being prosecuted twice for the same crime.

[d] Surplusage and Variances

On occasion, an indictment will contain language that is neither relevant nor material to the essential elements of the alleged crime. As noted above, this excess language is considered to be *surplusage*, which the defendant may move to strike in advance of the trial. In terms of trial strategy, this is the sensible course of action because the prosecutor may be allowed to read to the jury the entire indictment, including the surplus allegations. To the extent that the excess language may prejudice the defendant, courts routinely strike surplusage.

Assume, for example, that the government alleges a conspiracy to sell stolen bonds and states that the bonds in question were stolen. At trial, the government concedes that it cannot prove that the bonds actually were stolen. If the defendant claims that this constitutes a fatal variance (and therefore the conviction for conspiracy to sell bonds should be overturned), how should the court rule? In *United States v. Hughes*, 766 F.2d 875 (5th Cir. 1985), the court affirmed the conviction, holding that proof of the fact that the bonds were stolen was not essential to the conviction. Accordingly, the allegation in the indictment was mere surplusage and not material to the essential elements of the crime.

[e] Lesser Included Offenses

Another type of a variance issue arises when a defendant is indicted for one offense and yet convicted of a lesser included offense. Similarly, a defendant may be indicted as a principal but found guilty as an accessory. In both instances, it has been held that adequate notice is given the accused and therefore the variance is permissible. *See People v. Garrison*, 765 P.2d 419 (Cal. 1989). Of course, this analysis requires very close attention to the question of what constitutes a lesser included offense. For example, in *People v. Schmidt*, 533 N.E.2d 898 (Ill. 1989), the defendant was indicted for burglary but was convicted of theft. Because theft was not considered to be a lesser included offense of burglary, the conviction was overturned.

Problem 7-7. Fatal Variances

1. The defendant is indicted for the offense of carrying a .357 revolver during the commission of certain drug trafficking crimes. Evidence at trial suggests that the gun carried was, in fact, not a revolver but a sawed-off shotgun. The defendant's asserted defense at trial was that he was a drug user and not a drug dealer. Under these circumstances, is the variance fatal?

2. Defendant is charged with mail fraud and making a false statement to the Securities and Exchange Commission. It was alleged that the activity was connected to a scheme to "defraud and obtain money and property by false and fraudulent pretenses and representations." The indictment further alleged that the scheme began in February 2000. It also identified the exact mailings in question. At trial, however, the government was able to prove that the alleged scheme actually began in August 2000. Is this a case of fatal variance?

[6] Challenging an Indictment

[a] Introduction

A defense attorney may attempt to challenge the indictment prior to trial. This is usually accomplished through a motion to dismiss under Federal Rule of Criminal

Procedure 12(b) or a comparable state rule or statute. While this Rule does not specifically list the grounds upon which an indictment may be dismissed, a number of states specify grounds in detail. For example, New York allows a motion to dismiss the indictment because of a defective indictment, defective proceeding, and (among others) because "[t]he evidence before the grand jury was not legally sufficient to establish the offense charged. . . ." N.Y. Crim. Proc. Law § 210.20(1) (a–c). Another common requirement, included in Federal Rule 52(a), is that the accused must establish that the error prejudiced the defendant in some way.

There are many reasons why courts are hesitant to afford relief when a motion to dismiss is filed. Objections to grand jury proceedings could frustrate the expeditious administration of grand jury investigations. Another consideration is the notion of grand jury secrecy, previously discussed. When a defense attorney moves for dismissal of the indictment because something allegedly occurred inside the grand jury room, in all likelihood he or she will seek more information to buttress the claim. Obviously, disclosure of such information breaches the secrecy principle.

[b] Challenges Frequently Litigated

In addition to explicit statutory bases upon which motions to dismiss indictments may be made, the most frequently litigated issues are (a) selection of grand jurors, (b) bias by grand jurors, (c) grand jury misfeasance, (d) evidentiary challenges, (e) prosecutorial misconduct, and (f) unauthorized presence. These will be treated very briefly below. For more detailed analysis, *see* Beale et al., Grand Jury Law and Practice, *supra*, Ch. 9.

Selection of grand jurors. As described above, every jurisdiction has rules regulating the selection of grand jurors. In addition, the Constitution, particularly the Equal Protection Clause, establishes standards for selecting grand jurors. *See Rose v. Mitchell*, 443 U.S. 545 (1979). Violation of either the statute or the Constitution can engender a challenge to an indictment. This matter is considered more fully in Chapter 13, where challenges to jurors are discussed in detail.

Grand juror bias. Contrary to the language found in the petit jury guarantee of the Sixth Amendment to the United States Constitution, the Fifth Amendment grand jury guarantee contains no impartiality requirement. While the United States Supreme Court has not directly ruled on the question whether a grand juror must be unbiased, in *Beck v. Washington*, 369 U.S. 541 (1962), the Court intimated that the Fourteenth Amendment Due Process Clause may require "the state, having once resorted to a grand jury procedure, to furnish an unbiased grand jury." The facts presented in *Beck*, however, involved no showing of prejudice; therefore, the Court's pronouncement is of questionable precedential value. Other cases also hint at the need for an unbiased grand jury.

Considerable authority exists for the proposition, however, that the defendant is *not* entitled to an unbiased grand jury. Even where a court allows a challenge based upon grand jury bias, it may require an actual showing of bias on the part of named jurors. Since it may be extremely difficult to acquire this information because of grand jury secrecy, such claims are unlikely to succeed.

Juror misfeasance. Assume that the defendant somehow learns that the federal grand jury issued an indictment after only two minutes of deliberation. Defendant now desires to challenge the indictment on the ground that the grand jurors failed to perform their duty; that is, they could not have meaningfully deliberated in that short a period of time. Hence, the defendant's right to be charged by indictment has been infringed. Similar to the case in which a challenge is based upon prosecutorial misconduct, the defendant making this challenge first confronts the strong presumption of regularity of grand jury proceedings. In *United States v. Gower*, 447 F.2d 187 (5th Cir. 1971), the fact that grand jurors spent approximately 45 minutes considering the defendant's case was not deemed to be sufficient proof of failure to perform grand jurors' duty.

Evidentiary challenges. Based upon the two major Supreme Court cases previously discussed (*Costello* and *Calandra*), most courts will not permit an indictment to be successfully challenged on the ground of either the nature or the sufficiency of the evidence presented to and considered by the grand jury. These cases stress deference to the investigative function of the grand jury. Also, the cases reflect a disinclination to sanction any procedure that may result in significant delay prior to trial.

While a majority of states follow the *Costello* rule (either by case law or by statute), many states permit some review of either the nature or sufficiency of evidence heard by the grand jury. In some of these states, the defendant has a broad right to inspect the grand jury transcript in order to intelligently present such an evidentiary challenge. Even where the majority *Costello/Calandra* rule is followed, are there any circumstances in which an evidentiary challenge can be brought successfully? Two cases of this sort have been recognized: the knowing presentation of perjured testimony to a grand jury and a case in which the indictment is based on no evidentiary findings whatsoever.

If a prosecutor knowingly presents perjured testimony to the grand jury, a number of courts have permitted challenges to the indictment. Sometimes, this is called the "misconduct exception" to *Costello*. The indictment may be dismissed only if the perjured testimony is "material" to the finding of probable cause. *United States v. Vallie*, 284 F.3d 917 (8th Cir. 2002). One court described the materiality standard as whether the false declaration "has a tendency to influence, impede, or hamper the grand jury from pursuing its investigation." *United States v. Percell*, 526 F.2d 189, 190 (9th Cir. 1975).

A government attorney offering perjured testimony or false evidence to a grand jury also risks disciplinary sanctions for professional misconduct. Disciplinary Rule 7-102(a)(4) of the ABA Model Code of Professional Responsibility provides that a lawyer shall not "knowingly use perjured testimony or false evidence." Similarly, Rule 3.3(a)(3) of the Model Rules of Professional Conduct provides that a lawyer shall not knowingly "offer evidence that the lawyer knows to be false."

Occasionally it is alleged that the indictment should be dismissed because the grand jury did not consider any legal evidence in making its probable cause determination. While the United States Supreme Court has not ruled directly on this question, it may be helpful to recall Justice Burton's concurring opinion in *Costello*: "It seems to me if it is shown that the grand jury had before it no substantial or rationally persuasive evidence upon which to base its indictment, that indictment should be quashed." *Costello*, 350 U.S. at 364. It may be very difficult for defense counsel to gather support for a motion to dismiss on this ground because of grand jury secrecy.

A federal statute bars evidence obtained through illegal electronic surveillance from being presented to a grand jury. 18 U.S.C. §§ 2510 *et seq*. An indictment based on unlawful wiretapping could be dismissed for the violation.

Prosecutorial misconduct. An indictment may be dismissed because of any of the following various types of prosecutorial misconduct in the grand jury proceedings.

1. *Inflaming grand jury.* This form of misconduct typically refers to questions or comments by the prosecutor designed to improperly influence the grand jury. Although a grand jury must be unbiased, inflammatory remands rarely result in dismissal of an indictment because of the lack of prejudice to the accused.

2. *Stating personal views.* Many jurisdictions consider it objectionable for a prosecutor to express a personal opinion on such matters as the sufficiency of the evidence or the credibility of a particular witness. Some jurisdictions disagree with this notion, however, apparently on the basis of the prosecutor's advisory role.

3. *Testifying before the grand jury.* Based on the ethical norm that lawyers should not act as both advocates and witnesses in the same hearing, many jurisdictions view as improper a prosecutor acting as a witness in a grand jury session. Of course, the prosecutor is often an informal witness when he or she summarizes the available evidence.

4. *Unauthorized presence.* It is impermissible to allow simultaneous presence and testimony of multiple witnesses. Similarly, persons other than grand jurors may not be present during deliberations and voting. But a violation of secrecy may not result in dismissal because of the harmless error rule.

5. *Rendering improper or inadequate legal advice.* The prosecutor may be asked to render an opinion as to whether certain conduct constitutes a criminal offense. The prosecutor's inaccurate response may be grounds for dismissal of the indictment.

6. *Conflict of interest.* Prosecutorial misconduct may occur in a case in which a prosecutor who has previously represented the accused in connection with a related matter is now presenting a matter against that individual before the grand jury.

7. *Use of grand jury for an improper purpose.* While this category is vague, courts have indicated that it would be improper to utilize a grand jury to gather evidence for a pending civil or criminal proceeding, induce a witness to commit perjury, or harass a witness. *United States v. Apperson*, 441 F.3d 1162 (10th Cir. 2006) (grand

jury process is abused when prosecutor uses it for the primary purpose of strengthening government's case on pending indictment or as substitute for discovery). On the other hand, the grand jury may be used to gather evidence for new charges.

8. *Secrecy violations.* As previously discussed, prosecutors are generally prohibited from disclosing testimony given by grand jury witnesses. When a prosecutor discloses this information prior to issuance of an indictment, it has been suggested that the indictment should be dismissed. Nonetheless, it appears that most courts will not grant such a motion unless the secrecy violation creates a reasonable likelihood of prejudice to the defendant.

9. *Selective prosecution.* A decision to prosecute based on improper grounds such as race, gender, ethnicity, political affiliation, or as retaliation for the exercise of a constitutional right. *See* Chapter 2.

10. Unreasonable delay. The indictment may have been rendered so late that it was in violation of due process or the relevant statute of limitations. *See* Chapter 12.

For more detailed consideration of prosecutorial misconduct claims, *see* WAYNE R. LAFAVE ET AL., *supra*, §§ 15.6 & 15.7 (4th ed. 2017); BEALE ET AL., GRAND JURY LAW AND PRACTICE, *supra*, Ch. 9.

[c] The Problem of Prejudice

Ordinarily, errors occurring during the grand jury process are challenged after the accused has been indicted, tried, and convicted. Thus, the appellate courts are presented with an unusual situation. A rule of grand jury procedure has been violated but the accused nevertheless received a fair trial and was found guilty beyond a reasonable doubt. The question, then, is whether the grand jury error was so egregious that it should cause the subsequent conviction to be overturned, and, if not, what remedy is appropriate?

In general, "all but most serious grand jury errors are mooted by conviction." *United States v. Brennick*, 405 F.3d 96 (1st Cir. 2005). The Supreme Court held that an indictment should be dismissed for constitutional reasons if it contains "a defect so fundamental that it causes the grand jury no longer to be a grand jury, or the indictment no longer to be an indictment." *Midland Asphalt Corp., v. United States*, 489 U.S. 802 (1989).

In *United States v. Mechanik*, 475 U.S. 66 (1986), two government agents testified at the same time before a federal grand jury, in violation of Rule 6(d)'s provision that only the "witness being questioned" may be present at a grand jury proceeding. The grand jury indicted and the defendants were convicted in a jury trial of drug and conspiracy offenses. Defense counsel discovered the irregularity after the trial had begun and immediately filed a motion to dismiss the indictment. The trial judge took the motion under advisement, then rejected the motion to dismiss after the jury returned a guilty verdict. The Court of Appeals reversed the conviction, irrespective of the presence or absence of prejudice, because of the Rule 6(d) violation.

The United States Supreme Court then reversed the Court of Appeals, reinstating the conviction. The Supreme Court noted that the reversal of a criminal conviction engenders substantial social costs, including the time, energy, and other resources needed to conduct the second trial, the psychological harm to the victim who must relive the event, and the difficulties caused by the passage of time and its effect on memories and the dispersion of witnesses. Because of these concerns, Rule 52(a) of the Federal Rules of Criminal Procedure provides that errors not affecting substantial rights must be disregarded. This principle also applies to "any error, defect, irregularity, or variance" occurring before a grand jury. When the petit jury found the defendants guilty beyond a reasonable doubt, according to *Mechanik*, this

> rendered harmless any conceivable error in the charging decision that might have flowed from the violation [of Rule 6(d)]. In such a case, the society costs of retrial after a jury verdict of guilty are far too substantial to justify setting aside the verdict simply because of an error in the earlier grand jury proceedings.

Id. at 73.

Notes

1. After *Mechanik*, is there *any* remedy for a violation of grand jury procedures after the accused is convicted by a petit jury? Since the error is unlikely to be discovered until after the criminal trial, doesn't *Mechanik* essentially hold that any mistake is harmless error?

2. *Mechanik* involved an attack on an indictment *after* the accused was convicted by a petit jury. In *Bank of Nova Scotia v. United States*, 487 U.S. 250 (1988), the Supreme Court addressed whether a federal trial court may invoke its supervisory power to dismiss an indictment for prosecutorial misconduct in a grand jury investigation, when it is contended that the misconduct did not influence the grand jury to indict. In *Bank of Nova Scotia*, the trial court concluded that the prosecution had engaged in various forms of misconduct regarding operation of the grand jury that ultimately indicted the defendant bank. The Supreme Court evaluated the purported conduct but in the end deemed it non-prejudicial, not affecting the grand jury's decision to indict. According to the Court:

> In considering the prejudicial effect of the foregoing instances of alleged misconduct, we note that these incidents occurred as isolated episodes in the course of a 20-month investigation, an investigation involving dozens of witnesses and thousands of documents. In view of this context, those violations that did occur do not, even when considered cumulatively, raise a substantial question, much less a grave doubt, as to whether they had a substantial effect on the grand jury's decision to charge.
>
> Errors of the kind alleged in these cases can be remedied adequately by means other than dismissal. For example, a knowing violation of Rule 6 may be punished as a contempt of court. In addition, the court may direct

> a prosecutor to show cause why he should not be disciplined and request the bar or the Department of Justice to initiate disciplinary proceedings against him. The court may also chastise the prosecutor in a published opinion. Such remedies allow the court to focus on the culpable individual rather than granting a windfall to the unprejudiced defendant.

Id. at 263. Dismissal of an indictment, the Court stated, is warranted only when the government's conduct prejudiced the grand jury in its decision to indict:

> The prejudicial inquiry must focus on whether any violations had an effect on the grand jury's decision to indict. If violations did substantially influence this decision, or if there is grave doubt that the decision to indict was free from such substantial influence, the violations cannot be deemed harmless. The record will not support the conclusion that petitioners can meet this standard. The judgment of the Court of Appeals is affirmed.

Id.

Dissenting, Justice Marshall wrote that "[g]iven the nature of grand jury proceedings, Rule 6 violations can be deterred and redressed effectively only by a per se rule of dismissal. Today's decision reduces Rule 6 to little more than a code of honor that prosecutors can violate with virtual impunity." *Id.* at 264–65 (Marshall, J., dissenting).

3. *Burden of proof.* The Court in *Bank of Nova Scotia* held that the harmless error rule applies to most errors in grand jury proceedings. Who has the burden of proof? Must the defendant prove that there was harm or does the prosecution have to prove there was no harm?

4. *Proof of harm limited by grand jury secrecy.* Recall that grand jury proceedings are usually secret. This means that the defendant will not know who testified or what evidence the grand jury considered. If the burden of proving harm is on the defendant, how will he or she satisfy this?

5. *Substantial effect?* The Court holds that the many errors did not raise a substantial question or even a grave doubt about whether they had a substantial effect on the grand jury's decision. Do you agree? Did the Court have enough information to decide this? Would you have preferred more data?

For an unusual case finding that the *Bank of Nova Scotia* standard was met, *see United States v. Breslin*, 916 F. Supp. 438 (E.D. Pa. 1996) (holding that prosecutorial misconduct warranted dismissal of the indictment without prejudice, thereby allowing the government to present the case "to another grand jury and start with a clean slate").

6. *Remedies other than dismissal.* The Court in *Bank of Nova Scotia* suggested that there are remedies other than dismissal that are adequate to remedy the errors. These include contempt of court, professional discipline, and public chastisement. Do you agree that these are adequate under the circumstances? Would dismissal be appropriate *in addition*? Would it matter if it were dismissal with or without prejudice?

7. *Presumed prejudice. Bank of Nova Scotia* also indicated that there are some situations where no prejudice need be proven because the error was "fundamental." In such cases prejudice is presumed. Note that the two examples involve errors in the selection of grand jurors. Can you think of other situations where the "fundamental error" approach is appropriate?

F. Time for Reform?

While commentators continue to question whether the modern grand jury should be retained, the fact remains that it is constitutionally required in felony cases in federal prosecutions and in a significant number of states. Short of abolition efforts through the time-consuming process of amending constitutions, should statutory measures be adopted to revise the grand jury process?

Hyde Amendment. In 1997, Representative Henry Hyde, Chairman of the House Judiciary Committee, successfully sponsored legislation allowing individual and small businesses that were grand jury targets and subject to "bad faith, vexatious or frivolous" federal prosecutions to file motions to recoup their costs in defending against those prosecutions. This law became known as the Hyde Amendment. For background on this law, *see* Amanda K. Branch, *Hyde in Plain Sight—Back to Basics with the Hyde Amendment*, 33 REV. LITIGATION 371 (2014). *See also United States v. Campbell*, 134 F. Supp. 2d 1104, 1107 (C.D. Cal. 2001), *aff'd*, 291 F.3d 1169 (9th Cir. 2002) (covering attorney fees in the event of exoneration).

Grand Jury Bill of Rights. The National Association of Criminal Defense Lawyers, echoing an American Bar Association proposal, has proffered a "Grand Jury Bill of Rights" which argues that the following rules and procedures should be followed by federal prosecutors when seeking indictments:

(1) A grand jury witness that has not received immunity should have the right to be accompanied by counsel during his or her appearance.

(2) Prosecutors should not intentionally withhold clearly exculpatory information from a grand jury.

(3) Prosecutors should not present evidence to the grand jury that they know to be inadmissible at trial because a trial court ruled on its admissibility.

(4) A grand jury target or subject should have the right to testify before the grand jury. A grand jury target should also be permitted to provide written information to the grand jury foreperson for consideration by the grand jury.

(5) Grand jury witnesses should be allowed to receive a transcript of their own testimony.

(6) The grand jury should not name a person in an indictment as an unindicted co-conspirator.

(7) All non-immunized subjects or targets called before a grand jury should receive *Miranda* warnings.

(8) Grand jury subpoenas ordinarily should be issued at least 72 hours before the scheduled appearance.

(9) Grand jurors should receive meaningful instructions concerning the charges they are to consider.

(10) Prosecutors should not call before a grand jury any subject or target who has stated that he or she intends to invoke the constitutional privilege against self-incrimination.

With which recommendations do you agree? Disagree? Assuming that it would be constitutional to do so, should prosecutors have the option to charge either by indictment or by information?

Grand jury's own counsel. Another suggestion is that the prosecutor should be replaced as the grand jury's lawyer by counsel who represents the grand jury rather than the prosecution. This lawyer would be a buffer between the grand jury and the prosecution, advise the grand jury on the law, and provide them with information, such as evidence presented by the prosecutor was seized illegally and could not be used at trial. Susan W. Brenner, *The Voice of the Community: A Case for Grand Jury Independence*, 3 VA. J. SOC. POL'Y & L. 67 (1995).

For more proposals on ways in which the grand jury system might be improved, *see* Roger A. Fairfax, *Grand Jury 2.0: Toward a Functional Makeover of the Ancient Bulwark of Liberty*, 19 WM. & MARY BILL OF RTS. J. 339 (2010).

Chapter 8

Joinder and Severance

A. Introduction

Questions of joinder and severance may arise when a person commits more than one crime or when two or more people join together to engage in criminal activity. For example, assume that *A* and *B* conspire together and rob the Superior Convenient Mart. Assume further that *A*, acting alone and without the knowledge of *B*, also robbed the Minit Save Convenient Market the following week. *B* was not involved in any way in the second heist.

The prosecutor will have to decide several questions. The first is whether *A* and *B* can be indicted or tried together or separately. The second is whether *A* can be indicted or tried at the same time for the Superior robbery and the Minit Save robbery, or whether the two robberies will have to be handled separately. Finally, can both defendants and both robberies be joined in one indictment or trial, or will there have to be two or even three proceedings?

American criminal procedure analyzes these issues in terms of the closely related concepts of *joinder* and *severance. Joinder* is the process of joining two people or crimes together into one indictment or trial. *Severance* is the process of undoing a joinder. After a severance, the crimes or people would be tried separately.

Returning to the crimes of *A* and *B*, there are a number of possibilities. If there were total trial joinder (which is unlikely) in the above hypothetical, there would be one trial: *A* and *B* would be tried for the robbery of the Superior Mart and, during that same trial, *A* would also be tried for the robbery of the Minit Save Market. Another possibility is that *A* and *B* would be tried together for the robbery of the Superior Mart and *A* would be tried at another proceeding for the crime at the Minit Save. Still another possible arrangement is that *A* would face two trials: one for the robbery of each convenience store; *B* would be tried alone at a third proceeding for the theft at the Superior Mart.

B. Policies

Joinder and severance questions initially involve two often conflicting policies: efficiency and fairness. In an effort to conserve scarce human and physical resources, judges and prosecutors (and sometimes defense counsel) often prefer to join crimes and defendants together and have one trial. For example, in the above hypothetical, in order to resolve the Superior Mart case, it would be more efficient to have a trial in which *A* and *B* were co-defendants, as opposed to having two trials, one for each defendant. At the joint trial, everyone would save time.

The judge would have to preside over only one proceeding. The prosecutor would have to appear at only one trial. If one lawyer represents both *A* and *B* (which is unlikely because of a substantial possibility of a conflict of interest), it would save professional time if the lawyer had to participate in only one trial. Since the prosecution's witnesses are probably the same in the cases against both *A* and *B*, these witnesses and some defense witnesses who would testify for both defendants would welcome the opportunity to testify only once. Other savings also could be realized. The courtroom, court clerks, bailiffs, and the like could be used for other proceedings if only one trial were held for *A* and *B*. The obvious efficiencies inherent in virtually all joint trials have led courts to favor joinder.

Even though joinder may be efficient in many cases, it does not necessarily serve the cause of fairness. In *Drew v. United States*, 331 F.2d 85, 88 (D.C. Cir. 1964), the court observed:

> The argument against joinder [of offenses] is that the defendant may be prejudiced for one or more of the following reasons: (1) he may become embarrassed or confounded in presenting separate defenses; (2) the jury may use the evidence of one of the crimes charged to infer a criminal disposition on the part of the defendant from which is found his guilt of the other crime or crimes charged; or (3) the jury may cumulate the evidence of the various crimes charged and find guilt when, if considered separately, it would not so find. A less tangible, but perhaps equally persuasive, element of prejudice may reside in a latent feeling of hostility engendered by the charging of several crimes as distinct from only one. Thus, in any given case the court must weigh prejudice to the defendant caused by the joinder against the obviously important considerations of economy and expedition in judicial administration.

C. Effects of Joinder

Social scientists have studied the issue of joinder and severance. The results of one extensive study are summarized in Andrew D. Leipold, *How the Pretrial Process Contributes to Wrongful Convictions*, 42 Am. Crim. L. Rev. 1123 (2005). This study looked at various aspects of the pre-trial process and analyzed their impact on convictions and how these processes can hamper a defense. The study reviewed the trials of more than 20,000 federal defendants from 1997 through 2001. The conviction rates from these trials show a trend toward a higher rate of conviction when multiple counts or defendants are joined. Defendants who were tried alone on a single count had a 66% conviction rate, but when they were tried on more than one count, "the defendant was more likely to be convicted of something . . . [and] also more likely to be convicted of the most serious charge." Defendants tried on two charges were convicted of all counts in 72% of the cases, and the most serious count in 82%. When the trial was of three or more charges, defendants were convicted of all counts in 78% of the trials, and of the most serious count in 88%.

The same trend was found when multiple defendants were tried together. Defendants who stood trial alone and went to judgment on the most serious charge had a conviction rate of 73%, which increased to 83% when the defendant was joined with at least one other defendant. When both defendants and offenses were joined, defendants charged with multiple counts had a higher conviction rate than those charged with a single count (85% to 77%), though the numbers were similar for defendants charged with multiple counts regardless of whether they were joined with other defendants.

Although suggestive, the author notes that these numbers do not *prove* that joinder of counts or defendants causes unjust treatment of defendants. Why not? The study was further analyzed and expanded in Andrew D. Leipold & Hossein A. Abbasi, *The Impact of Joinder and Severance on Federal Criminal Cases: An Empirical Study*, 59 VAND. L. REV. 349 (2006).

D. Strategic Considerations

Counsel faced with the possibility of joint trials must carefully weigh the wisdom of requesting a severance. Defense counsel may seek a severance because, as the above studies show, a joinder could increase the chance of a conviction. There are several reasons why this might be so. For instance, sometimes evidence admissible against *X* in a joint trial of *X* and *Y* would be inadmissible in a separate trial against *Y*. Defense counsel for *Y* may move for a severance in order to keep the jury in *Y's* case from hearing this damaging proof.

A severance motion may have other beneficial effects as well. A severance may permit the defendant to testify in one case and remain silent in the other. It may also avoid presenting seemingly inconsistent defenses to the same jury. Assume a defendant is charged with two robberies. She maintains she had an alibi for the first and was too drunk to formulate the intent for the second. While a jury presented with only one of these defenses may be persuaded to accept the defense, a jury presented with both may find neither persuasive or even plausible.

In addition, since a severance motion requires the prosecution to devote time to answer the motion and, if the motion is granted, additional resources commanded by two or more trials, it is possible that a severance motion could induce a prosecutor to offer the defendant a better deal during plea bargaining negotiations. Conversely, the government's initial decision to join offenses or offenders may have been prompted by a prosecutor's desire to obtain an advantage during plea bargaining negotiations.

Another possible defense advantage in seeking a severance is that the motion process may provide discovery. The judge at the pretrial hearing on the severance motion may require the state to disclose some of its trial proof in order to establish the prerequisites for joinder. For example, the prosecutor may have to inform the court of the government's proof of a "common scheme or plan," as required by Rule 8(a) for the joinder of offenses. This information, helpful to the defense, may have been unavailable through normal discovery processes.

On the other hand, defense counsel may prefer that two crimes or defendants be tried at the same time. If two defendants are tried together and represented by different counsel (or, rarely, even the same counsel), the combined resources of the clients may permit additional investigators and experts to be hired to assist both defendants. If two lawyers are involved, they can split up legal research and drafting tasks where the clients are pursuing compatible theories.

Joinder of two or more offenses may also be advantageous to the defense, especially if a guilty plea is likely. A single judge will handle the consolidated cases and may be more likely to give concurrent sentences on all charges.

What if the government's case is much stronger as to one charge than the other? In many cases, defense counsel would prefer severance so that the defendant is not so tainted by the strong charge that the jury cannot fairly consider the weak charge. Sometimes, however, the opposite effect may seem possible: in presenting an obviously weak charge, the prosecutor may so lose credibility with the jury that the jury is unable or unwilling to appreciate the strength of the other charge.

Notes

1. *Partial waiver of jury trial.* An unusual situation occurs when the defendant wants a jury trial for some charges and a bench trial for others. Is consolidation appropriate? There are several possibilities. A court might permit a consolidation in this scenario. The judge would resolve the bench-tried issues and the jury handles the others, or the judge would order a jury trial on all the issues. Another approach is for the court to disapprove of this procedure and grant a severance of the jury and bench cases. To prevent defense counsel from manipulating the severance rules by waiving a jury trial on some issues, a number of locales permit this severance only with the prosecutor's approval.

2. *Dual juries.* Another option, used in a small number of cases in which two defendants are joined, is for the trial court to seat *two* juries, one for each defendant. The jury for defendant *A* is excluded from the courtroom during testimony not admissible against this defendant, but admissible against defendant *B*. Appellate courts have tolerated this device. *See, e.g., Wilson v. Sirmons*, 536 F.3d 1064 (10th Cir. 2008).

The many practical problems with dual juries were noted in the Oklahoma City bombing case, *United States v. McVeigh*, 169 F.R.D. 362, 371 (D. Colo. 1996), where the trial court ordered severance of the defendants' trials because the government intended to use several statements of one of the defendants against him but not anyone else. The court rejected all possible mechanisms for remedying the problem, finding that the difficulty of administering the solutions would counteract any efficiency achieved by a joint trial. With respect to the possibility of seating two juries, Judge Matsch observed:

> The possibility of a joint trial with separate juries has been considered. Conceptually, that is a convenient solution. Logistically, it is impracticable. If 6 alternate jurors were seated with each jury, the courtroom would have to accommodate 36 jurors for most of the trial. Moreover, the use of two juries would . . . not relieve the prejudice to each of the defendants from their antagonistic defenses requiring different tactics and strategies during the trial proceedings. It is reasonable to anticipate a need for extensive hearings outside the presence of the jury to consider conflicting defense objections and requests for cautionary instructions during the presentation of the evidence, including arguments about whether both juries can hear particular testimony or see certain exhibits. The resulting delays would interrupt the rhythm and flow of the proceedings and risk unforeseeable adverse consequences.

E. Joinder and Severance Rules

[1] Introduction

In the federal system, joinder and severance are governed by Rules 8, 13, and 14, which should be read and applied together. In general terms, Rule 8 details when offenses (Rule 8(a)) and defendants (Rule 8(b)) may be joined in an indictment or information. Although Rule 13 describes when offenses and defendants may be tried at the same time, it contains no separate standard for either. Rather, Rule 13 indicates that crimes or defendants may be *tried* together if, under Rule 8, they could have been *indicted* together. If offenses or defendants are properly joined under Rules 8 or 13, the trial court has the discretion under Rule 14 to grant a severance if joinder would cause prejudice to either a defendant or the government.

Note that in some situations *both* 8(a) (joinder of crimes) and 8(b) (joinder of defendants) could apply. This could occur when *A* and *B* work together to carry out a series of bank robberies or drug transactions. Which rule is used to assess joinder? The answer is 8(b), not 8(a). The two are deemed mutually exclusive. If more than one defendant is to be indicted or tried, Rule 8(b) provides the standards for joinder.

State statutes and rules on joinder and severance often resemble the federal rules. Indeed, state courts sometimes look to the federal case law for guidance in interpreting their own joinder and severance provisions. *See, e.g., State v. Foster*, 839 N.W.2d 783, 837 (Neb. 2013) ("Because of [the] similarities between the state and federal rules . . . we find federal case law to be instructive in determining when severance should be granted.").

[2] Joinder of Offenses

Rule 8(a) covers joinder of offenses and does not limit the number of crimes that may be joined. Looking more carefully at Rule 8, it is clear that the standard for joinder of offenses differs from that for joinder of defendants. Joinder of offenses is possible if any of three criteria is satisfied. First, Rule 8(a) permits joinder if the crimes are of the *same or similar character.* This means that a defendant could be indicted in a single indictment for two robberies or several drug sales. Second, joinder of offenses is possible if the crimes were based on the *same act or transaction.* Third, joinder is permissible if the crimes were *connected with or constitute parts of a common scheme or plan.* The third approach would permit joinder of an auto theft, robbery, and homicide that were part of a grand scheme to steal a car to use in robbing a bank, during which robbery a homicide occurred. In most situations, joinder requires the crimes to have been committed in the same jurisdiction.

United States v. Jawara

474 F.3d 565 (9th Cir. 2007)

[In December 2000, Haji Jawara executed an INS application for asylum in which he claimed to be a native of Sierra Leone. Three years later . . . it was discovered that Haji Jawara was a second name used by Mohamed Jawara, and that in 1999 Mohamed Jawara had submitted applications for a visa and a social security number in which he claimed Gambia as his birthplace. The following year, Jawara approached a friend for help in finding a citizen to marry an acquaintance for immigration purposes, not knowing that his friend was a paid informant working with federal law enforcement authorities. In June 2004, the informant met Jawara and they discussed the mechanics of a potential sham marriage. Some months later, the informant had another meeting with Jawara at which Jawara sought his help in finding a wife for himself. Both meetings were recorded.

A grand jury indicted Jawara on one count of fraud related to immigration documents and one count of conspiracy to commit marriage fraud. . . . A forensic document examiner testified [at trial] that Jawara's Sierra Leone documents were counterfeit. The informant testified that . . . he and Jawara had spoken about document fraud for immigration purposes. The meeting recordings were played for the jury.

At trial, Jawara testified that his real name was Haji, he was born in Sierra Leone, and Mohamed Jawara was the name of his Gambian cousin whose passport he borrowed to enter the United States. He admitted using Mohamed Jawara's passport and name to obtain various identity cards in the United States. Jawara acknowledged several falsehoods in his asylum application, but maintained that he was unaware of the falsehoods at the time the application was filed because aside from providing copies of his Sierra Leone documents, he had no role in preparing the application and did not read it before signing. Jawara maintained that the informant initiated the fraudulent marriage idea.]

McKeown, Circuit Judge.

Mohamed Jawara . . . appeals from his convictions for document fraud related to his personal asylum application and conspiracy to commit marriage fraud to avoid the immigration laws. . . . Jawara argues the two counts were improperly joined under Rule 8(a). Alternatively, he argues that even if the initial joinder was proper, the district court should have severed the counts under Rule 14 because the joinder was prejudicial.

Rule 8(a) provides for joinder of offenses against a single defendant in the indictment if one of three conditions is satisfied. . . .

Rule 14 permits the district court to "order separate trials of counts" at its discretion "[i]f the joinder of offenses . . . in an indictment . . . appears to prejudice a defendant." . . . Thus, even if joinder is permissible under Rule 8, a party who feels prejudiced by joinder may move to sever pursuant to [Rule] 14.

We take the view that "[b]ecause Rule 8 is concerned with the propriety of joining offenses in the indictment, the validity of the joinder is determined solely by the allegations in the indictment." *United States v. Terry*, 911 F.2d 272, 276 (9th Cir. 1990). . . .

Because Rule 14 is available as a remedy for prejudice that may develop during the trial, Rule 8 has been broadly construed in favor of initial joinder. . . . Nonetheless, the joinder decision warrants scrutiny, and Rule 14 should not be viewed as a backstop or substitute for the initial analysis required under Rule 8(a). At least one of Rule 8(a)'s three conditions must be satisfied for proper joinder, and those conditions, although phrased in general terms, are not infinitely elastic. . . . In Jawara's case, the government invokes two of the three bases for joinder: that the counts formed part of a "common scheme or plan" to engage in immigration fraud, and that the counts were of a "similar character."

[While we] have not specifically defined the requisite nexus for a "common scheme or plan" . . . courts generally permit joinder under this test where the counts grow out of related transactions. Stated another way, we ask whether "[c]ommission of one of the offenses either depended upon or necessarily led to the commission of the other; proof of the one act either constituted or depended upon proof of the other." *United States v. Halper*, 590 F.2d 422, 429 (2d Cir. 1978). . . .

Restricting our inquiry to the allegations in the . . . indictment, nothing suggests such a nexus between the two counts. The document fraud count describes acts—knowingly making false statements on an asylum application—that were completed as of December 23, 2000. The marriage fraud conspiracy count describes very different acts—the two meetings between Jawara and a "cooperating witness . . ."—that occurred several years later, on June 24, 2004 and November 13, 2004. The document fraud charge makes no reference to the "cooperating witness" that is central to the marriage fraud charge, and the marriage fraud charge makes no reference to the asylum application that is central to the document fraud charge. Aside from the subject matter of immigration, the . . . indictment does not offer a discernible link between the two offenses or suggest any overlapping evidence. No plan or common scheme links the charges nor can any commonality be inferred from the indictment.

... Here, there is no direct connection between the acts other than Jawara's participation in both events. For example, the false statements were not made to bolster or help conceal the marriage fraud conspiracy, nor can it be said that the marriage fraud conspiracy flowed from the document fraud crime.... [T]he alleged acts underlying the two offenses had no temporal connection and were separated by several years.

The more difficult question is the government's alternate basis for joinder—that the offenses are of a "similar character" because they relate to immigration fraud....

[We consider the] immediate question: does the fact that the two offenses relate to immigration fraud make them of a "similar character" for joinder purposes? ...

We consider it appropriate to consider factors such as the elements of the statutory offenses, the temporal proximity of the acts, the likelihood and extent of evidentiary overlap, the physical location of the acts, the modus operandi of the crimes, and the identity of the victims in assessing whether an indictment meets the "same or similar character" prong of Rule 8(a). The weight given to a particular factor will depend on the specific context of the case and the allegations in the indictment. But the bottom line is that the similar character of the joined offenses should be ascertainable—either readily apparent or reasonably inferred—from the face of the indictment. Courts should not have to engage in inferential gymnastics or resort to implausible levels of abstraction to divine similarity. Thus, where the government seeks joinder of counts on the basis of "same or similar character," it crafts a barebones indictment at its own risk.

Applying this inquiry to the indictment here, it is apparent that the two counts are not of the "same or similar character." The indictment alleges two different statutory violations requiring proof of different elements. The underlying acts alleged in the indictment are separated by three-and-a-half years.... The lack of any temporal connection is all the more significant because the counts do not stem from common events. As for potential evidentiary overlap ... the cooperating witness whose centrality to the marriage fraud charge is obvious from the indictment, is notably absent from the document fraud charge; nor is any other evidentiary link ascertainable from the indictment. The indictment evinces no similar mode of operation with respect to the two crimes—lying about being from Sierra Leone on an asylum application is vastly different from facilitating or procuring meetings with prospective marriage candidates. The counts do not involve related geographic locations or related victims of the fraud. Ultimately, the only similarity discernible from the indictment is that both counts involve immigration. Such a vague thematic connection cannot, in and of itself, justify joinder.

The immigration document fraud charge is, in essence, a perjury claim related to Jawara's national origin. The other charge stems from an arrangement to facilitate sham marriages. The proof is in the framing. We interpret "similar" to mean something beyond facial similarity of subject matter. Looking at the allegations in the indictment, including any reasonable inferences of the connections and similarities that maybe drawn about these two counts, we hold that the counts do not qualify as "same or similar" under Rule 8.

According to the Supreme Court, our inquiry does not end here. "A violation of Rule 8 'requires reversal only if the misjoinder results in actual prejudice because it had a substantial and injurious effect or influence in determining the jury's verdict.'" *Terry*, 911 F.2d at 277 (quoting *United States v. Lane*, 474 U.S. 438, 449 (1986)). This standard . . . is less exacting than Rule 14's "manifest prejudice" standard.

In *Lane*, the Supreme Court considered a variety of factors in resolving that misjoinder under Rule 8 did not have a "substantial and injurious" effect on the jury's verdict, including the "overwhelming evidence of guilt shown," the provision of a "proper limiting instruction . . . admonish[ing] the jury to consider each count and defendant separately," and the likelihood that evidence admitted on the misjoined count would have been admissible in a separate trial as evidence of intent. . . . The Court also refused to "necessarily assume that the jury misunderstood or disobeyed" the district court's limiting instruction, and noted that the evidence as to one count "was distinct and easily segregated from evidence" relating to the other counts.

After carefully reviewing the trial record as a whole, we are comfortable in our analysis that misjoinder did not have a "substantial and injurious" effect on the verdict. A number of factors support this conclusion. We begin with the fact that the district court instructed the jury to treat the charges separately. . . . In addition, the evidence of guilt was overwhelming as to both counts. . . . Given the strength of the individual cases, we do not confront a situation where prejudice might stem from a disparity of evidence—i.e., a weak case joined with a strong case.

Finally, for many of the same reasons that we determined the charges are not similar—the differences in applicable statute, modes of operation, evidence, and time frame—the jury likewise would have had no difficulty distinguishing between the charges and the evidence. . . . The issues in this four-day trial were relatively simple, and the evidence central to the document fraud count—the asylum application, the Sierra Leonean identity documents . . . —was distinct and easily segregated from evidence central to the marriage fraud count—the recordings and [witness] testimony.

In claiming prejudice as a result of the joinder, Jawara offers the general assertion that "evidence of alleged material misstatements in an asylum application would not have been admissible against [him] in a separate trial on the charge of conspiracy to commit marriage fraud, and vice versa." We have observed that one of the ways that joinder of offenses may prejudice a defendant is that the jury may use the evidence of one of the crimes charged to infer a criminal disposition on the part of the defendant from which is found his guilt of the other crime or crimes charged. Jawara does not point to any specific "inadmissible" evidence in support of this assertion. Even if some of the evidence would not have been cross-admissible in separate trials, it is likely that the jury was able to "compartmentalize the evidence" in light of the other factors we have described.

In the absence of prejudice, reversal is not required. Since Jawara has not established that he was prejudiced by the violation of Rule 8, he cannot satisfy the burden of demonstrating "manifest prejudice" under Rule 14. . . .

Reinhardt, Circuit Judge, dissenting from the judgment.

[Judge Reinhardt dissented from the majority on the issue of harmless error in the misjoinder. He found that the evidence with respect to falsifying immigration documents was not overwhelming and that the critical issue with respect to this charge was Jawara's credibility—if the jury believed Jawara's testimony, it would have acquitted him of that charge.]

In the vast majority of cases, and especially in cases in which a defendant's credibility is the crucial issue, the most prejudicial evidence the prosecution can present—perhaps aside from a confession—is testimony establishing that the defendant has committed other serious crimes and is a bad person generally. Evidence of other crimes is particularly damning when the other crimes, as in this case, are of the same general type (here, immigration offenses) as the offense with which the defendant is charged. . . .

Prejudice can arise even more readily than in the average case when there is misjoinder of a crime that would be particularly disturbing to the average juror. Conspiring to violate the immigration laws by aiding a number of aliens to remain in the country unlawfully and obtain permanent resident status would be highly offensive to many jurors these days. . . . [T]he jury likely was influenced, in determining whether Jawara was guilty of submitting his own fraudulent immigration document, by its conclusion that he had in fact conspired to commit immigration fraud to aid others over an extended period of time. . . .

[Furthermore, by] hearing far stronger evidence on the conspiracy charge than the document fraud charge, the jury may have experienced the human tendency to draw a conclusion which is impermissible in the law: because he did it before, he must have done it again.

Although the majority relies heavily on its technical arguments that the district court's error was mitigated by the instruction that the jury consider the counts separately . . . and that the jury could compartmentalize the evidence as to each charge, these factors, while not irrelevant, are hardly sufficient to overcome the overwhelming actual prejudice created in this case by joinder with the conspiracy charge.

For these reasons, I would find the improper joinder prejudicial, at least with respect to the document fraud charge.

Notes

1. *Applying Rule 8(a).* An application of Rule 8(a) often requires a detailed look at the facts of a case, meaning that appellate precedents are of limited value.

2. *Same or similar character.* Rule 8(a) permits joinder of crimes that are of the same or similar character. Many relevant factors were listed in *Jawara.* Because of the possibility that crimes of the same or similar character may actually be unrelated to one another and proof of them will involve totally different witnesses, severance in this situation is more readily ordered under Rule 14's generic authority to sever crimes because of the potential prejudice of joinder and the reduced administrative efficiencies in a joint trial.

3. *Same act or transaction.* Rule 8(a) also permits joinder of crimes that "are based on the same act or transaction." A fact-specific inquiry is necessary. Some courts ask whether the offenses come from the same sequence of events. Ordinarily this means that the crimes will have some common relationship that is described in the indictment.

4. *Connected with or constitute parts of a common scheme or plan.* The last joinder alternative under Rule 8(a) is for crimes connected with or part of a common scheme or plan. Often the commonality is established by proof of a common purpose or that the offenses shared parties, time, and location. *See, e.g., United States v. Dominguez,* 226 F.3d 1235 (11th Cir. 2000) (filing fraudulent mortgage application, designed to hide drug proceeds, properly joined with drug trafficking charges; government presented evidence that one charge was motive for other charge although nothing in indictment tied the two sets of charges together); *United States v. Nettles,* 476 F.3d 508 (7th Cir. 2007) (upholding joinder of counterfeiting and plan to blow up a federal building since former was done to obtain money for latter). *But cf. Walker v. Commonwealth,* 770 S.E.2d 197 (Va. 2015) (four charges covering four drug sales made by defendant not properly joined as part of "common scheme or plan," even though the four sales were made to the same buyer in same neighborhood for similar amounts of money over a period of 13 days).

5. *Misjoinder in* Jawara. The court in *Jawara* found that the document fraud crime was unrelated to the marriage conspiracy count. Yet in both instances Jawara was attempting to procure legal status to stay in the U.S. (first applying for a visa, then asylum, then meeting with the informant to acquire a wife for himself for immigration purposes). Could these instances of conduct be considered a "common scheme or plan" of immigration fraud to obtain legal status for himself in the U.S.? What about these acts being of a "similar character" for the same reason?

6. *Prejudice.* The majority and dissent disagree on whether Jawara was prejudiced by the joinder. Was the majority or the dissent correct in its analysis? Was it probable that the jury was able to keep the two charges and evidence separate during deliberations? Would a jury find Jawara's attempted marriage fraud "particularly disturbing" or "highly offensive" as the dissent claims? Would Jawara have been convicted of both counts if there had been separate trials?

7. *Rule 8 versus Rule 14.* In *United States v. Terry,* 911 F.2d 272 (9th Cir. 1990), cited in *Jawara,* the court indicated that defendants seeking relief under Rules 8 and 14 must engage in different motion practices. The Motion for Relief under Rule 8

need not be renewed at the end of the trial, but a Motion for Severance under Rule 14 must be renewed or it is waived. The court reasoned:

> The rationale behind the renewal requirement in the Rule 14 context is inapplicable to Rule 8. A Rule 14 motion must be renewed in order to allow the trial court to assess whether the joinder was prejudicial and to prevent a defendant from deliberately failing to make a meritorious motion and waiting to see what verdict the jury returns.
>
> A Rule 8 motion, in contrast to Rule 14, disputes the propriety of joining charges in the indictment. Rather than being decided at the discretion of the lower court judge it permits joinder only under certain specific circumstances.... Because the propriety of a Rule 8 joinder is determined solely by the initial allegations of the indictment, there is no need to assess what actually happened in the trial.... [I]t is unnecessary to renew a Rule 8 misjoinder objection to preserve it for appeal....

8. *Focus on indictment.* The *Jawara* opinion, following a common approach, holds that the trial court is to assess the propriety of a misjoinder by looking "solely" to the allegations in the indictment. This means that a knowledgeable prosecutor, who drafts an indictment, should be able to include the necessary facts to make joinder of crimes or defendants very likely. If you were the prosecutor drafting the indictment in the *Jawara* case, what would you include to maximize the chances that a joinder would be permitted?

9. *Effect of acquittal.* If a jury acquits a defendant of one of several crimes joined under Rule 8(a), it does not mean that joinder was improper or that the convictions on the remaining joined offenses should be reversed for prejudice. Rather than assume the convictions were the product of prejudice, appellate courts often reason the acquittal proves the opposite—the jury was able to consider each crime on its own merits.

10. *State laws.* State laws on the joinder of offenses tend to be quite similar to Rule 8(a). The most common notable divergence relates to the possibility of joinder based on the similar character of two charged offenses. While this is permitted in the federal system, only about half of the states have adopted the pertinent language from Rule 8(a). Wayne R. LaFave et al., Criminal Procedure § 17.1(b) (5th ed. 2009). In other states, it may be more difficult for prosecutors to join together offenses that are not directly related to one another. On the other hand, if a state in this camp interprets its "common scheme or plan" language broadly, there may not be much practical difference between its joinder law and that of the federal system.

Consider *Farmer v. State*, 405 P.3d 114 (Nev. 2017). Farmer was employed as a nursing assistant at a hospital. The state charged him with multiple sexual offenses based on five incidents in which he touched the breasts or genitals of five female patients at the hospital over a two-month period. Over Farmer's objection, the trial judge held that the five incidents were properly joined under the "common scheme or plan" prong of Nevada law, which lacked a "similar character" option. The state supreme court later affirmed in a 4–3 decision, determining that Farmer had "a scheme to use his position . . . to access unusually vulnerable victims and exploit them under the guise of providing medical care." *Id.* at 121. However, the dissenters argued that the majority had effectively approved joinder on the basis of the similarity of the offenses, suggesting that the majority had identified a "mere thematic similarity" among the offenses rather than identifying a sufficiently concrete unifying purpose behind the offenses. "If our Legislature had intended to allow for joinder based on the similarity of offenses, the Legislature could have done so as provided for in the federal rules." *Id.* at 126 (Stiglich, J., dissenting).

In a few states, joinder law diverges in other important respects from Rule 8(a). For instance, a handful of states have adopted so-called mandatory joinder provisions. Consider this portion of Colorado's Rule 8:

> *(a)(1) Mandatory Joinder [of Offenses].* If several offenses are actually known to the prosecuting attorney at the time of commencing the prosecution and were committed within his judicial district, all such offenses upon which the prosecuting attorney elects to proceed must be prosecuted by separate counts in a single prosecution if they are based on the same act or series of acts arising from the same criminal episode. Any such offense not thus joined by separate count cannot thereafter be the basis of a subsequent prosecution. . . .

Is this a good policy?

Similarly, some states permit *defendants* to request the joinder of offenses. *See, e.g.*, Ariz. R. Crim. P. 13.3 (either party may file a motion requesting a joinder of offenses or defendants); Mass. R. Crim. P. 9(a)(4) ("Upon the written motion of a defendant, or with his written consent, the trial judge may join for trial two or more charges of unrelated offenses upon a showing that failure to try the charges together would constitute harassment or unduly consume the time or resources of the parties."). The American Bar Association also supports giving defendants an opportunity to request joinder. Standards for Crim. J., Std. 13-2.3(a) (2d ed. Supp. 1986). Do you think this is good policy?

11. *Double jeopardy.* In some cases, the legal permissibility or strategic desirability of joining offenses may be affected by the constitutional prohibition on double jeopardy. The Supreme Court's double jeopardy jurisprudence provides that a defendant may not be tried or punished twice for the same offense. However, as we will see when we consider the double jeopardy jurisprudence in more detail in Chapter 15, it is not always easy or intuitive to determine when two offenses are considered the "same" for double jeopardy purposes. In addition, the Double Jeopardy Clause has been interpreted to include a collateral estoppel principle. Under this principle, if a prosecutor goes to trial on one charge and loses, the prosecutor may be barred from initiating a new case against that defendant involving a separate, but related, crime. In some situations, concerns about collateral estoppel may make it more strategically desirable for the prosecutor to join all related charges in

one case. Again, we will consider the collateral estoppel doctrine in more detail in Chapter 15.

Problem 8-1. A Thief Is a Thief Is a Thief

Kerry was arrested for two crimes: robbery (defined as theft by use of force) of a convenience food market and shoplifting from a department store. Because of a heavy trial docket caused by inadequate numbers of lawyers in the district attorney's office, the prosecutor would like to join the two offenses in a single indictment and trial. Under Rule 8(a), are the two crimes of the same or similar character? What facts should the prosecutor seek to discover in order to prove that they satisfied the "connected together" and "common scheme or plan" requirement of Rule 8(a)?

[3] Joinder of Defendants

Joinder of defendants, governed by Rule 8(b), is similar to but more restrictive than the provisions in Rule 8(a) for joinder of offenses. Joinder of defendants is permissible only if they participated in the *same act or transaction or series of acts or transactions constituting the crime(s)*. Thus, *X* and *Y* could not be joined together in the same indictment simply because they both robbed the Safelock Bank. There must be some connection between the offenders. Under Rule 8(b), *X* and *Y* could be included in the same indictment only if they both participated in the same robbery. In other words, if *A* and *B together* carried out the Safelock Bank job, they could be indicted together. If *X* and *Y* conspired to rob the Safelock Bank, a joint indictment and trial under Rule 8(b) would be likely for both the conspiracy and substantive offenses stemming from the conspiracy. But if each did an independent crime without the participation of the other, then a joint indictment would not be permissible under Rule 8(b). Each would have to be indicted and tried separately. For a general discussion about the wisdom and difficulties of trying defendants together, *see* Paul Marcus, *Re-Evaluating Multiple-Defendant Criminal Prosecutions*, 11 Wm. & Mary Bill Rts. J. 67 (2002).

The necessary connection for Rule 8(b) joinder typically involves a conspiracy allegation. Although a separate conspiracy count is not technically required for the joinder of defendants, prosecutors may be more inclined to include such a count in order to make the appropriateness of joinder seem clearer.

Most fact patterns provide a straightforward application of Rule 8(b). For example, in *United States v. Satterfield*, 548 F.2d 1341 (9th Cir. 1977), Satterfield was indicted, jointly tried (over his objection), and convicted with Merriweather for five bank robberies. The joinder issue arose because the indictment alleged Merriweather was involved in all five robberies, but that Satterfield participated in only two. In addition, the indictment failed to allege a common plan or scheme. The appellate court concluded (in an opinion by future Supreme Court Justice Anthony Kennedy) that joinder for trial under these circumstances was improper because Satterfield had been "substantially prejudiced" by the strong evidence against

Merriweather for all five robberies "in the precise manner against which rule 8(b) seeks to protect." 548 F.2d at 1346.

In the next case, consider whether the court misapplied Rule 8(b).

United States v. Walker

657 F.3d 160 (3d Cir. 2011)

[The Walker brothers, Barron and Barry, were indicted for cocaine possession, criminal conspiracy, possession of a firearm in furtherance of drug trafficking, attempted robbery, and possession of a firearm in furtherance of the robbery. In addition, Barry was charged with escaping from custody and possession with intent to distribute cocaine. The prosecutor voluntarily dismissed the charge of possession of a firearm by a prohibited person. Before trial, the trial judge denied Barron's motion to sever for misjoinder based upon the escape charge and the additional drug charge against Barry. At trial, the brothers were found guilty of all charges.]

Pollak, District Judge [sitting by designation].

Rule 8(b) governs the joinder of defendants in federal criminal cases. . . . In construing this rule, this court has followed the Supreme Court in recognizing [that] "joint trials 'promote efficiency and serve the interests of justice by avoiding the scandal and inequity of inconsistent verdicts.'" *United States v. Urban*, 404 F.3d 754, 775 (3d Cir. 2005) (quoting *Zafiro v. United States*, 506 U.S. 534, 537 (1993)). . . .

Under Rule 8(b), "[i]t is not enough that defendants are involved in offenses of the same or similar character; there must exist a transactional nexus in that the defendants must have participated in 'the same act or transaction, or in the same series of acts or transactions,' before joinder of defendants in a multiple-defendant trial is proper." *United States v. Jimenez*, 513 F.3d 62, 82–82 (3d Cir. 2008). Where charges leveled against only a single defendant "arose directly" from her participation in a common illicit enterprise which led to charges against that defendant and co-defendants, we have held that all of the charges may be considered part of the same series of acts, rendering joinder proper under Rule 8(b). *United States v. Riley*, 621 F.3d 312, 334 (3d Cir. 2010) ("In this case, it was Riley's failure to report income earned from the land fraud scheme that led to her Tax Fraud Counts. Because the tax evasion arose directly from the land fraud proceeds, it was in the interest of judicial efficiency to join these claims.").

Barron Walker argues that joinder was improper because the first [three] counts of the indictment, including the conspiracy count, only covered conduct occurring before May 31, 2007, while the escape and additional drug charges against Barry Walker were both based on conduct occurring in July 2007. While a conspiracy count *may* serve as a link justifying the joinder of various substantive offenses, joinder may still be proper in the absence of a conspiracy count covering the time period for every substantive offense if those substantive offenses were part of the same series of transactions. In this case, the two escape-related charges against Barry Walker were properly joined because they arose directly from the earlier drug, conspiracy, and gun charge[ ]. In so holding, we agree with the analysis of Rule 8(b) by the district court in *United States v. Avila*:

> [T]he government may charge escape-related crimes alongside underlying offenses if the two are closely related to one another. This nexus depends upon the temporal proximity between the offenses, whether the defendant escaped to evade prosecution for the underlying offense, and whether the defendant was in custody for the underlying offense at the time of the flight.

610 F. Supp. 2d 391, 395 (M.D. Pa. 2009).

Barry Walker's evident purpose in escaping from pretrial detention was to evade prosecution for the offenses charged in the first . . . counts of the indictment. If it were not for the underlying offenses, Walker would not have been arrested and then able to escape from custody. Similarly, the additional drug charge arose directly from the initial charges, because at the time of Walker's re-arrest and the discovery of cocaine on his person the police were searching for him in an effort to return him to custody so that he could be tried for the . . . charges then pending against him. We note, in addition, that the short span of time between the initial offenses and the two charges against Barry Walker—a period of a little over a month—further suggests that the various charges were part of the same series of transactions. Accordingly, we conclude that the defendants were properly joined pursuant to Rule 8(b).

Notes

1. *Not all counts.* As illustrated by *Walker*, Rule 8(b) does not require that each defendant be charged in every count, although the rule requires that defendants joined in an indictment have shared a common activity. Barron and Barry both engaged in most of the criminal activity alleged, but Barry alone also was charged with two additional crimes.

2. *Retroactive correction of misjoinder.* Since the validity of a joinder of defendants is essentially determined by the allegations in the indictment, what happens if the proof at trial does not support the linkage described in the indictment? For example, assume that *A* and *B* are indicted for conspiracy to commit fraud and four counts of fraud. The jury acquits on the conspiracy charge. Is joinder of the substantive fraud charges still permissible? Most courts uphold the joinder's propriety as assessed by the indictment, not trial, unless the defendants can establish the prosecutor's bad faith in preparing the indictment.

Problem 8-2. By the Time We Get to Boston

Sam and Oliver each owned a small business in Boston. Sam ran a barber shop and Oliver owned a dry cleaning store. They were arrested after an anonymous informant telephoned the police and reported that they had committed insurance fraud. Within a week before the informant's tip, both of their businesses had burned down. Each was insured by the All Safe Insurance Company. Both Sam and Oliver filed claims for damages caused by the fires.

The local prosecutor believes that Sam and Oliver worked together to defraud the All Safe Insurance Company and would like to indict and try them together under Rule 8(b). What facts should the prosecutor seek to establish?

[4] Discretionary Relief from Prejudicial Joinder

Federal Rules 8(a) and (b) are quite liberal and permit joinder in many situations, but compliance with Rule 8 does not necessarily end matters. Either the government or defense counsel can request a severance pursuant to Rule 14.

The criteria are vague. Rule 14 authorizes a severance if either side is "prejudiced" by the joinder, but does not define prejudice or provide guidance in the logic the court is to follow. Often Rule 14 is read as authorizing a court to balance the likelihood of prejudice against the interests of judicial economy. Prejudice is frequently said to require more than an increased likelihood that the defendant would be acquitted without joinder. One court, for example, said that the defendant can obtain a severance if he or she can show an inability to obtain a fair trial. *United States v. Serpico*, 320 F.3d 691 (7th Cir. 2003). Another court, *United States v. Foutz*, 540 F.2d 733, 736 (4th Cir. 1976), summarized the required proof of prejudice in joinder of offense cases as follows:

> [T]hree sources of prejudice are possible which may justify the granting of a severance under Rule 14: (1) the jury may confuse and cumulate the evidence, and convict the defendant of one or both crimes when it would not convict him of either if it could keep the evidence properly segregated; (2) the defendant may be confounded in presenting defenses, as where he desires to assert his privilege against self-incrimination with respect to one crime but not the other; or (3) the jury may conclude that the defendant is guilty of one crime and then find him guilty of the other because of his criminal disposition.

United States v. Davis

397 F.3d 173 (3d Cir. 2005)

Sloviter, Circuit Judge.

We have before us the appeal of defendants Kevin Davis, Kevin A. Minnis, and Reginal Scott, who were tried together and who were each found guilty by the jury of both possession of cocaine base or crack with intent to distribute in violation of 21 U.S.C. § 841(a)(1) and possession of a firearm during and in relation to an underlying drug felony in violation of 18 U.S.C. § 924(c)(1)(A).

Two police officers traveling in South Philadelphia in an unmarked car saw six or seven shots fired from the passenger side of a black Honda automobile one block in front of them on 17th and Annin streets. The officers immediately activated their lights and siren, and pursued the Honda when the Honda did not stop. Within a few minutes, a marked police car also joined the chase led by the fleeing vehicle as it traveled at a high rate of speed, passed a number of red lights and stop signs, and on several occasions drove the wrong way on one-way streets. The police cars never lost sight of the Honda, and they eventually forced it to stop. All four doors immediately opened and the passengers attempted to exit.

Officer Brook, one of the officers in the marked car, testified that he observed Reginal Scott exit from the back passenger seat and Kevin Davis emerge from the front passenger seat. According to Officer Brook, Scott initially put up his hands and surrendered, but then began inching away from the car. At the same time, Davis attempted to flee on foot and Officer Brook pursued him. According to Officer Brook, Davis pointed his firearm at him and he then fired one shot and hit Davis. A pistol was recovered from the area where Davis fell. Davis was then taken to the hospital by Officers Haines and Thomas who recovered from Davis $169.00 in cash and one plastic baggie containing nineteen zip-lock packets of cocaine base.

Officer Bucceroni, who was with Officer Brook, observed Kevin Minnis exiting the vehicle with a semi-automatic firearm in his right hand. Officer Bucceroni instructed Minnis to drop the firearm. After he complied the officer retrieved the weapon, placed Minnis under arrest, and, in the search incident to the arrest, recovered twelve packets containing cocaine base. At approximately the same time, Officer Dawsonia, who arrived on the scene after responding to the radio call for assistance, was instructed to stop Scott who had been slowly attempting to inch away. Upon hearing this instruction, Scott threw a handgun onto the ground and was arrested by Officer Dawsonia, who searched Scott and recovered forty-four packets of cocaine base from his pocket. Ballistics tests later confirmed that the firearm recovered from Scott was the weapon fired at 17th and Annin Streets.

Defendants were convicted following a jury trial on the drug and weapons charges referred to above.... Defendants filed a timely appeal.

[The appellate court first rejected Scott's argument that he was improperly joined with his codefendants under Rule 8(b).] Scott also argues that he was prejudiced by this joinder. In determining whether severance is appropriate, we have stated that "[a] claim of improper joinder under Fed.R.Crim.P. 14 must 'demonstrate clear and substantial prejudice.'" *United States v. Gorecki*, 813 F.2d 40, 43 (3d Cir. 1987). In determining whether severance should have been granted, we review the District Court's decision for abuse of discretion; in the absence of an affirmative showing of an abuse of discretion, this court will not interfere with the Rule 14 determinations made by the District Court. *United States v. Somers*, 496 F.2d 723, 730 (3d Cir. 1974).

Scott argues that he was extremely prejudiced by being joined with Kevin Davis, who fled the scene and allegedly attempted to fire at a police officer. However, we held in *Somers* that "a defendant is not entitled to a severance merely because evidence against a co-defendant is more damaging than the evidence against the moving party." *Id.* The issue is not whether the evidence against a co-defendant is more damaging but rather whether the jury will be able to "compartmentalize the evidence as it relates to separate defendants in view of its volume and limited admissibility."

Id. In this case, the facts are relatively simple; all the events occurred in a single evening; there are only three defendants; and there are no overly technical or scientific issues. Therefore, we conclude that the jury could reasonably have been expected to compartmentalize the evidence as it related to each individual defendant.

Scott also contends that he was prejudiced because he wished to present exculpatory evidence from Davis and Minnis, who could confirm that he was not in the black Honda on the night of his arrest. We have held that "[b]are assertions that co-defendants will testify are insufficient" to warrant separate trials. *United States v. Boscia*, 573 F.2d 827, 832 (3d Cir. 1978). Four factors need be considered: "(1) the likelihood of co-defendant's testifying; (2) the degree to which such testimony would be exculpatory; (3) the degree to which the testifying co-defendants could be impeached; [and] (4) judicial economy." *Id.* In addition, we have held that a defendant's claim that his co-defendants would testify on his behalf must be supported by the record, and the record must show more than simply the defendant's "request for declaration of [his co-defendants'] intent to testify." *United States v. Gonzalez*, 918 F.2d 1129, 1137 (3d Cir. 1990).

Applying the *Boscia* factors, the District Court found that Scott presented no evidence that the other defendants would testify and that even if they did testify, "their testimony could be seriously impeached." In addition, the Court believed that such testimony would have little exculpatory value and was outweighed by concerns for judicial economy.

Affirmed.

Notes

1. *Discretion and burden of proof.* The trial judge is given wide discretion in ruling on severance issues. On appeal the trial judge's decision is reviewed under the forgiving standard of whether there was an "abuse of discretion." A person requesting severance under Rule 14 has the burden of proof. Often this burden is characterized as being quite substantial. *See, e.g.*, *United States v. Mitchell*, 484 F.3d 762 (5th Cir. 2007) (defendant seeking severance from codefendants bears burden of showing specific and compelling prejudice that resulted in unfair trial).

2. *Jury instructions to limit use of evidence.* Sometimes prejudice may be present or possible, but severance is denied because the court can minimize or eliminate the harm by giving curative jury instructions that are usually viewed as effective in ensuring that the jury can perform in a fair, unbiased way. *See United States v. Riley*, 621 F.3d 312 (3d Cir. 2010) (prejudice that might have occurred was cured by jury instructions to consider each count separately and to return a separate verdict for each defendant).

3. *Timing of motion.* In order to permit the trial court to rule on a severance motion before the trial begins, the motion should be filed well before that date. A severance motion filed after trial has begun can be denied because of the tardy filing. Of course, the motion can be filed during trial if the reasons for it first surface

during proof. Statutes, court rules, or local practice in some jurisdictions mandate that severance petitions be filed by a specific time in the proceedings. For example, a jurisdiction may require filing five days before trial. Rule 12(b)(3)(D) of the Federal Rules of Criminal Procedure requires severance motions under Rule 14 to be filed "before trial."

4. *Exculpatory testimony from codefendant.* What should be the result when one codefendant wants a severance in order to require a codefendant to provide exculpatory evidence? Consider the following factors in the context of two defendants who are willing to testify for each other in separate trials, sometimes known as "alibi-swapping." The defendant seeking a severance initially must show that she has a bona fide need for the codefendant's testimony, the substance of that testimony, its exculpatory nature and effect, and the likelihood that the codefendant in fact would testify. If the defendant succeeds, the court balances the significance of the exculpatory testimony in relation to the defendant's theory of the case, how much prejudice would exist in the absence of the testimony, the effect on judicial economy, and the timeliness of the motion. *See, e.g., United States v. Catalan-Roman*, 585 F.3d 453 (1st Cir. 2009).

5. *Mutually antagonistic defenses.* Although it is difficult to generalize about the situations meriting a severance under Rule 14, examples of successful reasons supporting a severance include mutually antagonistic defenses by two defendants, i.e., acceptance of one defendant's defense would preclude acquittal of the other defendant.

Zafiro v. United States

506 U.S. 534 (1993)

Justice O'Connor delivered the opinion of the Court.

. . . Gloria Zafiro, Jose Martinez, Salvador Garcia, and Alfonso Soto were accused of distributing illegal drugs in the Chicago area, operating primarily out of Soto's bungalow in Chicago and Zafiro's apartment in Cicero, a nearby suburb. One day, government agents observed Garcia and Soto place a large box in Soto's car and drive from Soto's bungalow to Zafiro's apartment. The agents followed the two as they carried the box up the stairs. When the agents identified themselves, Garcia and Soto dropped the box and ran into [Zafiro's] apartment. The agents entered the apartment in pursuit and found the four petitioners in the living room. The dropped box contained 55 pounds of cocaine. [Agents also found cocaine, heroin, marijuana, and cash in the apartment.]

The four petitioners were indicted and brought to trial together. At various points during the proceeding, Garcia and Soto moved for severance, arguing that their defenses were mutually antagonistic. Soto testified that he knew nothing about the drug conspiracy. He claimed that Garcia had asked him for a box, which he gave Garcia, and that he (Soto) did not know its contents until they were arrested. Garcia did not testify, but his lawyer argued that Garcia was innocent: The box belonged to Soto and Garcia was ignorant of its contents.

Zafiro and Martinez also repeatedly moved for severance on the ground that their defenses were mutually antagonistic. Zafiro testified that she was merely Martinez's girlfriend and knew nothing of the conspiracy. She claimed that Martinez stayed in her apartment occasionally, kept some clothes there, and gave her small amounts of money. Although she allowed Martinez to store a suitcase in her closet, she testified, she had no idea that the suitcase contained illegal drugs. Like Garcia, Martinez did not testify. But his lawyer argued that Martinez was only visiting his girlfriend and had no idea that she was involved in distributing drugs.

The District Court denied the motions for severance. [After conviction, all but Zafiro appealed, claiming] that the District Court abused its discretion in denying their motions to sever. (Zafiro did not appeal the denial of her severance motion, and thus, her claim is not properly before this Court.) [The Court of Appeals affirmed the convictions because the defendants had not suffered prejudice from the denial of a severance.] We granted the petition for certiorari and now affirm the judgment of the Court of Appeals.

Rule 8(b) states that "two or more defendants may be charged in the same indictment or information if they are alleged to have participated in the same act or transaction or in the same series of acts or transactions constituting an offense or offenses." There is a preference in the federal system for joint trials of defendants who are indicted together. Joint trials play a vital role in the criminal justice system. They promote efficiency and serve the interests of justice by avoiding the scandal and inequity of inconsistent verdicts. For these reasons, we repeatedly have approved of joint trials. But Rule 14 recognizes that joinder, even when proper under Rule 8(b), may prejudice either a defendant or the Government. Thus, the Rule provides,

> [i]f it appears that a defendant or the government is prejudiced by a joinder of . . . defendants . . . for trial together, the court may order an election or separate trials of counts, grant a severance of defendants or provide whatever other relief justice requires.

. . . [P]etitioners urge us to adopt a bright-line rule, mandating severance whenever codefendants have conflicting defenses. We decline to do so. Mutually antagonistic defenses are not prejudicial per se. Moreover, Rule 14 does not require severance even if prejudice is shown; rather, it leaves the tailoring of the relief to be granted, if any, to the district court's sound discretion.

We believe that, when defendants properly have been joined under Rule 8(b), a district court should grant a severance under Rule 14 only if there is a serious risk that a joint trial would compromise a specific trial right of one of the defendants, or prevent the jury from making a reliable judgment about guilt or innocence. Such a risk might occur when evidence that the jury should not consider against a defendant and that would not be admissible if a defendant were tried alone is admitted against a codefendant. . . . Conversely, a defendant might suffer prejudice if essential exculpatory evidence that would be available to a defendant tried alone were unavailable in a joint trial. The risk of prejudice will vary with the facts in each case, and district courts may find prejudice in situations not discussed here. . . .

Turning to the facts of this case, we note that petitioners do not articulate any specific instances of prejudice. Instead they contend that the very nature of their defenses, without more, prejudiced them. Their theory is that when two defendants both claim they are innocent and each accuses the other of the crime, a jury will conclude (1) that both defendants are lying and convict them both on that basis, or (2) that at least one of the two must be guilty without regard to whether the Government has proved its case beyond a reasonable doubt.

As to the first contention, it is well settled that defendants are not entitled to severance merely because they may have a better chance of acquittal in separate trials. . . . While an important element of a fair trial is that a jury consider *only* relevant and competent evidence bearing on the issue of guilt or innocence, a fair trial does not include the right to exclude relevant and competent evidence. A defendant normally would not be entitled to exclude the testimony of a former codefendant if the district court did sever their trials, and we see no reason why relevant and competent testimony would be prejudicial merely because the witness is also a codefendant.

As to the second contention, the short answer is that petitioners' scenario simply did not occur here. . . . [E]ven if there were some risk of prejudice, here it is of the type that can be cured with proper instructions, and "juries are presumed to follow their instructions." The District Court properly instructed the jury that the Government had "the burden of proving beyond a reasonable doubt" that each defendant committed the crimes with which he or she was charged. The court then instructed the jury that it must "give separate consideration to each individual defendant and to each separate charge against him. Each defendant is entitled to have his or her case determined from his or her own conduct and from the evidence [that] may be applicable to him or to her." . . . These instructions sufficed to cure any possibility of prejudice.

Rule 14 leaves the determination of risk of prejudice and any remedy that may be necessary to the sound discretion of the district courts. Because petitioners have not shown that their joint trial subjected them to any legally cognizable prejudice, we conclude that the District Court did not abuse its discretion in denying petitioners' motions to sever.

Justice Stevens, concurring in the judgment.

. . . Joinder is problematic in cases involving mutually antagonistic defenses because it may operate to reduce the burden on the prosecutor, in two general ways. First, joinder may introduce what is in effect a second prosecutor into a case, by turning each codefendant into the other's most forceful adversary. Second, joinder may invite a jury confronted with two defendants, at least one of whom is almost certainly guilty, to convict the defendant who appears the more guilty of the two regardless of whether the prosecutor has proven guilt beyond a reasonable doubt as to that particular defendant. Though the Court is surely correct that this second risk may be minimized by careful instructions insisting on separate consideration of the evidence as to each codefendant, the danger will remain relevant to the prejudice inquiry in some cases.

. . . For the reasons discussed above, however, I think district courts must retain their traditional discretion to consider severance whenever mutually antagonistic defenses are presented. . . .

Notes

1. *Deference to trial judge.* Since decisions under Rule 14 involve a heavy dose of the trial judge's discretion, appellate courts are quite deferential to the lower court's ruling. Does this make sense? What information will the trial court need to assess whether there was prejudice? Is this any different than a trial court's decision about the meaning of words in a statute, where little or no deference is given the trial court's ruling?

2. *Standard of prejudice.* What is the standard of "prejudice" in *Zafiro*? Must the defendants prove actual prejudice? Must they prove that the result *would* have been different had a severance been granted? That it *might* have been different? How would they prove this?

3. *Spillover evidence.* A common ground for a Rule 14 motion is the concern that "spillover" evidence, admissible against one or more defendants, but not against others, will be improperly used against the latter offenders. Was this risk adequately considered in *Zafiro*?

4. *Mutually antagonistic defenses. Zafiro* follows the traditional view that mutually antagonistic defenses are grounds for a discretionary severance under Rule 14 if the necessary prejudice is shown. In these cases, ordinarily the jury will be forced to believe one defendant and disbelieve another. The typical pattern is that each defendant offers a defense to his or her charge but supports the guilt of the other defendant. Why should this typical factfinding process be grounds for a severance under Rule 14?

5. *Jury instructions. Zafiro* also suggests that jury instructions can often cure problems arising from mutually antagonistic defenses and other joinder problems. Do you agree? Can a jury really obey such instructions? Note that the *Zafiro* Court found that the curative instructions "sufficed to cure any possibility of prejudice." Do you agree?

6. *A constitutional right to severance?* Severance is normally analyzed as a subconstitutional matter involving the interpretation and application of Rule 14. However, at least one court has indicated that the general constitutional right to a fair trial may in some circumstances require severance even if Rule 14 does not. *See United States v. Shkreli*, 260 F. Supp. 3d 247 (E.D.N.Y. 2017). The government charged two defendants with various counts of business fraud, and the codefendants moved to sever their trials. Although their defenses involved considerable blame-shifting, the court determined that they were not so mutually antagonistic as to require severance

under Rule 14. *See id.* at 254 ("Defendants' defenses are not mutually antagonistic because they do not require a jury to find one defendant guilty if that jury accepts the other defendant's defense."). The court also rejected one defendant's claim that he would suffer spillover prejudice from some of the evidence expected to be used against his codefendant, noting that the evidence would likely be admissible against both even if they were tried separately. *Id.* at 255.

However, the court nonetheless ruled that constitutional considerations required severance, relying particularly on one defendant's stated intention to function as a "second prosecutor" against the other. "[Defendant] Greebel's counsel intends to assert a defense that will be an 'echo chamber' for the prosecution by presenting evidence of multiple instances of [defendant] Shkreli's purported lies, deceptions, and misrepresentations. In addition, Greebel's counsel plans to present evidence, even if the government does not, that Shkreli lied to Greebel and other attorneys and investors. . . . Through such double prosecution of Shkreli by the government and Greebel, there is a serious risk that the jury would be prevented from making a reliable judgment about guilt or innocence even with limiting instructions by the court." *Id.* at 256. Note how the court's "second prosecutor" point dovetails with the concurring opinion of Justice Stevens in *Zafiro*. If this is accepted as a basis for severance, though, is it too easy for defendants to obtain separate trials, contrary to the government's legitimate interest in preventing largely redundant proceedings? Defendants often attempt to shift blame to their codefendants, thereby becoming in some sense a second prosecutor. If that dynamic did not require severance in *Zafiro*, why should it in *Shkreli*? The court in *Shkreli* suggested that the key difference lay in the contention by one defendant (Shkreli) that no crime occurred, while codefendant Greebel was going to actively support the government's position that there had been a criminal fraud. *Id.* at 257. More commonly in blame-shifting cases, there is no dispute that a crime has occurred; the only real question is who should be held criminally liable for the offense. But do the unusual features of *Shkreli* really warrant different treatment by the court?

7. *Severance and the right to remain silent.* If a defendant exercises his or her right to remain silent at trial, the prosecutor is not permitted to comment negatively on the defendant's failure to testify. But what if two defendants are indicted together and plan to present antagonistic defenses, only one plans to testify, and counsel for the testifying defendant would like to comment negatively on the codefendant's silence—does that require severance of the trials? Courts have handled this difficult issue in different ways, but some have held that defense counsel may be prohibited from commenting on a codefendant's silence, which removes the basis for severance. *See, e.g., United States v. Morales-Guanill*, 77 F. Supp. 3d 258, 263 (D. Puerto Rico 2015). Note, however, that such an order may be in tension with the testifying defendant's constitutional right to present a defense—the defendant is deprived of what might be a powerful argument in his or her favor.

8. *Severance and the right to confront accusers.* As we will see in Chapter 14, the Sixth Amendment Confrontation Clause gives defendants a right to cross-examine

their accusers, which generally prohibits the use of hearsay evidence against a defendant. However, an awkward problem may arise in multidefendant cases when one defendant has made an inculpatory out-of-court statement, such as a confession given to police investigators, but then refuses to testify at trial. In general, a defendant's own out-of-court statement can be used against that defendant notwithstanding the Confrontation Clause, but what if the statement also incriminates a codefendant? Use of the hearsay confession against the codefendant would violate the Confrontation Clause. How can the two defendants be tried together if a key item of evidence against one cannot be used against the other?

This scenario is called a *Bruton* problem, recalling the name of the case in which the Supreme Court established new restrictions on the use of one defendant's out-of-court statements in a joint trial. We will consider *Bruton* in more detail in Chapter 14. For now, suffice it to say that the existence of a *Bruton* problem may provide support for severing the trials of codefendants.

9. *State law.* A few states give defendants a right to severance in various circumstances. *See, e.g.*, ALA. CODE § 15-14-20 (joined defendants "may be tried either jointly or separately, as either may elect"); GA. CODE ANN. § 17-8-4 (capital defendants have right to severance; severance discretionary for other defendants); TEX. PENAL CODE § 3.04 (right to severance of offenses joined because they arose from same criminal episode); *Markee v. State*, 494 S.E.2d 551 (Ga. Ct. App. 1997) (right to severance of crimes joined solely because of same or similar character).

Problem 8-3. "We Can't Go on Like This"

An information charged Carl Hurst and Kerri Belker with manslaughter in the death of their one-year-old daughter. An autopsy revealed that the baby died from blows to the upper part of her body with a flat instrument, such as a belt. After the baby's death, both Hurst and Belker claimed that the baby had fallen down the stairs. Belker also told the police that Hurst had repeatedly struck his baby with a belt. While denying that she had ever used a belt on the baby, Belker admitted that on the day the baby died she had spanked the baby with a shoe.

1. If the defendants move for separate trials, what information supports their motion?

2. If the motion to sever is denied, how should you as an appellate judge rule on Hurst's appeal after his conviction if at trial Belker testified on her own behalf and put the blame directly and exclusively on Hurst?

Problem 8-4. Lawyer's Advice

Smith and Phillips were sports agents who represented football players. They secured some of their player-clients by paying cash bonuses, no-interest loans and sports cars, then signing the athletes to secret postdated contracts while the players were still members of their college football teams. Since college rules bar such contracts, the understanding was that each player would lie about the contracts until the end of the player's college eligibility. Before beginning their business venture, Smith and Phillips consulted Lowell, a lawyer specializing in sports law. Each provided her with a significant amount of confidential information.

Smith and Phillips are scheduled to be tried for mail fraud, stemming from the players' lies on routine forms the players mailed to the NCAA in which they denied signing any contracts with sports agents. At the trial, Smith plans to argue that he is not guilty of mail fraud because he had no intent to defraud, one of the elements of mail fraud. He maintains that he was told by Lowell, his attorney, that the scheme was legal. To prove this, Smith plans to call Ms. Lowell as a crucial defense witness.

Phillips' attorney has decided that it would be unwise for Phillips to rely on the advice-of-counsel defense. It is feared that Lowell's testimony will likely include confidential information that Phillips provided Lowell. Accordingly, the lawyer has filed, pursuant to Rule 14, a Motion to Sever, arguing that Smith's defense will force Phillips to assert the same advice-of-counsel defense and that this will have negative consequences for Phillips because privileged communications will probably be revealed by Lowell. What result?

Problem 8-5. Booze Brothers

Four people were indicted for conspiracy to violate the revenue laws in that they were involved in making and transporting illegal whiskey. The one-count indictment alleged the following facts. On January 6, Defendants *A* and *B* were arrested for transporting 90 gallons of untaxed spirits. After the arrest, they went to Defendant *C*'s house to sleep. On July 19, Defendant *C* drove a heavily loaded truck near Defendant *D*'s house. The truck, no longer loaded, was seen an hour later traveling away from *D*'s house, where an illegal still was located the same day. Twenty thousand pounds of sugar, used to make moonshine whiskey, were found at the still.

Was joinder correct under Rule 8(b)? If so, should there be a severance under Rule 14?

Assume also that the indictment contained other counts: In Count Two, *A* and *B* were charged with the substantive offense of transporting untaxed whiskey. In Count Three, *C* and *D* were charged with the crime of illegal manufacture of intoxicating liquors. Was joinder correct under Rule 8(a)? Under Rule 8(b)? Should there be a severance under Rule 14? If a severance is appropriate, which defendant(s) and crime(s) should be severed?

Chapter 9

Motion Practice in Criminal Cases

A. Introduction

Motion practice is a very important facet of criminal representation. Although many cases are won or lost on the basis of motion practice, it is often ignored in law school and is described in only the most general terms in the rules of criminal procedure. This chapter focuses primarily on pretrial motion practice and the strategic and ethical questions it raises (see discussion at end of Chapter 14 of post-verdict motions). For additional information regarding the myriad motions that may be filed in a criminal case, including grounds for motions and an examination of governing legal principles, *see* James A. Adams & Daniel D. Blinka, Pretrial Motions in Criminal Prosecutions (4th ed. 2008).

A motion is a formal request for a judge to issue an order. The requested order may direct a clerk or someone else to do or not do something (such as give counsel access to a sealed file), or may regulate some future aspect of the case (perhaps excluding certain proof at trial), or may even end the case (see *dispositive motions*, below). More than one motion can be filed at the same time. Sometimes, counsel will file motions in the alternative. If Motion A is not granted, then counsel asks for relief under Motion B. The danger of alternative motions, of course, is that the dual approach may undercut the strength of the argument for each motion. The court may get the feeling that counsel is not serious about either motion.

Once made, a motion triggers a series of events. The opposing counsel is given an opportunity to respond (perhaps arguing that the motion should be denied for certain specific reasons), and often the judge will rule on the motion (perhaps granting or denying all or part of it, or postponing a decision).

Motions can be filed by the prosecutor or defense counsel, and sometimes by other people as well. For example, a witness may file a motion to quash a subpoena issued to compel the witness to testify at trial.

B. Functions of Motions—Dispositive and Tactical

[1] Types of Motions

Some defense motions (generally referred to as *dispositive motions*) may seek to dismiss charges, ending the case against the defendant. Examples of dispositive motions include motions to dismiss for insufficient evidence usually brought at the close of the prosecution's case in chief (sometimes called a *Motion for Directed Verdict of Acquittal*), or on grounds such as *statute of limitations*, *double jeopardy*, or a fatal flaw in the indictment. Some motions, while not technically dispositive (not automatically requiring dismissal by themselves), nonetheless turn out to be dispositive in effect—for example, a *Motion to Suppress* evidence which if granted will leave the prosecution without sufficient evidence to sustain the charge(s).

Other motions, in contrast, seek to gain some tactical advantage at or before trial, e.g., to permit discovery, or to limit the evidence that will be used at trial. For obvious reasons, the prosecution may only bring tactical motions, but not dispositive motions, in criminal cases.

[2] Functions of Motions

Motions serve a number of important functions. Some are the product of legal rules requiring that certain motions be made and foreclosing some options if the motions are not made. Others stem from strategic considerations aside from legal requirements.

[a] Obtain Specific Result

The most obvious reason for making a motion is to obtain a court ruling on the matter raised in the motion. For example, if defense counsel wants the court to try two defendants in separate trials rather than one trial, a counsel should file a *Motion to Sever Defendants* in order to obtain a court ruling on this request.

[b] Prerequisite to Raising Certain Legal Issues

Some important issues in criminal cases can only be raised by written motion. The failure to file the appropriate motion may preclude the party from obtaining a court order that might have been given if correct motion practice had been followed.

[c] Preserve Issue for Appeal

If a party does not formally request a court ruling on an issue, ordinarily the party cannot later appeal the fact that the court made no such ruling. Often the issue is considered to have been *waived* or *forfeited*. Thus, a motion, even though denied, may keep an issue alive for presentation to an appellate court. *See, e.g.*, *United States v. Yousef*, 327 F.3d 56 (2d Cir. 2003) (failure to file pretrial suppression motion bars later consideration of issue of involuntary confession).

Two closely related, tragic cases illustrate the importance of preserving an issue for appellate review. In August 1974, John Eldon Smith and his wife Rebecca Smith Machetti were involved in a double murder of Rebecca's former husband and the former husband's new wife. The homicides were committed to obtain life insurance proceeds. John and Rebecca were tried in state court for the murders in separate trials in the same Georgia county a few weeks apart in early 1975. Both were convicted and sentenced to death. The juries for both trials were selected in a way that underrepresented women, in violation of decisions by the United States Supreme Court. Rebecca's attorney raised the issue of the invalid jury selection process at an early stage of the proceedings and a federal appellate court eventually overturned her conviction. *Machetti v. Linahan*, 679 F.2d 236 (11th Cir. 1982).

John's attorney, on the other hand, was unaware of the United States Supreme Court's decisions, the most important of which was decided five days before John's trial, indicating that the Georgia jury selection procedure was unconstitutional. Consequently, he did not raise the issue of the invalid jury selection process until eight years later, after Rebecca's convictions had been set aside by a federal appellate court. She was retried and received a life sentence. Her husband was not as fortunate. Under Georgia law, a defendant's challenge to jury composition had to be made when, or before, the jury is "put upon him." Because John's lawyer failed to make a timely objection to the unconstitutionally selected jury, he waived the issue under Georgia law and both Georgia and federal courts refused to intervene because of this waiver. *Smith v. Kemp*, 715 F.2d 1459 (11th Cir. 1983). John Smith was executed by Georgia authorities on December 15, 1983. *See generally* Stephen B. Bright, *Death by Lottery—Procedural Bar of Constitutional Claims in Capital Cases Due to Inadequate Representation of Indigent Defendants*, 92 W. Va. L. Rev. 679 (1990).

[d] Counter Prosecutor's Claim of Inadvertent Mistake

Defendants sometimes appeal their convictions (rarely successfully) alleging that they were harmed ("prejudiced") by prosecutorial misconduct. Sometimes a prosecutor's motivation for making a comment or taking an action, later held to be inappropriate or legally unfounded, is a factor that will be considered by an appellate court in determining whether to reverse a conviction because of the prosecutor's error. Similarly, a trial judge may consider whether the motives for a defense counsel's harmful errors in representation were proper (e.g., simple inadvertence) or improper (e.g., the result of counsel's conflict of interest with representing another client) in deciding whether to order a mistrial for serious trial error by counsel.

A motion may set the stage for a later argument that adversary counsel's motivations were unacceptable or at least suspect. For example, defense counsel may file a motion requesting a court order that the prosecution not do certain things. Even though the motion may be denied as premature, it will set the stage for a trial or appellate court reversal if the subject of the motion actually happens. To illustrate, assume that defense counsel fears that a prosecutor or prosecution witness will refer to evidence (perhaps a baggie of drugs) that has been ruled inadmissible as the result of a successful Motion to Suppress. Counsel may file a Motion to Prohibit the Prosecution from Referring Directly or Indirectly to Suppressed Evidence. Some judges might deny the motion as too speculative (no one knows whether the prosecution will actually engage in this unethical behavior or whether a witness will venture into forbidden topics). But if during the trial the prosecutor or a prosecution witness actually does make a reference to the suppressed evidence, even an "unsuccessful" motion will make it unlikely that either the trial or appellate court will view such behavior as inadvertent.

[e] Provide Discovery

As discussed in Chapters 1 and 10, in most jurisdictions discovery is quite limited in criminal cases. Depositions are rare and interrogatories nonexistent. Some witnesses may refuse to speak with lawyers for the other side until after they have testified on direct examination. Sometimes motion practice may provide a little discovery for both sides. If, for example, the defense files a motion, the prosecution's response may provide an indication of the prosecution's view of the case. The judge's ruling on the motion may also provide insight into the judge's attitude toward the case. If there is a hearing on the motion, counsel may learn something about the other side's evidence and view of the case and may get to hear and cross-examine witnesses or, if hearsay evidence is presented, at least to find something out about the information that some likely witnesses have. On rare occasions, counsel will use a motion hearing to give friendly witnesses experience testifying and to assess those witnesses' credibility in advance of trial.

[f] Assist in Planning Trial Strategy

Some motions are used to assist in planning trial strategy. For example, assume that defense counsel files a pretrial motion to exclude certain evidence that could be used in cross-examining one of the defense's key witnesses, perhaps even the defendant. If the motion is granted and the evidence barred, counsel may decide to call that person as a witness since the harmful impeaching proof cannot be used. But if the motion is denied and the harmful evidence is admissible to impeach, counsel may elect to proceed without benefit of that witness's testimony. This sophisticated motion practice should help enhance counsel's ability to plan an effective presentation of the client's case at trial.

[g] Affect Plea Bargaining

Since the great majority of criminal cases are resolved by guilty pleas, serious attention to motion practice may contribute to the defendant's ability to obtain a better plea offer from the prosecutor. Zealous (but not frivolous) motion practice demonstrates to the prosecutor that defense counsel is willing to "go to the mat" on this case. The prosecutor may dread that a time-consuming, protracted series of procedural hurdles and hearings, with uncertain outcomes, is ahead. In too many American jurisdictions, prosecutors are overworked. They have far more cases scheduled than they can handle except in a most perfunctory way. When an overworked prosecutor is deluged with defense motions and faces the prospect of a fight over matters considered by the prosecutor to be trivial or not worth the time to deal with them, a natural response may be to offer an attractive deal so that the defendant will plead guilty and the motions will not have to be answered, and a motion hearing can be avoided, conserving limited prosecutorial resources. A caveat against *over*zealousness is in order here—it is also possible that an avalanche of dubious motions might stiffen a prosecutor's resolve and harden the prosecution's position as to the motions themselves and as to the case's ultimate disposition.

Defense motion practice may also encourage negotiations by creating or exposing weaknesses in the prosecution's case. For example, a Motion to Suppress Defendant's Confession may, if granted, severely reduce the likelihood of a conviction and therefore encourage the prosecutor to make an attractive offer in order to avoid the risk of an acquittal or hung jury. Similarly, if the court erroneously denies a defense motion and thereby creates a viable appellate issue, the prosecution may be willing to agree to a minimal sentence so that it does not have to risk a lengthy appellate process followed by a retrial.

[h] Educate Participants in the Case

Motions not only seek a result, they also educate those persons involved in the motion practice. In addition to putting the prosecutor "on notice" that counsel intends to vigorously defend the case, motion practice can also educate the judge about key legal and strategic issues the defense intends to present. For example, if a judge is not familiar with a technical facet of the case, a motion dealing with that issue will force the judge to learn about the issue before it arises in court. This may make it easier for counsel to obtain favorable evidentiary rulings and to present the case at trial. Finally, motion practice may help educate the client. It tells the client that counsel is aggressively pursuing the case and may make the client feel better about the quality of counsel's services and the fairness of the proceeding.

[i] Protect Attorney from Malpractice Action

Today, lawyers, like physicians, always face the possibility of a malpractice action. Good motion practice may help prevent or defeat malpractice claims. An attorney who files appropriate motions has created a documented record of efforts to represent the accused competently. Incompetent representation may also subject derelict counsel to professional discipline. Motion practice may help prove that the lawyer zealously protected the client's rights.

On the other hand, poor motion practice can provide strong evidence of incompetent representation. Counsel may be required to explain why certain motions were not filed (especially if a court determines that a motion not filed would have been filed by any competent counsel), or were drafted incompetently.

[j] Gain Time to Further Prepare Case

As discussed below, an ethical attorney should not file motions as a pretext to delay a pending criminal trial (unless, of course, the motion specifically addresses that issue; an example would be a Motion for a Continuance, discussed below). Nevertheless, sometimes a motion will have the effect of delaying criminal proceedings by requiring time to permit the other lawyers and the judge an opportunity to respond and rule on the motion. This delay may sometimes be a beneficial by-product of motion practice.

C. Form of Motions

There is surprisingly little law that describes the form of motions. Often the best way to find out what a motion is supposed to look like is to study motions that have been successfully used in the court where the motion will be filed. Prosecution, public defender, and private law offices typically have "motion banks" that counsel contemplating bringing a motion for the first time can consult to learn the form and content of motions that have been brought in previous cases. Local rules of court (state and federal) should also be carefully consulted, for they may establish time limits for filing and serving motions, rules for such important matters as the length and propriety of supporting documents, the need for a pre-filing conference with opposing counsel, the need for a written response to a motion, and the procedures used in hearings on motions.

[1] Written or Oral

Although many motions can be made either in writing or orally, some must be in writing. Rule 47 of the Federal Rules of Criminal Procedure, for example, states: "A motion—except when made during a trial or hearing—must be in writing, unless the court permits the party to make the motion by other means." Rule 12 reinforces this by providing that pretrial motions "may be written or oral at the discretion of the judge."

A written motion has many advantages. It provides a formal record that the motion was made and it provides accurate notice to all parties of the content of the motion. It also allows counsel to draft the motion carefully so that it includes the proper requests. This ensures that the right issue is raised and therefore preserved for appellate review. An oral motion, on the other hand, does permit counsel to respond quickly to a fast-moving situation during the course of a hearing or trial and calls for the other side to respond with little time for reflection. Since appellate courts may refuse to review an issue not properly raised at trial, a lawyer making an oral motion should make sure that the court reporter accurately preserves the motion and the court's ruling.

[2] Content of Motions

Criminal procedure rules are surprisingly silent on the content of motions. Many questions are simply not addressed by court rule. Local rules and custom determine the acceptable content of a motion, but some generalizations are possible because motions are usually quite similar irrespective of the jurisdiction.

In general terms, a motion should contain a clear statement of what is requested and why it is requested. More particularly, the motion will ordinarily contain the following 10 parts:

1. *Court where filed.* At the top of most motions is a statement of the court in which the motion is filed. For example, the motion may indicate that it is filed in the United States District Court for the Southern District of New York. This helps counsel and court clerks keep track of motions filed in different courts.

2. *Style or Caption of case (names of parties).* Near the top of the motion, counsel should include the names of the parties. Ordinarily in a criminal case, one of the parties will be a government entity (State of *X* or United States of America) and the other will be one or more defendants. For example, a motion may be styled:

UNITED STATES OF AMERICA

vs.

JONATHAN BLAIR DOE

This is crucial in ensuring that the motion is considered in the correct case and filed in the correct folder.

3. *Case number.* The court clerk's office assigns each criminal case a unique number. This facilitates record keeping in a potentially confusing situation where thousands of cases may be active at the same time and many defendants have the same or similar names or face multiple charges. Counsel filing a motion should insert the case number near the top of the motion.

4. *Title that summarizes content of motion.* In most jurisdictions, somewhere near the top of each motion is a sparsely worded title indicating the substance of the motion. This helps distinguish one document from another in cases where many items are filed. While this statement should be brief, it must be sufficiently inclusive to be helpful. For example, a motion titled simply "Motion" does not provide adequate guidance. A better title would be "Motion to Sever Offenses" or "Motion to Suppress Product of Unconstitutional Search" or "Motion to Reduce Bail."

5. *Statement of relief requested and the party requesting it.* The heart of a motion is contained in the first paragraph of the body of the document. This indicates which party is making the request and includes a conclusory statement of the relief sought. In some locales this paragraph begins with a stilted (and unnecessary) opening line such as, "Comes now the Defendant Jonathan Blair Doe by and through counsel Elizabeth Adams. . . ." A more modern, plain-English rendition, less painful to read, is, "Defendant Jonathan Blair Doe moves the court for an order. . . ."

After the party making the request is identified, the motion may contain a recitation of the authority permitting the motion to be made. For example, the motion may indicate that the motion is made "pursuant to Rule 47 of the Rules of Criminal Procedure."

The next item is a summary statement of the relief requested. This should be sufficiently precise to indicate exactly what order is sought. For example, the motion may indicate that the defendant is moving to have the defendant's case severed from that of a co-defendant. The relief requested must be described with great care to avoid waiving matters not mentioned in the motion. *See, e.g, United States v. Mathison*, 157 F.3d 541 (8th Cir. 1998) (motion to sever offenses does not constitute motion to sever one codefendant).

6. *Statement of underlying facts.* Sometimes the motion will include a brief statement of facts underlying the motion. One or more affidavits or other documents may also be attached to the motion. Rules of criminal procedure are usually silent on whether the motion must adhere to the usual civil standard of being stated "with particularity." This factual description will provide background for the judge to use in ruling on the motion. Some lawyers prefer to disclose as few facts and theories as possible in order to avoid providing adversary counsel with discovery. If some or all of the underlying facts are not in dispute, the motion should so state, or the moving party may even seek the other side's agreement to submit a more formal "Stipulation of Undisputed Facts" to the court.

For both tactical and ethical reasons, the facts must be stated accurately, for counsel may have to prove them if a hearing is held to determine whether the motion should be granted. For example, in a Motion to Dismiss Because of the Statute of Limitations, the motion may include a brief recitation of such facts as the alleged date of the crime and the date of the indictment. A copy of the indictment may be attached to the motion.

7. *Statement of reasons why entitled to relief.* The motion must also include a brief statement about why the relief requested should be granted. If there are several grounds for granting the motion, counsel should include them all and number them sequentially (leading, of course, with those grounds that counsel believes to be the strongest). For example, if a motion is brought to exclude the defendant's confession to the police, the Motion to Exclude the Defendant's Confession may argue that the confession should be barred because it was obtained in violation of the Fifth Amendment's self-incrimination guarantee, the Fourteenth Amendment's Due Process Clause, and the Sixth Amendment's right to counsel. Often counsel will include a citation to the key provisions of law (e.g., statutes, rules, or cases) supporting the request, but in most courts citation to authority should be quite brief in the motion itself. A more detailed *memorandum of law*, described below, should be attached to the motion to provide a fuller justification for the requested court order.

8. *Concluding paragraph.* Many lawyers include a final paragraph summarizing once again the relief sought. For example, the motion may state, "For the reasons given, the defendant Jonathan Blair Doe moves for an order that his case be severed from that of co-defendant."

9. *Signed by lawyer offering the motion.* Usually motions must be signed by the attorney filing them. Some courts even refuse to accept unsigned motions. Beneath the lawyer's signature, virtually every motion includes the name (and often the address, email, and telephone number) of the attorney filing it. This *signature block*

provides a quick way for the court and adversary counsel to identify the maker of the motion and to contact the lawyer if necessary. This may be especially helpful in cases involving many defendants and numerous lawyers, or where there is a need for prompt court action.

10. *Indication of service on opposing party.* In most jurisdictions, a lawyer who files a motion with a court has the responsibility of providing a copy to the other lawyers in the case. To prove that service on all lawyers was made, frequently a *certificate of service* will be included at the end of a motion, indicating that a copy of the motion was mailed, faxed, emailed, or hand delivered to one or more lawyers whose names and addresses are listed in this part of the motion.

D. Supporting Documents

Since a motion is usually quite conclusory and contains few facts and citations to relevant cases, rules, statutes, and constitutional provisions, often counsel will want to submit an affidavit and/or a brief or memorandum in support of the motion. These documents provide the court with more detailed information and authorities and may be instrumental in obtaining a favorable ruling on the motion.

Although these supporting affidavits, memoranda, and briefs are common in many jurisdictions, they may be virtually unregulated by formal court rules. Sometimes local rules will prescribe some of the process (perhaps by establishing standards for the size of the paper or font used for the memorandum or brief, or limits on the number of pages that can be submitted in support of a motion). Usually, however, informal local practice establishes the parameters of this facet of motion practice.

[1] Affidavit

An *affidavit* is a sworn statement. It provides facts or expert opinions helpful or necessary in resolving the motion. An affidavit may be made by a party or anyone else, including an expert or even a lawyer. The only limit is that the *affiant* (the person who signs and swears to the affidavit) must be competent to testify as a witness. Affidavits are signed under penalty of perjury and usually also signed ("*attested*") by a notary. Although it is hearsay, an affidavit may be admissible to support a motion because the formal rules of evidence usually do not apply to motion hearings. Rule 47(b) of the Federal Rules of Criminal Procedure specifically provides that a motion "may be supported by affidavit." Rule 47(d) states that an affidavit should be served on all parties at the same time as the motion it supports.

An affidavit has several advantages. First, it provides the court with important factual information that has been carefully scrutinized by counsel submitting it. Second, it does so in a way that cannot be cross-examined by opposing counsel. Thus, a criminal defendant can submit an affidavit without having to take the stand at a hearing on a motion. On occasion, a judge may permit the motion to be resolved on the basis of facts submitted in affidavits by both sides. This procedure may avoid the discovery and delay that might result if the judge holds a full evidentiary hearing on the motion.

Because of the lack of detailed rules regulating this facet of motion practice, there is significant confusion about what is appropriate to include in an affidavit. For the reasons stated above, counsel may prefer to rely on an affidavit rather than a live witness. But such so-called "speaking motions" may be held impermissible since they are a substitute for live testimony at a hearing.

Use of affidavits in motion practice. Proper use of affidavits generally depends on the issue raised in a given motion. Except in unusual cases, affidavits should not be permitted to counter the allegations in an indictment. The government is entitled to prove its case through direct and cross examination and other evidence. On the other hand, if the issue can be resolved by undisputed facts, affidavits may be an appropriate and sufficient source of factual data. This is especially true for legal (as opposed to factual) issues.

For example, in *United States v. J.R. Watkins Co.*, 16 F.R.D. 229 (D. Minn. 1954), the court held that a motion to dismiss for violation of the statute of limitations can be resolved on the basis of affidavits and exhibits. However, that court also held, to the contrary, that the defendant's motion opposing the government's characterization of facts alleged in the indictment (that the defendant's use of a code number constituted a "representation" and therefore violated federal requirements mandating the provision of certain information) must be resolved at trial rather than through affidavits because it is the factual heart of the prosecution.

Sealed affidavit. On rare occasions, counsel may be placed in the difficult position of needing to file an affidavit, yet fearing that doing so will adversely affect the case. For example, defense counsel may believe that a defense motion should be supported by an affidavit from a key defense witness. But if the affidavit is filed and read by the prosecutor, important defense strategy will be revealed and the prosecutor may get significant discovery about a defense witness's likely testimony at trial. In this situation, the defense counsel can file a *sealed affidavit* and a motion requesting the court to consider the affidavit ex parte, without disclosure to the prosecution. Since some judges are reluctant to permit ex parte affidavits, counsel seeking to offer one may elect first to file a Motion to File a Sealed Affidavit. This motion may trigger a hearing on the issue and result in a ruling that itself could be a ground for appeal.

[2] Supporting Memoranda and Briefs

A *memorandum* or *brief* contains legal argument and authorities in support of a motion. They may also include details about the procedural history of the case. These are especially appropriate for motions that raise questions of law and need supporting legal arguments and citations to relevant authorities. Memoranda and briefs are written by an advocate for a particular position and are rarely neutral in their approach.

Form varies markedly. The form of memoranda and briefs varies considerably among lawyers and jurisdictions. Some are quite lengthy, while others consist of a short summary of arguments and authorities. State or local rules of court may place page or size limits on these documents, and may require them in certain situations. Sometimes counsel will attach copies of relevant rules, cases, and statutes to the memorandum.

Sometimes these items will be combined. A motion may be filed, accompanied by a memorandum which includes an appendix containing an affidavit. In some courts, the memorandum and affidavit may be filed after the motion is filed. The needs of each case and the rules and preferences of the court will determine when and what items, if any, are submitted with a motion.

[3] Proposed Order

In many jurisdictions, counsel will submit a *proposed order* with the motion. This is a draft of a court order that implements the motion. The trial judge may sign the draft order (or one based on the draft order) if the motion is granted. Many courts prefer that the draft order be signed by all lawyers in the case, indicating it has been approved by all parties. This ensures that the order is accurate, acceptable, and virtually immune from appellate reversal. Obviously, the procedure of submitting a draft order saves the court time. It also gives counsel a chance to affect the exact wording of the judge's decree.

E. Sample Motion

The following sample motion illustrates what a typical motion looks like. The parts of the motion are bracketed in bold. In this case, Jonathan Blair Doe is a police officer charged with multiple cocaine sales. Because of Doe's job, the local and national media have covered the crime in great detail, decrying corruption by public officials. Investigative reporters have combed the crime scene, interviewed every possible person in the case, and heavily covered every legal proceeding. For the past five months, the local papers have published daily stories on some facet of the case.

UNITED STATES DISTRICT COURT FOR THE EASTERN DISTRICT OF STATALINA [Court]

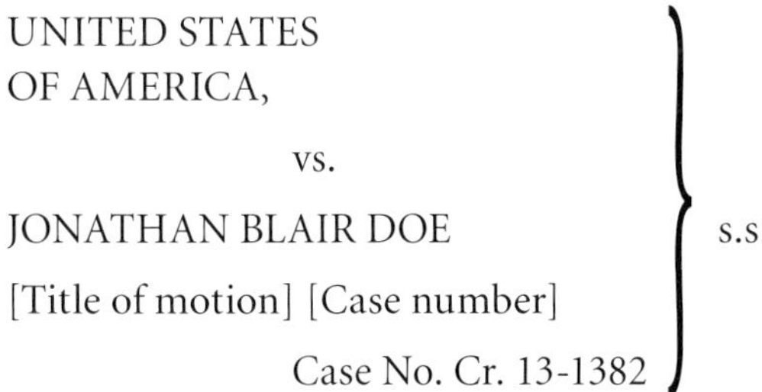

UNITED STATES
OF AMERICA,

vs.

JONATHAN BLAIR DOE

[Title of motion] [Case number]

Case No. Cr. 13-1382

s.s.:

MOTION FOR EXCLUSION OF PUBLIC FROM PRELIMINARY HEARING

[Relief requested]

The Defendant Jonathan Blair Doe moves the court for an order excluding the general public from a Preliminary Hearing in the instant case set for August 3, 20XX, at 1:30 P.M.

[Underlying facts and reasons motion should be granted]

In support of this motion, the defendant states:

1. That there will be extensive press coverage of this hearing, and

2. Evidence that will not be admitted at trial will be introduced and reported, and

3. That this press coverage will make it substantially probable that the defendant will be unable to have a fair trial because the extensive publicity will make it impossible to select an unbiased jury, and

4. That no reasonable alternatives exist to protect the defendant's rights to a fair trial. *Press-Enterprise Co. v. Superior Court*, 478 U.S. 1 (1986).

[**Concluding paragraph**]

THEREFORE, defendant respectfully moves this Court to order that the above-described preliminary hearing be closed to the general public and that attendance be limited to the defendant, legal counsel for all parties, the judge, necessary court officers, and witnesses permitted to remain in the courtroom pursuant to the Statalina Rules of Evidence.

____

Date
[**Signature block**]

____

Pat Ferguson
Attorney for Defendant,
Jonathan Blair Doe
Ferguson & Mancuso
2317 Main Street
Center, Statalina 37924
Tel. (234)567-8910

[**Proof of service**]

Certificate
I hereby certify that on July 18, 20XX, I mailed a copy of the foregoing Motion to the United States Attorney for the Eastern District of Statalina, Federal Court House, 239 Court Street, Center, Statalina 37924.

____

Pat Ferguson

Notes

1. *Additional information.* Although this Motion for Exclusion of Public from Preliminary Hearing does contain both facts and a citation to a leading case, more information may be helpful to the court. Accordingly, many lawyers would at least file a memorandum. Since this particular motion has constitutional overtones, a legal brief, titled "Memorandum of Law in Support of Defendant's Motion for Exclusion of Public from Preliminary Hearing," would be essential to educate the judge and persuade him or her to rule in the defendant's favor. This document would present the legal arguments and authorities supporting the defendant's motion.

One or more affidavits may also be attached so that the court has more detailed information about such matters as the quantity and quality of publicity to date, the precise evidence that is likely to be introduced at the preliminary hearing but unavailable at the trial, and the practical pitfalls of other methods of controlling the dissemination of information about the preliminary hearing. The prosecution, of course, would have an opportunity to file its *memorandum in opposition*, containing its counterarguments, before the judge rules on the motion.

2. *Ruling on motion.* If you were the judge, would you grant the defendant's motion? If not, what additional information would change your mind? How should the information be furnished? In an affidavit? Memorandum? Hearing?

3. *Role of third parties.* Should the press be able to intervene in opposition to the defendant's motion? If so, what limits should there be on interventions by third parties? Should the victim be permitted to express an opinion as to the presence of the press? If so, how should the victim's opinion be presented to the court?

F. Procedure

[1] Timing and Waiver

Motions can be made before, during, or after a criminal trial. Sometimes court rules mandate that certain motions be filed at or before a specified time in the proceedings. These time limits must be explored carefully and taken seriously. Failure to adhere to them can constitute a waiver or forfeiture of the issue the motion addresses. Fed. R. Crim. P. 12(c)(3).

Under Federal Rule of Criminal Procedure 12(b)(2), a motion to dismiss for lack of jurisdiction "may be made at any time while the case is pending." Rule 12(b)(3), in contrast, states that virtually all other "defenses, objections, and requests must be raised by pretrial motion if the basis for the motion is then reasonably available and the motion can be determined without a trial on the merits," or be deemed waived or forfeited. Specifically included under this rule are motions that allege the following:

(A) a defect in instituting the prosecution, including:

(i) improper venue;

(ii) preindictment delay;

(iii) a violation of the constitutional right to a speedy trial;

(iv) selective or vindictive prosecution; and

(v) an error in the grand-jury proceeding or preliminary hearing;

(B) a defect in the indictment or information, including:

(i) joining two or more offenses in the same count (duplicity);

(ii) charging the same offense in more than one count (multiplicity);

(iii) lack of specificity;

(iv) improper joinder; and

(v) failure to state an offense;

(C) suppression of evidence;

(D) severance of charges or defendants under Rule 14; and

(E) discovery under Rule 16.

However, the waiver rule is not absolute; the court has the discretion to refuse to find that an issue has been waived because of an untimely motion. *See* Rule 12(c)(3): "If a party does not meet the deadline for making a Rule 12(b)(3) motion, the motion is untimely. But a court may consider the defense, objection, or request if the party shows good cause." Common reasons offered to excuse a late motion include that counsel was too busy to complete and file the motion (a reason that is unlikely to be viewed with favor by the trial judge), counsel rendered ineffective assistance or, despite due diligence, counsel was unaware of the defect addressed in the motion.

Notes

1. *Pretrial motions.* The requirement of an early filing is designed to facilitate the use of a single hearing on all motions in the case and to permit the court and the parties time to implement any court decision.

The list of motions that must be filed in advance of trial should not be read exclusively. Even when a rule does not require a pretrial motion, many judges prefer or require that motions affecting a trial be filed sufficiently in advance of the trial to permit the parties to prepare for it if the motion is granted or denied. Thus, when possible, certain motions should be filed before a trial even though no court rule so states. Examples include a motion for a continuance (discussed in detail later in this chapter), for support services during trial, for special trial arrangements (such as letting two counsel present closing argument, permitting the client to serve as co-counsel, permitting the defense to argue last), or narrowing the scope of the trial by eliminating certain issues or evidence.

2. *Post-trial motions.* Just as some motions must be filed before trial, other motions must be filed after the trial has ended in order for the issue to be properly preserved for appeal. These vary among the jurisdictions, but include such motions (discussed in Chapter 14) as a motion for judgment of acquittal, motion in arrest of judgment, and motion for a new trial.

3. *In-trial motions.* Still other motions are filed at key junctures during trial. For example, when the prosecution rests after presenting its case, the defense often moves for judgment of acquittal, alleging that the prosecution has not met its burden of producing evidence sufficient to prove guilt beyond a reasonable doubt. *See* Fed. R. Crim. P. 29(a).

4. *Tactical considerations in timing of motions.* If counsel has a choice of when to file a particular motion, there are many tactical considerations to take into account. An early filing may engender an early resolution, which may or may not be desired. For example, an unresolved issue may be more of a plea bargaining advantage than one that was rejected in an early motion process. Conversely, an early pretrial motion may prompt an early decision and the greater possibility of an interlocutory appeal by the losing side.

[2] Filing

A motion and its supporting documents must be *filed* with the court. This means that they must be filed electronically or presented to the court clerk who usually will make an official docket entry that the item was submitted and will write or stamp on the item the date and time it was filed. Usually the clerk then routinely sends the motion to the file, the judge, or another appropriate location.

[3] Service

Motions, in addition to being filed with the court clerk, must be *served* on all other parties. Since in criminal cases where motions are used, all parties will probably be represented by counsel, service on a party's lawyer is sufficient. Although the legal system sometimes provides that the court clerk performs service on all parties, in most jurisdictions service on other parties is the responsibility of the party filing the motion. Ordinarily the motion itself will indicate the persons who were served with copies. Service is usually accomplished by delivering or mailing a copy of the motion to opposing counsel's office. Many courts also permit service by electronic means. *See, e.g.*, Fed. R. Crim. P. 49(e) (permitting service of motions and certain other papers to be filed, signed or verified by electronic means).

Timing of service. Rule 47(c) requires that a party serve a written motion (other than one that the court may hear ex parte) at least seven days before the hearing date, unless a rule or court order sets a different period. For good cause, the court may set a different period upon ex parte application. Rule 47(d) requires any supporting affidavits to be served together with the motion. The responding party must serve any supporting affidavit at least one day before the hearing on the motion, unless the court permits later service.

[4] Response by Other Parties

The rules of criminal procedure are quite sketchy on the issue of what happens after a motion is filed and served on all parties. The general rule is that a party does not have to file a written response to a motion, but some courts have adopted local rules that require a written response, or at least a fair opportunity to submit a response, to some or all motions. If no written reply is necessary, the party can wait until the hearing and respond orally. Even if no written response is required, all parties have the option of providing one. They can file a responsive pleading entitled, for example, "Government's Opposition to Defendant's Motion to Dismiss Indictment." As noted above, supporting memoranda and affidavits may also be included in these responsive pleadings, and must be served on all parties and filed with the court.

Because of their heavy caseloads, some prosecutors do not respond in writing to some or all motions. Their practice is to wait until the motion hearing to respond orally. Since many criminal defendants will plead guilty before the motion hearing is held, many defense motions are never answered by the prosecution. The issues they present become moot when the defendant pleads guilty. However, the prosecution may be conceding a tactical or psychological advantage to the defense if it seeks to oppose a well-crafted and well-supported written defense motion only with on-the-spot oral argument, especially where the issues raised by the motion are complex or involve constitutional questions.

[5] Amendment and Withdrawal of Motions

As counsel gets further into case preparation, new information and ideas may suggest that a motion that has been filed is no longer adequate. Counsel may want to amend the original motion or withdraw it altogether. Rules regulating motion practice rarely deal with the propriety of amending or withdrawing motions. Because of this lack of direction, in most jurisdictions motions can be freely amended or withdrawn at the court's discretion, at least before a motion hearing.

An amended motion (for example, one which adds an additional ground for relief) should be filed and served in the same way as the original. Similarly, counsel may have a change of strategy or enter a deal with the prosecution that makes it necessary to withdraw a motion. The notice of withdrawal must also be filed and served on all parties. Sometimes courts will refuse to permit withdrawal of a motion after a hearing on the motion has commenced.

[6] Burden of Proof

Irrespective of the type of motion, the general rule, subject to few exceptions, is that the movant has the burden of establishing the merits of the motion. *See, e.g.,*

United States v. Briscoe, 896 F.2d 1476 (7th Cir. 1990) (defendants' motions for severance were properly denied because they did not sustain their burden of proving joinder caused actual prejudice); *United States v. Trumpower*, 546 F. Supp. 2d 849 (E.D. Cal. 2008) (party moving for a deposition has burden of proving witness will be unavailable at trial).

The matter becomes more complex when the motion addresses constitutional issues. To some extent, the difficulty is caused by the lack of an authoritative resolution of many burden of proof issues in criminal constitutional law. Although a detailed analysis of this area of constitutional law is beyond the scope of this book, a few examples illustrate this murky area. For example, when the defendant files a motion to suppress evidence allegedly seized in violation of the Fourth Amendment, the general rule is that the defendant has the burden of proof of challenging a search based on a warrant, but the prosecution has the burden where the search was conducted without a warrant. *See, e.g.*, *United States v. Jones*, 374 F. Supp. 2d 143 (D.D.C. 2005). In other areas, the defendant has been given the burden of proof. *See, e.g.*, *Wayte v. United States*, 470 U.S. 598 (1985), discussed in Chapter 2, (on motion to dismiss for selective prosecution, defendant has burden of proving discriminatory enforcement of criminal laws).

Surprisingly, there is little law describing exactly what standard of proof must be met. For many motions raising non-constitutional matters, the issue is especially difficult because state jurisdictions are generally free to resolve them using their own policies. Some motions raise questions of law, as to which there may be a clear answer governed by the Constitution or a federal or state statute. Appellate courts reviewing rulings on motions that raise questions of law usually apply a *de novo* standard of review—the appellate court is free to review the motion judge's ruling "anew," and determine for itself whether the ruling was correct or erroneous.

Many other motions, however, address themselves not to clearly governing rules of law, but rather to the *discretion* of the court. Most "housekeeping" rulings on motions regarding the timing and manner of presentation of evidence at the trial fall into this category. Appellate courts are extremely reluctant to reverse discretionary rulings, and typically will only (and rarely) do so if they find that the trial court's decision on the motion was an "abuse of discretion." *See, e.g.*, *United States v. Nettles*, 476 F.3d 508 (7th Cir. 2007) (abuse of discretion standard used to review decision on transfer of case for trial under Rule 21); *United States v. Walker*, 657 F.3d 160 (3d Cir. 2011) (motion to sever offenses or defendants under Rule 14; also reviewed under abuse of discretion standard).

The few cases on point often indicate that many motions can be sustained if the party who has the burden of proof provides sufficient evidence to satisfy the preponderance of evidence test. *See, e.g.*, *Missouri v. Seibert*, 542 U.S. 600, 608 n.1 (2004) (prosecution bears the burden of proving, at least by a preponderance of the evidence, defendant's waiver of *Miranda* rights and the voluntariness of defendant's confession); *Medina v. California*, 505 U.S. 437 (1992) (not unconstitutional for state to allocate to the defense the burden of persuasion on issue of defendant's competency to stand trial).

[7] Hearing

Law and practice are quite murky with regard to the procedures following the filing of a motion. The typical procedure is that a hearing on the motion is available, although many jurisdictions' criminal procedure rules may not mandate a hearing. Local court rules may often provide for a hearing on some or all motions. Sometimes counsel must request a hearing. Such requests should be in writing to facilitate appellate review. By custom or local rule, in some courts a lawyer notifies opposing counsel of an intent to argue a particular motion at a specific future motion hearing. This practice allows counsel to determine the sequence of consideration of motions. Of course the court must consent to the hearing time and date.

Scheduling hearing. Some judges have a "motion day" on which they conduct hearings on motions. Many judges in criminal cases automatically schedule motion hearings for a set time before trial. Perhaps the most sophisticated approach is the *omnibus hearing*, a wide-ranging hearing used in some jurisdictions. Scheduled automatically a number of days before each criminal trial, the omnibus hearing tries to resolve all outstanding motions by all parties and to deal with many other administrative matters that will speed up the criminal process.

Often informal. Motion hearings are usually quite informal, although their exact contours differ markedly among jurisdictions and judges. Usually oral argument by counsel is permitted but not required. Counsel submitting the motion may argue why it should be granted. Opposing counsel may then argue why it should be denied. The court may permit the parties to take turns until no one has anything else to say. The court can ask for the parties to provide a brief on certain legal issues.

At some motion hearings, especially where the outcome of the motion may depend on the court's determination of certain facts (e.g., a motion to suppress, where the actions and knowledge of the officer who seized the contested evidence are in dispute), the court will hold an *evidentiary hearing*, where both parties can present witnesses and physical evidence. Where determination of facts is not crucial to the outcome of the motion, counsel may simply summarize the relevant facts or rely on affidavits submitted with the motion or response. One benefit of an evidentiary hearing on a motion is that it may provide an opportunity for both sides to preview the likely trial testimony of witnesses who testify at the motion hearing. Where facts are not in dispute and there is no need for an evidentiary hearing, the hearing on the motion is simply an opportunity for the lawyers to offer oral and written arguments in support of their positions.

[8] Ruling by Court

As strange as it may seem, on occasion a motion is filed, perhaps a hearing is held, and no decision on it is ever reached. The court may "take the matter under advisement" or simply refuse or forget to render a decision. When this occurs, appellate review of the issue is virtually foreclosed. Counsel submitting a motion must ensure that a decision is made on the motion if counsel wants to preserve the issue for appellate review. Whenever possible, counsel should urge the judge to indicate why the judge denied or granted a motion. Any such ruling on a motion should be on the record so the appellate court has a clear understanding of what happened and why. Rule 12(d) provides that "[w]hen factual issues are involved in deciding a motion, the court must state its essential findings on the record."

Counsel will usually prefer that the court make a prompt ruling on a motion so counsel can plan for other motions or proceedings that will be affected by the ruling. Rule 12(d) of the Federal Rules of Criminal Procedure clearly indicates that a pretrial motion should be determined before trial unless a later determination is needed "for good cause." Some judges delay such decisions in order to obtain more information. For example, they may postpone until trial the decision on a pretrial motion asking that evidence be excluded as too prejudicial. The judge may feel that the motion cannot be assessed without an understanding of how this evidence will complement other evidence and affect the outcome of the trial. No such delay is permissible, however, "if a party's right to appeal is adversely affected." Fed. R. Crim. P. 12(d).

The difficulty that counsel can sometimes encounter in obtaining a ruling on a pretrial motion was highlighted in *Luce v. United States*, 469 U.S. 38 (1984). The defendant had filed a pretrial motion to exclude evidence of his prior criminal conviction. Presumably, the defendant would testify if the impeaching conviction were barred, but would not testify if it were admissible. The district court denied the motion and the defendant did not testify at trial, where he was convicted of various drug offenses. The United States Supreme Court held that the defendant was not entitled to appellate review of the trial court's denial of the motion to exclude the conviction. The Court stated,

> [H]ad petitioner testified and been impeached by evidence of a prior conviction ... [t]he Court of Appeals would then have had a complete record detailing the nature of petitioner's testimony, the scope of the cross-examination, and the possible impact of the impeachment on the jury's verdict.
>
> A reviewing court is handicapped in any effort to rule on subtle evidentiary questions outside a factual context.... Any possible harm flowing from a district court's *in limine* ruling permitting impeachment by a prior conviction is wholly speculative. The ruling is subject to change when the case unfolds, particularly if the actual testimony differs from what was contained in the defendant's proffer.... When the defendant does not testify, the reviewing court also has no way of knowing whether the government would have sought to impeach with the prior conviction.... Even if these difficulties could be surmounted, the reviewing court would still face the question of harmless error.... Were *in limine* rulings under [Federal Rules of Evidence] Rule 609(a) reviewable on appeal, almost any error would result in the windfall of automatic reversal; the appellate court could not logically term "harmless" an error that presumptively kept the defendant

> from testifying. Requiring that a defendant testify in order to preserve Rule 609(a) claims [dealing with the admissibility of prior criminal convictions to impeach] will enable the reviewing court to determine the impact any erroneous impeachment may have had in light of the record as a whole; it will also tend to discourage making such motions solely to "plant" reversible error in the event of conviction.

Id. at 41–42.

Notes

1. *Impact of Luce on planning.* What effect will *Luce* have on defense planning for trial? For prosecution planning?

2. *Motion in limine.* The *Luce* opinion makes reference to the district court's ruling *in limine*. A motion *in limine*, meaning literally, in Latin, a motion brought "at the threshold" of trial, asks the judge to make a ruling about the conduct of the trial. Common motions *in limine* include a motion to sequester witnesses, to allow a defendant in custody to appear in trial in civilian clothing instead of a jail uniform, or to preclude or limit the other side from questioning witnesses about certain subjects. These motions are often heard at the pretrial conference (*see* Rule 17.1 of the Federal Rules of Criminal Procedure) rather than during the trial itself, so as to anticipate and resolve contested procedural issues in advance of the trial and thereby minimize interruptions in the presentation of evidence during the trial, and to let the parties know in advance what kinds of questioning of witnesses will or will not be permitted.

3. *Luce and other types of motions. Luce* dealt with one kind of motion: suppressing evidence of a prior criminal conviction. Does the Court's logic in *Luce* apply to other motions as well? Could a trial court use *Luce* to delay ruling on a Motion to Dismiss Because of the Statute of Limitations? What about a Motion to Dismiss Because of Extensive, Harmful Pretrial Publicity That Makes a Fair Trial Impossible?

[9] Appeal from Adverse Ruling

The law regulating appeals of unsuccessful motions is quite complex and beyond the scope of this book. Nevertheless, a few general principles should be kept in mind. Often appeals of motions are governed by the rules of appellate procedure rather than the rules of criminal procedure. The appellate rules ordinarily permit appeals of final orders and, in the discretion of the appellate court, interlocutory appeals. These principles are interpreted to place severe limits on the appeal of unsuccessful motions in criminal cases.

The general approach is that unsuccessful motions may not be appealed until after the defendant is convicted. The alleged erroneous rulings on motions are considered as part of the normal appellate review process. For example, if the court erroneously denies a defense motion to exclude certain evidence, ordinarily the appellate courts will not hear the appeal of the decision on the motion until the defendant is convicted and appeals. On appeal, the allegedly wrongful admission of evidence against the defendant will be one ground used to challenge the conviction.

A few motions are reviewable by an *interlocutory appeal* to an appellate court before the defendant is convicted. Often the motions for which interlocutory review is allowed are specified in a statute or appellate rule. For example, federal law provides that a criminal defendant denied release pending trial can appeal the detention decision to the Court of Appeals. *See* 18 U.S.C. § 3145(c). Similarly, another federal statute lists several situations where the government can appeal successful defense motions. *See* 18 U.S.C. § 3731 (government can appeal granting of defense motion to dismiss indictment or information, suppressing or excluding evidence or requiring the return of seized property, and granting release of a person pending trial; all subject to double jeopardy limitations).

G. Varieties of Motions

The list of motions that can be filed in criminal cases is limited only by the imagination of counsel. Virtually any topic can be addressed. To give a sense of the variety and scope of motions in criminal cases, the descriptive titles of some that have been filed in actual criminal cases are listed below.

Motions seeking dismissal. A Motion to Dismiss a criminal prosecution can be based on a number of grounds. Examples include Motions to Dismiss for Failure to State a Criminal Offense, because Statute is Unconstitutional, for Lack of Jurisdiction, for Improper Venue, for Denial of Speedy Trial, for Delay in Returning Indictment, for Failure to Prosecute, for Prejudicial Pretrial Delay, because Barred by Statute of Limitations, because of Immunity From Prosecution, because Barred by Double Jeopardy Clause, for Violation of Ex Post Facto Clause, for Prosecutorial Misconduct, for Insufficient Indictment, for Grand Jury Abuse, for Illegally Constituted Grand Jury, for Loss or Destruction of Indispensable Evidence, for Failure to Honor Grant of Immunity, for Prejudicial Pretrial Publicity, for Failure to Grant a Preliminary Hearing, and for Judgment of Acquittal.

Motions affecting evidence. Counsel may file a written motion in order to obtain a ruling on an evidentiary issue. Often these evidentiary motions are filed as motions *in limine*, which, in most jurisdictions, are made and ruled on before the start of the trial. These can include motions *in limine* to exclude or to admit evidence. Examples are: Motions to Suppress Unconstitutionally Seized Evidence, to Bar Reference to Past Convictions, to Produce an Incarcerated Witness, to Exclude a Coconspirator's Statement, to Disclose the Existence of Electronic Surveillance, to Permit Defendant to Testify in Narrative Style, and to Permit Introduction of Results of a Polygraph Test.

Motions affecting pretrial proceedings. Pretrial proceedings may also be addressed by motions. For example, a lawyer may file a Motion for a Prompt Preliminary

Hearing, or a Speedy Grand Jury Hearing, to Intervene in a Grand Jury Proceeding, to Exclude Evidence from the Grand Jury or the Preliminary Hearing, and to Testify Before the Grand Jury.

Motions affecting trial procedure. Virtually any aspect of the trial can be altered by court order responding to a motion. These requests can include such motions as a Motion to Withdraw Guilty Plea, to Sever Counts, to Sever Defendants, to Change Venue, to Disqualify the Judge, to Disqualify the Prosecutor, to Disqualify Defense Counsel, to Disqualify an Improperly Selected Jury, to Grant a Continuance, to Permit the Defendant to Appear Without Shackles, to Have the Defendant's Mother Sit at Counsel's Table, to Exclude the Media from the Trial (or certain proceedings, such as a suppression hearing), to Interrogate Potential Jurors Individually Rather than as a Group, to Preclude Discriminatory Use of Peremptory Challenges, for Additional Peremptory Challenges, for Daily Transcripts, and for a Written Jury Charge.

Motions involving defendant's activities. If the defendant wants the court to modify a previous order to facilitate new activities or alter conditions of release or confinement, various motions can be filed. These include motions to Grant Bail, to Change the Conditions of Release, to Lower the Amount of Bail, to Quash Arrest Warrant, to Travel Out of State to Interview a Witness, to Transfer Cells, to Receive Medicine While Incarcerated, to Increase Opportunities to Meet with Defense Counsel, and to be Present at All Hearings.

Motions to assist in gathering evidence. Many aspects of the process of gathering information for use in preparing for trial or another proceeding merit a motion in order to obtain a court order. Examples of these motions are a Motion to Produce a Witness in Government Control for Purposes of Interview, to Compel a Witness to Be Interviewed by Defense Counsel, to Grant Immunity to Defense or Prosecution Witness, to Inspect Jencks Act Material (discussed in Chapter 10), to Grant a Protective Order, to Order a Mental Examination of the Defendant (or a named witness or the victim), to Have a List of Prosecution (or Defense) Witnesses, for State Paid Investigator (or forensic expert, handwriting expert, etc.), for a Bill of Particulars (to get more information about the allegations; discussed in Chapter 7), for Discovery and Inspection (Rule 16 motion), for Disclosure of Evidence Favorable to Accused, to Reveal the Deal (disclosure of any government promises to prosecution witnesses), for Demographic Information about Potential Jurors, and to Inspect the Grand Jury Minutes.

H. Requesting a Continuance: Via Formal Motion, or Informal Practice?

A detailed discussion of all criminal motions is beyond the scope of this book. Nevertheless, to provide a better understanding of motion practice, this section will describe one motion, the Motion for a Continuance, as an illustration of motion practice.

[1] Continuances, Generally

A Motion for a Continuance is a request for a postponement of a scheduled trial, hearing, or other proceeding. If counsel for one party wants a continuance, in many jurisdictions that matter is worked out informally between the lawyers. The lawyer seeking the postponement will contact the other lawyers who, as a matter of professional courtesy, will often agree to the postponement and may even try to agree on an alternate day that is convenient for both sides and the court. The court's calendar clerk is then notified of the lawyers' agreement and will routinely reschedule the matter at a time acceptable to everyone.

In order to facilitate efficient use of both human and physical resources and to permit adequate preparation in criminal cases, hearings are often scheduled days or weeks in advance. Not uncommonly, the judge or one or more lawyers finds that the scheduled hearing date is inconvenient or impossible to meet. A *continuance* or postponement (in some jurisdictions referred to as an *adjournment*) may be sought by some or all parties, or by the judge him- or herself.

There are virtually no limits on the grounds that can support a Motion for a Continuance. Typical grounds include counsel's conflict with another case scheduled at the same time; illness of counsel, the defendant, or a witness; newly discovered evidence; incomplete expert evaluation of the defendant or evidence; incomplete investigation; inadequate time to complete legal research; and active, intense media coverage that makes a fair trial unlikely at that time. Sometimes a judge will grant a continuance because an earlier trial ran longer than anticipated and the courtroom and judge are simply unavailable on the scheduled date. Obviously, illness of the judge, prosecutor, or defense counsel may prompt a continuance. Other typical reasons for a continuance include a lawyer's inability to attend because he or she is also scheduled to appear at that time in another courtroom in another case; one or more lawyers has not had time to adequately prepare for the hearing; a key witness or the defendant is ill or absent; the defendant wants to fire the defense lawyer and hire another lawyer who needs time to prepare; or either side needs time to have an expert witness conduct a scientific test or to locate or analyze evidence that has just been discovered.

If a continuance is needed because the judge cannot or will not be available, he or she simply reschedules the hearing as part of the court's inherent authority to control its docket. Unless a rule of criminal procedure or a statute, such as a speedy trial law, would be violated by the judge's postponement, no hearing is necessary, although a brief meeting or telephone conference may be held to reschedule at a time convenient to the lawyers and parties. If the continuance is sought by either the prosecutor or defense attorney, the judge may or may not hold a hearing on whether to order the continuance, depending on the reasons given for the requested delay.

Though continuances are granted frequently and sometimes routinely, many judicial decisions deny a motion for continuance in the interest of providing speedy justice, except where the moving party shows a compelling need for the continuance.

When a formal Motion for a Continuance is used, courts prefer that the motion be filed well before the scheduled hearing, although often the delay is sought because of an unexpected last-minute matter and advance filing of the motion is impossible. Advance filing lets the court efficiently handle its calendar by scheduling another matter in place of the postponed one.

Judges have inherent authority and discretion to control their dockets. Speedy trial statutes, however, may put some limits on the judge's discretion to grant a continuance. *See* Chapter 12. These statutes often establish time limits for various proceedings. *See, e.g.*, 18 U.S.C. § 3161 *et seq.* Unless these time limits are waived by the defendant, the court cannot grant a continuance in violation of the speedy trial statute.

[2] Standards for Continuance

Because most continuances issues involve factual issues, there is little helpful law on the issue of when and whether a continuance should be granted or denied. The appellate decisions virtually always involve appeals by criminal defendants who were convicted after their requests for continuance were denied. Defendants rarely appeal the granting of a continuance for the prosecution (a notable exception being where the prosecution seeks multiple continuances for an arresting officer who has repeatedly failed to appear for court proceedings). There are few, if any, cases where the prosecution appeals the granting or denial of a continuance motion.

The decision to grant or deny a continuance motion is ordinarily left to the discretion of the judge, who controls the court calendar. The exercise of this discretion is rarely overturned on appeal. Appellate courts routinely ask whether the denial of a continuance was an "abuse of discretion." They also inquire whether the defendant can prove that the denial caused him or her "actual prejudice," a showing that is quite difficult to make. *See, e.g., United States v. Allmon*, 500 F.3d 800 (8th Cir. 2007) (trial courts have "broad discretion" in ruling on continuance; reversal only for abuse of discretion and prejudice caused by denial).

This is well illustrated by *McFadden v. Cabana*, 851 F.2d 784 (5th Cir. 1988), in which a Mississippi prisoner tried to overturn a robbery conviction via a federal habeas corpus petition. He and three others were indicted on September 16. Over the next three days, his public defender attorney filed a motion for a continuance, contending that there would be an alibi defense and that the public defender, who had three trials scheduled on the three days immediately before McFadden's trial, did not have adequate time to prepare. The continuance motion was denied and the one-day trial was held on September 26, only 10 days after the indictment. Four eyewitnesses testified for the prosecution. The three defense witnesses testified about a lineup that was overly suggestive. Defense counsel offered no alibi witness. The defendant was convicted and given a life sentence. The Court of Appeals, despite what it regarded as the "unseemly haste" with which the defendant was forced to trial, upheld the denial of habeas relief because McFadden could not prove that the denial of the continuance was prejudicial.

Do you agree with the result in *McFadden v. Cabana*? Did the "unseemly haste" with which the defendant was tried render his trial so fundamentally unfair as to amount to a denial of due process, even without a showing of actual prejudice?

Some jurisdictions have statutes, court rules, or local practices that purport to restrict the granting of a continuance. The American Bar Association's Standards Relating to Criminal Justice express this more limited approach:

> The court should grant a continuance only upon a showing of good cause and only for so long as is necessary. In ruling on requests for continuances, the court should take into account not only the request or consent of the prosecution or defense, but also the public interest in timely resolution of cases.

Standards for Criminal Justice: Speedy Trial and Timely Resolution of Criminal Cases § 12-4.5: Court responsibility for management of calendars and caseloads (3d ed. 2006). This requirement of showing good cause for a continuance is also reflected in state statutes. *See, e.g.*, Cal. Penal Code § 1050 (e) (continuances granted only for "good cause"; convenience or stipulation of parties alone insufficient).

A few jurisdictions list the factors to be considered. *See, e.g.*, Ga. Code Ann. § 17-8-23 *et seq.* (continuance authorized for absence of party, counsel, witness, or Attorney General, for attendance at General Assembly or state Board of Human Resources, or active duty with National Guard). In rare situations, a statute places time limits on various procedures and may dictate when the limits may be exceeded, thus placing limits on the grant of a continuance.

As discussed above, courts have broad discretion in granting or denying continuances. *See, e.g., United States v. Flynt*, 756 F.2d 1358 (9th Cir. 1985). To bring a successful abuse-of-discretion challenge on appeal, a party must show that the denial was "arbitrary or unreasonable." *Id. Flynt* sets forth four factors that are relevant in reviewing a denial of a continuance for abuse of discretion: (1) the requester's diligence in preparing for trial; (2) the likely utility of the continuance, if granted; (3) the inconvenience to the court and the other side; and (4) prejudice from the denial.

Notes

1. *Factors.* Courts considering motions for continuance typically use a "laundry list" of factors. Should the factors articulated in *Flynt* be given equal weight? Are there additional factors that should be taken into account?

2. *Diligence.* Should a court take into consideration the fact that a defendant is proceeding *pro se*, or is limited by psychological problems or seeming lack of mental competence? *See United States v. Pope*, 841 F.2d 954 (9th Cir. 1988). Applying the *Flynt* factors, the court in *Pope* found that the denial of a severely mentally ill defendant's request for continuance for him to obtain new counsel, asserting that his lawyer had been negligent in obtaining a psychiatric evaluation that could assist him in the preparation of his defense, was an abuse of discretion. The appellate court found that Pope "did the best he could to help himself," despite his own

psychological limitations and his counsel's lack of diligence, and ruled that the denial of his request for continuance was an abuse of discretion.

3. *Inconvenience to other parties.* Another *Flynt* factor is inconvenience to the opposing parties and all witnesses. A court may have to balance the putative harm to one party if continuance should be denied versus the potential inconvenience to the other side and to witnesses.

4. *Special procedures to reduce need for continuance.* In some jurisdictions, courts have developed a special stipulation-type procedure designed to reduce the need for continuances in cases where a witness needed by either side is unavailable. When a continuance motion is filed for this reason, the adverse party can admit that the witness, if produced, would testify as described in the continuance motion. The court may then deny the continuance as being unnecessary, and inform the jury that both sides agree what the witness would have said. Sometimes the court may also condition the denial of the motion on the adverse party's admission that the absent witness's evidence was true. *See, e.g.*, La. Code Crim. Proc. Ann. art. 710 (following ALI Code of Crim. Proc. § 303); Ind. Stat. Ann. § 35-36-7-1.

5. *Actual prejudice.* The key factor is whether the defendant would suffer actual prejudice unless a continuance were ordered. General allegations are routinely rejected. The party seeking a contested continuance must articulate specifically how the case would be prejudiced without a continuance. This may be very difficult in some cases, especially since often a continuance actually benefits the defendant.

I. Ethical Facets of Motion Practice

There is no doubt that counsel must conduct competent motion practice as necessary if the client is to be represented effectively. The American Bar Association, for example, recommends that defense counsel routinely consider all procedural steps that can be taken in good faith, including the filing of necessary and appropriate motions. Standards for Criminal Justice § 4-3.7(f) (4th ed. 2015). As noted above, issues and opportunities can be lost if proper motions are not made in a timely manner.

The failure to file appropriate motions can constitute *ineffective assistance of counsel* in violation of the Sixth Amendment. However, if a motion is not pursued because of a trial tactic, usually the failure will not constitute ineffective assistance. The United States Supreme Court has recognized that "[o]ften the interests of the accused are not advanced by challenges that would only delay the inevitable date of prosecution . . . or by contesting all guilt." *Tollett v. Henderson*, 411 U.S. 258, 268 (1973). More specifically, "The decision whether or not to make various pretrial motions is a matter of trial tactics generally not reviewable under a claim of ineffective assistance. Moreover, counsel is not required to make futile or frivolous motions." *United States v. Ritch*, 583 F.2d 1179, 1182 (1st Cir. 1978). In *Strickland v. Washington*, 466 U.S. 668 (1984), discussed below, the Supreme Court established general standards for assessing whether defense counsel's representation satisfied the Sixth Amendment's guarantee of "the effective assistance of counsel."

Because of the virtually unlimited array of possible motions, counsel must decide which ones to pursue. To some lawyers, the issue is made easier by the fact that engaging in motion practice may, by itself, give defense counsel some leverage in plea negotiations and additional time to prepare the case. These benefits may create a significant ethical or tactical dilemma, as counsel may have to resolve difficult questions about the extent of motion practice it should pursue in a particular case. Should counsel file discovery motions to obtain information not required to be disclosed by existing law in the jurisdiction? Should counsel seek release on bail in a capital case where such motion stands no chance of success but where the hearing on it may provide some needed discovery into the prosecution's case?

The ethical precepts of the legal profession are not very helpful on these issues. The two widely recognized sets of rules detailing professional standards, although vague, focus on two issues: good faith and frivolousness. A lawyer must file motions in good faith and may not file frivolous motions.

Model Code of Professional Responsibility. The American Bar Association approved the Model Code of Professional Responsibility in 1969, which was widely adopted by American jurisdictions. Canon 6 states that "A lawyer should represent a client competently." Canon 7 makes it more emphatic: "A lawyer should *represent a client zealously within the bounds of the law*" (emphasis added). More particularly, a client is entitled "to seek any lawful objective through legally permissible means, and to present for adjudication any lawful claim, issue, or defense." (EC 7-1) If there is any doubt about what the law allows, "a lawyer should resolve in favor of his client doubts as to the bounds of the law." (EC 7-3) Thus, the attorney is to be an aggressive advocate for the client. But how far can counsel go in arguing what is permissible? The Model Code is helpful in a general way. The lawyer's conduct is permissible "if the position taken is supported by the law or is supportable by a good faith argument for an extension, modification, or reversal of the law." (EC 7-4).

The key concept is *good faith.* The contrasting principle is frivolousness. Counsel may not, consistent with the Model Code, assert "a position in litigation that is frivolous." (EC 7-4) More specifically, DR 7-102 states that a lawyer cannot "assert a position, conduct a defense, delay a trial, or take other action on behalf of his client when he knows or when it is obvious that such action would serve merely to harass or maliciously injury another." The lawyer also may not "[k]nowingly advance a claim or defense that is unwarranted under existing law, except that he may advance such claim or defense if it can be supported by good faith argument for an extension, modification, or reversal of existing law." *Id.*

Model Rules of Professional Conduct. In response to significant criticisms of the Model Code, the American Bar Association adopted the Model Rules of Professional Conduct in 1983, then substantially updated them in 2002. A majority of American jurisdictions have now adopted all or part of the Model Rules in lieu of the Model Code. The new Rules, however, are no more helpful than the Model Code on the issue of the ethics of motion practice. The same themes of requiring good faith and barring frivolous motions are present. Rule 3.1 states that a lawyer cannot "bring or defend a proceeding, or assert or controvert an issue therein, unless there is a basis for doing so that is not frivolous, which includes a good faith argument for an extension, modification or reversal of existing law." The Comment to this section explains that an action is frivolous "if the lawyer is unable either to make a good faith argument on the merits of the action taken or to support the action taken by a good faith argument for an extension, modification or reversal of existing law." A more specific reference to frivolous motion practice is in Rule 3.4: "A lawyer shall not . . . (d) in pretrial procedure, make a frivolous discovery request or fail to make reasonably diligent effort to comply with a legally proper discovery request by an opposing party."

The Model Rules also address the issue of delay. Rule 3.2 states that "[a] lawyer shall make reasonable efforts to expedite litigation consistent with the interests of the client." The Comment to Rule 3.2 explains that an action done solely for the purpose of delay is improper:

> The question is whether a competent lawyer acting in good faith would regard the course of action as having some substantial purpose other than delay. Realizing financial or other benefit from otherwise improper delay in litigation is not a legitimate interest of the client.

See also Standards for Criminal Justice §4-1.9(b) (4th ed. 2015) (defense counsel should use procedural devices that will cause delay only where there is a legitimate basis for their use). Bear in mind, however, that unless affirmatively adopted or enacted by statute, case law, or formal rulemaking in a given jurisdiction, all these model rules and standards, though they may be persuasive and well-considered, are aspirational only and do not carry the force of law.

Note

The two-prong Strickland test for ineffective assistance of counsel. In *Strickland v. Washington*, 466 U.S. 668 (1984) the United States Supreme Court established a twofold test to determine whether criminal defense counsel was ineffective in violation of the Sixth Amendment. The test, described in greater detail below and in Chapters 11 and 17, focuses on the quality of the lawyer's work and the effects of alleged deficiencies in the representation. *Strickland* involved a convicted murderer who received three death sentences. The defendant challenged the effectiveness of defense counsel's decisions to withhold certain proof during the sentencing hearing.

The first prong of the *Strickland* test states that the client-defendant must prove that counsel's performance was deficient. This requires showing that counsel made errors so serious that counsel was not functioning as the "counsel" guaranteed by the Sixth Amendment. "When a convicted defendant complains of the ineffectiveness of counsel's assistance, the defendant must show that counsel's representation fell below an objective standard of reasonableness." 466 U.S. at 687–688. What kinds of errors in motion practice might satisfy this test? Would your answer be affected by the *Strickland* Court's guidance that "the court could recognize that counsel is strongly presumed to have rendered adequate assistance and made all significant decisions in the exercise of reasonable professional judgment[?]" 466 U.S. at 690.

The second prong of *Strickland* looks at the consequences of the ineffective counsel. The key is the defendant's burden of proving prejudice.

> Second, the defendant must show that the deficient performance prejudiced the defense. This requires showing that counsel's errors were so serious as to deprive the defendant of a fair trial, a trial whose result is reliable.

466 U.S. at 687.

More particularly:

> The defendant must show that there is a reasonable probability that, but for counsel's unprofessional errors, the result of the proceeding would have been different. A reasonable probability is a probability sufficient to undermine confidence in the outcome.

Id. at 694.

What kinds of errors in motion practice are likely to rise to the level of "prejudice" as defined in *Strickland*? Counsel's defective representation that results in an increase in a prison term is prejudicial under *Strickland. See Glover v. United States*, 531 U.S. 198 (2001). *See also Hinton v. Alabama*, 134 S. Ct. 1081 (2014) (counsel's failure to move for additional funds to replace inadequate expert for indigent client held to be deficient performance under first prong of *Strickland*; remanded for determination of prejudice under *Strickland* second prong).

J. Communicating with the Other Side

A motion for continuance, discussed earlier in this chapter, is but one of many possible examples where it may be of significant benefit (and in some cases, a matter of practical necessity) for either the prosecution or defense to use informal channels of communication with the other side (the conversation can be designated beforehand, if necessary, as "off the record") before filing a formal motion. A lot can be worked out through discussion and stipulation between the parties or, even if a formal motion and court order are required, via an *assented to* (sometimes called *agreed motion*), or at least *unopposed* motion. Sometimes the cooperation is reflected in a motion signed by both counsel who jointly ask for the relief requested in the motion.

Establishing credibility in the value of a lawyer's word and a reputation for veracity, reasonableness, and reciprocity can serve both the attorney and the client very well in achieving desired results on motions, especially those that might not be particularly controversial. Being reasonable when your opponent seeks a time extension makes it all the more likely that your opponent will be reasonable in return when and if you find yourself in a similar position.

Judges usually prefer not to decide any more than they have to. An assented to motion relieves the judge of having to decide who wins and who loses the motion. Also, oftentimes when presented with a motion for decision, the judge will ask the moving party, "Have you discussed this with the other side?" Counsel can look foolish taking up the court's time with a formal motion where a phone call might have sufficed, or where the other side might have assented if asked. Unless doing so might somehow compromise the defense (and the same goes for prosecution motions), it is usually better, at least with relatively routine, housekeeping-type motions that are not likely to be opposed, to talk to the other side first.

Chapter 10

Discovery, Disclosure, and Preservation

A. Introduction

This chapter deals with three critically important and related issues: the defense or prosecution's right to gather factual information from the other side, each party's duty to disclose information to the other side, and each party's duty to preserve evidence it obtains on its own. These matters are important because they affect trial preparation and conduct as well as decisions in guilty plea negotiations. Assume that the defendant is charged with vehicular homicide after a hit-and-run incident. The prosecution has photographed, measured, and preserved (using a plaster cast) tire prints from the car that struck the victim. If the defense can get access to the photographs, measurements, and casts of the prints, it can have its own expert examine them to assess whether they match the tires on the defendant's car. Moreover, if the prosecution has had an expert conduct these tests, the defense would benefit considerably if permitted to read the expert's written report and to depose the expert regarding the expert's assessment of the similarity between the tire prints at the scene and those from the defendant's vehicle. The prosecution would also like to get access to any tire print information the defense counsel has gathered. If the prosecution were satisfied that the tire prints at the scene matched those on the defendant's car, perhaps the prosecution would insist on a stiff sentence during plea negotiations. Conversely, if the prosecution believed that the tire prints did not match those of the defendant, perhaps the case would be dropped.

B. Discovery and Disclosure: In General

[1] Civil and Criminal Discovery

The law of discovery in criminal cases differs markedly from that in civil cases. In general terms, criminal discovery is far more limited than civil discovery. Much less information must be disclosed to the other side. For example, most jurisdictions severely limit depositions in criminal cases while routinely permitting them in civil cases. Similarly, interrogatories are often unknown in criminal cases but are quite prevalent in civil cases. The usual explanation, to be explored at the end of this chapter, is that the criminal defendant cannot be trusted with much information about the prosecution's case because the accused will tamper with the evidence or witnesses, or will commit or suborn perjury. Another explanation for some differences is that the Fifth Amendment bars some discovery by the prosecution, but does not limit discovery by the defense.

The substantial differences between civil and criminal discovery have led both prosecutors and defense lawyers to attempt to use the more liberal civil discovery procedures in order to obtain information for use in a criminal case. This practice is theoretically not difficult because many crimes are also torts or other civil actions. It is clear, however, that courts will not permit civil discovery to be used as a subterfuge for criminal discovery. *See, e.g.*, *Application of Eisenberg*, 654 F.2d 1107 (5th Cir. 1981) (defendant cannot use civil discovery as disguised "back door" attempt at criminal discovery; preindictment deposition not permitted); *United States v. Tison*, 780 F.2d 1569 (11th Cir. 1986) (government similarly barred from bringing a civil action to generate discovery for a criminal case). The possibility or existence of criminal charges does not *per se* bar legitimate civil discovery in a civil case, but sometimes courts stay discovery in civil cases until completion of all related criminal proceedings.

In some situations where both civil and criminal actions are possible, special procedural rules have been formulated to resolve questions about the proper scope of discovery. *See, e.g.*, 15 U.S.C. § 1312 (extensive discovery, called civil investigative demands, available in antitrust cases before filing of either civil or criminal antitrust proceedings); 18 U.S.C. § 1345(b) (civil injunctions authorized in certain fraud and banking violations; discovery governed by civil procedure rules until indictment returned, then criminal procedure discovery rules applicable).

The issue of discovery is also addressed in legal areas that could be characterized as either criminal or civil. For example, discovery in habeas corpus proceedings by state prisoners attacking convictions on federal constitutional grounds is governed by the federal rules of civil procedure (with some judicial discretion), while discovery for federal prisoners attacking federal convictions is governed by either civil or criminal discovery rules. *Compare* Rules Governing § 2254 Cases, Rule 6 *with* Rules Governing § 2255 Cases, Rule 6.

[2] Formal versus Informal Discovery

One trend in criminal procedure, discussed below, is for rules of discovery to be codified in a jurisdiction's statutes or rules of criminal procedure. In addition, some important judicial decisions mandate discovery in certain situations. These rules, statutes and judicial decisions provide a mechanism of *formal discovery*, often involving written motions and responses, and sometimes closely supervised by a judge.

While these methods of discovery are quite important, there is also another method of discovery that may have an even greater actual impact. In many jurisdictions, discovery occurs routinely through an *informal discovery* system that has developed. Often the product of continuing relationships between prosecutors and defense counsel, the informal processes facilitate the sharing of information without resort to the formal discovery processes authorized by rules and statutes. One example is the so-called *open file* practice. A prosecutor may routinely give defense counsel access to most or all of the information available to the prosecution. Another model is for the prosecutor and defense counsel to exchange information about the case, perhaps in an informal telephone call or chat in the courthouse corridor.

[3] Trend Toward Mutuality

Discovery in criminal cases is ordinarily reciprocal. In most situations, if one side must turn over something to the other side, the other side must reciprocate. The primary limits on this approach are constitutional, particularly the Fifth Amendment privilege against self-incrimination which limits the materials the defense must furnish the prosecution.

[4] Overview of Discovery and Disclosure Law

In general terms, discovery and disclosure are governed by three sources of rules, each discussed in greater detail below. First, the United States Constitution itself mandates certain disclosure. Second, formal discovery in criminal cases is governed, in perhaps every jurisdiction, by statutes or court rules that are designed to avoid surprise. As discussed below, these rules usually give the prosecution and defense counsel the right to obtain specified information from the other side. Typically, the two sides will exchange information about physical evidence, expert testimony, and prior statements of witnesses. Often the prosecution or defense must also provide the other side with advance notice of certain proof or theories to be used at trial. The rules may also require disclosure of the names of witnesses to be used at trial, and may embrace a limited right to depose friendly and hostile witnesses. The third source of discovery and disclosure rules is the trial court's inherent authority to regulate many facets of the practice of criminal proceedings. Some judges use this authority to issue orders requiring the disclosure of information, such as the names and addresses of witnesses who will be called to testify at trial, even though that information is not covered by discovery statutes or rules of criminal procedure.

C. Discovery and Disclosure: Constitutional Issues

It has often been held that there is no constitutional right to discovery. While this is true in the most general sense, in several situations the Constitution does create a right to discovery or at least raises questions about a right to discovery.

[1] Discovery by the Defendant

The due process guarantee in the Fifth and Fourteenth Amendments gives the criminal accused the right to a fair trial. In some situations, a fair trial is possible only if the accused is accorded some discovery from the prosecution. The leading case, *Brady v. Maryland*, engendered the so-called "*Brady* Rule," and materials required to be disclosed by the prosecution to the defense are commonly known as "*Brady* materials."

Brady v. Maryland

373 U.S. 83 (1963)

Opinion of the Court By Mr. Justice Douglas, Announced By Mr. Justice Brennan.

Petitioner and a companion, Boblit, were found guilty of murder in the first degree and were sentenced to death, their convictions being affirmed by the Court of Appeals of Maryland....

... Their trials were separate, petitioner being tried first. At his trial Brady took the stand and admitted his participation in the crime, but he claimed that Boblit did the actual killing. And, in his summation to the jury, Brady's counsel conceded that Brady was guilty of murder in the first degree, asking only that the jury return that verdict "without capital punishment." Prior to the trial petitioner's counsel had requested the prosecution to allow him to examine Boblit's extrajudicial statements. Several of those statements were shown to him; but one dated July 9, 1958, in which Boblit admitted the actual homicide, was withheld by the prosecution and did not come to petitioner's notice until after he had been tried, convicted, and sentenced, and after his conviction had been affirmed.

Petitioner moved the trial court for a new trial based on the newly discovered evidence that had been suppressed by the prosecution. Petitioner's appeal from a denial of that motion was dismissed by the Court of Appeals without prejudice to relief under the Maryland Post Conviction Procedure Act....

We agree with the Court of Appeals that suppression of this confession was a violation of the Due Process Clause of the Fourteenth Amendment....

This ruling is an extension of *Mooney v. Holohan*, 294 U.S. 103 (1935), where the Court ruled on what nondisclosure by a prosecutor violates due process:

> It is a requirement that cannot be deemed to be satisfied by mere notice and hearing if a state has contrived a conviction through the pretense of a trial which in truth is but used as a means of depriving a defendant of liberty through a deliberate deception of court and jury by the presentation of testimony known to be perjured. Such a contrivance by a state to procure the conviction and imprisonment of a defendant is as inconsistent with the rudimentary demands of justice as is the obtaining of a like result by intimidation.

used to convict the defendant was false. The Court noted the well-established rule that "a conviction obtained by the knowing use of perjured testimony is fundamentally unfair, and must be set aside if there is any reasonable likelihood that the false testimony could have affected the judgment of the jury." Although this rule is stated in terms that treat the knowing use of perjured testimony as error subject to harmless-error review, it may as easily be stated as a materiality standard under which the fact that testimony is perjured is considered material unless failure to disclose it would be harmless beyond a reasonable doubt. The Court in *Agurs* justified this standard of materiality on the ground that the knowing use of perjured testimony involves prosecutorial misconduct and, more importantly, involves "a corruption of the truth-seeking function of the trial process."

At the other extreme is the situation in *Agurs* itself, where the defendant does not make a *Brady* request and the prosecutor fails to disclose certain evidence favorable to the accused. . . .

The third situation identified by the Court in *Agurs* is where the defense makes a specific request and the prosecutor fails to disclose responsive evidence. . . .

[Noting that subsequent cases reformulated the *Agurs* tests, the *Bagley* Court adopted the test articulated in *Strickland v. Washington*, 466 U.S. 668 (1984), to cover all three types (i.e., "no request," "general request," and "specific request") of claimed prosecutorial failure to disclose evidence favorable to the accused: evidence is "material only if there is a *reasonable probability that, had the evidence been disclosed to the defense, the result of the proceeding would have been different.*" A "reasonable probability" was defined as "a probability sufficient to undermine confidence in the outcome."]

The Government suggests that a materiality standard more favorable to the defendant reasonably might be adopted in specific request cases. The Government notes that an incomplete response to a specific request not only deprives the defense of certain evidence, but also has the effect of representing to the defense that the evidence does not exist. In reliance on this misleading representation, the defense might abandon lines of independent investigation, defenses, or trial strategies that it otherwise would have pursued.

We agree that the prosecutor's failure to respond fully to a *Brady* request may impair the adversary process in this manner. And the more specifically the defense requests certain evidence, thus putting the prosecutor on notice of its value, the more reasonable it is for the defense to assume from the nondisclosure that the evidence does not exist, and to make pretrial and trial decisions on the basis of this assumption. This possibility of impairment does not necessitate a different standard of materiality, however, for under the *Strickland* formulation the reviewing court may consider directly any adverse effect that the prosecutor's failure to respond might have had on the preparation or presentation of the defendant's case. The reviewing court should assess the possibility that such effect might have occurred in light of the totality of the circumstances and with an awareness of the difficulty of reconstructing in a post-trial proceeding the course that the defense and the trial would have taken had the defense not been misled by the prosecutor's incomplete response.

In the present case, we think that there is a significant likelihood that the prosecutor's response to respondent's discovery motion misleadingly induced defense counsel to believe that O'Connor and Mitchell could not be impeached on the basis of bias or interest arising from inducements offered by the Government.... While the Government is technically correct that the blank contracts did not constitute a "promise of reward," the natural effect of these affidavits would be misleadingly to induce defense counsel to believe that O'Connor and Mitchell provided the information in the affidavits, and ultimately their testimony at trial recounting the same information, without any "inducements."

... Accordingly, we reverse the judgment of the Court of Appeals and remand the case to that court for a determination whether there is a reasonable probability that, had the inducement offered by the Government to O'Connor and Mitchell been disclosed to the defense, the result of the trial would have been different.

JUSTICE POWELL took no part in the decision of this case.

JUSTICE WHITE, with whom THE CHIEF JUSTICE and JUSTICE REHNQUIST join, concurring in part and concurring in the judgment [opinion omitted].

[JUSTICE STEVENS' AND MARSHALL'S dissenting opinions are omitted.]

Notes

1. *Uniform standard.* Justice Blackmun's plurality opinion in *Bagley* establishes a uniform standard for reviewing the "no request," "general request," and "specific request" cases. How does that standard differ from the one used for the knowing use of perjured testimony? How does it differ from *Agurs*? *Bagley* held that exculpatory and impeachment evidence are the same for *Brady* purposes. Do you agree?

2. *Standard based on request. Bagley* provides that the "reasonable probability" test applies to appeals in cases where the defense made a specific request for materials. Yet recall that Justice Blackmun's opinion observes that nondisclosure after a specific disclosure request might be more misleading than that after no request or a general request. Moreover, nondisclosure after a specific request involves greater prosecutorial carelessness or even intentional misrepresentation. Was *Bagley* right in lumping together the appellate review standards for specific request, no request, and general request cases?

Under *Bagley*'s "unified standard," favorable evidence is material if there is a "reasonable probability" that, had the evidence been disclosed to the defense, the result of the proceeding would have been different. Many courts, despite *Bagley*, still distinguish between the specific, general, and no request situations. One court observed:

> As the specificity of the defendant's request increases, a lesser showing of materiality will suffice to establish a [*Brady*] violation.

United States v. Anderson, 31 F. Supp. 2d 933, 940 (D. Kan. 1998). Is this interpretation of "materiality" consistent with *Bagley*?

3. Kyles. In *Kyles v. Whitley*, 514 U.S. 419 (1995), the United States Supreme Court held that this materiality standard is defined in terms of the cumulative effect of all suppressed evidence favorable to the defense, not the evidence considered item-by-item. Justice Souter, writing for the majority, emphasized four aspects of materiality under *Bagley*:

First, a showing of materiality does not require demonstration by a preponderance of evidence that disclosure of the suppressed evidence would have resulted ultimately in the defendant's acquittal; the question is whether the defendant received a fair trial resulting in a verdict worthy of confidence.

Second, *Bagley* is not a sufficiency of evidence test in that the accused must demonstrate that after discounting for evidence that should have been disclosed but was not, there was not enough evidence left to convict. Rather, the accused must show that the favorable evidence could reasonably be taken to put the case in such a different light as to undermine confidence in the verdict.

Third, once a reviewing court has found constitutional error under *Bagley*, there is no need for further harmless-error review; no such error could be deemed harmless since the accused did not receive a fair trial worthy of confidence.

And fourth, as stated above, materiality is defined in terms of suppressed evidence considered collectively, not item-by-item. Thus, the prosecution must gauge the likely net effect of all *Brady* evidence and make disclosure when the point of "reasonable probability" is reached. As a subsequent decision noted, until that point, there is no *Brady* violation. *Strickler v. Greene*, 527 U.S. 263 (1999) (there is never a *Brady* violation unless nondisclosure was so serious that there is a reasonable probability the suppressed evidence would have produced a different result).

4. *Failure to satisfy the materiality standard.* In *Turner v. United States*, 137 S. Ct. 1885 (2017), the prosecution's theory was that a large group had murdered the victim but no defendant rebutted the prosecution's group attack theory. After their convictions became final, defendants claimed that the prosecution had withheld evidence at trial that was material to their guilt. The evidence included the identity of a lone man seen running into the alley after the murder and stopping near the victim's body. The Supreme Court held that the withheld evidence was not material, citing *Agurs*, by looking at the withheld evidence "in the context of the entire record." Because virtually every witness at trial agreed that a group killed the victim, it was not reasonably probable that the withheld evidence could have led to a different result at trial.

5. *Duty to correct concealment of Brady materials.* Another U.S. Supreme Court *Brady* decision analyzes and applies the major decisions (*Brady, Bagley, Kyles, and Strickler*) to a Texas death penalty case. In *Banks v. Dretke*, 540 U.S. 668 (2004), Justice Ginsburg, writing for the Court, provides this succinct overview:

> Petitioner Delma Banks, Jr., was convicted of capital murder and sentenced to death. Prior to trial, the State advised Banks's attorney there would be

no need to litigate discovery issues, representing: "[W]e will, without the necessity of motions[,] provide you with all discovery to which you are entitled." Despite that undertaking, the State withheld evidence that would have allowed Banks to discredit two essential prosecution witnesses. The State did not disclose that one of those witnesses was a paid police informant, nor did it disclose a pretrial transcript revealing that the other witness' trial testimony had been intensively coached by prosecutors and law enforcement officers.

Furthermore, the prosecution raised no red flag when the informant testified, untruthfully, that he never gave the police any statement and, indeed, had not talked to any police officer about the case until a few days before the trial. Instead of correcting the informant's false statements, the prosecutor told the jury that the witness "ha[d] been open and honest with you in every way," and that his testimony was of the "utmost significance." Similarly, the prosecution allowed the other key witness to convey, untruthfully, that his testimony was entirely unrehearsed. Through direct appeal and state collateral review proceedings, the State continued to hold secret the key witnesses' links to the police and allowed their false statements to stand uncorrected.

Ultimately, through discovery and an evidentiary hearing authorized in a federal habeas corpus proceeding, the long-suppressed evidence came to light. The District Court granted Banks relief from the death penalty, but the Court of Appeals reversed. In the latter court's judgment, Banks had documented his claims of prosecutorial misconduct too late and in the wrong forum; therefore he did not qualify for federal-court relief. We reverse that judgment. When the police or prosecutors conceal significant exculpatory or impeaching material in the State's possession, it is ordinarily incumbent on the State to set the record straight.

6. *Cumulative evidence.* In light of the Court's decisions in *Bagley* and *Kyles*, lower courts have attempted to delineate what cumulative amount of evidence constitutes materiality under the *Brady* standard. In *United States v. Sipe*, 388 F.3d 471 (5th Cir. 2004), the Fifth Circuit Court of Appeals struggled with this question in a case involving the conviction of a Border Patrol Agent on charges that the agent used excessive force while arresting a Mexican national who entered the United States illegally. The *Sipe* court, in a 2–1 decision, upheld the trial court's decision to grant defendant's motion for a new trial, stating, in part, "[e]ven if none of the nondisclosures [by the government] standing alone could have affected the outcome, when viewed cumulatively in the context of the full array of facts, we cannot disagree with the conclusion of the district judge that the government's nondisclosures undermined confidence in the jury's verdict." While the court noted that "[u]nquestionably, there is sufficient evidence to support a finding of guilt in this case," it concluded that "[g]iven the closeness of this case based solely on those facts presented at trial, the government's failure to disclose copious amounts of evidence casting doubt upon the credibility of almost all of the key witnesses severely undermines our confidence in the outcome of this case."

7. *Special case of perjury; the "harmless beyond a reasonable doubt" standard.* Justice Blackmun's opinion in *Bagley* characterized the perjury cases as following the traditional harmless error standard of review (any reasonable likelihood that the false testimony could have affected the jury's decision). He then said this "may as easily be stated as a materiality standard under which the fact that testimony is perjured is considered material unless failure to disclose it would be harmless beyond a reasonable doubt." Implicit in this language is the recognition that use of perjured testimony perverts a trial's search for truth in a more pernicious way that does not necessary happen in the other three classes of materials (specific request, no request, general request). Therefore, perjured testimony ought to be reviewed under a stricter standard.

8. *Promise of leniency and impeachment: Giglio.* In *Giglio v. United States*, 405 U.S. 150 (1972), a key government witness in a forged money order case falsely testified that he had not been promised leniency in exchange for his testimony. The prosecutor repeated this statement during closing argument. Later it was discovered that, unknown to the prosecuting attorney, another prosecutor had promised the witness leniency. The Supreme Court reversed because the prosecution's nondisclosure of important impeachment proof violated due process. Many lawyers now use the expression "*Giglio* materials" in referring to proof that would help impeach a government witness by establishing a deal for leniency in exchange for testimony. Isn't *Giglio* just an application of *Brady, Agurs, Bagley*, and *Kyles*?

9. *Inadmissible Brady evidence.* Assume that the prosecution searches its files and finds information that would be helpful to the defense but which would be inadmissible at trial. If the government does not disclose this information, what result under *Bagley* and *Brady*?

If the information in the government's files would likely be inadmissible, but could lead to admissible evidence if defense investigators used it well, *Brady* and *Bagley* may require disclosure. *See United States v. Sipe*, 388 F.3d 471 (5th Cir. 2004) (evidence may be inadmissible but still material for *Brady* purposes). What if the evidence were inadmissible but could somehow help the defense formulate its trial strategy?

The United States Supreme Court addressed some of these questions in *Wood v. Bartholomew*, 516 U.S. 1 (1995). The defendant sought habeas relief based upon the prosecutor's failure to turn over results of a polygraph examination of a key witness. Though the polygraph information was inadmissible even for impeachment under state law, the Ninth Circuit Court of Appeals reversed the conviction, reasoning that the withholding of such information might have had an adverse effect on pretrial preparation by the defense. In a *per curiam* reversal, the Supreme Court characterized the lower court's decision as a misapplication of *Brady* jurisprudence. The Court explained that evidence is "material" under *Brady* only where there exists a "reasonable probability" that had the evidence been disclosed the result at trial would have been different. Concluding that any adverse impact on the defendant in the present case was little more than speculative, the Court declined to grant habeas relief.

10. *Information defense could have obtained or did know about.* What if the prosecution withholds material *Brady* information that the defense could obtain on its own? *See United States v. Rodriguez*, 162 F.3d 135 (1st Cir. 1998) (prosecutor must disclose *Brady* information if defense could not obtain the information through reasonable diligence, but defense "knew full well" of witness' long prior criminal record, therefore no *Brady* violation for government's nondisclosure of its notice of intention to seek enhanced recidivist penalties for that witness).

A similar result occurs if defendant knew of the *Brady* materials. *See, e.g., United States v. Runyan*, 290 F.3d 223 (5th Cir. 2002) (no *Brady* violation when defendant already had possession of defendant's computer).

11. *Prosecutor's dilemma.* How does a prosecutor know whether evidence is subject to disclosure under *Brady*? While some *Brady* proof is obvious, other such evidence is not. To know what to disclose, must the prosecutor anticipate the defenses that might be raised?

If you were a prosecutor, would you adopt an open file rule to satisfy *Brady*? An open file policy may satisfy *Brady* if the *Brady* materials are actually disclosed. *See, e.g., United States v. Pelullo*, 399 F.3d 197 (3d Cir. 2005) (*Brady* satisfied if necessary materials are in file or papers that are given to defense; prosecution has no duty to point out *Brady* materials); *Smith v. Secretary, DOC*, 50 F.3d 801 (10th Cir. 1995) (open file practice is inadequate if *Brady* materials are not included because they were given orally or were in a police file).

12. *Types of Brady information.* What types of information are covered by *Brady*? Clearly evidence that is favorable to the defense on issues of guilt or punishment or that would assist in cross-examining prosecution witnesses. There are countless illustrations. *See, e.g., Paradis v. Arave*, 130 F.3d 385 (9th Cir. 1997) (location of crime to establish lack of jurisdiction); *Banks v. Reynolds*, 54 F.3d 1508 (10th Cir. 1995) (identity of another person suspected of committing the offense); *United States v. Wilson*, 135 F.3d 291 (4th Cir. 1998) (information contradicting government's theory of case).

More recently, in *Cone v. Bell*, 556 U.S. 449 (2009), the Supreme Court held that allegations that the government had improperly suppressed information relating to the defendant's drug addiction at the time of two homicides, although not material to his unsuccessful insanity defense, were potentially material to the issue of his punishment and death sentence. By a 7 to 2 vote, the Court remanded the defendant's habeas corpus petition to the federal district court for a determination of whether there was a "reasonable probability" that the outcome of the defendant's sentencing proceedings would have been different if the trial jury had heard the allegedly suppressed evidence. The Court in *Cone* also noted that while *Brady* requires disclosure of *material* evidence favorable to the defense, ethical standards and rules may impose broader disclosure obligations on prosecutors.

13. *False information.* What if the prosecutor believes the possibly exculpatory evidence is false? *See United States v. Alvarez*, 86 F.3d 901 (9th Cir. 1996) (prosecutor should turn over evidence believed false; criminal trial will resolve truthfulness).

14. *Timing of Brady disclosure.* When must the prosecution turn over *Brady* material? What if it waits until the eve of trial, so that the defense cannot have full use of it in planning and investigating the defense? In *United States v. Coppa*, 267 F.3d 132 (2d Cir. 2001), a lower court's ruling that *immediate* disclosure of *Brady* material is required upon the defendant's request was overturned. Rather, such material must be disclosed in time for its effective use at trial or at a plea proceeding. Additionally, however, the Second Circuit Court of Appeals added that the time required "for effective use" will depend on the likely materiality of that evidence (characterized as a predictive "result-affecting test") and the particular circumstances of the case. The same court also discussed the question of timing of disclosures in *Leka v. Portuondo*, 257 F.3d 89 (2d Cir. 2001), holding that *Brady* material (a former police officer's observation of the crime that cast doubt upon the prosecutor's theory) disclosed three days before trial was "too little [the disclosure consisted only of the officer's name and address, and] too late," and therefore merited "suppression" under *Brady*.

The conflict between the timeliness of disclosure of *Brady* and Rule 26.2 (*Jencks*) materials is discussed later in this chapter.

15. *Effect of guilty plea.* Should *Brady* material be disclosed if the accused pleads guilty? Will such disclosure increase the accuracy of fact-finding during plea proceedings in court? The Supreme Court rejected these claims in *United States v. Ruiz*, 536 U.S. 622 (2002) (discussed further in Chapter 11), holding that the prosecution may constitutionally require the defendant to waive the right under *Brady* to receive impeachment evidentiary materials prior to pleading guilty.

Ruiz implicitly recognized the distinction between exculpatory and impeachment evidence when it noted that Ruiz's plea agreement provided that the prosecutor would disclose "any information establishing the factual innocence of the defendant." 536 U.S. at 631. From that reference, lower courts have speculated that the Court would find a Due Process violation where prosecutors failed to disclose exculpatory information to a defendant before he enters a guilty plea. *See McCann v. Mangialardi*, 337 F.3d 782, 788 (7th Cir. 2003). State courts have declined to extend *Ruiz*. *See, e.g., State v. Huebler*, 275 F.3d 91 (Nev. 2012); *Buffey v. Ballard*, 782 S.E.2d 204 (W.Va. 2015).

16. *Who is the "government"?* The prosecution represents the "government," which includes many different agencies and departments. Obviously *Brady* applies to information physically in the files in the prosecution's office. *Kyles v. Whitley*, 514 U.S. 419, 437 (1995), held that the prosecutor under *Brady* also has a duty to seek out evidence known to the police or any other persons acting on the government's behalf in the case. This means that disclosure is required even if no prosecutor has actual knowledge of the *Brady* materials. *See, e.g., United States v. Kearns*, 5 F.3d 1251 (9th Cir. 1993) (destruction by police of written agreement for witness to cooperate, without disclosing it to prosecution, arguably violated *Brady*, but dismissal of charges not justified where less drastic sanctions would have sufficed).

Similarly, *Brady* also applies to promises made by individual prosecutors, whether or not other prosecutors knew of the promise. *See Giglio v. United States*, 405 U.S. 150 (1972) (one prosecutor, apparently without informing other prosecutors, promised a witness immunity in exchange for testimony; a promise by one prosecutor is attributed to the government and must be disclosed to the defense).

Do *Bagley* and *Brady* also apply to data in files of all other government agencies involved somehow in the case or only to those agencies directly investigating the case? Recall that *Kyles v. Whitley*, discussed above, imposes on the prosecutor a duty "to learn of any favorable evidence known to the others acting on the government's behalf in the case, including the police." *Kyles*, 514 U.S. at 437. Does it extend to data in files of government agencies having no obvious connection with the investigation? In a court's possession? Does it extend across the borders between state and federal agencies or between agencies of different states or localities or countries? *See* Peter J. Henning, *Defense Discovery in White Collar Criminal Prosecutions*, 15 GA. ST. U. L. REV. 601, 616 (1999) (arguing that the definition of "government" under *Brady* is not as broad as that for discovery under Rule 16, discussed later in this chapter; *Brady* only reaches the prosecutor's office and other government offices "closely allied with the investigation" because a broader definition "would be disruptive to the [offices'] operations without much benefit to ensuring the fairness of the trial"). Do you agree with Professor Henning?

17. *Independent source. Brady* requires the prosecution to turn over exculpatory and impeachment proof. Does it also require the government to seek such proof from independent sources? *See Commonwealth v. Beal*, 709 N.E.2d 413 (Mass. 1999) (*Brady* only requires disclosure of information in possession of prosecutor and those subject to prosecutor's control; prosecutor need not interrogate rape victim to assist defendant in obtaining new exculpatory information).

18. *Brady codified.* Some jurisdictions have attempted to codify *Brady*. *See, e.g.*, Ariz. R. Crim. P. 15.1(b)(8) (by 30 days after arraignment, state must provide defendant with all "material or information which tends to mitigate or negate the defendant's guilt" or punishment); Md. R. Crim. P. 4-262(d) (same); Mont. Code Ann. § 46-15-322(1)(e) (same).

19. *Variations from Bagley under state constitutions.* States are ordinarily free to interpret their state constitutions to allow greater constitutional protections than analogous provisions of the federal constitution. In *People v. Vilardi*, 555 N.E.2d 915 (N.Y. 1990), the New York Court of Appeals interpreted the New York due process clause as rejecting the "lesser protections of *Bagley*" and following the analysis outlined in *Agurs.* The *Vilardi* case involved the government's failure to disclose an expert's report that had been specifically requested by the defense. The New York Court of Appeals held that under its state's constitution the correct standard of materiality was whether there was a "reasonable possibility" that nondisclosure "contributed to the verdict." How does this test differ from *Bagley*? Do you think the New York Court of Appeals was correct when it said that this test would better encourage the prosecution to comply with its discovery obligations?

The New Hampshire Supreme Court, relying upon its state constitution, concluded that *Bagley* places too severe a burden on defendants, and therefore held that where a defendant is able to show that favorable exculpatory evidence has been knowingly withheld by the prosecution, the burden shifts to the state to prove beyond a reasonable doubt that the undisclosed evidence would not have affected the verdict. *New Hampshire v. Laurie*, 653 A.2d 549 (N.H. 1995). The case was remanded for a new trial because the conviction depended upon the testimony of a particular detective and the prosecutor failed to turn over the detective's employment records (which may have affected the verdict because they reflected negatively upon the detective's character and credibility).

20. *Comparable ethical standards.* Model Rule of Professional Conduct 3.8(d) requires prosecutors to "make timely disclosure to the defense of all evidence or information known to the prosecutor that tends to negate the guilt of the accused or mitigates the offense, and, in connection with sentencing, disclose to the defense and to the tribunal all unprivileged mitigating information known to the prosecutor." ABA Formal Opinion 09-454 (2009), states that this obligation differs from obligations under *Brady* or state law, noting that the obligation includes not only "evidence," but also inadmissible "information," has no materiality exception, and requires disclosure at an early point. By way of contrast, in *Disciplinary Counsel v. Kellogg-Martin*, 923 N.E.2d 125 (Ohio 2010), the court refused to interpret the ethical standard to impose a broader obligation than *Brady* and state discovery law.

21. *Brady not applicable to post-conviction proceedings.* In *District Attorney's Office for Third Judicial District v. Osborne*, 557 U.S. 52 (2009), the Supreme Court refused to extend *Brady* to post-conviction proceedings, ruling that a defendant who collaterally seeks to attack his conviction via habeas corpus has no due process right to obtain post-conviction access to DNA evidence within the state's possession. Osborne sought access to Alaska's DNA evidence some years after his conviction in the hope that more modern state-of-the-art DNA testing methods might exonerate him. Since habeas corpus petitioners have already been found guilty (as opposed to trial defendants, who are presumptively innocent), the Court determined that a more lenient test than the *Brady* standard should apply to the defendant's claimed constitutional entitlement of access to potentially exculpatory evidence—i.e., whether state post-conviction discovery procedures are so fundamentally and "facially inadequate" as to violate due process. The Court went on to conclude that

Osborne had failed to show that Alaska's available post-conviction procedures for discovery were so inadequate.

22. *Remedy for Brady violation: new trial or dismissal?* In United States v. Kohring, 637 F.3d 895 (9th Cir. 2011), the appellate court agreed that the failure of the government to disclose that its witness was under criminal investigation, combined with the suppression of thousands of pages of potentially exculpatory documents and other discovery violations by the government, viewed cumulatively, amounted to a violation of *Brady* that required reversal of the defendant's conviction. The court majority observed that remand for new trial is the "usual remedy" for *Brady* violations, but that the extreme remedy of reversal and dismissal with prejudice may be appropriate in cases of flagrant, bad faith *Brady* violations by the government. The majority in *Kohring* concluded that there was insufficient evidence of bad faith under the facts presented, and that the usual remedy of a new trial was appropriate. In an interesting contrast of views, partially dissenting Judge Fletcher concluded that "flagrant prosecutorial misconduct" had occurred, and that therefore the court should have exercised its supervisory power and ordered dismissal of the indictment in order to "preserve judicial integrity" and to "deter future misconduct" by the prosecution. 637 F.3d at 913.

23. *Is Brady an unfulfilled promise?* Some commentators express the view that the principles of fairness underlying the *Brady* rule have been undermined by the *Bagley* materiality requirement, and by alleged prosecutorial practices such as routinely and reflexively denying the existence of any exculpatory information in response to *Brady* motions. *See, e.g.*, Eugene Cerruti, *Through the Looking-Glass at the* Brady *Doctrine: Some New Reflections on White Queens, Hobgoblins, and Due Process*, 94 Ky. L.J. 211 (2005–2006):

> The *Brady* doctrine, as developed by the Supreme Court, has never lived up to its billing. It begins with the right idea—fundamental fairness requires state disclosure of exculpatory information to the criminal defendant—but then immediately cabins and compromises that idea. The only consistent and compelling explanation for the unprincipled reductions of the doctrine is an unreconstructed fear of the hobgoblins of an earlier era regarding the dangers of disclosure to overly zealous defense counsel. *Brady* is now best understood as a rule of prosecutorial privilege rather than a rule of disclosure.

In your view, should prosecutors be legally and ethically obligated to disclose, upon request by the defense, *all* potentially exculpatory information, without regard to the prosecutor's opinion as to whether or not such information is materially exculpatory? *See* Bruce A. Green, *Federal Criminal Discovery Reform: A Legislative Approach*, 64 Mercer L. Rev. 639 (2013).

The most recent decisions of the Supreme Court reflect the Court's continuing and even heightened concern that prosecutors fairly and properly comply with their constitutional obligations under *Brady* and *Bagley*.

Smith v. Cain

132 S. Ct. 627 (2012)

Chief Justice Roberts delivered the opinion of the Court.

The State of Louisiana charged petitioner Juan Smith with killing five people during an armed robbery. At Smith's trial a single witness, Larry Boatner, linked Smith to the crime. Boatner testified that he was socializing at a friend's house when Smith and two other gunmen entered the home, demanded money and drugs, and shortly thereafter began shooting, resulting in the death of five of Boatner's friends. In court Boatner identified Smith as the first gunman to come through the door. He claimed that he had been face to face with Smith during the initial moments of the robbery. No other witnesses and no physical evidence implicated Smith in the crime.

The jury convicted Smith of five counts of first-degree murder. The Louisiana Court of Appeal affirmed Smith's conviction. The Louisiana Supreme Court denied review, as did this Court.

Smith then sought postconviction relief in the state courts. As part of his effort, Smith obtained files from the police investigation of his case, including those of the lead investigator, Detective John Ronquillo. Ronquillo's notes contain statements by Boatner that conflict with his testimony identifying Smith as a perpetrator. The notes from the night of the murder state that Boatner "could not . . . supply a description of the perpetrators other then [*sic*] they were black males." Ronquillo also made a handwritten account of a conversation he had with Boatner five days after the crime, in which Boatner said he "could not ID anyone because [he] couldn't see faces" and "would not know them if [he] saw them." And Ronquillo's typewritten report of that conversation states that Boatner told Ronquillo he "could not identify any of the perpetrators of the murder."

Smith requested that his conviction be vacated, arguing, *inter alia*, that the prosecution's failure to disclose Ronquillo's notes violated this Court's decision in *Brady v. Maryland*, 373 U.S. 83 (1963). The state trial court rejected Smith's *Brady* claim, and the Louisiana Court of Appeal and Louisiana Supreme Court denied review. We granted certiorari, and now reverse.

Under *Brady*, the State violates a defendant's right to due process if it withholds evidence that is favorable to the defense and material to the defendant's guilt or punishment. The State does not dispute that Boatner's statements in Ronquillo's notes were favorable to Smith and that those statements were not disclosed to him. The sole question before us is thus whether Boatner's statements were material to the determination of Smith's guilt. We have explained that "evidence is 'material' within the meaning of *Brady* when there is a reasonable probability that, had the evidence been disclosed, the result of the proceeding would have been different." *Cone v. Bell*, 556 U.S. 449, 469–470 (2009). A reasonable probability does not mean that the defendant "would more likely than not have received a different verdict with the evidence," only that the likelihood of a different result is great enough to "undermine[ ] confidence in the outcome of the trial." *Kyles v. Whitley*, 514 U.S. 419, 434 (1995).

We have observed that evidence impeaching an eyewitness may not be material if the State's other evidence is strong enough to sustain confidence in the verdict. That is not the case here. Boatner's testimony was the *only* evidence linking Smith to the crime. And Boatner's undisclosed statements directly contradict his testimony: Boatner told the jury that he had "[n]o doubt" that Smith was the gunman he stood "face to face" with on the night of the crime, but Ronquillo's notes show Boatner saying that he "could not ID anyone because [he] couldn't see faces" and "would not know them if [he] saw them." Boatner's undisclosed statements were plainly material.

The State and the dissent advance various reasons why the jury might have discounted Boatner's undisclosed statements. They stress, for example, that Boatner made other remarks on the night of the murder indicating that he could identify the first gunman to enter the house, but not the others. That merely leaves us to speculate about which of Boatner's contradictory declarations the jury would have believed....

The judgment of the Orleans Parish Criminal District Court of Louisiana is reversed, and the case is remanded for further proceedings not inconsistent with this opinion.

It is so ordered.

[JUSTICE THOMAS's dissenting opinion is omitted.]

Note

At oral argument in *Cain*, almost all the Justices (except for the sole dissenter) pressed the Assistant District Attorney who argued the case, albeit without success, to confess to *Brady* error in the non-disclosure of the exculpatory statements at issue there. In the immediately preceding term, the Court by a 5–4 vote denied civil relief under 42 U.S.C. § 1983 to a criminal defendant who had been wrongfully convicted by the same district attorney's office of murder and attempted armed robbery and spent 14 years on death row before exoneration after an exculpatory blood type test which had been deliberately suppressed at trial by the prosecutor came to light one week before the defendant's scheduled execution. *Connick v. Thompson*, 536 U.S. 51 (2011). Writing for the four dissenters, Justice Ginsburg stated:

> [T]he evidence demonstrated that misperception and disregard of *Brady's* disclosure requirements were pervasive in Orleans Parish.... *Brady*, this Court has long recognized, is among the most basic safeguards brigading a criminal defendant's fair trial right. [citations omitted]. Vigilance in superintending prosecutors' attention to *Brady*'s requirement is all the more important for this reason: A *Brady* violation, by its nature, causes suppression of evidence beyond the defendant's capacity to ferret out. Because the absence of the withheld evidence may result in the conviction of an

> innocent defendant, it is unconscionable not to impose reasonable controls impelling prosecutors to bring the information to light.

536 U.S. at 80, 105–106. More recently, in *Wearry v. Cain*, 136 S. Ct. 1002 (2016), the prosecutor's failure to disclose witness statements casting doubt on the credibility of the state's main witness was held to violate Due Process, because those statements were sufficient to undermine confidence in the verdict.

If cases presenting blatant *Brady* violations continue to come before the Supreme Court, might the Court in the light of the sentiments and holdings in *Cain*, *Thompson*, and *Wearry*, be receptive in future cases to imposing stronger disclosure requirements on prosecutors, or stronger remedies for willful *Brady* violations?

[2] Discovery by the Government

As the cases above suggest, the United States Constitution provides the criminal defendant with a due process right to discovery in a narrow category of situations. Perhaps in an effort to counteract the impact of defense discovery, in recent years many jurisdictions have created rules of criminal procedure that provide the *government* with a right to discover certain items possessed by or known to the defense. Such efforts raise serious constitutional issues because the accused, unlike the government, is protected by the Fifth Amendment's right of silence and the Sixth Amendment's guarantee of the assistance of counsel.

[a] Defenses

Williams v. Florida

399 U.S. 78 (1970)

Mr. Justice White delivered the opinion of the Court.

Prior to his trial for robbery in the State of Florida, petitioner filed a "Motion for a Protective Order," seeking to be excused from the requirements of Rule 1.200 of the Florida Rules of Criminal Procedure. That rule requires a defendant, on written demand of the prosecuting attorney, to give notice in advance of trial if the defendant intends to claim an alibi, and to furnish the prosecuting attorney with information as to the place where he claims to have been and with the names and addresses of the alibi witnesses he intends to use. In his motion petitioner openly declared his intent to claim an alibi, but objected to the further disclosure requirements on the ground that the rule "compels the Defendant in a criminal case to be a witness against himself" in violation of his Fifth and Fourteenth Amendment rights. The motion was denied.... Petitioner was convicted as charged and was sentenced to life imprisonment.... We granted certiorari.

Florida's notice-of-alibi rule is in essence a requirement that a defendant submit to a limited form of pretrial discovery by the State whenever he intends to rely at trial on the defense of alibi. In exchange for the defendant's disclosure of the witnesses he proposes to use to establish that defense, the State in turn is required to notify the defendant of any witnesses it proposes to offer in rebuttal to that defense. Both sides are under a continuing duty promptly to disclose the names and addresses of additional witnesses bearing on the alibi as they become available. The threatened sanction for failure to comply is the exclusion at trial of the defendant's alibi evidence—except for his own testimony—or, in the case of the State, the exclusion of the State's evidence offered in rebuttal of the alibi.

In this case, following the denial of his Motion for a Protective Order, petitioner complied with the alibi rule and gave the State the name and address of one Mary Scotty. Mrs. Scotty was summoned to the office of the State Attorney on the morning of the trial, where she gave pretrial testimony. At the trial itself, Mrs. Scotty, petitioner, and petitioner's wife all testified that the three of them had been in Mrs. Scotty's apartment during the time of the robbery. On two occasions during cross-examination of Mrs. Scotty, the prosecuting attorney confronted her with her earlier deposition in which she had given dates and times that in some respects did not correspond with the dates and times given at trial. Mrs. Scotty adhered to her trial story, insisting that she had been mistaken in her earlier testimony. The State also offered in rebuttal the testimony of one of the officers investigating the robbery who claimed that Mrs. Scotty had asked him for directions on the afternoon in question during the time when she claimed to have been in her apartment with petitioner and his wife.

We need not linger over the suggestion that the discovery permitted the State against petitioner in this case deprived him of "due process" or a "fair trial." Florida law provides for liberal discovery by the defendant against the State, and the notice-of-alibi rule is itself carefully hedged with reciprocal duties requiring state disclosure to the defendant. Given the ease with which an alibi can be fabricated, the State's interest in protecting itself against an eleventh-hour defense is both obvious and legitimate. Reflecting this interest, notice-of-alibi provisions, dating at least from 1927, are now in existence in a substantial number of States. The adversary system of trial is hardly an end in itself; it is not yet a poker game in which players enjoy an absolute right always to conceal their cards until played. We find ample room in that system, at least as far as "due process" is concerned, for the instant Florida rule, which is designed to enhance the search for truth in the criminal trial by insuring both the defendant and the State ample opportunity to investigate certain facts crucial to the determination of guilt or innocence.

Petitioner's major contention is that he was "compelled . . . to be a witness against himself" contrary to the commands of the Fifth and Fourteenth Amendments because the notice-of-alibi rule required him to give the State the name and address of Mrs. Scotty in advance of trial and thus to furnish the State with information useful in convicting him. No pretrial statement of petitioner was introduced at trial; but armed with Mrs. Scotty's name and address and the knowledge that she was to be petitioner's alibi witness, the State was able to take her deposition in advance of trial and to find rebuttal testimony. Also, requiring him to reveal the elements of his defense is claimed to have interfered with his right to wait until after the State had presented its case to decide how to defend against it. We conclude, however, as has apparently every other court that has considered the issue, that the privilege against self-incrimination is not violated by a requirement that the defendant give notice of an alibi defense and disclose his alibi witnesses.[14]

The defendant in a criminal trial is frequently forced to testify himself and to call other witnesses in an effort to reduce the risk of conviction. When he presents his witnesses, he must reveal their identity and submit them to cross-examination which in itself may prove incriminating or which may furnish the State with leads to incriminating rebuttal evidence. That the defendant faces such a dilemma demanding a choice between complete silence and presenting a defense has never been thought an invasion of the privilege against compelled self-incrimination. The pressures generated by the State's evidence may be severe but they do not vitiate the defendant's choice to present an alibi defense and witnesses to prove it, even though the attempted defense ends in catastrophe for the defendant. However "testimonial" or "incriminating" the alibi defense proves to be, it cannot be considered "compelled" within the meaning of the Fifth and Fourteenth Amendments.

Very similar constraints operate on the defendant when the State requires pretrial notice of alibi and the naming of alibi witnesses. Nothing in such a rule requires the defendant to rely on an alibi or prevents him from abandoning the defense; these matters are left to his unfettered choice.... Response to that kind of pressure by offering evidence or testimony is not compelled self-incrimination transgressing the Fifth and Fourteenth Amendments.

In the case before us, the notice-of-alibi rule by itself in no way affected petitioner's crucial decision to call alibi witnesses or added to the legitimate pressures leading to that course of action. At most, the rule only compelled petitioner to accelerate the timing of his disclosure, forcing him to divulge at an earlier date information that the petitioner from the beginning planned to divulge at trial. Nothing in the Fifth Amendment privilege entitles a defendant as a matter of constitutional right to await the end of the State's case before announcing the nature of his defense, any more than it entitles him to await the jury's verdict on the State's case-in-chief before deciding whether or not to take the stand himself.

Petitioner concedes that absent the notice-of-alibi rule the Constitution would raise no bar to the court's granting the State a continuance at trial on the ground of surprise as soon as the alibi witness is called. Nor would there be self-incrimination problems if, during that continuance, the State was permitted to do precisely what it did here prior to trial: take the deposition of the witness and find rebuttal evidence.

---

14. We emphasize that this case does not involve the question of the validity of the threatened sanction, had petitioner chosen not to comply with the notice-of-alibi rule. Whether and to what extent a State can enforce discovery rules against a defendant who fails to comply, by excluding relevant, probative evidence is a question raising Sixth Amendment issues which we have no occasion to explore. It is enough that no such penalty was exacted here.

But if so utilizing a continuance is permissible under the Fifth and Fourteenth Amendments, then surely the same result may be accomplished through pretrial discovery, as it was here, avoiding the necessity of a disrupted trial. We decline to hold that the privilege against compulsory self-incrimination guarantees the defendant the right to surprise the State with an alibi defense. . . .

Mr. Justice Black, with whom Mr. Justice Douglas joins, concurring in part and dissenting in part.

. . . The Court also holds that a State can require a defendant in a criminal case to disclose in advance of trial the nature of his alibi defense and give the names and addresses of witnesses he will call to support that defense. This requirement, the majority says, does not violate the Fifth Amendment prohibition against compelling a criminal defendant to be a witness against himself. Although this case itself involves only a notice-of-alibi provision, it is clear that the decision means that a State can require a defendant to disclose in advance of trial any and all information he might possibly use to defend himself at trial. This decision, in my view, is a radical and dangerous departure from the historical and constitutionally guaranteed right of a defendant in a criminal case to remain completely silent, requiring the State to prove its case without any assistance of any kind from the defendant himself. . . .

[The dissent of Justice Marshall is omitted.]

Notes

1. *Unanswered questions.* In clearly stating that the Fifth Amendment's self-incrimination provision and the Due Process Clause do not bar at least some pretrial disclosure to the prosecution, *Williams* resolved a number of doubts about the validity of the trend toward requiring the defense to disclose information to the prosecution before trial. But *Williams* did not answer all questions.

For example, the Florida provision requires the defense to disclose the names and addresses of defense alibi witnesses. Would the Fifth Amendment or Due Process Clause be violated if the rule also required disclosure of the expected *content* of the defense witness's alibi testimony?

What if the defense had to notify the prosecution of an intent to use self-defense and to list the witnesses on this issue? What if a rule required each side to provide an "open file" to the other side? Would this be constitutional?

2. *Non-reciprocal alibi rule.* Note that *Williams* considered a Florida provision involving the reciprocal exchange of information about alibi witnesses. Would *Williams* also uphold a state rule mandating that the defense disclose data about its alibi witnesses to the prosecution, but not requiring that the prosecution provide the same information to the defense? In *Wardius v. Oregon*, 412 U.S. 470 (1973), the defendant refused to comply with Oregon's notice-of-alibi defense that required the defense to disclose alibi witnesses, but did not obligate the state to disclose its

rebuttal witnesses. The Supreme Court in *Wardius* held that alibi disclosure rules violate due process unless the defendant also is given information about the prosecution's case. The Court observed:

> In the absence of a strong showing of state interests to the contrary, discovery must be a two-way street. The State may not insist that trials be run as a "search for truth" so far as defense witnesses are concerned, while maintaining "poker game" secrecy for its own witnesses. It is fundamentally unfair to require a defendant to divulge the details of his own case while at the same time subjecting him to the hazard of surprise concerning refutation of the very pieces of evidence which he disclosed to the State.

Id. at 475. Does *Wardius* also support an argument in favor of reciprocal discovery for the *prosecution*?

3. *State variations.* Since *Williams*, many states have enacted statutes or court rules requiring the defense to notify the prosecution of an intent to use a particular defense, such as alibi, insanity, duress, intoxication, and the like. These rules are discussed in greater detail later in this chapter.

[b] Work Product

United States v. Nobles

422 U.S. 225 (1975)

Mr. Justice Powell delivered the opinion of the Court.

In a criminal trial, defense counsel sought to impeach the credibility of key prosecution witnesses by testimony of a defense investigator regarding statements previously obtained from the witnesses by the investigator. The question presented here is whether in these circumstances a federal trial court may compel the defense to reveal the relevant portions of the investigator's report for the prosecution's use in cross-examining him....

Respondent was tried and convicted on charges arising from an armed robbery of a federally insured bank. The only significant evidence linking him to the crime was the identification testimony of two witnesses, a bank teller and a salesman who was in the bank during the robbery....

In the course of preparing respondent's defense, an investigator for the defense interviewed both witnesses and preserved the essence of those conversations in a written report. When the witnesses testified for the prosecution, respondent's counsel relied on the [investigator's] report in conducting their cross-examination. Counsel asked the bank teller whether he recalled having told the investigator that he had seen only the back of the man he identified as respondent. The witness replied that he did not remember making such a statement. He was allowed, despite defense counsel's initial objection, to refresh his recollection by referring to a portion of the investigator's report. The prosecutor also was allowed to see briefly the relevant portion of the report. The witness thereafter testified that although the report indicated that he told the investigator he had seen only respondent's back, he in fact had seen more than that and continued to insist that respondent was the bank robber.

The other witness acknowledged on cross-examination that he too had spoken to the defense investigator. Respondent's counsel twice inquired whether he told the investigator that "all blacks looked alike" to him, and in each instance the witness denied having made such a statement. The prosecution again sought inspection of the relevant portion of the investigator's report, and respondent's counsel again objected. The court declined to order disclosure at that time, but ruled that it would be required if the investigator testified as to the witnesses' alleged statements from the witness stand. The court further advised that it would examine the investigator's report in camera and would excise all reference to matters not relevant to the precise statements at issue.

After the prosecution completed its case, respondent called the investigator as a defense witness. The court reiterated that a copy of the report, inspected and edited in camera, would have to be submitted to Government counsel at the completion of the investigator's impeachment testimony. When respondent's counsel stated that he did not intend to produce the report, the court ruled that the investigator would not be allowed to testify about his interviews with the witnesses.

The Court of Appeals for the Ninth Circuit . . . found that the Fifth Amendment prohibited the disclosure condition imposed in this case. . . . Decisions of this Court repeatedly have recognized the federal judiciary's inherent power to require the prosecution to produce the previously recorded statements of its witnesses so that the defense may get the full benefit of cross-examination and the truth-finding process may be enhanced. At issue here is whether, in a proper case, the prosecution can call upon that same power for production of witness statements that facilitate "full disclosure of all the [relevant] facts."

In this case, the defense proposed to call its investigator to impeach the identification testimony of the prosecution's eyewitnesses. It was evident from cross-examination that the investigator would testify that each witness' recollection of the appearance of the individual identified as respondent was considerably less clear at an earlier time than it was at trial. It also appeared that the investigator and one witness differed even as to what the witness told him during the interview. The investigator's contemporaneous report might provide critical insight into the issues of credibility that the investigator's testimony would raise. It could assist the jury in determining the extent to which the investigator's testimony actually discredited the prosecution's witnesses. If, for example, the report failed to mention the purported statement of one witness that "all blacks looked alike," the jury might disregard the investigator's version altogether. On the other hand, if this statement appeared in the contemporaneously recorded report, it would tend strongly to corroborate the investigator's version of the interview and to diminish substantially the reliability of that witness' identification.

It was therefore apparent to the trial judge that the investigator's report was highly relevant to the critical issue of credibility. In this context, production of the report might substantially enhance "the search for truth." We must determine whether compelling its production was precluded by some privilege available to the defense in the circumstances of this case.

... In this instance disclosure of the relevant portions of the defense investigator's report would not impinge on the fundamental values protected by the Fifth Amendment. The court's order was limited to statements allegedly made by third parties who were available as witnesses to both the prosecution and the defense. Respondent did not prepare the report, and there is no suggestion that the portions subject to the disclosure order reflected any information that he conveyed to the investigator. The fact that these statements of third parties were elicited by a defense investigator on respondent's behalf does not convert them into respondent's personal communications. Requiring their production from the investigator therefore would not in any sense compel respondent to be a witness against himself or extort communications from him.

We thus conclude that the Fifth Amendment privilege against compulsory self-incrimination, being personal to the defendant, does not extend to the testimony or statements of third parties called as witnesses at trial. The Court of Appeals' reliance on this constitutional guarantee as a bar to the disclosure here ordered was misplaced.

... Respondent contends further that the work-product doctrine exempts the investigator's report from disclosure at trial. While we agree that this doctrine applies to criminal litigation as well as civil, we find its protection unavailable in this case.

[The Court reaffirmed the validity of the work-product doctrine, announced in *Hickman v. Taylor*, 329 U.S. 495 (1947), as providing a privileged area within which lawyers in both civil and criminal cases can analyze and prepare their clients' cases without disclosing the lawyers' mental processes. The Court also observed that the work-product doctrine provides protection both before and during the trial, and reaches materials prepared by the attorney and agents for the attorney.]

... We need not, however, undertake here to delineate the scope of the doctrine at trial, for in this instance it is clear that the defense waived such right as may have existed to invoke its protection.

The privilege derived from the work-product doctrine is not absolute. Like other qualified privileges, it may be waived. Here respondent sought to adduce the testimony of the investigator and contrast his recollection of the contested statements with that of the prosecution's witnesses. Respondent, by electing to present the investigator as a witness, waived the privilege with respect to matters covered in his testimony....

Finally, our examination of the record persuades us that the District Court properly exercised its discretion in this instance. The court authorized no general "fishing expedition" into the defense files or indeed even into the defense investigator's report. Rather, its considered ruling was quite limited in scope, opening to prosecution scrutiny only the portion of the report that related to the testimony the investigator would offer to discredit the witnesses' identification testimony. The court further afforded respondent the maximum opportunity to assist in avoiding unwarranted disclosure or to exercise an informed choice to call for the investigator's testimony and thereby open his report to examination.

The court's preclusion sanction was an entirely proper method of assuring compliance with its order. Respondent's argument that this ruling deprived him of the Sixth Amendment rights to compulsory process and cross-examination misconceives the issue. The District Court did not bar the investigator's testimony. It merely prevented respondent from presenting to the jury a partial view of the credibility issue by adducing the investigator's testimony and thereafter refusing to disclose the contemporaneous report that might offer further critical insights. The Sixth Amendment does not confer the right to present testimony free from the legitimate demands of the adversarial system. . . .

[The *Nobles* Court also held that Rule 16 of the Federal Rules of Criminal Procedure did not bar the trial court from requiring disclosure of the defense's investigatory report.]

Notes

1. *Mutual work product waiver.* Consistent with *Williams v. Florida*, the Court in *Nobles* stressed that pretrial discovery serves the important interest of finding the truth. Accordingly, *Nobles* held that in extreme situations, the Fifth Amendment does not limit pretrial disclosure of defense investigators' reports of interviews with potential witnesses. In order to facilitate the finding of the "truth," would the Court also have approved a rule requiring disclosure of the defendant's statements to a defense investigator?

2. *Good cause for work product waiver. Nobles* also found a waiver of the work-product rule. That rule has always been flexible, permitting disclosure of most work-product when there is good cause. Was there good cause here? Could the government have obtained the same information by carefully interviewing these witnesses or by questioning them during the trial? *See generally* Rand L. Koler, Note, 16 Santa Clara L. Rev. 391 (1976).

D. Preservation of Evidence

In many criminal cases, the police and other investigatory agencies and the defense will gather evidence that could be used for or against the accused at trial. Because of *Brady v. Maryland,* and the rules of criminal procedure, discussed *infra*, sometimes this evidence must be turned over to the other side before trial. The other side may want to conduct its own scientific tests to ascertain whether the evidence could help its case. The most common example may be drugs found at the defendant's home. Both the defense and prosecution may want to have the drugs chemically analyzed by their own independent experts to determine the precise content of the substance. While the rules of criminal procedure and constitutional law will generally permit this, the analysis is only possible if the items have been preserved. The matter is made more complicated by the fact that the first analysis of the substance may destroy or alter it so that subsequent analyses are impossible. In such cases, the first analysis may reveal a chemical composition that is devastating to the other side, which cannot conduct its own independent tests of the now-destroyed or altered substance. Must efforts be made to preserve such evidence?

Arizona v. Youngblood

488 U.S. 51 (1988)

Chief Justice Rehnquist delivered the opinion of the Court.

[A jury convicted defendant Youngblood of child molestation, sexual assault, and kidnapping. The ten-year-old victim was abducted from a carnival and sexually assaulted numerous times. After being released, the victim was taken to a hospital where a "sexual assault kit" was used routinely to obtain evidence for police use. Saliva, hair, blood, and microscopic samples were taken from the victim. His underwear and tee shirt were also obtained by the police but were not refrigerated.

The defendant was later identified from a photograph and arrested. The police criminologist who processed the data in the sexual assault kit testified that he determined that a sexual assault occurred, but he and other police experts testified that other tests were unsuccessful in detecting blood group substances. A police criminologist also was unable to obtain useful information from semen stains on the victim's underwear and tee shirt.]

... Respondent's principal defense at trial was that the boy had erred in identifying him as the perpetrator of the crime. In this connection, both a criminologist for the State and an expert witness for respondent testified as to what might have been shown by tests performed on the samples shortly after they were gathered, or by later tests performed on the samples from the boy's clothing had the clothing been properly refrigerated. The court instructed the jury that if they found the State had destroyed or lost evidence, they might "infer that the true fact is against the State's interest."

The jury found respondent guilty as charged, but the Arizona Court of Appeals reversed the judgment of conviction. It stated that "when identity is an issue at trial and the police permit the destruction of evidence that could eliminate the defendant as the perpetrator, such loss is material to the defense and is a denial of due process." The Court of Appeals concluded on the basis of the expert testimony at trial that timely performance of tests with properly preserved semen samples could have produced results that might have completely exonerated respondent. The Court of Appeals reached this conclusion even though it did "not imply any bad faith on the part of the State." The Supreme Court of Arizona denied the State's petition for review, and we granted certiorari. We now reverse.

. . . Our most recent decision in this area of the law, *California v. Trombetta*, 467 U.S. 479 (1984), arose out of a drunk driving prosecution in which the State had introduced test results indicating the concentration of alcohol in the blood of two motorists. The defendants sought to suppress the test results on the ground that the State had failed to preserve the breath samples used in the test. We rejected this argument for several reasons: first, the officers here were acting in 'good faith and in accord with their normal practice'; second, in the light of the procedures actually used the chances that preserved samples would have exculpated the defendants were slim; and, third, even if the samples might have shown inaccuracy in the tests, the defendants had 'alternative means of demonstrating their innocence.' In the present case, the likelihood that the preserved materials would have enabled the defendant to exonerate himself appears to be greater than it was in *Trombetta*, but here, unlike in *Trombetta*, the State did not attempt to make any use of the materials in its own case in chief."

Our decisions in related areas have stressed the importance for constitutional purposes of good or bad faith on the part of the Government when the claim is based on loss of evidence attributable to the Government. . . . [I]n *United States v. Valenzuela-Bernal*, 458 U.S. 858 (1982), we considered whether the Government's deportation of two witnesses who were illegal aliens violated due process. We held that the prompt deportation of the witnesses was justified "upon the Executive's good-faith determination that they possess no evidence favorable to the defendant in a criminal prosecution."

The Due Process Clause of the Fourteenth Amendment, as interpreted in *Brady*, makes the good or bad faith of the State irrelevant when the State fails to disclose to the defendant material exculpatory evidence. But we think the Due Process Clause requires a different result when we deal with the failure of the State to preserve evidentiary material of which no more can be said than that it could have been subjected to tests, the results of which might have exonerated the defendant. Part of the reason for the difference in treatment is found in the observation made by the Court in *Trombetta* that "[w]henever potentially exculpatory evidence is permanently lost, courts face the treacherous task of divining the import of materials whose contents are unknown and, very often, disputed." Part of it stems from our unwillingness to read the "fundamental fairness" requirement of the Due Process Clause as imposing on the police an undifferentiated and absolute duty to retain and to preserve all material that might be of conceivable evidentiary significance in a particular prosecution. We think that requiring a defendant to show bad faith on the part of the police both limits the extent of the police's obligation to preserve evidence to reasonable bounds and confines it to that class of cases where the interests of justice most clearly require it, i.e., those cases in which the police themselves by their conduct indicate that the evidence could form a basis for exonerating the defendant. We therefore hold that unless a criminal defendant can show bad faith on the part of the police, failure to preserve potentially useful evidence does not constitute a denial of due process of law.

In this case, the police collected the rectal swab and clothing on the night of the crime; respondent was not taken into custody until six weeks later. The failure of the police to refrigerate the clothing and to perform tests on the semen samples can at worst be described as negligent. None of this information was concealed from respondent at trial, and the evidence—such as it was—was made available to respondent's expert who declined to perform any tests on the samples. The Arizona Court of Appeals noted in its opinion—and we agree—that there was no suggestion of bad faith on the part of the police. It follows, therefore, from what we have said, that there was no violation of the Due Process Clause.

The Arizona Court of Appeals also referred somewhat obliquely to the State's "inability to quantitatively test" certain semen samples with the newer P-30 test. If the court meant by this statement that the Due Process Clause is violated when the police fail to use a particular investigatory tool, we strongly disagree. The situation here is no different than a prosecution for drunk driving that rests on police observation alone; the defendant is free to argue to the finder of fact that a breathalyzer test might have been exculpatory, but the police do not have a constitutional duty to perform any particular tests. The judgment of the Arizona Court of Appeals is reversed and the case remanded for further proceedings not inconsistent with this opinion.

Justice Blackmun, with whom Justice Brennan and Justice Marshall join, dissenting.

The Constitution requires that criminal defendants be provided with a fair trial, not merely a "good faith" try at a fair trial. Respondent here, by what may have been nothing more than police ineptitude, was denied the opportunity to present a full defense. That ineptitude, however, deprived respondent of his guaranteed right to due process of law. In reversing the judgment of the Arizona Court of Appeals, this Court, in my view, misreads the import of its prior cases and unduly restricts the protection of the Due Process Clause. An understanding of due process demonstrates that the evidence which was allowed to deteriorate was "constitutionally material," and that its absence significantly prejudiced respondent. Accordingly, I dissent.

Notes

1. *Importance of unpreserved evidence.* In *Youngblood*, what is the relationship between the government's good faith and the importance (materiality) to the defendant of the lost evidence? If the government acted in good faith but the evidence could have definitely exonerated the accused, would *Youngblood* excuse the loss of the evidence? What if the government in bad faith destroyed the evidence but the evidence would have been of virtually no use to the defense?

2. *Inculpatory evidence.* Assume that evidence is subjected to scientific analysis and the results provide strong proof that the defendant is guilty. Must the evidence be preserved under *Youngblood* so that the defendant can have an independent

analysis conducted that could prove the defendant innocent? *See, e.g., United States v. Gibson*, 963 F.2d 708 (5th Cir. 1992) (80 pounds of marijuana destroyed; lab samples and photographs preserved; no error absent proof of bad faith by government).

The trial court's inherent authority to control the proceedings is probably broad enough to permit it to order preservation for this purpose in appropriate cases. Moreover, some prosecutors routinely provide the defense with a sample of the evidence, whenever possible, to facilitate scientific analysis. *See also* Standards for Criminal Justice § 11-3.2 (3d ed. 1996) (either party intending to destroy or transfer from its possession any discoverable objects or information must so notify the other party; either party should be permitted to evaluate or test discoverable physical evidence in the other party's possession, subject to appropriate court orders).

3. *Practical problems.* What practical problems would result had *Youngblood* required the preservation of any evidence that could exonerate the defendant?

4. *Proof of bad faith.* How could defense counsel ever prove bad faith when a law enforcement official disposed of evidence that may have helped the accused if it had been viewed? *See, e.g., United States v. Zaragoza-Moreira*, 780 F.3d 971 (9th Cir. 2015) (bad faith when Homeland Security agent knew exculpatory value of video but did not prevent it from being destroyed).

5. *Pending discovery request.* Assume that a defendant charged with possession of cocaine files a motion for discovery of physical evidence the government intends to use at his trial. Prior to the time for response, the defendant (who has been released on bond) fails to appear and remains a fugitive for more than 10 years. Upon his renewed request, the government responds by establishing that the evidence (cocaine) had been destroyed in good faith pursuant to established police procedures. Would a court violate *Youngblood* by dismissing criminal charges? Yes, answered the U.S. Supreme Court in *Illinois v. Fisher*, 540 U.S. 544 (2004). In a *per curiam* decision, the Court stated, "[w]e have never held or suggested that the existence of a pending discovery request eliminates the necessity of showing bad faith on the part of police." The Court also responded to a related argument by clarifying that the bad-faith requirement does not depend on the "centrality of the contested evidence;" it depends only upon the "distinction between 'material exculpatory' evidence and 'potentially useful' evidence."

6. *Remedy for bad faith.* If it is established that the government destroyed evidence in bad faith, should the conviction be reversed automatically or should a "harmless error" analysis be performed?

7. *State variations.* A number of states do not follow *Youngblood*'s bad faith approach. Relying on state law, they impose a higher standard on the prosecution's duty to preserve evidence. Most use a balancing test. *See, e.g., State v. Tiedemann*, 162 P.2d 1106 (Utah 2007) (in loss or destruction of evidence cases, the Utah state constitution's due process clause requires that a court evaluate "the reason for the destruction or loss of the evidence, including the degree of negligence or culpability on the part of the State; and the degree of prejudice to the defendant in light of the

materiality and importance of the missing evidence in the context of the case as a whole, including the strength of the remaining evidence"). *But see Collins v. Commonwealth*, 951 S.W.2d 569 (Ky. 1997) (following *Youngblood*'s bad faith requirement as a matter of state constitutional law).

8. *Duty to gather evidence.* If *Trombetta* and *Youngblood* require the prosecution to preserve obviously exculpatory evidence in some cases, do they impose a duty on the police to *gather* exculpatory proof? Most courts have not gone so far as to require that the government obtain exculpatory evidence. In *Miller v. Vasquez*, 868 F.2d 1116 (9th Cir. 1989), the court noted that a "bad faith failure to collect potentially exculpatory evidence would violate the due process clause." That viewpoint has been described as "an aberration." *White v. Tamlyn*, 961 F. Supp. 1047 (E.D. Mich. 1997).

The American Bar Association has gone further than the cases demand. "A prosecutor should not intentionally avoid pursuit of evidence because he or she believes it will damage the prosecution's case or aid the accused." STANDARDS FOR CRIMINAL JUSTICE § 3-3.11(c) (3d ed. 1993). Although this passage could be read as not mandating a *search* for pro-defense evidence, the commentary to this section makes it clear that the "duty of the prosecutor is to acquire all the relevant evidence without regard to its impact on the success of the prosecution." *Id.* cmt. Does this mean that the prosecution must continue looking for evidence after it has gathered enough to convict the accused?

E. Access to Witnesses and Other Evidence

Both prosecution (and the police and other law enforcement officials) and defense counsel will often attempt to interview potential witnesses to find out what happened, to locate other witnesses and evidence, and to prepare for guilty plea negotiations and trial. The usual format is for a police investigator or the lawyer prosecuting or defending the case to contact possible witnesses. Sometimes the task is as simple as placing a telephone call to a crime witness and asking what the witness saw. Often, particularly for key witnesses, a personal interview will be held. The session may be held at such locations as the witness's home or job, or at the police station or defense lawyer's office. Often it will be tape recorded.

Absent a court order (which is rare), a crime witness (or anyone else, for that matter) does not have to speak with either the prosecution or defense representatives. When a witness will not voluntarily talk with the prosecution or defense, either lawyer may use a subpoena to require the witness to appear and provide information at a preliminary hearing or trial. In addition, the prosecution can also subpoena a witness to testify before a grand jury. The use of a subpoena in such cases may be dangerous, however, if the witness, whose testimony is not known, testifies in a way harmful to the side that issued the subpoena. Accordingly, it is better to interview the witness informally before deciding whether to subpoena the witness to testify at a formal hearing.

Another way to compel a potential witness to provide pretrial information is the deposition, discussed later in this chapter. While some jurisdictions allow a potential witness in a criminal case to be deposed, usually it is permissible only in extraordinary circumstances by court order. *See* Fed. R. Crim. P. 15.

[1] Ethical and Professional Restrictions

In an adversary system, sometimes one side would prefer that the other side not contact the first side's witnesses before trial. For example, the prosecutor may prefer that defense counsel not conduct pretrial interviews of police officers who may be prosecution witnesses at trial. Since gathering pretrial information may be critical to adequate trial preparation, the ethical standards of the legal profession severely limit a lawyer's efforts to prevent adversary counsel from conducting a full pretrial investigation of the case. Rule 3.4(a) of The Model Rules of Professional Conduct provides that a lawyer must not "unlawfully obstruct another party's access to evidence or unlawfully alter, destroy or conceal a document or other material having potential evidentiary value." She also must "not counsel or assist another person to do any such act."

A lawyer also must not ask anyone "other than a client to refrain from voluntarily giving relevant information to another party unless the person is a relative or an employee or other agent of a client, and the lawyer reasonably believes that the person's interests will not be adversely affected by refraining from giving such information."

Moreover, the American Bar Association's Standards for Criminal Justice provide specific guidance for both prosecutors and defense counsel. The Standards bar lawyers both from discouraging or obstructing communication between prospective witnesses and counsel for the other side. More specifically, a prosecutor "should not" and "it is unprofessional conduct" for defense counsel to advise any person or cause any person (other than a defense lawyer's client) to be advised to decline to give to counsel for the other side "information which such person has the right to give." STANDARDS FOR CRIMINAL JUSTICE §§ 3-3.1(d) (prosecutor), 4-4.3(d) (defense counsel) (3d ed. 1993).

[2] Constitutional Restrictions

Just as the ethical standards of the legal profession bar a lawyer from preventing a non-client from talking with counsel for the other side, the United States Constitution also has been read as barring such conduct by the *prosecution*. In general terms, the criminal defense lawyer has a right to attempt to interview potential witnesses without unreasonable interference by either the police or the prosecuting attorneys. This right has been attributed to a number of constitutional provisions: the Due Process Clause, the Sixth Amendment right to the effective assistance of counsel, and the Sixth Amendment right to compulsory process. In order to establish a due process or Sixth Amendment violation, however, a defendant who has been denied access to potential witnesses by the government must show that the denial has been prejudicial—i.e., that the missing witnesses would have provided material testimony favorable to the defense. *See, e.g., United States v. Valenzuela-Bernal*, 458 U.S. 858 (1982) (no constitutional violation where defendant could not show prejudice from deportation of potential witnesses).

[3] Other Restrictions

In addition, some courts use their inherent authority to supervise the practice of criminal defense counsel to restrict interference with access to potential witnesses. *See generally Gregory v. United States*, 369 F.2d 185 (D.C. Cir. 1966).

Statutes in a few jurisdictions also forbid interference with an investigation. *See, e.g.*, Ark. R. Crim. P. 19.1 (neither prosecutor nor defense counsel shall advise persons other than the defendant to refrain from discussing the case with opposing counsel or from showing opposing counsel any relevant information).

[4] Remedy

What happens when one side improperly impedes access to information? In extreme cases, if the government's impropriety affected the fairness of the proceeding, perhaps dismissal would be appropriate. Of course, contempt of court and professional ethical sanctions are also possible. Another possibility is to adjust the discovery rules to offset the harm. *See, e.g., United States v. Carrigan*, 804 F.2d 599 (10th Cir. 1986) (court invoked its inherent authority to supervise its own proceedings in order to assure fair administration of justice and permitted defense to depose a government witness, beyond the normal scope of criminal discovery rules, where government had attempted to discourage its witnesses from talking to defense counsel).

Problem 10-1. Do What You Want to Do

Margaret was the victim of a street robbery. A young man held a knife to her throat and threatened to kill her unless she gave him her purse. She readily complied and he ran away. Margaret gave the police a detailed description of the robber, and Seth Brownlow was arrested a month later and charged with the robbery.

Defense counsel has begun the investigation. Obviously, she would like to interview Margaret, the victim and primary government witness. Margaret has called the prosecutor to ask for advice. She wants to know to what extent she must cooperate with the defense lawyer's investigator who has just called her to schedule an interview.

Assess the validity of the following advice the prosecutor gave Margaret.

1. "You do not have to talk to anyone."

2. "You do not have to talk to anyone. If you want to talk to someone and would like for me to be present, let me know and I'll be there to help you."

3. "You do not have to talk to anyone. If you do, I would like to be present."

4. "You do not have to talk to anyone, but you are free to do so. If you do talk to the defense, they will try to use what you say against you at trial."

5. "The defense will try to trick you with their questions, but you don't have to cooperate with them."

F. Specific Modes of Discovery

As noted at the first of this chapter, discovery in criminal cases is restricted in most jurisdictions. Consequently, both sides must avail themselves of the few avenues of discovery permitted by the rules of criminal procedure. Some discovery occurs as the by-product of various pretrial proceedings where information about the case is disclosed as an essential part of the process. Examples include hearings on bail, suppression of evidence under Rule 41(h), venue, and jury selection, as well as preliminary hearings and grand jury proceedings. There are also a number of provisions that specifically authorize discovery.

[1] Bill of Particulars

As described more fully in Chapter 7, an indictment or information should provide the accused with sufficient information about the charges so that counsel can prepare for trial and assert the double jeopardy guarantee if the same case is charged again. If an indictment contains too few facts to satisfy these goals, the rules of criminal procedure ordinarily permit the accused to file a Motion for a Bill of Particulars, which is a formal request for more information about the charges. *See* Fed. R. Crim. P. 7(f).

If the court orders the prosecution to comply with the request or the government does so voluntarily, the prosecution will submit a written document providing more information about the crime. For example, if an indictment for armed robbery does not indicate where and when the robbery occurred, defense counsel may file a Motion for a Bill of Particulars to force the prosecution to disclose this information. The prosecution's response could provide defense counsel with some discovery about the case. Absent some detailed information about the offense, the defendant may find it difficult or impossible to defend. Returning to the armed robbery hypothetical, the defendant cannot investigate a possible alibi until he or she knows where and when the alleged robbery occurred.

Note that the Bill of Particulars is not mutual. The defense requests it from the government, but the government is not authorized to demand one from the defense. Should the rules of criminal procedure require the defense to inform the prosecution of details of the defense's likely proof? For example, should the defense have to tell the prosecution what its approach will be (such as arguing criminal insanity, alibi, prosecution witnesses are lying, or self-defense)?

Some discovery rules are reciprocal. If the defense requests and receives certain items, it is then obligated to turn over similar items to the prosecution. The Bill of Particulars could follow this model. If the defense sought a Bill of Particulars, it would have to inform the prosecution of its likely defenses. Would this make sense?

[2] Notice to the Other Side

A significant trend in American criminal law is to minimize trial surprises by requiring the parties to provide one another with some information about their case. Obviously the indictment serves this purpose since it informs the defendant of the charges and some of the facts to be addressed at trial.

[a] Evidence Rules

The rules of evidence occasionally provide some discovery in criminal cases. Perhaps the best examples are rape shield laws, which limit the proof that is admissible about the sexual assault victim's sexual history. Typically, these rules bar the defendant in sexual assault cases from introducing some data about the victim's sexual past unless the accused first notifies the prosecution (and sometimes the victim as well) of the intent to use such evidence. *See, e.g.*, Fed. R. Evid. 412 (c)(1). Usually the notice also includes an "offer of proof" that summarizes the evidence to be introduced. It may also include the names and addresses of witnesses on the issue. According to the United States Supreme Court, the rape shield notice provisions serve a number of purposes, including protecting the government against a surprise at trial. Once notified that certain evidence will be introduced, the prosecutor now has some understanding of the defense theory and can investigate the alleged facts to determine their veracity. *See Michigan v. Lucas*, 500 U.S. 145 (1991).

Other rules of evidence also mandate notice to the other side. *See, e.g.*, Fed. R. Evid. 807 ("residual" hearsay exception available only if adverse party given advance notice of intent to offer the evidence and name and address of declarant); 609(b) (convictions more than 10 years old may be used to impeach if proponent gives adverse party advance written notice of intent to use such evidence); 404(b) (upon request of defendant, prosecution intending to use evidence of other crimes, wrongs, or acts to prove such issues as intent or motive must ordinarily give the defense advance notice of the nature of such evidence).

[b] Alibi

Just as the rules of evidence require notice to the other side if certain proof is to be used, the rules of criminal procedure mandate notice to the other side if certain defenses are used.

As previously seen in *Williams v. Florida*, many jurisdictions require the defense to notify the prosecution if the defense intends to use an alibi defense. This prevents surprise at trial and permits both sides to investigate the alibi defense and gather proof to counter the other side's witnesses. It also facilitates more predictable court scheduling as it may remove a ground for a government request for a continuance shortly before trial to permit the government to prepare for unexpected alibi testimony.

Without advance notice of an intent to use an alibi defense, the prosecution will find it difficult to cross-examine defense alibi witnesses and provide proof that the alibi witnesses are mistaken or lying. Assume, for example, that the accused is charged with committing a one-person bank robbery in San Francisco. Of course the prosecution must prove beyond a reasonable doubt that the accused was the person who robbed that particular bank. Assume further that the defendant will assert at trial that she was in Los Angeles at a rock concert at the moment of the robbery in San Francisco. Unless the prosecution knows in advance of this alibi defense, it will be limited to proving presence in San Francisco. It will not have a real opportunity to prove that the defendant was not in Los Angeles by producing witnesses to testify that there was no record that defendant purchased a ticket to the concert, stayed at a hotel in Los Angeles, charged gas or anything else in Los Angeles on her credit card, visited her best friend who lives in Los Angeles, and the like.

Rule 12.1 of the Federal Rules of Criminal Procedure mandates notice. The rule is triggered by a written "demand" by the government, but the defendant cannot initiate the rule's reciprocal discovery process. If the government does not initiate the notice process, Rule 12.1 is inapplicable and neither side is obligated to follow its procedures. In such cases, the defense may offer a full alibi defense without providing any alibi notice to the government.

Why would the government initiate the Rule 12.1 process? What does it have to gain? To lose? When would it choose to not do so in a case where an alibi defense is possible? If you were the United States Attorney, would you routinely provide a Rule 12.1 demand notice in every case? Note that some courts have held that the government cannot request a continuance because of a surprise alibi defense if it does not provide the "demand" required by Rule 12.1. If the required demand is made, both sides have a continuing duty to supply the names of witnesses identified later.

Rule 12.1 requires the parties to exchange information about alibi witnesses but not other witnesses. Thus, Rule 12.1 is an exception to the general, though not universal, rule that parties in a criminal case need not exchange a list of witnesses to be called at trial. If the accused relies on an alibi, often the alibi witnesses are the only defense witnesses since the defendant claims to know nothing about the event and does not dispute that it happened. On the other hand, the prosecution will have witnesses both to prove the crime and disprove the alibi. This means that the defense must disclose its main and perhaps only witnesses, but the prosecution need disclose only some of its witnesses. Is this fair?

The witnesses to be disclosed include government witnesses both placing the defendant at the crime scene as well as those rebutting defense alibi witnesses, perhaps establishing that the defendant was not where the alibi witnesses claimed.

Under the Crime Victims' Rights Act, judges have discretion under Rule 12.1(b)(1)(B) to protect victims by withholding from disclosure a victim's address and telephone number, and to fashion a reasonable alternative disclosure procedure that both allows for preparation of the defense and also protects the victim's privacy interests.

Courts use the sanction of exclusion when the defendant does not either provide a timely response or respond at all before trial. *See, e.g., United States v. Day*, 524 F.3d 1361 (D.C. Cir. 2008). Of course, this penalty does not apply to the defendant, who need not be mentioned in the exchange of witnesses under Rule 12.1. How much value is an alibi defense when only the defendant testifies and there is no corroboration?

In *Taylor v. Illinois*, 484 U.S. 400 (1988), the Supreme Court held there are some limits on barring a defense witness from testifying as a sanction for violation of a discovery order. In *Taylor*, when the defense did not list a particular person on its court-ordered witness list, the trial judge refused to allow the witness to testify. While the Supreme Court upheld this order, it noted that the compulsory process guarantee of the Sixth Amendment gives the criminal accused the right to present favorable witnesses to the jury. This right severely limits a trial judge's authority to bar such witnesses as a sanction for discovery violations. The trial court should find out the reason for noncompliance. If the noncompliance was willful and motivated by a desire to obtain a tactical advantage, it may be appropriate to bar the witness from testifying. On the other hand, if the harm of noncompliance could be cured by a continuance, the court should consider this alternative. The Supreme Court in *Taylor* noted that sanctions for noncompliance with discovery should be resolved on a case-by-case basis, giving appropriate weight to the defendant's right to present witnesses.

In deciding whether exclusion of a witness is proper for noncompliance with Rule 12.1, the court looks at a number of factors, including the prejudice caused by the failure to disclose, any evidence of actions mitigating the prejudice, the reason for nondisclosure, and the weight of evidence of guilt. *See United States v. Burkhalter*, 735 F.2d 1327 (11th Cir. 1984).

Prejudice would be difficult to prove if the unidentified witness were known to the other side, such as when the witness was already named on a list of trial witnesses (as some judges require) or had identified the defendant in a line up where defense counsel was present. Intentional withholding, on the other hand, will be viewed with extreme disfavor and may well lead to the exclusion of the unidentified witness, even without a showing of prejudice.

[c] Mental Condition Defense

Just as many rules of criminal procedure mandate notice of alibi, a large number establish a somewhat complex procedure when the defendant intends to use a defense, such as insanity, that is based on a mental disease or defect. The overall purpose of these rules is to provide the prosecution with an opportunity to have the defendant examined before trial by a neutral expert. If there were no such rules, the defense could surprise the prosecution at trial by raising, without prior indication, the insanity defense and producing defense experts who testify that the accused was insane. The prosecution would not have had a chance to have its own experts examine the accused and may find it difficult to counter the defense proof, especially in jurisdictions where the defendant must raise the insanity defense and then the prosecution has the burden of proving that the accused was sane.

Federal Rule 12.2, "Notice of an Insanity Defense; Mental Examination," applies whenever the defense intends to raise a defense based on insanity (Rule 12.2(a)) or to use an expert on a "mental disease or defect or any other mental condition . . . bearing upon the issue of . . . guilt" (Rule 12.2(b)).

The reciprocal notice provisions of Rule 12.2 are triggered by the defense's written notice of intent to rely upon an insanity defense or to use expert testimony to the effect that the defendant's mental condition affected guilt. The key to Rule 12.2 is that it authorizes the court to order the defendant to undergo a mental examination. The exam is to be conducted by a psychiatrist or clinical psychologist. The defendant can be committed to a mental institution for a short period of time to facilitate the examination. The examining expert must prepare a written report which is given to all parties and the court. Rule 16(a)(1)(F), discussed below, also requires disclosure of reports of scientific tests. Moreover, Rules 16(a)(1)(G) and 16(b)(1)(C) often mandate disclosure of a summary of expert testimony to be presented on the defendant's mental condition.

Since the government pays for these compelled mental examinations, sometimes the defense files a notice under Rule 12.2 in order to obtain a free evaluation. This is especially likely if the defendant has too few assets to hire independent mental health professionals for a private evaluation.

During the mental examination ordered pursuant to Rule 12.2, the defendant may well discuss the crime at issue, other crimes that have not been discovered, and other issues that may be relevant to either guilt or the sentence. If disclosed in court, this information could lead the defendant to be convicted of the case at hand as well as others not yet filed. Despite these significant self-incrimination concerns, courts have consistently held that this mandated examination does not violate the defendant's Fifth Amendment rights. Rule 12.2(c) eliminates most of the Fifth Amendment concerns by providing that any statement the defendant gives during the exam, any testimony of the examining expert based on that statement, and any fruit of the defendant's statement are inadmissible on any matter other than the mental condition at issue.

Nevertheless, some defense counsel will encourage their clients undergoing a Rule 12.2 evaluation to avoid discussions of criminal activity. A few defense lawyers have even asked the court's permission to attend the evaluation sessions to protect their client's interests. *See, e.g.*, *United States v. Cohen*, 530 F.2d 43 (5th Cir. 1976) (defense counsel not entitled to attend evaluation).

Failure to comply with Rule 12.2 can cause drastic consequences for the defense. If notice is not given under Rule 12.2(a) and (b), the defendant may be barred from offering an insanity defense or an expert witness on the defendant's mental condition. A similar result may occur if the defendant refuses to participate in a court-ordered evaluation.

Problem 10-2. Mental Issues

1. Assume that defendant *X* is charged with the "knowing and willful attempt to evade federal income taxes." Defense counsel would like to call a psychiatrist to testify that the defendant was "too stupid to understand the intricacies of the reporting requirements under the federal tax laws." Must defense counsel provide notice under Rule 12.2? *See United States v. Edwards*, 90 F.R.D. 391 (E.D. Va. 1981) (notice requirements of Rule 12.2 apply to "stupidity" defense).

2. Defendant *Y* is charged with selling drugs to a police undercover agent. *Y*'s defense is entrapment. *Y* maintains that she had no predisposition to sell drugs and was entrapped by a government agent who overcame her resistance by repeatedly offering her large sums of money to obtain a small quantity of drugs for the agent. *Y* plans to call a clinical psychologist to testify that the defendant's psychological characteristics and subnormal intelligence combined to make *Y* particularly susceptible to persuasion and psychological pressure. Must defense counsel provide notice under Rule 12.2? *See United States v. Hill*, 655 F.2d 512 (3d Cir. 1981) (holding the rule's notice requirement inapplicable to expert testimony relative to defense of entrapment). *But see United States v. Sullivan*, 919 F.2d 1403 (10th Cir. 1990) (notice requirement held applicable to mental condition evidence in entrapment defenses).

3. Defendant *Z* was charged with perjury and obstructing justice for lying to a grand jury about a bid-rigging in which she denied involvement. As a defense, *Z* would like to call a physician to testify that, at the time of the grand jury hearing, she was taking medicine for a benign tumor. The medicine caused a short-term memory loss and therefore she had no criminal intent when she falsely denied involvement in the bid-rigging. Assume that no notice was provided by the defense attorney under Rule 12.2. As Assistant United States Attorney, what arguments would you make in support of your claim that the physician's testimony should not be allowed? *See United States v. Cervone*, 907 F.2d 332 (2d Cir. 1990); *United States v. Kim*, 303 F. Supp. 2d 150 (D. Conn. 2004) (good cause not shown for late disclosure of proffered expert witness; proffered expert testimony relative to defendant's history of family abuse and mental illness as explanation for defendant's criminal activity disallowed).

[d] Other Notice Rules

Following the well-recognized lead of Rules 12.1 and 12.2, some jurisdictions have recognized a need to prevent surprise for other defenses at trial. For example, Rule 12.3 of the Federal Rules of Criminal Procedure requires the defense to notify the prosecution of an intent to "assert a defense of actual or believed exercise of public authority on behalf of a law enforcement agency or federal intelligence agency at the time of the alleged offense." The notice must identify the agency and personnel involved and when the authority existed. The government then becomes obligated to admit or deny the existence of the public authority identified in the defendant's notice. Both sides must then exchange the names and addresses of witnesses on this issue.

Other jurisdictions have gone much further than the federal government. Arizona represents one of the most expansive approaches to the disclosure of defenses:

> Within the time specified in Rule 15.2(d), the defendant shall provide a written notice to the prosecutor specifying all defense as to which the defendant intends to introduce evidence at trial, including, but not limited to, alibi, insanity, self-defense, defense of others, entrapment, impotency, marriage, insufficiency of a prior conviction, mistaken identity, and good character. The notice shall specify for each listed defense the persons, including the defendant, whom the defendant intends to call as witnesses in support of each listed defense.

Ariz. R. Crim. P. 15.2(b). *See also* Ark. R. Crim. P. 18.3 (disclose nature of any defense to be used at trial and witnesses on that issue); Ill. Sup. Ct. R. 413(d) (any defenses); Mass. R. Crim. P. 14(b)(3) (disclosure of defense based upon license, claim of authority or ownership, or exemption). Do you agree with the Arizona approach? Should it be reciprocal, requiring the prosecution to disclose its theories and witnesses? Would it make sense to limit this disclosure to surprise witnesses or theories? Do you think it will speed up, slow down, or not affect the trial process?

[3] Depositions

While depositions are a common and important feature of discovery in civil cases, they are rare or nonexistent in criminal cases in most jurisdictions. When permitted in criminal cases by court rule or statute, often they are limited to unusual situations. The federal approach, embraced in Rule 15, is typical.

Rule 15 makes it clear why depositions are so rare in federal criminal cases. They are available only by court order "to preserve testimony for trial" and the trial court is given significant discretion in deciding whether to issue the order.

Depositions are only authorized to "preserve testimony for trial." This limitation is widely interpreted as barring a deposition simply for discovery. Ordinarily the person deposed will likely be unavailable for trial.

Consistent with the preference against the use of depositions in criminal cases, Rule 15 places two significant limits on depositions. Rule 15(a) states that a deposition is authorized only in "exceptional circumstances" in the "interests of justice." The party requesting the deposition has the burden of establishing that this test is satisfied. The trial judge is given great discretion in deciding whether to order the deposition.

Although there is no generally recognized definition of these terms, courts consider the facts of each case and look at four factors: the importance of the testimony, the likelihood that the witness will be able to testify personally at trial, the financial and other costs that would be saved by the deposition, and the fact the witness is that of the party taking the deposition.

Some states are less restrictive in their allowance of depositions in criminal cases. But there are routinely more restrictions than are present in civil cases. *See*, e.g, Ariz. R. Crim. P. 15.3 (depositions permissible if party shows that deponent's testimony is material to case, to prepare a defense, or investigate the offense and deponent was not witness at preliminary hearing and will not grant personal interview); Colo. R. Crim. P. 15(a) (deposition permissible if deponent may be unable to attend hearing and deposition necessary to prevent injustice); Tex. Crim. Proc. Code Ann. § 39.02 (deposition for "good reason").

Although Federal Rule 15(a) is titled "depositions," it reaches further than that. It not only can compel a party's witness to appear for deposition, it also can require the witness to bring "any designated book, paper, document, record, recording, or other material not privileged."

Federal Rule 15 outlines the procedures to be followed in those rare cases where a deposition is taken in a criminal case. According to Rule 15(b), the party seeking the deposition must notify the other parties of the time and place of the deposition. The defendant has a right to attend the deposition in person.

Rule 15(c) provides that the government may be ordered to pay the expenses of a deposition requested by either the government or an indigent defendant. But the government does not pay lawyer's fees of retained defense counsel for depositions requested by the government.

Rule 15(f) provides that these depositions are admissible "as provided by the Federal Rules of Evidence." Thus a deposition can be admissible for several purposes. First, if the deponent is unavailable at trial, as defined by the rules of evidence, the deposition may be admissible as substantive evidence through the former testimony hearsay exception in Rule 804(b)(1). Second, if the declarant testifies at trial, the deposition can be used as substantive evidence as a prior inconsistent statement. Third, the deposition is admissible to impeach or contradict the deponent's trial testimony.

[4] Pretrial Discovery: Statements, Tests, Objects, Etc.

The primary focus of pretrial discovery in criminal cases is on providing access to some statements, tests, and objects in the possession of the other side. Usually these rules are reciprocal: if one side must give *X* proof (perhaps a copy of a scientific test of the weapons used in the crime) to the other side, the requesting party must give *Y* proof (a copy of its own tests of the weapon) to the party who provided *X* proof.

Under federal law, Rule 16 gives each side rights to some such information before trial. This rule does not, however, give defense counsel total access to the prosecution's files. In reading Rule 16, note both what is and what is not included.

[a] Overview

Rule 16 is the primary criminal procedure rule regulating pretrial discovery. The general features are outlined below and discussed in greater detail in subsequent subsections.

In general terms, Rule 16 establishes a regime of *mutual discovery*. This obligates each side to provide the other with information after certain procedures are followed. The defendant begins the Rule 16 discovery process by making a *request* for the prosecution to turn over specified categories of information. These categories are the defendant's own statements and criminal record, relevant documents and objects, requests of examinations and tests, and information about expert witnesses to be used at trial.

Once the prosecution complies with the defendant's requests, the defendant must turn over the same type of information to the prosecution. The defendant, however, need not disclose his or her own statements or criminal record. Each side is under a continuing duty to disclose information acquired after the initial compliance with discovery.

Certain information is not subject to disclosure under Rule 16. This includes work product of either side, defendant's statements in the possession of the defense, and the identity of confidential informants. Rule 16 gives the court the authority to issue a protective order to avoid discovery abuses. The trial judge has discretion in ordering sanctions for discovery violations.

[b] Statements

[i] Defendant's Statements in Prosecution's Possession

The rules of criminal procedure routinely authorize pretrial disclosure of the defendant's own statements and sometimes also mandate disclosure of those of other defendants or even of all witnesses. This disclosure should facilitate trial preparation as it alerts the defense to key evidence available to the prosecution. It may also assist in locating new witnesses or evidence.

Federal Rule 16(a)(1), typical of most discovery rules, gives the defense a right to inspect and copy four types of prior statements of the defendant that are relevant to the case:

> (1) relevant written or recorded statements of the defendant which the government has in its possession, custody or control and knows or should know about (through "due diligence");
>
> (2) the substance of any oral statement by the defendant, made to a known government agent during interrogation, which the government intends to offer in evidence;
>
> (3) the portion of any written record containing the substance of any relevant oral statement made by the defendant during interrogation to a known government agent; and

(4) recorded statements the defendant made to a grand jury relating to the instant offense.

It must be noted that this discovery is triggered by "request" of the defendant, usually in a discovery "motion" or "request" filed before trial. Virtually all states also require disclosure of the defendant's statements in government possession. *See, e.g.*, N.Y. Crim. Proc. Law § 240.20(1)(a) (defendant's statement to public servant engaged in law enforcement activity or person under that person's direction or in cooperation with that person). Some even require disclosure of the names of witnesses to the defendant's statements. *See, e.g.*, Ill. Sup. Ct. R. 412(a)(i).

Note the severe limitations of Federal Rule 16. While it does give the accused access to many of his or her own statements, it does not provide discovery of all of them. For example, it does not reach statements which the government has in its possession but could not, through due diligence, find. This may occur because many federal agencies may be involved in an investigation and the communication between them may be poor.

Rule 16(a)(1) also does not require disclosure of the substance of oral statements the defendant made outside of interrogation or to people who conducted an interrogation but the accused did not know were government agents. This result is not changed if the government agent made a written memorandum of the oral statements. For example, if the defendant confessed to a neighbor who told an FBI agent who wrote a memorandum describing the neighbor's information, Rule 16 does not mandate disclosure of the agent's memorandum. But if the government has obtained a written version or a recording of such statements, they must be disclosed under Rule 16(a)(1)(B). *See State v. Vanderford*, 980 S.W.2d 390 (Tenn. Crim. App. 1997) (state court's interpretation of provision identical to Rule 16 that audio recording of conversation between defendant and "wired" undercover agent is discoverable if the defendant's statements to agent are "relevant" to the crime charged; statements on audio tape here found not relevant).

The American Bar Association recommends broader discovery of a criminal defendant's statements. The prosecution must give the defendant all written and oral statements of the defendant that are within the possession or control of the prosecution and that relate to the subject matter of the offense charged. Standards for Criminal Justice § 11-2.1(a) (3d ed. 1996). Is this model superior to the federal one?

[ii] Defendant's Statements in Defense Counsel's Possession

While Federal Rule 16(a) requires the government to give the defendant copies of virtually all of the defendant's statements the prosecution has, the discovery is not mutual. Because of concerns about the lawyer-client privilege, the self-incrimination protection of the Fifth Amendment, and the guarantee of counsel in the Sixth Amendment, Rule 16 does not obligate the defense to provide the prosecution with copies of statements made by the defendant or actual or potential witnesses. Disclosure may be required under Rule 26.2, however, if the defendant or witness testifies.

[iii] Third Parties' Statements

Finally, Rule 16 does not cover statements of persons (except for experts, as described below) other than the accused. Thus, the defendant may not discover statements of witnesses or codefendants unless exculpatory and disclosure is required by *Brady v. Maryland*, supra. Of course if the statements are recordings of the defendant speaking to a third person, the recording is covered by Rule 16(a)(1). But note that Rule 16(a)(1)(C) does include statements by various representatives of an organizational defendant, such as a corporation or labor union.

A number of states expand their discovery rules to include statements of third persons. *See, e.g.*, Ala. R. Crim. P. 16.1(b) (defense entitled to discover statements of codefendants and accomplices); Ariz. R. Crim. P. 15.1(b) (statements of state's witnesses and of all people to be tried with defendant); N.Y. Crim. Proc. Law § 240.20(1)(a) (statements of defendant and jointly tried codefendant).

[iv] Recommendations

The American Bar Association recommends broader discovery of witnesses' statements. The prosecution must give the defense the names, addresses, and relevant written statements of all persons known to the prosecution to have information concerning the offense charged. It must also identify the persons it intends to call as witnesses. Standards for Criminal Justice § 11-2.1(a)(ii) (3d ed. 1996). The defense, according to the ABA, need only disclose the names, addresses, and statements of witnesses it intends to call as witnesses for its case-in-chief; statements of defense witnesses used solely to impeach a prosecution witness need not be disclosed until after the witness has testified at trial. *Id.* § 11-2.2(a)(i). Rule 26.2, discussed below, mandates disclosure of a witness's statement after the witness has testified on direct examination.

[c] Tests

Rule 16 establishes reciprocal discovery for the reports of physical or mental examinations and other scientific tests or experiments. Note that Rule 16(a)(1)(F) focuses on "results or reports" of tests. It does not appear to reach log notes and other internal lab documents from which the report was written, yet these documents may be critical if the report is to be re-evaluated by other experts. *See United States v. Uzenski*, 434 F.3d 690 (4th Cir. 2006). Rule 16(a)(1)(E) may reach these items, however, if they form the basis for expert testimony. *United States v. W.R. Grace*, 233 F.R.D. 586 (D. Mont. 2005) (court-ordered pretrial disclosure of documents underlying government's test results).

Test results. Upon request by the defendant, the government must provide the "results or reports" to the defense if available (including through "due diligence") to the government and which the government intends to use at trial or which are material to the defense's trial preparation. Once the government complies with this request, it is entitled to ask the defendant for the same access to results or reports in the control or possession of the defendant if the defense intends to introduce them as evidence or which were prepared by an expert the defense intends to call as a defense witness. Note that the standards for prosecution and defense differ slightly. The defense receives various reports that are "material" to "trial preparation," but the prosecution receives only those related to proof to be used at trial. What is the practical effect of these differing approaches? Why are the standards different? Should they be the same?

Rule 16 does not appear to limit the type of tests subject to discovery. However, the rules do not subject purely oral reports to discovery, nor does it obligate the government to conduct tests.

Work product. Since some of the data covered by this provision are also included in the work-product rule, Rule 16 creates an exception to the work-product rule. If the defense asks for the government's test results, the defense is viewed as waiving the work-product protection for its own test results. The defense does not have to disclose such data, however. Since the entire process is started by the "request" of the defense, the defense can opt to forego this facet of discovery under Rule 16. This means that under Rule 16 the defense does not always have access to test and related results in the government's file, but it also does not have to disclose such items in its own file.

[d] Summary of Expert Witnesses' Testimony

Rule 16(a)(1)(G) partially rejects the view that one side's expert witnesses can surprise the other side. The rule requires disclosure of (1) an intent to rely on expert opinion testimony; the (2) content and (3) bases of that testimony; and (4) the qualifications of the expert witness. This rule is designed to reduce the need for continuances and to permit expert opinion testimony to be evaluated by both effective cross-examination and the use of counter testimony by other experts.

This rule follows the pattern of other portions of Rule 16. It is triggered by a defense request. Once the prosecution complies, the defense must give reciprocal disclosure of defense expert witnesses. This means that the defense can avoid disclosing information about its own experts by refusing to request data about prosecution expert witnesses.

The government's responsibility is to give information that is either material to the preparation of the defense or intended for use in the government's case-in-chief (but not rebuttal).

This provision must be read in conjunction with Rule 16(a)(1)(F), which requires disclosure of various test reports. Sometimes, an expert will testify without having prepared a report covered by Rule 16(a)(1)(F). Rule 16 now mandates pretrial disclosure of both the expert's reports and a summary of the expert's testimony. If the expert changes his or her view, the new opinion ordinarily must be provided under Rule 16 and, sometimes, *Brady*.

[e] Documents and Objects

Rule 16 also creates a reciprocal discovery process for various documents and tangible objects, such as books, papers, photographs, buildings, and places. These items must be in the government's possession, custody, or control. They may have been obtained by a search warrant. Since many documents important to the defense may not be in the *prosecutor's* files, how far does the definition of "government" reach to require disclosure of items in various agency files? *See* Peter J. Henning, *Defense Discovery in White Collar Criminal Prosecutions*, 15 GA. STATE U. L. REV. 601, 618 (1999) (arguing for a broad reading of "government" because Rule 16 is designed to provide discovery).

Material to defense preparation or used as government proof at trial. To be discoverable by the defense, documents and objects must be material to the preparation of the defense, intended for use as evidence by the government, or belong to or be obtained from the defendant.

Does the phrase "material to the preparation of the defendant's defense" include allegations of selective prosecution? The United States Supreme Court answered that question in *United States v. Armstrong*, 517 U.S. 456 (1996), discussed in Chapter 2. According to Chief Justice Rehnquist, writing for the Court:

> Respondents argue that documents "within the possession . . . of the government" that discuss the government's prosecution strategy for cocaine cases are "material" to respondents' selective-prosecution claim. Respondents argue that the Rule applies because any claim that "results in nonconviction " if successful is a "defense" for the Rule's purposes, and a successful selective-prosecution claim has that effect.
>
> We reject this argument, because we conclude that in the context of Rule 16 "the defendant's defense" means the defendant's response to the Government's case-in-chief. . . . If "defense" means an argument in response to the prosecution's case-in-chief, there is a perceptible symmetry between documents "material to the preparation of the defendant's defense," and, in the very next phrase, documents "intended for use by the government as evidence in chief at the trial."
>
> If this symmetry were not persuasive enough, paragraph (a)(2) of Rule 16 establishes beyond peradventure that "defense" in section (a)(1)[E] can refer only to defenses in response to the Government's case-in-chief. Rule 16(a)(2), as relevant here, exempts from defense inspection "reports, memoranda, or other internal government documents made by the attorney for the government or other government agents in connection with the investigation or prosecution of the case."
>
> Under Rule 16(a)(1)[E], a defendant may examine documents material to his defense, but, under Rule 16(a)(2), he may not examine Government work product in connection with his case. If a selective-prosecution claim is a "defense," Rule 16(a)(1)(C) gives the defendant the right to examine Government work product in every prosecution except his own. Because respondents' construction of "defense" creates the anomaly of a

> defendant's being able to examine all Government work product except the most pertinent, we find their construction implausible. We hold that Rule 16(a)(1)[E] authorizes defendants to examine Government documents material to the preparation of their defense against the Government's case-in-chief, but not to the preparation of selective-prosecution claims.

Documents not covered. This required disclosure of "documents" does not include statements of other witnesses (covered by Rule 26.2) or government work product.

Defendant's items. Rule 16(a)(1)(E) requires the government to disclose items belonging to or obtained from the defendant. Note compliance is not based on either use at trial by the government or material to the defense.

Reciprocity. Under Rule 16(b)(1)(A), after the government complies with the defense's request for this tangible proof, the defense must provide the government with access to the same items in the defendant's possession, custody, or control and which the defendant intends to use as evidence in chief. Again, note that the defense gets items "material" to "preparation of the defense," but the government receives only items which the defense intends to use as evidence in its case-in-chief.

The reciprocal discovery process is begun by the "request" of the defense. If the defendant does not want to be compelled to turn over this kind of information to the prosecution, the defendant can opt not to request it from the prosecution under Rule 16.

Mechanics of discovery. For documents and tangible objects covered by Rule 16, the other side is entitled "to inspect and copy or photograph" the items. Ordinarily the two sides, without court involvement, work out the details of this process using common sense and professional courtesy. For example, the prosecution may copy the documents for the defense.

Sometimes the mechanics of this discovery become complicated. Since one side may be concerned about chain of custody, loss, or spoliation of evidence, inspection and copying may have to be done under supervision in a restricted environment. Other restrictions may also be appropriate depending on the particular circumstances. *See, e.g., United States v. Horn*, 187 F.3d 781 (8th Cir. 1999) (trial court correctly denied defendant's request to copy pornographic video tapes, which were contraband; defendant limited to having expert view the tapes); *United States v. Hsu*, 185 F.R.D. 192 (E.D. Pa. 1999) (defendant entitled to limited disclosure of documents protected as trade secrets).

[f] Prior Criminal Record

Record of defendant. Under Rule 16(a)(1)(D), upon request by the defense, the prosecution must provide the defense with a copy of the defendant's criminal record if that record is in the possession, custody, or control of the government and its existence is known or could be known through due diligence. It does not require disclosure of pending or likely criminal charges.

Note that this rule is not reciprocal. The defendant need not supply the government with a copy of the defendant's record. This means that Rule 16 does not require the defendant to inform the prosecution about criminal convictions, such as those from other states, that are not in the prosecutor's files.

Record of witnesses. Federal Rule 16 does not require disclosure of the criminal record of witnesses, though *Brady v. Maryland*, discussed earlier in this chapter, does compel such disclosure to assist in impeaching government witnesses.

Some state provisions, however, require the prosecution to disclose the prior criminal record of prosecution witnesses. *See, e.g.*, Ariz. R. Crim. P. 15.1(d)(1) and (2) (state must "make available to the defendant of the prior felony convictions of witnesses whom the prosecutor expects to call at trial" in both felony and misdemeanor cases); Minn. R. Crim. P. 9.01 subd. 1(1)(a) (prosecution must inform defendant of prior conviction record of witnesses prosecution intends to call at trial). Does *Brady* require this as a matter of constitutional law?

Record of jurors. What about the criminal records of prospective jurors? *See State v. Thompson*, 985 S.W.2d 779 (Mo. 1999) (state need not disclose arrest records of venire persons absent showing of pending charges against one or that there could have been a leniency deal or threat to one).

ABA Recommendations. The American Bar Association recommends substantial defense discovery of criminal records. The prosecution should disclose any record of prior convictions, pending charges, or probationary status of the defendant and any codefendant. The same is true for the information about any witness (of any party) if the information is known to the prosecution and may be used to impeach the witness. Standards for Criminal Justice § 11-2.1(a)(vi) (3d ed. 1996).

[g] Witness List

Rule 16 does not require either side in advance of trial to provide the other with a list of witnesses, other than those who have provided expert assistance with tests and the like. Some federal courts, however, utilize their inherent authority to regulate criminal discovery and require each side to inform the other side of its likely witnesses. Some federal courts even have a "standing order" requiring the exchange of witness lists. *See, e.g.*, *United States v. Combs*, 267 F.3d 1167 (10th Cir. 2001). Others refuse to order such disclosure in typical cases but occasionally will mandate disclosure when there is a "compelling need" for it.

Many states now require or permit pretrial disclosure of the names and addresses of witnesses to be called at trial. *See, e.g.*, Ariz. R. Crim. P. 15.1(b)(1) (pretrial disclosure of names, addresses, and statements of witnesses to be called in case-in-chief; defense need not list defendant or provide defendant's statements); Ill. Sup. Ct. Rules 412, 413 (pretrial disclosure of names, addresses, and statements of prosecution and defense witnesses); Mass. R. Crim. P. 14(a)(1)(A) (automatic discovery of names and addresses of prosecution's prospective witnesses). Some rules specifically embrace rebuttal witnesses.

Capital cases. A separate federal statute requires disclosure of the names and addresses of government witnesses who will testify in a federal trial for treason or other capital offenses. 18 U.S.C. § 3432. This law is not reciprocal; it does not obligate the defense to provide the government with a list of defense witnesses. Since both treason and capital cases are rare in federal courts, this provision is infrequently used.

Policy issue. Should witness lists be exchanged in all criminal trials? Why or why not? Recall that federal law already requires disclosure of *some* witnesses (e.g., experts). Would pretrial disclosure of all witnesses provide a trial more likely to reach the truth? What about also requiring disclosure of the *content* of a witness's likely testimony?

[h] Person's Physical Characteristics

Sometimes a person's physical characteristics may be an important part of proof. For example, a criminal defendant may have left blood stains at a crime scene. The prosecution will seek a court order compelling the accused to provide a blood sample.

Inherent authority. Rule 16 does not mention discovery of the defendant's physical characteristics. But federal and state courts often use their inherent authority to require a witness or other person to submit to various tests. *See, e.g., United States v. Benn*, 476 F.2d 1127 (D.C. Cir. 1973) (using its inherent authority, court may order mentally disabled witness to submit to psychiatric examination for assessing her competency or credibility).

State variations. Some state provisions specifically authorize discovery of the defendant's physical characteristics. *See, e.g.*, N.Y. Crim. Proc. Law 240.40(2) (prosecutor may obtain court order requiring defendant to appear in line-up, speak for identification, be fingerprinted, pose for photograph (but not reenact the event), provide handwriting sample, submit to a bodily physical inspection or medical examination, or permit the taking of an array of physical samples, such as hair, blood, saliva, or urine).

The defendant may be able to affect the fairness of some identification procedures. In *Moore v. Illinois*, 434 U.S. 220, 230 n.5 (1977), the Supreme Court noted that the trial court has the discretion to grant a criminal accused's request that an in-court indentification be conducted in a way that is not unduly suggestive of guilt. This issue is also discussed in Chapter 6.

[i] Other Information

State discovery provisions mandate discovery of various information not covered by Rule 16. Some of these are designed to alert the defendant to possible issues to address or to possible sources of information. Examples of the data required to be disclosed to the defense are: the use of electronic surveillance, Ariz. R. Crim. P. 15.1(b)(9); the use of an informant, Ariz. R. Crim. P. 15.1(b)(11); whether the state has any material or information provided by a confidential informant, Fla. R. Crim. P. 3.220(b)(1)(G); the existence of a search warrant, Ariz. R. Crim. P. 15.1(b)(10); the relationship a state witness has to the prosecution (for example, whether the witness is on probation, a paid informant, or a government employee), Ark. R. Crim. P. 17.1(b)(iii); names and addresses of all persons known to prosecutor to have information relevant to the crime or a defense, Fla. R. Crim. P. 3.220(b)(1)(A); a prosecution witness's pretrial identification of the defendant, Md. R. Crim. P. 4-263(a)(2); and information indicating entrapment, Wash. Super. Ct. Crim. R. 4.7(a)(2)(iii).

Arizona's rules authorize a prosecutor, upon a showing of "substantial need ... for material or information not otherwise covered" by the rules of criminal discovery and an inability "without undue hardship to obtain the substantial equivalent by other means," to obtain a court order requiring "any person to make such material or information available to the prosecutor." Ariz. R. Crim. P. 15.2(g).

See also Standards for Criminal Justice § 11-2.1 (3d ed. 1996) (prosecution must disclose the relationship between the prosecution and any of its witnesses; information about lineups and other identifications; materials relating to searches in which prosecution evidence was obtained; and if there was electronic surveillance of the defendant's conversations or premises).

[j] Information Not Subject to Disclosure

Work product. Rule 16 and most state rules of criminal procedure routinely list information that is not subject to disclosure under the general discovery provision. The most common example is work-product information. *See, e.g.*, Fed. R. Crim. P. 16(a)(2). Note that this provision extends to documents made by the prosecuting attorney "or any other government agent investigating or prosecuting the case." *See United States v. Robinson*, 439 F.3d 777 (8th Cir. 2006) (Rule 16 does not require disclosure of agent-generated internal tax liability computations because they were reports created for investigation). The concept of a government agent investigating the case could even extend to local police investigating a case when their reports were later shared with federal law enforcement authorities. *United States v. Fort*, 472 F.3d 1106 (9th Cir. 2007).

The ban also extends to work product of the defendant's attorney or agent. Rule 16(b)(2). Of course the ban on work-product disclosure is not absolute, since Rule 16 itself mandates some such disclosure by both sides.

Informant's identity. In some cases courts are permitted to protect the identity of law enforcement informants. The Supreme Court, recognizing the need to encourage people to provide information about criminal activity, has held the government possesses a *qualified privilege* to withhold such information. The privilege does not apply if the information would be helpful to the defense or essential to a fair trial. *Roviaro v. United States*, 353 U.S. 53 (1957). *Roviaro*, however, articulated a federal evidentiary, not a constitutional, rule. *McCray v. Illinois*, 386 U.S. 300 (1967).

The defense has the burden of establishing that the informant's identity is helpful or essential. *See, e.g., United States v. Hollis*, 245 F.3d 671 (8th Cir. 2001). Disclosure is more likely to be required if the informant actually participated in the crime rather than simply provided a tip to the police. Some state provisions also ban disclosure of the names of government informants if disclosure would risk either the informant's health or operational effectiveness. *See, e.g.*, Ariz. R. Crim. P. 15.4(b)(2); Mont. Code Ann. §46-15-324(3).

Grand jury testimony. Another category of nondiscoverable evidence relates to grand jury testimony not otherwise authorized to be disclosed. *See, e.g.*, Ore. Rev. Stat. §135.855(1)(c).

Problem 10-3. You Show Me Yours, I'll Show You Mine

Barret was killed when a bomb planted in his car exploded while the car was parked in Barret's garage. Defendant D, a tall (6' 2") man with long black hair, was arrested and charged with the homicide. Defense counsel is now assessing what proof is discoverable under Rule 16.

1. After the explosion, a team of government investigators carefully sifted through the rubble and took 32 bags of materials to the FBI. laboratory for analysis.

a. Are the 32 bags discoverable under Rule 16? Do you need any additional facts to answer this question. If so, what are they? *See United States v. Esquivel*, 755 F. Supp. 434 (D.D.C. 1990).

b. If the 32 bags are discoverable under Rule 16, how would this be accomplished? Should the prosecution simply deliver the bags to defense counsel? Obviously, taking a photograph of the outside of the 32 bags would be of little help. What should defense counsel do?

c. Assume that defense counsel utilized Rule 16 to obtain the contents of the 32 bags. Assume further that both defense and prosecution had them analyzed by their own experts, who have submitted written reports detailing their findings.

i. The prosecution's expert submitted a report to the prosecutor indicating that the explosion was caused by dynamite triggered by a wind-up alarm clock. Is the defense entitled to a copy of this report under Rule 16? Reread Rule 16(a)(1)(E) and (F). Do you need additional facts to answer this question?

ii. Assume that the report by the prosecution expert has been turned over to the defense under Rule 16. Assume also that the defense expert has submitted a report to defense counsel indicating that a new photographic process revealed that the clock used to trigger the explosion contained fingerprints. An Appendix to the report included a photograph of the fingerprints. Defense counsel fears that the fingerprints belong to Defendant D. Must defense counsel give a copy of the expert's report, including the Appendix, to the prosecution pursuant to Rule 16(b)(1)(B)?

iii. Assume that the prosecution's expert witness told the prosecutor about what the witness will say at trial. Is the defense entitled to know about the substance of

In order to facilitate the pretrial determination of the admissibility of discoverable evidence, Rule 12(b)(4)(B) authorizes the defendant to request the government to provide notice of its intent to use, as evidence in chief at trial, evidence the defendant may be entitled to discover under Rule 16. The Rule 12(b)(4)(B) mechanism assists both the defense and prosecution in planning for trial and will help reduce the number of mid-trial suppression hearings that disrupt the orderly process of the trial. Note that subdivision (b)(4)(B) does not deal with evidence to be used in rebuttal or on cross-examination.

Because Rule 12(b)(4)(B) is written in general terms, it is not clear what constitutes compliance. What if the government responds that the defense should assume all items disclosed under Rule 16 would be used during the prosecution's case-in-chief? In *United States v. Gullo*, 672 F. Supp. 99 (W.D. N.Y. 1987), the court upheld this response. What if the government responds that it has provided the defense with "open file" discovery? *See United States v. Anderson*, 416 F. Supp. 2d 110 (D.D.C. 2006) (open file policy does not satisfy Rule 12(b)(4) because it does not specify what evidence the prosecution intends to use).

United States v. Ishak, 277 F.R.D. 156 (E.D. Va. 2011) noted that Rule 12(b)(4)(B) is limited to "notice of evidence that the government intends to use only insofar as that notice would provide the defendant with sufficient information to file the necessary suppression motions. . . . In this respect, the Rule was not designed to aid the defendant in ascertaining the government's trial strategy, but only in effectively bringing suppression motions before trial. . . . In sum, the Rule does not require the government to disclose its exhibit and witness list at this time." What if the evidence is clearly admissible? Must the prosecution still provide it under 12(b)(4)(B) upon the defendant's timely request?

The sanction for government noncompliance with Rule 12(b)(4)(B) is reversal of a conviction if the defendant can prove prejudice by the noncompliance. *See United States v. de la Cruz-Paulino*, 61 F.3d 986 (1st Cir. 1995).

A similar provision, Rule 12(b)(4)(A), authorizes the government to give notice to the defendant of the government's intention to use specified evidence (whether or not discoverable under Rule 16) at trial. Although there is no similar rule permitting the defense to provide the government with pretrial notice of defense proof, surely the typical "unwritten" court procedures permit the defense to do so in order to obtain a pretrial ruling on the matter.

Protective order. Although Rule 16 makes it likely that some important evidence will be shared with the other side before trial, it also contains a procedure to protect against the possible misuse of the disclosures. Rule 16(d)(1) provides that the court may, "for good cause, deny, restrict, or defer discovery or inspection, or grant other appropriate relief." The court is given no guidance in determining when this protective order should be given or how it should be structured. In those unusual cases where confidential information justifies the protective order,

Rule 16(d)(1) permits the court to issue the protective order after an ex parte process. The record of the ex parte process should be preserved for possible appellate review.

Rule 16(d) is vague on the contents of the protective order. Apparently it can do two things. First, it can limit the information otherwise available under Rule 16. Thus, it could be used to protect trade secrets or the identity of government witnesses whose safety could be jeopardized by discovery, or to prevent the abuse of criminal discovery to aid a civil case. Second, it can order the defendant or others to refrain from contacting witnesses or otherwise tampering with witnesses. Do you think the latter would be effective in protecting witnesses from abuse by the defendant personally or through the defendant's "friends"?

Both civil and criminal remedies may also be available to protect witnesses. *See, e.g.*, 18 U.S.C. § 1512 (crime to tamper with witness); 42 U.S.C. § 1985 (civil rights action for conspiracy to interfere with witness). State provisions also routinely authorize the court to place limits on discovery on a case-by-case basis. *See, e.g.*, N.Y. Crim. P. Law § 240.50.

[5] Pretrial and Trial Discovery: Subpoena

Federal Rule 17(c) deals with the processes for obtaining and serving subpoenas for evidence and documents. While ordinarily this rule has primary application in obtaining an item's presence at trial or another proceeding, it also has a limited role in pretrial discovery.

Rule 17 provides a formal method for both sides to issue subpoenas in criminal cases. Its availability to the criminal accused satisfies the Sixth Amendment's right to compulsory process.

Rule 17 follows the traditional view that parties obtain a subpoena from the court clerk. To preserve the parties' right to conduct their own case, Rule 17 specifically authorizes the clerk to provide subpoenas in blank, to be filled in and served by the party issuing the subpoenas. Service under Rule 17(d) may be made by a Marshal or any adult who is not a party.

The subpoena under Rule 17 may compel attendance at any criminal proceeding, including trial, deposition, and various hearings (such as suppression, preliminary, and grand jury). But Rule 17 does not authorize a subpoena for a witness to attend a private interview with a government agent. *See, e.g.*, *United States v. Villa-Chaparro*, 115 F.3d 797 (10th Cir. 1997).

Rule 17(c) directs production of various items "before the court at any time prior to the trial when they are to be offered into evidence" and authorizes the court to permit the parties and their attorneys to inspect the items when produced. While Rule 16 mandates discovery of some items in the *government's* possession, custody, or control, it does not apply to items in the hands of private parties. Can the defense lawyer subpoena such items for delivery to the court and inspection, say, five months before the trial date?

The Supreme Court has answered "sometimes." In *United States v. Nixon*, 418 U.S. 683 (1974), a prosecutor issued a Rule 17(c) subpoena to President Nixon to produce certain tape recordings and documents involving the President's conversations with various aides. The items could be evidence in a trial scheduled of other people in five months. Rejecting the President's motion to quash the subpoena, the Supreme Court held that Rule 17(c) permitted such subpoenas in limited circumstances. The *Nixon* Court first noted that precedent had established that Rule 17(c) was designed to expedite a trial by providing a time and place before trial for the parties to inspect the subpoenaed items; it was "not intended to provide a means of discovery for criminal cases." *Id.* at 698. The Court also favorably cited prior case law limiting Rule 17(c) to cases where the items are not procurable in advance of trial by due diligence, the party needs the pretrial inspection to prepare for trial and avoid a trial delay, and the subpoena is issued in good faith, not as a fishing expedition. Accordingly, the person seeking the subpoena must establish that the items subpoenaed are described with specificity, are relevant to the trial, and contain admissible evidence.

Rule 17(c)(3) provides "a protective mechanism when the defense subpoenas a third party to provide personal or confidential information about a victim." Advisory Committee Notes (2008). Unless exceptional circumstances exist, the victim must be notified before the defense may use a subpoena to seek such information about her background. In addition, judicial approval is necessary for the subpoena to issue. *See United States v. Bradley*, 675 F.3d 1021 (7th Cir. 2012) (no abuse of discretion by trial court in refusing to find exceptional circumstances justifying foregoing the notice requirement to the victim).

Rule 17(h) specifies that a subpoena may not be issued for a statement of a witness or prospective witness. Witness statements are generally covered by Rule 26.2, discussed below.

A subpoena is a court order. Rule 17(g) makes failure to abide by the subpoena punishable as contempt of court under Rule 42.

[6] In-trial Discovery: Statements of Witnesses (*Jencks*)

Nothing in the Federal Rules of Criminal Procedure or those of most states provides generally for the pretrial discovery of statements by all witnesses. In 1957 the United States Supreme Court exercised its supervisory power over federal courts and required disclosure of prior statements of government witnesses to facilitate impeachment by the criminal accused. *Jencks v. United States*, 353 U.S. 657 (1957). Congress responded by enacting 18 U.S.C. § 3500, known as the Jencks Act, which requires the government to disclose to defense counsel statements made by government witnesses who testify at trial. But this disclosure does not occur until after the witness has testified on direct examination. This last-minute disclosure is justified on the theory that if disclosure were earlier, the criminal accused may try to harm the witness or otherwise affect the witness's testimony or tailor defense proof to counter the prosecution witness's testimony.

Rule 26.2 of the Federal Rules of Criminal Procedure, added in 1979, repeats most of the Jencks Act. It was included in the rules of criminal procedure because of a belief that procedural rules should be readily available in a complete package of provisions rather than scattered throughout both the rules of criminal procedure and various separate statutes. *See generally* Ellen S. Podgor, *Criminal Discovery of Jencks Witness Statements: Timing Makes a Difference*, 15 GA. STATE U. L. REV. 651 (1999).

Rule 26.2 provides a minimal level of discovery of witnesses' statements by requiring disclosure of such statements after a witness has testified on direct examination. Thus, it is a departure from the traditional view that such statements are not discoverable, perhaps because part of counsel's work-product.

Several features of Rule 26.2 are important. Unlike the Jencks Act, Rule 26.2 requires disclosure by both the defense and the prosecution of any statement, whether inculpatory, exculpatory, or neither, but it does not mandate that any statements be memorialized at all or in any specific way. Either side may request and receive relevant statements made by the other side's witnesses after the witness has completed direct examination. But Rule 26.2 is not identical for the two sides. The rule does not mandate disclosure to the prosecution of prior statements by the defendant.

Rule 26.2(g) applies at sentencing, suppression hearings, detention hearings, and, important for discovery purposes, preliminary examinations. Of course, the prosecutor (and defense lawyer on rare occasions when defense witnesses are called at a preliminary examination) can avoid compliance with Rule 26.2's disclosure requirement at preliminary examinations for Witness X's statement by not calling Witness *X* at the preliminary examination.

Another difference in the treatment of prosecution and defense is in the sanctions for noncompliance. If Rule 26.2 is violated by either side's failure to produce a witness's statement, the authorized sanction differs for the two sides. The court is required by Rule 26.2(e) to order the testimony of that witness stricken from the record. In addition, if the government was at fault, the court must declare a mistrial "if justice so requires." Rule 26.2 does not specifically permit the court to declare a mistrial for the defendant's failure to comply with Rule 26.2, but it may have the inherent authority to do so anyway in extraordinary situations.

Rule 26.2 answers several practical problems that arise regularly. Sometimes a witness will provide a written statement dealing with many facts and issues, some of which the witness mentions on direct examination. Rule 26.2(c) permits the court, *in camera*, to review the statement and excise the irrelevant parts before the statement is turned over to the other side.

Since Rule 26.2 deals with statements by the witness, if the statement also contains remarks by other people, the latter's comments need not be produced under Rule 26.2. In addition, Rule 26.2 does not authorize one side to peruse the other side's records to determine whether the records contain a witness's statement. Each side is obligated to review its own records to assess whether it has a statement covered by Rule 26.2.

Rule 26.2(f) defines "statement" as including a written statement made by the witness that was signed or adopted or approved by the witness, a "substantially verbatim" recital of a witness's oral statement that was recorded contemporaneously, and a grand jury statement. This definition does not include an investigator's rough notes or brief summary of a witness' statement, mingled with the investigator's opinions. *See United States v. Wright*, 540 F.3d 833 (8th Cir. 2008). Statements made by the government investigator in his notes that reflect his interpretations or impressions do not qualify as statements.

Rule 26.2 covers statements in the "possession" of a party. For the prosecution, this may include various government agencies. *See, e.g., United States v. Moore*, 452 F.3d 382 (5th Cir. 2006) (Bureau of Prisons, irrespective of whether statement's existence was known to anyone in entire Justice Department outside of BOP); *Cole v. State*, 835 A.2d 600 (Md. 2003) (police department internal affairs division).

Timing of disclosure. Another practical problem is caused by the timing of disclosure under Rule 26.2. What if a prosecution witness provides the prosecution with a 100-page statement and then testifies for four days on direct examination at trial? As soon as the direct exam is completed, the prosecution gives the defense a copy of the lengthy statement. Obviously, it will take defense counsel hours to read and digest this statement and think about how to use it in cross-examining the witness.

Rule 26.2(d) specifically authorizes the trial court to grant a recess in the trial to facilitate the defense's need for time to review the witness's statement. But many defense counsel report that courts apply subtle and sometimes blatant pressure to "get on with it" to avoid delays in the proceedings. This judicial encouragement may cause some defense counsel to rush reading the statement and preparing for its use on cross-examination. A defense counsel's failure to ask for an adequate continuance or recess so he or she has time to read the Rule 26.2 statement may cause an appellate court to reject an appeal on the basis of the inadequate time.

Although some courts reject the notion that they have the authority, either under the rule or under their inherent authority, to order early release of *Jencks* materials, some lawyers (with not-so-subtle judicial encouragement) may voluntarily provide early access to Rule 26.2 statements. In *United States v. Mariani*, 7 F. Supp. 2d 556 (M.D. Pa 1998), for example, the prosecutor agreed to provide these statements one week before trial.

In *United States v. Suarez*, 2010 U.S. Dist. LEXIS 112097 (D.N.J. Oct. 19, 2010), the trial court determined that text messages between FBI agents and government witnesses constituted discoverable Jencks Act materials that should have been (but which were not) preserved prior to trial for possible disclosure to the defense. Finding no bad faith in the deletion of the text messages in question, the court denied the defendants' motion to strike the testimony of the cooperating witnesses. Rather, the court determined that a much less drastic sanction against the government would be appropriate in the interest of justice—i.e., a permissive instruction allowing but not requiring the jury to infer from the government's failure to preserve the text messages that the contents of the deleted messages would have been favorable to the defendants.

States routinely adopt a version of Federal Rule 26.2. Sometimes it is more expansive. *See, e.g.*, N.Y. Crim. P. Law § 240.45 (defendant entitled to government witnesses' prior statements before prosecutor's opening argument at trial; prosecution entitled to defendant's witnesses' statements before defense counsel presents defense evidence in chief).

In some cases, *Jencks* material and *Brady* material overlap. For example, a *Jencks* statement may constitute exculpatory or impeachment evidence; if so, it constitutes *Brady* material as well. *Brady* materials are ordinarily disclosed before trial to permit adequate trial preparation. When this dual coverage occurs, courts differ as to the timing of disclosure. Some hold that *Brady*'s pretrial disclosure rule must be followed in the event of *Brady/Jencks* overlap, *see, e.g., United States v. Starusko*, 729 F.2d 256 (3d Cir. 1984); others find that the Rule 26.2 *Jencks* procedures prevail, *see, e.g., United States v. Causey* [and Jeffrey Skilling and Kenneth Lay—the Enron securities fraud prosecution], 356 F. Supp. 2d 681 (S.D. Tex. 2005). Still other courts adopt a middle ground. *See, e.g., United States v. Beckford*, 962 F. Supp. 780 (E.D. Va. 1997) (adopting a balancing approach and holding that except in limited circumstances, disclosure of evidence constituting both *Brady* and *Jencks* material need not occur earlier than as provided by the Jencks Act). *See generally* Ellen S. Podgor, *Criminal Discovery of Jencks Witness Statements: Timing Makes a Difference*, 15 Ga. State U. L. Rev. 651, 673 (1999).

Problem 10-4. To Give Or Not to Give, That Is the Question

You are the prosecutor in a bank fraud case involving misrepresentation of the value of assets listed on the defendant's loan application. Your first witness, Sally Lightner, is President of the First State Bank that was the victim of the scam. President Lightner has just completed her direct examination, during which she described the loan procedures used by the bank and the falsehoods in the defendant's loan application. The defense has filed a Motion for Production of Witness Statements Under Rule 26.2. You have carefully reviewed your files and have found several items that could possibly be covered by the defense's motion. Assuming that each related to Lightner's direct testimony at the trial, which of the following must you disclose to the defense under Rule 26.2?

1. President Lightner was interviewed two times by investigators from your office.

a. Agent A visited Lightner at her office at the bank after Lightner called your office to report the scam. The session lasted 45 minutes. Agent A made handwritten notes of Lightner's description of the offense. The notes cover two handwritten pages in Agent A's notebook and generally summarize Lightner's information. Are Agent A's handwritten notes covered by Rule 26.2?

> Would your answer be different if the notes were 20 pages in length?
>
> What if Agent A concluded the interview by saying, "Let me see if I have everything." He then spent five minutes summarizing the data in his notes. He then asked Lightner, "Is this basically it?" She responded, "Yes, that's about it." Are his notes now discoverable under Rule 26.2?

b. Agent A returned to his office where he dictated a 10-page memorandum describing the interview with Ms. Lightner. He used his handwritten notes to supplement his memory of the interview. Is the 10-page memorandum covered by Rule 26.2? Is the tape recording he dictated?

c. Four days after the interview, Agent A received a letter from President Lightner. The letter said that after the interview she remembered several facts that she had forgotten to mention. The letter then detailed the information omitted during the interview. Is the letter discoverable under Rule 26.2?

d. Agent B conducted the second interview with Lightner a month before trial. Agent B recorded the entire interview. Must the entire recording be turned over to the defense under Rule 26.2?

> Assume that during Agent B's interview with Lightner, the bank's Vice President was called and asked to participate in the last half of the interview. The Vice President agreed to do so and participated in the interview. Assume that Lightner and the Vice President spoke for about the same length of time while jointly interviewed and that this portion of the interview lasted about 30 minutes. Is this part of the recording discoverable under Rule 26.2?

2. You have carefully prepared for trial. Your trial notebook includes a section for each witness. In the section labeled "Lightner," you summarize her likely testimony in two typed pages. Should you disclose these two pages to the defense pursuant to Rule 26.2?

[7] Grand Jury Evidence

An important principle of American law, discussed more fully in Chapter 7, is that grand jury proceedings are generally regarded as secret. Accordingly, transcripts of grand jury hearings are usually deemed secret. Of course, defense counsel would love to have access to these transcripts, for key government witnesses will testify both before the grand jury and later at trial. A witness's grand jury testimony would likely provide important information about the witness's trial testimony and could also be used to impeach the witness at trial and to gather other information that might benefit the defense. This information is particularly desirable when the grand jury witness refuses to talk about the case with defense counsel or a defense investigator.

The rules of criminal procedure often provide some flexibility in the dissemination of transcripts of testimony before the grand jury. Federal law, for example, specifically authorizes their disclosure to the prosecution to assist in preparing for trial. Moreover, there is some flexibility that permits the court to order disclosure to defense counsel.

Rule 6 authorizes the trial judge to order disclosure of grand jury transcripts, most federal courts do so only upon a showing of a "particularized need" which outweighs the policy of grand jury secrecy. *Pittsburgh Plate Glass Co. v. United States*, 360 U.S. 395 (1959).

Rule 26.2(f) of the Federal Rules of Criminal Procedure also authorizes disclosure of grand jury testimony. After a witness testifies on direct, the other side is entitled to a copy of the witness's prior statements, including those made before a grand jury.

Rule 16(a)(1)(B)(iii) authorizes a defendant to discover his or her own grand jury testimony. This provision will rarely be invoked, however, because defendants rarely testify before a grand jury.

Some state rules are more liberal, authorizing pretrial disclosure of grand jury statements, *see, e.g.*, Mass R. Crim. P. 14(a)(1)(ii) (defendant to receive relevant written or recorded statements of grand jury witnesses), and the identities of grand jury witnesses, *see, e.g.*, Minn. R. Crim. P. 9.01, subd. 1(1)(c) (names and addresses of grand jury witnesses).

[8] Court's Inherent Authority to Order Disclosure

Although the rules of criminal procedure do not accord full discovery in criminal cases, the courts have some inherent authority to extend discovery beyond that specifically authorized in the rules. This inherent authority is used routinely by some judges and sparingly by others. One area in which it has been used is to remedy interference by one side with the other side's access to potential witnesses. *See, e.g., United States v. Carrigan*, 804 F.2d 599 (10th Cir. 1986).

Some states have essentially codified the court's inherent authority to order discovery by authorizing the court to order discovery beyond that mandated by the discovery rules. *See, e.g.*, Ark. R. Crim. P. 17.4(a) (court may require disclosure to defense counsel of other information material to preparation of the defense); Ill. Sup. Ct. Rules 412(h), 413(e) (reasonable disclosure to either side of relevant material not covered by discovery rules).

[9] Other Sources and Limits of Discovery

[a] Electronic Surveillance

A federal statute provides that in any trial, hearing, or other proceeding, including grand jury hearings, a party claiming that evidence is inadmissible because it was procured through illegal electronic surveillance of that party is entitled to have the opponent of the claim affirm or deny the occurrence of the alleged wrongful act. 18 U.S.C. § 3504. The party alleging the illegality must make a prima facie showing of electronic surveillance (usually through an affidavit), and then the government must affirm or deny that the illegal surveillance occurred.

This statute can be illustrated by assuming that Defendant D believes that her phone was illegally tapped by the police and that some of her conversations were used to obtain evidence against her. She cannot prove it because she cannot locate the wiretap, perhaps because government technicians had removed it. Under § 3504, Defendant D can assert that there was an illegal wiretap of her house telephone. The government must then affirm or deny the wiretap. Ordinarily, the government's response is in the form of a written document entitled something like "Answer to Defendant's Motion Pursuant to 18 U.S.C. § 3504." The government will most likely attach affidavits from appropriate government officials detailing the presence or absence of the illegal wiretap.

[b] Freedom of Information Act

Another source of discovery is the Freedom of Information Act (F.O.I.A.), 5 U.S.C. § 552. Some states have similar "open records laws." The federal F.O.I.A. law provides the public with a right of access to various federal government materials. It also mandates procedures for obtaining this information. In order to avoid interference with law enforcement activities, some data are excluded from discovery under the F.O.I.A. Statutes also exempt materials from release under the Act. *See, e.g., Fund for Constitutional Government v. National Archives and Records Service*, 656 F.2d 856 (D.C. Cir. 1981) (Rule 6 of Federal Rules of Criminal Procedure exempts federal grand jury matters from release under the Freedom of Information Act).

Case law has shown a judicial reluctance to allow the F.O.I.A. as a substitute for the more rigorous requirements of discovery under the Federal Rules of Criminal Procedure. *See, e.g., United States v. United States District Court*, 717 F.2d 478 (9th Cir. 1983).

[c] National Security

On rare occasions the government will argue it cannot comply with a pretrial discovery request because of national security concerns. Courts routinely try to accommodate those concerns by reviewing the discovery request in an ex parte setting and making feasible adjustments in the discovery compliance. *See* Classified Information Procedures Act, 18 U.S.C. App. § 4. Courts seek to balance the defendant's need for the information against the government's need to keep the data from being revealed.

Often the court will accommodate both sides by permitting the government to summarize or redact the information. In *United States v. O'Hara*, 301 F.3d 563 (7th Cir. 2002), for example, the court redacted sensitive documents in a manner that still disclosed *Brady* materials.

If disclosure is needed because redaction or other remedies are inadequate, the court will order it. To avoid a dismissal for refusing to obey the court-ordered discovery, the government may be forced to drop charges.

[10] Remedies for Violation of Discovery Order

Rules requiring disclosure of information also authorize the trial judge to take various steps when disclosure is improperly withheld. Because these violations of the discovery rules may be based on unique facts or have consequences unique to the case, both the discovery rules and appellate courts usually give the trial judge discretion in fashioning an appropriate remedy.

Federal Rule 16(d)(2) is typical. If a party does not comply with Rule 16, a court may order that discovery or inspection occur under prescribed conditions, grant a continuance, prohibit the offending party from introducing the undisclosed evidence, or enter any order that is just under the circumstances.

Other discovery rules also deal with sanctions for their violation. The general pattern is to authorize, but not require, the court to exclude evidence. For example, if either side fails to comply with the notice of alibi requirements in Federal Rule of Criminal Procedure 12.1, the court may exclude the testimony of an undisclosed witness, other than the defendant. Fed. R. Crim. P. 12.1(e).

Courts routinely look at the particular facts of the case in deciding what sanction to apply. "In addition to preventing surprise, other factors considered before a witness preclusion sanction is employed to enforce discovery rules are: the effectiveness of less severe sanctions, the materiality of the testimony to the outcome of the case, prejudice to the other party caused by the testimony, and the evidence of bad faith in the violation of the discovery rules." *United States ex rel. Enoch v. Hartigan*, 768 F.2d 161, 163 (7th Cir. 1985).

As in civil cases, intentional nondisclosure is treated more harshly than negligent nondisclosure. Occasionally, the government's outrageous misconduct amounts to a due process violation and persuades the trial court to dismiss the charged offenses with prejudice. *United States v. Chapman*, 524 F.3d 1073 (9th Cir. 2008). Even without a due process issue, the court may dismiss under its supervisory powers. *Id.*

The harmless error rule is also used in deciding the proper sanction for a violation of a discovery rule. If the government's failure to disclose was of little consequence, the error will usually not cause a reversal of a conviction. On the other hand, if the nondisclosure actually made it impossible for the other side to investigate an issue or obtain proof, the court may bar evidence or even declare a mistrial. *See, e.g., United States v. Buchbinder*, 796 F.2d 910 (7th Cir. 1986) (in violation of Rule 12.2, defendant failed to provide notice of intent to use an expert; trial court properly excluded defense expert witness on issue of mental condition because defense's failure to give notice deprived government of opportunity to have defendant examined by government psychiatrist; nonexpert proof on mental condition permitted).

It is arguably unconstitutional to bar the defendant from testifying because defense counsel did not provide adequate disclosure of a witness list or a particular defense. The defendant may have a right to testify that cannot be abridged through counsel's error. Some decisions have also held that it is unconstitutional to bar defense witnesses from testifying as a sanction for the defense's failure to comply with a discovery rule. *See, e.g., Taylor v. Illinois*, 484 U.S. 400 (1988) (while upholding the exclusion of a defense witness, the Court discussed limits on barring defense witnesses because of a violation of a discovery rule) (discussed *supra*). If important defense evidence is barred because of defense counsel's discovery errors, this could constitute ineffective assistance of counsel in violation of the Sixth Amendment. *See Commonwealth v. Sena*, 709 N.E.2d 1111 (Mass. 1999).

In general, a trial judge's decision on discovery is deemed *interlocutory* and not subject to pretrial appellate review. Appellate courts use the abuse of discretion standard in reviewing the trial judge's decision. Some cases do allow the government to appeal if the court excludes evidence because of the government's failure to provide discovery. *See, e.g., United States v. Golyansky*, 291 F.3d 1245 (10th Cir. 2005).

Problem 10-5. "Don't Punish Me. I'm Just the Client."

Following a search of his home that uncovered a large quantity of heroin, defendant O'Brien was indicted for heroin trafficking. Pursuant to the state's rules providing for reciprocal discovery, O'Brien's lawyer agreed to provide the prosecutor with the names and addresses of witnesses the defense intended to call at trial. By the time the trial was to begin, the prosecutor had not received the names of any defense witnesses. At trial, during its case-in-chief, the prosecution called a state-employed chemist who identified the substance seized from O'Brien's home as heroin, a controlled substance under state law. On cross-examination, defense counsel tried to establish that the chemist's testing could not distinguish heroin from a synthetic substance that the defense argued does not qualify as a controlled substance under state law. When defense counsel called three out-of-state chemists to testify that the seized substance is not a controlled substance under state law, and that the testing procedures used by the state's chemist were defective, the prosecutor asked the trial judge to bar the chemists from testifying because their names and addresses had not been disclosed by defense counsel. The court granted the motion, and the jury subsequently convicted the defendant as charged.

1. Assess the trial court's ruling to prevent any of the chemists from testifying as a sanction for failing to comply with the prior reciprocal agreement.

2. If defense counsel's failure to comply was deliberate and his attempts to overturn his conviction have failed, should O'Brien seek post-conviction relief for his counsel's ineffective assistance?

[11] Ethical Issues in Discovery

While some ethical issues have already been discussed in this chapter, several others bear mention. Lawyers are held to high ethical standards in the area of discovery. As noted earlier in this chapter, the Model Rules of Professional Conduct deal in considerable detail with discovery. They not only ban obstructing adversary counsel's access to evidence, they also prohibit falsifying evidence, disobeying an obligation imposed by court rules (unless the court rules are openly challenged), making a frivolous discovery request, and failing to make a reasonably diligent effort to comply with a proper discovery request by adversary counsel. Model Rules of Professional Conduct Rule 3.4 (1983). *See also* STANDARDS FOR CRIMINAL JUSTICE §§ 3–3.11(b) (3d ed. 1993) (prosecutor must make reasonably diligent effort to comply with proper discovery request), 4-4.5 (same for defense counsel).

G. A Better System

[1] Arguments Against Extensive Discovery in Criminal Cases

Now that you are familiar with discovery in criminal cases, you have seen how less extensive it is than that allowed in civil cases. These differences may be surprising because in other areas, such as the right to free counsel for indigents, criminal procedure offers more protection for the defendant than does civil procedure. To a large extent, the greater protections given the criminal accused in many areas of criminal procedure are based on the theory that these protections are appropriate since the defendant's life or liberty (as opposed to the civil defendant's money) is at stake. Several rationales are repeated commonly for limiting the scope of discovery in criminal cases.

[a] Harm or Intimidate Witnesses

Perhaps the most prevalent argument is that extensive discovery would allow the criminal accused to learn the identity and likely testimony of prosecution witnesses. To avoid conviction, the accused would intimidate or harm these witnesses to prevent or alter their trial testimony. This risk may also deter some potential witnesses from agreeing to testify or even providing the prosecution with information. There is some evidence that this fear is real, although we do not know its extent or whether it is confined to certain types of cases. A federal prosecutor reported that a survey of United States Attorneys found more than 700 instances of witness intimidation, assault, or assassination. Edward S.G. Dennis, Jr., *The Discovery Process in Criminal Prosecutions: Toward Fair Trials and Just Verdicts*, 68 WASH. U. L.Q. 63, 65 (1990).

[b] Commit or Suborn Perjury

A related argument is that the accused would learn the likely prosecution evidence and then tailor his or her own testimony or that of other defense witnesses to meet the likely government evidence. While this possibility is also present in civil cases, for some reason it is rarely discussed.

[c] Violate Adversary Process

A third argument is that full discovery would undermine the adversary process, particularly if disclosure were not identical for both sides. Some adherents of this view note that the burden of proof in criminal cases weighs heavily against the government, yet the defendant can withhold critical information, helpful to the prosecution, because of the protection of the Fifth Amendment. If the defendants had full discovery of the government's file plus the advantages of a "tilted" burden of proof, the resulting adversary process would not be a fair one for both sides. Judge Learned Hand observed in an often-quoted passage:

> Under our criminal procedure the accused has every advantage. While the prosecution is held rigidly to the charge, he need not disclose the barest outline of his defense. He is immune from question or comment on his silence; he cannot be convicted when there is the least fair doubt in the minds of any of the twelve. Why in addition he should in advance have the whole evidence against him to pick over at his leisure, and to make his defense, fairly or foully, I have never been able to see.

United States v. Garsson, 291 F. 646, 649 (S.D.N.Y. 1923).

One suggestion to improve the existing system is to create a presumption *in favor of* early and full discovery by the defendant. Under this model, the government must provide full disclosure unless it could demonstrate to the court that there really is a danger that the defendant will tamper with evidence, intimidate witnesses, or commit perjury. When the government satisfies this standard, the trial court would restrict discovery only to the extent necessary to avoid the dangers established by the government's proof. *See* H. Lee Sarokin & William E. Zuckerman, *Presumed Innocent? Restrictions on Criminal Discovery in Federal Court Belie This Presumption*, 43 RUT. L. REV. 1089, 1090 (1991). Do you agree with this approach? Are there any problems with it?

The intimidation and perjury theories assume the worst type of defendant while ignoring the role of counsel. According to a distinguished jurist, Judge Frankel, the perjury theory overlooks

> that it is a lawyer who ordinarily moves for discovery, representing that he has a proper purpose for what is on its face a responsible professional request.... [We should not abandon the presumption] that members of our bar behave regularly and refrain from suborning perjury.

United States v. Projansky, 44 F.R.D. 550 (S.D.N.Y. 1968). Do you agree?

Another argument is that more discovery in criminal cases would facilitate plea bargaining (and therefore help alleviate crowded dockets) by giving the defendant a good sense of the strength of the government's case that will be presented if there is a trial. Will an increase in discovery in criminal cases lead to more guilty pleas? If so, is this progress for the American criminal justice system? *See* H. Lee Sarokin

& William E. Zuckerman, *Presumed Innocent? Restrictions on Criminal Discovery in Federal Court Belie This Presumption*, 43 RUTGERS L. REV. 1089 (1991) (arguing in favor of more criminal discovery).

[2] More Disclosure: The California Model

Since little of the law of discovery in criminal cases is mandated by the Constitution, jurisdictions have considerable leeway in fashioning their discovery rules. While most jurisdictions have laws that resemble the federal approach, a few jurisdictions have considerably broadened the scope of discovery in criminal cases.

A popular example is the California discovery process, added by the Crime Victim's Justice Reform Act through a citizen's initiative in 1990. *See generally* Deborah Glynn, *Proposition 115: The Crime Victims Justice Reform Act*, 22 PAC. L. J. 1010 (1991). To a large extent, these rules were a reaction to California judicial decisions severely limiting discovery by the prosecution in criminal cases.

California Penal Code

§ 1054.1. *Prosecuting attorney; disclosure of materials to defendant*

> The prosecuting attorney shall disclose to the defendant or his or her attorney all of the following materials and information, if it is in the possession of the prosecuting attorney or if the prosecuting attorney knows it to be in the possession of the investigating agencies:
>
> (a) The names and addresses of persons the prosecutor intends to call as witnesses at trial.
>
> (b) Statements of all defendants.
>
> (c) All relevant real evidence seized or obtained as a part of the investigation of the offenses charged.
>
> (d) The existence of a felony conviction of any material witness whose credibility is likely to be critical to the outcome of the trial.
>
> (e) Any exculpatory evidence.
>
> (f) Relevant written or recorded statements of witnesses or reports of the statements of witnesses whom the prosecutor intends to call at the trial, including any reports or statements of experts made in conjunction with the case, including the results of physical or mental examinations, scientific tests, experiments, or comparisons which the prosecutor intends to offer in evidence at the trial.

§ 1054.2. *Disclosure of address or telephone number of victim or witness; prohibition; exception*

> (a)(1) Except as provided in paragraph (2), no attorney may disclose or permit to be disclosed to a defendant, members of the defendant's family,

or anyone else, the address or telephone number of a victim or witness whose name is disclosed to the attorney pursuant to subdivision (a) of Section 1054.1, unless specifically permitted to do so by the court after a hearing and a showing of good cause.

(2) Notwithstanding paragraph (1), an attorney may disclose or permit to be disclosed the address or telephone number of a victim or witness to persons employed by the attorney or to persons appointed by the court to assist in the preparation of a defendant's case if that disclosure is required for that preparation. Persons provided this information by an attorney shall be informed by the attorney that further dissemination of the information, except as provided by this section, is prohibited.

(3) Willful violation of this subdivision by an attorney, persons employed by the attorney, or persons appointed by the court is a misdemeanor.

(b) If the defendant is acting as his or her own attorney, the court shall endeavor to protect the address and telephone number of a victim or witness by providing for contact only through a private investigator licensed by the Department of Consumer Affairs and appointed by the court or by imposing other reasonable restrictions, absent a showing of good cause as determined by the court.

§ 1054.3. *Defense counsel; disclosure of information to prosecution*

The defendant and his or her attorney shall disclose to the prosecuting attorney:

(a) The names and addresses of persons, other than the defendant, he or she intends to call as witnesses at trial, together with any relevant written or recorded statements of those persons, or reports of the statements of those persons, including any reports or statements of experts made in connection with the case, and including the results of physical or mental examinations, scientific tests, experiments, or comparisons which the defendant intends to offer in evidence at the trial.

(b) Any real evidence which the defendant intends to offer in evidence at the trial.

§ 1054.5. *Criminal cases; discovery orders; informal request; testimony of witnesses; prohibition*

. . . .

(b) Before a party may seek court enforcement of any of the disclosures required by this chapter, the party shall make an informal request of opposing counsel for the desired materials and information. If within 15 days the opposing counsel fails to provide the materials and information requested, the party may seek a court order. Upon a showing that a party has not complied with Section 1054.1 or 1054.3 and upon a showing that the moving party complied with the informal discovery procedure provided in this subdivision, a court may make any order necessary to enforce the provisions of this chapter, including, but not limited to, immediate disclosure, contempt proceedings, delaying or prohibiting the testimony of a witness or the presentation of real evidence, continuance of the matter, or any other lawful order. Further, the court may advise the jury of any failure or refusal to disclose and of any untimely disclosure.

(c) The court may prohibit the testimony of a witness pursuant to subdivision (b) only if all other sanctions have been exhausted. The court shall not dismiss a charge pursuant to subdivision (b) unless required to do so by the Constitution of the United States.

Notes

1. While California mandates extensive pretrial discovery, it has not adopted an open-file rule that requires each side to turn over its entire file to the other. What would be wrong with an open-file rule? Wouldn't it speed up the trial process and promote the ascertainment of truth by eliminating surprise at trial and providing each side with its best opportunity to present its case?

2. Examine the California discovery rules. Do they mandate that California law enforcement authorities *gather* exculpatory evidence? Should they?

3. What if both sides conduct extensive investigation and find witnesses helpful to the other side. Must the prosecution give the defense this information? Does the defense have to do so for the prosecution? Do you agree with this result?

4. Should this discovery process apply even to misdemeanors?

5. Which do you prefer—the California discovery process or the system under the federal rules?

Chapter 11

Pleas and Plea Bargaining

A. Introduction

Criminal cases, like civil cases, rarely go to trial. Where civil litigation typically is resolved by settlement, criminal cases are resolved in overwhelming proportion, in both state and federal courts, by the process of *plea bargaining*, which results in a negotiated *guilty plea*. The Supreme Court observed recently that 97% of federal convictions and 94% of state convictions are the result of guilty pleas. *Lafler v. Cooper*, 566 U.S. 156, 170 (2012) (discussed later in this chapter). In this chapter we will explore the processes, the constitutional constraints, and the policy concerns surrounding plea bargaining in our nation's courts.

The criminal defendant who pleads guilty admits responsibility for one or more of the crimes charged (perhaps in the form of a lesser included offense), agrees to be punished in accordance with the criminal laws, and waives the right to trial and other procedural rights under the Fifth and Sixth Amendments.

As starkly stated recently by the Supreme Court in the companion decision to *Lafler*:

> [P]lea bargains have become . . . central to the administration of the criminal justice system. . . . Ours is for the most part a system of pleas, not a system of trials. . . . [Plea bargaining] is not some adjunct to the criminal justice system; it *is* the criminal justice system.

Missouri v. Frye, 566 U.S. 134, 144 (2012). Even if this proposition is a bit of an exaggeration, still it is indisputable that to understand the American criminal justice system, one must understand the process of plea bargaining.

B. Plea Options Available to the Defendant

In federal cases and in almost all of the states, a defendant may enter one of three pleas to a criminal charge: not guilty, *nolo contendere*, or guilty. *E.g.*, Fed. R. Crim. P. 11(a)(1). In addition, some jurisdictions also allow the separate plea of "not guilty by reason of insanity" or "guilty but mentally ill." *See, e.g.*, Ohio R. Crim. P. 11(A); Mich. R. Crim. P. 6.303, 6.304. New York does not allow the plea of *nolo contendere* "as a matter of right," while Illinois only allows the *nolo* plea for those defendants charged with a violation of the state income tax law. *See* N.Y. Crim. Proc. Law § 220.10; ILCS ch. 725, art. 113-4.1.

[1] Plea of Not Guilty

By pleading not guilty, the defendant requires the government to prove its case, thereby placing in issue each material element specified in the indictment. This plea also preserves many constitutional rights, including the right to jury trial, the privilege against self-incrimination, and the right to confront one's accusers.

A plea of not guilty is a legal assertion of rights, rather than a sworn statement of fact. Therefore, a defendant who is guilty of the crime(s) charged but pleads not guilty in order to exercise his or her right to trial by jury, does *not* thereby commit an act of perjury.

[2] Plea of *Nolo Contendere* (No Contest)

A plea of *nolo contendere*, like a plea of guilty, involves a waiver of the right to a trial and other related procedural rights. Fed. R. Crim. P. 11(b)(1)(F). A *nolo* plea is a formal declaration that the defendant will not contest the charge and it has the same legal effect as a guilty plea in terms of its finality. Therefore, judgment following entry of a *nolo contendere* plea is a criminal conviction which sometimes may be admitted as evidence in other proceedings where the fact of conviction has legal, perhaps decisive, significance.

In contrast to the plea of guilty, however, the legal consequences of a *nolo* plea differ in one critical respect. In most jurisdictions, the *nolo* plea may not be used in a later civil case as proof of the fact that the defendant committed the offense, *see* Fed. R. Evid. 803(22). That is, the plea of *nolo* may not be used as direct evidence of liability in a civil suit. In fact, some jurisdictions even provide that the plea of no contest may not be used against the defendant in any subsequent civil or criminal proceeding. *See, e.g.*, Ohio R. Crim. P. 11(B)(2). This feature explains why a person facing both civil and criminal proceedings might prefer to plead *nolo contendere* to resolve the criminal matter without compromising subsequent civil proceedings.

A defendant does not have an absolute right to plead *nolo contendere*. In federal cases, the *nolo* plea requires the consent of the court and "such a plea shall be accepted by the court only after due consideration of the views of the parties and the interest of the public in the effective administration of justice." Fed. R. Crim. P. 11(a)(3). This rule has been construed to vest the trial judge with broad discretion to refuse to accept a *nolo* plea. *See United States v. David E. Thompson, Inc.*, 621 F.2d 1147 (1st Cir. 1980) (district court did not abuse its discretion in rejecting a *nolo* plea in a criminal antitrust action where entry of the plea would have deprived the victims of the antitrust conspiracy of a significant opportunity in subsequent civil actions to benefit from the government's efforts). Most states follow the same rule. Many judges are reluctant to permit *nolo* pleas since this plea leaves unresolved the issue of actual responsibility for the crime.

A minority of jurisdictions do not permit a *nolo* plea. *See, e.g., Corbin v. State*, 713 N.E.2d 906 (Ind. Ct. App. 1999) (*nolo* pleas not permitted because guilty plea in Indiana requires admission of crime charged).

[3] Plea of Guilty

By pleading guilty, the defendant consents to entry of a judgment of conviction without trial and jury verdict. Although a plea of guilty is usually entered before trial, it may also be entered at any point during trial before the jury returns its verdict.

The guilty plea waives the right to be tried by a jury and also the defendant's other constitutional trial-related rights, including the right to the assistance of trial counsel, the right to confront and cross-examine adverse witnesses, and the privilege against compelled self-incrimination. Fed. R. Crim. P. 11(b)(1)(F). Consequently, before accepting a plea of guilty and a waiver of these rights, the court must determine that the accused is acting voluntarily and understands the charges. The plea itself is an admission of guilt and the accepted plea is essentially a criminal conviction. The judge's only remaining tasks are to enter judgment and impose sentence. As discussed later in this chapter, a guilty plea may be based on *North Carolina v Alford*, 400 U.S. 25 (1970). The defendant in an *Alford* plea acknowledges that there is sufficient evidence to convict him, but nonetheless still maintains his innocence.

C. The Plea Bargaining Process

Virtually all attorneys involved in the criminal justice system—whether a prosecutor or defense attorney, whether federal or state—participate in plea bargaining. Simply put, plea bargaining is a form of plea negotiation in which the prosecutor agrees to make certain concessions in exchange for the defendant's guilty or *nolo contendere* plea. Both the government and the defendant may benefit from a negotiated resolution of the case. First, a trial on the merits is time consuming and potentially expensive for the government, for defendants, and even for trial jurors. Second, there is a considerable amount of unpredictability as to the outcome of a criminal trial. Both prosecution and defense may prefer the certainty of the guilty plea, which establishes guilt as well as the level of criminal culpability. Third, even if the defendant is convicted at trial, the sentence imposed by the court may exceed what the defendant expected or may be less than the prosecution thinks is appropriate. Hence, a bargained-for sentence may be seen as beneficial to both sides by virtue of the certainty and finality it provides to all concerned, including not only the prosecution and defense attorneys but also the crime victim, the police, the public, and the defendant himself.

In federal criminal cases, there are essentially four types of plea agreements available: (1) charge agreements; (2) recommendation agreements; (3) specific sentence agreements; and (4) fact stipulation agreements.

[1] Charge Agreements

A charge agreement is one in which the prosecution agrees that the defendant will plead guilty to one or more specific charges in exchange for the prosecutor's assent to dismiss other pending charges. If this kind of agreement is reached prior to the issuance of an indictment, the prosecution agrees not to pursue one or more particular charges (sometimes referred to as placing the other charges *on file*). If the agreement is reached following indictment, the prosecution agrees to dismiss or reduce one or more existing charges.

Example 1. The prosecution accepts defendant A's agreement to plead guilty to involuntary manslaughter where the original charge was second-degree murder.

Example 2. Defendant B has been indicted for robbery, burglary, and two counts of receiving and concealing stolen property. He could enter an agreement to plead guilty to robbery (the most serious of his charges) in exchange for the prosecutor's agreement to dismiss the burglary and the receiving and concealing charges.

[2] Recommendation Agreements

A recommendation agreement is one in which the defendant agrees to plead guilty in exchange for the prosecutor's willingness either to recommend a particular sentence or not to resist or oppose a sentence recommendation made by the defense. In federal cases, the agreement may entail precise commitments—perhaps from both prosecution and defense—regarding departures from the sentence or sentencing range prescribed by the federal sentencing guidelines.

Return to Example 2 involving Defendant B, who was indicted for robbery, burglary, and two counts of receiving and concealing stolen property. Perhaps he would agree to plead guilty to all four crimes if the prosecution will recommend to the judge that he be given a sentence of 10 years in prison for the robbery and three-year prison sentences each for the other three offenses, all to be served concurrently with the 10-year robbery sentence. If (as is likely) the recommendation is accepted by the judge, Defendant B will have served all four sentences by the time he completes the 10-year term for robbery.

[3] Specific Sentence Agreements

Similar to a recommendation agreement, a specific sentence agreement entails a guilty plea in exchange for an agreement from the prosecution that a particular sentence or sentencing range is the appropriate disposition, or that a specific sentencing guideline or factor should or should not apply. *See* Fed. R. Crim. P. 11(c)(1)(C).

While the judge may (and usually does) choose to abide by such an agreement, the court has the authority to reject the specific agreed-upon sentence. In that event, the defendant is allowed to withdraw the guilty plea. Withdrawals of guilty pleas are discussed in further detail later in this chapter.

Returning again to Example 1 regarding Defendant A assume that the plea agreement involved a specific (as opposed to a recommended) 10-year sentence for robbery, with the other three sentences to be served concurrently. If the judge accepts the deal, Defendant A will be sentenced to the 10-year term in accordance with the agreement. If the judge refuses to accept the agreement, perhaps believing it to be too lenient, Defendant A has the option of withdrawing his plea and going to trial on all four charges (of course, this entails a substantial risk that if he is convicted, the sentence will be more than what could be negotiated in a plea agreement the court would accept).

[4] Fact Stipulation Agreements

A fact stipulation agreement, while not a traditional form of plea negotiation, is a separate agreement in which pertinent facts and circumstances surrounding the offense are agreed upon. These agreements are contemplated by federal sentencing guidelines, and their purpose is to stipulate specific facts that the federal judge relies upon to support the particular sentence within statutory and guideline ranges. For a more detailed discussion of fact bargaining under federal sentencing guidelines, *see* Tony Garoppolo, *Fact Bargaining: What the Sentencing Commission Hath Wrought*, 10 BNA Criminal Practice Manual 405 (1996), and William L. Gardner & Davis S. Rifkind, *A Basic Guide to Plea Bargaining Under the Federal Sentencing Guidelines*, 7 CRIM. JUST. 14 (Summer, 1992). For a critical view, arguing that some fact stipulations between prosecution and defense (such as an agreement to treat a repeat offender as a first offender for sentencing purposes) may inappropriately, even fraudulently, shield certain relevant facts from the sentencing judge's view, see the *cri de coeur* of one federal district judge:

> The most repugnant of the [Justice] Department's tactics is to lie to the Court in order to induce a guilty plea. This is the process known as "fact bargaining." It occurs when a departmental attorney "swallows the drugs" or "the gun" as the case may be, i.e., fails to report to the probation officer in rendering its descriptions of offense conduct (and then later fails to bring to the attention of the Court) relevant evidence that may affect the [federal sentencing g]uidelines calculation in order to reduce that calculation to secure a disposition to which it and defense counsel have agreed. This, of course, is flat-out illegal.

United States v. Green, 346 F. Supp. 2d 259, 278 (D. Mass. 2004) (Young, C.J.), vacated *sub nom. United States. v. Yeje-Cabrera*, 430 F.3d 1 (1st Cir. 2005).

[5] Plea Bargaining Variations

[a] Conditional Pleas

A *conditional plea* is designed to make it possible for the defendant to enter a guilty plea yet preserve an important adverse pretrial motion ruling for appellate review. It is specifically authorized by Federal Rule of Criminal Procedure 11(a)(2):

> **Conditional Plea.** With the consent of the court and the government, a defendant may enter a conditional plea of guilty or nolo contendere,

> reserving in writing the right to have an appellate court review an adverse determination of a specified pretrial motion. A defendant who prevails on appeal may then withdraw the plea.

Essentially, when a conditional guilty plea is accepted by the court, the defendant reserves the right to appeal the denial of an adverse pretrial motion. If the appellate court affirms the pretrial ruling, the guilty plea stands. If the appellate court upholds the defendant's claim, however, the guilty plea may then be withdrawn.

1. *Hypothetical.* Assume a case in which the defendant's apartment is searched by a police officer without a search warrant. As a result of this search, cocaine is found and the defendant is charged with possession of cocaine. The defense attorney files a pretrial suppression motion arguing that the search was unlawful and the drugs should be excluded from evidence. Without this evidence, the prosecution's case is so weak that the charges would likely be dismissed. Assume also that defense counsel's suppression motion is denied by the trial judge, but the defense attorney believes that the appellate court will probably exclude the evidence. The general rule is that a guilty plea waives all non-jurisdictional defects in the case. Therefore, if the defendant wishes to preserve the evidentiary issue for review by an appellate court, he or she cannot plead guilty; the case must go to trial.

In this hypothetical, however, assume that the defendant enters a conditional guilty plea, reserving the right to appeal the issue of the admissibility of the cocaine. If the appeal is unsuccessful, the defendant's plea is valid and will subject him or her to the criminal sanctions agreed to in the plea bargain. On the other hand, if the appeal is successful and the evidence is ruled inadmissible, the defendant's plea can be withdrawn and, if it is, the prosecution has the option of dropping the charges, setting the case for trial, or engaging in further plea bargaining.

2. *Mutual benefit.* Both defense and prosecution may benefit from a conditional plea. The defendant benefits by not having to go to trial in order to appeal an important issue, such as the admissibility of a confession. The prosecution gains by avoiding the waste of time that would occur if the defendant went through a trial, then successfully appealed and had the conviction overturned. The prosecution would then have to launch a second trial if it could not work out a deal or did not want to drop charges.

3. *Legal basis.* Many states also allow conditional pleas. *See, e.g.*, Mich. Court Rule 6.301(C)(2). *See generally Neuhaus v. People*, 289 P.3d 19 (Colo 2012) (survey showed 10 jurisdictions allow conditional pleas by statute, 16 by court rule, two by judicial decision; Colorado Supreme Court refused to allow conditional plea without legislative authorization). The courts of South Dakota and Rhode Island have held, on jurisdictional grounds, that such pleas are invalid and unenforceable in the absence of an underlying state statute or court rule. *See State v. Rondell*, 791 N.W.2d 641 (S.D. 2010); *State v. Keohane*, 814 A.2d 327 (R.I. 2003). In other words, in some states conditional pleas are proper and enforceable only if they are affirmatively authorized under state law.

4. *Written agreement approved by prosecution and court.* Rule 11(a)(2) states that the conditional plea can be made only with the consent of the court and the government (i.e., the prosecution). The defendant is required to file a written document reserving the right to appeal an adverse ruling on a specific pretrial motion. This document should describe the precise issue that will be appealed. This unusual requirement of a *written* conditional plea assures that the government acquiesced in the precise plea, and leaves a clear record that both prosecution and defense considered the plea to be conditional. Further, it allows both the trial and appellate courts to know precisely which issues are reserved for appeal. If the defendant succeeds on appeal, the defendant is allowed to withdraw the guilty plea.

5. *Appellate court's limited information.* When the defendant enters a conditional plea and then pursues appellate review of a pretrial motion, the trial record will be limited to those matters considered at the pretrial stage along with the record of the conditional guilty plea. Thus, the appellate court will not have the full trial record normally available to it when reviewing a lower court's ruling. For this reason, it has been suggested that the conditional plea is inappropriate. Do you agree?

6. *Conditional pleas: pro and con.* The conditional plea actually gives the defendant the best of both worlds: the defendant is permitted to seek review of an adverse pretrial ruling yet is not required to undergo the time, expense, and risk involved in a full trial on the merits. Since the plea negotiation process entails the waiver or forfeiture of many significant constitutional rights, why shouldn't appellate review also be one of those rights waived by guilty plea? Stated differently, is it not fair to require the defendant who desires appellate review to "jump through the hoop" of trial on the merits?

Notwithstanding the criticism that the conditional plea strikes at the notion of finality in the criminal process, many courts and commentators applaud this procedure. Indeed, in *Lefkowitz v. Newsome*, 420 U.S. 283 (1975), the United States Supreme Court indicated its approval of a New York conditional plea statute as a procedure "which permits a defendant to obtain appellate review of certain pretrial constitutional claims without imposing on the state the burden of going to trial."

[b] Agreements for Cooperation

A somewhat different form of plea bargaining has emerged in recent years: the "agreement for cooperation." Unlike traditional plea bargaining, this form of agreement contemplates a favorable disposition for the defendant in exchange for cooperation with the prosecution, usually in the form of testimony against other defendants. The late Professor Graham Hughes described this compact as one involving "contested issues that must be negotiated, sometimes for months, and that eventually are embodied in letter agreements that range from the fairly straightforward to the extremely complicated."

As Professor Hughes also explains, cooperation agreements entail a very precise description of the cooperation promised by the defendant as well as a clear delineation of the scope of immunity or nature of the plea bargain benefit extended by the prosecution. Subsequent litigation between the contracting parties necessarily hinges upon the very terms of the contract. Graham Hughes, *Agreements for Cooperation in Criminal Cases*, 45 VAND. L. REV. 1 (1992). This issue will be explored later in this chapter in *Ricketts v. Adamson*, 483 U.S. 1 (1987).

Sometimes a cooperation agreement may be accompanied by a *consistency agreement*, which obligates the defendant to testify against others in a way that is consistent with the offender's prior statements. Since these provisions discourage the defendant from recanting or altering the earlier statement that may have been incomplete or untruthful, consistency agreements are disfavored in many courts. *See, e.g., State v. Kayer*, 984 P.2d 31 (Ariz. 1999) (agreements that oblige the defendant to testify truthfully and completely are valid, but those that oblige the defendant to testify to certain stipulated facts are not).

[c] Bargaining for Unusual Sentencing Provisions

Sometimes, judges, prosecutors, and defense attorneys use the plea bargaining process to reach results in individual cases that allow for unusual punishments or sentencing results that are not specifically provided for under the sentencing laws. For example, an agreed upon guilty plea may require the defendant to stay out of certain cities or geographical areas, engage in unpaid charitable contributions or labors, enter the armed services (if the military is willing to induct the defendant), or to undergo certain "scarlet letter" punishments (such as wearing a confessional sandwich-board in a public place or writing a public letter of apology for the crime).

Views differ on the appropriateness of bargaining for particular sentencing outcomes that fall outside the express provisions of the sentencing laws. On the one hand, Professor Joseph A. Colquitt, *Ad Hoc Plea Bargaining*, 75 TULANE L. REV. 695, 699 (2001), argues that such ad hoc settlements are outside the law and must be controlled:

> Prosecutors and defense attorneys should not be allowed to assume the legislative functions of defining crimes and establishing the types and ranges of punishments. Giving them the option to settle criminal cases through the use of ad hoc alternatives to legal punishments does precisely that. They establish the law of the locale rather than apply the laws of the state. Moreover, the "punishments" they negotiate most often fail to address penological goals. Ad hoc justice commonly leaves much to be desired.

On the other hand, as discussed in Chapter 16, courts have broad discretionary powers to fashion specific conditions of probation appropriate to the facts and circumstances of each particular case, and often impose these kinds of individualized alternative sanctions as conditions of probation.

D. Plea Bargaining Policy Considerations Pro and Con: Necessary Evil, Necessary Good, or Just Plain Evil?

Opinions about the value and fairness of plea bargaining differ sharply. To oversimplify somewhat, views on plea bargaining tend to fall into three schools of thought. Some view plea bargaining itself as inherently unfair, compromising of justice, and even unconstitutional. Others regard it as a kind of necessary evil without which the criminal justice system would grind to a halt, but which should be subject to close legislative and judicial oversight. Still others regard the plea bargaining process as not only necessary, but also one which tends to yield fair and just results when the adversary system works properly. This section of the chapter explores these contrasting viewpoints, and although somewhat more space is given to the "cons" than the "pros" of plea bargaining, students are encouraged to think for themselves and come to their own conclusions after reading these materials. Students should consider also whether the potential evils of plea bargaining can adequately be addressed by procedurally "policing" the process, or whether plea bargaining should be severely limited or abolished altogether.

[1] Administrative Convenience/Necessity

Many persons—judges and advocates included—maintain that plea bargaining in our society is a necessary part of the criminal justice system. This argument rests upon two assumptions. First, without plea bargaining, it is argued, many criminal defendants will have little incentive to plead guilty and will insist on a trial. Second, we have inadequate resources (prosecutors, defense attorneys, judges, courtrooms, *etc.*) to conduct a full trial in every criminal case. We would have to devote massive additional funding to the criminal justice system if many more defendants demanded all the rights guaranteed by the Constitution. This would be a waste of resources, it is argued, since most defendants in fact are guilty and the proof against them is overwhelming. These arguments are buttressed by the fact that currently there is roughly one trial for every 10 or more guilty pleas. What would happen to our already overburdened system if a much larger percentage of criminal defendants elected to face trial rather than plead guilty?

In recent years, some jurisdictions have tested this argument by attempting to ban plea bargaining altogether (isolated jurisdictions within the states of Texas, Michigan, and New York, and state-wide in Alaska, among others). The few empirical studies that have examined those efforts suggest that bargaining prohibitions have not caused courts and criminal justice officials to be overwhelmed. In Alaska, where the State Attorney General banned plea negotiations in 1975 (but recognized possible exceptions to the ban where suspects exchange helpful information), a study found that (1) defendants continued to plead guilty at about the same rate as before the ban, (2) the rate of trials increased, but the number of trials remained low, and (3) conviction rates changed very little. Other studies have found that such bans produced increases in sentencing severity, especially for minor offenses. As to the hypothesis that banning plea bargaining would substantially disrupt the criminal justice system (through increased trial rates, case backlogs, and lengthened case processing times), none of these adverse effects occurred (except in New York, according to one study). *See* Sandra Shane-Dubow, Alice P. Brown & Erik Olsen, Sentencing Reform in the United States: History, Content, and Effect (1985); Michael H. Tonry, Sentencing Reform Impacts (1987).

Where plea bargaining has been "eliminated," two important points must be kept in mind. First, banning the practice of plea bargaining does not preclude a defendant from pleading guilty to the charge(s) without any agreement for leniency from the prosecution, and asking for "the mercy of the court"—a so-called "naked plea." Second, some commentators believe that prohibiting explicit plea bargaining will never eliminate "implicit plea bargaining," defined as an informal understanding among prosecutors, defense attorneys, and judges that a guilty defendant who enters a plea of guilty should and will receive a reduced sentence. Similarly, banning plea bargaining could have the effect of shifting the exercise of discretion to a less visible stage of the criminal case. For example, California's attempt to ban plea bargaining through a constitutional amendment ("Proposition 8") did not produce that result. Rather, it had the effect of encouraging guilty pleas at earlier stages of the process than before. This result led one commentator to observe: "Paradoxically, . . . Proposition 8 strengthened plea bargaining rather than eliminating it." Candace McCoy, Politics and Plea Bargaining: Victims' Rights in California 179 (1993).

[2] Fair and Accurate Results

Many people believe that our current plea bargaining system produces results that are both unfair and inaccurate. The charge of unfairness is premised upon the assertion that the offender who negotiates a "sweet deal" may receive an inappropriately lenient sentence. The "accuracy" concern rests upon the contention that the enticement to plead guilty may be so attractive that an innocent defendant will plead guilty rather than face the possibility of a false conviction at trial. While the latter hypothesis is difficult to test, some commentators assert that a significant number of legally innocent defendants are persuaded to enter pleas of guilty. On the assumption that a prosecutor's reputation may be based upon the conviction rate, sometimes a very favorable plea bargain may be offered to avoid the possibility of an acquittal. *See* Albert W. Alschuler, *The Prosecutor's Role in Plea Bargaining*, 36 U. Chi. L. Rev. 50, 59 (1968) (one prosecutor interviewed by Professor Alschuler admitted, "when we have a weak case for any reason, we'll reduce to almost anything rather than lose."). The late Professor H. Richard Uviller, while defending plea bargaining as a necessary aspect of the criminal justice system, offers a proposal for insuring fair and accurate results from the plea bargaining process. Specifically, he recommends that for each defendant, a conference should be held among opposing counsel and the presiding judge "during which the individual case is fully evaluated on its special merits and an appropriate sentence settled upon" if possible. H. Richard Uviller, VIRTUAL JUSTICE: THE FLAWED PROSECUTION OF CRIME IN AMERICA 177, 198 (1996).

[3] Disparity

Another concern about plea bargaining is that it may contribute to sentencing disparity as similar defendants receive different sentences. Evidence suggests that sentencing disparities result from differential plea bargaining rather than from real distinctions in offenders or offenses. It is well established that defendants who bargain for a plea receive lower sentences than those who are convicted at trial. For example, in 1986, among state felony defendants convicted after a trial, the average sentence was 145 months; the comparable figure for defendants who pled guilty was 72 months. Robert E. Scott & William J. Stuntz, *Plea Bargaining as Contract*, 101 YALE L.J. 1909 (1992). Similarly, defendants who plead guilty in federal court receive sentences from 25 to 75 percent lower than the sentences imposed on comparable defendants convicted at trial. Stephen J. Schulhofer, *Plea Bargaining as Disaster*, 101 YALE L.J. 1979, 1993 (1992).

As noted later in this chapter, the United States Supreme Court has held that the Constitution does not bar sentencing defendants who plead guilty to a lesser sentence than those who go to trial. *Brady v. United States*, 397 U.S. 742 (1970). Those who plead are rewarded for accepting their responsibility, saving government resources, and sparing victims and witnesses the burdens and anxieties of testifying at trial. Conversely, it is widely held that the trial court cannot penalize defendants who go to trial by giving them a longer sentence. Of course, it is difficult for some to understand how the longer sentence following a trial is not, in essence, a penalty for exercising an important constitutional right.

Consider the following recommendations of the American Bar Association:

> (a) The fact that a defendant has entered a plea of guilty . . . should not, by itself alone, be considered by the court as a mitigating factor in imposing sentence. It is proper for the court to approve or grant charge and sentence concessions to a defendant who enters a plea of guilty . . . when consistent with governing law. . . .
>
> (b) The court shall not impose upon a defendant any sentence in excess of that which would be justified by any of the protective, deterrent, or other purposes of the criminal law because the defendant has chosen to require the prosecution to prove guilt at trial rather than to enter a plea of guilty . . .

STANDARDS FOR CRIMINAL JUSTICE § 14-1.8 (3d ed. 1999).

The potential for both disparity and dishonesty is inherent in a wide-open system of plea bargaining. With respect to the crime of conviction, similarly situated offenders who have committed identical crimes may not be treated identically. They may bargain for different charges or sentences, or one may demand a trial and receive a harsher sentence than the co-defendant who pleads guilty. One commentator has characterized this aspect of plea bargaining as "willful mislabeling" which has "turned our criminal statistics into a pack of lies." John H. Langbein, *On the Myth of Written Constitutions: The Disappearance of Criminal Jury Trial*, 15 HARV. J.L. & PUB. POL'Y 119, 125 (1992) (examples cited by Professor Langbein include the person who commits murder but who is "pretended to have committed manslaughter" and the person whose "real crime" was child molesting but is convicted of loitering around a schoolyard).

On the other hand, it would be naive to believe that simply eliminating plea bargaining would cure the long-standing and well-documented sentencing disparities that have existed in state and federal courts. See Chapter 16 for a fuller discussion of the issues surrounding disparity in sentencing practices and of various efforts to reduce unwarranted disparities.

[4] Invisibility

Because plea negotiation is essentially a process that occurs in private and replaces the public trial, it is an invisible procedure that may keep information away from the public. Many commentators believe that there is a strong public interest in full, open and public inquiry and adjudication. An example frequently cited in this context is the murder plea accepted from James Earl Ray, who was charged with killing Rev. Martin Luther King, Jr. Society's interest in discovering the facts about the assassination of a public figure may arguably be frustrated by private plea discussions and the absence of a public trial. Professor Abraham Goldstein argues that the public interest in a public trial is so strong in some cases that judges should not be allowed to "deny the public [the] educative and deterrent role that attaches to a contested and visible public trial." Abraham S. Goldstein, *Converging Criminal Justice Systems: Guilty Pleas and the Public Interest*, 49 S.M.U.L. REV. 567 (1996). In these cases, if:

> the trial judge determines that the public interest requires a public airing of the facts culminating in a criminal charge, he should do one of two things: (1) he should reject the plea and insist on the prosecution putting its witnesses on record, with the defendant either challenging those witnesses or acquiescing in what they have said; or (2) if he decides to accept a guilty plea, he should follow the English practice and require a presentation, in open court, of the testimony of the principal witnesses and such stipulations of fact as make a contested trial inappropriate.

[5] Effect upon Counsel

With the realization that relatively few criminal cases go to trial, routine plea bargaining may encourage lackadaisical preparation by both prosecution and defense lawyers. Since the case will likely be settled by a plea bargain, too many lawyers wait until the eve of trial to "work up" the case. If there is no trial, they save the time they would have devoted to a full investigation of all the factual and legal issues in the case. This means that they will engage in plea negotiations without having fully explored these matters. Yet, they cannot know the strengths and weaknesses of their case without a full investigation prior to plea negotiations. To the extent that either prosecution or defense attorneys engage in this less-than-zealous representation, the possibility of an inappropriate guilty plea is heightened. In addition, defense counsel's sloppy pre-plea preparation may violate the defendant's Sixth Amendment right to effective counsel as well as the lawyer's professional obligation to provide competent legal assistance.

[6] Overcharging

The plea negotiation process can be a complicated, time consuming, give-and-take procedure. Given the high probability that a criminal charge will be bargained "down," the initial "asking price" in plea negotiations is the prosecutor's determination of the initial charges. It has been suggested that many prosecutors inflate those charges, a practice called "overcharging." Albert W. Alschuler, *The Prosecutor's Role in Plea Bargaining*, 36 U. Chi. L. Rev. 50, 85 (1968).

One way for the prosecutor to raise the ante in plea bargaining is to multiply the number of accusations against a single defendant. Professor Alschuler refers to this practice as "horizontal overcharging." *Id.* For example, the defendant alleged to have committed an armed robbery may be charged with robbery, assault, and possessing unlawful weapons; the maximum possible sentence may be in excess of 50 years in prison. The objective is to use the lengthy possible sentence to convince the defendant to plead guilty to a few of the charges in exchange for a dismissal of the others. Somewhat ironically, even where the defendant succeeds in persuading the prosecutor to dismiss some of the additional counts, very little actual benefit may be realized. This is because consecutive sentences are rare and also because the sentencing judge may take into account the dismissed charge(s) in determining the sentence.

Another prosecutorial strategy is "vertical overcharging," the practice of charging a single offense at a high level and then bargaining for a plea to a lesser included or lower offense. *Id.* at 86. Many defense attorneys believe that vertical overcharging occurs as a matter of course in homicide cases. Prosecutors defend the practice of vertical overcharging because facts and circumstances may emerge between the initial charge and trial that would warrant a finding of guilt as to the crime charged. If the initial charge is set at a level that does not adequately gauge the defendant's culpability, a guilty plea may be entered to the lower offense, with the result that an "inaccurate" judgment will have been entered. Whatever their motivations, prosecutors often charge the "highest and most" that the evidence permits. *Id.* at 88–89. *See also* Donald G. Gifford, *Meaningful Reform of Plea Bargaining: The Control of Prosecutorial Discretion*, 1983 U. Ill. L. Rev. 37, 47–49.

One may well ask the question, exactly what is overcharging? Is charging the "highest and most" really overcharging? Is it "overcharging" to bring charges at the highest level that the prosecutor in good faith believes are potentially sustainable given the facts and the law, and then let a jury sort it out if the plea bargaining process is unsuccessful? Or does overcharging consist in bringing more, or more serious charges, than the prosecutor in good faith believes can be sustained at trial? Definitions and views of overcharging may vary, but ethically, the existence of *probable cause* and a good faith assessment of "tryability" set the limit on the number and severity of charges a prosecutor may responsibly bring.

[7] The Views of Police and Crime Victims

Depending on the policies and practices of prosecutors' offices, the plea bargaining process may either include or exclude the possibility that the views of police and crime victims will be taken into consideration in the negotiation of an agreed-upon guilty plea. Views among police and crime victims also differ. Some police may see their front-line law enforcement efforts being undermined by prosecutors who they think are too eager and willing to bargain out a "good" case and accept lenient punishment. Others, especially at the administrative level, may appreciate that plea bargaining, by eliminating unnecessary trials, enables police agencies to keep their personnel "on the street" more and tied up in court less.

Similarly, some crime victims see a trial as part of their own healing process and their opportunity to confront the person who injured them and to affect the outcome of the case. Such victims may feel excluded by a plea bargaining process that does not take seek their views prior to disposition. Others, in contrast, may appreciate being spared by a guilty plea from having to undergo the rigors and sometimes the re-inflicted trauma of the crime that can result from having to testify and undergo cross examination at trial. Many prosecutors' offices now have victims' assistance units, which not only provide victims with access to therapeutic services, but also operate to ensure that victims' views are heard and taken appropriately into consideration in the plea bargaining process.

[8] Plea Bargaining Seen as Furthering Justice

In addition to the utilitarian justifications for plea bargaining mentioned in the preceding discussion (conserving limited police, judicial, prosecution, and defense resources, and sparing victims the potential trauma of having to testify at trial and pretrial proceedings and being confronted again by those who injured them), plea bargaining is also sometimes seen as a means to achieve justice while protecting the rights and interests of all concerned. *See Bordenkircher v. Hayes*, 434 U.S. 357, 361–362 (1978) (discussed later in this chapter) ("[T]he guilty plea and the often concomitant plea bargain are important components of this country's criminal justice system. Properly administered, they can benefit all concerned."); *Id.* at 372 (Powell,

J., dissenting) ("The plea-bargaining process. . . . normally affords genuine benefits to defendants as well as to society.").

For an interesting refutation of plea bargaining criticisms, especially the notion that it coerces unacceptable numbers of innocent defendants to plead guilty, *see* Michael Young, *In Defense of Plea-Bargaining's Possible Morality*, 40 OHIO N. L. REV. 251 (2013). Based on data from the Innocence Project (see Chapter 17 discussion of Actual Innocence), the rate of "innocent conviction" is no worse for defendants who plead guilty than for those convicted after a jury trial, i.e., there is no "innocence problem" inherent in plea bargaining, compared with jury trials. In contrast, *see* William Ortman, *Probable Cause Revisited*, 68 STAN. L. REV. 551 (2016), positing that there *is* an innocence problem inherent in plea bargaining that is exacerbated by what the author believes to be an unduly low (and historically wrong) standard for determining probable cause in grand jury decisions to indict, or in prosecutors' decisions to initiate felony charges by filing an "information" (see Chapter 7 for fuller discussion).

Implicit in the assumption of Justice Stewart and the *Bordenkircher* majority that the plea bargaining process is being "properly administered," is the notion that the adversary system is functioning properly—with fair and competent judges, prosecutors, and defenders. Experienced and conscientious practitioners have a good sense of the "market value" range of reasonable outcomes for a given offense considered in light of the defendant's personal background and prior criminal history. According to this "market value" view, the plea negotiation process in a properly functioning adversary system appropriately takes into account the relative strengths and weaknesses of the prosecution and defense cases, and results in outcomes that, on the whole, do justice to defendants, victims, and society.

Of course, this idealized notion of the adversary system can (and sometimes does) tend to break down in the real world, as observed by some of the skeptics of plea bargaining cited above. Therefore, federal and state rules have been developed (*see, especially*, Federal Rule of Criminal Procedure 11's detailed procedural requirements, emulated by many states) which are aimed at "policing" the system to provide the greatest possible degree of procedural fairness and transparency to the processes and the outcomes of plea bargaining.

Procedural justice. Social psychology research has established that a fair process may matter as much to the acceptance of a legal decision as does the substance of the decision. *See generally* Michael M. O'Hear, *Plea Bargaining and Procedural Justice*, 42 GA. L. REV. 407 (2008). Thus, a litigant—for example, a criminal defendant—may be willing to accept a decision that is perceived to be *substantively* unjust if the decisionmaker acted in a way that was seen as *procedurally* just. Moreover, the research suggests that perceptions of procedural justice can contribute more generally to a person's respect for the law and the legal system. Is this something that prosecutors should think about during plea negotiations? If so, how might prosecutors best assure that defendants perceive the plea bargaining process to be fair? Note that a layperson's sense of what makes for a fair process might not correspond exactly with what lawyers mean by "due process." The social psychology research has identified four factors that can be important to lay perceptions of procedural justice: the people who are affected by a decision (for instance, the prosecutor's decision about what plea offer to make) should have an opportunity to tell their side of the story before the decision is rendered; the decisionmaker should be unbiased, honest, and principled; the decisionmaker should actually consider the input offered by others; and the decisionmaker should exhibit basic courtesy to others. Of course, judges normally try to adhere to these ideals, but, as prosecutors have gained more power over sentencing outcomes through their plea bargaining decisions, it is perhaps increasingly important for prosecutors also to attend to procedural justice.

E. Plea Bargaining: Constitutional Issues

[1] Introduction

It may be surprising to know that plea bargaining was not officially "discovered" until about 1921. Before that time there were no records in existence to document the extent to which plea bargaining was occurring in either state or federal cases. Indeed, some of the early nineteenth-century cases suggest that any inducement to secure a guilty plea from the accused was prohibited. One author has concluded that "early American decisions exhibited judicial disdain for plea bargaining." Jay Wishingrad, *The Plea Bargain in Historical Perspective*, 23 BUFF. L. REV. 499, 525 (1974). Professor George Fisher, on the other hand, describes plea bargaining in the nineteenth century, observing that "individual prosecutors [at that time] found a personal and political advantage in securing the easy victories that plea bargaining afforded. [P]rosecutors may have believed that the more clandestinely they could secure those victories, the better." George Fisher, *Plea Bargaining's Triumph*, 109 YALE L.J. 857, 935–36 (2000).

Nonetheless, it is widely believed that various forms of plea bargaining were practiced long before the adoption of statutes and rules explicitly sanctioning the plea negotiation process. We can speculate, however, that, due to the fear that judges would not accept guilty pleas resulting from the negotiation process, prosecutors, defense attorneys, and defendants routinely may have withheld information about their deals from the judges (or perhaps, in some cases, flatly misrepresented the truth) in order to secure judicial acceptance of negotiated pleas.

In recent years, however, plea bargaining has "come out of the closet" as a recognized facet of the American criminal justice system. To some extent, this recognition is the product of judicial decisions that have "constitutionalized" some of the procedures involved in guilty pleas. Once guilty pleas became subject to judicial scrutiny, it was no longer possible to pretend that they did not exist or to downplay their prevalence and importance. In the 1970s, the Supreme Court, somewhat belatedly, came to acknowledge not only the existence of plea bargaining, but also its central role in the criminal justice system, and the need to assure that plea bargaining procedures do not bargain away fundamental fairness. *See, e.g., Santobello v. New York*, 404 U.S. 257 (1971); *Blackledge v. Allison*, 431 U.S. 63 (1977).

[2] Does Plea Bargaining Impermissibly Burden the Exercise of the Constitutional Right to Trial by Jury?

Despite having had several possible occasions on which to hold the plea bargaining system unconstitutional, the Supreme Court has not come close to doing so, as the following cases illustrate.

In *United States v. Jackson*, 390 U.S. 570 (1968), three defendants were indicted by a federal grand jury and charged with kidnapping under the Federal Kidnapping Act, which provided:

> whoever knowingly transports in interstate . . . commerce, any person who has unlawfully . . . kidnapped . . . and held for ransom . . . shall be punished (1) by death if the kidnapped person has not been liberated unharmed, and if the verdict of the jury shall so recommend, or (2) by imprisonment for any term of years or for life, if the death penalty is not imposed.

Because the statute authorized the death penalty only if a *jury* so recommended, this allowed a defendant to avoid the death penalty by waiving a jury trial and facing the possibility of a conviction after a bench trial or a guilty plea. The Supreme Court held that this death penalty provision imposed an impermissible burden on the exercise of the defendant's constitutional right to trial by jury. Therefore, the Court invalidated the death penalty provision in the kidnapping statute, but also held it severable from the rest of the statute. Accordingly, the Court ruled that Jackson could be retried under the kidnapping statute but not put to death if convicted on retrial. Justice Stewart explained:

> Under the Federal Kidnapping Act . . . the defendant who abandons the right to contest his guilt before a jury is assured that he cannot be executed; the defendant ingenious enough to seek a jury acquittal stands forewarned that, if the jury finds him guilty and does not wish to spare his life, he will die. . . . The inevitable effect of any such provision, is of course, to discourage assertion of the Fifth Amendment right not to plead guilty and to deter exercise of the Sixth Amendment right to demand a jury trial. If the provision had no other purpose or effect than to chill the assertion of constitutional rights by penalizing those who choose to exercise them, then it would be patently unconstitutional.

Id. at 581.

Jackson left open at least the possibility that plea bargaining may unconstitutionally chill or penalize a defendant's exercise of the right to trial by jury, insofar as a prosecutor's plea offer may discourage the accused from asserting that right (because of the real or perceived likelihood of a more severe sentence if the defendant rejects the plea offer and goes to trial). Such a claim was presented squarely to the Supreme Court two years later.

Brady v. United States

397 U.S. 742 (1970)

Mr. Justice White delivered the opinion of the Court.

In 1959, petitioner was charged with kidnaping in violation of 18 U.S.C. § 1201(a) [the statute quoted above]. Since the indictment charged that the victim of the kidnaping was not liberated unharmed, petitioner faced a maximum penalty of death if the verdict of the jury should so recommend. Petitioner, represented by competent counsel throughout, first elected to plead not guilty. Apparently because the trial judge was unwilling to try the case without a jury, petitioner made no serious attempt to reduce the possibility of a death penalty by waiving a jury trial. Upon learning that his codefendant, who had confessed to the authorities, would plead guilty and be available to testify against him, petitioner changed his plea to guilty. His plea was accepted after the trial judge twice questioned him as to the voluntariness of his plea. Petitioner was sentenced to 50 years' imprisonment, later reduced to 30.

In 1967, petitioner sought relief . . . claiming that his plea of guilty was not voluntarily given because § 1201(a) operated to coerce his plea, because his counsel exerted impermissible pressure upon him, and because his plea was induced by representations with respect to reduction of sentence and clemency. . . . [The District Court and Court of Appeals denied relief.] . . .

We granted certiorari to consider the claim that the Court of Appeals was in error in not reaching a contrary result on the authority of this Court's decision in *United States v. Jackson*, 390 U.S. 570 (1968). We affirm.

. . . Brady contends that *Jackson* requires the invalidation of every plea of guilty entered under that section, at least when the fear of death is shown to have been a factor in the plea. Petitioner, however, has read far too much into the *Jackson* opinion.

The Court made it clear in *Jackson* that it was not holding § 1201(a) inherently coercive of guilty pleas: "the fact that the Federal Kidnaping Act tends to discourage defendants from insisting upon their innocence and demanding trial by jury hardly implies that every defendant who enters a guilty plea to a charge under the Act does so involuntarily."

. . . Plainly, it seems to us, *Jackson* ruled neither that all pleas of guilty encouraged by the fear of a possible death sentence are involuntary pleas nor that such encouraged pleas are invalid whether involuntary or not. *Jackson* prohibits the imposition of the death penalty under § 1201(a), but that decision neither fashioned a new standard for judging the validity of guilty pleas nor mandated a new application of the test theretofore fashioned by courts and since reiterated that guilty pleas are valid if both "voluntary" and "intelligent."

. . . Central to the plea and the foundation for entering judgment against the defendant is the defendant's admission in open court that he committed the acts charged in the indictment. He thus stands as a witness against himself and he is shielded by the Fifth Amendment from being compelled to do so—hence the minimum requirement that his plea be the voluntary expression of his own choice. But the plea is more than an admission of past conduct; it is the defendant's consent that judgment of conviction may be entered without a trial—a waiver of his right to trial before a jury or a judge. Waivers of constitutional rights not only must be voluntary but must be knowing, intelligent acts done with sufficient awareness of the relevant circumstances and likely consequences. On neither score was Brady's plea of guilty invalid.

... Petitioner, advised by competent counsel, tendered his plea after his codefendant, who had already given a confession, determined to plead guilty and became available to testify against petitioner. It was this development that the District Court found to have triggered Brady's guilty plea.

... The record before us also supports the conclusion that Brady's plea was intelligently made. He was advised by competent counsel, he was made aware of the nature of the charge against him, and there was nothing to indicate that he was incompetent or otherwise not in control of his mental faculties; once his confederate had pleaded guilty and became available to testify, he chose to plead guilty, perhaps to ensure that he would face no more than life imprisonment or a term of years. Brady was aware of precisely what he was doing when he admitted that he had kidnaped the victim and had not released her unharmed.

It is true that Brady's counsel advised him that § 1201(a) empowered the jury to impose the death penalty and that nine years later in *United States v. Jackson*, the Court held that the jury had no such power as long as the judge could impose only a lesser penalty if trial was to the court or there was a plea of guilty. But these facts do not require us to set aside Brady's conviction.

Often the decision to plead guilty is heavily influenced by the defendant's appraisal of the prosecution's case against him and by the apparent likelihood of securing leniency should a guilty plea be offered and accepted. Considerations like these frequently present imponderable questions for which there are no certain answers; judgments may be made that in the light of later events seem improvident, although they were perfectly sensible at the time. The rule that a plea must be intelligently made to be valid does not require that a plea be vulnerable to later attack if the defendant did not correctly assess every relevant factor entering into his decision. A defendant is not entitled to withdraw his plea merely because he discovers long after the plea has been accepted that his calculus misapprehended the quality of the State's case or the likely penalties attached to alternative courses of action.... A plea of guilty triggered by the expectations of a competently counseled defendant that the State will have a strong case against him is not subject to later attack because the defendant's lawyer correctly advised him with respect to the then existing law as to possible penalties but later pronouncements of the courts, as in this case, hold that the maximum penalty for the crime in question was less than was reasonably assumed at the time the plea was entered.

... Although Brady's plea of guilty may well have been motivated in part by a desire to avoid a possible death penalty, we are convinced that his plea was voluntarily and intelligently made and we have no reason to doubt that his solemn admission of guilt was truthful. Affirmed.

Notes

1. *Brady's contemporary: Parker.* In *Parker v. North Carolina*, 397 U.S. 790 (1970), decided the same day as *Brady*, the United States Supreme Court followed the *Brady* analysis. Parker pled guilty to burglary in the first degree. Under the then-applicable North Carolina statute, the maximum penalty available in the event of a plea of guilty was life imprisonment, whereas the death penalty could have been imposed had he elected to contest the criminal charge. Parker also claimed that his guilty plea was invalid because it was the product of a coerced confession he had given to the police shortly after his arrest. This claim was rejected because "even if Parker's counsel was wrong in his assessment ... [that Parker's confession was admissible in a trial], it does not follow that his error was sufficient to render the plea unintelligent and entitle Parker to disavow his admission in open court that he committed the offense with which he was charged." After assessing the facts related to Parker's confession and guilty plea, the Court concluded that the lawyer's advice to Parker "was well within the range of competence required of attorneys representing defendants in criminal cases."

Justice Brennan, joined by Justices Douglas and Marshall, dissented in *Parker.* In their opinion, Parker would be entitled to relief "if he can demonstrate that the unconstitutional capital punishment scheme was a significant factor in his decision to plead guilty." The same Justices concurred in *Brady*, however, because of the findings made below that his decision to plead guilty rested upon bases other than the Kidnapping Act.

2. *Unconstitutional conditions.* The concept of "unconstitutional conditions" has been described as prohibiting the government from conditioning the grant of a benefit on the recipient's willingness to forego the exercise of a constitutional right. It has been suggested that the plea bargaining process unlawfully coerces defendants to surrender important constitutional rights in exchange for sentencing leniency, and that judges routinely and unconstitutionally impose significantly harsher sentences on convicted defendants who go to trial than on those who plead guilty (the so-called "trial penalty"), but these arguments have not found judicial acceptance. For a thoughtful analysis of this issue, see Thomas R. McCoy & Michael J. Mirra, *Plea Bargaining as Due Process in Determining Guilt*, 32 Stan. L. Rev. 887 (1980).

[3] Plea Bargaining and Competent Counsel

In *Brady*, the United States Supreme Court emphasized that the defense attorney in that case had met the standard of competent counsel. The question of an attorney's effective representation in the context of plea bargaining also was addressed in *McMann v. Richardson*, 397 U.S. 759 (1970). The defendant there challenged his guilty plea in a collateral proceeding by asserting that the plea had been motivated by a prior coerced confession. Finding that the plea of guilty was not open to such attack, the United States Supreme Court emphasized that the plea had been tendered after an assessment of the case by the defendant's attorney. Therefore, the question whether the plea was subject to attack depends upon ". . . whether that advice was within the range of competence demanded of attorneys in criminal cases." Whether the petitioner's attorney met that standard, however, was left "to the good sense and discretion of the trial courts with the admonition . . . that judges should strive to maintain proper standards of performance by attorneys."

Not until 1984, in *Strickland v. Washington*, 466 U.S. 668 (1984), did the United States Supreme Court establish the constitutional standard for judging claims of attorney incompetency. The following year, in the excerpted case below, the Court evaluated the application of *Strickland* to the guilty plea process.

Hill v. Lockhart

474 U.S. 52 (1985)

Justice Rehnquist delivered the opinion of the Court.

Petitioner William Lloyd Hill pleaded guilty in the Arkansas trial court to charges of first-degree murder and theft of property. More than two years later he sought federal habeas relief on the ground that his court-appointed attorney had failed to advise him that, as a second offender, he was required to serve one-half of his sentence before becoming eligible for parole. [The District Court and Court of Appeals denied relief.]

. . . . We affirm the judgment of the Court of Appeals for the Eighth Circuit because we conclude that petitioner failed to allege the kind of prejudice from the allegedly incompetent advice of counsel that would have entitled him to a hearing.

. . . Our concern in *McMann v. Richardson*, 397 U.S. 759 (1970), with the quality of counsel's performance in advising a defendant whether to plead guilty stemmed from the more general principle that all "defendants facing felony charges are entitled to the effective assistance of competent counsel." Two Terms ago, in *Strickland v. Washington*, 466 U.S. 668 (1984), we adopted a two-part standard for evaluating claims of ineffective assistance of counsel. There, citing *McMann*, we reiterated that "[w]hen a convicted defendant complains of the ineffectiveness of counsel's assistance, the defendant must show that counsel's representation fell below an objective standard of reasonableness." We also held, however, that "[t]he defendant must show that there is a reasonable probability that, but for counsel's unprofessional errors, the result of the proceeding would have been different." This additional "prejudice" requirement was based on our conclusion that "[a]n error by counsel, even if professionally unreasonable, does not warrant setting aside the judgment of a criminal proceeding if the error had no effect on the judgment."

Although our decision in *Strickland v. Washington* dealt with a claim of ineffective assistance of counsel in a capital sentencing proceeding, and was premised in part on the similarity between such a proceeding and the usual criminal trial, the same two-part standard seems to us applicable to ineffective-assistance claims arising out of the plea process. Certainly our justifications for imposing the "prejudice" requirement in *Strickland v. Washington* are also relevant in the context of guilty pleas:

> The government is not responsible for, and hence not able to prevent, attorney errors that will result in reversal of a conviction or sentence. Attorney errors come in an infinite variety and are as likely to be utterly harmless in a particular case as they are to be prejudicial. They cannot be classified according to likelihood of causing prejudice. Nor can they be defined with sufficient precision to inform defense attorneys correctly just what conduct to avoid. Representation is an art, and an act or omission that is unprofessional in one case may be sound or even brilliant in another. Even if a defendant shows that particular errors of counsel were unreasonable, therefore, the defendant must show that they actually had an adverse effect on the defense.

In addition, we believe that requiring a showing of "prejudice" from defendants who seek to challenge the validity of their guilty pleas on the ground of ineffective assistance of counsel will serve the fundamental interest in the finality of guilty pleas we identified in *United States v. Timmreck*, 441 U.S. 780 (1979):

> Every inroad on the concept of finality undermines confidence in the integrity of our procedures; and, by increasing the volume of judicial work, inevitably delays and impairs the orderly administration of justice. The impact is greatest when new grounds for setting aside guilty pleas are approved because the vast majority of criminal convictions result from such pleas. Moreover, the concern that unfair procedures may have resulted in the conviction of an innocent defendant is only rarely raised by a petition to set aside a guilty plea.

We hold, therefore, that the two-part *Strickland v. Washington* test applies to challenges to guilty pleas based on ineffective assistance of counsel. In the context of guilty pleas, the first half of the *Strickland v. Washington* test is nothing more than a restatement of the standard of attorney competence already set forth in *Tollett v. Henderson* 411 U.S. 258 (1973), and *McMann v. Richardson*. The second, or "prejudice," requirement, on the other hand, focuses on whether counsel's constitutionally ineffective performance affected the outcome of the plea process. In other words, in order to satisfy the "prejudice" requirement, the defendant must show that there is a reasonable probability that, but for counsel's errors, he would not have pleaded guilty and would have insisted on going to trial.

In many guilty plea cases, the "prejudice" inquiry will closely resemble the inquiry engaged in by courts reviewing ineffective-assistance challenges to convictions obtained through a trial. For example, where the alleged error of counsel is a failure to investigate or discover potentially exculpatory evidence, the determination whether the error "prejudiced" the defendant by causing him to plead guilty rather than go to trial will depend on the likelihood that discovery of the evidence would have led counsel to change his recommendation as to the plea. This assessment, in turn, will depend in large part on a prediction whether the evidence likely would have changed the outcome of a trial.

... In the present case the claimed error of counsel is erroneous advice as to eligibility for parole under the sentence agreed to in the plea bargain. We find it unnecessary to determine whether there may be circumstances under which erroneous advice by counsel as to parole eligibility may be deemed constitutionally ineffective assistance of counsel, because in the present case we conclude that petitioner's allegations are insufficient to satisfy the *Strickland v. Washington* requirement of "prejudice." Petitioner did not allege in his habeas petition that, had counsel correctly informed him about his parole eligibility date, he would have pleaded not guilty and insisted on going to trial. He alleged no special circumstances that might support the conclusion that he placed particular emphasis on his parole eligibility in deciding whether or not to plead guilty. Indeed, petitioner's mistaken belief that he would become eligible for parole after serving one-third of his sentence would seem to have affected not only his calculation of the time he likely would serve if sentenced pursuant to the proposed plea agreement, but also his calculation of the time he likely would serve if he went to trial and were convicted.

Because petitioner in this case failed to allege the kind of "prejudice" necessary to satisfy the second half of the *Strickland v. Washington* test, the District Court did not err in declining to hold a hearing on petitioner's ineffective assistance of counsel claim. The judgment of the Court of Appeals is therefore affirmed.

[The concurring opinion of JUSTICE WHITE, joined by JUSTICE STEVENS, is omitted.]

Notes

1. *Counsel's questionable recommendations.* Most cases involving competency of counsel in the plea bargaining context concern attorneys who recommended acceptance of a plea bargain in the face of facts indicating either (1) the bargain was not especially favorable to the accused or (2) the case should have proceeded to trial on the merits. How would (or should) a reviewing court ascertain whether defense counsel has rendered competent assistance under the *Lockhart* standard?

In *Lee v. United States,* 137 S. Ct. 1958 (2017), the defendant, a native of South Korea, had lived in the United States for 35 years as a lawful permanent resident. After being indicted for drug possession, his attorney repeatedly assured him that he would not face deportation if he pled guilty. Contrary to his attorney's advice, however, Lee's guilty plea made him subject to mandatory deportation under the federal Immigration and Nationality Act. Lee moved to vacate the conviction, asserting that his attorney had provided ineffective assistance. Both attorney and client testified at a hearing on his motion that deportation was the determinative issue in Lee's decision to plead guilty. Lee stated that he would have rejected any plea leading to deportation and gone to trial instead.

Following *Lockhart*, the Court held that the defendant had established a reasonable probability that he would have rejected the plea had he known that it would lead to mandatory deportation and remanded for further proceedings, thus giving Lee the opportunity to show, under both prongs of *Strickland*, that his attorney's erroneous advice violated the his Sixth Amendment right to effective assistance. *Id.* at 1969. As to the argument of dissenting Justice Thomas, that Lee should be denied relief because he had no viable defense to his drug possession charge and therefore could not demonstrate prejudice under *Strickland*, Chief Justice Roberts' majority opinion found demonstrable prejudice from the fact that Lee's ill-counseled guilty plea had subjected him to the *certainty* of deportation, whereas going to trial and improbably seeking an acquittal (described by the Chief Justice as "throwing a 'Hail Mary'") might have given him at least a slim *possibility* of avoiding deportation. *Id.* at 1967. Does the result in *Lee* suggest that challenging guilty pleas by attacking the competency of counsel's advice might be less of a "Hail Mary" than previously thought?

2. *Types of ineffective assistance claims.* One commentator has noted that ineffective assistance of counsel claims in the plea bargaining context can be categorized as follows: (1) the attorney failed to inform the defendant of the plea offer altogether; (2) the attorney offered no advice regarding the wisdom of accepting or rejecting the plea; (3) inaccurate information was provided by the lawyer; or (4) the attorney coerced the defendant into either accepting or rejecting a plea offer. This commentator urges attorneys to adopt a client-centered counseling strategy, whereby they are obligated to listen to their client and ensure that the client assumes an active and primary role in making decisions about their case. *See* Steven Zeidman, *To Plead or Not to Plead: Effective Assistance and Client-Centered Counseling*, 39 B.C.L. Rev. 841 (1998). Courts tend, however, to look very skeptically at well-worn after-the-fact ineffective assistance claims by remorseful defendants that "my lawyer made me do it."

3. *Advice regarding collateral consequences of a guilty plea.* In an earlier case with facts strikingly similar to *Lee v. United States*, the Supreme Court in *Padilla v. Kentucky*, 559 U.S. 356 (2010), held the *Strickland* ineffective assistance standard applicable to claims of counsel's failure to properly advise a client that pleading guilty would render him subject to mandatory deportation. In that case, counsel allegedly advised Padilla, a lawful permanent resident of the United States for more than 40 years who had served honorably with the U.S. Armed Forces in Vietnam, that he did not have to worry about the effect of pleading guilty to drug transportation charges on his immigration status "since he had been in the country for so long." In fact, the Court found, pleading guilty to the drug offense made Padilla's deportation "virtually mandatory" under existing immigration law.

Accepting Padilla's averments as true, the Court found a duty to correctly advise one's client where, as here, the removal consequences of a plea of guilty are "truly clear." Counsel's erroneous advice, under the facts alleged, met the first (deficient performance) prong of *Strickland*, and the Court remanded for a determination of whether Padilla can meet the second prong (resulting prejudice). The Court reasoned that any competent attorney, even one who is not schooled in the complexities of immigration law, could have easily learned of the deportation consequence by simply reading the text of the applicable statute. However, in cases where the deportation consequences of a particular plea are "unclear or uncertain," the Court stated in *dicta* that defense counsel "need do no more than advise a noncitizen client that pending criminal charges may carry a risk of adverse immigration consequences."

Relying on *Padilla*, the Eleventh Circuit reached a similar conclusion in *Bauder v. Dep't. of Corrections*, 619 F.3d 1272 (11th Cir. 2010), with respect to a claim by a habeas corpus petitioner that his attorney's erroneous advice, that his plea of guilty to a charge of stalking could not be the basis for a later civil commitment as a sexually violent predator, amounted to ineffective assistance of counsel that would void his guilty plea. The court affirmed the conclusion of the court below, that counsel's "affirmative misadvice" regarding this particular collateral consequence of Bauder's guilty plea was adequate grounds for habeas relief.

In both *Padilla* and *Bauder*, the collateral consequences (deportation and civil commitment as a sexually violent predator, respectively) were, as the Supreme Court stated in *Padilla*, "close[ly] connect[ed] to the criminal process." Can you think of other kinds of collateral consequences of a guilty plea as to which courts might be likely to make exceptions to the general rule that a defendant need not be advised in advance of the collateral consequences of pleading guilty? *See, e.g., Calvert v. State*, 342 S.W.3d 477 (Tenn. 2011) (counsel's failure to advise defendant that his contemplated plea of guilty to violent sexual felony charges would subject him to mandatory lifetime community supervision held to be deficient performance, and ineffective assistance of counsel, under the two-pronged *Strickland* standard); *Webb v. State*, 334 S.W.3d 126 (Mo. 2011) (defendant claimed counsel erroneously advised him prior to guilty plea that he would be eligible for parole after serving 40% of contemplated sentence, whereas correct percentage was actually 85%; held, defendant entitled to evidentiary hearing on claim of ineffective assistance). What about possible termination of parental rights as a consequence of a guilty plea? *See* Note, *Ensuring Effective Counsel for Parents: Extending* Padilla *to Termination of Parental Rights Proceedings*, 42 Hofstra L. Rev. 303 (2013).

4. Padilla *held not retroactive.* In *Chaidez v. U.S.*, 568 U.S. 342 (2013), the Supreme Court held that *Padilla* is not to be applied retroactively—i.e., only defendants whose ineffective assistance claims arose after *Padilla* was decided may benefit from that decision. Principles of retroactivity are discussed below in Chapter 17.

5. *Advice concerning appeal.* As discussed in Chapter 17, defense attorneys are strongly advised to consult with the defendant after conviction regarding the possibility of pursuing an appeal. If counsel fails to follow the defendant's instructions with respect to an appeal by failing to file a notice of appeal, then counsel performs in a professionally unreasonable manner, as the Supreme Court held in *Roe v. Flores-Ortega*, 528 U.S. 470 (2000) (applying *Strickland v. Washington* to such a claim). Must a defense attorney consult with his or her client about an appeal, as a constitutional matter, in *every* case? Not according to the Court in *Flores-Ortega*. That duty exists only when counsel has reason to think that his or her client has reasonably demonstrated an interest in appealing or that a rational defendant would want to appeal. The court noted, however, that it would be "highly relevant" to that inquiry as to whether the conviction followed trial or a guilty plea:

> [This is important, although not determinative,] both because a guilty plea reduces the scope of potentially appealable issues and because such a plea may indicate that the defendant seeks an end to judicial proceedings. Even in cases when the defendant pleads guilty, the court must consider such factors as whether the defendant received the sentence bargained for as a part of the plea and whether the plea expressly reserved or waived some or all appeal rights.

Id. at 1036.

Justice Ginsburg, who concurred in part and dissented in part, noted that after a defendant pleads guilty or is convicted, the Sixth Amendment "hardly ever" permits defense counsel to walk away, leaving the defendant uncounseled about his or her appeal rights.

6. *Showing prejudice.* Although the Court in *Lockhart* determined that the petitioner had failed, under the facts he alleged, to establish prejudice under the second prong of the *Strickland* test, the opinion of the Court, per Justice Rehnquist, finds that the right to effective assistance of counsel is "also relevant in the context of guilty pleas." In the following two companion cases from 2012, a sharply divided Court determined that the defendants had shown the required *Strickland/Lockhart* prejudice where, in one case, defense counsel failed to inform the defendant of the prosecutor's advantageous plea offer, and in the other case, defense counsel had misadvised the defendant to reject a favorable plea offer based on counsel's undisputedly erroneous assessment that the evidence was insufficient to convict him of assault with intent to murder. The fundamental split among the Justices in these significant cases revolves around the question of whether a properly conducted trial, free of reversible error, renders irrelevant any alleged prejudice to the defendant as a result of counsel's deficient assistance during the course of plea negotiations.

Lafler v. Cooper

566 U. S. 156 (2012)

Justice Kennedy delivered the opinion of the Court.

. . . Here, the favorable plea offer was reported to the client but, on advice of counsel, was rejected. . . . [A]fter the plea offer had been rejected, there was a full and fair trial before a jury. After a guilty verdict, the defendant received a sentence harsher than that offered in the rejected plea bargain. The instant case comes to the Court with the concession that counsel's advice with respect to the plea offer fell below the standard of adequate assistance of counsel guaranteed by the Sixth Amendment,. . . .

I

On the evening of March 25, 2003, respondent pointed a gun toward Kali Mundy's head and fired. From the record, it is unclear why respondent did this, and at trial it was suggested that he might have acted either in self-defense or in defense of another person. In any event the shot missed and Mundy fled. Respondent followed in pursuit, firing repeatedly. Mundy was shot in her buttock, hip, and abdomen but survived the assault.

Respondent was charged under Michigan law with assault with intent to murder, possession of a firearm by a felon, possession of a firearm in the commission of a felony, misdemeanor possession of marijuana, and for being a habitual offender. On two occasions, the prosecution offered to dismiss two of the charges and to recommend a sentence of 51 to 85 months for the other two, in exchange for a guilty plea. In a communication with the court respondent admitted guilt and expressed a willingness to accept the offer. Respondent, however, later rejected the offer on both occasions, allegedly after his attorney convinced him that the prosecution would be unable to establish his intent to murder Mundy because she had been shot below the waist. On the first day of trial the prosecution offered a significantly less favorable plea deal, which respondent again rejected. After trial, respondent was convicted on all counts and received a mandatory minimum sentence of 185 to 360 months' imprisonment.

[R]espondent argued his attorney's advice to reject the plea constituted ineffective assistance. The trial judge rejected the claim, and the Michigan Court of Appeals . . . rejected the claim of ineffective assistance of counsel on the ground that respondent knowingly and intelligently rejected two plea offers and chose to go to trial. The Michigan Supreme Court denied respondent's application for leave to file an appeal.

Respondent then filed a petition for federal habeas relief, [and] the District Court granted a conditional writ. To remedy the violation, the District Court ordered "specific performance of [respondent's] original plea agreement, for a minimum sentence in the range of fifty-one to eighty-five months."

The United States Court of Appeals for the Sixth Circuit affirmed, [and we] granted certiorari.

II

A

. . . In this case all parties agree the performance of respondent's counsel was deficient when he advised respondent to reject the plea offer on the grounds he could not be convicted at trial. In light of this concession, it is unnecessary for this Court to explore the issue.

The question for this Court is how to apply [*Strickland v. Washington*'s] prejudice test where ineffective assistance results in a rejection of the plea offer and the defendant is convicted at the ensuing trial.

B

. . . [Respondent] maintains that, absent ineffective counsel, he would have accepted a plea offer for a sentence the prosecution evidently deemed consistent with the sound administration of criminal justice. The favorable sentence that eluded the defendant in the criminal proceeding appears to be the sentence he or others in his position would have received in the ordinary course, absent the failings of counsel. If a plea bargain has been offered, a defendant has the right to effective assistance of counsel in considering whether to accept it. If that right is denied, prejudice can be shown if loss of the plea opportunity led to a trial resulting in a conviction on more serious charges or the imposition of a more severe sentence.

. . . [H]ere the question is not the fairness or reliability of the trial but the fairness and regularity of the processes that preceded it, which caused the defendant to lose benefits he would have received in the ordinary course but for counsel's ineffective assistance.

. . . The fact that respondent is guilty does not mean he was not entitled by the Sixth Amendment to effective assistance or that he suffered no prejudice from his attorney's deficient performance during plea bargaining.

. . . [P]etitioner's . . . arguments amount to one general contention: a fair trial wipes clean any deficient performance by defense counsel during plea bargaining. That position ignores the reality that criminal justice today is for the most part a system of pleas, not a system of trials. Ninety-seven percent of federal convictions and ninety-four percent of state convictions are the result of guilty pleas. . . .

C

Even if a defendant shows ineffective assistance of counsel has caused the rejection of a plea leading to a trial and a more severe sentence, there is the question of what constitutes an appropriate remedy. That question must now be addressed.

. . . The specific injury suffered by defendants who decline a plea offer as a result of ineffective assistance of counsel and then receive a greater sentence as a result of trial can come in at least one of two forms. In some cases, the sole advantage a defendant would have received under the plea is a lesser sentence. This is typically the case when the charges that would have been admitted as part of the plea bargain are the same as the charges the defendant was convicted of after trial. In this situation the court may conduct an evidentiary hearing to determine whether the defendant has shown a reasonable probability that but for counsel's errors he would have accepted the plea. If the showing is made, the court may exercise discretion in determining whether the defendant should receive the term of imprisonment the government offered in the plea, the sentence he received at trial, or something in between.

In some situations it may be that resentencing alone will not be full redress for the constitutional injury. If, for example, an offer was for a guilty plea to a count or counts less serious than the ones for which a defendant was convicted after trial, or if a mandatory sentence confines a judge's sentencing discretion after trial, a resentencing based on the conviction at trial may not suffice. In these circumstances, the proper exercise of discretion to remedy the constitutional injury may be to require the prosecution to reoffer the plea proposal. Once this has occurred, the judge can then exercise discretion in deciding whether to vacate the conviction from trial and accept the plea or leave the conviction undisturbed.

In implementing a remedy in both of these situations, the trial court must weigh various factors; and the boundaries of proper discretion need not be defined here. Principles elaborated over time in decisions of state and federal courts, and in statutes and rules, will serve to give more complete guidance as to the factors that should bear upon the exercise of the judge's discretion. At this point, however, it suffices to note two considerations that are of relevance.

First, a court may take account of a defendant's earlier expressed willingness, or unwillingness, to accept responsibility for his or her actions. Second, it is not necessary here to decide as a constitutional rule that a judge is required to prescind (that is to say disregard) any information concerning the crime that was discovered after the plea offer was made. The time continuum makes it difficult to restore the defendant and the prosecution to the precise positions they occupied prior to the rejection of the plea offer, but that baseline can be consulted in finding a remedy that does not require the prosecution to incur the expense of conducting a new trial.

Petitioner argues that implementing a remedy here will open the floodgates to litigation by defendants seeking to unsettle their convictions. Petitioner's concern is misplaced. Courts have recognized claims of this sort for over 30 years, and yet there is no indication that the system is overwhelmed by these types of suits or that defendants are receiving windfalls as a result of strategically timed *Strickland* claims. In addition, the "prosecution and the trial courts may adopt some measures to help ensure against late, frivolous, or fabricated claims after a later, less advantageous plea offer has been accepted or after a trial leading to conviction." *Missouri v. Frye*. . . .

III

Respondent has satisfied *Strickland*'s two-part test. Regarding performance, . . . the fact of deficient performance has been conceded by all parties. The case comes to us on that assumption, so there is no need to address this question.

As to prejudice, respondent has shown that but for counsel's deficient performance there is a reasonable probability he and the trial court would have accepted the guilty plea. In addition, as a result of not accepting the plea and being convicted at trial, respondent received a minimum sentence 3 1/2 times greater than he would have received under the plea. The standard for ineffective assistance under *Strickland* has thus been satisfied.

As a remedy, the District Court ordered specific performance of the original plea agreement. The correct remedy in these circumstances, however, is to order the State to reoffer the plea agreement. Presuming respondent accepts the offer, the state trial court can then exercise its discretion in determining whether to vacate the convictions and resentence respondent pursuant to the plea agreement, to vacate only some of the convictions and resentence respondent accordingly, or to leave the convictions and sentence from trial undisturbed. Today's decision leaves open to the trial court how best to exercise that discretion in all the circumstances of the case.

The judgment of the Court of Appeals for the Sixth Circuit is vacated, and the case is remanded for further proceedings consistent with this opinion.

It is so ordered.

JUSTICE SCALIA, with whom JUSTICE THOMAS joins, and with whom THE CHIEF JUSTICE joins as to all but Part IV, dissenting.

. . . [T]he Court today opens a whole new field of constitutionalized criminal procedure: plea-bargaining law. The ordinary criminal process has become too long, too expensive, and unpredictable, in no small part as a consequence of an intricate federal Code of Criminal Procedure imposed on the States by this Court in pursuit of perfect justice. The Court now moves to bring perfection to the alternative in which prosecutors and defendants have sought relief. . . . And it would be foolish to think that "constitutional" rules governing *counsel*'s behavior will not be followed by rules governing the *prosecution*'s behavior in the plea-bargaining process that the Court today announces "'*is* the criminal justice system,'" *Frye*. Is it constitutional, for example, for the prosecution to withdraw a plea offer that has already been accepted? Or to withdraw an offer before the defense has had adequate time to consider and accept it? Or to make no plea offer at all, even though its case is weak—thereby excluding the defendant from "the criminal justice system"?

. . .

III

It is impossible to conclude discussion of today's extraordinary opinion without commenting upon the remedy it provides for the unconstitutional conviction. It is a remedy unheard-of in American jurisprudence—and, I would be willing to bet, in the jurisprudence of any other country.

The Court requires Michigan to "reoffer the plea agreement" that was rejected because of bad advice from counsel. That would indeed be a powerful remedy—but for the fact that Cooper's acceptance of that reoffered agreement is not conclusive. Astoundingly, "the state trial court can then *exercise its discretion* in determining whether to vacate the convictions and resentence respondent pursuant to the plea agreement, to vacate only some of the convictions and resentence respondent accordingly, *or to leave the convictions and sentence from trial undisturbed*." *Ibid.* (emphasis added).

Why, one might ask, require a "reoffer" of the plea agreement, and its acceptance by the defendant? If the district court finds (as a necessary element, supposedly, of *Strickland* prejudice) that Cooper *would have accepted* the original offer, and would thereby have avoided trial and conviction, why not skip the reoffer-and-reacceptance minuet and simply leave it to the discretion of the state trial court what the remedy shall be? The answer, of course, is camouflage. Trial courts, after all, *regularly* accept or reject plea agreements, so there seems to be nothing extraordinary about their accepting or rejecting the new one mandated by today's decision. But the acceptance or rejection of a plea agreement that has no status whatever under the United States Constitution is worlds apart from what this is: "discretionary" specification of a remedy for an unconstitutional criminal conviction.

To be sure, the Court asserts that there are "factors" which bear upon (and presumably limit) exercise of this discretion—factors that it is not prepared to specify in full, much less assign some determinative weight. "Principles elaborated over time in decisions of state and federal courts, and in statutes and rules" will (in the Court's rosy view) sort all that out. I find it extraordinary that "statutes and rules" can specify the remedy for a criminal defendant's unconstitutional conviction. Or that the remedy for an unconstitutional conviction should *ever* be subject *at all* to a trial judge's discretion. Or, finally, that the remedy could *ever* include no remedy at all....

IV

...The Court today embraces the sporting-chance theory of criminal law, in which the State functions like a conscientious casino-operator, giving each player a fair chance to beat the house, that is, to serve less time than the law says he deserves. And when a player is excluded from the tables, his *constitutional rights* have been violated. I do not subscribe to that theory. No one should, least of all the Justices of the Supreme Court.

...Today...the Supreme Court of the United States elevates plea bargaining from a necessary evil to a constitutional entitlement. It is no longer a somewhat embarrassing adjunct to our criminal justice system; rather, as the Court announces in the companion case to this one, "'it *is* the criminal justice system.'" *Frye*, at 1407, (quoting approvingly from Scott & Stuntz, *Plea Bargaining as Contract*, 101 YALE L.J. 1909, 1912 (1992)). Thus, even though there is no doubt that the respondent here is guilty of the offense with which he was charged; even though he has received the exorbitant gold standard of American justice—a full-dress criminal trial with its innumerable constitutional and statutory limitations upon the evidence that the prosecution can bring forward, and ... the requirement of a unanimous guilty verdict by impartial jurors; the Court says that his conviction is invalid because he was deprived of his *constitutional entitlement* to plea-bargain....

...The result in the present case is the undoing of an adjudicatory process that worked *exactly* as it is supposed to. Released felon Anthony Cooper, who shot repeatedly and gravely injured a woman named Kali Mundy, was tried and convicted for his crimes by a jury of his peers, and given a punishment that Michigan's elected representatives have deemed appropriate. Nothing about that result is unfair or unconstitutional. To the contrary, it is wonderfully just, and infinitely superior to the trial-by-bargain that today's opinion affords constitutional status. I respectfully dissent.

JUSTICE ALITO, dissenting.

... If a defendant's Sixth Amendment rights are violated when deficient legal advice about a favorable plea offer causes the opportunity for that bargain to be lost, the only logical remedy is to give the defendant the benefit of the favorable deal. But such a remedy would cause serious injustice in many instances, as I believe the Court tacitly recognizes. The Court therefore eschews the only logical remedy and relies on the lower courts to exercise sound discretion in determining what is to be done.

Time will tell how this works out. The Court, for its part, finds it unnecessary to define "the boundaries of proper discretion" in today's opinion. In my view, requiring the prosecution to renew an old plea offer would represent an abuse of discretion in at least two circumstances: first, when important new information about a defendant's culpability comes to light after the offer is rejected, and, second, when the rejection of the plea offer results in a substantial expenditure of scarce prosecutorial or judicial resources....

Lafler discusses the obligation of counsel to provide sound advice about whether or not to accept a plea offer. Its companion case deals with the more fundamental issue whether counsel has a duty even to inform the defendant of an outstanding plea offer by the prosecution.

Missouri v. Frye

566 U.S. 134 (2012)

JUSTICE KENNEDY delivered the opinion of the Court.

The right to counsel is the right to effective assistance of counsel. See *Strickland v. Washington*, 466 U.S. 668 (1984). This case arises in the context of claimed ineffective assistance that led to the lapse of a prosecution offer of a plea bargain, a proposal that offered terms more lenient than the terms of the guilty plea entered later. The initial question is whether the constitutional right to counsel extends to the negotiation and consideration of plea offers that lapse or are rejected. If there is a right to effective assistance with respect to those offers, a further question is what a defendant must demonstrate in order to show that prejudice resulted from counsel's deficient performance....

I

[Frye was charged with the *felony* of driving with a revoked license, after three prior offenses. The maximum term of imprisonment was four years. Three months later, the prosecutor sent Frye's counsel a choice of two plea bargain offers, neither of which was communicated to Frye. One offer included a recommendation of a ten-day jail sentence, and the other provided for imprisonment for ninety days, on reduced *misdemeanor* charges. Both offers were withdrawn when the prosecutor's "expiration date" passed. After another six weeks, Frye pled guilty to the felony charge *without* a plea agreement, and he was sentenced to three years in prison.]

Frye filed for postconviction relief in state court. He alleged his counsel's failure to inform him of the prosecution's plea offer denied him the effective assistance of counsel. At an evidentiary hearing, Frye testified he would have entered a guilty plea to the misdemeanor had he known about the offer.

A state court denied the postconviction motion, but the Missouri Court of Appeals reversed. It determined that Frye met both of the requirements for showing a Sixth Amendment violation under *Strickland*. First, the court determined Frye's counsel's performance was deficient because the "record is void of any evidence of any effort by trial counsel to communicate the Offer to Frye during the Offer window." The court next concluded Frye had shown his counsel's deficient performance caused him prejudice because "Frye pled guilty to a felony instead of a misdemeanor and was subject to a maximum sentence of four years instead of one year."

To implement a remedy for the violation, the court deemed Frye's guilty plea withdrawn and remanded to allow Frye either to insist on a trial or to plead guilty to any offense the prosecutor deemed it appropriate to charge. This Court granted certiorari.

II

A

. . . With respect to the right to effective counsel in plea negotiations, a proper beginning point is to discuss two cases from this Court considering the role of counsel in advising a client about a plea offer and an ensuing guilty plea. *Hill v. Lockhart*, 474 U.S. 52 (1985); and *Padilla v. Kentucky*, 559 U.S. 356 (2010).

. . . In *Hill*, the decision turned on the second part of the *Strickland* test. There, a defendant who had entered a guilty plea claimed his counsel had misinformed him of the amount of time he would have to serve before he became eligible for parole. But the defendant had not alleged that, even if adequate advice and assistance had been given, he would have elected to plead not guilty and proceed to trial. Thus, the Court found that no prejudice from the inadequate advice had been shown or alleged. *Hill, supra*, at 60.

In *Padilla*, the Court again discussed the duties of counsel in advising a client with respect to a plea offer that leads to a guilty plea. *Padilla* held that a guilty plea, based on a plea offer, should be set aside because counsel misinformed the defendant of the immigration consequences of the conviction. The Court made clear that "the negotiation of a plea bargain is a critical phase of litigation for purposes of the Sixth Amendment right to effective assistance of counsel." . . .

Ninety-seven percent of federal convictions and ninety-four percent of state convictions are the result of guilty pleas. The reality is that plea bargains have become so central to the administration of the criminal justice system that defense counsel have responsibilities in the plea bargain process, responsibilities that must be met to render the adequate assistance of counsel that the Sixth Amendment requires in the criminal process at critical stages. . . . In today's criminal justice system, therefore, the negotiation of a plea bargain, rather than the unfolding of a trial, is almost always the critical point for a defendant.

B

The inquiry then becomes how to define the duty and responsibilities of defense counsel in the plea bargain process. . . . The alternative courses and tactics in negotiation are so individual that it may be neither prudent nor practicable to try to elaborate or define detailed standards for the proper discharge of defense counsel's participation in the process.

This case presents neither the necessity nor the occasion to define the duties of defense counsel in those respects, however. Here the question is whether defense counsel has the duty to communicate the terms of a formal offer to accept a plea on terms and conditions that may result in a lesser sentence, a conviction on lesser charges, or both.

This Court now holds that, as a general rule, defense counsel has the duty to communicate formal offers from the prosecution to accept a plea on terms and conditions that may be favorable to the accused. Any exceptions to that rule need not be explored here, for the offer was a formal one with a fixed expiration date. When defense counsel allowed the offer to expire without advising the defendant or allowing him to consider it, defense counsel did not render the effective assistance the Constitution requires.

Though the standard for counsel's performance is not determined solely by reference to codified standards of professional practice, these standards can be important guides. The American Bar Association recommends defense counsel "promptly communicate and explain to the defendant all plea offers made by the prosecuting attorney," ABA Standards for Criminal Justice, Pleas of Guilty 14–3.2(a) (3d ed. 1999), and this standard has been adopted by numerous state and federal courts over the last 30 years. The standard for prompt communication and consultation is also set out in state bar professional standards for attorneys.

The prosecution and the trial courts may adopt some measures to help ensure against late, frivolous, or fabricated claims after a later, less advantageous plea offer has been accepted or after a trial leading to conviction with resulting harsh consequences. First, the fact of a formal offer means that its terms and its processing can be documented so that what took place in the negotiation process becomes more clear if some later inquiry turns on the conduct of earlier pretrial negotiations. Second, States may elect to follow rules that all offers must be in writing, again to ensure against later misunderstandings or fabricated charges. See N.J. Ct. Rule 3:9–1(b) (2012) ("Any plea offer to be made by the prosecutor shall be in writing and forwarded to the defendant's attorney"). Third, formal offers can be made part of the record at any subsequent plea proceeding or before a trial on the merits, all to ensure that a defendant has been fully advised before those further proceedings commence.

Here defense counsel did not communicate the formal offers to the defendant. As a result of that deficient performance, the offers lapsed. Under *Strickland*, the question then becomes what, if any, prejudice resulted from the breach of duty.

C

To show prejudice from ineffective assistance of counsel where a plea offer has lapsed or been rejected because of counsel's deficient performance, defendants must demonstrate a reasonable probability they would have accepted the earlier plea offer had they been afforded effective assistance of counsel. Defendants must also demonstrate a reasonable probability the plea would have been entered without the prosecution canceling it or the trial court refusing to accept it, if they had the authority to exercise that discretion under state law. To establish prejudice in this instance, it is necessary to show a reasonable probability that the end result of the criminal process would have been more favorable by reason of a plea to a lesser charge or a sentence of less prison time.

This application of *Strickland* to the instances of an uncommunicated, lapsed plea does nothing to alter the standard laid out in *Hill.* In cases where a defendant complains that ineffective assistance led him to accept a plea offer as opposed to proceeding to trial, the defendant will have to show "a reasonable probability that, but for counsel's errors, he would not have pleaded guilty and would have insisted on going to trial." *Hill*, 474 U.S., at 59 . . . Unlike the defendant in *Hill*, Frye argues that with effective assistance he would have accepted an earlier plea offer (limiting his sentence to one year in prison) as opposed to entering an open plea (exposing him to a maximum sentence of four years' imprisonment). In a case, such as this, where a defendant pleads guilty to less favorable terms and claims that ineffective assistance of counsel caused him to miss out on a more favorable earlier plea offer, *Strickland*'s inquiry into whether "the result of the proceeding would have been different," 466 U.S., at 694, requires looking not at whether the defendant would have proceeded to trial absent ineffective assistance but whether he would have accepted the offer to plead pursuant to the terms earlier proposed.

In order to complete a showing of *Strickland* prejudice, defendants who have shown a reasonable probability they would have accepted the earlier plea offer must also show that, if the prosecution had the discretion to cancel it or if the trial court had the discretion to refuse to accept it, there is a reasonable probability neither the prosecution nor the trial court would have prevented the offer from being accepted or implemented. This further showing is of particular importance because a defendant has no right to be offered a plea. In at least some States, including Missouri, it appears the prosecution has some discretion to cancel a plea agreement to which the defendant has agreed. The Federal Rules, some state rules including in Missouri, and this Court's precedents give trial courts some leeway to accept or reject plea agreements. So in most instances it should not be difficult to make an objective assessment as to whether or not a particular fact or intervening circumstance would suffice, in the normal course, to cause prosecutorial withdrawal or judicial non-approval of a plea bargain. The determination that there is or is not a reasonable probability that the outcome of the proceeding would have been different absent counsel's errors can be conducted within that framework.

III

These standards must be applied to the instant case.... On this record, it is evident that Frye's attorney did not make a meaningful attempt to inform the defendant of a written plea offer before the offer expired. The Missouri Court of Appeals was correct that "counsel's representation fell below an objective standard of reasonableness."

There appears to be a reasonable probability Frye would have accepted the prosecutor's original offer of a plea bargain if the offer had been communicated to him, because he pleaded guilty to a more serious charge, with no promise of a sentencing recommendation from the prosecutor.

The Court of Appeals failed . . . to require Frye to show that the first plea offer, if accepted by Frye, would have been adhered to by the prosecution and accepted by the trial court. Whether the prosecution and trial court are required to do so is a matter of state law, and it is not the place of this Court to settle those matters. . . . In Missouri, it appears "a plea offer once accepted by the defendant can be withdrawn without recourse" by the prosecution. The extent of the trial court's discretion in Missouri to reject a plea agreement appears to be in some doubt.

We remand for the Missouri Court of Appeals to consider these state law questions, because they bear on the federal question of *Strickland* prejudice. If, as the Missouri court stated here, the prosecutor could have canceled the plea agreement, and if Frye fails to show a reasonable probability the prosecutor would have adhered to the agreement, there is no *Strickland* prejudice. Likewise, if the trial court could have refused to accept the plea agreement, and if Frye fails to show a reasonable probability the trial court would have accepted the plea, there is no *Strickland* prejudice. In this case, given Frye's new offense for driving without a license on December 30, 2007, there is reason to doubt that the prosecution would have adhered to the agreement or that the trial court would have accepted it at the January 4, 2008, hearing, unless they were required by state law to do so.

It is appropriate to allow the Missouri Court of Appeals to address this question in the first instance. The judgment of the Missouri Court of Appeals is vacated, and the case is remanded for further proceedings not inconsistent with this opinion.

It is so ordered.

Justice Scalia, with whom The Chief Justice, Justice Thomas, and Justice Alito join, dissenting.

. . .

While the inadequacy of counsel's performance in this case is clear enough, whether it was prejudicial (in the sense that the Court's new version of *Strickland* requires) is not. The Court's description of how that question is to be answered on remand is alone enough to show how unwise it is to constitutionalize the plea bargaining process. Prejudice is to be determined, the Court tells us, by a process of retrospective crystal ball gazing posing as legal analysis. First of all, of course, we must estimate whether the defendant *would have accepted* the earlier plea bargain. Here that seems an easy question, but as the Court acknowledges, it will not always be. Next, since Missouri, like other States, permits accepted plea offers to be withdrawn by the prosecution (a reality which alone should suffice, one would think, to demonstrate that Frye had no entitlement to the plea bargain), we must estimate whether the prosecution *would have withdrawn* the plea offer. And finally, we must estimate whether the trial court *would have approved* the plea agreement. These last two estimations may seem easy in the present case, since Frye committed a new infraction before the hearing at which the agreement would have been presented; but they assuredly will not be easy in the mine run of cases.

. . . [A]fter today's opinions there will be cases galore, so the Court's *assumption* would better be cast as an optimistic *prediction* of the certainty that will emerge, many years hence, from our newly created constitutional field of plea bargaining law. Whatever the "boundaries" ultimately devised (if that were possible), a vast amount of discretion will still remain, and it is extraordinary to make a defendant's constitutional rights depend upon a series of retrospective mindreadings as to how that discretion, in prosecutors and trial judges, *would have been* exercised. . . .

Notes and Questions

1. *Disastrous defense advice or failure to advise?* Which fact scenario is more likely to recur: the *Frye* defense counsel's failure to communicate a plea offer, or the *Lafler* defense counsel's faulty advice about whether to accept a prosecutor's offer? Which of the scenarios is more troubling? Are your answers the same for both questions?

Unlike counsel in these two cases, *competent* criminal defense lawyers do understand these critical aspects of representing the accused: to convey a plea offer to the client, *and* to offer the client solid advice about whether or not to accept the offer. Without these basic tenets, what would the right to counsel mean?

2. *All-important prosecutorial discretion?* The Court in both cases cites statistics showing the practical dominance of plea bargaining. If the Court believes that the modern justice system is not one of trials but of pleas, is it elevating the importance of prosecutorial discretion to new heights? For example, a defense counsel may be able to persuade the trial judge to sentence the defendant to a minimum sentence, but that defendant may not serve *any* time if counsel persuades the prosecutor to reduce or drop the original charge.

3. *Making and protecting the record?* Speaking of practicalities, how will these opinions affect how prosecutors deal with defense counsel and defendants, how

defense counsel deal with clients, and how both sides memorialize their actions concerning plea bargains? Prosecutors may send plea offers in writing or enter them in the court record to ensure that the offers are communicated to the defense side of the case. Defense counsel may write memos to the client file describing the nature of their advice. Judges too may want the record to show that an offer was made, as well as the defense response or rejection.

4. *Protesting too much?* Did Justice Scalia exaggerate in his *Frye* dissent when he accused the Court of fabricating a new procedural right to engage in plea bargaining, and/or when he predicted that *Frye* and *Lafler* will lead to the Court prescribing standards of prosecutorial behavior? Since the *Bordenkircher* and *Santobello* decisions (discussed in this chapter), the Court has been prescribing prosecutorial norms for more than three decades. Is Justice Scalia correct in suggesting that any time a defendant, via plea bargaining, receives less than the maximum sentence allowed by law, the defendant is "beat[ing] the house, that is, [by] serv[ing] less time than the law says he deserves"? *See* Albert W. Alschuler, Lafler *and* Frye, *Two Small Band-aids for a Festering Wound*, 51 DUQ. L. REV. 674 (2013) (an emphatic response of "No!").

5. *Bringing plea bargaining out of the "gray market."* "For many years, plea bargaining has been a gray market.... The Supreme Court has usually treated plea bargaining as an afterthought, doing little to regulate it." Stephanos Bibas, *Incompetent Plea Bargaining and Extrajudicial Reforms*, 126 HARV. L. REV. 150 (2012). Professor Bibas predicts that while not actually operating to overturn many plea bargaining convictions, *Lafler* and *Frye* will more indirectly benefit the quality of the criminal justice system by bringing the gray market out into the open, subject to effective-assistance review, and also by placing both prosecutors and defense counsel on their mettle in the plea bargaining process. "[E]ven prosecutors and defendants have strong incentives to collaborate in explaining, promoting, and bulletproofing plea bargains." Bibas concludes, and predicts, "*Lafler* and *Frye* stand to improve criminal justice.... [W]hile far from panaceas for sloth, ineptitude, and overwork [that sometimes attend plea bargaining lawyering], ... they do provide a remedy for some of the worst incompetence[.]"

[4] Plea Bargaining and Vindictiveness

Plea bargaining involves a give-and-take process among participants who often have unequal bargaining power. One of the advantages the prosecution has is its ability to control the charges against the defendant. Ordinarily, the defendant knows the charges before the plea bargaining process begins. But sometimes the prosecution has not sought an indictment for all *possible* charges. In order to secure an advantage during plea negotiations, can the prosecution threaten to bring new charges against the defendant or others if the defendant does not accept a certain deal? If the defendant yields to pressure and accepts the deal rather than face additional charges, can he or she later invalidate the plea because it was coerced and therefore involuntary?

Bordenkircher v. Hayes

434 U.S. 357 (1978)

MR. JUSTICE STEWART delivered the opinion of the Court.

The question in this case is whether the Due Process Clause of the Fourteenth Amendment is violated when a state prosecutor carries out a threat made during plea negotiations to reindict the accused on more serious charges if he does not plead guilty to the offense with which he was originally charged.

The respondent was indicted by a grand jury on a charge of uttering a forged instrument in the amount of $88.30, an offense then punishable by a term of 2 to 10 years in prison. After arraignment, Hayes, his retained counsel, and the Commonwealth's Attorney met in the presence of the Clerk of the Court to discuss a possible plea agreement. During these conferences the prosecutor offered to recommend a sentence of five years in prison if Hayes would plead guilty to the indictment. He also said that if Hayes did not plead guilty and "save the court the inconvenience and necessity of a trial," he would return to the grand jury to seek an indictment under the Kentucky Habitual Criminal Act, which would subject Hayes to a mandatory sentence of life imprisonment by reason of his two prior felony convictions.

Hayes chose not to plead guilty, and the prosecutor did obtain an indictment charging him under the Habitual Criminal Act. It is not disputed that the recidivist charge was fully justified by the evidence, that the prosecutor was in possession of this evidence at the time of the original indictment, and that Hayes' refusal to plead guilty to the original charge was what led to his indictment under the habitual criminal statute.

[A jury found Hayes guilty of uttering a forged instrument and of having two prior felonies, resulting in a life sentence as an habitual criminal. After an unsuccessful appeal, Hayes filed for federal habeas corpus. The District Court denied his petition, but the Sixth Circuit Court of Appeals reversed the conviction, holding that the prosecutor violated *Blackledge v. Perry*, 417 U.S. 21 (1974), by engaging in the vindictive exercise of prosecutorial discretion.]

It may be helpful to clarify at the outset the nature of the issue in this case. While the prosecutor did not actually obtain the recidivist indictment until after the plea conferences had ended, his intention to do so was clearly expressed at the outset of the plea negotiations. Hayes was thus fully informed of the true terms of the offer when he made his decision to plead not guilty. This is not a situation, therefore, where the prosecutor without notice brought an additional and more serious charge after plea negotiations relating only to the original indictment had ended with the defendant's insistence on pleading not guilty. As a practical matter, in short, this case would be no different if the grand jury had indicted Hayes as a recidivist from the outset, and the prosecutor had offered to drop that charge as part of the plea bargain.

The Court of Appeals nonetheless drew a distinction between "concessions relating to prosecution under an existing indictment," and threats to bring more severe charges not contained in the original indictment—a line it thought necessary in order to establish a prophylactic rule to guard against the evil of prosecutorial vindictiveness. Quite apart from this chronological distinction, however, the Court of Appeals found that the prosecutor had acted vindictively in the present case since he had conceded that the indictment was influenced by his desire to induce a guilty plea. The ultimate conclusion of the Court of Appeals thus seems to have been that a prosecutor acts vindictively and in violation of due process of law whenever his charging decision is influenced by what he hopes to gain in the course of plea bargaining negotiations.

We have recently had occasion to observe: "[W]hatever might be the situation in an ideal world, the fact is that the guilty plea and the often concomitant plea bargain are important components of this country's criminal justice system. Properly administered, they can benefit all concerned." *Blackledge v. Allison*, 431 U.S. 63 (1977).

. . . [I]n *North Carolina v. Pearce*, 395 U.S. 711 (1969) [limiting sentence that could be imposed in a second trial after defendant successfully appealed a conviction in the first trial] and *Blackledge v. Perry* [limiting charges that can be filed after a defendant exercises the right to seek a trial *de novo* in a higher court] the Court was dealing with the State's unilateral imposition of a penalty upon a defendant who had chosen to exercise a legal right to attack his original conviction—a situation "very different from the give-and-take negotiation common in plea bargaining between the prosecution and defense, which arguably possess relatively equal bargaining power." The Court has emphasized that the due process violation in cases such as *Pearce* and *Perry* lay not in the possibility that a defendant might be deterred from the exercise of a legal right but rather in the danger that the State might be retaliating against the accused for lawfully attacking his conviction.

To punish a person because he has done what the law plainly allows him to do is a due process violation of the most basic sort, and for an agent of the State to pursue a course of action whose objective is to penalize a person's reliance on his legal rights is "patently unconstitutional." But in the "give-and-take" of plea bargaining, there is no such element of punishment or retaliation so long as the accused is free to accept or reject the prosecution's offer.

Plea bargaining flows from "the mutuality of advantage" to defendants and prosecutors, each with his own reasons for wanting to avoid trial. Defendants advised by competent counsel and protected by other procedural safeguards are presumptively capable of intelligent choice in response to prosecutorial persuasion, and unlikely to be driven to false self-condemnation. Indeed, acceptance of the basic legitimacy of plea bargaining necessarily implies rejection of any notion that a guilty plea is involuntary in a constitutional sense simply because it is the end result of the bargaining process. By hypothesis, the plea may have been induced by promises of a recommendation of a lenient sentence or a reduction of charges, and thus by fear of the possibility of a greater penalty upon conviction after a trial.

. . . It is not disputed here that Hayes was properly chargeable under the recidivist statute, since he had in fact been convicted of two previous felonies. In our system, so long as the prosecutor has probable cause to believe that the accused committed an offense defined by statute, the decision whether or not to prosecute, and what charge to file or bring before a grand jury, generally rests entirely in his discretion. Within the limits set by the legislature's constitutionally valid definition of chargeable offenses, "the conscious exercise of some selectivity in enforcement is not in itself a federal constitutional violation" so long as "the selection was [not] deliberately based upon an unjustifiable standard such as race, religion, or other arbitrary classification."

... There is no doubt that the breadth of discretion that our country's legal system vests in prosecuting attorneys carries with it the potential for both individual and institutional abuse. And broad though that discretion may be, there are undoubtedly constitutional limits upon its exercise. We hold only that the course of conduct engaged in by the prosecutor in this case, which no more than openly presented the defendant with the unpleasant alternatives of forgoing trial or facing charges on which he was plainly subject to prosecution, did not violate the Due Process Clause of the Fourteenth Amendment. [Reversed]

Mr. Justice Blackmun, with whom Mr. Justice Brennan and Mr. Justice Marshall join, dissenting.

I feel that the Court, although purporting to rule narrowly ... is departing from, or at least restricting, the principles established in [*Pearce* and *Perry*]. If those decisions are sound and if those principles are salutary, as I must assume they are, they require, in my view, an affirmance, not a reversal, of the judgment of the Court of Appeals in the present case.

... The Court now says ... that this concern with vindictiveness is of no import in the present case, despite the difference between five years in prison and a life sentence, because we are here concerned with plea bargaining where there is give-and-take negotiation, and where, it is said, "there is no such element of punishment or retaliation so long as the accused is free to accept or reject the prosecution's offer." Yet in this case vindictiveness is present to the same extent as it was thought to be in *Pearce* and in *Perry*; the prosecutor here admitted that the sole reason for the new indictment was to discourage the respondent from exercising his right to a trial. Even had such an admission not been made, when plea negotiations, conducted in the face of the less serious charge under the first indictment, fail, charging by a second indictment a more serious crime for the same conduct creates "a strong inference" of vindictiveness. ... I therefore do not understand why, as in *Pearce*, due process does not require that the prosecution justify its action on some basis other than discouraging respondent from the exercise of his right to a trial.

It might be argued that it really makes little difference how this case, now that it is here, is decided. The Court's holding gives plea bargaining full sway despite vindictiveness. A contrary result, however, merely would prompt the aggressive prosecutor to bring the greater charge initially in every case, and only thereafter to bargain. The consequences to the accused would still be adverse, for then he would bargain against a greater charge, face the likelihood of increased bail, and run the risk that the court would be less inclined to accept a bargained plea. Nonetheless, it is far preferable to hold the prosecution to the charge it was originally content to bring and to justify in the eyes of its public.

Even if overcharging is to be sanctioned, there are strong reasons of fairness why the charges should be presented at the beginning of the bargaining process, rather than as a filliped threat at the end. First, it means that a prosecutor is required to reach a charging decision without any knowledge of the particular defendant's willingness to plead guilty; hence the defendant who truly believes himself to be innocent, and wishes for that reason to go to trial, is not likely to be subject to quite such a devastating gamble since the prosecutor has fixed the incentives for the average case.

Second, it is healthful to keep charging practices visible to the general public, so that political bodies can judge whether the policy being followed is a fair one. Visibility is enhanced if the prosecutor is required to lay his cards on the table with an indictment of public record at the beginning of the bargaining process, rather than making use of unrecorded verbal warnings of more serious indictments yet to come.

Finally, I would question whether it is fair to pressure defendants to plead guilty by threat of reindictment on an enhanced charge for the same conduct when the defendant has no way of knowing whether the prosecutor would indeed be entitled to bring him to trial on the enhanced charge. Here, though there is no dispute that respondent met the then-current definition of a habitual offender under Kentucky law, it is conceivable that a properly instructed Kentucky grand jury . . . in response to the same considerations that ultimately moved the Kentucky Legislature to amend the habitual offender statute, would have refused to subject respondent to such an onerous penalty for his forgery charge. There is no indication in the record that, once the new indictment was obtained, respondent was given another chance to plead guilty to the forged check charge in exchange for a five-year sentence.

Mr. Justice Powell, dissenting.

Although I agree with much of the Court's opinion, I am not satisfied that the result in this case is just or that the conduct of the plea bargaining met the requirements of due process.

. . . There may be situations in which a prosecutor would be fully justified in seeking a fresh indictment for a more serious offense. The most plausible justification might be that it would have been reasonable and in the public interest initially to have charged the defendant with the greater offense. In most cases a court could not know why the harsher indictment was sought, and an inquiry into the prosecutor's motive would neither be indicated nor likely to be fruitful. In those cases, I would agree with the majority that the situation would not differ materially from one in which the higher charge was brought at the outset.

But this is not such a case. Here, any inquiry into the prosecutor's purpose is made unnecessary by his candid acknowledgment that he threatened to procure and in fact procured the habitual criminal indictment because of respondent's insistence on exercising his constitutional rights. . . .

The plea-bargaining process, as recognized by this Court, is essential to the functioning of the criminal-justice system. It normally affords genuine benefits to defendants as well as to society. And if the system is to work effectively, prosecutors must be accorded the widest discretion, within constitutional limits, in conducting bargaining. This is especially true when a defendant is represented by counsel and presumably is fully advised of his rights. Only in the most exceptional case should a court conclude that the scales of the bargaining are so unevenly balanced as to arouse suspicion. In this case, the prosecutor's actions denied respondent due process because their admitted purpose was to discourage and then to penalize with unique severity his exercise of constitutional rights. Implementation of a strategy calculated solely to deter the exercise of constitutional rights is not a constitutionally permissible exercise of discretion. I would affirm the opinion of the Court of Appeals on the facts of this case.

Notes

1. *Impact of* Bordenkircher. The United States Supreme Court in *Bordenkircher* found no due process violation even though there was clear evidence that the prosecutor sought the new indictment for the purpose of dissuading the defendant from exercising his right to a trial. Are you satisfied with the treatment of this issue by the majority? If you are persuaded by the dissenters that relief should have been provided, would such a holding exacerbate the "overcharging" phenomenon discussed earlier? Would such a holding also have the effect of influencing prosecutors to falsely state reasons for plea agreement concessions?

2. *Package deal.* In a separate footnote, the *Bordenkircher* majority noted that tying an individual defendant's guilty plea together with other individuals' pleas "might pose a greater danger of inducing a false guilty plea by skewing the assessment of the risks a defendant must consider." *Bordenkircher*, 434 U.S. at 364 n.8. This concern arises in a "package deal" plea agreement. Under these agreements, as one court explained:

> [S]everal confederates plead together and the government gives them a volume discount—a better deal than each could have gotten separately. Consistent with the package nature of the agreement, defendants' fates are often bound together: If one defendant backs out, the deal's off for everybody. This may well place additional pressure on each of the participants to go along with the deal despite misgivings they might have.

United States v. Caro, 997 F.2d 657, 658–59 (9th Cir. 1993).

Does this mean that a package deal plea agreement is *per se* impermissible? In *Caro*, the Court found one such agreement invalid because the trial judge failed to conduct a "careful examination" into whether the confederates had pressured Caro into accepting the plea agreement. Furthermore, the court held that since the real issue was one of voluntariness, the error could not be found harmless.

The Minnesota Supreme Court announced special rules for acceptance and withdrawal of package deal (or, in its words, "wired") plea agreements. The state must inform the trial judge of the details of such agreements, and the court must conduct a further inquiry (focusing upon such factors as (1) the degree to which the defendant was influenced to plead by the state's offer of leniency to a third party, and (2) the strength of the factual basis for the plea) to determine the plea's voluntariness. *Minnesota v. Danh*, 516 N.W.2d 539 (Minn. 1994). *See also People v. Fiumefreddo*, 626 N.E.2d 646 (N.Y. 1993) (third party's benefit from plea bargain is one factor in assessing whether plea was voluntary; special procedures unnecessary).

3. *Impermissible discrimination.* Toward the end of the majority opinion, the *Bordenkircher* Court alludes to the fact (discussed in Chapter 2 of this book) that selectivity in enforcement of the criminal law is constitutionally permissible so long as the selection is not "based upon an unjustifiable standard such as race, religion, or other arbitrary classification." It is widely recognized that prosecutors possess broad discretion regarding whether or not to negotiate with an individual defendant with respect to a plea agreement. Additionally, the terms of such agreements lie within that same discretion. This means that in some instances, similarly situated defendants who have committed very similar crimes are dealt with in dissimilar ways by prosecutors. In such a situation, it is possible that the defendant will raise the claim that the disparity in treatment was based upon race, sex, national origin, religion, or some other impermissible classification.

Rarely are discrimination claims presented in the context of plea bargaining, and it is extremely difficult for such a claim to succeed. For example, in *United States v. Moody*, 778 F.2d 1380 (9th Cir. 1985), several defendants were charged with conspiracy to import a controlled substance. While one defendant was permitted to plead, two others were not allowed to do so. They asserted that this was impermissibly discriminatory, offering to show that the other defendant, who was given a favorable plea bargain, was actually more culpable than the two who were not. Recognizing that a defendant has no constitutional right to a plea bargain, the appellate court held that there was no connection between the defendants' race or any other impermissible factor and the prosecutor's refusal to plea bargain. In order to prevail, a defendant must show that he or she was singled out because of race or some other arbitrary classification, and that such treatment was intentional. The defendants' assertions in *Moody* were too vague to establish a prima facie case of discrimination.

By contrast, impermissible gender-based discrimination in plea bargaining was initially found in *United States v. Redondo-Lemos*, 955 F.2d 1296 (9th Cir. 1992). Defendant, charged with possession with intent to distribute marijuana, was offered a plea agreement in which the prosecutor would recommend the minimum statutory imprisonment of five years. The United States District Court judge, finding that the United States Attorney's Office was treating this male defendant differently from other similarly situated female defendants (who were receiving sentences of approximately 18 months), held that the equal protection guarantee required that the defendant's sentence be reduced to 18 months. The Ninth Circuit Court of Appeals reversed and remanded, requiring further hearings to allow the prosecutor to present non-gender-based reasons for the perceived discriminatory treatment. After the remand hearing and appeal back to the Ninth Circuit, however, that court ultimately determined that the government had "amply demonstrated that it acted on the basis of . . . non-discriminatory criteria." *United States v. Redondo-Lemos*, 27 F.3d 439 (9th Cir. 1994).

Procedurally, a defendant should raise a claim of plea bargaining discrimination prior to trial, and submit evidence in support of the challenge that is as precise and specific as possible. *See e.g., United States v. Bernal-Rojas*, 933 F.2d 97 (1st Cir. 1991) (the claim of impermissible discrimination was vague and failed to establish a prima facie case; in addition, challenge was not raised until the sentencing phase of the trial).

4. *Statutory benefits for entering plea.* In *Corbitt v. New Jersey*, 439 U.S. 212 (1978), the defendant was tried and convicted of murder in the first degree and received a mandatory life prison sentence. If he had entered a nolo plea to the same charge, however, his sentence could have been either life imprisonment or a term of not more than 30 years. The defendant claimed that this sentencing scheme constituted an unconstitutional burden upon his right to trial by jury. The United States Supreme Court rejected that contention, holding that it was permissible for New Jersey to encourage a guilty plea by offering a benefit in return for the plea. The Court also found "no difference of constitutional significance between *Bordenkircher* and this case":

> There, as here, the defendant went to trial on an indictment that included a count carrying a mandatory life term under the applicable state statutes. There, as here, the defendant could have sought to counter the mandatory penalty by tendering a plea. In *Bordenkircher*, as permitted by state law, the prosecutor was willing to forgo the habitual criminal count if there was a plea, in which event the mandatory sentence would have been avoided. Here, the state law empowered the judge to impose a lesser term either in connection with a plea bargain or otherwise. In both cases, the defendant gave up the possibility of leniency if he went to trial and was convicted on the count carrying the mandatory penalty. In *Bordenkircher*, the probability or certainty of leniency in return for a plea did not invalidate the mandatory penalty imposed after a jury trial. It should not do so here, where there was no assurance that a plea would be accepted if tendered, and, if it had been, no assurance that a sentence less than life would be imposed. Those matters rested ultimately in the discretion of the judge, perhaps substantially influenced by the prosecutor and the plea-bargaining process permitted by New Jersey law.

Id. at 221–222.

5. *Capital cases.* Does *Bordenkircher* apply in death penalty cases? In *State v. Mann*, 959 S.W.2d 503 (Tenn. 1997), the Tennessee Supreme Court answered this question in the affirmative. There, the court found that the defendant's constitutional rights had not been violated by the government's decision to seek the death penalty after the defendant had rejected a plea offer of life imprisonment. Following the rejection of that offer, the defendant was convicted of premeditated first degree murder, aggravated rape and aggravated burglary, and was sentenced to death. Noting that *Bordenkircher* applies even to situations in which the death penalty ultimately is imposed, the court reasoned:

> A defendant who pleads guilty extends a substantial benefit to the criminal justice system, and in exchange, the State is entitled to extend a less harsh sentence than might otherwise be given. Likewise, if a plea offer is rejected, the State may prosecute the defendant to the fullest extent possible and seek whatever punishment is appropriate under the law.

[5] Waiver Limitations?

May the prosecutor, as a part of the plea bargain, demand that the defendant waive the right to appeal? If so, what protections remain for the defendant if the court fails to apply the proper sentence? Does the waiver bar a claim of ineffective assistance of counsel? Consider the following case.

Jones v. United States

167 F.3d 1142 (7th Cir. 1998)

Cudahy, Circuit Judge.

On March 3, 1995 a jury convicted Shawn Jones of conspiring to distribute cocaine and marijuana.... After trial and prior to sentencing, Jones entered into a cooperation agreement with the government, which contained a waiver of his rights to appeal and to file a habeas motion under **18 U.S.C. § 2255**. The district court subsequently sentenced Jones to 144 months imprisonment, five years of supervised release and a mandatory special assessment of $100. Notwithstanding the waiver, Jones ... moved under § 2255 [habeas corpus] to vacate, set aside or correct his sentence. The issue here is whether a cooperation agreement that waives the right to file a [habeas] petition under § 2255 bars a defendant from arguing that he received ineffective assistance of counsel when negotiating the agreement or that the agreement was involuntary.... [T]he district court denied the motion.

We have routinely held that a defendant may waive the right to a direct appeal as part of a written plea agreement. See *United States v. Wooley*, 123 F.3d 627 (7th Cir. 1997) ("the right to appeal is a statutory right, and like other rights—even constitutional rights—which a defendant may waive, it can be waived in a plea agreement"). The validity of an appeal waiver rests on whether it is "express and unambiguous" and whether ... it was made "knowingly and voluntarily." [In accepting a plea agreement] the court is not required to conduct a specific dialogue with the defendant concerning the appeal waiver, so long as the record contains sufficient evidence to determine whether the defendant's acceptance of the waiver was knowing and voluntary.

We have recognized that the right to appeal survives where the agreement is involuntary, or the trial court relied on some constitutionally impermissible factor (such as race), or . . . the sentence exceeded the statutory maximum. [Other] circuits have held that a plea agreement waiver cannot bar an appeal based on the Sixth Amendment right to effective counsel.

. . . Justice dictates that a claim of ineffective assistance of counsel in connection with the negotiation of a cooperation agreement cannot be barred by the agreement itself. . . . To hold otherwise would deprive a defendant of an opportunity to assert his Sixth Amendment right to counsel where he had accepted the waiver in reliance on delinquent representation. Similarly, where a waiver is not the product of the defendant's free will—for example, where it has been procured by government coercion or intimidation—the defendant cannot be said to have knowingly and voluntarily relinquished his rights. It is intuitive that in those circumstances the waiver is ineffective against a challenge based on involuntariness.

. . . [W]e cannot approve the district court's determination that the waiver was effective and we hold that Jones was entitled to file a [habeas] petition under § 2255 challenging the cooperation agreement on the grounds of involuntariness and ineffective assistance of counsel.

[The court did, however, affirm the district court's decision to deny the petitioner's motion to vacate the sentence. The Court of Appeals found that the petitioner failed to adequately specify his claims of ineffective assistance of counsel and involuntariness.]

Notes

1. *Appeal sentence severity.* Where the appeal relates to the severity of the sentence, rather than the integrity of the bargain, and the sentence falls within statutory guidelines, most courts hold that such a waiver is valid and enforceable. *See, e.g., In re Acosta*, 480 F.3d 421 (6th Cir. 2007) (appeal of the determination of degree of culpability may be waived).

2. *Public policy concerns.* The Second Circuit Court of Appeals as well as district courts in both Massachusetts and the District of Columbia have refused to enforce such waivers on the ground that they are contrary to public policy. *See United States v. Goodman*, 165 F.3d 169 (2d Cir. 1999) (refusing to enforce a broad waiver of appeal including the right to appeal from an upward departure from the applicable United States Sentencing Guidelines, which would subject the defendant to risk of sentencing error or abuse). *But see United States v. Montano*, 472 F.3d 1202 (10th Cir. 2007) (upholding waiver of plea condition in plea agreement). Consider Judge Gertner's opinion in *United States v. Perez*, 46 F. Supp. 2d 59 (D. Mass. 1999):

> In a guideline regime that presumes that the correct guideline sentence is a fair sentence, a sentence based on mistake is plainly unfair. Moreover, in a guideline regime that emphasizes rational pre-sentence investigations and sentencing hearings, that seeks to stem unwarranted disparities in sentence through a reasonable analysis at the trial court level and through appellate review of sentencing, the suppression of the right to appeal judicial errors is anathema.
>
> Despite the attraction of the idea of maximizing a defendant's power by allowing him to sell whatever he has, the market for plea bargains, like every other market, should not be so deregulated that the conditions essential to assuring basic fairness are undermined.
>
> ... In finding the "syllogism" that runs from the premise that defendants can waive various constitutional rights to the conclusion that defendants can waive the statutory right to appeal a sentence overlooks both the significance of sentence appeals in the criminal justice system, and the limits on the waivability of rights. Second, I find that there is a due process problem with pressuring defendants, in a plea bargain setting, to waive their appeal rights. Third, I find that appeal waiver clauses are inconsistent with and would systematically undermine, the Congressional intent in drafting the Sentencing Reform Act of 1984. Fourth, I find that there are contractual problems with appeal waivers in plea bargains. Fifth, I find that the government's interest in enforcing appeal waivers is not very substantial.
>
> ... In addition, allowing appeals waivers would have a cost in terms of the development of appellate law necessary to clarify how the guidelines should be applied.
>
> ... There is also a more insidious systemic effect. If appeals waivers are generally accepted, then the baseline for cooperation will shift so that only a defendant who has something exceptionally valuable for the government will be able to maintain his right to appeal. Rather than seeing waiver of appeal rights as a bargaining chip, defendants will have to bargain for the ability to keep it.
>
> ... There is an additional problem of systemic distortion which arises from the fact that many appeal waivers ... are asymmetrical; the defendant waives appeal rights which the government does not waive.

3. *Rule 11's appeal waiver rule.* Federal Rule of Criminal Procedure 11(b) contains the following provision relating to plea waivers:

> (b)(1) *Advising and Questioning the Defendant.* Before the court accepts a plea of guilty or nolo contendere, ... the court must address the defendant personally in open court [and] ... inform the defendant of, and determine that the defendant understands, the following:

....

(N) the terms of any plea-agreement provision waiving the right to appeal or to collaterally attack the sentence.

4. *Other waivers. Jones* and *United States v. Hahn*, 359 F.3d 1315 (10th Cir. 2004), hold that a claim of ineffective assistance of counsel in connection with the negotiation of a cooperation agreement cannot be barred by the agreement itself. *Accord United States v. Smith*, 640 F.3d 580 (4th Cir. 2011) (plea of guilty does not waive or bar later claim of ineffective assistance of counsel).

Are there other rights that can never be waived? In *United States v. Ruiz*, 536 U.S. 622 (2002), the United States Supreme Court unanimously held that it was constitutionally permissible for the government to insist as a part of a plea bargain that the defendant waive the right to receive "impeachment information relating to any informants or other witnesses [and] information supporting any affirmative defense the defendant raises if the case goes to trial." Noting that this particular agreement still obligated the government to provide information establishing the defendant's factual innocence, the Court found it "difficult to distinguish, in terms of importance, (1) a defendant's ignorance of grounds for impeachment of potential witnesses . . . from (2) the varying forms of ignorance [in such cases as *United States v. Brady* (quality of state's case); *McMann v. Richardson*, 397 U.S. 759 (1970) (admissibility of a confession); *Broce v. United States*, 488 U.S. 93 (1989) (a potential defense), or *Tollett v. Henderson*, 411 U.S. 258 (1973) (a potential constitutional infirmity in the grand jury proceeding)]." The Court also observed that a contrary rule could "significantly" interfere with the plea bargaining process itself.

F. Procedures

Now that plea bargaining is a visible part of the criminal justice system, statutes and rules exist in virtually all jurisdictions pertaining to the way in which guilty pleas—whether the result of bargaining or not—are to be accepted. The first procedural step in the plea process (guilty or not guilty) is the arraignment, governed by Rule 10.

[1] Arraignment

The exact nature of an arraignment varies among the jurisdictions, but in general terms it presents the defendant with formal notice of the charges (indictment or information for felonies), allows the defendant to plead (guilty, not guilty, or *nolo contendere* in most locales), and schedules trial (if the defendant pleads not guilty) or sentencing (if the plea is guilty or *nolo contendere*). *See, e.g.*, Fed. R. Crim. P. 10(a). The defendant may choose to waive arraignment. Fed. R. Crim. P. 10(b).

Notes

1. *Enters no plea.* If the defendant refuses to enter a plea at the arraignment, the court will treat it as if the defendant pled "not guilty" and will schedule trial.

2. *Right to counsel.* The Sixth Amendment guarantee of counsel extends to an arraignment. *Fellers v. United States*, 540 U.S. 519 (2004). Thus, a judge who sees a defendant who is not represented by counsel at an arraignment should inquire whether the defendant wants a lawyer or is willing to waive counsel.

3. *Informing defendant of charges.* A primary function of the arraignment is to inform defendant of the charges, usually by providing the defendant or defense counsel with a copy of the indictment or information. While Rule 10 technically requires the court to *read* the indictment to the defendant or at least to summarize the "substance of the charge," ordinarily this process is waived or simply not offered if the defendant in fact has received a copy of the indictment or information.

4. *Waiver of defendant's presence.* Rule 10 specifically authorizes an indicted defendant (or one facing misdemeanor charges by a filed information) to waive personal appearance at an arraignment. The waiver must be signed by both the defendant and defense counsel. It must state that the defendant received a copy of the indictment or information and pleads not guilty. The court is not obligated to accept the waiver and can require the defendant to be physically present for the arraignment.

5. *Waiver of arraignment.* While Rule 10 specifically allows defendant to waive presence at an arraignment, it does not permit waiver of the arraignment itself.

6. *Videoconferencing.* Any arraignment may be held by videoconferencing if the defendant consents. Rule 10(c).

7. *Rule 11 applies if sentence imposed at arraignment.* If the defendant pleads not guilty, or simply refuses to enter any plea, the court will ordinarily set the case for trial. On the other hand, if the defendant pleads guilty or *nolo contendere* at the arraignment, the court may accept the plea and then either schedule a sentencing hearing in the future or impose sentence at that time. If a sentence is to be imposed, the court must follow the detailed requirements of Federal Rule of Criminal Procedure 11, below, which governs all federal cases and has been the model for most state provisions.

[2] Rule 11

By far the most important rule of criminal procedure is Rule 11, which governs—sometimes in great detail—the conduct of proceedings where defendant pleads guilty or nolo contendere. It should be studied carefully since it affects more than 90% of criminal defendants.

Rule 11. *Pleas*

(a) Entering a Plea.

(1) ***In General.*** A defendant may plead not guilty, guilty, or (with the court's consent) nolo contendere.

(2) *Conditional Plea.* With the consent of the court and the government, a defendant may enter a conditional plea of guilty or nolo contendere, reserving in writing the right to have an appellate court review an adverse determination of a specified pretrial motion. A defendant who prevails on appeal may then withdraw the plea.

(3) *Nolo Contendere Plea.* Before accepting a plea of nolo contendere, the court must consider the parties' views and the public interest in the effective administration of justice.

(4) *Failure to Enter a Plea.* If a defendant refuses to enter a plea or if a defendant organization fails to appear, the court must enter a plea of not guilty.

(b) Considering and Accepting a Guilty or Nolo Contendere Plea.

(1) *Advising and Questioning the Defendant.* Before the court accepts a plea of guilty or nolo contendere, the defendant may be placed under oath, and the court must address the defendant personally in open court. During this address, the court must inform the defendant of, and determine that the defendant understands, the following:

(A) the government's right, in a prosecution for perjury or false statement, to use against the defendant any statement that the defendant gives under oath;

(B) the right to plead not guilty, or having already so pleaded, to persist in that plea;

(C) the right to a jury trial;

(D) the right to be represented by counsel—and if necessary have the court appoint counsel—at trial and at every other stage of the proceeding;

(E) the right at trial to confront and cross-examine adverse witnesses, to be protected from compelled self-incrimination, to testify and present evidence, and to compel the attendance of witnesses;

(F) the defendant's waiver of these trial rights if the court accepts a plea of guilty or nolo contendere;

(G) the nature of each charge to which the defendant is pleading;

(H) any maximum possible penalty, including imprisonment, fine, and term of supervised release;

(I) any mandatory minimum penalty;

(J) any applicable forfeiture;

(K) the court's authority to order restitution;

(L) the court's obligation to impose a special assessment;

(M) [the court's obligation to calculate the sentencing guideline range and to consider possible departures and other sentencing factors]; and

(N) the terms of any plea-agreement provision waiving the right to appeal or to collaterally attack the sentence.

(2) *Ensuring That a Plea Is Voluntary.* Before accepting a plea of guilty or nolo contendere, the court must address the defendant personally in open court and determine that the plea is voluntary and did not result from force, threats, or promises (other than promises in a plea agreement).

(3) *Determining the Factual Basis for a Plea.* Before entering judgment on a guilty plea, the court must determine that there is a factual basis for the plea.

(c) **Plea Agreement Procedure.**

(1) *In General.* An attorney for the government and the defendant's attorney, or the defendant when proceeding pro se, may discuss and reach a plea agreement. The court must not participate in these discussions. If the defendant pleads guilty or nolo contendere to either a charged offense or a lesser or related offense, the plea agreement may specify that an attorney for the government will:

(A) not bring, or will move to dismiss, other charges;

(B) recommend, or agree not to oppose the defendant's request, that a particular sentence or sentencing range is appropriate or that a particular provision of the Sentencing Guidelines, or policy statement, or sentencing factor does or does not apply (such a recommendation or request does not bind the court); or

(C) agree that a specific sentence or sentencing range is the appropriate disposition of the case, or that a particular provision of the Sentencing Guidelines, or policy statement, or sentencing factor does or does not apply (such a recommendation or request binds the court once the court accepts the plea agreement).

(2) *Disclosing a Plea Agreement.* The parties must disclose the plea agreement in open court when the plea is offered, unless the court for good cause allows the parties to disclose the plea agreement in camera.

(3) *Judicial Consideration of a Plea Agreement.*

(A) To the extent the plea agreement is of the type specified in Rule 11(c)(1)(A) or (C), the court may accept the agreement, reject it, or defer a decision until the court has reviewed the pre-sentence report.

(B) To the extent the plea agreement is of the type specified in Rule 11(c)(1)(B), the court must advise the defendant that the defendant has no right to withdraw the plea if the court does not follow the recommendation or request.

(4) *Accepting a Plea Agreement.* If the court accepts the plea agreement, it must inform the defendant that to the extent the plea agreement is of the type specified in Rule 11(c)(1)(A) or (C), the agreed disposition will be included in the judgment.

(5) *Rejecting a Plea Agreement.* If the court rejects a plea agreement containing provisions of the type specified in Rule 11(c)(1)(A) or (C), the court must do the following on the record and in open court (or, for good cause, in camera):

(A) inform the parties that the court rejects the plea agreement;

(B) advise the defendant personally that the court is not required to follow the plea agreement and give the defendant an opportunity to withdraw the plea; and

(C) advise the defendant personally that if the plea is not withdrawn, the court may dispose of the case less favorably toward the defendant than the plea agreement contemplated.

. . . .

(h) **Harmless Error.** A variance from the requirements of this rule is harmless error if it does not affect substantial rights.

[3] Requirement of a Record

In order to facilitate appellate review, Rule 11(g) requires a verbatim record of the plea proceeding. Assuming acceptance of the plea, the court must inform the defendant that disposition provided for in the plea agreement, per Rule 11(c)(4), "will be included in the judgment."

Constitutional basis for requiring a record. There is also a constitutional dimension to the requirement of a guilty plea acceptance record. Since a guilty plea serves to relinquish several fundamental constitutional rights, the guilty plea proceeding must ensure that the defendant's abandonment of those rights is voluntary and knowing. *See Boykin v. Alabama*, 395 U.S. 238 (1969) (a plea of guilty must be voluntary and knowing). Additionally, *Boykin* held that a waiver of constitutional rights cannot be presumed "from a silent record."

Absence of record. While the *Boykin* case may be interpreted to require that all guilty pleas be invalidated in the absence of an explicit record, this is not the uniform rule. For example, in *United States v. Ferguson*, 935 F.2d 862 (7th Cir. 1991), the defendant argued that his sentence could not be enhanced because of prior convictions since at least one of those convictions was based upon a guilty plea which was not entered voluntarily and knowingly. In support of his claim, he alleged that there was no transcript of the guilty plea proceeding in the Illinois state court. Noting that the defendant had not previously challenged his plea of guilty and also interpreting *Boykin* to permit the federal court to examine "custom, practice and law applicable to Illinois guilty pleas," the federal circuit court rejected his claim. It held that, despite the lack of a record of the guilty plea proceedings, the defendant had not satisfied his burden of proving that his prior conviction was unconstitutional. Illinois law, which is presumed to have been followed, mandated that the trial court explain fully the defendant's rights before accepting a plea. Moreover, the judgment of conviction entered after each guilty plea clearly stated that the defendant had been apprised of his rights. His prior conviction based upon a recordless guilty plea therefore was valid for the purpose of federal sentence enhancement.

Burden of proof. States may place the burden of proving a defective guilty plea on the person challenging the validity of a prior conviction based on the allegedly defective guilty plea. *Parke v. Raley*, 506 U.S. 20 (1992). In the absence of a record of the guilty plea, this burden will be difficult to satisfy.

[4] Disclosing Agreement in Open Court

Rule 11(c)(2) mandates that the plea agreement ordinarily must be disclosed "in open court" when the plea is offered. For "good cause," the agreement may be disclosed *in camera*. This requirement ensures that all parties and the judge understand the deal and allows the judge to decide whether to honor it.

[5] Role of Victim

Participate in plea process. In recent years, the victim's role in the plea bargaining process has expanded dramatically. Many states have statutory provisions that guarantee the victim certain rights in the plea bargaining context. Idaho's statute is a good example of the trend to enable victims to become much more active participants in the adjudication process. Idaho Code § 19-5306(1)(e) and (f) provides victims the right to "be advised of any proposed plea agreement by the prosecuting attorney prior to entering into a plea agreement in criminal or juvenile cases involving crimes of violence, sex crimes or crimes against children," and to be heard upon request at all guilty plea and sentencing hearings. Many states now allow victims to address the court through direct testimony at the time of plea or sentencing ("*victim allocution*") or via a "victim impact statement" in a presentence report. *See* Ariz. Rev. Stat. § 13-4423(A) ("On request of the victim, the victim has the right to be present and be heard at any proceeding in which a negotiated plea . . . will be presented to the court.").

Recommendations. These kinds of provisions mirror the recommendations made by a number of organizations. For example, the American Bar Association recommends: "The prosecuting attorney should make every effort to remain advised of the attitudes and sentiments of the victims . . . before reaching a plea agreement." Standards for Criminal Justice § 14-3.1(e) (3d ed. 1999). The 1992 Uniform Victims of Crime Act, promulgated by the National Conference of Commissioners on Uniform State Laws, recommends that all states enact legislation providing that: "To the extent practicable, the [prosecutor] shall confer with the victim before amending or dismissing a charge or agreeing to a [negotiated plea]. . . ." Commentary to this recommendation offers the following supporting rationale:

> Expanding the victim's role will . . . increase cooperation in the reporting of crimes and the prosecution of criminal offenders. Affording victims information concerning the crimes and any negotiated plea will lead to greater victim satisfaction with the criminal justice system which translates into greater cooperation of victims in the prosecution of criminal offenders.

For consideration of competing views regarding the expansion of the victim's role in the plea bargaining process, *see* Josephine Gittler, *Expanding the Role of the Victim in a Criminal Action: An Overview of Issues and Problems*, 11 PEPP. L. REV. 117 (1984); Sarah N. Welling, *Victim Participation in Plea Bargains*, 65 WASH. U.L.Q. 301 (1987); and Donald J. Hall, *Victims' Voices in Criminal Court: The Need for Restraint*, 28 AM. CRIM. L. REV. 233 (1991).

[6] Ensuring Voluntariness of Plea

Rule 11(b)(2) requires that the court determine that a plea of guilty or nolo contendere is voluntary and not the result of improper "false threats, or promises." The United States Supreme Court has held on numerous occasions that a guilty plea must be voluntary. *See, e.g., Brady v. United States*, 397 U.S. 742, 750 (1970) (a plea may not be produced "by actual or threatened physical harm or by mental coercion overbearing the will of the defendant"); *Godinez v. Moran*, 509 U.S. 389 (1993) (guilty plea decision must be "uncoerced").

Case-by-case determination. In determining the voluntariness of a plea, the trial judge must evaluate all of the surrounding circumstances on a case-by-case basis. For example, in *Manley v. United States*, 396 F.2d 699 (5th Cir. 1968), the appellate court interpreted Rule 11 to require that the trial judge determine the effect of narcotics administered to a defendant upon the voluntariness of his proffered plea. There, the trial court's finding of voluntariness was overturned. Interestingly, the appellate court noted that "generally the burden of proof is on a defendant to show that he was under the influence of a narcotic, but in the instant case that burden was shifted to the government because the Assistant United States Attorney had made an innocent misrepresentation that the defendant was not under the influence of narcotics at the time the guilty plea was proffered."

Judge's duty to probe. If there is any credible evidence that the defendant's proffered plea was not the product of free will, a more searching inquiry must be undertaken by the trial judge. For instance, in *Mack v. United States*, 635 F.2d 20 (1st Cir. 1980), the defendant was asked the standard series of questions surrounding the guilty plea, one of which was, "Is your plea entirely free and voluntary?" Mack answered, "Yes, it is." However, some time prior to that, in the context of an inquiry concerning competency to stand trial, Mack stated, "I would like to state that I am being pressured into making the plea. I am not doing it of my own free will." The First Circuit Court of Appeals concluded: "In view of Mack's earlier statement that he was pressured into making a plea, his subsequent answer should have triggered a deeper probe for the purpose of reconciling the clearly contradictory comments." *Id.* at 25.

Kinds of pressures argued to create involuntary plea. There is no shortage of reasons defendants give for seeking to overturn their plea as involuntary. The obvious ones, threats to harm the defendant physically, are rare. More common ones are threats of increased charges unless a plea is entered (not successful); threats to prosecute third parties, such as loved ones (relatives, friends, lovers) unless the defendant pleads (cases divided; sometimes unsuccessful if there is a good faith basis for believing the third party has committed a crime); and threats by the judge (successful if can be proven).

Standard of mental competence to plead. In *Godinez v. Moran*, 509 U.S. 389 (1993), the United States Supreme Court held that a defendant who is adjudged competent to stand trial is also competent to plead guilty. In so holding, the Court rejected the argument that the competency standard for pleading guilty or waiving the right to counsel should be a more demanding one than competency for standing trial. The test for both is whether the defendant has sufficient present ability to consult with defense counsel and has an understanding of the nature of the proceedings at hand.

If the judge, prosecutor, or defense counsel has a reason to question the defendant's competency, the judge should convene a hearing on the issue. The court has the authority to order the defendant to be examined by a mental health professional and both sides would be permitted to offer evidence at the competency hearing.

[7] Advice to Defendant: In General

Rule 11(b)(1) explicitly requires the judge to address the defendant personally and to inform the defendant of specific rights listed. These rights include full awareness of the nature of the charge and possible penalties, right to be represented by counsel, right to plead not guilty, right to jury trial, right to confront and cross-examine witnesses, right not to incriminate himself or herself, and consequences of statements made under oath.

By requiring that the court must personally address the defendant, Rule 11 aims to assure that the trial judge will be better able to ascertain that the plea is voluntary. Subdivisions (b)(1)(B)–(N) also assure that the defendant's waiver of rights when pleading guilty is both knowing and voluntary, in compliance with the standard articulated in *Boykin v. Alabama*, 395 U.S. 238 (1969).

Rule 11(b) requires the judge to do two things: (1) convey information specified in the Rule and (2) "determine that the defendant understands" all of the information communicated by the court. A finding that the defendant knows and understands the rights being waived provides the groundwork for one of the critically important constitutional aspects of the plea hearing: the determination that the defendant's plea of guilty is a knowing and intelligent one.

En masse pleas? May a judge accept simultaneous guilty pleas "*en masse*" from multiple defendants? It is not unusual for arrests and prosecutions for illegal entry into the United States to involve large numbers of defendants. The Ninth Circuit has upheld, albeit with some concerns, the practice of taking guilty pleas en masse from multiple defendants in such cases. In *United States v. Roblero-Solis*, 588 F.3d 692 (9th Cir. 2009) (47 defendants) and again in *United States v. Escamilla-Rojas*, 640 F.3d 1055 (9th Cir. 2011) (67 defendants), the court refused to invalidate such practices, but disapproved of plea colloquy that is limited merely to the defendants all answering "yes" simultaneously to the court's Rule 11(b)(1) questions:

> The adverb "personally," as used in Rule 11, indicates that "the judge's speech is to be person to person." *Roblero-Solis*, 588 F.3d at 700. As the advisory committee's note explains, this language was added to the rule to clarify that the court must address the defendant, rather than his counsel, in person. Although, the "rule speaks only of the defendant in the singular," it is not "rigid," and we have previously held that it does not strictly require the court to address each defendant *individually. Roblero-Solis, 588 F.3d at 700* (citing cases where small groups of co-conspirators have been addressed at once).
>
> Nevertheless, in *United States v. Roblero-Solis*, we rejected the idea "that the number of plea-takers may be indefinitely expanded without violation of Rule 11." *Id.* In *Roblero-Solis*, a magistrate judge both advised a group of forty-seven defendants en masse of their rights and questioned the defendants en masse to determine whether they understood the advisement. There, the transcript denoted only "general 'yes'" answers to the magistrate judge's questions, and the only question posed to the defendants individually was how each defendant would plead to his charge. We held that such procedure violated Rule 11(b)(1), because "no judge, however alert, could tell whether every single person in a group of 47 or 50 affirmatively answered her questions when the answers were taken at the same time." Instead, the court must erect a more individualized procedure "sufficient to show that *each* defendant pleaded voluntarily" and understood the consequences of such plea. *Id.* (emphasis added). [FN2, below.]
>
> FN2. We nevertheless affirmed the convictions in *Roblero-Solis*, concluding that the defendants in that case had failed to demonstrate that the Rule 11 deficiencies amounted to plain error.

Escamilla-Rojas, 640 F.3d at 1159–60. Subsequently, in *United States v. Arqueta-Ramos*, 730 F.3d 1133 (9th Cir. 2013), the same court, relying on *Escamalla-Rojas*, held that a U.S. Magistrate Judge's collective questioning of the defendant and other defendants charged with illegally entering the United States during a "streamlined" group plea proceeding (which combined defendants' initial appearances, guilty pleas, and sentencing hearings) was error requiring *vacatur* of the defendant's conviction.

[8] Knowing and Intelligent Plea

Because a guilty plea involves a waiver of many constitutional rights, the plea is constitutionally valid only if it is "knowing and intelligent." This means that the defendant must understand both the charges and the penalties.

[a] Understanding the Charge

[i] Judge's Duty to Inform

Before accepting a guilty plea, the judge must determine whether the defendant understands the charges. This standard is mandated by both Rule 11(b)(1) and the United States Supreme Court:

> [A plea of guilty] cannot support a judgment of guilt unless it was voluntary in a constitutional sense. And clearly the plea could not be voluntary in the sense that it constituted an intelligent admission that [the defendant] committed the offense unless the defendant received "real notice of the true nature of the charge against him, the first and most universally recognized requirement of due process."

Henderson v. Morgan, 426 U.S. 637 (1976).

In *Henderson*, the defendant pled guilty to second degree murder. At the sentencing hearing, the trial judge did not discuss the elements of that offense or the requirement of actual intent to cause death. Concluding that the defendant did not receive adequate notice of the offense to which he pled guilty, the United States Supreme Court held that "it is impossible to conclude that his plea to the unexplained charge of second degree murder was voluntary." The Court observed:

> Normally the record contains either an explanation of the charge by the trial judge, or at least a representation by defense counsel that the nature of the offense has been explained to the accused. Moreover, even without such an express representation, it may be appropriate to presume that in most cases defense counsel routinely explained the nature of the offense in sufficient detail to give the accused notice of what he is being asked to admit. This case is unique because the trial judge found as a fact that the element of intent was not explained to respondent.

Id. at 647.

Judge's actual performance: empirical evidence. Despite the clear language of Rule 11 (and similar state provisions) and the constitutional underpinning for it, a 1987 survey of felony-level judicial practices in six jurisdictions found that many judges simply fail to inform the defendant of the necessary matters. The average court time per felony plea was 9.9 minutes and per misdemeanor plea was 5.2 minutes. About three-quarters of the defendants were addressed individually by the judge. They were informed of their rights to the following degree: right to a jury trial (70% of defendants were informed); to confront witnesses (44%); to remain silent (38%). In more than half the cases it was noted that defense counsel had explained the rights to the defendant. The charges were explained to the defendant in almost 70% of the cases. In less than half the cases (48%) they were told the maximum possible sentence. The plea agreement's terms were entered in the record in 71% of the cases. The pleas were rejected in less than 2% of the cases. Interviews with defendants who had pled guilty showed that 80% said they understood what had been said about the charges and the rights they would waive. William F. McDonald, *Judicial Supervision of the Guilty Plea Process: a Study of Six Jurisdictions*, 70 JUDICATURE 203 (1987).

[ii] How Informed Must the Defendant Be?

While *Henderson* holds that a defendant must know certain information about the offense to which the guilty plea is addressed, the decision is unclear about how fully informed the defendant must be. It has been held, for example, that the mere reading of the indictment may be insufficient to inform the defendant of the charge. Similarly, simply asking the defendant if he or she understands the charge may not be enough. At least one court has suggested that the exchange between defendant and judge will vary from case to case depending upon the complexity of the charges and the relative sophistication of the defendant.

[iii] Role of Defense Counsel

Note that *Henderson* presumes that normally defense counsel informs the defendant of specific elements of the charges. Does this mean that the defense attorney may serve as a "substitute" for the judge with respect to compliance with Rule 11(b)? Courts have split on this question. In *Horsely v. United States*, 583 F.2d 670 (3d Cir. 1978), the trial judge asked the defendant, "Have you had an opportunity to go over [the indictment] with your attorney?" The defendant responded in the affirmative. There was nothing in the record to show that the elements of the offense had been explained by the judge. Therefore, notwithstanding the defendant's response, this was held to be error under Rule 11. The defendant's sentence was vacated and the plea withdrawn so that he could be permitted to plead anew.

By contrast, in *United States v. Butcher*, 926 F.2d 811 (9th Cir. 1991), the defendant's trial attorney testified that it was his "standard procedure . . . to advise his clients of the nature and elements of the offenses with which the defendant is charged and the possible defenses." The Ninth Circuit, citing *Henderson* for the proposition that "notice of the true nature of a charge does not require a description of every element of the offense," held that it was appropriate to rely upon the attorney's representations and therefore the plea was properly accepted.

[b] Understanding the Penalty

Rules 11(b)(1)(H)–(O) require that the defendant understand the penalties associated with the charge to which the plea is offered. The defendant must understand the mandatory minimum penalty, if any, and the maximum possible penalty, including the effect of any supervised release term. Advisory Committee Notes observe that "giving this advice tells a defendant the shortest mandatory sentence and also the longest possible sentence for the offense to which he is pleading guilty."

Rules 11(b)(1)(H)–(O) also mandate that the defendant be apprised in general that the court must consider any applicable federal sentencing guidelines, including the fact that the court may depart from them under some circumstances. This rule does not prohibit the trial judge from providing additional information about sentencing guidelines; rather, it sets forth only the minimum information that must be conveyed to the defendant by the court. The Advisory Committee Notes to Rule 11 explain:

> This requirement assures that the existence of guidelines will be known to a defendant before a plea of guilty . . . is accepted. Since it will be impracticable, if not impossible, to know which guidelines will be relevant prior to the formulation of a presentence report and resolution of disputed facts, the amendment does not require the court to specify which guidelines will be important or which grounds for departure might prove to be significant. . . . By giving the advice, the court places the defendant and defense counsel on notice of the importance that guidelines may play in sentencing and of the possibility of a departure from those guidelines. A defendant represented by competent counsel will be in a position to enter an intelligent plea.

Collateral consequences. Although a number of indirect or collateral consequences may flow from a judgment of guilty, Rule 11(b) does not require that such information be conveyed to the defendant. It has been held, for example, that the defendant need not be told of the loss of the right to vote. However, in *Padilla v. Kentucky*, 559 U.S. 356 (2010), discussed earlier in this chapter, the Supreme Court held that defense counsel must properly advise the defendant of clear deportation consequences prior to entering a guilty plea.

By way of contrast, *see People v. Harnett*, 945 N.E.2d 439 (N.Y. 2011), where the New York Court of Appeals regarded the distinction between "direct" and "collateral" consequences of guilty pleas to be crucial. There, the court held that the sentencing judge's failure to warn the defendant, prior to pleading guilty to sexual abuse, that he might as a consequence be subject to indefinite civil commitment under that state's Sex Offender Management and Treatment Act, did not render his guilty plea involuntary, unknowing, or fundamentally unfair. The court in *Harnett* drew a sharp distinction between *direct* consequences of a guilty plea (of which the defendant *must* be warned during plea colloquy) and *collateral* consequences (of which the failure to warn does not invalidate the plea). Despite the potentially serious consequence of indefinite (i.e., possible lifetime) civil commitment in *Harnett*, the court deemed it to be collateral rather than direct because it did not necessarily flow immediately or automatically from his plea. Do you agree? Do you see the distinction between a defendant seeking to void a guilty plea based on alleged failure of *counsel* to warn him of potential consequences (*Strickland* ineffective assistance of counsel standard governs), and alleged failure of the *court* to so warn (Rule 11 or comparable state rule, and due process requirement that pleas be knowing, intelligent, and voluntary, govern).

[c] Understanding the Defendant's Rights and the Fact of Waiver

Rule 11 provides an extensive laundry list of rights that the judge is to tell the defendant are available if he or she wants a trial and that those rights are waived by a plea. These include such fundamental rights as the right to plead not guilty, to have a jury trial, to be represented by counsel, and to confront and cross-examine witnesses at that trial.

[d] Inadmissibility of Statements Made in the Course of Plea Discussions

Statements during negotiations inadmissible. In order to encourage plea bargaining, Rule 11(f) and Federal Rule of Evidence 410 provide that statements made in the course of plea discussions between a criminal defendant and a prosecutor are inadmissible against the defendant if the defendant does not actually plead guilty or pleads guilty but then withdraws the guilty plea. Note, however, that these rules do not exclude such statements if the defendant *does* plead guilty. This means that the exclusionary rule in Rule 11(f) does not apply in most cases since the usual practice is for the defendant to enter a guilty plea after the plea negotiations.

Waiver of rule making plea discussion statements inadmissible. What if a prosecutor indicates to the defendant, represented by counsel, that plea negotiations can occur only if the defendant agrees that any statements made during the meeting could be used to impeach any contradictory testimony he or she might give at trial if the case proceeds that far? In response, the defendant and his or her attorney agree to proceed according to those terms. At the later trial, the prosecutor cross-examines the defendant about inconsistent statements made during the unsuccessful plea negotiations. In *United States v. Mezzanatto*, 513 U.S. 196 (1995), the United States Supreme Court held, under those facts, that absent some affirmative indication that the agreement was entered into unknowingly or involuntarily, "an agreement to waive the exclusionary provisions of the plea-statement Rules is valid and enforceable."

[e] Plea and Waiver of Fifth Amendment

A defendant who pleads guilty waives the Fifth Amendment with regard to the plea proceedings. He or she will "confess" in open court as part of the plea process. But does a guilty plea waive the privilege against self-incrimination in the sentencing phase of the case? In *Mitchell v. United States*, 526 U.S. 314 (1999), the Court held, by a 5 to 4 vote, that the plea does not operate as a waiver of the privilege at sentencing. In *Mitchell* the defendant pled guilty to three counts of distributing cocaine near a school ground and to conspiracy to distribute five or more kilograms of cocaine. At the plea colloquy, the U.S. District Court judge, while assessing whether there was a factual basis for the plea, asked her whether she had done the things to which she was pleading guilty. She admitted to doing "some of it," but reserved the right to contest the drug quantity under the conspiracy charge at sentencing. The Court accepted the guilty plea. At sentencing, she did not testify regarding the quantity of drugs. The sentencing judge concluded that her guilty plea waived her Fifth Amendment self-incrimination privilege and therefore the judge could draw an adverse inference from her silence at the sentencing hearing. In reversing, the U.S. Supreme Court explained:

> The Fifth Amendment by its terms prevents a person from being "compelled in any criminal case to be a witness against himself." To maintain that sentencing proceedings are not part of "any criminal case" is contrary to the law and to common sense. [In this case] the defendant was less concerned with the proof of her guilt or innocence than with the severity of her punishment. Petitioner faced imprisonment from one year upwards to life, depending on the circumstances of the crime. To say that she had no right to remain silent but instead could be compelled to cooperate in the deprivation of her liberty would ignore the Fifth Amendment privilege at the precise stage where, from her point of view, it was most important.

The Court also concluded that by drawing an adverse inference from Mitchell's silence, the sentencing judge imposed an impermissible burden on her attempt to exercise her privilege against self-incrimination.

The issue of a defendant's right not to testify under *Griffin v. Illinois*, 380 U.S. 609 (1965), and later cases is explored more fully in Chapter 13. It is worth noting here, however, that the dissenters in *Mitchell* argue vigorously that *Griffin* was erroneously decided. Justice Scalia, joined by the three other dissenters, would refuse to extend *Griffin* in any way—an argument raised again by Justices Thomas and Scalia in *Salinas v. Texas*, 570 U.S. 178, 191 (2013) (Thomas, J., concurring, would not extend *Griffin* to defendant's silence to pre-custodial police interview); Justice Thomas, dissenting in *Mitchell*, would take the further step of considering overruling *Griffin* and its progeny in an appropriate future case. 526 U.S. at 331; *see also* dissent of Scalia, J. at 341. The holdings of both *Griffin* and *Mitchell*, therefore, may be vulnerable in the future.

[9] Factual Basis

Purpose. Rule 11(b)(3) requires that the judge not accept a guilty plea without first determining that there is a *factual basis* for it. The court should ascertain that the conduct the defendant admits to having done constitutes the crime for which the defendant will plead. The purpose of the factual basis rule is to provide at least some assurance that the defendant actually is guilty of the charges. This procedure also is used to deny later motions seeking a reversal on the basis of innocence.

How determined. The Rule does not specify the particular kind of inquiry required, however. According to the Advisory Committee Notes, "[a]n inquiry might be made of the defendant, of the attorneys for the government and the defense, of the presentence report when one is available, or by whatever means is appropriate in a specific case." Sometimes a law enforcement officer or the victim will testify about the defendant's involvement in the crime.

A study of felony practices in six jurisdictions showed that the factual basis was determined most frequently (in 40% of the cases) by asking the defendant if he or she committed the offense. The factual basis was also established by having the prosecutor provide additional information about the crime (48% of the cases) and/or questioning the defendant about the offense (36%). William F. McDonald, *Judicial Supervision of the Guilty Plea Process: a Study of Six Jurisdictions*, 70 JUDICATURE 203 (1987).

Standard of certainty. Note that under Rule 11(b)(3) the court must make an inquiry "as shall satisfy it that there is a factual basis for the plea." In an unusual case, *United States v. Ventura-Cruel*, 356 F.3d 55 (1st Cir. 2003), the trial court accepted a guilty plea, then later rejected it when information at the subsequent sentencing hearing cast doubt on the defendant's guilt. The First Circuit upheld the court's decision based on concerns that there was inadequate factual basis for the plea.

Does the "satisfy" standard require proof beyond a reasonable doubt? By a preponderance of the evidence? By clear and convincing evidence? If the test is less rigorous than the usual criminal case standard of beyond a reasonable doubt, does this mean that the court would accept a guilty plea (and enter a judgment of conviction) on less convincing evidence than would be required for a criminal trial? Keep this question in mind as you read the next case, which deals with the question of whether a judge may accept a guilty plea in the face of the defendant's assertion of innocence.

Baseless pleas. Not all jurisdictions require a factual basis be established before a guilty or *nolo contendere* plea is accepted. And some require a factual basis but accept the plea itself as establishing the factual basis. This leads to a practice of what has been called "baseless pleas." It involves a plea to a crime often totally unrelated to the defendant's criminal actions. The purpose is to facilitate a sentence authorized for the nonexistent crime but barred or politically unacceptable for the actual offense. An excellent article by Mari Byrne, Note, *Baseless Pleas: A Mockery of Justice*, 78 FORDHAM L. REV. 2961 (2010), describes the case of a violent robber permitted to plead guilty to illegal recording of music. As long as the plea is voluntary, knowing, and acceptable to both sides and the judge, do you find any problems with the practice of permitting baseless pleas?

G. Guilty but Not Guilty?

North Carolina v. Alford

400 U.S. 25 (1970)

MR. JUSTICE WHITE delivered the opinion of the Court.

On December 2, 1963, Alford was indicted for first-degree murder, a capital offense under North Carolina law. The court appointed an attorney to represent him, and this attorney questioned all but one of the various witnesses who appellee said would substantiate his claim of innocence. The witnesses, however, did not support Alford's story but gave statements that strongly indicated his guilt. Faced with strong evidence of guilt and no substantial evidentiary support for the claim of innocence, Alford's attorney recommended that he plead guilty, but left the ultimate decision to Alford himself. The prosecutor agreed to accept a plea of guilty to a charge of second-degree murder, and on December 10, 1963, Alford pleaded guilty to the reduced charge.

Before the plea was finally accepted by the trial court, the court heard the sworn testimony of a police officer who summarized the State's case. Two other witnesses besides Alford were also heard. Although there was no eyewitness to the crime, the testimony indicated that shortly before the killing Alford took his gun from his house, stated his intention to kill the victim, and returned home with the declaration that he had carried out the killing. After the summary presentation of the State's case, Alford took the stand and testified that he had not committed the murder but that he was pleading guilty because he faced the threat of the death penalty if he did not do so.[3]

In response to the questions of his counsel, he acknowledged that his counsel had informed him of the difference between second-and first-degree murder and of his rights in case he chose to go to trial. The trial court then asked appellee if, in light of his denial of guilt, he still desired to plead guilty to second-degree murder and appellee answered, "Yes, sir. I plead guilty on—from the circumstances that he (Alford's attorney) told me." After eliciting information about Alford's prior criminal record, which was a long one, the trial court sentenced him to 30 years' imprisonment, the maximum penalty for second-degree murder.

Alford sought post-conviction relief in the state court. Among the claims raised was the claim that his plea of guilty was invalid because it was the product of fear and coercion. After a hearing, the state court in 1965 found that the plea was "willingly, knowingly, and understandingly" made on the advice of competent counsel and in the face of a strong prosecution case.

---

3. After giving his version of the events of the night of the murder, Alford stated: "I pleaded guilty on second degree murder because they said there is too much evidence, but I ain't shot no man, but I take the fault for the other man. We never had an argument in our life and I just pleaded guilty because they said if I didn't they would gas me for it, and that is all." In response to questions from his attorney, Alford affirmed that he had consulted several times with his attorney and with members of his family and had been informed of his rights if he chose to plead not guilty. Alford then reaffirmed his decision to plead guilty to second-degree murder: Q. (by Alford's attorney). "And you authorized me to tender a plea of guilty to second degree murder before the court?" A. "Yes, sir." Q. "And in doing that, that you have again affirmed your decision on that point?" A. "Well, I'm still pleading that you all got me to plead guilty. I plead the other way, circumstantial evidence; that the jury will prosecute me on—on the second. You told me to plead guilty, right. I don't—I'm not guilty but I plead guilty."

... State and lower federal courts are divided upon whether a guilty plea can be accepted when it is accompanied by protestations of innocence and hence contains only a waiver of trial but no admission of guilt.... [W]hile most pleas of guilty consist of both a waiver of trial and an express admission of guilt, the latter element is not a constitutional requisite to the imposition of criminal penalty. An individual accused of crime may voluntarily, knowingly, and understandingly consent to the imposition of a prison sentence even if he is unwilling or unable to admit his participation in the acts constituting the crime.

Nor can we perceive any material difference between a plea that refuses to admit commission of the criminal act and a plea containing a protestation of innocence when, as in the instant case, a defendant intelligently concludes that his interests require entry of a guilty plea and the record before the judge contains strong evidence of actual guilt. Here the State had a strong case of first-degree murder against Alford. Whether he realized or disbelieved his guilt, he insisted on his plea because in his view he had absolutely nothing to gain by a trial and much to gain by pleading. Because of the overwhelming evidence against him, a trial was precisely what neither Alford nor his attorney desired. Confronted with the choice between a trial for first-degree murder, on the one hand, and a plea of guilty to second-degree murder, on the other, Alford quite reasonably chose the latter and thereby limited the maximum penalty to a 30-year term. When his plea is viewed in light of the evidence against him, which substantially negated his claim of innocence and which further provided a means by which the judge could test whether the plea was being intelligently entered, its validity cannot be seriously questioned. In view of the strong factual basis for the plea demonstrated by the State and Alford's clearly expressed desire to enter it despite his professed belief in his innocence, we hold that the trial judge did not commit constitutional error in accepting it.[11]

Mr. Justice Brennan, with whom Mr. Justice Douglas and Mr. Justice Marshall join, dissenting.

... Today the Court makes clear that its previous holding [in *Brady v. United States*] was intended to apply even when the record demonstrates that the actual effect of the unconstitutional threat was to induce a guilty plea from a defendant who was unwilling to admit his guilt.

I adhere to the view that, in any given case, the influence of such an unconstitutional threat "must necessarily be given weight in determining the voluntariness of a plea." And, without reaching the question whether due process permits the entry

---

11. Our holding does not mean that a trial judge must accept every constitutionally valid guilty plea merely because a defendant wishes so to plead. A criminal defendant does not have an absolute right under the Constitution to have his guilty plea accepted by the court, although the States may by statute or otherwise confer such a right. Likewise, the States may bar their courts from accepting guilty pleas from any defendants who assert their innocence. Cf. Fed. Rule Crim. Proc. 11, which gives a trial judge discretion to "refuse to accept a plea of guilty...." We need not now delineate the scope of that discretion.

of judgment upon a plea of guilty accompanied by a contemporaneous denial of acts constituting the crime, I believe that at the very least such a denial of guilt is also a relevant factor in determining whether the plea was voluntarily and intelligently made. With these factors in mind, it is sufficient in my view to state that the facts set out in the majority opinion demonstrate that Alford was "so gripped by fear of the death penalty" that his decision to plead guilty was not voluntary but was "the product of duress as much so as choice reflecting physical constraint." . . .

Notes

1. *Discretion in accepting Alford plea.* As suggested in footnote 11 of *Alford*, trial judges have considerable discretion whether or not to accept a guilty plea from a defendant who asserts factual innocence. One commentator has observed that there are no standards for the acceptance and use of the *Alford* plea, which has led to excessive judge shopping. *See* Curtis J. Shipley, Note, *The Alford Plea: A Necessary But Unpredictable Tool for the Criminal Defendant*, 72 Iowa L. Rev. 1063 (1987). A few jurisdictions reject *Alford* and require an admission of guilt to the crime charged as a precondition to a valid guilty plea. *See, e.g. Sims v. State*, 873 N.E.2d 204 (Ind. Ct. App. 2007) (reversible error to accept guilty plea when defendant maintains his innocence).

2. *Encouraging lies?* Some have suggested that a defendant who asserts innocence while pleading guilty may not be amenable to correctional measures. If true, this notion argues in favor of having guilt or innocence established at the trial stage rather than by a guilty plea. If this practice were followed, however, would it encourage defendants to be less than candid at the plea hearing?

3. *Factual basis matching crime elements.* Under Rule 11(b) the court must find a "factual basis" before accepting a guilty plea. When an *Alford* plea is offered and the defendant essentially denies guilt, the factual basis still is necessary but will not be based on the defendant's own statements. Other sources, such as law enforcement or even the victim, may have to provide the necessary link between the defendant and the crime for which the plea will be entered.

Another issue sometimes confronted by courts in *Alford* plea cases is how closely the evidence establishing a factual basis must match the elements of the offense to which the plea is entered. For example, assume that the defendant is charged with aggravated robbery under a statute defining the offense as the "(1) intentional taking from the person of another property of any value by violence or putting the person in fear and (2) the robbery is accomplished with a deadly weapon or by display of any article used or fashioned to lead the victim to reasonably believe it to be a deadly weapon." As a result of plea negotiations, the defendant is permitted to plead guilty to the crime of simple robbery, which requires only the intentional taking of property by violence or putting the person in fear. At the plea hearing, the trial judge ascertains that the defendant actually accomplished the robbery by using a loaded pistol, satisfying the elements of aggravated robbery. A very strict interpretation of the factual basis requirement might lead the trial judge to reject the guilty plea because the facts established do not comport with the statutory definition of simple robbery. It appears, however, that most courts have little difficulty finding the guilty plea valid under these circumstances. The Supreme Court of California has suggested that the appropriate test in this context is whether the defendant's guilty plea (to an uncharged offense) is "reasonably related to the defendant's conduct." *People v. Jackson*, 694 P.2d 736, 742 (Cal. 1985).

4. *Should judge accept an Alford plea?* The decision whether or not to accept a proffered *Alford* plea may place some judges in a moral/ethical quandary. If you were the judge, would you have any qualms about accepting a plea of guilty from a defendant who still protested his or her innocence? On the other hand, would you have qualms about rejecting a proffered *Alford* plea and as a result, subjecting the defendant to enhanced punishment (possibly even including exposure to the death penalty, as was the circumstance in the *Alford* case itself)?

H. Breach of Plea Agreement

Given the contractual nature of plea agreements, at times either the prosecutor or defendant may refuse or fail to comply with certain terms of the bargain. The American Bar Association states plainly that "The prosecutor should comply with, and make good faith efforts to have carried out, the government's obligations. The prosecutor should construe agreement conditions and evaluate the defendant's performance including cooperation, in a good-faith and responsible manner." CRIMINAL JUSTICE STANDARDS FOR THE PROSECUTION FUNCTION 3–5.7(d) (4th ed. 2015). When compliance is questioned, a determination must be made whether a breach occurred and, if it did, what remedy is appropriate.

Santobello v. New York

404 U.S. 257 (1971)

MR. CHIEF JUSTICE BURGER delivered the opinion of the Court.

We granted certiorari in this case to determine whether the State's failure to keep a commitment concerning the sentence recommendation on a guilty plea required a new trial.

[The defendant agreed to plead guilty to a gambling crime which carried a maximum sentence of one year imprisonment, and the prosecutor agreed to make no recommendation as to the sentence. Following a series of delays, defendant appeared for sentencing. At that time, a different prosecutor than the one who had negotiated the plea appeared for the state and recommended the maximum one-year sentence. Defense counsel immediately objected, but the prosecutor asserted that there was no record to support the defendant's claim of a no-sentence-recommendation promise by the state. In subsequent proceedings, however, the state no longer contested the fact that the earlier promise had been made.]

... This record represents another example of an unfortunate lapse in orderly prosecutorial procedures, in part, no doubt, because of the enormous increase in the workload of the often understaffed prosecutor's offices. The heavy workload may well explain these episodes, but it does not excuse them. The disposition of criminal charges by agreement between the prosecutor and the accused, sometimes loosely called "plea bargaining," is an essential component of the administration of justice. Properly administered, it is to be encouraged. If every criminal charge were subjected to a full-scale trial, the States and the Federal Government would need to multiply by many times the number of judges and court facilities.

Disposition of charges after plea discussions is not only an essential part of the process but a highly desirable part for many reasons. It leads to prompt and largely final disposition of most criminal cases; it avoids much of the corrosive impact of enforced idleness during pre-trial confinement for those who are denied release pending trial; it protects the public from those accused persons who are prone to continue criminal conduct even while on pretrial release; and, by shortening the time between charge and disposition, it enhances whatever may be the rehabilitative prospects of the guilty when they are ultimately imprisoned.

... This phase of the process of criminal justice, and the adjudicative element inherent in accepting a plea of guilty, must be attended by safeguards to insure the defendant what is reasonably due in the circumstances. Those circumstances will vary, but a constant factor is that when a plea rests in any significant degree on a promise or agreement of the prosecutor, so that it can be said to be part of the inducement or consideration, such promise must be fulfilled.

On this record, petitioner "bargained" and negotiated for a particular plea in order to secure dismissal of more serious charges, but also on condition that no sentence recommendation would be made by the prosecutor. It is now conceded that the promise to abstain from a recommendation was made, and at this stage the prosecution is not in a good position to argue that its inadvertent breach of agreement is immaterial. The staff lawyers in a prosecutor's office have the burden of "letting the left hand know what the right hand is doing" or has done. That the breach of agreement was inadvertent does not lessen its impact.

We need not reach the question whether the sentencing judge would or would not have been influenced had he known all the details of the negotiations for the plea. He stated that the prosecutor's recommendation did not influence him and we have no reason to doubt that. Nevertheless, we conclude that the interests of justice and appropriate recognition of the duties of the prosecution in relation to promises made in the negotiation of pleas of guilty will be best served by remanding the case to the state courts for further consideration. The ultimate relief to which petitioner is entitled we leave to the discretion of the state court, which is in a better position to decide whether the circumstances of this case require only that there be specific performance of the agreement on the plea, in which case petitioner should be resentenced by a different judge, or whether, in the view of the state court, the circumstances require granting the relief sought by petitioner, i.e., the opportunity to withdraw his plea of guilty. We emphasize that this is in no sense to question the fairness of the sentencing judge; the fault here rests on the prosecutor, not on the sentencing judge.

The judgment is vacated and the case is remanded for reconsideration not inconsistent with this opinion.

[Justice Douglas concurred, arguing that the trial court should decide the remedy for the government's error, but the defendant's preference should be given great weight since the prosecutor violated the defendant's right in breaching the plea bargain. Justice Marshall, joined by Justices Brennan and Stewart, concurred in part and dissented in part. He believed that the defendant should be permitted to withdraw the plea, which was the relief requested. The government had taken no action in reliance on the plea and would suffer no harm from having to go to trial.]

In the *Santobello* case, there was little doubt that the plea agreement had been breached by the prosecution. Sometimes it is not clear whether a breach—either by the government or by the defendant—took place.

Ricketts v. Adamson

483 U.S. 1 (1987)

Justice White delivered the opinion of the Court.

The question for decision is whether the Double Jeopardy Clause bars the prosecution of respondent for first-degree murder following his breach of a plea agreement under which he had pleaded guilty to a lesser offense, had been sentenced, and had begun serving a term of imprisonment. The Court of Appeals for the Ninth Circuit held that the prosecution of respondent violated double jeopardy principles and directed the issuance of a writ of habeas corpus. We reverse.

In 1976, Donald Bolles, a reporter for the *Arizona Republic*, was fatally injured when a dynamite bomb exploded underneath his car. Respondent was arrested and charged with first-degree murder in connection with Bolles' death. Shortly after his trial had commenced, while jury selection was underway, respondent and the state prosecutor reached an agreement whereby respondent agreed to plead guilty to a charge of second-degree murder and to testify against two other individuals—Max Dunlap and James Robison—who were allegedly involved in Bolles' murder. Specifically, respondent agreed to "testify fully and completely in any Court, State or Federal, when requested by proper authorities against any and all parties involved in the murder of Don Bolles. . . ." The agreement provided that "[s]hould the defendant refuse to testify or should he at any time testify untruthfully . . . then this entire agreement is null and void and the original charge will be automatically reinstated."[1]

1. The agreement further provided that, in the event respondent refused to testify, he "will be

The parties agreed that respondent would receive a prison sentence of 48–49 years, with a total incarceration time of 20 years and 2 months. In January 1977, the state trial court accepted the plea agreement and the proposed sentence, but withheld imposition of the sentence. Thereafter, respondent testified as obligated under the agreement, and both Dunlap and Robison were convicted of the first-degree murder of Bolles. While their convictions and sentences were on appeal, the trial court, upon motion of the State, sentenced respondent. In February 1980, the Arizona Supreme Court reversed the convictions of Dunlap and Robison and remanded their cases for retrial. This event sparked the dispute now before us.

The State sought respondent's cooperation and testimony in preparation for the retrial of Dunlap and Robison. On April 3, 1980, however, respondent's counsel informed the prosecutor that respondent believed his obligation to provide testimony under the agreement had terminated when he was sentenced. Respondent would again testify against Dunlap and Robison only if certain conditions were met, including, among others, that the State release him from custody following the retrial.[2]

The State then informed respondent's attorney on April 9, 1980, that it deemed respondent to be in breach of the plea agreement. On April 18, 1980, the State called respondent to testify in pretrial proceedings. In response to questions, and upon advice of counsel, respondent invoked his Fifth Amendment privilege against self-incrimination.

[After the State filed a new information charging respondent with first-degree murder, respondent filed a motion to quash the information on grounds of a double jeopardy violation. The Arizona Supreme Court rejected the challenge, holding that the plea agreement "by its very terms waives the defense of double jeopardy if the agreement is violated."]

. . . Respondent was then convicted of first-degree murder and sentenced to death.

. . . We may assume that jeopardy attached at least when respondent was sentenced in December 1978, on his plea of guilty to second-degree murder. Assuming also that under Arizona law second-degree murder is a lesser included offense of first-degree murder, the Double Jeopardy Clause, absent special circumstances, would have precluded prosecution of respondent for the greater charge on which he now stands convicted. The State submits, however, that respondent's breach of the plea arrangement

---

subject to the charge of Open Murder, and if found guilty of First Degree Murder, to the penalty of death or life imprisonment requiring mandatory twenty-five years actual incarceration, and the State shall be free to file any charges, not yet filed as of the date of this agreement."

2. Respondent's other conditions—which he characterized as "demands"—included that he be held in a nonjail facility with protection during the retrials, that he be provided with new clothing, that protection be afforded his ex-wife and son, that a fund be provided for his son's education, that he be given adequate resources to establish a new identity outside Arizona following his release from custody, and that he be granted "full and complete immunity for any and all crimes in which he may have been involved."

to which the parties had agreed removed the double jeopardy bar to prosecution of respondent on the first-degree murder charge. We agree with the State.

... The agreement specifies in two separate paragraphs the consequences that would flow from respondent's breach of his promises. Paragraph 5 provides that if respondent refused to testify, "this entire agreement is null and void and the original charge will be automatically reinstated." (emphasis added). Similarly, Paragraph 15 of the agreement states that "[i]n the event this agreement becomes null and void, then the parties shall be returned to the positions they were in before this agreement." Respondent unquestionably understood the meaning of these provisions.

... The terms of the agreement could not be clearer: in the event of respondent's breach occasioned by a refusal to testify, the parties would be returned to the status quo ante, in which case respondent would have no double jeopardy defense to waive. And, an agreement specifying that charges may be reinstated given certain circumstances is, at least under the provisions of this plea agreement, precisely equivalent to an agreement waiving a double jeopardy defense.

... We are also unimpressed by the Court of Appeals' holding that there was a good-faith dispute about whether respondent was bound to testify a second time and that until the extent of his obligation was decided, there could be no knowing and intelligent waiver of his double jeopardy defense. But respondent knew that if he breached the agreement he could be retried, and it is incredible to believe that he did not anticipate that the extent of his obligation would be decided by a court. Here he sought a construction of the agreement in the Arizona Supreme Court, and that court found that he had failed to live up to his promise. The result was that respondent was returned to the position he occupied prior to execution of the plea bargain: he stood charged with first-degree murder. Trial on that charge did not violate the Double Jeopardy Clause.

... Finally, it is of no moment that following the Arizona Supreme Court's decision respondent offered to comply with the terms of the agreement. At this point, respondent's second-degree murder conviction had already been ordered vacated and the original charge reinstated. The parties did not agree that respondent would be relieved from the consequences of his refusal to testify if he were able to advance a colorable argument that a testimonial obligation was not owing. The parties could have struck a different bargain, but permitting the State to enforce the agreement the parties actually made does not violate the Double Jeopardy Clause. [Reversed]

Justice Brennan, with whom Justice Marshall, Justice Blackmun, and Justice Stevens join, dissenting.

The critical question in this case is whether Adamson ever breached his plea agreement. Only by demonstrating that such a breach occurred can it plausibly be argued that Adamson waived his rights under the Double Jeopardy Clause.

... Without disturbing the conclusions of the Arizona Supreme Court as to the proper construction of the plea agreement, one may make two observations central to the resolution of this case. First, the agreement does not contain an explicit waiver of all double jeopardy protection.

... Second, Adamson's interpretation of the agreement—that he was not required to testify at the retrials of Max Dunlap and James Robison—was reasonable. Nothing in the plea agreement explicitly stated that Adamson was required to provide testimony should retrials prove necessary....

... This Court has yet to address in any comprehensive way the rules of construction appropriate for disputes involving plea agreements. Nevertheless, it seems clear that the law of commercial contract may in some cases prove useful as an analogy or point of departure in construing a plea agreement, or in framing the terms of the debate. It is also clear, however, that commercial contract law can do no more than this, because plea agreements are constitutional contracts. The values that underlie commercial contract law, and that govern the relations between economic actors, are not coextensive with those that underlie the Due Process Clause, and that govern relations between criminal defendants and the State. Unlike some commercial contracts, plea agreements must be construed in light of the rights and obligations created by the Constitution.

... Of course, far from being a commercial actor, Adamson is an individual whose "contractual" relation with the State is governed by the Constitution. The determination of Adamson's rights and responsibilities under the plea agreement is controlled by the principles of fundamental fairness imposed by the Due Process Clause. To grant to one party—here, the State—the unilateral and exclusive right to define the meaning of a plea agreement is patently unfair. Moreover, such a grant is at odds with the basic premises that underlie the constitutionality of the plea-bargaining system. Guilty pleas are enforceable only if taken voluntarily and intelligently. It would be flatly inconsistent with these requirements to uphold as intelligently made a plea agreement which provided that, in the future, the agreement would mean whatever the State interpreted it to mean. Yet the Court upholds today the equivalent of such an agreement. The logic of the plea-bargaining system requires acknowledgment and protection of the defendant's right to advance against the State a reasonable interpretation of the plea agreement.

This right requires no exotic apparatus for enforcement. Indeed, it requires nothing more than common civility. If the defendant offers an interpretation of a plea agreement at odds with that of the State, the State should notify the defendant of this fact, particularly if the State is of the view that continued adherence to defendant's view would result in breach of the agreement. If the State and the defendant are then unable to resolve their dispute through further discussion, a ready solution exists—either party may seek to have the agreement construed by the court in which the plea was entered. By following these steps the State would have placed far fewer demands on the judicial process than were in fact imposed here, and would have fulfilled its constitutional obligation to treat all persons with due respect.

The unfairness of the Court's decision does not end here. Even if one assumes, arguendo, that Adamson breached his plea agreement by offering an erroneous interpretation of that agreement, it still does not follow that the State was entitled to retry Adamson on charges of first degree murder. As the Court acknowledges, immediately following the decision of the Arizona Supreme Court adopting the State's construction of the plea agreement, Adamson sent a letter to the State stating that he was ready and willing to testify. At this point, there was no obstacle to proceeding with the retrials of Dunlap and Robison; each case had been dismissed without prejudice to refiling, and only about one month's delay had resulted from the dispute over the scope of the plea agreement. Thus, what the State sought from Adamson—testimony in the Dunlap and Robison trials—was available to it.

... The Court's decision flouts the law of contract, due process, and double jeopardy. It reflects a world where individuals enter agreements with the State only at their peril, where the Constitution does not demand of the State the minimal good faith and responsibility that the common law imposes on commercial enterprises, and where, in blind deference to state courts and prosecutors, this Court abdicates its duty to uphold the Constitution. I dissent.

Notes

1. *Need for careful drafting.* The *Ricketts* case underscores the significance of drafting precise plea agreements. Note, for example, that the plea agreement did not explicitly state that the defendant was required to testify in any future proceedings that might take place after appellate review. A number of commentators have asserted that Adamson's interpretation of the agreement was a reasonable one. *See* Graham Hughes, *Agreements for Cooperation in Criminal Cases*, 45 Vand. L. Rev. 1 (1992); Mark V. Tushnet, *The Politics of Executing the Innocent: The Death Penalty in the Next Century?*, 53 U. Pitt. L. Rev. 261, 263 (1991) (noting, sarcastically, that the United States Supreme Court apparently believes that "the death penalty is an appropriate sanction for breach of contract"). Professor Tushnet points out, however, that Adamson ultimately was spared the death penalty through some "bizarre" developments that occurred after the case was remanded to the Ninth Circuit Court of Appeals. *Id.* at 264, n.8.

2. *Interpretation of plea agreements and the role of contract law.* Is the commercial contract analogy the appropriate one in deciding whether or not a breach of a plea agreement has occurred? In many breach-of-plea-bargain cases, courts address a variety of contract concepts, such as inducements to bargain, expectations of the parties, and receipt of benefit of the bargain. *See In re Alfro*, 180 F.3d 372 (2d Cir. 1999) (plea agreements are interpreted under contract law but there are unique due process concerns for fairness and procedural safeguards).

In *United States v. Wood*, 378 F.3d 342 (4th Cir. 2004), the court observed:

> The law governing the interpretation of plea agreements is an "amalgam of constitutional, supervisory, and private [contract] law concerns. In

> most cases, contract principles will be wholly dispositive because neither side should be able, any more than would be private contracting parties, unilaterally to renege or seek modification simply because of uninduced mistake or change of mind. A plea agreement, however, is not simply a contract between two parties. It necessarily implicates the integrity of the criminal justice system and requires the courts to exercise judicial authority in considering the plea agreement and in accepting or rejecting the plea. Consequently, we hold the Government to a greater degree of responsibility than the defendant (or possibly than would be either of the parties to commercial contracts) for imprecisions or ambiguities in plea agreements."

3. *Construe against government.* A number of courts have observed that ambiguities in the plea agreement should be construed against the government due to the unequal bargaining power between the government and the defendant. *See, e.g., United States v. Vaval*, 404 F.3d 144 (2d Cir. 2005) (plea agreements construed against government; government's conduct must comport with highest standards of fairness). *See also United States v. Frownfelter*, 626 F.3d 549 (10th Cir. 2010), where after entry of a plea of guilty to an indictment charging theft of government funds, the presentence report and the prosecution both mischaracterized the misdemeanor offense as a felony. Despite the defendant's objection, the district court sentenced the defendant as a felon. Denouncing the indictment as "poorly drafted" and the plea agreement as "botched," the appellate court vacated the felony conviction and remanded for entry of a misdemeanor conviction and sentence. The court pointedly rejected the government's argument that the plea should be voided altogether and the charges reinstated on the contract-based grounds of frustration of purpose and mutual mistake, stating, "We decline the invitation to rescue the government from its own blunder." *Id.* at 551.

4. *Too vague to enforce.* A plea agreement may involve such vague terms that all or part of it is unenforceable. *See, e.g., State v. Nason*, 981 P.2d 866 (Wash. Ct. App. 1999) (defendant pled guilty on agreement that "no other charges will be filed"; applying contract principle of lack of mutual assent, court found this language ambiguous and refused to bar new charges for conduct unknown to prosecutor at time of plea).

5. *Sentence recommendations.* A large number of plea bargain breach cases involve situations related to promises from the government concerning sentencing recommendations. In *United States v. Brummett*, 786 F.2d 720 (6th Cir. 1986), the plea agreement provided that the government would make no recommendation as to the sentence. At the sentencing hearing, however, the prosecutor stated that while no specific recommendation would be made, "a lengthy incarceration" was necessary because of the defendant's criminal behavior. Because the prosecutor did not make a "specific" recommendation, the court held that there was no breach of the plea agreement.

By contrast, in *United States v. Crusco*, 536 F.2d 21 (3d Cir. 1976), the government agreed to take no position at the sentencing hearing. When the hearing was held, however, the prosecutor attacked the defendant's character and reputation and also provided details as to the defendant's criminal record. On these facts, the court ruled that the government had breached the agreement: "We see the government's characterization [of the defendant] as a transparent effort to influence the severity of [the defendant's] sentence." *Id.*, at 26. *See also United States v. Johnson*, 187 F.3d 1129 (9th Cir. 1999) (plea agreement said government would recommend a four-level enhancement for possession of firearm but would not recommend any other enhancement or departure; condition violated when prosecutor introduced victim impact statement in attempt to increase sentence).

6. *Require prosecutor to be "enthusiastic"?* In *United States v. Benchimol*, 471 U.S. 453 (1985), a per curiam decision, the United States Supreme Court reviewed a case in which the government had agreed to recommend probation with restitution in exchange for the defendant's guilty plea. At the sentencing hearing, the defense attorney informed the judge that the presentence report erroneously stated that the government would "stand silent." The Assistant United States Attorney remarked that the defense attorney had made an "accurate representation" in so correcting the presentence report. A lower court found that the government had breached the agreement because the government attorney "made no effort to explain [the recommendation] but rather left an impression with the court of less-than-enthusiastic support for leniency." Reversing that decision, the United States Supreme Court found no breach:

> It may well be that the Government in a particular case might commit itself to "enthusiastically" make a particular recommendation to the court, and it may be that the Government in a particular case might agree to explain to the court the reasons for the Government's making a particular recommendation. But respondent does not contend, nor did the Court of Appeals find, that the Government had in fact undertaken to do either of these things here. The Court of Appeals simply held that as a matter of law such an undertaking was to be implied from the Government's agreement to recommend a particular sentence. But our view of Rule 11 is that it speaks in terms of what the parties in fact agree to, and does not suggest that such implied-in-law terms as were read into this agreement by the Court of Appeals have any place under the Rule. [*Id.* at 455]

[1] Remedies for Breach of Plea Agreement

[a] Breach by Defendant

Recall *Santobello's* discussion of the question of remedy. Where the defendant breaches the plea agreement, the prosecution no longer is required to uphold its end of the bargain. Thus, the government may re-charge the defendant and proceed to trial. And, as noted in *Ricketts*, the defendant's breach also removes a double jeopardy bar to prosecution of the defendant on a higher charge than the one to which the defendant initially pled guilty.

[b] Breach by Government

When the prosecutor breaks the plea agreement, however, there are three options available to the court. First, the court may view the breach as not meriting any remedy. Second, specific performance of the agreement can be demanded, meaning that the defendant insists upon full compliance with the plea agreement. Third, the defendant may be allowed to withdraw the plea.

[i] No Remedy Necessary for Breach

Many cases hold that the defendant is entitled to relief whenever the government breaches the plea agreement after the plea is entered, irrespective of whether the defendant suffers prejudice. The government is held to a high standard of integrity. In two situations, however, some courts have held no remedy is needed despite the government's breach.

De minimis harm. In some situations the government or court commits a technical violation of the plea agreement but the defendant suffers no real harm and gets essentially what was expected in the bargain. No remedy is ordered. In *Paradiso v. United States*, 689 F.2d 28 (2d Cir. 1982), for example, the defendant entered a plea bargain that sentences would run concurrently rather than consecutively and would not total more than 10 years. Although the trial judge sentenced him to serve the two sentences consecutively, the Court of Appeals imposed no remedy for the breach of the agreement because the total number of years did not exceed 10, which was characterized as the real essence of the plea agreement.

Government later remedies the breach. In a few unusual cases, the government breaches a plea agreement then later "cures" it by subsequent action that satisfies the defendant's expectations in making the deal. For example, in *United States v. Brody*, 808 F.2d (2d Cir. 1986), the plea agreement obligated the government to tell the court of the defendant's cooperation with law enforcement, but at sentencing the prosecution did not do so. Nevertheless, at a subsequent hearing on a motion to reduce sentence, the prosecution complied with the agreement. No remedy was ordered because the defendant received the benefit he had bargained for in the plea agreement.

[ii] Specific Performance

When specific performance is deemed the proper remedy for the government's breach of a plea agreement, the case is routinely remanded to the trial court to implement the agreement. As suggested in *Santobello*, the new sentencing should occur before a different judge and the prosecutor would then be compelled to adhere to the plea agreement in full. It should be noted, however, that some courts have questioned whether reassignment to a different judge is required in all cases. *See, e.g., State v. Bracht*, 573 N.W.2d 176 (S.D. 1997) (cases cited in dissenting opinion).

In federal cases, it appears that specific performance is the remedy usually ordered by trial judges. Appellate courts routinely defer to the trial judge's decision. *See United States v. Moscahlaidis*, 868 F.2d 1357 (3d Cir. 1989). However, in order to obtain specific performance through federal habeas corpus relief, a state prisoner must prove that the state court error was so serious that the state ruling went beyond fairminded disagreement. *See Kernan v. Cuero*, 138 S. Ct. 4 (2017).

What factors should a trial judge use in deciding upon the appropriate remedy? Some states, influenced by Justice Douglas's concurring opinion in *Santobello*, hold that the defendant's preference should be given considerable weight. *Brooks v. Narick*, 243 S.E.2d 841 (W. Va. 1978). For more on remedies for broken plea agreements, *see* Peter Westen & David Westin, *A Constitutional Law of Remedies for Broken Plea Bargains*, 66 Cal. L. Rev. 471 (1978).

[iii] Withdrawal of Guilty Plea

The other remedy available to the defendant is to withdraw the guilty plea, returning both the government and the defendant to their original positions. *See* Subsection J., *infra*.

[2] Specifying Remedy in Plea Agreement

As discussed earlier, plea agreements must be as thorough and precise as possible. The agreement should also include the issue of remedy in the event of breach. For a good example of such a written agreement, *see United States v. Jefferies*, 908 F.2d 1520 (11th Cir. 1990) (the plea agreement contained a provision that any breach of the agreement by defendants for failure to forfeit identified property would (1) not relieve the defendants of their obligation to continue in their original plea of guilty, (2) permit the government to reinstate and proceed with other identified criminal charges, and (3) permit the government to "instigate and proceed with any prosecution of any other offenses now known to the government."). *See also Jones v. Commonwealth*, 995 S.W.2d 363 (Ky. 1999) (defendant violated valid plea agreement that required him to appear for sentencing hearing or prosecutor would recommend sentence of 20 years instead of 6).

I. Effect of Rule 11 Violations

Rule 11 obligates the court to perform a litany of specific tasks. Common experience teaches that any such comprehensive rule will be violated on occasion, whether accidentally or purposefully. What is the legal effect of a trial judge's failure to comply with every detail of Rule 11? One approach would be to hold that any violation, however slight or unintentional, invalidates the guilty plea. While this result could be rationalized as technically appropriate, it could be seen as unjust because guilty pleas would be invalidated for technical reasons when the defendant was not actually misled about anything. For example, assume that the trial judge did not apprise the defendant of the mandatory minimum penalty in a case in which the defendant had agreed to plead guilty and receive a sentence that far exceeded the minimum penalty. Should the defendant's plea be invalidated because of that minor and seemingly irrelevant oversight?

[1] Harmless Error: Defense Objection

Rule 11(h) establishes the harmless error standard, specifying that a variance from Rule 11 procedures which "does not affect substantial rights" shall be considered harmless error. In other words, such minor errors are not grounds for invalidating or undoing the plea. The rule does not define the meaning of "substantial rights"; that is left to the courts. This short provision is very important because it means that literal word-for-word compliance with all Rule 11 provisions is not necessarily required.

The difficult judicial task is to ascertain circumstances in which noncompliance with Rule 11 affected substantial rights and will result in vacating the defendant's conviction and remanding for new proceedings. The Tenth Circuit Court of Appeals has held that the appropriate standard is whether the failure to comply with Rule 11 "had a significant influence on [the defendant's] decision to plead guilty." *United States v. Barry*, 895 F.2d 702, 704 (10th Cir. 1990).

If the defendant objected to the court's Rule 11 violation, the burden is on the government to prove the error was harmless. *See United States v. Davila*, 569 U S. 597 (2013). Some Rule 11 errors have been deemed of sufficient magnitude that they were not harmless. *See, e.g., United States v. Harrington*, 354 F.3d 178 (2d Cir. 2004) (failure to apprise defendant of restitution possibility not harmless if restitution ordered).

With respect to Rule 11 violations raised on direct appeal, the Advisory Committee Notes (1983 amendment) provide:

> ... [I]t is fair to say that the kinds of Rule 11 violations which might be found to constitute harmless error upon direct appeal are fairly limited. Illustrative are: where the judge's compliance with subdivision (c)(1) was not absolutely complete, in that some essential element of the crime was not mentioned, but the defendant's responses clearly indicate his awareness of that element; where the judge's compliance with subdivision (c)(2) was erroneous in part in that the judge understated the maximum penalty somewhat, but the penalty actually imposed did not exceed that indicated in the warnings; and where the judge completely failed to comply with subdivision (c)(5), which of course has no bearing on the validity of the plea itself.

As the Advisory Committee Notes to Rule 11 also make clear, however, the harmless error rule is not to be construed by trial judges as an invitation to be sloppy in conducting Rule 11 proceedings: "[Rule 11(h)] makes no change in the responsibilities of the judge at Rule 11 proceedings, but instead merely rejects the extreme sanction of automatic reversal." The Advisory Committee concludes with a reiteration of the importance of compliance with Rule 11:

> ... [t]houghtful and careful compliance with Rule 11 best serves the cause of fair and efficient administration of criminal justice, as it will help reduce the great waste of judicial resources required to process the frivolous attacks

> on guilty plea convictions that are encouraged, and are more difficult to dispose of, when the original record is inadequate. It is, therefore, not too much to require that, before sentencing defendants to years of imprisonment, district judges take the few minutes necessary to inform them of their rights and to determine whether they understand the action they are taking.

[2] Plain Error: No Objection by Defense

Assume that a Rule 11 violation is committed by the U.S. District Court judge during the plea colloquy. Assume, further, that the defendant fails to lodge a contemporaneous objection thereto. After the guilty plea is accepted and the defendant is sentenced, an appeal is filed. By what standard is the appellate court to ascertain whether the defendant is entitled to relief?

In *United States v. Dominguez Benitez*, 542 U.S. 74 (2004), the Supreme Court held that because no objection was made at the time of the error, appellate courts may correct a plain error only under Rule 52(b). This provision allows for a correction of a "plain error that affects substantial rights" (see fuller discussion of the plain error doctrine in Chapter 17). This, in turn, means that the defendant "is obliged to show a reasonable probability that, but for the error, he would not have entered the plea." The Court noted that because of the error, "probability of a different result is sufficient to undermine confidence in the outcome of the proceeding."

Under this standard, plain error has been found in a fairly small number of cases. Courts look at the "totality of circumstances" in the entire record to determine whether the defendant has satisfied his or her burden of proof. For example, in *United States v. Martinez*, 289 F.3d 1023 (7th Cir. 2002), the trial judge violated Rule 11 by not informing defendant of the maximum possible sentence or the elements of two drug offenses. Nevertheless, the Seventh Circuit found no plain error since the prosecutor had informed the defendant of the maximum sentence, the court told defendant of the nature (though not the elements) of the charge, the defendant, represented by two lawyers, agreed that the government could prove its case, and defendant told the judge that he understood the charges and consequences of pleading guilty.

[3] Collateral Attack

Whether relief will be granted for failure to comply fully with Rule 11 procedures may hinge upon the way in which relief is sought. For example, the defendant may pursue a collateral attack upon the plea pursuant to 28 U.S.C. § 2255. Such an action was brought in *United States v. Timmreck*, 441 U.S. 780 (1979), where the trial judge had failed to inform the defendant of a mandatory special parole term following imprisonment. Since the error did not result in a "complete miscarriage of justice" or in a proceeding "inconsistent with the rudimentary demands of fair procedure," relief was denied. The United States Supreme Court also noted that Timmreck's claim was one of a "technical violation" of Rule 11 and that the claim could have been raised on direct appeal.

J. Finality

[1] Withdrawal of Plea

Federal Rule of Criminal Procedure 11 (d) and (e), reprinted verbatim here because of their importance, govern the withdrawal of guilty pleas:

> (d) **Withdrawing a Guilty or Nolo Contendere Plea.** A defendant may withdraw a plea of guilty or nolo contendere:
>
> > (1) before the court accepts the plea, for any reason or no reason; or
> >
> > (2) after the court accepts the plea, but before it imposes sentence if:
> >
> > (A) the court rejects a plea agreement under Rule 11(c)(5); or
> >
> > (B) the defendant can show a fair and just reason for requesting the withdrawal.
>
> (e) **Finality of a Guilty or Nolo Contendere Plea.** After the court imposes sentence, the defendant may not withdraw a plea of guilty or nolo contendere, and the plea may be set aside only on direct appeal or collateral attack.

[a] Withdrawal by Defendant

[i] Type of Plea

Sometimes a defendant who has entered into a plea agreement will desire to withdraw the guilty plea either for the purpose of proceeding to trial or for the purpose of trying to negotiate a more favorable agreement. Whether or not the defendant will be allowed to do so requires careful attention to Rules 11(c), (d), and (e) and 32(d), and to the exact nature of the plea. Under Rule 11(c)(1), the government, in exchange for the defendant's guilty plea, may agree to do any one or more of the following three options: move for dismissal of other charges, make a non-binding recommendation for a particular sentence, or agree that a specific sentence is appropriate. Rule 11(c) requires close attention to the type of agreement specified because if the agreement is of the type specified in subdivision (c)(3)(B) [a non-binding recommendation for a particular sentence], "the court must advise the defendant that the defendant has no right to withdraw the plea if the court does not follow the recommendation or request."

As to the other types of agreements, however, the court must either accept or reject the agreement "so that it may be determined whether the defendant shall receive the bargained-for concessions or shall instead be afforded an opportunity to withdraw his plea." Notes of Advisory Committee on Rules (1979 Amendment).

[ii] Before or After Imposition of Sentence

A defendant may seek to get out of a guilty plea at any of three times.

Before entering plea. If the defendant works out a deal with the prosecution but has a change of mind before actually entering the plea in court, he or she may back out of the deal for any reason.

After plea entered but before judge accepts it and imposes sentence. After the defendant enters a plea in court but before the court accepts it and imposes sentence, Rule 11(d)(2)(B) provides that the court may permit withdrawal if the defendant shows any "fair and just reason," discussed below.

After judge accepts plea and imposes sentence. In contrast, the rules change once the judge has accepted the plea and imposed sentence. Federal Rule of Criminal Procedure 11(e) provides, "After the court imposes sentence, the defendant may not withdraw a plea of guilty or nolo contendere, and the plea may be set aside only on direct appeal or collateral attack."

This rule recognizes the clear dichotomy between pre-sentence and post-sentence motions to withdraw the guilty plea. In the former instance, the defendant's motion to withdraw the plea is governed by the "fair and just reason" standard, as opposed to the more restrictive standard applicable to relief sought under § 2255 (federal post-conviction relief): "a fundamental defect which inherently results in a complete miscarriage of justice or an omission inconsistent with the rudimentary demands of fair procedure."

[iii] Fair and Just Reason to Withdraw

If defendant seeks to withdraw a plea after it is made and accepted but before the judge imposes sentence, the defendant has the burden of showing a "fair and just" reason for withdrawal of the plea. Recognizing that this standard is inexact, Notes of the Advisory Committee (1983 amendment) observed:

> Whether the [defendant] has asserted his legal innocence is an important factor to be weighed, as is the reason why the defenses were not put forward at the time of the original pleading. The amount of time which has passed between the plea and the motion must also be taken into account.
>
> If the defendant establishes such a reason, it is then appropriate to consider whether the government would be prejudiced by withdrawal of the plea. Substantial prejudice may be present for a variety of reasons [citing cases in which physical evidence had been discarded, the chief government witness had died, other defendants with whom defendant had been joined for trial had already been tried in a lengthy trial, and the fact that prosecution had dismissed more than 50 witnesses who had traveled long distances for the trial].

[iv] State Variations

State rules governing the withdrawal of guilty pleas vary significantly with regard to: (1) at what point during the criminal process withdrawal is allowed, and (2) the standard for allowing withdrawal. Consistent with the federal model, most states utilize a more demanding withdrawal standard after sentencing than when the motion to withdraw is filed before sentence is imposed.

[v] Deferral of Decision on Permitting Withdrawal

On occasion, a judge will accept a guilty plea (finding, of course, that the defendant was acting knowingly, voluntarily, and intelligently, and that there was a factual basis for the plea) but defer a decision on whether to accept the plea *agreement* until after completion of a presentence report. Assume that a defendant moves to withdraw the guilty plea *before* the trial judge has ruled on whether to accept the plea agreement. Does the defendant have an absolute right to do so, or must he or she provide a "fair and just reason" for the withdrawal as required by Rule 11(d)(2)(B)? The Supreme Court ruled unanimously in *United States v. Hyde*, 520 U.S. 670 (1997), that Rule 11(d)(2)(B) (formerly Rule 32 (e)) governs and thus the defendant cannot withdraw the plea "simply on a lark."

Notes

1. *Absolute right to withdraw plea before acceptance by court.* Under Rule 11(d)(1) a defendant may withdraw a plea "for any reason or for no reason" before the court accepts it. Courts therefore have no discretion to deny a motion to withdraw a guilty plea brought prior to its acceptance by the court, and regard this right as absolute. *United States v. Mendez-Santana*, 645 F.3d 822 (6th Cir. 2011), in accord with three other circuits. Because of the lack of any discretion under Rule 11(d)(1) to deny a motion to withdraw a guilty plea prior to its acceptance by the court, such denials are reviewed under a *de novo* standard. *Id.*

2. *Review of ruling on Rule 11(d)(2)(B) motion for abuse of discretion.* In *United States v. Bonilla*, 637 F.3d 980 (9th Cir. 2011), the defendant, after pleading guilty to firearms charges but before imposition of sentence, moved unsuccessfully in the district court to withdraw his plea on the ground that his counsel had not first informed him that he would most likely be deported as a consequence of his plea. The Ninth Circuit applied an abuse of discretion standard of review to the district court's denial of the defendant's motion, holding that his attorney's failure to advise him of the immigration consequences of his guilty plea provided a "fair and just reason" for withdrawal under Rule 11(d)(2)(B), and that the denial of his motion amounted to an abuse of discretion by the district court. The court also observed, "as we have recently explained, the 'fair and just' standard is generous and must be applied liberally." 637 F.3d at 983.

[b] Withdrawal by Prosecution

[i] Before Plea Entered

A different question—not addressed in the Federal Rules of Criminal Procedure—is whether the prosecution is allowed to withdraw a plea offer before the plea is entered in court. In *Mabry v. Johnson*, 467 U.S. 504 (1984), the defendant was tried and convicted on charges of burglary, assault, and murder. After the murder conviction was set aside by the state supreme court, plea negotiations ensued. The prosecutor proposed that in exchange for a plea of guilty to the charge of accessory after felony murder, the prosecutor would recommend a sentence of 21 years to be served *concurrently* with the burglary and assault sentences. The next day, the defendant's lawyer called the prosecutor to convey his acceptance of the offer but "was told that a mistake had been made" and the prosecutor therefore withdrew the offer. Instead, the prosecutor now proposed to recommend the sentence of 21 years to be served *consecutively* to the other sentences. Ultimately, the defendant accepted the prosecutor's second offer.

Following the district court's dismissal of his habeas corpus petition, defendant appealed to the Eighth Circuit Court of Appeals, which reversed. The Circuit Court concluded that "'fairness' precluded the prosecution's withdrawal of a plea proposal once accepted by respondent." A unanimous United States Supreme Court reversed. Citing *Santobello v. New York*, the Court acknowledged that when the prosecution breaches its promise with respect to an *executed* plea agreement, the defendant pleads guilty on a false premise and therefore the conviction cannot stand. This case, however, is fundamentally different:

> *Santobello* demonstrates why respondent may not successfully attack his plea of guilty. Respondent's plea was in no sense induced by the prosecutor's withdrawn offer; unlike Santobello, who pleaded guilty thinking he had bargained for a specific prosecutorial sentencing recommendation which was not ultimately made, at the time respondent pleaded guilty he knew the prosecution would recommend a 21-year consecutive sentence. Respondent does not challenge the District Court's finding that he pleaded guilty with the advice of competent counsel and with full awareness of the consequences—he knew that the prosecutor would recommend and that the judge could impose the sentence now under attack. Respondent's plea was thus in no sense the product of governmental deception; it rested on no "unfulfilled promise" and fully satisfied the test for voluntariness and intelligence.

Thus, because it did not impair the voluntariness or intelligence of his guilty plea, respondent's inability to enforce the prosecutor's offer is without constitutional significance. Neither is the question whether the prosecutor was negligent or otherwise culpable in first making and then withdrawing his offer relevant. The Due Process Clause is not a code of ethics for prosecutors; its concern is with the manner in which persons are deprived of their liberty. Here respondent was not deprived of his liberty in any fundamentally unfair way. Respondent was fully aware of the likely consequences when he pleaded guilty; it is not unfair to expect him to live with those consequences now. *Id.*

[ii] Exception for Detrimental Reliance

Although the government may withdraw from a plea deal any time until the plea is entered, a few cases hold the government may not do so if the defendant detrimentally relied on the deal.

[2] Conditional Pleas

The conditional plea, discussed earlier in this chapter, is governed by Rule 11(a)(2). It allows a defendant to plead guilty while reserving an issue for appeal. If the appeal is successful, the defendant may withdraw the plea.

[3] Post-Conviction Review

In the absence of a conditional plea that expressly preserves the issue for appeal, a later challenge to a conviction or sentence following a guilty plea may be difficult and limited to a few issues. Recall that one of the critical consequences of a guilty plea is that the accused forgoes a number of rights, such as the rights to confront accusers and, in more serious cases, to have a jury trial. Rule 11 is designed to ensure—and provide a written record—that the waiver of these various rights is knowing, intelligent, and voluntary. If the plea is knowing, intelligent, and voluntary, the defendant is thereafter barred from raising most issues on appeal or through various collateral remedies such as habeas corpus or post-conviction relief procedures. The obvious rationale is that the defendant has the option of waiving these rights and has done so in order to obtain an advantage during plea negotiations. Although post-conviction procedures are discussed in more detail in Chapter 17, this section provides a few general principles that are uniquely applicable to legal challenges launched by criminal defendants who have pled guilty.

Ordinarily, a person convicted of a crime has a right to appeal the case to an appellate court in that jurisdiction. These appeals must be taken within a relatively short time from the conviction. After that time, the only remedy is some sort of post-conviction "collateral" proceeding, such as habeas corpus or a state post-conviction relief procedure. Often the latter are limited to constitutional or jurisdictional issues.

Appeal. Under both state and federal procedure, the defendant may file a direct appeal from the judgment of guilt based upon the guilty plea. Usually this must be done relatively promptly after the conviction. The applicable statute normally specifies the grounds upon which the appeal can be based. In many respects, the direct appeal from a plea conviction in a federal case is the most desirable form of post-conviction review:

> Direct appeal is . . . the most advantageous route for challenging a federal conviction [because of] the potential for reversal on a showing of error of less than constitutional, jurisdictional, or fundamental magnitude [and because the defendant] is entitled to both court-appointed counsel and necessary transcripts.

Paul D. Borman, *The Hidden Right to Direct Appeal from a Federal Plea Conviction*, 64 Cornell L. Rev. 319, 371 (1979).

General waiver rule. As the result of a long series of judicial decisions, it has been held that a person who pleads guilty waives appeal or collateral relief on most issues, including many not covered specifically in the waiver provisions of Rule 11. *See, e.g.*, *United States v. Tolson*, 988 F.2d 1494 (7th Cir. 1993) (defendant who voluntarily and intelligently pled guilty to marijuana conspiracy cannot appeal the facts of the indictment for that crime). *But see United States v. Morales-Martinez*, 496 F.3d 356 (5th Cir. 2007) (recognizing authority in some jurisdictions for a narrower waiver which treats guilty pleas as an admission of only those facts necessary to support conviction). As discussed earlier, the plea agreement itself may contain a specific provision in which the accused agrees to waive an appeal. Generally such waivers are upheld.

Knowing and voluntary exception. In the context of a habeas corpus case, the United States Supreme Court expressed the general waiver rule and discussed an exception in *Tollett v. Henderson*, 411 U.S. 258, 267 (1973):

> When a criminal defendant has solemnly admitted in open court that he is in fact guilty of the offense with which he is charged, he may not thereafter raise independent claims relating to the deprivation of constitutional rights that occurred prior to the entry of the guilty plea. He may only attack the voluntary and intelligent character of the guilty plea by showing that the advice he received from counsel was not within the standards [of competency for a criminal defense attorney].

Although *Tollett* specifically dealt with federal habeas corpus relief, the principles in it are often cited as providing limits on direct appeals. *See, e.g., United States v. Cortez*, 973 F.2d 764 (9th Cir. 1992) (guilty plea may constitute waiver of right to appeal ruling on selective prosecution grounds, citing *Tollett*). Thus, *Tollett* and other decisions permit the defendant to attack the guilty plea if the "voluntary and intelligent" standards are not met. The reason is that the plea itself is invalid if the defendant was coerced into pleading or did so with inadequate knowledge or legal assistance. *See, e.g., United States v. Brady*, 397 U.S. 742 (1970) (plea upheld because facts show it was knowing and intelligent); *McMann v. Richardson*, 397 U.S. 759 (1970) (upholding plea of guilty based on reasonably competent advice of counsel that confession was admissible; plea was intelligent and habeas corpus hearing denied).

Jurisdiction exception. Other decisions have added another exception: the defendant who pled guilty may also attack certain jurisdictional defects in the proceeding. *See United States v. Broce*, 488 U.S. 563 (1989) (person entering guilty plea may still appeal that the trial court had no power to enter the conviction or impose the sentence). In addition, *Class v. United States*, 138 S. Ct. 798 (2018), relied upon *Broce* in holding 6–3 that a guilty plea does not per se prevent a defendant from challenging the constitutionality of the statute of conviction on direct appeal.

Statute of limitations. Although it is not clear exactly what jurisdictional defects are preserved after a guilty plea, the statute of limitations is often listed as one that is. However, a waiver of the statute of limitations is permissible if specific. *See, e.g., United States v. Del Percio*, 870 F.2d 1090 (6th Cir. 1989) (specific waiver of statute of limitations upheld). When, one might ask, would it be in the defendant's interest to waive a statute of limitations provision? Given the general rule that misdemeanor offenses carry shorter statutes of limitations periods than felonies, a defendant charged with a felony may seek a charge reduction to a lesser-included—but time-barred—misdemeanor. A plea of guilty under such circumstances could necessitate a specific statute of limitations waiver.

Failure to recuse. Another defect that may be preserved after a guilty plea is a denial of a recusal motion where the trial judge's impartiality is questioned (discussed more fully in Chapter 13, Part B). The federal circuit courts are divided on this issue. *Compare United States v. Chantal*, 902 F.2d 1018 (1st Cir. 1990) (holding that the guilty plea was not a waiver of the right to appeal a denied recusal motion), *with United States v. Patti*, 337 F.3d 1317 (11th Cir. 2003) (holding that this issue is not preserved where the recusal motion is based upon 28 U.S.C. § 455(a)). One commentator argues that federal courts should recognize that an unconditional guilty plea is not *a per se* waiver of the defendant's right to disqualify the judge when the judge's impartiality is reasonably in question. *See* Nancy B. Pridgen, Note, *Avoiding the Appearance of Bias: Allowing a Federal Criminal Defendant to Appeal a Denial of a Recusal Motion Even After Entering an Unconditional Guilty Plea*, 53 Vand. L. Rev. 983 (2000).

K. Ethical Issues

Plea bargaining generates a number of important—and often unrecognized—issues for the judge, prosecutor, and defense lawyer. As one would expect, often there are no clear answers to the important questions about what is ethical and what is not.

[1] Judge

[a] Majority Rule: Judge Barred from Participating in Plea Discussions

In most jurisdictions, the role of the judge in plea bargaining is clear: the judge is barred from participating in the process. Rule 11(c)(1) of the Federal Rules of Criminal Procedure states unequivocally that "[t]he court must not participate in [plea negotiation] discussions." A presidential commission summarized the judge's role:

> The judge's function is to insure the appropriateness of the correctional disposition reached by the parties and to guard against any tendency of the prosecution to overcharge or to be excessively lenient.... The judge's role is not that of one of the parties to the negotiation, but that of an independent examiner to verify that the defendant's plea is the result of an intelligent and knowing choice and not based on misapprehension or the product of coercion.

President's Commission on Law Enforcement and Administration of Justice, The Challenge of Crime in a Free Society 167 (1967).

Rationale. Several reasons are given for this ban. A defendant who refuses to plead guilty despite the judge's involvement in the negotiations may believe that a fair trial or a fair sentence is impossible by that same judge whose desire for a negotiated sentence was thwarted. Similarly, the judge's position of power by itself may give him or her sufficient clout to convince the defendant to plead guilty, irrespective of actual guilt or innocence. Judicial involvement in plea bargaining may also make it impossible for the judge to determine objectively whether a plea was voluntary, since the judge may have participated in the alleged coercive process. Finally, the judge who actively participates in plea bargaining may shift from neutral decision-maker to advocate for a side or disposition. This would alter the traditional role of neutrality that is a hallmark of the American judiciary. It would leave the defendant with the impression that the judge is simply another arm of the prosecution trying to convince the defendant to accept a lengthy prison term. *See generally* Albert W. Alschuler, *The Judge's Role in Plea Bargaining, Part I*, 76 COLUM. L. REV. 1059 (1976).

No automatic reversal of conviction or vacatur of plea. In *United States v. Davila*, 569 U.S. 597 (2013), a U.S. Magistrate Judge rather blatantly violated Rule 11(c)(1) by advising a tax fraud defendant at an *in camera* hearing (with no prosecutor present) that the government "held all the marbles" with respect to sentencing and that the defendant's only hope for sentencing leniency was to "come to the cross, Brother" (i.e., confess and accept responsibility for his guilt). Three months after this hearing, the defendant pled guilty. Despite this conceded violation of Rule 11(c)(1) that the Supreme Court characterized as "indeed beyond the pale," the Court rejected a rule of automatic plea vacatur for all violations of that rule's prohibition of judicial involvement in plea discussions, and remanded for an assessment of the full record to determine whether Davila's "substantial rights" had been violated.

[b] Minority View: Permit Judicial Involvement in Plea Discussions

While Rule 11 appears to bar judges from involvement in any plea discussions, the Notes of the Advisory Committees on Rules indicate that Rule 11 bars only judicial involvement in plea discussions that lead to a plea agreement. After the agreement is announced in court, the judge is not prohibited from discussing it with the parties. It is not clear, however, to what extent the court should become involved in resolving ambiguities or suggesting specific changes in the deal that the parties worked out.

While Rule 11's ban on judicial participation represents the prevailing view, there are several other approaches that permit much greater involvement by the judge. North Carolina, for example, specifically authorizes the judge to participate in plea discussions. N.C. Gen. Stat. § 15a-1021 (a). This provision was adopted to facilitate the expeditious resolution of criminal cases. North Carolina judges use this authority frequently, sometimes forcefully encouraging plea negotiations the day before trial or even during the trial. *See generally* Norman Lefstein, *Plea Bargaining and the Trial Judge: the New ABA Standards, and the Need to Control Judicial Discretion*, 59 N.C. L. REV. 477, 486 (1981). *See also* Ill. Sup. Ct. R. 402(d) (trial judge may not initiate plea discussions, but may participate in them). A few jurisdictions also authorize the parties to submit a proposed deal to the judge for an advisory opinion as to whether the bargain will be accepted. Ill. Sup. Ct. R. 402; N.C. Gen. Stat. § 15A-1021(c).

The American Bar Association has recommended greater judicial participation in plea bargaining than is permitted by Rule 11. Under the Bar Association's proposals, the judge is specifically authorized to play a limited, non-directive role in discussions between the prosecutor and defense counsel if the two are unable to reach agreement on a plea and both request the judge's participation. Upon request of the parties, the judge is allowed to evaluate a proposed plea agreement and "may indicate whether the court would accept the terms as proposed and if relevant, indicate what sentence would be imposed." Nonetheless, this standard holds to the view that a judge "should not ordinarily participate in plea negotiation discussions among the parties" and "should not . . . communicate to the defendant . . . that a plea agreement should be accepted or that a guilty plea should be entered." STANDARDS FOR CRIMINAL JUSTICE § 14-3.3 (3d ed. 1999).

[2] Lawyers

Plea negotiations create a number of ethical issues for both the prosecution and the defense lawyer.

[a] Duty to Explore Possibility of a Plea?

Both the prosecutor and defense attorney will ordinarily benefit from exploring the possibility of a guilty plea, although "there is no constitutional right to plea bargain; the prosecutor need not do so if he prefers to go to trial." *Weatherford v. Bursey*, 429 U.S. 545, 561 (1977). The American Bar Association specifically recommends that "[t]he prosecutor should be open, at every stage of a criminal matter, to discussions with defense counsel concerning disposition of charges by guilty plea or other negotiated disposition." CRIMINAL JUSTICE STANDARDS FOR THE PROSECUTION FUNCTION, Standard 3-5.6(a) (4th Ed. 2015). Neither side, however, should enter plea negotiations without first becoming familiar with the case, including the available evidence. This may mean deferring plea discussions until after formal and informal discovery has occurred. The ABA makes a similar recommendation for defense counsel. CRIMINAL JUSTICE STANDARDS FOR THE DEFENSE FUNCTION, Standards 4-6.1(a) and 4-6.2 (a) (4th Ed. 2015).

[b] Negotiations

[i] Zealous Advocate

During negotiations, each advocate has an important duty to represent the client zealously. The MODEL RULES OF PROFESSIONAL CONDUCT provide that "[a] lawyer must also act with commitment and dedication to the interests of the client and with zeal in advocacy upon the client's behalf." Model Rules of Professional Conduct

Rule 1.3 cmt. (2013). Similarly, the Model Code of Professional Responsibility states that "[a] lawyer shall not intentionally ... fail to seek the lawful objectives of his clients through reasonably available means permitted by law and the Disciplinary rules." MODEL CODE OF PROFESSIONAL RESPONSIBILITY DR 7-101A (1969).

These guidelines mean that both prosecutors and defense lawyers should try to advance their clients' interests in plea discussions, although these interests will differ for the two sides. The prosecutor has a unique role in the criminal justice adversary system. According to the American Bar Association, "[t]he prosecutor is an administrator of justice, an advocate, and an officer of the court; the prosecutor's office should exercise sound discretion and independent judgment in the performance of the prosecution function." STANDARDS FOR CRIMINAL JUSTICE FOR THE PROSECUTION FUNCTION, Standard 3-1.2 (4th ed. 2015). Defense counsel, on the other hand, is ordinarily not described as an "administrator of justice." Defense counsel's duty is to "act zealously within the bounds of the law and applicable rules to protect the client's confidences and the unique liberty interests that are at stake in criminal prosecution." STANDARDS FOR CRIMINAL JUSTICE FOR THE DEFENSE FUNCTION, Standard 4-1.4(a) (4th ed. 2015). For a thorough treatment of general negotiation principles as they apply to the plea bargaining of criminal cases, *see* Rodney J. Uphoff, *The Criminal Defense Lawyer as Effective Negotiator: A Systemic Approach*, 2 CLIN. L. REV. 73 (1995).

[ii] Candor

Although attorneys all must be zealous advocates, there are serious limitations on the actions they may take. In the context of plea negotiations, a key restriction is the obligation for both the prosecutor and defense lawyer to be truthful. Both the Model Rules and the Model Code prohibit a lawyer from knowingly making a false statement of law or material fact to anyone during the course of representation. MODEL RULES OF PROFESSIONAL CONDUCT Rule 4.1(a) (2013); MODEL CODE OF PROFESSIONAL RESPONSIBILITY DR 7-102(A)(5) (1969).

However, the American Bar Association appears to apply this standard differently to the prosecution and the defense. Both sides must avoid falsehood and deception, but *compare*, STANDARDS FOR THE PROSECUTION FUNCTION, Standard 3-1.4(a) (4th Ed. 2015) (prosecutor has a "heightened duty of candor in light of prosecutor's public responsibilities, broad authority and discretion"), *with* STANDARDS FOR THE DEFENSE FUNCTION, Standard 4-1.4 (4th Ed. 2015) ("counsel's duty of candor may be tempered by competing ethical and constitutional obligations").

The duty of candor can be difficult in negotiations when each side may try to ignore or "favorably shade" its own weaknesses and to emphasize its strong points while denigrating those of the adversary. Puffery in negotiations has long been tolerated, while outright lying is impermissible. *See*, for example, *People v. Jones*, 375 N. E. 2d 41 (N.Y. 1978), in which no due process violation was found where the state failed to disclose during plea negotiations that it had received information that the complaining witness had died. The court noted that there was no claim of affirmative misrepresentation, and that the undisclosed information did not involve exculpatory evidence. Do these ordinary negotiation tactics violate the lawyer's ethical duty of candor? The Model Rules of Professional Conduct try to address this concern by providing a flexible definition of "facts."

> Under generally accepted conventions in negotiation, certain types of statements ordinarily are not taken as statements of material facts. Estimates of price or value placed on the subject of a transaction and a party's intentions as to an acceptable settlement of a claim are in this category. . . .

Model Rules of Professional Conduct Rule 4.1 com. (2013).

A shorthand way of analyzing this issue is to view some such statements as *fact* and others as *opinion*. Even this dichotomy, however, may be imprecise in particular instances.

An increasing number of commentators have addressing issues relating to instances in which an innocent person is wrongfully convicted. Some suggest that prosecuting attorneys should be more mindful of these injustices and should temper their adversarial tendencies. *See* Abbe Smith, *Can You Be A Good Person and A Good Prosecutor?* 14 Geo. J. Legal Ethics 355, 390 (2001) (describing several instances in which the prosecutor's desire for victory "wins out over matters of procedural fairness, such as disclosure"); Bennett L. Gershman, *The Prosecutor's Duty to Truth*, 14 Geo. J. Legal Ethics 309, 316 (2001) (noting numerous instances of wrongful convictions and asserting that a prosecutor has an obligation not to proceed with a prosecution "without being personally convinced of the defendant's guilt").

Problem 11-1. Do I Have a Deal for You

John Hobart and Francine Pickens are charged with burglary and theft of a painting from the Seaside Art Gallery. The indictment alleges the two entered the gallery during normal business hours, then hid in a storeroom until midnight when they took an original McClintock watercolor worth $5500 from a gallery wall and exited through a fire door.

1. You represent Hobart in plea negotiations with the prosecutor. Do the following statements violate ethical norms?

    a. "You have no case against my client."

        i. Assume that defense counsel does not know the strength of the government's case.

        ii. What if you are convinced the government has an airtight case against your client and that the chances of a conviction approach 100% if there is a trial?

    b. "My client did not take the painting from the wall; Pickens did."

        i. Assume that your client told you in confidence that he did take the painting from the wall.

ii. What if you do not know who took the painting? Your client refuses to tell you despite your persistent questioning. Would it matter if you did not ask?

c. "My client will agree to nothing more than a one-year prison term. We go to trial for anything more."

i. Assume that your client told you that he would accept the best deal you can get for him.

ii. What if your client told you that he would accept no more than a three-year prison sentence, but would prefer a maximum of one year in prison?

2. You are now the Assistant District Attorney prosecuting the case. Do the following statements violate ethical norms?

a. "We have an eyewitness who saw your client [Hobart] take the painting."

i. Assume that there is no such eyewitness.

ii. What if you, the prosecutor, are confident that you will eventually induce Pickens to testify against Hobart (and state that she saw Hobart take the painting), but so far Pickens has refused to discuss the case with you?

b. "My boss said I have to get five years from your client."

i. Assume that you and your boss (the District Attorney) have never discussed this case.

ii. Although you and the District Attorney have never discussed this case, you honestly believe that the D.A. would insist upon a minimum of five years' incarceration.

[c] Defense Counsel's Obligation to Client

Plea negotiations present the defense attorney with special ethical obligations with regard to relations with the client. Defense counsel should keep the client "reasonably and currently informed" about disposition negotiations and should "promptly communicate to the client every plea offer." Standards for the Defense Function, Standards 4-3.9(a) and 4-5.1(c) (4th ed. 2015). Failure to apprise the defendant of an offer may constitute ineffective assistance of counsel under the Sixth Amendment, *Missouri v. Frye*, 566 U.S. 134 (2012), discussed earlier in this chapter.

The client should also be told the lawyer's professional opinion of the likely outcome of the case and the ramifications of possible plea deals. The defense attorney must be sensitive to the fact that the ultimate decision whether to plead guilty or to proceed to trial rests with the client. Yet the way in which the attorney conveys information to the client (*i.e.*, "I'm positive that a jury will return a guilty verdict") can (and most certainly does on occasion) dictate the client's "choice." Additionally, defense counsel may be called upon by the client to make the decision (*i.e.*, "I'm not the lawyer … you are. You tell me what to do.").

Significant issues arise where the attorney faces possible conflicts of interest. An obvious one is when defense counsel represents two or more defendants during plea negotiations. Sometimes the deal may require one to testify against the other or to accept a greater punishment than the other. While separate defense counsel for both defendants is best, if the defendants want to be represented by the same lawyer, there must be complete candor so that each defendant is fully apprised of the situation. Sometimes the conflict of interest will cause a reversal for ineffective assistance of counsel. *See Burden v. Zant*, 498 U.S. 433 (1991) (counsel representing two alleged murderers negotiated immunity for one to testify against the other; reversal ordered).

Another source of conflict is between the interests of the present client and that of future clients. For example, a busy criminal defense lawyer may engage in routine plea negotiations with a prosecutor several times a week on various unrelated cases. The defense lawyer may be tempted not to "upset the apple cart" by having heated negotiations on a particular case. If the prosecutor were angered, future discussions on other cases may be compromised. Of course, this may violate the defense lawyer's ethical duty to represent each client with undivided loyalty.

[d] Prosecution's Contact with Defendant

If a prosecutor knows the defendant is represented by counsel, the prosecutor must not engage in plea negotiations directly with the client unless defense counsel specifically consents or the law or court authorize the communication. *See* Model Rules of Professional Conduct Rule 4.2 (2013); Model Code of Professional Responsibility DR 7-104(A)(1). Such discussions should ordinarily take place only with defense counsel. The defendant need not be personally present for the negotiation.

If the defendant has waived counsel, the prosecution may negotiate directly with the defendant. To protect against claims of undue influence or overreaching by the prosecutor, the American Bar Association recommends that the prosecutor make and preserve a record of negotiations with an uncounseled defendant. Standards for the Defense Function, Standard 3-5.6(b) (4th ed. 2015).

Chapter 12

Time Limitations

A. Introduction

After the police identify a particular person as having committed a crime, there may be considerable delay between the date of the crime (or identification of the alleged criminal) and the date of various proceedings. For example, assume that a crime was committed in January 2018. The accused could be identified shortly afterward or years after the offense. After being identified, he or she may be arrested anywhere from days to years later. Other legal proceedings may also be held promptly or after considerable delay. The prosecution could obtain an indictment shortly after the culprit was identified or years afterward. Similarly, the trial and sentencing could occur shortly after the crime or indictment, or years after one or both.

One could easily imagine a robbery occurring in 2018, an arrest (following an extensive investigation) made in 2019, an indictment in 2020, and a trial in 2021. Although there may be valid reasons why each of these events occurred when it did, the significant time between the crime, formal charges, and the trial may cause considerable problems for both the defense and the prosecution. The defendant may have spent months or years in jail awaiting trial. Moreover, evidence for both sides may have disappeared or become less reliable as memories fade and witnesses become difficult to trace. The public itself may lose confidence in a judicial system that takes so long to discharge its important responsibilities.

Because of these important concerns, American law has long placed some limits on these delays. In general terms, some proceedings cannot be delayed too long without offending statutes, procedural rules, or state and federal constitutional guarantees. Delays between the commission of the crime and the institution of formal charges are often referred to as *pre-accusation delays* and are addressed principally through state and federal statutes of limitations. These requirements place pressure on the police to expedite investigations and to institute formal processes in a timely fashion.

Delays in convening a trial are addressed explicitly by the Sixth Amendment's speedy trial provision that "[i]n all criminal prosecutions, the accused shall enjoy the right to a speedy and public trial." Virtually all state constitutions have similar speedy trial guarantees. In addition, a variety of state and federal statutes and rules of procedure establish precise time limitations for formal charges and trials. These rules bar the prosecution from indefinitely postponing trials and other criminal proceedings. Finally, the Due Process Clause places general limits on delays in every portion of the criminal justice process, but its most significant impact is restricted to pre-accusation and post-conviction phases of the criminal case.

B. Pre-Accusation Delays

We first turn to the question of limits on the time between the commission of the crime and the defendant's arrest or the filing of criminal charges. For example, assume that Harry commits arson on February 1, 2018, is arrested on January 1, 2019, and is indicted on February 1, 2019. There has been an 11-month delay between the crime and the arrest, and a 12-month delay between the crime and the indictment. Has this delay violated any constitutional or statutory provisions?

In general, there are two legal limits on such delays: statutes of limitations and the Due Process Clause. You might think that the Speedy Trial Clause of the Sixth Amendment would also have something to say about these timing issues, but note below what the Supreme Court teaches about the clause in *United States v. Marion*.

[1] General Approaches: Speedy Trial, Statutes of Limitation, and Due Process

United States v. Marion

404 U.S. 307 (1971)

Justice White delivered the opinion of the Court.

This appeal requires us to decide whether dismissal of a federal indictment was constitutionally required by reason of a period of three years between the occurrence of the alleged criminal acts and the filing of the indictment.

On April 21, 1970, the two appellees were indicted and charged in 19 counts with operating a business known as Allied Enterprises, Inc., which was engaged in the business of selling and installing home improvements such as intercom sets, fire control devices, and burglary detection systems. Allegedly, the business was fraudulently conducted and involved misrepresentations, alterations of documents, and deliberate nonperformance of contracts. The period covered by the indictment was March 15, 1965, to February 6, 1967; the earliest specific act alleged occurred on September 3, 1965, the latest on January 19, 1966.

On May 5, 1970, appellees filed a motion to dismiss the indictment "for failure to commence prosecution of the alleged offenses charged therein within such time as to afford (them their) rights to due process of law and to a speedy trial under the Fifth and Sixth Amendments to the Constitution of the United States."

... Appellees moved to dismiss because the indictment was returned "an unreasonably oppressive and unjustifiable time after the alleged offenses." They argued that the indictment required memory of many specific acts and conversations occurring several years before, and they contended that the delay was due to the negligence or indifference of the United States Attorney in investigating the case and presenting it to a grand jury. No specific prejudice was claimed or demonstrated. The District Court judge dismissed the indictment for "lack of speedy prosecution" at the conclusion of the hearing and remarked that since the Government must have become aware of the relevant facts in 1967, the defense of the case "is bound to have been seriously prejudiced by the delay of at least some three years in bringing the prosecution that should have been brought in 1967, or at the very latest early 1968."

... Appellees do not claim that the Sixth Amendment [right to a speedy trial] was violated by the two-month delay between the return of the indictment and its dismissal. Instead, they claim that their rights to a speedy trial were violated by the period of approximately three years between the end of the criminal scheme charged and the return of the indictment; it is argued that this delay is so substantial and inherently prejudicial that the Sixth Amendment required the dismissal of the indictment. In our view, however, the Sixth Amendment speedy trial provision has no application until the putative defendant in some way becomes an "accused," an event that occurred in this case only when the appellees were indicted on April 21, 1970.

The Sixth Amendment provides that "[i]n all criminal prosecutions, the accused shall enjoy the right to a speedy and public trial...." On its face, the protection of the Amendment is activated only when a criminal prosecution has begun and extends only to those persons who have been "accused" in the course of that prosecution. These provisions would seem to afford no protection to those not yet accused, nor would they seem to require the Government to discover, investigate, and accuse any person within any particular period of time.

... It is apparent also that very little support for appellees' position emerges from a consideration of the purposes of the Sixth Amendment's speedy trial provision, a guarantee that this Court has termed "an important safeguard to prevent undue and oppressive incarceration prior to trial, to minimize anxiety and concern accompanying public accusation and to limit the possibilities that long delay will impair the ability of an accused to defend himself." Inordinate delay between arrest, indictment, and trial may impair a defendant's ability to present an effective defense. But the major evils protected against by the speedy trial guarantee exist quite apart from actual or possible prejudice to an accused's defense. To legally arrest and detain, the Government must assert probable cause to believe the arrestee has committed a crime. Arrest is a public act that may seriously interfere with the defendant's liberty, whether he is free on bail or not, and that may disrupt his employment, drain his financial resources, curtail his associations, subject him to public obloquy, and create anxiety in him, his family and his friends.... So viewed, it is readily understandable that it is either a formal indictment or information or else the actual restraints imposed by arrest and holding to answer a criminal charge that engage the particular protections of the speedy trial provision of the Sixth Amendment.

Invocation of the speedy trial provision thus need not await indictment, information, or other formal charge. But we decline to extend that reach of the amendment to the period prior to arrest. Until this event occurs, a citizen suffers no restraints on his liberty and is not the subject of public accusation: his situation does not compare with that of a defendant who has been arrested and held to answer. Passage of time, whether before or after arrest, may impair memories, cause evidence to be lost, deprive the defendant of witnesses, and otherwise interfere with his ability to defend himself.

But this possibility of prejudice at trial is not itself sufficient reason to wrench the Sixth Amendment from its proper context. Possible prejudice is inherent in any delay, however short; it may also weaken the Government's case.

The law has provided other mechanisms to guard against possible as distinguished from actual prejudice resulting from the passage of time between crime and arrest or charge. . . . [Statutes of limitations] represent legislative assessments of relative interests of the State and the defendant in administering and receiving justice; they "are made for the repose of society and the protection of those who may (during the limitation) . . . have lost their means of defence." These statutes provide predictability by specifying a limit beyond which there is an irrebuttable presumption that a defendant's right to a fair trial would be prejudiced.

. . . [I]t is appropriate to note here that the statute of limitations does not fully define the appellees' rights with respect to the events occurring prior to indictment. Thus, the Government concedes that the Due Process Clause of the Fifth Amendment would require dismissal of the indictment if it were shown at trial that the pre-indictment delay in this case caused substantial prejudice to appellees' rights to a fair trial and that the delay was an intentional device to gain tactical advantage over the accused. However, we need not, and could not now, determine when and in what circumstances actual prejudice resulting from pre-accusation delays requires the dismissal of the prosecution. Actual prejudice to the defense of a criminal case may result from the shortest and most necessary delay; and no one suggests that every delay-caused detriment to a defendant's case should abort a criminal prosecution. To accommodate the sound administration of justice to the rights of the defendant to a fair trial will necessarily involve a delicate judgment based on the circumstances of each case. It would be unwise at this juncture to attempt to forecast our decision in such cases.

. . . The 38-month delay between the end of the scheme charged in the indictment and the date the defendants were indicted did not extend beyond the period of the applicable statute of limitations here. Appellees have not, of course, been able to claim undue delay pending trial, since the indictment was brought on April 21, 1970, and dismissed on June 8, 1970. Nor have appellees adequately demonstrated that the pre-indictment delay by the Government violated the Due Process Clause. No actual prejudice to the conduct of the defense is alleged or proved, and there is no showing that the Government intentionally delayed to gain some tactical advantage over appellees or to harass them. Appellees rely solely on the real possibility of prejudice inherent in any extended delay: that memories will dim, witnesses become inaccessible, and evidence be lost. In light of the applicable statute of limitations, however, these possibilities are not in themselves enough to demonstrate that appellees cannot receive a fair trial and to therefore justify the dismissal of the indictment. Events of the trial may demonstrate actual prejudice, but at the present time appellees' due process claims are speculative and premature. Reversed.

Justice Douglas, with whom Justice Brennan and Justice Marshall join, concurring in the result.

I assume that if the three-year delay in this case had occurred after the indictment had been returned, the right to a speedy trial would have been impaired and the indictment would have to be dismissed. I disagree with the Court that the guarantee does not apply if the delay was at the pre-indictment stage of a case.

... The Sixth Amendment, to be sure, states that "the accused shall enjoy the right to a speedy and public trial." But the words "the accused," as I understand them in their Sixth Amendment setting, mean only the person who has standing to complain of prosecutorial delay in seeking an indictment or filing an information. The right to a speedy trial is the right to be brought to trial speedily which would seem to be as relevant to pre-indictment delays as it is to post-indictment delays.

... Undue delay may be as offensive to the right to a speedy trial before as after an indictment or information. The anxiety and concern attendant on public accusation may weigh more heavily upon an individual who has not yet been formally indicted or arrested for, to him, exoneration by a jury of his peers may be only a vague possibility lurking in the distant future. Indeed, the protection underlying the right to a speedy trial may be denied when a citizen is damned by clandestine innuendo and never given the chance promptly to defend himself in a court of law. Those who are accused of crime but never tried may lose their jobs or their positions of responsibility, or become outcasts in their communities.

The impairment of the ability to defend oneself may become acute because of delays in the pre-indictment stage. Those delays may result in the loss of alibi witnesses, the destruction of material evidence, and the blurring of memories. At least when a person has been accused of a specific crime, he can devote his powers of recall to the events surrounding the alleged occurrences. When there is no formal accusation, however, the State may proceed methodically to build its case while the prospective defendant proceeds to lose his.

... In the present case, two to three years elapsed between the time the District Court found that the charges could and should have been brought and the actual return of the indictment. The justifications offered were that the United States Attorney's office was "not sufficiently staffed to proceed as expeditiously" as desirable and that priority had been given to other cases.... But on the bare bones of this record I hesitate to say that the guarantee of a speedy trial has been violated. Unless appellees on remand demonstrate actual prejudice, I would agree that the prosecution might go forward. Hence I concur in the result.

[2] Statutes of Limitation

[a] Purpose

While *Marion* recognized that there may be due process protections with respect to pre-charge delay, it stressed the importance of statutes of limitations insofar as they operate "to guard against possible . . . prejudice resulting from the passage of time between crime and arrest or charge." The Court noted:

> The purpose of a statute of limitations is to limit exposure to criminal prosecution to a certain fixed period of time following the occurrence of those acts the legislature has decided to punish by criminal sanctions. Such a limitation is designed to protect individuals from having to defend themselves against charges when the basic facts may have become obscured by the passage of time and to minimize the danger of official punishment because of acts in the far-distant past. Such a time limit may also have the salutary effect of encouraging law enforcement officials promptly to investigate suspected criminal activity.

404 U.S. at 323.

[b] Illustrative Statutes of Limitation

Almost all states have precise statutes of limitations specifying the time periods within which a criminal prosecution must be brought. Generally, the length of the limitation period increases with the seriousness of the crime. *See, e.g.*, Cal. Pen. Code Ann. §§ 799–802 (offenses punishable by death—no limit; offenses punishable by eight years' imprisonment or more—six-year limit; most other felonies—three-year limit; most misdemeanors—one-year limit); Tex. Code Crim. Pro. art. 12.01 (murder or manslaughter—no limit; certain sexual assaults—10-year limit; theft and burglary—five-year limit; all other felonies—three-year limit). Many jurisdictions have no statutes of limitations applicable to capital crimes. Often, there are generic statutes setting time limitations based upon the classification of offenses. *See, e.g.*, Model Penal Code § 1.06 (1)-(2) (no limitation for murder; six-year limit for a felony of the first degree; three-year limit for any other felony; two-year limit for a misdemeanor; six-month limit for a petty misdemeanor or violation).

[c] Procedural Issues

If the statute of limitations has run, the crime can no longer be prosecuted, irrespective of the strength of the prosecution's case against the accused. Thus, the statute of limitations is a defense to criminal prosecution, and is usually raised formally in a motion to dismiss. The burden of persuasion, however, generally is on the government, which must prove beyond a reasonable doubt that the statute of limitations was not violated.

[d] Periods Calculated; Tolling

Usually the statute of limitations begins to run when the crime is committed, and ends when either an arrest is made or an indictment or information is issued. According to statute or case law, the running of the statute of limitations is *tolled* or stopped during various periods, such as when the existence of the crime is hidden or when the accused is out of state.

What of "continuing offenses"—crimes like kidnapping, which are viewed as ongoing even after all the elements of the crime have been performed? As we saw in Chapter 3, determining whether a charged offense is continuing can be crucial to the venue analysis in some cases, and the same is true of the statute of limitations analysis. Consider, for instance, the facts of *Toussie v. United States*, 397 U.S. 112 (1970). Toussie was required to register for the military draft when he turned 18 in 1959, but he never did so. Later, in 1967, he was criminally charged with failure to register. Since the offense was subject to a five-year statute of limitations, the charge against Toussie would be time-barred unless the offense were regarded as continuing in nature. The Supreme Court ruled in Toussie's favor, based chiefly on two considerations: the registration statute did not clearly indicate that it was intended to create a continuing offense, and there was "nothing inherent in the act of registration itself which makes failure to do so a continuing crime." *Id.* at 122. The Court distinguished earlier cases holding that a conspiracy continued for as long as the conspirators committed overt acts in furtherance of the plot, noting that "each day's acts bring a renewed threat of the substantive evil Congress sought to prevent." *Id.*

Statutes of limitations commonly handle fraud cases in a distinctive way, providing greater flexibility for the start date if the victim does not immediately realize that a crime has been committed. *See, e.g.*, Iowa Code § 802.5 (establishing that prosecution of fraud offenses may commence after normal three-year limit as long as prosecution begins "within one year after the discovery of the offense by an aggrieved party"). What if the victim discovers that a fraud has been committed, but does not know the identity of the perpetrator—does that start the clock ticking on the statute of limitations? Yes, said the Iowa Supreme Court in *State v. Tipton*, 897 N.W.2d 653, 683 (Iowa 2017). However, very few other states have addressed this question under their laws. *See id.*

Child sex abuse cases raise particular concerns in relation to statutes of limitations, given the special difficulties that the victims may have in understanding the nature of what has been done to them and alerting the authorities. All 50 states have now adopted special tolling provisions to deal with these sorts of cases. *See* Wayne R. LaFave et al., Criminal Procedure § 18.5 (a) (5th ed. 2009).

[e] Waiver

Some states will permit a waiver of a statute of limitations defense when the defendant agrees to plead guilty to a crime that is time-barred. For example, in *Cowan v. Superior Court*, 926 P.2d 438 (Cal. 1996), the defendant, charged with three murders, entered into a plea agreement whereby he would plead no contest to one count of voluntary manslaughter. Because the statute of limitations had run on that crime, the trial court set aside the guilty plea prior to sentencing. However, the California Supreme Court held that the guilty plea was valid so long as the defendant's waiver of the statute of limitations was knowing, intelligent, voluntary, and made for the defendant's benefit after consultation with counsel.

[3] Due Process

United States v. Lovasco

431 U.S. 783 (1977)

Justice Marshall delivered the opinion of the Court.

We granted certiorari in this case to consider the circumstances in which the Constitution requires that an indictment be dismissed because of delay between the commission of an offense and the initiation of prosecution.

On March 6, 1975, respondent was indicted for possessing eight firearms stolen from the United States mails, and for dealing in firearms without a license. The offenses were alleged to have occurred between July 25 and August 31, 1973, more than 18 months before the indictment was filed. Respondent moved to dismiss the indictment due to the delay.

The District Court conducted a hearing on respondent's motion at which the respondent sought to prove that the delay was unnecessary and that it had prejudiced his defense. In an effort to establish the former proposition, respondent presented a Postal Inspector's report on his investigation that was prepared one month after the crimes were committed, and a stipulation concerning the post-report progress of the probe. The report stated, in brief, that within the first month of the investigation respondent had admitted to Government agents that he had possessed and then sold five of the stolen guns, and that the agents had developed strong evidence linking respondent to the remaining three weapons. The report also stated, however, that the agents had been unable to confirm or refute respondent's claim that he had found the guns in his car when he returned to it after visiting his son, a mail handler, at work. The stipulation into which the Assistant United States Attorney entered indicated that little additional information concerning the crimes was uncovered in the 17 months following the preparation of the Inspector's report.

To establish prejudice to the defense, respondent testified that he had lost the testimony of two material witnesses due to the delay. The first witness, Tom Stewart, died more than a year after the alleged crimes occurred. At the hearing respondent claimed that Stewart had been his source for two or three of the guns. The second witness, respondent's brother, died in April 1974, eight months after the crimes were completed. Respondent testified that his brother was present when respondent called Stewart to secure the guns, and witnessed all of respondent's sales. Respondent did not state how the witnesses would have aided the defense had they been willing to testify.[4]

The Government made no systematic effort in the District Court to explain its long delay. The Assistant United States Attorney did expressly disagree, however, with defense counsel's suggestion that the investigation had ended after the Postal Inspector's report was prepared.

... Following the hearing, the District Court filed a brief opinion and order. The court found that by October 2, 1973, the date of the Postal Inspector's report, "the Government had all the information relating to defendant's alleged commission of the offenses charged against him," and that the 17-month delay before the case was presented to the grand jury "had not been explained or justified" and was "unnecessary and unreasonable." The court also found that "(a)s a result of the delay defendant has been prejudiced by reason of the death of Tom Stewart, a material witness on his behalf." Accordingly, the court dismissed the indictment [and the Eighth Circuit Court of Appeals affirmed].

... Respondent seems to argue that due process bars prosecution whenever a defendant suffers prejudice as a result of preindictment delay. To support that proposition respondent relies on the concluding sentence of the Court's opinion in *Marion* where, in remanding the case, we stated that "(e)vents of the trial may demonstrate actual prejudice, but at the present time appellees' due process claims are speculative and premature." But the quoted sentence establishes only that proof of actual prejudice makes a due process claim concrete and ripe for adjudication, not that it makes the claim automatically valid. Indeed, two pages earlier in the opinion we expressly rejected the argument respondent advances here: "(W)e need not ... determine when and in what circumstances actual prejudice resulting from preaccusation delays requires the dismissal of the prosecution. Actual prejudice to the defense of a criminal case may result from the shortest and most necessary delay; and no one suggests that every delay-caused detriment to a defendant's case should abort a criminal prosecution." Thus *Marion* makes clear that proof of prejudice is generally a necessary but not sufficient element of a due process claim, and that the due process inquiry must consider the reasons for the delay as well as the prejudice to the accused.

... It requires no extended argument to establish that prosecutors do not deviate from "fundamental conceptions of justice" when they defer seeking indictments until they have probable cause to believe an accused is guilty; indeed it is unprofessional conduct for a prosecutor to recommend an indictment on less than probable cause. It should be equally obvious that prosecutors are under no duty to file

4. Respondent admitted that he had not mentioned Stewart to the Postal Inspector when he was questioned about his source of the guns. He explained that this was because Stewart "was a bad tomato" and "was liable to take a shot at me if I told (on) him." Respondent also conceded that he did not mention either his brother's or Stewart's illness or death to the Postal Inspector on the several occasions in which respondent called the Inspector to inquire about the status of the probe.

charges as soon as probable cause exists but before they are satisfied they will be able to establish the suspect's guilt beyond a reasonable doubt.

It might be argued that once the Government has assembled sufficient evidence to prove guilt beyond a reasonable doubt, it should be constitutionally required to file charges promptly, even if its investigation of the entire criminal transaction is not complete. Adopting such a rule, however, would have many of the same consequences as adopting a rule requiring immediate prosecution upon probable cause.

First, compelling a prosecutor to file public charges as soon as the requisite proof has been developed against one participant on one charge would cause numerous problems in those cases in which a criminal transaction involves more than one person or more than one illegal act. In some instances, an immediate arrest or indictment would impair the prosecutor's ability to continue his investigation, thereby preventing society from bringing lawbreakers to justice. In other cases, the prosecutor would be able to obtain additional indictments despite an early prosecution, but the necessary result would be multiple trials involving a single set of facts. Such trials place needless burdens on defendants, law enforcement officials, and courts.

Second, insisting on immediate prosecution once sufficient evidence is developed to obtain a conviction would pressure prosecutors into resolving doubtful cases in favor of early and possibly unwarranted prosecutions. The determination of when the evidence available to the prosecution is sufficient to obtain a conviction is seldom clear-cut, and reasonable persons often will reach conflicting conclusions. . . .

Finally, requiring the Government to make charging decisions immediately upon assembling evidence sufficient to establish guilt would preclude the Government from giving full consideration to the desirability of not prosecuting in particular cases.

. . . In our view, investigative delay is fundamentally unlike delay undertaken by the Government solely "to gain tactical advantage over the accused," *United States v. Marion*, 404 U.S. at 324, precisely because investigative delay is not so one-sided. Rather than deviating from elementary standards of "fair play and decency," a prosecutor abides by them if he refuses to seek indictments until he is completely satisfied that he should prosecute and will be able promptly to establish guilt beyond a reasonable doubt. Penalizing prosecutors who defer action for these reasons would subordinate the goal of "orderly expedition" to that of "mere speed," *Smith v. United States*, 360 U.S. 10 (1959). This the Due Process Clause does not require. We therefore hold that to prosecute a defendant following investigative delay does not deprive him of due process, even if his defense might have been somewhat prejudiced by the lapse of time.

In the present case, the Court of Appeals stated that the only reason the Government postponed action was to await the results of additional investigation. Although there is, unfortunately, no evidence concerning the reasons for the delay in the record, the court's "finding" is supported by the prosecutor's implicit representation to the District Court, and explicit representation to the Court of Appeals, that the investigation continued during the time that the Government deferred taking action against respondent. The finding is, moreover, buttressed by the Government's repeated assertions in its petition for certiorari, its brief, and its oral argument in this Court, "that the delay was caused by the government's efforts to identify persons in addition to respondent who may have participated in the offenses." We must assume that these statements by counsel have been made in good faith. In light of this explanation, it follows that compelling respondent to stand trial would not be fundamentally unfair. The Court of Appeals therefore erred in affirming the District Court's decision dismissing the indictment.

In *Marion* we conceded that we could not determine in the abstract the circumstances in which preaccusation delay would require dismissing prosecutions. More than five years later, that statement remains true. Indeed, in the intervening years so few defendants have established that they were prejudiced by delay that neither this Court nor any lower court has had a sustained opportunity to consider the constitutional significance of various reasons for delay. We therefore leave to the lower courts, in the first instance, the task of applying the settled principles of due process that we have discussed to the particular circumstances of individual cases. We simply hold that in this case the lower courts erred in dismissing the indictment. Reversed.

[The dissent of Justice Stevens is omitted.]

Notes

1. *Charge dismissed, then reinstituted.* How should *Marion* and *Lovasco* apply when there is a formal charge brought, then dismissed, and later the defendant is formally charged again? In *United States v. Loud Hawk*, 474 U.S. 302 (1986), an indictment was issued in late 1975, but was dismissed in March 1976. The government appealed the dismissal order and made it clear that it desired to prosecute the defendant. Due to various interlocutory appeals, the defendant was not reindicted until more than seven years had elapsed. In a five-to-four decision, the United States Supreme Court held that the time during which the indictment was dismissed was to be excluded from the length of delay considered under the speedy trial guarantee. This ruling was based upon the earlier case of *United States v. MacDonald*, 456 U.S. 1 (1982), holding that the time between the dismissal of military charges and the subsequent indictment on civilian charges is not to be considered in determining whether a speedy trial violation occurred.

2. *Defendant's proof of pre-charge delay.* In applying the *Marion* due process standard to pre-charge delays, most courts require the defendant to prove (1) actual prejudice and (2) malicious prosecutorial intent (based upon the suggestion that there must be a "showing that the Government intentionally delayed to gain some tactical advantage over [the defendant] or to harass [the defendant]"). *See United States v. Crouch*, 84 F.3d 1497 (5th Cir. 1996) (expressly adopting that standard and noting that "[a] significant majority of our sister circuits appear to now follow the same rule"); *but see Howell v. Barker*, 904 F.2d 889 (4th Cir. 1990) (minority view, holding that where the defendant establishes prejudice, there is no absolute requirement that the defendant also must prove improper prosecutorial motive).

Under the demanding *Marion* standard, it is exceedingly difficult for defendants to prove prejudice based on claims that (1) the defendant's or witness's memories have faded, *see, e.g., United States v. Brown*, 498 F.3d 523 (6th Cir. 2007); (2) discovery of witnesses is precluded, *see, e.g., United States v. Wright*, 343 F.3d 849 (6th Cir. 2003); or (3) loss of evidence has resulted, *see, e.g., United States v. Gulley*, 526 F.3d 809 (5th Cir. 2008).

3. *Some state standards less exacting.* Contrary to the *Marion* standard, recognized by a majority of states, some courts have adopted a less exacting standard. Under this approach, once the defendant has demonstrated actual prejudice, a balancing test is used, weighing prejudice to the defendant against the prosecutor's reasons for delay.

In *State v. Cyr*, 588 A.2d 753 (Me. 1991), the defendant was indicted for arson five years after the crime had been committed (within the six-year statute of limitations). This was also five years after the investigation had been completed and during which time no new evidence was found, no new studies were conducted, and no new witnesses or statements regarding the fire were available to authorities. Cyr moved to dismiss the indictment, but the trial judge reserved judgment until after trial. Following his conviction, the court determined that the defendant had established actual and unjustifiable prejudice as a result of the pre-indictment delay and granted the motion to dismiss the indictment. The Supreme Court of Maine affirmed, noting that during this period of delay, the state had misplaced several pieces of evidence that possessed exculpatory value. Because the state had offered no reason for the delay in seeking the indictment, dismissal on due process grounds was affirmed.

Problem 12-1. "What Is Taking You People So Long?"

In July 2009, Mucker gave the Cincinnati, Ohio, District Attorney's Office a statement implicating Denney and Mucker's husband Ross, in a liquor store robbery-murder, which she claimed to have watched from her apartment window. She also claimed that husband Ross, wounded in his right leg, had returned to the apartment with $200 and the decedent's gun. Shortly thereafter, local officials recovered the decedent's gun in rusted condition from the apartment and photographed recent gunshot scars on Ross's right leg.

Early in 2011, Florida police notified the Cincinnati sheriff that a Shawna Cotter had accused two other men of the same robbery-murder: one of these men was in custody in Florida for beating Cotter, and the other was in custody in Ohio. The sheriff, who had previously interviewed Cotter about the liquor store robbery-murder, concluded that her allegations against the other two were fabricated.

In January 2014, a grand jury indicted Ross and Denney after receiving Mucker's testimony and the photograph of Ross's leg. In response to a subsequent defense motion to dismiss because of preindictment delay, the prosecutor argued that Mucker's 2009 statement suggested that she may have been an accomplice; if so, state law required her testimony to be corroborated. Finally, the prosecutor said that her office had viewed Mucker's credibility as uncertain because the sheriff had promised her immunity. The judge denied the motion to dismiss.

At trial, Ross testified that during the robbery, he and his brother were in Mucker's apartment. Ross's brother died in 2013. Denney testified that at the time of the liquor store robbery he was in another bar talking to the owner and a bartender. The owner died in 2013, and the bartender died shortly after the robbery. Denney could not recall the other people in the bar. The prosecutor informed the court that the investigator who first interviewed Mucker had died in September 2013.

After Ross and Denney were convicted of felony murder, how should an appellate court rule on their claim of pre-charge delay?

C. Post-Accusation Delays

Post-accusation delays are those between the arrest or filing of formal charges and the trial. Both constitutional and statutory speedy trial provisions place limits on the extent of these delays. For example, an accused could be indicted in 2018 but not tried until 2020 or 2021, with the delay caused by an infinite variety of circumstances. At one end of the spectrum, the accused may have escaped shortly after being indicted, causing delay of the trial until the escapee was apprehended. On the other hand, trial could have been delayed because judicial or prosecutorial resources were committed to other trials involving other defendants, because the prosecution needed more time to investigate this offense, because the prosecution was waiting for an important witness to recover from a serious illness, because the defense lawyer was ill or had requested the delays, or because the case got lost in an overloaded system with far too few prosecutors and inadequate records. Both constitutional and statutory speedy trial provisions limit the permissibility of these delays.

[1] Constitutional Speedy Trial Guarantee

In *Klopfer v. North Carolina*, 386 U.S. 213 (1967), the United States Supreme Court held that the Sixth Amendment right to speedy trial applies to the states through the Due Process Clause of the Fourteenth Amendment. It was not until 1972, however, that the Court, in the next case, addressed the two most significant questions related to that guarantee: (1) by what standard is a court to determine whether the right to a speedy trial has been violated, and (2) what remedy is required for such a violation?

Barker v. Wingo

407 U.S. 514 (1972)

Justice Powell delivered the opinion of the Court.

[Barker was indicted September 15, 1958, in connection with a double homicide. Because the state wanted to obtain the testimony of his co-defendant, Manning, the decision was made to proceed first against Manning. Assuming Manning's conviction, he would then be available to testify against Barker. This strategy resulted in a series of some sixteen continuances of Barker's trial, to which Barker did not object. Because of various difficulties (mistrials and reversals of convictions), Manning's convictions did not occur until late 1962.]

In February 1963, the first term of court following Manning's final conviction, the Commonwealth moved to set Barker's trial for March 19. But on the day scheduled for trial, it again moved for a continuance until the June term. It gave as its reason the illness of the ex-sheriff who was the chief investigating officer in the case. To this continuance, Barker objected unsuccessfully.

The witness was still unable to testify in June, and the trial, which had been set for June 19, was continued again until the September term over Barker's objection. This time the court announced that the case would be dismissed for lack of prosecution if it were not tried during the next term. The final trial date was set for October 9, 1963. On that date, Barker again moved to dismiss the indictment, and this time specified that his right to a speedy trial had been violated. The motion was denied; the trial commenced with Manning as the chief prosecution witness; Barker was convicted and given a life sentence.

. . . The right to a speedy trial is generically different from any of the other rights enshrined in the Constitution for the protection of the accused. In addition to the general concern that all accused persons be treated according to decent and fair procedures, there is a societal interest in providing a speedy trial which exists separate from, and at times in opposition to, the interests of the accused. The inability of courts to provide a prompt trial has contributed to a large backlog of cases in urban courts which, among other things, enables defendants to negotiate more effectively for pleas of guilty to lesser offenses and otherwise manipulate the system. In addition, persons released on bond for lengthy periods awaiting trial have an opportunity to commit other crimes. It must be of little comfort to the residents of Christian County, Kentucky, to know that Barker was at large on bail for over four years while accused of a vicious and brutal murder of which he was ultimately convicted. Moreover, the longer an accused is free awaiting trial, the more tempting becomes his opportunity to jump bail and escape. Finally, delay between arrest and punishment may have a detrimental effect on rehabilitation.

. . . A second difference between the right to speedy trial and the accused's other constitutional rights is that deprivation of the right may work to the accused's advantage. Delay is not an uncommon defense tactic. As the time between the commission of the crime and trial lengthens, witnesses may become unavailable or their memories may fade. If the witnesses support the prosecution, its case will be weakened, sometimes seriously so. And it is the prosecution which carries the burden of proof. Thus, unlike the right to counsel or the right to be free from compelled self-incrimination, deprivation of the right to speedy trial does not per se prejudice the accused's ability to defend himself.

Finally, and perhaps most importantly, the right to speedy trial is a more vague concept than other procedural rights. It is, for example, impossible to determine with precision when the right has been denied. We cannot definitely say how long is too long in a system where justice is supposed to be swift but deliberate. As a consequence, there is no fixed point in the criminal process when the State can put the defendant to the choice of either exercising or waiving the right to a speedy trial.

... The amorphous quality of the right also leads to the unsatisfactorily severe remedy of dismissal of the indictment when the right has been deprived. This is indeed a serious consequence because it means that a defendant who may be guilty of a serious crime will go free, without having been tried. Such a remedy is more serious than an exclusionary rule or a reversal for a new trial, but it is the only possible remedy.

Perhaps because the speedy trial right is so slippery, two rigid approaches are urged upon us as ways of eliminating some of the uncertainty which courts experience in protecting the right. The first suggestion is that we hold that the Constitution requires a criminal defendant to be offered a trial within a specified time period. The result of such a ruling would have the virtue of clarifying when the right is infringed and of simplifying courts' application of it. Recognizing this, some legislatures have enacted laws, and some courts have adopted procedural rules which more narrowly define the right.

... But such a result would require this Court to engage in legislative or rule-making activity, rather than in the adjudicative process to which we should confine our efforts. We do not establish procedural rules for the States, except when mandated by the Constitution. We find no constitutional basis for holding that the speedy trial right can be quantified into a specified number of days or months. The States, of course, are free to prescribe a reasonable period consistent with constitutional standards, but our approach must be less precise.

The second suggested alternative would restrict consideration of the right to those cases in which the accused has demanded a speedy trial. Most States have recognized what is loosely referred to as the "demand rule," although eight States reject it. It is not clear, however, precisely what is meant by that term. Although every federal court of appeals that has considered the question has endorsed some kind of demand rule, some have regarded the rule within the concept of waiver, whereas others have viewed it as a factor to be weighed in assessing whether there has been a deprivation of the speedy trial right. We shall refer to the former approach as the demand-waiver doctrine. The demand-waiver doctrine provides that a defendant waives any consideration of his right to speedy trial for any period prior to which he has not demanded a trial. Under this rigid approach, a prior demand is a necessary condition to the consideration of the speedy trial right.

Such an approach, by presuming waiver of a fundamental right from inaction, is inconsistent with this Court's pronouncements on waiver of constitutional rights. The Court has defined waiver as "an intentional relinquishment or abandonment of a known right or privilege."

... In excepting the right to speedy trial from the rule of waiver we have applied to other fundamental rights, courts that have applied the demand-waiver rule have relied on the assumption that delay usually works for the benefit of the accused and on the absence of any readily ascertainable time in the criminal process for a defendant to be given the choice of exercising or waiving his right. But it is not necessarily true that delay benefits the defendant. There are cases in which delay appreciably harms the defendant's ability to defend himself. Moreover, a defendant confined to jail prior to trial is obviously disadvantaged by delay as is a defendant released on bail but unable to lead a normal life because of community suspicion and his own anxiety.

The nature of the speedy trial right does make it impossible to pinpoint a precise time in the process when the right must be asserted or waived, but that fact does not argue for placing the burden of protecting the right solely on defendants. A defendant has no duty to bring himself to trial; the State has that duty as well as the duty of insuring that the trial is consistent with due process. Moreover, for the reasons earlier expressed, society has a particular interest in bringing swift prosecutions, and society's representatives are the ones who should protect that interest.

... We reject, therefore, the rule that a defendant who fails to demand a speedy trial forever waives his right. This does not mean, however, that the defendant has no responsibility to assert his right. We think the better rule is that the defendant's assertion of or failure to assert his right to a speedy trial is one of the factors to be considered in an inquiry into the deprivation of the right. Such a formulation avoids the rigidities of the demand-waiver rule and the resulting possible unfairness in its application. It allows the trial court to exercise a judicial discretion based on the circumstances, including due consideration of any applicable formal procedural rule. It would permit, for example, a court to attach a different weight to a situation in which the defendant knowingly fails to object from a situation in which his attorney acquiesces in long delay without adequately informing his client, or from a situation in which no counsel is appointed. It would also allow a court to weigh the frequency and force of the objections as opposed to attaching significant weight to a purely pro forma objection.

In ruling that a defendant has some responsibility to assert a speedy trial claim, we do not depart from our holdings in other cases concerning the waiver of fundamental rights, in which we have placed the entire responsibility on the prosecution to show that the claimed waiver was knowingly and voluntarily made. Such cases have involved rights which must be exercised or waived at a specific time or under clearly identifiable circumstances, such as the rights to plead not guilty, to demand a jury trial, to exercise the privilege against self-incrimination, and to have the assistance of counsel. We have shown above that the right to a speedy trial is unique in its uncertainty as to when and under what circumstances it must be asserted or may be deemed waived. But the rule we announce today, which comports with constitutional principles, places the primary burden on the courts and the prosecutors to assure that cases are brought to trial. We hardly need add that if delay is attributable to the defendant, then his waiver may be given effect under standard waiver doctrine, the demand rule aside.

We, therefore, reject both of the inflexible approaches—the fixed-time period because it goes further than the Constitution requires; the demand-waiver rule because it is insensitive to a right which we have deemed fundamental. The approach we accept is a balancing test, in which the conduct of both the prosecution and the defendant are weighed.

A balancing test necessarily compels courts to approach speedy trial cases on an ad hoc basis. We can do little more than identify some of the factors which courts should assess in determining whether a particular defendant has been deprived of his right. Though some might express them in different ways, we identify four such factors: length of delay, the reason for the delay, the defendant's assertion of his right, and prejudice to the defendant.

The length of the delay is to some extent a triggering mechanism. Until there is some delay which is presumptively prejudicial, there is no necessity for inquiry into the other factors that go into the balance. Nevertheless, because of the imprecision of the right to speedy trial, the length of delay that will provoke such an inquiry is necessarily dependent upon the peculiar circumstances of the case. To take but one example, the delay that can be tolerated for an ordinary street crime is considerably less than for a serious, complex conspiracy charge.

Closely related to length of delay is the reason the government assigns to justify the delay. Here, too, different weights should be assigned to different reasons. A deliberate attempt to delay the trial in order to hamper the defense should be weighted heavily against the government. A more neutral reason such as negligence or overcrowded courts should be weighted less heavily but nevertheless should be considered since the ultimate responsibility for such circumstances must rest with the government rather than with the defendant. Finally, a valid reason, such as a missing witness, should serve to justify appropriate delay.

We have already discussed the third factor, the defendant's responsibility to assert his right. Whether and how a defendant asserts his right is closely related to the other factors we have mentioned. The strength of his efforts will be affected by the length of the delay, to some extent by the reason for the delay, and most particularly by the personal prejudice, which is not always readily identifiable, that he experiences. The more serious the deprivation, the more likely a defendant is to complain. The defendant's assertion of his speedy trial right, then, is entitled to strong evidentiary weight in determining whether the defendant is being deprived of the right. We emphasize that failure to assert the right will make it difficult for a defendant to prove that he was denied a speedy trial.

A fourth factor is prejudice to the defendant. Prejudice, of course, should be assessed in the light of the interests of defendants which the speedy trial right was designed to protect. This Court has identified three such interests: (i) to prevent oppressive pretrial incarceration; (ii) to minimize anxiety and concern of the accused; and (iii) to limit the possibility that the defense will be impaired. Of these, the most serious is the last, because the inability of a defendant adequately to prepare his case skews the fairness of the entire system. If witnesses die or disappear during a delay, the prejudice is obvious. There is also prejudice if defense witnesses are unable to recall accurately events of the distant past. Loss of memory, however, is not always reflected in the record because what has been forgotten can rarely be shown.

We have discussed previously the societal disadvantages of lengthy pretrial incarceration, but obviously the disadvantages for the accused who cannot obtain his release are even more serious. The time spent in jail awaiting trial has a detrimental impact on the individual. It often means loss of a job; it disrupts family life; and it enforces idleness. Most jails offer little or no recreational or rehabilitative programs. The time spent in jail is simply dead time. Moreover, if a defendant is locked up, he is hindered in his ability to gather evidence, contact witnesses, or otherwise prepare his defense. Imposing those consequences on anyone who has not yet been convicted is serious. It is especially unfortunate to impose them on those persons who are ultimately found to be innocent. Finally, even if an accused is not incarcerated prior to trial, he is still disadvantaged by restraints on his liberty and by living under a cloud of anxiety, suspicion, and often hostility.

We regard none of the four factors identified above as either a necessary or sufficient condition to the finding of a deprivation of the right of speedy trial. Rather, they are related factors and must be considered together with such other circumstances as may be relevant. In sum, these factors have no talismanic qualities; courts must still engage in a difficult and sensitive balancing process. But, because we are dealing with a fundamental right of the accused, this process must be carried out with full recognition that the accused's interest in a speedy trial is specifically affirmed in the Constitution.

The difficulty of the task of balancing these factors is illustrated by this case, which we consider to be close. It is clear that the length of delay between arrest and trial—well over five years—was extraordinary. Only seven months of that period can be attributed to a strong excuse, the illness of the ex-sheriff who was in charge of the investigation. Perhaps some delay would have been permissible under ordinary circumstances, so that Manning could be utilized as a witness in Barker's trial, but more than four years was too long a period, particularly since a good part of that period was attributable to the Commonwealth's failure or inability to try Manning under circumstances that comported with due process.

Two counterbalancing factors, however, outweigh these deficiencies. The first is that prejudice was minimal. Of course, Barker was prejudiced to some extent by living for over four years under a cloud of suspicion and anxiety. Moreover, although he was released on bond for most of the period, he did spend 10 months in jail before trial. But there is no claim that any of Barker's witnesses died or otherwise became unavailable owing to the delay. The trial transcript indicates only two very minor lapses of memory—one on the part of a prosecution witness—which were in no way significant to the outcome.

More important than the absence of serious prejudice, is the fact that Barker did not want a speedy trial. Counsel was appointed for Barker immediately after his indictment and represented him throughout the period. No question is raised as to the competency of such counsel. Despite the fact that counsel had notice of the motions for continuances, the record shows no action whatever taken between October 21, 1958, and February 12, 1962, that could be construed as the assertion of the speedy trial right. On the latter date, in response to another motion for continuance, Barker moved to dismiss the indictment. The record does not show on what ground this motion was based, although it is clear that no alternative motion was made for an immediate trial. Instead the record strongly suggests that while he hoped to take advantage of the delay in which he had acquiesced, and thereby obtain a dismissal of the charges, he definitely did not want to be tried.

... We do not hold that there may never be a situation in which an indictment may be dismissed on speedy trial grounds where the defendant has failed to object to continuances. There may be a situation in which the defendant was represented by incompetent counsel, was severely prejudiced, or even cases in which the continuances were granted *ex parte*. But barring extraordinary circumstances, we would be reluctant indeed to rule that a defendant was denied this constitutional right on a record that strongly indicates, as does this one, that the defendant did not want a speedy trial. We hold, therefore, that Barker was not deprived of his due process right to a speedy trial. Affirmed.

[The concurring opinion of Justice White is omitted.]

Notes

1. *Demand by defendant.* One of the important factors to be weighed in the balance is, according to *Barker*, "the defendant's assertion of his right [to a speedy trial]." While *Barker* makes clear that it is not absolutely essential that the defendant "demand" a speedy trial, the Court observed that finding a violation in the absence of such a demand will be "difficult for a defendant to prove."

Barker leaves some questions about the demand unanswered. For example, is the defendant expected to assert the right each time that it could have been raised? *See United States v. Abad*, 514 F.3d 271 (2d Cir. 2008) (failing to consistently raise the speedy trial issue is weighed against the defendant). Is the timing of the assertion important? *See United States v. Hopkins*, 310 F.3d 145 (4th Cir. 2002) (waiting until five days before trial weighs against the defendant).

2. *Length of delay.* Regarding length of delay, *Barker* assumed that "delay ... can be tolerated [more so] for a serious, complex conspiracy charge [than] an ordinary street crime." How persuasive are these examples? Is it not probable that many conspiracy cases are far *less* complex in terms of case preparation than street crimes?

A delay in excess of one year is often regarded as presumptively prejudicial to the defendant's rights, as noted in *Doggett v. United States*, 505 U.S. 647 (1992). Some courts treat shorter delays in the same manner. *Compare United States v. Woolfolk*, 399 F.3d 590 (4th Cir. 2005) (eight-month delay triggers *Barker* balancing test), *with United States v. Titlbach*, 339 F.3d 692 (8th Cir. 2003) (eight-month delay not sufficient).

3. *Reasons for delay.* Another *Barker* factor is the reason offered by the government to justify a delay. The burden is on the prosecution to articulate an acceptable reason for the delay. *United States v. Seltzer*, 595 F.3d 1170 (10th Cir. 2010). As to crowded dockets, lower courts have followed *Barker*'s suggestion that the prosecution must bear "ultimate responsibility" for such "institutional delays." On the other hand, delays attributable to the defendant are not weighed against the prosecution.

Sometimes a trial is delayed for a considerable period because of interlocutory appeals from pretrial decisions. How should that kind of delay be factored into the balance? In *United States v. Loud Hawk*, 474 U.S. 302 (1986), the United States Supreme Court explicitly adopted the *Barker* test to determine the extent to which appellate time consumed in the review of pretrial motions should weigh towards a speedy trial claim. While recognizing that a 90-month delay was presumptively prejudicial, the Court in *Loud Hawk* found no speedy trial violation because an interlocutory appeal was deemed to be "ordinarily . . . a valid reason that justifies the delay." Factors to be considered in this context include the strength of the government's position on the issue appealed, the importance of the issue and the seriousness of the underlying offense.

4. *Prejudice.* In explaining the balancing test, *Barker* declared that no one factor is "either a necessary or sufficient condition to the finding of a deprivation of the right of speedy trial." However, it noted that the most significant harm is the possibility the defense will be impaired. On the facts presented in *Barker*, two factors were considered to be detrimental to Barker's claim of a violation: (1) prejudice was deemed to be "minimal," and (2) Barker apparently did not desire a speedy trial. The second factor (absence of demand) was considered to be the "more important" of the two. Assume that a defendant is able to demonstrate serious prejudice due to post-accusation delays attributable to the government (for example, the government delayed the defendant's trial until after a key defense witness was deported from the country and the government had knowledge that a prompt trial would have allowed the witness to testify). In that kind of case, should not the presence of demonstrable prejudice be sufficient, alone, for a finding of a speedy trial violation?

5. *Missed rehabilitative opportunity.* If an addicted defendant is unable to participate in a drug treatment program because of the pendency of a criminal charge, does that count as prejudice under the *Barker* test? Yes, concluded the Montana Supreme Court in *State v. Mayes*, 384 P.3d 102 (Mt. 2016). The state charged Mayes with a felony related to drug use and held him in jail for 279 days between the time of his arrest and the resolution of his case. Although Mayes had been accepted into

a community-based drug treatment program, he was unable to participate in it due to his pretrial incarceration. Although the Montana Supreme Court noted that the state's alleged interference with a defendant's merely "speculative prospects for rehabilitation" might not count as prejudice, Mayes' missed opportunity was sufficiently definite to weigh against the state under *Barker. Id.*, ¶ 19. Indeed, the prejudice against Mayes was great enough, and the state's justification for the delay—"a backlog at the State Crime Lab and an unexplained failure to timely submit [evidence to the Lab]"—weak enough, that dismissal of the charge against Mayes was required. *Id.*, ¶ 25.

6. *Revocation of probation or parole.* Although separate from "criminal prosecutions" protected by the Sixth Amendment's speedy trial guarantee, revocation proceedings for probation or parole are governed by due process requirements. Thus, the final revocation of parole hearing "must be tendered within a reasonable time after the parolee is taken into custody." *Morrissey v. Brewer*, 408 U.S. 471 (1972). A delay in a parolee's final revocation hearing could result in the proceeding taking place much later than when, and in an entirely different jurisdiction from where, the violation of a parole condition occurred. *Morrissey* reasoned that "due process would seem to require that some minimal inquiry be conducted at or reasonably near the place of the alleged parole violation or arrest and as promptly as convenient after arrest while information is fresh and sources are available."

7. *Interlocutory appeal.* Assume that you represent a person whose trial has been delayed repeatedly, notwithstanding your persistent insistence upon speedy trial. After six continuances, you file a motion for dismissal of the indictment under *Barker*, but the trial judge denies the motion. It is your position at that time that the judge erroneously weighed the *Barker* factors and that appellate review of that decision should be pursued immediately, thereby avoiding the time and cost associated with trial on the merits. Do you (or should you) have a right to an interlocutory appeal?

The United States Supreme Court answered "no" in *United States v. MacDonald*, 435 U.S. 850 (1978), holding that federal circuit courts have no jurisdiction to hear such claims prior to trial. Accordingly, the defendant was required to proceed to trial, reserving appellate review of the speedy trial issue until after verdict. The Court emphasized that "resolution of a speedy trial claim necessitates a careful assessment of the particular facts of the case [and therefore such claims] are best considered only after the relevant facts have been developed at trial." Additionally, the Court rejected the notion that the speedy trial guarantee encompasses a right not to be tried. In the Court's words, "it is the delay before trial, not the trial itself, that offends against the [right to] a speedy trial."

8. *When does the clock start to run?* The *Barker* test requires a calculation of how much time has passed between accusation and trial, but it is not always clear when exactly a person becomes an "accused" for purposes of the Speedy Trial Clause. In *Marion*, the Supreme Court indicated that the clock starts to run at the time of arrest, indictment, or information, whichever comes first. But what about the filing of a prearrest criminal complaint? Lower courts have adopted varying answers to this

question. *See, e.g., Butler v. Mitchell*, 815 F.3d 87, 90 (1st Cir. 2016) ("[A] Massachusetts criminal complaint, standing alone, is not the public, official accusation that the Sixth Amendment requires."); *United States v. Richardson*, 780 F.3d 812 (7th Cir. 2015) (holding that federal felony complaint does not start Sixth Amendment clock, even when served along with detainer on defendant in jail facing state charges); *State v. Wright*, 404 P.3d 166 (Alaska 2017) (noting Alaska precedent indicating that state constitution's speedy-trial clock starts to run with filing of complaint; raising, but not answering, question of whether the pertinent statement was merely dicta); *People v. Mirenda*, 174 Cal. App. 4th 1313, 1327 (Cal. Ct. App. 2009) ("Unlike federal law, however, this state has extended the [state constitutional speedy-trial] right to the preindictment and prearrest stage, holding that it attaches . . . after a complaint has been filed.").

Doggett v. United States

505 U.S. 647 (1992)

Justice Souter delivered the opinion of the Court.

In this case we consider whether the delay of 8 1/2 years between petitioner's indictment and arrest violated his Sixth Amendment right to a speedy trial. We hold that it did.

On February 22, 1980, petitioner Marc Doggett was indicted for conspiring with several others to import and distribute cocaine. Douglas Driver, the Drug Enforcement Administration's principal agent investigating the conspiracy, told the United States Marshal's Service that the DEA would oversee the apprehension of Doggett and his confederates. On March 18, 1980, two police officers set out under Driver's orders to arrest Doggett at his parents' house in Raleigh, North Carolina, only to find that he was not there. His mother told the officers that he had left for Colombia four days earlier.

To catch Doggett on his return to the United States, Driver sent word of his outstanding arrest warrant to all United States Customs stations and to a number of law enforcement organizations. He also placed Doggett's name in the Treasury Enforcement Communication System (TECS), a computer network that helps Customs agents screen people entering the country, and in the National Crime Information Center computer system, which serves similar ends. The TECS entry expired that September, however, and Doggett's name vanished from the system.

In September 1981, Driver found out that Doggett was under arrest on drug charges in Panama and, thinking that a formal extradition request would be futile, simply asked Panama to "expel" Doggett to the United States. Although the Panamanian authorities promised to comply when their own proceedings had run their course, they freed Doggett the following July and let him go to Colombia, where he stayed with an aunt for several months. On September 25, 1982, he passed unhindered through Customs in New York City and settled down in Virginia. Since his return to the United States, he has married, earned a college degree, found a steady job as a computer operations manager, lived openly under his own name, and stayed within the law.

Doggett's travels abroad had not wholly escaped the Government's notice, however. In 1982, the American Embassy in Panama told the State Department of his departure to Colombia, but that information, for whatever reason, eluded the DEA, and Agent Driver assumed for several years that his quarry was still serving time in a Panamanian prison. Driver never asked DEA officials in Panama to check into Doggett's status, and only after his own fortuitous assignment to that country in 1985 did he discover Doggett's departure for Colombia. Driver then simply assumed Doggett had settled there, and he made no effort to find out for sure or to track Doggett down, either abroad or in the United States. Thus Doggett remained lost to the American criminal justice system until September 1988, when the Marshal's Service ran a simple credit check on several thousand people subject to outstanding arrest warrants and, within minutes, found out where Doggett lived and worked. On September 5, 1988, nearly 6 years after his return to the United States and 8 1/2 years after his indictment, Doggett was arrested.

He naturally moved to dismiss the indictment, arguing that the Government's failure to prosecute him earlier violated his Sixth Amendment right to a speedy trial.... The Magistrate found that the delay between Doggett's indictment [February 1980] and arrest [September 1988] was long enough to be "presumptively prejudicial," that the delay "clearly [was] attributable to the negligence of the government," and that Doggett could not be faulted for any delay in asserting his right to a speedy trial, there being no evidence that he had known of the charges against him until his arrest. The Magistrate also found, however, that Doggett had made no affirmative showing that the delay had impaired his ability to mount a successful defense or had otherwise prejudiced him. In his recommendation to the District Court, the Magistrate contended that this failure to demonstrate particular prejudice sufficed to defeat Doggett's speedy trial claim.

[The District Court and Court of Appeals denied relief. Doggett then entered a conditional guilty plea under Federal Rule of Criminal Procedure 11(a)(2), expressly reserving the right to appeal his ensuing conviction on the speedy trial claim.]

... On its face, the Speedy Trial Clause is written with such breadth that, taken literally, it would forbid the government to delay the trial of an "accused" for any reason at all. Our cases, however, have qualified the literal sweep of the provision by specifically recognizing the relevance of four separate enquiries: whether delay before trial was uncommonly long, whether the government or the criminal defendant is more to blame for that delay, whether, in due course, the defendant asserted his right to a speedy trial, and whether he suffered prejudice as the delay's result.

The first of these is actually a double enquiry. Simply to trigger a speedy trial analysis, an accused must allege that the interval between accusation and trial has crossed the threshold dividing ordinary from "presumptively prejudicial" delay, since, by definition, he cannot complain that the government has denied him a "speedy" trial if it has, in fact, prosecuted his case with customary promptness. If the accused makes this showing, the court must then consider, as one factor among several, the extent to which the delay stretches beyond the bare minimum needed to trigger judicial examination of the claim. This latter enquiry is significant to the speedy trial analysis because, as we discuss below, the presumption that pretrial delay has prejudiced the accused intensifies over time. In this case, the extraordinary 8 1/2 year lag between Doggett's indictment and arrest clearly suffices to trigger the speedy trial enquiry. . . . [1]

As for *Barker*'s second criterion, the Government claims to have sought Doggett with diligence. The findings of the courts below are to the contrary, however, and we review trial court determinations of negligence with considerable deference. . . . While the Government's lethargy may have reflected no more than Doggett's relative unimportance in the world of drug trafficking, it was still findable negligence, and the finding stands.

The Government goes against the record again in suggesting that Doggett knew of his indictment years before he was arrested. Were this true, *Barker*'s third factor, concerning invocation of the right to a speedy trial, would be weighed heavily against him. But here again, the Government is trying to revisit the facts. At the hearing on Doggett's speedy trial motion, it introduced no evidence challenging the testimony of Doggett's wife, who said that she did not know of the charges until his arrest, and of his mother, who claimed not to have told him or anyone else that the police had come looking for him.

. . . The Government is left, then, with its principal contention: that Doggett fails to make out a successful speedy trial claim because he has not shown precisely how he was prejudiced by the delay between his indictment and trial.

We have observed in prior cases that unreasonable delay between formal accusation and trial threatens to produce more than one sort of harm, including "oppressive pretrial incarceration," "anxiety and concern of the accused," and "the possibility that the [accused's] defense will be impaired" by dimming memories and loss of exculpatory evidence. Of these forms of prejudice, "the most serious is the last, because the inability of a defendant adequately to prepare his case skews the fairness of the entire system." Doggett claims this kind of prejudice, and there is probably no other kind that he can claim, since he was subjected neither to pretrial detention nor, he has successfully contended, to awareness of unresolved charges against him.

The Government answers Doggett's claim by citing language in three cases, *United States v. Marion*, 404 U.S. 307 (1971), *United States v. MacDonald*, 456 U.S. 1 (1982), and *United States v. Loud Hawk*, 474 U.S. 302 (1986), for the proposition that the Speedy Trial Clause does not significantly protect a criminal defendant's interest in

1. Depending on the nature of the charges, the lower courts have generally found postaccusation delay "presumptively prejudicial" at least as it approaches one year. We note that, as the term is used in this threshold context, "presumptive prejudice" does not necessarily indicate a statistical probability of prejudice; it simply marks the point at which courts deem the delay unreasonable enough to trigger the *Barker* enquiry.

fair adjudication. In so arguing, the Government asks us, in effect, to read part of *Barker* right out of the law, and that we will not do.

. . . As an alternative to limiting *Barker*, the Government claims Doggett has failed to make any affirmative showing that the delay weakened his ability to raise specific defenses, elicit specific testimony, or produce specific items of evidence. Though Doggett did indeed come up short in this respect, the Government's argument takes it only so far: Consideration of prejudice is not limited to the specifically demonstrable, and, as it concedes, affirmative proof of particularized prejudice is not essential to every speedy trial claim. *Barker* explicitly recognized that impairment of one's defense is the most difficult form of speedy trial prejudice to prove because time's erosion of exculpatory evidence and testimony "can rarely be shown." . . . Thus, we generally have to recognize that excessive delay presumptively compromises the reliability of a trial in ways that neither party can prove or, for that matter, identify. While such presumptive prejudice cannot alone carry a Sixth Amendment claim without regard to the other *Barker* criteria, it is part of the mix of relevant facts, and its importance increases with the length of delay.

This brings us to an enquiry into the role that presumptive prejudice should play in the disposition of Doggett's speedy trial claim. We begin with hypothetical and somewhat easier cases and work our way to this one.

Our speedy trial standards recognize that pretrial delay is often both inevitable and wholly justifiable. The government may need time to collect witnesses against the accused, oppose his pretrial motions, or, if he goes into hiding, track him down. We attach great weight to such considerations when balancing them against the costs of going forward with a trial whose probative accuracy the passage of time has begun by degrees to throw into question. Thus, in this case, if the Government had pursued Doggett with reasonable diligence from his indictment to his arrest, his speedy trial claim would fail. Indeed, that conclusion would generally follow as a matter of course however great the delay, so long as Doggett could not show specific prejudice to his defense.

The Government concedes, on the other hand, that Doggett would prevail if he could show that the Government had intentionally held back in its prosecution of him to gain some impermissible advantage at trial. That we cannot doubt. *Barker* stressed that official bad faith in causing delay will be weighed heavily against the government and a bad-faith delay the length of this negligent one would present an overwhelming case for dismissal.

Between diligent prosecution and bad-faith delay, official negligence in bringing an accused to trial occupies the middle ground. While not compelling relief in every case where bad-faith delay would make relief virtually automatic, neither is negligence automatically tolerable simply because the accused cannot demonstrate exactly how it has prejudiced him.

. . . Although negligence is obviously to be weighed more lightly than a deliberate intent to harm the accused's defense, it still falls on the wrong side of the divide between acceptable and unacceptable reasons for delaying a criminal prosecution once it has begun. And such is the nature of the prejudice presumed that the weight we assign to official negligence compounds over time as the presumption of evidentiary prejudice grows. Thus, our toleration of such negligence varies inversely with its protractedness, and its consequent threat to the fairness of the accused's trial. Condoning prolonged and unjustifiable delays in prosecution would both penalize many defendants for the state's fault and simply encourage the government to gamble with the interests of criminal suspects assigned a low prosecutorial priority. . . .

To be sure, to warrant granting relief, negligence unaccompanied by particularized trial prejudice must have lasted longer than negligence demonstrably causing such prejudice. But even so, the Government's egregious persistence in failing to prosecute Doggett is clearly sufficient. The lag between Doggett's indictment and arrest was 8 1/2 years, and he would have faced trial 6 years earlier than he did but for the Government's inexcusable oversights. . . . When the Government's negligence thus causes delay six times as long as that generally sufficient to trigger judicial review, and when the presumption of prejudice, albeit unspecified, is neither extenuated, as by the defendant's acquiescence, nor persuasively rebutted,[4] the defendant is entitled to relief. [Reversed and remanded.]

Justice O'Connor, dissenting.

. . . The only harm to petitioner from the lapse of time was potential prejudice to his ability to defend his case. We have not allowed such speculative harm to tip the scales. Instead, we have required a showing of actual prejudice to the defense before weighing it in the balance. . . .

Justice Thomas, with whom The Chief Justice and Justice Scalia join, dissenting.

. . . [T]he Speedy Trial Clause's core concern is impairment of liberty. Whenever a criminal trial takes place long after the events at issue, the defendant may be prejudiced in any number of ways. But "[t]he Speedy Trial Clause does not purport to protect a defendant from all effects flowing from a delay before trial."

. . . A lengthy pretrial delay, of course, may prejudice an accused's ability to defend himself. But . . . prejudice to the defense is not the sort of impairment of liberty against which the Clause is directed. "Passage of time, whether before or after arrest, may impair memories, cause evidence to be lost, deprive the defendant of witnesses, and otherwise interfere with his ability to defend himself. But this possibility of prejudice at trial is not itself sufficient reason to wrench the Sixth Amendment from its proper context." Even though a defendant may be prejudiced by a pretrial delay, and even though the government may be unable to provide a valid justification for that delay, the Clause does not come into play unless the delay impairs the defendant's liberty.

---

4. While the Government ably counters Doggett's efforts to demonstrate particularized trial prejudice, it has not, and probably could not have, affirmatively proved that the delay left his ability to defend himself unimpaired.

. . . [P]rejudice to the defense stems from the interval between crime and trial, which is quite distinct from the interval between accusation and trial. If the Clause were indeed aimed at safeguarding against prejudice to the defense, then it would presumably limit all prosecutions that occur long after the criminal events at issue. A defendant prosecuted 10 years after a crime is just as hampered in his ability to defend himself whether he was indicted the week after the crime or the week before the trial—but no one would suggest that the Clause protects him in the latter situation, where the delay did not substantially impair his liberty, either through oppressive incarceration or the anxiety of known criminal charges. . . . The initiation of a formal criminal prosecution is simply irrelevant to whether the defense has been prejudiced by delay.

. . . So engrossed is the Court in applying the multifactor balancing test set forth in *Barker* that it loses sight of the nature and purpose of the speedy trial guarantee set forth in the Sixth Amendment. The Court's error [is] . . . in its failure to recognize that the speedy trial guarantee cannot be violated—and thus *Barker* does not apply at all—when an accused is entirely unaware of a pending indictment against him.

. . . Today's opinion, I fear, will transform the courts of the land into boards of law-enforcement supervision. For the Court compels dismissal of the charges against Doggett not because he was harmed in any way by the delay between his indictment and arrest,[6] but simply because the Government's efforts to catch him are found wanting. . . . By divorcing the Speedy Trial Clause from all considerations of prejudice to an accused, the Court positively invites the Nation's judges to indulge in ad hoc and result-driven second-guessing of the government's investigatory efforts. Our Constitution neither contemplates nor tolerates such a role. I respectfully dissent.

Notes

1. *Meanings of prejudice.* Take note of how Justice Souter has characterized the issue of "prejudice" in two different ways. First, prejudice is a component of the finding that the interval between accusation and trial was not prompt enough. Second, it is a separate factor for consideration as the delay lengthens. Does it seem logical to you that prejudice is necessarily a part of the "initial delay" analysis? Could the defendant satisfy the first "prejudice" test without any proof of prejudice to his or her case?

2. *Negligence v. bad faith.* Did the Court provide any helpful guidance with respect to the distinction between "bad-faith government delay" and "negligent government delay"? The importance of such a distinction is clearly underscored in that

---

6. It is quite likely, in fact, that the delay benefitted Doggett. At the time of his arrest, he had been living an apparently normal, law-abiding life for some five years—a point not lost on the District Court Judge, who, instead of imposing a prison term, sentenced him to three years' probation and a $1000 fine. Thus, the delay gave Doggett the opportunity to prove what most defendants can only promise: that he no longer posed a threat to society. There can be little doubt that, had he been tried immediately after his cocaine-importation activities, he would have received a harsher sentence.

portion of the opinion noting that "where bad-faith delay [occurs], relief [is] virtually automatic."

The line between negligence and bad faith is not always clear. What if the police force were so shorthanded it could not investigate cases in a timely fashion? Is this negligence or bad faith? If this police force refused to prod politicians for more resources, would "bad faith" be present? To avoid a bad faith finding, would the police have to reassign officers from traffic and other responsibilities to ensure timely investigations? If the lack of resources persists, at some point is there "bad faith"? Would it be bad faith or negligence to assign a case to an incompetent detective who failed to investigate the case despite knowledge of the offender's identity?

3. *Effect of delay caused by defendant or defense counsel.* The *Barker* Court explicitly recognized that a prosecution-requested delay of a defendant's trial because of a missing witness would normally be justified. How are delays caused by the *defense* to be weighed under *Barker*'s four-factor analysis? In *Doggett*, the Court framed one of the *Barker* factors as an assessment of "whether the government or the criminal defendant is more to blame" for the delay. In *Vermont v. Brillon*, 556 U.S. 81 (2009), the Court applied the same principle to delays caused by defense counsel (whether retained or appointed), and refused to weigh against the state a delay caused by the failure of a succession of six assigned lawyers to move the defendant's case forward. The Court in *Brillon* also, unsurprisingly, weighed the defendant's own disruptive behavior—firing his first attorney on the eve of trial and threatening the life of his third attorney—heavily against him. The Court suggested one possible exception (not presented by the facts in that case) to the general rule that delays caused by assigned counsel's lack of diligence are chargeable against the defendant: situations where there is a "systemic breakdown in the public defender system." Do you think that a defendant asserting a Sixth Amendment speedy trial violation should have to suffer the consequences of delays caused by the actions or omissions of appointed counsel?

Chronic underfunding is often said to hamper the quality of representation provided through public defender systems in the United States. Are there jurisdictions in which such underfunding is so bad as to constitute the sort of "systemic breakdown" to which the Court alluded in *Brillon*? The question came up, but was not answered on the merits, in *Boyer v. Louisiana*, 569 U.S. 238 (2013). The Court initially agreed to hear the case in light of a seven-year delay between Boyer's arrest and trial, but then dismissed *certiorari* as improvidently granted. Four justices dissented from this decision. Writing for the dissenters, Justice Sotomayor argued that the Court should have addressed the implications of Louisiana's "funding crisis" for the speedy trial rights of defendants. She reasoned:

> Where a State has failed to provide funding for the defense and that lack of funding causes a delay, the defendant cannot reasonably be faulted. *See Barker*, 407 U. S., at 531. Placing the consequences of such a delay squarely on the State's shoulders is proper for the simple reason that an indigent defendant has no control over whether a State has set aside funds to pay his lawyer or

> fund any necessary investigation. The failure to fund an indigent's defense is not as serious as a deliberate effort by a State to cause delay. *Ibid.* But States routinely make tradeoffs in the allocation of limited resources, and it is reasonable that a State bear the consequences of these choices.

Id. at 246 (Sotomayor, J., dissenting).

The constitutionality of underfunded public defender systems has been challenged in many jurisdictions, but typically under the Sixth Amendment right to counsel. For an argument that the right to a speedy trial might also be a promising basis for attacking underfunding, *see* Emily Rose, Note, *Speedy Trial as a Viable Challenge to Chronic Underfunding in Indigent-Defense Systems*, 113 MICH. L. REV. 279 (2014).

4. *Source of prejudice.* Do you agree with Justice Thomas's statement in his *Doggett* dissent that "the initiation of a formal criminal prosecution is simply irrelevant to whether the defendant has been prejudiced by delay"? If you disagree, how would you respond to his observation that "prejudice to the defense stems from the interval between crime and trial, which is quite distinct from the interval between accusation and trial"?

5. *Rebutting presumption of prejudice.* Justice Souter in *Doggett* acknowledged that the government may be able to defeat a speedy trial claim if it could "persuasively rebut" the presumption of prejudice. Footnote 4, however, appears to make it next to impossible for the government to carry this burden. In *United States v. Shell*, 974 F.2d 1035 (9th Cir. 1992), the Court of Appeals found that a five-year delay between indictment and arrest was attributable to the government's negligence (the defendant's file had been misplaced and the government thereafter made no attempt to locate him), creating a strong presumption of prejudice. The government attempted to "persuasively rebut" the presumption of prejudice by pointing to the fact that the defendant actually conceded that "most of the essential witnesses and documentary evidence [were] still available." While the court acknowledged that *Doggett* "did not define precisely what type of evidence must be shown to rebut the presumption," it concluded that the government failed to meet that burden.

6. *Remedy for speedy trial violation.* In *Barker*, the Supreme Court held that the remedy for a speedy trial violation is dismissal of the indictment. Writing for the Court, Justice Powell characterized the remedy as an "unsatisfactorily severe remedy . . . because it means that a defendant who may be guilty of a serious crime will go free, without having been tried." Nonetheless, he declared this to be "the only possible remedy." Do you agree?

Problem 12-2. Should the Defendant Complain?

After the police discover a dead body on January 1, 2012, the police focused their attention on Harry Amos, Mary Beak, Ronald Page, and Joe Donnelly. Donnelly died within a month, and shortly thereafter, Beak told the grand jury a story implicating Amos and Donnelly in the killing. On March 30, the grand jury indicted Amos for murder. In April, Beak gave Amos's appointed lawyer a sworn statement exonerating Amos, and on May 1, she again exonerated Amos at a court hearing. Five days before Amos's trial was scheduled to begin on May 3, the prosecutor asked for and obtained a continuance because of Beak's inconsistent statements. In June, the prosecutor obtained a second continuance, and in October she obtained an indefinite continuance. Explaining her actions, the prosecutor later said that she did not want to see Amos acquitted of a killing he committed.

Between January and October 2013, Amos's lawyer filed four motions demanding to have Amos brought to trial. Noting the prosecutor's belief that the case could not be tried in the foreseeable future, the court discharged Amos's appointed lawyer. The court never ruled on Amos's speedy trial motions.

In January 2014, a newly elected prosecutor rescheduled Amos's trial for March. In February 2014, the police arrested Beak for perjury. When Beak responded by vouching for the reliability of her earlier grand jury statement implicating Amos and Donnelly, the prosecutor said that he would drop the perjury charge. At Amos's trial in March, Beak invoked the Fifth Amendment on the advice of counsel. After the prosecutor's case-in-chief, Amos called Ronald Page as a defense witness. Page at first claimed a memory loss, but after being declared a hostile witness, he also refused to testify on Fifth Amendment grounds. The jury convicted Amos of murder.

On appeal, how should the appellate court rule on Amos's claim that he was deprived of his Sixth Amendment right to a speedy trial?

[2] Statutes and Rules of Procedure

Although the Sixth Amendment's speedy trial guarantee has been effective in some cases to compel prompt criminal proceedings, the *Barker* factors may be difficult for the accused to establish. Often, for example, the defendant will not have demanded a speedy trial and cannot prove prejudice by the delay. The result is a system of delayed criminal proceedings that, as *Barker* noted, deprives the public of its interest in the timely resolution of criminal cases.

Because the constitutional speedy trial guarantee has not substantially eliminated delays in criminal proceedings, both federal and state legislative bodies have passed statutory speedy trial laws establishing maximum time limits for various proceedings in criminal cases. The next few sections describe three such efforts: the federal speedy trial statute, state speedy trial provisions, and a uniform act that facilitates prompt resolution of criminal charges against people imprisoned in other jurisdictions.

[a] The Federal Speedy Trial Act

The Speedy Trial Act, which governs only federal criminal prosecutions, establishes precise time limits for processing a federal criminal case. First, the information or indictment must be filed within 30 days of arrest or service of summons. Second, the trial must take place within 70 days of the filing of the formal charge (information or indictment) or 70 days from the date on which the defendant appears before a judicial officer, whichever is later. Various "tolling" provisions apply to dismissals of the indictment, mistrials, etc. A variety of matters that occur prior to trial also are excluded from the stated time limits. In the event of a violation of the statute, the case against the defendant is dismissed either with or without prejudice. The Act is codified at 18 U.S.C. §§ 3161, 3162, 3164, and 3173.

Notes

1. *No trial before 30 days.* Examine § 3161(c)(2), which is designed to protect against the defendant's trial commencing in a "too speedy" fashion. (Consider, for instance, the discussion of *McFadden v. Cabana* in Chapter 9, in which a robbery defendant was forced to go to trial only 10 days after his indictment.) Congress has declared, in effect, that forcing a person to trial in less than 30 days after first appearance would be fundamentally unfair due to the presumed inability of the accused and counsel to adequately prepare for trial.

2. *Indictment or information within 30 days of arrest or summons.* Note that the general rule is that an information or indictment must be filed within 30 days of the date the defendant was arrested or summoned *in connection with such charges.* 18 U.S.C. § 3161(b). Arrest for another charge may not trigger the speedy trial clock. *See, e.g, United States v. Congdon*, 54 Fed. Appx. 636 (9th Cir. 2002) (arrest for state parole violation does not start the 30-day Speedy Trial Act clock).

3. *Trial within 70 days of filing information or indictment or of appearance before judicial officer where charge is pending.* The second significant deadline is that the trial must be commenced within 70 days of the filing of the information or indictment or the date the defendant first appeared before a judicial officer in the court where the information or indictment is pending, *whichever is last.* 18 U.S.C. § 3161(c). Thus, if the government begins the process by obtaining an indictment and the defendant is then arraigned on that indictment (a frequent sequence in federal cases), the 70-day period begins to run at the arraignment.

4. *Exclusions from time periods.* Section 3161(h) contains an extensive list of exclusions from the calculation of the 30- and 70-day deadlines.

a. *Continuance.* It is routine in a criminal case for one or even both sides to request a continuance that will postpone a Speedy Trial Act deadline. For example, the accused may assert that there has been insufficient time to prepare for trial. This is especially true when there has been a change of attorneys between the initial charge and trial. Normally, the newly appointed or retained lawyer will file a motion for a continuance, arguing that it would be unfair to try the defendant because of inadequate time to prepare the case.

Section 3161(h)(7)(A) authorizes the trial court to grant a continuance on its own motion or that of either the government or defense if the court makes a finding that the "ends of justice" outweigh the "best interest of the public and the defendant in a speedy trial." The time of the continuance is not counted in assessing whether the trial, information, or indictment was timely. Although the Speedy Trial Act was adopted in part to eliminate open-ended ends-of-justice continuances or delays, judges may grant those delays that are reasonably related to the needs of the case. *See, e.g., United States v. Sabino*, 307 F.3d 446 (6th Cir. 2002). Note that this rule only applies when the judge makes a finding on the record that the ends-of-justice reasons for the continuance outweigh the countervailing interests in a speedy trial. When the judge fails to make these findings, the harmless error rule is inapplicable, meaning that the time of the continuance is not excluded from the time limits of the Speedy Trial Act. *Zedner v. United States*, 547 U.S. 489 (2006).

Notwithstanding the flexibility of the ends-of-justice provision, note that § 3161(h)(7)(C) bars the granting of a continuance "because of general congestion of the court's calendar, or lack of diligent preparation or failure to obtain available witnesses on the part of the attorney for the government."

b. *Mental competency.* Periods of time needed to determine the defendant's mental competency are not counted under the Speedy Trial Act. 18 U.S.C. § 3161(h)(1)(a). There is no time limit for this delay. Likewise, periods during which the defendant was mentally incompetent or physically unable to attend trial are not counted. 18 U.S.C. § 3161(h)(4).

c. *Interlocutory appeal.* The Speedy Trial Act also excludes delays caused by pursuit of an interlocutory appeal by either side. 18 U.S.C. § 3161 (h)(1)(C).

d. *Motions.* The filing of a pretrial motion by either the prosecution or defense stops the running of the Speedy Trial Act clock. Periods between the filing of a motion and its disposition by the court are not counted. 18 U.S.C. § 3161 (h)(1)(D). The Supreme Court in *United States v. Tinklenberg*, 563 U.S. 647 (2011), held that Congress intended this exclusion to be "automatic," and not dependent on a case-specific determination of whether the motion actually caused, or was expected to cause, delay of a trial.

In *Bloate v. United States*, 559 U.S. 196 (2010), the Court observed that certain periods of delay under § 3161(h) are "automatically excludable" from the 70-day post-indictment time limit for commencement of trial, while other delays are excludable *only* if the court makes case-specific written findings under subsection (h)(7)(A) that the "ends of justice" in ordering a delay or continuance "outweigh the best interests of the public and the defendant in a speedy trial." The Court held, narrowly, that a request of new defense counsel, appointed shortly after plea negotiations broke down, for additional time to prepare pretrial motions, "is not automatically excludable under subsection (h)(1)," but is rather subject to the required "ends of justice" finding under subsection (h)(7)(A).

e. *Plea agreements.* To encourage guilty pleas, the Speedy Trial Act excludes delays resulting from the court's consideration of a proposed plea agreement. 18 U.S.C. § 3161(h)(1)(G).

8. *Dismissal with or without prejudice.* Under § 3162, the trial judge is to consider specific factors in determining whether a violation of the Act should result in a dismissal of charges "with or without prejudice." If dismissed "with prejudice," the government is barred from refiling the case. If "without prejudice," on the other hand, the government may refile the case as long as the statute of limitations has not elapsed.

In *United States v. Taylor*, 487 U.S. 326 (1988), the district court dismissed the indictment against the defendant with prejudice due to a violation of the Speedy Trial Act. In a 6-to-3 decision, the United States Supreme Court held that the trial judge committed error by failing to consider all of the factors listed in the Act. Additionally, the majority found that the factors relied upon were not adequately supported by factual findings or evidence in the record. Therefore, even though the Court recognized that "ordinarily, a trial judge is endowed with great discretion to make decisions concerning trial schedules and to respond to abuse and delay where appropriate," the decision was reversed.

In *Taylor*, the district court apparently dismissed the indictment with prejudice because dismissal without prejudice "would tacitly condone the government's behavior." As to the effectiveness (or ineffectiveness) of dismissal without prejudice, Justice Blackmun stated for the Court:

> Dismissal without prejudice is not a toothless sanction: It forces the Government to obtain a new indictment if it decides to reprosecute, and it exposes the prosecution to dismissal on statute of limitations grounds. Given the burdens borne by the prosecution and the effect of delay on the Government's ability to meet those burdens, substantial delay well may make reprosecution, even if permitted, unlikely.

487 U.S. at 342.

9. *Waiver of deadlines.* The Speedy Trial Act provides specific deadlines but by many actions the defendant may essentially "waive" those deadlines, such as by filing a motion that is taken under advisement. The Supreme Court has held that the Speedy Trial Act contains no provision authorizing the defendant to formally waive the deadlines. Rather, the issue is handled by a continuance motion, as described above. *United States v. Zedner*, 547 U.S. 489 (2006).

Timely motion to dismiss to avoid waiver. Section 3162(a)(2) provides that a defendant who seeks to dismiss charges because of a Speedy Trial Act violation must file an appropriate motion before trial or entry of a guilty or *nolo contendere* plea. Failure to file this motion in a timely fashion constitutes a waiver of the right to dismiss charges for the violation. The Supreme Court in *United States v. Zedner*, 547 U.S. 489, 502–03 (2006), explained the purpose of this time limit:

> First, § 3162(a)(2) assigns the role of spotting violations of the Act to defendants—for the obvious reason that they have the greatest incentive to perform this task. Second, by requiring that a defendant move before the trial starts or a guilty plea is entered, § 3162(a)(2) both limits the effects of a dismissal without prejudice (by ensuring that an expensive and time-consuming trial will not be mooted by a late-filed motion under the Act) and prevents undue defense gamesmanship.

10. *Role of victim.* The traditional rule is that the victim plays no role in decisions concerning speedy trial. Modern victims' rights laws, however, change this in some locales. The federal Crime Victims' Rights Act, 18 U.S.C. § 3771, gives federal crime victims many rights, including the right to "timely notice of any public court proceeding," the right not to be excluded from any such proceeding, and the right to "proceedings free from unreasonable delay." The statute gives victims standing to assert these right in federal court. Though the statute is vague about the victim's participation in matters involving trial or other delays, it has been held that the Act gives victims the right to be notified of, and to attend and be heard in court proceedings about trial delays.

Problem 12-3. Justice Delayed

1. P. Stamp, a postal service employee, was arrested and charged on June 10 with felony mail theft and the misdemeanor of opening mail without authority. Allegedly, Stamp had taken a ring from a package he was to deliver. He was promptly arraigned and then released after he entered a plea of not guilty. Nothing further occurred until July 31, when the government made an ex parte motion for dismissal of the charges. The United States magistrate granted the motion. The government admitted that the delay was caused by simple oversight; no other excuse was proffered. Thereafter, an information was filed, charging Stamp with the misdemeanor offense.

a. With respect to the 51-day delay, was the Speedy Trial Act of 1974 violated?

b. If you conclude that there was a violation, should the dismissal (July 31) have been with or without prejudice?

2. Harry Woods, indicted by a federal grand jury on the charge of distributing eight ounces of cocaine, was brought to trial 90 days after indictment. He moved for dismissal of the charge with prejudice, though he was unable to identify specific ways in which his defense would be prejudiced by the 90-day delay. The Assistant U.S. Attorney, while acknowledging a violation of the Speedy Trial Act, asserted that (1) the government did not purposely delay matters, but was "merely lax" in pursuing Woods' case; (2) Woods suffered no prejudice; and (3) the action should not be dismissed with prejudice because of the seriousness of the offense and the "impact of reprosecution on administration of the Act and justice in general."

a. If you were the trial judge, how would you rule? Would your answer change if it were proven that the United States Attorney's Office in that district frequently violated the Speedy Trial Act?

b. How should the trial judge evaluate the "impact of reprosecution on the Act and justice in general" factor? Is this nothing more than another way to weigh the seriousness of the underlying crime?

3. James "Peewee" May was arrested January 5, following a search of his residence in which contraband was discovered. On February 22, the same year, a federal grand jury returned a six-count indictment, charging May with federal narcotics and firearms offenses. This indictment was dismissed without prejudice four weeks later at the government's request during an ex parte hearing before a magistrate. The next day, March 20, May was reindicted. Following reindictment, May filed a motion asserting that the initial indictment should have been dismissed with prejudice because of the 47-day delay between arrest and indictment.

a. The trial judge inquires of the Assistant U.S. Attorney why the indictment was not obtained within 30 days of May's arrest. The attorney offered no explanation whatsoever. As defense counsel, what is the significance of the government's failure to explain the delay?

b. Should the length of delay be factored into the court's analysis? If so, how?

[b] State Speedy Trial Provisions

With the exception of New York, all state constitutions guarantee to the accused the right to a speedy trial. Slightly less than one-half of the states also have statutory provisions establishing precise time limitations and remedies for speedy trial violations. These laws vary markedly, and it appears that very few states have modeled their statutes after the Speedy Trial Act of 1974.

In Florida, for example, the defendant is entitled, absent "exceptional circumstances" to be tried within 90 days if the charge is a misdemeanor or 175 days if the charge is a felony. Additionally, special provisions are applicable if the defendant serves a "Demand for Speedy Trial" upon the prosecution. Fla. R. Crim. Pro. 3.191. Other states, such as North Carolina, use less precise time limits. N.C. Crim. Pro. § 15-10 (upon the defendant's demand, if the defendant is not "indicted and tried at the second term of the court, he shall be discharged from his imprisonment").

State laws also diverge over the question of whether court congestion can be a valid basis for delaying trial. While some statutes adopt the federal approach and specifically declare that court congestion cannot justify the continuance of a trial, other statutes take the opposite position. Still other speedy trial laws adopt a compromise position, such as limiting congestion-based delays to a maximum of 30 days. *See* Daniel Hamburg, *A Broken Clock: Fixing New York's Speedy Trial Statute*, 48 Colum. J. L. & Soc. Problems 223, 256–57 (2015).

[c] The Imprisoned Defendant

On occasion, the defendant formally charged with commission of a criminal offense is in prison for another crime at the time of the charge. If the defendant is incarcerated in an institution within that geographic jurisdiction, it is relatively easy to proceed against that defendant on those pending charges. Every jurisdiction has adopted procedures enabling a prisoner to be transported to another location in the same jurisdiction to participate in various proceedings involving unresolved criminal charges. It is more complicated when the defendant is incarcerated in another jurisdiction, as in the next case.

Smith v. Hooey

393 U.S. 374 (1969)

Justice Stewart delivered the opinion of the Court.

In *Klopfer v. North Carolina*, 386 U.S. 213 (1967), this Court held that, by virtue of the Fourteenth Amendment, the Sixth Amendment right to a speedy trial is enforceable against the States as "one of the most basic rights preserved by our Constitution." The case before us involves the nature and extent of the obligation imposed upon a State by that constitutional guarantee, when the person under the state criminal charge is serving a prison sentence imposed by another jurisdiction.

In 1960 the petitioner was indicted in Harris County, Texas, upon a charge of theft. He was then, and still is, a prisoner in the federal penitentiary at Leavenworth, Kansas. Shortly after the state charge was filed against him, the petitioner mailed a letter to the Texas trial court requesting a speedy trial. In reply, he was notified that "he would be afforded a trial within two weeks of any date (he) might specify at which he could be present." Thereafter, for the next six years, the petitioner, "by various letters, and more formal so-called 'motions,'" continued periodically to ask that he be brought to trial. Beyond the response already alluded to, the State took no steps to obtain the petitioner's appearance in the Harris County trial court. Finally, in 1967, the petitioner filed in that court a verified motion to dismiss the charge against him for want of prosecution. No action was taken on the motion.

... There can be no doubt that if the petitioner in the present case had been at large for a six-year period following his indictment, and had repeatedly demanded that he be brought to trial, the State would have been under a constitutional duty to try him. And Texas concedes that if during that period he had been confined in a Texas prison for some other state offense, its obligation would have been no less. But the Texas Supreme Court has held that because petitioner is, in fact, confined in a federal prison, the State is totally absolved from any duty at all under the constitutional guarantee. We cannot agree.

... At first blush it might appear that a man already in prison under a lawful sentence is hardly in a position to suffer from "undue and oppressive incarceration prior to trial." But the fact is that delay in bringing such a person to trial on a pending charge may ultimately result in as much oppression as is suffered by one who is jailed without bail upon an untried charge. First, the possibility that the defendant already in prison might receive a sentence at least partially concurrent with the one he is serving may be forever lost if trial of the pending charge is postponed. Secondly, under procedures now widely practiced, the duration of his present imprisonment may be increased, and the conditions under which he must serve his sentence greatly worsened, by the pendency of another criminal charge outstanding against him.

And while it might be argued that a person already in prison would be less likely than others to be affected by "anxiety and concern accompanying public accusation," there is reason to believe that an outstanding untried charge (of which even a convict may, of course, be innocent) can have fully as depressive an effect upon a prisoner as upon a person who is at large. . . .

Finally, it is self-evident that "the possibilities that long delay will impair the ability of an accused to defend himself" are markedly increased when the accused is incarcerated in another jurisdiction. Confined in a prison, perhaps far from the place where the offense covered by the outstanding charge allegedly took place, his ability to confer with potential defense witnesses, or even to keep track of their whereabouts, is obviously impaired. And, while "evidence and witnesses disappear, memories fade, and events lose their perspective," a man isolated in prison is powerless to exert his own investigative efforts to mitigate these erosive effects of the passage of time.

Despite all these considerations, the Texas Supreme Court has said that the State is under no duty even to attempt to bring a man in the petitioner's position to trial, because "(t)he question is one of power and authority and is in no way dependent upon how or in what manner the federal sovereignty may proceed in a discretionary way under the doctrine of comity." Yet Texas concedes that if it did make an effort to secure a federal prisoner's appearance, he would, in fact, "be produced for trial in the state court."

. . . [W]e think the Texas court was mistaken in allowing doctrinaire concepts of "power" and "authority" to submerge the practical demands of the constitutional right to a speedy trial.

. . . Upon the petitioner's demand, Texas had a constitutional duty to make a diligent, good-faith effort to bring him before the Harris County court for trial.

[The concurring opinions of JUSTICES BLACK, HARLAN and WHITE are omitted.]

Notes

1. *Federal defendant in state prison: Speedy Trial Act.* Where a defendant in a pending federal criminal case is also serving a state prison sentence on other charges, the Speedy Trial Act of 1974 has a specific provision for having the prisoner tried in a timely manner in federal court. Under § 3161(j), the federal prosecutor may either attempt to have the defendant temporarily transferred from state to federal custody for purposes of trial, or may lodge a "detainer" with the appropriate prison official requesting that official to advise the defendant of the defendant's right to demand trial. If the defendant then informs the prison official that he or she does, in fact, desire a trial, notice is to be forwarded promptly to the federal prosecutor who must then seek to obtain the defendant's presence for trial.

2. *State defendant incarcerated in another state: pretrial problems.* While the federal Speedy Trial Act provides guidance for federal prosecutors involved in cases where there are outstanding criminal charges against a prisoner, it has no bearing on state prosecutions of out-of-state prisoners. Assume, for example, that Karen goes on an interstate crime spree. She commits a murder in State A and a kidnaping

in State B, where she is apprehended. She is also indicted for the murder in State A. Assume also that Karen is tried, convicted, and sentenced to a 20-year prison term in State B for the kidnapping. While the law enforcement officials in State B may be satisfied because Karen is punished for violating State B's criminal laws, officials in State A will want to prosecute Karen for the homicide committed in that state. The problem is that Karen may be incarcerated in State B for the next 20 years. If the prosecutors in State A wait for 20 years to begin the trial against Karen, key government witnesses may be unavailable and a conviction impossible. Constitutional speedy trial rights may also be violated. Karen, too, may prefer that the charges in State A be resolved. She may fear losing a defense during the 20-year period or may prefer to get the State A charges resolved and, if convicted, seek to get concurrent sentences on the two charges (letting her earn credit for State A and State B sentences at the same time). How should a prosecutor in State A proceed with the outstanding murder charges against Karen?

3. *Extradition.* One statutory solution is that the law enforcement officials in State A can obtain Karen's presence in State A by utilizing extradition proceedings involving the governors of both states. *See* Uniform Criminal Extradition Act. But the extradition process sometimes is slow and cumbersome. In general terms, the process is begun when the governor of a state from which the defendant fled makes a written demand on the governor of the state where the fugitive is found. The initial application is ordinarily made by a local prosecutor who asks the governor to make a formal demand for extradition. The demand states that the person is a fugitive who is charged with a crime in the demanding state. This suffices to establish probable cause of the crime in the demanding state. A judge in the "asylum" state may then order the defendant arrested and held until further proceedings authorize the defendant to be taken to the demanding state.

4. *Interstate Agreement on Detainers (IAD).* In order to simplify the process of getting a prisoner in one jurisdiction to a trial in another, 48 states, the District of Columbia, and the federal government have adopted the Interstate Agreement on Detainers (IAD). *See generally* Leslie W. Abramson, *The Interstate Agreement on Detainers: Narrowing Its Availability and Application*, 21 N. Eng. J. Crim. Civ. Conf. 1 (1995).

A *detainer*, used frequently throughout the country, is a request by one criminal justice agency addressed to another such agency that is incarcerating a particular individual. The detainer asks the incarcerating agency to notify the former agency before the prisoner is released or to hold the prisoner until the requesting agency can obtain the legal right to take the prisoner into its custody. This latter procedure is referred to as a *hold* in some jurisdictions.

The IAD provides that when an individual is indicted for a crime in one jurisdiction, yet is imprisoned in another, the prisoner can be transported to the demanding state (the "requesting jurisdiction") as long as both jurisdictions are parties to the agreement. Extradition procedures are not used.

Under the IAD's procedures, the requesting jurisdiction sends the appropriate detainer to the prospective defendant. The IAD's provisions are then activated to deal with an "untried indictment, information, or complaint" (but not an arrest warrant, sentencing proceeding, or parole or probation violation). Upon receipt of the detainer, the prisoner has the option of demanding speedy trial. If this option is exercised, the prisoner must communicate a written demand to the prison warden, who sends it to both the prosecuting attorney and the appropriate court in the jurisdiction filing the detainer. Trial must be held within 180 days of the date the demand is delivered to the court and the prosecutor. Trial must also be within 120 days of the prisoner's arrival in the requesting state.

If the prisoner is returned to the sending state before trial is held, under the IAD the indictment, information, or complaint in the requesting state must be dismissed with prejudice in the requesting state. *Alabama v. Bozeman*, 533 U.S. 146 (2001) (under IAD prisoner brought from federal prison to Alabama where he had an initial appearance and counsel was appointed, then he was returned to the federal prison; Alabama was barred from returning prisoner to Alabama for trial because once prisoner was in Alabama under the IAD's "anti-shuttling" provision, he had to be kept there until the trial was completed).

D. Post-Conviction Delays

[1] Delay Between Conviction and Sentencing

Does the Speedy Trial Clause have implications for the timing of post-conviction proceedings, such as sentencing hearings? No, said the Supreme Court in *Betterman v. Montana*, 136 S. Ct. 1609 (2016). The Court held that the speedy trial guarantee "protects the accused from arrest or indictment through trial, but does not apply once the defendant has been found guilty at trial or has pleaded guilty to criminal charges." *Id.* at 1612. The defendant in *Betterman* had waited more than 14 months for his sentencing after he pled guilty to a bail-jumping charge. In refusing to evaluate this delay under the Speedy Trial Clause, the Court emphasized the wording of the Clause—noting the traditional meaning of "trial" as a proceeding to determine guilt—and the primary historical purpose of the clause as a mechanism to protect presumptively innocent defendants from lengthy periods of pretrial detention, stigma, and anxiety. Since a convicted defendant awaiting sentencing is no longer presumptively innocent, such a defendant stands outside the core concern of the Clause. However, the Court suggested, in cases of "inordinate delay in sentencing . . . a defendant may have other recourse, including in appropriate circumstances, tailored relief under the Due Process Clauses of the Fifth and Fourteenth Amendments." *Id.* Betterman himself had not preserved a due process challenge, so the Court had no occasion in his case to clarify the due process standards for assessing post-conviction delays.

[2] Delay Between Conviction and Appellate Review

Perhaps the most visible post-conviction delay is the delay in obtaining appellate review of the verdict of conviction, sentence, or both. Indeed, delays in the appellate process are sometimes so extreme that prisoners serve their full sentences before their appeals are even considered. Reasons for significant delays range from overcrowded appellate court dockets to the failure of court reporters to prepare transcripts of trials, without which appellate review is impossible.

As indicated by *Betterman*, the very language of the Sixth Amendment suggests that the Speedy Trial Clause has no application to post-conviction appellate review. However, relying on other constitutional provisions, a number of courts have found due process and equal protection rights to a speedy criminal appeal. For instance, the First Circuit has held:

> Extreme delay in the processing of an appeal may amount to a due process violation, and delays caused by court reporters are attributable to the government for purposes of determining whether a defendant has been deprived of due process. However, mere delay, in and of itself will not give rise to a due process infraction. The defendant must show prejudice. Furthermore, as the Supreme Court has said in the context of pre-indictment delay, even proof of actual prejudice does not make a due process claim automatically valid. The court must consider the reasons for the delay as well as the prejudice to the defendant. The showing of prejudice is therefore a threshold requirement. The prejudice must be such as to render the proceedings fundamentally unfair.

United States v. DeLeon, 444 F.3d 41, 56–57 (1st Cir. 2006) (internal quotation marks and citations omitted).

In *United States v. Johnson*, 732 F.2d 379, 382 (4th Cir. 1984), the court, applying the *Barker* test, concluded that a two-year delay in preparation of the transcript "may have violated due process" but ruled that the defendant was not entitled to release because his appeal had been heard and found lacking in merit.

Is the *Barker v. Wingo* test (discussed at the beginning of this chapter) appropriate in the context of appellate delay? Even if the test applies, is the *Barker* dismissal remedy appropriate? Professor Mark Arkin argues for a "sliding scale of remedies," including such alternatives as ordering release of the defendant if the appeal is not heard within a relatively short period, ordering release of the defendant on bail pending resolution of the appeal, or reducing the defendant's sentence in proportion to the length of the appellate delay. Marc Arkin, *Speedy Criminal Appeal: A Right Without a Remedy*, 74 MINN. L. REV. 437 (1990).

[3] Delay Between Imposition and Execution of Sentence

Once the defendant is convicted and the sentence is imposed, it can be expected in most cases that the defendant will begin serving the sentence within a relatively short period of time. Due to jail and prison overcrowding, however, there may be a significant delay between the sentencing decision and its actual execution. When this occurs, are there legal constraints upon such delays?

There appears to be no uniform constitutional standard applied in such cases. Nonetheless, some courts have granted relief to the defendant upon due process grounds. *See, e.g., People v. Levandoski*, 603 N.W.2d 831 (Mich. Ct. App. 1999) (based upon a totality of circumstances approach, including fact that defendant requested that he be allowed to serve his 90-day sentence, five-year delay "is inconsistent with fundamental principles of liberty and justice").

In addition to due process and statutory rights, delays in the execution of a sentence might conceivably implicate the Eighth Amendment prohibition on cruel and unusual punishments. The possibility has been argued most forcefully in connection with capital cases, in which there is routinely a gap of 10 years or more between the imposition of a death sentence and its execution. Justice Breyer, for instance, has signaled that he views exceptionally long waits on death row as cruel and unusual punishment. For instance, in *Foster v. Florida*, the defendant had spent 27 years on death row. In dissenting from the denial of *certiorari* in the case, Breyer wrote, "Foster has endured an extraordinarily long confinement under sentence of death, a confinement that extends from late youth to later middle age. The length of this confinement has resulted partly from the State's repeated procedural errors. Death row's inevitable anxieties and uncertainties have been sharpened by the issuance of two death warrants and three judicial reprieves. If executed, Foster, now 55, will have been punished both by death and also by more than a generation spent in death row's twilight. It is fairly asked whether such punishment is both unusual and cruel." 537 U.S. 990, 991 (2002) (Breyer, J., dissenting from denial of *certiorari*). However, Breyer's view has thus far found little support among the other justices or in the lower courts, reflecting a tendency to see delays in capital cases as the defendant's fault. *See* Russell L. Christopher, *The Irrelevance of Prisoner Fault for Excessively Delayed Executions*, 72 Wash. & Lee L. Rev. 3 (2015).

Chapter 13

Jury Trial

A. Overview

One of the features that distinguishes the American criminal justice process is the role of the *petit jury*, a body of (usually) 12 people who resolve most fact issues in a criminal trial. As described more fully in *Duncan v. Louisiana*, reproduced below, the jury serves a number of important functions. It gives the populace an opportunity to be involved in criminal justice decisions while adding a measure of legitimacy to the process by allowing citizens, not politicians, to make those decisions.

Since the United States Supreme Court "constitutionalized" the jury process by holding that the states and the federal government must accord the criminal accused a jury trial in all but the least serious cases, the details of the jury trial have become an important focus of American criminal procedure. To some extent, rules of criminal procedure provide the working framework for analysis. This chapter discusses these important issues, and provides answers to the following questions.

The first issue, and one often ignored, is what decisions must the jury make? This requires an analysis of the roles of both the jury and the judge. Another key issue is when does the criminal defendant have a right to a jury trial? Is there this right in every case, even the most minor? A related issue is waiver. If the accused has a right to a jury trial, can this right be waived even if the government wants a jury trial?

There are also numerous procedural issues. While a criminal jury is ordinarily comprised of 12 people, can there be a jury of 15 or 7 or 3? Another set of issues concerns the procedures used to select a particular jury. Who is eligible for jury service and how is each juror chosen? What are the limits on counsel's ability to exclude an individual juror from hearing a case? Once a jury is chosen, how does it operate? May individual jurors take notes or ask questions of a witness? When may a judge require jurors to be *sequestered*, or kept separate from their families during the trial?

B. Issues Tried by Jury

[1] Questions of Fact and Law

The short-hand, though not completely accurate, rule is that the jury decides questions of fact and the judge decides questions of law. *E.g.*, 725 ILCS 5/115-4 ("Questions of law shall be decided by the court and questions of fact by the jury").

Although the exact details of the division of responsibilities between judges and jury are beyond the scope of this book, the true picture is quite complex.

The jury actually performs two interrelated functions. First, it decides what the facts are that relate to the question of guilt or innocence. Second, it decides whether those facts satisfy the legal standards at issue in the case (sometimes this is called applying the law to the facts). For example, assume that the defendant is charged with store burglary in violation of a state statute that defined the crime as "the unlawful entry of a business at night with the intent to commit a felony therein." The jury would listen to the evidence and decide such issues as: (1) did any part of the defendant enter the store, (2) did the defendant have permission to enter, (3) was the building used as a business, (4) what time did the event occur, and (5) what was the defendant's intent at the time of the event.

After resolving these factual issues, the jury would then turn to its second task: deciding whether the facts it found satisfied the elements of the crime. For example, assume that the jury believed witnesses who testified that the entry occurred at 8:45 p.m. Since the burglary statute covered only entries that occur "at night," the jury would have to decide whether 8:45 p.m. was "at night."

How would the jury know whether 8:45 p.m. is "night"? One of the judge's responsibilities is to decide which law is applicable and to instruct the jury on that law, including relevant definitions. Returning to the burglary case, the jury instructions would tell the jury about this statute and may define some of the key terms, including "at night." The jury would then use the statute and the judge's definitions to decide whether an 8:45 p.m. entry occurred "at night" under the burglary law.

Although this pattern is typical, the situation is frequently much more complex. Often the judge also decides questions of fact because some factual questions are not within the jury's responsibilities. In virtually all jurisdictions, the judge imposes the sentence. This means that ordinarily (with some important exceptions) the judge decides both questions of law and fact relevant solely to the sentence. For example, if the jury finds the defendant guilty of the business burglary, the determination of the appropriate sentence may require the judge to ascertain such facts as the defendant's background, likely success if released on probation, employment possibilities, and acceptance of responsibility. The judge may hear witnesses and examine various documents in making these factual determinations.

[2] Fact Questions Jury May Not Address

In some unusual circumstances, a jury is not permitted to resolve factual questions. In *Jackson v. Denno*, 378 U.S. 368 (1964), the Supreme Court struck down a New York procedure that essentially let the jury decide whether a confession was voluntary (and therefore admissible) at the same time it decided guilt or innocence. The Court was critical of the fact that it was impossible to know whether the jury actually dealt with the issue of voluntariness and whether it ignored the confession if the confession was deemed involuntary. To eliminate the possibility that the jury will misuse an involuntary confession, the Court indicated that voluntariness can be decided by the trial judge, another judge, or another jury; it cannot be resolved by the "convicting" jury. *Id.* at 391 n.19. *See also Commonwealth v. Miller*, 865 N.E.2d 825 (Mass. Ct. App. 2007) (judge must determine voluntariness of confession before submitting it to jury).

[3] Mixed Fact-Law Questions

Complex issues may arise in determining mixed questions of law and fact. For example, in *United States v. Gaudin*, 515 U.S. 506 (1995), the Supreme Court held that the question of the "materiality" of a defendant's allegedly false statement, an element of the offense in issue, must be submitted to a jury for determination. Characterizing the issue of materiality as a mixed question of law and fact, the Court explained that the jury's constitutional responsibility "is not merely to determine facts, but to apply the law to those facts and draw the ultimate conclusion of guilt or innocence."

C. Right to a Jury Trial

There are two possible sources of a right to a jury trial. The most obvious is the United States Constitution's Sixth Amendment, as discussed below in the leading case, *Duncan v. Louisiana*. The second source is statutory.

[1] Sixth Amendment

Until 1968 it was not known whether the Sixth Amendment's right to a jury trial was applicable to the states. In *Duncan v. Louisiana*, the United States Supreme Court resolved this issue but left open a number of important questions about the scope of the criminal accused's right to a jury trial.

Duncan v. Louisiana

391 U.S. 145 (1968)

MR. JUSTICE WHITE delivered the opinion of the Court.

Appellant, Gary Duncan, was convicted of simple battery.... Under Louisiana law simple battery is a misdemeanor, punishable by a maximum of two years' imprisonment and a $300 fine. Appellant sought trial by jury, but because the Louisiana Constitution grants jury trials only in cases in which capital punishment or imprisonment at hard labor may be imposed, the trial judge denied the request. Appellant was convicted and sentenced to serve 60 days in the parish prison and pay a fine of $150. Appellant [unsuccessfully] sought review in the Supreme Court of Louisiana, asserting that the denial of jury trial violated rights guaranteed to him by the United States Constitution. . . . [A]ppellant sought review in this Court, alleging that the Sixth and Fourteenth Amendments to the United States Constitution secure the right to jury trial in state criminal prosecutions where a sentence as long as two years may be imposed.

. . . Appellant was 19 years of age when tried. While driving on Highway 23 in Plaquemines Parish on October 18, 1966, he saw two younger cousins engaged in a conversation by the side of the road with four white boys. Knowing his cousins, Negroes who had recently transferred to a formerly all-white high school, had reported the occurrence of racial incidents at the school, Duncan stopped the car, got out, and approached the six boys. At trial the white boys and a white onlooker testified, as did appellant and his cousins. The testimony was in dispute on many points, but the witnesses agreed that appellant and the white boys spoke to each other, that appellant encouraged his cousins to break off the encounter and enter his car, and that appellant was about to enter the car himself for the purpose of driving away with his cousins. The whites testified that just before getting in the car appellant slapped Herman Landry, one of the white boys, on the elbow. The Negroes testified that appellant had not slapped Landry, but had merely touched him. The trial judge concluded that the State had proved beyond a reasonable doubt that Duncan had committed simple battery, and found him guilty.

The Fourteenth Amendment denies the States the power to "deprive any person of life, liberty, or property, without due process of law." In resolving conflicting claims concerning the meaning of this spacious language, the Court has looked increasingly to the Bill of Rights for guidance; many of the rights guaranteed by the first eight Amendments to the Constitution have been held to be protected against state action by the Due Process Clause of the Fourteenth Amendment.

. . . The test for determining whether a right extended by the Fifth and Sixth Amendments with respect to federal criminal proceedings is also protected against state action by the Fourteenth Amendment has been phrased in a variety of ways in the opinions of this Court. The question has been asked whether a right is among those "fundamental principles of liberty and justice which lie at the base of all our civil and political institutions," *Powell v. State of Alabama*, 287 U.S. 45, (1932); whether it is "basic in our system of jurisprudence," *In re Oliver*, 333 U.S. 257, 273 (1948); and whether it is "a fundamental right, essential to a fair trial," *Gideon v. Wainwright*, 372 U.S. 335, 343–344 (1963). The claim before us is that the right to trial by jury guaranteed by the Sixth Amendment meets these tests. . . . [W]e hold that the Fourteenth Amendment guarantees a right of jury trial in all criminal cases which—were they to be tried in a federal court—would come within the Sixth Amendment's guarantee. Since we consider the appeal before us to be such a case, we hold that the Constitution was violated when appellant's demand for jury trial was refused.

The history of trial by jury in criminal cases has been frequently told. It is sufficient for present purposes to say that by the time our Constitution was written, jury trial in criminal cases had been in existence in England for several centuries and carried impressive credentials traced by many to Magna Carta. Its preservation and proper operation as a protection against arbitrary rule were among the major objectives of the revolutionary settlement which was expressed in the Declaration and Bill of Rights of 1689.

. . . The Constitution itself, in Art. III, § 2, commanded: "The Trial of all Crimes, except in Cases of Impeachment, shall be by Jury; and such Trial shall be held in the State where the said Crimes shall have been committed."

Objections to the Constitution because of the absence of a bill of rights were met by the immediate submission and adoption of the Bill of Rights. Included was the Sixth Amendment which, among other things, provided: "In all criminal prosecutions, the accused shall enjoy the right to a speedy and public trial, by an impartial jury of the State and district wherein the crime shall have been committed."

The constitutions adopted by the original States guaranteed jury trial. Also, the constitution of every State entering the Union thereafter in one form or another protected the right to jury trial in criminal cases.

Even such skeletal history is impressive support for considering the right to jury trial in criminal cases to be fundamental to our system of justice, an importance frequently recognized in the opinions of this Court.

. . . Jury trial continues to receive strong support. The laws of every State guarantee a right to jury trial in serious criminal cases; no State has dispensed with it; nor are there significant movements underway to do so.

. . . The guarantees of jury trial in the Federal and State Constitutions reflect a profound judgment about the way in which law should be enforced and justice administered. A right to jury trial is granted to criminal defendants in order to prevent oppression by the Government. Those who wrote our constitutions knew from history and experience that it was necessary to protect against unfounded criminal charges brought to eliminate enemies and against judges too responsive to the voice of higher authority. The framers of the constitutions strove to create an independent judiciary but insisted upon further protection against arbitrary action. Providing an accused with the right to be tried by a jury of his peers gave him an inestimable safeguard against the corrupt or overzealous prosecutor and against the compliant, biased, or eccentric judge. If the defendant preferred the commonsense judgment of a jury to the more tutored but perhaps less sympathetic reaction of the single judge, he was to have it. Beyond this, the jury trial provisions in the Federal and State Constitutions reflect a fundamental decision about the exercise of official power—a reluctance to entrust plenary powers over the life and liberty of the citizen to one judge or to a group of judges. Fear of unchecked power, so typical of our State and Federal Governments in other respects, found expression in the criminal law in this insistence upon community participation in the determination of guilt or innocence. The deep commitment of the Nation to the right of jury trial in serious criminal cases as a defense against arbitrary law enforcement qualifies for protection under the Due Process Clause of the Fourteenth Amendment, and must therefore be respected by the States.

Of course jury trial has its weaknesses and the potential for misuse. We are aware of the long debate, especially in this century, among those who write about the administration of justice, as to the wisdom of permitting untrained laymen to determine the facts in civil and criminal proceedings.... Yet, the most recent and exhaustive study of the jury in criminal cases concluded that juries do understand the evidence and come to sound conclusions in most of the cases presented to them and that when juries differ with the result at which the judge would have arrived, it is usually because they are serving some of the very purposes for which they were created and for which they are now employed.

The State of Louisiana urges that holding that the Fourteenth Amendment assures a right to jury trial will cast doubt on the integrity of every trial conducted without a jury. Plainly, this is not the import of our holding. Our conclusion is that in the American States, as in the federal judicial system, a general grant of jury trial for serious offenses is a fundamental right, essential for preventing miscarriages of justice and for assuring that fair trials are provided for all defendants. We would not assert, however, that every criminal trial—or any particular trial—held before a judge alone is unfair or that a defendant may never be as fairly treated by a judge as he would be by a jury. Thus we hold no constitutional doubts about the practices, common in both federal and state courts, of accepting waivers of jury trial and prosecuting petty crimes without extending a right to jury trial....

Louisiana's final contention is that even if it must grant jury trials in serious criminal cases, the conviction before us is valid and constitutional because here the petitioner was tried for simple battery and was sentenced to only 60 days in the parish prison. We are not persuaded. It is doubtless true that there is a category of petty crimes or offenses which is not subject to the Sixth Amendment jury trial provision and should not be subject to the Fourteenth Amendment jury trial requirement here applied to the States. Crimes carrying possible penalties up to six months do not require a jury trial if they otherwise qualify as petty offenses. But the penalty authorized for a particular crime is of major relevance in determining whether it is serious or not and may in itself, if severe enough, subject the trial to the mandates of the Sixth Amendment.... In the case before us the Legislature of Louisiana has made simple battery a criminal offense punishable by imprisonment for up to two years and a fine. The question, then, is whether a crime carrying such a penalty is an offense which Louisiana may insist on trying without a jury.

... In determining whether the length of the authorized prison term or the seriousness of other punishment is enough in itself to require a jury trial, we ... refer to objective criteria, chiefly the existing laws and practices in the Nation. In the federal system, petty offenses are defined as those punishable by no more than six months in prison and a $500 fine. In 49 of the 50 States crimes subject to trial without a jury, which occasionally include simple battery, are punishable by no more than one year in jail.... We need not, however, settle in this case the exact location of the line between petty offenses and serious crimes. It is sufficient for our purposes to hold that a crime punishable by two years in prison is, based on past and contemporary standards in this country, a serious crime and not a petty offense. Consequently, appellant was entitled to a jury trial and it was error to deny it. [Reversed]

[The concurring opinions of JUSTICES BLACK and FORTAS are omitted, as is the dissenting opinion of JUSTICE HARLAN.]

Note

Jury trial in absence of Constitutional right? Does a United States District Court have the authority to grant a defendant's request for a jury trial even where it is not constitutionally mandated? The *Duncan* Court found that the defendant was not entitled to a jury trial under the Constitution because the offense was a petty offense (but did not define the category, which the *Baldwin* Court eventually did, *see infra*). Nevertheless, noting that there is "some authority" to support such a request, in *United States v. Greenpeace*, 314 F. Supp. 2d 1252 (S.D. Fla. 2004), despite the lack of a constitutional right to a jury trial, the trial judge granted the request over the government's objection "as a matter of judicial discretion," but commented that this was done because the case was "unusual" and "would benefit from a jury's collective decision-making."

[a] Petty Offenses: Six-Month Rule

The Supreme Court in *Duncan* acknowledged that the constitutional right to a jury trial does not apply to "petty offenses," but did not indicate precisely where the line would be drawn. The key concept is how "serious" the offense is. This is determined by the sanction authorized for the crime. Although it would seem easy to assess whether the crime was serious or petty, the issue is more complex than it would appear. Criminal statutes do not always characterize sanctions in a way consistent with the Supreme Court's categories, as discussed below.

In *Dyke v. Taylor Implement Co.*, 391 U.S. 216, 220 (1968), decided the same day as *Duncan*, the Court held that "a six-month jail sentence is short enough to be 'petty'." On the other hand, the plurality opinion in *Baldwin v. New York*, 399 U.S. 66, 69 (1969), held that no offense is petty "where imprisonment for more than six months is authorized." Note that the key is the sentence that is *authorized;* not the one actually imposed. Similarly, as *Blanton, infra*, makes clear, a mandatory period of incarceration short of six months does not change a petty offense into a serious one.

Presumption and flexibility. Although the six-month dividing line is easy to apply on its face, the Supreme Court actually provided a more flexible test. In *Blanton v. City of North Las Vegas*, 489 U.S. 538 (1989), discussed further below, the Supreme Court reiterated its six-month holding but then indicated that actually there is only a *presumption* that a maximum sentence of six months or less is a petty offense for which the Constitution does not mandate a jury trial. The key to overcoming this presumption is for the defendant to convince the court that the additional authorized penalties (beyond the six-month maximum sentence) are so severe that "they clearly indicate a legislative determination that the offense is a serious one." *See, e.g., United States v. Stanfill El*, 714 F.3d 1150 (9th Cir. 2013).

State variations. Some state constitutions extend the right to a jury trial explicitly to misdemeanors. *See, e.g.*, W. Va. Const. art. 3, 14; Wyo. Const. art. 1, § 9. *See also* Standards for Criminal Justice § 15-1.1 (3d ed. 1996) (jury trial should be available to either the defendant or the state if confinement in jail or prison may be imposed); American Bar Association, Principles for Juries and Jury Trials, Prin. 1(B) (same).

Right to jury v. right to counsel. It should be noted that the standards for determining the right to a jury trial differ from those triggering the right to counsel. The Supreme Court held that "an indigent defendant is entitled to court-appointed *counsel* under the Sixth Amendment even in petty offense" cases—at least where actual imprisonment (even for one day) is involved. *Argersinger v. Hamlin*, 407 U.S. 25 (1972).

[b] Aggregate Sentence Exceeding Six Months

Should a defendant be accorded a constitutional right to a jury trial in a prosecution for multiple petty offenses where the aggregate sentence authorized for the offenses exceeds six months' imprisonment? Justice O'Connor, speaking for the 7–2 majority in *Lewis v. United States*, 518 U.S. 322 (1996), answered the question "no," reasoning as follows:

> Here, by setting the maximum authorized prison term at six months, the legislature categorized the offense of obstructing the mail as petty. The fact that the petitioner was charged with two counts of a petty offense does not revise the legislative judgment as to the gravity of that particular offense, nor does it transform the petty offense into a serious one, to which the jury trial right would apply.
>
> . . . Petitioner directs our attention to *Codispoti v. Pennsylvania*, 418 U.S. 506 (1974), for support for the assertion that the "aggregation of multiple petty offenses renders a prosecution serious for jury trial purposes." *Codispoti* is inapposite. There, defendants were each convicted at a single, non-jury trial for several charges of criminal contempt. The Court was unable to determine the legislature's judgment of the character of that offense, however, because the legislature had not set a specific penalty for criminal contempt. In such a situation, where the legislature has not specified a maximum penalty, courts use the severity of the penalty actually imposed as the measure of the character of the particular offense. Here, in contrast, we need not look to the punishment actually imposed, because we are able to discern Congress' judgment of the character of the offense.

Id. at 327.

[c] Probation

What happens if the defendant is sentenced to a jail term of more than six months, but the sentence is suspended and the defendant is placed on probation?

Is he or she entitled to a jury trial since no incarceration is actually imposed? In *Alabama v. Shelton*, 535 U.S. 654 (2002), the Court held that the possibility of incarceration of more than six months if probation is revoked entitles the defendant to a jury trial even though he or she is not initially incarcerated.

[d] Other Sanctions

While the six-month incarceration rule provides a fairly clear dividing line in cases where imprisonment is authorized, the line becomes fuzzy when other sanctions are present. Is the right to a jury trial triggered by sanctions other than incarceration? The issue is difficult because often more than one of these sanctions are imposed instead of, or in addition to, a short period of imprisonment.

In *Blanton v. City of North Las Vegas*, 489 U.S. 538 (1989), the defendant was convicted of driving under the influence and received a number of "punishments." The Court reaffirmed that it would assess whether a case was "petty" by looking at how serious society regarded the offense. Society's value of it would be determined after examining all the penalties accompanying the conviction, especially the maximum possible period of incarceration. Fines and probation were characterized as involving a significant loss of freedom, though not nearly as severe as incarceration.

Like *Duncan*, the Court in *Blanton* refused to hold that a prison term of six months or less automatically meant that the crime was "petty," but:

> . . . we do find it appropriate to presume for purposes of the Sixth Amendment that society views such an offense as "petty." A defendant is entitled to a jury trial in such circumstances only if he can demonstrate that any additional statutory penalties, viewed in conjunction with the maximum authorized period of incarceration, are so severe that they clearly reflect a legislative determination that the offense in question is a "serious" one. This standard, albeit somewhat imprecise, should ensure the availability of a jury trial in the rare situation where a legislature packs an offense it deems "serious" with onerous penalties that nonetheless "do not puncture the 6-month incarceration line."

Id. at 543.

Applying these principles, the *Blanton* Court held that the defendants were not entitled to a jury trial despite having to endure adverse collateral consequences, discussed below. Since the maximum possible incarceration for them was less than six months, the Court found a "presumption" that the offense was petty. The Court dismissed as "not constitutionally determinative" the fact that the defendant may have to serve a minimum of two days' incarceration; the proper focus was on the maximum, not the minimum incarceration period.

Loss of driver's license. The *Blanton* defendant argued that his DUI offense was not petty because one of his sanctions was the loss of a driver's license for 45–90 days. Measuring the severity of this sanction against that of six months in prison, the Court held that the license suspension was irrelevant if it ran concurrently with the prison term. Even if it did not, however, the Court held that the license loss was not "that significant as a Sixth Amendment matter, particularly when a restricted license may be obtained after only 45 days." *Blanton*, 489 U.S. at 544 n.9.

Attend counseling. The *Blanton* defendant also complained that he would have to attend an alcohol abuse education course as part of his sentence. The Supreme Court dismissed this complaint as "*de minimis*."

Community service. Another penalty in *Blanton* was that the accused could have been ordered to perform 48 hours of community service dressed in clothing identifying him as a DUI offender. The Court also found this unpersuasive since it was less embarrassing and onerous than six months in jail.

Additional charges as repeat offender. The accused in *Blanton* also argued that he was entitled to a jury trial because he would face additional sanctions if convicted in the future as a recidivist DUI offender under state law. The Supreme Court noted that DUI recidivist penalties are commonplace, but essentially held that the issue was moot since the accused did not face such penalties. A footnote made it clear that the Court in *Blanton* did not consider whether a repeat offender facing enhanced penalties had a valid constitutional objection based on the absence of a jury trial in a previous DUI conviction. *Blanton*, 489 U.S. at 545 n.12.

Fine. The defendant in *Blanton* faced a maximum fine of $1000. He argued that this was sufficient to make the crime a "serious" offense, even though the maximum prison term was six months. The *Blanton* Court rejected the claim, noting only that the $1000 figure "was well below the $5000 level set by Congress in its most recent definition of a 'petty' offense." *Blanton*, 489 U.S at 544 (*citing* 18 U.S.C. § 1 (1982)).

What amount of fine is sufficient to entitle the accused to a jury trial? In *Muniz v. Hoffman*, 422 U.S. 454 (1975), a local labor union was fined $10,000 for criminal contempt under the Labor Management and Relations Act. This was the maximum authorized by the applicable statute; a prison term was not permissible. Noting that fines and imprisonment should be analyzed differently because of their differences in risk and deprivation, the Court held that the union was not entitled to a jury trial. The Court analyzed the extent of risk to the union and found that the deprivation was not of "such magnitude" that a jury was required. Since the union has 13,000 dues-paying members, the $10,000 fine did not work such a hardship as to merit Sixth Amendment protection. On the other hand, a $52,000,000 criminal contempt fine against a union is clearly a "serious contempt" entitling the union to a jury trial. *United Mine Workers v. Bagwell*, 512 U.S. 821 (1994) (court noted it had not specified the precise difference between a "serious" and "petty" criminal contempt sanction).

Muniz did not indicate whether a $10,000 fine would be sufficient to trigger the right to a jury trial for an individual. Would it matter whether the defendant were wealthy or poor? Does this make sense considering the purposes for the jury trial articulated in *Duncan v. Louisiana*?

When a statutory scheme has a flexible maximum fine based on certain facts, such as the amount of loss, the Supreme Court has held that only a jury can determine these facts unless the jury is waived. *Southern Union Co. v. United States*, 567 U.S. 343 (2013) (illegal storage of mercury punished by statute setting maximum fine of $50,000 per day of violation; jury must determine number of days law violated since this determines the maximum amount of the permissible fine).

Restitution. When a defendant is subject to a court order to pay restitution to the crime victim, the payment of restitution does not elevate a petty crime into a serious one. *See, e.g., United States v. Stanfill El*, 714 F.3d 1150 (9th Cir. 2013) (restitution does not impose additional punishment; merely recognizes debt that defendant already owes the victim).

Court and related costs. Sometimes the actual out-of-pocket costs far exceed the formal fine in a criminal case. Courts distinguish between court and related costs, and fines. The costs are not computed in assessing the right to a jury. *See, e.g., State v. Washington*, 498 So. 2d 136 (La. Ct. App. 1986) (special DWI costs and reinstatement fees were costs, not fines).

Register as sex offender. The cases are split whether the obligation to register as a sex offender is sufficient to render a petty sex offense into a serious one meriting jury trial. *See, e.g., Fushek v. State*, 183 P.3d 536 (Ariz. 2008) (yes); *Thomas v. United States*, 942 A.2d 1180 (D.C. App. 2008) (no).

Deportation. The possibility that a person convicted of a petty offense will be deported does not make the underlying petty offense a "serious" one that triggers a jury trial. *See, e.g., Fretes-Zarate v. United States*, 40 A.3d 374 (D.C. 2012).

[e] Juvenile Cases

Although *Duncan v. Louisiana, supra*, held that the Sixth Amendment guaranteed a jury trial in non-petty criminal cases, the Supreme Court subsequently held that the Sixth Amendment does not apply to juveniles adjudicated in juvenile court (as opposed to being tried in adult court). Justice Blackmun's plurality opinion in *McKeiver v. Pennsylvania*, 403 U.S. 528 (1971), reasoned that a juvenile delinquency proceeding is neither civil nor criminal. In addition, fundamental fairness as guaranteed by the Due Process Clause does not require a jury trial in such proceedings, for accurate fact finding is possible without a jury trial. Moreover, the plurality opinion expressed concern about the danger of turning the proceeding into an adversary trial rather than an intimate, informal protective proceeding if the formalities of a Sixth Amendment trial were mandated.

[f] De Novo Cases

Just as the Sixth Amendment does not guarantee a jury trial in juvenile cases, it also does not bar a jurisdiction from using a two-tiered trial system in which no jury is provided for the first trial, but the accused has an absolute right to a second trial before a jury. In *Ludwig v. Massachusetts*, 427 U.S. 618 (1976), the Supreme Court considered the constitutionality of the Massachusetts "two-tiered" system. In this state, a person charged with a misdemeanor or certain felonies has the option of first being tried in a bench trial. If convicted, the offender may appeal to a higher court where he has the right to receive a jury trial *de novo*.

The Supreme Court in *Ludwig* held that this procedure did not violate the Sixth Amendment by unduly burdening the accused's right to be tried by a jury. The Court found that the possibility of a second trial before a jury satisfied the need to protect an individual from government oppression. Moreover, the Court found that the two-tiered system did not place an unreasonable financial burden on the accused who could essentially waive the first trial and proceed directly to the jury trial.

Problem 13-1. I'd Like a Box of Twelve, Please

Defendant Sheila Banks was arrested leaving a large department store with a new watch secreted in a new purse. Surveillance cameras clearly show her taking the watch from a display case and the purse from a display on another floor, then leaving the store without paying. She was in jail for three days until her uncle paid her bail.

Since the value of each item was under $500, the state had the option of charging Banks with a "violation" or a misdemeanor for the two crimes. If a misdemeanor, the state concedes Banks would have been entitled to a jury trial, but since the state opted to charge her with two violations, one for each item, the state contends she is not entitled to a jury trial.

Under state law, a violation carries a maximum fine of $500 and no more than six months of jail time, while a misdemeanor carries a potential jail term of six months and one day with a maximum $500 fine.

Defendant Banks requested a jury trial for the two violations. The court refused to order a jury trial and she was convicted of both violations. She was fined $300 for each violation and given no jail time. Unfortunately, Banks was fired from her position as a school teacher as soon as the school board learned of the convictions. Without a job, her house was foreclosed and she was evicted, moving to a homeless shelter run by a local church.

1. If you were an appellate judge, would you rule that defendant Banks was entitled to a jury trial under the United States Constitution?

2. Would your answer change if she were sentenced to four months in jail for each violation, making a total jail term of eight months?

3. What if the fine were $2000 for each violation (a total of $4000) in addition to any jail time? *See State v. Fuller*, 287 P.3d 1263 (Or. Ct. App. 2012).

[2] Court Rules

The federal rules of criminal procedure are surprisingly silent on the question of when a jury trial is authorized. In the federal system, the matter is resolved by the

Constitution rather than by the rules of criminal procedure, which are not helpful on the issue. Rule 23(a), however, prescribes a jury trial unless the defendant waives that right in writing and the prosecution and trial judge approve.

D. Waiver of Jury Trial

Although the Sixth Amendment gives the criminal accused in non-petty offense cases a right to a jury trial, a jury trial actually occurs in surprisingly few cases. A national survey of felonies resolved in state courts found that a jury trial was held in only 4% of the cases (94% of all defendants pled guilty; of the 6% who went to trial, a third opted for a bench trial). United States Dept. of Justice, Sourcebook of Criminal Justice Statistics Online, www.albany.edu/sourcebook/pdf/t5462006.pdf (accessed Sept. 18, 2013).

It is clear that the "knowing, intelligent, and voluntary" standard is applicable to waivers of a jury trial. *See, e.g.*, *Schneckloth v. Bustamonte*, 412 U.S. 218, 237 (1973) ("knowing and intelligent" standard applies to waiver of jury trial). The trial judge has the responsibility for gathering the information necessary to determine whether this standard is satisfied. The Supreme Court has suggested that the trial court should not accept a waiver of jury trial "as a matter of rote, but with sound and advised discretion, with an eye to avoid unreasonable or undue departures from that mode [the jury] of trial." *Patton v. United States*, 281 U.S. 276, 312–13 (1930).

The government has the burden of proving a knowing and voluntary waiver. This means the prosecutor should monitor the waiver process to ensure that a valid waiver can be proven if later challenged. In one case, for example, there was considerable evidence that the accused had an exceptionally low IQ at the time he waived jury trial. The appellate court held that the trial judge should have conducted "an in-depth colloquy" that delved into such issues as whether the defendant understood a jury is comprised of 12 people, the defendant may participate in jury selection, jury verdicts must be unanimous, and the court would decide guilt or innocence if a jury is waived. *United States v. Preston*, 706 F.3d 1106 (9th Cir. 2013).

Rule 23(a) and similar rules in many states permit the accused to waive a jury trial. Frequently, these rules also permit *both* the court and the government (or just the government), without stating reasons, to block the waiver and require the case to be tried by a jury. This is somewhat anomalous since the right to a jury trial is designed to protect the *accused* from government oppression. Nevertheless, in *Singer v. United States*, 380 U.S. 24, 36 (1965), the Supreme Court upheld this rule in a mail fraud case in which the accused wanted to waive a jury trial but the government objected and the case was tried before a jury.

The *Singer* Court did recognize that there may be unusual situations where the accused's interests in a fair trial could require that the accused's waiver of a jury trial be implemented despite the government's desire to impanel a jury. The Court noted:

> We need not determine in this case whether there might be some circumstances where a defendant's reasons for wanting to be tried by a judge alone are so compelling that the Government's insistence on trial by jury would result in the denial to a defendant of an impartial trial. Petitioner argues that there might arise situations where "passion, prejudice . . . public feeling" or some other factor may render impossible or unlikely an impartial trial by jury.

Id. at 37.

Contrast with waiver of counsel. By contrast, it should be noted that the Supreme Court has held that a defendant has the right to waive *counsel* even if the government objects. The Sixth Amendment guarantees the right to self-representation. *Faretta v. California*, 422 U.S. 806 (1975). Does the difference in approaches between waiver of jury trial and waiver of counsel make sense?

State variations. Approximately half of the states allow prosecutors to either directly request jury trials or to override the defendant's waiver as was done in *Singer.* By contrast, some states provide the defendant with a unilateral and absolute right to a bench trial. *See People v. Brown*, 988 N.E.2d 706 (Ill. App. Ct. 2013) (state law gives defendants right to a bench trial; defendant, convicted by a jury, unsuccessfully argued he did not waive his right to a bench trial).

[1] Form of Waiver

In writing. Rule 23 provides specifically that a waiver of a jury trial must be in writing. Many state provisions are identical. *See, e.g.*, Ariz. R. Crim. P. 18.1(b) (waiver of jury trial must be in writing or in open court). This requirement is designed to assure that the accused is aware of the right to a jury and that the decision to waive it is unequivocal and documented. But what happens when counsel (usually) or the accused orally waives a jury trial without also doing so in writing? If the accused knew of the right to a jury trial and consented to the waiver, the waiver will be upheld despite the lack of written documentation. *United States v. Johnson*, 306 Fed. Appx. 305 (2009). Any other resolution would let the accused agree orally to be tried by the court and then, if convicted, successfully appeal the lack of a written jury waiver. Should the prosecuting lawyer and the judge ensure that an oral waiver of a jury trial is not accepted?

By defendant personally. The right to a jury trial is considered so important that the vast majority of decisions hold that the defendant, not defense counsel, must personally waive it. *See, e.g., United States v. Babul*, 476 F.3d 498 (7th Cir. 2007).

[2] Recommendations

The American Bar Association recommends that any case where confinement is possible be tried by a jury unless waived by the accused with the prosecutor's consent. The court should accept a waiver only after the defendant is advised in open court of the right to a jury, including the consequences of a waiver, and the accused personally waives jury trial in writing or in open court. American Bar Association, Principles for Juries and Jury Trials, Prin. 1 (2005).

Problem 13-2. I Sort of Didn't Want a Jury

Marybeth is facing trial for submitting false loan applications to buy a $5 million, 12-bedroom home. Thinking that a jury may not view her favorably because of the lavish house she bought, she and her lawyer decided to waive a jury and risk trial by Judge Clement Farnsworth IV, who lives in a huge house and had inherited a fortune from his father.

At the hearing where the jury was waived, Marybeth's lawyer told judge Farnsworth that "my client and I thought waiving a jury would be a good idea and have great trust in a bench trial by your honor."

Judge Farnsworth asked Marybeth if she agreed with this statement by counsel. Marybeth said, "Yep, I sort of want you to handle the case and my lawyer thought it was a good idea." Judge Farnsworth then said, "OK. We'll have a bench trial."

1. Is this adequate proof that there was a voluntary and knowing waiver of Marybeth's right to a jury trial?

2. If not, what should Judge Farnsworth have done?

3. If you were the prosecutor, would you have done anything after Marybeth's statement and the judge's decision?

E. Jury Size

Generally, a jury in a criminal case is comprised of 12 people, perhaps with a few alternates available for emergencies. Federal Rule 23(b) prescribes a jury of 12, unless the trial court approves a written stipulation to proceed with fewer than 12.

Notes

1. *States approve smaller juries.* A significant minority of jurisdictions authorize juries of less than 12 for some or all criminal cases. *See, e.g.*, Fla. R. Crim. P. 3.270 (jury of 12 in capital cases, six in all other criminal cases). Often a 12-person jury is used in serious cases (usually felonies) and a six-person jury is convened for less serious ones (usually misdemeanors).

2. *Limits on reduction in number of jurors.* Does the Sixth Amendment permit a jury of less than 12? If so, how small can a criminal jury be? Could a state permit a jury of three, as happens in some European countries where three people (including a judge and two laypeople) decide guilt or innocence?

In *Williams v. Florida*, discussed in *Ballew v. Georgia*, below, the United States Supreme Court upheld a Florida statute providing a six-person jury in all but capital cases (where a 12-person jury was authorized). *Ballew* addressed the question whether a jury of less than six was permissible under the Sixth Amendment.

Ballew v. Georgia

435 U.S. 223 (1977)

Mr. Justice Blackmun announced the judgment of the Court and delivered an opinion in which Mr. Justice Stevens joined.

This case presents the issue whether a state criminal trial to a jury of only five persons deprives the accused of the right to trial by jury guaranteed to him by the Sixth and Fourteenth Amendments. Our resolution of the issue requires an application of principles enunciated in *Williams v. Florida*, 399 U.S. 78 (1970), where the use of a six-person jury in a state criminal trial was upheld against similar constitutional attack.

[Petitioner Ballew, manager of an adult theater in Atlanta, was convicted of two misdemeanor counts of distributing obscene materials after his theater exhibited a film. He was convicted by a jury of five persons, consistent with Georgia law providing a five-person jury in misdemeanor cases, that deliberated only thirty-eight minutes. Petitioner's motion for a twelve-person jury was denied. He was sentenced to two concurrent one-year sentences, both suspended upon payment of a $2000 fine. The petitioner lost appeals in Georgia state courts and applied for certiorari in the United States Supreme Court.]

The Fourteenth Amendment guarantees the right of trial by jury in all state non-petty criminal cases. *Duncan v. Louisiana*, 391 U.S. 145 (1968). The Court in *Duncan* applied this Sixth Amendment right to the States because "trial by jury in criminal cases is fundamental to the American scheme of justice." The right attaches in the present case because the maximum penalty for violating § 26-2101, as it existed at the time of the alleged offenses, exceeded six months' imprisonment.

In *Williams v. Florida*, the Court reaffirmed that the "purpose of the jury trial ... is to prevent oppression by the Government." ... This purpose is attained by the participation of the community in determinations of guilt and by the application of the common sense of laymen who, as jurors, consider the case.

Williams held that these functions and this purpose could be fulfilled by a jury of six members.... Rather than requiring 12 members, then, the Sixth Amendment mandated a jury only of sufficient size to promote group deliberation, to insulate members from outside intimidation, and to provide a representative cross-section of the community. Although recognizing that by 1970 little empirical research had evaluated jury performance, the [*Williams*] Court found no evidence that the reliability of jury verdicts diminished with six-member panels. Nor did the Court anticipate significant differences in result, including the frequency of "hung" juries. Because the reduction in size did not threaten exclusion of any particular class from jury roles, concern that the representative or cross-section character of the jury would suffer with a decrease to six members seemed "an unrealistic one." As a consequence, the six-person jury was held not to violate the Sixth and Fourteenth Amendments.

... [*Williams* and later cases] generated a quantity of scholarly work on jury size. These writings do not draw or identify a bright line below which the number of jurors would not be able to function as required by the standards enunciated in *Williams*. On the other hand, they raise significant questions about the wisdom and constitutionality of a reduction below six. We examine these concerns:

First, recent empirical data suggest that progressively smaller juries are less likely to foster effective group deliberation. At some point, this decline leads to inaccurate fact-finding and incorrect application of the common sense of the community to the facts.... As juries decrease in size, then, they are less likely to have members who remember each of the important pieces of evidence or argument. Furthermore, the smaller the group, the less likely it is to overcome the biases of its members to obtain an accurate result.... Groups also exhibited increased motivation and self-criticism. All these advantages, except, perhaps, self-motivation, tend to diminish as the size of the group diminishes.

... Second, the data now raise doubts about the accuracy of the results achieved by smaller and smaller panels. Statistical studies suggest that the risk of convicting an innocent person (Type I error) rises as the size of the jury diminishes.

... Third, the data suggest that the verdicts of jury deliberation in criminal cases will vary as juries become smaller, and that the variance amounts to an imbalance to the detriment of one side, the defense.

... That a five-person jury may return a unanimous decision does not speak to the questions whether the group engaged in meaningful deliberation, could remember all the important facts and arguments, and truly represented the sense of the entire community.

... Georgia [also] submits that the five-person jury adequately represents the community because there is no arbitrary exclusion of any particular class. We agree that it has not been demonstrated that the Georgia system violates the Equal Protection Clause by discriminating on the basis of race or some other improper classification. But the data outlined above raise substantial doubt about the ability of juries truly to represent the community as membership decreases below six. If the smaller and smaller juries will lack consistency, as the cited studies suggest, then the sense of the community will not be applied equally in like cases. Not only is the representation of racial minorities threatened in such circumstances, but also majority attitude or various minority positions may be misconstrued or misapplied by the smaller groups.

... With the reduction in the number of jurors below six creating a substantial threat to Sixth and Fourteenth Amendment guarantees, we must consider whether any interest of the State justifies the reduction. We find no significant state advantage in reducing the number of jurors from six to five.

. . . The point that is to be made, of course, is that a reduction in size from six to five or four or even three would save the States little. They could reduce slightly the daily allowances, but with a reduction from six to five the savings would be minimal. If little time is gained by the reduction from 12 to 6, less will be gained with a reduction from 6 to 5. . . .

Petitioner, therefore, has established that his trial on criminal charges before a five-member jury deprived him of the right to trial by jury guaranteed by the Sixth and Fourteenth Amendments. [Reversed]

[The concurring opinions of JUSTICES STEVENS, WHITE, and BRENNAN are omitted.]

MR. JUSTICE POWELL, with whom THE CHIEF JUSTICE and MR. JUSTICE REHNQUIST join, concurring in the judgment.

. . . I do not agree . . . that every feature of jury trial practice must be the same in both federal and state courts. . . .

Notes

1. *Why not five? Ballew* holds that a jury of six is permissible but a jury of five is not. Do the Court's reasons convince you that this is the correct place to draw the line? Can you think of a situation in which a jury of less than six persons may be permissible? *See* Colo. Rev. Stat. Ann. § 13-10-114 (providing that juries in municipal courts shall consist of a minimum of three and a maximum of six, persons). Is this constitutional? Is additional information needed to address this question?

2. *What happened between* Ballew *and* Williams? *Williams*, decided in 1970, held that a six-person jury was constitutionally permissible. But *Ballew*, in 1977, held that a five-person jury was not. What happened between 1970 and 1977 to convince the Court that six was the bottom limit on jury size? If the Court in *Williams* had the same empirical data as it had in *Ballew*, do you think it would have accepted a six-person jury? If not, where would it have drawn the line?

3. *Size and diversity.* As the jury decreases in size from twelve to six, the likelihood of minority jurors decreases substantially. *See generally* Shari Seidman Diamond *et al.*, *Achieving Diversity on the Jury: Jury Size and the Peremptory Challenge*, 6 J. EMPIR. LEGAL STUDIES 425 (2009) (civil trial data). Is this a good reason by itself to retain the traditional 12-person jury?

4. *ABA recommendations.* The American Bar Association recommends the traditional 12-person rule for serious offenses. STANDARDS FOR CRIMINAL JUSTICE § 15-1.1(a) and (b) (3d ed. 1996) (jury should consist of 12 persons, except a jury of 6 to 11 persons may be provided if the maximum possible penalty is confinement for six months or less); AMERICAN BAR ASSOCIATION, PRINCIPLES FOR JURIES AND JURY TRIALS, Prin. 3 (2005) (same).

[1] Waiver of Full Jury

In most jurisdictions, including the federal system pursuant to Rule 23(b), the accused has a right to a jury of a certain size but is permitted to waive that right and submit to a trial by a smaller jury. *See, e.g.*, Ark. Stat. Ann. § 16-32-202 (jury composed of 12 people, but parties may agree to lesser number in non-felonies). Before accepting a waiver, the court must ensure that both defense counsel and the accused agree to the smaller jury.

Although a jury of five or fewer members would violate *Ballew*, could the defendant waive a jury of six and agree to be tried by a jury of five or less? This could happen if a jury of six started a case, then one or more jurors had to quit for a legitimate reason, such as illness or a family death. Recall that a defendant may waive a jury trial, so why should the accused be barred from waiving a jury comprised of six members and submit to trial by a jury of five or fewer jurors?

[2] Alternate Jurors

Irrespective of the size of the trial jury, every jurisdiction also provides a mechanism for selecting and using *alternate jurors*. Ordinarily from one to four alternate jurors may be selected, depending on the likely length of the trial. The trial court is usually given the discretion whether to select alternate jurors and how many should be taken. The usual rule is that the alternate jurors are selected in the same manner as the trial jury and hear the same evidence as the trial jury, sometimes even sitting in the jury box during the trial.

Identifying alternates before trial begins. Ordinarily the alternate jurors are identified as such throughout the trial. When alternate jurors are specifically identified, as in the federal system under Rule 24(c), and a regular juror must be replaced, the replacement juror is selected either randomly from the alternate jurors or in the order of a number given each alternate juror (for example, if there are two alternate jurors, one of them would be "Alternate Juror One," the other "Two." Alternate One would be the first replacement juror).

Not identifying alternates and regular jurors until just before deliberation. In some jurisdictions, however, the alternates and regular jurors are not identified as one or the other, and are selected as one jury of, for example, 15 people. Shortly before the jury retires, the judge randomly "deselects" the alternates and sends the remaining jurors to the jury room to deliberate. This novel approach is designed to keep alternate jurors interested in the trial since no juror knows whether he or she is a regular or alternate juror until after final jury instructions. *See* Standards for Criminal Justice, § 15-2.9(a) (3d ed. 1996); American Bar Association, Principles for Juries and Jury Trials, Prin. 11(G)(2) (2005) (status of jurors as regular or alternate jurors should be determined by random selection at the time for jury deliberation). Ordinarily, the alternate jurors are dismissed when the trial jury retires to consider its verdict, though in many locales the court may keep them until verdict in case a regular juror must be replaced during deliberations.

Notes

1. *Great judicial discretion.* The trial court is given great discretion in deciding whether and when to replace a regular juror with an alternate juror. Usually

the decision will be reversed on appeal only if the defendant can show prejudice. *See, e.g., United States v. Walker*, 479 Fed. Appx. 329, 2012 U.S. App. LEXIS 14155 (11th Cir. July 11, 2012) (judge's decision to replace juror overturned only if defendant can show bias or prejudice).

2. *Illustrations of reasons to replace juror.* To illustrate the variety of reasons for empaneling an alternate juror, the following reasons were held to be acceptable in a brief survey of state and federal appellate decisions: the regular juror lied while answering questions during voir dire; the juror slept through some of the testimony; the juror's employer submitted a letter indicating that the juror was desperately needed to inspect an Air Force Base; the juror received anonymous telephone calls concerning the trial; the juror tried to contact a defendant; the juror was 10 minutes late to trial; in mid-trial the juror indicated that she had already formed an opinion as to guilt; a juror surreptitiously used a cell phone during trial; a juror's parents-in-law had worked for the defendant, a local politician, in elections; juror said she felt distressed, was losing sleep, could not focus, and was incapable of thinking or making a decision; and perhaps the most shocking of all, a juror was masturbating in the jury room during a break when other jurors were present.

3. *Role of alternates who replace regular jurors.* If an alternate juror is substituted for a regular juror, the alternate essentially becomes a regular juror and is subject to exactly the same rules and rights as the other trial jurors. The alternate will vote and discuss the case as any other juror.

4. *Role of alternate jurors who do not replace regular jurors.* In most jurisdictions, alternates who do not replace a regular juror are dismissed, completing their involvement in the case. Alternate jurors ordinarily do not accompany the regular jury to the jury room during deliberations or participate in jurors' discussions about the case. *See, e.g., United States v. Beasley*, 464 F.2d 468 (10th Cir. 1972) (reversal because alternate juror went with trial jury to jury room and participated in vote to select foreperson). If an alternate juror does attend the deliberations without participating in them, the conviction will be reversed only if the defendant can show prejudice. *United States v. Olano*, 507 U.S. 725 (1993).

F. Selection of Jurors

Some lawyers believe that the most important procedural facet of a criminal trial is the selection of the jurors. For many reasons, this process has come under increased scrutiny in recent years, resulting in tighter controls over a process that used to be subject to little meaningful appellate review.

Jury pool. The process starts with the *jury pool*, a large group of people who could be part of a jury. This theoretically includes all eligible jurors in the jurisdiction. Federal law provides that jurors should be randomly selected from a fair cross section of the community. 28 U.S.C. § 1861. Each federal district must have a written plan that implements this policy and ensures that there is no discrimination against people because of various ethnic and economic reasons. 28 U.S.C. § 1863. Failure to adhere to proper selection procedures can result in the dismissal of an indictment. 28 U.S.C. § 1867(d).

Sources of jury pool. People are selected for the jury pool from various lists, including voting lists, lists of driver's license holders, and tax rolls. Sometimes special efforts are made to obtain the names of persons in groups not adequately represented in the usual sources.

Venire. Often, a computer selects a number, perhaps 100–500 people, who constitute the *venire*. Individuals selected then receive a letter or summons that directs them to appear at the courthouse at a specified date and hour.

Process for selecting petit jury. Members of the venire are subjected to a process that will produce the *petit jury*, a jury of from six to 12 persons, plus alternates, who will decide the outcome of the case. First, venire members, perhaps in groups of from 25 to 50 persons, will be asked general questions to ascertain whether they qualify for jury service. This process, often referred to as the *voir dire*, is conducted by the judge and, in most jurisdictions, counsel for both sides. During this time, the judge can eliminate some members of the jury pool *for cause*—a reason why the person cannot (e.g., physical or mental problems, childcare or equivalent responsibilities, job responsibilities) or should not (e.g., related to a party or lawyer in the case, such strong feelings about the case or the legal system that he or she cannot render a fair decision) serve as a juror. For example, if a potential juror is pregnant and likely to have a baby in a few weeks, she may be excluded from the panel. Similarly, if a potential juror is the spouse of the prosecutor in the case, he or she will be excluded.

Lawyers may still exclude some of the remaining jurors through a *peremptory* challenge, discussed in detail later in this chapter. This challenge permits the lawyer for each party to exclude a fixed number of potential jurors. For example, in some jurisdictions each party's lawyer in a felony case may exclude up to eight potential jurors for virtually any reason.

Compensation. Jurors are paid a daily fee for their service, plus mileage costs for travel. *See, e.g.*, 28 U.S.C. § 1871 (federal jurors paid $40 per day, travel allowance, and subsistence allowance in some circumstances). Many states provide paltry fees, sometimes as little as two dollars per day. *See, e.g.*, S.C. Code Ann. § 14-7-1370 (jury pay varies by county, with jurors in certain counties paid two dollars per day).

[1] Eligibility for Jury Service

Virtually any adult is eligible to serve as a juror. Federal law is typical, providing that a person is eligible for jury service if the person is a citizen, 18 years old, a resident of the district for one year, sufficiently capable in English to speak and fill out a questionnaire, or mentally or physically capable of serving, or if the person has a felony criminal record or pending felony charges and civil rights have not been restored. 28 U.S.C. § 1865. *See also* AMERICAN BAR ASSOCIATION, PRINCIPLES FOR

Juries and Jury Trials, Prin. 2 (2005) (for juror eligibility, persons must be at least age 18, a U.S. citizen, a resident of the proper geographical district, and able to communicate in English if no satisfactory interpreter is available, and must not have been convicted of a felony and in actual confinement or under parole or probation or court supervision).

States may require the juror to be a citizen of the state and the county with jurisdiction in the case. Some also bar people who are related to a party or attorney within a specified degree, will be a witness in the case, served on the grand jury that indicted the defendant, served on a prior jury in the same case, or have a material interest in the outcome of the case. *See, e.g.*, Ark. Stat. Ann. § 16-31-102; S.C. Code Ann. § 14-7-830.

The accused has a right to be tried by a jury from the district or county where the crime was committed. This affects juror eligibility by limiting the geographical area from which jurors may be selected. *See supra* Chapter 3.

If an ineligible juror serves and participates in the rendering of the verdict, the defendant may challenge the validity of the verdict. However, some jurisdictions have enacted statutes that uphold the verdict unless the juror lied during questioning on voir dire. *See*, e.g., Ark. Stat. Ann. § 16-31-107.

[2] The Fair Cross Section Requirement

The Sixth Amendment ensures that a criminal case shall be tried before "an impartial jury of the State and district wherein the crime shall have been committed." The language has been interpreted to require a degree of community representativeness. As the Supreme Court put it:

> [the process of selecting a jury] must always accord with the fact that the proper functioning of the jury system, and, indeed, our democracy itself, requires that the jury be a "body truly representative of the community," and not an organ of any special group or class . . . [O]fficials charged with choosing federal jurors may exercise some discretion to the end that competent jurors may be called. But they must not allow the desire for competent jurors to lead them into selections which do not comport with the concept of the jury as a cross-section of the community.

Glasser v. United States, 315 U.S. 60, 85–86 (1942) (citation omitted). The fair cross section requirement serves several purposes: it ensures "that the common sense judgment of the community will act as a hedge against overzealous prosecutions"; preserves "public confidence in the criminal justice system"; and furthers "the notion that participation in the administration of justice is part of one's civic responsibility." *United States v. Berry*, 71 F.3d 1269, 1273–74 (7th Cir. 1995).

In addition to the fair cross section requirement, based in the Sixth Amendment, the Equal Protection Clause of the Fourteenth Amendment prohibits the rejection or selection of jurors on the basis of race, gender, or other suspect classification.

Like equal protection claims in other areas, a challenge must first establish that the procedure employed resulted in statistical underrepresentation or intent to discriminate, which the government can then seek to rebut. *See, e.g., United States v. Esquivel*, 75 F.3d 545 (9th Cir. 1996). Federal statutory law also provides that no citizen shall be excluded from federal jury service because of the person's race, color, religion, sex, national origin, or economic status. 28 U.S.C. § 1862.

The two constitutional requirements share an overlapping goal of ensuring a fair and representative jury. They are animated by different goals, however. An equal protection challenge seeks to root out discrimination, whereas a fair cross section challenge seeks to ensure use of a jury that is representative of the community. A key difference lies in the category of individuals affected; as noted, an equal protection claim addresses alleged discrimination on the basis of race, gender, or other suspect classification, whereas a fair cross section claim does not. *See, e.g., United States v. Esquivel*, 75 F.3d 545, 725 (9th Cir. 1996) (noting that, unlike an equal protection claim, a prima facie "fair cross section violation does not require the [petitioner] to prove discriminatory intent or require that the [petitioner] be a member of the distinct, excluded group").

A key question when litigating any case is whether an individual has standing to bring a claim. The next case addresses the standing question in the context of the fair cross section requirement.

Taylor v. Louisiana

419 U.S. 522 (1975)

Mr. Justice White delivered the opinion of the Court.

[Appellant was sentenced to death for aggravated kidnaping. He argued that the jury venire deprived him of his Sixth Amendment right to a trial by a jury that was representative of the community. Louisiana law provided that a woman should not be selected for jury service unless she had previously filed a written declaration of her desire to be subject to jury service. The Supreme Court accepted the case to consider whether the Louisiana system deprived the appellant of his Sixth Amendment right to an impartial jury trial.]

... The Louisiana jury-selection system does not disqualify women from jury service, but in operation its conceded systematic impact is that only a very few women, grossly disproportionate to the number of eligible women in the community, are called for jury service. In this case, no women were on the venire from which the petit jury was drawn. The issue we have, therefore, is whether a jury-selection system which operates to exclude from jury service an identifiable class of citizens constituting 53% of eligible jurors in the community comports with the Sixth and Fourteenth Amendments.

[The Court held that Taylor, a male, had standing to challenge the exclusion of women on the criminal jury that convicted him, as he was entitled to a jury drawn from a fair cross section of the community.]

. . . The background against which this case must be decided includes our holding in *Duncan v. Louisiana*, 391 U.S. 145 (1968), that the Sixth Amendment's provision for jury trial is made binding on the States by virtue of the Fourteenth Amendment. Our inquiry is whether the presence of a fair cross section of the community on venires, panels, or lists from which petit juries are drawn is essential to the fulfillment of the Sixth Amendment's guarantee of an impartial jury trial in criminal prosecutions.

. . . We accept the fair-cross-section requirement as fundamental to the jury trial guaranteed by the Sixth Amendment and are convinced that the requirement has solid foundation. The purpose of a jury is to guard against the exercise of arbitrary power—to make available the commonsense judgment of the community as a hedge against the overzealous or mistaken prosecutor and in preference to the professional or perhaps overconditioned or biased response of a judge. *Duncan v. Louisiana*. This prophylactic vehicle is not provided if the jury pool is made up of only special segments of the populace or if large, distinctive groups are excluded from the pool. Community participation in the administration of the criminal law, moreover, is not only consistent with our democratic heritage but is also critical to public confidence in the fairness of the criminal justice system.

. . . We are also persuaded that the fair-cross-section requirement is violated by the systematic exclusion of women, who in the judicial district involved here, amounted to 53% of the citizens eligible for jury service. This conclusion necessarily entails the judgment that women are sufficiently numerous and distinct from men and that if they are systematically eliminated from jury panels, the Sixth Amendment's fair-cross-section requirement cannot be satisfied.

. . . There remains the argument that women as a class serve a distinctive role in society and that jury service would so substantially interfere with that function that the State has ample justification for excluding women from service unless they volunteer, even though the result is that almost all jurors are men.

. . . The States are free to grant exemptions from jury service to individuals in case of special hardship or incapacity and to those engaged in particular occupations the uninterrupted performance of which is critical to the community's welfare. It would not appear that such exemptions would pose substantial threats that the remaining pool of jurors would not be representative of the community. A system excluding all women, however, is a wholly different matter. It is untenable to suggest these days that it would be a special hardship for each and every woman to perform jury service or that society cannot spare any women from their present duties. This may be the case with many, and it may be burdensome to sort out those who should be exempted from those who should serve. But that task is performed in the case of men, and the administrative convenience in dealing with women as a class is insufficient justification for diluting the quality of community judgment represented by the jury in criminal trials.

. . . It should also be emphasized that in holding that petit juries must be drawn from a source fairly representative of the community we impose no requirement that petit juries actually chosen must mirror the community and reflect the various distinctive groups in the population. Defendants are not entitled to a jury of any particular composition, but the jury wheels, pools of names, panels, or venires from which juries are drawn must not systematically exclude distinctive groups in the community and thereby fail to be reasonably representative thereof. [Reversed]

Mr. Chief Justice Burger concurs in the result.

Mr. Justice Rehnquist, dissenting.

... Absent any suggestion that appellant's trial was unfairly conducted, or that its result was unreliable, I would not require Louisiana to retry him (assuming the State can once again produce its evidence and witnesses) in order to impose on him the sanctions which its laws provide.

Notes

1. *Challenge to array. Taylor* and other cases permit what has been called a challenge to the *array.* Sometimes this is referred to as a challenge to the *panel* (this ambiguous term may also refer to a challenge to the *venire* or to the individual body of 12 or so jurors sitting in an individual case). This alleges that the jury pool is somehow defective because it does not include certain groups. Proof of this defect requires considerable demographic data to show that the jury pool is statistically unrepresentative. In order to enable the judge to cure any defects, some jurisdictions require that such challenges be made before the jury is sworn. *See, e.g.,* N.Y. Crim. Pro. Law § 270.10 (challenge to panel must be made before jury selection begins; otherwise issue is waived).

2. *Does the requirement apply to petit juries?* Would there be a Sixth Amendment violation if the particular jury that tried the defendant contained no minorities, but the original venire contained a fair representation of all groups in the community? What if the venire contained a definite underrepresentation of a minority group, but the jury that tried the accused was representative of the community?

3. *Validity of basic qualifications. Duran v. Missouri,* 439 U.S. 357 (1979) clearly permits jurisdictions to establish qualifications for jurors. These are routinely upheld as not violating the fair cross section requirement.

4. *Exemptions from jury service.* Note that *Taylor* specifically authorizes a jurisdiction to exempt from jury service people who have a special hardship or incapacity or who work in "particular occupations the uninterrupted performance of which is critical to the community's welfare," *E.g.,* physicians, veterinarians, teachers, and judges. A federal statute excludes from federal jury service active duty armed forces personnel; police and fire officers; and various officials of the executive, legislative, and judicial departments. 28 U.S.C. § 1863.

State statutes contain similar provisions, plus other categories. *See, e.g.,* Iowa Code §§ 607A.5 and 607A.6 (automatically excludes person solely responsible for daily care of permanently disabled person in their home; discretionary excuses for hardship, inconvenience, or public necessity); N.J. Stat. Ann. §2B:20-10 (exemptions include those with obligations to care for a sick, aged or infirm dependent or a minor child, those providing highly specialized health care service, teachers during school terms, volunteer firefighters and members of volunteer first aid or rescue squads).

The American Bar Association and a growing number of states reject these occupational (and other) exemptions to jury service in order to provide maximum inclusiveness and representativeness. *See* American Bar Association, Principles for Juries and Jury Trials, Prin. 2 (jury service should not be denied or limited because of occupation).

5. *Allocation and burden of proof.* In *Duren v. Missouri*, 439 U.S. 357 (1979), the Court struck down a Missouri rule that automatically exempted from jury service any woman who requested an exemption. The decision clarified how a fair cross-section violation is proved. The Court in *Duren* held that:

> In order to establish a prima facie violation of the fair-cross-section requirement, the defendant must show (1) that the group alleged to be excluded is a "distinctive" group in the community; (2) that the representation of this group in venires from which juries are selected is not fair and reasonable in relation to the number of such persons in the community; and (3) that this underrepresentation is due to systematic exclusion of the group in the jury-selection process. . . . [O]nce the defendant has made a prima facie showing of an infringement of his constitutional right to a jury drawn from a fair cross section of the community, it is the State that bears the burden of justifying this infringement by showing attainment of a fair cross section to be incompatible with a significant state interest.

Id. at 364, 368.

a. *Distinctive group. Duren* requires proof that a distinctive group was underrepresented. Why is this a requirement? If the underlying problem is the denial of an impartial jury, what difference does it make whether the views that were underrepresented stemmed from a distinctive group? Would there still be a problem if there were no liberals on the jury, irrespective of whether liberals are a distinctive group? What about homosexuals?

What would make a group a "distinctive group"? Must it be distinct in an objective way? Must its members have internal cohesion or be identified as a separate group by society? In *Lockhart v. McCree*, 476 U.S. 162 (1986), the Supreme Court made a minimal effort to define "distinctive group." In holding that persons with strong anti-death penalty views are *not* part of a distinctive group, the Court stated:

> The essence of a "fair-cross-section" claim is the systematic exclusion of "a distinctive group in the community" [citation to *Duren*]. In our view, groups defined solely in terms of shared attitudes that would prevent or substantially impair members of the group from performing one of their

> duties as jurors . . . are not "distinctive groups" for fair-cross-section purposes. . . .

Id. at 174, 176–77.

Clearly, certain groups qualify as "distinctive groups." *See, e.g., United States v. Kleifgen*, 557 F.2d 1293 (9th Cir. 1977) (blacks and males are cognizable groups; young people, less educated people, and unemployed people are not cognizable groups); *State v. Couture*, 482 A.2d 300 (Conn. 1984), *cert. denied*, 469 U.S. 1192 (1985) (Hispanics are distinctive group); *United States v. Gelb*, 881 F.2d 1155 (2d Cir. 1989) (Jews are cognizable group).

But what about less identifiable groups? In *Lockhart*, the Court held that those strongly opposed to the death penalty did not comprise a distinctive group. *See also United States v. Salamone*, 800 F.2d 1216 (3d Cir. 1986) (members of National Rifle Association not distinctive group). *See also State v. Rogers*, 562 S.E.2d 859 (N.C. 2002) (people over age 65 are not a distinctive group but may be excused because of their age on a case-by-case basis; people between 18 and 29 are not a distinctive group).

b. *Fair and reasonable representation.* In order to make the venire a fair and reasonable representation of the community, is it necessary that the percentage of people in each "distinctive group" be exactly the same in both the venire and the community? If not, how great a difference is permissible? *See United States v. Test*, 550 F.2d 577 (10th Cir. 1976) (fact that disparity is statistically significant does not mean it is legally significant); *Anderson v. Casscles*, 531 F.2d 682 (2d Cir. 1976) (although county had 4% black population and jury venire had only 2%, difference insufficient to constitute unreasonable representation).

In its most recent fair-cross section case, *Berghuis v. Smith*, 559 U.S. 314 (2010), the Court rejected any specific test for assessing a distinctive group's underrepresentation.

c. *Systematic exclusion.* What is the relationship between a "systematic exclusion" and an intentional exclusion? Can a systematic exclusion, barred by *Duren*, be unintentional? What if an accidental computer error excluded a particular group of people? Why is systematic exclusion even an issue? If the concern is the composition of the jury (or even the venire), should it matter whether a group was systematically excluded if it was, in fact, absent from the jury or venire?

d. *Significant state interest. Duren* holds that a state can justify the fair cross-section violation by proving that the attainment of a fair cross section is incompatible with a significant state interest. What type of significant state interest would justify this constitutional violation? Would requiring jurors to be proficient in English be impermissible discrimination against Hispanics? *See People v. Eubanks*, 266 P.3d 301 (Cal. 2011) (no) (also no cross-section violation for various hardship exclusions such as financial burden, day care problems, medical concerns not tied to an appointment, and prior jury service).

Why should a significant *state* interest be permitted to justify the violation of the *defendant's* right to a jury comprised of a fair cross section of the community?

[3] Voir Dire Procedures: In General

Trial courts are generally given significant discretion in fashioning procedures for selecting the panel of jurors who will sit on a particular case.

[a] Names and Addresses of Potential Jurors; Anonymous Juries

Lawyers preparing for the jury selection process often prefer to examine a list of the names and addresses of the venire prior to the voir dire process. This enables them to prepare questions appropriate for individual jurors and by providing some minimal demographic data. For example, a person's address may tell something about the person's financial status and ethnicity. Sometimes a statute or court rule will authorize the exchange of this information. *See, e.g.,* 18 U.S.C. § 3432 (capital defendant usually entitled to names and addresses of potential jurors no later than three days before trial); 28 U.S.C. § 1867 (f) (setting forth circumstances under which access to jury records should be granted); Ariz. R. Crim. P. 18.3 (parties furnished with names and biographical information about each potential juror; comment states this includes names, addresses, occupation, and age of both juror and spouse, employer's names and addresses, number of years employed, marital status and number and age of children, length of residence in state and county, ownership of real estate, education, experience as law enforcement officer, previous juror service, and courses in law that were taken); ABA STANDARDS FOR CRIMINAL JUSTICE § 15-2.2(a)(1) (3d ed. 1996) (before voir dire, court and counsel should receive data pertinent to the jurors' qualifications, including name, sex, age, residence, marital status, education level, occupation and occupational history, employment address, previous service as a juror, and present or past involvement as a party to civil or criminal litigation).

Anonymous jury. In general, however, the trial court is given the discretion whether to release this information and proceed with an "anonymous jury." Many state and federal courts have expressly approved the use of the anonymous jury under limited circumstances. *See United States v. Edmond*, 52 F.3d 1080 (D.C. Cir. 1995) (the district court could decide *sua sponte* that an anonymous jury was necessary; court should look to five factors to determine necessity of jury anonymity: (1) defendant's involvement in organized crime, (2) defendant's participation in a group with the capacity to harm jurors, (3) defendant's past attempts to interfere with the judicial process, (4) the potential that, if convicted, the defendant will suffer a lengthy incarceration and substantial monetary penalties, and (5) extensive publicity that could enhance the possibility that jurors' names would become public and expose them to intimidation or harassment).

Even though every federal circuit court addressing this question has expressly approved the use of the anonymous jury in appropriate cases, it has been noted that empaneling such a jury "is a drastic measure, which should be undertaken only in limited and carefully delineated circumstances." *See, e.g., United States v. Sanchez*, 74 F.3d 562 (5th Cir. 1996) (holding that the district court abused its discretion in empaneling an anonymous jury because there was no factual showing to support the conclusion that anonymity was warranted).

A compromise: releasing jurors' names to defense counsel but using numbers to identify jurors during trial. In order to permit defense counsel to investigate and question potential jurors, a few courts have released demographic information to counsel but forbid counsel to further release the identifying information and require that during the trial all jurors be referred to by number rather than name. In *United Sates v. Hager*, 721 F.3d 167 (4th Cir. 2013), this procedure was approved. Do you think it creates a possibility that the use of numbers will prejudice the jurors against the accused, perhaps by getting the signal that the accused is dangerous and that the jurors or their families are at risk? Would this risk be alleviated if the jury were instructed (as occurred in *Hager*) that the use of numbers should not interfere with the presumption of innocence?

[b] Juror Questionnaire

Content. In some courts, potential jurors are required to fill out a questionnaire ranging from a page or two to as many as 70 pages. The questions ask about various demographic data (age, gender, home address, job, marital status, education), exposure to information about the crime, and perhaps attitudes about events or people. The judge and the lawyers then use these completed questionnaires when selecting jurors.

Significant judicial discretion. Trial courts ordinarily are given the discretion whether to use questionnaires (although they are mandatory in some jurisdictions) and what questions may be included in the questionnaire. *See, e.g., United States v. McDade*, 929 F. Supp. 815 (E.D. Pa. 1996) (refusing to permit several questions to be asked of prospective jurors because of privacy concerns); *United States v. Serafini*, 57 F. Supp. 2d 108 (M.D. Pa. 1999) (district court excluded questions from defendant questionnaire relating to prospective jurors' place of birth, race, marital status, health, political party affiliation, ownership of stock, income, religious affiliation, government employment or security clearance, television programs watched, membership in social or business organizations, and other personal questions, holding them to be intrusive and not linked to the issues of the case or juror ability to be fair).

[c] Expert Consultation

Since the 1970s, some lawyers have used "jury selection experts" or "trial consultants" to assist in jury selection. While some of these experts may be characterized as fortune tellers, others have more traditional credentials, such as a doctorate in psychology and extensive experience. Some lawyers believe that such experts can be of material assistance in selecting jurors most likely to be amenable to their arguments.

These experts perform a range of services. Sometimes they help draft and interpret written juror questionnaires and assess community attitudes toward the defendant or certain issues. They may conduct telephone surveys which will help them prepare a *juror profile*, a study that correlates juror characteristics, attitudes, and verdict preferences. They may also be present at the voir dire proceeding and offer suggestions to counsel about questions to ask or jurors to select.

[4] Questioning Potential Jurors: The Voir Dire Process

Judge and/or lawyers. While potential jurors are interrogated in every jurisdiction, the process varies considerably. Judges routinely ask questions of the venire, usually assembled in a group of 25–100 people. Often judges ask counsel for both sides to suggest questions for the judge to ask. These questions generally focus on obvious reasons why a particular juror should not serve in this case. Thus, potential jurors are asked whether their health or job would prevent service. They are also asked about their relationship with the parties, witnesses, lawyers, or to the case. Other topics may also be explored.

Many judges also permit the defense lawyer and the prosecutor to question jurors. In order to expedite the process, judges may limit the number of questions or the time each lawyer has. *See* Standards for Criminal Justice § 15-2.4 (3d ed. 1996) (voir dire should be conducted initially by judge, but counsel should be permitted a reasonable opportunity to question jurors directly, both as a panel and individually; individual voir dire [discussed after Rule 24] should be permitted when the juror is to be asked about sensitive matters or prior exposure to potentially prejudicial material). *See* C.J. Williams, *To Tell You the Truth, Federal Rule of Criminal Procedure 24(a) Should be Amended to Permit Attorneys to Conduct Voir Dire of Prospective Jurors*, 67 S.C.L. Rev. 35 (2015) (jurors are more candid with attorneys than with judges, and attorneys are better questioners).

Sometimes court rules indicate whether lawyers are permitted to question potential jurors. Some specifically permit both the prosecutor and defense counsel to question potential jurors. *See, e.g.*, Fla. R. Crim. P. 3.300(b). Rule 24(a) leaves the matter to the judge's discretion.

Note

Individual or group. Besides the question of who should interrogate the prospective jurors, the judge also must decide whether the questions are more appropriately posed to groups of jurors or to the individual jurors. In the latter situation, each potential juror is brought into the courtroom to be questioned by the judge and perhaps the defense lawyer and the prosecutor. The other jurors are not present. Because *individual voir dire* (sometimes called *sequestered voir dire*) is more time consuming than *group voir dire*, most judges prefer the latter. They may question many jurors at one time, then break the potential jurors into smaller groups for more intensive questioning. One fairly obvious situation in which sequestered voir dire is preferred, however, is when questions are to be asked of prospective jurors about their exposure to publicity about the case, as discussed above. Some states that still use the death penalty require individual voir dire for jury selection.

[5] Types of Challenges: Cause and Peremptory

Potential jurors are subject to two kinds of challenges or grounds for exclusion. A *challenge for cause* is a claim that a potential juror is disqualified from service because of an inability to serve or a bias that would prevent the juror from being fair. Although the judge decides whether a potential juror is to be excluded for cause, often a defense attorney or prosecutor asks the judge to exclude the juror on this basis. Either side may challenge a juror for cause. The reasons for this challenge must be given so that the judge can determine whether the juror should be excused.

A *peremptory challenge*, discussed later in this chapter, is a decision by a party's lawyer that a particular juror should not serve on the jury. Ordinarily, each side is given a limited number of peremptory challenges which can be exercised for virtually any reason. Often, lawyers will try to preserve their few peremptory challenges by asking the judge to disqualify a juror for cause. If the juror is removed for cause, the lawyer is able to have the juror excused without spending a peremptory challenge.

[6] Challenges for Cause

Although frequently the rules of criminal procedure do not mention challenges for cause, this challenge is an important facet of the jury selection process in every jurisdiction. There are few limits on the grounds that can be used for a challenge for cause and no limit on the number of jurors who can be struck for cause. Sometimes the grounds for a challenge for cause are stated in general terms. *See, e.g.*, Ariz. R. Crim. P. 18.4 (challenge for cause when there is "reasonable ground to believe that a juror cannot render a fair and impartial verdict").

A small number of states have adopted statutes pertaining to challenges for cause and have set forth precise reasons or grounds that permit excusing jurors from service. *See, e.g.*, Fla. Stat. § 913.03 (identifying 12 grounds upon which such challenges may be based).

There are actually two general bases for challenge for cause: an inability to perform the necessary functions and a bias that could compromise the juror's ability to decide the case impartially.

[a] Inability to Serve

Jury service requires both physical and mental activities, and a potential juror may be disqualified because he or she is not able to perform the necessary functions.

Physical or mental capacity. A person who does not have the physical or mental capacity to perform the services required of a juror can be excluded (or excused) for cause. This includes a potential juror whose mental incompetence means the juror cannot understand or deliberate the issues. *See, e.g.*, Ind. Code § 35-37-1-5; N.J. Stat. Ann. § 2B:23-11.

Understanding of law. A juror may also be disqualified for cause if he or she is unable to grasp the legal principles at issue. However, it is difficult to assess this ground for exclusion since ordinarily jurors are not instructed in depth about the law until the end of the trial. *See United States v. Vera*, 701 F.2d 1349 (11th Cir. 1983) (although potential juror indicated confusion about burden of proof in criminal case, trial court did not err in barring voir dire of juror on this issue when court asked general questions about the law and gave clear jury instructions about the burden of proof).

Understanding English. A potential juror may be excused for cause if he or she cannot adequately understand English. Sometimes this is expressed in terms of reading, understanding, and speaking (so juror can communicate with other jurors during deliberations) English. A few jurisdictions alleviate this somewhat by providing translators for non-English speaking jurors.

Lying in response to voir dire questions. A juror who lied during voir dire may be excused for that reason alone.

[b] Possible Bias

A juror must be fair. The Sixth Amendment guarantees a jury trial by an impartial jury. According to the Supreme Court:

> . . . [T]he right to jury trial guarantees the criminally accused a fair trial by a panel of impartial, "indifferent" jurors. The failure to accord an accused a fair hearing violates even the minimal standards of due process.

Irvin v. Dowd, 366 U.S. 717, 722 (1961).

Implied (implicit) and actual bias. The process of questioning and excluding potential jurors is the primary vehicle for ensuring that a jury panel is comprised of unbiased people. There are actually two types of challenges for cause based on bias: implied bias and actual bias. *Implied bias* permits an assumption that a potential juror is so likely to be biased that disqualification is appropriate. *Actual bias* involves proof that a particular juror would be biased in a particular case. Actual bias is often difficult to prove since the juror may state during voir dire that he or she will put aside all biases and decide the case on its merits. Sometimes actual bias is detected through circumstantial evidence. If actual bias is discovered during the voir dire process, the court must excuse the juror for cause. *United States v. Rhodes*, 177 F.3d 963 (9th Cir. 1999). Some courts find actual bias when a juror lies in response to questions during voir dire and a truthful answer would have led to the juror being excused for cause. *See, e.g., Hatten v. Quarterman*, 570 F.3d 595 (5th Cir. 2009).

According to most courts, the key determination is actual rather than implied bias. The trial court should ask whether *this* potential juror is biased. Questions during the voir dire process should address this issue. Ordinarily, a person should not be excluded for cause simply because of the possibility of bias. In exceptional cases, however, some judges are willing to exclude a potential juror for implied bias. *See Smith v. Phillips*, 455 U.S. 209, 222 (1982) (in some situations it may be appropriate to use implied bias to dismiss a juror for cause; examples include a juror who is an employee of the prosecuting agency, is a close relative of a trial participant, or was a witness or otherwise involved in the criminal transaction).

In implied bias cases, some courts use an "average person" test, asking whether an average person in a similar situation would feel prejudice. *See, e.g., United States v. Haynes*, 398 F.2d 980 (2d Cir. 1968) (examples of implied bias include a juror who has served on jury that convicted another defendant in prior case involving same transaction, kinship to the defendant, or interest in the proceeding).

Government employment. Since the government is a party in every criminal prosecution, it has been alleged that a government employee should be barred from jury service because of likely bias. In *Dennis v. United States*, 339 U.S. 162 (1950), the United States Supreme Court rejected this argument in a case involving an avowed communist who was charged with failure to obey a subpoena from the House Un-American Activities Committee. The Court refused to presume that all government employees were too biased to serve as criminal jurors.

Of course, the *Dennis* Court also recognized that a government employee could be excluded for cause upon proof that the particular juror would not be fair in *this* case. *See, e.g., United States v. Apodaca*, 666 F.2d 89 (5th Cir. 1982) (potential juror and her husband had worked for F.B.I.; she knew how much investigation went into grand jury case; she might give more credence to prosecution; it would have been prudent and reasonable to exclude this juror for cause, but no error because juror said she could be impartial).

Exposure to pretrial publicity. A frequent allegation is that a particular juror or an entire panel of jurors should be excluded for cause because of their exposure to pretrial publicity. The argument is that the potential jurors cannot be bias-free because their minds were polluted by publicity.

In the leading case, *Irvin v. Dowd*, 366 U.S. 717 (1961), the defendant was sentenced to death for six murders in a small community. The local news media extensively publicized the crimes and the defendant's confessions. The trial court denied the defendant's motions for a continuance and a change of venue. The Supreme Court reversed, holding that the accused was denied a fair trial by the massive pretrial publicity and the impact it had on the jurors. However, the Court was careful to note that knowledge of a crime alone is insufficient to render a potential juror unqualified to serve. The key is whether the juror can be fair:

> [A]n important case can be expected to arouse the interests of the public in the vicinity, and scarcely any of those best qualified to serve as jurors will not have formed some impression or opinion as to the merits of the case. This is particularly true in criminal cases. To hold that the mere existence

> of any preconceived notion as to the guilt or innocence of an accused, without more, is sufficient to rebut the presumption of a prospective juror's impartiality would be to establish an impossible standard. It is sufficient if the juror can lay aside his impression or opinion and render a verdict based on the evidence presented in court.

Id. at 722–23.

Feelings about this case. A juror may be excluded for cause for having such strong feelings about the case that impartiality is unlikely. For example, if a juror felt strongly that no one was insane, he or she should be disqualified for cause in a case in which the insanity defense is asserted. *See, e.g., United States v. Allsup*, 566 F.2d 68 (9th Cir. 1977).

Relationship to party, lawyer, witness, victim, or crime. Another ground for exclusion for cause is the juror's relationship to a person, entity, or some other facet of the case that could cause the juror to be biased. Examples: the potential juror in a bank robbery case was an employee of the bank that was robbed; a cab driver was excluded in a case where a cab driver was robbed and killed; jurors were related to defense counsel or had used his professional services; jurors were acquainted with the defendant; juror was "close friends" with each defendant; juror had a pastoral and professional relationship with several members of defendant's family; a juror's parents-in-law had worked for the defendant's election (the defendant was a public official charged with voter bribery); a juror's involvement in prior similar litigation; a juror in a drug case had sons serving prison terms for drug-related crimes; a juror was the presiding judge's mother; and a peace officer was employed by the same police department that investigated the crime at issue

Membership in organization. Sometimes a potential juror is a member of an organization that represents views somehow related to the case. Ordinarily, such membership alone is insufficient to prove actual bias and justify exclusion for cause. *See, e.g., United States v. Salamone*, 800 F.2d 1216 (3d Cir. 1986) (juror's membership in National Rifle Association insufficient to exclude juror for cause in case involving illegal firearms).

Prior jury service. If a potential juror has already served on a jury in the same or a similar case, the juror can be excluded for cause if the earlier experience somehow creates actual bias. In general, prior service on unrelated matters, if coupled with a juror's statement about the ability to be fair, does not merit being excused for cause.

Some courts are willing to infer bias if the prior service occurred quite near in time to the present case. *See, e.g., United States v. Franklin*, 700 F.2d 1241 (10th Cir. 1983) (jurors who, between the time of their selection as a juror and actual trial, have served on another jury involving similar legal or factual issues or the same government witnesses can be dismissed for cause).

Courts are more likely to grant a challenge for cause if the potential jurors sat on a previous case involving the same transaction or witnesses at issue in the current case. Similarly, a challenge for cause is routinely granted if the potential jurors participated in a previous case in which the current defendant was convicted. *See, e.g.*, *Graham v. State*, 258 S.W.3d 201 (Tex. App. 2008) (juror was member of grand jury that indicted defendant; excusal for cause proper).

Rehabilitation. Exclusion is not necessarily automatic for most varieties of juror bias. The court may find the juror acceptable if the court believes the juror can set aside the bias and render a fair and impartial verdict. In this situation, the lawyer for the side that would benefit from the juror's "leaning" will likely want the juror retained. The lawyer will make serious efforts to convince the court that the juror's bias is not fatal to jury service because, despite it, the juror can be fair and impartial in this case.

Often courts will look closely at the relationship and the juror's response to questions to determine whether the bias will actually impair the juror's impartiality *See, e.g.*, *United States v. Tab*, 259 Fed. Appx. 684 (6th Cir. 2007) (juror had met shooting victim's father many years ago and was certain it would not affect his judgment); *United States v. Brown*, 540 F.2d 364 (8th Cir. 1976) (citizens of St. Louis not automatically barred for cause in case of fraud against City of St. Louis and its citizens; must be proof of actual bias); *Ex Parte Killingworth*, 82 So. 3d 761 (Ala. 2010) (fact juror knew victim or members of victim's family does not automatically disqualify juror; issue is whether juror can be fair and impartial); *Johnson v. State*, 642 S.E.2d 170 (Ga. App. 2007) (juror knew wife of police officer victim but said she could be fair); *State v. Hopkins*, 908 So. 2d 1265 (La. App. 2005) (juror formed an opinion about the case because of previous grand jury service that taught her there was an evidentiary basis for the charges, but was acceptable because she said she would hold the state to its burden of proof).

Problem 13-3. I Like Cops

In a murder case where police testimony about a confession is critical prosecution evidence, Frank Jackson was a potential juror, questioned as follows by the District Attorney:

Q. Mr. Jackson, police officers will testify in this case. Will you give their testimony more credence than that of any other witness?

A. I think I would automatically believe the testimony of a police officer unless the evidence showed it was untrue.

Q. Would your opinion change if I [the prosecutor] told you this was not a good policy because the officer may be wrong,

A. No, I would believe the police officer. . . . Now, I might lower how I view his testimony. But as you said, he may be wrong and not know he is wrong. . . . I do believe that a police officer believes what he says.

Q. Would you see a problem with that if jurors said to themselves, well, it doesn't matter what they testify to or what the other evidence shows, since he is a police officer I'm going to automatically believe whatever he says.

A. Well, yeah. I think I was trying to say, though, I believe—I accept his testimony as he believes it.

Q. All right.

A. Then I would rank it as to where I would place it in my decision.

Q. To the extent that police officers are scheduled to testify in this trial, if we put a police officer on the stand, would you be able to assess that police officer's credibility and testimony as they testify in an individual and fair manner?

A. I can try.

Q. Would you be able to wait until their testimony was completed before you formed a decision as far as how credible they are or how truthful they are or their testimony as a whole, how much weight you're going to give their testimony?

A. I believe so, yes.

Q. So when I bring it back around, would you just automatically believe a police officer that comes in to testify before you've heard everything they've said?

A. I would go under the assumption of believing him when he starts because of his position.

Q. With that in place, how would you treat a police officer's testimony if we were to present it?

A. Still I would have to accept it as being the truth until something that I hear or whatever objects to that—subjects that to question.

1. What is the District Attorney trying to do here? Could this explain why the *prosecutor* suggested that police officers may be wrong sometimes?

2. The defense has moved to have Mr. Jackson excused for cause. What argument should defense counsel make?

3. How should the judge rule on the motion to excuse Jackson? *See State v. Dorsey*, 74 So.3d 603 (La. 2011).

[c] Unique Procedures in Death Penalty Cases

In a typical criminal case, each lawyer may seek to have the most questionable jurors excused for cause, thus preserving the lawyer's peremptory challenges for use on other jurors. The same procedure applies in death penalty cases, with a slightly different twist.

Jury selection procedures in death penalty cases are unique. During the voir dire process, potential jurors are asked the same questions as jurors in any other criminal case, plus others about their views of the death penalty. The latter questions are important since the capital case jury typically decides whether the accused is guilty and, if so, imposes the sentence.

Sometimes the voir dire process reveals that a potential juror has strong feelings about the death penalty. This may mean that the person has reservations about the ultimate punishment. When a juror indicates anti-death penalty sentiments, often the prosecutor will ask that the juror be excused for cause. The defense lawyer, on the other hand, will fight exclusion for two reasons. First, the defense lawyer would like to fill the jury box with people who oppose the death penalty. During jury deliberations these people may vote and argue against the death penalty and may also be more amenable to defense arguments on guilt or innocence. Second, if the juror is to be excused, defense counsel would like to force the prosecution to exercise one of its precious peremptories rather than having the juror excused for cause.

"Witherspoon *excludables.*" In the early leading case, *Witherspoon v. Illinois*, 391 U.S. 510 (1968), an Illinois statute authorized exclusion for cause of any juror in a death penalty case who had "conscientious scruples against capital punishment." During the jury selection process in *Witherspoon*, the trial judge said, "[l]et's get these conscientious objectors out of the way, without wasting any time on them." He then excluded 47 potential jurors because of their views of the death penalty. Thirty-nine of these acknowledged having "conscientious or religious scruples against the infliction of the death penalty" or against its infliction "in a proper case." The defendant objected to the exclusions, arguing that a jury selected in this manner was not a random cross-section of the community and was biased in favor of conviction. The Supreme Court agreed. "[W]e hold that a sentence of death cannot be carried out if the jury that imposed or recommended it was chosen by excluding veniremen for cause simply because they voiced general objections to the death penalty or expressed conscientious or religious scruples against its infliction." *Id.* at 521–523.

Adams' *modifications of Witherspoon.* In *Adams v. Texas*, 448 U.S. 38 (1980), the Supreme Court established a slightly different test that indicated that jurors in capital cases can be excluded if they are unwilling to apply the law:

> [Case law] establishes the general proposition that a juror may not be challenged for cause based on his views about capital punishment unless those views would prevent or substantially impair the performance of his duties as a juror in accordance with his instructions and his oath. The State may insist, however, that jurors will consider and decide the facts impartially and conscientiously apply the law as charged by the court.

Id. at 45.

Subsequent cases dealt with whether a particular juror's responses on voir dire were sufficient to excuse that juror for cause. In those cases, often both the questions asked and answers given were poorly focused. In *Wainwright v. Witt*, 469 U.S. 412 (1985), a potential juror was excused for cause after the following colloquy occurred between the juror and the prosecutor:

> Prosecutor: Do you have any religious beliefs or personal beliefs against the death penalty?
>
> Juror: . . . I am afraid of being a little personal, but definitely not religious.
>
> Prosecutor: Now, would that interfere with you sitting as a juror in this case?

Juror: I am afraid it would.

Prosecutor: . . . Would it interfere with judging the guilt or innocence of the Defendant in this case?

Juror: I think so.

Prosecutor: . . . Your Honor, I would move for cause at this point.

The defendant appealed, partially on the theory that this juror should not have been excluded for cause because the juror did not indicate that she would *automatically* vote against the death penalty.

The Supreme Court in *Witt* affirmed *Adams* in an opinion that stressed the need to give the trial court discretion in deciding whether to exclude a juror for cause.

> Determinations of juror bias cannot be reduced to question-and-answer sessions which obtain results in the manner of a catechism. What common sense should have realized experience has proved: many veniremen simply cannot be asked enough questions to reach the point where their bias has been made "unmistakably clear"; these veniremen may not know how they will react when faced with imposing the death sentence, or may be unable to articulate, or may wish to hide their true feelings. . . . [T]here will be situations where the trial judge is left with the definite impression that a prospective juror would be unable to faithfully and impartially apply the law. . . . [T]his is why deference must be paid to the trial judge who sees and hears the juror.

Id. at 424–25.

Although the trial judge has great discretion in deciding whether a particular juror should be excused for cause and what questions may be asked on voir dire, the Supreme Court held that the judge, if requested by counsel, must ask whether a potential juror would automatically vote for the death penalty if the defendant were found guilty of capital murder. *Morgan v. Illinois*, 504 U.S. 719 (1992).

Supreme Court's summary of death penalty juror rules. In *Uttecht v. Brown*, 551 U.S. 1, 9 (2007), the Court summarized its *Witherspoon-Adams* decisions:

> These precedents establish at least four principles of relevance here. First, a criminal defendant has the right to an impartial jury drawn from a venire that has not been tilted in favor of capital punishment by selective prosecutorial challenges for cause. Second, the State has a strong interest in having jurors who are able to apply capital punishment within the framework state law prescribes. Third, to balance these interests, a juror who is substantially impaired in his or her ability to impose the death penalty under the state-law framework can be excused for cause; but if the juror is not substantially impaired, removal for cause is impermissible. Fourth, in determining whether the removal of a potential juror would vindicate the State's interest without violating the defendant's right, the trial court makes a judgment

> based in part on the demeanor of the juror, a judgment owed deference by reviewing courts.
>
> . . . Deference to the trial court is appropriate because it is in a position to assess the demeanor of the venire, and of the individuals who compose it, a factor of critical importance in assessing the attitude and qualifications of potential jurors.

Conviction-prone jury. In *Lockhart v. McCree*, 476 U.S. 162 (1986), the Supreme Court squarely faced a related question: whether *Witherspoon* and *Adams*, by excluding potential jurors with strong anti-death penalty sentiments, produced an unconstitutional conviction-prone jury. Assuming for purposes of argument that the voir dire process in capital cases does produce a "somewhat more" conviction-prone jury, the Court in *Lockhart* rejected the defendant's allegation that the "death-qualification" process violated the Sixth Amendment's cross-section requirement. The Court held that groups, such as "*Witherspoon* excludables," who are defined solely in terms of shared attitudes that would prevent or substantially impair their members from performing their duties as jurors, are not a "distinctive group" for purposes of the Sixth Amendment's fair cross-section requirement. Further, the fair cross-section requirement, according to *Lockhart*, applies only to the venire; it does not apply to petit juries and it does not guarantee that a particular petit jury will reflect the composition of the community at large. *Id.* at 180. Do you agree?

Racial impact of death qualification voir dire. Findings from a study of death qualification voir dire in capital cases show a tendency of death qualification to exclude a disproportionate percentage of African-American potential jurors. Aliza Cover, *The Eighth Amendment's Lost Jurors: Death Qualification and Evolving Standards of Decency*, 92 IND. L.J. 113 (2016).

Remedy for erroneous exclusion of capital juror. In *Gray v. Mississippi*, 481 U.S. 648 (1987), the Court held that the erroneous exclusion for cause of a capital juror because of that juror's anti-death penalty views is not subject to "harmless error" analysis. In other words, there should be an automatic reversal of any death sentence imposed by a jury from which a potential juror was excused in violation of *Witherspoon* and *Adams*.

The Court in *Ross v. Oklahoma*, 487 U.S. 81 (1988) held that *Gray* was limited to the erroneous exclusion of a juror; it did not apply to the erroneous seating of a pro-death juror who was later removed by peremptory challenge. The *Ross* Court noted, however, that the case would have been reversed had the pro-death juror been seated as a juror and had the defendant preserved the issue for appeal.

Problem 13-4. Are They Keepers?

You are a judge in a state murder case where the defendant is charged with shooting at a member of a rival gang in a drive-by shooting. A four-year-old child was killed by one of the bullets defendant allegedly fired during the event. At the capital trial, assess whether the following potential jurors should be dismissed for cause:

1. William Prentiss, a 22-year-old carpenter, answered a question that he thought that the defendant should take the stand and prove he is innocent.

Judge Wilson interjected, "Mr. Prentiss, the defendant does not have to take the stand or prove he is innocent. Do you understand this?" The record did not reflect anyone answered the judge's question.

The prosecutor then asked Prentiss if he understood that the government has the burden of proving each element of the crime beyond a reasonable doubt. Prentiss said, "That's OK with me."

The prosecutor then asked, "If the government failed to prove an element, wouldn't you acquit the defendant?" Prentiss responded, "Yep, if it's proven."

The prosecutor followed up with, "if the facts warrant it and the law permits it, could you join the other 11 jurors and vote guilty knowing it would lead to this man's death?" Prentiss replied, "Yep."

Prosecutor again, "Mr. Prentiss, can you be fair and impartial to both sides in this case." Prentiss said, "Yep, sir. But I want to know why and how he did it, killed that child."

a. Based solely on the above questions and answers, if you were defense counsel would you seek to have this juror excused for cause? Assuming you wanted this to occur, what questions would you ask?

b. If you were the prosecutor, how would you rehabilitate this juror so the court would not dismiss him for cause.

c. If you were the judge, would you dismiss juror Prentiss under *Adams* for cause? Would you ask more questions first? *See Franklin v. Anderson*, 434 F.3d 412 (6th Cir. 2006).

2. Catherine Crosby was a 53-year-old department store clerk. On voir dire, when asked by defense counsel whether she would lean toward a death penalty since a child was killed, she said, "I probably would, but can't say definitely."

a. Should the court dismiss juror Crosby for cause under the *Adams* approach?

b. If you were a prosecutor, what questions would you ask to "rehabilitate" this juror so the court would not dismiss her for cause (forcing the defense to use one of its precious peremptory challenges).

[7] Peremptory Challenges

As noted above, a potential juror may be excluded by two types of challenges: cause and peremptory. While a challenge for cause is based on something that makes the juror incapable of serving, a peremptory challenge is one that traditionally requires no articulated reason whatsoever. Whether based upon an objective reason falling short of excusal for cause or some intuitive judgment, the peremptory challenge is used when the lawyer believes that the juror might favor the opposing side or not favor his or her own side.

In general terms, a peremptory challenge is a way for the parties to achieve an impartial jury. Since the peremptory challenge is not guaranteed by the Constitution, jurisdictions have much leeway in fashioning the peremptory challenge process.

[a] Number of Peremptory Challenges

Number varies with severity of crime. Today, court rules or statutes often prescribe both the number of peremptory challenges and the procedures used to exercise them. In general terms, more peremptory challenges are permitted for more serious crimes. Often the two sides are given the same number of peremptory challenges. *See, e.g.,* Ariz. R. Crim. P. 18.4(c) (both sides get same number: 10 in capital cases, six in cases in Superior Court, two in non-record courts); Ill. Rev. Stat. ch. 38, para. 5/115-4 (defendant has 20 in capital case, 10 in other cases where imprisonment in penitentiary is possible, and five in all other cases; where there are multiple defendants, each has 12, 6, and 3, respectively; prosecution is allowed same number as all defendants combined).

More for defense. Sometimes the defense is given more than those allotted the prosecution. *E.g.,* Mich. Code Crim. P. 768.13 (in capital case, defendant has 20 peremptories, prosecutor has 15).

Trial judge's discretion to increase. In many jurisdictions the trial judge is given the discretion to increase the number of peremptory challenges in unusual cases, such as those that have engendered significant pretrial publicity. Additional peremptory challenges are usually provided in multi-defendant trials. *See, e.g.,* Ill. Rev. Stat.ch. 38, para. 5/115-4. The American Bar Association recommends that peremptory challenges should be allowed in all cases and in equal number to both sides. The court should have the authority to increase the number of peremptories when necessary. Standards for Criminal Justice § 15-2.6 (3d ed. 1996); Principles for Juries and Jury Trials, Prin. 11(D) (2005) (same).

Some jurisdictions require the party seeking additional peremptories (virtually always the defense) to establish prejudice without the additional challenges. *See, e.g., State v. Cruz,* 181 P.3d 196 (Ariz. 2008) (extensive media coverage merits additional peremptory challenges if defendant can show prejudice).

The federal approach is typical. Rule 24(b) allocates 20 peremptory challenges to each side in a death penalty case, six peremptories for the government and 10 peremptories for the defense in other felony trials, and three challenges for each side in trials involving crimes punishable by fine and/or imprisonment.

[b] Procedures for Peremptory Challenges

Jurisdictions differ markedly in the procedures used for the exercise of peremptory challenges. Because there is no constitutional right to peremptory challenges, the Court has held that states providing peremptory challenges confer a benefit "beyond the minimum requirements of fair jury selection,[] and thus retain discretion to design and implement their own systems." *Rivera v. Illinois*, 556 U.S. 148, 157–58 (2009). Ordinarily, peremptory challenges are made after challenges for cause have been made. Two of the most prevalent models are the "strike" and "challenge" approaches.

"Strike" system. One model, called the "strike" system, involves the selection of 12 jurors from the larger venire. Sometimes the entire venire or a portion of it is first questioned to determine if the members should be challenged for cause. Twelve (sometimes the number of alternate jurors and the number of peremptory challenges are added to the 12) potential jurors are then randomly selected from the venire and provisionally seated as jurors in the case. The judge (and sometimes counsel for both sides) interrogates these provisional jurors. Each side may then attempt to have one or more of the 12 potential jurors excused for cause. At this point, counsel for both sides are permitted to exercise peremptory challenges to remove any objectionable jurors remaining from the original panel of 12 provisional jurors. Jurors remaining after all challenges have been made are selected to try the case. In some jurisdictions a new provisional juror is seated immediately after a provisional juror has been "struck." This means that there are always 12 "provisional" jurors. The process continues until the jury panel has the requisite number of jurors. The American Bar Association recommends the strike system. PRINCIPLES FOR JURIES AND JURY TRIALS, Prin. 11(D)(4) (2005).

"Challenge" system. Under the "challenge" system, the prosecutor randomly selects 12 potential jurors from the venire, exercises challenges for cause and peremptory challenges, and arrives at a panel of 12. The defense then takes this potential panel, exercises its challenges for cause and peremptory challenges, and adds more jurors (subject, of course, to challenges) until the defense has a panel of 12. This panel is then examined by the prosecutor, who may challenge for cause or use peremptory challenges to pare the number lower than 12. The process continues until a panel of 12 jurors, acceptable to both the government and the defendant, is selected.

Anonymous exercise of peremptory challenges. A growing number of jurisdictions have adopted procedures to ensure that potential jurors do not know which side exercised a peremptory challenge. This approach is designed to avoid any adverse reactions to a side's decision to excuse a particular juror. *See* PRINCIPLES FOR JURIES AND JURY TRIALS, Prin. 11(E)(1) (2005) (all challenges to potential jurors should be addressed to the court outside the presence of the jury, so jury panel is not aware of nature or basis of challenge or party making challenge).

[c] Grounds for Peremptory Challenges

Traditionally, there were no legal limits on the grounds for exercising peremptory challenges. Sometimes this vague approach was summarized as permitting a peremptory challenge "for any reason or no reason." Lawyers often used hunches based on experience to decide whether to accept or exclude a particular juror. The details of a case may suggest whether a particular potential juror should be excluded by peremptory challenge. Sometimes the reasons for exercising a peremptory challenge reflect the lawyer's hunches about a juror's predisposition. *See, e.g.*, Shamena Anwar et al., *The Role of Age in Jury Selection and Trial Outcomes*, 57 J. L. & ECON. 1001 (2014) (prosecutors more likely to use peremptory challenges to exclude younger potential jurors, and defense attorneys are more likely to exclude older potential jurors, who are more likely to convict). For example, some prosecutors would not accept a juror who wore a bow tie (too independent), or who belonged to a certain ethnic group (too liberal) or the same racial or religious group as the defendant (too likely to identify with the defendant). Similarly, some criminal defense lawyers would use peremptory challenges to exclude potential jurors with a law enforcement background (too likely to believe police officer witnesses) or a government job (too likely to believe in "the system" and feel threatened by criminals). The next case established a "new" tradition.

Batson v. Kentucky

476 U.S. 79 (1986)

JUSTICE POWELL delivered the opinion of the Court.

This case requires us to reexamine that portion of *Swain v. Alabama*, 380 U.S. 202 (1965), concerning the evidentiary burden placed on a criminal defendant who claims that he has been denied equal protection through the State's use of peremptory challenges to exclude members of his race from the petit jury.

Petitioner, a black man, was indicted in Kentucky on charges of second-degree burglary and receipt of stolen goods. On the first day of trial in Jefferson Circuit Court, the judge conducted voir dire examination of the venire, excused certain jurors for cause, and permitted the parties to exercise peremptory challenges. The prosecutor used his peremptory challenges to strike all four black persons on the venire, and a jury composed only of white persons was selected. Defense counsel moved to discharge the jury before it was sworn on the ground that the prosecutor's removal of the black veniremen violated petitioner's rights under the Sixth and Fourteenth Amendments to a jury drawn from a cross section of the community, and under the Fourteenth Amendment to equal protection of the laws. Counsel requested a hearing on his motion. Without expressly ruling on the request for a hearing, the trial judge observed that the parties were entitled to use their peremptory challenges to "strike anybody they want to." The judge then denied petitioner's motion, reasoning that the cross-section requirement applies only to selection of the venire and not to selection of the petit jury itself.

[After being convicted on both counts, petitioner appealed to the Kentucky Supreme Court, alleging that the prosecutor's use of peremptory challenges violated the Sixth Amendment cross-section requirement, the Kentucky Constitution, and the Equal Protection Clause's prohibition of a pattern of racially discriminatory peremptory challenges. The Kentucky Supreme Court affirmed, holding that a fair cross-section argument must establish systematic exclusion of a group of jurors from the venire rather than from a single jury.] We granted certiorari and now reverse.

In *Swain v. Alabama*, this Court recognized that a "State's purposeful or deliberate denial to Negroes on account of race of participation as jurors in the administration of justice violates the Equal Protection Clause." We reaffirm the principle today.

... [T]he State's privilege to strike individual jurors through peremptory challenges, is subject to the commands of the Equal Protection Clause. Although a prosecutor ordinarily is entitled to exercise permitted peremptory challenges "for any reason at all, as long as that reason is related to his view concerning the outcome" of the case to be tried, the Equal Protection Clause forbids the prosecutor to challenge potential jurors solely on account of their race or on the assumption that black jurors as a group will be unable impartially to consider the State's case against a black defendant.

... [A] defendant may establish a prima facie case of purposeful discrimination in selection of the petit jury solely on evidence concerning the prosecutor's exercise of peremptory challenges at the defendant's trial. To establish such a case, the defendant first must show that he is a member of a cognizable racial group, and that the prosecutor has exercised peremptory challenges to remove from the venire members of the defendant's race. Second, the defendant is entitled to rely on the fact, as to which there can be no dispute, that peremptory challenges constitute a jury selection practice that permits "those to discriminate who are of a mind to discriminate." *Avery v. Georgia*, 345 U.S. at 562. Finally, the defendant must show that these facts and any other relevant circumstances raise an inference that the prosecutor used that practice to exclude the veniremen from the petit jury on account of their race. This combination of factors in the empaneling of the petit jury, as in the selection of the venire, raises the necessary inference of purposeful discrimination.

In deciding whether the defendant has made the requisite showing, the trial court should consider all relevant circumstances. For example, a "pattern" of strikes against black jurors included in the particular venire might give rise to an inference of discrimination. Similarly, the prosecutor's questions and statements during voir dire examination and in exercising his challenges may support or refute an inference of discriminatory purpose. These examples are merely illustrative. We have confidence that trial judges, experienced in supervising voir dire, will be able to decide if the circumstances concerning the prosecutor's use of peremptory challenges creates a prima facie case of discrimination against black jurors.

Once the defendant makes a prima facie showing, the burden shifts to the State to come forward with a neutral explanation for challenging black jurors. Though this requirement imposes a limitation in some cases on the full peremptory character of the historic challenge, we emphasize that the prosecutor's explanation need not rise to the level justifying exercise of a challenge for cause. But the prosecutor may not rebut the defendant's prima facie case of discrimination by stating merely that he challenged jurors of the defendant's race on the assumption—or his intuitive judgment—that they would be partial to the defendant because of their shared race.... The prosecutor therefore must articulate a neutral explanation related to the particular case to be tried. The trial court then will have the duty to determine if the defendant has established purposeful discrimination.

... While we recognize, of course, that the peremptory challenge occupies an important position in our trial procedures, we do not agree that our decision today will undermine the contribution the challenge generally makes to the administration of justice. The reality of practice, amply reflected in many state-and federal-court opinions, shows that the challenge may be, and unfortunately at times has been, used to discriminate against black jurors. By requiring trial courts to be sensitive to the racially discriminatory use of peremptory challenges, our decision enforces the mandate of equal protection and furthers the ends of justice. In view of the heterogeneous population of our Nation, public respect for our criminal justice system and the rule of law will be strengthened if we ensure that no citizen is disqualified from jury service because of his race.

... In those States applying a version of the evidentiary standard we recognize today, courts have not experienced serious administrative burdens, and the peremptory challenge system has survived. We decline, however, to formulate particular procedures to be followed upon a defendant's timely objection to a prosecutor's challenges.[24]

In this case, petitioner made a timely objection to the prosecutor's removal of all black persons on the venire. Because the trial court flatly rejected the objection without requiring the prosecutor to give an explanation for his action, we remand this case for further proceedings. If the trial court decides that the facts establish, prima facie, purposeful discrimination and the prosecutor does not come forward with a neutral explanation for his action, our precedents require that petitioner's conviction be reversed.

Justice Marshall, concurring.

... The decision today will not end the racial discrimination that peremptories inject into the jury-selection process. That goal can be accomplished only by eliminating peremptory challenges entirely.

... The inherent potential of peremptory challenges to distort the jury process by permitting the exclusion of jurors on racial grounds should ideally lead the Court to ban them entirely from the criminal justice system....

Justice Rehnquist, with whom The Chief Justice joins, dissenting.

... In my view, there is simply nothing "unequal" about the State's using its peremptory challenges to strike blacks from the jury in cases involving black

24. In light of the variety of jury selection practices followed in our state and federal trial courts, we make no attempt to instruct these courts how best to implement our holding today. For the same reason, we express no view on whether it is more appropriate in a particular case, upon a finding of discrimination against black jurors, for the trial court to discharge the venire and select a new jury from a panel not previously associated with the case, or to disallow the discriminatory challenges and resume selection with the improperly challenged jurors reinstated on the venire.

defendants, so long as such challenges are also used to exclude whites in cases involving white defendants, Hispanics in cases involving Hispanic defendants, Asians in cases involving Asian defendants, and so on. This case-specific use of peremptory challenges by the State does not single out blacks, or members of any other race for that matter, for discriminatory treatment. Such use of peremptories is at best based upon seat-of-the-pants instincts, which are undoubtedly crudely stereotypical and may in many cases be hopelessly mistaken. But as long as they are applied across-the-board to jurors of all races and nationalities, I do not see—and the Court most certainly has not explained—how their use violates the Equal Protection Clause.

Nor does such use of peremptory challenges by the State infringe upon any other constitutional interests. The Court does not suggest that exclusion of blacks from the jury through the State's use of peremptory challenges results in a violation of either the fair-cross-section or impartiality component of the Sixth Amendment. And because the case-specific use of peremptory challenges by the State does not deny blacks the right to serve as jurors in cases involving nonblack defendants, it harms neither the excluded jurors nor the remainder of the community.

[The dissenting opinion of Chief Justice Berger and the concurring opinions of JUSTICES WHITE, STEVENS, and O'CONNOR are omitted.]

Notes

1. *Standing expanded to non-members of excluded group.* Recall that *Batson* was an equal protection case involving a black defendant who objected to a prosecutor's use of peremptory challenges to exclude potential black jurors. Subsequent decisions have dealt with other racial and ethnic combinations. In *Powers v. Ohio*, 499 U.S. 400 (1991), the Supreme Court applied *Batson* to a case where the prosecutor exercised peremptory challenges to exclude six black potential jurors in the trial of a white defendant. The Court noted that *Batson* was based in part on the Equal Protection Clause's role in recognizing the potential juror's opportunity to participate in the administration of the criminal justice system. Thus, the defendant has standing to enforce the juror's equal protection right to serve even if he or she is not the same race as those excluded.

2. *Extended to defense challenges. Batson* dealt with a *prosecutor's* use of race-based peremptory challenges. Although several of the *Batson* Justices opined that the equal protection analysis applied as well to race-based peremptory challenges by *defense counsel*, the matter was not finally resolved until *Georgia v. McCollum*, 505 U.S. 42 (1992). The Court held that the Equal Protection Clause bars defense counsel from using race-based peremptory challenges, reasoning along lines suggested in *Powers* that the Equal Protection Clause protects potential jurors from discrimination on the basis of race.

3. *Civil cases.* Although the focus in this section is *Batson*'s impact upon the conduct of jury selection in criminal cases, it is noteworthy that the Court also held that *Batson* applies equally to civil cases. *Edmonson v. Leesville Concrete Co.*, 500 U.S. 614 (1991).

4. *Gender. Batson* held that the Equal Protection Clause barred race-based peremptory challenges. But what about the validity of peremptory challenges based on classifications other than race?

In *J.E.B. v. Alabama ex rel. T.B.*, 511 U.S. 127 (1994), the Supreme Court held that *Batson*'s equal protection analysis forbids intentional discrimination on the basis of gender. *J.E.B.* involved a civil paternity case where the state used its peremptory challenges to remove male potential jurors, leaving an all-female jury. The Supreme Court specifically rejected arguments that gender-based peremptory challenges are permissible because members of one sex may be more sympathetic to a particular party or argument. According to the Supreme Court, such gender-based stereotypes are barred as a justification for the exercise of peremptory challenges.

The *J.E.B.* decision was careful to note, however, that it was not eliminating all peremptory challenges. Such challenges are permissible to secure a fair trial. Moreover,

> [p]arties may also exercise their peremptory challenges to remove from the venire any group or class of individuals normally subject to "rational basis" review. Even strikes based on characteristics that are disproportionately associated with one gender could be appropriate, absent a showing of pretext.

Id. at 143.

5. *Standard to assess whether a "group" is covered by* Batson. Standards utilized in deciding whether a particular group is subject to equal protection under *Batson* are unclear. One court held that a *Batson* challenge could succeed if the proponent proves that the group is definable and limited by a clearly definable factor; a common thread of attitudes, ideas or experiences runs through the group; and there exists a community of interests among the members such that the group's interest cannot be adequately represented if the group is excluded from the jury selection process. *United States v. Sgro*, 816 F.2d 30 (1st Cir. 1987), *cert. denied*, 484 U.S. 1063 (1988) (Italian-Americans are not cognizable racial group).

6. *Groups covered by* Batson. *Batson* has been held to apply to the other groups. *See, e.g., Hernandez v. New York*, 500 U.S. 352 (1991) (Latinos or Hispanics); *United States v. Mitchell*, 502 F.3d 931 (9th Cir. 2007) (Native Americans); *Fields v. People*, 732 P.2d 1145 (Colo. 1987) (Spanish surnamed people).

7. *Groups not covered by* Batson. In contrast, other courts have held certain groups outside *Batson*'s limitations. *See, e.g. J.E.B. v. Alabama, ex rel. T.B.*, 511 U.S. 127 (1994) (persons with military experience [disproportionately men] and nurses [disproportionately women]); *United States v. Watson*, 483 F.3d 750, 754 (10th Cir. 2007) (disability); *United States v. Maxwell*, 473 F.3d 868, 872 (8th Cir. 2007) (teacher).

8. *Rational basis review.* Some courts have also held that groups subject to "rational basis" review fall outside *Batson*'s limitations. *See, e.g., United States v. Watson*, 483 F.3d 828 (D.C. Cir. 2007) (disability); *Webber v. Strippit*, 186 F.3d 907 (8th Cir.

1999) (age). *But see* Mary Lynch, *The Application of Equal Protection to Prospective Jurors with Disabilities: Will Batson Cover Disability-Based Strikes*, 57 Alb. L. Rev. 289 (1993) (discussing the confusion about whether and how to apply *Batson*'s equal protection analysis beyond race and arguing it should be extended to cover those with disabilities).

9. *Religion.* In *State v. Davis*, 504 N.W.2d 767 (Minn. 1993), the Minnesota Supreme Court held that *Batson* does not apply to religion-based challenges. The United States Supreme Court denied a writ of certiorari, but a dissenting opinion authored by Justice Thomas maintained that "no principled reason immediately appears for declining to apply *Batson* to any strike based on a classification that is accorded heightened scrutiny under the Equal Protection Clause." *Davis v. Minnesota*, 511 U.S. 1115, 1117 (1994).

In *United States v. Somerstein*, 959 F. Supp. 592 (E.D.N.Y. 1997), the United States District Court adopted Justice Thomas' reasoning, and held that *Batson* applies to religious classifications (in that particular case, persons of the Jewish faith). But the *Somerstein* court noted:

> [B]efore a Court applies *Batson* to a challenge on religious grounds, there must be a determination as to whether the religion of the juror is relevant to the issues of the case. Generally, the religion of a juror is not relevant to the jury selection process, in the legal sense. . . . In this case, the defendants are kosher caterers specializing in making kosher affairs, and they are accused of criminal conduct in connection with an alleged scheme to defraud their employees' benefit funds. Based on the particular and unique facts of this case, in which, arguably, the religious element is intertwined in the criminal charges, the Court rules that the religion of the jurors would be relevant as a foundation for a *Batson* challenge.

Id. at 595–596.

10. *Eliminating Peremptory Challenges?* Justice Marshall's *Batson* concurrence cautioned that race-based and gender-based discrimination would survive *Batson* and the continued use of peremptory challenges. He advocated abolition of peremptory challenges. Twenty years later, in *Rice v. Collins*, 546 U.S. 333 (2006), Justices Breyer and Souter agreed that Justice Marshall's view had been proven correct. If peremptory challenges were no longer available, would or should their demise alter the nature or number of challenges for cause?

[d] Batson *Step One: Prima Facie Case*

Recall that *Batson* held that the person claiming an equal protection violation must first establish a prima facie case of purposeful discrimination. A successful showing raises an inference of purposeful discrimination.

There are many ways of establishing a prima facie case. Courts look at all the facts to assess whether there is an inference of purposeful discrimination. These include such facts as the questions and statements made during voir dire of all potential jurors, the pattern of peremptory challenges (including how potential jurors who answered questions the same way were treated), the nature and facts of the crime, statements and actions inferring motivation, the race (or other minority status) of the defendant and the victim and the witnesses, and the composition of the venire and the jury that was actually seated. Generally, no single factor is dispositive.

An obvious example of a prima facie case is a prosecutor who uses peremptory challenges to exclude only black jurors. But a challenge to the only Hispanic on the venire also may be sufficient. *See United States v. De Gross*, 913 F.2d 1417 (9th Cir. 1990) (prima facie case established where Hispanic defendant was charged with illegal importation of Mexicans and prosecutor used peremptory challenge to remove only Hispanic on the jury).

Most decisions indicate that a prima facie case is not established when any black jurors sit on the trial jury. *See, e.g., United States v. Dawn*, 897 F.2d 1444 (8th Cir. 1990) (prosecutor used six of seven peremptory challenges to exclude blacks; no prima facie case); *United States v. Dennis*, 804 F.2d 1208 (11th Cir. 1986) (prosecutor used four peremptory challenges, three of which excluded blacks; no prima facie case because two black jurors were not excluded although government had remaining peremptory challenges; no inference of purposeful discrimination).

Standard of prima facie. Is it permissible for a state to require at step one (prima facie case) that the objecting party must show that it is "more likely than not" that the other party's peremptory challenges, if unexplained, were based on impermissible group bias? In *Johnson v. California*, 545 U.S. 162 (2005), the U.S. Supreme Court held that such a standard was "at odds with the prima facie inquiry mandated by *Batson*." Turning to the facts of this case, the Court found that a prima facie case had been established where the prosecutor removed all three prospective black jurors peremptorily.

[e] Batson *Step Two: Neutral Explanation or Pretext*

Once the defendant has offered a prima facie case, under *Batson* the burden shifts to the government to offer a race neutral explanation. The government need not present its reasons until after a prima facie case has been made and many prosecutors delay giving such reasons because they do not want to give the defense information that the defense could use to bolster the prima facie proof. However, to facilitate appellate review, some appellate courts strongly recommend that the prosecutor offer an explanation even if the defense does not make out a prima facie case. *See, e.g., People v. Zambrano*, 163 P.3d 4 (Cal. 2007).

One of the main practical problems is assessing the constitutional validity of an explanation given for excluding members of identifiable groups from a jury. The concern is whether the lawyer's "neutral" explanation is actually pretextual—i.e., a race-neutral reason given to cover the true race-based justification for exclusion of certain potential jurors.

In *Hernandez v. New York*, 500 U.S. 352 (1991), the government used four peremptory challenges to exclude potential Latino jurors. The prosecutor said that he excluded two of them because he was uncertain whether they would be able to accept a Spanish interpreter's official translation since both possible jurors spoke Spanish themselves. Following *Batson*'s three-step analysis (defendant's prima facie showing of race-based peremptory challenge, prosecutor's burden of establishing a race-neutral explanation, and defendant's burden of proving purposeful discrimination), the Court, without a majority opinion, upheld the use of the peremptory challenges. Noting that *Batson* held that the trial court's decision on discriminatory intent is to be accorded great deference by appellate courts, Justice Kennedy's plurality opinion in *Hernandez* found that the trial court was not clearly erroneous when it decided that the prosecutor's reason for excluding the two Latino jurors was not pretextual.

Hernandez is important for two reasons. First, it demonstrates how much deference is given to the trial court's decision on whether the prosecutor used a race-based motive. Second, it illustrates the importance of establishing discriminatory intent under *Batson*. There is no doubt that the two jurors were excused because their Latin heritage made them fluent in Spanish. But since they were excused because of their language skills rather than their ethnicity, the Supreme Court upheld the jury selection process. *Hernandez* focused upon the question whether the prosecutor's proffered reason for excluding jurors was pretextual.

Notes

1. *I can't remember.* What if the defendant makes out a prima facie case (step one) and the burden then shifts to the prosecutor (step two) who cannot recall why the peremptory challenge at issue was made? In *Yee v. Duncan*, 463 P.3d 893 (9th Cir. 2006), the court held that the lack of explanation is evidence of purposeful discrimination, but the defendant must still meet the step three burden of establishing the motive for the challenge. Looking at the entire record, the *Yee* court found that there was a neutral explanation for the use of the peremptory challenge (the juror had served previously on a jury that considered an issue somewhat similar to one in the instant case).

2. *Illustrations of race neutral explanations.* An informal survey of recent cases found the following to be accepted as race neutral explanations for a peremptory challenge of a member of a distinctive group: prior shoplifting conviction, concerns juror could grasp intricacies of accomplice liability, juror had eyes closed during part of voir dire, juror had son who she thought had been mistreated by the justice system, juror appeared upset during selection process, juror's answers to written questionnaire differed from answers given in court during voir dire and raised questions about juror's mental capacities, and a juror's experience as a counselor.

Perhaps the best example of the variety of acceptable excuses is presented by two cases. In one, both the trial and appellate courts approved a peremptory exercised because a potential juror avoided eye contact with the prosecution. *United States v. Cartlidge*, 808 F.2d 1064 (5th Cir. 1987). In the other, the trial and appellate courts upheld a peremptory challenge that was based on a potential juror's too frequent eye contact. *United States v. Mathews*, 803 F.2d 325 (7th Cir. 1986) ("[H]e spent a great deal of time examining me in a way which I felt was in the end becoming rather hostile."). Other reasonable explanations may include a juror's work with substance abusers, lack of education, or difficulty answering questions. *Rodriguez v. Senkowski*, 2004 U.S. Dist. LEXIS 3975 (S.D.N.Y. 2004)

[f] Batson *Step Three: Purposeful Discrimination*

Step three of *Batson* involves an assessment of whether, considering the government's "neutral explanation" (step two), there was purposeful discrimination. The burden is on the party (the defendant ordinarily) objecting to the use of the peremptory challenge. If the prosecutor's "neutral explanation" is considered to be pretextual, there is an "inference of discriminatory content." *Snyder v. Louisiana*, 552 U.S. 472, 485 (2008).

In *Miller-El v. Dretke*, 545 U.S. 231 (2005), the Supreme Court rejected the state court's conclusion that the prosecutor did not violate *Batson* when only one of the 20 black members of the 108-person panel served as a juror, and 10 were excused by the state's peremptory challenges. Justice Souter wrote for the majority.

> If a prosecutor's proffered reason for striking a black panelist applies just as well to an otherwise-similar nonblack who is permitted to serve, that is evidence tending to prove purposeful discrimination to be considered at *Batson's* third step. . . .
>
> The prosecution used its second peremptory strike to exclude Billy Jean Fields, a black man who expressed unwavering support for the death penalty. . . . [The Prosecutor] represented that Fields said he would not vote for death if rehabilitation was possible. . . . If, indeed, Fields's thoughts on rehabilitation did make the prosecutor uneasy, he should have worried about a number of white panel members he accepted with no evident reservations. . . . [N]onblack jurors whose remarks on rehabilitation could well have signaled a limit on their willingness to impose a death sentence were not questioned further and drew no objection, but the prosecution expressed apprehension about a black juror's belief in the possibility of reformation even though he repeatedly stated his approval of the death penalty and testified that he could impose it according to state legal standards even when the alternative sentence of life imprisonment would give a defendant (like everyone else in the world) the opportunity to reform. . . .
>
> In sum, when we look for nonblack jurors similarly situated to Fields, we find strong similarities as well as some differences. But the differences seem far from significant, particularly when we read Fields's *voir dire* testimony in its entirety. Upon that reading, Fields should have been an ideal juror in the eyes of a prosecutor seeking a death sentence, and the prosecutors' explanations for the strike cannot reasonably be accepted. . . .
>
> . . . The next body of evidence that the State was trying to avoid black jurors is the contrasting *voir dire* questions posed respectively to black

> and nonblack panel members, on two different subjects. First, there were the prosecutors' statements preceding questions about a potential juror's thoughts on capital punishment. Some of these prefatory statements were cast in general terms, but some followed the so-called graphic script, describing the method of execution in rhetorical and clinical detail. It is intended, Miller–El contends, to prompt some expression of hesitation to consider the death penalty and thus to elicit plausibly neutral grounds for a peremptory strike of a potential juror subjected to it, if not a strike for cause. If the graphic script is given to a higher proportion of blacks than whites, this is evidence that prosecutors more often wanted blacks off the jury, absent some neutral and extenuating explanation. . . . Of the 10 non-blacks whose questionnaires expressed ambivalence or opposition, only 30% received the graphic treatment. But of the seven blacks who expressed ambivalence or opposition, 86% heard the graphic script. As between the State's ambivalence explanation and Miller–El's racial one, race is much the better, and the reasonable inference is that race was the major consideration when the prosecution chose to follow the graphic script.

Id. at 241, 242, 245, 247, 255, 260.

Notes

1. *Prosecutor's challenges generally upheld.* Trial and appellate courts rarely find that a prosecutor's decision to remove a juror through the exercise of a peremptory challenge was motivated by discriminatory intent. Courts tend to accept prosecutors' "neutral explanations" to justify striking jurors. Some courts even presume that the prosecution used the challenges in a constitutional manner. *See, e.g., People v. Zambrano*, 163 P.3d 4 (Cal. 2007). *But see Foster v. Chatman*, 136 S. Ct. 1737 (2016) (reversing conviction because prosecutor in capital case used peremptory challenges to exclude all four black jurors; providing detailed analysis of impermissible reasons for exclusion of each juror and rejecting the proffered race-neutral reasons).

Reasoned basis. Given the fact that a prosecutor will not readily admit an outright violation of *Batson*, upon what bases may courts conclude that a prosecutor acted with a discriminatory purpose? The explanation offered must present a reasoned basis for the juror's removal. *See, e.g., United States v. Horsley*, 864 F.2d 1543 (11th Cir. 1989) (prosecutor struck only black juror; only explanation was that he "just got a feeling about him"; *Batson* held to be violated); *see also People v. Jackson*, 623 N.Y.S.2d 881 (App. Div. 1995) (*Batson* violation where prosecutor's reasons for challenging juror was that he did not "feel comfortable" with her and because juror worked as a counselor who assisted the unemployed in finding jobs she might be unduly sympathetic towards the unemployed defendant; the court determined these arguments to be vague and unrelated to the case since the defendant's employment status would not be introduced into the case and such status did not relate to the specific circumstances of the case).

In *Snyder v. Louisiana*, 552 U.S. 472 (2008), the prosecutor used peremptory challenges to remove all five black jurors. Noting that *Batson* would be violated if even one juror were struck for racial reasons, the Supreme Court reversed a murder conviction because one black juror was removed, according to the prosecutor, because he seemed "nervous" and was a student teacher concerned about missing some mandatory training. The Supreme Court discounted the "nervous" explanation for lack of a lower court finding, then reversed because of the student-teaching explanation. Noting that the record simply did not support the conclusion that the standard teaching duties were of significant concern to the juror, the Supreme Court held sufficient evidence of discriminatory intent, based on the prosecutor's implausible explanations, to merit overturning the conviction.

Only striking some members of distinctive group while accepting others. When a lawyer uses one or more peremptory challenges to excuse member(s) of a distinctive group but does not use them to strike other members of the same group so that the trial jury does have members of this group, many courts view this as an indication that the lawyer did not act with discriminatory purpose, especially if the lawyer did not use all of his or her peremptory challenges. On the other hand, when the juror who is struck is the only member of a distinctive group, courts are often skeptical of the justification for the action, though it may be upheld if a good reason is given for the strike.

[g] Procedural Issues in Implementing Batson

Timing of Batson *objection.* Another issue is when a *Batson*-based issue must be raised. Some jurisdictions require counsel to make *Batson* objections after the jury is selected and before the jurors are sworn in order to allow the trial judge to cure the problem and ensure that the jury is properly selected. The United States Supreme Court has characterized this as a "sensible rule." *Ford v. Georgia*, 498 U.S. 411 (1991).

Record of violation. In order to launch a successful *Batson* challenge, there must be a record sufficient to establish a prima facie case. Counsel should ensure that the record accurately reflects the races of both the jurors who were seated and excluded as well as documenting other characteristics given as grounds for exclusion, questions that were asked of the jurors on voir dire, information about the jurors available to the party who excluded them, and any other information about the reasons for the use of peremptory challenges. While the record must be sufficient, it need not be perfect. For strikes based on the potential juror's demeanor, the trial judge may sustain the strike even if the judge did not personally observe the objectionable demeanor that precipitated a lawyer's exercise of a peremptory challenge. *Thaler v. Haynes*, 559 U.S. 43 (2010) (upholding peremptory challenge of juror whose demeanor was "somewhat humorous" and "not serious," and whose body language "had belied her 'true feeling.'"). For an article suggesting that the voir dire process be videotaped in order to provide a record for assessing such neutral reasons as "eye contact," *see* Mimi Samuel, *Focusing on* Batson: *Let the Cameras Roll*, 74 Brook. L. Rev. 95(2008).

Deprivation of peremptory challenge: erroneous denial of challenge for cause. What if the court erroneously denies a challenge for cause for Juror X and therefore forces the defendant to exercise a peremptory challenge to exclude that juror? If the defendant uses all available peremptory challenges, the court's erroneous decision on Juror X essentially deprives the defendant of the opportunity to use a peremptory challenge against Juror Y. Although this judicial error may force the defendant to be tried by a juror who would otherwise have been excluded, the Supreme Court in *Ross v. Oklahoma*, 481 U.S. 81 (1988), held that the error is not of constitutional dimension. The focus must be on whether the 12 jurors who heard the case were impartial. "So long as the jury that sits is impartial, the fact that the defendant had to use a peremptory challenge to achieve that result does not mean the Sixth Amendment was violated." *See also United States v. Martinez-Salazar*, 528 U. S. 304 (2000) (same as *Ross* under Federal Rule 24(b)). *Martinez-Salazar* held that reversal may be appropriate if the trial court deliberately misapplied the law to force the defendants to use a peremptory challenge or if the final jury included a juror who should have been excluded for cause.

Deprivation of peremptory challenge: wrongful denial. Just as the Constitution is probably not violated by the erroneous denial of a challenge for cause, it is also not likely to be infringed by the wrongful denial of a peremptory challenge. In *Rivera v. Illinois*, 556 U.S. 148 (2009), a state trial judge erroneously refused to permit the defense to use one of its peremptory challenges to exclude a particular juror. The judge mistakenly ruled that the exclusion of the female African-American juror would violate *Batson* because of race and gender discrimination. Noting that the U.S. Constitution does not require peremptory challenges, the Supreme Court held that the wrongful denial of a peremptory challenge, by itself, does not offend the Constitution. State law determines the consequences of the wrongful denial. Accordingly, the defendant's conviction was upheld by the U.S. Supreme Court because under Illinois law the defendant could obtain a reversal only by showing prejudice, which was impossible because the jury that convicted the defendant was fully qualified and its members were not subject to challenge for cause.

Wrongful granting of peremptory challenge. When a court erroneously accepts a *Batson* challenge, thus seating a juror despite adversary counsel's attempts to exclude the juror by exercising a peremptory challenge, many courts ask whether the jury that was seated was fair. If so, the *Batson* error is ignored. Other courts, however, reverse a conviction on the theory that the jury, including the juror who should have been excluded by a peremptory challenge, was sufficiently tainted to deny the accused a fair trial. *See, e.g., State v. Edwards*, 682 S.E.2d 820 (S.C. 2009).

Need to use all peremptory challenges. In some jurisdictions, an accused, arguing that the conviction was rendered by a jury that was not impartial, may appeal the presence of an objectionable juror only if the accused had used all available peremptory challenges and was therefore unable to exclude the objectionable juror. This process is viewed as fair because it requires the accused to take positive steps to ensure the jury was impartial. The Supreme Court has approved state law following this process, *Ross v. Oklahoma*, 487 U.S. 81, 90 (1988), but has refused to require it as a prerequisite to a claim that the accused was denied a fair trial because forced to use a peremptory challenge to remove a juror who should have been removed for cause. *United States v. Martinez-Salazar*, 528 U. S. 304 (2000).

Problem 13-5. The Lawyer's Craft or the Crafty Lawyer

In the last 14 years, Assistant District Attorney Vickie Miles has conducted approximately 100 jury trials. She was assigned the prosecution of Frank Benton, a 39-year-old, white, unemployed construction worker, charged with robbing a K Mart of $2700. The robber wore a paper bag on his head with large eye holes cut out. Defendant Benton claims that he was not the robber. He maintains that the afternoon of the crime he was asleep at his girlfriend's apartment. The girlfriend will probably corroborate the alibi. The K Mart clerk, the victim of the robbery, has identified Benton, who briefly removed the bag from his head when he jumped into his car and drove away. Benton was found with $1700 cash in his pocket. Benton and the clerk are white.

During jury selection, prosecutor Miles used only six of her eight peremptory challenges. Five of the six excused black jurors. The sixth excused a white lawyer. The jury that was selected included 10 white jurors and two black jurors. The county was 38% black. The venire was 35% black.

Defense counsel cited *Batson* in challenging the prosecutor's use of the peremptory challenges.

1. Based solely on the above information, has the defense established a prima facie case under *Batson*? If not, what additional information would make this a prima facie case?

Would your answers change if the defendant Benton was black instead of white? If the K Mart witness was black? Why should the race of the defendant or the witnesses matter under *Batson*? Is the race of the *prosecutor* relevant?

2. Assuming that a prima facie case were established, assess the acceptability of the following explanations given by Assistant District Attorney Miles for dismissing the five black jurors:

a. "Juror A was a 32-year-old construction worker. I felt that he would identify too closely with the defendant because of the similarities in their age and occupation."

b. "Juror B had this Afro hairstyle. My experience is that I have a hard time convincing this type of person, irrespective of the race of the people in the case."

c. "Juror C dropped out of school in the fourth grade, was working as a dishwasher, and I felt that he could not understand the issues in the case."

d. "Juror D, a 50-year-old mechanical engineer, had a traffic ticket last year. Although he stated that it would not affect his view of law enforcement, I felt that he would be hostile to our police witnesses who worked for the same police department that gave Juror D a ticket last year. My experience is that engineers don't like it when a cop pulls them over, blue lights flashing, and gives them a hard time about speeding."

e. "I have been trying cases for a long time. I have interviewed literally thousands of jurors, have spent thousands of hours discussing jury selection with other prosecutors, have attended many seminars on the issue, and have watched many juries perform. In my professional opinion, based on my intuition that has proven to be right on many occasions, I felt that Juror E would be prone to accept this phony alibi defense. He just seemed to me to be a bit gullible. I don't know what it was. There was something about the way he answered the question and looked around the room."

Would your answer change if the prosecutor said that she excluded Juror E because the research she read showed that black jurors are more likely to favor the defense (irrespective of the defendant's race) and disbelieve white police officers (the officers in this case are all white) than are white jurors? Assume *arguendo* that the prosecutor has correctly summarized the available research.

[8] Ethical Issues

Defense attorneys and prosecutors have the opportunity to learn jurors' names and addresses and question them for possible bias. Accordingly, there is always a possibility that the defense lawyer (or defendant) or prosecutor could attempt to influence the juror's performance or unwittingly harass the juror or the juror's family. For example, someone could attempt to sway a potential juror's view of the case so that, if selected, the person would favor one side. A number of ethical rules specifically prohibit lawyers from engaging in such conduct.

The American Bar Association's various professional guidelines specifically limit lawyers in their dealings with both potential and actual jurors. Contact with potential jurors is severely restricted. The Standards of Criminal Justice state that when pretrial investigation of possible jurors is conducted, defense counsel should ensure that the jurors are not harassed or unduly embarrassed, and their privacy is respected. Whenever possible, the investigation should be restricted to existing records and sources of information. Standards of Criminal Justice §4-7.3(c)(4th ed. 2005). Disciplinary Rule 7-108(A) of the Model Code of Professional Responsibility also addresses the issue of contact with *potential* jurors.

> Before the trial of a case a lawyer connected therewith shall not communicate with or cause another to communicate with anyone he knows to be a member of the venire from which the jury will be selected for the trial of the case.

A similar rule bars contact with jurors *during trial.*

During the trial of a case:

> (1) A lawyer connected therewith shall not communicate with or cause another to communicate with any member of the jury.

> (2) A lawyer who is not connected therewith shall not communicate with or cause another to communicate with a juror concerning the case.

Model Code of Prof'l Responsibility DR 7-108(B). *See also* Standards for Criminal Justice § 4-7.3 (3d ed. 1993) (defense counsel should not intentionally communicate privately with potential or impaneled jurors; the reality or appearance of such communications should be avoided). *Id.* § 3-6.3 (same for prosecutor); Principles for Juries and Jury Trials, Prin. 13(E) (4th ed. 2005) (during trial, jurors should be instructed that parties are permitted to communicate with jurors only in open court with opposing parties present).

The Model Code of Professional Responsibility also prohibits conduct that directly or indirectly causes a vexatious or harassing investigation of a venireperson, juror, or a member of either's family. Model Code of Prof'l Responsibility DR 7-108(E). A lawyer must also report to the court any improper conduct towards or by a juror or venireperson. *Id.* at DR 7-108(G).

The Model Rules of Professional Conduct are far less specific than either the Model Code or the Standards for Criminal Justice. The Model Rules simply provide that a lawyer shall not influence or communicate with a prospective or sitting juror by illegal means. Model Rules of Prof'l Conduct r. 3.5 (1983).

G. Removal of Juror

Sometimes unexpected developments occur after the jury is sworn, and a juror must be removed and perhaps replaced by an alternate juror. Rules of criminal procedure often provide for this possibility, but they rarely describe the grounds for removal of a juror. Instead, they focus on procedural matters such as the minimum number of jurors that can hear the case or the process of replacing original jurors with alternate jurors.

Federal Rule 23 generally requires that a jury consist of 12 people. With the written approval of both the parties and the court, the trial may proceed with a jury of fewer than 12 persons. A jury of fewer than 12 may return a verdict if the court finds good cause to excuse a juror.

[1] Grounds for Removal

Although there are no limits on the grounds for removal of a sworn juror, generally jurors are removed because they may not be impartial or they cannot physically or mentally complete the work on the case. Trial courts are given great discretion in these decisions.

Impartiality. A common example of removal because of impartiality concerns is when a juror is exposed to prejudicial publicity about aspects of the case not introduced as evidence. *See, e.g., United States v. Williams*, 568 F.2d 464 (5th Cir. 1978) (jurors saw news program about defendant's previous convictions). Other illustrations where jurors have been removed because of partiality include: the only Hispanic juror expressed concerns that he would be blamed for a verdict against an Hispanic defendant; juror expressed an inability to render a verdict because of her religious convictions; a juror disclosed that his parents-in-law had worked for the defendant's election campaign; shortly before retiring for deliberations a juror put a hand on defendant's shoulder and smiled; a juror, in violation of the court's instructions to the jury, had spoken to defendant's family, defense counsel, and defendant himself; in the middle of a trial, a juror indicated she had a strong prejudice against wiretapping and could not render a fair verdict if wiretapping evidence was used; a juror was concerned that he might be guilty of the crime with which the defendant was charged; and a juror's daughter received a threatening telephone call.

Sometimes statutes provide grounds for removing a juror. *See, e.g.,* Ind. Code Ann. § 35-37-2-3 (juror shall be removed if juror has personal knowledge of fact material to the case).

Inability to perform duties. Jurors are also removed if they cannot perform their duties. The broad category encompasses difficulties caused by physical and mental challenges as well as schedule conflicts. Illustrative federal cases have approved the removal of jurors on grounds of the illness of a juror or a close relative; the juror's need to attend a close relative's funeral in a distant city; hardship due to a juror suddenly being given custody of three young children; a job-related emergency; absence because of a religious holiday; an inability to remain awake during the testimony; an inability to concentrate because of concerns about missing a scheduled airplane flight; tardy arrival in court after testimony had commenced; arriving for jury service in a state of intoxication; inability to communicate or understand English; and an inability to hear testimony or to read and write.

Lying. Another ground for removal is the discovery that the juror gave false answers during voir dire. *See, e.g., State v. Tatum,* 506 So. 2d 584 (La. Ct. App. 1987) (juror's failure to disclose mental illness constitutes grounds for dismissal of the juror). *Cf. McDonough Power Equipment, Inc. v. Greenwood,* 464 U.S. 548 (1984) (to obtain new trial on basis of juror's false answers during voir dire, party must demonstrate that a correct response would have provided a challenge for cause).

Refusal to follow law. Jurors can also be dismissed if they refuse to apply the law or follow the court's instructions. *See, e.g., United States v. Martinez,* 481 Fed. Appx. 604, 2012 U.S. App. LEXIS 15023 (11th Cir. 2012) (juror stated she was unable to reach a verdict because she did not personally observe the defendant commit the offense).

[2] Procedural Issues

In the ordinary case a judge will conduct a hearing, outside the presence of the jury, before removing a juror and seating an alternate juror. Lawyers for both sides usually are permitted to speak. In some cases, witnesses or affidavits will be considered. For example, if a juror's partiality is at issue, the juror may appear as a witness at the removal hearing.

At this hearing the key concern is whether the juror can render an impartial decision. The trial court will inquire whether *this* juror's fairness has been compromised. *See Smith v. Phillips*, 455 U.S. 209, 217 (1982) (during trial, juror applied for job as investigator with prosecutor's office; trial court should not have dismissed the juror without inquiring into this juror's actual bias).

If a juror is removed, the issue is whether the juror will be replaced by an alternate, assuming an alternate juror is available. If the removal occurs before deliberations, an alternate juror is virtually always used. Once deliberations have begun, courts are hesitant to substitute with an alternate juror, who will have missed the early deliberations and may have been dismissed when the jury retired. In some jurisdictions, the usual remedy is for the deliberations to continue with one less juror.

Under Rule 23(b) of the Federal Rules of Criminal Procedure, the court can permit an 11-person jury to decide the case if a juror is removed after deliberations have begun. In other jurisdictions, a jury of 12 (or some other number) is required unless the defendant consents (or both parties consent) to a trial by a smaller jury. Absent such consent, if a juror is removed during the deliberations, the trial judge must order a mistrial. *See* Chapter 15.

H. Pre-Deliberation Processes

The rules of criminal procedure deal with only a small number of the details of the jury process. In the absence of concrete guidance in court rules or statutes, trial courts are given great discretion in structuring the jury's activities. This section deals with three issues: notetaking by jurors during the trial, questions by jurors during trial, and sequestration of jurors.

These issues are important tools in a national effort to improve both jury performance and juror satisfaction. The latter is of considerable interest because juror "no-shows" are all too frequent in a criminal justice system that depends on citizen participation in the jury process. *See* Julianna Chomos et al., *Increasing Juror Satisfaction: A Call to Action for Judges and Researchers*, 59 Drake L. Rev. 707 (2010–2011) (discussing notetaking and juror questions as a possible solution to juror stress in order to increase juror satisfaction).

[1] Notetaking by Jurors

While it is likely that a juror's memory may be incapable of recalling accurately the testimony of all witnesses at trial, relatively few jurors ask whether they may take notes during the proceedings, and courts are divided on whether notetaking by jurors is permissible. Accordingly, jurors do not take notes during trial in most jurisdictions. This is in sharp contrast to a law student who would justifiably feel outraged if not permitted to take notes during law school classes, or a judge or lawyer who would insist on being permitted to take notes during trial.

Comparing a criminal jury that was permitted to take notes with one that was not, a researcher found that notetaking did not increase deliberation time, but jurors allowed to take notes rated the quality of their deliberations higher than those who could not take notes. The notetaking jurors also indicated that their cases were less difficult to decide, they placed less reliance on other jurors, half took more notes at the beginning of trial than at the end, and most reported that they participated more actively in deliberations because of the availability of their notes. Victor E. Flango, *Would Jurors Do a Better Job if They Could Take Notes?*, 63 JUDICATURE 436 (1980). *See also* Steven Penrod & Larry Hever, *Tweaking Commonsense: Assessing Aids to Jury Decision Making*, 3 PSYCHOL. PUB. POL'Y & LAW 259, 271 (1997) (reviewing literature pertaining to notetaking studies and concluding there are some advantages and no disadvantages).

There are some reasons to forbid notetaking by jurors. Notetaking could divert the attention of the jurors from the testimony so that they do not hear critical testimony or do not focus enough on the witness's demeanor. The notes may emphasize one feature of the case over other equally or more important ones. The notes of some jurors may be inaccurate. This would provide erroneous information to all the jurors. In addition, the author of the notes may, through stubbornness, insist on the accuracy of the notes despite the strong contrary memory or notes of other jurors. There may be a conflict in the notes of various jurors. Counsel, in picking a jury, would become concerned with a potential juror's notetaking ability. The best notetaker could become the most influential juror. A juror might purposely falsify notes. Notes may contain information about evidence that has been ruled inadmissible. *See* W. Steckler, *Management of the Jury*, 28 F.R.D. 190, 195–96 n.20 (1960).

In addition, after the verdict, a juror's notes may be read by counsel or the news media and destroy jury secrecy and public confidence in the process. When a juror's notes conflict with another juror's memory of testimony, the written version may carry more weight with the other jurors. If, as is likely, a juror takes more and better notes early in the trial and tapers off as the trial progresses, the party who presents testimony early in the trial may have an advantage since there will be a better record of that party's evidence. Notetaking is unnecessary because of the availability of the trial record. During trial, it may not be obvious to the juror what facts are most relevant to the case so a significant amount of time may be spent taking unnecessary notes.

Although notetaking by jurors is rare, in most jurisdictions courts have the discretion to permit it in both simple and complex cases. Of course, jurors are free to refuse to take notes during the trial. A conviction will only be reversed if somehow notetaking was an abuse of discretion. Often the courts ask whether the accused was prejudiced by the notetaking, a standard that is virtually impossible to establish. In some jurisdictions, notetaking by jurors is specifically authorized by state law. *See, e.g.*, Ariz. R. Crim. P. 18.6 (court must instruct jurors that they may take notes; court provides notetaking materials; bailiff destroys notes after verdict); Iowa Code § 813.2, Rule 18(e) (jurors may take notes during testimony; jurors must destroy notes at end of deliberations). Other jurisdictions bar notetaking. *See, e.g.*, Pa. R. Crim. P. 1113 (jurors not permitted to take notes during course of trial).

Some decisions hold that a judge may or should instruct the jury on the proper use of notes. The Fifth Circuit suggested the following instruction:

> The court will permit jurors to take notes during the course of the trial. You of course are not obliged to take any notes, and some feel that the taking of notes is not helpful because it may distract you so that you do not hear and evaluate all of the evidence. If you do take notes, do not allow notetaking to distract you from the ongoing proceedings.
>
> Your notes should be used only as memory aids. You should not give your notes precedence over your independent recollection of the evidence. If you do not take notes, you should rely on your own independent recollection of the proceedings and you should not be influenced by the notes of other jurors. I emphasize that notes are not entitled to any greater weight than the recollection or impression of each juror as to what the testimony may have been.

United States v. Rhodes, 631 F.2d 43, 46 n.3 (5th Cir. 1980).

[2] Juror Notebooks

Another "jury reform" is to authorize courts to provide jurors with notebooks to use in organizing their materials, such as their own notes, exhibits, and written jury instructions. Although courts have long had the discretion to permit this practice, only recently has it been included in recommendations for improving jury performance. Principles for Juries and Jury Trials, Prin. 13 (2005).

[3] Juror's Questioning of Witnesses, Lawyers, or Judge

The usual role of a juror during the trial is as a passive observer who watches and listens and is often cautioned against discussing the case with anyone, including other jurors, until the jury is sent to deliberate. But what if the juror has a question to ask of a witness, the judge, or a lawyer? Taking the easiest possibility, what if a juror does not hear an important statement by a soft-spoken witness? Can the juror interrupt the witness and ask the witness to repeat the testimony? Or what if the witness was vague or ambivalent in responding to a question by counsel? Can the juror ask a pointed question? What if no one asks about an issue the juror thinks is important? Can the juror ask a witness, lawyer, or judge about the matter? Similarly, what if a juror simply does not understand a jury instruction? Can the juror ask the judge for clarification?

Because of the obvious advantages in permitting jurors to avoid misunderstandings or partial understandings, virtually all jurisdictions hold that the judge has the discretion to permit questions by jurors. *See generally United States v. Rawlings*, 522 F.3d 403 (D.C. Cir. 2008) (noting advantages and disadvantages of juror questions, suggesting procedures for courts to use if they allow juror questions; and noting that all federal circuits that had decided the issue recognize that trial judges have the discretion to permit such questions).

There are a number of advantages in permitting jurors to ask questions. An empirical study of actual trials where jurors were or were not permitted to ask questions substantiated a number of the possible advantages of juror questions. It found that in trials where jurors could ask questions of witnesses, the jurors were more satisfied that they had ample evidence to reach a responsible verdict. Interestingly, the study also found that there were fewer than three questions asked by all jurors combined in an average trial. Lawyers objected to only 17% of the jurors' questions, and jurors reported that the objections did not anger them. Larry Heuer & Steven Penrod, *Increasing Jurors' Participation in Trials*, 12 LAW & HUM. BEHAV. 231 (1988).

A minority of jurisdictions ban juror questions. *See, e.g., Morrison v. State*, 845 S.W.2d 882 (Tex. Ct. App. 1992). *See generally* Kara Lundy, Note, *Juror Questions of Witnesses: Questioning the United States Criminal Justice System*, 85 MINN. L. REV. 2007 (2001) (arguing that juror questioning of witnesses should not be permitted because it destroys the jurors' impartiality).

To the extent that the disadvantages of allowing jurors to ask questions are valid, measures may alleviate these concerns. Jurors' questions about evidence should be framed in a neutral way and limited to clarifications of the evidence that was presented. At the beginning of trial, the court should establish specific time and manner requirements for jurors' questions. Jurors' questions may be communicated in writing or orally, but written questions are preferred. Written questions should be addressed to the judge, who will propound them to the witness if appropriate. A juror's questions to a witness should be asked after the witness has testified but before the witness has left the stand. The judge should conduct a jury-out hearing to discuss the propriety of jurors' questions. Michael A. McLaughlin, Note, *Questions to Witnesses and Notetaking by the Jury as Aids in Understanding Complex Litigation*, 18 NEW ENG. L. REV. 687 (1983).

The American Bar Association has taken no stand on the issue. *See* PRINCIPLES FOR JURIES AND JURY TRIAL, Prin. 13(B) (2005) (saying that in deciding whether to permit jurors to ask questions, courts should consider the historic reasons for disapproving the practice as well as the experience of those jurisdictions that have allowed it).

Notes

1. Do you think that jurors should be permitted to ask questions during the trial? If so, do you agree with the above recommendations for procedures to minimize the risks of this practice?

2. What about a system that permitted jurors to ask questions, but only in written form addressed to the judge, who would (1) disclose it to the parties, (2) confer with the parties or hold a hearing outside the presence of the jury, (3) decide whether the question in its current or a revised form is permissible, (4) personally ask the question or permit a party to do so, and (5) permit parties to ask follow up questions of the witness? Would this cure most of the problems associated with jurors' questions? *See* PRINCIPLES FOR JURIES AND JURY TRIAL, Prin. 13(B) (2005) (recommending this procedure if a judge decides to permit juror questions of witnesses).

[4] Sequestration of Jurors

Just as a trial judge ordinarily is given great discretion in deciding whether jurors may take notes or ask questions during a trial, the court is also given significant leeway in deciding whether a jury should be *sequestered*—housed and fed away from home during the trial and deliberations. Sequestration is widely viewed as an extreme measure that should be employed only when other methods would be ineffective at ensuring a fair trial.

While both the prosecutor and defense counsel may argue for or against sequestration, in most jurisdictions the decision is that of the judge alone and can be made despite protests from one or both parties. *See, e.g.*, Ind. Code Ann. § 35-37-2-4 (jurors may separate at end of court day unless judge finds sequestration necessary to assure a fair trial).

In some locales, however, judicial decisions or court rules mandate sequestration in some circumstances. *See, e.g.*, La. Code Crim. P. Art. 791 (in a capital case, jury must be sequestered after being sworn unless both sides waive sequestration; in a non-capital case, jury must be sequestered during deliberations unless waived).

The purpose of sequestration is to prevent the jurors' opinions from being contaminated by contact with outside people or information. It is used most frequently in cases engendering significant media coverage. During sequestration a juror's access to newspapers, and radio and television news broadcasts is controlled to prevent the communication of information about the trial or other matters that might affect the jurors' impartiality.

During sequestration, jurors ordinarily eat as a group in restaurants, attend movies and other recreational activities, and sleep in a motel, all at government expense and under government supervision. One or more bailiffs usually stay in the same motel as the jurors and chaperone the jurors throughout the day. Because of the expense and inconvenience involved, sequestration is rarely ordered.

In cases where sequestration is ordered, the trial judge has discretion to determine its parameters. Often the jurors will receive a special jury instruction before their break. This directs them to avoid any outside influences or communications about the case. *See, e.g.*, *United States v. Barrett*, 505 F.2d 1091, 1110 (7th Cir. 1974) (court may permit selected jurors to return home after voir dire and before they are sworn in, even where sequestration is to be the rule in trial).

If a jury is to be sequestered, the usual practice is for the court to decide this before voir dire and to include the possibility of sequestration in its screening questions. A juror who could not be away from home at night would be eliminated for cause. Ordinarily, a jury is sequestered for the entire trial, including deliberations, although a court may order sequestration for only part of the process, such as during deliberations only.

Appeals resulting from a trial court's refusal to grant a motion to sequester are reviewed under an abuse of discretion standard. Appellants must prove that the failure to sequester "resulted in actual prejudice to his or her right to a fair trial." *United States v. Floyd*, 81 F.3d 1517, 1528 (10th Cir. 1996).

Irrespective of the court's decision on sequestration, the accused can rarely prove prejudice; there are virtually no appellate reversals on this issue unless sequestration is made mandatory by statute or court rule. If the jury is not sequestered, the court's jury instructions against outside influence are usually viewed as adequate to prevent prejudice. *See, e.g., State v. Cruz*, 181 P.3d 196 (Ariz. 2008).

The American Bar Association recommends that courts have the discretion to order sequestration, but notes that the costs and adverse impact on jurors' lives "weigh against its use in almost all cases." PRINCIPLES FOR JURIES AND JURY TRIALS, Prin. 15(E) cmt. (2005) (Comment). When sequestration is ordered, it should be as juror-friendly as possible, perhaps limited to only particular parts of the trial, such as deliberations. Jurors should be involved in forming the sequestration rules and the jurors' experience should be monitored so that jury concerns are brought to the court's attention. Post-trial counseling may be needed. *Id.* For a critical look at sequestration, *see* James P. Levine, *The Impact of Sequestration on Juries*, 79 JUDICATURE 266, 272 (1996).

Chapter 14

Trial

A. Public Trial

[1] Constitutional Right

The Sixth Amendment to the Constitution provides that "the accused shall enjoy the right to a . . . public trial." This right, extended to the states, establishes a strong presumption in favor of criminal trials being open to the public. Since the defendant's Sixth Amendment right to a public trial is personal to the defendant, it confers no general right of access to the press or members of the community. The First Amendment, however, protects press coverage and will be discussed below.

The Supreme Court has recognized that the public trial guarantee serves many important functions. It helps ensure that judges, lawyers, witnesses, and jurors will perform their various functions more responsibly when those tasks are carried out in public view rather than in secret proceedings. Additionally, a public trial is thought to encourage witnesses to come forward and also to discourage perjury. Finally, the public trial guarantee has an educative effect upon the public and is thought to be an effective restraint upon the possible abuse of judicial power.

[2] Extended Meaning of "Trial"

While the Sixth Amendment public trial guarantee does not apply to juvenile proceedings, it extends to all criminal proceedings and goes beyond the actual trial. For example, the Court in *Waller v. Georgia*, 467 U.S. 39 (1984), held that the right applies to a pretrial hearing to suppress wrongfully seized evidence. It also applies to documents filed in a case. With respect to the trial, the right to a public trial extends to impaneling the jury, opening statements, all facets of presentation of evidence, closing arguments, jury instructions, and final verdict. It also applies to jury selection. *Presley v. Georgia*, 558 U.S. 209 (2010).

[3] *Waller's* Four Requirements for Permitting Total or Partial Closure

The defendant's right to a public and open trial is not absolute. There is a *presumption of openness*. While this presumption is characterized as *strong*, it can be overcome. According to the leading case, *Waller v. Georgia*, 467 U.S. 39 (1984), the presumption is overcome only by establishing four points:

> [1] an overriding interest that is likely to be prejudiced [by a public trial], [2] the closure must be no broader than necessary to protect that interest, [3] the trial court must consider reasonable alternatives to closing the proceeding, and [4] it must make findings adequate to support the closure.

Notes

1. *Judicial findings.* Before a trial court excludes some or all of the public from a hearing, *Waller* requires that it make findings identifying the interest served by the closure and the alternatives considered in lieu of closure. This ensures the court addresses the issues and facilitates appellate review.

2. *Closely circumscribed closure rules.* If all or part of the proceeding is closed to some or all of the public, the court must fashion the closure as narrowly as possible to achieve the objectives that merit closure.

3. *Illustration of application of* Waller *elements.* In *Smith v. Hollins*, 448 F.3d 533 (2d Cir. 2006), the trial court ordered the drug defendant's brother and sister either to sit behind a screen or leave the courtroom during the testimony of an undercover agent. The court was concerned that the agent's safety and future usefulness would be compromised if the brother and sister could see the agent. While recognizing the the safety of the agent as a legitimate government concern, the appellate court held that the trial court's ruling violated the defendant's right to a public trial. The trial court should have made the necessary findings that the screen-or-exclusion rule was necessary. The appellate court noted that other relatives were permitted to remain in the courtroom in full view of the undercover agent-witness, so the agent's identity was easily ascertainable by the brother and sister. Also, the court held that a defendant's relatives deserve special consideration in allowing them to attend the trial.

[4] Illustrations of Permissible Trial Closures

Reasons accepted by courts ordering total or partial closure of trials are the following:

(1) *Welfare of crime victim.* Courts consider the victim's age, psychological makeup, and nature of the offense when considering whether to order a total or partial closure of proceedings (discussed more specifically in the next section). *See, e.g., Richardson v. State*, 990 So. 2d 247 (Miss. Ct. App. 2008) (upholding exclusion of public during testimony of 11-year-old sex abuse victim to avoid embarrassment and emotional disturbance; defendant remained in courtroom during child's testimony).

While the victim's welfare may occasionally justify excluding the public from a trial, it will virtually never justify excluding the victim. Rule 60 of the Federal Rules of Criminal Procedure and victims' rights legislation in many states specifically give the victim a right to attend a public court proceeding. The court may exclude the victim only if the court finds by clear and convincing evidence that the victim's testimony would be materially altered if the victim heard other testimony at that hearing. Any decision to exclude the victim must occur only after reasonable alternatives to exclusion have been considered and the court has made "every effort to permit the fullest attendance possible" by the victim. Fed. R. Crim. P. 60(a)(2). The prosecutor and the victim are given the right to enforce this rule. *See* Paul G. Cassell, *Treating Victims Fairly: Integrating Victims into the Federal Rules of Criminal Procedure*, 2007 Utah L. Rev. 861 (2008).

(2) *Protection of witness from threatened harm. See, e.g., People v. Frost*, 790 N.E.2d 1182 (N.Y. 2003) (closure of courtroom during several witnesses' testimony did not violate defendant's Sixth Amendment rights where court held pretrial hearing to determine whether closure was necessary and where witnesses produced evidence relating to their extreme fear of testifying in open court); *Longus v. State*, 968 A.2d 140 (Md. Ct. Spec. App. 2007) (exclusion of two people during testimony of witness whom the two had threatened and who was afraid to testify in their presence).

(3) *Protection of an undercover agent's identity.* Courts may take administrative steps to protect the identity of an undercover agent. This is deemed important to protect the agent's well-being and to permit continued employment in subsequent criminal investigations. *See, e.g., Rodriguez v. Miller*, 537 F.3d 102 (2d Cir. 2007).

Another approach is to permit particular persons to attend a trial only if they submit to an obscured view. *See, e.g., People v. Hargett*, 293 A.D.2d 757 (N.Y. App. Div. 2002) (closure of courtroom to general public and use of blackboard to block view of defendant's family did not violate defendant's right to a public trial; undercover officer-witness testified that he feared for his safety and that of his team which was still working in the area where the defendant's relatives lived).

But absolute exclusion is impermissible for this purpose unless the closure is necessary to protect the safety of the agents and the integrity of their ongoing investigations. *People v. Akaydin*, 258 A.D.2d 466 (N.Y. App. Div. 1999).

(4) *National security concerns.* National security concerns represent a paramount public interest that may justify trial closure. *See, e.g., N. Jersey Media Group, Inc. v. Ashcroft*, 308 F.3d 198 (3d Cir. 2002) (newspapers did not have a First Amendment right to access deportation hearings that were determined by the Attorney General to present significant national security concerns).

(5) *Court security concerns. See, e.g, People v. Perez*, 245 A.D.2d 71 (N.Y. App. Div. 1997) (screening of spectators permitted as security precaution).

(6) *Practical reasons related to space.* For obvious practical reasons, some persons desiring to attend a public trial may be excluded due to the lack of available seating. *See, e.g., United States v. Shryock*, 342 F.3d 948 (9th Cir. 2003) (Sixth Amendment precludes the indiscriminate exclusion of the public from a criminal trial, but recognizes that some persons may be barred when exclusion is justified by lack of space). Courts must be creative in assessing alternatives when courtroom space is limited. For example, in *Presley v. Georgia*, 588 U.S. 209 (2010), the trial court excluded the lone person watching jury selection due to a fear that the individual would have to mingle with potential jurors seated in some of the gallery seats and that there

would not be enough room for potential jurors to sit. The Supreme Court found a Sixth Amendment violation and noted that the trial judge could have reserved one or more rows of seats for the public, divided the jury panel into smaller groups to decrease the number in the courtroom at any one time, or instructed jurors not to interact with audience members.

(7) *Practical reasons related to orderly proceedings.* Courts routinely uphold short-term closures, such as to prevent interruptions during opening and closing statements or jury instructions. *See, e.g., United States v. Scott*, 564 F.3d 34 (1st Cir. 2009).

(8) *Exclusion because of particular attributes of person excluded.* Courts routinely uphold the exclusion of people for misbehavior or other reasons that may compromise a fair trial. *See, e.g., Andrade v. State*, 246 S.W.3d 217 (Tex. App. 2007) (exclusion of one of defendant's lawyers for arguing with judge; court has authority to control behavior of people in courtroom); *State v. Momah*, 171 P.3d 1064 (Wash. App. 2007) (exclusion of disruptive spectator). *See generally* Stephen Smith, *The Right to a Public Trial and Closing the Courtroom to Disruptive Spectators*, 93 WASH. U. L. REV. 235 (2015) (collecting cases that are divided over whether the *Waller* factors must be considered for disruptive spectators).

(9) *Not actually a "closure."* The right to public trial does not mean the public has a right to see exactly the same information as the trial participants. For example, documents and exhibits do not have to be shown to the spectators. *See, e.g., United States v. Boyle*, 700 F.3d 1138 (8th Cir. 2012) (turning off only television monitor visible to spectators during showing of sexually explicit video in child sex abuse case was not a trial closure; right to a public trial means a right to attend a trial and report what was observed, which occurred here).

[5] Remedy for Violation of Right to Public Trial

The remedy for violation of the right to a public trial depends on when the objection is raised. If an objection is made at trial and the issue is raised on direct appeal, the defendant generally is entitled to "automatic reversal" regardless of the error's actual "effect on the outcome." If instead, the defendant raises the issue later in an ineffective assistance claim, the defendant must show either a reasonable probability of a different outcome or that the violation was so serious as to render the trial fundamentally unfair.

[a] Prejudice Not Required

Waller v. Georgia, supra, held that if the public trial right is infringed, the defendant is not required to prove actual prejudice to obtain relief. The Court reasoned that it may well be impossible for the defendant to establish actual prejudice because of the nature of the right to a public trial. By contrast, it is interesting to note that if a defendant alleges ineffective assistance of counsel, a showing of prejudice is required. Does the "no-prejudice" public trial rule, however, require that the defendant receive a new trial whenever his or her right to a public trial is violated?

[b] Trivial Error Exception

Not every minor error in according a defendant a public trial is recognized as violating the Sixth Amendment. Courts have held that errors characterized as *trivial* do not merit any remedy. Thus, in *Peterson v. Williams*, 85 F.3d 39 (2d Cir. 1996), the appellate court found that the trial court had made a trivial error in inadvertently keeping the courtroom closed to the public beyond the time needed to protect the identity of an undercover agent. The failure to reopen the court was not noticed until after the next witness, the defendant, had testified briefly. On the other hand, the Supreme Court reversed a conviction on Sixth Amendment grounds when the only observer in the courtroom was excluded from jury selection. *Presley v. Georgia*, 588 U.S. 209 (2010).

[c] Flexible Remedy Appropriate to Violation

In *Waller*, the Court refused to adopt the rule that a new trial was necessary whenever the right to a public trial was violated. Rather, the Court held that the remedy "should be appropriate to the violation." *Waller* involved evidence from wiretaps and searches that was used in a gambling trial. Before trial, the court held a suppression hearing in accordance with the defendant's motion to exclude this evidence. At the prosecutor's request, the trial court restricted attendance at the suppression hearing, and permitted only the parties, lawyers, court personnel, and witnesses to attend the hearing. The exclusion was authorized because of a Georgia statute that rendered evidence obtained from a wiretap inadmissible at trial if the wiretap proof was unnecessarily published. Defendant's motion to suppress was denied in part and defendant was later convicted. The Supreme Court in *Waller* held that the public trial guarantee was violated when the public was excluded from the suppression hearing. In determining the remedy for this error, the Court held that since the closure order related to the suppression hearing, a new trial would be required only if the new public suppression hearing resulted in a material change in the position of the parties, such as the suppression of material evidence that was not suppressed at the defendant's first trial. Does this remedy make sense? Why should a different ruling on *suppression* issues determine whether there will be a new *trial*?

[d] Illustrations of Remedy for Denial of Public Trial

Federal and state lower court decisions strongly support the *Waller* proposition that the remedy for a public trial violation "should be appropriate to the violation." *See People v. Martin*, 949 N.E.2d 491 (N.Y. 2011) (defendant's public trial right was violated when trial judge closed the courtroom to the defendant's father during voir dire; remedy is a new trial); *P.M.M. v. State*, 762 So. 2d 384 (Ala. Crim. App. 1999) (court's closure of courtroom to the public for the duration of the entire trial is a violation of public trial right; remedy in this case, explicitly citing *Waller*, is a new trial); *People v. Guevara*, 135 A.D.2d 566 (N.Y. App. Div. 1987) (the appropriate remedy for a violation of the defendant's right to a public trial at the pretrial stage is not a new trial but a new public suppression hearing).

Problem 14-1. You Had Me at Hello

Judge Martha Tolliver was presiding over a drug conspiracy trial that had been going on for two days when she looked into the audience and saw a man in the third row typing on a cell phone. She stopped the trial, excused the jury, and instructed the man to rise. She asked him if he was sending a text message on his cell phone. He responded, "Yes I was. Frankly, I was bored and needed to tell my brother about our plans tonight."

1. May Judge Tolliver have all spectators, including the cell phone texter, excluded from the courtroom for the rest of the trial? What about excluding only the texter?

2. What other options should Judge Tolliver consider under *Waller? See State v. Tucker*, 290 P.3d 1248 (Ariz. Ct. App. 2012).

3. May Judge Tolliver direct that all cell phones and similar items in the courtroom be turned off, and exclude any spectator who violates this directive?

Problem 14-2. But There Are Guards with Guns

Assume a state permits some criminal cases to be heard in a room in a maximum security prison. For security reasons, the public and press are not permitted to attend. If Terry, a prisoner with a long sentence, is tried in this prison room for assaulting another prisoner, have his Sixth Amendment rights to a public trial been violated? What should the trial judge do to protect Terry's rights? *See Lilly v. State*, 365 S.W.3d 321 (Tex. Crim. App. 2012).

[6] Press Controls

The Sixth Amendment's public trial guarantee appears to be a right given only to the defendant. If that were the case, then logically the defendant could choose to waive that right and thereby deny public access to the trial. Stated differently, if the defendant possessed unlimited control (via waiver) of the public trial right, in some cases both the public and the press would be denied access to one of the most important functions of our government.

It was not until *Richmond Newspapers, Inc. v. Virginia*, 448 U.S. 555 (1980), that the United States Supreme Court explicitly recognized a right of the public under both the First and Fourteenth Amendments to attend criminal trials. While acknowledging that the First Amendment rights of the public and representatives of the press are not absolute, the plurality opinion held that "absent an overriding interest articulated in findings, the trial of a criminal case must be open to the public." In condemning the trial judge's action of clearing the courtroom (upon motion of the defendant and without objection from the prosecution), the opinion explained:

> The First Amendment, in conjunction with the Fourteenth, . . . share a common core purpose of assuring freedom of communication on matters

> relating to the functioning of government. Plainly it would be difficult to single out any aspect of government of higher concern and importance to the people than the manner in which criminal trials are conducted. . . .
>
> . . . [T]he conduct of trials "before as many of the people as chose to attend" was regarded as one of "the inestimable advantages of a free English constitution of government." . . . Free speech carries with it some freedom to listen. . . . What this means in the context of trials is that the First Amendment guarantees of speech and press, standing alone, prohibit government from summarily closing courtroom doors which had long been open to the public at the time that Amendment was adopted.
>
> . . . We hold that the right to attend criminal trials is implicit in the guarantees of the First Amendment; without the freedom to attend such trials, which people have exercised for centuries, important aspects of freedom of speech and "of the press could be eviscerated."
>
> [W]e return to the closure order challenged by appellants. . . . Despite the fact that this was the fourth trial of the accused, the trial judge made no findings to support closure; no inquiry was made as to whether alternative solutions would have met the need to ensure fairness; there was no recognition of any right under the Constitution for the public or press to attend the trial. . . . There was no suggestion that any problems with witnesses could not have been dealt with by their exclusion from the courtroom or their sequestration during the trial. Nor is there anything to indicate that sequestration of the jurors would not have guarded against their being subjected to any improper information. All of the alternatives admittedly present difficulties for trial courts, but none of the factors relied on here was beyond the realm of the manageable. Absent an overriding interest articulated in findings, the trial of a criminal case must be open to the public.

Id. at 575, 576, 580–581.

Notes

Note that *Richmond Newspapers* recognized a First Amendment right of the *public* to attend criminal trials, yet it was the *press* that sought access to the proceeding. In one case, the judge barred the media from the voir dire examinations of prospective jurors held in the robing room but provided for the release of these transcripts with the juror's names redacted. The appellate court vacated that decision, finding that the district court did not have enough evidence to warrant a closed-court voir dire. *ABC, Inc. v. Stewart*, 360 F.3d 90 (2d Cir. 2004).

Does the Court in *Richmond Newspapers* suggest the right of the press *is the same as* that of the public? If not, could a judge exclude the press but not the general public from all or part of a criminal trial? What about the reverse? Could it exclude the public but not the press? *See Stephens v. State*, 405 S.E.2d 483 (Ga. 1991) (holding it was reversible error to exclude the public because of insufficient findings therefor; error not ameliorated by allowing media representatives to attend); *but see Drummond v. Houk*, 761 F. Supp. 2d 638 (N.D. Ohio 2010) (raising possibility that Sixth Amendment would not be violated if the general public were excluded but the press permitted to attend the trial and the *Waller* factors were satisfied).

Under what circumstances might it be permissible to bar both members of the press and public from the defendant's trial?

Globe Newspaper Co. v. Superior Court

457 U.S. 596 (1982)

Justice Brennan delivered the opinion of the Court.

[A Massachusetts statute[1] required that trial judges exclude the press and the public from the courtroom during testimony given by victims of specified sexual offenses when victims are under the age of eighteen. The trial judge, over objections both by Globe Newspaper and the defendant, ordered that the courtroom be closed. The prosecution attempted to distance itself from the trial court's order, stating that the closure decision was made on the court's own motion and not at the request of the prosecution. The United States Supreme Court held that the trial judge's decision was a violation of *Richmond Newspapers* right of access to criminal trials.]

The state interests asserted to support Massachusetts statute § 16A, though articulated in various ways, are reducible to two: the protection of minor victims of sex crimes from further trauma and embarrassment; and the encouragement of such victims to come forward and testify in a truthful and credible manner.

... We agree with appellee that the first interest—safeguarding the physical and psychological well-being of a minor—is a compelling one. But as compelling as that interest is, it does not justify a *mandatory* closure rule, for it is clear that the circumstances of the particular case may affect the significance of the interest. A trial court can determine on a case-by-case basis whether closure is necessary to protect the welfare of a minor victim. Among the factors to be weighed are the minor victim's age, psychological maturity and understanding, the nature of the crime, the desires of the victim, and the interests of parents and relatives. Section 16A, in contrast, requires closure even if the victim does not seek the exclusion of the press and general public, and would not suffer injury by their presence. In the case before us, for example, the names of the minor victims were already in the public record, and the record indicates that the victims may have been willing to testify despite the

1. Massachusetts General Laws Annotated, ch. 278, § 16A (West 1981): "At the trial of a complaint or indictment for rape, incest, carnal abuse or other crime involving sex, where a minor under eighteen years of age is the person upon, with or against whom the crime is alleged to have been committed, ... the presiding judge shall exclude the general public from the courtroom, admitting only such persons as may have a direct interest in the case."

presence of the press. If the trial court had been permitted to exercise its discretion, closure might well have been deemed unnecessary. In short, § 16A cannot be viewed as a narrowly tailored means of accommodating the State's asserted interest: That interest could be served just as well by requiring the trial court to determine on a case-by-case basis whether the State's legitimate concern for the well-being of the minor victim necessitates closure. Such an approach ensures that the constitutional right of the press and public to gain access to criminal trials will not be restricted except where necessary to protect the State's interest.

... For the foregoing reasons, we hold that § 16A, as construed by the Massachusetts Supreme Judicial Court, violates the First Amendment to the Constitution.[27]

[The concurring and dissenting opinions are omitted.]

Notes

1. *Press exclusion. Richmond* and *Globe* established that the public and the press have a right of access to criminal trials. When the First Amendment right of access to criminal proceedings is competing with the right of the accused to a fair trial, the proceedings may be closed only if specific findings are made that 1) there is a substantial probability that defendant's right to fair trial will be prejudiced by publicity that closure could prevent; and 2) reasonable alternatives to closure cannot adequately protect the defendant's fair trial rights. *Press-Enterprise Co. v. Superior Court (Press-Enterprise II)*, 478 U.S. 1 (1986).

2. *Particular proceedings.* Subsequent decisions dealt with access to other parts of the judicial process. In *Press-Enterprise Co. v. Superior Court (Press-Enterprise I)*, 464 U.S. 501 (1984), the Supreme Court indicated that a newspaper reporter had a right of access, guaranteed by the First Amendment, to the voir dire examination of trial jurors. Two years later, in *Press-Enterprise Co. v. Superior Court* (*Press-Enterprise II*), 478 U.S. 1 (1986), the right of access guarantee was extended to preliminary hearings (at least as then conducted in California), with the admonition that such proceedings could not be closed to the press unless specific findings were made on the record demonstrating that closure was essential to preserve higher values and that such closure was narrowly tailored to serve those interests.

3. *ABA recommendations.* The American Bar Association has adopted a comprehensive policy that recognizes the right of public and press access to "criminal matters" and makes suggestions for how each participant should interact with the media. Criminal Justice Standards on Fair Trial, and Public Discourse (4th ed. 2013). As a general principle, "the public presumptively should have access

27. We emphasize that our holding is a narrow one: that a rule of mandatory closure respecting the testimony of minor sex victims is constitutionally infirm. In individual cases, and under appropriate circumstances, the First Amendment does not necessarily stand as a bar to the exclusion from the courtroom of the press and general public during the testimony of minor sex-offense victims. But a mandatory rule, requiring no particularized determinations in individual cases, is unconstitutional.

to all judicial proceedings, related documents and exhibits, and any record made thereof" not required to be confidential. Standard 8-5.2 Nonetheless, a closure order may be issued, after notice and opportunity to be heard, if the court finds that (1) a substantial probability that public access would pose more harm "to the fairness of the trial or other overriding interest" than the defendant's or public's interest in public access, (2) the closure order will effectively prevent or substantially lessen such harm, and (3) there is no less restrictive alternative available to prevent that harm. *Id.*

4. *Gag order.* While criminal courts find it virtually impossible to exclude the press from hearings, it may be possible to limit the information the press receives by imposing a *gag order* on lawyers and other participants. A typical gag order involves the trial judge barring certain people from discussing the case out of court. It is enforceable through contempt of court. The gag order should be narrowly tailored and specific to withstand vagueness and First Amendment concerns. *See, e.g., United States v. Aldawsari*, 683 F.3d 660 (8th Cir. 2012) (court order barring the parties, their representatives, and attorneys of record from communicating with the news media about the case is upheld only when the government can establish the restrained activity presents a clear and present danger or serious and imminent threat to a protected competing interest such as a fair trial or national security and the order is narrowly drawn and the least restrictive means available).

5. *Ethical considerations.* Even if there is no gag order limiting counsel's access to the media, various ethical rules bar a lawyer from at least some contact with the media to avoid trying a case in the press rather than the courtroom. *See, e.g.*, Model Rules of Prof'l Conduct r. 3.6 (lawyers participating in investigation or litigation of a matter "shall not make an extrajudicial statement that the lawyer knows or reasonably should know will be disseminated by means of public communications and will have a substantial likelihood of materially prejudicing an adjudicative proceeding in the matter"; some exceptions exist permitting limited press contact).

6. *Sixth and First Amendment rights to attend: same or different?* Recall that *Waller v. Georgia* held that the Sixth Amendment gave the *criminal accused* the right to a public trial and *Press- Enterprise* gave the *public* a First Amendment right to attend criminal trials. Still unanswered is the question whether the extent of the defendant's Sixth Amendment right is the same as the public's First Amendment right to attend. *Presley v. Georgia*, 588 U.S. 209 (2010). Does it matter that defendant's right is based on ensuring a fair trial? On the other hand, surely a fair trial is possible—and occurs frequently—even if no one is in the audience during all or part of the proceedings.

[7] Electronic Access

Federal courts. A separate issue frequently arising in the context of the First Amendment right of access to criminal trials is the extent to which electronic access (by means of cameras, recording devices, etc.) is allowed. Federal courts have consistently denied requests for televising criminal trials. In addition, Rule 53 of the

Federal Rules of Criminal Procedure specifically bans taking photographs during judicial proceedings and broadcasting of such proceedings from the courtroom. Courts have held that this rule violates no right of the defendant. *See, e.g., United States v. Hastings*, 695 F.2d 1278 (11th Cir.), *cert. denied*, 461 U.S. 931 (1983); Katherine Geldmacher, *Behind Closed Doors: Why the Federal Judiciary's Decision to Keep Cameras Out of District Courts Was a Mistake*, 30 GEO. J. LEGAL ETHICS 753 (2017).

State courts. In contrast to the federal trend, one study found that cameras are allowed in criminal courtrooms to some degree in every American state and many foreign countries. Forty-four states allow trial and appellate courts to be covered by television. Some require the consent of all parties. Other American states limit television to appellate cases. Kyo Ho Youm, *Cameras in the Courtroom in the Twenty-First Century: The U.S. Supreme Court Learning from Abroad?*, 2012 B.Y.U. L. REV. 1989. The Supreme Court has specifically held that courtroom cameras in the states do not violate due process even when the defendant objects to the coverage. *Chandler v. Florida*, 449 U.S. 560 (1981).

ABA recommendations. The American Bar Association condemns unregulated camera coverage of criminal cases, but endorses judicially supervised coverage so long as the coverage is done "in a manner that will be unobtrusive, will not distract or otherwise adversely affect witnesses, jurors, or other trial participants, and will not otherwise interfere with the administration of justice." STANDARDS FOR CRIMINAL JUSTICE §8-5.6 (4th ed. 2013). *See also* PRINCIPLES FOR JURIES AND JURY TRIALS, Prin. 7(C) (if cameras are allowed in court, should not be allowed to show jurors' faces).

Impact of television coverage. How would cameras affect judges' behavior? Lawyers'? By educating the public about the judiciary, including what judges look like, could the cameras increase security risks? Increase citizens' sense that the judicial system is transparent and fair? Provide access to proceedings for people, such as those working full time or disabled, who cannot otherwise attend the hearings?

B. Judge: Disqualification/Recusal

[1] Right to Impartial Judge

A bedrock principle of the American judicial system is that the judge presiding at trial must be neutral and unbiased. Only if the judge is impartial can a person accused of crime be afforded the requisite fairness guaranteed by the Due Process Clause of the United States Constitution. *See Tumey v. Ohio*, 273 U.S. 510 (1927) ("It . . . deprives a defendant in a criminal case of due process of law to subject his liberty or property to the judgment of a court, the judge of which has a direct, personal, substantial pecuniary interest in reaching a conclusion against him in his case.").

Under the Due Process Clause, recusal is based on an objective standard. *Williams v. Pennsylvania*, 136 S. Ct. 1188 (2016). Recusal is required "when the likelihood of bias on the part of the judge 'is too high to be constitutionally tolerated.'"

Id. (requiring recusal when a Justice of the Pennsylvania Supreme Court, considering a post-conviction petition in a capital case, had been the district attorney who personally approved seeking the death penalty at the trial level). In *Rippo v. Baker*, 137 S. Ct. 905 (2017), a convicted state defendant sought state post-conviction relief, claiming that the state trial judge could not impartially try his case because the judge himself was a suspect in a federal criminal investigation. The Court held that the state court failed to use the standard required for years by case precedent, i.e., "whether the risk of bias was too high to be constitutionally tolerable."

While bias based upon a pecuniary interest is relatively obvious, the Supreme Court has also recognized that the requirement of judicial impartiality can be infringed where the judge has a personal, though not pecuniary, interest in the proceedings. In *Taylor v. Hayes*, 418 U.S. 488 (1974), for example, the Court held that contempt charges against a defense attorney should have been heard by a judge other than the one who had observed the "attorney's behavior that gave rise to the charges." The defense attorney in *Taylor*, while defending a person charged with double murder, was held in contempt eight times and given prison sentences that totaled more than four years. Although the Supreme Court found that the defendant's conduct did not constitute a personal attack on the judge, the circumstances created a likelihood of judicial bias or at least the appearance of bias.

[2] Statutes Related to Judge Disqualification

[a] Federal

Two statutes directly address the disqualification of a district court judge in a federal criminal trial. One, 28 U.S.C. § 144, allows for a peremptory challenge of judges; the other, 28 U.S.C. § 455, involves self-disqualification. Because grounds for judicial disqualification in 28 U.S.C. § 455 and 28 U.S.C. § 144 are so similar, they may be considered together.

Peremptory challenge. The federal peremptory challenge procedure in 28 U.S.C. § 144 allows a party to a proceeding who believes that the trial judge is in any way personally prejudiced to file an affidavit, setting out in detail the facts and reasons supporting the belief that bias exists. Once the affidavit is filed, disqualification is *mandatory*—hence the notion that this is a "peremptory" challenge statute. Indeed, the statute explicitly leaves nothing to the discretion of the challenged judge; he or she is immediately disqualified and another judge must be appointed.

The seminal case under this statute is *Berger v. United States*, 255 U.S. 22 (1920). Defendants, charged with violations of the Espionage Act, asserted by affidavit that the trial judge held strong anti-German beliefs and therefore would be biased against them because of their German origin. The challenged judge denied the motion for disqualification. The United States Supreme Court recognized that the district court judge may determine whether the affidavit, on its face, is sufficient under the statute. Having once done so, however, the judge is not permitted to rule on the truth of the matters alleged; they must be assumed as true. The *Berger* decision means that the party seeking to disqualify a judge is entitled to the disqualification if the statutory requirements are met with respect to the appropriate affidavit.

Because the statute is weighed heavily in favor of recusal, the filing requirements are strictly construed. *See, e.g.*, *United States v. Sykes*, 7 F.3d 1331 (7th Cir. 1993) (holding recusal not required because the affidavit had "procedural and substantive shortcomings"); *Levine v Gerson*, 334 F. Supp. 2d 376 (S.D.N.Y. 2003) (unlike 28 U.S.C. § 455 self-disqualification, which may be invoked by motion of party or by judge *sua sponte*, 28 U.S.C. § 144 self-disqualification is triggered by an affidavit of a party). This affidavit must be accompanied by certificate of counsel of record, and pursuant to § 144, the district judge must recuse himself if the affidavit states that the judge has personal bias or prejudice either for or against one of parties and it provides facts and reasons supporting the statement that prejudice or bias exists. The affidavit must show an objectionable inclination or disposition of the judge; it must give fair support to a charge of a bent of mind that may prevent or impede impartiality of judgment.

Self-disqualification. Self-disqualification under 28 U.S.C. § 455 directs the federal trial judge to recuse in any case in which the judge's "impartiality might reasonably be questioned." The remainder of the statute catalogs specific reasons for disqualification, including personal bias toward one of the parties or instances in which the trial judge may have served as an attorney for one of the parties at an earlier date. This statute permits the judge either to disqualify without motion from either party or disqualify after a party has moved for recusal. *See* Leslie W. Abramson, *Appearance of Impropriety: Deciding When the Judge's Impartiality "Might Reasonably Be Questioned,"* 14 Geo. J. Legal Ethics 55 (2000).

By focusing on circumstances in which the trial judge should recuse when his or her impartiality might *reasonably* be questioned, the statute creates an objective rather than a subjective standard. For example, in *Liljeberg v. Health Services Acquisition Corp.*, 486 U.S. 847 (1988), the United States Supreme Court held that the district court judge, who had a financial interest in the matter but was unaware of this interest, should have been disqualified because an objective observer would have questioned the judge's ability to judge impartially.

At one time, the appellate courts construed this self-disqualification statute to require that the judge's bias or prejudice *must* be directed *against the defendant*, personally, and also must be extra-judicial in nature. More recently the United States Supreme Court has articulated a somewhat different interpretation of the federal recusal statutes. In *Liteky v. United States*, 510 U.S. 540, 554 (1994), the Court held that while an extra-judicial source of prejudice is *a* factor in determining whether the trial judge should be disqualified, extra-judicial prejudice is neither mandatory nor sufficient on its own:

> The fact that an opinion held by a judge derives from a source outside judicial proceedings is not a *necessary* condition for "bias or prejudice" recusal,

> since predispositions developed during the course of a trial will sometimes (albeit rarely) suffice. Nor is it a *sufficient* condition for "bias or prejudice" recusal, since *some* opinions acquired outside the context of judicial proceedings . . . will *not* suffice.

Id. at 554. Accordingly, the Supreme Court held that the district court judge acted properly in denying the disqualification motion (which relied on events that had occurred during an earlier trial and which involved one of the defendants before the same judge). In sum, courts have held recusal to be appropriate when the judge expresses personal bias concerning the outcome of the case at issue and when the judge has a direct personal bias or fiduciary interest in the outcome of case. However, when the alleged interest of the judge is not direct, but is remote, contingent, or speculative, it is not the kind of interest that reasonably brings into question the judge's impartiality. *Levine v. Gerson*, 334 F. Supp. 2d 376 (S.D.N.Y. 2003). Similarly, short-temperedness alone does not require recusal. *Jacobson v. Everson*, 2005 U.S. Dist. LEXIS 24792 (W.D. Wis. 2005).

[b] States

Many states, including California and New York, have adopted statutes modeled after the federal statute, 28 U.S.C. § 455. The main difference between the state and federal systems with respect to judicial recusal is treatment of the peremptory challenge issue. According to *United States v. Escobar*, 803 F. Supp. 611 (E.D.N.Y. 1992), only 19 states allowed peremptory challenges of the judge. In California and many other jurisdictions a party may use one peremptory challenge per case. Cal. Civ. Proc. Code § 170.6 (prejudice because counsel believes cannot have fair trial).

Problem 14-3. Yuk! It's Judge Smuthers!

You represent a woman charged with drunk driving in a national park where United States law applies. Your client had consumed seven beers at her campsite and had a blood-alcohol level of 0.22, which is very high. The case is assigned to Judge Smuthers, known to be especially harsh when dealing with drunk drivers since his niece was killed by one a few years ago.

1. Should you seek a peremptory challenge under 28 U.S.C. § 144 by filing the necessary affidavit? If so, what would you include in it? Should you take into consideration that applying for a peremptory challenge may anger Judge Smuthers and the other federal judges who do not like to be peremptorily challenged because they think they can be fair-minded in all cases?

What if you have other similar cases pending before Judge Smuthers and you are concerned he may retaliate against you by being difficult in future cases. Does it matter who would replace Judge Smuthers after he leaves the case pursuant to your peremptory challenge?

2. Should you file a motion asking Judge Smuthers to self-disqualify himself?

3. If you were Judge Smuthers, would you remove yourself from this case because your objectivity may reasonably be challenged? From all drunk driving cases? If so, for how long?

C. Defendant's Presence at Trial

[1] Scope of Right to Attend

Defendants in all criminal cases have the right to attend their criminal trials. They should be situated in the courtroom so that they can consult with their counsel and see and hear the proceedings. Sources of this right include common law, constitutional guarantees (such as due process and the Sixth Amendment right of confrontation), and statutory rules of procedure.

[a] General Rule: Broad Right to Attend

Federal Rule 43 requires the presence of the defendant at the initial appearance, arraignment, time of plea, and every stage of the trial including the impaneling of the jury and the return of the verdict, and at the imposition of sentence. Notwithstanding this relatively clear language, a number of cases, state and federal, have addressed the question whether particular aspects of the criminal trial require the presence of the defendant. *See generally* Eugene L. Shapiro, *Examining an Underdeveloped Constitutional Standard: Trial in Absentia and the Relinquishment of a Criminal Defendant's Right to be Present*, 96 MARQ. L. REV. 591 (2012).

[b] Proceedings Where There Is Right to Attend

The United States Supreme Court has declared that the defendant's right of presence applies to any proceeding or portion thereof that "has a relation, reasonably substantial, to the fullness of his opportunity to defend against the charge. . . ." *Snyder v. Massachusetts*, 291 U.S. 97, 105 (1934) (holding no constitutional violation occurred where the defendant was not permitted to be present at jury view of murder scene). This includes jury selection, jury instructions, rereading testimony to the jury, return of the verdict, and sentencing.

[c] Proceedings Where There Is No Right to Attend

Courts have found that a defendant does not have a right to be present during purely legal aspects of a trial. Thus, case law holds that the defendant has no right to be present at various in-chamber conferences, bench conferences conducted outside the jury's hearing, conferences and rulings on jury instructions, and other matters relating principally to questions of law rather than questions of fact. *See, e.g., United States v. Gonzales-Flores*, 701 F.3d 112, 119 (4th Cir. 2012) (defendant did not have a right to be present at a hearing on a motion in limine on a discovery issue, a legal proceeding that "turns on questions to which a defendant's contribution is apt to be more marginal than at the trial and sentencing proceedings at which a defendant's presence is a must"); *State v. Swoopes*, 166 P.3d 945 (Ariz. Ct. App. 2007) (defendant did not have a right to be present when trial judge answered question from jury during deliberations; judge did not read testimony back to the jury or provide it with any factual information in the case, but rather, he merely provided a legal answer to jurors' question).

In *United States v. Gagnon*, 470 U.S. 522 (1985), for example, the district court judge, in the presence of the defendant's attorney, conferred in chambers with a juror over the possibility that the juror may have been prejudiced against the defendant. Emphasizing that this encounter "was a short interlude in a complex trial," and that the defendant could not have gained anything by attending the encounter, the Court held that his Fifth Amendment due process rights were not violated.

[d] Waiver

It is well accepted that in most situations a defendant may waive presence at trial as long as the waiver is voluntary and knowing. Rule 43(b) authorizes an organization (such as a corporation) or a misdemeanor defendant to waive presence. As discussed later in this chapter, the defendant may sometimes waive presence by fleeing or disruptive behavior.

Waivers also may occur by acquiescence or specific acts and may waive presence for only part of a trial. For example, in *State v. Newman*, 738 N.W.2d 887 (N.D. 2007), the defense counsel specifically approved the procedure by which the judge alone met with an errant juror (because of an unauthorized cell phone use) and then with the rest of the jurors. The court found the defendant had knowingly and voluntarily waived his presence when defendant was present when the procedure was discussed and acquiesced in it.

[e] Harmless Error

When a defendant's right to be present is violated, courts ordinarily assess whether the error was harmless. One theme is that defense counsel's participation, despite defendant's absence, sometimes renders the violation harmless and without remedy. The outcome depends on the type of proceeding and the length of the defendant's absence.

The United States Supreme Court has noted that the defendant's right to be present at the criminal trial is based, in large measure, on the defendant's right to confront and cross-examine the accuser. In *Kentucky v. Stincer*, 482 U.S. 730 (1987), the defendant was not present during a competency hearing to determine whether two children, who were the victims of the alleged crime, were competent to testify. The hearing was held in the judge's chambers. Finding no Confrontation Clause violation, the Supreme Court approached the issue by asking whether the exclusion of the defendant from the hearing interfered with his opportunity for effective cross-examination. No such interference was found because both of the witnesses appeared and testified later in open court, subject to full and complete cross-examination.

Justice Marshall, joined by Justices Brennan and Stevens, dissented in *Stincer*. He asserted that the physical presence of the defendant enhances reliability of the fact finding process. He noted that "it is both functionally inefficient and fundamentally unfair to attribute to the defendant's attorney complete knowledge of the facts which the trial judge, in the defendant's involuntary absence, deems relevant to the competency determination."

Notes

1. *Medicated defendant.* Could a defendant be both present and not present at the same time? What if the defendant were physically present but heavily medicated so that the defendant's mind was fuzzy and he or she was unable to remember the trial or consult with counsel? *Riggins v. Nevada*, 504 U.S. 127 (1992), is the seminal case on the subject. The defendant in *Riggins* was being treated for a psychiatric disorder by means of an extremely high dose of antipsychotic medication that caused drowsiness, confusion, and possibly severe interference with mental processes. Citing the Sixth and Fourteenth Amendments, the defendant requested that he be allowed to refrain from taking the medication for the duration of his trial. First, he said that the calm, sedate appearance caused by the medication interfered with his ability to present an insanity defense. Second, he claimed that the medicine interfered with his thought processes and his ability to mentally follow the trial and consult with his counsel.

Once a defendant raises a claim that forced administration of medication affects his constitutional rights to a fair trial, the state must prove that the "treatment with antipsychotic medication [is] medically appropriate and, considering less intrusive alternatives, essential for the sake of [the defendant's] own safety or the safety of others." *Id.* at 135. The defendant's conviction was reversed because the trial court had not made the necessary findings to support the forced administration of medication.

Competence to stand trial. Can a court order administration of medication against a defendant's will in order to *make* him or her competent to stand trial? The United States Supreme Court, in *Sell v. United States*, 539 U.S. 166 (2003), held that

> the Constitution permits the government involuntarily to administer antipsychotic drugs to a mentally ill defendant facing serious criminal charges in order to render that defendant competent to stand trial, but only if the treatment is medically appropriate and substantially likely to render the defendant competent to stand trial, is substantially unlikely to have side effects that may undermine the fairness of the trial, and, taking account of less intrusive alternatives, is necessary significantly to further important governmental trial-related interests.

Id. at 179. *See also United States v. Loughner*, 672 F.3d 731, 767 (9th Cir. 2012) (if medication involuntarily administered to the defendant for purposes of prison safety was not capable on its own of rendering the defendant competent for trial, then additional medication could be forced upon the defendant under *Sell*).

2. *Accommodations for disabled defendants.* Obviously courts must make reasonable accommodations for defendants with disabilities to enable them to hear and see the proceedings and communicate with counsel. *See, e.g., Zumberge v. State*, 236 P.3d 1028 (Wyo. 2010) (hearing impaired defendant). Defense counsel should monitor the situation and make specific requests for appropriate accommodations. *See* Americans with Disabilities Act of 1990, 42 U.S.C. §§ 12101 *et seq.*

3. *Right to be absent.* While Rule 43 confers a right of presence, is it inconsistent with a right to be absent? Many statutes mandate the defendant's presence in capital cases. But what if the defendant wants to be absent, perhaps for political or tactical reasons? While the defendant can be forced to appear for purposes of identification, some courts have held the state cannot force a defendant to attend some proceedings if there is a knowing and voluntary waiver of presence. *See, e.g., Nixon v. State*, 572 So. 2d 1336 (Fla. 1990) (defendant will not be forced to attend his capital trial if his actions or the means to ensure his presence would prejudice him in the eyes of the jury). Does this approach adequately consider the interests of the court and the public?

4. *Video technology.* Is the right of presence satisfied when the defendant views the proceedings and communicates with those in the courtroom from a remote location, using videoconferencing? Recent advances in technology have allowed for the increased use of videoconferencing in trials, enabling the defendant to participate in the trial proceedings without being physically present. Many states authorize a wide range of court proceedings by videoconferencing when the defendant is incarcerated.

In federal criminal cases, teleconferencing is permitted at the initial appearance and the arraignment if the defendant consents (Fed. R. Crim. P. 5(f) and 10(c)). Rule 43 specifically approves of presence-by-video in these proceedings. Benefits of the videoconferencing technique include reduced consumption of time and resources in moving an incarcerated defendant to the courthouse from distant facilities, increased security in proceedings that are open to the public, and efficient handling of cases. However, the use of videoconferencing may place constraints (e.g., distorting normal communication between the defendant and counsel) on the judicial process that detrimentally affect criminal defendants, outweighing any perceived benefits of the technology. *See* Anne Bowen Poulin, *Criminal Justice and Videoconferencing Technology: The Remote Defendant*, 78 Tulane L. Rev. 1089 (2004).

[2] The Escaping Defendant

While Rule 43 literally mandates the presence of defendant at certain critical stages of the criminal case, under some circumstances, discussed below, it also permits a trial to proceed in the defendant's absence. *Crosby v. United States*, 506 U.S. 255 (1993), explored whether Federal Rule of Criminal Procedure 43 permits the trial in absentia of a defendant who absconds prior to trial and is absent at its beginning. The Court held that the "language, history, and logic of Rule 43 support a straightforward interpretation that prohibits the trial in absentia of a defendant who is not present at the beginning of trial."

Case law recognizes that the Due Process and Confrontation Clauses confer a right of the defendant to attend various proceedings, but also approve of a knowing and voluntary waiver of that right by a voluntary absence. *See, e.g., United States v. Sharp*, 1993 CMA LEXIS 112 (Sept. 27, 1993) (defendant who voluntarily absented himself after arraignment could be tried in absentia even without being notified of exact trial date); *Pinkney v. State*, 711 A.2d 205 (Md. 1998) (state and federal constitution permit trial court to conduct a trial in defendant's absence where defendant was aware of time and place of trial and judge determines that absence was voluntary). Some courts recognize a presumption that a waiver of presence was valid when the accused purposefully absents herself from the courtroom, *see, e.g., State v. Bracken*, 382 S.W.3d 206 (Mo. Ct. App. 2012).

Allowing defendant to explain absence. An absent defendant at some feasible time should be allowed to give a reason to ensure that the absence was knowing and voluntary. *See, e.g., Tweedy v. State*, 845 A.2d 1215 (Md. 2004) (error not to have at least allowed defendant an opportunity to show good reason for his absence during sentencing); *Robinson v. Commonwealth*, 837 N.E.2d 241 (Mass. 2005) (if a defendant does not appear at a scheduled hearing on a motion to suppress, the judge should determine whether the defendant's absence was voluntary by making a reasonable inquiry into the circumstances surrounding the defendant's failure to appear).

Court's options when defendant is absent. While Rule 43 permits a court to proceed with the trial if the defendant waives presence, the court has the option of declaring a mistrial or granting a continuance (perhaps to await the defendant's capture or return).

Taylor v. United States, 414 U.S. 17 (1973) involved a claim by the defendant, who had voluntarily absented himself during trial, that such voluntary absence, alone, cannot be construed as an effective waiver of his right to be present. In a *per curiam* ruling in which that claim was rejected, the Court found that his absence was the product of his voluntary choice and that it was not necessary in establishing waiver that the defendant be expressly warned by the trial court of the consequences of his absence. The Court, however, did not abandon the requirement that a waiver of presence must be "knowing and voluntary." Rather it held that it "seemed incredible" that the defendant would not have known the trial would continue in his absence.

What should be the result if the court believes the defendant really did not know the consequences of flight? Could *Taylor* be viewed as creating a rebuttable presumption of this knowledge? Rule 43(c)(1) provides the defendant may waive presence by voluntary absence "regardless of whether the court informed the defendant of an obligation to remain during trial." Does this deal with the issue whether an absent defendant knew the trial would proceed?

[3] The Disruptive Defendant

Illinois v. Allen

397 U.S. 337 (1970)

Mr. Justice Black delivered the opinion of the Court.

[The defendant, charged with armed robbery, refused court-appointed counsel and was allowed by the trial judge to proceed *pro se*—but only if the appointed lawyer remained at trial "to protect the record." During voir dire, the defendant was admonished to confine the examination to pertinent matters.]

... At that point, the petitioner started to argue with the judge in a most abusive and disrespectful manner. At last, and seemingly in desperation, the judge asked appointed counsel to proceed with the examination of the jurors. The petitioner continued to talk, proclaiming that the appointed attorney was not going to act as his lawyer. He terminated his remarks by saying, "When I go out for lunchtime, you're (the judge) going to be a corpse here." At that point he tore the file which his attorney had and threw the papers on the floor. The trial judge thereupon stated to the petitioner, "One more outbreak of that sort and I'll remove you from the courtroom." This warning had no effect on the petitioner. He continued to talk back to the judge, saying, "There's not going to be no trial, either. I'm going to sit here and you're going to talk and you can bring your shackles out and straight jacket and put them on me and tape my mouth, but it will do no good because there's not going to be no trial." After more abusive remarks by the petitioner, the trial judge ordered the trial to proceed in the petitioner's absence. The petitioner was removed from the courtroom. The voir dire examination then continued and the jury was selected in the absence of the petitioner.

After a noon recess and before the jury was brought into the courtroom, the petitioner, appearing before the judge, complained about the fairness of the trial and his appointed attorney. He also said he wanted to be present in the court during his trial. In reply, the judge said that the petitioner would be permitted to remain in the courtroom if he "behaved (himself) and (did) not interfere with the introduction of the case." The jury was brought in and seated. Counsel for the petitioner then moved to exclude the witnesses from the courtroom. The (petitioner) protested this effort on the part of his attorney, saying: "There is going to be no proceeding. I'm going to start talking and I'm going to keep on talking all through the trial. There's not going to be no trial like this. I want my sister and my friends here in court to testify for me." The trial judge thereupon ordered the petitioner removed from the courtroom.

After this second removal, Allen remained out of the courtroom during the presentation of the State's case-in-chief, except that he was brought in on several occasions for purposes of identification. During one of these latter appearances, Allen responded to one of the judge's questions with vile and abusive language. After the prosecution's case had been presented, the trial judge reiterated his promise to Allen that he could return to the courtroom whenever he agreed to conduct himself properly. Allen gave some assurances of proper conduct and was permitted to be present through the remainder of the trial, principally his defense, which was conducted by his appointed counsel.

. . . Although mindful that courts must indulge every reasonable presumption against the loss of constitutional rights, we explicitly hold today that a defendant can lose his right to be present at trial if, after he has been warned by the judge that he will be removed if he continues his disruptive behavior, he nevertheless insists on conducting himself in a manner so disorderly, disruptive, and disrespectful of the court that his trial cannot be carried on with him in the courtroom. Once lost, the right to be present can, of course, be reclaimed as soon as the defendant is willing to conduct himself consistently with the decorum and respect inherent in the concept of courts and judicial proceedings.

It is essential to the proper administration of criminal justice that dignity, order, and decorum be the hallmarks of all court proceedings in our country. The flagrant disregard in the courtroom of elementary standards of proper conduct should not and cannot be tolerated. We believe trial judges confronted with disruptive, contumacious, stubbornly defiant defendants must be given sufficient discretion to meet the circumstances of each case. No one formula for maintaining the appropriate courtroom atmosphere will be best in all situations. We think there are at least three constitutionally permissible ways for a trial judge to handle an obstreperous defendant like Allen: (1) bind and gag him, thereby keeping him present; (2) cite him for contempt; (3) take him out of the courtroom until he promises to conduct himself properly.

Trying a defendant for a crime while he sits bound and gagged before the judge and jury would to an extent comply with that part of the Sixth Amendment's purposes that accords the defendant an opportunity to confront the witnesses at the trial. But even to contemplate such a technique, much less see it, arouses a feeling that no person should be tried while shackled and gagged except as a last resort. Not only is it possible that the sight of shackles and gags might have a significant effect on the jury's feelings about the defendant, but the use of this technique is itself something of an affront to the very dignity and decorum of judicial proceedings that the judge is seeking to uphold. Moreover, one of the defendant's primary advantages of being present at the trial, his ability to communicate with his counsel, is greatly reduced when the defendant is in a condition of total physical restraint. . . .

. . . [I]f the defendant is determined to prevent any trial, then a court in attempting to try the defendant for contempt is still confronted with the identical dilemma that the Illinois court faced in this case. And criminal contempt has obvious limitations as a sanction when the defendant is charged with a crime so serious that a very severe sentence such as death or life imprisonment is likely to be imposed. In such a case the defendant might not be affected by a mere contempt sentence when he ultimately faces a far more serious sanction. Nevertheless, the contempt remedy should be borne in mind by a judge in the circumstances of this case.

Another aspect of the contempt remedy is the judge's power, when exercised consistently with state and federal law, to imprison an unruly defendant such as Allen for civil contempt and discontinue the trial until such time as the defendant promises to behave himself. This procedure is consistent with the defendant's right to be present at trial, and yet it avoids the serious shortcomings of the use of shackles and gags. It must be recognized, however, that a defendant might conceivably, as a matter of calculated strategy, elect to spend a prolonged period in confinement for contempt in the hope that adverse witnesses might be unavailable after a lapse of time. A court must guard against allowing a defendant to profit from his own wrong in this way.

The trial court in this case decided under the circumstances to remove the defendant from the courtroom and to continue his trial in his absence until and unless he promised to conduct himself in a manner befitting an American courtroom. As we said earlier, we find nothing unconstitutional about this procedure. Allen's behavior was clearly of such an extreme and aggravated nature as to justify either his removal from the courtroom or his total physical restraint. Prior to his removal he was repeatedly warned by the trial judge that he would be removed from the courtroom if he persisted in his unruly conduct, and . . . the record demonstrates that Allen would not have been at all dissuaded by the trial judge's use of his criminal contempt powers. Allen was constantly informed that he could return to the trial when he would agree to conduct himself in an orderly manner. Under these circumstances we hold that Allen lost his right guaranteed by the Sixth and Fourteenth Amendments to be present throughout his trial.

. . . [Reversed]

MR. JUSTICE BRENNAN, concurring.

. . . I would add only that when a defendant is excluded from his trial, the court should make reasonable efforts to enable him to communicate with his attorney and, if possible, to keep apprised of the progress of his trial. Once the court has removed the contumacious defendant, it is not weakness to mitigate the disadvantages of his expulsion as far as technologically possible in the circumstances.

[The separate opinion by JUSTICE DOUGLAS is omitted.]

Notes

1. *Pro se disruptive defendant.* What will a court do with a disruptive defendant who chooses to proceed *pro se*? The fact of self-representation must be considered in selecting the appropriate sanction. In *Biglari v. State*, 847 A.2d 1239 (Md. Ct. Spec. App. 2004), defendant fired his counsel during trial and represented himself. When defendant was taken from the courtroom due to his disruptive behavior, the trial judge erred in not giving him the chance to return upon a promise to behave properly. After instructing the jury, the trial court should have: (1) sent the jury to the jury room, (2) brought defendant into the courtroom, (3) told defendant he could object to the instructions, and (4) told defendant, if he promised to behave properly, he could give a closing argument and stay in the courtroom for closing argument.

In another illustrative case, the *pro se* defendant was removed from the courtroom for inappropriate conduct and was denied the opportunity to exercise peremptory challenges. Finding that this gave the prosecution an unfair advantage, the court reversed the conviction and held that the defendant's Sixth Amendment rights were violated. *People v. Cohn*, 160 P.3d 336 (Colo. Ct. App. 2007). The court suggested that a trial judge facing a contumacious *pro se* defendant could appoint standby counsel to take over if necessary or could allow the defendant to participate by remote video technology.

2. *Shackles.* As noted in *Allen*, shackling (defined by one court as all forms of hand-cuffs, leg irons, restraining belts, and the like) a defendant in the courtroom may be highly prejudicial to the accused. In *Deck v. Missouri*, 544 U.S. 622 (2005), the Supreme Court held that it is not permissible to shackle a convicted offender during the penalty phase of a capital case unless such use is justified by "an essential state interest."

Electronic shackles. Are other methods, such as electronic shackling, which is undetectable, allowed? *See, e.g., United States v. Moore*, 651 F.3d 30 (D.C. Cir. 2011) (use of stun belt not abuse of discretion when trial judge considered 11 factors before deciding to impose stun belt, all of which favored the stun belt's use).

By contrast, the Supreme Court of Indiana held in *Wrinkles v. State*, 749 N.E.2d 1179 (Ind. 2001), that stun belts may not be used on Indiana defendants. *See also Gonzalez v. Pliler*, 341 F.3d 897 (9th Cir. 2003) (forcing defendant to wear stun belt improper when the only reason was that judge heard from bailiff that the defendant had a "bit of an attitude"). Courts will analyze this need carefully because of the ramifications of a stun belt. In one case, the court remanded after it determined it was prejudicial error to require the defendant to wear a stun belt absent a "manifest need" and there was a reasonable probability that the error affected the trial's outcome by affecting the defendant's demeanor during his crucial testimony. *People v. Mar*, 52 P.3d 95 (Cal. 2002).

3. *Jury instructions concerning restraints.* If a criminal accused is physically restrained in the jurors' presence, should the judge instruct the jurors that the restraint should not be considered in assessing credibility or determining guilt? *See* Standards for Criminal Justice § 15-3.2(d) (4th ed. 2005) (yes). Could this make matters worse?

If shackles are prejudicial, what about large numbers of police officers standing near the defendant during trial? *See Middlebrooks v. State*, 363 S.E.2d 39 (Ga. Ct. App. 1987) (not ground for automatic mistrial).

4. *Prison or jail clothing.* The Supreme Court has held that the government cannot, consistent with due process, "compel an accused to stand trial before a jury while dressed in identifiable prison clothes." *Estelle v. Williams*, 425 U.S. 501, 512 (1976). However, relief may be denied if no juror saw the clothing, if there was

a very strong reason for it, or if the error was harmless since the jury was fully aware of defendant's status as a prisoner. Defense counsel should arrange for civilian clothing to be brought to court, perhaps by defendant's family, and should seek a court order when necessary to have the defendant properly clothed during the trial.

Problem 14-4. Outta Here

You, a judge in a busy criminal court, have been assigned the case of Ben Simon who is charged with assaulting an officer stemming from an encounter with a police officer responding to a bar fight. Trial is scheduled to begin in two days.

1. Your clerk just received a telephone call from Simon's defense lawyer indicating that Simon is in the hospital after an automobile accident. He is scheduled for surgery tomorrow to repair a broken leg. What should you do about the trial to begin in two days? If you were the prosecutor, should you press the judge to hold the trial as scheduled?

2. You decide to postpone the trial. In how many days or weeks should you schedule it to begin? What steps should you take?

3. You schedule it to begin in a month and defense counsel is so notified. The day before the new trial date your office received a call from the same defense lawyer who informed your clerk that Simon, discharged from the hospital a few weeks ago, is not to be found. What should you do? Conduct the trial as scheduled? Postpone it—for how long?

4. You decide to go ahead with the trial as scheduled and Simon shows up a few minutes before the trial is to start, then leaves the court house without telling anyone his whereabouts or plans. What should you do?

5. Simon returns to the courtroom two hours later, very drunk. Defense counsel asks you to postpone the case for six months. Should you go on with the trial as scheduled? Postpone?

6. You postpone it for a day. The next day Simon appears as scheduled, asks to fire his lawyer and conduct the hearing himself, and gets very upset when you try to tell him how unwise it would be for him to defend himself. He spits at his lawyer and gives the finger to the jury. What should you do?

D. Burden of Proof

[1] Crime Elements: Beyond a Reasonable Doubt

The burden of proof is a critical issue. The side having the burden may lose the case simply because it cannot satisfy this burden. The matter is especially important if the standard to be met is high, such as beyond-a-reasonable-doubt.

It was not until 1970 that the United States Supreme Court explicitly held that the Due Process Clause "protects the accused against conviction except upon proof beyond a reasonable doubt of every fact necessary to constitute the crime with which he is charged." *In re Winship*, 397 U.S. 358, 364 (1970). Noting that the reasonable doubt standard plays a "vital role" in the criminal case, the Court in *Winship* characterized the standard as a "prime instrument for reducing the risk of convictions resting on factual error."

Though the *Winship* Court acknowledged the beyond a reasonable doubt standard's significance to criminal jurisprudence, the Court has never put forth a precise definition of reasonable doubt. As a result, numerous definitions have been proposed. Some courts even choose to withhold any formal definition, leaving the jury to decide the term's boundaries with common sense. Generally, however, it has been characterized as doubt that prevents one from being firmly convinced of a defendant's guilt. This doubt should be based on evidence or lack of evidence and not conjecture or imagination.

While *Winship* establishes an important burden of proof principle for elements of a crime, it does not answer the question whether some evidentiary burdens can be placed upon the *defendant*. For example, could a state require the defendant to prove by a preponderance of the evidence that he or she was "acting in the heat of passion on sudden provocation" so as to reduce a murder charge to manslaughter? The United States Supreme Court held in *Mullaney v. Wilbur*, 421 U.S. 684 (1975), that it could not. This result meant the government had to prove *absence* of provocation beyond a reasonable doubt.

Two years later, however, the Supreme Court upheld a state statute that required the defendant to prove extreme emotional disturbance by the civil "preponderance" standard in order to reduce a murder charge to manslaughter. *Patterson v. New York*, 432 U.S. 197 (1977). The *Patterson* Court reasoned that under New York homicide law, second degree murder required the government to prove beyond a reasonable doubt that the defendant intended to and did cause death. As an affirmative defense, the defendant could reduce a murder to the lesser crime of manslaughter by proving that he or she acted "under the influence of extreme emotional disturbance." Finding that the government's proof of intent and causation for second degree murder did not negate extreme emotional disturbance, the Court held that allocating proof of the latter to the accused did not violate *Mullaney v. Wilbur*. Some, including the *Patterson* dissenters, find it difficult to reconcile the two cases. *See* Luis E. Chiesa, *When an Offense Is Not an Offense: Rethinking the Supreme Court's Reasonable Doubt Jurisprudence*, 44 Creighton. L. Rev. 647 (2011). For an insightful article on jurors understanding of the beyond-a-reasonable-doubt standard, *see* Casey Reynolds, *Implicit Bias and the Problem of Certainty in the Criminal Standard of Proof*, 37 Law & Psychol. Rev. 229 (2013).

[2] Defenses: Wide Variation

After *Patterson*, the government can require the defendant to prove various defenses. Often these are characterized as "affirmative defenses" under state law. In

Smith v. United States, 568 U.S. 106 (2013), a unanimous Supreme Court, citing *Patterson*, noted that "[w]hile the Government must prove beyond a reasonable doubt every fact necessary to constitute the crime with which the defendant is charged, *proof of the nonexistence of all affirmative defenses has never been constitutionally required*" (emphasis added).

Generally, the defendant may be responsible for proving defenses such as insanity, self-defense, or duress. The standard of proof in such cases usually is a preponderance of the evidence. In some jurisdictions there is a "burden-shifting." The defendant must first offer *some proof* of the defense's existence (sometimes referred to as meeting the burden of production or presenting a *prima facie* case or meeting the burden of going forward). The burden then shifts to the government to prove that the defense does not exist either to a beyond a reasonable doubt or lesser standard. For example, in a jurisdiction where the insanity defense is subject to a burden-shifting procedure, a defendant who wants to assert this defense must offer some proof of its existence. This burden could be satisfied by expert testimony that the defendant has a serious mental illness that impedes the defendant's ability to discern right from wrong behavior. Since the defendant has now satisfied the burden of production, the burden of proof shifts to the government to disprove the insanity defense, perhaps by a preponderance of evidence or even by proof beyond a reasonable doubt. Likely the government would also offer expert testimony or materials prepared by experts to meet its burden.

[3] Presumptions and Inferences

In some cases, the prosecution has attempted to lighten its burden of proof of the elements of a crime by using a presumption authorized by statute or case law. For example, in a homicide case, the prosecutor may seek to have the jury instructed that the defendant's state of mind can be proven through the use of a presumption based upon certain proven physical acts of the defendant. Such a proposed instruction might be phrased as follows: "A person is presumed to intend the natural and probable consequences of his or her acts."

In *Francis v. Franklin*, 471 U.S. 307 (1985), however, the United States Supreme Court held that such an instruction creates an unconstitutional presumption, improperly relieving the government of its burden of proving the defendant's mental state (an element of the crime) beyond a reasonable doubt. The Court characterized the quoted language as having "undeniably created an unconstitutional burden-shifting presumption with respect to the element of intent," and therefore violating the Due Process Clause.

Since *Francis*, the government must rely on "permissive inferences" rather than burden-shifting presumptions. For example, the jury is now instructed, "You may infer that the defendant intended to kill from the fact (if so found beyond a reasonable doubt) that she aimed her weapon at the victim, and fired the shots that caused the victim's death."

E. Order of Proof

After the judge and lawyers select a jury and the judge informs the jury of the formal charges (often by reading the indictment), the prosecution begins presentation of its case-in-chief.

[1] Opening Statements

Unless the prosecution waives its option (which rarely occurs), the first step in a trial is for the prosecution to give an opening statement. The prosecution's goal is to present an overview of the alleged offense, the government's theory of the case, and the evidence it will offer to establish guilt beyond a reasonable doubt.

The defense ordinarily will respond with its own opening statement, sketching its theory of the case and the proof it intends to offer. In some courts the defense is permitted to delay its opening statement until after the prosecution has presented its proof.

[2] Prosecution's Proof

The prosecution then presents its case "in chief" to satisfy its responsibility of proving guilt beyond a reasonable doubt. This may consist of testimonial evidence, such as testimony from the victim, other witnesses to the crime, and experts. It may also include physical evidence, such as drugs found in defendant's pocket, clothing found at the scene of the offense, the weapon used to commit the crime, and various documents. For example, if the defendant has confessed to the offense yet is denying guilt at trial, the confession is generally offered by presenting testimony from the police officer who obtained the defendant's statement. Sometimes, a written or videotaped version of the admission will accompany the officer's testimony. The defendant is entitled under the Sixth Amendment to confront and cross-examine the government's witnesses, as discussed in the next section. The prosecution "rests its case" once it has presented all of its evidence.

[3] Defense Motion for Acquittal

The defense attorney may then move for an acquittal, asserting that the government has failed to offer sufficient proof of the defendant's guilt to satisfy the beyond-a-reasonable-doubt standard. Rule 29 provides procedures for acquittal motions.

When considered at the close of the government's case under Rule 29(a), a motion for judgment of acquittal asks the trial judge to ascertain whether a jury could, based upon the evidence presented by the government, find guilt beyond a reasonable doubt. If at that point, that particular evidentiary standard has been met, the motion will be denied and the defendant will have the opportunity to present evidence. As provided in Rule 29(b), the judge may decide to delay a decision on the motion until after the return of a verdict (discussed in further detail at the end of this chapter).

[4] Defendant's Proof

The defense has the right to "rest" and present no contradictory evidence whatsoever in response to the government's proof. This option, while sometimes risky, is chosen in cases in which the defense attorney believes that the government's evidence fails to satisfy the beyond-a-reasonable-doubt standard. The defendant is entitled to remain completely silent under the Fifth Amendment self-incrimination privilege. Ordinarily, however, the defense will present the same kind of evidence offered by the prosecution (witnesses, physical evidence, etc.).

[5] Rebuttal Proof

Most judges permit the government to offer rebuttal evidence to respond to new evidence or theories presented by defendant's proof. The defense may also be permitted to introduce rebuttal proof if the prosecutor's rebuttal raises new issues.

[6] Closing Arguments

Upon completion of prosecution and defense evidence, both prosecution and defense are allowed to present summations or closing arguments to the trier of fact. Indeed, the Supreme Court held in *Herring v. New York*, 422 U.S. 853, 865 (1975), that denying defense counsel the opportunity to present a closing argument in a non-jury criminal trial is a violation of the Sixth Amendment assistance of counsel guarantee. During closing argument, each side will summarize its own evidence, question the reliability or meaning of the other side's proof, and try to convince the trier of fact that the necessary burden of proof has or has not been satisfied.

Prosecution may have two. In many American jurisdictions, as exemplified by Rule 29.1 of the Federal Rules of Criminal Procedure, the prosecution actually gets to make *two closing arguments*. The prosecutor makes the first closing argument. The defense lawyer makes the second closing argument. Then the prosecutor is permitted to rebut the defendant's argument. This order means that the prosecution gets the last chance to influence the trier of fact. John B. Mitchell, *Why Should the Prosecutor Get the Last Word*, 27 Am. J. Crim. L. 139 (2000); *see also* Mark Spottswood, *Ordering Proof: Beyond Adversarial and Inquisitorial Trial Structures*, 83 Tenn. L. Rev. 291 (2015) (proposing a new method of ordering proof).

Legal limits. The trial court is given broad discretion in controlling the content, duration, and form of closing argument. For example, appellate courts have upheld a trial court's discretion on whether to permit counsel in closing argument to read from a trial transcript, to give a jury instruction correcting defense counsel's legal analysis in closing argument, to limit inflammatory remarks, and to set time limits for each side.

Many appellate courts have addressed the propriety of prosecutors' closing arguments (inflammatory, expressing personal opinions of guilt, etc.), but reversal is rare even when error is found. The harmless error doctrine is relied upon to uphold convictions in such instances. *See Darden v. Wainwright*, 477 U.S. 168 (1986) (finding prosecutor's closing argument deserved "condemnation" but reversal not ordered because trial not fundamentally unfair).

[7] Jury Instruction and Verdict

After both sides complete their closing arguments, the judge instructs the jury (discussed later in this chapter) and, after deliberation, the jury returns to the courtroom with its verdict.

F. Defendant's Right to Testify

The United States Constitution contains no explicit guarantee of the right to testify on one's own behalf. While the notion of the right to "take the stand" appears to be unquestioned, this principle was not definitively established by the United States Supreme Court until *Rock v. Arkansas*, 483 U.S. 44 (1987). There, the defendant was charged with manslaughter in the death of her husband. When she could not remember the details of the shooting incident, her attorney suggested that she submit to hypnosis to refresh her memory. After hypnosis, she could remember some of the details concerning the incident. Upon learning of the hypnosis sessions, the prosecutor filed a motion to exclude the defendant's testimony. The motion was granted by the state court on the ground that under Arkansas law hypnotically-refreshed testimony is always unreliable.

The United States Supreme Court held that the state's "per se rule" of inadmissibility infringed impermissibly on the defendant's right to testify on her own behalf. The Court stated that a defendant has "the right to take the witness stand and to testify in his or her own defense." Sources of this right include: (1) the Fifth Amendment's Due Process Clause, (2) the Sixth Amendment's Compulsory Process Clause, (3) the Sixth Amendment's right to self-representation, and (4) the Fifth Amendment's self-incrimination privilege (as a "corollary" thereto).

Defendant's personal decision. The decision whether or not to testify must be made by the defendant personally. Defense counsel may make a recommendation about the decision but cannot make the decision for the accused. A defendant who elects to testify automatically waives the Fifth Amendment's right to remain silent. This waiver must be knowing and voluntary. *See, e.g., United States v. Gillenwater*, 717 F.3d 1070 (9th Cir. 2013).

Polygraph evidence. Many jurisdictions do not admit evidence of polygraph tests because of concerns about the accuracy of the tests and the undue weight juries may place on the results. But what if the defendant wants to introduce evidence about having taken a polygraph test? In contrast to *Rock*, the United States Supreme Court has ruled that a defendant is not denied the right to present a defense where, by reason of an evidentiary rule, results of polygraph examinations (favorable to the accused) are inadmissible. *United States v. Scheffer*, 523 U.S. 303 (1998). While acknowledging that individual jurisdictions may reach differing conclusions as to whether polygraph results should be admitted, the per se rule of exclusion (Military Rule of Evidence 707) was found to serve legitimate interests in the criminal trial process. Because Rule 707 did not preclude the defendant from introducing any factual evidence (other than the unreliable polygraph proof) pertaining to guilt or innocence, this case was distinguished from *Rock* because there, the defendant was barred from testifying in her own behalf. Justice Stevens dissented, asserting that a categorical rule that prohibits the admission of polygraph evidence in all cases, no matter how reliable or probative, is unconstitutional.

It should be noted that a minority of states do admit polygraph evidence, sometimes only if all the parties stipulate to its admissibility.

Risks of cross-examination. A defendant facing the strategic issue whether or not to testify must carefully assess the risks associated with the cross-examination process. Many persons accused of crime elect not to testify on their own behalf because cross-examination by the prosecutor may disclose past criminal activity of the accused. *See* Fed. R. Evid. 609. In this sense, then, a defendant does not have an absolutely "unfettered" right to testify. Some states depart from the federal model and place tighter limits on the prosecutor's ability to cross-examine defendants with prior crimes evidence. Montana has gone farther than any state in completely disallowing impeachment by prior conviction evidence. Mont. R. Rev. Rule 609 ("For the purpose of attacking the credibility of a witness, evidence that the witness has been convicted of a crime is not admissible.").

Procedural hurdles. The defendant's right to testify may also be impeded by various procedural rules. For example, in *Brooks v. Tennessee*, 406 U.S. 605 (1972), a Tennessee statute required that a defendant "desiring to testify shall do so before any other testimony for the defense is heard." The United States Supreme Court found this statute to be an infringement of due process:

> Whether the defendant is to testify is an important tactical decision as well as a matter of constitutional right. By requiring the accused and his lawyer to make that choice without an opportunity to evaluate the actual worth of their evidence, the statute restricts the defense—particularly counsel—in the planning of its case. Furthermore, the penalty for not testifying first is to keep the defendant off the stand entirely, even though as a matter of professional judgment his lawyer might want to call him later in the trial. The accused is thereby deprived of the "guiding hand of counsel" in the timing of this critical element of his defense.

Id. at 612–613.

G. Defendant's Right to Not Testify

Under the Fifth Amendment the criminal accused has a right to refuse to testify. But does this mean a defendant cannot suffer adverse legal consequences from the decision to remain silent? The Supreme Court addresses one form of harm in the next case.

Griffin v. California

380 U.S. 609 (1965)

Mr. Justice Douglas delivered the opinion of the Court.

Petitioner was convicted of murder in the first degree after a jury trial in a California court. He did not testify at the trial on the issue of guilt, though he did testify at the separate trial on the issue of penalty. The trial court instructed the jury on the issue of guilt, stating that a defendant has a constitutional right not to testify. But it told the jury:

> As to any evidence or facts against him which the defendant can reasonably be expected to deny or explain because of facts within his knowledge, if he does not testify or if, though he does testify, he fails to deny or explain such evidence, the jury may take that failure into consideration as tending to indicate the truth of such evidence and as indicating that among the inferences that may be reasonably drawn therefrom those unfavorable to the defendant are the more probable.

It added, however, that no such inference could be drawn as to evidence respecting which he had no knowledge. It stated that failure of a defendant to deny or explain the evidence of which he had knowledge does not create a presumption of guilt nor by itself warrant an inference of guilt nor relieve the prosecution of any of its burden of proof.

... The question ... [is whether] the comment rule, approved by California, violates the Fifth Amendment.

We think it does. It is in substance a rule of evidence that allows the State the privilege of tendering to the jury for its consideration the failure of the accused to testify. No formal offer of proof is made as in other situations; but the prosecutor's comment and the court's acquiescence are the equivalent of an offer of evidence and its acceptance.

... [C]omment on the refusal to testify is a remnant of the "inquisitorial system of criminal justice," which the Fifth Amendment outlaws. It is a penalty imposed by courts for exercising a constitutional privilege. It cuts down on the privilege by making its assertion costly. It is said, however, that the inference of guilt for failure to testify as to facts peculiarly within the accused's knowledge is in any event natural and irresistible, and that comment on the failure does not magnify that inference into a penalty for asserting a constitutional privilege. What the jury may infer, given no help from the court, is one thing. What it may infer when the court solemnizes the silence of the accused into evidence against him is quite another.

... We ... hold that the Fifth Amendment, in its direct application to the Federal Government and in its bearing on the States by reason of the Fourteenth Amendment, forbids either comment by the prosecution on the accused's silence or instructions by the court that such silence is evidence of guilt. Reversed.

The Chief Justice took no part in the decision of this case.

[Justice Harlan concurred and Justices Stewart and White dissented.]

Notes

1. Griffin*'s application to indirect comments.* Either direct or indirect references to a defendant's choice not to testify may constitute a Fifth Amendment violation. The test used to determine whether there was a *Griffin* violation is whether the language used was (1) manifestly intended to be or (2) was of such a character that the jury would naturally and necessarily take it to be a comment on the defendant's failure to testify. *Ben-Yisrayl v. Davis*, 431 F.3d 1043 (7th Cir. 2005).

Courts agree on the general standard that should be applied, but results vary on what comments are proper and improper. In *Ben-Yisrayl v. Davis*, above, in closing arguments, the prosecutor referred to the defendant's confession, and then further went on to state that "[n]o one freely and voluntarily confesses to a murder unless they're guilty. Let the Defendant tell you why somebody would freely and voluntarily confess." The court reversed the conviction because the jury could have believed that the prosecutor was arguing that because of defendant's failure to testify as to why he would confess, the inference to be drawn is that his confession was true.

Compare that comment to the language in *United States v. Porter*, 687 F.3d 918 (8th Cir. 2012), where the prosecutor stated in closing argument:

> There was one witness provided by the defense, Mr. Porter, Raymond Porter. ... He was not there that night. ... Who was there? The defendant, and also two police officers, and they [two police officers] testified unequivocally to what they saw that night.

The court ruled that the prosecutor's comment was not an improper comment on defendant's failure to testify because the statements referred to the testimony of others and not of the defendant.

2. *Invocation of* Miranda*'s right to remain silent.* It is well established that no negative inference can be drawn against a defendant for exercising Fifth Amendment rights at trial or sentencing. *United States v. Ronquillo*, 508 F.3d 744 (5th Cir. 2007). This extends to the prosecutor's trying to discredit the defendant's trial testimony by bringing out the defendant's assertion of *Miranda* rights after arrest. But a defendant's silence when interrogated before arrest and before being given *Miranda* rights may be commented on by the prosecution at trial. *Salinas v. Texas*, 570 U.S. 178 (2013).

3. *Jury instructions on silence.* If the defendant chooses not to testify, no inference can be drawn from the silence. But can the judge instruct the jury to give the defendant's decision no significance? In *Lakeside v. Oregon*, 435 U.S. 333 (1978), over the defendant's objection, the trial judge instructed the jury as follows:

> Under the laws of this state a defendant has the option to take the witness stand to testify in his or her own behalf. If a defendant chooses not to testify, such a circumstance gives rise to no inference or presumption against the defendant, and this must not be considered by you in determining the question of guilt or innocence.

The defense counsel argued that the effect of such a jury instruction was like "waving a red flag in front of the jury." The Supreme Court rejected the claim, holding that the giving of such an instruction over the defendant's objection does not violate *Griffin*; nor does it violate the Fifth Amendment self-incrimination guarantee. The Court explained: "The petitioner's argument would require indulgence in two very doubtful assumptions: First, that the jurors have not noticed that the defendant did not testify and will not, therefore, draw adverse inferences on their own; second, that the jurors will totally disregard the instruction, and affirmatively give weight to what they have been told not to consider at all. Federal constitutional law cannot rest on speculative assumptions so dubious as these." *Id.* at 340.

Entitlement to no-inference instruction. While *Lakeside* addresses the question of the propriety of giving a "no adverse inference instruction," it does not address the question whether a defendant is *entitled* to such an instruction. In *Carter v. Kentucky*, 450 U.S. 288 (1981), the United States Supreme Court held that state trial judges have a constitutional obligation, upon proper request, to give such an instruction. In that case, the defendant had requested that the jury be told that "the defendant is not compelled to testify and the fact that he does not cannot be used as an inference of guilt and should not prejudice him in any way."

4. *Sentencing.* The Court also held in *Mitchell v. United States*, 526 U.S. 314 (1999), that *Griffin*'s no-adverse-inference rule also applies to defendants who do not testify at a sentencing hearing. *Mitchell* was decided by a 5–4 majority, and several of the dissenters called *Griffin* into question and indicated a willingness to reconsider it in the future.

Although the Supreme Court in *Mitchell* declined to adopt an exception to the *Griffin* rule for the criminal sentencing phase, the Court has recognized that the Fifth Amendment does not forbid adverse inferences against parties to civil actions when they refuse to testify in response to probative evidence offered against them. *Baxter v. Palmigiano*, 425 U.S. 308 (1976). This also includes habeas corpus cases, in which a petitioner's refusal to testify in habeas proceedings is relevant to the district court's credibility determination. *Latif v. Obama*, 677 F.3d 1175 (D.C. Cir. 2012).

5. *Comment on fact defendant testified after hearing government witnesses.* Assume that the defendant testifies after having heard the government's witnesses testify. During closing argument, the government's attorney calls the jury's attention to

this fact, suggesting that the defendant's credibility should be questioned because of the opportunity afforded him to tailor his testimony to that of the witnesses. Is the prosecutor's argument prohibited by *Griffin*? The Supreme Court held in *Portuondo v. Agard*, 529 U.S. 61 (2000), that it would not "extend" *Griffin* to this practice. It reasoned that (1) *Griffin* prohibits a prosecutor from urging the jury to do something that it is not permitted to do, whereas here the jury is "perfectly entitled" to do what it was invited to do; and (2) *Griffin* prohibits comments that suggest that the defendant's silence is evidence of guilt, whereas here the comments concerned the defendant's credibility as a witness.

6. *Otherwise improper prosecution comments may be invited by the defense.* In *United States v. Robinson*, 485 U.S. 25 (1988), the Supreme Court held that the *Griffin* prohibition does not apply where the prosecutor's reference to the defendant's opportunity to testify is a fair response to a claim made by defendant or his counsel. Because defense counsel asserted in closing argument that the government did not allow the defendant to tell his side of the story, the Court found no Fifth Amendment violation for the prosecutor to point out that defendant had the right and opportunity to testify.

7. *Missing witness rule.* In many jurisdictions, the so-called "missing witness" rule permits a side during closing argument to comment on the fact that the other side did not call an obvious witness. This rule permits the court to instruct the jury that it may infer the witness would have testified adversely to the party that did not call the obvious witness. The rule even extends to a witness mentioned by a defendant who chose to testify.

8. Debate about prosecutorial comment on the defendant's failure to testify continues. *See, e.g.*, Jeffrey Bellin, *Reconceptualizing the Fifth Amendment Prohibition of Adverse Comment on Criminal Defendants' Silence*, 71 Ohio St. L.J. 229 (2010); Ted Sampsell-Jones, *Making Defendants Speak*, 93 Minn. L. Rev. 1327 (2009).

Problem 14-5. But the Defendant Did Not Respond

In a lengthy murder trial in which the defendant did not testify, is it permissible for the prosecutor to say to the jury during final summation:

1. "You heard the evidence in this case and may have noticed that the prosecution's theory of this hideous murder and the prosecution's evidence were uncontradicted." *People v. Euell*, 969 N.E.2d 935 (Ill. App. Ct. 2012).

2. "The defendant has a right to call witnesses and to present them in this trial. But here the defendant produced no one to testify that defendant was not at the scene of the murder."

3. "You'd think the defense would put on anyone who could shed light on what happened that night."

4. Assume that a police officer testified about a confession defendant made shortly after being arrested. During cross-examination of the officer, defense counsel suggested that the officer had either misheard the defendant or was lying about the content of the confession. During closing argument, may the prosecutor tell the jury that "you have been given no evidence to contradict the accuracy of the officer's recollection of the confession?" *United States v. Burroughs*, 465 Fed. Appx. 530, 2012 U.S. App. LEXIS 5276 (6th Cir. March 9, 2012).

H. Defendant's Access to Evidence and Compulsory Process

[1] Constitutional Right to Offer Witnesses

The Sixth Amendment provides, in part, that "in all criminal prosecutions, the accused shall enjoy the right . . . to have compulsory process for obtaining witnesses in his favor." In *Washington v. Texas*, 388 U.S. 14, 19 (1967), the United States Supreme Court held that this guarantee was a fundamental element of due process of law:

> The right to offer the testimony of witnesses, and to compel their attendance, if necessary, is in plain terms the right to present a defense, the right to present the defendant's version of the facts as well as the prosecution's to the jury so it may decide where the truth lies. [The defendant] . . . has the right to present his own witnesses to establish a defense.

While jurisdictions may establish rules excluding some evidence from criminal trials, statutes and court rules interfering with the defendant's right to present evidence may be held unconstitutional. For example, in *Washington v. Texas*, a Texas statute denied the accused the opportunity to present the testimony of an alleged accomplice, Fuller, who "would have testified that [Washington] pulled at him and tried to persuade him to leave, and that [Washington] ran before Fuller fired the fatal shot [in the murder case]." The statute provided that persons charged or convicted as co-participants in the same crime could not testify for one another, although there was no bar to their testifying for the state. Under these circumstances, the Supreme Court held that the defendant's compulsory process rights had been denied.

Chambers v. Mississippi. Six years later, the Court again evaluated rules of procedure and evidence that limited defense proof and, again, found their application a violation of due process. Defendant Chambers, charged with murdering a police officer, attempted to present evidence that a third person (McDonald) actually committed the offense. Under Mississippi's "voucher rule" and its hearsay rule, however, the defense was unable to cross-examine McDonald or to present witnesses who would have testified that McDonald was responsible for the murder. While reaffirming that states possess the power to establish "their own criminal trial rules," the Court held that the exclusion of this "critical evidence . . . denied [Chambers] a trial in accord with traditional and fundamental standards of due process." *Chambers v. Mississippi*, 410 U.S. 284, 302 (1973).

Many illustrations of Chambers *rule.* The critical principle behind *Chambers v. Mississippi* is that the defendant is entitled to present a full defense even if doing so would violate evidence and other rules. For example, the Supreme Court reversed a death sentence because the defendant was denied the right to introduce evidence that a third party had committed the crime. *Holmes v. South Carolina*, 547 U.S. 319 (2006) (defendant's constitutional right to present a complete defense cannot be denied by evidence rules that are arbitrary or disproportionate to the interests they are to serve; state evidence law barred weak defense evidence of third person's guilt in face of strong forensic evidence of guilt).

Chambers *rule not absolute.* A number of decisions have upheld limits on defense evidence. For example, in *Nevada v. Jackson*, 569 U.S. 505 (2013), the Court upheld a trial court's decision to bar extrinsic evidence that the woman whom the defendant allegedly raped had made a false complaint that he had also raped her previously. The Court noted that state and federal rule makers have broad latitude in establishing evidence rules excluding some evidence from trial.

[2] Subpoena Process

An important right of the criminal accused, guaranteed by the Sixth Amendment, is the right "to have compulsory process for obtaining witnesses in his favor." Federal Rule 17 and similar rules in all jurisdictions implement this critical procedure by providing a mechanism for both sides to subpoena witnesses. Recall that subpoenas as part of a grand jury investigation are discussed in Chapter 7, *supra*.

Rule 17 requires the court clerk to issue a subpoena *in blank* so that the prosecutor or defense counsel may fill in the blank subpoena and serve it without letting the other side know about the subpoena. This process is consistent with the limited discovery of potential adverse witnesses in criminal cases.

Rule 17(c)(1) authorizes a subpoena to order the witness to bring various items, but not statements of witnesses covered by Rules 16 (expert) and 26.2 (after witness testifies, witness's statement must be released to adverse party).

While a person receiving a subpoena must comply or face possible contempt of court charges, Rule 17(c) authorizes a person to file a *motion to quash* the subpoena as being *unreasonable or oppressive*. The motion could be granted if the subpoena requests a large number of documents, costs too much to comply with, or is too broad. As noted in Chapter 7, the subpoenaed person may assert a privilege, such as the Fifth Amendment's self-incrimination ban.

What happens if a subpoenaed witness is deported before trial? In *United States v. Valenzuela-Bernal*, 458 U.S. 858 (1982), the defendant was indicted for transporting an illegal alien in violation of federal law. Two of the three passengers who admitted that they were illegally in the country were immediately deported to Mexico after an Assistant United States Attorney concluded that they possessed no evidence material to the prosecution or defense. The defendant moved to dismiss the indictment, claiming that their deportation violated his Fifth Amendment right to due process and his Sixth Amendment right to compulsory process for obtaining favorable witnesses. A third passenger was detained to provide a non-hearsay basis for establishing that the defendant had violated the federal statute. The motion was denied and the defendant was convicted.

The United States Supreme Court held that prompt deportation of witnesses determined by the government to possess no material evidence was justified by practical considerations (i.e., overcrowded detention facilities and related budgetary limitations). The Court concluded that "[t]he mere fact that the Government deports such witnesses is not sufficient to establish a violation of the Compulsory Process Clause of the Sixth Amendment or the Due Process Clause of the Fifth Amendment. A violation of these provisions requires some showing that the evidence lost would be both material and favorable to the defense." *Id.* at 872–73.

Do you agree with the majority in *Valenzuela-Bernal*? Would your view change if the government had deported the two passengers after learning that they could provide testimony helpful to the defense? If you believe the government should not have been permitted to deport these potential defense witnesses, what should it have done? Kept the two in jail until trial (recall they were in the country illegally)? Released them but monitored their whereabouts? If the witnesses had been released, would the government have to allow them to work (recall they were in the country illegally)? If not, how would they have supported themselves?

Indigent defendants have special procedures for obtaining expert testimony using subpoenas under Rule 17(b) (in an insanity defense case, for example), while a non-indigent would be financially unable to obtain the same kind of expert testimony. Note the defendant's burden of proving that the expert's services are "necessary to an adequate defense" under Rule 17(b). Trial courts have wide discretion in determining when the defendant has met this burden, and the standard of review is abuse of discretion. These determinations are extremely fact-specific.

Due process may require the appointment of a state-paid expert to assist the defense in unusual cases. *See, e.g., Ake v. Oklahoma*, 470 U.S. 68 (1985) (state must pay for psychiatric examination of indigent criminal defendant whose sanity was seriously in question).

Problem 14-6. She Said He's Outside

Albert and Bruce are out on a Friday night two days before their marine unit is to be deployed overseas. They part ways around midnight. At one in the morning Albert gets a phone call from his close friend Debra. He claims that Debra told him she was scared because her ex-husband Charlie was outside her house in his car, but she did not want Albert to call the police or come over.

The next morning Bruce is arrested and charged with murdering Debra who was killed in her house about 3:00 a.m. that same morning. Bruce and Debra had been having a secret romance for several months.

1. Bruce's defense lawyer tries to block Albert from being deployed so Albert can testify about Debra's telephone call. Do you think he would be successful? What arguments would you make for Bruce? How would you respond if you were the prosecutor?

2. Assume Albert is not deployed and is prepared to testify about the conversation with Debra possibly linking ex-husband Charlie with the homicide. The prosecutor objects on hearsay grounds and the court upholds the objection, banning Albert's testimony about Debra's statements that Charlie was outside her house. If Bruce is convicted, what arguments would you make on appeal concerning the banned hearsay?

I. The Right to Cross-Examine and Confront Witnesses

[1] Cross-Examination

In *Pointer v. Texas*, 380 U.S. 400 (1965), the United States Supreme Court held that the Sixth Amendment gives the accused in a criminal case both the right to confront witnesses and, as a necessary corollary, the right of cross-examination. While this principle is considered essential to a fundamentally fair trial, numerous issues arise with respect to limitations upon the cross-examination right.

Scope of cross-examination: limited and wide-open approaches. Under the Federal Rules of Evidence and in a majority of states, cross-examination is restricted to matters testified to by the witness on direct examination and to issues of credibility. *See* Fed. R. Evid. 611(b). This is often called the *limited* or *federal* approach.

Approximately 15 states, on the other hand, adopt the so-called *wide open* approach in which the witness may be cross-examined about any subject relevant to any of the issues in the entire case, including facts related solely to the cross-examiner's own case or to an affirmative defense. In some of those jurisdictions, the trial judge may, in the interest of justice, limit the scope of cross-examination with respect to matters not testified to on direct. *See, e.g.*, Ky. R. Evid. 611(b).

Constitutionality of limits on cross-examination. Are statutes or court rulings that impose limits on cross-examination constitutionally permissible? In *Delaware v. Van Arsdall*, 475 U.S. 673, 679 (1986), the United States Supreme Court ruled that appropriate limitations may be imposed. "[T]rial judges retain wide latitude insofar as the Confrontation Clause is concerned to impose reasonable limits on such cross-examination based on concerns about, among other things, harassment, prejudice, confusion of the issues, the witness' safety, or interrogation that is repetitive or only marginally relevant."

Name and address of witness. The Supreme Court has held that the accused is entitled under the Sixth Amendment to cross-examine an informer who was the principal prosecution witness as to his actual name and address. *Smith v. Illinois*, 390 U.S. 129, 131 (1968).

Disguised witness. What if a witness rightfully fears retaliation if he or she testifies and is identified? Can the witness testify while wearing a disguise, such as a fake goatee and moustache and a wig? *See Morales v. Artuz*, 281 F.3d 55 (2d Cir. 2002) (sunglasses permitted); *Smith v. Graham*, 2012 U.S. Dist. LEXIS 89468 (S.D.N.Y. May 7, 2012) (yes if fear justified).

Nondisclosure order. Sometimes the court compromises on releasing the identity of a witness by issuing a nondisclosure order releasing the information to defense counsel but forbidding further release of the name, even to the accused.

Confidential information. What if the defendant wants to impeach a key government witness by using confidential information, such as mental health records or medical records? It is obvious that in this situation the defendant's right to confront prosecution witnesses may conflict with a witnesses' interest in privacy. A common resolution is for the trial court to review the records *in camera* and balance the competing interests.

Confidential informant. The Supreme Court held in *Roviaro v. United States*, 353 U.S. 53 (1957), on the facts of the case that the government was obligated to disclose to the defense the name of an informer-eyewitness. Unlike the traditional informer privilege that protects disclosure, the informer here was the only participant in the transaction charged, other than the defendant. The Court noted its balancing process, weighing the "public interest in protecting the flow of information against the individual's right to prepare his defense."

Status as probationer. Similarly, in *Davis v. Alaska*, 415 U.S. 308 (1974), the Court held that the trial court erred in refusing to allow the defendant to cross-examine a key prosecution witness to show that the witness had been placed on probation following an adjudication of juvenile delinquency. The state claimed that cross-examination had been properly restricted because of its interest in protecting the anonymity of juvenile offenders. The defense desired to pursue this line of questioning, however, in the hopes that it would show that the government had control over the witness's post-testimony freedom. While the Court acknowledged that states may implement policies to protect juvenile offenders, such an interest was outweighed, on the facts of this case, by the defendant's Sixth Amendment right to cross-examine the witness to determine whether the witness was biased.

Notes

1. *Trial remedy for violation of right to impeach witness: strike direct testimony.* What if a defendant is unable to effectively cross examine a government witness because the witness refuses to answer pertinent questions or the court refuses to release necessary information, such as the name of the prosecution witness? Many cases hold that the direct testimony may be stricken since it cannot be adequately tested by cross-examination.

2. *Appellate remedy for violation of right to impeach witnesses.* Assume that a defendant is denied the right to impeach a witness through appropriate cross-examination

questioning. Following conviction, must the appellate court automatically reverse or is such an error subject to harmless error analysis? In *Delaware v. Van Arsdall*, 475 U.S. 673 (1986), the Court rejected a *per se* reversal rule, holding that a multi-factored harmless-error analysis applies that includes consideration of "the importance of the witness' testimony in the prosecution's case, whether the testimony was cumulative, the presence or absence of evidence corroborating or contradicting the testimony of the witness on material points, the extent of cross-examination otherwise permitted, and, of course, the overall strength of the prosecution's case." *Id.* at 684.

3. *Limits on cross-examination of victims of sexual assault.* Almost all jurisdictions, including the federal government, have *rape shield* laws restricting the defendant's ability to cross-examine rape victims with regard to evidence of past sexual history. Rule 412 of the Federal Rules of Evidence, following the pattern established by state statutes, disallows such evidence but recognizes situations in which such inquiry will be allowed, such as where the past sexual behavior was with a person other than the accused and is offered by the defendant to explain the source of semen or injury to the victim.

Problem 14-7. Did I Solve the Problem?

You are a state legislator concerned about child sex abuse cases getting dismissed because the child refuses to testify. You have an idea how to ameliorate at least some of the trauma the child faces. You propose a statute in which both the prosecutor and defense lawyer prepare a set of interrogatories for the child victim. A social worker then asks the child the questions in a comfortable setting designed to put the child at ease. The entire session is videotaped and played at trial in lieu of the child's live testimony. The first time the procedure is used, defense counsel objects on confrontation grounds. Do you think your statute will survive the challenge? Why or why not? *See Coronado v. State*, 351 S.W.3d 315 (Tex. Crim. App. 2011).

[2] Confrontation

The preceding section related to cross-examination assumes that a witness has testified for the prosecution and is physically available for cross-examination. In most instances, testimony from a witness deemed favorable to the prosecution will be presented in "live" form. On occasion, however, testimony is offered in a way that effectively deprives the defendant of the right to confront the witness physically.

A literal interpretation of the Confrontation Clause of the Sixth Amendment would require the physical presence of all adverse witnesses. As this section of the chapter demonstrates, the Sixth Amendment does not require actual presence of witnesses in all cases.

Both confrontation and cross-examination issues may arise in those instances in which the government seeks to offer testimonial evidence from a person not physically testifying in open court. Sometimes a witness is not brought to open court in order to protect him or her from real or perceived harm (for example, child witnesses). More commonly, the government may seek to offer hearsay testimony under circumstances in which a witness is not physically available to testify at trial.

[a] "In-Court" Testimony and the Confrontation Clause

Maryland v. Craig

497 U.S. 836 (1990)

JUSTICE O'CONNOR delivered the opinion of the Court.

This case requires us to decide whether the Confrontation Clause of the Sixth Amendment categorically prohibits a child witness in a child abuse case from testifying against a defendant at trial, outside the defendant's physical presence, by one-way closed circuit television. . . .

[Defendant Craig was indicted for various sex offenses against a six-year-old girl who attended a kindergarten and prekindergarten center owned and operated by the defendant.]

In March 1987, before the case went to trial, the State sought to invoke a Maryland statutory procedure that permits a judge to receive, by one-way closed circuit television, the testimony of a child witness who is alleged to be a victim of child abuse. To invoke the procedure, the trial judge must first "determin[e] that testimony by the child victim in the courtroom will result in the child suffering serious emotional distress such that the child cannot reasonably communicate." Md. Cts. & Jud. Proc. Code Ann. § 9-102(a)(1)(ii) (1989). Once the procedure is invoked, the child witness, prosecutor, and defense counsel withdraw to a separate room; the judge, jury, and defendant remain in the courtroom. The child witness is then examined and cross-examined in the separate room, while a video monitor records and displays the witness's testimony to those in the courtroom. During this time the witness cannot see the defendant. The defendant remains in electronic communication with defense counsel, and objections may be made and ruled on as if the witness were testifying in the courtroom.

In support of its motion invoking the one-way closed circuit television procedure, the State presented expert testimony that the named victim as well as a number of other children who were alleged to have been sexually abused by Craig, would suffer "serious emotional distress such that [they could not] reasonably communicate," § 9-102(a)(1)(ii), if required to testify in the courtroom. . . .

Craig objected to the use of the procedure on Confrontation Clause grounds, but the trial court rejected that contention, concluding that although the statute "take[s] away the right of the defendant to be face to face with his or her accuser," the defendant retains the "essence of the right of confrontation," including the right to observe, cross-examine, and have the jury view the demeanor of the witness. The trial court further found that, "based upon the evidence presented . . . the testimony of each of these children in a courtroom will result in each child suffering serious emotional distress . . . such that each of these children cannot reasonably communicate." The trial court then found the named victim and three other children competent to testify and accordingly permitted them to testify against Craig via the one-way closed circuit television procedure.

[Craig was convicted by a jury on all counts, but the Maryland appellate court reversed, holding that the showing made by the state was insufficient to reach the threshold required by *Coy* for invocation of the statute. The U.S. Supreme Court granted certiorari.]

... [I]n *Coy v. Iowa*, [487 U.S. 1012 (1988)], we expressly "le[ft] for another day... the question whether any exceptions exist" to the "irreducible literal meaning of the Clause: 'a right to meet face to face all those who appear and give evidence at trial.'" The procedure challenged in *Coy* involved the placement of a screen that prevented two child witnesses in a child abuse case from seeing the defendant as they testified against him at trial. In holding that the use of this procedure violated the defendant's right to confront witnesses against him, we suggested that any exception to the right "would surely be allowed only when necessary to further an important public policy"—i.e., only upon a showing of something more than the generalized, "legislatively imposed presumption of trauma" underlying the statute at issue in that case. We concluded that "[s]ince there ha[d] been no individualized findings that these particular witnesses needed special protection, the judgment [in the case before us] could not be sustained by any conceivable exception." Because the trial court in this case made individualized findings that each of the child witnesses needed special protection, this case requires us to decide the question reserved in *Coy*.

The central concern of the Confrontation Clause is to ensure the reliability of the evidence against a criminal defendant by subjecting it to rigorous testing in the context of an adversary proceeding before the trier of fact. The word "confront," after all, also means a clashing of forces or ideas, thus carrying with it the notion of adversariness....

As this description indicates, the right guaranteed by the Confrontation Clause includes not only a "personal examination," but also "(1) insures that the witness will give his statements under oath—thus impressing him with the seriousness of the matter and guarding against the lie by the possibility of a penalty for perjury; (2) forces the witness to submit to cross-examination, the 'greatest legal engine ever invented for the discovery of truth'; [and] (3) permits the jury that is to decide the defendant's fate to observe the demeanor of the witness in making his statement, thus aiding the jury in assessing his credibility."

... [W]e have never insisted on an actual face-to-face encounter at trial in every instance in which testimony is admitted against a defendant. Instead, we have repeatedly held that the Clause permits, where necessary, the admission of certain hearsay statements against a defendant despite the defendant's inability to confront the declarant at trial.... Thus, in certain narrow circumstances, "competing interests, if 'closely examined,' may warrant dispensing with confrontation at trial."

. . . Maryland's statutory procedure, when invoked, prevents a child witness from seeing the defendant as he or she testifies against the defendant at trial. We find it significant, however, that Maryland's procedure preserves all of the other elements of the confrontation right: The child witness must be competent to testify and must testify under oath; the defendant retains full opportunity for contemporaneous cross-examination; and the judge, jury, and defendant are able to view (albeit by video monitor) the demeanor (and body) of the witness as he or she testifies. Although we are mindful of the many subtle effects face-to-face confrontation may have on an adversary criminal proceeding, the presence of these other elements of confrontation — oath, cross-examination, and observation of the witness' demeanor — adequately ensures that the testimony is both reliable and subject to rigorous adversarial testing in a manner functionally equivalent to that accorded live, in-person testimony. These safeguards of reliability and adversariness render the use of such a procedure a far cry from the undisputed prohibition of the Confrontation Clause: trial by *ex parte* affidavit or inquisition.

. . . We likewise conclude today that a State's interest in the physical and psychological well-being of child abuse victims may be sufficiently important to outweigh, at least in some cases, a defendant's right to face his or her accusers in court. That a significant majority of States have enacted statutes to protect child witnesses from the trauma of giving testimony in child abuse cases attests to the widespread belief in the importance of such a public policy.

. . . In sum, we conclude that where necessary to protect a child witness from trauma that would be caused by testifying in the physical presence of the defendant, at least where such trauma would impair the child's ability to communicate, the Confrontation Clause does not prohibit use of a procedure that, despite the absence of face-to-face confrontation, ensures the reliability of the evidence by subjecting it to rigorous adversarial testing and thereby preserves the essence of effective confrontation. Because there is no dispute that the child witnesses in this case testified under oath, were subject to full cross-examination, and were able to be observed by the judge, jury, and defendant as they testified, we conclude that, to the extent that a proper finding of necessity has been made, the admission of such testimony would be consonant with the Confrontation Clause.

[The Maryland Court of Appeals appeared to have rested its conclusion on the trial court's failure to observe the child witness' behavior in the defendant's presence and also its failure to explore less restrictive alternatives to the use of the closed circuit television procedure. The Supreme Court declined to establish, as a matter of federal constitutional law, that any such categorical evidentiary prerequisite was necessary for the use of the closed circuit television procedure. But because the Maryland appellate court held that the trial judge had not made the requisite finding of necessity required by Maryland law, the case was vacated and remanded for further proceedings.]

Justice Scalia, with whom Justice Brennan, Justice Marshall, and Justice Stevens join, dissenting.

Seldom has this Court failed so conspicuously to sustain a categorical guarantee of the Constitution against the tide of prevailing current opinion. The Sixth Amendment provides, with unmistakable clarity, that "[i]n all criminal prosecutions, the accused shall enjoy the right . . . to be confronted with the witnesses against him." The purpose of enshrining this protection in the Constitution was to assure that none of the many policy interests from time to time pursued by statutory law could overcome a defendant's right to face his or her accusers in court. . . .

Because the text of the Sixth Amendment is clear, and because the Constitution is meant to protect against, rather than conform to, current "widespread belief," I respectfully dissent.

According to the Court, "we cannot say that [face-to-face] confrontation [with witnesses appearing at trial] is an indispensable element of the Sixth Amendment's guarantee of the right to confront one's accusers. . . . Whatever else it may mean in addition, the defendant's constitutional right "to be confronted with the witnesses against him" means, always and everywhere, at least what it explicitly says: the "right to meet face to face all those who appear and give evidence at trial."

Notes

1. *Shield between defendant and witness.* Assume that a state statute allows a child victim to testify by way of closed-circuit television if it is determined by the judge that in-court testimony "will result in the child's suffering serious emotional distress." If the judge decides that the child would not suffer such distress if testifying in the presence of the *jury* so long as she could not observe the *defendant*, would it be constitutionally permissible to erect a shield between the defendant and the witness as a "modified courtroom setup" to avoid use of the closed-circuit television procedure? In *People v. Lofton*, 740 N.E.2d 782 (Ill. 2000), the Illinois Supreme Court held that this procedure violated the defendant's right to confrontation under both the United States and Illinois Constitutions:

> Here the defendant's ability to observe the manner of the witness while testifying could have prejudiced him by limiting his ability to suggest lines of examination to his attorney that might have been indispensable to effective cross-examination. Unlike the use of one-way closed-circuit television provided for by the legislature . . . and found permissible in *Craig*, the barricade . . . erected [between the witness and the accused] precluded the defendant from seeing her while she testified.

Id. at 794. Does it seem sensible that trial judges should be limited to either "full" in-court testimony, consistent with *Coy*, or the closed-circuit television "out of court" procedure authorized by *Craig*?

2. *Effect on defendant's communications with defense counsel.* If the witness is to testify outside the physical presence of the defendant and defense counsel, the process must ensure that the defendant can communicate effectively with defense counsel during the testimony. *See, e.g.*, *United States v. Miguel*, 111 F.3d 666 (9th Cir.

1997) (rejecting procedure by which child sex abuse victim gave deposition in presence of judge and lawyer with defendant watching on television but unable to communicate with defense lawyer; violates defendant's right to contemporaneous communication with his lawyer).

3. *Federal legislative response to* Craig. Shortly after *Craig*, Congress enacted 18 U.S.C. § 3509 under which a court may order that a child witness testify "in a room outside the courtroom . . . televised by a 2-way closed circuit television." This procedure requires the trial court to determine that "the child is unable to testify in open court in the presence of the defendant" because "of fear" or "a substantial likelihood, established by expert testimony, that the child would suffer emotional trauma from testifying." In *United States v. Etimani*, 328 F.3d 493 (9th Cir. 2003), the statute was held constitutional and properly applied; the court also rejected the defendant's argument that the statute required that the television monitor be located directly in the child's field of vision while the child testified.

4. *Suggested alternate means of taking child testimony.* Although many states have enacted legislation to comply with the strict constitutional standards set forth in *Maryland v. Craig*, no formal structure is given to attorneys and courts as to when and under what circumstances alternative means of taking child testimony should take place. To remedy this, the National Conference of Commissioners on Uniforms State Laws proposed the Uniform Act on Taking Testimony of Children by Alternative Methods. The act applies to all children under the age of 13 who may be called as witnesses in either criminal or noncriminal proceedings. It gives direction and structure across state jurisdictions for handling particularly vulnerable child witnesses, while aiming to strike a balance between protecting the interests of child witnesses and the rights of parties. The Uniform Act has been adopted by a few states and is being considered in others.

[b] "Out-of-Court" Testimony and the Confrontation Clause

Crawford v. Washington, 541 U.S. 36 (2004), addresses both the admission of hearsay evidence and the Sixth Amendment right of confrontation. The Court held that, because pretrial interrogation of a crime victim was to establish a past crime, its admission deprived the defendant of the opportunity to confront the witness who was unavailable for trial. Because law school courses in Evidence explore *Crawford* and its progeny as restrictions on the admissibility of out-of-court hearsay, this book's coverage of the right of confrontation concentrates on in-court testimony.

J. After the Proof: Moving Toward a Verdict

[1] Jury Instructions

The general rule, subject to some exceptions, is that the judge resolves questions of law and the jury decides questions of fact. Since jurors are not necessarily trained in law, they must be told of their duties and the applicable law. This is the responsibility of the judge. In every jurisdiction, judges will inform jurors of their duties and the applicable law several times during a trial. Often the judge instructs the jury at the beginning of trial, perhaps one or more times during the trial, and at the end of closing arguments by counsel. In some jurisdictions, jurors are also given a handbook that explains their functions and the administrative details of jury service.

[a] Content

Jury instructions in criminal cases address two issues: routine administrative matters and the laws the jurors are to apply when deciding questions of fact. The first category tells jurors such information as when the trial will resume, where the jurors are to dine or sleep, and that they are not to discuss the case with anyone until deliberations begin.

The second category—the law jurors are to apply—includes both general and specific legal principles. The general ones, expressed in identical language in many trials, inform the jury of the burden of proof, the presumption of innocence, and the like. Specific jury instructions relate to the crime being tried. For example, if the offense is a homicide where the accused has raised self-defense, the jury instructions will virtually always deal with the elements of homicide, various lesser included offenses, and self-defense.

[i] Comment on the Evidence

In the federal system and some states, the trial judge is permitted to comment on the evidence. A small number of states permit the court to summarize or comment on the evidence if both the defense attorney and prosecutor so request. *See, e.g.*, Mo. Rev. Stat. § 546.380.

In the leading Supreme Court case, *Quercia v. United States*, 289 U.S. 466, 468 (1933), the defendant testified and denied involvement with the illegal drug transactions at issue in the case. The jury instructions included the judge's observations:

> You may have noticed, Mr. Foreman and gentlemen, that he [the defendant] wiped his hands during his testimony. It is rather a curious thing, but that is almost always an indication of lying. Why it should be so we don't know, but that is the fact. I think that every single word that man [the defendant] said, except when he agreed with the Government's testimony, was a lie.

On appeal, the Supreme Court reversed the conviction because the judge's remarks were not based on the evidence. The Court observed:

> In charging the jury, the trial judge . . . may not assume the role of a witness. He may analyze and dissect the evidence, but he may not either distort it or add to it. . . . This court has . . . emphasized the duty of the trial judge to use great care that an expression of opinion upon the evidence [should not mislead or be one-sided or contain deductions or theories not warranted by the evidence.]

Id. at 469–70.

Many jurisdictions disagree with the federal approach and bar the judge from commenting on the evidence. *See, e.g.*, Ga. Code Ann. § 17-8-57 (error for trial judge to express or intimate opinion as to what has or has not been proved or as to guilt; violation "shall" cause a reversal of conviction and granting of new trial). The American Bar Association standards for jury instructions specify, "The instructions should not contain comments by the court reflecting the court's personal belief regarding credibility of certain witnesses, evidentiary value of specific items of evidence, or the guilt or innocence of the defendant." Standards for Criminal Justice § 15-4.4(a) (3d ed. 1996).

Notes

1. *Fair trial.* Which approach do you favor? Can the defendant get a fair trial if the *judge* tells the jury that a defense witness or even the defendant lied?

2. *Jury instructions on judge's comments.* Note that *Quercia* states that the judge must inform the jury that it, not the judge, decides questions of fact. Is this statement adequate to overcome the impact of the judge's comment on the case?

Problem 14-8. The Judicious Judge Jones

Fred was charged with bank robbery in New York City on December 6. He testified that he was in Los Angeles the day of the robbery. Defense witnesses Allison and Abraham testified that Fred was with them in Los Angeles that day. Barbara and Benjamin, the tellers who were actually robbed, made an in-court identification of Fred as the New York robber. They had previously described the robber to police and had picked Fred from a lineup at the police station.

At the conclusion of the trial, Judge Jones gave the following jury instructions in pertinent part:

> . . . You have heard lots of conflicting testimony today and you are to rely on all you know about the witnesses to determine whom to believe. You are to consider the witness's interests in the case as well as everything else you observed and heard in court. You are not bound by any of my comments; you are the sole judges of the credibility of witnesses.

Assess each of the following additional instructions in a jurisdiction that follows the federal approach and permits the judge to comment on the evidence but bars the judge from "going too far":

1. "You have probably heard more than one person commit perjury during this trial."

2. "The testimony of eyewitnesses is significant evidence that should be given much weight."

3. "Recall that during the cross-examination of Allison, she admitted that she was just released from a three-year prison term for embezzlement. I think this casts a huge shadow over her credibility."

4. "I think these two bank tellers are very brave to go through the ordeal of the robbery and then to come in here and relive it."

5. "I admire public-spirited citizens like Barbara and Benjamin who are helping us today."

[ii] Lesser-Included Offenses

The jury instructions in criminal cases will detail the elements of the offense(s) with which the defendant is charged. They may also include those of *lesser-included* crimes. Federal law is typical. Federal Rule 31(c) states that a defendant may be found guilty of "an offense necessarily included in the offense charged; an attempt to commit the offense charged; or an attempt to commit an offense necessarily included in the offense charged, if the attempt is an offense in its own right."

A jury may only convict or acquit a person of the criminal charges contained in the jury instructions. Therefore, the definition of a lesser-included offense is important to both prosecution and defense since it defines the scope of possible criminal liability and indicates what jury instructions should be given.

Assume that the defendant is charged with first degree murder. If the jury is only instructed on this crime, it will have only two choices: guilty or innocent of first degree murder. If there is insufficient proof of first degree murder, the defendant must be acquitted. On the other hand, if other crimes (such as second degree murder, voluntary manslaughter, and involuntary manslaughter) are lesser-included offenses of first degree murder and are included as options in the jury instructions, the jury will have a choice of four offenses. Perhaps the jury will acquit the defendant of first degree murder but convict him or her of voluntary manslaughter.

Notes

1. *Trial judge's options.* The most widely recognized rule is that the court has the inherent authority to charge the jury on lesser-included offenses. Another approach is that the court *must* do so if the lesser- included crime is established by the evidence. *See, e.g., United States v. Cooper*, 714 F.3d 873 (5th Cir. 2013). A third view, the so-called "party autonomy" rule, gives either the defendant or prosecution the right to have a lesser-included instruction if the evidence supports guilt of the lesser offense. *See, e.g., Wiggins v. State*, 902 A.2d 1110 (Del. 2006).

California adopts still another approach: a court is barred from instructing the jury on a lesser-included crime that was not charged in the pleadings unless the prosecution agrees. This approach is based on the principle that prosecutor has the sole discretion to decide who and what to charge. *See, e.g., People v. Valentine*, 143 Cal. App. 4th 1383 (2006). Do you agree with this unusual approach to jury instructions on less-included crimes?

After years of uncertainty about the proper test for determining what is a lesser-included offense, the Supreme Court resolved the matter. In *Schmuck v. United States*, 489 U.S. 705 (1989), the Court adopted the "elements" test. "Under this test, one offense is not 'necessarily included' in another unless the elements of the lesser offense are a subset of the elements of the charged offense. Where the lesser offense requires an element not required for the greater offense, no instruction is to be given under Rule 31(c)."

2. *Permutations. Schmuck* says that the lesser offense may not require an element not required for the greater offense. What if the greater offense requires an element not required in the lesser offense? For example, assume one contains elements A, B, C, X, and Y, but the other contains only elements A, B, and C. Can the less serious offense be a lesser-included offense under *Schmuck*?

3. *Identical crimes.* Sometimes a legislature will enact virtually identical crimes with different punishments but neither is lesser included in the other. What if the prosecutor chooses to prosecute the defendant under the more serious one? If the two offenses require identical proof, can the defendant successfully request a lesser-included crime instruction for the less serious one under Rule 31(c)? *See Berra v. United States*, 351 U.S. 131 (1956). This issue is discussed in Chapter 2 in connection with *United States v. Batchelder*, 442 U.S. 114 (1979), where the Supreme Court upheld a prosecutor's discretion to charge a defendant under either of two overlapping criminal statutes.

4. *Tactical issues.* The possibility of a lesser-included crime instruction raises a number of tactical considerations. The prosecution in a murder case may think it has a weak first degree murder case and may prefer a jury instruction on lesser-included offenses in addition to first degree murder. This may enable the government to get a conviction for some offense rather than an acquittal on the only charge. Similarly, the defense may prefer to give the jury an alternative to the serious offense of first degree murder, perhaps hoping that the jury will show mercy when there is sufficient proof of first degree murder to convict.

On the other hand, it is also possible that neither side will want the jury instructed on lesser-included crimes. Perhaps the prosecution believes it has a strong case for first degree murder and does not want the defendant to be convicted of a lesser offense. The defense may also prefer to roll the dice in a case in which it believes it has a defense to first degree murder but not to a lesser-included offense.

5. *Illustration of* Schmuck*'s approach.* Assume that the defendant is charged with violating 18 U.S.C. § 2113(a), which makes it a federal offense to "by force and violence, or by intimidation, [take] . . . any . . . thing of value [from a] bank." Assume that § 2113(b) provides for lesser penalties in the case of an individual who "takes and carries away, with intent to steal or purloin, [anything] of value exceeding $1,000 [from a] . . . bank." Is the defendant entitled to a jury instruction on the lesser offense if the defendant's contention at trial is that he or she did not take any of the bank's money "by force and violence, or by intimidation?"

In *Carter v. United States*, 530 U.S. 255 (2000), the Supreme Court applied the "elements test" from *Schmuck* and held that § 2113(b) was not a lesser included offense of § 2113(a) because it required three elements not required for conviction under Subsection (a). As the Court explained,

> First, whereas Subsection (b) requires that the defendant act "with intent to steal or purloin," Subsection (a) contains no similar requirement. Second, whereas Subsection (b) requires that the defendant "tak[e] and carr[y] away" the property, Subsection (a) only requires that the defendant "tak[e]" the property. Third, whereas the first paragraph of Subsection (b) requires that the property have a "value exceeding $1,000" Subsection (a) contains no valuation requirement.

Id. at 262.

In dissent, Justice Ginsburg, joined by Justices Stevens, Souter, and Breyer, observed that at common law, larceny was considered a lesser-included offense of robbery. Therefore, she concluded that "Congress did not depart from that traditional understanding when it [adopted the relevant federal statutes]."

Problem 14-9. I'm Innocent, But of What?

1. Keith is charged with two crimes. Crime 1 contains elements X, Y and Z. Crime 2 contains only elements X and Y. Assume that elements X and Y are the same for both offenses.

a. Is Crime 2 lesser-included in Crime 1 according to *Schmuck*?

b. Could Crime 1 be lesser-included in Crime 2?

c. Would your answer to the above questions change if:

> Crimes 1 and 2 were punished exactly the same? What if Crime 1 were punished more severely than Crime 2? What if the reverse: Crime 2 were punished more severely than Crime 1?

2. Heather was arrested after an undercover agent reported that she had marijuana in her house. After a search revealed marijuana there, she was charged with the crime of possession of marijuana with intent to distribute, as follows:

> *State Statute § 44-101 — Possession with Intent*
>
> Except as otherwise authorized by law, it is unlawful for any person knowingly or intentionally to manufacture, distribute, or dispense, or possess with intent to manufacture, distribute, or dispense, marijuana.
>
> The punishment is 3–5 years in prison.

During trial, two police detectives testified that they searched Heather's apartment and found two tons of baled marijuana in her basement. They also found two small packets of rolling papers, containing a total of 100 sheets. An undercover agent testified that Heather offered to sell him 500 pounds of marijuana.

The judge indicated that she would charge the jury under State Statute § 44-101, possession with intent. Heather has filed a motion requesting that the jury also be instructed on State Statute § 44-201, simple possession.

> *State Statute § 44-201 — Simple Possession*

> Except as otherwise authorized by law, it is unlawful for any person knowingly or intentionally to possess marijuana.
>
> The punishment is not more than one year in prison.

a. Is simple possession (§44-201) a lesser-included offense of the crime of possession with intent (§44-101) under the inherent relationship approach? The *Schmuck* elements view?

b. Should the judge grant Heather's motion and instruct the jury on simple possession as well as possession with intent?

i. Assume that Heather testified at trial, admitted purchasing the marijuana from someone named Juan whose address and whereabouts are unknown, and stated that her intent was to burn the marijuana so that the youth of the area would not be harmed by it. Should this affect the decision whether to give the instruction on simple possession?

ii. Changing the facts, assume that the detectives had found two pounds of marijuana instead of two tons and that Heather did not testify at trial. Should the judge give the requested jury instruction on simple possession?

[2] Jury Instruction Procedures

[a] Overview

In general terms, it is the judge's responsibility to prepare and give jury instructions, but lawyers for prosecution and defense are also involved. Before the instructions are given, the attorneys are usually permitted—sometimes encouraged—to request that specific instructions be given and to screen the judge's proposed instructions for possible error.

The rules of criminal procedure routinely describe at least part of the process. Federal Rule 30(a) states that any party "may request in writing that the court instruct the jury on the law as specified in the request." Logically, that request is circulated to all parties and can be made no later than the close of the evidence. Before closing arguments, the court informs the parties about its ruling on the request.

While the court instructs the jury before and/or after the closing arguments, any party objecting to an instruction or the failure to agree to the request for an instruction "must inform the court of the specific objection and the grounds for the objection *before* the jury retires to deliberate." Generally, a failure to object precludes appellate review.

Notes

1. *Many unanswered questions.* Rule 30 leaves many questions about jury instructions unanswered. For example, jury instructions are given orally. Can they also be "reduced to writing" and given the jurors for use during deliberations? Must the court conduct a hearing on proposed jury instructions or can the court simply

rule on the proposals without according either side an opportunity to argue its case in an oral argument? If a lawyer wants the judge to instruct the jury on a certain topic, must that lawyer provide the court with the precise language to use or can the lawyer simply request a jury instruction on a particular topic? Are oral requests for a particular instruction valid?

2. *Advance copy of instructions for counsel.* Many states require the judge to provide counsel with a written copy of the jury instructions before they are read to the jury in order to ensure that counsel has the opportunity to carefully review the instructions and to facilitate informed objections. Note that Rule 30 does not require the judge to provide counsel with a written copy or to inform counsel of the exact instructions to be given, making it difficult for counsel to carefully scrutinize the judge's work and suggest any changes before the instructions are read.

[b] Timing of Jury Instructions

Instruction at beginning of trial. At the beginning of the trial, the court may provide basic information about the proceedings and some administrative matters, e.g., information about the law to be applied in the case.

Instructions during trial. The court may also instruct the jury during the trial, e.g., the court may tell the jury that certain evidence is to be used for one purpose but not another, that certain erroneously admitted testimony should be ignored, and that argument of counsel is not evidence.

Before or after closing argument. Rule 30 specifically requires the court to instruct the jury before or after closing arguments, or at both times. Some recent jury reform proposals suggest that judges depart from the traditional rule (jury instructions are given *after* closing arguments) and give jury instructions regarding the applicable law prior to closing arguments. This practice is designed to help jurors better understand the closing arguments and to provide the attorneys a context from which to argue how the law in the case relates to the facts. Of course, the court is free and likely to instruct the jury at other times.

After closing arguments for both sides, the court's final instructions tell the jury about the applicable laws and jury procedures. To ensure a fair opportunity to object and to participate fully in the trial, all jury instructions should be given in the presence of counsel for all parties and the defendant personally. Ordinarily, this is no problem because the necessary people are already in the jury room during the trial. Sometimes an instruction is given in the defendant's absence, however, but this error is usually deemed "harmless error" and of little consequence to the outcome of the case.

[c] Written or Oral

At common law, jurors were only given oral instructions. Noting that written instructions help jurors process and comprehend the instructions as well as recall and apply them, the American Bar Association recommends that each juror be given a written copy of the jury instructions to use while the court instructs the jury and during deliberations. PRINCIPLES FOR JURIES AND JURY TRIALS, Prin. 14(B) and comment.

Empirical data. Research has shown that there are considerable advantages in providing the jury with a written copy of the oral instructions. One study reported that juries with written instructions, when compared with those that had to rely on oral instructions, were more efficient, conducted better deliberations, appeared to be less confused about the law, spent less time trying to understand the instructions, concentrated more on relevant facts and accurate application of the law, and felt better about the quality of their decisions. Robert F. Forston, *Sense and Non-Sense: Jury Trial Communication*, 1975 B.Y.U. L. REV. 601.

[d] Pattern Jury Instructions

American jurisdictions routinely have *pattern jury instructions* which ordinarily have been prepared by a panel of judges and lawyers and are used throughout the jurisdiction. Sometimes they are approved by the state Supreme Court. These pattern instructions spare trial judges the responsibility of drafting their own jury instructions in criminal cases. For example, a judge trying a robbery case may use pattern jury instructions for such issues as the definition of robbery, the burden of proof, and the responsibility of each juror to decide the case without regard to bias or prejudice.

Because the pattern instructions have been used in many trials and upheld by appellate courts, trial judges feel "safe" using them since they will very likely withstand appellate challenge. While these pattern jury instructions do make a judge's job easier, in some situations the judge must alter the pattern instructions to fit unique features of the case at hand. And lawyers for both sides may suggest altering all or portions of the pattern instructions to suit their case or even to take account of recent case or statutory developments.

[e] Judicial Discretion

The court is not obligated to accept counsel's proposed jury instructions. The court may reject the proposed instructions altogether or accept counsel's suggestion that a jury instruction on a certain topic be given, then write and use its own version of the instruction on that issue. In order to permit counsel to discuss jury instructions during the closing argument, Rule 30 requires the judge to inform counsel of its ruling on jury instruction requests before the closing argument.

[3] Closing Arguments

The closing argument is an attorney's last chance to speak to the jury before deliberation. The purpose of closing arguments, or summation, is for each attorney to tie together the evidence into a coherent story, counter the other side's arguments, and help the jury to apply the law to that evidence. Although the jury has already heard all the evidence before closing arguments begin, prosecution and defense attorneys know that their arguments, both in content and style of delivery, can have a tremendous psychological impact upon the jurors, and therefore influence the verdict. The great power of closing arguments mandates restrictions to govern the types of arguments that are permissible from both the defense and the prosecution.

Trial judges have immense discretion to control their form and content. Appellate reversal for abuse of discretion is rare.

Time limits. Trial courts often set time limits on closing arguments. *See, e.g., United States v. Jamal*, 246 Fed. Appx. 351 (6th Cir. 2007) (upholding 45-minute per side for closing argument); *Dorsey v. State*, 646 S.E.2d 713 (Ga. App. 2007) (upholding trial court giving additional time to conclude closing argument); *United States v. Holt*, 493 Fed. Appx. 515 (5th Cir. 2012) (despite 27-hour trial over three days, 25 witnesses, 164 wiretap sessions, and about 200 exhibits, trial judge's decision to limit defendant's closing arguments to five minutes was upheld though the court of appeals expressed "strong disagreement" with the severe time limit; defense lawyer did not request additional time or inform the court what arguments the lawyer was precluded from making because of the five-minute limit). A few states even establish time limits. *See, e.g.*, Ga. Code Ann. § 17-8-73 (closing argument limited to one hour for each side in non-capital case and two hours in capital case).

Reversal for prejudice. A prosecutor's error in closing argument, such as intentionally referring to facts not in evidence, will cause a reversal only if the court finds it impeded the defendant's right to a fair trial. *See, e.g., Garcia v. State*, 246 S.W.3d 121 (Tex. App. 2007) (error in prosecutor's closing argument reversed only if "extremely or manifestly improper"); *United States v. Tafolla-Gonzalez*, 393 Fed. Appx. 502 (9th Cir. 2010) (prosecutor's closing argument improperly referred to information not introduced during the trial, but was harmless error because of overwhelming evidence of defendant's guilt). If the trial judge gave a curative jury instruction, often the error is deemed non-prejudicial on the theory that the jury follows the jury instructions.

The American Bar Association's standards place reasonable limits on closing arguments. The ABA Standards for Criminal Justice Standards for the Prosecution Function, § 3-6.8 contains the standards for prosecutors. While the prosecutor may argue reasonable inferences from the evidence, she cannot intentionally misstate the evidence or mislead the jury about which inferences to draw from that evidence. She cannot express her personal belief about the testimony or the defendant's guilt, nor can she make arguments that are either calculated to appeal to the jury's prejudices or divert them from its duty to decide the case on the evidence. The standards for defense attorneys in are nearly identical. For other related standards, *see* Model Rules of Prof'l Conduct r. 3.3(a)(1); 3.4(e); 4.1 (1983); National District Attorneys' Association, Nat'l Prosecution Standard 85.1 (2d ed. 1991).

Defense "opening the door" in its closing argument. Since the doctrine of double jeopardy prevents most government appeals, the majority of applicable cases deal with impropriety by the prosecution. However, some courts have indirectly addressed impermissible closing arguments by the defense. If the defense counsel "opens the door" by using impermissible questioning or arguments, many courts will allow the prosecution to respond in like kind during rebuttal.

[4] Jury Deliberations

Retire to jury room. After the closing arguments and the jury instructions, the jury leaves the courtroom and goes to the jury room to begin deliberations. Only the jurors are permitted in this room, although a court officer may be nearby to assist the jury and to prevent others from disturbing the jurors. Alternate jurors should not be present during deliberations.

Alternate jurors. In many jurisdictions, alternate jurors are discharged once deliberations begin. Under the federal approach, however, alternate jurors may be detained during deliberations. Fed. R. Crim. P. 24(e)(3). If alternate jurors do attend and observe the deliberations, the case will be reversed only if prejudice is shown. *See United States v. Olano*, 507 U.S. 725 (1993).

Under supervision of court officer. Sometimes jurors eat meals in the jury room or go to a nearby restaurant. In the latter case, they are under the direct supervision of a court officer to ensure that they are not subjected to outside influences and information, and do not discuss the case before instructed to do so by the judge.

Select foreperson. Often the jury's first task is to select a "foreperson" or leader to organize the jury's work and serve as a liaison with court officers and the judge. The latter function includes communicating with the judge on matters such as the need to have certain jury instructions repeated or explained, to have the transcript of certain testimony read to the jury, and to report the jury's decisions. Often there is no prescribed method of selecting a foreperson; the jury can decide for itself the procedures to use.

Exhibits in jury room. Often a statute or court rule will permit jurors to take into the jury room all or part of the papers and exhibits, such as maps or physical objects, admitted in evidence in the case. These items may be studied by jurors and used in their deliberations. Exceptions are frequently made for depositions that were read into evidence and for some other documents and items (such as the murder weapon) that could be dangerous. These are not permitted in the jury room because of a fear the jury will give them too much weight when compared with oral testimony that is not available for scrutiny in the jury room. Sometimes exhibits in the form of books are not permitted because of concern the jurors will use pages not introduced into evidence. In some locales, jurors are also given copies of the indictment and the jury instructions. Sometimes the parties may agree to add or remove items available to the jury.

Reviewing proof presented during trial. During deliberations, jurors may find they cannot remember or they disagree about the content of evidence admitted during the trial. They are routinely permitted to ask the judge if they may review the questionable proof. For example, they may seek to rehear a 911 recording played during trial or have a witness's testimony read from the transcript. The judge should receive such requests from the foreperson in open court on the record. Both sides are allowed to comment on whether and how the request should be granted. Although the judge is ordinarily given the discretion to grant or deny the request, a minority of jurisdictions require the judge to approve the request if possible. The court may instruct the jury not to give undue weight to the repeated evidence. If the jury's request for a review of oral evidence is approved, the court will order the clerk or someone else to read the pertinent portions of the transcript to the jury.

Juror's experiments. Jurors may attempt experiments with evidence presented at trial. In general, such efforts are impermissible since the experiment is not subject to adversarial testing and may be misleading. Some experiments are upheld, though the reasoning is sometimes strained. *See, e.g., State v. Pease*, 163 P.3d 985 (Ak. App. 2007) (upholding jury experiment to look out jury room window to see if a person could recognize another person at 200 feet, but improper to leave court house to perform same experiment; not reversible error because did not deny defendant a fair trial).

Continued plea negotiations during deliberations. Sometimes the accused and the prosecutor continue plea negotiations during the trial. Since neither side may want to risk a jury's decision, they may work out a deal while the jury is in the jury room deliberating. The American Bar Association recommends in such cases that the jury be dismissed, without rendering a verdict, as soon as the plea is accepted. If a verdict has been decided, the court should not accept it. STANDARDS FOR CRIMINAL JUSTICE § 15-5.5 (3d ed. 1996).

[5] Verdict

[a] In General

The essential purpose of a trial is the resolution of the issues. The *verdict*, the decision of the jury or judge as to guilt, accomplishes this. The verdict states whether the defendant is guilty or innocent of each charge (or lesser-included offense). Rule 31 of the Federal Rules of Criminal Procedure sketches some of the procedural facets of the verdict. In most states, the jury must return a unanimous verdict in open court.

When there are multiple defendants or multiple counts for any defendant, the jury may return a verdict about any defendant or any count where its verdict is unanimous. If a jury is unable to agree on a verdict on any counts, the court may declare a mistrial on those counts. A jury may return a guilty verdict on the offense charged, an attempt to commit that charge, and or an attempt to commit an offense included in the offense charged.

A party may request or the court may poll the jurors individually. If the poll shows a lack of unanimity, the court may order the jury to deliberate further or declare a mistrial and discharge the jury.

Notes

1. *Announcement of verdict.* Rule 31 answers some, but not all, questions about the return of the verdict. Ordinarily in open court, the judge asks whether the jury has agreed on a verdict. Then, the foreperson orally, in writing, or both, informs the court or the court clerk of the jury's decision. The defendant has a right to be present at this time.

2. *General verdict.* The usual practice is that the jury issues a *general verdict*, which is a simple "guilty" or "not guilty" decision on each count. The jury does not articulate any reasons for its conclusions.

3. *Special verdicts.* On occasion, a *special verdict* is used in criminal cases. This verdict requires the jury to answer specific factual questions in addition to resolving the allegations in each count. Usually, the special verdict requires the jury to state whether particular elements were present or absent, then to state its conclusion on guilt or innocence.

The Federal Rules of Criminal Procedure do not discuss a special verdict in a criminal case tried by a jury, but Rule 23(c) authorizes it in non-jury cases when requested before the finding of guilty or not guilty. Some state provisions authorize a special verdict in jury cases. *See, e.g.*, Cal. Penal Code §§ 1150 & 1152 (special verdict permissible in felony cases when jury is in doubt as to legal consequences of proven facts; jury specifically states proven facts and then court draws conclusions of law).

A special verdict is quite helpful to jurors in organizing their discussions and decisions, but criminal courts do not make use of it frequently. The primary argument against the special verdict is that it provides the jury with so much specific guidance that it impinges on the jury's independence in exercising jury nullification and could tilt the scales in favor of conviction. *See generally United States v. Spock*, 416 F.2d 165 (1st Cir. 1969). In some situations, however, a special verdict is essential. For example, if a defendant is charged with conspiracy or attempt to commit several felonies, to assure proper sentencing if the defendant is convicted, the jury must indicate which felony the defendant conspired or attempted to commit. Similarly, in some jurisdictions the quantity of drugs or the amount of money stolen must be included in the verdict in order to impose sentences and assess the amount of restitution. This is especially important because of recent Supreme Court decisions, discussed in Chapter 16, requiring the jury, not judge, to make certain factual determinations affecting sentences. *See United States v. Booker*, 543 U.S. 220 (2005).

A special verdict could also be significant in establishing a collateral estoppel claim, since it is crucial to know precisely what facts were found in an earlier criminal case. *See Ashe v. Swenson*, 397 U.S. 436 (1970), discussed in Chapter 15. Finally, a special verdict is often required in capital cases where the sentencing jury must list such facts as the specific aggravating and mitigating factors it found.

Counsel desiring a special verdict should make a timely request, perhaps even suggesting the exact questions the jury should be asked. Failure to request a special verdict may be deemed a waiver of the issue and make appellate reversal unlikely on this claim.

4. *Correction or amendment of a verdict.* Sometimes a jury verdict in a criminal case is ambiguous, not responsive to the judge's instructions, or incorrect in not accurately representing the jury's decision. Examples include a failure to resolve all charges, a guilty verdict to a crime with which the defendant had not been charged, a failure to specify which degree of murder the defendant committed, and a failure to sign the correct verdict form. In such cases, ordinarily the court can simply send the jury back to the jury room to correct the error. If the jury has been discharged, however, usually the trial court cannot reconvene the panel and will declare a mistrial.

After a verdict of acquittal is accepted, the Double Jeopardy Clause bars further proceedings even if the verdict was in error. *See, e.g., State v. Taylor*, 544 So. 2d 1387 (Miss. 1989) (after jury verdict of acquittal was ordered filed, jury was polled and one juror disagreed with the acquittal; court ordered jury to retire for additional deliberations and jury found defendant guilty as charged; conviction reversed).

[6] Unanimity

The traditional American view is that a jury in a criminal case consists of 12 people who must vote unanimously in order to convict or acquit a defendant. In federal prosecutions, the jury verdict must be unanimous to avoid a mistrial. Fed. R. Crim. P. 31(a). If the jury is not unanimous, under this view there is a *hung jury* or a *deadlocked jury*, and the trial judge may declare a mistrial.

[a] Due Process and Equal Protection

Although the rule requiring a unanimous jury has a long history, it is not mandated by the constitution. In *Johnson v. Louisiana*, 406 U.S. 356 (1972), the defendant was convicted after a 9–3 vote by a 12-person jury, consistent with Louisiana criminal procedure that provided for a guilty verdict if 9 of the 12 jurors voted for conviction. The Supreme Court upheld the conviction against both due process and equal protection challenges. The non-unanimous verdict did not offend the Due Process Clause because there was nothing in the record to suggest that the nine jurors who voted guilty did not listen to the dissenting jurors and did not apply the court's instruction on the meaning of guilty beyond a reasonable doubt. Moreover, the fact that three jurors voted against conviction does not mean that there was not proof beyond a reasonable doubt.

The Supreme Court also held that Louisiana's less-than-unanimous procedure did not violate the Equal Protection Clause, even though Louisiana law mandated a unanimous verdict in capital cases and certain lesser felonies where a five-person jury was authorized. The Supreme Court reasoned that the Louisiana legislature's choice to save money by using smaller juries in less serious cases served a rational purpose. The defendant argued that the Louisiana procedure made it easier to convict in a non-unanimous 12-person jury than in a unanimous five-person jury, but the Supreme Court found no constitutional violation. Do you agree that this difference is not of constitutional dimension? Recall that the 12-person jury is used in more serious cases than the five-person jury.

[b] Sixth Amendment

Although *Johnson* resolved the issue whether the Due Process and Equal Protection Clauses would permit a non-unanimous verdict, the companion case dealt with the more difficult question whether the Sixth Amendment permitted this practice.

Apodaca v. Oregon

406 U.S. 404 (1972)

MR. JUSTICE WHITE announced the judgment of the Court in an opinion in which THE CHIEF JUSTICE, MR. JUSTICE BLACKMUN, and MR. JUSTICE REHNQUIST joined.

[The three defendants were convicted of various offenses in separate Oregon state trials. Two of them were convicted by a 10–2 jury vote and one by an 11–1 vote, consistent with Oregon law authorizing a conviction by no less than 10–2. Each defendant claimed that the Sixth Amendment barred a conviction by a non-unanimous jury verdict.]

In *Williams v. Florida*, 399 U.S. 786 (1970), we had occasion to consider a related issue: whether the Sixth Amendment's right to trial by jury requires that all juries consist of 12 men. After considering the history of the 12-man requirement and the functions it performs in contemporary society, we concluded that it was not of constitutional stature. We reach the same conclusion today with regard to the requirement of unanimity.

. . . As we observed in *Williams*, one can draw conflicting inferences from this legislative history. . . . And, as in *Williams*, our inability to divine "the intent of the Framers" when they eliminated references to the "accustomed requisites" requires that in determining what is meant by a jury we must turn to other than purely historical considerations.

Our inquiry must focus upon the function served by the jury in contemporary society. As we said in *Duncan*, the purpose of trial by jury is to prevent oppression by the Government by providing a "safeguard against the corrupt or overzealous prosecutor and against the compliant, biased, or eccentric judge." [*Duncan v. Louisiana*, 391 U.S. 145, 156 (1968).] "Given this purpose, the essential feature of a jury obviously lies in the interposition between the accused and his accuser of the commonsense judgment of a group of laymen. . . ." A requirement of unanimity, however, does not materially contribute to the exercise of this commonsense judgment. . . . In terms of this function we perceive no difference between juries required to act unanimously and those permitted to convict or acquit by votes of 10 to two or 11 to one. Requiring unanimity would obviously produce hung juries in some situations where nonunanimous juries will convict or acquit. But in either case, the interest of the defendant in having the judgment of his peers interposed between himself and the officers of the State who prosecute and judge him is equally well served.

[The opinion rejected the claim that a unanimous verdict is essential to protect an asserted Sixth Amendment's guarantee of proof of guilt beyond a reasonable doubt. The Sixth Amendment does not embrace the beyond-reasonable-doubt guarantee, which is part of due process.]

Petitioners also cite quite accurately a long line of decisions of this Court upholding the principle that the Fourteenth Amendment requires jury panels to reflect a cross section of the community. They then contend that unanimity is a necessary precondition for effective application of the cross-section requirement, because a rule permitting less than unanimous verdicts will make it possible for convictions to occur without the acquiescence of minority elements within the community.

There are two flaws in this argument. One is petitioners' assumption that every distinct voice in the community has a right to be represented on every jury and a right to prevent conviction of a defendant in any case. All that the Constitution forbids, however, is systematic exclusion of identifiable segments of the community from jury panels and from the juries ultimately drawn from those panels; . . .

We also cannot accept petitioners' second assumption — that minority groups, even when they are represented on a jury, will not adequately represent the viewpoint of those groups simply because they may be outvoted in the final result. They will be present during all deliberations, and their views will be heard. We cannot assume that the majority of the jury will refuse to weigh the evidence and reach a decision upon rational grounds, just as it must now do in order to obtain unanimous verdicts, or that a majority will deprive a man of his liberty on the basis of prejudice when a minority is presenting a reasonable argument in favor of acquittal. We simply find no proof for the notion that a majority will disregard its instructions and cast its votes for guilt or innocence based on prejudice rather than the evidence. [Affirmed.]

Mr. Justice Douglas, with whom Mr. Justice Brennan and Mr. Justice Marshall concur, dissenting.

. . . I dissent from this radical departure from American traditions.

The Constitution does not mention unanimous juries. Neither does it mention the presumption of innocence, nor does it say that guilt must be proved beyond a reasonable doubt in all criminal cases. Yet it is almost inconceivable that anyone would have questioned whether proof beyond a reasonable doubt was in fact the constitutional standard.

. . . I had similarly assumed that there was no dispute that the Federal Constitution required a unanimous jury in all criminal cases. . . . Today the bases of those cases are discarded and two centuries of American history are shunted aside.

The result of today's decisions is anomalous: though unanimous jury decisions are not required in state trials, they are constitutionally required in federal prosecutions [by *Andres v. United States*, 333 U.S. 740 (1948)]. How can that be possible when both decisions stem from the Sixth Amendment?

. . . I would construe the Sixth Amendment, when applicable to the States, precisely as I would when applied to the Federal Government.

The plurality approves a procedure which diminishes the reliability of a jury. First, it eliminates the circumstances in which a minority of jurors (a) could have rationally persuaded the entire jury to acquit, or (b) while unable to persuade the majority to acquit, nonetheless could have convinced them to convict only on a lesser-included offense. Second, it permits prosecutors in Oregon and Louisiana to enjoy a conviction-acquittal ratio substantially greater than that ordinarily returned by unanimous juries.

The diminution of verdict reliability flows from the fact that nonunanimous juries need not debate and deliberate as fully as must unanimous juries. As soon as the requisite majority is attained, further consideration is not required either by Oregon or by Louisiana even though the dissident jurors might, if given the chance, be able to convince the majority. . . . Indeed, if a necessary majority is immediately obtained, then no deliberation at all is required in these States. . . .

The new rule also has an impact on cases in which a unanimous jury would have neither voted to acquit nor to convict, but would have deadlocked. In unanimous-jury States, this occurs about 5.6% of the time. Of these deadlocked juries, Kalven and Zeisel [in THE AMERICAN JURY (1966)] say that 56% contain either one, two, or three dissenters. In these latter cases, the majorities favor the prosecution 44% (of the 56%) but the defendant only 12% (of the 56%). Thus, by eliminating these deadlocks, Louisiana wins 44 cases for every 12 that it loses, obtaining in this band of outcomes a substantially more favorable conviction ratio (3.67 to 1) than the unanimous-jury ratio of slightly less than two guilty verdicts for every acquittal. By eliminating the one-and-two-dissenting-juror cases, Oregon does even better, gaining 4.25 convictions for every acquittal. While the statutes on their face deceptively appear to be neutral, the use of the non-unanimous jury stacks the truth-determining process against the accused. Thus, we take one step more away from the accusatorial system that has been our proud boast.

It is my belief that a unanimous jury is necessary if the great barricade known as proof beyond a reasonable doubt is to be maintained. . . .

. . . Suppose a jury begins with a substantial minority but then in the process of deliberation a sufficient number changes to reach the required 9:3 or 10:2 for a verdict. Is not there still a lingering doubt about that verdict? Is it not clear that the safeguard of unanimity operates in this context to make it far more likely that guilt is established beyond a reasonable doubt? . . .

[JUSTICE BLACKMUN's concurring opinion stated that a less-than-unanimous verdict system is constitutional even though it is unwise.

JUSTICE POWELL concurred in the judgment. He argued that a less-than-unanimous verdict does not offend the Due Process Clause because it is not fundamental to the essentials of a jury trial. The jury's function of guarding against arbitrary law enforcement is preserved with or without a unanimous jury verdict requirement. Minority perspectives are not unconstitutionally compromised under the Oregon system because there is no evidence that jurors in Oregon will not listen to all views before rendering a decision.

JUSTICES BRENNAN's dissent argued that a unanimous jury requirement means that minority views will have to be taken seriously, which is not necessary in a non-unanimous jurisdiction.

JUSTICES MARSHALL and STEWART also wrote dissenting opinions.]

Notes

1. *Protection against government oppression.* The plurality opinion in *Apodaca* suggested that a non-unanimous jury could protect against government oppression, but had little empirical support for this assertion. Do you think this protection is as likely in a non-unanimous jurisdiction, such as one that permitted guilt to be determined by a 9–3 vote?

2. *Effect on deliberations.* What effect do you think a non-unanimous model will have on jury deliberations? Will they be shorter or longer than under a unanimous approach? More or less heated? Will minority views be given more or less respect? Will more innocent people be convicted? More guilty people acquitted? *See* Aliza Kaplan & Amy Saack, *Overturning* Apodaca v. Oregon *Should Be Easy: Nonunanimous Jury Verdicts in Criminal Cases Undermine the Credibility of Our Justice System*, 95 OR. L. REV. 1 (2016).

3. *Effect on compromises.* Will there be more, less, or the same number of compromises in a non-unanimous and a unanimous jury system? Is this good? Do you agree that compromises on guilt or innocence (which usually means guilt for a lesser included crime) are appropriate in the criminal justice system?

4. *Size v. unanimity.* Recall that in *Williams v. Florida* and *Ballew v. Georgia*, both discussed earlier in this chapter, the Supreme Court held that juries in state courts do not have to consist of 12 people, but they cannot have less than six. Combining these cases with *Apodaca*, what is the relationship between jury size and jury unanimity? Could a state have a jury of six people and require only a two-thirds vote for conviction (thus a person could be convicted by a vote of 4–2)?

In *Burch v. Louisiana*, 441 U.S. 130 (1979), the Supreme Court invalidated obscenity convictions obtained by a 5–1 vote of jurors, as authorized by Louisiana law. Finding the issue to be "a close one," the Supreme Court held that conviction by a non-unanimous six-member jury violated the accused's Sixth Amendment right to a jury trial. The Court stated that "conviction for a nonpetty offense by only five members of a six-person jury presents a similar threat to preservation of the substance of the jury trial guarantee and justifies our requiring verdicts rendered by six-person juries to be unanimous." *Id.* at 138.

Do you agree with the Supreme Court in *Burch*? If a verdict of 9 of 12 jurors (75%) is valid, what is wrong with a verdict of five of six jurors (83%)? Will it be less reflective? Less accurate? Recall that the Supreme Court upheld a unanimous verdict by a six-person jury. Is an almost-unanimous verdict by five of six jurors less likely to protect against government oppression? Less likely to involve the community in the decision and the process?

5. The American Bar Association recommends a unanimous verdict in all jury cases. Recall the ABA also recommends a jury of 12 for serious offenses (more than six months' confinement) unless the parties, with court approval, stipulate that the jury shall consist of a smaller number, though not smaller than six. However, the ABA also states that, at any time before verdict, the parties, with court approval, may stipulate to a non-unanimous jury verdict so long as it is made clear the number of concurring jurors required for the verdict to be valid. PRINCIPLES FOR JURIES AND JURY TRIALS Prin. 4 (2005).

6. *What must be unanimous?* Does the right to a unanimous jury verdict mean, literally, that the jurors must agree unanimously about each and every fact in dispute? In *Richardson v. United States*, 526 U.S. 813 (1999), the Supreme Court held that in a federal criminal prosecution under the "Continuing Criminal Enterprise" statute, the jurors must agree unanimously on the specific drug violations constituting the "continuing series of [drug law] violations." In so holding, however, the Court noted that in some instances factual disagreements are permissible. It explained:

> ... [A] federal jury need not always decide unanimously which of several possible sets of underlying brute facts make up a particular element, say, which of several possible means the defendant used to commit an element of the crime. Where, for example, an element of robbery is force or the threat of force, some jurors might conclude that the defendant used a knife to create the threat; others might conclude he used a gun. But that disagreement—a disagreement about means—would not matter as long as all 12 jurors unanimously concluded that the Government had proved the necessary related element, namely that the defendant had threatened force.

Id. at 817.

[7] Deadlock

Hung jury and mistrial. Recall that a jury in a criminal case can acquit or convict a defendant of a crime only if the jury returns a verdict that meets a specific vote standard. Usually this means that the jury must be unanimous, although a less-than-unanimous verdict is permissible in some jurisdictions. Assuming that a jurisdiction requires a unanimous vote, what happens if the jury is deadlocked 11–1 in favor of conviction? The jury is a *hung jury* and the court must order a mistrial. The prosecution is free to retry the defendant since the Double Jeopardy Clause does not bar a retrial after a hung jury, as discussed in Chapter 15. Since the defendant was neither convicted nor acquitted, he or she is in a state of limbo, where further prosecution is possible but frequently not conducted.

"Dynamite" or Allen *charge.* What should the judge do when the foreperson reports that the jury is deadlocked? Often the court inquires whether further deliberations would be fruitful or a waste of time. Sometimes the court also gives an additional jury instruction, often referred to as an *Allen charge* or *dynamite charge.* This instruction was approved in substance by the United States Supreme Court in *Allen v. United States*, 164 U.S. 492, 501 (1896). The Court noted that jurors "should examine the question submitted with candor, and with a proper regard and deference to the opinions of each other; . . . [A] dissenting juror should consider whether his doubt was a reasonable one which made no impression upon the minds of so many men, equally honest, equally intelligent with himself."

Opponents of the *Allen* charge essentially characterize it as judicial intimidation of the hold-outs. This coercion deprives the accused (and the state) of the opportunity for a hung jury, sometimes characterized as an important safeguard against conviction of innocent persons. It also may deflect the jurors from focusing on the evidence to considering the need to reach a decision on something. *See generally* Emil J. Bove III, Note, *Preserving the Value of Unanimous Criminal Jury Verdicts in Anti-Deadlock Instructions*, 97 Geo. L.J. 251 (2008) (discussing ways to minimize judge's influence over jury deliberations).

Because of these concerns, a number of jurisdictions have limited the *Allen* charge or do not use it. Other jurisdictions permit the *Allen* charge to be given only one time, not repeatedly to the same jury, or only during the regular jury instructions and not during deliberations. *See, e.g.*, Wash. Crim. R. Lim. Juris. 6.15(e)(2) (after jury begins deliberations, court shall not instruct jury on need for agreement, consequences of no agreement, or the length of time the jury will be required to deliberate).

ABA alternate instruction. The American Bar Association has recommended an alternative to the *Allen* instruction. *See* American Bar Association, ABA Standards for Criminal Justice: Discovery and Trial by Jury § 15-5.4 (3d ed. 1996). A growing number of jurisdictions have adopted the ABA's recommendation. *See, e.g., Commonwealth v. Mitchell*, 943 S.W.2d 625 (Ky. 1997). Yet other jurisdictions have embraced the ABA's recommendation while retaining some aspects of the *Allen* model. *See, e.g., State v. Howard*, 537 N.E.2d 188 (Ohio 1989) (approving an instruction that incorporates aspects of both *Allen* and the ABA model, but specifically requesting that jurors on *both sides* of the issue reconsider their views).

In *Lowenfield v. Phelps*, 484 U.S. 231, 241 (1988), the Supreme Court, noting that a criminal defendant "is entitled to the uncoerced verdict" of a jury, approved use of an instruction that paraphrased the American Bar Association's recommendation.

> When you enter the jury room it is your duty to consult with one another to consider each other's views and to discuss the evidence with the objective of reaching a just verdict if you can do so without violence to that individual judgment.

> Each of you must decide the case for yourself but only after discussion and impartial consideration of the case with your fellow jurors. You are not advocates for one side or the other. Do not hesitate to reexamine your own views and to change your opinion if you are convinced you are wrong but do not surrender your honest belief as to the weight and effect of evidence solely because of the opinion of your fellow jurors or for the mere purpose of returning a verdict.

Id. at 235.

Notes

1. *Allen or ABA.* Compare the *Allen* and the ABA instructions. Is the ABA approach less coercive? Is it coercive at all? Should either be given? Does either put too much pressure on an individual juror to yield the juror's individual view to that of the majority?

2. *When to give.* How is a trial court to know whether to give an *Allen*-type instruction? One method is for the court to poll the jurors to determine whether additional deliberations would be fruitless or worthwhile. *Lowenfield v. Phelps*, 484 U.S. 231 (1988). Is this process coercive? In *Brasfield v. United States*, 272 U.S. 448 (1926), the Supreme Court held that polling a deadlocked jury to ascertain the numerical division of the jurors is an automatic ground for reversal.

Most state courts, however, have determined that *Brasfield* does not apply to the states either because it is an interpretation of a federal procedural rule or was a ruling based upon the Supreme Court's supervisory authority over federal courts. *See State v. Fowler*, 322 S.E.2d 389 (N.C. 1984); *Scoggins v. State*, 726 So. 2d 762 (Fla. 1999).

3. *Determining coercion.* In *State v. Fowler*, 322 S.E.2d 389 (N.C. 1984), the court held that the trial judge who polled the jury on its numerical division but who requested not to be told whether the majority was for acquittal or conviction was not unduly coercive. On the other hand, in *State v. McCrimmon*, 927 P.2d 1298 (Ariz. 1996), the trial judge was found to have coerced the verdict where, after polling the jury, the judge repeatedly asked the lone dissenter in private whether she could reach a verdict.

4. *Partial verdict.* If the jury cannot agree on the verdict for all the defendants, it may report a verdict on some of the defendants and be a hung jury on the others. In some cases the jury may deliberate for some time, then report to the court that it has reached a verdict on some defendants (without indicating which defendants) and is deadlocked on others. Defense counsel may then request an instruction, telling the jurors that they may return a partial verdict. Most appellate courts hold that the trial judge need not give this instruction, but must not indicate that a partial verdict is unacceptable. *See, e.g., United States v. Burke*, 700 F.2d 70 (2d Cir. 1983). *See* Jessie D. Shields, *On the Subject of Partial Verdicts: A Series of Practical Questions Answered for District Court Judges*, 88 Temp. L. Rev. 579 (2016).

Problem 14-10. When Is Enough, Enough?

Dorothy was tried for two bank robberies that occurred on the same day. The only issue was identity. Tellers at both banks identified Dorothy as the lone robber. Dorothy and her alibi witnesses claimed that she was in another town the day of the robberies. Three hours after the jury began deliberations, it returned to the courtroom and the foreperson gave the judge a note which read, "We are unable to agree on a verdict on both counts because of insufficient evidence."

1. The judge then asked the foreperson how the vote was split. You are Dorothy's attorney. Would you object to the judge's question? If so, on what basis? Would you object if the judge asked, "Are you closer to a unanimous verdict on one count than on the other?"

2. The judge then gave additional jury instructions. Assess the validity of each.

a. "Ladies and gentlemen. You have got to reach a decision in this case." *See Jenkins v. United States*, 380 U.S. 445 (1965).

b. "Ladies and gentlemen. This is an important case, a very important one. The taxpayers of our state have paid a lot to have it tried. They pay me, the prosecutor, all the court personnel you see, the costs of maintaining this beautiful courthouse, your expenses, everything. In addition, there is a tremendous backlog of cases in our jurisdiction. If you fail to reach a verdict, we may have to retry this case at considerable expense and delay. Now I have done my job. I have tried to be as fair as I could. Now you must do your job so we can get on with the business of our criminal justice system." *See United States v. Rey*, 811 F.2d 1453 (11th Cir. 1987).

[8] Jury Justice or Nullification

American juries generally operate in secrecy. Their deliberations are conducted in private and individual jurors ordinarily cannot be questioned about the jury's processes or the juror's personal views or vote. Moreover, during the trial, lawyers for both sides may try to appeal to the jurors' emotions and common sense. It should not be surprising that on occasion a jury does what has been called *jury justice*—renders a verdict that is not justified by the evidence but was influenced by reasons of fairness or prejudice, or some arbitrary factor. Of course jury justice can be used to favor either the defendant or the government. Jury justice favoring the accused is often referred to as *jury nullification*.

Jury justice can take several forms. The obvious one is a conviction or acquittal on all charges, but jury justice may also produce a conviction for a lesser crime or on some but not all charges. Assume, for example, the defendant is a woman charged with intentional murder of her husband, for which there is clearly proof of guilt beyond a reasonable doubt. She killed with repeated doses of a slow-acting poison that she discovered while reading an article entitled, "How to Kill Without Being Caught." Manslaughter is a lesser-included crime. It is possible that despite the evidence, a jury will acquit the defendant of murder and convict her of manslaughter because of sympathy for her and an antipathy for the deceased victim, who had beaten the defendant many times during a long marriage but had not beaten her for several months before his death.

There are many reasons juries might exercise their nullification powers, including disagreement with the crime, punishment, or application of the law in the particular case. A more politically interesting rationale is a jury's exercise of nullification powers to send a message, such as by acquitting the environmentalists who trespass on lawn to protest a new strip mine that is opposed by the local populace.

Today, most jurisdictions conclude that jury justice is inconsistent with many important legal principles. Jurors are instructed to follow the law, to be fair to all sides, and to base their decision on the evidence presented at trial. If a jury acquits a defendant because he or she was poor or uneducated, because the victim deserved the beating, or because the jury disliked the prosecutor, critics argue that the rule of law is compromised and the jury is not performing its proper functions.

Despite these concerns, American courts have consistently held that jury justice is permissible if it results in leniency. In the leading case, the Supreme Court observed:

> The main reason ordinarily assigned for a recognition of the right of the jury, in a criminal case, to take the law into their own hands, and to disregard the directions of the court in matters of law, is that the safety and liberty of the citizen [defendant] will be thereby more certainly secured.

Sparf v. United States, 156 U.S. 51, 106 (1895).

[a] Jury Instructions on Nullification

If jury nullification is part of the American criminal justice system (perhaps because there is nothing that can be done when it happens), should jurors be instructed on it as part of the routine package of jury instructions outlining the jury's duties? Obviously defense counsel would prefer that such instructions be given. One requested the following:

> If you feel strongly about the values involved in this case [alleging failure to file tax returns], so strongly that your conscience is aroused, then you may, as the conscience for the community, disregard the strict requirements of the law. You should disregard the law only if the requirements of the law cannot justly be applied in this case. By disregarding the law, you may use your common sense judgment and find a verdict according to your conscience.

Following the traditional view, the court refused defense counsel's request. *United States v. Powell*, 955 F.2d 1206, 1213 (9th Cir. 1992).

Majority view: reject nullification instruction. The usual reason for rejecting such jury instructions is a fear that "anarchy would result from instructing the jury that it may ignore the requirements of the law." *Id.* Another court noted that a "[jury] instruction on nullification would have undermined the impartial determination of justice based on law." *United States v. Krzyske*, 836 F.2d 1013 (6th Cir. 1988).

Minority view: permit nullification instruction. A distinct minority of jurisdictions permit jury instructions on nullification. *See, e.g., State v. Mayo*, 480 A.2d 85 (N.H. 1984) (nullification instructions discretionary).

Impact of nullification instruction. The presence or absence of jury nullification instructions appears to affect both the content and the outcome of jury deliberations. One study shows that when a jury is instructed that it has the discretion to apply the law to the facts, the jury is more prone to acquit sympathetic defendants and more likely to convict unsympathetic ones. If the nullification suggestion occurs in counsel's argument and is countered by adversary counsel's objection, the jury generally is not swayed toward nullification. Irwin A. Horowitz, *Jury Nullification: The Impact of Judicial Instructions, Arguments, and Challenges on Jury Decision Making*, 12 L. & HUM. BEHAV. 439 (1988). Might a nullification instruction lead to increased incidence of hung juries? *See* Paula L. Hannaford-Agor & Valerie P. Hans, *Nullification at Work? A Glimpse from the National Center for State Courts Study of Hung Juries*, 78 CHI. KENT L. REV. 1249 (2003).

Policy dilemma. The refusal to instruct on jury nullification creates an anomaly that reflects the criminal justice system's conflicted approach to the issue. While American law permits jury nullification in order to protect the citizen from the state, in most jurisdictions it simultaneously bars a jury instruction on the issue. Does this conflicting approach make sense?

[b] Argument by Counsel on Nullification

Even if jury instructions do not include guidance on jury nullification, can defense counsel use closing argument to ask the jury to disregard the law and acquit the accused? Most courts do not permit this form of argument, reasoning that it would violate the rule that the jury is to apply the law contained in the jury instructions. *See, e.g., United States v. Trujillo*, 714 F.2d 102 (11th Cir. 1983).

A minority of courts do permit defense counsel to discuss jury nullification in closing argument. *See, e.g., United States v. Krzyske*, 836 F.2d 1013 (6th Cir. 1988); *State v. Mayo*, 480 A.2d 85 (N.H. 1984). When defense counsel makes an emotional appeal on behalf of the defendant, however, is there any way to prevent an indirect appeal for jury nullification? *See generally* Christopher C. Schwan, Comment, *Right Up to the Line: The Ethics of Advancing Nullification Arguments to the Jury*, 29 J. LEGAL PROF. 293 (2005) (techniques lawyers may use).

[c] Other Procedural Aspects of Jury Justice

The possibility of jury nullification influences many procedural facets of the criminal trial. Since jury nullification is technically a violation of the jurors' oaths, many judges will attempt to limit the information that could influence jurors to ignore the judge's instruction and render a jury-justice verdict. Lawyers for both sides, on the other hand, may attempt to provide the jury with information that would promote jury justice for one side or against the other side.

Jury selection. The possibility of jury justice influences the jury-selection process. For example, the defense lawyer might seek jurors who will be empathetic toward the defendant and sufficiently independent to ignore the judge's jury instructions, and might reject jurors who will rigidly apply the law and have little sympathy for the defendant.

Evidence. Jury nullification might also affect the evidence that is offered and the court's ruling on objections. For example, in order to elicit sympathy for the accused, the defense lawyer may attempt to introduce evidence about the victim's bad character and the defendant's good character. The prosecution may file a motion *in limine* to exclude it, arguing that this evidence should be excluded if its only relevance is jury nullification.

[d] Recent Jury Nullification Proposals

In 1995, ten legislatures introduced measures to require that trial judges instruct juries on their nullification right. *See* David C. Brody, Sparf *and* Dougherty *Revisited: Why the Court Should Instruct the Jury of Its Nullification Right*, 33 Am. Crim. L. Rev. 89 (1995) (evaluating the opposing arguments and articulating both a model instruction and procedures a trial court can take when nullification might be an issue).

[9] Inconsistent Verdicts

Sometimes a jury returns *inconsistent verdicts*—multiple verdicts that are inconsistent with one another. The inconsistency may be one of two kinds: *multiple-count inconsistency* or *multiple-defendant inconsistency.* A multiple-count inconsistency may arise when a defendant is charged with a compound crime, a crime based upon the commission of another crime. For example, a defendant could be charged with possessing cocaine with the intent to distribute and also with the offense of using a telephone to commit that offense. The telephone count is a compound crime in that it has as an element the commission of a separate crime, the possession of cocaine. A jury could acquit the defendant of the possession charge but convict him or her of using a telephone to commit the possession offense. The jury, then, has effectively said that the defendant is both guilty and not guilty of the crime of possession; it has produced an inconsistent verdict.

An example of a multiple-defendant inconsistency is the case of a defendant and his or her co-defendant charged with committing the crime of conspiracy (requiring an agreement between at least two people to commit an illegal act). The jury could acquit one defendant of conspiracy while convicting the other, thereby producing an inconsistent verdict. *See* Eric L. Muller, *The Hobgoblin of Little Minds? Our Foolish Law of Inconsistent Verdicts*, 111 Harv. L. Rev. 771 (1998) (discussing these hypotheticals in detail).

In *United States v. Powell*, 469 U.S. 57 (1984), the Supreme Court held that inconsistent verdicts do not offend the Constitution. The Court reasoned:

> The rule that the defendant may not upset such a verdict embodies a prudent acknowledgment of a number of factors. First, . . . inconsistent verdicts—even verdicts that acquit on a predicate offense while convicting on the compound offense—should not necessarily be interpreted as a windfall to the Government at the defendant's expense. It is equally possible that the jury, convinced of guilt, properly reached its conclusion on the compound offense, and then through mistake, compromise, or lenity, arrived at an inconsistent conclusion on the lesser offense. But in such situations the Government has no recourse if it wishes to correct the jury's error; the Government is precluded from appealing or otherwise upsetting such an acquittal by the Constitution's Double Jeopardy Clause.
>
> . . . We . . . reject, as imprudent and unworkable, a rule that would allow criminal defendants to challenge inconsistent verdicts on the ground that in their case the verdict was not the product of lenity, but of some error that worked against them. Such an individualized assessment of the reason for the inconsistency would be based either on pure speculation, or would require inquiries into the jury's deliberations that courts generally will not undertake. . . .
>
> Finally, we note that a criminal defendant already is afforded protection against jury irrationality or error by the independent review of the sufficiency of the evidence undertaken by the trial and appellate courts. This review should not be confused with the problems caused by inconsistent verdicts. Sufficiency-of-the-evidence review involves assessment by the courts of whether the evidence adduced at trial could support any rational determination of guilty beyond a reasonable doubt. This review should be independent of the jury's determination that evidence on another count was insufficient.

Id. at 64–67.

Notes

1. *Inconsistent verdict and jury nullification.* Does *Powell* reaffirm the propriety of jury nullification?

2. *Fairness. Powell* focuses on the likelihood that inconsistent verdicts result from jury leniency. But it also recognizes that the inconsistent results could also stem from prejudice or error. Do you think *Powell* provides adequate assurances that criminal defendants will not be convicted of crimes because a jury was prejudiced or simply mistaken?

3. *Jury instructions.* If inconsistent verdicts are not reversible error, should the jury be instructed that it may return inconsistent verdicts?

4. *Collateral estoppel.* When *Powell* held that inconsistent verdicts do not invalidate either verdict, it created a significant block to the use of collateral estoppel in

certain circumstances. As discussed more fully in Chapter 15, collateral estoppel would prevent a subsequent trial of the same issue that resulted in an acquittal in an earlier trial. But if there is an inconsistent verdict when a jury convicted the defendant of one count and acquitted on the other count, *Powell* indicates that the doctrine of collateral estoppel is inapplicable to invalidate the conviction. *See generally* Anne Bowen Poulin, *Collateral Estoppel in Criminal Cases: Reuse of Evidence After Acquittal*, 58 U. Cin. L. Rev. 1, 39–48 (1989).

5. *State variations.* Some state courts apply state law to reverse inconsistent verdicts. In *DeSacia v. State*, 469 P.2d 369 (Alaska 1970), the Alaska Supreme Court reversed a conviction involving inconsistent verdicts because state law required a minimal degree of reasonableness in a jury's decision. Similarly, in *State v. Peters*, 855 S.W.2d 345 (Mo. 1993), the Missouri Supreme Court found no error where the trial judge ordered the jury to deliberate further after it returned an inconsistent verdict.

[10] Impeachment of Jury Verdict

If a jury convicts the defendant of a crime, he or she may decide to challenge the verdict. Several possible grounds relate to the jury processes. The range of possible misconduct is vast. Examples include allegations that a juror was biased (and perhaps also lied during voir dire), drunk, insane, bribed, or asleep through the trial or deliberations; that jurors used outside information, such as a newspaper or book, in their deliberations; that during deliberations someone, other than a juror, spoke with a juror about the case; and that jurors misunderstood the jury instructions.

The defendant may allege that one or more such problems caused the jury to perform in a way that violated due process or the Sixth Amendment's jury-trial guarantee of a competent jury. The Supreme Court has held that the criminal defendant has a right to a tribunal that is both impartial and mentally competent to afford a hearing. *Tanner v. United States*, 483 U.S. 107, 126 (1987).

Another theory is that some jury processes violated the accused's Sixth Amendment right to confront the accusers. *See, e.g., Rushen v. Spain*, 464 U.S. 114 (1983) (ex parte communications between the judge and a juror, never reported to either counsel, may violate confrontation right); *Parker v. Gladden*, 385 U.S. 363 (1966) (defendant's right of confrontation was violated when bailiff told several jurors during deliberations that defendant was guilty and Supreme Court would correct any error if defendant were found guilty).

The convicted defendant has a difficult burden of proving prejudice. *See, e.g., United States v. Taliaferro*, 558 F.2d 724 (4th Cir. 1977) (defendant unable to prove prejudice when jurors consumed liquor during meal eaten while jury deliberating); *United States v. Tanner*, 483 U.S. 107 (1987) (jurors' consumption of drugs and alcohol during trial and deliberations is not considered "outside influence" warranting hearing to determine whether defendant was prejudiced).

[a] Bias and Lies During Voir Dire

In *McDonough Power Equipment, Inc. v. Greenwood*, 464 U.S. 548 (1984), a civil case involving injuries caused by a lawnmower, a juror did not disclose during voir dire that a member of his family had suffered a severe accidental injury, despite being questioned on that point. Assuming that the juror did not intend to mislead counsel during voir dire, the Supreme Court established a standard of review: "[A] party must first demonstrate that a juror failed to answer honestly a material question on *voir dire*, and then further show that a correct response would have provided a valid basis for a challenge for cause." *Id.* at 556.

The *Greenwood* court remanded the case to apply the new test. This standard was applied to reverse a conviction where the juror lied about knowing the defendant and prior involvement in litigation. *United States v. Perkins*, 748 F.2d 1519 (11th Cir. 1984) (emphasizing that the juror gave false answers during voir dire). *Cf. State v. Thomas*, 830 P.2d 243 (Utah 1992) (applying *Greenwood* but holding that juror's partiality is key consideration, rather than her intent as in *Perkins*).

[b] The Problem of Proof

Even if a juror misbehaved and the error would cause the verdict to be overturned, there may be no way of proving it. In order to protect jurors from harassment and to encourage finality in judicial proceedings, American courts have traditionally barred jurors from testifying about most facets of the deliberations. The usual rule is that jurors may not testify about "internal" jury processes. This is read as barring their testimony about the deliberative process. A juror can be questioned about "external" influences, such as contact with outsiders or the use of evidence not introduced during the trial. Federal Rule of Evidence 606(b) is typical, stating in part that "a juror may not testify about any statement made or incident that occurred during the jury's deliberations." However, a juror may testify about extraneous prejudicial information or outside influences improperly brought to the jury's attention, or a mistake being made in entering the verdict on the verdict form.

Notes

1. *Illustrations of impermissible topics.* Courts interpreting Rule 606(b) have held that after a verdict, jurors are not competent to testify about the following misconduct that occurred during deliberations or the trial: a juror was intoxicated or asleep; the judge's jury instructions were coercive or not followed; the jurors hurried their deliberations in order to finish quickly; and a juror feared government recriminations if the juror voted to acquit. *See Tanner v. United States*, 483 U.S. 107 (1987) (the court cannot inquire into jurors' drug and alcohol use during trial).

2. In *Pena-Rodriguez v. Colorado*, 137 S. Ct. 855 (2017), the Supreme Court held that "where a juror makes a clear statement indicating that he or she relied on racial stereotypes or animus to convict a criminal defendant, the Sixth Amendment requires that the [general] no-impeachment rule give way in order to permit the trial court to consider the evidence of the juror's statement and any resulting denial of the jury trial guarantee." *Id.* at 869.

[c] Attorney's Post-Trial Contact with Jurors

After a jury verdict, counsel for the losing (and sometimes winning) party may be interested in learning about what happened during the jury's deliberations. One reason is simply to improve counsel's performance in the next trial by getting feedback on various facets of the trial. For example, a lawyer might be interested in learning whether a particular witness or closing argument was effective. A second reason for inquiring into the jury's processes is to determine whether there is any ground to reverse the judgment. Recall that reversal is possible for some malfeasance in the jury room.

To achieve these goals, counsel has to communicate with the jurors. This may pose few practical problems since the trial lawyers likely have the jurors' names and addresses. The problem, of course, is that during this communication the jurors may feel harassed or intimidated, and jurors may be less than candid during jury deliberations because of the concern that their comments will be the subject of aggressive post-trial inquiries by trial counsel.

Because of these fears, many jurisdictions have adopted rules limiting counsel's post-trial contact with the trial jurors. A common example is a court rule barring lawyers from having post-trial contact with jurors without court permission, which is given after a showing of "good cause." Other rules permit such contacts only in open court under the judge's supervision and/or only after notice to adversary counsel or the court.

Another approach is to encourage the court to permit lawyer-juror contact after the trial is over. *See, e.g.*, PRINCIPLES FOR JURIES AND JURY TRIALS, Prin. 18 (after trial, court should instruct jurors they have a right to discuss or not discuss the case with anyone; court should ordinarily permit the parties to contact jurors after the end of the juror's term of jury service).

Surprisingly, the various ethical and professional standards contain relatively few restrictions on counsel's post-trial contact with jurors. The most comprehensive discussion is provided by the American Bar Association's Defense Function, which states that "[a]fter discharge of the jury from further consideration of a case, defense counsel should not intentionally make comments to or ask questions of a juror for the purpose of harassing or embarrassing the juror in any way which will tend to influence judgment in future jury service. If defense counsel believes that the verdict may be subject to legal challenge, he or she may properly, if no statute or rule prohibits such course, communicate with jurors to determine whether such challenge may be available." STANDARDS FOR CRIMINAL JUSTICE: PROSECUTION & DEFENSE FUNCTION §4-7.3(c) (3d ed. 1993). There is a similar standard for prosecutors. *Id.* §3-5.4(c).

The Model Rules of Professional Conduct bar an attorney from using means designed to embarrass, delay or burden a former juror, or that violate the person's legal rights. Model Rules of Prof'l Conduct r. 4.4 (1983). For a critical discussion of restrictions on post-trial contact by attorneys with jurors, *see* Benjamin M. Lawsky, Note, *Limitations on Attorney Postverdict Contact with Jurors: Protecting the Criminal Jury and Its Verdict at the Expense of the Defendant*, 94 Colum. L. Rev. 1950 (1994) (concluding that such limitations tread on a criminal defendant's Sixth Amendment rights by impeding discovery of jury misconduct).

[11] Non-Jury Verdicts

If a criminal defendant waives a jury or is not entitled to one because the case is considered to be a "petty crime," the trial will be conducted by the judge. In such cases, it is often said that the judge's responsibility is to weigh the evidence, determine the credibility of witnesses, and find the facts. Although the judge may render a decision any time after final argument, usually the decision on guilt or innocence comes quite quickly after the closing arguments. The judge may delay imposing sentence until a later date to permit both sides and the probation department to gather information about the offense and the defendant and to explore sentencing alternatives.

In most jurisdictions, the court simply pronounces whether the defendant is guilty or innocent on each count. Federal Rule 23(c) also gives both sides a right to request that the judge make a *specific finding* of fact prior to the judge returning a general verdict of guilt or innocence.

A request made after the general verdict is issued is considered untimely and a waiver of the right to a special verdict. Of course, the judge is free to provide specific findings even without a request by either side. Since Rule 23 states that the specific findings may be made orally, they are usually made at the same time the general verdict is announced in open court.

This request should be made in especially complex cases where it is possible the judge may misunderstand the issues or base the conviction on an erroneous finding of fact. It will greatly facilitate appellate review since it will provide the appellate court with data about the logic used by the trial court.

K. Motions after Guilty Verdict

Just as numerous motions may be filed with the court before and during a criminal trial, the defendant may submit motions after a verdict of guilty has been returned either by the jury or the trial judge. In some jurisdictions, the failure to file an appropriate motion after a guilty verdict may preclude an assertion of certain arguments on appeal. Counsel should carefully assess all possible motions, with particular emphasis on the subject matter germane to each motion and specified time limitations.

[1] Motion for Judgment of Acquittal

A motion for judgment of acquittal must be granted if "the evidence is insufficient to sustain a conviction." Fed. R. Crim. P. 29. In most jurisdictions, this motion is made routinely by the defense after the prosecution has presented its proof but may also be made at the close of the defendant's proof and even after the jury has been discharged following its return of a guilty verdict. Even if the motion is made at or before the close of all the evidence, the court may reserve ruling on the motion, submit the case to the jury, and then make the appropriate ruling after the jury returns a guilty verdict or is discharged without returning a verdict. Usually, a post-verdict motion for judgment of acquittal may be made even if an earlier motion was not submitted by counsel. Federal Rule 29 is typical.

If the trial court grants an acquittal motion, the double jeopardy guarantee usually bars a government appeal of the motion. When an acquittal motion is granted after a jury verdict of guilt, however, the government is permitted an appeal in order to demonstrate error by the trial court in granting the acquittal motion. If the government prevails, its requested relief is reinstatement of the guilty verdict. *See United States v. Martin Linen Supply Co.*, 430 U.S. 564 (1977).

A Rule 29 motion may be made or renewed within 14 days after a guilty verdict or the jury is discharged, whichever is later. Does a federal district court have authority to grant such a motion if it is filed one day late? Rule 45 now permits federal courts to consider untimely motions under Rule 29 if the delay results from "excusable neglect."

[2] Motion for New Trial

This motion may encompass a wider range of issues than the motion for judgment of acquittal. In federal criminal cases, this motion is governed by Rule 33. Due to the vague standard enunciated in Rule 33 ("interest of justice"), a wide range of errors may be specifically alleged. According to one commentator, bases for a new trial include prosecutorial misconduct, prejudicial exposure of jurors to news accounts, incorrect jury instructions, improper introduction of evidence, and misconduct of the jury. *See* James C. Cissell, Federal Criminal Trials § 13-1(b) (7th ed. 2012).

The defendant bears the burden of persuasion in a motion for new trial, but the court does not construe the evidence in the light most favorable to the prosecution. Rather, the court may evaluate the credibility and weight of the evidence for itself. *See* Cissell, *supra*, § 13.1.

Rule 33 also authorizes a court to order a new trial because of "newly discovered evidence." In federal cases, an exacting test must be satisfied before a judge will grant a new trial on this ground: the evidence must not have been known to the defendant at the time of the trial, the newly discovered evidence must be material to the issues involved, and the evidence must be so significant that it probably would produce an acquittal. *See* Cissell, *supra*, § 13-1(a) (7th ed. 2012). Note that the period in which such a motion under Rule 33 can be made is three years, as opposed to 14 days for a Rule 29 motion for a judgment of acquittal.

[3] Motion in Arrest of Judgment

This post-verdict motion, which can be granted even after a plea of guilty, is usually limited to very precise matters. The granting of such a motion renders the judgment void. In federal criminal cases, this is governed by Federal Rule 34.

In addition, some jurisdictions provide for a longer period in which such a motion may be filed. *See* Tenn. R. Crim. P. 34 (providing that such a motion may be made orally in open court, but requiring that it be reduced to writing and filed within 30 days of pronouncement of sentence).

Because the issues addressed in this motion are quite technical, in many jurisdictions the motion can be resolved by reviewing the record without regard to the evidence. For example, if the motion alleges that the indictment charges no offense, this defect can be assessed by reviewing the indictment and does not depend on the proof in the case.

Chapter 15

Double Jeopardy

A. General Overview

The Fifth Amendment to the United States Constitution provides that "no person shall . . . be subject for the same offence to be twice put in jeopardy of life or limb. . . ." In *Benton v. Maryland*, 395 U.S. 784, 794 (1969), this guarantee was held applicable to the states through the Fourteenth Amendment because it "represents a fundamental idea in our constitutional heritage." Noting that virtually every state has some form of double jeopardy prohibition (either by state constitution or by common law), the *Benton* Court explained:

> [T]he underlying idea . . . is that the State with all its resources and power should not be allowed to make repeated attempts to convict an individual for an alleged offense, thereby subjecting him to embarrassment, expense, and ordeal and compelling him to live in a continuing state of anxiety and insecurity, as well as enhancing the possibility that even though innocent he may be found guilty. This underlying notion has from the very beginning been part of our constitutional tradition. Like the right to trial by jury, it is clearly fundamental to the American scheme of justice.

Id. at 796 (citation omitted).

The Supreme Court has observed repeatedly that the double jeopardy guarantee consists of three separate constitutional protections:

> It protects against a second prosecution for the same offense after acquittal. It protects against a second prosecution for the same offense after conviction. And it protects against multiple punishments for the same offense.

North Carolina v. Pearce, 395 U.S. 711, 717 (1969).

Notice that the same key phrase lies at the heart of each of the three protections: "same offense." Although the concept may initially seem straightforward, much of the voluminous case law on the Double Jeopardy Clause focuses on the question of whether two charged offenses were the "same" for constitutional purposes.

B. "Same Offense"

[1] *Blockburger* Test

If one criminal episode subjects a defendant to charges under various criminal statutes, what determines whether or not the defendant is being charged twice with the "same offense"? For example, assume that the prosecutor believes that Carol robbed the ABC Liquor Store and killed the clerk who reached beneath the counter to get a shotgun. Does the Double Jeopardy Clause permit Carol to be convicted of both robbery and murder, or only one of the two? Does it matter whether the theory of murder is felony-murder, using the robbery as the predicate felony? What about convicting her of both attempted murder (for pointing her pistol at the clerk) and murder (for pulling the trigger)? The answer depends on the meaning of "same offense" in the Fifth Amendment.

The double jeopardy analysis requires an examination of the elements of the two crimes and the alleged conduct sought to be proven to satisfy those elements. Courts routinely note that "separate statutory crimes need not be identical—either in constituent elements or in actual proof—in order to be the same [offense] within the meaning of the [double jeopardy] prohibition." *Brown v. Ohio*, 432 U.S. 161, 164 (1977).

The current rule is the so-called *Blockburger* test:

> [W]here the same act or transaction constitutes a violation of two distinct statutory provisions, the test to be applied to determine whether there are two offenses or only one, is whether each provision requires proof of a fact which the other does not.

Blockburger v. United States, 284 U.S. 299, 304 (1932). Under this test, a court examines the elements of the two crimes. If *each* requires proof of a fact that the other does not, the two crimes are not the "same offense," even if there is considerable overlap in their elements. On the other hand, if one crime requires the *same* evidence as another, the two are the "same offense." (Some commentators reject the term "same evidence" as misleading and argue "same elements" is a more accurate standard.)

For example, under this "same elements" or "same evidence" test, the Supreme Court *in Brown v. Ohio, supra*, held that the crime of joyriding (taking or operating a vehicle without the owner's consent) and auto theft (joyriding with an intent to permanently deprive the owner of possession) are the "same offense" for double jeopardy purposes and therefore the defendant may not be convicted of both crimes for a single vehicle taking. Auto theft requires proof of a fact (intent to permanently deprive the owner of the vehicle) that joyriding does not; but joyriding does not require proof of a fact beyond those required for auto theft. Therefore, since the greater offense (auto theft) is the "same offense" for double jeopardy purposes as the lesser offense (joyriding), double jeopardy bars conviction or punishment for both.

Here are a few other illustrative results under *Blockburger.* First, air piracy and boarding an aircraft with explosives are not the "same offense." Each requires proof of a distinctive fact: the latter requires proof of bringing an explosive device aboard a plane, while the former requires proof of exercising control over the plane. Second, possession of narcotics with intent to sell is the same offense as the lesser-included crime of possession of narcotics, Third, petty theft is the same offense as "robbery by sudden snatching" for the same incident. Fourth, possession of cocaine and attempted possession of the same cocaine are the same offense. Finally, "assault while attempting to rob" is a lesser-included crime to (and hence the same offense as) "armed robbery."

Problem 15-1. Drugs . . . More Drugs

Hubert Putt harvested a small amount of marijuana from his back-yard garden. One Tuesday he distributed the contraband to Betty Dyal, an undercover police officer, in exchange for $25. He was immediately arrested. Subsequently, he was charged with (1) unlawful cultivation of marijuana, (2) possession of marijuana, (3) possession with intent to sell marijuana, and (4) unlawful sale of marijuana.

Would the Double Jeopardy Clause permit Putt to be convicted on all four counts? Could Putt be convicted of more than one offense? If so, which ones? Would it help to have the precise wording of any of the relevant criminal statutes?

What if each of the four counts was alleged to have been committed on a different date—would that affect your analysis?

Notes

1. *Unit of prosecution.* What if a person robs two people who are waiting together at a bus stop—can the person be prosecuted for two robberies or would this violate the Double Jeopardy Clause? Or what if a defendant secretly opened a cash register and took two $20 bills. Would the crime be one or two larcenies? Courts resolve this common dilemma by applying what is sometimes called a *unit of prosecution* test. It involves an assessment of legislative intent. How did the legislature define the scope of conduct for the particular criminal statute? This can be an important question when a defendant is charged with multiple counts of violating the same statute.

The issue can be tricky. For instance, imagine a criminal suspect who escapes from police custody and runs away. If the police give chase and apprehend the suspect several blocks away, might there be multiple charges for the crime of "eluding a police officer?" *Compare People v. McMinn*, 412 P.3d 551 (Colo. Ct. App. 2013) (permitting multiple charges of eluding a police officer, even from a single episode, if there were discrete acts of eluding, each constituting a new volitional departure in the defendant's course of conduct), *with Washington v. State*, 28 A.3d 164 (Md. Ct. Spec. App. 2011) (holding that eluding charges were for same offense even though defendant tried to escape police officer in a vehicle and then on foot).

In the robbery illustration above, courts routinely find that the legislature intended for each robbery to be a separate offense. The unit of prosecution is a single victim. The same is true for multiple assaults or homicides. Each victim of a violent offense represents a separate crime.

On the other hand, the theft case would be one larceny on the theory that the legislature meant to aggregate the thefts that occur from one victim in one transaction. *See also In re Snow*, 120 U.S. 274 (1887) (for crime of cohabiting with more than one woman, unit of prosecution is the plural cohabitation; double jeopardy violated when defendant was convicted of multiple counts of plural cohabitation for living with seven women, at same time, as his wives); *Bell v. United States*, 349 U.S. 81 (1955) (for crime of transporting a woman in interstate commerce for prostitution, unit of prosecution is act of transporting; transporting two women at same time is only one crime); *United States v. Grimes*, 702 F.2d 460 (8th Cir. 2012) (for crime of making repeated harassing telephone calls, unit of prosecution is an "episode" or "impulse" consisting of a number of calls in close temporal proximity; each call is not a separate unit of prosecution). *But see State v. Green*, 172 P.3d 1213 (Kan. Ct. App. 2007) (defendant engaged in identity theft by using another person's name to open, or charge items to, credit accounts in several stores; each account was a separate crime under Kansas identity theft law).

2. *Burden of proof.* The general rule is that a defendant asserting a double jeopardy claim must establish a *prima facie* case. The burden then shifts to the government to establish that the offenses are separate. *See, e.g., United States v. Delgado*, 256 F.3d 264 (5th Cir. 2001) (defendant failed to establish a *prima facie* case that a prior conspiracy conviction was for the same conspiracy now on trial).

[2] Same Transaction/Lesser-Included Offense Analysis in Successive Prosecutions

Blockburger readily answers the "same offense" question for most criminal prosecutions, but there can be complications. In this section, we particularly consider problems in relation to *successive prosecutions*.

[a] More Serious First

The Supreme Court has observed that for offenses that are the same offense under *Blockburger*, "the sequence of the two trials for the greater and the lesser offense is immaterial." *Jeffers v. United States*, 432 U.S. 137, 151 (1977). For example, in *Harris v. Oklahoma*, 433 U.S. 682 (1977), the defendant, charged in connection with the killing of a grocery store clerk in the course of a robbery by his companion, was convicted of felony-murder (the more serious) in an Oklahoma state court. The robbery was the predicate felony. At a later date, he was brought to trial and convicted on a separate information of robbery (the less serious) with firearms for the same grocery store robbery. Proof of the robbery had been used to establish the intent necessary for the felony-murder conviction in his first trial. In a *per curiam* opinion, the United States Supreme Court held that the second trial was barred by the Double Jeopardy Clause: "When ... conviction of a greater crime, murder, cannot be had without conviction of the lesser crime, robbery with firearms, the Double Jeopardy Clause bars prosecution for the lesser crime after conviction of the greater one."

[b] Less Serious First

[i] General Rule: More Serious Barred

In *Harris*, the more serious crime, murder, was tried first. What if the less serious is first? In *Illinois v. Vitale*, 447 U.S. 410 (1980), a juvenile was convicted of failing to reduce speed to avoid an accident in violation of state law. The day after this traffic conviction, a petition was filed in juvenile court charging him with two counts of involuntary manslaughter (two children were killed as a result of the incident giving rise to the earlier charges). The state supreme court affirmed the dismissal of the second petition, concluding that the manslaughter cases in juvenile court were barred by the double jeopardy guarantee because of the earlier traffic conviction. The United States Supreme Court observed that "if, as a matter of Illinois law, a careless failure to slow is always a necessary element of manslaughter by automobile, then the two offenses are the 'same' under *Blockburger*." The Court explained:

> It may be that to sustain its manslaughter case the State may find it necessary to prove a failure to slow or to rely on conduct necessarily involving such failure; it may concede as much prior to trial. In that case, because Vitale has already been convicted for conduct that is a necessary element of the more serious crime for which he has been charged, his claim of double jeopardy would be substantial under . . . [*Harris v. Oklahoma*].

Id. at 420.

The *Vitale* Court remanded the case for the Illinois courts to resolve uncertainties over the precise relationship between the two charged offenses under Illinois law.

[ii] Exceptions

While the general rule is that a defendant convicted of a lesser-included offense may not later be prosecuted for the greater offenses, there are several exceptions.

Subsequent events. One exception is when all the events needed for the greater crime have not occurred when the prosecution for the lesser-included crime began. This could occur if the defendant were convicted of assault, then the victim dies. Prosecution for the homicide is permissible despite the previous assault conviction. *See Diaz v. United States*, 223 U.S. 442 (1912).

Late discovery of facts necessary for the greater crime. The later discovery of facts necessary for the greater crime, despite due diligence, may also be an exception permitting prosecution for the greater offense. *Jeffers v. United States*, 432 U.S. 137, 151 (1977).

Subsequent proceedings at defendant's request. Another exception is when the defendant successfully moves for separate trials on the lesser and greater crimes. *Id.* After having sought the second trial, the defendant can hardly complain that the trial violates his or her double jeopardy rights.

[c] Criticisms

The *Blockburger* test has been harshly criticized as overly formalistic and easily manipulated by prosecutors in order to gain the sorts of unfair tactical advantages that the Double Jeopardy Clause was intended to prevent. *See, e.g.,* Akhil Reed Amar, *Double Jeopardy Law Made Simple*, 106 YALE L.J. 1807 (1997) (characterizing *Blockburger* as "a mess, legally and logically" and arguing that "we [can] do better"); Anne Bowen Poulin, *Double Jeopardy Protection from Successive Prosecution: A Proposed Approach*, 92 GEO. L.J. 1183 (2004) (proposing rejection of *Blockburger* in favor of a test that balances interests of the government against the defendant's double jeopardy interests).

For a brief interval in the early 1990s, the Supreme Court itself moved away from *Blockburger* and adopted a more flexible "same-conduct" test. The breakthrough came in *Grady v. Corbin*, 495 U.S. 508 (1990). Corbin had been involved in an automobile accident that killed one person and injured another. He was issued two traffic tickets, one for the misdemeanor of driving while intoxicated and the other for failing to keep to the right of the median. He appeared in a town justice court and pled guilty to the two traffic tickets. The presiding judge was not informed of the fatality or an impending homicide investigation. Later, in connection with the same accident, Corbin was charged by a grand jury with reckless manslaughter, criminally negligent homicide, and third-degree reckless assault. A bill of particulars specified the acts upon which the prosecution would rely to prove these charges: (1) operating a motor vehicle in an intoxicated condition, (2) failing to keep to the right of the median, and (3) driving too fast for the weather and road conditions.

In sustaining Corbin's double jeopardy challenge, a slim 5–4 majority of the Supreme Court concluded that a comparison of the elements of two offenses, under *Blockburger*, did not sufficiently protect defendants from the burdens of multiple trials:

> If *Blockburger* constituted the entire double jeopardy inquiry in the context of successive prosecutions, the State could try Corbin in four consecutive trials for failure to keep right of the median, for driving while intoxicated, for assault, and for homicide. The State could improve its presentation of proof with each trial, assessing which witnesses gave the most persuasive testimony, which documents had the greatest impact, and which opening and closing arguments most persuaded the jurors. Corbin would be forced either to contest each of these trials or to plead guilty to avoid the harassment and expense.
>
> Thus, a subsequent prosecution must do more than merely survive the *Blockburger* test. . . . [T]he Double Jeopardy Clause bars any subsequent prosecution in which the government, to establish an essential element of offense charged in that prosecution, will prove conduct that constitutes an offense for which the defendant has already been prosecuted. The critical inquiry is what conduct the State will prove, not the evidence the State will use to prove that conduct.

Id. at 520–21.

The new "same-conduct" test did not last long. The replacement of Justice Thurgood Marshall with Justice Clarence Thomas in 1991 splintered the *Grady* majority. Two years later, in *United States v. Dixon*, 509 U.S. 688 (1993), the Court formally put *Grady* to rest. Writing for the new majority, Justice Antonin Scalia—a *Grady* dissenter—emphasized considerations of history and tradition: "Unlike *Blockburger* analysis, whose definition of what prevents two crimes from being the 'same offence,' U.S. Const., Amdt. 5, has deep historical roots and has been accepted in numerous precedents of this Court, *Grady* lacks constitutional roots. The 'same-conduct' rule it announced is wholly inconsistent with earlier Supreme Court precedent and with the clear common-law understanding of double jeopardy." *Id.* at 704.

Notes

1. *What's the right result*? Put aside for a moment the question of which legal test should be employed. Do you think there was something fundamentally unfair about the second (homicide) prosecution of Corbin? Did the second case truly implicate the concerns that underlie the Double Jeopardy Clause? What arguments do you see on both sides of the question?

2. *What's the right test?* What do you see as the relative strengths and weaknesses of the *Blockburger* and same-conduct tests?

3. *State variations.* The double jeopardy protections under a state constitution may be more extensive than those guaranteed by the federal constitution. This has occurred in the context of the *Grady-Dixon* dichotomy. For example, in *State v. Lessary*, 865 P.2d 150 (Haw. 1994), Hawaii's high court adopted a minority position and ruled that under the state constitution's Double Jeopardy Clause, *Grady* "is necessary to afford adequate double jeopardy protection," and rejected the *Dixon* holding as one that "does not adequately protect individuals from [double jeopardy]."

One study published in 2017 found that 27 states use some version of the *Dixon* (*Blockburger*) test. Rebecca A. Delfino, *Prohibition on Successive Prosecutions for the Same Offense—In Search of the "Goldilocks Zone": The California Approach to a National Conundrum*, 54 Am. Crim. L. Rev. 423, 431 (2017). Five states more broadly bar successive prosecutions of charges arising from the same transaction or course of conduct. *Id.* at 433. Four states focus on the defendant's intentions and objectives as the key variable. *Id.* at 435. Thirteen states use a variety of multifactor tests. *Id.* at 436. The law in the final state, California, is characterized as messy and unsettled. *See id.* at 450 ("[T]he cases in the last decade illustrate inconsistent and increasingly arbitrary applications of [California's established double jeopardy] tests—and a tendency to ignore the tests entirely.").

[3] Collateral Estoppel

The double jeopardy guarantee not only bars retrial after a conviction or acquittal, it may also bar a second prosecution that would require relitigation of *issues* resolved in the defendant's favor in a prior prosecution. This principle, sometimes referred to as *collateral estoppel* or *issue preclusion*, was recognized by the Supreme Court in *Ashe v. Swenson*, 397 U.S. 436 (1970). In that case, Ashe was charged with the armed robbery of several individuals, each of whom was engaged in a poker game at the time of the robbery. Ashe was tried on the charge of robbing only one of the victims (Knight), but was found not guilty "due to insufficient evidence" (the evidence that Ashe was one of the three or four alleged robbers was described as "weak"). Six weeks later, Ashe was tried again—this time for the robbery of another named victim (Roberts) at the poker game—and was found guilty. The United States Supreme Court reversed:

> Where a previous judgment of acquittal was based upon a general verdict, as is usually the case, this [collateral estoppel or issue preclusion] approach requires a court to "examine the record of a prior proceeding, taking into account the pleadings, evidence, charge, and other relevant matter, and conclude whether a rational jury could have grounded its verdict upon an issue other than that which the defendant seeks to foreclose from consideration."
>
> . . . Straightforward application of the federal rule to the present case can lead to but one conclusion. For the record is utterly devoid of any indication that the first jury could rationally have found that an armed robbery had not occurred, or that Knight had not been a victim of that robbery. The single rationally conceivable issue in dispute before the jury was whether the petitioner had been one of the robbers. And the jury by its verdict found that he had not. The federal rule of law, therefore, would make a second prosecution for the robbery of Roberts wholly impermissible.
>
> The ultimate question to be determined . . . is whether this established rule of federal law is embodied in the Fifth Amendment guarantee against double jeopardy. We do not hesitate to hold that it is. For whatever else that constitutional guarantee may embrace, it surely protects a man who has been acquitted from having to "run the gantlet" a second time.
>
> The question is not whether Missouri could validly charge the petitioner with six separate offenses for the robbery of the six poker players. It is not whether he could have received a total of six punishments if he had been convicted in a single trial of robbing the six victims. It is simply whether, after a jury determined by its verdict that the petitioner was not one of the robbers, the State could constitutionally hale him before a new jury to litigate that issue again.
>
> After the first jury had acquitted the petitioner of robbing Knight, Missouri could certainly not have brought him to trial again upon that charge. Once a jury had determined upon conflicting testimony that there was at least a reasonable doubt that the petitioner was one of the robbers, the State could not present the same or different identification evidence in a second prosecution for the robbery of Knight in the hope that a different jury

> might find that evidence more convincing. The situation is constitutionally no different here, even though the second trial related to another victim of the same robbery. For the name of the victim, in the circumstances of this case, had no bearing whatever upon the issue of whether the petitioner was one of the robbers.
>
> In this case the State in its brief has frankly conceded that following the petitioner's acquittal, it treated the first trial as no more than a dry run for the second prosecution: "No doubt the prosecutor felt the state had a provable case on the first charge and, when he lost, he did what every good attorney would do—he refined his presentation in light of the turn of events at the first trial." But this is precisely what the constitutional guarantee forbids.

Id. at 444–47 (citations omitted).

Notes

1. *Collateral estoppel as supplement to* Blockburger. Note the relationship between the *Blockburger* same-elements test and collateral estoppel: collateral estoppel can sometimes bar a second prosecution that would be permissible under *Blockburger.* This means that *Blockburger* is not the only standard for determining whether successive prosecutions are permissible under the Double Jeopardy Clause.

2. *One-way street.* Collateral estoppel bars the government from relitigating a fact that was the basis of an acquittal, but it does not stop the *defendant* from relitigating a fact that was the basis of an earlier conviction.

3. *Burden of establishing collateral estoppel.* The party arguing that collateral estoppel bars a second proceeding has the burden of demonstrating that the issue in the second trial was actually decided in that party's favor in the first proceeding. *See United States v. Rigas*, 605 F.3d 194 (3d Cir. 2010) (stating this is a "heavy burden"). Does this allocation of the burden make sense? Should it be the government's job to ensure that a citizen is not put "twice in jeopardy" since the government made the decision to proceed in both the first and second cases?

4. *Issues actually resolved in first trial.* The application of collateral estoppel requires a close analysis of the issues actually resolved in the first trial. The Supreme Court characterized collateral estoppel as barring "relitigation of determinations necessary to the ultimate outcome of a prior proceeding." *Bobby v. Bies*, 556 U.S. 825, 829 (2009). The facts in *Ashe* strongly suggest that the issue of identity was resolved in the acquittal, but in the usual case it may be far more difficult to assess exactly what facts were resolved in an earlier decision. To make it clear what facts were found by a jury that acquitted the defendant, Professor Amar recommends that the defendant be permitted to request a specific verdict after an acquittal. Akhil Reed Amar, *Double Jeopardy Law Made Simple*, 106 Yale L.J. 1807, 1829 (1997).

Assume that a person enters the United States without declaring to customs officials that he or she is in possession of valuable jewelry. Thereafter, this person is acquitted of charges of violating a federal statute that prohibited "willfully and knowingly, with intent to defraud the United States," smuggling those items into the country. The federal government then institutes a civil forfeiture action under a statute that requires that the government need only prove that the property was brought into the country without the required declaration; that is, there is no requirement of proving mens rea. Under those circumstances, should the civil forfeiture action be barred under the *Ashe* collateral estoppel principle?

In *One Lot Emerald Cut Stones and One Ring v. United States*, 409 U.S. 232 (1972), the United States Supreme Court held that the forfeiture action was allowed. First, the Court noted that the doctrine of collateral estoppel itself would not bar the forfeiture proceeding because the earlier criminal acquittal did not resolve the key issues in the later forfeiture action. The acquittal on the criminal charge may have been based on a finding that the defendant's act was done without the requisite intent. Because the civil forfeiture action does not require a finding of intent, "the criminal acquittal may not be regarded as a determination that the property was not unlawfully brought into the United States, and the forfeiture proceeding will not involve an issue previously litigated and finally determined between these parties."

Additionally, the Court in *One Lot* declared that the difference in the burden of proof in criminal and civil cases precludes application of collateral estoppel to bar a civil proceeding because of a previous finding in a criminal case. The criminal acquittal means only that the trier of fact did not find guilt beyond a reasonable doubt. It is not a finding on whether a fact was proven by the civil preponderance-of-the-evidence standard. Finally, the Court held that the Double Jeopardy Clause was inapplicable because it reaches only successive *criminal* prosecutions, not a criminal prosecution followed by a civil action.

5. *Inconsistent verdicts.* If it is difficult to utilize collateral estoppel in a general verdict case because of an inability to ascertain the precise issues resolved, it is virtually impossible to do so when the jury has reached logically inconsistent verdicts of guilty on some counts and not guilty on others. *See, e.g., United States v. Powell*, 469 U.S. 57, 68 (1984) (once it is established a jury reached inconsistent verdicts, "established principles of collateral estoppel—which are predicated on the assumption that the jury acted rationally and found certain facts in reaching its verdict—are no longer useful"). This reasoning holds even if the guilty verdict is overturned on appeal on non-double-jeopardy grounds—the acquittal verdict is still denied any collateral estoppel force if the remaining count is retried after the defendant's successful appeal. *Bravo-Fernandez v. United States*, 137 S. Ct. 352 (2016).

6. *One trial, two decisionmakers.* In *State v. Johnson*, 70 A.3d 168 (Conn. App. Ct. 2013), the defendant was charged with three crimes. A jury acquitted him on two: murder and carrying a pistol without a permit, but he was convicted at the same trial by a judge of criminal possession of a revolver (he waived the jury on this count). He argued that the jury acquittal on the carrying-a-pistol count triggered collateral estoppel that barred the judge-only conviction for criminal possession of the same pistol. The appellate court rejected the argument since collateral estoppel applies only when

there are successive trials, not when, as here, there was one trial though two decision-makers. Do you agree that this resolution serves the policies of double jeopardy?

Problem 15-2. Birth Pains

William Blaine was tried for two crimes: willful possession of an unlawfully issued birth certificate with intent to defraud (Count I), and willfully making false statements on a passport application for purposes of obtaining a passport (Count II).

Blaine is an attorney who, according to government proof, made false representations to obtain a certified copy of a birth certificate in the name of Harold Linden. He also obtained a fake social security number in Linden's name. Blaine then used these two items to obtain a United States passport for his client, a Canadian citizen named Timothy Wiggins. The passport bore the name Harold Linden but the photo of Timothy Wiggins, permitting Wiggins to use it.

At trial, defendant Blaine argued lack of intent because he actually believed his client Timothy Wiggins was really Harold Linden. The jury acquitted him of Count I (birth certificate) and could not reach a verdict on Count II (passport). The government then obtained another indictment for conspiracy (with Wiggins) to make false statements in a passport application. Should the second prosecution be barred by collateral estoppel? *See United States v. White*, 936 F.2d 1326 (D.C. Cir.), *cert. denied*, 502 U.S. 942 (1991).

C. Multiple Punishments

Just as the Double Jeopardy Clause prohibits the government from convicting a person more than once for the same offense, the guarantee also proscribes multiple punishments for the same offense. For example, a defendant may not be convicted of robbery and sentenced to 10 years in prison, then convicted again (at the same or a subsequent trial) for exactly the same crime and given another 10-year sentence. This would involve double punishment for the same offense. Of course, the judge could achieve the same result by imposing a 20-year sentence for the first robbery conviction, but only if such a prison term were authorized by statute for a single robbery.

[1] Multiple Punishment in Single Trial

Sometimes a person is charged with several offenses in one trial. What are the limits on multiple punishments? As the following case concludes, the analysis may not necessarily follow the *Blockburger* same-elements test.

Missouri v. Hunter

459 U.S. 359 (1983)

Chief Justice Burger delivered the opinion of the Court.

[The defendant and two accomplices robbed a supermarket. During the robbery, the defendant struck the store manager with the butt of a revolver and shot at a police officer at the scene. The defendant was convicted under Missouri law of (1) first-degree robbery and (2) armed criminal action. (A third charge is not relevant.) First-degree robbery is defined under Missouri law as feloniously taking property from another's person or presence by violence to the person or by putting the person in fear of immediate injury. The second crime, armed criminal action, is defined as the use of a dangerous weapon to commit a felony. The Missouri legislature specified that the penalty for armed criminal action is a prison term of not less than three years, to be served in addition to the punishment imposed for the felony (here, robbery) for which the weapon was used. The defendant was sentenced to 10 years in prison for robbery and 15 years for armed criminal action.]

On appeal the defendant claimed that a sentence for both robbery and armed criminal action violated double jeopardy.

... The Double Jeopardy Clause is cast explicitly in terms of being "twice put in jeopardy." We have consistently interpreted it "to protect an individual from being subjected to the hazards of trial and possible conviction more than once for an alleged offense." *Burks v. United States*, 437 U.S. 1, 11 (1978), *quoting Green v. United States*, 355 U.S. 184, 187 (1957). Because respondent has been subjected to only one trial, it is not contended that his right to be free from multiple trials for the same offense has been violated. ... With respect to cumulative sentences imposed in a single trial, the Double Jeopardy Clause does no more than prevent the sentencing court from prescribing greater punishment than the legislature intended.

In *Whalen v. United States*, 445 U.S. 684 (1980), we addressed the question whether cumulative punishments for the offenses of rape and of killing the same victim in the perpetration of the crime of rape was contrary to federal statutory and constitutional law. A divided Court relied on *Blockburger v. United States*, 284 U.S. 299 (1932), in holding that the two statutes in controversy proscribed the "same" offense. The opinion in *Blockburger* stated: "The applicable rule is that where the same act or transaction constitutes a violation of two distinct statutory provisions, the test to be applied to determine whether there are two offenses or only one, is whether each provision requires proof of a fact which the other does not."

In *Whalen* we also noted that *Blockburger* established a rule of statutory construction in these terms:

> "The assumption underlying the rule is that Congress *ordinarily* does not intend to punish the same offense under two different statutes. Accordingly, where two statutory provisions proscribe the 'same offense,' they are construed not to authorize cumulative punishments *in the absence of a clear indication of contrary legislative intent.*" (emphasis added).

We went on to emphasize the qualification on that rule:

> "[W]here the offenses are the same ... cumulative sentences are not permitted, *unless elsewhere specially authorized by Congress.*" *Id.*, at 693 (emphasis added).

It is clear, therefore, that the result in *Whalen* turned on the fact that the Court saw no "clear indication of contrary legislative intent." Accordingly, under the rule of statutory construction, we held that cumulative punishment could not be imposed under the two statutes.

. . . Here, the Missouri Supreme Court has construed the two statutes at issue as defining the same crime. In addition, the Missouri Supreme Court has recognized that the legislature intended that punishment for violations of the statutes be cumulative. We are bound to accept the Missouri court's construction of that State's statutes.

. . . Our analysis and reasoning in *Whalen v. United States*, 445 U.S. 684 (1980) . . . [leads] inescapably to the conclusion that simply because two criminal statutes may be construed to proscribe the same conduct under the *Blockburger* test does not mean that the Double Jeopardy Clause precludes the imposition, in a single trial, of cumulative punishments pursuant to those statutes. . . .

Where, as here, a legislature specifically authorizes cumulative punishment under two statutes, regardless of whether those two statutes proscribe the "same" conduct under *Blockburger*, a court's task of statutory construction is at an end and the prosecutor may seek and the trial court or jury may impose cumulative punishment under such statutes in a single trial. [Reversed]

Justice Marshall, with whom Justice Stevens joins, dissenting.

The Double Jeopardy Clause forbids either multiple prosecutions or multiple punishment for "the same offence." Respondent was convicted of both armed criminal action and the lesser included offense of first-degree robbery, and he was sentenced for both crimes. Had respondent been tried for these two crimes in separate trials, he would plainly have been subjected to multiple prosecutions for "the same offence" in violation of the Double Jeopardy Clause.[1] For the reasons stated below, I do not believe that the phrase "the same offence" should be interpreted to mean one thing for purposes of the prohibition against multiple prosecutions and something else for purposes of the prohibition against multiple punishment.

. . . A State has wide latitude to define crimes and to prescribe the punishment for a given crime. For example, a State is free to prescribe two different punishments (e.g., a fine and a prison term) for a single offense. But the Constitution does not permit a State to punish as two crimes conduct that constitutes only one "offence" within the meaning of the Double Jeopardy Clause. For whenever a person is subjected to the risk that he will be convicted of a crime under state law, he is "put in jeopardy of life or limb." If the prohibition against being "twice put in jeopardy" for "the same offense" is to have any real meaning, a State cannot be allowed to convict a defendant two, three, or more times simply by enacting separate statutory

1. The Double Jeopardy Clause would have forbidden multiple prosecutions regardless of which charge was brought first, and regardless of whether the first trial ended in a conviction or an acquittal.

provisions defining nominally distinct crimes. If the Double Jeopardy Clause imposed no restrictions on a legislature's power to authorize multiple punishment, there would be no limit to the number of convictions that a State could obtain on the basis of the same act, state of mind, and result.

... [T]he entry of two convictions and the imposition of two sentences cannot be justified on the ground that the legislature could have simply created one crime but prescribed harsher punishment for that crime. This argument incorrectly assumes that the total sentence imposed is all that matters, and that the number of convictions that can be obtained is of no relevance to the concerns underlying the Double Jeopardy Clause.

When multiple charges are brought, the defendant is "put in jeopardy" as to each charge. To retain his freedom, the defendant must obtain an acquittal on all charges; to put the defendant in prison, the prosecution need only obtain a single guilty verdict. The prosecution's ability to bring multiple charges increases the risk that the defendant will be convicted on one or more of those charges. The very fact that a defendant has been arrested, charged, and brought to trial on several charges may suggest to the jury that he must be guilty of at least one of those crimes. Moreover, where the prosecution's evidence is weak, its ability to bring multiple charges may substantially enhance the possibility that, even though innocent, the defendant may be found guilty on one or more charges as a result of a compromise verdict. The submission of two charges rather than one gives the prosecution "the advantage of offering the jury a choice—a situation which is apt to induce a doubtful jury to find the defendant guilty of the less serious offense rather than to continue the debate as to his innocence." *Cichos v. Indiana*, 385 U.S. 76, 81 (1966) (Fortas, J., dissenting from dismissal of certiorari).

The Government's argument also overlooks the fact that, quite apart from any sentence that is imposed, each separate criminal conviction typically has collateral consequences, in both the jurisdiction in which the conviction is obtained and in other jurisdictions. The number of convictions is often critical to the collateral consequences that an individual faces. For example, a defendant who has only one prior conviction will generally not be subject to sentencing under a habitual offender statute.

Furthermore, each criminal conviction itself represents a pronouncement by the State that the defendant has engaged in conduct warranting the moral condemnation of the community. Because a criminal conviction constitutes a formal judgment of condemnation by the community, each additional conviction imposes an additional stigma and causes additional damage to the defendant's reputation.

... In light of these considerations, the Double Jeopardy Clause cannot reasonably be interpreted to leave legislatures completely free to subject a defendant to the risk of multiple punishment on the basis of a single criminal transaction.... Since the Double Jeopardy Clause limits the power of all branches of government, including the legislature, there is no more reason to treat the [*Blockburger*] test as simply a rule of statutory construction in multiple-punishment cases than there would be in multiple-prosecution cases.

Notes

1. *What is* Hunter *saying?* Recall that the Double Jeopardy Clause is read to bar "multiple punishments for the same offense." In *Hunter*, is the Supreme Court saying the two sentences (1) are not "multiple punishment," (2) are not for the "same offense," or (3) something else?

2. *Changing the* Hunter *facts.* In *Hunter* the defendant was convicted of first-degree robbery and armed criminal action in a single trial. What if he were first convicted of the robbery, then at a later trial convicted of armed criminal action, and given a consecutive sentence to be served on completion of the robbery sentence. Would this offend *Blockburger*? Would this offend *Hunter*? Would your answer change if it were clearly established that the legislature intended for there to be successive prosecutions?

Revisit the policies behind the Double Jeopardy Clause. Are they served if consecutive trials are barred, but multiple charges for the "same offense" in the same trial are permitted?

3. *State legislature defines double jeopardy?* After *Hunter*, the resolution of some double jeopardy issues will depend largely on state legislative intent. Is it fair to say that *Hunter* lets a state legislature define the meaning of "same offense" in the federal double jeopardy guarantee?

4. *Legislative intent.* How clear must legislative intent be to resolve a multiple punishment issue under *Hunter*? The rule of lenity is sometimes used in criminal cases when legislative intent is unclear. This rule resolves ambiguities in favor of the accused. Should this rule ever be used to resolve double jeopardy issues? *See, e.g.*, *State v. O'Brien*, 267 P.3d 422 (Wash. Ct. App. 2011) (statute punishing bail jumping is ambiguous about unit of prosecution when offender fails to appear multiple times; rule of lenity applied to make unit a failure to appear even after multiple court orders to do so).

If *Blockburger* is a rule of statutory construction, when does it apply in multiple punishment cases? If legislative intent is clear? Unclear? When there is a slight indication that multiple punishments are permissible? Impermissible? In a number of jurisdictions, *Blockburger* is used to ascertain legislative intent when that intent cannot be determined through other means. *See, e.g., United States v. Perez-Gonzalez*, 455 F.3d 39 (1st Cir. 2006) (in multiple punishment case involving single trial, *Blockburger* test is used to determine legislative intent when other indicia of legislative intent are unclear).

Some legislatures have enacted statutes to express their intent in this area. *See, e.g.*, Kan. Stat. Ann. § 21-5109 (if same conduct constitutes more than one crime, defendant may be prosecuted for each crime, but may not be convicted of more than one); Ohio Rev. Code § 2941.25 (where same conduct by defendant can be construed to constitute two or more allied offenses of similar import, defendant may be convicted of [and punished for] only one).

5. *Multiple punishment intended.* Many cases after *Hunter* have found a legislative intent allowing multiple punishments. *See, e.g., United States v. Patel*, 370 F.3d 108 (1st Cir. 2004) (double jeopardy did not bar imposition of multiple punishments for arson and causing fire to commit mail fraud); *Birr v. Shillinger*, 894 F.2d 1160 (10th Cir.1990) (consecutive sentences for felony murder and underlying felony); *Branham v. Gay*, 2011 U.S. Dist. LEXIS 135624 (D. Ariz.) (legislature intended separate crimes for multiple assaults against same victim during same episode).

6. For critical assessments of *Hunter, see* Carissa Byrne Hessick & F. Andrew *Hessick, Double Jeopardy as a Limit on Punishment*, 97 CORN. L. REV. 45 (2011) (arguing that double jeopardy should bar some sentencing enhancements based on other convictions); Anne Bowen Poulin, *Double Jeopardy and Multiple Punishment: Cutting the Gordian Knot*, 77 U. COLO. L. REV. 595 (2006); George C. Thomas III, *Multiple Punishments for the Same Offense: The Analysis after* Missouri v. Hunter, 62 WASH. U. L.Q. 79 (1984).

Problem 15-3. Don't Be A Lamb

Lamb, who worked for a drug-trafficking operation run by Hernandez, stole a quantity of meth from his employer. Two days later, police discovered Lamb's body, dead from multiple gunshots to the head at close range. Hernandez fled the country, but federal prosecutors charged one of his associates, Olgin, in connection with the killing. The charges included conspiracy to possess with intent to distribute a controlled substance (Count 1), using or carrying a firearm in relation to a drug trafficking crime in violation of 18 U.S.C. § 924(c)(1)(A) (Count 2), and causing death through the use of a firearm in relation to a drug trafficking crime in violation of 18 U.S.C. § 924(j) (Count 3). A jury found Olgin guilty as to all three counts. The sentencing judge imposed a separate prison term for each count, all to run consecutively. Olgin now appeals on double jeopardy grounds.

Do you think it was permissible for the judge to impose separate sentences for Counts 1 and 2? Counts 2 and 3? Here is the relevant statutory language:

18 U.S.C. § 924(c)(1)(A)

> [A]ny person who, during and in relation to any crime of violence or drug trafficking crime . . . for which the person may be prosecuted in a court of the United States, uses or carries a firearm . . . shall, in addition to the punishment provided for such crime of violence or drug trafficking crime[,] be sentenced to a term of imprisonment of not less than 5 years. . . .

18 U.S.C. § 924(j)

> A person who, in the course of a violation of subsection (c), causes the death of a person through the use of a firearm, shall . . . be punished by death or by imprisonment for any term of years or for life. . . .

The facts of this problem are adapted from *United States v. Gonzales*, 841 F.3d 339 (5th Cir. 2016). The *Gonzales* court agreed with Olgin that cumulative punishment should not have been imposed under the two subsections of 18 U.S.C. § 924, but noted that there was contrary authority in the Eleventh Circuit. *See id.* at 355 (discussing *United States v. Julian*, 633 F.3d 1250 (11th Cir. 2011)).

[2] What Is Punishment?

Difficult double jeopardy questions can arise when two sanctions are imposed for the same conduct, but the sanctions are not similar to one another. If both sanctions are considered to be criminal punishments, then double jeopardy rights may be implicated. However, many sanctions are instead considered to be merely civil penalties. Unfortunately, the line between criminal punishment and civil penalty has not always been drawn with clarity by the courts.

For instance, in *Hudson v. United States*, 522 U.S. 93 (1997), the defendants used their bank positions to arrange a series of loans to a third individual in violation of banking statutes and regulations. Thereafter, the Office of the Comptroller of Currency (OCC) imposed monetary penalties and occupational debarment on the defendants. Later, these defendants were indicted for numerous federal crimes, all of which rested on the lending transactions that had formed the basis for the prior administrative actions brought by the OCC. The defendant argued that the criminal indictment was additional punishment in violation of double jeopardy. The Supreme Court disagreed, holding that double jeopardy did not bar the subsequent criminal proceedings because the monetary penalties and debarment were civil in nature.

The proper approach, according to *Hudson*, is two-fold:

1. The trial court must ask whether the particular punishment is civil or criminal, a determination at least initially which is a matter of statutory construction. The court must determine whether the legislature indicated expressly or impliedly a preference for one or the other label. The statute's text and structure are to be assessed.

2. In cases where the legislature has indicated an intention to establish a civil penalty, the court assessing a double jeopardy claim must inquire whether the statutory scheme was so punitive in purpose or effect as to transform an intended civil remedy into a criminal penalty.

Applying this approach (sometimes called the "intent-effects test"), *Hudson* held that the Double Jeopardy Clause was not offended since Congress intended for the regulatory penalties to be civil and these sanctions were not so punitive that they were rendered criminal punishment. The fact that the civil penalties were meant to deter certain conduct does not make them criminal in nature.

Notes

1. Hudson *factors.* The Supreme Court's *Hudson* decision listed factors to be used in deciding whether the statutory scheme is so punitive to be deemed punishment irrespective of the legislature's intent. The factors are whether the sanction (1) involves an affirmative disability or restraint; (2) has historically been regarded as a punishment; (3) requires a finding of scienter; (4) will promote traditional punishment aims of retribution and deterrence; (5) applies to behavior that is already a crime; (6) can reasonably have an alternative purpose; and (7) appears excessive in relation to the alternative purpose assigned to it. *Hudson*, 522 U.S. at 99. Do you think these factors are helpful in assessing whether a sanction is civil or criminal?

2. *Non-criminal "crimes."* Some jurisdictions have a category of very minor offenses considered to be "infractions" or some other category rather than crimes. Usually the maximum penalty is a small fine. These infractions may be deemed civil and do not implicate double jeopardy protections. *See, e.g., State v. Jiminez-Jaramill*, 38 A.3d 239 (Conn. Ct. App. 2012) (trial court erroneously dismissed public disturbance case; retrial permissible because under state law the offense is an "infraction," not considered a criminal offense since only sanction was $75 fine); *State v. Jenson*, 184 P.3d 1194 (Or. Ct. App. 2008) (possession of less than ounce of marijuana is not a "crime," so double jeopardy does not bar subsequent criminal action for intoxicated driving for same event).

3. *Illustrative cases.* Cases applying the criminal/noncriminal distinction involving "civil" sanctions vary considerably according to the precise laws involved, but the sanctions are usually found to be civil. *See, e.g., City of South Milwaukee v. Kester*, 830 N.W.2d 710 (Wis. Ct. App. 2013) (defendant charged under city ordinance with maintaining a civil nuisance by being a convicted sex offender living in a residence within 1000 feet of an elementary school; nuisance ordinance is regulatory, not punitive, and does not violate double jeopardy as additional punishment for his prior sex offense conviction); *State v. Hunt*, 727 S.E.2d 584 (N.C. Ct. App. 2012) (adding civil no-contact order to prison term for rape does not offend double jeopardy); *People v. Taylor*, 985 N.E.2d 648 (Ill. App. Ct. 2013) (bond forfeiture judgment is civil); *Treece v. Wilson*, 212 Fed. Appx. 948, 2007 U.S. App. LEXIS 6 (11th Cir.) (suspension of social security benefits during incarceration is civil). *But see State v. McKenzie*, 736 S.E.2d 591 (N.C. Ct. App. 2013) (a one-year suspension of a commercial truck driving license for intoxicated driving is punitive and bars a later conviction for drunk driving for same incident).

4. *Taxes.* While *Hudson* addresses the double jeopardy analysis in civil fine cases, does the same analysis apply to taxing schemes? In *Department of Revenue of Montana v. Kurth Ranch*, 511 U.S. 767 (1994), the Supreme Court found that a state tax did count as punishment for double jeopardy purposes. The taxpayer defendants had pled guilty to drug charges related to marijuana plants found during a raid of their farm by Montana law enforcement officers. Thereafter, the State Revenue Department brought a second action to collect a state tax imposed upon "the possession and storage of dangerous drugs," and collected only after "any state or federal fines or forfeitures have been satisfied." The amount of the tax was either 10% of the assessed market value of the drugs or a specified amount depending upon the particular drug in question. Additionally, taxpayers were obligated to file a return within 72 hours of their arrest; indeed, taxpayers had no obligation to file a return or to pay any tax until they were arrested.

The defendants challenged the tax in bankruptcy proceedings. The bankruptcy court, noting that the assessment on the marijuana harvest resulted in a tax eight times the product's market value, held that it was a form of double jeopardy.

In the Supreme Court, Justice Stevens' majority opinion concluded that the state drug tax was "a concoction of anomalies too far-removed in crucial respects from a standard tax assessment to escape characterization as punishment for the purpose of Double Jeopardy analysis." He pointed out, for example, that the state tax is conditioned on the commission of a crime, is exacted only after the taxpayer has been arrested, and is levied on goods that the taxpayer neither owns nor possesses when the tax is imposed. He concluded:

> This drug tax is not the kind of remedial sanction that may follow the first punishment of a criminal offense. Instead, it is a second punishment . . . and therefore must be imposed during the first prosecution or not at all. The proceeding Montana initiated to collect a tax on the possession of drugs was the functional equivalent of a successive criminal prosecution that placed the Kurths in jeopardy a second time "for the same offense."

Id. at 784.

5. *Forfeiture.* Forfeiture laws establish processes by which the government can take ownership of property that was used in the commission of a crime (for instance, a car used to transport drugs illegally across the border) or that constitutes the fruit of a crime (for instance, the cash acquired through illegal drug sales). In many cases, such laws give the government the option of accomplishing forfeiture through a civil lawsuit, rather than requiring the government to initiate a criminal proceeding with its higher burdens of proof and other distinctive features. Should civil forfeiture be considered a form of punishment for double jeopardy purposes? The Supreme Court held to the contrary in *United States v. Ursery*, 518 U.S. 267 (1996), applying the intent-effects test to an important federal civil forfeiture law. State courts have similarly found that state forfeiture laws do not trigger double jeopardy rights. *See, e.g., State v. 2002 Chevrolet Trail Blazer*, 155 So. 3d 547 (La. Ct. App. 2013); *Childers v. State Dept. of Management Services*, 989 So. 2d 716 (Fla. Dist. Ct. App. 2008).

6. *Civil commitment.* Since the early 1990s, many states have adopted or expanded laws that provide for the indefinite involuntary civil commitment of certain sexual offenders, even after they have completed their prison sentences. The Supreme Court indicated that such civil commitments would not generally run afoul of the Double Jeopardy Clause in *Kansas v. Hendricks*, 521 U.S. 346 (1997).

7. *Deportation.* Deportation is widely considered to be a civil penalty and not affected by a criminal prosecution for the same conduct that caused the deportation. For an argument that this analysis is due for some reconsideration, *see* Aaron S. Haas, *Deportation and Double Jeopardy After* Padilla, 26 Geo. Immigr. L.J. 121 (2011) (arguing that recent developments in the civil-criminal distinction suggest deportation may be sufficiently punitive to trigger double jeopardy protection).

8. *Sentence enhancement.* As we will see in the next chapter, judges normally have broad discretion to consider a wide array of factors in selecting a sentence within the

applicable statutory range. Sometimes a judge will take into account criminal conduct of which the defendant has not been formally convicted. For instance, a defendant may be convicted for a single drug sale, subject to a statutory range of one to five years. Based on the circumstances of that particular sale, the judge might be inclined to impose a sentence of two years. However, if the judge has reliable information that the defendant completed dozens of additional, uncharged sales, the judge might decide to impose the maximum of five years as better reflecting the true seriousness of the defendant's overall course of conduct. Indeed, in some jurisdictions, such consideration of "relevant conduct" may be required of the sentencing judge. What if the government then separately charges some of the relevant conduct that has already been used to enhance the defendant's sentence in the first case—would that be a double jeopardy violation? The Supreme Court held otherwise in *Witte v. United States*, 515 U.S. 389 (1995). The same formalistic logic—for double jeopardy purposes, a sentence constitutes "punishment" only as to the offense of conviction—also serves to protect "three strikes and you're out" and other recidivism laws from double jeopardy challenge. When a defendant receives a much longer sentence as a result of two prior convictions, the added length of the prison term in the new case is simply not seen as a second round of punishment for the earlier convictions.

D. When Does Jeopardy Attach?

Just as it is critically important to determine whether a defendant has been twice charged with the "same offence," it is equally important to determine, for double jeopardy purposes, if jeopardy has "attached" to the defendant's case. The double jeopardy protection is inapplicable until jeopardy attaches. For example, assume that a defendant is indicted and the case is set for trial. Two days before the trial is to begin, the trial judge orders that the case be dismissed. Thereafter, the defendant is indicted a second time for the exact same offense. The defendant now files a motion to dismiss on the ground that a trial for the crime in the second indictment is barred by the Double Jeopardy Clause. Should the judge grant the motion to dismiss?

Fortunately—for law students, anyway—the case law provides relatively clear answers to the question of when jeopardy attaches. In the following case, you can see a good illustration of the Supreme Court's insistence on maintaining a bright-line rule in this area.

Martinez v. Illinois

572 U.S. 883 (2014)

Per Curiam.

The trial of Esteban Martinez was set to begin on May 17, 2010. His counsel was ready; the State was not. When the court swore in the jury and invited the State to present its first witness, the State declined to present any evidence. So Martinez moved for a directed not-guilty verdict, and the court granted it. The State appealed, arguing that the trial court should have granted its motion for a continuance. The question is whether the Double Jeopardy Clause bars the State's attempt to appeal in the hope of subjecting Martinez to a new trial.

The Illinois Supreme Court manifestly erred in allowing the State's appeal, on the theory that jeopardy never attached because Martinez "was never at risk of conviction." 2013 IL 113475, ¶ 39. Our cases have repeatedly stated the bright-line rule that "jeopardy attaches when the jury is empaneled and sworn." *Crist v. Bretz,* 437 U.S. 28, 35 (1978). There is simply no doubt that Martinez was subjected to jeopardy. And because the trial court found the State's evidence insufficient to sustain a conviction, there is equally no doubt that Martinez may not be retried. . . .

I

A

The State of Illinois indicted Martinez in August 2006 on charges of aggravated battery and mob action against Avery Binion and Demarco Scott. But Martinez's trial date did not arrive for nearly four years.

The story picks up for present purposes on July 20, 2009, when the State moved to continue an August 3 trial date because it had not located the complaining witnesses, Binion and Scott. The State subpoenaed both men four days later, and the court rescheduled Martinez's trial to September 28. But the State sought another continuance, shortly before that date, because it still had not found Binion and Scott. The court rescheduled the trial to November 9, and the State reissued subpoenas. But November 9 came and went (the court continued the case when Martinez showed up late) and the trial was eventually delayed to the following March 29. In early February, the State yet again subpoenaed Binion and Scott. When March 29 arrived, the trial court granted the State another continuance. It reset the trial date for May 17 and ordered Binion and Scott to appear in court on May 10. And the State once more issued subpoenas.

On the morning of May 17, however, Binion and Scott were again nowhere to be found. At 8:30, when the trial was set to begin, the State asked for a brief continuance. The court offered to delay swearing the jurors until a complete jury had been empaneled and told the State that it could at that point either have the jury sworn or move to dismiss its case. When Binion and Scott still had not shown up after the jury was chosen, the court offered to call the other cases on its docket so as to delay swearing the jury a bit longer. But when all these delays had run out, Binion and Scott were still nowhere in sight. The State filed a written motion for a continuance, arguing that it was "unable to proceed" without Binion and Scott. The court denied that motion:

> "The case before the Court began on July 7, 2006. In two months we will then be embarking upon half a decade of pending a Class 3 felony. Avery Binion, Jr., and Demarco [Scott] are well known in Elgin, both are convicted felons. One would believe that the Elgin Police Department would

> know their whereabouts. They were ordered to be in court today. The Court will issue body writs for both of these gentlemen.
>
> "In addition, the State's list of witnesses indicates twelve witnesses. Excluding Mr. Scott and Mr. Binion, that's ten witnesses. The Court would anticipate it would take every bit of today and most of tomorrow to get through ten witnesses. By then the People may have had a chance to execute the arrest warrant body writs for these two gentlemen.
>
> "The Court will deny the motion for continuance. I will swear the jury in in 15, 20 minutes. Perhaps you might want to send the police out to find these two gentlemen."

After a brief recess, the court offered to delay the start of the trial for several more hours if the continuance would "be of any help" to the State. But when the State made clear that Binion and Scott's "whereabouts" remained "unknown," the court concluded that the delay "would be a further waste of time." The following colloquy ensued:

> "THE COURT: . . . It's a quarter to eleven and [Binion and Scott] have not appeared on their own will, so I'm going to bring the jury in now then to swear them.
>
> . . .
>
> "[The Prosecutor]: Your Honor, just so your Honor is aware, I know that it's the process to bring them in and swear them in; however, the State will not be participating in the trial. I wanted to let you know that.
>
> "THE COURT: Very well. We'll see how that works."

The jury was then sworn. After instructing the jury, the court directed the State to proceed with its opening statement. The prosecutor demurred: "Your Honor, respectfully, the State is not participating in this case." After the defense waived its opening statement, the court directed the State to call its first witness. Again, the prosecutor demurred: "Respectfully, your Honor, the State is not participating in this matter." The defense then moved for a judgment of acquittal:

> "[Defense Counsel]: Judge, the jury has been sworn. The State has not presented any evidence. I believe they've indicated their intention not to present any evidence or witnesses. Based on that, Judge, I would ask the Court to enter directed findings of not guilty to both counts, aggravated battery and mob action.
>
> "THE COURT: Do the People wish to reply?
>
> "[The Prosecutor]: No, your Honor. Respectfully, the State is not participating.
>
> "THE COURT: The Court will grant the motion for a directed finding and dismiss the charges."

B

The State appealed, arguing that the trial court should have granted a continuance. Martinez responded that the State's appeal was improper because he had been acquitted. The Illinois Appellate Court sided with the State, holding that jeopardy had never attached and that the trial court had erred in failing to grant a continuance.

The Illinois Supreme Court granted review on the jeopardy issue and affirmed. 2013 IL 113475. It began by recognizing that "[g]enerally, in cases of a jury trial, jeopardy attaches when a jury is empaneled and sworn, as that is the point when the defendant is '"put to trial before the trier of the facts."'" *Id.,* ¶ 23 (quoting *Serfass v. United States,* 420 U.S. 377, 394 (1975)). But it reasoned that under this Court's precedents, "'"rigid, mechanical" rules'" should not govern the inquiry into whether jeopardy has attached. 2013 IL 113475, ¶ 24 (quoting *Serfass, supra,* at 390). Rather, it opined, the relevant question is whether a defendant "was '"subjected to the hazards of trial and possible conviction."'" 2013 IL 113475, ¶ 24 (quoting *Serfass, supra,* at 391).

Here, the court concluded, Martinez "was never at risk of conviction"—and jeopardy therefore did not attach—because "[t]he State indicated it would not participate prior to the jury being sworn." 2013 IL 113475, ¶ 39. And because Martinez "was not placed in jeopardy," the court held, the trial "court's entry of directed verdicts of not guilty did not constitute true acquittals." *Id.,*¶ 40. . . .

II

This case presents two issues. First, did jeopardy attach to Martinez? Second, if so, did the proceeding end in such a manner that the Double Jeopardy Clause bars his retrial? Our precedents clearly dictate an affirmative answer to each question.

A

There are few if any rules of criminal procedure clearer than the rule that "jeopardy attaches when the jury is empaneled and sworn." *Crist,* 437 U.S., at 35; *see also United States v. Martin Linen Supply Co.,* 430 U.S. 564, 569 (1977). . . .

The Illinois Supreme Court misread our precedents in suggesting that the swearing of the jury is anything other than a bright line at which jeopardy attaches. . . .

. . . Martinez was subjected to jeopardy because the jury in his case was sworn.

B

. . . The remaining question is whether the jeopardy ended in such a manner that the defendant may not be retried. Here, there is no doubt that Martinez's jeopardy ended in a manner that bars his retrial: The trial court acquitted him of the charged offenses. "Perhaps the most fundamental rule in the history of double jeopardy jurisprudence has been that '[a] verdict of acquittal . . . could not be reviewed . . . without putting [a defendant] twice in jeopardy, and thereby violating the Constitution.'" *Martin Linen, supra,* at 571.

"[O]ur cases have defined an acquittal to encompass any ruling that the prosecution's proof is insufficient to establish criminal liability for an offense." *Evans v. Michigan*, 133 S. Ct. 1069, 1074-1075 (2013). And the trial court clearly made such a ruling here. After the State declined to present evidence against Martinez, his counsel moved for "directed findings of not guilty to both counts," and the court "grant[ed] the motion for a directed finding." That is a textbook acquittal: a finding that the State's evidence cannot support a conviction.

The Illinois Supreme Court thought otherwise. . . . The court went on to "note that, in directing findings of not guilty," the trial court "referred to its action as a 'dismissal' rather than an acquittal." *Ibid.* Under our precedents, however, that is immaterial: "[W]e have emphasized that what constitutes an 'acquittal' is not to be controlled by the form of the judge's action"; it turns on "whether the ruling of the judge, whatever its label, actually represents a resolution . . . of some or all of the factual elements of the offense charged." *Martin Linen,* 430 U.S., at 571.

Here, as in *Evans* and *Martin Linen,* the trial court's action was an acquittal because the court "acted on its view that the prosecution had failed to prove its case." *Evans,* 133 S. Ct., at 1078. And because Martinez was acquitted, the State cannot retry him.

III

The functional rule adopted by the Illinois Supreme Court is not necessary to avoid unfairness to prosecutors or to the public. On the day of trial, the court was acutely aware of the significance of swearing a jury. It repeatedly delayed that act to give the State additional time to find its witnesses. It had previously granted the State a number of continuances for the same purpose. And, critically, the court told the State on the day of trial that it could "move to dismiss [its] case" before the jury was sworn. Had the State accepted that invitation, the Double Jeopardy Clause would not have barred it from recharging Martinez. Instead, the State participated in the selection of jurors and did not ask for dismissal before the jury was sworn. . . . Here, the State knew, or should have known, that an acquittal forever bars the retrial of the defendant when it occurs after jeopardy has attached. The Illinois Supreme Court's holding is understandable, given the significant consequence of the State's mistake, but it runs directly counter to our precedents and to the protection conferred by the Double Jeopardy Clause. [Reversed.]

Notes

1. *A troubling outcome?* The Supreme Court's *per curiam* opinion treats *Martinez* as an exceptionally easy case. But note the end result: a defendant who was charged with a violent felony escapes any meaningful trial of the charge—and hence any possibility of punishment, no matter how clearly his guilt could have been established if the state's witnesses had shown up to testify. No wonder the Supreme Court characterized the lower court's effort to introduce more flexibility into the jeopardy test as "understandable, given the significant consequence of the State's mistake."

2. *A line too bright?* In some respects, bright-line rules of procedure make life easier for judges, lawyers, and law students. But such rules almost inevitably come at the cost of troubling results in some cases. You might see *Martinez* itself as an illustration. Does the more flexible rule suggested by the Illinois Supreme Court seem preferable to you? In answering this question, you might consider how much of a bind the bright-line rule really creates for prosecutors. What could the prosecutor in *Martinez* have done differently to avoid the double jeopardy problem? After *Martinez*, would you expect many other defendants to be able to avoid trial altogether because the state's witnesses temporarily go AWOL?

3. *Whose ox is really gored?* Because of the way *Martinez* played out, you might get the impression that the rule for jeopardy-attachment is a boon for defendants, but in some cases the unfairness might go the other way. For instance, what if the trial judge in *Martinez* had granted the state's motion for yet another continuance before the jury was sworn? That would have resulted in a *sixth* trial date, with still no double jeopardy consequences for the state. Indeed, as far as double jeopardy law is concerned, trials could be scheduled and continued indefinitely so long as a jury was never sworn—potentially creating significant expense and anxiety for the defendant as preparations are made for each successive trial date. Don't forget, too, that the defendant may be stuck in a jail cell for the entire time before trial. Should the Double Jeopardy Clause provide greater protections for defendants (and defense counsel) who prepare diligently and show up on a trial date ready to go? This might be a good time to review the time-limitation doctrines covered in Chapter 12—do they obviate any need for the Double Jeopardy Clause to help defendants who can't get their trial dates to stick?

4. *A bright-line rule for bright-line rules?* In *Martinez*, the Supreme Court insisted on a bright-line rule for one double-jeopardy question (when does jeopardy attach), but rejected a bright-line rule for another double-jeopardy question (whether the trial judge must use the label "acquittal" for his or her order to be treated as an acquittal). In some areas of double jeopardy law (as with criminal procedure more generally), the Supreme Court has embraced bright-line rules, while in other areas the Court has opted for more flexible legal standards. The debate about the *Grady* same-conduct test, discussed earlier in this chapter, reflects this tension in the double jeopardy jurisprudence: in *Grady*, the Court opted for a more flexible approach to defining "same offense," but then just two years later decided to go back to the brighter-line formalism of *Blockburger*. Does the Court need a bright-line rule to help it decide when bright-line rules should be adopted?

5. *Cases without a jury. Martinez* reaffirms the long-standing rule for jury-trial cases that jeopardy does not attach until the jury is selected and sworn (sometimes expressed as "empaneled and sworn"); termination of the case prior to that time does not afford the defendant any double jeopardy protection. What about other sorts of cases? In a bench trial, jeopardy does not attach until the first witness for the prosecution is sworn. *See, e.g., Serfass v. United States*, 420 U.S. 377, 388 (1975).

Meanwhile, in guilty plea cases, jeopardy attaches when the defendant's plea is accepted and a judgment of guilt is subsequently entered.

E. Reprosecution Following Dismissal or Acquittal

[1] Acquittal by Jury

[a] Bar to Retrial

A jury verdict of not guilty (i.e., an acquittal) carries absolute finality for double jeopardy purposes and therefore bars a retrial on the same issue in the same jurisdiction. The state is not normally even entitled to appeal the acquittal. The United States Supreme Court's strong adherence to this principle is reflected in *United States v. DiFrancesco*:

> The Constitutional protection against double jeopardy unequivocally prohibits a second trial following an acquittal, for the "public interest in the finality of criminal judgments is so strong that an acquitted defendant may not be retried even though the acquittal was based upon an egregiously erroneous foundation." If the innocence of the accused has been confirmed by a final judgment, the Constitution conclusively presumes that a second trial would be unfair.
>
> . . . This is justified on the ground that, however mistaken the acquittal may have been, there would be an unacceptably high risk that the Government, with its superior resources, would wear down a defendant, thereby "enhancing the possibility that even though innocent he may be found guilty."

449 U.S. 117, 129–30 (1980) (citations omitted).

Acquittal contrary to proof or otherwise improper. As suggested by *DiFrancesco*, sometimes it may appear that an acquittal is flatly contrary to the government's proof or is otherwise improper. For example, in *Fong Foo v. United States*, 369 U.S. 141, 143 (1962), the judge thought the prosecutor had committed misconduct and the government's proof lacked credibility. The court then improperly ordered the jury to acquit. The Supreme Court agreed that the trial judge's actions in directing an acquittal were erroneous, but held that the acquittal produced a final decision and future proceedings were barred by double jeopardy.

Implied acquittal. What if the defendant is charged with both a greater offense (such as felony murder during an armed robbery) and a lesser included one (armed robbery), and the jury convicts the defendant of the lesser without reaching a verdict on the greater? Can the defendant be reprosecuted in a second trial for the greater? Using the doctrine of *implied acquittal*, many courts hold that the jury's silence as to the greater charge is deemed to be an acquittal of that charge and bars a later prosecution for it. *See, e.g.*, *Brazzel v. Washington*, 491 F.3d 976, 981 (9th Cir. 2007). The result is different if the jury announces it is deadlocked on the first (greater) charge; retrial is then permissible on that charge as discussed below.

Acquittal as final resolution. While ordinarily it is clear when a jury acquits on a particular charge, in *Blueford v. Arkansas*, 566 U.S. 599 (2012), the foreperson reported to the court that the jury was unanimous against guilt on both capital and first-degree murder but was deadlocked on the lesser charge of manslaughter. The judge ordered the jury to continue deliberations, then later ordered a mistrial when no progress was made. Despite the foreperson's indication of unanimity about the two most serious charges, the Supreme Court held double jeopardy does not bar retrial on them since the foreperson was deemed to have given only a progress report, not a final decision, and the jury was free to reconsider its initial decisions on the two most serious charges. For double jeopardy purposes, an acquittal is a final resolution, not an interim assessment that the jury is free to reconsider.

[b] Exception in Interests of Justice

[i] Fraud or Intimidation

Should an acquittal obtained through fraud bar a subsequent prosecution for the same offense? The general rule is that the acquittal still bars the retrial. Based upon an analysis of the policies underlying the Double Jeopardy Clause, Professor David Rudstein agrees with this conclusion, "even though that acquittal may have been the result of bribery, blackmail, intimidation, or other improper conduct on the part of the accused or with her knowledge and acquiescence." David S. Rudstein, *Double Jeopardy and the Fraudulently-Obtained Acquittal*, 60 Mo. L. Rev. 607 (1995). Do you agree?

[ii] Newly Discovered Evidence

What if the defendant is acquitted, then newly discovered evidence (perhaps DNA) becomes available and clearly establishes guilt? Should double jeopardy prevent a retrial? The general rule in the United States is that retrial is barred, though perhaps a prosecution for perjury is possible if the defendant testified falsely and the statute of limitations for perjury has not run.

A 2003 English law now grants an exception to its double jeopardy protection in this situation when there is "new and compelling evidence." This rule was applied in a case in which a man was acquitted of murdering a baby but later confessed. Using the 2003 law, the government obtained a retrial based on the man's post-acquittal confessions. The man eventually pled guilty and received a mandatory life sentence. *See* Kenneth G. Coffin, *Double Take: Evaluating Double Jeopardy Reform*, 85 Notre Dame L. Rev. 771 (2010); Kyden Creekpaum, Note, *What's Wrong with a Little More Double Jeopardy? A 21st Century Recalibration of an Ancient Individual*

Right, 44 AM. CRIM. L. REV. 1179 (2007) (arguing for constitutional amendment permitting retrial for newly discovered evidence).

If retrial for new evidence is permitted, what limits would you put on it? Would the evidence have to be decisive or could it just be "strong" or "better than was offered at trial?" Would you adopt the English "new and compelling" standard? Would you require that the evidence not have been available at trial had the government made good faith efforts to find it?

[2] Acquittal by Judge

Noting that the Double Jeopardy Clause does not distinguish between jury and non-jury trials, the Supreme Court treats directed acquittals entered by the judge the same as a jury verdict of not guilty. *Sanabria v. United States*, 437 U.S. 54 (1978).

What is an acquittal? According to the Supreme Court in *Evans v. Michigan*, 133 S. Ct. 1069 (2013), an "acquittal" is "any ruling that the prosecution's proof is insufficient to establish criminal liability for the offense." Putting it another way, the *Evans* Court said an acquittal is "a ruling by the court that the evidence is insufficient to convict," or "a factual finding that necessarily establishes the criminal defendant's lack of culpability." An acquittal is distinguished from a mistrial or dismissal which is the product of a procedural problem rather than a decision as to guilt or innocence. As we saw in *Martinez v. Illinois*, an acquittal may occur even if the judge does not use the magic word "acquittal." The nature of the trial court's decision does not turn on the "form of the trial court's actions" but rather whether it serves substantive purposes or procedural ones. *Evans, Id.* at 1078.

Erroneous acquittal. A judge's acquittal may take many forms, such as entering a judgment of acquittal or directing the jury to acquit. The acquittal is unreviewable even if erroneous. In *Evans,* the Supreme Court noted illustrations of erroneous acquittals that are unreviewable: (1) an acquittal for lack of evidence when the court erroneously excluded the necessary evidence, and (2) an acquittal based on a mistaken understanding of what evidence would suffice to sustain a conviction or what elements had to be proven. In *Evans* itself, a judge gave a directed verdict of acquittal based on an erroneous understanding of the elements of the crime. The defendant was charged with burning real property. The judge mistakenly thought that the property had to be a dwelling. When there was no proof that it was a dwelling, the court granted the defense motion to acquit. The Supreme Court, while recognizing that the acquittal was an error, nevertheless held that double jeopardy barred retrial for this same crime.

Judge grants acquittal after jury convicts. This situation is to be contrasted, however, with the rare case in which a judge enters a judgment of acquittal *after* the jury has returned a verdict of guilty. In that instance, the government is permitted to appeal the judge's acquittal. If the government prevails, the appellate court is permitted to reinstate the jury verdict of guilty. *United States v. Jenkins*, 420 U.S. 358 (1975). As explained in *United States v. Scott*, 437 U.S. 82 (1978), a judgment of acquittal bars the government from an appeal only when, if the government wins its appeal, a second trial would be necessitated. Since this is not the case where a jury first returns a verdict of guilty and then the judge orders an acquittal, the government's appeal is allowed. The appeal simply restores the jury's original guilty verdict.

[3] Dismissal by Judge

A *dismissal* of the criminal charges (as opposed to an *acquittal*) by the judge normally presents no double jeopardy constraint on reprosecution because dismissals normally occur prior to the attachment of jeopardy. But what should be the result if a trial judge dismisses criminal charges *after* empaneling and swearing in the jury? In such circumstances, as we saw in *Martinez v. Illinois*, an order of dismissal is *sometimes* treated as the functional equivalent of an acquittal for double jeopardy purposes.

By contrast, in *United States v. Scott*, 437 U.S. 82 (1978), the trial judge granted the defendant's motion to dismiss two counts on the ground of prejudicial pretrial delay; this came during trial and at the close of all the evidence. The Supreme Court refused to treat this dismissal as an acquittal; accordingly, the government was permitted to appeal the dismissal and, if successful on appeal, to reprosecute the defendant. Distinguishing between a judge's acquittal versus dismissal during trial, the Supreme Court noted:

> [A] defendant is acquitted only when the ruling of a judge, whatever its label, actually represents a resolution [in the defendant's favor], correct or not, of some or all of the factual elements of the offense charged.
>
> ... [T]he defendant, by deliberately choosing to seek termination of the proceedings against him on a basis unrelated to factual guilt or innocence ... suffers no injury cognizable under the Double Jeopardy Clause. ...

437 U.S. at 97–99.

Timing can be everything in distinguishing between an acquittal and a dismissal. In *Serfass v. United States*, 420 U.S. 390 (1975), the district court granted the defendant's pretrial motion to dismiss, ruling in the defendant's favor on an affirmative defense after previewing evidence that the defendant would have presented in support of his defense at trial. The defendant argued that this ruling was the functional equivalent of an acquittal, thus precluding appellate review. However, the Supreme Court rejected this argument, reasoning that jeopardy had never attached. Since the defendant had not waived his right to a jury trial, and no jury had yet been sworn, the trial judge's decision did not count as an acquittal for double jeopardy purposes.

Similarly, in *United States v. Sanford*, 429 U.S. 9 (1976), another trial judge's favorable ruling on the merits of a defense proved to have no double jeopardy consequences. In *Sanford*, the defendants' trial ended with a hung jury and the declaration of a mistrial. Four months later, while the government was preparing for a retrial, the defendants moved to dismiss on the basis of a consent defense. The trial judge granted the motion. However, the Supreme Court ruled that the case was controlled by *Serfass*—even though one trial had already occurred, the defendants' motion still had to be treated as a pretrial motion to dismiss in light of the jury's failure to reach a verdict and the impending start of a new trial. By contrast, in another case, *United States v. Martin Linen Supply Co.*, 430 U.S. 564 (1977), there was also trial that ended in a hung jury and then a judge's ruling in the defendant's favor, but this time the Double Jeopardy Clause barred the government's appeal. What distinguished *Sanford*? In *Martin Linen*, unlike the earlier case, the defendants filed their motion within seven days of the jury's discharge pursuant to the requirements of Rule 29(c) for a post-trial judgment of acquittal.

Note that the defendant's success with a post-trial motion may normally be appealed by the government without any double jeopardy problem if the trial ended with a guilty verdict, in contrast to the hung juries in *Sanford* and *Martin Linen*. In the former scenario, a reversal on appeal simply results in a reinstatement of the jury's verdict of guilt, rather than a retrial; in that sense, there is no impermissible second round of jeopardy for the defendant. *United States v. Wilson*, 420 U.S. 332 (1975).

F. Retrial Following Mistrial: "Manifest Necessity" and the Issue of Defendant's Consent

[1] Manifest Necessity: Hung Jury and Other Circumstances

It occasionally happens that, after jeopardy has attached, a criminal case fails to end in a final judgment. This occurs when the trial judge declares a *mistrial,* either with or without the defendant's consent. In a mistrial, unlike a dismissal, the court simply ends the trial without dismissing the criminal charges.

The United States Supreme Court has long held that trial judges may declare a mistrial over the objection of the defendant without double jeopardy consequences whenever there is *manifest necessity* for the mistrial. For instance, in *United States v. Perez*, 22 U.S. 579 (1824), the Supreme Court recognized that when a trial ends in the declaration of a mistrial because of a "hung jury" (hopelessly deadlocked and unable to reach a verdict), such manifest necessity exists and double jeopardy does not preclude retrial.

Manifest necessity may also exist when there has been a serious procedural error at trial that cannot easily be remedied. As explained in *Illinois v. Somerville*, 410 U.S. 458 (1973), the *Perez* doctrine of manifest necessity reflects the notion that trial judges should not be pressed into proceeding with a case all the way to conviction when an obvious procedural error makes appellate reversal a certainty. The "ends of justice" are not served by wasting government resources on what is apt to prove a pointless trial.

To determine whether or not the "manifest necessity" standard is met, some courts require the trial judge to determine whether or not effective alternatives to a mistrial are present. Many courts say that mistrial should be a last resort. Often counsel will be asked to suggest alternatives to a mistrial. Counsel's failure to do so may be used by appellate courts to conclude that no reasonable alternatives existed.

United States v. Jorn, 400 U.S. 470 (1971), illustrates some of the considerations that may affect that manifest necessity analysis. The defendant was charged with assisting in the preparation of fraudulent income tax returns. At trial the prosecutor called as a witness the taxpayer whose return the defendant allegedly had aided in preparing. The trial judge refused to permit the witness to testify until he had consulted an attorney. The judge then discharged the jury, thereby aborting the trial, to give the witness time to talk with counsel. When the case was later set for retrial before another jury, the defendant moved for dismissal on the ground of double jeopardy. Dismissal was granted and the United States Supreme Court affirmed in a case that produced no majority opinion. Writing for a plurality, Justice Harlan explained:

> It is apparent from the record that no consideration was given to the possibility of a trial continuance; indeed, the trial court acted so abruptly in discharging the jury that, had the prosecutor been disposed to suggest a continuance, or the defendant to object to the discharge of the jury, there would have been no opportunity to do so. When one examines the circumstances surrounding the discharge of this jury, it seems abundantly apparent that the trial judge made no effort to exercise a sound discretion to assure that, taking all the circumstances into account, there was a manifest necessity for the *sua sponte* declaration of this mistrial. Therefore, we must conclude that in the circumstances of this case, [defendant's] reprosecution would violate the double jeopardy provision of the Fifth Amendment.

Id. at 487.

Notes

1. *Burden of proof.* After a mistrial, the government usually has the burden of establishing that there was manifest necessity when it seeks to retry a defendant for the same charges unresolved by the mistrial.

2. *Illustrations.* Some examples of what has been found to constitute manifest necessity include: death, illness, or absence of a judge, juror, lawyer, or the defendant; judge's disqualification of himself mid-trial because surprising testimony made it appear the judge could not be impartial; ineffective assistance of defense counsel; defense counsel's mid-trial discovery of a serious conflict of interest; and defense counsel's repeated violations of a court order prohibiting referral to inadmissible evidence.

Some examples of situations *not* found to constitute manifest necessity include: improper opening statement that could have been cured by a clarifying jury instruction; docket overcrowding and unexpectedly long trial; unavailability of government witness who was available later in trial and whose testimony could have been provided by a supervisor instead; and the government's desire to gather more evidence.

3. *AWOL prosecution witnesses.* Recall the facts of *Martinez v. Illinois*. The prosecutor was unable to secure the presence of two key government witnesses on the day of trial, but the jury was sworn in anyway. The judge then dismissed the charges at the defendant's behest. What if the judge had instead declared a mistrial? Would that present circumstances of "manifest necessity" such that a retrial would be permissible? The Supreme Court indicated to the contrary in a footnote: "once jeopardy has attached, the absence of witnesses generally does not constitute the kind of '"extraordinary and striking circumstanc[e]"' in which a trial court may exercise discretion to discharge the jury before it has reached a verdict." 134 S. Ct. at 2076 n.4.

4. *Deadlocked jury.* The trial court's decision to declare a mistrial because of a deadlocked jury is accorded great deference by appellate courts and usually constitutes manifest necessity, permitting a retrial on the same charges. The trial judge is conventionally thought to be in the best position to assess the many relevant factors in deciding whether a just verdict is possible.

The Supreme Court has noted that trial courts declaring a mistrial because of a deadlocked jury don't even have to state on the record all the factors that influenced the decision. Moreover, there is no "minimum period of time" the jury must deliberate and the judge need not "question the jurors individually, . . . consult with (or obtain the consent of) either the prosecutor or defense counsel," or "issue a supplementary jury instruction . . . or consider any other means of breaking the impasse." *Renico v. Lett*, 559 U.S. 766 (2010).

5. *Deadlocked jury and collateral estoppel.* When a hung jury causes a judge to declare a mistrial, there is normally no double jeopardy significance to the trial. But what if the defendant faced trial on multiple counts and the jury deadlocked on only some of the counts, acquitting on the others? And, further, what if the jury's acquittal verdicts necessarily decided in the defendant's favor some fact that was critical to the remaining counts — does the collateral estoppel aspect of double jeopardy law block retrial of those remaining counts? As we saw in the collateral estoppel material earlier in this chapter, the Supreme Court generally denies any estoppel force to trials with inconsistent verdicts. However, in *Yeager v. United States*, 557 U.S. 110 (2009), the Court distinguished the partially deadlocked jury from the normal situation of inconsistent verdicts, holding that collateral estoppel could preclude retrial of the counts on which the jury hung.

6. *Enough is enough.* Although double jeopardy does not bar retrials after a hung jury, a court may have the inherent authority to dismiss subsequent prosecution in the interests of "fair play," "substantial justice," or the like. *See, e.g., State v. Kyles*, 706 So. 2d 611 (La. Ct. App. 1998) (refusing to use its inherent authority to dismiss fifth murder prosecution following several mistrials); *State v. Abbati*, 493 A.2d 513 (N.J. 1985) (recognizing and discussing inherent authority).

Do you agree that using inherent authority to bar later trials is an appropriate judicial decision? Or could the separation of powers doctrine suggest this is a prosecutorial, not judicial, decision? In exercising its inherent authority, should a court consider the strength of the prosecution's case? Or focus on the harm to the defendant? Or something else?

[2] Defendant Requests or Consents to Mistrial: No Provocation

Where the *defendant* moves for a mistrial, reprosecution usually is allowed and manifest necessity is not required. The Court in *United States v. Dinitz*, 424 U.S. 600 (1976), noted that it is basically the defendant's decision whether (1) to continue the trial, notwithstanding the alleged judicial or prosecutorial error, or (2) to ask for a mistrial and therefore surrender the right to have the matter determined by the first jury.

What constitutes consent? Whether a retrial is permissible may depend on whether the accused requested the mistrial. The easy case is when the defendant—alone or joined by the prosecution—formally requests the mistrial. But what if the defense lawyer is silent or fails to object to the mistrial? Many courts hold that this does not constitute consent. *See, e.g., Dawson v. State*, 979 So. 2d 1099 (Fla. Dist. Ct. App. 2008) (defense counsel stated "the defense has no position" when court considered whether to declare a mistrial; defense did not consent to mistrial); *Pierson v. State*, 398 S.W.3d 406 (Tex. App. 2013) (consent will not be inferred from silent record).

Other courts are more flexible, finding consent when the defendant "sits silently by and does not object" to the mistrial when there is a fair opportunity to do so. *See, e.g., United States v. El-Mezain*, 664 F.3d 467 (5th Cir. 2011) (consent to mistrial may be express or implied through failure to make timely and explicit objection to mistrial); *Marte v. Vance*, 480 Fed. Appx. 83, 2012 U.S. App. LEXIS 9480 (2d Cir.) (defendants implicitly consented to mistrial by saying they did not want to be heard when judge announced intent to declare mistrial and asked for counsel's views). However, even if the defendant must affirmatively signal non-consent to the mistrial, no particular wording is required. *See United States v. Lara-Ramirez*, 519 F.3d 76 (1st Cir. 2008) (no consent; defense counsel urged alternatives to mistrial, giving "unmistakable notice of objection to mistrial," even though never using words "I object").

In some jurisdictions, a statute may set forth the requirements relating to consent. *See* Colo. Rev. Stat. Ann. § 18-1-301(2)(a) (consent is a waiver of objection to mistrial; defendant is deemed to consent unless objections to mistrial are on the record at time of court order of mistrial).

Must defendant personally consent? If consent to a mistrial constitutes a waiver of double jeopardy (which is the usual rule), can defense counsel waive it or must the defendant personally do so? Most courts conclude the decision is for defense counsel as part of professional judgment, but a minority view is that the waiver must be knowing, intelligent, and voluntary and can only be done by the accused personally. *See generally Nero v. District of Columbia*, 936 A.2d 310 (D.C. 2007) (reviewing authorities and concluding that the decision to move for mistrial is within defense counsel's discretion and may be made over the defendant's objection). Which view do you think is best?

Withdrawal of consent. What if a defendant requests, or consents to, a mistrial, but then withdraws the request or consent after the mistrial is granted? Courts routinely reject the withdrawal. *See, e.g., Tinsley v. Million*, 399 F.3d 796 (6th Cir. 2005) (defense counsel moved and argued for mistrial, then objected when mistrial granted). However, if the withdrawal of consent is made before the mistrial is ordered, the defendant is not deemed to have consented. *See, e.g., Weston v. Kernan*, 50 F.3d 633 (9th Cir. 1995) (prior to court's ruling on mistrial, defense clarified that his motion was for mistrial with prejudice; no consent to mistrial without prejudice).

[3] Defendant Provoked to Request or Consent to Mistrial

What should be the result if the defendant is provoked into requesting a mistrial because of some intentional misbehavior on the part of the prosecuting attorney? The Supreme Court held that a different rule applies in that instance:

> The Double Jeopardy Clause does protect a defendant against governmental actions intended to provoke mistrial requests and thereby to subject defendants to the substantial burdens imposed by multiple prosecutions. It bars retrials where "bad-faith conduct by judge or prosecutor" threatens the "harassment of an accused by successive prosecutions or declarations of a mistrial so as to afford the prosecution a more favorable opportunity to convict" the defendant.

United States v. Dinitz, 424 U.S. 600, 611 (1976). Whether the prosecutor intended to provoke a mistrial is a question decided by the judge, not the jury.

How workable is the standard requiring intentional provocation? Assume that a witness for the prosecution is asked by defense counsel on cross examination whether the witness had ever filed a criminal complaint against the accused (so as to establish the witness's bias against the defendant). After the witness has admitted filing a complaint, the prosecutor on redirect examination now seeks to rehabilitate the witness by eliciting reasons why such a complaint may have been filed against the defendant. The following colloquy occurs:

> Prosecutor: Have you ever done business with [the defendant]?
>
> Witness: No, I have not.
>
> Prosecutor: Is that because he is a crook?

At that point, the defendant's motion for a mistrial is granted by a trial judge. Would retrial of the defendant be barred by the Double Jeopardy Clause?

These facts were at issue in *Oregon v. Kennedy*, 456 U.S. 667 (1982). A state trial court found that "it was not the intention of the prosecutor in this case to cause a mistrial," and therefore permitted retrial of the defendant. A state appellate court disagreed, however, concluding that retrial was barred because the prosecutor's conduct was "overreaching"—notwithstanding the fact that the appellate court accepted the finding that the prosecutor did not actually intend to cause a mistrial. The United States Supreme Court rejected the appellate court's analysis and adopted a standard that focuses on the intent of the prosecutor: "Only where the governmental conduct in question is intended to 'goad' the defendant into moving for a mistrial may a defendant raise the bar of double jeopardy to a second trial after having succeeded in aborting the first on his own motion." *Id.* at 676.

The Court in *Kennedy* explained why the "prosecutorial intent" standard was preferable to a more generalized standard of "bad faith conduct" or "harassment":

> The difficulty with the more general standards which would permit a broader exception than one based merely on intent is that they offer virtually no standards for their application. Every act on the part of a rational prosecutor during a trial is designed to "prejudice" the defendant by placing before the judge or jury evidence leading to a finding of his guilt. Given the complexity of the rules of evidence, it will be a rare trial of any complexity in which some proffered evidence by the prosecutor or by the defendant's attorney will not be found objectionable by the trial court. Most such objections are undoubtedly curable by simply refusing to allow the proffered evidence to be admitted, or in the case of a particular line of inquiry taken by counsel with a witness, by an admonition to desist from a particular line of inquiry.
>
> More serious infractions on the part of the prosecutors may provoke a motion for mistrial on the part of the defendant, and may in the view of the trial court warrant the granting of such a motion. The "overreaching" [or harassment] standard . . . would add another classification of prosecutorial error, one requiring dismissal of the indictment, but without supplying any standard by which to assess that error.
>
> By contrast, a standard that examines the intent of the prosecutor, though certainly not entirely free from practical difficulties, is a manageable standard to apply. It merely calls for the court to make a finding of fact. Inferring the existence or nonexistence of intent from objective facts and circumstances is a familiar process in our criminal justice system.

Id. at 674–75. Because the Oregon trial court found that the prosecutor's conduct culminating in the termination of the trial was not intended to provoke the defendant into moving for a mistrial, no double jeopardy violation occurred.

Notes

1. *Proof of intent to provoke.* The defendant has the difficult task of meeting the burden of proving that the judge or prosecutor intended to provoke a motion for a mistrial. Factors courts look at include the tone and manner of the judge's or prosecutor's improper actions, the response to the defendant's mistrial motion (did the

state strongly oppose it?), the strength of the state's cases (no intent for mistrial if case strong), and any motive for the judge's or state's action.

The difficulty of proving intent explains why few cases hold the government actually did goad the defense into requesting a mistrial. The cases finding the improper intent involve egregious government misconduct. *See, e.g., Anderson v. State*, 645 S.E.2d 647 (Ga. Ct. App. 2007) (prosecutor knowingly elicited testimony that defendant refused to answer police questions and requested a lawyer).

2. *Goading by the judge.* In rare situations, a judge's intentional goading of defense counsel to request a mistrial may trigger double jeopardy protections against a retrial, but the standards seem quite high. *See, e.g., Lee-Thomas v. United States*, 921 A.2d 773 (D.C. 2007) (trial court strongly suggested defense counsel's trial representation was deficient and that the defense request a mistrial, which the defense did; court's motives were not improper goading of defense since intent was to benefit defendant's right to a fair trial).

3. *State rejection of "intentional goading" test.* Interestingly, the Supreme Court of Oregon later considered the issue under the Oregon Constitution and rejected the United States Supreme Court's test of "intentional provocation of mistrials." *Oregon v. Kennedy*, 666 P.2d 1316 (Or. 1983). The Oregon Supreme Court observed that the "intentional provocation" test has two significant shortcomings. First, in focusing only upon the behavior of prosecutors, the focus is too limited because other officials (judges, bailiffs, or other courthouse officials) could also cause a mistrial or a reversal. Second, a finding of "intentional provocation" would likely constitute contempt of court and could also lead to disbarment or other discipline as a violation of professional standards. Given the possible invocation of additional penalties against the offending prosecutor, "that places too heavy a burden on the inference that a defendant must ask a judge to draw from the objective conduct and circumstances." *Id.* at 1326.

In its place, the following standard was adopted:

> [R]etrial is barred by [the Oregon Constitution] when improper official conduct is so prejudicial to the defendant that it cannot be cured by means short of a mistrial, and if the official knows that the conduct is improper and prejudicial and either intends or is indifferent to the resulting mistrial or reversal. When this occurs, it is clear that the burden of a second trial is not attributable to the defendant's preference for a new trial over completing the trial infected by an error. Rather, it results from the state's readiness, though perhaps not calculated intent, to force the defendant to such a choice.

See also People v. Batts, 68 P.3d 357 (Cal. 2003) (retrial barred if "prosecutorial misconduct deprived the defendant of a reasonable prospect of an acquittal"); *State v. Rogan*, 984 P.2d 1231 (Haw. 1999) (retrial barred if prosecutorial misconduct was so egregious, from an objective standpoint, as to deny the defendant a fair trial); *Commonwealth v. Grider*, 390 S.W.3d 803 (Ky. App. 2012) (retrial barred if conduct giving rise to mistrial order was precipitated by bad faith, overreaching, or some other fundamentally unfair action of the prosecutor or court).

Problem 15-4. Pizzo's Decapitated Rodent

Sam Stevens was charged with theft of valuable construction equipment. Paul Pizzo, a crucial government witness, was to testify that Stevens had made incriminating comments to him about the crime. The prosecutor referred to this expected testimony in his opening statement, though he knew that Pizzo might be hesitant to testify.

On the third day of the trial, Pizzo's attorney, Rachel Rich, informed the prosecutor that Pizzo would refuse to testify "whether or not he was granted immunity." Specifically, Pizzo was concerned about the well-being of his family. He had received telephone threats and found a decapitated rodent left at his door. When Pizzo was called to the stand, he refused to testify. The prosecutor offered immunity and explained to Pizzo that he was now obligated to answer all questions truthfully. Still, he refused to answer. After being held in contempt and jailed, Pizzo again was called to testify. Again, he refused to testify.

Conceding that without Pizzo's testimony there was insufficient evidence to convict, the prosecutor moved for a mistrial. The trial judge granted the motion and denied the defendant's motion for a judgment of acquittal. Stevens was re-indicted, and his attorney moved to dismiss the indictment on double jeopardy grounds.

What arguments should defense counsel make in support of the motion? How should those arguments be countered by the prosecutor? If you were judge, how would you rule? *See United States v. Stevens*, 177 F.3d 579 (6th Cir. 1999).

G. Reprosecution Following Conviction and Reversal

[1] Conviction Reversed on Appeal; General Approach

If the defendant's trial ends in conviction, the defendant may pursue an appeal (or some other post-conviction remedy) to set aside the guilty verdict on the basis of an alleged error at trial. If the defendant's appeal succeeds and the conviction is overturned, the Double Jeopardy Clause does not prevent the government from prosecuting the defendant a second time. As explained in *United States v. DiFrancesco*, 449 U.S. 117, 131 (1980):

> It would be a high price indeed for society to pay were every accused granted immunity from punishment because of any defect sufficient to constitute reversible error in the proceedings leading to conviction. To require a criminal defendant to stand trial again after he has successfully invoked a statutory right of appeal to upset his first conviction is not an act of governmental oppression of the sort against which the Double Jeopardy Clause was intended to protect.

[2] Exception: Reversal for Insufficiency of Evidence

In *Burks v. United States*, the United States Supreme Court recognized that retrial of the convicted defendant is *not* allowed when the basis for appellate reversal is insufficiency of the evidence. The contrast was explained as follows:

> [R]eversal for trial error, as distinguished from evidentiary insufficiency, does not constitute a decision to the effect that the government has failed to prove its case. As such, it implies nothing with respect to the guilt or innocence of the defendant....
>
> The same cannot be said when a defendant's conviction has been overturned due to a failure of proof at trial, in which case the prosecution cannot complain of prejudice, for it has been given one fair opportunity to offer whatever proof it could assemble. Moreover, such an appellate reversal means that the government's case was so lacking that it should not have been *submitted* to the jury. Since we necessarily afford absolute finality to a jury's *verdict* of acquittal—no matter how erroneous its decision—it is difficult to conceive how society has any greater interest in retrying a defendant when, on review, it is decided as a matter of law that the jury could not properly have returned a verdict of guilty.

437 U.S. 1, 15–16 (1978).

Reversal for weight of evidence. Sometimes the basis for appellate court reversal is expressed in terms of *weight* of the evidence rather than *legal sufficiency* of the evidence. In *Tibbs v. Florida*, the state supreme court had overturned the defendant's conviction on this basis (in the court's words, "the evidence, although sufficient to support the jury's verdict, did not fully persuade the court of Tibbs' guilt"). In this instance, the United States Supreme Court concluded that double jeopardy would *not* bar a retrial. As the Court explained:

> While [reversal of a conviction] based on the weight of the evidence... fails to implicate the policies supporting *Burks*, it does involve the usual principles permitting retrial after a defendant's successful appeal. Just as the Double Jeopardy Clause does not require society to pay the high price of freeing every defendant whose first trial was tainted by prosecutorial error, it should not exact the price of immunity for every defendant who persuades an appellate panel to overturn an error-free conviction and give him a second chance at acquittal. Giving the defendant this second opportunity, when the evidence is sufficient to support the first verdict, hardly amounts to governmental oppression of the sort against which the Double Jeopardy Clause was intended to protect.

475 U.S. 31, 44 (1982).

Notes

1. *Weight v. sufficiency—what?* Considering the policies underlying the Double Jeopardy Clause, does it make sense to you that a reversal because of the *sufficiency* of evidence prevents retrial but a reversal because of the *weight* of evidence does not?

2. *Conviction on lesser-included offense.* Assume that a defendant is charged with aggravated robbery, a class A felony, but is convicted of the lesser-included offense of robbery, a class B felony. If the defendant successfully appeals the robbery conviction on a ground other than evidence sufficiency, is the government allowed to charge him or her once again with aggravated robbery? Normally, the jury's verdict of guilt on the lesser-included offense is treated as an implicit acquittal as to the greater offense of aggravated robbery. Accordingly, the Double Jeopardy Clause bars reinstatement of the greater charge on retrial. *See Green v. United States*, 355 U.S. 184 (1957).

3. *Greater sentence on retrial.* With regard to sentencing, it is usually permissible to impose a more severe sentence following conviction on retrial. This is not permissible, however, when the harsher sentence is based on judicial or prosecutorial vindictiveness. *See North Carolina v. Pearce*, 395 U.S. 711 (1969) (discussed in Chapter 2).

4. *Government appeal of sentence.* The Double Jeopardy Clause does not bar the government from seeking appellate review of a *sentence*. In *United States v. DiFrancesco*, 449 U.S. 117 (1980), the Supreme Court held that increasing a sentence on appeal does not violate double jeopardy because imposition of the lesser sentence is not tantamount to an "implied acquittal" of the greater sentence.

5. *Retrial after completion of sentence.* It can take some time for a defendant to get his or her conviction overturned on appeal. What if the defendant actually finishes serving his sentence before the appeals process plays out—is retrial permissible at that point? *See State v. Jordan*, 716 A.2d 1004 (Me. 1998) (no double jeopardy bar).

6. *Serious prosecutorial misconduct.* Even if a prosecutor's trial behavior was egregiously improper and a conviction is overturned on that basis on appeal, the defendant will still be subject to retrial. That, at any rate, appears to be the general rule. However, in a few states, the courts analogize this situation to a mistrial intentionally provoked by the government. These courts bar a retrial if a conviction is reversed because of intentional government misconduct or use some other similar standard. *See, e.g., State v. Jorgenson*, 10 P.3d 1177 (Ariz. 2000) (retrial barred when conviction reversed because of the state's "egregiously intentional improper conduct"); *State v. Rogan*, 984 P.2d 1231 (Haw. 1999) (retrial barred if prosecutor made highly prejudicial error that was so egregious, from an objective standpoint, it clearly denied a defendant the right to a fair trial; prosecutor made racist comments in closing argument); *State v. Breit*, 930 P.3d 792 (N.M. 1996) (retrial barred if official misconduct is so unfairly prejudicial it cannot be cured without mistrial or motion for new trial, and official knew the conduct was improper and prejudicial,

and the official intended to provoke a mistrial or acted in willful disregard of the resulting mistrial, new trial, or reversal).

H. Reprosecution by a Separate Sovereign

[1] General Rule: Prosecution Permitted by Different Sovereigns

It is not uncommon that a single criminal episode violates the laws of more than one jurisdiction. For example, a serious drug offense ordinarily is punishable by both state and federal authorities. Although it may seem that prosecution by both would be "double jeopardy," the Double Jeopardy Clause does not prohibit prosecution by a state simply because the accused has been convicted or acquitted of the same offense by a federal court or another state's court. *Abbate v. United States*, 359 U.S. 187 (1959); *Bartkus v. Illinois*, 359 U.S. 121 (1959). This principle of double jeopardy law is known as "the dual sovereignty" or "separate sovereign" doctrine. Its underlying rationale was explained by the Supreme Court in *Heath v. Alabama*:

> The dual sovereignty doctrine is founded on the common-law conception of crime as an offense against the sovereignty of the government. When a defendant in a single act violates the "peace and dignity" of two sovereigns by breaking the laws of each, he has committed two distinct "offences." . . . Consequently, when the same act transgresses the laws of two sovereigns, "it cannot be truly averred that the offender has been twice punished for the same offence; but only that by one act he has committed two offences, for each of which he is justly punishable."

474 U.S. 82, 88 (1985) (citations omitted).

Another rationale for the dual sovereignty rule is the fear that without it a person could escape fair punishment by obtaining a lenient sentence in one jurisdiction and thereby barring other jurisdictions from imposing more appropriate sanctions. The scenario becomes more compelling if it is hypothesized that the lenient jurisdiction is where the defendant, a politically influential person, lives and receives "home cooking" by a politically sensitive judge who is facing reelection.

Notes

1. *Sham exception.* Although the separate sovereign doctrine generally makes it possible for different jurisdictions to convict a person for the same crime, there is authority suggesting that the Double Jeopardy Clause would be violated if one of the jurisdictions were a "tool" or "cover" for a prosecution by the other jurisdiction. A defendant asserting the sham prosecution argument has the burden of establishing that one sovereign was so dominated, controlled, or manipulated by the other that the former is not acting of its own volition. This is difficult to establish since courts routinely hold that interjurisdictional cooperation in investigating and apprehending an alleged criminal is desirable and does not render a prosecution by either entity a "sham." *See Bartkus*, 359 U.S. at 123.

2. *Doctrine criticized.* The separate sovereign doctrine has been strongly criticized. Justice Black, dissenting in *Abbate* and *Bartkus*, protested that "double prosecutions for the same offense are . . . contrary to the spirit of our free country." He continued:

> The Court [in *Bartkus*] takes the position that a second trial for the same act is somehow less offensive if one of the trials is conducted by the Federal Government and the other by a State. [F]rom the standpoint of the [defendant], this notion is too subtle for me to grasp. If double punishment is what is feared, it hurts no less for two "sovereigns" to inflict it than one.

Bartkus, 359 U.S. at 150, 155 (Black, J., dissenting).

3. *Federal government's policy.* Under the *Petite* policy (so named because the policy was mentioned by the United States Supreme Court in *Petite v. United States*, 361 U.S. 529 (1960)), United States attorneys will generally not initiate or continue a federal prosecution following a state prosecution based upon substantially the same act unless there is substantial federal interest, prior state prosecution left that interest unvindicated, and there is sufficient evidence for a federal conviction and a compelling reason for doing so. This internal policy constraint, which now appears as §9-2.031 in the United States Attorneys' Manual, is not constitutionally mandated and is not enforceable against the government by the accused.

One prominent federal interest which has sometimes persuaded the United States government to prosecute, even after a defendant has been acquitted or not charged at all in state court, has been the vindication of civil rights. On occasion, the Department of Justice has investigated and prosecuted certain acts which constitute criminal federal civil rights violations, as well as crimes under state law. Examples include the prosecution of Los Angeles police officers in the 1990s for the beating of Rodney King after he was in handcuffs and not resisting arrest, the investigation of the murderers of civil rights workers in Mississippi in the 1960s, and prosecution of the fatal bombing of an African-American church in Birmingham, Alabama, in the same era. These cases suggest that the dual sovereignty doctrine can be used by one jurisdiction to correct the errors of another.

4. *Imminent demise of the doctrine?* On June 28, 2018, the United States Supreme Court granted certiorari in *Gamble v. United States* (No. 17-646) for the purpose of deciding whether the separate sovereign doctrine should be overruled. As this book was going to press, the case had not yet been scheduled for oral argument.

[2] Different Units of Same Government

Where separate prosecutions are pursued by different units of the *same government*, however, the double jeopardy prohibition applies. For example, a court-martial trial bars a successive trial for the same crime in a federal district court. *Grafton v. United States*, 206 U.S. 333 (1907). Similarly, successive municipal (or county) and state prosecutions are barred. *See Waller v. Florida*, 397 U.S. 387 (1970) (observing that cities are not separate sovereigns, but rather are "subordinate governmental instrumentalities" of the state).

In *United States v. Lara*, 541 U.S. 193 (2004), the Court held that a tribal court's prosecution of a non-member Native American was "in its capacity of a separate sovereign." Thus the Double Jeopardy Clause did not bar the federal government from prosecuting the defendant for essentially the same offense (assaulting a federal officer).

What about Puerto Rico? This island "commonwealth" has its own constitution and other attributes of sovereignty, but remains a territory of the United States. Should Puerto Rico be considered a separate sovereign from the federal government for double jeopardy purposes? The Supreme Court answered to the contrary in *Puerto Rico v. Sanchez Vallee*, 136 S. Ct. 1863 (2016). Based on the same illegal gun sales, the defendants faced firearms charges simultaneously in federal court and in Puerto Rico's commonwealth court system. They pled guilty to the federal charges and then moved to dismiss the charged violation of Puerto Rico law on double jeopardy grounds. The trial court granted their motion, and the United States Supreme Court affirmed this decision. Although the Court acknowledged the "Commonwealth's wide-ranging self-rule," *id.* at 1876, the Court emphasized that the sovereignty test for double jeopardy purposes depends on history, not practical autonomy. After reviewing the historical development of Puerto Rico's constitution, which was adopted under the authority of a federal law, the Court concluded, "Because the ultimate source of Puerto Rico's prosecutorial power is the Federal Government—because when we trace that authority all the way back, we arrive at the doorstep of the U.S. Capitol—the Commonwealth and the United States are not separate sovereigns." *Id.*

Imagine an offense committed partly in Puerto Rico and partly in Florida. For instance, the defendant might have kidnapped a victim in Puerto Rico and transported the victim to Florida. Could the defendant be made to face kidnapping charges in both a state court in Florida and a commonwealth court in Puerto Rico? How about a federal court in Florida and a commonwealth court in Puerto Rico? A federal court in Florida and a federal court in Puerto Rico?

[3] Two States

Does the dual sovereignty doctrine permit successive prosecutions by two states? In *Heath v. Alabama*, 474 U.S. 82 (1985), the Supreme Court answered "yes." There, a resident of Alabama arranged for the kidnapping and murder of his wife. The kidnapping occurred in Alabama. The homicide victim's body was found in an automobile in Georgia, where it was later established the murder actually took place. Both Georgia and Alabama law enforcement officials pursued investigations, and ultimately the defendant was arrested by Georgia authorities. He pled guilty in Georgia to a murder charge in exchange for a sentence of life imprisonment. Approximately three months later, an Alabama grand jury returned an indictment against the defendant for the capital offense of murder during a kidnapping. The defendant's double jeopardy objection to the Alabama indictment was rejected on the basis of the dual sovereignty doctrine. Thereafter, he was convicted in Alabama of "murder during a kidnapping" in the first degree and received a death sentence.

The United States Supreme Court affirmed the Alabama death sentence. Justice O'Connor explained that the dual sovereignty doctrine applies fully to successive prosecutions by two states. Next, she turned to the defendant's argument that the dual sovereignty principle should be restricted to cases where both jurisdictions can demonstrate that allowing only one entity to exercise jurisdiction over the defendant will interfere with the unvindicated interests of the second entity.

> This balancing of interests approach . . . cannot be reconciled with the dual sovereignty principle. . . . If the States are separate sovereigns, as they must be under the definition of sovereignty which the Court consistently has employed, the circumstances of the case are irrelevant.
>
> . . . Foremost among the prerogatives of sovereignty is the power to create and enforce a criminal code. To deny a State its power to enforce its criminal laws because another State has won the race to the courthouse "would be a shocking and untoward deprivation of the historic right and obligation of the States to maintain peace and order within their confines."

Id. at 92–93 (citation omitted).

Writing in dissent, Justice Marshall maintained:

> Where two States seek to prosecute the same defendant for the same crime in two separate proceedings, the justifications found in the federal-state context for an exemption from double jeopardy constraints simply do not hold. Although the two States may have opted for different policies within their assigned territorial jurisdictions, the sovereign concerns with whose vindication each State has been charged are identical. Thus, in contrast to the federal-state context, barring the second prosecution would still permit one government to act upon the broad range of sovereign concerns that have been reserved to the States by the Constitution. The compelling need in the federal-state context to subordinate double jeopardy concerns is thus considerably diminished in cases involving successive prosecutions by different States.

Id. at 100–01 (Marshall, J., dissenting).

Notes

1. *State rejection of doctrine.* A significant number of states have rejected the dual sovereignty doctrine either under a state statute or state constitutional provisions. For example, *People v. Morgan*, 785 P.2d 1294 (Colo. 1990), characterized the dual sovereignty doctrine as "harsh." The Colorado statute, applied in that case, provides:

> If conduct constitutes an offense within the concurrent jurisdiction of this state and of the United States, or another state, or of a municipality, a prosecution in any other of these jurisdictions is a bar to a subsequent prosecution in this state [if] the first prosecution resulted in a conviction or an acquittal . . . and the subsequent prosecution is based on the same conduct. . . .

Colo. Rev. Stat. § 18-1-303 (1999). *See also* Cal Penal Code § 656; 720 Ill. Comp. Stat. Ann. 5/3-4; Wash. Rev. Code 10.43.040.

2. *Foreign country.* The separate sovereign doctrine also permits prosecutions by a United States governmental unit and a foreign country. *See, e.g., United States v. Ducuara De Saiz*, 2013 WL 781909 (11th Cir.).

Problem 15-5. Double Trouble?

Tiffany needed money to support a serious cocaine addiction. Her solution was to rob wealthy people who walk their dogs late at night. One night she was prowling Seaside Street in an affluent part of town and saw Nathan (a retired federal judge) with his poodle. Tiffany quietly walked up behind Nathan and stuck a loaded .45 in his back, saying "Give me your wallet and your phone or you will be dead in 30 seconds."

Nathan complied without turning around. Tiffany then smacked him over the head with the pistol and ran away. She did not know that Nathan had a weak heart. Walker Jones, a late-night jogger, saw the encounter and called 911. Nathan died from a heart attack in the ambulance on the way to the emergency room.

Police, alerted by the 911 caller's description of the assailant, arrested Tiffany four blocks away. Nathan's wallet was in her backpack. Suspecting that Tiffany was responsible for a number of robberies of affluent elderly dog-walkers, the state prosecutor decided to be quite aggressive. Tiffany has been charged in state court with: (1) first-degree (intentional) murder, (2) second-degree (reckless) murder, (3) involuntary (negligent) manslaughter, (4) armed robbery, and (5) attempted murder.

a. At Tiffany's jury trial in state court, the judge forgets to swear in any witnesses. The first government witness is Walker the jogger. He testifies about the robbery and describes the assailant. Has jeopardy attached yet?

b. Assume that the jury convicts Tiffany of all five crimes. Would this violate the Double Jeopardy Clause?

c. Changing the facts, assume that defense counsel gets in a series of arguments with the trial judge. After the judge overrules an objection to the admissibility of critical hearsay evidence, a frustrated defense counsel says, "Perhaps, your honor, I should speak more slowly and use shorter words next time I make an objection." The judge's face turns red. The judge turns to the jury and yells, "This trial is over; go home." The judge then storms out of the courtroom. The prosecutor decides to schedule a second trial but only for the manslaughter and armed robbery charges. Would double jeopardy permit a second trial under these circumstances?

d. Changing the facts, assume that the jury convicts Tiffany of armed robbery and involuntary (negligent) homicide, is deadlocked on attempted murder, and acquits on first- and second-degree murder. The prosecutor is unhappy. Will the Double Jeopardy Clause permit a retrial of Tiffany for first- and second-degree murder and attempted murder? Would it matter if the acquittal had been by the judge in a bench trial rather than by a jury?

e. Tiffany's defense lawyer appeals the involuntary manslaughter conviction. Would double jeopardy permit a retrial for involuntary manslaughter in the following situations?

(i) The appellate court reverses on the ground that the trial judge erroneously admitted hearsay evidence in violation of Tiffany's confrontation rights.

(ii) The appellate court excludes the hearsay evidence, then reverses because there was not enough admissible evidence remaining in the case to satisfy guilt beyond a reasonable doubt.

f. Assume that the robbery violated a federal statute punishing violent acts, including armed robbery, against active or retired federal judges. Would double jeopardy be violated if Tiffany were prosecuted in a federal court for the same armed robbery for which she was convicted in the state proceeding? What about trying her in federal court for intentional murder of a federal judicial officer (recall she had been acquitted of intentional murder in state court)?

Chapter 16

Sentencing

A. Nature of the Decision

Up to this point, the court procedures we have considered have been mostly directed to a single decision: a determination of the defendant's guilt as to the charged offense or offenses. If the decision is "not guilty" across the board, then—thanks to the double jeopardy protections covered in Chapter 15—court proceedings in the case are normally at an end. In most cases, though, the defendant is convicted of *something*, even if only of a lesser offense than what was initially charged. The finding of guilt by a judge or jury at the end of a trial, or—as is more common—the defendant's entry of a guilty plea, initiates a new phase of the criminal process. Now, the defendant's presumption of innocence is gone, and the procedural protections afforded the defendant are weakened. With guilt established, the court focuses on the question of what punishment should be imposed in response to the defendant's criminal conduct.

Traditionally, sentencing has been seen as preeminently a *judicial* decision. Whatever the offense of conviction, the statute defining the offense will normally specify a *range* of potential penalties, and it is up to the judge to select a sentence from within that range. For instance, federal law makes it a crime knowingly to aim a laser pointer at an aircraft, with an authorized punishment of no more than five years in prison and a fine of no more than $250,000. 18 U.S.C. §§ 39A, 3571(b). When sentencing a person convicted of this crime, the judge might decide that a $1,000 fine and no prison would be an appropriate punishment, or might go near the other extreme with, say, a four-year prison term and a $200,000 fine. Obviously, the judge's choice of a sentence at the top of the range, the bottom of the range, or somewhere in between can have enormous, life-altering consequences for the defendant.

This momentous decision will be informed by a variety of considerations, including the general *purposes of punishment*, case-specific *sentencing factors*, and *plea bargaining dynamics*. We explore these considerations in turn below.

[1] Purposes of Punishment

Why do we have criminal punishments at all? In a nation that professes strong commitments to liberty and equality, does it seem odd to empower some citizens operating within the court system to take away the freedom—not to mention the property and sometimes even the lives—of certain of their fellow citizens?

Whether and how punishment can be justified has been debated by philosophers for centuries. *See, e.g.*, Why Punish? How Much? A Reader on Punishment (Michael Tonry, ed. 2010). Different schools of thought have emphasized different purposes that ought to be served by punishment, such as deterring antisocial conduct or giving the offender his or her just deserts. While the theoretical debates can seem daunting, students may take some comfort in knowing that few judges and lawyers are philosophical purists. Rather, practitioners typically take a *pragmatic, eclectic* approach to punishment, giving priority to different purposes according to the perceived needs of different cases.

The most widely recognized purposes of punishment can be divided into four categories: (1) general deterrence, (2) individualized control of dangerous people, (3) just deserts, and (4) victim restoration.

[a] General Deterrence

Punishing someone for doing something undesirable serves as a threat to others who might consider doing the same thing. Assuming some degree of visibility and reliability in penalizing the individuals who commit a particular crime, the deterrent message of punishment likely reduces the frequency of that crime. This effect is known as *general deterrence.*

Although long-recognized and frequently invoked as a purpose of punishment, general deterrence is subject to a number of important limitations. For instance, deterrent threats may have little or no effect in preventing crimes as to which the risk of apprehension is low. Likewise, it is difficult to deter conduct that does not result from a rational process of weighing costs and benefits, such as impulsive behavior in circumstances of severe mental illness or intoxication. In addition, there is the challenge of "marginal deterrence." If punishments are too severe for some misconduct, there may be perverse incentives created for offenders to engage in even worse behavior. Thus, if rape is always punished by death, then rapists will be more likely to kill their victims—this reduces the risk of apprehension without any corresponding risk of greater punishment. Deterrence theorists thus argue that there should normally be some marginally greater punishment for each marginal increase in the severity of a person's criminal conduct.

[b] Individualized Control

When a person is punished for committing a crime, the deterrent message goes not only to society at large, but also to the specific offender. Once punished, the offender can usually expect an even greater penalty for committing more crimes in the future. To whatever extent the offender is scared away from further crime (that is, from recidivism), we say that punishment has achieved *specific* deterrence—deterrence of a specific individual.

This concept of specific deterrence points to a broader category of justifications for punishment. When a person once commits a crime, we might imagine that the person presents an unusually high risk of future crime. After all, the offender has seemingly revealed something disturbing or threatening about his or her character. Punishment can be thought of as a way to address the presumed dangerousness of those who have been found guilty of committing crimes in the past. Viewed in this light, the sentence can function as a sort of individualized control—a mechanism to manage the risks posed by individuals who are unable or unwilling to refrain from certain kinds of socially undesirable behavior.

Punishment operates as individualized control to the extent that it achieves specific deterrence, but punishment can also accomplish individualized control in two other ways. First, punishment may physically *incapacitate* the offender. To appreciate the conceptual distinction between specific deterrence and incapacitation, imagine an offender convicted for the first time. At sentencing, the judge says, "I'm giving you probation now, but if you mess up again, you can expect to go to prison for sure." The sentence is an attempt to achieve specific deterrence, but it does not physically prevent the offender from committing more crimes. If the offender does commit another crime and is sent to prison, then we enter the realm of incapacitation.

Second, punishment may be used as a tool to force the offender into *rehabilitative treatment*. Again, it may be helpful to see a conceptual distinction between specific deterrence and rehabilitation. Imagine a thief who steals in order to support an addiction to gambling. At sentencing, the judge says, "I am giving you probation on the condition that you enter and stick with a treatment program for gambling." If the program is successful, the offender will stop stealing—not necessarily because of a fear of punishment (specific deterrence), but because the underlying motivation for stealing has been alleviated (rehabilitation).

As with general deterrence, there are important limitations on the extent to which the goal of individualized control can justify punishment. Past conduct does not necessarily predict future conduct, especially when the past conduct was a first-time occurrence. The fact that a person has once committed a crime may only very slightly increase the odds that he or she will commit more crimes in the future. It is thus doubtful that individualized control can justify much punishment of first-time offenders. Even when it comes to repeat offenders, the goal of mitigating individual dangerousness hardly justifies unlimited punishment. Because most offenders naturally age out of crime-committing, long-term incapacitation is rarely called for. Comm. on Causes and Consequences of High Rates of Incarceration, Nat'l Research Council of the Nat'l Academies, The Growth of Incarceration in the United States: Exploring Causes and Consequences 155–56 (2014). Meanwhile, it is important to realize that rehabilitative treatment can be very helpful with some offenders, but useless for others. Edward J. Latessa & Christopher Lowenkamp, *What Works in Reducing Recidivism?*, 3 U. St. Thomas L.J. 521 (2006).

[c] Just Deserts (Retribution)

General deterrence and individualized control are often characterized as *utilitarian* or *instrumental* purposes of punishment. When punishment is imposed to achieve these purposes, the offender's suffering is not seen as a desirable end in itself, but rather as a cost that must be borne by the offender in the name of some greater social good. However, when it comes to some crimes, punishment may appear to be the right thing to do even without regard to the possibility that future crimes may thereby be avoided. It may seem, in other words, that the offender simply *deserves* to experience some suffering.

Imagine a murderer who is shot in the back by police while making his getaway, leaving him permanently paralyzed from the neck down. The killing was deliberate and cold-blooded, and there is no question of the defendant's guilt. Should he be executed for his crime? His medical condition removes individualized control as a justification for punishment. Assume further that the death penalty would carry no general deterrence benefits (a view that is consistent with much, but not all, of the social scientific research on the question). Despite the absence of any clear instrumental benefit, there are probably many people who would view execution as the murderer's just desert—and hence as an appropriate sentence to be imposed upon the murderer's conviction. If a sentence succeeds in "evening the scales of justice," is any other purpose or justification required?

Doing justice in this sense (sometimes called "retribution") may seem in principle an appropriate purpose of punishment, but translating the just deserts ideal into specific sentences in particular cases has proven difficult. At first blush, just deserts would seem to call for "eye for an eye"-type sentences, but, with the possible exception of capital punishment for murderers, there seem few crimes that lend themselves in a satisfactory way to such treatment. Raping the rapist, forcing drugs on the drug dealer, stealing from the (likely indigent) thief—all such sentences present serious ethical and practical difficulties.

The difficulties may be somewhat less if we think about desert in *relative*, rather than *absolute*, terms. Under this approach, we should try to ensure that the harshest punishments are reserved for the most blameworthy crimes, with proportionately less severe sentences for proportionately less blameworthy offenses. For instance, we would not need to figure out how many years in prison would in some abstract sense constitute the "just" punishment for unarmed robbery, so long as we made sure that the sentences for unarmed robbery are generally less severe than those for armed robbery and more severe than those for simple theft. But note that some crimes defy easy comparison. Which is worse, for instance, the alleyway mugging that nets $100 or the slick fraud that nets $100,000? Violent crimes are conventionally regarded as worse than nonviolent, but even that generalization may not always hold.

A great deal more could be said about the complex and controversial subject of just deserts, but, for now, note one final point: while doing justice can be thought of as a *purpose* of punishment, it can also be seen as a *constraint* on punishment. The hypothetical of the quadriplegic murderer raises the question of whether punishment can be justified on desert grounds in the absence of any instrumental benefits, but the reverse scenario can also be imagined. What if punishment is undeserved, but would nonetheless be socially beneficial? For instance, it is sometimes observed that punishing an innocent scapegoat may have just as much deterrent benefit as punishing the truly guilty. If the authorities could prevent crime by executing a person they know to be innocent, would they be justified in doing so? Certainly not, if desert serves as a constraint on punishment.

That illustration may seem a little too easy. After all, there are few people who would openly support executing the innocent. Consider a more difficult case. Spray-painting graffiti on public property is a criminal offense in a particular town, carrying a maximum penalty of six months in jail. Normally, the judges in town merely impose a fine of $500 for this offense, which is more than enough to offset the cost of cleaning up the vandalized property. Recently, however, there has been an irritating surge of graffiti in town, and Judge Jane Smith decides that she is going to do something about the problem. The next graffiti defendant who appears before her is a 17-year old with no prior arrests of any sort—a popular kid who plays quarterback for the local high school. He pleads guilty, expecting the standard fine. But, in order to "send a message to all the other kids in town," Judge Smith instead sentences the defendant to six months in jail. Does that seem an appropriate punishment in light of the considerations we have covered so far?

Among other things, you might think about the risk that a disproportionately severe sentence may backfire. Is it possible that the defendant's classmates will lose respect for the legal system as a result of the sentence? If so, would that be a serious concern? *See* Paul H. Robinson & John M. Darley, *The Utility of Desert*, 91 Nw. U. L. Rev. 453 (1997) (arguing that desert-based sentences enhance public respect for the legal system and thereby promote utilitarian crime-control objectives).

[d] Victim Restoration

Although not all crimes have readily identifiable victims, many do. In some cases, addressing the needs of victims might constitute an appropriate purpose of punishment. To be sure, it is commonly said that the criminal justice system exists primarily to serve *public* interests in crime control and just punishment, and not the *private* interests of individual victims. And, of course, many crimes are also torts, which means that civil litigation may be available to vindicate victim interests. On the other hand, civil remedies can be expensive and time-consuming to pursue, and many offenders lack the resources to satisfy a tort judgment. Given these limitations on the civil side, as well as a growing social sensitivity to the deep psychological harm that can be caused by violent and sexual offenses in particular, there has been more focus in recent years on serving victim needs in the criminal process, including at the sentencing stage. This has included an increased use of restitution (financial compensation for victims) as a routine component of the sentence. But there are also nonfinancial victim needs that can be addressed at sentencing. For instance, a sentence might be designed so as to alleviate a victim's fear of revictimization, most bluntly by incarcerating the defendant on a long-term basis. From a victim's perspective, there might also be an important symbolic dimension to the sentence, with a stiff punishment seen as a sort of official vindication—a definitive, public statement that the victim did *not* deserve whatever happened to him or her.

To the extent that serving victims is seen as an important purpose of punishment, does that necessarily dictate greater severity? Contrary to popular perceptions, victims and offenders are not always locked in a zero-sum game with diametrically opposed interests. For instance, in cases of assault, the offender and the victim are commonly known to one another, often as members of the same family, household, or neighborhood. In such cases, the victim sometimes prefers to see the offender receive some sort of community-based rehabilitative treatment rather than being sent to jail, especially if treatment is seen as more likely to prevent repeat offending over the long run. Additionally, offenders are more likely to be able to pay restitution if they are allowed to remain in the community.

Restorative justice as alternative paradigm for meeting victim needs. If it is recognized that the needs and wishes of victims are not necessarily opposed to those of offenders in all respects, then conventional, adversarial sentencing processes may seem unhelpful or even counterproductive for the victim in some cases. This insight has spurred the development of "restorative justice" (RJ) processes for some types of cases in some jurisdictions. A leading RJ theorist has described the basic approach this way: "Restorative justice is a process to involve, to the extent possible, those who have a stake in the specific offense and collectively identify and address harms, needs, and obligations, in order to heal and put things as right as possible." Howard Zehr, The Little Book of Restorative Justice 37 (2002).

The theory of RJ can be implemented in a variety of different ways. Two leading approaches are victim-offender dialogues and group conferencing. Dialogues involve a face-to-face, mediated conversation between the victim and the offender, in which both sides have an opportunity to discuss the offense and its aftermath. The offender may come to a deeper understanding of the consequences of his actions and may wish to offer an apology. However, the offender is not required to apologize, and nor is the victim obligated to accept any apology that is offered. The two sides might also try to come to an agreement about how the offender can make amends. For instance, if the offender has vandalized the victim's property, the offender might agree to repair the damage.

Group conferencing, the second major type of RJ process, adds community representatives to the mix. They are able to describe the broader "ripple effects" of a crime that carry beyond the immediate victim. For instance, in a residential burglary case, the conference might include not only the burglar and the victimized homeowner, but also neighbors who now feel more fearful about threats to their homes. In any event, all participants in the conference are able to share their perspectives. As with victim-offender dialogues, successful group conferences may culminate with an offer and acceptance of apology and an agreement about how the offender can make amends.

RJ processes can be used as a response to any sort of harm, including non-criminal harms, and many RJ programs have now been set up in schools, universities, and other settings that are not connected to the criminal justice system. Within the criminal justice system, RJ processes can be structured as a pretrial or precharge diversion from conventional prosecution, or may be set up as a post-conviction alterative or supplement to conventional sentencing. Either way, both victim and offender must normally consent before a matter is referred by a prosecutor or a judge to an RJ program. After referral, if no agreement is reached through the RJ process for the offender to make amends, do you think that the matter should be returned to court for conventional prosecution and punishment, or does that place too much pressure on the offender to offer insincere apologies and make empty promises to do better in the future?

In general, victims and offenders alike give higher marks to RJ than to conventional court processing. Erik Luna & Barton Poulson, *Restorative Justice in Federal Sentencing: An Unexpected Benefit of* Booker?, 37 McGeorge Law Review 787, 799 (2006). Why do you think that victims might prefer RJ? Offenders? In practice, RJ processes are usually only available for juvenile offenses and low-level property crimes. If it would mean more positive experiences for victims, do you think that RJ should be made available for more serious types of crime?

[e] Implementing Competing Purposes

Because there is considerable analytical imprecision to all of the basic purposes of punishment, clear, stark contradictions in their implementation—e.g., the defendant unquestionably "deserves" a prison term, but the victim's interests would undoubtedly best be served by probation and restitution—are probably more common in law school hypotheticals than real-life practice. Still, key concepts like dangerousness and desert are not entirely lacking in practical meaning, and lawyers and judges will inevitably perceive some degree of tension between different purposes of punishment in some cases. However, despite the difficulties that can arise in reconciling competing objectives, the law generally provides little clear guidance about how to prioritize or balance the various purposes of punishment, leaving the matter squarely in the lap of the sentencing judge. Similarly, the judge is usually given a great deal of freedom in deciding what *sentencing factors* should be given the most weight in trying to achieve the purposes of punishment, a topic to which we turn next.

[2] Sentencing Factors

Sentencing factors are the factual considerations that a judge takes into account in deciding how best to advance the relevant purposes of punishment in a particular case. For instance, the defendant's criminal history is among the most commonly considered and heavily weighted sentencing factors. The factor has an obvious, important relationship with the goal of identifying and effectively controlling the convicted defendants who are the most dangerous. With that purpose in mind, defendants who have extensive criminal histories are more likely as a result to receive sentences that involve significant incapacitation.

There are a multitude of potential sentencing factors in any given case. They are often divided into the categories of *offense characteristics* and *offender characteristics*. Commonly considered offense characteristics include:

- Was the victim physically harmed, and, if so, how badly?
- How great was the victim's monetary loss?
- How vulnerable was the victim?
- Was the victim also at fault in a significant way?
- Did the offender carry or use a weapon in connection with the offense?
- Was there some degree of justification for the offender's actions, even if not enough to establish a full defense to criminal liability?
- Did the offender know that he or she was breaking the law?
- Did the offender intend to cause harm?

In addition to criminal history, commonly considered offender characteristics include:

- Does the offender have a job?
- What are the offender's skills and educational accomplishments?
- Is the offender a primary caregiver for dependent children?
- Does the offender suffer from an addiction or mental illness?
- Has the offender taken responsibility for the offense?
- Does the offender have a positive record of volunteer work or charitable contributions?

Sentencing factors can also be divided into those that are *aggravating* (i.e., tend to call for a more severe sentence) and those that are *mitigating* (i.e., tend to call for a more lenient sentence). Interestingly, there are a number of commonly discussed factors that can be treated as either aggravating or mitigating, depending on the values of the judge and the penal purposes sought to be served. For instance, imagine a middle-class defendant with a good job who has been convicted of tax evasion. A judge considering whether to impose a sentence of imprisonment might view the defendant's job as a mitigating factor that cuts against prison because stable employment generally indicates a low risk of recidivism and increases the likelihood of eventual compensation for the victim (here, the government) if the defendant is kept in the community. On the other hand, viewed through the lens of just deserts, the defendant's job might be viewed as an aggravating factor: arguably, a defendant with a privileged social status and a comfortable lifestyle who breaks the law is more blameworthy than a defendant who acts under the pressure of more desperate circumstances. Additionally, there may be a particularly powerful deterrent message when a "white-collar" defendant is sent to prison and thereby loses good employment and middle-class status.

Despite the wide discretion traditionally given to sentencing judges regarding such matters, there are a few factors that are generally regarded as off-limits, including the defendant's race, religion, and ethnic background. Some see the defendant's sex, age, and economic status in the same light, although these factors can present more difficult problems. For instance, should the defendant's pregnancy be taken into account by a sentencing judge? Many would intuitively think that an important consideration, e.g., in deciding whether the defendant should be given a sentence of incarceration that lasts through her due date. On the other hand, giving a break to pregnant defendants does represent a sort of sex discrimination—only female defendants can benefit from this practice. We've already touched on some of the difficulties surrounding economic class in the example of the middle-class tax evader. What about age? Imagine three defendants, each convicted of drunk-driving in separate incidents. Each has one prior conviction in the past year for the same offense, but no other criminal history. The first is 20 years old, the second 40, and the third 60. Same sentence for each? If not, who should get the most severe sentence and why?

[3] Plea Bargaining

As we saw in Chapter 11, plea bargaining is a controversial practice, but extremely common now in the United States—and arguably necessary for busy courts that could not possibly conduct trials in any more than a small fraction of the criminal cases brought by prosecutors. In any event, plea bargaining often exerts a powerful influence at sentencing. Indeed, from the defendant's standpoint, the whole point of plea bargaining is normally to secure a lower sentence than would be imposed otherwise.

Plea bargains can affect sentences in several different ways. Most directly, if the prosecutor, in return for the defendant's guilty plea to one charge, either dismisses or declines to file another charge, then the applicable statutory sentencing range will be affected. This kind of deal controls the parameters within which the judge will exercise his or her sentencing discretion. In addition to, or in lieu of, such a "charge bargain," a plea deal may include a promise from the prosecutor to recommend (or at least not to oppose) a particular sentence sought by the defendant. A good example of such a deal appeared in *Santobello v. New York* (excerpted in Chapter 11). To be sure, the prosecutor's sentencing recommendations are not formally binding on the judge, but they often influence the judge's thinking about the case. If nothing else, judges have an incentive to go along with bargained-for recommendations because, if they do not, defendants will be less likely to enter into plea deals, which could greatly increase the judge's caseload pressures.

Plea deals might also affect the sentence in other ways. For instance, the prosecutor might agree not to present certain information or arguments in court that might lead the sentencing judge to find an aggravating factor or to reject a mitigating factor. By way of illustration, a prosecutor might charge a defendant with a single drug sale, but have information suggesting that the defendant made several additional, uncharged drug sales on other occasions—a persistent course of criminal conduct that would normally be regarded as an aggravating factor at sentencing.

However, in return for the defendant's guilty plea to the one sale, the prosecutor might agree not to seek a longer sentence on the basis of the other sales.

Plea bargaining considerations can also influence the sentence even if there is no express deal between the prosecutor and the defendant. The same caseload pressures that encourage judges to defer to express plea agreements may also create incentives for judges to ensure that defendants who go to trial generally receive harsher sentences than those who plead guilty (with or without a deal). The resulting differences in punishment could be labeled a "trial penalty" or a "plea benefit," but either way the effect is clear: defendants are less likely to take their chances at trial. For this reason, the practice is sometimes called "implicit plea bargaining."

Closely related to plea bargains are the sorts of cooperation agreements noted in Chapter 11. In such deals, a defendant or prospective defendant agrees to assist the government in the investigation or prosecution of another suspect, often with the explicit or implicit expectation of a reduced sentence in return. Again, sentencing judges will be inclined to honor such expectations to the extent that they wish to encourage other defendants to enter into such deals in the future.

Problem 16-1. Purposes and Factors in Practice

Consider the following facts from *United States v. Stevens*, 29 F. Supp. 2d 592 (D. Alaska 1998).

> Donald G. Stevens ("Stevens") was charged in an indictment with one count of possession of child pornography in violation of 18 U.S.C. § 2252A(a)(5)(B), a class D felony. Stevens entered a plea of guilty without a plea agreement and proceeded to sentencing. The maximum penalty is five years imprisonment and a $250,000 fine....
>
> THE OFFENSE
>
> On September 26, 1997, Stevens took his laptop computer to John Martinson who operates a computer repair business. Stevens had been having difficulty with his computer's "mouse pad," which Martinson repaired. Martinson apparently performs an additional service for his customers, whether requested or not, whereby he searches the computers left in his care for computer viruses. The test Martinson performs requires him to review files kept on the computer's hard drive. During his inspection, Martinson found what he suspected were image files containing child pornography. Martinson was concerned that there were over four-hundred such images. Martinson initially copied these files to his hard disk but on advice of the police, he transferred the files to a zip disk and destroyed the images on his own hard drive. In the meantime, Martinson sabotaged Stevens' computer to prevent him from erasing the images. Martinson initially contacted the Anchorage Police Department and the case was eventually assigned to the Federal Bureau of Investigation.

The FBI obtained a search warrant for Stevens' computer and was able to access the files previously discovered by Martinson. Many of the files depict pre-teenage children.... There are images of very young children engaging in bestiality and various sadomasochistic activities in apparent distress. The conduct depicted could cause severe physical pain to the youthful participants. Experience teaches that the risk of psychological and emotional injury is even greater. The FBI found no additional evidence of child pornography in Stevens' residence except the computer images on his hard drive.

All of the images were obtained through "chat rooms" on America Online ("AOL"), to which Stevens subscribed. Stevens apparently became interested in the scope of material available through the chat rooms and took the time to learn the necessary codes and passwords to access those chat rooms specializing in child pornography. Stevens' modus operandi was to enter the chat room and transmit the single message "list me" in answer to code messages posted in the chat rooms. Other participants having pornography to distribute would read this message and in response, Stevens' "screen name" would be added to a mailing list and he would receive bulk e-mails of images, many of which would qualify as child pornography, from other participants in the chat rooms. It does not appear that Stevens ever actively participated in the activities of the chat room by soliciting particular images or discussing his collection with other participants.

... A preponderance of the evidence would therefore indicate that each of the images collected by Stevens originated and was probably produced prior to 1977, over eighteen years before Stevens first downloaded pornography in 1995. Thus there is no evidence that any of the images depict individuals who were under the age of eighteen at the time Stevens downloaded their image.

... There is no evidence that Stevens attempted to contact any person depicted in any of the images, or ever learned or attempted to learn the identity of any such person. Furthermore, there is no evidence that Stevens corresponded with anyone representing that he or she was currently producing child pornography or currently abusing children.

THE OFFENDER

Stevens was born in West Stewartstown, New Hampshire, on February 25, 1951. He was forty-seven years old at the time of sentencing. He has no criminal record. Stevens has never been married and has no children. He is currently living with Suzanne Eusden, whom he met at a mountaineering club meeting in New Hampshire twenty-seven years ago. They have lived together for eight years. At sentencing it was mentioned that Stevens had previous short term relationships lasting up to a year with other women, but the details are sketchy. It does not appear that Stevens ever sought out women with children for relationships. In fact, Stevens indicates that he does not wish to be married and have children because it would interfere with his freedom.

Stevens graduated from high school and attended college for two years earning an Associate of Science degree in Forestry. Most recently, Stevens has worked steadily as a longshoreman in Whittier, Alaska. He also has a part time business caring for privately owned boats in Whittier. Stevens has invested successfully in the stock market and has a net worth of over $350,000. He purchased his computer in 1995 in part to monitor his stock holdings. . . .

1. What purposes of punishment seem most pertinent in sentencing Stevens?

2. What factors seem most important to you? How are those factors connected to any of the purposes of punishment? Which are aggravating and which are mitigating?

3. If you were the prosecutor, how would you argue for a sentence of imprisonment? If you were Stevens' lawyer, how would you argue for probation?

4. If you were the judge, what sentence would you impose? Federal law mandates that the "court shall impose a sentence sufficient, but not greater than necessary, to comply with the [general] purposes [of punishment]." 18 U.S.C. § 3553(a). Does your sentence meet that standard?

B. Sentencing Options

American jurisdictions have adopted a significant array of sentencing options. The following sections provide a brief sketch of many of these options and the legal limits on them.

[1] Death Penalty

The death penalty has long been a part of the American sentencing system, although it has been virtually abandoned in most other developed countries. Today, the death penalty remains a legally permissible sentencing option for a narrow set of aggravated homicide cases in about two-thirds of American states, as well as in the federal system.

The practice of capital punishment in the United States is governed by a remarkably intricate body of constitutional and statutory law. An entire course could easily be devoted to the subject. We can provide only the barest introduction by highlighting a few key points.

First, modern death penalty statutes have been shaped by a line of United States Supreme Court cases beginning with *Furman v. Georgia*, 408 U.S. 238 (1972). A badly divided Court was unable to produce a majority opinion in *Furman*, but the practical upshot of the case seemed to be that all or most death penalty statutes in existence at the time were in violation of the Eighth Amendment's prohibition of "cruel and unusual punishments." After *Furman*, states immediately set about enacting revised death penalty laws in an effort to get into compliance with the new Eighth Amendment jurisprudence. At the time, there was considerable doubt about whether *any* capital punishment scheme could pass constitutional muster. However, in *Gregg v. Georgia*, 428 U.S. 153 (1976), the Court did uphold one of the new approaches, which was then replicated in many other states. Since *Gregg*, the Court has remained relatively active in supervising state use of capital punishment—relative, that is, in comparison to the Court's more deferential approach to state *noncapital* sentencing policies. "Death is different," as a number of justices have observed in varying ways over the years. *See, e.g., Furman*, 408 U.S. at 306 (Stewart, J., concurring) ("The penalty of death differs from all other forms of criminal punishment, not in degree but in kind. It is unique in its total irrevocability.").

Second, the basic thrust of *Furman*, *Gregg*, and their progeny has been to strike a balance between two objectives that are in some tension with one another. On the one hand, the Court insists that the capital sentencing decision must involve an individualized weighing of mitigating and aggravating circumstances. For instance, in *Woodson v. North Carolina*, 428 U.S. 280 (1976), and *Roberts v. Louisiana*, 428 U.S. 325 (1976), the Court invalidated mandatory death penalty statutes that required capital punishment for all first-degree murders. The Court has similarly rejected efforts to restrict the defendant's ability to present mitigating information at sentencing. *See, e.g., Lockett v. Ohio*, 438 U.S. 586 (1978). On the other hand, the Court has tried to promote consistency in capital sentencing decisions, resulting partly from long-standing concerns about racial disparities in the administration of the death penalty. As the Court indicated in *Eddings v. Oklahoma*, the death penalty must be imposed "fairly, and with reasonable consistency, or not at all." 455 U.S. 104, 112 (1982). Reflecting this consistency objective, modern death penalty statutes identify particular aggravating circumstances and require that at least one be found in order to make a defendant eligible for capital punishment. There also tend to be a variety of special procedural protections in capital cases, such as a right to obtain review of the sentence in the state supreme court.

Do you think the goals of individualization and consistency can be satisfactorily reconciled? By the end of his career, Justice Harry Blackmun—who had dissented in *Furman* and joined the majority in *Gregg*—decided they could not. *See Callins v. Collins*, 510 U.S. 1141, 1144 (1994) (Blackmun, J., dissenting from denial of certiorari) ("Experience has taught us that the constitutional goal of eliminating arbitrariness and discrimination from the administration of death can never be achieved without compromising an equally essential component of fundamental fairness—individualized sentencing." (citations omitted)).

Third, in a notable series of Eighth Amendment decisions since 2002, the Court has significantly narrowed the classes of offenders and offenses that are constitutionally eligible for the death penalty. The leading cases have been *Atkins v. Virginia*, 536 U.S. 304 (2002) (prohibiting death sentence for intellectually disabled defendants); *Roper v. Simmons*, 543 U.S. 1 (2005) (prohibiting death sentence for defendants who were under the age of 18 at the time of offense); and *Kennedy v. Louisiana*, 554 U.S. 407 (2008) (prohibiting death sentence for rape of a child and likely for any other nonhomicide offense). The decisions reflect the view that the Cruel and Unusual Punishments Clause includes a proportionality component, and, in turn, that the constitutional proportionality requirement limits capital punishment to the "worst of the worst"—the most damaging offenses perpetrated by the most culpable offenders. *See* Michael O'Hear, The Failed Promise of Sentencing Reform 153–54 (2017).

Since *Furman* and *Gregg*, the Supreme Court has addressed many other notable aspects of the death penalty. *See, e.g.,* *Enmund v. Florida*, 458 U.S. 782 (1982) (death sentence must be based on defendant's own conduct and culpability, not just accomplice's); *Ford v. Wainwright*, 477 U.S. 399 (1986) (no execution of the insane); *McCleskey v. Kemp*, 481 U.S. 279 (1987) (upholding death sentence despite statistical evidence showing racial disparities in its application); *Glossip v. Gross*, 135 S. Ct. 2726 (2015) (upholding particular lethal injection protocol as method of execution). For a more detailed exploration of the capital punishment case law, *see* Linda E. Carter, Ellen S. Kreitzberg & Scott Howe, Understanding Capital Punishment (3d ed. 2010). For a fascinating, behind-the-scenes look at the pivotal *Furman* and *Gregg* cases, *see* Evan J. Mandery, A Wild Justice: The Death and Resurrection of Capital Punishment in America (2013).

One final point should be made: capital punishment in the United States seems in long-term decline, and now has very limited practical importance in much of the nation. The number of death sentences peaked in 1996 and fell by more than three-quarters over the next 18 years. O'Hear, *supra*, at 150. Similarly, the number of executions peaked in 1999 and then fell by nearly two-thirds over the next 15 years. It is estimated that there were only 39 new death sentences imposed in the entire United States in 2017. Death Penalty Information Center, The Death Penalty in 2017: Year End Report (2018). By way of comparison, nearly 12,000 individuals were arrested for non-negligent homicide offenses the previous year, Fed. Bureau of Investigation, Crime in the United States, 2016, tbl. 18 (2017), suggesting that, even for the "worst of the worst," death sentences have become quite unusual. Indeed, as a matter of law or practice, the death penalty appears largely moribund in many states, with just eight states accounting for more than three-quarters of the nation's death row population. Death Penalty Information Center, *supra*, at 3. Sizeable states like New York, Illinois, Michigan, New Jersey, and Washington have either banned the death sentence altogether or impose it so infrequently in practice as to have single-digit death row populations. Even within active death penalty states, there are wide county-to-county variations in the likelihood that a convicted killer will face capital punishment. For instance, in 2017, one-third of all new death sentences in the United States came from just three counties—one each in California, Nevada, and Arizona. *Id.* at 2.

Are these trends good news or not? There remains a vigorous debate about whether and under what circumstances the death penalty can be justified based on the purposes of punishment discussed earlier in this chapter.

[2] Incarceration

Incarceration is the standard sentencing disposition in cases of serious crime in the United States. This is most dramatically so in the federal system, where more than 90% of sentenced defendants in 2016 received a term of imprisonment. U.S. Sent'ing Comm'n, Sourcebook of Federal Sentencing Statistics, 2016, tbl. 12. Incarceration sentences are also common in state systems. For instance, in large urban counties in 2009, fully three-quarters of the defendants convicted of a felony were sentenced to incarceration. Brian A. Reaves, U.S. Dep't of Justice, Felony Defendants in Large Urban Counties, 2009 — Statistical Tables 29 (2013).

Incarceration might involve a sentence to prison or to jail. State prisons are normally reserved for offenders sentenced to more than one year behind bars. Jails, which are typically operated at the local level of government, hold offenders with shorter sentences, as well as the defendants who are detained while awaiting trial or sentencing. Among convicted felony offenders in urban counties, 42% received prison sentences in 2009, while 33% were sent to jail. *Id.*

Average sentence lengths vary considerably by offense type. For instance, among those convicted of murder in urban counties, the median prison term was 360 months (30 years). By contrast, the median sentence for rape was 120 months; robbery, 60 months; theft, 24 months; and drug offenses, 24 months.

American prison terms tend to be unusually long by global standards. As a result, the United States has a much higher per capita rate of imprisonment than other Western, democratic nations. For instance, the American rate is about four times higher than that of the United Kingdom, and 10 times higher than that of the Scandinavian nations. Michael O'Hear, The Failed Promise of Sentencing Reform xvii (2017). The current American rate is also about five times higher than it was before it entered a sustained period of growth in the final quarter of the twentieth century. *Id.* at xiv.

"Mass incarceration" in the United States falls especially heavily on African-Americans and Hispanics. For instance, the incarceration rate for non-Hispanic black men is more than six times higher than it is for non-Hispanic white men. Meanwhile, the Hispanic rate is about two and half times greater than that of non-Hispanic whites. Comm. on Causes and Consequences of High Rates of Incarceration, Nat'l Research Council of the Nat'l Academies, The Growth of Incarceration in the United States: Exploring Causes and Consequences

93 (2014). Many researchers have attempted to determine whether and to what extent such disparities can be explained by reference to legally relevant variables, such as differences in average offense severity or criminal history among different racial groups. The results have been recently summarized this way: "A sizable literature has long shown and continues to show that blacks are more likely than whites to be confined awaiting trial (which increases the likelihood that an incarcerative sentence will be imposed), to receive incarcerative than community sentences, and to receive longer sentences. Racial differences at each stage are typically modest, but their cumulative effect is significant." *Id.* at 93–94.

There is also a rich research literature on the experience and long-term consequences of a prison sentence. Generalizations are difficult due to the wide variation among institutions (for instance, with respect to programming opportunities for inmates, prevalence of gangs, and disciplinary practices), as well as the wide variation among inmates (for instance, with respect to prior experience with incarceration, mental and physical health, and family support). Still, there can be no doubt that the adjustment to prison life can be extremely socially and psychologically challenging for many inmates; that opportunities for education, employment, vocational training, and high-quality rehabilitative programming behind bars are often in short supply; and that a protracted separation from family, friends, school, and work can have a detrimental impact that extends far beyond the length of the prison term itself. Of particular concern may be research indicating that imprisonment tends to *increase* recidivism risk, *id.* at 193–95, and that the incarceration of a parent tends to harm children in a variety of ways, including leading to reduced educational attainment and increased rates of juvenile delinquency, *id.* at 271–74.

Depending on the jurisdiction and the offense, a prison sentence could be either *determinate* or *indeterminate.* With a determinate sentence, the release date can be readily determined at the time of sentencing. If the judge says five years, for instance, then the defendant will serve five years, with perhaps just a modest discount for good behavior behind bars. With an indeterminate sentence, the defendant's actual release date will depend in large part on decisions made after the sentence is imposed, typically by an executive agency called a parole board. Indeterminate sentencing systems can be set up in different ways. For instance, in some jurisdictions, the judge imposes a sentence in the form of a range, say, three to five years. The parole board then decides on a release date within the range, based in part on the inmate's disciplinary record, completion of programming behind bars, and general readiness for release. In other jurisdictions, the judge imposes a particular term of years, but the parole board is empowered to release inmates before the expiration of their terms. In such jurisdictions, the law commonly prescribes a minimum and maximum percentage of the sentence that must be served before parole release.

Eighth Amendment constraints. As interpreted by the United States Supreme Court, the Constitution imposes few limits on the length of a prison term. *Solem v. Helm,* 463 U.S. 277 (1983), is one of the very few cases in which the Court has overturned a prison sentence as excessively severe. The facts were indeed extreme: Helm was given a sentence of life in prison without the possibility of parole for passing a bad check for $100. Although he did have several prior felony convictions, each was for a nonviolent offense that the Court characterized as "relatively minor." *Id.* at 296–97. The Court thus concluded that Helm's life sentence violated the proportionality principle implicit in the Cruel and Unusual Punishments Clause. In a subsequent line of cases, though, the Court indicated that it would overturn a prison sentence only in circumstances of "gross disproportionality." Thus, for instance, in *Ewing v. California*, 538 U.S. 11 (2003), the Court upheld an indeterminate sentence of 25 years to life that was imposed for what was essentially a shoplifting offense—the defendant attempted to slip out of a pro shop with three golf clubs concealed in his pants. Do you think *Ewing* really is distinguishable from *Solem*? Does it matter to your analysis that Ewing's criminal history included prior convictions for battery, robbery, and unlawful possession of a firearm?

Curiously, though, the Court has recently adopted new restrictions on life terms for *juvenile* offenders, building on its earlier decision barring the death penalty for younger offenders. More specifically, in *Graham v. Florida*, 560 U.S. 48 (2010), the Court held that the Eighth Amendment prohibits sentencing juveniles to life without parole for nonhomicide offenses. The Court observed:

> [L]ife without parole is the second most severe penalty permitted by law.... It is true that a death sentence is unique in its severity and irrevocability; yet life without parole sentences share some characteristics with death sentences that are shared by no other sentences. The State does not execute the offender sentenced to life without parole, but the sentence alters the offender's life by a forfeiture that is irrevocable. It deprives the convict of the most basic liberties without hope of restoration, except perhaps by executive clemency—the remote possibility of which does not mitigate the harshness of the sentence.... [T]his sentence means the denial of hope; it means that good behavior and character improvement are immaterial; it means that whatever the future might hold in store for the mind and spirit [of the convict], he will remain in prison for the rest of his days.

Id. at 70.

Comparing juveniles who did not kill or intend to kill to adult murderers, the Court determined that the former have a "twice diminished moral culpability"—both because their crimes are less severe and because they have diminished maturity and decisionmaking ability. Twice diminished culpability left these offenders unsuitable for the second most severe penalty.

The Court also found the practice of sentencing nonhomicide juvenile defendants to life without parole to be so "exceedingly rare" that "it is fair to say that a national consensus has developed against it." *Id.* at 67. The Court concluded, "A State is not required to guarantee eventual freedom to a juvenile offender convicted of a nonhomicide crime. What the State must do, however, is give defendants like

Graham some meaningful opportunity to obtain release based on demonstrated maturity and rehabilitation." *Id.* at 75.

Two years later, in *Miller v. Alabama*, 576 U.S. 460 (2012), the Court extended *Graham* to bar the mandatory imposition of life-without-parole sentences on *any* juvenile—even those convicted of homicide offenses. Under *Miller*, a juvenile murderer may still be sent to prison for life, but only through an exercise of judicial sentencing discretion. We will consider mandatory sentences and *Miller* in more detail below.

Although the federal Cruel and Unusual Punishment Clause is not likely to lead to appellate reversal of lengthy sentences outside the juvenile context, occasionally a state constitution's own cruel and unusual punishment clause (or an equivalent provision) will result in a successful challenge to a harsh sentence. *See, e.g., People v. Bullock*, 485 N.W.2d 866 (Mich. 1992) (mandatory life-without-parole sentence for possessing 650 grams of cocaine mixture violated state constitution's prohibition against cruel *or* unusual punishment); *State v. Barker*, 410 S.E.2d 712 (W. Va. 1991) (life sentence for repeat offender, with no history of crimes involving personal violence, violated provision of state constitution requiring proportionality in punishment). *See also* Stanley E. Adelman, *Towards an Independent State Constitutional Jurisprudence, or, How to Disagree with the Supreme Court and How Not To*, 2002 Ark. L. Notes 1 (available on Lexis and WestLaw) (discussing *Bullock* and ways in which a court may interpret its state's cognate constitutional provision differently from the way the Supreme Court has interpreted the analogous provision of the federal constitution).

One final note about the Eighth Amendment and incarceration: while the Cruel and Unusual Punishments Clause imposes few constraints on the *length* of prison terms, there is an entirely separate line of Eighth Amendment cases that establish a number of constitutional requirements regarding the *conditions* of confinement, such as the requirement that inmates be provided with health care for serious medical conditions. *See, e.g., Estelle v. Gamble*, 429 U.S. 27 (1976). A rich and important topic, the field of prisoner rights mostly lies beyond the scope of this book.

[3] Semi-Incarceration

Incarceration in America is expensive and prisons and jails are often filled to or beyond their designed capacity. Moreover, incarceration can separate an offender from his or her family and job, reducing the likelihood of rehabilitation. Because of these concerns, there are now a number of semi-incarceration punishments that involve the deprivation of liberty, but not to the same extent as incarceration.

[a] House Arrest

One sanction is *house arrest* or *home confinement*, although it is more often used for pretrial detainees than convicted criminals. The offender, usually a nonviolent person with a minimal criminal history, is required to remain at home during a certain period, such as six months, or during certain hours each day. For example, an offender could be required to be at home during all hours that he or she is not at work.

Electronic monitoring. To ensure that the offender does not leave home during the restricted periods, an electronic monitoring (EM) system may be used. For many years, the dominant EM technology was the radio frequency system. In such a system, the offender wears a transmitter, typically as an ankle "bracelet," while a receiver is placed in the home. If the offender strays too far from the receiver, then connection with the transmitter is lost, and the supervising agency is automatically notified. Since 2000, the radio frequency system has been eclipsed by the rival GPS system, which permits continuous tracking of the offender's whereabouts. GPS monitoring is much more adaptable to enforcing restrictions on where an offender can go outside the home, which has contributed to a rapid increase in EM use, including use for purposes other than enforcing home confinement. For instance, for sex offenders, GPS monitoring can be used to enforce prohibitions on visiting schools and playgrounds. Reflecting the popularity of such uses, between 2005 and 2015, the number of offenders on EM grew from about 53,000 to more than 125,000. Pew Charitable Trusts, Use of Electronic Offender-Tracking Devices Expands Sharply (2016). Over the same time period, the GPS share of the EM market grew from less than 6% to more than 70%.

Evaluation. The concept of house arrest has many appealing features. It saves the state or local government money since offenders pay their own expenses. Moreover, it relieves overcrowded jails and prisons. The downside, of course, is that the offender is not subject to secure confinement and retains some ability to commit new crimes. It may also be perceived as too lenient, making it inappropriate for retributive or deterrent purposes. Another issue is that "house" arrest may not be available for homeless defendants or those who cannot afford to pay the fees for the EM system. If such defendants are disqualified from house arrest and incarcerated as a result, does that amount to an unfair socioeconomic disparity in punishment?

[b] Halfway House

Another common punishment is an order that the offender reside in a *halfway house*, ordinarily a relatively small residential facility where offenders live when not at work or in a therapeutic or educational program. The American Bar Association recommends what it characterizes as "intermittent confinement in a facility"—one that allows the defendant to leave for "employment, education, vocational training, or other approved purpose, but requires the offender to return to the facility for specified hours or period, such as nights or weekends." Standards for Criminal Justice § 18-3.19(a) (3d ed. 1994). While in the halfway house, the offender's behavior is monitored by staff, and residents may be required to participate in group or individual therapy sessions. A halfway house may be an attractive option for offenders in need of some structure and supervision but who have a job or other responsibilities that they should not have to forego. Many jurisdictions also use halfway houses as a way station between prison and outright release.

[4] Probation

Probation may be the most common punishment imposed by American judges in criminal cases. It is routinely used for misdemeanors. Even in felony cases, some research indicates that probation is used about one-quarter of the time. BRIAN A. REAVES, U.S. DEP'T OF JUSTICE, FELONY DEFENDANTS IN LARGE URBAN COUNTIES, 2009—STATISTICAL TABLES 29 (2013).

[a] Suspended Execution or Imposition of Sentence

Traditionally, a person is placed on probation in one of two ways. The sentencing judge may *suspend execution* of a sentence or *suspend imposition* of the sentence and put the offender on probation. If the court suspends execution of the sentence, it imposes a prison sentence, then suspends the actual service of the prison term and releases the offender on probation. If the offender successfully completes probation, the prison term is never served. If the court suspends imposition of a sentence, it places the offender on probation without actually imposing a prison sentence (sometimes called a sentence to *straight probation*). If the offender violates probation, the court then imposes a prison term as if the offender had never been on probation. The primary difference between the two approaches is that, in case of a probation violation, the court may be bound by the original prison sentence it imposed in the suspended execution model, but there are no such limits in the suspended imposition model. The American Bar Association recommends that judges should not utilize the suspended execution procedure. STANDARDS FOR CRIMINAL JUSTICE § 18-7.3(e) (3d ed. 1994).

[b] Limits on Probation

Many jurisdictions impose limits on probation. For example, this sanction may be unavailable for more serious offenses. Another common limit is that an offender cannot be on probation for more than a fixed number of years, such as eight or ten years. The reason for this limit is that at some stage the offender should be ready to live crime-free without government supervision. If a probationer has not violated the conditions of release during this period, scarce probation resources could better be devoted to more recent offenders.

[c] Probation Conditions

A probationer is ordinarily obligated to adhere to a list of *probation conditions*. Conditions may number 10 to 20, or even more. Common conditions include: (1) violate no criminal law, (2) hold a job, (3) support dependents, and (4) report for regular counseling visits with a probation officer. The American Bar Association recommends that any such restrictions "have a reasonable relationship to the individual's current offense and criminal history," and may include such matters as making restitution to the victim, maintaining residence in a prescribed area, submitting to random drug or alcohol testing, or performing specified public or community service. STANDARDS FOR CRIMINAL JUSTICE § 18-3.13(d) (3d ed. 1994).

Split confinement combines incarceration and probation. The offender first serves a short prison or jail term, then is released on probation for the remainder of the sentence. This gives the offender an unpleasant experience without long-term removal from family and job.

Courts have wide discretion to impose probation conditions which are reasonably related to legitimate penological goals. *See, e.g., United States v. Rearden*, 349 F.3d 608 (9th Cir. 2003) (defendant convicted of sending child pornography over the Internet; condition prohibiting him from accessing the Internet without prior approval of probation officer upheld as reasonably related to penological goals of deterrence, rehabilitation, and public protection); *State v. Oakley*, 629 N.W.2d 200 (Wis. 2001) ("deadbeat dad" sentenced to probation for nonsupport of nine children he had fathered by four different women; condition prohibiting him from fathering another child unless he could first demonstrate ability to support all his children upheld as reasonably related to rehabilitative purposes of probation and to societal goal of assuring financial support to children, despite partial infringement on constitutional right to procreate).

However, some conditions of probation (and parole as well) have been struck down as not reasonably related to the proper goals of supervision, as unauthorized by the probation statute, or as violating a constitutional guarantee. *See, e.g., United States v. Evans*, 155 F.3d 245 (3d Cir. 1998) (court cannot order reimbursement of defense counsel's fees as condition of probation); *Commonwealth v. Pike*, 701 N.E.2d 951 (Mass. 1998) (condition banishing probationer from state held violative of right to interstate travel and not reasonably related to correctional purposes); *Inouye v. Kemna*, 504 F.3d 705 (9th Cir. 2007) (parole officer violated Establishment Clause of the First Amendment by ordering Buddhist parolee, as a condition of parole, to attend a 12-step drug treatment program that required participation in meetings that had "substantial religious component," and then recommending revocation of parole because parolee refused to participate).

Shame sentences. So-called "shame sentences," requiring probationers to wear self-condemning signboards in public, write public letters of apology, or wear clothing or post signs warning the public that they are criminal offenders have been particularly controversial, and judicial opinion has been mixed. *Compare United States v. Gementera*, 379 F.3d 596 (9th Cir. 2004) (upholding condition requiring convicted mail thief to wear a signboard outside post office saying, "I stole mail. This is my punishment."), *with People v. Letterlough*, 655 N.E.2d 146 (N.Y. 1995) (striking down probation condition requiring convicted drunk driver to affix a fluorescent sign stating "convicted dwi" to any vehicle he drives).

Sometimes an offender is ordered to apologize to the victim, While this may appear sensible, the practice is not without significant opponents. What do you think the objections are? *See* Nick Smith, *Against Court-Ordered Apologies*, 16 New Crim. L. Rev. 1 (2013).

[d] Revocation

If the offender violates a condition of release, the court may respond in any of a number of ways, including reprimanding the probationer and warning against future violations, or modifying the terms of probation. The court's ultimate response, though, is to *revoke probation*, sending the offender to jail or prison. But there are limits on this process. For instance, in *Bearden v. Georgia*, 461 U.S. 660 (1983), the Supreme Court held that the Due Process Clause's fundamental fairness guarantee bars a sentencing court from automatically revoking probation for the failure to comply with a condition of release requiring the payment of money. If the probationer willfully refused to pay or make sufficient efforts to get the necessary funds, incarceration may be ordered at the probation revocation hearing. But if the offender could not pay despite reasonable efforts to do so, the court must consider alternate measures.

According to *Gagnon v. Scarpelli*, 411 U.S. 778 (1973), probationers enjoy a conditional liberty that cannot be taken away without certain due process protections. Before probation can be revoked, the offender is usually entitled to a preliminary and final hearing. The preliminary revocation hearing is to determine whether there is probable cause to believe that the probationer violated release conditions. The final revocation proceeding is to determine whether probation should be revoked. The defendant has a qualified right to counsel and to present evidence at both proceedings. *See generally* Neil P. Cohen, The Law of Probation and Parole (2d ed. 1999).

[5] Fines

Fines have long been a sanction for violation of criminal law and are used routinely in Western Europe. Since a fine is paid to a state agency, it differs markedly from restitution, paid to the crime victim as compensation. A fine serves several penal purposes. If sufficiently severe, it may satisfy retribution and could be both a general and special deterrent. The obvious problem with fines is that they may discriminate against the poor. The other side of the coin is that they may favor the wealthy who can afford to pay. The American Bar Association recommends that legislatures not set minimum fines for any offense; fine amounts should be set by utilizing one or more of the following factors: (1) the defendant's income and assets, (2) the amount of the victim's loss or the offender's gain, and (3) the "difficulty of detection of the offense." Standards for Criminal Justice § 18-3.16(b) & (c) (3d ed. 1994).

Day fines. Many countries have adopted the Scandinavian *day-fine*, a fine based on the amount of money a person makes in a day. Thus, a particular offender may be required to pay a day fine equivalent to the earnings of 100 days of work. It can be argued that the day fine system is fair to both rich and poor since it punishes them equally, despite differences in the amount of their particular fines. *See generally* T. Lappi-Seppala, *Fines in Europe, in* Encyclopedia of Criminology and Criminal Justice (G. Bruinsma & D. Weisburd eds., 2013).

Fines as revenue-generator. Along with court fees, forfeiture, and restitution, fines are part of an increasingly burdensome set of "legal financial obligations" (LFOs) that are routinely imposed on criminal defendants. LFOs have drawn criticism on several grounds, not the least of which is the potentially devastating economic impact they can have on poor and working-class families. There are also concerns that LFOs may create conflicts of interest for criminal justice officials who have become dependent on the revenue generated by these financial consequences. Do you see how LFOs might potentially warp the decisions of prosecutors or judges in some cases? *See generally* Wayne A. Logan & Ronald F. Wright, *Mercenary Criminal Justice,* 2014 U. Ill. L. Rev. 1175.

[6] Community Service

If sentenced to community service, the offender is ordered to spend a set number of hours, for example, 100, working at no pay for a public or charitable purpose. Examples include picking up trash in a park, working in a hospital emergency room, painting the houses of elderly citizens, repairing roads or playgrounds, and speaking to school groups about the dangers of drugs. This sentencing option, used extensively in Britain, has many advantages. It not only provides a valuable service to the people or agency receiving the free work, it aids rehabilitation, at least in theory, by teaching the offender about the needs of the community and making the offender feel a part of the collective enterprise of citizenship. If sufficiently rigorous, it also could deter future criminality and satisfy the need for retribution.

Community service is not without costs. It requires human and financial resources for supervision, equipment, supplies, and insurance. Community service workers could also perform jobs that would otherwise be done by paid public or private employers, thus increasing employment problems for some law-abiding citizens. It also raises questions about liability for injuries caused by the offender (e.g., negligent use of a shovel causing injury to a co-worker) or to the offender (e.g., back injury incurred performing community service).

[7] Forfeiture

Another sentencing option is a *forfeiture* of property. In general, forfeiture laws provide for the taking of two types of property. First, a court may order the forfeiture of property used in the commission of a particular offense. For instance, a car, boat, or house used for illegal drug activities can be ordered to be forfeited to the government. Second, a court may order the forfeiture of proceeds of illegal activity, such as the money earned from drug sales.

Constitutional limits. Forfeitures can present significant constitutional issues. For instance, in *United States v. Bajakajian*, 524 U.S. 321 (1998), the Supreme Court applied the Eighth Amendment's Excessive Fines Clause to strike down a forfeiture. The case involved a man who was apprehended leaving the United States with $357,144 in his luggage, in violation of a federal statute requiring reporting of currency in excess of $100,000 taken out of the country. A lower court authorized forfeiture of the $357,144 in accordance with federal law. The Supreme Court held that the forfeiture violated the Excessive Fines Clause since the forfeiture was punitive rather than remedial and bore no relationship to the injury suffered by the government. Had the government suffered some injury and the forfeiture been designed to reimburse the government for that loss or had the defendant been involved in a separate offense such as money laundering or tax evasion, the Court indicated that the forfeiture may have been sustained.

By contrast, the Court has indicated that civil forfeitures in general do not constitute punishment and therefore do not implicate the Double Jeopardy Clause. Such forfeitures are viewed as actions against the property rather than actions against the owner. *United States v. Ursery*, 518 U.S. 267 (1996). Additionally, the Court has upheld the forfeiture of drug proceeds that were to have been used to pay for criminal defense counsel. *Caplin & Drysdale, Chartered v. United States*, 491 U.S. 617 (1989).

Procedural issues. Forfeitures create a number of unique procedural difficulties, some stemming from the fact that property subject to forfeiture can be transferred to others or may be owned at least in part by several people. Statutes routinely permit a court to order that property subject to forfeiture not be transferred to other persons. There are also provisions to protect the interests of non-criminals who own an interest in property subject to forfeiture. *See, e.g.*, 18 U.S.C. § 1963. Finally, the Due Process Clause requires that, absent exigent circumstances, the government in a civil forfeiture case cannot seize real property without first providing the owner notice and an opportunity to be heard. *See United States v. James Daniel Good Real Property*, 510 U.S. 43 (1993) (due process violated when 4 1/2 years after marijuana seized from defendant's home, government obtained ex parte forfeiture warrant for this home and surrounding four acres); *cf. Bennis v. Michigan*, 516 U.S. 442 (1996) (due process not offended when car, jointly owned by husband and wife, was forfeited because of husband's use of it with prostitute; wife accorded opportunity to contest forfeiture).

Rule 32.2 of the Federal Rules of Criminal Procedure sets out procedures applicable to forfeitures, including notice of intended forfeiture, determination of whether property is subject to forfeiture (entitling either the government or the defendant to have the question of forfeitability decided by the trial jury), the conduct of forfeiture hearings, entry of preliminary and final forfeiture orders, and seizure of property ordered forfeited.

[8] Restitution

Restitution is compensation provided to the victim by the offender for the harm he or she caused. For example, a burglar may be sentenced to repay the value of the items taken (e.g., $750) plus the cost of replacing a door damaged in the entry (e.g., $200). Restitution may also be authorized for such amounts as lost wages, medical costs, and even pain and suffering. Jurisdictions routinely permit victim restitution to be a sentencing alternative, often in combination with other sanctions. Indeed, in some cases, restitution is required by law.

The American Bar Association recommends that restitution should be limited "to the greater of the benefit to [the defendant] or actual loss to [the victim]." Victims seeking exemplary, punitive damages, or consequential damages, such as pain and suffering or loss of profits, should be limited to civil remedies.

Procedural issues. The amount of restitution should be set only after a hearing in which the accused has an opportunity to offer proof on the value of the losses for which restitution is authorized. The procedure becomes more complicated if there are multiple offenders, particularly if some have not been apprehended or have no resources to pay a restitution order. The issue is what share each offender must pay.

Theoretical basis. Although restitution is now an accepted part of sentencing, its theoretical basis is often ignored. One approach is the notion that restitution is actually not punishment at all. If X steals Y's lawn mower, is it punishment if X is ordered to return the lawn mower? After all, the lawn mower never belonged to X, the thief. Another view is that restitution is rehabilitative or restorative in that it forces the offender to come to grips with and repair the harm he or she caused. It can also be argued that restitution contributes to deterrence since it conveys the message that the criminal will not profit from the offense.

[9] Concurrent versus Consecutive Sentences

If an offender is convicted of more than one crime, the sentencing judge will determine whether the sentence for the separate crimes will be served concurrently or consecutively. A *concurrent sentence* is one that is served at the same time as another sentence. A *consecutive sentence* is one that is served after completion of another sentence. For example, assume that an offender is convicted of two burglaries and sentenced to five years in prison on each. If the sentences are concurrent, the offender will be released after serving a maximum of five years. On the other hand, if the sentences are consecutive, the offender will serve the sentence for one burglary after completing the sentence for the other (a total of 10 years maximum). The sentencing judge ordinarily determines whether sentences are to be consecutive or concurrent. Some sentencing statutes or case law provide factors for the court to use in making this determination, while other legislation may mandate that consecutive sentences be imposed for certain offenses. By and large, concurrent sentences tend to be the "rule" in practice, and consecutive sentences the exception.

[10] Collateral Consequences

The true impact of punishment in a given case cannot be understood without appreciating the increasingly complex and burdensome web of "collateral consequences" that now follow a criminal conviction. Collateral consequences are not formally part of the sentence—that is what makes them "collateral"—but they may constitute a large part of what an offender perceives his or her punishment to be. The specifics vary widely from state to state. Thus, for instance, depending on the state and the offense of conviction, an offender might experience:

- loss of basic civil rights, including the right to vote, serve on a jury, and possess a firearm;
- loss of eligibility for student loans, subsidized housing, and other government benefits;
- deportation, if the defendant is not a U.S. citizen;
- suspension of driver's license; and/or
- disqualification from work in a multitude of different fields.

Sometimes such consequences last only as long as the offender is serving his or her sentence, but some consequences in some states may last for years after the sentence is over—potentially, indeed, for the rest of the offender's life.

Collateral consequences have grown especially severe for those convicted of sexual offenses. These individuals must commonly register and regularly update various types of personal information, including home address, in publicly accessible databases. They also increasingly face restrictions on where they can live. The evidence that such collateral consequences may help to reduce sexual recidivism is slim, at best. *See, e.g.,* Jeff A. Bouffard & LaQuana N. Askew, *Time-Series Analyses of the Impact of Sex Offender Registration and Notification Law Implementation and Subsequent Modifications on Rates of Sexual Offenses,* __ CRIME & DELINQUENCY __ (forthcoming).

There are concerns that collateral consequences have grown excessively severe and counterproductive for many offenders. For instance, restrictions on employment and housing may seriously impair an offender's ability to reintegrate into society and thereby potentially increase recidivism risk. Do you think there is ever a good justification for *lifetime* collateral consequences? Should sentencing judges have some control over which collateral consequences are applied to which offenders and how long they last? *See generally* NAT'L ASS'N OF CRIM. DEFENSE LAWYERS, COLLATERAL DAMAGE: AMERICA'S FAILURE TO FORGIVE OR FORGET IN THE WAR ON CRIME (2014).

C. Mechanisms to Guide or Restrict the Judge's Sentencing Discretion

Over the final quarter of the twentieth century, American sentencing laws were substantially modified as a result of sustained criticism of the wide discretion traditionally enjoyed by sentencing judges. Criticism came from both the political left and the political right. In general, those on the left were most concerned about the potential for unfair discrimination ("unwarranted disparities") among defendants who were convicted of similar offenses, particularly with respect to race and economic class. Meanwhile, critics on the right tended to focus on what they saw as excessive lenience on the part of many judges.

These criticisms dovetailed with a number of other developments in the 1970s and 1980s. For instance, American crime rates were relatively high throughout that period, which tended to make politicians and voters more skeptical about the competence of criminal justice officials, including sentencing judges, and more willing to embrace major changes to their roles. In addition, researchers were increasingly raising concerns about the effectiveness of rehabilitative programs for offenders. This mattered for the debate about the judicial role at sentencing, since one of the perceived benefits of discretion had been the judge's ability to assess the rehabilitative needs of each offender on an individualized basis. We might note, too, a general atmosphere of public mistrust of "activist" judges in the wake of politically controversial decisions in such areas as school desegregation, abortion, and procedural rights for criminal defendants. Finally, many jurisdictions were shifting from indeterminate to determinate sentencing systems, that is, eliminating the possibility of parole release for prisoners. This move took away a traditional check on the power of the sentencing judge—the parole board—and seemed to call for tighter regulation of judicial sentencing decisions by other means.

The critique of judicial discretion resulted in two distinct types of reforms, sentencing guidelines and mandatory minimums. Both remain significant parts of the overall American sentencing landscape today, albeit with much state-to-state variation in their structure and importance. We will first consider guidelines in more detail, and then move to mandatory minimums.

[1] Sentencing Guidelines

Traditionally, the defendant's conviction of a particular offense subjects the defendant to punishment somewhere within a wide statutory range. There might be several years, or even *decades*, between the bottom and top of the range. Sentencing guidelines are designed to provide judges with a significantly narrower range, or even a specific sentence, within the broader statutory range. Typically, this is done by identifying certain commonly recurring sentencing factors, such as criminal history, and giving them a particular weight. After determining which guidelines factors are present in a particular case, the judge can then apply a formula or matrix to calculate the guidelines range or sentence. For instance, a defendant convicted of perjury in federal court would face a statutory sentencing range of zero to five years in prison. However, if the defendant pled guilty and had no significant criminal history, the federal sentencing guidelines would indicate a much narrower range of 10 to 16 months. Assuming that federal judges normally adhere to the guidelines, one would expect much greater consistency in the sentencing of federal perjury cases than if the guidelines did not exist. We will take a closer look at the federal guidelines below.

Most guidelines systems can be categorized as *presumptive* or *advisory.* (The terms *mandatory* and *voluntary* are also sometimes used to describe the same concepts.) In a presumptive system, the sentencing judge is required to impose a sentence within the guidelines range unless there is some special consideration present that justifies a *departure* (which could be either *upward* or *downward* from the guidelines range). In an advisory system, the judge may be required to calculate the guidelines range, but is free to sentence outside the range. Perhaps not surprisingly, presumptive guidelines have generally proven more effective at changing sentencing practices and reducing disparities than advisory guidelines. COMM. ON CAUSES AND CONSEQUENCES OF HIGH RATES OF INCARCERATION, NAT'L RESEARCH COUNCIL OF THE NAT'L ACADEMIES, THE GROWTH OF INCARCERATION IN THE UNITED STATES: EXPLORING CAUSES AND CONSEQUENCES 75–78 (2014). In all, 26 states, plus the federal government, adopted sentencing guidelines between 1970 and 2004, although several guidelines systems have been repealed or substantially changed over the years. *See* John F. Pfaff, *The Future of Appellate Sentencing Review:* Booker *in the States*, 93 MARQ. L. REV. 683 (2009). More recently, the Supreme Court's decision in *Blakely v. Washington*, 542 U.S. 296 (2004), considered in more detail below, has discouraged states from establishing new presumptive systems. A handful of states do retain their presumptive guidelines, while a few other jurisdictions, including the federal system, have developed what might best be characterized as presumptive-advisory hybrids. *See* RICHARD S. FRASE, JUST SENTENCING: PRINCIPLES AND PROCEDURES FOR A WORKABLE SYSTEM 124–25 (2013).

In most guidelines jurisdictions, the guidelines are written and then revised as necessary by a *sentencing commission*, usually comprised of representatives of various criminal justice stakeholder groups. Commission members may include judges, prosecutors, law enforcement and corrections officials, public defenders, academics, legislators, and members of the general public. The commission may have as few as seven members or as many as two dozen. Usually it will have a professional staff to aid in drafting and researching.

The following two sections of this chapter describe the guidelines in use in Minnesota and the federal system. Both sets of guidelines aim to reduce unwarranted sentencing disparity, but they are structured in markedly contrasting ways. As you read these sections, make note of the ways you find these systems to be both similar and different from one other.

[a] Minnesota

In 1978, Minnesota became the first jurisdiction to appoint a sentencing commission. In designing the state's guidelines system, the Minnesota Sentencing Guidelines Commission's work was characterized by several features:

> The Minnesota Commission made a number of bold policy decisions. First, it decided to be "prescriptive" and explicitly to establish its own sentencing priorities.... Second, the Commission decided to de-emphasize imprisonment as a punishment for property offenders and to emphasize

> imprisonment for violent offenders. . . . Third, in order to attack sentencing disparities, the Commission established very narrow sentencing ranges (for example 30–34 months, or 50–58 months) and to authorize departures from guideline ranges only when "substantial and compelling" reasons were present. Fourth, the Commission elected to adopt "just deserts" as the governing premise of its policies concerning who receives prison sentences. Fifth, the Commission chose to interpret an ambiguous statutory injunction that it take correctional resources into "substantial consideration" as a mandate that its guidelines not increase prison population beyond existing capacity constraints. This meant that the Commission had to make deliberate trade-offs in imprisonment policies. If the Commission decided to increase the length of prison terms for one group of offenders, it either had to decrease prison terms for another group or to shift the "in/out" line and divert some group of prisoners from prison altogether. Sixth, the Commission forbade consideration at sentencing of many personal factors—such as education, employment, marital status, living arrangements—that many judges believed to be legitimate. This decision resulted from a policy that sentencing decisions not be based on factors that might directly or indirectly discriminate against minorities, women, or low income groups.

Michael H. Tonry, Sentencing Reform Impacts 48 (1987).

The Minnesota guidelines system has been modified in various respects over the years, but much of the original design remains intact. For a more complete overview and evaluation of the first quarter-century of the Minnesota system, *see* Richard S. Frase, *Sentencing Guidelines in Minnesota, 1978–2003*, 32 Crime & Just. 131 (2005). The more recent history is recounted in Richard S. Frase & Kelly Lyn Mitchell, *Why Are Minnesota's Prison Populations Continuing to Rise in an Era of Decarceration?*, 30 Fed. Sent'ing Rptr. 114 (2017).

The current version of the Minnesota guidelines can be viewed at the website of the Minnesota Sentencing Guidelines Commission: https://mn.gov/sentencing-guidelines/guidelines/. Focus particularly on the "Standard Grid." The guidelines instruct:

> The presumptive sentence for a felony conviction is found in the appropriate cell on the applicable Grid located at the intersection of the criminal history score (horizontal axis) and the severity level (vertical axis). The conviction offense determines the severity level. The offender's criminal history score is computed according to [§ 2.B of the guidelines]. For cases contained in cells outside of the shaded areas, the sentence should be executed. For cases contained in cells within the shaded areas, the sentence should be stayed unless the conviction offense carries a mandatory minimum sentence.
>
> Each cell on the Grids provides a fixed sentence duration. Minn. Stat. § 244.09 requires that the Guidelines provide a range for sentences that

> are presumptive commitments. For cells above the solid line, the Guidelines provide both a fixed presumptive duration and a range of time for that sentence. . . . The shaded areas of the grids do not display ranges. If the duration for a sentence that is a presumptive commitment is found in a shaded area, the standard range—15 percent lower and 20 percent higher than the fixed duration displayed—is permissible without departure, provided that the minimum sentence is not less than one year and one day, and the maximum sentence is not more than the statutory maximum.

Minnesota Sent'ing Guidelines Comm'n, Minnesota Sentencing Guidelines and Commentary § 2.C.1 (2017).

What is the presumptive sentence to be imposed on an unarmed first-time offender convicted of residential burglary of an unoccupied dwelling? Does it seem fair?

[b] Federal Guidelines

The federal sentencing guidelines are quite different from those of Minnesota and other American jurisdictions. In general terms, they are more complex, rely more on incarceration as the sanction of choice, involve more factors, and require a somewhat more complicated mathematical calculation to determine the appropriate sentence. *See generally* Thomas W. Hutchison *et al.*, Federal Sentencing Law and Practice (2014 ed.); Michael M. O'Hear, *The Original Intent of Uniformity in Federal Sentencing*, 74 U. Cin. L. Rev. 749, 780 (2006).

Development. Prior to the guidelines, federal sentences were indeterminate, i.e., subject to parole release. Federal judges had great discretion in assigning a sentence, while the United States Parole Board determined the prisoner's actual release date. The indeterminate structure was strongly criticized on the bases that it (1) was based on a rehabilitative model that had proved to be unsuccessful, (2) facilitated sentencing disparity among federal judges, and (3) produced a lack of certainty (and "honesty") about when a federal offender would be released from prison.

Congress rejected the traditional sentencing system in 1984 when it passed the Sentencing Reform Act, which created the seven-member United States Sentencing Commission and charged it with drafting presumptive guidelines. The law also abolished parole and established a determinate system in which the offender is to serve virtually all of the sentence imposed by the judge.

The United States Sentencing Commission employed a rather different approach to drafting its guidelines than its Minnesota counterpart had. The Commission chose not to adopt any particular overriding purpose of punishment, but instead to base its sentencing recommendations primarily on past averages. O'Hear, *supra*, at 780. Where the Commission chose to deviate from past practices, it was normally to *increase* the sentences for certain categories of offenders, including white-collar, drug, and violent offenders. *Id.* at 775–76, 783. Thus, in contrast to Minnesota, the Commission gave little weight to keeping the federal prison population within existing capacity constraints. Not surprisingly, the federal population grew quickly under the guidelines, with the federal prison system surpassing those of Texas and California to become the nation's largest prison system by 2002. MICHAEL O'HEAR, THE FAILED PROMISE OF SENTENCING REFORM 109 (2017). Along the way, the percentage of convicted federal defendants receiving probation fell by one-third and average prison terms nearly doubled. *Id.*

Despite loud, persistent criticism of the new system from lower-court judges, the United States Supreme Court upheld the federal guidelines against a constitutional challenge based on non-delegation and separation-of-powers doctrines. *Mistretta v. United States*, 488 U.S. 361 (1989).

Now "advisory" only. As discussed in more detail below, the Supreme Court purported to convert the federal guidelines from presumptive to advisory in *United States v. Booker*, 543 U.S. 220 (2005). However, it is important to appreciate that sentencing judges must still calculate and consider the guidelines range. In light of these requirements, as well as the unusual system of appellate review for sentences that has developed post-*Booker*, the federal guidelines might best be characterized today as a presumptive-advisory hybrid.

[i] Procedure Under Federal Guidelines: In General

In order to determine a sentence under the federal guidelines, one must consult a thick manual of several hundred pages. In general terms, the sentence can only be ascertained after calculating two numbers: the *offense level* and the *criminal history* category. Both of these numbers are determined only after a sometimes lengthy process of adding and subtracting points for various factors. When the two items are computed, the sentence can be determined by consulting a two-dimensional matrix, the "Sentencing Table." The offense level is the vertical category and the criminal history category is the horizontal category. To assist in applying these complex rules, the Guidelines include "Application Notes" that provide detailed explanations of various sections.

The current version of the guidelines, contained in the regularly updated *Guidelines Manual*, can be found at the Commission's website: https://www.ussc.gov/guidelines. The Sentencing Table can be found in Part 5.A.

[ii] Offense Level

In order to use the federal guidelines, the first step is to determine the offense level. If you know the statute that was violated, an appendix to the *Manual* will point you to a specific guideline for the offense. This guideline will supply a "base offense level."

For example, assume that an offender is convicted of burglary of a post office, in violation of 18 U.S.C. § 2115. The appendix indicates that the proper guideline is § 2B2.1. What is the base offense level for this crime?

Specific offense characteristics. The next step is to add the "Specific Offense Characteristics" to the base offense level. This involves fine-tuning of the base offense level based on factors that the Sentencing Commission thought sufficiently important to affect the sentence. Returning to our post office burglary hypothetical, assume that the offender used a firearm. How would that affect the offense level? Now go back to the Sentencing Table. Assuming he or she is a first-time offender, what would the applicable guidelines range be? Does this seem fair?

Adjustments. The next step is to make further "adjustments" to the offense level. Chapter Three of the guidelines contains the key provisions. For example, there is a victim-related adjustment. Under § 3A1.1, if the victim is unusually vulnerable because of age, the offense level is increased by two points. Similar adjustments are also authorized if the victim was a public official or was physically restrained.

Other categories of adjustments relate to the offender's role in the offense (levels added if the defendant played an organizing or leading role in a crime involving numerous people and levels deducted if the offender's role was minor); the abuse of a position of public or private trust; the use of special skills in the crime; the obstruction of justice during the case's processing; and the creation of a substantial risk of death or serious bodily injury while fleeing.

There are special rules for calculating the offense level in cases involving multiple counts. The offense level is also reduced if the defendant accepts responsibility for the offense and has timely provided information on his or her involvement in the crime or timely notified authorities of the intent to plead guilty.

Real offense sentencing: relevant conduct. A controversial aspect of the guidelines is called "real offense" sentencing. The drafters of the federal guidelines opted to focus as much as possible on the defendant's actual conduct in committing the crime. Accordingly, the guidelines permit the court to use "relevant conduct" in determining the defendant's offense level. "Relevant conduct" includes the defendant's acts and reasonably foreseeable acts of others involved in the crime, whether or not these other acts were charged as crimes.

For example, in *United States v. Crawford*, 991 F.2d 1328 (7th Cir. 1993), the defendant entered a plea of guilty to the crime of possession with intent to distribute marijuana. In determining the base offense level, the judge considered both the 875 pounds of marijuana that the defendant admitted he "off-loaded" plus an additional 736 pounds of marijuana which was never actually delivered (it was described as having been "under negotiation" between an accomplice and a police informant). The base level calculation was affirmed because the record established that the defendant participated in the negotiations for the purchase of the 736 pounds. In other words, the "relevant conduct" approach permitted the sentencing court to rely upon facts (i.e., the additional marijuana) as to which the defendant was not convicted.

The American Bar Association recommends that sentences should not be based upon the "real offense"; rather, the sentence should reflect the "offense of conviction," which should be "fixed by the charges proven at trial or established as the factual basis for a plea of guilty or nolo contendere." STANDARDS FOR CRIMINAL JUSTICE § 18-3.6 (3d ed. 1994). Similarly, the Minnesota guidelines specifically reject the "real offense" sentencing approach, and their accompanying Commentary suggests that sentencing on the basis of an offense other than the offense "of record" for which the defendant was actually convicted, is ethically questionable. No state has emulated this aspect of the federal guidelines.

Acquittal. The United States Supreme Court has held that a sentencing court may even consider conduct of which a jury acquitted a defendant if the government proves that conduct by a preponderance of the evidence. In *United States v. Watts*, 519 U.S. 148 (1997), the Court reasoned that the use of relevant conduct, even if the subject of a prior acquittal, does not impose punishment in violation of the Double Jeopardy Clause.

[iii] Criminal History

After determining the offense level, the next step is to consult Chapter Four of the *Manual* to calculate the defendant's criminal history score. For example, under § 4A1.1, an offender receives three points for each prior sentence of imprisonment exceeding 13 months, two points for each one at least 60 days long, and one point for each other prior sentence. Two points are also added if the current offense was committed while the offender was on release on probation, parole, and the like, and another one or two if the defendant committed the instant offense less than two years after release from imprisonment, while in prison, or while in escape status.

There are specific rules for calculating the point scores for juvenile offenses, expunged convictions, and other variations. Under § 4A1.3, the court is also authorized to depart from the formula for calculating the criminal history category if the ordinary formula would inadequately reflect the seriousness of the defendant's criminal history or risk of recidivism. There are especially harsh provisions in § 4B1.1 if the offender is a "career offender"—someone facing punishment for a violent felony or drug crime who has two prior convictions for such offenses.

[iv] Departures and Variances

The guidelines include an elaborate set of rules regarding the circumstances under which a judge may "depart" from the guidelines range. *See* Guidelines Pts. 5H, 5K. These portions of the guidelines identify a multitude of sentencing factors and, for each, specifically indicate whether the factor is an encouraged, discouraged, or prohibited basis for departure. In general, the guidelines tend to discourage or prohibit the consideration of mitigating offender circumstances, such as a disadvantaged upbringing, family responsibilities, and military or other types of public service.

Prior to *Booker*, the federal appellate courts tended to play an active role in restricting departures and enforcing limitations on the consideration of various mitigating factors. When *Booker* overturned the presumptive character of the guidelines, much of this large body of case law was rendered obsolete. However, the appellate courts continue to play a role in reviewing decisions to sentence outside the guidelines range (now often labeled "variances" instead of "departures," in recognition of the change in legal standards under *Booker*).

In the 2016 fiscal year, about half (48.6%) of federal sentences were within the guidelines range. U.S. SENT'ING COMM'N, SOURCEBOOK OF FEDERAL SENTENCING STATISTICS, 2016, tbl. N. Only 2.4% were above the range, while about 49 percent were below. Most of the downward departures and variances were supported by the prosecutor, presumably pursuant to a plea deal or cooperation agreement. By way of comparison, in the years immediately before *Booker*, about 70% of federal sentences were within the guidelines range. MICHAEL O'HEAR, THE FAILED PROMISE OF SENTENCING REFORM 116 (2017).

Substantial assistance. The single most important departure ground, used in about 11% of all cases, is the defendant's *substantial assistance* to the authorities in the investigation or prosecution of another offender. Since §5K1.1 indicates that this departure can only be given if the government requests it, federal defendants often have powerful incentives to turn on coconspirators or otherwise work with their prosecutors.

Review of sentences for "reasonableness." Under *Booker* and its progeny, federal sentences are now reviewed for reasonableness by the appellate courts (a standard often equated with abuse of discretion). This is meant to be more lenient than the pre-*Booker* standard under which departures were evaluated. Accordingly, below-range sentences are now upheld more frequently than they were in the old system, but there have also been instances of reversal even under the more deferential standard.

For examples of below-range sentences affirmed since *Booker, see United States v. Munoz-Nava*, 524 F.3d 1137 (10th Cir. 2008) (significant downward departure for defendant convicted of possession of heroin with intent to distribute upheld on basis of defendant's long and consistent work history and sole support of young child and ailing elderly parents, absence of a prior felony record; sentence that ordered stringent post-release supervision conditions held to appropriately reflect the seriousness of the offense and to provide "just punishment"); *United States v. Pauley*, 511 F.3d 468 (4th Cir. 2008) (downward departure for possessor of images of child pornography upheld as furthering rehabilitation and diminishing likelihood of reoffending under court-imposed counseling requirements, and on basis of defendant's remorse and possession of a relatively small number of photographs, which did not show child's face). *But see United States v. Livesay*, 525 F.3d 1081 (11th Cir. 2008) (downward variance for defendant in high-profile health care fraud conspiracy, from range of 78–97 months imprisonment to 60 months of probation with the first six months served as home detention, held *not* justified by the fact that the defendant had repudiated the conspiracy early on and cooperated with prosecutors; sentencing judge held to have inadequately stated reasons for departure); *United States v. Williams*, 524 F.3d 209 (2d Cir. 2008) (downward variance from guideline range held *not* justified by sentencing judge's view that prosecution for sale of crack cocaine should have been in state, not federal, court, and that the federal sentence should be adjusted to approximate sentence that could have been expected from state court).

[v] Continuing Controversy and Future Uncertainty

The federal guidelines remain a subject of considerable debate. Most commentators prefer the current to the pre-*Booker* system, although some in Congress and the Department of Justice would clearly like to restore the fully presumptive character of the guidelines. (Do you see why prosecutors might be inclined to favor the old system?) On the other end of the critical spectrum, there are those who argue that *Booker* and its progeny did not go far enough in changing the federal sentencing system. Certainly, if you are troubled by the complexity or severity of the guidelines, you might well object to the ongoing requirement that judges calculate and consider the guidelines range in each case. You might also note that the increase in below-guideline sentences has not resulted in much apparent softening of punishment. Indeed, the average length of federal sentences actually slightly *increased* in the wake of *Booker*. MICHAEL O'HEAR, THE FAILED PROMISE OF SENTENCING REFORM 116 (2017).

What do you think are the most problematic aspects of the current system? Based on what you have seen of them, do you prefer the Minnesota or the federal guidelines?

[c] Ex Post Facto

The operation of presumptive sentencing systems can give rise to *ex post facto* problems. The Constitution bars both Congress and the states from passing an *ex post facto* law. U.S. Const. art I, §§ 9, 10. This provision is designed to prevent legislatures from passing vindictive legislation and to provide potential lawbreakers with fair warning about what conduct is criminal and about penalties. A law violates the *ex post facto* provision if it is (1) retrospective, applying to events occurring before the new law took effect, and (2) disadvantageous to the offender. *Weaver v. Graham*, 450 U.S. 24, 29 (1981).

Not every law that causes a criminal defendant to suffer a disadvantage, however, offends this provision. The Supreme Court has distinguished between disadvantageous changes affecting *procedure* and those altering *substantial personal rights.* The *ex post facto* provision was not designed to limit the legislature's prerogative of altering both remedies and procedures which do not involve matters of substance. *Dobbert v. Florida*, 432 U.S. 282, 293 (1977).

Sentencing procedures. The *ex post facto* provision can be involved any time a change in sentencing rules is applied to an offender who committed a crime before the new provisions were enacted. In *Miller v. Florida*, 482 U.S. 423 (1987), the defendant committed a sexual battery at a time when Florida law authorized a presumptive sentence of three to four years in prison. By the time he was sentenced, Florida law had increased the presumptive sentence to somewhere between five and seven years in prison. Using the new guidelines, the sentencing judge gave the defendant a seven-year sentence. The Supreme Court held that the *Ex Post Facto* Clause was violated because the sentence substantially increased the offender's punishment for conduct occurring before the new law was effective. The Court refused to find the change, which only increased the penalty for sexual battery, merely "procedural" and hence outside the *ex post facto* guarantee.

Conversely, in *Dobbert v. Florida*, 432 U.S. 282 (1977), the defendant committed a murder at a time when Florida law provided that the penalty for murder was death unless the jury recommended mercy. At the time of the trial, however, the law was changed so that the jury merely advised the judge about the penalty; it could no longer veto the death penalty by a recommendation of mercy. The *Dobbert* Court held that the change was merely procedural, and therefore not barred by the *ex post facto* guarantee because it only altered the methods used to determine whether the death penalty was imposed; it did not change the "quantum of punishment attached to the crime." *Id.* at 294. According to the *Dobbert* Court, the new Florida procedures did not change the definition of the crime or the amount of proof necessary for guilt.

Increased sentences resulting from changes to guidelines. In *Peugh v. United States*, 133 S. Ct. 2072 (2013), the defendant was sentenced in 2010 for acts of bank fraud that took place in 1999 and 2000. Federal sentencing guidelines in effect at the time of Peugh's criminal acts called for a sentencing range from 30 to 37 months. However, the sentencing judge imposed a term of 70 months imprisonment, applying a 2009 amendment to the guidelines that called for a range of 70 to 87 months. The Supreme Court found *Miller v. Florida* controlling and held, 5–4, that Peugh's increased sentence under the more stringent guideline violated the *Ex Post Facto* Clause. In a majority opinion by Justice Sotomayor, the Court reasoned that even though *Booker* and later decisions had rendered the guidelines advisory, the guideline change in this case still strongly affected the sentencing decision by placing the defendant at a significantly higher risk (which was in fact realized) of receiving a longer sentence. Therefore, the Court concluded that the "animating principles" of the *Ex Post Facto* Clause had been violated, and that the defendant was entitled to be sentenced under the guideline that was in effect at the time he committed his crime.

[2] Mandatory Minimums

Mandatory minimum statutes dictate that the sentences for a given class of offenses or offenders include some specified penalty, thus eliminating the discretion of judges as to that penalty. A minimum could involve any sort of penalty. For instance, a statute might specify that individuals convicted of driving while intoxicated must be sentenced to perform at least 100 hours of community service. However, in public policy conversations, "mandatory minimum" normally refers to a mandatory minimum prison term. For instance, consider 18 U.S.C. § 924(c)(1)(A), a statute that was partially reprinted in above in Problem 15-3. This law requires a five-year prison term for defendants who are convicted of carrying or using a firearm during and in relation to a crime of violence or a drug trafficking offense, to be imposed in addition to the sentence for the predicate offense. Thus, the judge might have discretion about a prison sentence for the underlying crime of violence or drug trafficking offense, but would not have discretion as to the § 924(c)(1)(A) count. The overall prison term in a § 924(c)(1)(A) case, adding together the sentences for all of the counts, might be five years (the minimum) or possibly much greater than five years.

Mandatory minimums are sometimes confused with presumptive sentencing guidelines, and, in truth, they can function in practice in quite similar ways. In general, though, minimums can be differentiated from guidelines in several respects. First, minimums are legislatively enacted statutes, while guidelines are normally developed and promulgated by a sentencing commission. Second, minimums are adopted on an *ad hoc* basis in response to legislative concerns about particular offenses or offenders, while guidelines are intended to deal with broad classes of offenses and offenders in a coherent way pursuant to a more-or-less consistently applied methodology. (Once adopted, though, it should be acknowledged that guidelines are subject to *ad hoc* amendments that may diminish their coherence.) Third, guidelines tend to have greater flexibility in their application than minimums. For instance, as we saw with the federal system even in its pre-*Booker* form, there was a departure mechanism built into the guidelines that was used in nearly one-third of cases. To be sure, some minimums in some jurisdictions are subject to "safety valve" provisions that permit the judge to disregard the minimum in some cases, but the eligibility criteria tend to be more demanding than guidelines departure provisions. *See, e.g.*, 18 U.S.C. § 3553(f) (establishing safety valve for federal drug minimums for defendants who have little criminal history and satisfy four additional criteria).

If differentiated in these ways, guidelines and minimums seem to embody quite distinct ideas about how best to regulate judicial sentencing discretion. However, despite some philosophical tension between the approaches, jurisdictions can and do maintain sets of guidelines and minimums side by side. The federal system supplies a good example. Section 924(c)(1)(A) is just one of many minimums adopted by Congress. Indeed, in 2016, more than one-fifth of sentenced federal defendants were convicted of a crime that carried a mandatory minimum. U.S Sent'ing Comm'n, Overview Of Mandatory Minimum Penalties in the Federal Criminal Justice System 6 (2017). Note that when a minimum requires a sentence above the otherwise-applicable guidelines range, the minimum trumps the range.

Like guidelines, mandatory minimums are often controversial. Supporters believe that they send an effective deterrent message and ensure that dangerous offenders are incapacitated. Critics respond that there is little evidence to support the claimed crime-reducing benefits of minimums. Erik Luna, *Mandatory*

Minimums, *in* Reforming Criminal Justice: Punishment, Incarceration, and Release 117 (Erik Luna ed., 2017). Critics further argue that minimums tend to produce disproportionately severe sentences to the extent that they assign a heavy weight to just one aggravating factor without regard to countervailing mitigating circumstances. Critics also point out that minimums do not truly reduce discretion in sentencing, but rather transfer discretion from judges to prosecutors, who are normally able to control the application of minimums through their charging and plea bargaining decisions. The debate raises important questions about the relative merits of prosecutorial versus judicial control over the severity of punishment. What is your view of the advisability of minimums? For instance, should Congress repeal § 924(C)(1)(A)? Does your answer depend on whether there is a good set of sentencing guidelines in place to regulate judicial discretion by other means? (And what, in your opinion, would make a set of guidelines good?)

Minimums have been challenged numerous times on constitutional grounds. Of particular interest are claims that that certain minimums violate the Eighth Amendment proportionality principle. As we noted earlier in this chapter, the Supreme Court has held that mandatory *death* sentences violate the Constitution; in a capital case, individualized sentencing is required, and the defendant must be given an opportunity to present mitigating circumstances for consideration by the sentencer. However, the Court has steadfastly declined to transpose this rule from the capital to the noncapital context—even in cases involving truly draconian mandatory prison terms. For instance, in *Harmelin v. Michigan*, 501 U.S. 957 (1991), the Court upheld a mandatory life without parole ("LWOP") sentence imposed for a drug possession offense. Finally, though, the Court seemed to extend the individualization requirement at least a little way into the noncapital area in a case that we touched on earlier:

Miller v. Alabama

567 U.S. 460 (2012)

Justice Kagan delivered the opinion of the Court.

The two 14-year-old offenders in these cases were convicted of murder and sentenced to life imprisonment without the possibility of parole. In neither case did the sentencing authority have any discretion to impose a different punishment. State law mandated that each juvenile die in prison even if a judge or jury would have thought that his youth and its attendant characteristics, along with the nature of his crime, made a lesser sentence (for example, life with the possibility of parole) more appropriate. Such a scheme prevents those meting out punishment from considering a juvenile's "lessened culpability" and greater "capacity for change," *Graham v. Florida*, 560 U.S. 48, and runs afoul of our cases' requirement of individualized sentencing for defendants facing the most serious penalties. We therefore hold that mandatory life without parole for those under the age of 18 at the time of their crimes violates the Eighth Amendment's prohibition on "cruel and unusual punishments."

I

A

In November 1999, petitioner Kuntrell Jackson, then 14 years old, and two other boys decided to rob a video store. En route to the store, Jackson learned that one of the boys, Derrick Shields, was carrying a sawed-off shotgun in his coat sleeve. Jackson decided to stay outside when the two other boys entered the store. Inside, Shields pointed the gun at the store clerk, Laurie Troup, and demanded that she "give up the money." Troup refused. A few moments later, Jackson went into the store to find Shields continuing to demand money. At trial, the parties disputed whether Jackson warned Troup that "[w]e ain't playin'," or instead told his friends, "I thought you all was playin'." When Troup threatened to call the police, Shields shot and killed her. The three boys fled empty-handed.

Arkansas law gives prosecutors discretion to charge 14-year-olds as adults when they are alleged to have committed certain serious offenses. The prosecutor here exercised that authority by charging Jackson with capital felony murder and aggravated robbery. Jackson moved to transfer the case to juvenile court, but after considering the alleged facts of the crime, a psychiatrist's examination, and Jackson's juvenile arrest history (shoplifting and several incidents of car theft), the trial court denied the motion, and an appellate court affirmed. A jury later convicted Jackson of both crimes. Noting that "in view of [the] verdict, there's only one possible punishment," the judge sentenced Jackson to life without parole. . . .

Following *Roper v. Simmons*, 543 U.S. 551 (2005), in which this Court invalidated the death penalty for all juvenile offenders under the age of 18, Jackson filed a state petition for habeas corpus. He argued, based on *Roper*'s reasoning, that a mandatory sentence of life without parole for a 14–year–old also violates the Eighth Amendment. The circuit court rejected that argument and granted the State's motion to dismiss. While that ruling was on appeal, this Court held in *Graham v. Florida* that life without parole violates the Eighth Amendment when imposed on juvenile nonhomicide offenders. After the parties filed briefs addressing that decision, the Arkansas Supreme Court affirmed the dismissal of Jackson's petition. . . .

B

Like Jackson, petitioner Evan Miller was 14 years old at the time of his crime. Miller had by then been in and out of foster care because his mother suffered from alcoholism and drug addiction and his stepfather abused him. Miller, too, regularly used drugs and alcohol; and he had attempted suicide four times, the first when he was six years old.

One night in 2003, Miller was at home with a friend, Colby Smith, when a neighbor, Cole Cannon, came to make a drug deal with Miller's mother. The two boys followed Cannon back to his trailer, where all three smoked marijuana and played drinking games. When Cannon passed out, Miller stole his wallet, splitting about \$300 with Smith. Miller then tried to put the wallet back in Cannon's pocket, but

Cannon awoke and grabbed Miller by the throat. Smith hit Cannon with a nearby baseball bat, and once released, Miller grabbed the bat and repeatedly struck Cannon with it. Miller placed a sheet over Cannon's head, told him "I am God, I've come to take your life," and delivered one more blow. The boys then retreated to Miller's trailer, but soon decided to return to Cannon's to cover up evidence of their crime. Once there, they lit two fires. Cannon eventually died from his injuries and smoke inhalation.

Alabama law required that Miller initially be charged as a juvenile, but allowed the District Attorney to seek removal of the case to adult court. The D.A. did so, and the juvenile court agreed to the transfer after a hearing. Citing the nature of the crime, Miller's "mental maturity," and his prior juvenile offenses (truancy and "criminal mischief"), the Alabama Court of Criminal Appeals affirmed. The State accordingly charged Miller as an adult with murder in the course of arson. That crime (like capital murder in Arkansas) carries a mandatory minimum punishment of life without parole.

Relying in significant part on testimony from Smith, who had pleaded to a lesser offense, a jury found Miller guilty. He was therefore sentenced to life without the possibility of parole....

II

The Eighth Amendment's prohibition of cruel and unusual punishment "guarantees individuals the right not to be subjected to excessive sanctions." *Roper*, 543 U.S., at 560. That right, we have explained, "flows from the basic 'precept of justice that punishment for crime should be graduated and proportioned'" to both the offender and the offense. *Ibid.* (quoting *Weems v. United States*, 217 U.S. 349, 367 (1910)). As we noted the last time we considered life-without-parole sentences imposed on juveniles, "[t]he concept of proportionality is central to the Eighth Amendment." *Graham*, 560 U.S., at 59. And we view that concept less through a historical prism than according to "'the evolving standards of decency that mark the progress of a maturing society.'" *Estelle v. Gamble*, 429 U.S. 97, 102 251 (1976) (quoting *Trop v. Dulles*, 356 U.S. 86, 101 (1958) (plurality opinion)).

The cases before us implicate two strands of precedent reflecting our concern with proportionate punishment. The first has adopted categorical bans on sentencing practices based on mismatches between the culpability of a class of offenders and the severity of a penalty. So, for example, we have held that imposing the death penalty for nonhomicide crimes against individuals, or imposing it on mentally retarded defendants, violates the Eighth Amendment. *See Kennedy v. Louisiana*, 554 U.S. 407 (2008); *Atkins v. Virginia*, 536 U.S. 304 (2002). Several of the cases in this group have specially focused on juvenile offenders, because of their lesser culpability. Thus, *Roper* held that the Eighth Amendment bars capital punishment for children, and *Graham* concluded that the Amendment also prohibits a sentence of life without the possibility of parole for a child who committed a nonhomicide offense. *Graham* further likened life without parole for juveniles to the death penalty itself, thereby evoking a second line of our precedents. In those cases, we have prohibited mandatory imposition of capital punishment, requiring that sentencing authorities consider the characteristics of a defendant and the details of his offense before sentencing him to death. *See Woodson v. North Carolina*, 428 U.S. 280 (1976) (plurality opinion); *Lockett v. Ohio*, 438 U.S. 586 (1978). Here, the confluence of these two lines of precedent leads to the conclusion that mandatory life-without-parole sentences for juveniles violate the Eighth Amendment.

To start with the first set of cases: *Roper* and *Graham* establish that children are constitutionally different from adults for purposes of sentencing. Because juveniles have diminished culpability and greater prospects for reform, we explained, "they are less deserving of the most severe punishments." *Graham*, 560 U.S., at 68. Those cases relied on three significant gaps between juveniles and adults. First, children have a "'lack of maturity and an underdeveloped sense of responsibility,'" leading to recklessness, impulsivity, and heedless risk-taking. *Roper*, 543 U.S., at 569. Second, children "are more vulnerable ... to negative influences and outside pressures," including from their family and peers; they have limited "contro[l] over their own environment" and lack the ability to extricate themselves from horrific, crime-producing settings. *Ibid.* And third, a child's character is not as "well formed" as an adult's; his traits are "less fixed" and his actions less likely to be "evidence of irretrievabl[e] deprav[ity]." *Id.*, at 570. ...

Roper and *Graham* emphasized that the distinctive attributes of youth diminish the penological justifications for imposing the harshest sentences on juvenile offenders, even when they commit terrible crimes. Because "'[t]he heart of the retribution rationale'" relates to an offender's blameworthiness, "'the case for retribution is not as strong with a minor as with an adult.'" *Graham*, 560 U.S., at 71 (quoting *Tison v. Arizona*, 481 U.S. 137, 149 (1987)). Nor can deterrence do the work in this context, because "'the same characteristics that render juveniles less culpable than adults'"—their immaturity, recklessness, and impetuosity—make them less likely to consider potential punishment. *Graham*, 560 U.S., at 72 (quoting *Roper*, 543 U.S., at 571). Similarly, incapacitation could not support the life-without-parole sentence in *Graham*: Deciding that a "juvenile offender forever will be a danger to society" would require "mak[ing] a judgment that [he] is incorrigible"—but "'incorrigibility is inconsistent with youth.'" 560 U.S., at 72–73 (quoting *Workman v. Commonwealth*, 429 S.W.2d 374, 378 (Ky.App.1968)). And for the same reason, rehabilitation could not justify that sentence. Life without parole "forswears altogether the rehabilitative ideal." *Graham*, 560 U.S., at 74. It reflects "an irrevocable judgment about [an offender's] value and place in society," at odds with a child's capacity for change. *Ibid.* ...

Most fundamentally, *Graham* insists that youth matters in determining the appropriateness of a lifetime of incarceration without the possibility of parole. In the circumstances there, juvenile status precluded a life-without-parole sentence, even though an adult could receive it for a similar crime. And in other contexts as well, the characteristics of youth, and the way they weaken rationales for punishment, can render a life-without-parole sentence disproportionate. ...

But the mandatory penalty schemes at issue here prevent the sentencer from taking account of these central considerations. By removing youth from the balance—by subjecting a juvenile to the same life-without-parole sentence applicable to an adult—these laws prohibit a sentencing authority from assessing whether the law's harshest term of imprisonment proportionately punishes a juvenile offender. That contravenes *Graham*'s (and also *Roper*'s) foundational principle: that imposition of a State's most severe penalties on juvenile offenders cannot proceed as though they were not children.

And *Graham* makes plain these mandatory schemes' defects in another way: by likening life-without-parole sentences imposed on juveniles to the death penalty itself. Life-without-parole terms, the Court wrote, "share some characteristics with death sentences that are shared by no other sentences." 560 U.S., at 69. Imprisoning an offender until he dies alters the remainder of his life "by a forfeiture that is irrevocable." *Ibid.* (citing *Solem v. Helm*, 463 U.S. 277, 300–301 (1983)). And this lengthiest possible incarceration is an "especially harsh punishment for a juvenile," because he will almost inevitably serve "more years and a greater percentage of his life in prison than an adult offender." *Graham*, 560 U.S., at 70. The penalty when imposed on a teenager, as compared with an older person, is therefore "the same ... in name only." *Ibid.* All of that suggested a distinctive set of legal rules: In part because we viewed this ultimate penalty for juveniles as akin to the death penalty, we treated it similarly to that most severe punishment....

That correspondence—*Graham*'s "[t]reat[ment] [of] juvenile life sentences as analogous to capital punishment," 560 U.S., at ___ (ROBERTS, C.J., concurring in judgment)—makes relevant here a second line of our precedents, demanding individualized sentencing when imposing the death penalty. In *Woodson*, 428 U.S. 280, we held that a statute mandating a death sentence for first-degree murder violated the Eighth Amendment. We thought the mandatory scheme flawed because it gave no significance to "the character and record of the individual offender or the circumstances" of the offense, and "exclud[ed] from consideration ... the possibility of compassionate or mitigating factors." *Id.*, at 304. Subsequent decisions have elaborated on the requirement that capital defendants have an opportunity to advance, and the judge or jury a chance to assess, any mitigating factors, so that the death penalty is reserved only for the most culpable defendants committing the most serious offenses....

In light of *Graham*'s reasoning, these decisions too show the flaws of imposing mandatory life-without-parole sentences on juvenile homicide offenders. Such mandatory penalties, by their nature, preclude a sentencer from taking account of an offender's age and the wealth of characteristics and circumstances attendant to it. Under these schemes, every juvenile will receive the same sentence as every other—the 17–year–old and the 14–year–old, the shooter and the accomplice, the child from a stable household and the child from a chaotic and abusive one. And still worse, each juvenile (including these two 14–year–olds) will receive the same sentence as the vast majority of adults committing similar homicide offenses—but really, as *Graham* noted, a greater sentence than those adults will serve. In meting out the death penalty, the elision of all these differences would be strictly forbidden. And once again, *Graham* indicates that a similar rule should apply when a juvenile confronts a sentence of life (and death) in prison.

So *Graham* and *Roper* and our individualized sentencing cases alike teach that in imposing a State's harshest penalties, a sentencer misses too much if he treats every child as an adult. To recap: Mandatory life without parole for a juvenile precludes consideration of his chronological age and its hallmark features—among them, immaturity, impetuosity, and failure to appreciate risks and consequences. It prevents taking into account the family and home environment that surrounds him—and from which he cannot usually extricate himself—no matter how brutal or dysfunctional. It neglects the circumstances of the homicide offense, including the extent of his participation in the conduct and the way familial and peer pressures may have affected him. Indeed, it ignores that he might have been charged and convicted of a lesser offense if not for incompetencies associated with youth—for example, his inability to deal with police officers or prosecutors (including on a plea agreement) or his incapacity to assist his own attorneys. And finally, this mandatory punishment disregards the possibility of rehabilitation even when the circumstances most suggest it....

We therefore hold that the Eighth Amendment forbids a sentencing scheme that mandates life in prison without possibility of parole for juvenile offenders. *Cf. Graham*, 560 U.S., at 75 ("A State is not required to guarantee eventual freedom," but must provide "some meaningful opportunity to obtain release based on demonstrated maturity and rehabilitation"). By making youth (and all that accompanies it) irrelevant to imposition of that harshest prison sentence, such a scheme poses too great a risk of disproportionate punishment....

III

A

[The States] claim that *Harmelin v. Michigan*, 501 U.S. 957 (1991), precludes our holding. The defendant in *Harmelin* was sentenced to a mandatory life-without-parole term for possessing more than 650 grams of cocaine. The Court upheld that penalty, reasoning that "a sentence which is not otherwise cruel and unusual" does not "becom[e] so simply because it is 'mandatory.'" *Id.*, at 995. We recognized that a different rule, requiring individualized sentencing, applied in the death penalty context. But we refused to extend that command to noncapital cases "because of the qualitative difference between death and all other penalties." *Ibid.* According to Alabama, invalidating the mandatory imposition of life-without-parole terms on juveniles "would effectively overrule *Harmelin*."

We think that argument myopic. *Harmelin* had nothing to do with children and did not purport to apply its holding to the sentencing of juvenile offenders. We have by now held on multiple occasions that a sentencing rule permissible for adults may not be so for children....

[The States] next contend that because many States impose mandatory life-without-parole sentences on juveniles, we may not hold the practice unconstitutional. In considering categorical bars to the death penalty and life without parole, we ask as part of the analysis whether "'objective indicia of society's standards, as expressed in legislative enactments and state practice,'" show a "national consensus" against a sentence for a particular class of offenders. *Graham*, 560 U. S., at 61 (quoting *Roper*, 543 U. S., at 563). By our count, 29 jurisdictions (28 States and the Federal Government) make a life-without-parole term mandatory for some juveniles convicted of murder in adult court. The States argue that this number precludes our holding.

We do not agree; indeed, we think the States' argument on this score weaker than the one we rejected in *Graham*. For starters, the cases here are different from the typical one in which we have tallied legislative enactments. Our decision does not categorically bar a penalty for a class of offenders or type of crime—as, for example, we did in *Roper* or *Graham*. Instead, it mandates only that a sentencer follow a certain process—considering an offender's youth and attendant characteristics—before imposing a particular penalty. And in so requiring, our decision flows straightforwardly from our precedents: specifically, the principle of *Roper*, *Graham*, and our individualized sentencing cases that youth matters for purposes of meting out the law's most serious punishments. When both of those circumstances have obtained in the past, we have not scrutinized or relied in the same way on legislative enactments. . . .

In any event, the "objective indicia" that the States offer do not distinguish these cases from others holding that a sentencing practice violates the Eighth Amendment. In *Graham*, we prohibited life-without-parole terms for juveniles committing nonhomicide offenses even though 39 jurisdictions permitted that sentence. *See* 560 U.S., at 62. That is 10 more than impose life without parole on juveniles on a mandatory basis. And in *Atkins*, *Roper*, and *Thompson*, we similarly banned the death penalty in circumstances in which "less than half" of the "States that permit[ted] capital punishment (for whom the issue exist[ed])" had previously chosen to do so. *Atkins*, 536 U. S., at 342 (Scalia, J., dissenting) (emphasis deleted); *see id.*, at 313–315 (majority opinion); *Roper*, 543 U. S., at 564–565; *Thompson*, 487 U. S., at 826–827 (plurality opinion). So we are breaking no new ground in these cases. . . .

[The concurring opinion of Justice Breyer and the dissenting opinions of Chief Justice Roberts and Justices Thomas and Alito are omitted.]

Notes

1. *Juvenile sentencing, purposes of punishment, and the Constitution.* Based on *Miller*'s discussion of *Graham*, what considerations led the Supreme Court to ban juvenile life without parole (LWOP) sentences in nonhomicide cases? How did *Miller* extend *Graham*? What was the Court's reasoning? Are you persuaded? Do you see how the Court's reasoning in *Graham* and *Miller* gives constitutional significance to the general purposes of punishment discussed earlier in this chapter?

2. *Can* Miller *be contained?* The *Miller* Court distinguishes *Harmelin* based on the juvenile-adult distinction, but doesn't the logic of *Miller* cast doubt on the constitutionality of mandatory LWOP sentences in some adult cases, too? Youth is a mitigating factor of such profound importance, the Court seems to say, that it must always be considered by the sentencing judge before LWOP is imposed on a juvenile. But it is not clear that youth is *uniquely* important. Most obviously, there is intellectual disability. In the context of capital sentencing, the Court has treated youth and intellectual disability in a closely parallel manner, reasoning on similar grounds that the Eighth Amendment bans the death sentence for both juvenile offenses and offenses committed by the intellectually disabled. *See Atkins v. Virginia*, 536 U.S. 304 (2002) (intellectually disabled); *Roper v. Simmons*, 543 U.S. 1 (2005) (juveniles). How can these mitigating factors then be distinguished in the *noncapital* context? Similarly, the Court has banned the death penalty for certain defendants convicted of murder who had only a peripheral role in the offense. *Enmund v. Florida*, 458 U.S. 782 (1982). Might there be an argument that the Eighth Amendment prohibits mandatory LWOP for low-level accomplices? That is, just as *Miller* says that the judge must have discretion to consider juvenile status before imposing an LWOP sentence, the Eighth Amendment might also require consideration of a mitigating role in the offense. Can you think of any other mitigating factors that seem comparably weighty? Is juvenile status really of such distinctive importance as to warrant a different constitutional rule from every other mitigating circumstance in LWOP cases?

3. *What is a "life" sentence*? If a defendant is convicted on multiple counts in a single case, the sentences can be imposed to run consecutively, which may result in an extraordinarily long sentence to a term of years. For instance, after his conviction of sexually abusing seven individuals, Larry Nassar, the 54-year-old former doctor for the United States women's gymnastics team, was given an indeterminate sentence of 40 to 175 years. Scott Cacciola & Victor Matherjan, *Larry Nassar Sentencing: "I Just Signed Your Death Warrant,"* N.Y. Times, Jan. 24, 2018. Given his age and the fact that he had already received a 60-year determinate sentence in another case, there was no difficulty in viewing his sentence as the functional equivalent of LWOP. Indeed, to emphasize the near-certainty that Nassar would die in prison, the judge declared when imposing sentence, "I just signed your death warrant."

Nassar, of course, was not a juvenile, but sometimes young defendants do receive sentences that seem no less likely to keep them behind bars for the rest of their lives, even though not formally designated a "life" sentence. Should *Graham* and *Miller* apply to sentences that are the functional equivalent of LWOP? Lower courts have divided over this question. *See United States v. Mathurin*, 868 F.3d 921 (11th Cir. 2017) (discussing cases). If the Eighth Amendment protections are extended, it is hard to know where to draw the line. If the sentence will keep the defendant in prison for, say, 100 years, it is easy enough to characterize the punishment as LWOP. But what about 80 years or 60 years? Should the analysis include a consideration of the defendant's life expectancy? If so, how should life expectancy be calculated?

In *Mathurin*, the Eleventh Circuit faced an awkward constitutional problem in assessing a 685-month sentence imposed for an offense committed while the defendant was just 17 years old. If served in full, the sentence would keep Mathurin in prison until he was 74, which was within the life expectancy (77) of males of Mathurin's age. However, Mathurin was African-American, and he pointed out that the life expectancy of black males is four years less than the general life expectancy for men in the United States. Thus, he argued, if race were taken into account, the sentence would indeed exceed his projected life span. But can the Eighth Amendment analysis really differ based on the defendant's race? The Eleventh Circuit was able to dodge this question by bringing another factor into consideration: if Mathurin earned all of the available credit for good behavior in prison, he would be released at age 67—well within even his calculation of his life expectancy.

4. *What is life "without parole"? Graham* and *Miller* raise no problem for life sentences *per se*, provided that the defendant has an opportunity to earn release some time before death. The traditional means for providing such an opportunity would be parole. However, parole processes tend to be politicized, with parole boards averse to making controversial decisions. Thus, prisoners who were convicted of the most serious violent and sexual offenses often have great difficulty in gaining release no matter how persuasive their evidence of rehabilitation. For instance, California was long particularly notorious for its stinginess in granting parole. *See, e.g.*, W. David Ball, *Normative Elements of Parole Risk*, 22 Stan. L. & Pol'y Rev. 395 (2011) ("Just six parole-eligible murderers out of several thousand eligible were granted parole release during the tenure of Governor Gray Davis; by one recent estimate, each year the parole board finds only three percent of parole-eligible prisoners serving life sentences suitable for release, and only one percent are actually released after review by the full parole board and the governor."). Should such patterns be taken into account in determining the constitutionality of a life sentence? At some point, can't the practical difficulties of obtaining parole convert a nominally parole-eligible life sentence into the functional equivalent of LWOP?

On the other hand, there is a timing problem with such realism. It is hard to know at the time of sentencing what the state's parole practices will be many years or decades down the line when the defendant actually becomes eligible for release. Even California has become much more generous with parole grants in recent years. *See* Michael O'Hear, The Failed Promise of Sentencing Reform 196 (2017) (noting that Governor Jerry Brown had approved parole for 2,750 lifers by early 2016). Does adjudicating the constitutionality of a parole-eligible life sentence need to wait until the defendant has reached his or her eligibility date and actually been denied a few times?

Although *Graham* and *Miller* focus on the availability of parole release, there are also questions about the constitutional significance of other early-release mechanisms. For instance, what if a juvenile receives an LWOP sentence, but the state has a "geriatric release" program that permits elderly inmates to petition for release before the expiration of their terms—does the possibility of age-based release convert an otherwise impermissible juvenile LWOP sentence into a constitutionally acceptable life term? This was the situation the Supreme Court confronted in *Virginia v. LeBlanc*, 137 S. Ct. 1726 (2017). Although the Court did not provide a definitive ruling on the merits, the Court indicated that affirming the sentence did not reflect an "unreasonable" application of *Graham*. Similarly, in *Mathurin* (note 3 above), the Eleventh Circuit indicated that the availability of "good time" credits should be factored into the *Graham* analysis.

5. *Objective indicia*. Many of the Supreme Court's Eighth Amendment cases look to "objective indicia" to determine whether a challenged sentence violates the "evolving standards of decency" that are said to be protected by the ban on cruel and unusual punishments. *See, e.g., Atkins v. Virginia*, 536 U.S. 304, 312 (2002) ("Proportionality review under those evolving standards should be informed by objective factors to the maximum possible extent." (citation omitted)). Particularly important has been a determination of how many states ban the challenged type of sentence. *See id.* ("We have pinpointed that the clearest and most reliable objective evidence of contemporary values is the legislation enacted by the country's legislatures." (citation omitted)). The resulting state-counting exercises reflect a certain view of the Eighth Amendment—that the Amendment primarily serves to move outlier states into the nation's penal mainstream. Is this a sensible way to give content to the constitutional ban on cruel and unusual punishments?

In *Miller*, Alabama and Arkansas invoked the state-counting approach as favorable to them. They claimed, in effect, "We are not outliers in providing for mandatory juvenile LWOP, but part of the American mainstream." How did the Court respond? Note the Court's implicit concession that objective indicia had hardly provided strong support for the holdings in *Graham* and other recent Eighth Amendment cases. *Miller* may cast some doubt on the continued viability of the objective component of the Eighth Amendment analysis. Should we be concerned about such a development? *Cf.* Michael O'Hear, *Not Just Kid Stuff? Extending* Graham *and* Miller *to Adults*, 78 Mo. L. Rev. 1087 (2013) (suggesting that *Graham* and *Miller* may point the way to a more flexible, nuanced approach to assessing objective indicia that is less reliant on a simple tally of state laws).

D. Sentencing Procedures

Although the precise procedural details may vary from one jurisdiction to another, most sentencing decisions are based on a common model. With the exception of capital cases and the handful of states that routinely use juries for sentencing in noncapital felony cases, sentencing in America is done by the judge. Ordinarily, the sentence is decided after a *sentencing hearing*, which may occur immediately after the defendant's guilt is established or several days, weeks, or months later. At the hearing, the government will be represented by a prosecutor and the defendant by defense counsel, unless counsel has been waived. Usually the prosecution will speak first, perhaps even offering witnesses and sometimes advocating a certain sentence. Defense counsel may cross-examine government witnesses and present additional witnesses and documents. Often the rules of evidence do not apply at sentencing hearings, making hearsay evidence both admissible and frequently used. The traditional standard of proof on factual issues is the preponderance-of-the-evidence standard; although, as we will see, a recent line of cases indicates that the beyond-a-reasonable-doubt standard must sometimes be used.

[1] Data Used in Sentencing: Reports and Other Information

In order to arrive at a sentence that best serves the judge's sentencing goal(s) in a particular case, the court will often feel the need for more information than just the basic facts of the offense set forth in the charging document, especially if (as is common) there has been no trial and the defendant has been convicted by way of a guilty plea. For example, if the judge would like to impose a sentence designed to rehabilitate the offender, the court must have information about the defendant's social history in order to determine an appropriate sentence. A defendant with a fourth-grade education and a poor work record may be handled quite differently than one with a college degree and a lengthy employment history.

Courts typically obtain information about the defendant and the offense from three sources, as explained below and in the next subsection.

Written presentence report. First, the court will often have a *presentence report* prepared by a probation officer or the equivalent. The presentence report normally provides a social history of the offender, and may also include information about the crime, the effect on the victim, and the available sentencing options. In some jurisdictions, the author may even recommend a particular sentence to the judge.

Under the Federal Rules of Criminal Procedure, the presentence report may not include information that, if disclosed, might result in harm to the defendant or other persons, or that was obtained upon a promise of confidentiality. Fed. R. Crim. P. 32(d)(3). The American Bar Association recommends that presentence reports be confidential (not a part of a public record) but that they should be available to the parties; it also recommends that rules of procedure should provide that parties are "entitled . . . to copies of the written presentence report and any similar reports." STANDARDS FOR CRIMINAL JUSTICE §§ 18-5.6(a), 18-5.7(a) (3d ed. 1994).

Rules of criminal procedure routinely provide protections against inaccurate information used in sentencing decisions. The Federal Rules of Criminal Procedure are especially protective. The federal rules give defense counsel the right to attend any interview of the defendant by the probation officer conducting a presentence investigation. They also require the probation officer to disclose the presentence report to the defendant, defense lawyer, and the government more than a month before the sentencing hearing. Since some states do not mandate disclosure, the

American Bar Association recommends that states adopt rules of procedure entitling parties to "copies of the written presentence report and any similar reports." STANDARDS FOR CRIMINAL JUSTICE § 18-5.7(a) (3d ed. 1994). If the parties object to any facts in the report, the rules provide procedures and deadlines for resolving the problems. Fed. R. Crim. P. 32(f)-(g).

Information from lawyers and victim. The second source of information is the lawyers for both sides. Ordinarily, each side may submit its own presentence memorandum to the court, stressing information that may or may not be available from other sources. Sometimes the victim also is permitted to provide the court with information about his or her feelings about the crime and the possible sentence. The victim's information may be included in the presentence report or a separate document, or through live testimony at the sentencing hearing (sometimes referred to as *victim allocution*). For example, the federal Crime Victims' Rights Act gives victims "the right to be reasonably heard at any public proceeding . . . involving . . . sentencing." 18 U.S.C. § 3771(a)(4). Additional data may be presented during the trial or earlier proceedings. The defendant's prior criminal record (or "rap sheet") is also typically considered by the judge prior to sentencing the defendant.

The American Bar Association recommends that states adopt rules of procedure establishing mechanisms for providing notice to victims of "all important steps in the sentencing process." In addition to the victims' statements submitted in writing and attached to presentence reports, the ABA states that victims also should be permitted to make oral statements at sentencing hearings "concerning the physical, psychological, economic, or social effects of the offense on the victim or the victim's family." The ABA does not explicitly endorse the notion of permitting the crime victim to comment on the appropriate or recommended sentence. STANDARDS FOR CRIMINAL JUSTICE §§ 18-5.9(a), 5.10(a) & 5.11(a) (3d ed. 1994).

Victim impact evidence has been particularly controversial in capital sentencing hearings, in which there is a fear that the emotionally charged statements of family members of the deceased may inflame the jury and cause mitigation evidence to be disregarded. Nonetheless, some states permit the prosecution at the capital sentencing hearing to present evidence and jury arguments about the victim's uniqueness and the effect of the victim's loss on the family and community. In *Payne v. Tennessee*, 501 U.S. 808, 825 (1991), the Supreme Court held that the Constitution does not bar such practices. The "evidence about the victim and about the impact of the murder on the victim's family is relevant to the jury's decision as to whether or not the death penalty should be imposed." *Id.* at 827. Note, though, that *Payne* is somewhat limited. It does not authorize testimony about the "family members' characterizations and opinions about the crime, the defendant, and the appropriate sentence." *Id.* at 830 n.2.

[2] Sentencing Hearing

The third source of information is the *sentencing hearing*, an adversary proceeding in which both the prosecution and defense are permitted to provide the court with information relevant to the sentencing decision. Although procedures differ markedly among the jurisdictions, ordinarily the sentencing hearing is less formal than the trial. The rules of evidence may be inapplicable or only applied to some kinds of information. For example, some written reports may be admissible at a sentencing hearing though they would be inadmissible under the hearsay rule at a trial. Both sides may present witnesses. In a typical case, the defense may offer testimony from the defendant, members of the defendant's family, and character witnesses to talk about the defendant and the impact of a particular sentence. The defendant is accorded the right of *allocution* which permits him or her personally to address the judge in open court. If the defense counsel offers a plan for a probation sentence, a useful witness would be the person who has promised to employ the defendant if the court orders probation instead of prison. The prosecution's witnesses may include the victim, who can describe the crime, the extent of the loss or injury, and perhaps even comment on the appropriate sentence in some jurisdictions.

[3] Sentencing Factfinding and Constitutional Trial Rights

[a] Right to Confront Accusers

As we saw in Chapter 14, one of the defendant's most important trial rights is that of confrontation, including the right to cross-examine accusers in court. Does this right exist in sentencing hearings, too? No, the Supreme Court ruled in an important decision that set the tone for its jurisprudence on procedural rights at sentencing for half a century.

Williams v. New York

337 U.S. 241 (1949)

Justice Black delivered the opinion of the Court.

A jury in a New York state court found appellant guilty of murder in the first degree. The jury recommended life imprisonment, but the trial judge imposed sentence of death. In giving his reasons for imposing the death sentence the judge discussed in open court the evidence upon which the jury had convicted stating that this evidence had been considered in the light of additional information obtained through the court's "Probation Department, and through other sources." Consideration of this additional information was pursuant to § 482 of New York Criminal Code which provides:

> Before rendering judgment or pronouncing sentence the court shall cause the defendant's previous criminal record to be submitted to it, including any reports that may have been made as a result of a mental, psychiatric (sic) or physical examination of such person, and may seek any information that will aid the court in determining the proper treatment of such defendant.

The Court of Appeals of New York affirmed the conviction and sentence over the contention that as construed and applied the controlling penal statutes are in violation of the due process clause of the Fourteenth Amendment of the Constitution of the United States "in that the sentence of death was based upon information supplied by witnesses with whom the accused had not been confronted and as to whom he had no opportunity for cross-examination or rebuttal." . . .

The narrow contention here makes it unnecessary to set out the facts at length. The record shows a carefully conducted trial lasting more than two weeks in which appellant was represented by three appointed lawyers who conducted his defense with fidelity and zeal. The evidence proved a wholly indefensible murder committed by a person engaged in a burglary. The judge instructed the jury that if it returned a verdict of guilty as charged, without recommendation for life sentence, "The Court must impose the death penalty," but if such recommendation was made, "the Court may impose a life sentence." The judge went on to emphasize that "the Court is not bound to accept your recommendation."

About five weeks after the verdict of guilty with recommendation of life imprisonment, and after a statutory pre-sentence investigation report to the judge, the defendant was brought to court to be sentenced. Asked what he had to say, appellant protested his innocence. After each of his three lawyers had appealed to the court to accept the jury's recommendation of a life sentence, the judge gave reasons why he felt that the death sentence should be imposed. He narrated the shocking details of the crime as shown by the trial evidence, expressing his own complete belief in appellant's guilt. He stated that the pre-sentence investigation revealed many material facts concerning appellant's background which though relevant to the question of punishment could not properly have been brought to the attention of the jury in its consideration of the question of guilt. He referred to the experience appellant "had had on thirty other burglaries in and about the same vicinity" where the murder had been committed. The appellant had not been convicted of these burglaries although the judge had information that he had confessed to some and had been identified as the perpetrator of some of the others. The judge also referred to certain activities of appellant as shown by the probation report that indicated appellant possessed "a morbid sexuality" and classified him as a "menace to society." The accuracy of the statements made by the judge as to appellant's background and past practices were not challenged by appellant or his counsel, nor was the judge asked to disregard any of them or to afford appellant a chance to refute or discredit any of them by cross-examination or otherwise.

The case presents a serious and difficult question. The question relates to the rules of evidence applicable to the manner in which a judge may obtain information to guide him in the imposition of sentence upon an already convicted defendant. Within limits fixed by statutes, New York judges are given a broad discretion to decide the type and extent of punishment for convicted defendants. Here, for example, the judge's discretion was to sentence to life imprisonment or death. To aid a judge in exercising this discretion intelligently the New York procedural policy encourages him to consider information about the convicted person's past life, health, habits, conduct, and mental and moral propensities. The sentencing judge may consider such information even though obtained outside the courtroom from persons whom a defendant has not been permitted to confront or cross-examine. It is the consideration of information obtained by a sentencing judge in this manner that is the basis for appellant's broad constitutional challenge to the New York statutory policy.

Appellant urges that the New York statutory policy is in irreconcilable conflict with the underlying philosophy of a second procedural policy grounded in the due process of law clause of the Fourteenth Amendment. That policy as stated *In re Oliver*, 333 U.S. 257, 273, is in part that no person shall be tried and convicted of an offense unless he is given reasonable notice of the charges against him and is afforded an opportunity to examine adverse witnesses. That the due process clause does provide these salutary and time-tested protections where the question for consideration is the guilt of a defendant seems entirely clear from the genesis and historical evolution of the clause. *See, e.g., Chambers v. Florida*, 309 U.S. at 236–37.

Tribunals passing on the guilt of a defendant always have been hedged in by strict evidentiary procedural limitations. But both before and since the American colonies became a nation, courts in this country and in England practiced a policy under which a sentencing judge could exercise a wide discretion in the sources and types of evidence used to assist him in determining the kind and extent of punishment to be imposed within limits fixed by law. Out-of-court affidavits have been used frequently, and of course in the smaller communities sentencing judges naturally have in mind their knowledge of the personalities and backgrounds of convicted offenders. A recent manifestation of the historical latitude allowed sentencing judges appears in Rule 32 of the Federal Rules of Criminal Procedure. That rule provides for consideration by federal judges of reports made by probation officers containing information about a convicted defendant, including such information "as may be helpful in imposing sentence or in granting probation or in the correctional treatment of the defendant."

In addition to the historical basis for different evidentiary rules governing trial and sentencing procedures there are sound practical reasons for the distinction. In a trial before verdict the issue is whether a defendant is guilty of having engaged in certain criminal conduct of which he has been specifically accused. Rules of evidence have been fashioned for criminal trials which narrowly confine the trial contest to evidence that is strictly relevant to the particular offense charged. These rules rest in part on a necessity to prevent a time consuming and confusing trial of collateral issues. They were also designed to prevent tribunals concerned solely with the issue of guilt of a particular offense from being influenced to convict for that offense by evidence that the defendant had habitually engaged in other misconduct. A sentencing judge, however, is not confined to the narrow issue of guilt. His task within fixed statutory or constitutional limits is to determine the type and extent of punishment after the issue of guilt has been determined. Highly relevant—if not essential—to his selection of an appropriate sentence is the possession of the fullest information possible concerning the defendant's life and characteristics. And modern concepts individualizing punishment have made it all the more necessary that a sentencing judge not be denied an opportunity to obtain pertinent information by a requirement of rigid adherence to restrictive rules of evidence properly applicable to the trial.

Undoubtedly the New York statutes emphasize a prevalent modern philosophy of penology that the punishment should fit the offender and not merely the crime. The belief no longer prevails that every offense in a like legal category calls for an identical punishment without regard to the past life and habits of a particular offender. This whole country has traveled far from the period in which the death sentence was an automatic and commonplace result of convictions—even for offenses today deemed trivial. Today's philosophy of individualizing sentences makes sharp distinctions for example between first and repeated offenders. Indeterminate sentences, the ultimate termination of which are sometimes decided by nonjudicial agencies have to a large extent taken the place of the old rigidly fixed punishments. The practice of probation which relies heavily on non-judicial implementation has been accepted as a wise policy. Execution of the United States parole system rests on the discretion of an administrative parole board. Retribution is no longer the dominant objective of the criminal law. Reformation and rehabilitation of offenders have become important goals of criminal jurisprudence.

Modern changes in the treatment of offenders make it more necessary now than a century ago for observance of the distinctions in the evidential procedure in the trial and sentencing processes. For indeterminate sentences and probation have resulted in an increase in the discretionary powers exercised in fixing punishments. In general, these modern changes have not resulted in making the lot of offenders harder. On the contrary a strong motivating force for the changes has been the belief that by careful study of the lives and personalities of convicted offenders many could be less severely punished and restored sooner to complete freedom and useful citizenship. This belief to a large extent has been justified.

Under the practice of individualizing punishments, investigation techniques have been given an important role. Probation workers making reports of their investigations have not been trained to prosecute but to aid offenders. Their reports have been given a high value by conscientious judges who want to sentence persons on the best available information rather than on guesswork and inadequate information. To deprive sentencing judges of this kind of information would undermine modern penological procedural policies that have been cautiously adopted throughout the nation after careful consideration and experimentation. We must recognize that most of the information now relied upon by judges to guide them in the intelligent imposition of sentences would be unavailable if information were restricted to that given in open court by witnesses subject to cross-examination. And the modern probation report draws on information concerning every aspect of a defendant's life. The type and extent of this information make totally impractical if not impossible open court testimony with cross-examination. Such a procedure could endlessly delay criminal administration in a retrial of collateral issues.

The considerations we have set out admonish us against treating the due-process clause as a uniform command that courts throughout the Nation abandon their age-old practice of seeking information from out-of-court sources to guide their judgment toward a more enlightened and just sentence. New York criminal statutes set wide limits for maximum and minimum sentences. Under New York statutes a state judge cannot escape his grave responsibility of fixing sentence. In determining whether a defendant shall receive a one-year minimum or a twenty-year maximum sentence, we do not think the Federal Constitution restricts the view of the sentencing judge to the information received in open court. The due-process clause should not be treated as a device for freezing the evidential procedure of sentencing in the mold of trial procedure. So to treat the due-process clause would hinder if not preclude all courts—state and federal—from making progressive efforts to improve the administration of criminal justice.

[The dissenting opinions of JUSTICES MURPHY and RUTLEDGE are omitted.]

Notes

1. *An opinion from a different era.* Although Williams' argument focused particularly on his right to cross-examine his accusers, the Court's broadly worded opinion not only rejected Williams' claim, but also cast doubt more generally on procedural rights at sentencing. Writing for the Court, Justice Hugo Black embraced an informal approach to sentencing that sharply distinguished sentencing procedures from trial procedures. Notice how his reasoning seemed premised on the assumption that informality would normally *help* defendants, even though it may have hurt Williams himself. This assumption, in turn, rested on the belief that sentencing judges would use of the wealth of (hearsay) information contained in presentence reports to fashion *rehabilitative* sentences. Justice Black could not have foreseen the harshly punitive, anti-rehabilitative turn that American sentencing policies would take in the final quarter of the twentieth century. Perhaps he and his colleagues in the *Williams* majority would have seen a greater need for procedural formality if they had contemplated contemporary sentencing guidelines and mandatory minimums; in these systems, the judge's fact-finding normally serves to aggravate, not mitigate, the punishment. Still, *Williams* remains good law to this day, at least with respect to the specific confrontation right at issue in the case.

2. *A quick review of double jeopardy.* Williams' sentence was based, in part, on the judge's belief that he was responsible for 30 burglaries, all apparently uncharged. However, what if Williams had already been convicted and sentenced for all of those additional offenses? Would the Double Jeopardy Clause bar the judge in his murder case from taking the burglaries into account? The answer is no, as you may recall from Chapter 15. *See Witte v. United States*, 515 U.S. 389 (1995).

[b] Right to Jury Trial and Proof Beyond a Reasonable Doubt

[i] *Apprendi*

As legislatures adopted a swelling number of presumptive and mandatory sentencing laws in the 1970s and thereafter, the courts continued to embrace the relaxed approach to due process that was approved by *Williams*. In 2000, though, the Supreme Court finally attempted to impose some meaningful limitations on the informality, holding that a particular "sentence enhancement" under New Jersey law could not be applied unless either a jury found the necessary facts beyond a reasonable doubt or the defendant waived these procedural rights.

Apprendi v. New Jersey

530 U.S. 466 (2000)

Justice Stevens delivered the opinion of the Court.

[Following his arrest, Charles Apprendi admitted that he fired shots into the home of an African-American family. He also stated that he did not want the victims in the neighborhood "because they are black in color," although he later retracted that admission. In due course, he agreed to plead guilty to two firearms counts punishable by 5–10 years and another offense punishable by 3–5 years. The plea agreement allowed the State to request an "enhanced" sentence on the ground that the offense "was committed with a biased purpose," while Apprendi reserved the right to "challenge the hate crime sentence enhancement on the ground that it violates the United States Constitution." After a hearing, at which time several witnesses, including Apprendi himself, testified as to the "purpose" behind the shooting, the judge found by a preponderance of the evidence that Apprendi's actions were taken "with a purpose to intimidate" (i.e., the crime "was motivated by racial bias") and sentenced him to a 12-year term of imprisonment, to run concurrently with the other sentences.]

At stake in this case are constitutional protections of surpassing importance: the proscription of any deprivation of liberty without "due process of law," and the guarantee that "[i]n all criminal prosecutions, the accused shall enjoy the right to a speedy and public trial, by an impartial jury." Taken together, these rights indisputably entitle a criminal defendant to "a jury determination that [he] is guilty of every element of the crime with which he is charged, beyond a reasonable doubt."

... [O]ur reexamination of our cases in this area, and of the history upon which they rely, confirms the opinion that we expressed in *Jones* [*v. United States,* 526 U.S. 227 (1999)]. Other than the fact of a prior conviction, any fact that increases the penalty for a crime beyond the prescribed statutory maximum must be submitted to a jury, and proved beyond a reasonable doubt. With that exception, we endorse the statement of the rule set forth in the concurring opinions in that case: "[I]t is unconstitutional for a legislature to remove from the jury the assessment of facts that increase the prescribed range of penalties to which a criminal defendant is exposed. It is equally clear that such facts must be established by proof beyond a reasonable doubt."

The New Jersey statutory scheme that Apprendi asks us to invalidate allows a jury to convict a defendant of a second-degree offense based on its finding beyond a reasonable doubt that he unlawfully possessed a prohibited weapon; after a subsequent and separate proceeding, it then allows a judge to impose punishment identical to that New Jersey provides for crimes of the first degree based upon the judge's finding, by a preponderance of the evidence, that the defendant's "purpose" for unlawfully possessing the weapon was "to intimidate" his victim on the basis of a particular characteristic the victim possessed. In light of the constitutional rule explained above, and all of the cases supporting it, this practice cannot stand.

. . . [T]he New Jersey Supreme Court correctly recognized that it does not matter whether the required finding is characterized as one of intent or of motive, because "[l]abels do not afford an acceptable answer." That point applies as well to the constitutionally novel and elusive distinction between "elements" and "sentencing factors." Despite what appears to us the clear "elemental" nature of the factor here, the relevant inquiry is one not of form, but of effect—does the required finding expose the defendant to a greater punishment than that authorized by the jury's guilty verdict?[1]

. . . The New Jersey procedure challenged in this case is an unacceptable departure from the jury tradition that is an indispensable part of our criminal justice system.

[The concurring opinion of Justice Thomas and the dissenting opinions of Justices O'Connor and Breyer are omitted.]

Notes

1. *What's the big deal?* Why is *Apprendi* regarded as a minor revolution in American sentencing law? Does it help or hurt defendants?

2. *Waiver.* Does *Apprendi* mean that juries have to be involved in every sentencing decision in every state? Don't forget that criminal defendants plead guilty in the vast majority of felony cases. Part of the plea process involves a formal waiver of a jury trial. If the defendant waives a jury *trial*, does this also mean that there is a waiver of a jury's involvement in *sentencing*?

3. *Capital sentencing.* In *Ring v. Arizona*, 536 U.S. 584 (2002), the Supreme Court applied *Apprendi* to capital cases. Arizona law authorized the death penalty only

---

1. This is not to suggest that the term "sentencing factor" is devoid of meaning. The term appropriately describes a circumstance, which may be either aggravating or mitigating in character, that supports a specific sentence within the range authorized by the jury's finding that the defendant is guilty of a particular offense. On the other hand, when the term "sentence enhancement" is used to describe an increase beyond the maximum authorized statutory sentence, it is the functional equivalent of an element of a greater offense than the one covered by the jury's guilty verdict. Indeed, it fits squarely within the usual definition of an "element" of the offense.

when, after a conviction of first-degree murder, the judge (without a jury) found the presence of one or more aggravating circumstances. In Ring's case, the judge imposed the death penalty, finding that testimony at the sentencing hearing established two aggravating factors: that Ring was a major participant in the armed robbery that led to the killing and that he exhibited a reckless disregard or indifference for human life.

The Supreme Court overturned the death penalty, reasoning that under *Apprendi*'s reading of the Sixth Amendment, the determination regarding aggravating factors, and therefore the facts on which the life-or-death sentencing decision will depend, must be made by juries rather than judges. The Court reasoned from *Apprendi* that since life was the maximum penalty allowable on the basis of the jury's verdict of guilt standing alone, the ultimate penalty of death could only be imposed if the facts that lead to the imposition of the death penalty are found by the jury, not the judge. *Ring*, in effect, invalidated death penalty procedures in several other states which had assigned the finding of aggravating circumstances to the trial judge.

4. *Fines.* In *Southern Union v. United States*, 567 U.S. 343 (2012), the Supreme Court extended the *Apprendi* rule to the imposition of criminal fines. The Court determined that the district court, on the basis of the sentencing judge's own fact-finding, had improperly enhanced the defendant's criminal fine for environmental offenses beyond the maximum that could have been imposed on the basis of the jury's verdict or the defendant's admissions. The Court has not yet determined whether restitution or forfeiture orders that are made part of a criminal sentence are similarly subject to *Apprendi's* limitations. *See* William M. Acker, Jr., *The Mandatory Victims Restitution Act Is Unconstitutional. Will the Courts Say So After* Southern Union v. United States*?*, 64 Ala. L. Rev. 803 (2013).

5. *Criminal history.* Note one critically important "loophole" recognized in *Apprendi* itself: if a sentence enhancement depends on a defendant's prior convictions, the judge may perform the necessary fact-finding. This is no small matter, since sentencing laws very commonly call for increased punishment based on criminal history. Does this exception to *Apprendi* make any sense? Do you see any pertinent differences between a judge deciding what prior convictions the defendant has and a judge deciding, say, whether the defendant acted with a racial motive?

6. *Concurrent versus consecutive sentences.* In *Oregon v. Ice*, 555 U.S. 160 (2009), the Court held that the finding of facts (by judges rather than jurors) that underlie the imposition of consecutive, rather than concurrent, sentences for multiple offenses does not violate the Sixth Amendment right to trial by jury. In so doing, the Court refused to extend *Apprendi*, concluding that judicial factfinding in this context does not constitute "encroachment on the jury's traditional domain."

[ii] Application of *Apprendi* to Sentencing Guidelines

Perhaps the most important question left open by *Apprendi* was its application to presumptive sentencing guidelines, such as those used in Minnesota and in the federal system. If a fact increases the defendant's guidelines range, or is used by the judge to justify an upward "departure" above the range, can the judge find that fact, or is a jury necessary? On the one hand, such fact-finding does expose the defendant to increased punishment, just as occurred with the hate-crimes statute in *Apprendi*. On the other hand, guidelines sentencing operates within a statutory range; so long as an overarching statutory maximum remains in place and unchanged, you might argue that *Apprendi* is distinguishable. The *Apprendi* court itself indicated that fully discretionary sentencing could proceed without regard to the new procedural rights. In other words, in traditional, non-guidelines sentencing, the judge must select a sentence from within a wide sentencing range and is free to perform whatever fact-finding he or she wishes in making that selection. (Think, for instance, about the sentencing judge in *Williams* implicitly finding that the defendant had participated in 30 uncharged burglaries.) *Apprendi* changed nothing about the constitutionality of such practices in the context of a traditional discretionary system. One might argue that the fact-finding in a presumptive guidelines system is more closely analogous to fact-finding in a traditional system than it is to the fact-finding involved with the New Jersey hate-crimes law and similar statutes that raise the overall maximum punishment that can be imposed in a case.

However, the Supreme Court laid such arguments to rest in *Blakely v. Washington*, 542 U.S. 296 (2004). Blakely pled guilty in a Washington court to kidnapping his estranged wife. State law provided for a maximum sentence of 10 years for this offense, but Washington's presumptive guidelines prescribed a "standard range" of 49–53 months. The judge could sentence above the range, but only if he or she found that "substantial and compelling reasons" justified "an exceptional sentence." Washington law further identified a list of aggravating factors that could meet this legal standard for an upward departure. In Blakely's case, the judge did find one of the statutory aggravators, "deliberate cruelty," and thus imposed an above-range sentence of 90 months.

On appeal, the United States Supreme Court invalidated the enhanced sentence, holding that 53 months, not 10 years, was the "statutory maximum" for *Apprendi* purposes. More generally, the Court clarified that the maximum is the highest sentence that a judge may lawfully impose "*solely on the basis of the facts reflected in the jury verdict or admitted by the defendant.*" 542 U.S. at 303 (emphasis in original). In a presumptive system like Washington's, legal constraints on the judge's discretion confine the judge to the standard guidelines range unless some additional aggravating fact is found beyond those facts constituting the elements of the offense. Under *Blakely*, the defendant now has a Sixth Amendment right to a jury trial regarding such aggravating facts (such as the fact at issue in *Blakely* itself, that is, whether the defendant acted with "deliberate cruelty"). Since a judge, not a jury, made this determination as to Blakely, his sentence could not be elevated above the guidelines range on that basis.

At the same time, *Blakely* also made clear that the prosecution and defense may avoid jury factfinding in the sentencing process if the defendant executes a valid waiver of a jury trial and agrees to be sentenced by the court, or if both sides stipulate to the relevant enhancing facts. *See generally* Joanna Shepherd, Blakely's *Silver Lining: Sentencing Guidelines, Judicial Discretion, and Crime*, 58 HAST. L. J. 533 (2007).

Shortly after *Blakely*, to the surprise of few observers, the Supreme Court found that the federal guidelines system was also operating in violation of *Apprendi*. *United States v. Booker*, 543 U.S. 220 (2005), grew out of a drug trafficking case. A jury convicted Booker of possessing with the intent to distribute at least 50 grams of cocaine base (crack), which carried a statutory range of 10 years to life. The guidelines specified a range of 210–262 months for a person with Booker's criminal history who was convicted of trafficking in 50 grams of crack. However, at the sentencing hearing, a judge found by a preponderance of the evidence that Booker had actually possessed an additional 566 grams of crack and had obstructed justice. Taking into account this "relevant conduct," the judge calculated a revised guidelines range of 360 months to life and accordingly imposed a 30-year prison term.

Although the case did not technically involve an upward departure from the guidelines range, the Court held the sentence enhancement in *Booker* was not distinguishable for *Apprendi* purposes from the departure in *Blakely*. In *Booker*, as in *Blakely*, there was a standard guidelines range associated with the offense of conviction, the judge found certain aggravating facts to be present, and on the basis of those facts imposed a sentence above the top of the standard range. The finding of an *Apprendi* violation thus flowed in a straightforward way from the logic of *Blakely*.

What was not so straightforward was the remedy chosen by the Supreme Court for the violation. The Court framed the problem as one of "severability." The Sentencing Reform Act of 1984 authorized the creation of the federal guidelines and gave them legal force through a complex set of provisions. In light of *Apprendi* and *Blakely*, the provision requiring judges to adhere to the guidelines in most cases could no longer stand as written. Should the whole Act then be overturned, or would it be more consistent with legislative intent simply to sever the unconstitutional portions, leaving the guidelines system otherwise intact? A sharply divided Supreme Court chose the latter option. Thus, under *Booker*, as we have already noted, federal judges must still calculate and consider the guidelines range, but are not subject to all of pre-*Booker* limitations on departures. The *Booker* Court characterized the new system as "advisory," but retained appellate review of sentences for "reasonableness." As the post-*Booker* regime has taken shape, it has perhaps seemed less of a purely advisory system than a sort of presumptive-advisory hybrid.

Notes

1. *State responses to* Apprendi *and* Blakely. States with presumptive guidelines have responded to the *Apprendi* line of decisions in two ways. Some have added a second jury factfinding process after the determination of guilt. The jury reconvenes and decides whether statutory aggravating or enhancing factors are present. For example, if the jurisdiction authorized an enhanced sentence for the presence of a loaded weapon at a crime, the jury would first find guilt, then reconvene to

determine whether the defendant had a loaded weapon at the crime scene. The second approach is to replicate the *Booker* remedy, making state guidelines advisory rather than mandatory and thus eliminating the need to involve a jury in the sentencing process.

2. *California*. In *Cunningham v. California*, 549 U.S. 270 (2007), the Supreme Court applied the *Apprendi* line of reasoning to invalidate California's enhanced sentencing provisions enacted under its 1977 Determinate Sentencing Law. The statutory scheme, as implemented by court rules, required judges to sentence convicted felons to one of three terms (designated respectively as the "lower," the "middle," and the "upper") for any given crime. The middle term, also designated as the "presumptive" term, was to be imposed unless the judge found either that mitigating factors justified the lower term, or that aggravating factors justified the upper term. Assessing the presence or absence of these factors required the judge to engage in factfinding about the defendant and the offense.

Following *Apprendi* and its progeny, the Court held that Cunningham had been sentenced to the upper term on the basis of constitutionally impermissible factfinding by the sentencing judge: "Because the [California Determinate Sentencing Law] authorizes the judge, not the jury, to find facts permitting an upper term sentence, the system cannot withstand measurement under our Sixth Amendment precedent." *Id.* at 871.

3. *Appellate review in the federal system after* Booker. *Booker* established a new system of "reasonableness" review of federal sentences, but the Supreme Court's initial discussion of the system seemed to raise more questions than it answered. The Court has since returned to the subject on several occasions. In this line of cases, the Court has seemingly tried to strike a balance. On the one hand, the Court has wanted to preserve a meaningful role for the guidelines in federal sentencing. But, on the other hand, the Court has also wanted to move the intermediate courts of appeals away from the role of guidelines enforcers that they had played pre-*Booker*—a role that risks giving the guidelines more presumptive weight than is constitutionally permissible in the absence of jury fact-finding.

A trilogy of 2007 cases substantially clarified matters. First, in *Rita v. United States*, 551 U.S. 338 (2007), the Court held that when reviewing federal sentences for reasonableness, appellate courts *may* (but are not required to) apply a rebuttable presumption of reasonableness in favor of a sentence falling within a properly calculated guidelines range. However, the converse does not apply—appellate courts are *not* to presume that a sentence that falls *outside* of the guidelines is *unreasonable*.

Second, in *Kimbrough v. United States*, 552 U.S. 85 (2007), the Court indicated that a sentencing judge may deviate from a guidelines range even on the basis of a policy disagreement with the guidelines. After Kimbrough's conviction of crack cocaine and weapons offenses, the trial judge imposed a sentence of 15 years (the minimum allowable by statute), rather than adhering to the guideline range of 19 to 22 years, reflecting the judge's stated disagreement with the guidelines' highly controversial 100:1 crack-to-powder cocaine ratio (that is, treating one gram of crack as the equivalent of 100 grams of powder, which was widely criticized as racially discriminatory). On appeal, the Fourth Circuit reversed, holding that imposing a sentence "outside the guidelines range is *per se* unreasonable when it is based on a disagreement with the sentencing disparity for crack and powder cocaine offenses." However, the Supreme Court rejected this reasoning, determining that the Fourth Circuit's approach gave too much weight to the "advisory" guidelines.

Third, and finally, the Court further elaborated on the role of the guidelines in reasonableness review in *Gall v. United States*, 552 U.S. 38 (2007). In this case, the Court upheld as reasonable the sentencing judge's downward variance from the guidelines range of 30–37 months in prison to 36 months of probation. The judge had particularly cited the defendant's voluntary withdrawal from an ecstasy distribution conspiracy and the fact that he had lived productively and crime-free for years prior to being charged for his role in the conspiracy. The Supreme Court's opinion in *Gall* serves as a virtual primer both for sentencing courts in applying and varying from the federal guidelines, and for appellate courts in reviewing federal sentences:

> [A] district judge must give serious consideration to the extent of any departure from the Guidelines and must explain his conclusion that an unusually lenient or an unusually harsh sentence is appropriate in a particular case with sufficient justifications. . . .
>
> In reviewing the reasonableness of a sentence outside the Guidelines range, appellate courts may therefore take the degree of variance into account and consider the extent of a deviation from the Guidelines. We reject, however, an appellate rule that requires "extraordinary" circumstances to justify a sentence outside the Guidelines range. We also reject the use of a rigid mathematical formula that uses the percentage of a departure as the standard for determining the strength of the justifications required for a specific sentence.
>
> . . . [A] district court should begin all sentencing proceedings by correctly calculating the applicable Guidelines range. As a matter of administration and to secure nationwide consistency, the Guidelines should be the starting point and the initial benchmark. The Guidelines are not the only consideration, however. Accordingly, after giving both parties an opportunity to argue for whatever sentence they deem appropriate, the district judge should then consider all of the [statutory sentencing] factors to determine whether they support the sentence requested by a party. In so doing, he may not presume that the Guidelines range is reasonable. He must make an individualized assessment based on the facts presented. If he decides that an outside-Guidelines sentence is warranted, he must consider the extent of the deviation and ensure that the justification is sufficiently compelling to support the degree of the variance. We find it uncontroversial that a major departure should be supported by a more significant justification than a minor one. After settling on the appropriate sentence, he must adequately

> explain the chosen sentence to allow for meaningful appellate review and to promote the perception of fair sentencing....
>
> Regardless of whether the sentence imposed is inside or outside the Guidelines range, the appellate court must review the sentence under an abuse-of-discretion standard. It must first ensure that the district court committed no significant procedural error, such as failing to calculate (or improperly calculating) the Guidelines range, treating the Guidelines as mandatory, failing to consider the [statutory sentencing] factors, selecting a sentence based on clearly erroneous facts, or failing to adequately explain the chosen sentence—including an explanation for any deviation from the Guidelines range. Assuming that the district court's sentencing decision is procedurally sound, the appellate court should then consider the substantive reasonableness of the sentence imposed under an abuse-of-discretion standard. When conducting this review, the court will, of course, take into account the totality of the circumstances, including the extent of any variance from the Guidelines range.... It may consider the extent of the deviation, but must give due deference to the district court's decision that the [statutory] factors, on a whole, justify the extent of the variance. The fact that the appellate court might reasonably have concluded that a different sentence was appropriate is insufficient to justify reversal of the district court.

552 U.S. at 46–51.

Do you think the *Gall* formulation gives due regard to the constitutional rights recognized in *Apprendi* and *Blakely*? How might you argue to the contrary? Note that the Court in *Gall* might have simply said, "Advisory means advisory. Trial judges are free to select a sentence anywhere they wish within the statutory range, without regard to the guidelines. And, in reviewing the reasonableness of sentences, appellate courts may not use the guidelines as a benchmark." Would that have been a better approach? Do you think defense lawyers and prosecutors would tend to answer that question differently?

[iii] Application of *Apprendi* to Mandatory Minimums

In *Alleyne v. United States.*, 570 U.S. 99 (2013), the Supreme Court, applying the rationale of *Apprendi*, held that any fact which increases a mandatory minimum sentence is an "element that must be submitted to the jury." In that case, the trial judge imposed a mandatory minimum sentence of seven years on the basis of the judge's finding that the defendant had "brandished" a firearm in the course of a store robbery. The Court determined that enhancing the defendant's sentence in this manner, without submitting the "element" of "brandishing" to the jury to find beyond a reasonable doubt, violated the defendant's Sixth Amendment rights.

[4] Sentence Reduction by Trial Court

After a trial court imposes a sentence, most jurisdictions permit that same judge to reduce the sentence within a certain period after imposition. This practice is usually justified as permitting the court to receive new information or to reprocess old information. Many jurisdictions follow the former federal rule and permit the court to lower the sentence within 120 days of its imposition, although other time limits are also used. *See, e.g.*, Fla. R. Crim. P. 3.800(c) (60 days); Me. R. Crim. P. 35(c) (one year, on grounds that original sentence was influenced by a mistake of fact which existed at time of sentencing).

Should the rules be more flexible with respect to the timing of motions? For instance, a defendant who is several years into a lengthy term might be able to present compelling evidence of rehabilitation, but it would be too late to move for a reduced sentence in most jurisdictions. The question was not so important when most prisoners could obtain release from a parole board that was empowered to consider rehabilitative progress. However, in a jurisdiction that has embraced determinate sentencing, there would seem a greater need for judges to be able to revise sentences based on new information throughout the term of imprisonment. *See* Cecelia Klingele, *Changing the Sentence Without Hiding the Truth: Judicial Sentence Modification as a Promising Method of Early Release*, 52 Wm. & Mary L. Rev. 465 (2010).

In the federal courts, the judge may reduce a sentence for a defendant's substantial assistance in investigating or prosecuting another person. Ordinarily, the government must move for this reduction within one year after the sentence is imposed, but more time is possible when appropriate. Fed. R. Crim. P. 35(b).

Sometimes a court erroneously imposes a sentence that is not authorized by law. For example, the court could mistakenly impose a seven-year sentence on an offender when a five-year sentence was the maximum permitted by statute. Most jurisdictions permit this improper sentence to be corrected, even beyond the term permitted by rule or statute for a sentence reduction.

[5] Appellate Review

Despite the obvious importance of the judge's sentencing decision, appellate courts in many American jurisdictions have been reluctant to second-guess the trial judge's (or jury's) selection of a sentence. Prior to the adoption of the federal sentencing guidelines, federal courts simply refused to review most sentencing issues. Sometimes this refusal led to sweepingly broad statements. *See, e.g.*, *Dorszynski v. United States*, 418 U.S. 424, 431 (1974) ("[O]nce it is determined that a sentence is within the limitations set forth in the statute under which it is imposed, appellate review is at an end"). Nonetheless, even federal courts reviewed some issues in sentencing.

Many state courts continue to follow this tradition and refuse to overturn a trial court's sentence unless there has been an "abuse of discretion" or even a "gross abuse of discretion," standards that give great deference to the trial court's decision and rarely lead to an appellate reversal. *See generally* Michael O'Hear, *Appellate Review of Sentences: Reconsidering Deference*, 51 Wm. & Mary L. Rev. 2123 (2010).

The American Bar Association recommends that state legislatures authorize appellate courts to review sentences, at the initiative of either the defendant or the prosecution. The reviewing court should be authorized to (1) affirm the sentence, (2) reverse the sentence and remand to the original sentencing court for resentencing, or (3) "substitute for the sentence under review any other disposition that was available to the sentencing court." STANDARDS FOR CRIMINAL JUSTICE §§ 18-8.1(a), 8.3, 8.4(a) (3d ed. 1994).

The picture tends to be a bit different in jurisdictions with sentencing guidelines, especially presumptive guidelines. As we have seen, particularly in the pre-*Booker* federal system, appellate courts can take on the role of guidelines enforcers, ensuring that trial judges truly satisfy the applicable legal standards for departures. However, as we have also seen, rigorous enforcement of a guidelines system can create Sixth Amendment problems if the system does not include jury fact-finding for aggravating sentencing factors.

Can the government appeal a sentence as unduly lenient? Yes, in the federal system and in many states. And if the government succeeds in winning a resentencing, the Double Jeopardy Clause does not prevent a harsher punishment the second time around. *See United States v. DiFrancesco*, 449 U.S. 117 (1980).

[6] Good Time, Parole, and Supervised Release

The sentencing judge determines the sentence that the offender could serve, but in many jurisdictions, the judge only controls the outer limits of the sentence the defendant actually will serve. The exact length of time that the defendant will actually serve is usually determined by a mix of three factors. First, the judge sets the maximum (and sometimes minimum) sentence.

[a] Prison Credits

Second, the correctional authorities are usually authorized by statute to reduce that sentence by giving various forms of credit. For example, many jurisdictions give prisoners "good time" credits, which reduce the maximum (and sometimes minimum) sentence for good behavior while in prison. Other credits may be given for educational achievement (perhaps a sentence reduction for earning a high school, college, or vocational degree) and participation in certain prison programs (giving blood, fighting forest fires). Sometimes prison overcrowding problems also result in sentence reductions through an emergency release provision in state law.

[b] Parole

The third factor in determining the length of time that will actually be served is the parole process. As discussed earlier in this chapter, there was a movement toward determinate sentencing across the United States in the late twentieth century, but parole remains available today in most states, even if in less generous form than a generation ago.

Hearing. Ordinarily, the decision is made after a *parole hearing* in which the offender is present and provided an opportunity to argue in favor of release. Counsel is usually permitted but is not constitutionally required. The parole board will review the offense (perhaps including the views of the victim, prosecutor, and even sentencing judge), the offender's prison record, the recommendations of prison officials, and other relevant data. If the offender is paroled, he or she usually will serve the remainder of the sentence under the supervision of a *parole officer*, a state-paid counselor who in many jurisdictions also has police powers.

Conditions. The offender will be subject to various *parole conditions.* The conditions are similar to probation conditions and may include such items as committing no crimes, refraining from getting intoxicated, submitting to drug testing, holding a job, supporting dependents, meeting with a parole officer at regular intervals, remaining in a certain geographical area unless given permission to leave, and staying away from certain people (perhaps the victim of the original crime).

Revocation. Violation of a parole condition can cause the offender to be subject to revocation proceedings before the parole board (or sometimes the courts) and to be reincarcerated for all or part of the unexpired prison term. Due process requires that parolees, like probationers, be afforded a hearing prior to the revocation of their parole. Indeed, two hearings—a preliminary probable-cause-type hearing and a final revocation hearing—are often required under *Morrissey v. Brewer*, 408 U.S. 471 (1972). At the revocation hearing, the offender's rights are much less comprehensive than at a criminal trial. *See, e.g., Penn. Bd. of Probation v. Scott*, 524 U.S 357 (1998) (parole boards need not exclude evidence obtained in violation of the Fourth Amendment).

Supervised release. When parole is eliminated, the usual practice, as exemplified by the federal system, is to substitute a system of *supervised release.* Under this approach, at the time of the initial sentencing the offender is given both a prison term and a specific period of supervised release to be served after completing the prison term. *See* 18 U.S.C. § 3583. A person on supervised release, like a parolee, is subject to a number of release conditions. Violation of these terms of release can subject the releasee to another term of prison. The primary difference between supervised release and parole is that the judge, at the time of sentencing, determines the duration of supervised release while the parole board, a branch of the executive department, decides when the offender is to be paroled after considering the offender's behavior in prison. *See generally* Neil P. Cohen, The Law of Probation and Parole (2d ed. 1999); Fiona Doherty, *Indeterminate Sentencing Returns: The Invention of Supervised Release*, 88 N.Y.U. L. Rev. 958 (2013).

[7] Executive Sentencing Review: Clemency and Pardons

Although sentencing is normally regarded as the bailiwick of the judicial branch of government, the executive branch plays a role as well. For example, the executive branch ordinarily handles the parole granting process. Another area is executive clemency. Both federal and state constitutions authorize the executive to grant some form of *executive clemency. See generally* KATHLEEN DEAN MOORE, PARDONS: JUSTICE, MERCY AND THE PUBLIC INTEREST (1989).

The nomenclature for this process and procedural details vary considerably among jurisdictions and may include the terms *pardon, commutation, reprieve,* and *remission.* In general, federal or state constitutional provisions authorize the President or Governor to reduce all or part of a sentence, to delay implementation of a sentence, or to absolve the offender from all consequences of conviction. Sometimes the chief executive's decision must be based on the recommendation of a panel or board.

The Supreme Court has not mandated precise procedures that must be followed by an executive in considering an application for clemency. *See, e.g., Ohio Adult Parole Auth. v. Woodard,* 523 U.S. 272 (1998). Indeed, a gubernatorial or presidential grant or denial of clemency is typically not subject to any form of judicial review.

Although the various forms of executive clemency are seldom used in most jurisdictions, they have occasionally been relied on in some specific contexts. One use is to correct wrongful convictions, such as when new evidence shows that a long-time prisoner, perhaps now deceased, was actually innocent of the charges. Another is to spare judicial resources. For example, in some jurisdictions, when the death penalty statute was declared unconstitutional, the sentences of many capital offenders were commuted to life imprisonment, which obviated the need for a lot of resentencing hearings. A third use is to recognize unique circumstances that make a change in sentence appropriate. Thus, a life prisoner with terminal cancer may be given executive clemency to spend the last weeks of life at home, or an elderly prisoner with an exemplary prison record may be given executive clemency to shorten a very long sentence imposed 50 years earlier. *See* Carol Jacobsen et al., *Battered Women, Homicide Convictions, and Sentencing: The Case for Clemency,* 18 HAST. WOMEN'S L.J. 321 (2007).

Conditions of release. Sometimes a grant of executive clemency is given subject to the prisoner's adherence to a list of conditions of release, similar to parole and probation. For example, a governor may grant a pardon or commute a sentence on the condition that the released offender commit no more felonies, support dependents, and refrain from involvement in a certain business. A violation of such a condition can lead to a revocation of executive clemency and a return to prison.

Clemency decisions of governors and presidents are often politically charged and controversial. Examples include President Ford's pardon of former President Nixon even in the absence of any criminal prosecution of the former president, President Clinton's end-of-term pardons of several allegedly "well-connected" individuals, and President George W. Bush's commutation of the sentence of a former vice-presidential aide, Lewis I. "Scooter" Libby, sparing him from serving any period of imprisonment. *See generally* Margaret Love, *Reinventing the President's Pardon Power,* 20 FED. SENT'ING. RPTR. 5 (2007); Molly Gill, *Into the Bottomless*

Black Box: The Prisoner's Perspective on the Commutation Process, 20 FED. SENT'ING. RPTR. 16 (2007).

E. Ethical Issues in Sentencing

Sentencing, like every other issue in criminal practice, presents ethical issues for both the prosecutor and defense lawyer. The different responsibilities for the two create slightly different obligations.

[1] Defense Counsel

For the defense lawyer, recall that *Strickland v. Washington*, 466 U.S. 668 (1984), establishes the standard for the Sixth Amendment's guarantee of the effective assistance of counsel in sentencing matters. In *Strickland* the defendant was sentenced to death for three homicides. He sought to have the sentence overturned because of defense counsel's inadequate representation during the sentencing hearing. The Supreme Court held that the key consideration is "whether counsel's conduct so undermined the proper functioning of the adversarial process that the trial cannot be relied on as having produced a just result." The *Strickland* Court adopted a two-pronged test.

Deficient performance. First, the defendant must show that counsel's performance was "deficient." This means that defense counsel acted unreasonably under prevailing professional norms. Professional standards are guides but not dispositive. Counsel's conduct must be judged in the context of the particular case. There is a presumption that counsel was adequate.

Prejudice. The second *Strickland* prong is that counsel's deficient performance must have been prejudicial to the defense. Prejudice is presumed if counsel has an actual conflict of interest that adversely affected his or her performance. In other situations, the defendant can prove prejudice by showing a reasonable probability that, but for the lawyer's unprofessional errors, the result of the proceeding would have been different. Counsel's defective representation that results in an increase in a prison term is prejudicial under *Strickland*. *Glover v. United States*, 531 U.S. 198 (2001).

Applying this test in *Strickland*, the Supreme Court found no Sixth Amendment violation. The defendant, against the advice of defense counsel, had pled guilty. During the plea proceedings, the defendant accepted responsibility for the homicides, and stated he had no significant prior criminal record and was under extreme emotional disturbance at the time of the offense. The trial judge seemed sympathetic. At the subsequent sentencing hearing, defense counsel devoted little effort to finding character witnesses and did not request a psychiatric examination. The defense lawyer explained this as a strategic decision. Since helpful information was relayed to the seemingly sympathetic judge during the guilty plea procedure, counsel thought that it would be better to present no more information on those points at sentencing. He did not request a presentence report because he feared it would be harmful in its inclusion of the defendant's criminal history. By relying heavily on the earlier plea proceedings, defense counsel also prevented the prosecution from cross-examining the defendant and from bringing in pro-prosecution psychiatric expert testimony.

The Supreme Court found that counsel's performance was not ineffective under the two-pronged test. The decision to rely on the guilty plea procedure was professionally reasonable under the particular circumstances and the defendant could not prove that counsel's performance, even if deficient, was prejudicial.

The opposite result was reached in another extraordinary capital case involving a homicide during the course of a burglary. In *Horton v. Zant*, 941 F.2d 1449 (11th Cir. 1991), at the closing argument during the sentencing hearing the defense counsel actually told the jury:

> [T]he one you judge is not a very good person.... I ask you for the life of a worthless man. And, the prosecutor's closing made me hate my client. But then I... try to be reasonable about the whole situation; and I don't hate him as much... Mr. Briley [the prosecutor] has admirably told you just exactly why it is that Jimmy Lee [the defendant] has got to die. And it becomes my turn to try and explain to you why you don't have to say he's got to die.... I find my task virtually impossible.... Maybe Mr. Briley is right, maybe he is not. Maybe he ought to die, but I don't know.

Id. at 1462.

Defense counsel also introduced no mitigating evidence and called no witnesses at the sentencing proceeding on the mistaken theory that such evidence was only helpful in torture cases. The appellate court found defense counsel's performance at the sentencing hearing to be below the *Strickland* standard. *See also Lewis v. Lane*, 832 F.2d 1446 (7th Cir. 1987) (reversal for stipulating existence of four nonexistent prior felony convictions that affected sentence); *United States v. Phillips*, 210 F.3d 345 (5th Cir. 2000) (reversal because defense counsel did not correct erroneous application of sentencing guidelines that resulted in enhanced sentence).

Conflict of interest. Mickens v. Taylor, 535 U.S. 162 (2002), addressed the question, as articulated by Justice Breyer, whether the defendant may receive the death penalty "after [the state of Virginia] appointed to represent him as his counsel a lawyer, who at the time of the murder, was representing the very person Mickens was accused of killing." The majority expressed the issue somewhat differently. To them the question was "what a defendant must show in order to demonstrate a Sixth Amendment violation where the trial court fails to inquire into a potential conflict of interest about which it knew or reasonably should have known." Relying upon *Cuyler v. Sullivan*, 446 U.S. 335 (1980), the Court ruled that a defendant must demonstrate that a conflict of interest actually affected the adequacy of his representation. That is, prejudice under *Strickland* will be presumed only if the conflict sufficiently affected the attorney's performance. Here, because that finding had not been made and because the defendant did not establish prejudice, no relief was granted.

Failure to present mitigating evidence. In *Williams v. Taylor*, 529 U.S. 362 (2000), the Court held that a denial of effective assistance of counsel is established when attorneys fail to investigate and present substantial mitigating evidence during the sentencing phase of a capital murder trial. Simply stated, at the defendant's sentencing hearing, his lawyer failed to discover and present any significant mitigating evidence. Indeed, the defense attorney's closing argument was devoted to explaining that it was difficult to find a reason why the jury should spare Williams's life.

The Court found a Sixth Amendment violation under *Strickland*. The Court pointed out in considerable detail evidence that could have been discovered by the defense attorney that would have been relevant for mitigation purposes, and held that the failure to pursue this evidence could not be justified as a reasonable tactical decision. The Court further concluded that the lawyer's unprofessional service prejudiced the defendant within the meaning of *Strickland*:

> Mitigating evidence unrelated to dangerousness may alter the jury's selection of penalty, even if it does not undermine or rebut the prosecution's death-eligibility case. [The Virginia Supreme Court] failed to accord appropriate weight to the body of mitigation evidence available to trial counsel. . . . The entire postconviction record, viewed as a whole and accumulative of mitigation evidence presented originally, raised a "reasonable probability that the result of the sentencing proceeding would have been different" if competent counsel had presented and explained the significance of all the available evidence.

Id. at 398–99.

By contrast, the Court considered similar facts, but denied relief in *Wood v. Allen*, 558 U.S. 290 (2010). The Court observed in *Allen* that a failure to develop or present mitigating evidence at the penalty phase of a death penalty trial will not always be held to be ineffective assistance of counsel. And in that case, the Court upheld as "not unreasonable in light of the evidence presented" the state court's determination that the failure to present mitigating evidence of the defendant's mental deficiencies was the result of a strategic decision to focus on other defenses, rather than ineffective assistance of counsel.

In sum. In general, the cases interpreting the Sixth Amendment provide little specific guidance for the criminal defense lawyer at sentencing. The American Bar Association's Standards for Criminal Justice are only slightly more helpful. They obligate the defense attorney to become familiar with the available sentencing alternatives and the judge's sentencing practices, and to ensure that the court and prosecution have information helpful to the accused. Defense counsel at the sentencing hearing is acting as an advocate for the defendant. Accordingly, counsel "should present to the court any ground which will assist in reaching a proper disposition favorable to the accused." STANDARDS FOR CRIMINAL JUSTICE §4–8.1(b) (3d ed. 1993). The Commentary notes that at a sentencing hearing, defense counsel "is an advocate in a representative capacity participating in an adversary proceeding." Of course, the adversarial nature of the sentencing process does not authorize defense counsel to mislead the court or prosecution.

> Counsel may not present facts that are known to be false in a manner that creates an inference that they are true. Counsel may not, for example, present facts concerning the defendant's character that would suggest to the judge that the defendant does not have a prior record of crime if it is known that the defendant has such a record and that fact has not been disclosed to the court.

Id. §4–8.1 cmt. (3d ed. 1993).

[2] Prosecution

Given society's "get tough" attitude with respect to crime and punishment, a prosecutor may feel obligated to seek the most severe sentence possible in every case. This, it can be argued, is the prosecutor's function—to convey the sentiments of society through the criminal justice process. A prosecutor, especially one seeking re-election to office, could see and present this as evidence of prosecutorial effectiveness.

The American Bar Association's criminal justice standards squarely address this issue, declaring that the "severity of sentences imposed should not be used as a measure of a prosecutor's effectiveness." STANDARDS FOR CRIMINAL JUSTICE § 3-7.2(a) (4th ed. 2016). The standards go on to say that the "prosecutor should seek to assure that a fair and informed sentencing judgment is made, and to avoid unfair sentences and disparities." Id. § 3-7.2(c).

The ABA's standards also address how a prosecutor should function with respect to sentencing information:

> (a) The prosecutor should assist the court in obtaining complete and accurate information for use in sentencing, and should cooperate fully with the court's and staff's presentence investigations. The prosecutor should provide any information that the prosecution believes is relevant to the sentencing to the court and to defense counsel. A record of such information provided to the court and counsel should be made, so that it may be reviewed later if necessary. If material incompleteness or inaccuracy in a presentence report comes to the prosecutor's attention, the prosecutor should take steps to present the complete and correct information to the court and defense counsel.
>
> (b) The prosecutor should disclose to the defense and to the court, at or before the sentencing proceeding, all information that tends to mitigate the sentence and is known to the prosecutor, unless the prosecutor is relieved of this responsibility by a court order.

(c) Prior to sentencing, the prosecutor should disclose to the defense any evidence or information it provides, whether by document or orally, to the court or presentence investigator in aid of sentencing, unless contrary to law or rule in the jurisdiction or a protective order has been sought.

Id. § 3-7.3.

Note

Note that the ABA Standards impose an affirmative duty on the prosecutor to disclose information helpful to the defense relative to sentencing. Do they impose a similar duty on the defense lawyer (i.e., must he or she disclose evidence to the prosecution that would suggest a harsh sentence)? If not, what are the limits on the defense counsel's ability to keep harmful information secret?

Chapter 17

Post-Conviction Remedies

A. Introduction

After a criminal conviction (and occasionally even while charges are still pending), both the defendant and the prosecution may seek to have another court alter the conviction, sentence, or, less frequently, a judicial decision occurring before the conviction. Virtually every criminal conviction and sentence is subject to challenge by a complicated, often technical array of *post-conviction remedies*. For state offenders, sometimes both state and federal remedies are available.

This chapter provides a brief introduction to the primary post-conviction remedies and issues, but it is not designed as a complete treatment. *See generally* David G. Knibb, Federal Court of Appeals Manual (6th ed. 2013); Herbert Monte Levy, How to Handle an Appeal (4th ed. 2010); James S. Liebman & Randy Hertz, Federal Habeas Corpus Practice and Procedure (7th ed. 2016).

[1] Categories of Post-Conviction Remedies

[a] Direct Appeals and Collateral Challenges

In general, there are two types of post-conviction remedies: *direct appeals* and *collateral challenges*. A direct appeal requests a higher court to alter a lower court judge's ruling. Ordinarily, it is made shortly after the ruling or conviction and may be available "as a matter of right"—i.e., the higher court must entertain the appeal. "First instance" appeals, both state and federal, are allowed as matters of right.

Collateral challenges ordinarily are made after direct appeals have been exhausted and are often limited to certain issues, such as constitutional violations. Thus, collateral remedies may be available for a much narrower group of alleged errors than direct appeal. Collateral remedies, unlike direct appeals, are usually first sought from a trial court. Sometimes the various collateral remedies are referred to as "post-conviction" (as opposed to "appellate") remedies.

Procedural rules often dictate whether a convicted defendant will take a direct appeal or pursue collateral remedies. There may be a number of both statutory and common law collateral remedies theoretically available in a jurisdiction. Sometimes it is not clear whether the statutes have supplanted all or part of the common law remedies.

these lawsuits are successful when clearly established constitutional criminal procedural protections have been violated. *See, e.g., Monroe v. Pape*, 365 U.S. 167 (1961) (civil rights action for unreasonable search and seizure); *Robinson v. Solano County*, 278 F.3d 1007 (9th Cir. 2002) (officer pointing gun at head of unarmed, unresisting misdemeanor suspect constituted excessive force, actionable under § 1983); *Morgan v. Woessner*, 997 F.2d 1244 (9th Cir. *en banc* 1993) (unlawful airport detention not based on reasonable suspicion). *See generally* Joseph G. Cook & John L. Sobieski Jr., Civil Rights Actions (updated yearly).

[2] Federal and State Remedies

Both federal and state courts provide direct appeals and various remedies. The applicable procedure depends on whether the offender was convicted in a federal or state court.

Federal defendant. A criminal defendant convicted in a federal court will ordinarily pursue a federal direct appeal in the applicable United States Circuit Court of Appeals and may seek certiorari in the United States Supreme Court. If unsuccessful, the federal offender can file a § 2255 Motion to Vacate Sentence. 28 U.S.C. § 2255. A federal prisoner must use a § 2255 Motion rather than a habeas corpus petition if the former is available and adequate. *Id.* Both remedies are discussed below.

State defendant. A criminal defendant convicted in a state court will ordinarily take a direct appeal to the state's intermediate appellate court and then, if unsuccessful, to the state's highest court. The defendant can then ask the United States Supreme Court to review the state court's alleged violation of the federal laws applicable to the case.

After state direct appeal has been exhausted, the defendant may try both state and federal collateral procedures. Ordinarily, the state defendant will use the state collateral procedures first, although a state is not constitutionally required to offer state collateral remedies and the offender is not necessarily required to use them. After direct state appeals have been *exhausted*, the defendant may try federal collateral remedies, especially federal habeas corpus (per 28 U.S.C. § 2254, discussed below).

B. Direct Appeal

Both the criminal defendant and, to some extent, the prosecution may appeal certain judicial decisions in a criminal proceeding. The procedural requirements vary according to who is taking the appeal and at what point in the proceeding the appeal is sought.

In a criminal proceeding, the defendant usually appeals only after the court has ordered *final judgment*. This occurs after the court imposes sentence. In many jurisdictions, the prosecution may also appeal certain issues, though far fewer than the defendant. Usually the prosecution is authorized to appeal the sentence imposed on the defendant and decisions on some pretrial and post-trial motions. This limited appeal by the government does not conflict with the Double Jeopardy Clause of the Fifth Amendment to the United States Constitution. The Double Jeopardy Clause is discussed in Chapter 15.

Appellate review appears to be quite common in most countries. In England, although the right to appeal is well established, convictions are rarely overturned. Harry R. Dammer & Jay Albanese, Comparative Criminal Justice Systems (5th ed. 2014). In France, by contrast, criminal cases are appealed to the Court of Cassation. Although a court of last resort, this court, unlike the United States Supreme Court, does not have the authority to turn down cases.

While double jeopardy principles prohibit American prosecutors from appealing acquittals, such appeals are allowed in both Germany and Saudi Arabia. In the latter country, however, the appellate court is not permitted to overturn the judgment, but can only "return [it] for reconsideration to the lower court." *Id.* at 220.

[1] Limits on Appellate Review

[a] Mootness

As discussed further below with regard to habeas corpus, appellate courts will routinely dismiss a criminal appeal that has become *moot.* Although some decisions hold that this occurs when the defendant has completed service of the sentence, other decisions take a broader view of mootness and permit an appeal even after the sentence is served. In *Sibron v. New York*, 392 U.S. 40 (1968), the Supreme Court recognized that, for federal appellate purposes, a case is not moot in several post-sentence situations. First, it is not moot if it could not be appealed before expiration of the sentence. This rule is especially important for minor offenses where the sanctions are minimal. Second, and more importantly, a case is not moot in federal court if, under either state or federal law, additional penalties or disabilities could still be imposed because of the offense. In *Sibron*, the Court noted that the conviction being appealed could cause the offender to be impeached in a later case or have a sentence increased if he were to recidivate. *Sibron* virtually eliminated the doctrine of mootness in federal criminal appeals since some kind of disability is a possible consequence of virtually every criminal conviction. For example, a criminal conviction always raises the possibility that the accused will be denied a professional license, life or health insurance, a loan, the opportunity to run for certain elective offices, the right to serve on a jury, or the right to vote. *See, e.g.*, *Minnesota v. Dickerson*, 508 U.S. 366 (1993) (case not moot even though charges were dismissed under diversion program; dismissed charges could be used in future to increase sanction for future crime).

Many states have followed the *Sibron* approach, although some require proof that the appellant will suffer a particular disability from the conviction. The matter is more complicated if the offender has a previous conviction that could also cause some disability. Some states require the appellant to prove that the second conviction will have adverse consequences apart from those already caused by the first offense.

[b] Failure to Raise Issue at Trial and Plain Error

A maxim of appellate practice is that an appellate court will only consider an issue if it was first raised at trial. This maxim, commonly referred to as the *contemporaneous exception rule*, is often justified on the basis of either (1) a waiver or (2) forfeiture of the right to raise the issue on appeal. This widely recognized rule serves the policy of judicial efficiency. If the trial court corrects its own error or properly decides the issue in question, the time-consuming and expensive process of appellate reversal and retrial may be unnecessary. This serves society's interest in the prompt, efficient resolution of legal issues.

As with any rule barring appellate review, this rule has a number of exceptions that vary among the jurisdictions. One common exception is that at least some jurisdictional issues can be raised at any time, including on appeal. The theory is that the proceedings are void if the trial court had no jurisdiction over the case. Another exception is recognized where a procedural hurdle prevents raising an issue at trial. If a person is effectively barred from raising an issue at trial, appellate courts generally will overlook the failure and will hear the appeal.

The plain error rule. Many jurisdictions have a catch-all exception, permitting appellate courts to consider issues that were not raised at trial. Sometimes, the standard is expressed in terms of judicial economy (i.e., determining whether it would be more efficient for the appellate court to consider the issue despite the failure to bring it before the trial judge).

Federal appellate courts and most state courts are allowed to consider *plain errors or defects* affecting substantial rights that were not brought to the trial court's attention. Fed. R. Crim. P. 52(b). Often this is used to allow appeal of an issue that defense counsel negligently failed to raise properly at trial.

Some state plain error provisions limit the types of issues that are deemed "plain error," and some states do not recognize the plain error doctrine as a matter of their own law. *See Wicks v. State*, 606 S.W.2d 366 (Ark. 1980). While the federal rule is typical in not limiting the issues that can constitute plain error, the Supreme Court has stressed that the federal plain error rule should only be used sparingly to allow a defendant to pursue an issue on appeal that he or she did not properly raise at or before trial. Federal Rule of Criminal Procedure 52(b) simply states:

> **(b) Plain Error.** A plain error that affects substantial rights may be considered even though it was not brought to the court's attention.

Notes

1. *Error.* Rule 52(b) actually involves three issues. First, there must be an "error." This means that there must have been a deviation from a legal rule, and the right to complain about it was not waived by the failure to object at trial. A "waiver" occurs if the decision to not object was the product of an "intentional relinquishment or abandonment of a known right." *United States v. Olano*, 507 U.S. 725, 733 (1993) (quoting *Johnson v. Zerbst*, 304 U.S. 458, 464 (1938)). If there was no objection and no waiver, the matter is considered to be a "forfeiture" (rather than a waiver) under Rule 52(b). As explained by the Supreme Court, "[i]f a legal rule was violated . . . and if the defendant did not waive the rule, then there has been an 'error'; . . . despite the absence of a timely objection." *Id.* at 734.

2. *Plain.* The second issue under Rule 52(b) is whether the error was "plain," a word synonymous with the words "clear" or "obvious." *Olano*, 507 U.S at 734. This means that the mistake must have been clear under existing law. Rule 52(b) does not authorize reversal for errors that were based on law that did not exist at the time of the trial or at the time of initial appellate review, *see Henderson v. United States*, 568 U.S. 266 (2013), but are asserted under later case law. In other words, the plain error doctrine does not allow for retroactive application of later case law.

3. *Affecting substantial rights.* The third issue under Rule 52(b) is the most difficult for the defendant to establish. Rule 52(b) applies only to errors "affecting substantial rights." The Supreme Court has stated that "[n]ormally, although perhaps not in every case, the defendant must make a specific showing of prejudice to satisfy [this prong] of Rule 52(b)." *Olano*, 507 U.S. at 734. The alleged error "must have affected the outcome of the District Court proceedings." *Id.* Even if this prejudice test is satisfied, however, Rule 52(b) still does not require reversal. The express terms of the rule indicate that it is *discretionary* with the appellate court. According to the Supreme Court:

> The Court of Appeals should correct a plain forfeited error affecting substantial rights if the error "seriously affect[s] the fairness, integrity or public reputation of judicial proceedings."

Id. at 736, (quoting *United States v. Atkinson*, 297 U.S. 157, 160 (1936)). Some appellate decisions have held that the plain error should have been so important that it probably affected the outcome of the trial and a failure to correct it would result in a miscarriage of justice. *See also Puckett v. United States*, 556 U.S. 129 (2009) (plain error doctrine applied to forfeited claim where defendant tried to argue for the first time on appeal that government had violated the terms of the defendant's plea agreement; defendant failed to show substantial prejudice where prosecution at sentencing hearing withdrew from earlier agreement to recommend sentence reduction because defendant had committed a new crime while awaiting sentencing).

4. *Considered in context.* A plain error claim is usually considered in the context of the entire trial in order to assess the importance of the error. Accordingly, plain error claims are resolved on a case-by-case basis. Because of the difficulty of showing prejudice to the defendant, most plain error claims are rejected. *See, e.g.*, *United States v. Cotton*, 535 U.S. 625 (2002) (failure to allege quantity of cocaine in indictment for possession with intent to distribute; held erroneous but non-prejudicial); *United States v. Olano*, 507 U.S. 725 (1993) (alternate jurors attended

jury deliberations but did not participate); *United States v. Rena*, 981 F.2d 765 (5th Cir. 1993) (improper admission of cumulative evidence held not plain error).

5. *Plain error occasionally found.* In unusual cases, appellate courts do find plain error. *See, e.g., United States v. Carter*, 481 F.3d 601 (8th Cir. 2007) (plain error found where district court failed to impose a mandatory minimum sentence; error found to seriously affect substantial rights and the fairness, integrity, and public reputation of judicial proceedings, noting that "fairness concerns run both ways" and that prosecution, as well as defense, may invoke plain error rule on sentence appeal); *United States v. Watson*, 476 F.3d 1020 (D.C. Cir. 2007) (court's miscalculation of applicable federal sentencing guideline range held plain error which affected defendant's substantial rights); *but see Greenlaw v. United States*, 554 U.S. 237 (2008) (absent government appeal or cross-appeal of sentence, appellate court may not, on its own initiative, order increase in sentence based on plain error rule); *United States v. Hernandez*, 125 F.3d 859 (9th Cir. 1997, unpublished opinion) (prosecutor's comment on defendant's post-*Miranda* silence held plain error, but conviction still affirmed because evidence was sufficient to convict); *United States v. Mann*, 557 F.2d 1211 (5th Cir. 1977) (erroneous admission of unduly suggestive pretrial identification).

The decision of the Ninth Circuit in *Hernandez* is an apt illustration of the principle that reversal for plain error is not automatic, but rather is a matter committed to the court's discretion. The court there found all three required elements of the doctrine to be present, but denied relief in reliance on *Olano* because in its view, the error was not one that "seriously affected the fairness, integrity, or public reputation" of the proceedings in that case. Stated differently, "[only] if all three conditions are met, an appellate court may then exercise its discretion to notice a forfeited error." *Johnson v. United States*, 520 U.S. 461, 467 (1997) (internal quotations and citations omitted).

6. *Plain error applied to ex post facto claim.* In *United States v. Marcus*, 560 U.S. 258 (2010), the Supreme Court held that plain error analysis applies to a claim, raised for the first time on appeal, that the defendant was charged and convicted of forced labor and sex trafficking exclusively on the basis of conduct that predated enactment of the applicable statute (the Trafficking Victims Protection Act of 2000). The Second Circuit had held that under plain error review, "a retrial is necessary whenever there is any possibility, no matter how unlikely, that the jury could have convicted based exclusively on pre-enactment conduct." The Supreme Court rejected this approach, holding that *ex post facto* claims, like many other constitutional claims, may not be raised at any time and are not claims of "structural error" that require automatic reversal if meritorious. Rather, a belatedly raised *ex post facto* claim is subject to the four-part *Olano/Hernandez* analysis. The Court went on to conclude that the Second Circuit had failed to consider the third and fourth *Olano* factors (whether there was a reasonable probability that the error affected the outcome, and whether the error "seriously affect[ed] the fairness, integrity or public

reputation of judicial proceedings") in its plain error analysis. *Id.* at 262 (quoting from *Puckett v. United States*, 556 U.S. 129 (2009)). Therefore, the Court remanded the case for proper application of the four-part plain error test.

7. *Plain error applied to erroneous sentence calculation under U.S. Sentencing Guidelines.* In *Molina-Martinez v. United States*, 136 S. Ct. 1338 (2016), the defendant pleaded guilty to being unlawfully present in the United States after having been deported following an aggravated felony conviction. The sentencing court, unbeknownst to itself or to the prosecution or the defense, miscalculated the applicable sentencing range under the United States Sentencing Guidelines, and sentenced the defendant to 77 months imprisonment under a higher range than the correctly applicable range. The defendant first noticed the error during appeal to the Fifth Circuit, which refused to consider this newly raised issue. The Supreme Court applied *Olano*'s four-part analysis and determined that the defendant had not relinquished or abandoned the "unnoticed error," and remanded for resentencing, even though the defendant's 77-month sentence fell within *both* the original incorrectly applied range and the correct range.

Two years later, the Court applied *Molina-Martinez* in *Rosales-Mireles v. United States*, 138 S. Ct. 1897 (2018) by holding that a miscalculation of the correct guideline range at the time of sentencing calls for a court of appeals under Federal Rule of Criminal Procedure 52(b) to vacate the defendant's sentence under the plain error doctrine.

[c] Harmless Error and Automatic Reversal

If trials were required to be legally "perfect" in all respects, virtually every conviction would be reversed on appeal, resulting in the possibility of never-ending litigation and a paralyzed legal system. To prevent this absurd situation, every jurisdiction has adopted a *harmless error rule*, which means that trial errors will ordinarily not merit appellate reversal unless the error was somehow significant. The distinction between harmless errors and those sufficiently harmful to cause a reversal has produced varying standards and a vast amount of judicial and academic verbiage. Some errors are deemed so egregious that they will cause an *automatic reversal* without consideration of the actual impact on the proceedings, as discussed below.

The general rule followed in every jurisdiction is that a trial error that is "harmless" will not lead to appellate reversal. Federal Rule of Criminal Procedure 52(a), like Rule 52(b) (plain error), states this principle simply and generally:

> (a) Any error, defect, irregularity, or variance that does not affect substantial rights must be disregarded.

Notes

Sometimes it may be difficult to ascertain whether a particular error has affected substantial rights under this standard. The answer may depend upon whether the error was constitutional or not. Additionally, appellate courts typically will closely evaluate the entire case to assess the impact of the error. The harmless error rule applies to federal appeals and federal habeas corpus actions. *See Brecht v. Abrahamson*, 507 U.S. 619 (1993).

Nonconstitutional error. If the trial error at issue is one that does not involve a constitutional violation, the general standard of harmless error is expressed in many ways. One formulation is whether the error had a significant tendency to promote a guilty verdict. Another version is whether the error likely produced a guilty verdict.

There are myriad decisions where nonconstitutional errors have been deemed harmless. *See, e.g., United States v. Pridgen*, 518 F.3d 87 (1st Cir. 2008) (for nonconstitutional error, test is whether it is highly probable that the error did not affect the verdict; harmless error found when trial court may have erroneously excluded extrinsic evidence of a government witness's prior inconsistent statement).

In *United States v. Davila*, 569 U.S. 597 (2013) (discussed in Chapter 11), the trial judge improperly engaged in coercive plea discussions with the defendant, in violation of Federal Rule of Criminal Procedure 11(c)(1). Despite the clear violation of the Rule, the Supreme Court rejected a rule of automatic *vacatur* of guilty pleas obtained in violation of Rule 11(c)(1). Rather, the Court held that the defendant's motion to vacate his guilty plea was subject to the Rule 52(a) harmless error standard, and remanded for the lower courts to determine, in light of the full record, whether or not the defendant's "substantial rights" had been affected as a result of the Rule 11(c)(1) violation. The Court noted, however, that on remand "the prosecution bears the burden of showing harmlessness."

Constitutional error: In general. The rules change when the error is of constitutional dimension. In the leading case, *Chapman v. California*, 386 U.S. 18 (1967), the prosecutor violated the defendants' Fifth Amendment rights by commenting on their failure to testify at their joint trial for homicide. The petitioners argued that since the prosecutor deprived them of a constitutional right, the Supreme Court should reverse automatically and not apply harmless error analysis. The Court in *Chapman* agreed that there are some constitutional errors that merit automatic reversal, but also held that

> there may be some constitutional errors which in the setting of a particular case are so unimportant and insignificant that they can, consistent with the Federal Constitution, be deemed harmless, not requiring the automatic reversal of the conviction.

Id. at 22.

Trial v. "structural" errors. A key question is which constitutional violations are analyzed by harmless error standards and which result in automatic reversal without consideration of their impact. In *Arizona v. Fulminante*, 499 U.S. 279 (1991), the Court distinguished the two categories of errors by using a trial process-structure dichotomy. Constitutional violations merit harmless error analysis if they are "trial errors." This refers to an

> error which occurred during the presentation of the case to the jury, and which may therefore be quantitatively assessed in the context of other evidence presented in order to determine whether its admission was harmless beyond a reasonable doubt. In applying harmless-error analysis to these many different constitutional violations, the Court has been faithful to the belief that the harmless-error doctrine is essential to preserve the "principle that the central purpose of the criminal trial is to decide the factual question of the defendant's guilt or innocence, and promotes public respect for the criminal process by focusing on the underlying fairness of the trial rather than on the virtually inevitable presence of immaterial error.

Id. at 307–08 (quoting *Delaware v. Van Arsdall*, 475 U.S. 673, 681 (1986)).

Grave doubt regarding effect. In *O'Neal v. McAninch*, 513 U.S. 432 (1995), the United States Supreme Court further refined the harmless error standard in federal habeas corpus cases. In such cases, if the federal habeas judge is in "grave doubt" about whether a trial error of federal constitutional law had substantial and injurious effect or influence in determining the jury's verdict, the error is not harmless. This means that the risk of doubt is on the state, not the defendant. The Court rejected imposing a burden of proof on either party or using a presumption to resolve the issue.

Automatic reversal rule. The automatic reversal rule, on the other hand, is applied to errors that involve "structural defects in the constitution of the trial mechanism." *Fulminante*, 499 U.S. at 309. Such structural defects affect the framework within which the trial proceeds, as opposed to an error in the trial process itself. These structural errors violate a basic protection and defy measurement of their effect on a particular trial process. The Supreme Court has held that there is a strong presumption that constitutional errors are subject to the harmless error analysis. Which violations are in which category? The answers are not always intuitively obvious.

In *McCoy v. Louisiana*, 138 S. Ct. 1500 (2018), the Court in a 6–3 decision took the unusual step of ordering a new trial based on a structural error. During trial, defense counsel admitted to the jury that the defendant had committed the murders for which he was charged, based on the strategy that the admission was the best way to avoid the death penalty. That admission violated both the defendant's express instructions not to admit to the crimes, and the defendant's Sixth Amendment right to choose the objective of his defense. The latter violation was a structural error.

Constitutional error: harmless error analysis applied. Decisions after *Chapman v. California* have found that most constitutional violations are subject to harmless error analysis. *Fulminante*, 499 U.S. at 306–07, lists 17 examples of constitutional errors analyzed under the harmless error approach. Many involve errors in jury instructions, including overbroad jury instructions at a capital sentencing proceeding, an erroneous charge regarding a conclusive or rebuttable presumption, a misstatement of an element of the crime, and the failure to instruct on the presumption of innocence.

Other decisions cited in *Fulminante*, using harmless error analysis, deal with the erroneous admission or exclusion of evidence. Examples include the admission of evidence secured in violation of the Sixth Amendment right to counsel or the Fourth Amendment right to be free from an unreasonable search and seizure, and the exclusion of the defendant's testimony concerning the circumstances of a confession. *See, e.g., Hedgpeth v. Pulido*, 555 U.S. 57 (2008) (instructing jury on multiple theories of guilt, one of which is invalid, held subject to harmless error analysis, rather than structural error that would require automatic reversal).

Harmless error analysis has also been applied to errors in unduly restricting cross-examination on the issue of bias, improperly commenting on the defendant's silence, and the denial of counsel at a preliminary hearing.

In two 2015 decisions, the Supreme Court held that defense counsel's brief absence from trial and pretrial proceedings does not necessarily require automatic reversal. In *Davis v. Ayala*, 135 S. Ct. 2187 (2015), the Court held that any Sixth Amendment right-to-counsel violation resulting from the prosecution's ex parte (i.e., without defense counsel present) proffer of race-neutral reasons for its peremptory challenges striking all seven Hispanic and African-American prospective jurors during *voir dire* was harmless error, not requiring automatic reversal. Do you agree that the underlying claim in *Ayala*, that a right-to-counsel error during *voir dire* resulting in a *Batson* violation (see Chapter 13), should be subject to harmless error analysis? *See Arizona v. Fulminante*, 499 U.S. 279 (1991) (*Batson* errors require automatic reversal).

In *Woods v. Donald*, 135 S. Ct. 1372 (2015), the Court, *per curiam*, held that on habeas corpus review subject to the provisions of the Anti-Terrorism and Effective Death Penalty Act (discussed later in this chapter), the defendant's claim of ineffective assistance of counsel, stemming from his counsel's brief absence from the courtroom during a witness's testimony about his client's co-defendants, is not a structural error requiring automatic reversal, but instead is subject to harmless error review.

Harmless beyond a reasonable doubt. If the harmless error rule applies, what degree of harm must be shown before a conviction will be reversed? *Chapman v. California*, 386 U.S. 18 (1967), held that "before a federal constitutional error can be held harmless, the court must be able to declare a belief that it was harmless beyond a reasonable doubt." *Id.* at 24. Since the government benefitted from the alleged error, according to *Chapman* the government has the burden of proving "beyond a reasonable doubt that the error complained of did not contribute to the verdict obtained." *Id.* In assessing whether this test is satisfied, the reviewing court will look at the entire record *de novo.* If the appellate court cannot assess whether the error affected the trial, it is possible the error may be analyzed under the automatic-reversal standard rather than the harmless error rule. *See Sullivan v. Louisiana*, 508 U.S. 275 (1993). When the *Chapman* Court applied the harmless error test, it held that the prosecutor's improper comments about the defendant's silence at trial were not harmless beyond a reasonable doubt and reversed the conviction.

Constitutional error: no harmless error analysis—automatic reversal. Chapman v. California and later decisions have recognized that some constitutional violations are so egregious that they will always invalidate a criminal conviction, irrespective of proof of harm. As noted above, this category involves constitutional errors that relate to the structural integrity of the trial mechanism.

Arizona v. Fulminante, 499 U.S. 279 (1991), discussed above, listed a number of decisions holding that the constitutional errors were so fundamental that they were not subject to the harmless error approach. These include: the total deprivation of the right to trial counsel, the right to self-representation, and the right to a public trial, a biased judge, and the exclusion of members of the defendant's race from the grand jury. *See also United States v. Gonzalez-Lopez*, 548 U.S. 140 (2006) (erroneous disqualification of defendant's chosen trial counsel constitutes "structural error" requiring reversal of conviction, not subject to harmless error review; therefore "no additional showing of prejudice" is required); *Sullivan v. Louisiana*, 508 U.S. 275 (1993) (error in instructing jury on reasonable doubt causes automatic reversal without proof of harm).

Interestingly, *Fulminante* itself involved a 5–4 split, with the majority holding that harmless error analysis applies to the use of a coerced confession because it is a "trial process" rather than a "structural" error. Do you agree? If the use of a coerced confession is a "trial process" error subject to harmless error analysis, why is the exclusion of members of a person's race from the grand jury a structural error? Can't the grand jury error be "cured" by a subsequent fair trial using a properly selected trial jury where the accused is convicted by proof beyond a reasonable doubt?

[2] Appellate Structure

Article III of the Constitution allows for the creation of inferior courts, "as Congress may from time to time ordain and establish." U.S. Const. art. III. Congress, as we know, created in the federal system numerous trial courts as well as intermediate appellate courts to harmonize with the already-established Supreme Court. Most state systems have copied the federal model and provide intermediate courts between the lowest court and the Supreme Court. Generally, an intermediate court hears the first appeal in a criminal case.

In the relatively few states that do not have an intermediate appellate court, the first (and only) appeal goes directly to the state's highest court. In other states, some cases, such as death penalty cases, are appealed directly to the highest court, bypassing the intermediate appellate court. *E.g.*, N.Y. Crim. Proc. Law § 450.70; Idaho Code § 19-2827. Finally, some states' intermediate appellate courts have limited subject matter jurisdiction (e.g., civil cases are assigned to one appellate court and criminal cases to another). In most instances, decisions of each specialized appellate court may be appealed to the state's highest court.

[3] Types of Appeals by Criminal Defendant

[a] Appeals "As of Right"

Most appeals in criminal cases occur when a defendant appeals a conviction or sentence. Although the United States Supreme Court has long held that the constitution does not require a state to grant a criminal defendant an appeal, *Evitts v. Lucey*, 469 U.S. 387, 393 (1985), American jurisdictions routinely accord the defendant at least one "appeal as of right." Typically, the defendant must be informed of the right to appeal. *See, e.g.*, Fed. R. Crim. P. 32(j)(1). *See also* Fed. R. Crim. P. 58(c)(4) (appeals from misdemeanor convictions).

To some extent the concept of an "appeal as of right" is misleading, for not all convicted defendants who appeal actually receive full appellate consideration. In many jurisdictions an appellate court has the right to give a particular case less than full scrutiny via procedures such as summary affirmance with either only a brief opinion or no opinion at all, or deciding an appeal on the briefs only, without oral argument. The decision whether to grant full or truncated appellate review is generally based on whether the defendant has raised a substantial legal issue or, in some limited cases, a substantial factual issue that must be resolved by the appellate court. For example, an appellate court may give limited scrutiny to issues related to the sufficiency of evidence.

This right of appeal ordinarily does not extend in the same way to defendants who plead guilty or *nolo contendere* unless the jurisdiction has a conditional plea procedure. See Chapter 11 for a detailed discussion of conditional pleas. Also, the defendant who pleads guilty may, in some situations, be permitted to appeal the sentence imposed following the plea.

[i] The Decision Whether to Appeal

Although all convicted defendants have the right to file the notice of appeal once the conviction is final, many do not exercise that right because of the many factors that must be considered. The judge should inform the defendant of the right to appeal. Fed. R. Crim. P. 32(j)(1)(A), (B) (appeal conviction and sentence). Failure to provide this information is reversible error only if the defendant suffered prejudice. *Peguero v. United States*, 526 U.S. 23 (1999).

Defense counsel has an ethical obligation to explain all of these factors to the defendant to facilitate an informed decision of whether to appeal. The ultimate decision whether to appeal is made by the client. *See generally* American Bar Association, Standards for Criminal Justice §4-9.1(b) (4th ed. 2015).

One reason for foregoing an appeal, of course, is that the defendant is not dissatisfied with the result or has no real grounds to appeal. As discussed below, the defense attorney may consider the appeal "frivolous" and refuse to file it. Further, the defendant's appeal may be unsuccessful if it is based on an error that is "harmless," i.e., the error had no substantial effect on the outcome of the trial. Finally, the error alleged must have been preserved in the trial record or the error must be a "plain error."

Other factors that the defendant considering an appeal should explore are the wisdom of engaging a new attorney to handle the appeal, the costs of the appeal, and, most importantly, the possible adverse consequences of a *successful* appeal.

[ii] *North Carolina v. Pearce:* Harsher Sentence after Successful Appeal

An important factor in assessing whether to appeal is the possible result if the appeal is successful. Could the defendant actually be in *a worse* condition after winning the appeal? In *North Carolina v. Pearce*, 395 U.S. 711 (1969), the United States Supreme Court held that in some circumstances the defendant could actually receive a harsher sentence on retrial following a successful appeal or habeas corpus petition. *Pearce* involved several state defendants who were convicted of a crime and sentenced to prison. After their convictions were overturned on appeal, each was retried, convicted, and given a sentence that was harsher than that imposed in the first trial. Each defendant in *Pearce* filed a federal habeas corpus action alleging that the double jeopardy, equal protection, and due process guarantees bar the imposition of a more severe punishment after the retrial of a conviction that has been reversed.

The Supreme Court started its analysis by rejecting both the double jeopardy and equal protection claims. The Court noted that the federal Double Jeopardy Clause places no limit on the length of sentence following a retrial. After the first conviction is reversed by a higher court, the slate is "wiped clean" for purposes of double jeopardy and any lawful sentence may be imposed on retrial. The Court in *Pearce* also stated that equal protection is not violated if the defendant receives a harsher sentence on retrial. At the second trial, the offender could receive no sentence, a shorter sentence, the same sentence, or a longer sentence than imposed at the first trial. Because of these possibilities, the state has not established an invalid classification scheme for those who seek new trials.

Although the *Pearce* Court rejected the double jeopardy and equal protection arguments, it found part of the due process claim compelling. The Court held that the Due Process Clause prohibits the state from imposing a heavier sentence on retrial for the purpose of punishing those who use the courts to overturn a conviction. The harsher sanction creates a presumption of vindictiveness that the sentencing judge must overcome. According to *Pearce*:

> Due process of law, then, requires that vindictiveness against a defendant for having successfully attacked his first conviction must play no part in the sentence he receives after a new trial. And since the fear of such vindictiveness may unconstitutionally deter a defendant's exercise of the right to appeal or collaterally attack his first conviction, due process also requires that a defendant be freed of apprehension of such a retaliatory motivation on the part of the sentencing judge.

> In order to assure the absence of such a motivation, we have concluded that whenever a judge imposes a more severe sentence upon a defendant after a new trial, the reasons for his doing so must affirmatively appear. Those reasons must be based upon objective information concerning identifiable conduct on the part of the defendant occurring after the time of the original sentencing proceeding. And the factual data upon which the increased sentence is based must be made part of the record, so that the constitutional legitimacy of the increased sentence may be fully reviewed on appeal.

Id. at 725–26.

Notes

1. *Retroactivity. North Carolina v. Pearce* announced both substantive and procedure rules. The substantive rule is that due process bars actual judicial vindictiveness that results in a harsher sentence on retrial. The procedural rule establishes a rebuttable presumption that a harsher sentence is due to vindictiveness and must be justified on the basis of post-trial conduct. A subsequent Supreme Court decision held that the procedural rule is not retroactive. *Michigan v. Payne*, 412 U.S. 47 (1973). This rule was characterized as "prophylactic," designed to protect against possible vindictiveness. But *Pearce's* substantive rule banning retaliatory motivation in sentencing was considered a part of basic due process, not just a prophylactic rule, and was made retroactive. *Id.* at 55. Retroactivity principles are discussed in detail later in this chapter.

2. *Exceptions to Pearce: proof of vindictiveness.* The *Pearce* decision's concern with the possibility of vindictiveness has led subsequent Supreme Court decisions to create several exceptions where this possibility is either eliminated or minimized. According to the Supreme Court, *Pearce* applies only when there is a reasonable likelihood "that the increase in sentence is the product of actual vindictiveness on the part of the sentencing authority. Where there is no such reasonable likelihood, the burden remains upon the defendant to prove actual vindictiveness." *Alabama v. Smith*, 490 U.S. 794, 799 (1989). This means that the defendant can still bar the harsher sentence by proving this particular sentencing court was actually motivated by vindictiveness in imposing the harsher sentence.

3. *Harsher sentence imposed by jury.* Another exception to *Pearce* is when the second sentence is imposed by a jury rather than a judge. The issue appears infrequently today because the jury imposes sentences in very few American jurisdictions. In *Chaffin v. Stynchcombe*, 412 U.S. 17 (1973), a jury convicted the defendant of robbery and sentenced him to 15 years in prison. After his conviction was overturned because of an erroneous jury instruction, a second jury convicted him again and imposed a life sentence. The Supreme Court rejected the argument that the greater sentence was barred by *North Carolina v. Pearce.* The Court reasoned that *Pearce* did not apply because there is only a *de minimis* potential that the second jury's sentence was motivated by the vindictiveness barred by *Pearce.* Unlike a judge, a jury probably has no interest in discouraging appeals.

4. *First sentence imposed by jury, second by judge.* A third exception to *Pearce* was noted in a factually unique case when the first sentence was imposed by a jury and the harsher second sanction was exacted by a judge. In *Texas v. McCullough*, 475 U.S. 134 (1986), the defendant was convicted by a jury that sentenced him to 20 years in prison. After the trial judge granted the defendant's motion for a new trial, the defendant was convicted again by a jury but asked that the judge conduct the resentencing. The trial judge then sentenced the defendant to 50 years in prison. Based on these highly unusual facts, the Supreme Court held that *Pearce* did not bar a harsher sentence following the retrial.

First, the Court in *McCullough* found nothing in the record to suggest that this particular judge had a vindictive motive. The trial judge herself reversed the first conviction because of prosecutorial misconduct rather than judicial error. The Court refused to hold that this alone created the possibility that the trial judge would punish the defendant for bothering her with a second proceeding. Moreover, the defendant had asked the judge rather than the jury to impose the second sentence. This indicated that even the defense thought the judge capable of a fair decision. The mere fact that the defendant's desire to move for a new trial could be chilled by the possibility of a harsher sentence was rejected as an inadequate ground under *Pearce* to bar a greater sentence on retrial. Finally, even if *Pearce* applied, the Supreme Court in *McCullough* held that the trial court complied with *Pearce* in justifying the harsher sentence on new evidence about the crime that was not presented at the first trial. It should be noted that the new evidence was known to the authorities (though not the judge) at the first trial; the new material was not based on the defendant's conduct occurring after the trial. This is a subtle change from the *Pearce* Court's focus on the defendant's conduct *since* the first sentencing hearing.

5. *Harsher sentence after vacated guilty plea.* A related exception involves a harsher sentence imposed after a defendant pleads guilty, has the plea vacated, and is sentenced again after a trial. In *Alabama v. Smith*, 490 U.S. 794 (1989), the Supreme Court held that there is no presumption of vindictiveness when the first sentence followed a guilty plea but the second sentence occurred after a trial. The increased sanction is not likely to be the product of vindictiveness. Rather, the new sentence probably will be based on far more information (including the defendant's conduct during trial) than that available in the guilty plea proceeding. Also, the plea-based sentence may have been more lenient because of the defendant's willingness to accept responsibility for the crime.

6. *Different judges.* Some other courts have combined the Supreme Court decisions after *Pearce* to arrive at another exception: *Pearce* does not apply when different bodies or judges impose separate sentences because the chance of vindictiveness is minimal. *See, e.g., United States v. Lippert*, 740 F.2d 457 (6th Cir. 1984). Do you agree with the assumption that the chance of vindictiveness is remote when different judges impose the two sentences?

7. *Is the second sentence harsher?* One potential difficulty with implementing *Pearce* is determining whether the second sentence is actually harsher than the first. The

problem occurs when the two sentences are not expressed in the same "currency." For example, a three-year prison sentence is obviously harsher than a two-year prison sentence. But what about a three-year prison sentence versus a two-year jail term followed by five years on probation. The former sentence expires in three years while the latter will take seven years to complete. On the other hand, the former includes three years of incarceration while the latter demands only two. Which is harsher?

The problem is illustrated by *Gauntlett v. Kelley*, 658 F. Supp. 1483 (W.D. Mich. 1987), *aff'd*, 849 F.2d 213 (6th Cir. 1988), in which the defendant was convicted of several counts of child sex abuse. His first sentence was to five years' probation with the conditions that he must spend the first year in jail and submit to "chemical castration" for five years. After this sentence was overturned on appeal, the defendant was sentenced to a 5–15 year prison term. Assessing whether *Pearce* was violated because the second sentence was harsher than the first, the district judge candidly admitted that he did not know how to determine whether chemical castration was harsher than a substantial prison term. Since he could not conclude that it was harsher, he refused to find *Pearce v. North Carolina* applicable. Do you agree?

Comparing concurrent and consecutive sentences can also present difficulties in determining comparative severity. The Illinois Court of Appeals addressed this issue in *Illinois v. Walker*, 663 N.E.2d 148 (Ill. App. Ct. 1995). The defendant had initially been *consecutively* sentenced to 100 to 150 years for rape, 100 to 150 years for armed robbery and 19 to 20 years for attempted murder. After an appeal, the defendant received *concurrent* sentences of 100 to 300 years for each conviction. Illinois prohibited judges from imposing greater sentences on resentencing. The defendant argued and the court agreed that the increase in the defendant's sentences for his individual convictions was a violation of Illinois law, notwithstanding the fact that the total number of years he must actually serve did not increase.

8. *Prosecution's increase in charges at second trial. North Carolina v. Pearce* applies when a judge imposes a harsher sentence on retrial. Does it also apply to a *prosecutor* who, following a successful appeal, increases the charges that the appellant must face at the second trial? In *Blackledge v. Perry*, 417 U.S. 21 (1974), the defendant was charged with a misdemeanor assault stemming from a prison fight. After being convicted and receiving a six month sentence, he appealed the decision by requesting a trial *de novo* in accordance with state law. Prior to the new trial, the prosecutor obtained an indictment charging felony assault for the same fight that was the basis for the earlier misdemeanor conviction. He pled guilty to the new charge and was sentenced to five to seven years in prison. Citing *North Carolina v. Pearce*, the Supreme Court in *Blackledge* held that due process entitles an accused to pursue a statutorily-guaranteed right to a trial *de novo* without fear that the prosecution will retaliate by increasing the seriousness of the defendant's exposure at the second proceeding. This means that the *Pearce* presumption applies and the prosecution must explain a decision to increase the charges for defendants pursuing an appeal. *See also United States v. Goodwin*, 457 U.S. 368 (1982). Prosecutorial vindictiveness, including discussion of both *Blackledge* and *Goodwin*, is covered in Chapter 2.

Problem 17-1. When It Rains, It Pours

Fran was convicted of unarmed robbery. At the sentencing hearing, the government informed Judge Phillips that Fran had a charge of marijuana possession pending in another state. Since the marijuana charge had not been tried, Judge Phillips did not consider it and imposed a three-year sentence, with all but six months suspended. This means that Fran would serve six months in jail and then two-and-a-half years on probation.

Fran appealed the robbery case on a procedural issue and the conviction was overturned. She was convicted again on retrial in Judge Phillips' court. Between the first and second trials, Fran pleaded *nolo contendere* to the marijuana charge and was given a three-month jail term. After the second unarmed robbery conviction, Judge Phillips sentenced her to a five-year prison term. He noted for the record that the sentence was, in part, based on the recent marijuana conviction.

1. Does the five-year sentence violate *North Carolina v. Pearce? See Wasman v. United States*, 468 U.S. 559 (1984).

2. Changing the facts, what if Fran had been convicted of the marijuana charge before the first trial, but the prosecution did not discover the conviction until shortly before the second trial? Can it be used to justify a harsher sentence on retrial?

3. Changing the facts again, assume that the marijuana charges were still pending when the second sentence was imposed. Assume further that Judge Phillips ignored the pending charges in the first trial, but Judge Stein (who conducted the second trial) took them in consideration in imposing the five year sentence. While Judge Phillips had an informal policy of ignoring pending charges, Judge Stein considered them as some evidence of the defendant's rehabilitative potential. (Assume also that state law permitted both approaches.) Is *Pearce* violated?

[iii] Appellate Procedure

Trial motions. The defendant may file several post-trial motions before filing a notice of appeal. These include a Motion for a New Trial based on such grounds as new evidence or faulty jury instructions, a Motion for a Judgment of Acquittal, and a Motion for Arrest of Judgment. *See, e.g.*, Fed. R. Crim. P. 33 (motion for new trial), 34 (motion for arrest of judgment). These motions are discussed more fully in Chapters 9 and 13.

Notice of appeal. The usual formality for appealing a criminal case is to file a notice of appeal with the trial court. *See, e.g.*, Fed. R. App. P. 3(a). In the federal system, the defendant must file the notice of appeal with the clerk of the district court, who then transmits a copy to the appropriate Court of Appeals. Fed. R. App. P. 3(d). The court clerk also serves a copy of the notice of appeal on the defendant (defense counsel may have prepared it) and on the lawyer for each party other than the appellant.

In order to facilitate both finality and orderly procedures, court rules routinely establish a time-limit for filing a notice of appeal. In general, a notice of appeal in a federal case must be filed by a criminal defendant within 14 days after the entry of the judgment or order being appealed. Fed. R. App. P. 4(b). A federal defendant who exceeds the timely notice requirement may file a motion stating why the filing is late. The late defendant must show "excusable neglect" to justify the tardy filing, but the federal court will not allow an extension to reach beyond 30 days.

Some states allow the notice of appeal to be filed up to 20 and 30 days after judgment has been rendered. Ariz. R. Crim. P. 31.2(a)(2) (20 days); N.Y. Crim. Proc. Law §460.10 (30 days).

Some states do not require the defendant to file a notice of appeal in certain cases, most notably in capital cases. In Arizona, for example, if the defendant is sentenced to death, the clerk will automatically file the necessary notice with the court of appeals. Ariz. R. Crim. P. 31.2(b).

The exact information required to be included in the notice of appeal varies in every jurisdiction. Under federal procedure, the notice must designate the parties taking the appeal, the judgment appealed from, and the court to which the appeal is taken. Fed. R. App. P. 3(c).

Briefs. After the notice of appeal is served, the appellant must file a brief. *See, e.g.,* Fed. R. App. P. 28–32. The appellee may then file a reply brief. After the briefs are filed with the court, often both the appellant and the appellee are permitted to give oral arguments supporting their propositions. In an increasing number of cases, however, oral arguments are waived by the parties or not permitted by the court. *See* Fed. R. App. P. 34.

Once the court hears oral argument, it will enter an order disposing of the appeal. In some cases, there is a significant lapse of time between argument and final decision. See Chapter 12 for a discussion of the right to speedy trial as applied to the appellate process. A federal defendant who loses her appeal may ask the United States Supreme Court to review the case or may file a petition for rehearing in the same appellate court. Fed. R. App. P. 40. If the petition for rehearing is denied, or if it is successful but relief is still not granted, the defendant may seek permission for review from the Supreme Court.

Indigent defendants. Trial and appellate courts are required to make special arrangements to ensure that indigent defendants are not denied access to appellate processes because of their indigency. The right to appointed counsel is discussed below. *See, e.g., Draper v. Washington*, 372 U.S. 487 (1963) (invalidating state rule that free transcript is available to indigent defendant only if trial judge stated that appeal was not frivolous); *Burns v. Ohio*, 360 U.S. 252 (1959) (overturning rule that indigent defendants had to pay filing fee as prerequisite to filing notice of appeal); *Griffin v. Illinois*, 351 U.S. 12 (1956) (state must provide free transcript to indigent defendant if free transcript is only way to assure defendant has adequate and effective appeal).

[iv] Misdemeanor Appeals

Defendants convicted of a misdemeanor may also appeal, although few actually do. The procedure is generally the same as with felony convictions. *See, e.g.,* Fed. R.

Crim. P. 58(g)(2)(b). However, some jurisdictions require that the misdemeanor appeal first go to a higher-level trial court where the case may be tried *de novo* or, rarely, considered as an appeal. If relief is denied at this level, the defendant may appeal through the normal state appellate processes.

[v] Conditional Pleas

A conditional plea, discussed in Chapter 11, occurs when a criminal defendant pleads guilty while preserving for appeal issues raised at pretrial proceedings. Fed. R. Crim. P. 11(a)(2). Since the guilty plea serves as a final judgment, the defendant may then proceed with an appeal. The conditional plea is used frequently when a defendant desires to pursue appellate review of a denial of a motion to suppress important prosecution evidence.

[vi] Right to Counsel and Ethical Issues

Right to counsel. Since 1963, the Supreme Court has held that an indigent criminal accused has an equal protection right to appointed counsel at a first direct appeal as of right. However, the accused does not have a constitutional right to represent him- or herself at this appeal. *Martinez v. Court of Appeal of California*, 528 U.S. 152 (2000).

An appeal as of right, like every other facet of criminal practice, can raise important ethical issues for lawyers. *Douglas v. California*, 372 U.S. 353 (1963).

Standard of counsel's performance. In *Evitts v. Lucey*, 469 U.S. 387 (1985), the Court held that the Due Process Clause mandates that counsel on direct appeal meet the Sixth Amendment's standard of rendering *effective assistance.* In *Evitts*, the defendant was convicted of a drug offense and authorized his retained counsel to appeal. The appeal was dismissed when the retained lawyer failed to file certain required documents with the Kentucky Court of Appeals. After state courts refused to permit the appeal, the defendant filed a federal habeas corpus petition alleging that he had been denied the effective assistance of counsel guaranteed by the Sixth and Fourteenth Amendments. The Court agreed and granted relief and held that Due Process entitles a criminal accused to effective assistance of counsel on the first direct appeal. The Court noted that a defendant who has ineffective representation on appeal is no better off than one with no counsel at all.

Notes

1. *Standard of effectiveness of appellate counsel. Evitts* held that the accused on the first direct appeal is entitled to the effective assistance of counsel but did not specify how to assess whether this standard is satisfied. It is clear, however, that the total failure to appoint counsel for this appeal is reversible error. *Cf. Penson v. Ohio*, 488 U.S. 75, 88 (1988). Similarly, "nominal" counsel is inadequate.

According to *Evitts*, appellate counsel is necessary to ensure meaningful appellate review. This means that appellate counsel must assist in preparing and submitting a brief to the appellate court. *Evitts*, 469 U.S. at 394. But it does not mean that appellate counsel must advance every argument suggested by the defendant or even every arguable issue. *See also Jones v. Barnes*, 463 U.S. 745 (1983) (appellate counsel for indigent appellee need not raise every nonfrivolous issue that client wants raised; attorney must make professional evaluation of issues to raise; sometimes it is better to raise only solid issues and not include weaker ones).

As discussed in Chapters 9 and 11, the Sixth Amendment's test for ineffective assistance of counsel derives from *Strickland v. Washington*, 466 U.S. 668 (1984): the accused has a right to reasonably effective legal assistance. A defendant alleging ineffective assistance of counsel must show that counsel's representation fell below an objective standard of reasonableness, and the deficient representation prejudiced the defendant.

Cases after *Evitts* have been quite inconsistent in establishing the minimal standard of effectiveness for appellate counsel. Counsel is not usually expected to anticipate the course of future Supreme Court or other appellate caselaw, and failure to raise issues on appeal that became palpable only after a later change in caselaw has been held not to constitute ineffective assistance. *See, e.g., United States v. Barth*, 488 F. Supp. 2d 874 (D.N.D. 2007) (not ineffective assistance where counsel failed to anticipate and raise an objection to sentence enhancement based on *Blakely v. Washington* [see Chapter 16] prior to that decision—sometimes referred to as the "clairvoyance" principle); *Spence v. Nix*, 945 F.2d 1030 (8th Cir. 1991) (appellate counsel failed to file required motion, causing dismissal of state appeal on issue of voluntariness of guilty plea; no reversal because though counsel was deficient, there was no prejudice since even absent counsel's error, appeal challenge to guilty plea would not have succeeded on the merits); *Horne v. Trickey*, 895 F.2d 497 (8th Cir. 1990); *Lombard v. Lynaugh*, 868 F.2d 1475 (5th Cir. 1989) (appellate counsel's brief, which asserted that no arguable grounds for appeal exist but which failed to raise nonfrivolous appellate issues, held ineffective assistance of counsel on appeal). See discussion below of *Anders* briefs.

2. *Prejudice.* A key issue after *Evitts* is whether appellate counsel's poor performance can result in an order for a new appeal without proof that somehow the inadequate legal work caused prejudice. The problem is best exemplified if appellate counsel somehow failed to perfect the appeal, perhaps by missing a deadline or failing to file necessary forms. If the defendant must prove prejudice by the lack of an appeal, relief may turn on the likelihood that the appeal, if properly perfected, would have been successful.

Denial of counsel. The Supreme Court has held that a total denial of counsel on the first direct appeal is legally presumed to be prejudicial. This "casts such doubt on the fairness of the trial process, that it can never be considered harmless error." *Penson v. Ohio*, 488 U.S. 75, 88 (1988) (appellate counsel filed a timely notice of appeal but then filed a Certification of Meritless Appeal and participated no further in the appeal).

Failure to file notice of appeal. What happens if trial counsel does not file a notice of appeal, thereby foreclosing at least some appellate remedies? In *Roe v. Flores-Ortega*,

528 U.S. 470 (2000), trial counsel did not file a notice of appeal. In a subsequent habeas corpus action alleging ineffective assistance of counsel for this error, the Supreme Court held that there are three separate situations to assess under *Strickland* whether counsel was ineffective when there was a failure to file a notice of appeal. First, if the defendant specifically instructed defense counsel to file a notice of appeal, counsel's failure to do so is professionally unreasonable, satisfying the first prong of *Strickland*. The "prejudice" or second prong of *Strickland* is satisfied in such cases because the defendant was harmed since he or she would have taken an appeal had defense counsel performed as instructed.

Second, where the defendant explicitly tells defense counsel not to file an appeal, the defendant cannot later allege that counsel's performance was deficient. Third, where the defendant does not instruct defense counsel either to file an appeal or not, the issue turns on whether counsel discussed the issue with the defendant. *Roe* held that defense counsel has a constitutional and reasonable professional duty to consult with the defendant about an appeal when there is reason to think either that a rational defendant would want to appeal or that this particular defendant reasonably demonstrated to counsel that he or she was interested in appealing. If counsel violates this standard of reasonable professional performance, *Roe* permits a finding of ineffective assistance of counsel if there is a reasonable probability that, but for counsel's deficient performance, the defendant would have timely appealed. The *Roe* Court specifically held that the likely success of the appeal was not a factor in assessing prejudice.

Looking to the "prevailing law" to evaluate adequacy of representation. As elaborated in *Maryland v. Kulbicki*, 136 S. Ct. 2 (2015), *Strickland*-based claims of deficient representation are evaluated according to the law prevailing "as of the time of counsel's conduct," *Strickland*, 466 U.S. at 690, not in the light of later changes in the law. Therefore, the Court in held in *Kulbicki* that counsel in a 1995 murder trial was not deficient, under the first prong of *Strickland*, in failing to challenge the scientific validity of a method of ballistics analysis that was generally accepted and admissible at the time of trial, but that the Maryland courts 11 years later, in 2006, invalidated and held inadmissible. The Court in *Kulbicki* re-emphasized that the Sixth Amendment right to counsel requires "reasonable competence," but not "perfect advocacy." *Id.* (citing *Yarborough v. Gentry*, 540 U.S. 1 (2003)).

Other deficiencies. Courts are divided on whether lesser inadequacies by defense counsel require proof of prejudice before a habeas petition will be granted. *Compare Lombard v. Lynaugh*, 868 F.2d 1475 (5th Cir. 1989) (appellate counsel filed a two-page appellate brief which said that the defendant's conviction was valid and the appeal was without merit; no grounds to appeal were alleged; prejudice must be shown if appellate counsel simply failed to raise, brief, or argue specific issues on appeal, but no prejudice need be proven if there was actual or constructive complete denial of appellate counsel's assistance), *with Kimball v. State*, 490 A.2d 653 (Me. 1985) (must show that result of appeal would have been different but for counsel's lack of diligence).

Is it fair to say that *Anders* forces appellate defense lawyers to become advocates *against* their indigent clients? If so, doesn't it create a significant gap between the representation of the rich and the poor? Remember that *Anders* will have little impact on retained counsel. On the other hand, perhaps it doesn't matter. If defense counsel, whether retained or appointed, believes that there is no merit to an appeal, isn't it likely that the appeal would fail even if vigorously pressed by competent appellate counsel?

2. *Alternatives to Anders.* While *Anders* provides a detailed description of what counsel should do when he or she believes the appeal would be frivolous, in *Smith v. Robbins*, 528 U.S. 259 (2000), the Court held that the *Anders* procedure is not the only permissible one. States are free to adopt different procedures so long as those procedures adequately safeguard a defendant's right to appellate counsel. The *Smith* Court upheld a California procedure that differed from *Anders.* It requires that defense counsel, believing an appeal would be frivolous, must file a brief summarizing the factual and procedural history of the case, attesting that he or she has examined the record, explained the evaluation of the case to the client, given the client a copy of the brief, informed the client of the right to file a *pro se* supplemental brief, and requesting the court to examine independently the record for arguable issues. Unlike the *Anders* procedures, defense counsel need not explicitly indicate that the appeal is frivolous nor ask permission to withdraw; he or she may remain available to brief any issues the court directs to be briefed. Do you agree with the *Smith* Court that the California procedure adequately protects the defendant's right to appellate counsel?

3. *Content of Anders brief.* Note that the "*Anders* brief" described in *Anders* must include a statement of "anything in the record that might arguably support the appeal." It does not appear to require counsel to indicate *why* each of these issues lacks merit. Thus, *Anders* may not mandate inclusion of citations to cases or statutes suggesting the issues are not even arguably meritorious. Was this an important omission? Recall that the *Anders* brief is filed with a request to withdraw because the appeal is frivolous. Do you think that citations and arguments on the meritless nature of the issues are unnecessary? Or is more involved?

In *McCoy v. Court of Appeals*, 486 U.S. 429 (1988), the Supreme Court upheld a Wisconsin rule requiring that *Anders* briefs contain a discussion of why each issue lacks merit. This requirement, though not mandated by *Anders*, is permissible because it (1) may assist appellate counsel in finding support for an argument originally thought to be baseless, (2) will assist the appellate court in assessing whether counsel was diligent in investigating the case, and (3) will assist the appellate court in determining whether the appeal is actually frivolous. Do you agree with *McCoy*? Does it go too far in forcing lawyers to become advocates against their clients? Does it create a different standard for appellate consideration of rich and poor clients?

4. *Efforts to prepare Anders brief. Anders* did not specify what efforts counsel must expend before filing an *Anders* brief. In *McCoy v. Court of Appeals*, 486 U.S. 429, 438–39 (1988), the Supreme Court held lawyers to a high standard:

> The appellate lawyer must master the trial record, thoroughly research the law, and exercise judgment in identifying the arguments that may be

> advanced on appeal. In preparing and evaluating the case, and in advising the client as to the prospects for success, counsel must consistently serve the client's interest to the best of his or her ability. Only after such an evaluation has led counsel to the conclusion that the appeal is "wholly frivolous" is counsel justified in making a motion to withdraw. This is the central teaching of *Anders*.

Because counsel must "thoroughly research" as well as file an *Anders* brief, would it make more sense to require counsel to file a formal appellate brief rather than withdraw? Would this approach save time or waste time for both counsel and the court? *See Commonwealth v. Moffett*, 418 N.E.2d 585 (Mass. 1981) (suggesting that counsel's briefing even of "well nigh hopeless" issues would be more efficient for the court and less inimical to client's interests than filing an *Anders* brief; hopeless points should be stated as briefly and succinctly as possible; notice to court and client required if counsel is utterly unable to come up with even thinly arguable appellate issues).

5. The American Bar Association's *Standards for Criminal Justice* make the distinction between an appeal or a ground for appeal that is frivolous and one that lacks merit. STANDARDS FOR CRIMINAL JUSTICE §4-9.2. (4th ed. 2015). The *Standards* provide that appellate counsel is not permitted to withdraw because counsel believes the appeal lacks merit, but may do so if it is frivolous. Do you agree with this distinction? Could a court actually implement it? How would the court determine whether an appeal or issue is frivolous or simply without merit?

If appellate counsel believes that some issues are not frivolous but the client insists on including an issue that appellate counsel believes is frivolous, the ABA Standards counsel that:

> In this situation, it is proper for the lawyer to brief and argue the points he or she believes are supportable and tactically or strategically advisable to make and to omit the others.

Id., Commentary.

[b] Discretionary Appeals

[i] Appeal After a Direct Appeal as of Right: Supreme Court

Appeals after the initial appeal "as of right" are discretionary in most jurisdictions. The appellate court does not have to accept the case. If an intermediate appellate court upholds the conviction, interlocutory order, or denial of collateral relief, the defendant desiring another appeal often must file a petition, sometimes called a writ of *certiorari*, with the next higher court, usually the state supreme court, requesting the appeal be accepted.

This pattern is used in the federal system. The United States Supreme Court has discretion to decide what criminal cases it will hear. The Supreme Court's Rules state that a writ of *certiorari* will be granted only "for compelling reasons." These reasons generally involve a conflict among lower federal or sometimes state courts as to the interpretation of a federal law, or a lower court decision that conflicts with a Supreme Court decision or presents an issue that should be settled by the Supreme Court. Sup. Ct. R. 10.

Under federal procedure, the person seeking a writ of *certiorari* to overturn a Court of Appeals decision must file a petition for writ of *certiorari* in the United States Supreme Court within 90 days of the date the judgment is rendered or the date a petition for rehearing is denied. A Justice may extend the date the petition is due, but such an extension period cannot exceed 60 days. Sup. Ct. R. 13.

The content of the petition for *certiorari* is specified in detail in the Supreme Court's Rules. Sup. Ct. R. 14. A petition can be denied for failure to comply with these rules. In general terms, the petition for *certiorari* resembles an appellate brief that states the relevant issues and legal authorities in a way designed to convince the Court to grant the petition.

After a petition for *certiorari* is filed, the other side files a brief in opposition to the petition for a writ of *certiorari*. The petitioner can then file a reply brief to the brief in opposition. Sup. Ct. R. 15.

After consideration of the petition for a writ of *certiorari*, the United States Supreme Court enters an appropriate order. If the petition is granted, the Court will notify the interested parties and the case will be scheduled for briefing and oral argument. If the order is denied, the Supreme Court notifies the interested parties of the decision. Sup. Ct. R. 16.

[ii] Prior to Final Judgment: Interlocutory Appeals

In a criminal proceeding, the defendant ordinarily appeals only after conviction and sentencing. In this post-sentence appeal the defendant raises every available issue, including those raised unsuccessfully in pretrial motions. For example, many criminal defendants appeal their convictions on the ground that either an illegal confession or illegally seized physical evidence was admitted into evidence following an unsuccessful pretrial motion to suppress.

On occasion, however, the defendant wants an immediate appeal of a judge's decision on a pretrial motion (or even a decision made during trial). If the appeal is successful, it could alter the course of the trial or prevent it entirely. For example, in a drug case if a suppression motion is initially denied but then granted on appeal before the trial has begun, the prosecution may have to drastically alter the charges or even dismiss the case for lack of evidence.

As one would expect, courts do not welcome interlocutory appeals, for they can cause significant delay in processing a case and can play havoc with a judge's efforts to schedule cases. The Supreme Court has used strong language to express its negative feelings about interlocutory appeals:

> All our jurisprudence is strongly colored by the notion that appellate review should be postponed, except in certain narrowly defined circumstances, until after final judgment has been rendered by the trial court. This general policy

> against piecemeal appeals takes on added weight in criminal cases, where the defendant is entitled to a speedy resolution of the charges against him.

Will v. United States, 389 U.S. 90, 96 (1967). This preference has led to the so-called *final judgment* or *final order* rule, generally permitting appeals only after a final judgment. In the federal system, the courts of appeals have jurisdiction in appeals "from all final decisions" of district courts. 28 U.S.C. § 1291. According to the Supreme Court, a final judgment or decision in a criminal case occurs only after conviction and sentence. *Flanagan v. United States*, 465 U.S. 259, 263 (1984). Does the final judgment rule make sense? Whose interest does it serve? Does it have any relationship to the likelihood of a fair trial? Does it save judicial resources? Does it save prosecution or defense costs? Does it serve society's interest in the speedy resolution of criminal charges?

In unusual cases, virtually all jurisdictions have a procedure that authorizes *interlocutory appeals*. An interlocutory procedure occurs between the commencement of the case and the final judgment. Interlocutory appeals are actually authorized in two ways: by the collateral order doctrine and by statute. A third category, independent proceedings, is different in that it may not actually involve an interlocutory appeal. Each is discussed below.

Collateral order doctrine. The *collateral order doctrine*, derived from federal case law originally dealing with civil cases, permits, in federal criminal cases, the appeal of certain pretrial orders that are viewed as if they were final judgments. *See generally Cohen v. Beneficial Industrial Loan Corp.*, 337 U.S. 541 (1949) (civil case establishing collateral order doctrine).

The collateral order doctrine:

> considers as "final judgments," even though they do not "end the litigation on the merits," decisions "which finally determine claims of right separate from, and collateral to, rights asserted in the action, too important to be denied review and too independent of the cause itself to require that appellate jurisdiction be deferred until the whole case is adjudicated." To fall within the limited class of final collateral orders, an order must (1) "conclusively determine the disputed question," (2) "resolve an important issue completely separate from the merits of the action," and (3) "be effectively unreviewable on appeal from a final judgment."

Midland Asphalt Corp. v. United States, 489 U.S. 794, 798–99 (1989) (quoting *Cohen v. Beneficial Industrial Loan Corp., supra*, and *Coopers & Lybrand v. Livesay*, 437 U.S. 463 (1978)). The third prong is the most difficult to prove in criminal cases. It requires the appellant to convince the appellate court that the trial court's order involves "an asserted right the legal and practical value of which would be destroyed if it were not vindicated before trial." *United States v. MacDonald*, 435 U.S. 850 (1978).

Consistent with the general judicial hesitancy to permit interlocutory appeals, the collateral order doctrine is interpreted "with the utmost strictness" in criminal cases. Nevertheless, a few Supreme Court decisions do permit collateral order interlocutory appeals in such cases. *See, e.g.*, *Helstoski v. Meanor*, 442 U.S. 500 (1979) (motion to dismiss under Congressional Speech or Debate Clause is collateral order); *Abney v. United States*, 431 U.S. 651 (1977) (denial of motion to dismiss for double jeopardy is collateral order); *Stack v. Boyle*, 342 U.S. 1 (1951) (denial of bail is collateral order).

Most cases refuse to apply the collateral order exception. *See, e.g.*, *Midland Asphalt Corp. v. United States*, 489 U.S. 794 (1989) (denial of motion to dismiss because of improper disclosure of grand jury information not collateral order; is not completely separate from merits of action); *United States v. Hollywood Motor Car Co.*, 458 U.S. 263 (1982) (denial of motion to dismiss because of prosecutorial vindictiveness is not collateral order; is reviewable on appeal; court suggests collateral order rule extends to situations where there is a right not to be tried as opposed to a right to have charges dismissed); *United States v. MacDonald*, 456 U.S. 1 (1982) (denial of motion to dismiss because of speedy trial violation not collateral order; is reviewable on appeal).

Statutes. Statutes in most jurisdictions authorize an interlocutory appeal in limited circumstances. Typically, the accused must obtain the permission of a trial court or, occasionally, appellate judge before taking an interlocutory appeal. Some of these statutes present the court with a list of factors to consider in determining whether to permit an interlocutory appeal. In some circumstances, the government is granted more opportunities than the defendant to take an interlocutory appeal. Government appeals are discussed below.

Independent proceedings. On rare occasions a criminal case involves issues or people separate from the criminal case being tried. For example, the police may conduct a search and obtain property belonging to the defendant and third parties. The third parties file a motion to have their property returned to them. If the motion is denied, it may be immediately appealed if it is considered "independent of, and unaffected by, another litigation with which it happens to be entangled." *Radio Station WOW v. Johnson*, 326 U.S. 120, 126 (1945).

The leading case involved an attempt to appeal the denial of a motion to suppress in a drug case. In *DiBella v. United States*, 369 U.S. 121, 131–32 (1962), Justice Frankfurter observed, "[o]nly if the motion is solely for return of property and is in no way tied to a criminal prosecution *in esse* against the movant can the proceedings be regarded as independent." To illustrate, this test was satisfied where IRS agents seized bank records but the persons filing the suppression motion had not been arrested or indicted. Their action was deemed independent of any pending criminal case and the denial of the suppression motion could be appealed. *First National Bank of Tulsa v. Department of Justice*, 865 F.2d 217 (10th Cir. 1989).

[4] Appeals by the Government

With respect to appeals, the government in a criminal case is in an unusual situation. Because of the Double Jeopardy Clause, discussed in Chapter 15, it may not appeal acquittals in criminal cases. Moreover, concerns about government abuse and the citizen's right to face prosecution only once have led to the rule that "in the federal jurisprudence . . . appeals by the Government in criminal cases are something unusual, exceptional, not favored." *Carroll v. United States*, 354 U.S. 394, 400 (1957).

Although appeals by the government are not welcomed, they are permitted by statutes to a limited extent. Under federal law and in most states, statutes authorize the government to appeal a court order "dismissing an indictment or information or granting a new trial after verdict or judgment." 18 U.S.C. § 3731. *See also* Ill. Sup. Ct. Rule 604; N.Y. Crim. Proc. Law § 450.20. However, the government may not appeal this type of order if the "double jeopardy clause of the United States Constitution prohibits further prosecution." 18 U.S.C. § 3731. For example, this would occur if, after jeopardy attached, the case was dismissed because of the defendant's innocence.

The government in many jurisdictions is also permitted to appeal the sentence imposed on the defendant, *e.g.*, 18 U.S.C. § 3742(b); N.Y. Crim. Proc. Law § 450.30 (government may appeal only on ground that sentence is invalid as a matter of law), as well as many bail issues. 18 U.S.C. § 3731. The federal government is also often authorized to appeal an order suppressing or excluding evidence if the order is made before the defendant has been put in jeopardy, the appeal is not taken for purpose of delay, and the suppressed evidence is substantial proof of a fact material in the proceeding. 18 U.S.C. § 3731. The rationale behind allowing an interlocutory appeal in the pretrial motion context is that the government may have insufficient proof to continue the prosecution if it is unable to admit certain evidence at trial. *See also* Fla. Stat. Ann. § 924.071. Recall that the defendant, unlike the government, is often *not* permitted to appeal interlocutory orders. Does it make sense to permit the government, but not the defendant, to appeal interlocutory orders?

In general terms, the procedure that the government follows when appealing is much like that of the criminal defendant. *See generally* David G. Knibb, Federal Court of Appeals Manual (6th ed. 2013). There may be small differences that vary among the jurisdictions. In the federal system, for example, the government, unlike the criminal defendant, has 30 days to file its notice of appeal from a district court judgment. 18 U.S.C. § 3731.

C. Collateral Remedies

The best known, and most frequently invoked, collateral remedy is the writ of *habeas corpus*, discussed in detail below. For *state* prisoners, federal habeas entails seeking review in *federal* court of the constitutionality of the underlying conviction or sentence, after direct state appeals have been exhausted. The other significant collateral remedy, the writ of error *coram nobis*, in contrast, seeks relief (either before or after direct appeals are exhausted) from the court that originally imposed the conviction and sentence.

[1] *Coram Nobis*

The common law writ of error *coram nobis* (or its cousin *coram vobis*) still exists in the federal courts and many state jurisdictions, although it is used infrequently. *Coram nobis* is designed to permit a criminal conviction to be challenged because of a factual error detrimental to the defense. In *United States v. Morgan*, 346 U.S. 502 (1954), the United States Supreme Court held that federal *coram nobis* was a possible remedy for a state prisoner to use in challenging the validity of a prior federal conviction that was obtained in violation of the defendant's right to counsel. The Court stated:

> The writ of error *coram nobis* was available at common law to correct errors of fact. It was allowed without limitation of time for facts that affect the "validity and regularity" of the judgment and was used in both civil and criminal cases. While the occasions for its use were infrequent, no one doubts its availability at common law.... It has been used, in the United States, with and without statutory authority but always with references to its common law scope—for example, to inquire as to the imprisonment of a slave not subject to imprisonment, insanity of a defendant, a conviction on a guilty plea through the coercion of fear of mob violence, [and the] failure to advise of right to counsel.

See, e.g., People v. Chaklader, 24 Cal. App. 4th 407 (1994) (*coram nobis* relief available if guilty plea induced by mistake, fraud, or coercion), *but see, contra, Frazier v. State*, 495 S.W. 3d 246 (Tenn. 2016) (Tennessee *coram nobis* statute not available as a procedural vehicle to challenge a guilty plea); *Dugart v. State*, 578 So. 2d 789 (Fla. Dist. Ct. App. 1991) (*coram nobis* appropriate for ineffective assistance of trial counsel in providing misinformation about effect of plea); *State v. Cottingham*, 410 N.W.2d 498 (Neb. 1987) (*coram nobis* petition based on new evidence should be denied when new evidence was cumulative and probably would not have affected result).

The defendant and defense counsel must not have been negligent in failing to bring this fact to the judge's attention at trial. The writ will succeed if the factual error was so serious that, if known at trial, it would have prevented the conviction. For reasons that will make sense later in this chapter, *coram nobis* can be an important remedy for a prisoner who attacks a conviction for which he or she is not currently in custody. *See Chaidez v. United States*, 568 U. S. 342, 345 n.1 (2013) ("A petition for a writ of *coram nobis* provides a way to collaterally attack a criminal conviction for a person ... who is no longer 'in custody' and therefore cannot seek habeas relief[.]"). Some courts have characterized *coram nobis* as a remedy of last resort, meaning that it cannot be used if habeas corpus or some other collateral remedy is available. In some jurisdictions a *coram nobis* action will be dismissed if the petitioner had not previously used all available remedies to challenge the alleged error. *See, e.g., State v. Davis*, 515 N.W.2d 205 (S.D. 1994) (voluntary dismissal of direct appeal bars subsequent *coram nobis* action on issue raised in dismissed appeal). The procedures for using *coram nobis* vary considerably among the jurisdictions. In general, the writ first must be filed in the court where the conviction being challenged occurred.

[2] Habeas Corpus

[a] Nature and History of the Writ

The writ of habeas corpus, sometimes referred to as The Great Writ of Liberty or simply *The Great Writ*, exists under federal law and in many states, and is the primary vehicle (other than direct appellate review of a conviction or sentence) by which persons under confinement can challenge the constitutionality of their incarceration. As discussed later in this chapter, federal court habeas petitions are usually "collateral" attacks by state prisoners on their underlying convictions and/or sentences. However, the writ is also available for persons in federal custody. With origins extending to at least the twelfth century in England, habeas corpus has been an important judicial check on the government's actions in depriving its citizens of their liberty. *See Hamdi v. Rumsfeld*, 542 U.S. 507, 525 (2004) (habeas is a "critical check on the Executive ensuring that it does not detain individuals except in accordance with law," and citing, to the same effect, *I.N.S. v. St. Cyr*, 533 U.S. 289 (2001)); *see also* James S. Liebman & Randy Hertz, Federal Habeas Corpus Practice and Procedure (7th ed. 2016); Daniel J. Meador, Habeas Corpus and Magna Carta; Dualism of Power and Liberty (1966).

Civil action to produce petitioner. The phrase "habeas corpus" means "have or produce the body." Historically, and under the governing statutes and rules, a habeas petition is treated as a civil action, even though it is usually a collateral attack on a criminal conviction and/or sentence. The person bringing the petition is called the *petitioner*, or *applicant*, and the official who has custody over the petitioner, and to whom the writ is addressed, is called the *respondent*. In its essence, habeas corpus is a court order addressed to the respondent (usually the prison warden), to bring the petitioner before the court to determine the validity of the petitioner's confinement.

Habeas as a constitutionally protected procedure to obtain immediate release from unlawful confinement. In *Fay v. Noia*, 372 U.S. 391, 401–02 (1963), one of the leading Supreme Court habeas corpus precedents, the Court addressed the fundamental purpose of the Great Writ:

> Although in form the Great Writ is simply a mode of procedure, its history is inextricably intertwined with the growth of fundamental rights of personal liberty. For its function has been to provide a prompt and efficacious remedy for whatever society deems to be intolerable restraint. Its root principle is that in a civilized society, government must always be accountable to the judiciary for a man's imprisonment: if the imprisonment cannot be shown to conform with the fundamental requirements of law, the individual is entitled to his immediate release.

The Constitution recognizes this important role and provides that "[t]he privilege of the Writ of Habeas Corpus shall not be suspended, unless when in Cases of Rebellion or Invasion the public safety may require it." U.S. Const. art. 1, § 9 (the "Suspension Clause"). In *Hamdi v. Rumsfeld*, 542 U.S. 507 (2005), the Supreme Court held as a matter of due process that a United States citizen detained as an accused "enemy combatant" must be able to challenge that designation via habeas corpus. The Court in *Hamdi* reaffirmed the importance and the availability of habeas as a procedural mechanism for citizens to challenge the legality of their confinement:

> [A]bsent suspension, the writ of habeas corpus remains available to every citizen detained in the United States.

Id. at 525. In *Boumediene v. Bush*, 553 U.S. 723 (2008), the court extended the constitutional "privilege" of habeas corpus to "enemy combatants" being detained at the United States military detention facility in Guantanamo Bay, Cuba.

Availability of the writ to federal and state prisoners. Originally federal habeas corpus was limited to federal prisoners, but in 1867 the writ became available on a limited basis to state prisoners held in violation of selected federal constitutional provisions. Gradually, many of these limitations were removed, making the writ of habeas corpus a viable remedy for state prisoners claiming their state custody was in violation of the United States Constitution. By 1942, the Supreme Court was able to state that federal habeas corpus ". . . extends . . . to those exceptional cases where the conviction has been in disregard of the constitutional rights of the accused, and where the writ is the only effective means of preserving his rights." *Waley v. Johnston*, 316 U.S. 101, 105 (1942) (state prisoner can use federal habeas corpus to challenge custody resulting from coerced guilty plea).

Stone v. Powell *preclusion rule.* Despite the wording of the federal habeas corpus statute, not all federal constitutional violations are cognizable in federal habeas corpus. For policy reasons, the Supreme Court has held that habeas corpus relief is unavailable for certain constitutional claims. In *Stone v. Powell*, 428 U.S. 465 (1976), the Supreme Court held that a state prisoner is not constitutionally entitled to habeas corpus relief on the ground that evidence, obtained in an unconstitutional search or seizure, was introduced at trial. The key is whether the defendant was afforded "an opportunity for full and fair litigation" of the Fourth Amendment claim in state court. According to *Stone*, if this opportunity exists, the purpose of the "exclusionary rule" in deterring unlawful police conduct has been adequately served and the possibility of federal habeas corpus relief is unnecessary as an added deterrent or remedy.

The so-called "*Stone v. Powell* preclusion rule" has not been extended to other constitutional areas. Therefore, *Stone* did not lead to the complete destruction of access to habeas corpus, as some commentators had predicted. *See Kimmelman v. Morrison*, 477 U.S. 365 (1986) (*Stone* not extended to claims of Sixth Amendment violation of right to effective assistance of counsel); *Withrow v. Williams*, 507 U.S. 680 (1993) (not extended to *Miranda* violation); *Cardwell v. Taylor*, 461 U.S. 571

(1983) (suggesting *Stone* not extended to involuntary statements); *Rose v. Mitchell*, 443 U.S. 545 (1979) (not extended to discriminatory grand jury selection); *Jackson v. Virginia*, 443 U.S. 307 (1979) (not extended to claim that evidence was insufficient to convict). The *sui generis* nature of the ruling in *Stone* is probably best explained by the Court's continuing discomfort with the exclusionary rule (a topic which is beyond the scope of this book).

Federal and state habeas corpus. Although states have habeas corpus and related procedures, federal habeas corpus is the most important such remedy. Habeas corpus is a critical aspect of American procedures designed to protect the individual from government oppression. *See generally* Dallin H. Oaks, *Habeas Corpus in the States—1776–1865*, 32 U. Chi. L. Rev. 243 (1965).

Present statutory basis. The statutory authority for federal habeas corpus is now contained in 28 U.S.C. §§ 2241–2254 (for persons in state custody) and § 2255 (for persons in federal custody). Some procedural details are contained in Rules Governing Section 2254 Cases in the United States District Courts, originally adopted in 1977. In general terms, federal habeas corpus is available to a state (and sometimes federal) prisoner held in custody in violation of federal law.

[b] Twilight of the Great Writ?: The AEDPA

Despite the Supreme Court's often-expressed reverence for the Great Writ of Habeas Corpus, Congress (via the Antiterrorism and Effective Death Penalty Act of 1996), and the Supreme Court itself in recent decisions, have sharply limited the scope, availability, and efficacy of habeas relief. As discussed below, the Court has evolved towards a consensus that habeas corpus is truly extraordinary relief that is limited only to blatantly unconstitutional confinement, rather than merely a routine "second bite at the apple" to collaterally challenge state convictions and/or sentences.

AEDPA. In 1996 Congress passed the Antiterrorism and Effective Death Penalty Act ("AEDPA"), Pub. L. No. 104–132. This legislation significantly restricted prisoners' access to federal habeas corpus or relief under Section 2255, discussed below. AEDPA's major stated purpose was to make the death penalty more "effective" by cutting down on the time, often measured in decades, between the pronouncement and the actual execution of death sentences. However, despite the suggestion in the Act's title that it is targeted primarily at death penalty and terrorism cases, AEDPA's restrictions on habeas corpus relief apply to *all* federal habeas petitions filed after the Act's date, in both capital and non-capital cases and in both terrorism and non-terrorism cases alike. *Lindh v. Murphy*, 521 U.S. 320 (1997).

By design and in operation, AEDPA sharply curtails the availability of the writ in ways described in detail later in this chapter. As described by the Supreme Court in *Harrington v. Richter*, 562 U.S. 86 (2011), habeas corpus is a "'guard against *extreme* [emphasis added] malfunctions in the state criminal justice systems,' not just a substitute for ordinary error correction through appeal." *Id.* at 102–03 (quoting *Jackson v. Virginia*, 443 U.S. 307, (1979) (Stevens, J., concurring)).

AEDPA initially drew much scholarly criticism on both constitutional and policy grounds. *See, e.g.*, Marshall J. Hartman & Jeanette Nyden, *Habeas Corpus and the New Federalism After the Anti-Terrorism and Effective Death Penalty Act of 1996*, 30 J. Marshall L. Rev. 337 (1997); Mark Tushnet & Larry W. Yackle, *Symbolic Statutes and Real Laws: The Pathologies of the Antiterrorism and Effective Death Penalty Act and the Prison Litigation Reform Act*, 47 Duke L. J. 1 (1997); A.A. Kochan, Note, *The Antiterrorism and Effective Death Penalty Act of 1996: Habeas Corpus Reform?*, 52 Wash. U. J. Urb. & Contemp. L 399 (1997). However, in *Felker v. Turpin*, 518 U.S. 651 (1996), the United States Supreme Court upheld the constitutionality of AEDPA, noting that although the Act imposes new conditions on the Court's authority to grant relief, it does not deprive the Supreme Court of "jurisdiction to entertain original habeas petitions."

Supreme Court ambivalence about the writ. The opinion for the Court in *Harrington* by Justice Kennedy expresses the two sometimes contradictory and competing themes running throughout the Supreme Court's habeas corpus jurisprudence—on the one hand (and as expressed in the Suspension Clause of the Constitution, discussed above), reverence for the writ and the concern that its availability not be impaired, and on the other hand, concerns that federal habeas review of state convictions can violate principles of repose and finality, as well as notions of federal/state comity and state sovereignty and prerogatives:

> The writ of habeas corpus stands as a safeguard against imprisonment of those held in violation of the law. Judges must be vigilant and independent in reviewing petitions for the writ, a commitment that entails substantial judicial resources. Those resources are diminished and misspent, however, and confidence in the writ and the law it vindicates undermined, if there is judicial disregard for the sound and established principles that inform its proper issuance.

Harrington, 562 U.S. at 91–92. In recent years, the views of Justice Kennedy in his earlier dissent in *Harris v. Reed*, 489 U.S. 255, 282 (1989), have prevailed far more often than not in the Court's decision making:

> [F]ederal habeas review itself entails significant costs. It disturbs the State's significant interest in repose for concluded litigation, denies society the right to punish some admitted offenders, and intrudes on state sovereignty to a degree matched by few exercises of federal judicial authority.

[c] The Custody and Mootness Requirements

[i] Custody

The federal habeas corpus statute extends to a prisoner who is "in custody," a term that is not defined. 28 U.S.C. § 2241(c). The Supreme Court explained this limitation in *Hensley v. Municipal Court*, 411 U.S. 345, 351 (1973):

> The custody requirement of the habeas corpus statute is designed to preserve the writ of habeas corpus as a remedy for severe restraints on

> individual liberty. Since habeas corpus is an extraordinary remedy whose operation is to a large extent uninhibited by traditional rules of finality and federalism, its use has been limited to cases of special urgency, leaving more conventional remedies for cases in which the restraints on liberty are neither severe nor immediate.

In *Hensley*, a state offender, released on his own recognizance pending execution of sentence, challenged his conviction on various federal constitutional grounds. The Supreme Court found that he was in sufficient "custody" to satisfy federal habeas corpus even though he was not confined in an institution and was free to live at home and conduct a normal life. The Court noted that he was subject to restraints not shared by the general public and that he could be incarcerated as soon as a stay was removed.

Other decisions have further broadened the concept of "custody" beyond penal confinement to include a person who is on parole or probation, but not to a person sentenced to pay a fine or whose driver's license has been suspended. Custody also includes a prisoner incarcerated on one sentence who wishes to attack a consecutive sentence to be served at the completion of the first term. And it includes a prisoner, incarcerated for parole revocation, who files a habeas corpus petition attacking the revocation, then is released on parole. A person whose later sentence is enhanced by an allegedly constitutionally invalid prior sentence is also considered to be in sufficient custody from the prior sentence to use federal habeas corpus to attack that prior sentence. *Lackawanna County District Attorney v. Coss*, 532 U.S. 394 (2001). The petitioner's custody status is determined at the time of filing the petition. *Spencer v. Kemna*, 523 U.S. 1 (1998). *See also generally* Wayne A. Logan, *Federal Habeas in the Information Age*, 85 MINN. L. REV. 147 (2000) (considering whether the requirements and burdens imposed by sex offender registration and community notification laws qualify as "custody").

Query: Does *Hensley*'s rationale, limiting the concept of custody to "severe and immediate" restraints on liberty, make sense? If the defendant was convicted in violation of the constitution, why should it matter whether he or she is still in custody? Isn't it true that the government is responsible for the illegality that led to harm to the defendant's reputation and job prospects as well as other facets of his or her daily life?

[ii] Mootness

A federal habeas corpus petition will be dismissed if the issue is moot. The mootness rule is based on a lack of a "case or controversy" under Article III, § 2 of the Constitution. This provision requires the offender to have a stake in the outcome. Mootness is related to the concept of custody. A case often becomes moot once the offender is no longer in custody. It can become moot if the petitioner escapes from custody, is pardoned, or dies. But in *Carafas v. LaVallee*, 391 U.S. 234 (1968), the Court held that collateral consequences, such as an inability to hold a license because of a criminal conviction, were sufficient to keep a habeas petition from being deemed moot. Although the petitioner in *Carafas* had been unconditionally released from prison, the Supreme Court held that he could still challenge his conviction because it continued to cause consequences such as an inability to conduct certain businesses, vote, or serve as a juror. *But see Spencer v. Kemna*, 523 U.S. 1 (1998) (habeas corpus moot when parole violator released from prison and attacks parole revocation procedures; inadequate proof of collateral consequences).

[d] In Violation of Federal Law

[i] Federal Constitution, Statutes, or Treaties

Federal habeas corpus is available to a prisoner "in custody in violation of the Constitution or laws or treaties of the United States." 28 U.S.C. § 2241. This means that a state prisoner cannot use federal habeas corpus to challenge state custody without alleging a violation of federal law. Although technically the federal provision can be a treaty or statute, virtually always it is a federal constitutional provision.

Sometimes habeas corpus petitioners strain to turn a state court's error into a federal constitutional violation. *See, e.g., Estelle v. McGuire*, 502 U.S. 62 (1991) (even though state court erroneously admitted evidence in violation of state evidence law, Due Process Clause not necessarily violated); *Hill v. United States*, 368 U.S. 424 (1962) (failure to offer defendant opportunity to make statement before sentencing does not constitute due process violation authorizing collateral relief).

Harmless error. The harmless error doctrine, discussed earlier in this chapter, applies to habeas corpus cases. *See Calderon v. Coleman*, 525 U.S. 141 (1998); *Brecht v. Abrahamson*, 507 U.S. 619 (1993).

In *Wilson v. Corcoran*, 557 U.S. 952 (2010), and in other recent habeas corpus decisions, the Supreme Court has emphasized that federal habeas relief is available *only* for claims of unlawful custody resulting from violations of federal, not state, law: "[W]e have repeatedly held that federal habeas corpus relief does not lie for errors of state law [citations omitted]."

[ii] Actual Innocence: *Herrera*

An obvious habeas corpus claim is that the prisoner is actually innocent of the charges and therefore is being held unconstitutionally. The argument is that surely due process is violated if an innocent person is incarcerated for a crime he or she did not commit. Although in a just system the prisoner would eventually be freed if this were true, in *Herrera v. Collins*, 506 U.S. 390 (1993), the United States Supreme Court made it extremely difficult for such claims to prevail. The petitioner in *Herrera* was convicted of capital murder and, after unsuccessful state court appeals and habeas corpus proceedings, filed a federal habeas corpus petition alleging that recently acquired affidavits supported his claim of innocence. The Supreme Court denied relief, a plurality of the Court determining that an assertion of actual innocence does not raise a separate constitutional ground. The Court was concerned that any other holding would destroy finality and interfere with the comity-based principle that federal courts should not unduly interfere with the proceedings of state courts. Significantly, Herrera did not argue that his trial was constitutionally deficient; he argued that he was innocent. As discussed below, a strong showing of actual innocence may still enable a prisoner to seek habeas relief on an issue that should have been raised in an earlier proceeding.

Herrera did not go so far as to make a claim of actual innocence totally irrelevant (and insufficient as grounds for relief) to a habeas corpus petition in the absence of a separate claim of constitutional error. The Court assumed *arguendo* that in extraordinary cases a federal habeas corpus proceeding could be brought at any time if the prisoner could meet a very high standard of establishing actual innocence. The Court refused to specify the exact standard to be satisfied, but did indicate that it "would necessarily be extraordinarily high." *Id.* at 869. Justice Blackmun's dissent argued that a habeas corpus petition should be granted if the petitioner can prove that he or she is "probably innocent." *See generally* Arleen Anderson, *Responding to the Challenge of Actual Innocence Claims After Herrera v. Collins*, 71 Temp. L. Rev. 489 (1998); Kevin M. Zielke, Note, *The Governor, God, and the Great Writ of Habeas Corpus*, 1993 Det. C. L. Rev. 1393.

In *House v. Bell*, 547 U.S. 518 (2006), the Supreme Court determined that the federal habeas petitioner there, who had been convicted of murder and sentenced to death in state court, had proffered sufficient evidence of his likely innocence (especially including DNA evidence that semen found on the victim's clothing had come from her husband, rather than from the defendant as argued by the prosecution at trial, but also including other forensic and testimonial evidence that undermined the prosecution's circumstantial case) to warrant his habeas petition proceeding despite the fact that he had not raised this issue in a timely manner. The Court reiterated, however, that such a determination regarding likely actual innocence will only be made in those "rare" cases where the habeas petitioner meets the "extraordinarily high" requirement under *Herrera* of showing that reasonable trial jurors would likely have had a reasonable doubt of the petitioner's guilt had they heard the evidence presented later to the habeas court.

The Innocence Project and attempting to reopen old convictions on claims of innocence. First begun at Yeshiva University School of Law in 1992 and dedicated to seeking the exoneration of convicted persons who could be proved factually innocent by DNA testing, the Innocence Project is now a network of similar projects in law schools and universities in some 40 states. According to the Innocence Project's website (http://www.innocenceproject.org, most recently visited May 18, 2018) 356 persons have been exonerated in the United States in recent years on the basis of modern DNA testing technology, including 20 who had been sentenced to death. These individuals served an average of 14 years in prison before their exoneration and release. Many had been convicted at a time when DNA testing was either not available or when the available DNA testing technology had not yet attained its present enormous power either to convict or to exonerate, and had exhausted all their available direct and collateral post-conviction remedies. A prime example, discussed in Chapter 10, is *Arizona v. Youngblood*, 488 U.S. 51 (1988). There the Supreme Court upheld Youngblood's sexual assault conviction, rejecting his claim that the government's failure to properly preserve physical evidence required reversal; he was later represented by Innocence Project and exonerated in 2000 after DNA testing proved his innocence.

Many states now have enacted statutes or have judicial decisions requiring DNA testing in certain situations as part of their post-conviction relief process. If the jurisdiction has a time limitation for filing such claims, some states authorize their executive clemency process to obtain DNA testing. *See District Attorney's Office for Third Judicial District v. Osborne*, 557 U.S. 52 (2009) (Roberts, C.J.) (acknowledging DNA testing's "unparalleled ability both to exonerate the wrongly convicted and to identify the guilty," and noting that 46 states and the federal government now have statutes dealing with access to DNA evidence). In 2018, the American Bar Association adopted a resolution urging all jurisdictions "to enact legislation creating a substantive right and procedures for individuals to challenge their convictions by demonstrating that forensic evidence or testimony used to obtain their convictions has been undermined or discredited by reliable scientific research or technological advances."

Some prosecutors, invoking the need for finality, have vigorously opposed reopening convictions years after the fact to permit state-of-the-art DNA testing, while others, and some courts, have agreed to allow testing years after conviction, especially where life or death of the defendant may hang in the balance. The very effort to obtain later DNA testing can sometimes face insurmountable barriers. If the prosecution is unwilling to agree to a DNA test, the defendant may bring a habeas petition and seek a court order for DNA testing pursuant to the discovery procedures that apply to habeas corpus proceedings. Under a strict reading of *Herrera*, however, a *claim* of innocence is an insufficient ground on which to seek habeas relief absent a *showing* of probable innocence. Query, how does the habeas petitioner, who asserts innocence but does not have DNA testing or other strong evidence required to show probable innocence, avoid dismissal under *Herrera* at the outset and reach the discovery stage at which potentially exonerating DNA testing may be ordered and obtained?

Is there a constitutional right to post-conviction DNA testing or access to law enforcement DNA databases in furtherance of a claim of innocence? In Jason Kreag, *Letting Innocence Suffer: The Need for Access to the Law Enforcement Database*, 36 Cardozo L. Rev. 805 (2015), the author argues that convicted defendants retain a due process liberty interest to access evidence that can establish their innocence. Just as prosecutors and police disagree about convicted defendants' requests for DNA testing, they differ about requests for access to federal and state DNA databases in order to possibly match crime scene DNA evidence to an unknown "real culprit" (contrasting case histories discussed by author). Should courts recognize such a right?

In many cases, DNA testing done at the defendant's behest actually establishes guilt rather than innocence. Some commentators argue that the defendant should be penalized for obtaining the test that wasted both time and money. *See, e.g.*,

Gwendolyn Carroll, *Proven Guilty: An Examination of the Penalty-Free World of Post-Conviction DNA Testing*, 97 J. Crim. L. & Criminology 665 (2007) (recommending that prisoner lose good time prison credits for requesting DNA testing that confirms guilt). Do you think this is a good idea? What does a guilty prisoner facing the death penalty have to lose?

Also, as discussed later in this chapter, the severe limitations in AEDPA on bringing successive habeas petitions and on seeking federal habeas corpus relief on claims that have not been exhausted in the state courts may preclude a defendant from bringing a post-appellate habeas petition as a means to obtain potentially exculpatory DNA testing. In light of some very high-profile DNA-based exonerations in recent years (see the Innocence Project's website, above), judicial and prosecutorial resistance to allowing DNA testing to show possible actual innocence years after conviction appears to be softening somewhat. For example, in *Skinner v. Switzer*, 562 U.S. 521 (2011), discussed earlier in this chapter, the Supreme Court approved the use of a civil rights action under 42 U.S.C. § 1983 for injunctive relief as a vehicle for a death row prisoner to seek DNA testing that he claimed would eventually exonerate him. For an interesting and troubling empirical study of cases involving innocent people who were erroneously convicted, *see* Brandon L. Garrett, *Judging Innocence*, 108 Colum. L. Rev. 55 (2008). Professor Garrett suggests that although the *Osborne* decision "gingerly skirt[s]" the question of whether to recognize a federal constitutional right to relief based upon a substantial showing of actual innocence, "properly understood, the ruling places pressure on states to create meaningful avenues to prove innocence." Brandon L. Garrett, *DNA and Due Process*, 78 Fordham L. Rev. 2919 (2010).

Possible future modification of Herrera? In a very unusual procedural order, the Supreme Court, in *In re Davis*, 557 U.S. 952 (2009), took the exceedingly rare action of accepting *original* habeas corpus jurisdiction over a habeas petition which challenges the petitioner's death sentence based on a claim of actual innocence. The Court's order, while accepting original habeas jurisdiction, also transferred the petition to the Southern District of Georgia for hearing and determination on Davis' innocence claim, and directed the lower court to "receive testimony and make findings of fact as to whether evidence that could not have been obtained at trial clearly establishes petitioner's innocence."

The Court's unsigned procedural order was on a vote of 6–2, with Justice Souter having just retired from the Court, and newly-sworn Justice Sotomayor taking no part in the Court's consideration or decision on the petition. Of particular note is Justice Stevens' concurring opinion, joined by Justices Ginsburg and Breyer, expressing the views that "it is arguably unconstitutional to [bar habeas] relief for a death row inmate who has established his innocence," and, alternatively, that "it would be an atrocious violation of our Constitution and the principles upon which it is based to execute an innocent person" (internal quotes and citations omitted). These views of the concurring Justices are at least arguably at variance with the holding of *Herrera*, that a claim of innocence, by itself, does not raise a constitutional ground for habeas relief. Three other Justices (Chief Justice Roberts, and Justices Kennedy and Alito) voted with the majority, but without joining the Stevens concurrence. Might this seemingly obscure procedural order and 6–2 vote be a harbinger of the Court's willingness to reconsider and perhaps ultimately abandon or modify its much-criticized *Herrera* decision, and to open the door wider for habeas courts to give serious consideration to innocence claims?

Subsequent developments in the Davis case. After transfer of the habeas petition from the Supreme Court, the district court held, in agreement with the three concurring Supreme Court Justices, that execution of an innocent person, even one who had received a fair and error-free trial, violates the Eighth Amendment. The court went on, however, to hold Davis to a burden of establishing his innocence in the transferred evidentiary hearing by clear and convincing evidence, and concluded in a detailed opinion that Davis had fallen far short of meeting this burden. *In re Davis*, 2010 WL 3385081 (S.D. Ga. Oct. 8, 2010). The Eleventh Circuit then denied Davis's motion for a Certificate of Appealability and dismissed the appeal, and the Supreme Court denied certiorari. After last-ditch appeals and a final unsuccessful application for clemency from the state parole board, Troy Davis was executed by lethal injection by the State of Georgia on September 21, 2011. For an in-depth analysis of the facts and issues presented in *Davis* and a compelling argument that "free standing" claims of innocence should be cognizable in habeas corpus, *see* Sarah A. Mourer, *Gateway to Justice: Constitutional Claims to Actual Innocence*, 64 U. Miami L. Rev. 1279 (2010).

[e] Exhaustion of State Remedies

A long-standing principle in habeas corpus jurisprudence, called the *exhaustion requirement*, requires state prisoners, before being allowed to seek habeas corpus relief in *federal* court, to first challenge the legality of their confinement in *state* courts. A detailed examination of the exhaustion requirement follows.

[i] Federal Statutes and Rules Mandating Exhaustion

Accordingly, even if a state prisoner petitioning for federal habeas corpus relief adequately meets the requirements, discussed above, of showing "custody" that is "in violation of federal law," relief will be denied (subject to some narrow exceptions) unless the petitioner has satisfied the exhaustion requirement, *see* 28 U.S.C. § 2254(b) and (c). A petition for habeas corpus may be denied on the merits notwithstanding the failure of the petitioner to exhaust available state remedies, § 2254(b).

Deny petition even without exhaustion. Subsection 2254(b)(2) is an exception to the exhaustion rule, though not one that benefits the petitioner. The federal court is authorized to dismiss the habeas corpus petition even if the petitioner has not exhausted state remedies on all claims. This permits the federal court to dismiss patently frivolous petitions without burdening state courts with the need to act on the issues and without requiring the federal court to take the time to consider the case again at a future date after state remedies have been exhausted.

State may waive exhaustion. Subsection (b)(3) authorizes states to waive the exhaustion requirement, but the waiver must be express rather than implied.

[ii] Rationale for Exhaustion Requirement

The exhaustion requirement, based on principles of federalism and federal-state comity, is designed to enable state courts to play a role in enforcing federal law, especially the United States Constitution. It has been said that this will serve to minimize friction between state and federal systems of justice. Do you agree that the exhaustion rule helps reduce this friction? Could it actually aggravate it?

Another rationale for the exhaustion rule is to save federal court resources by providing federal courts with a complete record of the issue developed in a state court proceeding. Think about these rationales. Does the exhaustion rule actually save federal judicial resources, since the issue of exhaustion itself must be litigated by federal court? Could the exhaustion doctrine actually waste *state* judicial resources?

The importance of the exhaustion requirement is demonstrated by *Duckworth v. Serrano*, 454 U.S. 1 (1981), in which an Indiana state prisoner filed a federal habeas corpus petition alleging the ineffective assistance of counsel at his state murder trial. Before the state trial, a prosecution witness retained defense counsel to represent her at a later proceeding. This representation created an obvious conflict of interest for the defense counsel. The defendant did not raise the ineffective counsel issue on direct appeal to the Indiana Supreme Court or in a habeas corpus petition to a federal district court. It was first presented in a habeas corpus petition to the United States Court of Appeals. The Court of Appeals acknowledged that the issue had not been raised in a state forum or in the federal district court, but nevertheless reversed in order to conserve judicial resources since the matter was a "clear violation" of the defendant's Sixth Amendment rights. The Supreme Court reversed the Court of Appeals and dismissed the habeas petition for failure to exhaust state remedies, even if the habeas corpus petition raised a "clear violation" of defendant's constitutional rights. The Court feared that a "clear violation" exception would invite habeas corpus petitioners to bypass state procedures and file initially in federal court. The *Duckworth* Court observed that "it would be unseemly in our dual system of government for the federal courts to upset a state-court conviction without affording to the state courts the opportunity to correct a constitutional violation." *Id.* at 4.

[iii] Meaning of Exhaustion—"Fairly Presented" to State Courts

The exhaustion rule generally bars a state prisoner's habeas corpus action from proceeding in federal court unless the state court system has first been given the chance to rule on the federal constitutional claim presented in the federal habeas corpus petition. The claim raised on federal habeas must first have been *fairly presented* to the state court system, i.e., the defendant ordinarily must have meaningfully raised the federal issue in the state proceedings. *See Anderson v. Harless*, 459 U.S. 4 (1982) (defense counsel in state proceeding did not directly raise federal constitutional issue). If a habeas corpus petition contains some exhausted and some unexhausted claims, the petition should be dismissed until all claims have been exhausted. *Rose v. Lundy*, 455 U.S. 509 (1982).

Futility. The exhaustion requirement does not demand the impossible. If a federal issue was not raised in a state court because doing so would have been futile, the rule will be deemed satisfied. For example, no exhaustion is necessary if the identical issue was raised unsuccessfully by the petitioner or by another person before the state's highest court, and the state court has failed to issue a ruling despite the considerable passage of time. *See, e.g., House v. Mayo*, 324 U.S. 42 (1945). On the other hand, a recent change in state law may require submission of the issue once again to state courts.

[f] Procedures That Need Not Be Exhausted

If a state prisoner claiming to be held in custody in violation of the federal constitution has a direct appeal available in state court to raise an issue, the state remedy ordinarily must be pursued before federal habeas corpus is available. The prisoner must first have presented the state court system with the substance of the federal claim. But if the prisoner is unsuccessful in having the state court grant relief on the federal issue, he or she does not have to seek a writ of *certiorari* from the United States Supreme Court in order to have exhausted state remedies. State collateral remedies, such as state habeas corpus, need not ordinarily be pursued before a state prisoner can seek federal habeas relief if the issue was already raised on direct appeal in state courts. Similarly, when a state appellate court has been presented with a federal constitutional issue but has ignored it, state remedies may be deemed exhausted even if other state procedures may still be available. *See Castille v. Peoples*, 489 U.S. 346 (1989).

[g] Related Doctrines Dealing with Failure to Exhaust State Remedies

Failure to exhaust a habeas claim in state court will usually, but not always, bar consideration of the prisoner's claim in federal court. The Supreme Court has recognized several types of exceptions to the exhaustion rule. However, those exceptions have grown ever narrower in recent years, as discussed below, to the point where an unexhausted habeas claim has almost no chance of being ruled on by federal habeas courts.

A series of related doctrines, some grounded in statute and some based on the Supreme Court's habeas corpus jurisprudence, has provided further specificity to the traditional exhaustion requirement. All of these doctrines and rules, sometimes with only slight shades of difference between them, are variations on the same basic exhaustion theme—that federal habeas courts will not consider an unexhausted claim unless there is compelling reason to do so and a good reason why the claim was not presented and exhausted in state court.

[i] Deliberate Bypass

The "deliberate bypass" rule, prevalent in the 1960s and 1970s but now discarded, gave a federal judge the discretion to deny a habeas corpus petition to a state prisoner who intentionally failed to raise the federal issue in a state court. To cause the denial of a federal habeas corpus petition, the bypass of state remedies must have been intentional and knowing—"an intentional relinquishment or abandonment of a right or privilege." *See, e.g., McMann v. Richardson*, 397 U.S. 759 (1970) (guilty plea was deliberate bypass of issue whether plea was product of coerced confession).

[ii] Procedural Default: Cause and Prejudice

In place of the deliberate bypass rule, the Supreme Court came to adopt a more restrictive approach called the *procedural default* rule. Under this approach, failure to raise an issue at a state trial or to exhaust direct state appellate remedies, *whether deliberate or not*, is considered to be a procedural *waiver* of that issue, which will be excused by a federal habeas court only on a showing of "*cause and prejudice*" or a *fundamental miscarriage of justice*. The procedural default rule, with its extremely narrow exceptions, has had a devastating impact on the likelihood of a successful habeas corpus petition on an unexhausted issue.

Cause and prejudice. In order to excuse a failure to exhaust state remedies, a habeas corpus petitioner must show (1) some excusable *cause* for the procedural default, and (2) that it produced actual *prejudice*. For applications of this standard, *see, e.g., Bousley v. United States*, 523 U.S. 614 (1998) (cause and prejudice applicable to failure to use direct appeal to challenge voluntariness of guilty plea); *Keeney v. Tamayo-Reyes*, 504 U.S. 1 (1992) (cause and prejudice standard applied to excuse failure to develop material fact in state court proceedings); *Wainwright v. Sykes*, 433 U.S. 72 (1977) (defendant's failure to object to admission of confession at trial court, under Florida law, constituted a waiver of a later challenge in Florida courts; federal habeas corpus permissible only if defendant can prove cause and prejudice for failure to object); *Francis v. Henderson*, 425 U.S. 536 (1976) (failure to make timely objection to racial composition of grand jury, therefore barring state court consideration of issue, cognizable in federal habeas corpus only on showing of cause and prejudice for failure to make timely objection).

Cause. "Cause" for a procedural default ordinarily means that "some objective factor external to the defense impeded counsel's efforts to comply with the State's procedural rule." *Murray v. Carrier*, 477 U.S. 478, 488 (1986). Examples include an inability to comply because the factual or legal basis for invoking the procedural rule was not reasonably available to counsel, perhaps because of its novelty, or because officials somehow interfered with compliance with the state procedure. On the other hand, a defense attorney's ignorance or inadvertence is not deemed "cause" unless counsel's legal work is so poor that it violates the Sixth Amendment's guarantee of the effective assistance of counsel. Criminal defendants are generally considered to be responsible for their lawyers' actions. But when a defense lawyer's conduct is so deficient that it violates the Sixth Amendment, the Supreme Court has held that the harm is "external" to the accused and is somehow attributed to the state. *Coleman v. Thompson*, 501 U.S. 722 (1991) (lawyer filed late notice of appeal in state court, thereby barring consideration of issues raised in the appeal).

and when the adequacy and independence of a state legal ground is not clear, there is a presumption that there is no independent and adequate state ground. *Coleman v. Thompson*, 501 U.S. 722 (1991). To say the least, this is a murky area of habeas corpus jurisprudence.

Relationship of independent state ground to other exhaustion rules. The doctrines of independent and adequate state grounds and cause and prejudice (as well as cause and innocence) are, in actuality, part of the same formula. An adequate and independent state ground for finding a procedural default will bar federal habeas review of the federal claim unless the petitioner can establish either "cause and prejudice" or a "fundamental miscarriage of justice." *Harris v. Reed*, 489 U.S. 255, 262 (1989). In other words, a state procedural default that bars *state* review of a federal claim may also bar *federal* review of it unless cause and prejudice or a fundamental miscarriage of justice can be shown. *See Walker v. Martin*, 562 U.S. 307 (2011) (California's timeliness rule for state habeas corpus petitions, requiring petitioners to file known claims "as promptly as the circumstances allow," held to provide independent and adequate state ground to bar federal habeas review of belated ineffective assistance of counsel claim).

Most recent independent and adequate state ground decisions. See Johnson v. Lee, 136 S. Ct. 1802 (2016) (California rule consistent with rules in other states—barring *state* collateral review of "procedurally defaulted" claim presented for first time on state habeas petition which could have been raised on direct appeal—held independent and adequate ground to bar *federal* habeas review of same claim); *Kansas v. Carr*, 136 S. Ct. 633 (2016) (state supreme court determination based on the Eighth Amendment—that capital defendant was entitled to jury instruction that he need not prove mitigating circumstances beyond a reasonable doubt—held *not* to rest on independent state grounds, and therefore review (and eventual reversal) by U.S. Supreme Court was not precluded).

All of the successive elaborations on the exhaustion requirement discussed above, culminating in the AEDPA cause and innocence and miscarriage of justice rules, have increasingly made habeas relief virtually impossible to obtain for petitioners who have not fully presented and developed their claims (with the notable exception of claims of ineffective assistance of counsel) in state court, absent a strong showing of likely *miscarriage of justice*—in other words, it must be shown to be probable that a factually innocent defendant has been convicted.

[h] Effect of Previous Proceedings and Adjudications

A pervasive problem with federal habeas corpus is that prisoners frequently file repeated federal habeas corpus petitions raising the same issue or new issues that could have been presented in the first petition. A related problem is the effect of prior state adjudications of the same issues raised in a federal habeas corpus petition. To some extent these problems result from the historical principle that the doctrine of *res judicata* does not apply to a federal court's denial of habeas corpus relief. Despite this historical principle, however, the Supreme Court most recently has expressly given near-preclusive effect to state court decisions being challenged on federal habeas review: "[AEDPA] stops short of imposing a complete bar on federal court relitigation of claims already rejected in state proceedings." *Harrington v. Richter*, 562 U.S. 86, 102 (2011). Both of these problems raise important questions about the conservation of limited judicial resources and the respect (i.e., "*comity*") that should be accorded decisions on the same issue by other judges (sometimes from other jurisdictions).

Courts have often denied relief on successive habeas petitions that either allege the same old grounds as a previous petition or conjure up new, often fanciful grounds, as being an *abuse of the writ*. As discussed below, AEDPA has created procedures for weeding out repetitious and abusive petitions.

[i] Successive Petitions from the Same Prisoner

Successive petitions on the same issue. The changes in the federal habeas corpus statute enacted by AEDPA make it extremely difficult for a prisoner to obtain relief in a second habeas corpus petition on grounds already raised in a previous petition. *See* 28 U.S.C. § 2244. Dismissal for failure to exhaust does not, however, preclude the petitioner from seeking habeas relief again *after* the petitioner has gone back and exhausted available state remedies. *See Stewart v. Martinez-Villareal*, 523 U.S. 637 (1998) (later petition under such circumstance essentially seeks resolution of the first petition).

Successive petitions on different issues. AEDPA also makes it difficult to raise an issue in a second federal habeas corpus petition that was not raised in the first one. Following some earlier precedent, AEDPA makes it imperative that a person in custody bring all available claims in the first habeas petition; otherwise they will be deemed to be procedurally defaulted. *See* 28 U.S.C. § 2244(b)(2).

Refiling after dismissal for failure to exhaust. A habeas corpus petition filed after an earlier such petition was dismissed without adjudication on the merits because of a failure to exhaust state remedies is not a "second or successive" petition. *Slack v. McDaniel*, 529 U.S. 473 (2000).

Procedural hurdles to second petition: permission by court of appeals. As an added hurdle to the successful filing of a second habeas corpus petition, AEDPA now requires the applicant to receive permission to file the successive petition from a three-judge panel of the Court of Appeals. 28 U.S.C. § 2244. The three-judge panel, acting as a "gatekeeper," is under a strict 30-day time limit for rendering a decision on whether to authorize the filing of the second petition. Denial of permission is not subject to review by a petition for rehearing by the panel, or via a petition to the United States Supreme Court for a writ of *certiorari*.

This high procedural hurdle imposed by AEDPA has withstood constitutional attack. *See Felker v. Turpin*, 518 U.S. 651 (1996); Joseph T. Thai, *Recent Development*, 20 Harv. J. L. & Pub. Pol'y 605 (1997) (discussing *Felker*). *See also Calderon v. Thompson*, 523 U.S. 538 (1998) (appellate court *sua sponte* changing its mind and opting to revisit its own earlier decision denying habeas corpus relief to a state prisoner may do so only to avoid a miscarriage of justice).

Supreme Court's original habeas corpus jurisdiction. Prisoners, especially those who may be unable to surmount various procedural hurdles to having their petitions heard by the federal district courts, may petition the Supreme Court directly for a writ of habeas corpus, though such writs are granted only in exceptional circumstances. Sup. Ct. R. 20(4)(a); *Felker*, 518 U.S. at 665. In *In re Davis*, discussed earlier in this chapter, the Court accepted original habeas jurisdiction (albeit transferring the petition to the lower court for factfinding and decision on the death row petitioner's claim of actual innocence) in a procedural setting where a majority of the Justices apparently recognized that in the absence of the Court's extraordinary acceptance of original jurisdiction, the petitioner would have been put to death without ever receiving a full evidentiary airing of his colorable claim of actual innocence.

[ii] Prior Adjudications of the Same Issue in Other Cases

Prior Supreme Court adjudication of an issue. Habeas corpus law has long stated that a prior decision by the United States Supreme Court in the case is generally dispositive in a subsequent habeas corpus petition on the same point. The federal habeas corpus statute as amended by AEDPA now generally provides in 28 U.S.C. § 2244(c) that "a prior judgment of the Supreme Court of the United States on an appeal or review by a writ of *certiorari* at the instance of a prisoner of the decision of such State court, shall be conclusive as to all issues of fact or law [which were] actually adjudicated by the Supreme Court therein."

Prior state court adjudication of an issue: strong deference. The AEDPA amendments to habeas corpus law reflect a strong deference to state court adjudications. If a state court has resolved an issue against a person (perhaps in a direct appeal or a state post-conviction petition) who then files a federal habeas corpus petition addressing that same issue, the federal court must give the state court's decision great deference. Indeed, there is a presumption under AEDPA that the state court correctly resolved a factual issue, and the petitioner has a heavy burden of establishing that the state court decision was incorrect. *See Burt v. Titlow*, 517 U.S. 12 (2013), excerpted below, emphasizing the petitioner's burden under the AEDPA standard of "rebutting the state court's factual findings 'by clear and convincing evidence.'"

The prior-adjudication limits in 28 U.S.C. § 2254 are exceedingly strict:

. . . . . .

> (d) An application for a writ of habeas corpus on behalf of a person in custody pursuant to the judgment of a State court shall not be granted with respect to any claim that was adjudicated on the merits in State court proceedings unless the adjudication of the claim—

> (1) resulted in a decision that was contrary to, or involved an unreasonable application of, clearly established Federal law, as determined by the Supreme Court of the United States; or
>
> (2) resulted in a decision that was based on an unreasonable determination of the facts in light of the evidence presented in the State court proceeding.

(e)(1) In a proceeding instituted by an application for a writ of habeas corpus by a person in custody pursuant to the judgment of a State court, a determination of a factual issue made by a state court shall be presumed to be correct. The applicant shall have the burden of rebutting the presumption of correctness by clear and convincing evidence.

Notes

1. *Decision on federal law.* Note that this great degree of deference even embraces a state court's decision on *federal* law. A state court's reasonable, though arguably erroneous, application of a clearly established federal law appears to be able to withstand reversal in a habeas corpus action. *See, e.g., Knowles v. Mirzayance*, 556 U.S. 111 (2009) (state court rejection of ineffective assistance of counsel claim held neither contrary to, nor an unreasonable application of, clearly established federal law); *Waddington v. Sarausad*, 555 U.S. 179 (2009) (state court jury instruction, although arguably ambiguous and erroneous, held not an unreasonable application of clearly established federal law). Other recent examples (among many) of this highly deferential standard include *Berghuis v. Smith*, 559 U.S. 314 (2010) (state supreme court decision rejecting habeas petitioner's claim that jury was not drawn from a fair cross section of the community; same); *Smith v. Spisak*, 558 U.S. 139 (2010) (state supreme court decision upholding jury instructions on mitigation in penalty phase of capital case; same). However, federal habeas corpus may be granted if the state court arrived at a conclusion of law opposite that reached by the United States Supreme Court, or if the state court decided a case differently than the Supreme Court did on a set of materially indistinguishable facts. *Williams v. Taylor*, 529 U.S. 420 (2000).

In three decisions from the same term, the Supreme Court extended even further the extraordinary degree of deference that federal habeas courts owe to state court constitutional decisions. *See Cullen v. Pinholster*, 563 U.S. 170 (2011) (habeas relief foreclosed because state court *could have* reasonably concluded that *Strickland* requirements had not been met); *Premo v. Moore*, 562 U.S. 115 (2011) (state post-conviction court's conclusion that defense counsel had not rendered ineffective assistance by entering quick plea of no-contest, without having first moved to suppress petitioner's confession, also held not an unreasonable application of *Strickland* where, similarly, no prejudice was shown); *Harrington v. Richter*, 562 U.S. 86 (2011) (state court's determination that petitioner's counsel had not rendered ineffective assistance by failing to consult blood evidence experts held not an unreasonable application of *Strickland v. Washington*, given absence of any showing of prejudice from counsel's alleged failure). Even where the state court decision lacks any explanation, under *Harrington* and *Pinholster* the habeas petitioner must still show there was no reasonable basis for the state court to deny relief. A habeas court must "look through" the unexplained state denial to determine why habeas relief was denied. *Wilson v. Sellers*, 138 S. Ct. 1188 (2018). Further, the *Pinholster* decision limits federal habeas review to the record that was before the state court that previously adjudicated the petitioner's claim, 563 U.S. at 181, making it much more difficult than previously for a petitioner to introduce new evidence in support of his or her claim of unlawful conviction or imprisonment.

This trend, to limit the availability of habeas relief and to extend near-total deference to state court adjudications, continues with even greater intensity in the Supreme Court's most recent terms. In a welter of decisions, many of them via *per curiam* or unanimous or near-unanimous opinions written in very pointed language, the Court has reversed various circuit or district court grants of habeas relief because the lower federal court failed to accord adequate deference to state court findings of fact or applications of Supreme Court precedent on a great variety of substantive and procedural issues. *See, e.g., Virginia v. LeBlanc*, 137 S. Ct. 1726, 1729 (2017) (reversing Fourth Circuit for failure to afford adequate deference to state court ruling that Virginia's statutory scheme of "geriatric release" satisfies the requirement of *Graham v. Florida* (discussed in Chapter 16) that juvenile offenders may not be sentenced to life imprisonment without hope of parole or some form of release; state court ruling held "not objectively unreasonable" in light of current Supreme Court case law); *Kernan v. Hinajosa*, 136 S. Ct. 1603, 1606 (2016) (reversing Ninth Circuit for failure to review inmate's *ex post facto*-based habeas petition, challenging new state law that denied good-time sentence credits to gang members, through "AEDPA's deferential lens"); *Marshall v. Rodgers*, 569 U.S. 58 (2013) (*per curiam*), and *Johnson v. Williams*, 568 U.S. 289 (2012) (both reversing Ninth Circuit); *Parker v. Matthews*, 567 U.S. 37 (2012) (reversing Sixth Circuit); *Coleman v. Johnson*, 566 U.S. 650 (2012) (reversing Third Circuit); *Hardy v. Cross*, 565 U.S. 65 (2011) (reversing Seventh Circuit).

2. *"Doubly deferential" standard for habeas claims of ineffective assistance of counsel.* Consider the following emphatic recent language from the Supreme Court in *Burt v. Titlow*, 517 U.S. 12 (2013):

> When a state prisoner asks a federal court to set aside a sentence due to ineffective assistance of counsel . . . our cases require that the federal court use a "doubly deferential" standard of review that gives both the state court and the defense attorney the benefit of the doubt. *Cullen v. Pinholster*, 560 U.S. 170, 190 (2011). In this case, the Sixth Circuit failed to apply that doubly deferential standard by refusing to credit a state court's reasonable factual finding and by assuming that counsel was ineffective [in advising a defendant to withdraw a plea to manslaughter and to stand trial instead for murder, for which the defendant was then convicted and sentenced to a much longer term of imprisonment than the sentence offered under the earlier manslaughter plea agreement] where the record was silent. . . .

> [AEDPA] and *Strickland v. Washington*, 466 U.S. 668 (1984) do not permit federal judges to so casually second-guess the decisions of their state-court colleagues. . . .

Id. at 15. The Court added:

> AEDPA erects a formidable barrier to federal habeas relief for prisoners whose claims have been adjudicated in state court. AEDPA requires a "state prisoner [to] show that the state court's ruling . . . was so lacking in justification that there was an error . . . beyond any possibility for fairminded disagreement." "If this standard is difficult to meet, that is because it was meant to be." *Harrington v. Richter*, 562 U.S. 86, 102 (2011). We will not lightly conclude that a State's criminal justice system has experienced the "extreme malfunctio[n]" for which federal habeas relief is the remedy.

Id. at 19–20. See also Woods v. Etherton, 136 S. Ct. 1149 (2016) (claim of ineffective assistance of both trial and appellate counsel, based on their alleged failure to raise hearsay objections to testimony regarding anonymous tip that led to arrest and conviction for possession of cocaine with intent to deliver, rejected under the *Harrington/Burt* standard of "doubly deferential" review; reaffirming that habeas relief is to be denied unless "no fair minded jurist could disagree" that counsel had been ineffective).

In two more recent applications of *Richter*, the Court denied habeas relief because the error was not sufficiently serious. *Kernan v. Cuero*, 138 S. Ct. 4 (2017), held that, when a state court's failure to order specific performance of a plea agreement does not violate federal law, habeas corpus relief is unavailable. *Dunn v. Madison*, 138 S. Ct. 9 (2017) similarly held that state court determinations about a prisoner's competency to be executed were not "so lacking in justification" to be an error beyond any possibility for fair minded disagreement.

In your view, is the Supreme Court's recent consensus (as evidenced by such repeated, often stinging rebukes to "wayward" lower federal courts, most notably but not exclusively the Ninth Circuit), to subject only the most blatantly erroneous state court decisions to habeas review for constitutional error, a healthy manifestation of federal respect for state court adjudication and state prerogatives, or does it operate to diminish almost to irrelevancy The Great Writ of habeas corpus? For a critical view, *see* Jonathan M. Kirschbaum, *Supreme Court's Recent Decisions in* Richter *and* Pinholster *Further Tilt Playing Field Against State Prisoners Seeking Habeas Relief*, 89 CRIM. L. RPTR. 672 (2011).

How does one square the Court's limitation of habeas review in *Pinholster* to the record that was before the state court with the Court's own startling decision, discussed above, in *In re Davis*, 557 U.S. 952 (2009) (transferring the petition of a death row prisoner who claimed actual innocence to the federal district court and specifically directing that court to "receive testimony and make findings of fact as to whether evidence that could not have been obtained at trial clearly establishes petitioner's innocence")?

Overturned if unreasonable. A state court's decision applying federal law must be *both* erroneous and unreasonable. "Unreasonable application" of established federal law means that a state court either identified the correct legal rule but unreasonably applied it to the facts of the case, or unreasonably extended the legal principle to a new context that should not apply. Section 2254(d)(1) provides a remedy for instances in which a state court unreasonably *applies* Supreme Court precedent; it does not require state courts to *extend* that precedent or enable federal courts to treat the failure to do so as error. *See White v. Woodall*, 572 U.S. 415 (2014) (trial court refused to instruct jury in capital case not to draw any adverse inference from defendant's decision not to testify during the penalty phase).

In an extremely rare result on post-AEDPA habeas review, a 5–4 majority of the Supreme Court in *Brumfield v. Cain*, 135 S. Ct. 2269 (2015), held that a trial judge's rejection, without hearing, of a murder defendant's claim that he was "intellectually disabled" and therefore could not be executed under *Atkins v. Virginia*, 536 U.S. 304 (2002) (discussed in Ch. 16), was an "unreasonable determination of the facts in light of the evidence presented in the State court proceeding" under AEDPA. The majority found that the trial judge erred in denying the defense the opportunity to establish his claimed disability under *Atkins*. This decision stands in dramatic contrast to the many post-AEDPA habeas decisions discussed earlier, finding that the state court determinations at issue were *not* the result of either unreasonable determinations of fact or unreasonable applications of clearly established Supreme Court case law.

3. *Summing it all up.* The Supreme Court's demonstrated eagerness in its recent Terms—to grant *certiorari* and reverse grants of habeas review and relief by numerous lower federal courts—is dramatic evidence of the consensus it has now attained regarding the very limited scope of federal habeas review of state convictions and sentences. Even so, some areas of ambivalence and tension among the Justices concerning The Great Writ, discussed earlier in this chapter, still remain to be fully resolved. Despite AEDPA and the Court's ever-stricter habeas corpus jurisprudence, a sufficiently compelling showing of likely actual innocence, or the need to procure evidence that may prove innocence, may tweak the conscience of a federal habeas court, or the Supreme Court, to allow a habeas petition to proceed.

[iii] Retroactivity: *Teague*

Federal habeas corpus relief ordinarily is sought after a state court judgment has become final. Since the state trial and direct appellate decisions may have occurred years ago, the habeas petition may be based on legal developments occurring since the state decision, or a new theory that has not yet been accepted. For example, if the United States Supreme Court expands the scope of a constitutional provision, state prisoners convicted years before the new decision may argue that the new Supreme Court rule should cause their earlier state court conviction or sentence to be reversed. For habeas petitioners to be successful, however, the new decision will have to be applied retroactively—to convictions that were final before the new decision was announced. Recent Supreme Court decisions have greatly reduced the chances that a habeas corpus petitioner will be able to get relief based on a recent decision or a novel theory.

In a complicated set of sometimes inconsistent decisions, often marked by no majority opinion, the United States Supreme Court has severely limited the retroactive application of new decisions in habeas corpus cases. In the leading case, *Teague v. Lane*, 490 U.S. 1031 (1989), the petitioner's state conviction became final in 1983, several years before the Supreme Court decided in *Batson v. Kentucky*, 476 U.S. 79 (1986), that the Equal Protection Clause bars the use of peremptory challenges based on a potential juror's race. The habeas petitioner in *Teague* had been convicted by an all-white jury selected after the prosecutor had used his 10 peremptory challenges to exclude blacks.

There was no majority opinion in *Teague*, although Justice White's partial concurrence found the plurality's approach "acceptable." Justice O'Connor's plurality opinion noted that the retroactive application of new decisions severely interferes with the important value of finality in criminal cases. The plurality held that rules of constitutional criminal procedure resulting from new Supreme Court case law will ordinarily not be applied to cases that became final before the date of the new decision. The Court recognized two exceptions. First, a new rule would be retroactive if it placed certain conduct beyond the authority of the substantive criminal law (such as a new decision holding that it is a violation of due process to convict a drug addict of the crime of using narcotics). It should be obvious that this exception will rarely arise. The second *Teague* exception is also extremely unlikely to occur. New constitutionally required procedures apply retroactively if, without them, the likelihood of an accurate conviction is seriously diminished. The key question is whether the new procedure is a "watershed" rule of criminal procedure that alters our understanding of the "bedrock procedural elements" essential to the fairness of a trial. Under this standard, the Court in *Teague* held that *Batson* should be applied retroactively.

Application of Teague. Teague has been followed in subsequent Supreme Court decisions as if the plurality decision were a majority. *See Graham v. Collins*, 506 U.S. 461 (1993) (defining a "new rule" as one that breaks new ground, imposes a new obligation on either the "states or the federal government, or was not dictated by precedent existing at the time the petitioner's [state] conviction became final."). These "extremely narrow" exceptions to the general rule of nonretroactivity have made *Teague* an almost insurmountable obstacle to both direct appellants and habeas petitioners who seek retroactive application of new rules of criminal procedure.

In contrast, however, in *Montgomery v. Louisiana*, 136 S. Ct. 718 (2016), the Supreme Court read *Teague* as requiring courts to give retroactive effect to new *substantive rules* of constitutional law—a proposition that had not previously been clearly settled:

> The Court now holds that when a new substantive rule of constitutional law controls the outcome of a case, the Constitution requires state collateral

> review courts to give retroactive effect to that rule.... Substantive rules, then, set forth categorical constitutional guarantees that place certain criminal laws and punishments altogether beyond the State's power to impose.

Id. at 729. The Court in *Montgomery* went on to hold that its decision in *Miller v. Alabama*, 567 U.S. 460 (2012) (discussed in Chapter 16), forbidding the mandatory imposition of life-without-parole sentences on juvenile homicide offenders, announced a substantive rule of constitutional law that must be given retroactive effect.

Similarly, in *Welch v. United States*, 136 S. Ct. 1257 (2016), the Supreme Court determined (over a vigorous dissent from Justice Thomas) that its decision in *Johnson v. United States*, 135 S. Ct. 2251 (2015) (definition of prior "violent felony" in the residual clause of the Armed Career Criminal Act of 1984 held unconstitutionally vague in violation of due process), announced a substantive rule that is to be applied retroactively on collateral review. Query: in your view, do the *Montgomery* and *Welch* decisions flow directly and ineluctably from *Teague*, or do they signify an expansion of *Teague*'s general rule, subject only to "extremely narrow" exceptions of nonretroactivity?

When a habeas corpus petition is filed, the federal court will treat any question of retroactivity as a threshold issue to be resolved before considering the merits of the petition. If granting the relief requested in the petition would create or apply a new rule of constitutional law, the petition will be dismissed unless one of the above two rare *Teague* exceptions applies.

Teague and its progeny have greatly reduced the likelihood that a habeas corpus petition will succeed except in cases where the state courts have flatly misapplied Supreme Court precedents. It is now extremely difficult for the petitioner either to take advantage of recent constitutional decisions or to convince a habeas court to announce a new rule of constitutional criminal law. As a result, now a criminal defense lawyer must try to raise every possible new ground for relief (whether recently recognized or still merely theoretical) at or before trial, or on direct appeal within the state system, and even on petition for *certiorari* to the United States Supreme Court. Otherwise, it may be too late to raise the issue in a habeas corpus petition. In other words, it is possible to seek to break new doctrinal ground on direct appeal and *certiorari*, but nearly impossible to do so on habeas.

[i] Procedures

[i] Statute of Limitations

AEDPA changes in federal habeas corpus law drastically modify previous practice by establishing a one-year statute of limitations on filing most habeas corpus petitions. *See* 28 U.S.C. § 2244(d). The purpose of this change is to expedite the final resolution of habeas corpus petitions.

One-year time limit. In most cases, the offender will have one year from the date the conviction and sentence become final after the direct review process in state appellate courts. The precise impact of this standard is somewhat unclear. For example, when does the clock begin running if the defendant applies for *certiorari* in the United States Supreme Court after the state Supreme Court has refused to hear the case on direct appeal or has ruled against the defendant?

If the prisoner seeks state post-conviction relief after an unsuccessful direct appeal, the one-year limitation period is tolled while the state post-conviction matter is pending. However, if the petition for state post-conviction relief is itself untimely, then the one-year statute of limitations under AEDPA is not tolled. *See Wall v. Kholi*, 562 U.S. 545 (2011) (filing of state court motion to reduce sentence tolled one-year AEDPA statute of limitations); *Allen v. Siebert*, 552 U.S. 3 (2007) (federal habeas petitioner may not rely on "untimely filed" state post-conviction petition to toll AEDPA's one-year statute of limitations); *Pace v. DeGuglielmo*, 544 U.S. 408 (2005) (same result as in *Siebert*; statute not equitably tolled for period during which untimely petition for state post-conviction relief was pending prior to filing of federal habeas petition).

"Equitable tolling" of one-year statute of limitations based on attorney's extraordinary misconduct in failing to file timely petition. In *Holland v. Florida*, 560 U.S. 631 (2010) the Supreme Court recognized that the one-year statute of limitations is not an inflexible jurisdictional rule, but rather is subject in appropriate cases to "equitable tolling" where the habeas petitioner shows that he has been diligently pursuing his rights and that some extraordinary circumstance prevented timely filing of his petition. In this case, the Court recounted allegations of gross neglect by the attorney of a prisoner sentenced to death. The lawyer's misconduct extended over several years and arguably violated fundamental canons of professional responsibility, culminating in the failure of the attorney to file a petition for habeas corpus relief. After discovering his attorney's failure to file, the prisoner promptly filed his own, albeit untimely, *pro se* petition. The Court remanded the case for the Eleventh Circuit to determine, in the first instance, "whether the facts in the record entitle Holland to equitable tolling, or whether further proceedings, including an evidentiary hearing, might indicate that [Holland] should prevail." *Id.* at 654.

In *Maples v. Thomas*, 565 U.S. 266 (2012), the Court, relying on the *Holland* doctrine of allowing equitable tolling in extraordinary and compelling cases, found that the federal habeas petitioner there had shown sufficient "cause and prejudice" to justify his failure to file his petition for relief from his state court capital murder conviction and death sentence within the one-year statutory time limit. The Court determined that the petitioner himself had acted with due diligence but that his counsel had "abandoned his client without notice" at a critical juncture, causing the petitioner to miss the filing deadline.

This, and other recent decisions discussed in this chapter and in Chapter 16, appear to reflect a growing concern among the Justices to assure that sentences of death are arrived at by fair procedures and proceedings. *See, e.g., Christeson v. Roper*, 135 S. Ct. 891 (2015) (*per curiam*, but with two Justices dissenting) (statute of limitations for filing federal habeas was equitably tolled when the defendant's trial counsel missed a deadline for filing a habeas petition and the trial court later denied a motion to appoint substitute counsel to proceed with the habeas claim; trial counsel abandoned his client, had a conflict of interest, and could not have been expected to argue own incompetence).

Claim of actual innocence may overcome one-year habeas statute of limitations. In *McQuiggan v. Perkins*, 569 U.S. 383 (2013), a 5–4 majority of the Supreme Court held that a claim of actual innocence, if sufficiently strong and if brought with sufficient diligence, may overcome the one-year statute of limitations contained in 28 U.S.C. § 2244 for filing federal habeas challenges to state confinement. The Court reiterated, however, that a state prisoner raising a claim of actual innocence based on newly offered evidence must meet a very high threshold—i.e., a showing based on clear and convincing evidence, which will only arise in extraordinary cases, that "it is more likely than not that no reasonable juror would have convicted him in the light of the new evidence." *Id* at 399 (quoting from *Schlup v. Delo*, 513 U.S. 298, 327 (1995)). Presentation of "stale" evidence to collaterally attack a conviction and unexplained delay in presenting new evidence of innocence, the Court cautioned, may serve to undermine the credibility of a habeas petitioner's actual-innocence claim.

Equitable tolling for federal prisoner petitions to vacate sentence under 42 U.S.C. § 2255. As discussed later in this chapter, federal prisoners, under 42 U.S.C. § 2255, can seek the same habeas-type relief from unlawful confinement that state prisoners can under § 2254, subject to the same one-year statute of limitations that governs petitions by state prisoners. In *Ramos-Martinez v. United States*, 638 F.3d 315 (1st Cir. 2011), the court, without deciding the merits of the equitable tolling issue, held that under the reasoning of *Holland*, the one-year limitations period for § 2255 motions to vacate sentence was similarly subject to equitable tolling in appropriate extraordinary circumstances. The court remanded the matter for the district court to conduct an evidentiary hearing to determine the merits of the petitioner's equitable tolling claim.

Possible further reduced statute of limitations in certain states. An even shorter statute of limitations applies, theoretically, to habeas corpus petitions for review of death penalty convictions in states that have agreed to certain minimum standards for defense services in capital cases. *See* 28 U.S.C. § 2263 (in qualifying states, a federal habeas corpus petition involving a state capital case must be filed within 180 days of conclusion of direct review in state court). However, one author notes that as of 2005, no state had yet qualified for this reduced limitations period. *See* John H. Blume, *AEDPA: the "Hype" and the "Bite,"* 91 Cornell L. Rev. 259 (2006).

[ii] Written Procedures

In addition to the habeas corpus statute, 28 U.S.C. §§ 2241–2254, Congress has adopted a set of rules for federal habeas corpus proceedings. These Rules Governing Section 2254 Cases in the United States District Courts provide detailed information about habeas corpus petitions and other procedures.

[iii] Who May Bring

Ordinarily the person in custody brings the habeas corpus petition, but it can also be brought by someone else if the person in custody is unable to do so, perhaps because of age, physical condition, or circumstances of custody. *See* 28 U.S.C. § 2242(a) (petition may be signed and verified by the person seeking relief, "or by someone acting in his behalf"); *Hamdi v. Rumsfeld*, 542 U.S. 507 (2004) (habeas petition filed by father of petitioner, alleging son was being held incommunicado as alleged enemy combatant and therefore unable to file on his own behalf). If the petitioner is currently in custody, the respondent is the state official having custody over the petitioner. Usually this is the prison warden.

[iv] Petition

Form of petition. Because of the historical importance of the writ, courts have been very tolerant of habeas corpus petitions that lack technical perfection. This is especially true if, as is often the case, the petition is written and filed by an indigent prisoner. To assist in obtaining the proper information, some courts use a mandatory or permissive form that is designed to be completed with ease. A prisoner seeking to file a habeas corpus petition will be sent a blank form to fill out and return. This form often contains a laundry list of possible constitutional violations. It requires the petitioner to indicate whether he or she is complaining about each listed violation. Failure to raise an issue in this petition can be grounds to reject a later petition raising it.

The Rules Governing Section 2254 Cases provide a sample form used in many federal districts. Inadequate habeas corpus petitions can be amended. The petition must be in writing (it can be handwritten), signed, and verified by the petitioner. 28 U.S.C. § 2242. A petitioner unable to pay the usual filing fee in federal district court may seek permission to proceed *in forma pauperis*.

Content of petition. The habeas corpus petition must:

> allege the facts concerning the applicant's commitment or detention, the name of the person who has custody over him and by virtue of what claim or authority, if known.

28 U.S.C. § 2242.

[v] Issuance of Writ

Once a habeas corpus petition is filed, the court receiving it has two choices. First, it can dismiss the petition if "it appears from the application that the applicant or person detained is not entitled" to it. 28 U.S.C. § 2243. Second, it can "award the writ or issue an order directing the respondent to show cause why the writ should not be granted." *Id.* Contrary to popular belief, if the writ is issued, the prisoner is not immediately freed. All that happens is that the custodian, usually the warden or sheriff, must produce the prisoner in federal court for a hearing to assess the validity of the imprisonment. Habeas corpus petitions are given special priority on the court docket.

[vi] Answer and Reply

Unlike the usual civil procedure, a respondent named in a habeas corpus petition is not obligated to make any response unless ordered to do so by the court. If a writ or show cause order is issued, the custodian must file an "answer" which essentially explains the legal basis of the custody and why the writ should be denied. It must also deal with such procedural issues as whether the petitioner exhausted state remedies. It must describe what transcripts of other relevant proceedings are available and include relevant portions of available records. Rules Governing Section 2254 Proceedings, Rule 5.

[vii] Stay of State Court Proceedings

If a habeas corpus petitioner is currently engaged in state litigation, the federal judge before whom the habeas petition is pending has the authority to issue an order that stays the state court proceedings. 28 U.S.C. § 2251. This provision is designed to prevent state authorities from issuing an order that may be declared unconstitutional by a federal court.

[viii] Right to Counsel

As a general rule, there is no constitutional right to appointed counsel in either state or federal habeas corpus proceedings. *See, e.g., Pennsylvania v. Finley*, 481 U.S. 551 (1987) (no due process or equal protection right of counsel for indigent prisoners pursuing state habeas corpus relief). Virtually all jurisdictions, however, have a mechanism that gives a judge the discretion to appoint counsel in such cases. Federal law authorizes the appointment of counsel for indigent habeas corpus petitioners in some circumstances. *See, e.g.*, Rules Governing Section 2254 Cases, Rule 6 (appointment of counsel to assist in discovery); Rule 8(c) (appointment of counsel for evidentiary hearing).

[ix] Discovery

Although a federal habeas corpus action is technically a civil case, the Federal Rules of Civil Procedure are not applied as in normal civil cases. The rules of discovery do not apply, but federal courts can mandate some discovery in appropriate cases. Rules Governing Section 2254 Cases, Rule 6. According to the Supreme Court, in federal habeas corpus cases the federal courts are free to "fashion appropriate modes of procedure, by analogy to existing rules or otherwise in conformity with judicial usage." *Harris v. Nelson*, 394 U.S. 286, 299 (1969). For example, in *Ayestas v. Davis*, 138 S. Ct. 1080 (2018), the Court unanimously held that the denial of government funds to assist the petitioner in developing claims of ineffective assistance of trial and initial habeas counsel may be erroneous when the funding has a credible chance of enabling the petitioner to overcome "procedural default."

[x] Hearing

The usual rule is that unless the petition contains only issues of law or is dismissed on the basis of the petition and return, the federal district court or magistrate will convene an evidentiary hearing. As noted above, however, the 1996 AEDPA amendments severely limit evidentiary hearings when the applicant failed to develop the factual basis for the claim in state court. 28 U.S.C. § 2254(e)(2). If an evidentiary hearing is held, the prisoner is entitled to be present. 28 U.S.C. § 2243. The rules of evidence are somewhat relaxed at the hearing. The judge who conducted the original state trial may present a "certificate" that describes what happened at the trial. 28 U.S.C. § 2245. Evidence may include oral testimony, depositions, and if the judge permits, affidavits. Written interrogatories are permissible if affidavits are used. 28 U.S.C. § 2246. Judges are given great discretion in deciding whether to issue a subpoena for a witness.

In an unusual decision in a case involving many procedural twists and turns, the Supreme Court in *Wellons v. Hall*, 558 U.S. 220 (2010), held that the underlying claims of a prisoner sentenced to death (that the trial judge, jurors, and bailiff had committed prejudicial misconduct) were not procedurally barred on habeas corpus for failure to develop an adequate record in state court, where the petitioner had unsuccessfully made every effort to obtain discovery and adjudication on the issue in state court. The *per curiam* majority exercised the Court's "GVR" power (grant/vacate/remand), over strong dissents by Justices Scalia (joined by Thomas) and Alito (joined by Chief Justice Roberts), and directed the Eleventh Circuit to consider whether the petitioner's allegations of misconduct, together with the undisputed facts, warranted discovery and an evidentiary hearing.

No right to competence during federal habeas proceedings. The Supreme Court determined in *Ryan v. Valencia Gonzales*, 568 U.S. 57 (2013), that a habeas petitioner's alleged incompetence due to mental illness does not entitle the petitioner to a stay of habeas proceedings. The unanimous Court stated "Given the backward-looking, record-based nature of most federal habeas proceedings, counsel can generally provide effective representation to a habeas petitioner regardless of the petitioner's competence." *Id.* at 68. The Court also invoked "AEDPA's acknowledged purpose" to reduce delays in the execution of state and federal criminal sentences, especially in death penalty cases. *Id.* at 76 (citing *Schriro v. Landrigan*, 550 U.S. 465 (2007)).

[xi] Appeal

In a habeas corpus or § 2255 proceeding, the district judge's final order is subject to review by the appropriate court of appeals, but there is no appeal as of right. 28 U.S.C. § 2253(a). An appeal may be taken only if a circuit or district judge issues a *certificate of appealability* upon finding that the applicant has made a "substantial showing of the denial of a constitutional right." 28 U.S.C. § 2253(c)(2); Fed. R. App. P. 22(b). If the district court rejected the constitutional claim on its merits, this showing is satisfied if the applicant has established that "reasonable jurists would find the district court's assessment of the constitutional claims debatable or wrong." *Slack v.*

McDaniel, 529 U. S. 473, 484 (2000). But if the district court denied the habeas petition on procedural grounds without reaching the underlying constitutional claim, a certificate of appealability should issue if the petitioner shows "that jurists of reason would find it debatable whether the petition states a valid claim of a denial of a constitutional right and that jurists of reason would find it debatable whether the district court was correct in its procedural ruling." *Id.* Ordinarily the district judge will decide whether to issue the certificate. If that judge refuses to approve the certificate, the petitioner can ask the court of appeals to issue it. For example, in *Tharpe v. Sellers*, 138 S. Ct. 545 (2018), the Court held that the appellate court had wrongly denied a certificate of appealability. "Jurists of reason" could debate whether the murder defendant had shown that the state court's factual determination that the particular juror's presence on the jury did not prejudice his trial was wrong.

Because this certificate must state precisely which specific issue or issues satisfy this standard, 28 U.S.C. § 2253(c)(3), the court of appeals may permit an appeal on only some of the habeas corpus petition's issues. In *Gonzalez v. Thaler*, 566 U.S. 134 (2012), the Supreme Court held the specific-statement requirement of § 2253(c)(1) to be "mandatory" but not "jurisdictional." There, petitioner Gonzalez had failed to state specific grounds for his appeal in his application for a certificate of appealability from the district court's denial of his petition for habeas relief from his state court murder conviction. However, the state failed to raise this defect as a bar to his habeas appeal until the case reached the Supreme Court on *certiorari*. Under these circumstances, the Court determined that the Court of Appeals still had jurisdiction to adjudicate Gonzalez's appeal from the denial of his habeas petition. This unusual process is designed to limit severely the appeals in such cases by removing marginal cases from the appellate calendar. The habeas corpus petitioner has no right to be physically present at the appeal, but the United States Courts of Appeals have the discretion to order the defendant to be brought to the court for the hearing.

If the circuit court denies a certificate of appealability, the prisoner may ask the Supreme Court to review the denial. *Hohn v. United States*, 524 U.S. 236 (1998).

[3] Federal Prisoners: Motion to Vacate Sentence (§ 2255 Motion)

While federal habeas corpus is used primarily by state prisoners, a *Motion to Vacate Sentence* is used by federal prisoners to challenge the constitutionality of their incarceration. This motion is provided in 28 U.S.C. § 2255 and is ordinarily referred to as a § 2255 Motion. *See also* Rules Governing Section 2255 Proceedings for the United States District Courts. A § 2255 Motion involves virtually the same issues and procedures as federal habeas corpus. For example, the Motion is appropriate to challenge a federal prisoner's custody that is in violation of a federal constitutional or statutory provision. Section 2255 specifically provides that it, rather than federal habeas corpus, must be used unless a § 2255 Motion would be inadequate.

The § 2255 Motion is filed in the federal district court which imposed the sentence. The federal judge has the authority under this statute to vacate, set aside, or correct the federal sentence. This can result in an order discharging or resentencing the offender, or requiring a new trial. As with habeas corpus, the court can deny the Motion if the same issue was resolved in an earlier § 2255 Motion.

While a habeas corpus petition is filed in the federal district where the state offender is in *custody*, a § 2255 Motion is filed in the district where the *sentence was imposed*. This jurisdictional feature for § 2255 Motions was designed to alleviate caseload overcrowding in federal districts in which large federal prisons are located. It also recognized that the sentencing court, rather than the court where the prison is located, is more likely to have the records, witnesses, and knowledge necessary to process the motion efficiently. Since the prisoner filing the § 2255 Motion may be incarcerated in a federal prison far from the district where the sentence occurred, the statute states that the prisoner need not be present in person at any hearing on a § 2255 Motion.

Notes

1. *What's left of federal habeas corpus after AEDPA, Harrington, and Teague?* Under the 1996 AEDPA amendments to the federal habeas corpus laws, federal habeas relief is still possible, despite an adverse state court judgment on point, when the state judgment is contrary to clearly established federal law or involves an unreasonable application of clearly established federal law. 28 U.S.C. § 2254(d)(1). Also, under AEDPA, if a habeas petitioner has failed to develop the factual basis for a claim in *state* court, the federal court should not hold an evidentiary hearing on the issue unless the claim relies on a new rule of constitutional law that is retroactive. 28 U.S.C. § 2254(e)(2). Both of these sections suggest that some habeas petitioners, at least in theory, might still be able to benefit retroactively from rare new Supreme Court "watershed" decisions. Otherwise, the utility of habeas corpus relief appears now to be limited to curing blatantly erroneous state court applications of Supreme Court precedent.

For a wry view, that AEDPA did not live up to predictions that it would gut federal habeas corpus as an effective remedy because the Supreme Court's recent habeas corpus jurisprudence had already substantially eviscerated it, *see* John H. Blume, *AEDPA: the "Hype" and the "Bite,"* 91 Cornell L. Rev. 259 (2006) (noting that post-AEDPA habeas petitions have had the same rate of success in the Supreme Court as pre-AEDPA petitions, but that success rates post-AEDPA have declined in the lower federal courts).

2. *Claims of innocence in "closed" cases and DNA testing.* If you are representing a prisoner serving a long sentence or perhaps even facing the death penalty in a case dating back to a time when current state-of-the-art DNA testing procedures were not generally available, what strategies might you consider to try to get the prosecutor, the sentencing judge, or even a habeas court (despite all the obstacles previously discussed) to order or agree to a DNA test that might establish your client's actual innocence?

3. In your view, are the previously discussed constrictions in recent years on the availability of habeas relief, both pre- and post-AEDPA, excessively harsh and inappropriate diminutions on the utility and the stature of the Great Writ, or are they reasonable limitations that appropriately serve the interests of federalism, finality, efficiency, and prevention of abuse of The Great Writ? Do you think Congress could have struck a better balance—between the interest in preserving habeas corpus as an expeditious remedy for unlawful confinement and those countervailing interests—than the one it struck when it enacted AEDPA in 1996?

4. For an array of perspectives on the preceding question, *see, e.g.*, Joseph L. Hoffman & Nancy J. King, *Rethinking the Federal Role in State Criminal Justice*, 84 N.Y.U. L. Rev. 791 (2009) (federal habeas review wastes resources, is "failing and cannot be fixed," and should be eliminated except in capital cases—noting a success rate in noncapital cases of 0.34%); Sarah Russell, *Reluctance to Resentence: Courts, Congress, and Collateral Review*, 91 N.C. L. Rev. 79 (2012); Kent S. Scheidegger, *Habeas Corpus, Relitigation, and the Legislative Power*, 98 Colum. L. Rev. 888 (1998); Mark Tushnet and Larry W. Yackle, *Symbolic Statutes and Real Laws: The Pathologies of the Antiterrorism and Effective Death Penalty Act and the Prison Litigation Reform Act*, 47 Duke L.J. 1 (1997); Tung Yin, *A Better Mousetrap: Procedural Default as a Retroactivity Alternative to* Teague v. Lane *and the Antiterrorism and Effective Death Penalty Act of 1996*, 25 Am. J. Crim. L. 203 (1998); and Robert Weisberg, *A Great Writ While It Lasted*, 81 J. Crim. L. & Criminology 9 (1990) (best law review article title).

Index

[References are to pages.]

H

R

S

T